D0817466

CompTIA A+®
Certification Study Guide,
Eighth Edition

(Exams 220-801 & 220-802)

Jane Holcombe
Charles Holcombe

New York Chicago San Francisco Lisbon London Madrid
Mexico City Milan New Delhi San Juan Seoul Singapore Sydney Toronto

The McGraw·Hill Companies

Cataloging-in-Publication Data is on file with the Library of Congress

McGraw-Hill books are available at special quantity discounts to use as premiums and sales pro-
motions, or for use in corporate training programs. To contact a representative, please e-mail us at
bulksales@mcgraw-hill.com.

CompTIA A+® Certification Study Guide, Eighth Edition (Exams 220-801 & 220-802)

1234567890 DOC DOC 1098765432

ISBN: Book p/n 978-0-07-179577-7 and CD p/n 978-0-07-179579-1
of set 978-0-07-179580-7

MHID: Book p/n 0-07-179577-4 and CD p/n 0-07-179579-0
of set 0-07-179580-4

Sponsoring Editor	**Technical Editor**	**Production Supervisor**
Meghan Riley Manfre	Chris Crayton	George Anderson
Editorial Supervisor	**Copy Editor**	**Composition**
Patty Mon	Lisa McCoy	Cenveo Publisher Services
Project Editor	**Proofreader**	**Illustration**
LeeAnn Pickrell	Susie Elkind	Cenveo Publisher Services
Acquisitions Coordinator	**Indexer**	**Art Director, Cover**
Stephanie Evans	Karin Arrigoni	Jeff Weeks

ABOUT THE AUTHORS

Jane Holcombe, CompTIA A+, CompTIA Network +, CompTIA CTT+, and Microsoft MCSE, pioneered in the field of PC support training. She spent 20 years as an independent trainer, consultant, and course content author, creating and presenting courses on PC operating systems taught nationwide. She co-authored a set of networking courses for the consulting staff of a large network vendor. In the early 1990s, she worked with both Novell and Microsoft server operating systems, finally focusing on the Microsoft operating systems and achieving early MCSE certification, recertifying for new versions of Windows. Since 2001 she has been the lead author, in collaboration with her husband, of 10 books and numerous book chapters.

Charles Holcombe was a programmer of early computers in both the nuclear and aerospace fields. In his 15 years at Control Data Corporation, he was successively a programmer, technical sales analyst, salesman, and sales manager in the field marketing organization. At corporate headquarters, he ran the Executive Seminar program, served as corporate liaison to the worldwide university community, and was market development manager for Plato, Control Data's computer-based education system.

For the past 30 years, he has been an independent trainer and consultant, authoring and delivering training courses in many disciplines. He is a skilled writer and editor of books and online publications, and he collaborates with his wife, Jane, on many writing projects.

Together, Chuck and Jane Holcombe are a writing team who have authored *MCSE Guide to Designing a Microsoft Windows 2000 Network Infrastructure* (Course Technology) and both the *A+ Certification Press Lab Manual* and *Certification Press MCSE Windows 2000 Professional Lab Manual* (McGraw-Hill Professional). They authored three editions of *Survey of Operating Systems*, the first book in the Michael Meyers' Computer Skills series, and contributed chapters to *Mike Meyers' CompTIA A+ Guide to Managing and Troubleshooting PCs*, *CompTIA A+ Certification All-in-One Exam Guide, Fifth Edition*, and *Windows 2000 Administration* (McGraw-Hill Professional). They wrote several chapters for the Peter Norton *Introduction to Operating Systems, Sixth Edition* (McGraw-Hill), and have now authored three editions of the *CompTIA A+ Certification Study Guide*.

About the Contributors

Daniel Lachance, MCITP, MCTS, CNI, IBM Certified Instructor, CompTIA A+, CompTIA Network+, CompTIA Security+, is a technical trainer for Global Knowledge and has delivered classroom training in a wide variety of products for the past 17 years. Throughout his career, he has also developed custom applications and planned, implemented, troubleshot, and documented various network configurations.

Fred Shimmin, MCT, MCSE, MCSA, CTT+, CCA, worked for over 10 years as an independent contract training consultant at various Microsoft Authorized Training Centers and Chubb Computer Services. As the corporate training model changed to an online process, he worked for several years with a technical integration firm as a field engineer. He is currently employed as a manager of an IT infrastructure department for a major New Jersey healthcare organization.

About the Technical Editor

Chris Crayton, CompTIA A+, CompTIA Network+, MCSE, is an author, editor, technical consultant, and trainer. Chris has worked as a computer and networking instructor at Keiser University, as a network administrator for Protocol, an eCRM company, and as a computer and network specialist at Eastman Kodak. Chris has authored several print and online books on PC repair, CompTIA A+, CompTIA Security+, and Microsoft Windows. Chris has served as technical editor on numerous professional technical titles for leading publishing companies, including *CompTIA A+ Certification All-in-One Exam Guide*, *CompTIA A+ Certification Study Guide*, and *Mike Meyers' CompTIA A+ Certification Passport*.

About LearnKey

LearnKey provides self-paced learning content and multimedia delivery solutions to enhance personal skills and business productivity. LearnKey claims the largest library of rich streaming-media training content that engages learners in dynamic media-rich instruction complete with video clips, audio, full-motion graphics, and animated illustrations. LearnKey can be found on the Web at www.LearnKey.com.

CompTIA Approved Quality Content

It Pays to Get Certified

In a digital world, digital literacy is an essential survival skill. Certification proves you have the knowledge and skill to solve business problems in virtually any business environment. Certifications are highly valued credentials that qualify you for jobs, increased compensation, and promotion.

LEARN > **CERTIFY** > **WORK**

IT is Everywhere	IT Knowledge and Skills Get Jobs	Job Retention	New Opportunities	High Pay-High Growth Jobs
IT is mission critical to almost all organizations and its importance is increasing.	Certifications verify your knowledge and skills that qualifies you for:	Competence is noticed and valued in organizations.	Certifications qualify you for new opportunities in your current job or when you want to change careers.	Hiring managers demand the strongest skill set.
• 79% of U.S. businesses report IT is either important or very important to the success of their company	• Jobs in the high growth IT career field • Increased compensation • Challenging assignments and promotions • 60% report that being certified is an employer or job requirement	• Increased knowledge of new or complex technologies • Enhanced productivity • More insightful problem solving • Better project management and communication skills • 47% report being certified helped improve their problem solving skills	• 31% report certification improved their career advancement opportunities	• There is a widening IT skills gap with over 300,000 jobs open • 88% report being certified enhanced their resume

CompTIA A+ Certification Advances Your Career

- **The CompTIA A+ credential**—provides foundation-level knowledge and skills necessary for a career in PC repair and support.
- **Starting Salary**—CompTIA A+ Certified individuals can earn as much as $65,000 per year.
- **Career Pathway**—CompTIA A+ is a building block for other CompTIA certifications such as Network+, Security+ and vendor specific technologies.
- **More than 850,000**—individuals worldwide are CompTIA A+ certified.
- **Mandated/Recommended by organizations worldwide**—such as Cisco and HP and Ricoh, the U.S. State Department, and U.S. government contractors such as EDS, General Dynamics, and Northrop Grumman.
- **Some of the primary benefits individuals report from becoming CompTIA A+ certified are:**
    - More efficient troubleshooting
    - Improved career advancement
    - More insightful problem solving

CompTIA Career Pathway

CompTIA offers a number of credentials that form a foundation for your career in technology and that allow you to pursue specific areas of concentration. Depending on the path you choose to take, CompTIA certifications help you build upon your skills and knowledge, supporting learning throughout your entire career.

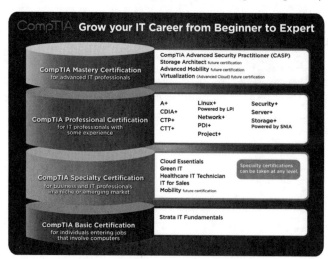

Steps to Getting Certified and Staying Certified

1. **Review exam objectives.** Review the certification objectives to make sure you know what is covered in the exam:
www.comptia.org/certifications/testprep/examobjectives.aspx
2. **Practice for the exam.** After you have studied for the certification, take a free assessment and sample test to get an idea what type of questions might be on the exam:
www.comptia.org/certifications/testprep/practicetests.aspx
3. **Purchase an exam voucher.** Purchase your exam voucher on the CompTIA Marketplace, which is located at: www.comptiastore.com
4. **Take the test!** Select a certification exam provider and schedule a time to take your exam. You can find exam providers at the following link:
www.comptia.org/certifications/testprep/testingcenters.aspx
5. **Stay Certified!** Continuing education is required. Effective January 1, 2011, CompTIA A+ certifications are valid for three years from the date of certification. There are a number of ways the certification can be renewed. For more information go to: http://certification.comptia.org/getCertified/steps_to_certification/stayCertified.aspx

Join the Professional Community

The free online IT Pro Community provides valuable content to students and professionals. Join the IT Pro Community:

http://itpro.comptia.org

Career IT job resources include:

- Where to start in IT
- Career assessments
- Salary trends
- U.S. job board

Join the IT Pro Community and get access to:

- Forums on networking, security, computing, and cutting-edge technologies
- Access to blogs written by industry experts
- Current information on cutting edge technologies
- Access to various industry resource links and articles related to IT and IT careers

Content Seal of Quality

This courseware bears the seal of CompTIA Approved Quality Content. This seal signifies this content covers 100 percent of the exam objectives and implements important instructional design principles. CompTIA recommends multiple learning tools to help increase coverage of the learning objectives.

AUTHORIZED

Why CompTIA?

- **Global recognition**—CompTIA is recognized globally as the leading IT nonprofit trade association and has enormous credibility. Plus, CompTIA's certifications are vendor-neutral and offer proof of foundational knowledge that translates across technologies.
- **Valued by hiring managers**—Hiring managers value CompTIA certification because it is vendor- and technology-independent validation of your technical skills.
- **Recommended or required by government and businesses**—Many government organizations and corporations (for example, Dell, Sharp, Ricoh, the U.S. Department of Defense, and many more) either recommend or require technical staff to be CompTIA certified.
- **Three CompTIA certifications ranked in the top 10**—In a study by DICE of 17,000 technology professionals, certifications helped command higher salaries at all experience levels.

How to Obtain More Information

Visit CompTIA online

Go to www.comptia.org to learn more about getting CompTIA certified.

Contact CompTIA

Please call 866-835-8020, ext. 5 or e-mail questions@comptia.org.

Join the IT Pro Community

Go to http://itpro.comptia.org to join the IT community to get relevant career information.

Connect with CompTIA

Find us on Facebook, LinkedIn, Twitter, and YouTube.

CAQC Disclaimer

The logo of the CompTIA Approved Quality Content (CAQC) program and the status of this or other training material as "Authorized" under the CompTIA Approved Quality Content program signifies that, in CompTIA's opinion, such training material covers the content of CompTIA's related certification exam.

The contents of this training material were created for the CompTIA A+ exams covering CompTIA certification objectives that were current as of the date of publication.

CompTIA has not reviewed or approved the accuracy of the contents of this training material and specifically disclaims any warranties of merchantability or fitness for a particular purpose. CompTIA makes no guarantee concerning the success of persons using any such "Authorized" or other training material in order to prepare for any CompTIA certification exam.

CONTENTS AT A GLANCE

CONTENTS

The objective of this Study Guide is to help you prepare for and pass the required exams so you can begin to reap the career benefits of CompTIA A+ certification. Because the primary focus of this book is to help you pass the exams, we don't always cover every aspect of the related technology. Some aspects of the technology are only covered to the extent necessary to help you understand what you need to know to pass the exams, but we hope this book will serve you as a valuable professional resource after your exams.

In This Book

This book is organized in such a way as to serve as an in-depth review for the 2012 CompTIA A+ exams: Exam 220-801 and Exam 220-802. Each chapter covers a major aspect of the exams, with an emphasis on the "why" as well as the "how to" of IT support in the areas of installation, configuration, and maintenance of devices, PCs, and software; networking and security/forensics; diagnosis, resolution, and documentation of common hardware and software issues; troubleshooting; virtualization; desktop imaging; and deployment.

On the CD-ROM

The CD-ROM contains additional tools to help you prepare for the exams. For more information on the CD-ROM, please see the "About the CD-ROM" appendix at the back of this book.

Exam Readiness Checklist

At the end of the Introduction, you will find two Exam Readiness Checklists. These tables have been constructed to allow you to cross-reference the official exam objectives with the objectives as they are presented and covered in this book. These checklists also allow you to gauge your level of expertise on each objective at the outset of your studies. This should allow you to check your progress and make sure you spend the time you need on more difficult or unfamiliar sections. References have been provided for the objective exactly as the vendor presents it, the section of the Study Guide that covers that objective, and a chapter and page reference.

In Every Chapter

We've created a set of chapter components that call your attention to important items, reinforce important points, and provide helpful exam-taking hints. Take a look at what you'll find in every chapter:

- Every chapter begins with the **Certification Objectives**—what you need to know in order to pass the section on the exams dealing with the chapter topic. The Certification Objective headings identify the objectives within the chapter, so you'll always know an objective when you see it!

- **Exam Watch** notes call attention to information about, and potential pitfalls in, the exams. These helpful hints reinforce your learning and exam preparation.

- **Step-by-Step Exercises** are interspersed throughout the chapters. These hands-on exercises allow you to get a feel for the real-world experience you need in order to pass the exams. They help you master skills that are likely to be an area of focus on the exams. Don't just read through the exercises; they are hands-on practice that you should be comfortable completing. Learning by doing is an effective way to increase your competency with a product.

- **On the Job** notes describe the issues that come up most often in real-world settings. They provide a valuable perspective on certification- and product-related topics. They point out common mistakes and address questions that have arisen from on-the-job discussions and experience.

- **Scenario & Solution** sections lay out problems and solutions in a quick-read format.

SCENARIO & SOLUTION

My computer is part of a large corporate network. What role is my desktop computer most likely playing in this network?	A large corporate network is a client/server network. A desktop PC in this network has the role of a client.
What is the protocol suite of the Internet?	The protocol suite of the Internet is TCP/IP.
I understand that NetBEUI is very easy to install and use. Why does our corporate internetwork not use it?	A corporate internetwork consists, by definition, of interconnected networks requiring a protocol suite routable between networks. NetBEUI, as a nonroutable protocol, is therefore not used.

■ The **Certification Summary** is a succinct review of the chapter and a restatement of salient points regarding the exams.

✓ ■ The **Two-Minute Drill** at the end of every chapter is a checklist of the main points of the chapter. It can be used for last-minute review.

Q&A ■ The **Self Test** offers multiple-choice questions similar to those found on the certification exams. The answers to these questions, as well as explanations of the answers, can be found at the end of each chapter. By taking the Self Test after completing each chapter, you'll reinforce what you've learned from that chapter while becoming familiar with the structure of the multiple-choice exam questions. The book does not include other types of questions that you may encounter on the exams.

Some Pointers

Once you've finished reading this book, set aside some time to do a thorough review. You might want to return to the book several times and make use of all the methods it offers for reviewing the material:

1. *Re-read all of the Two-Minute Drills,* or have someone quiz you. You also can use the drills as a way to do a quick cram before the exams.

2. *Review all the Scenario & Solutions* for quick problem solving.

3. *Complete the Exercises.* Did you do the exercises when you read through each chapter? If not, do them! These exercises are designed to cover exam topics, and there's no better way to get to know this material than by practicing. Be sure you understand why you are performing each step in each exercise. If there is something you are not clear on, re-read that section in the chapter.

4. *Retake the Self Tests.* Taking the tests right after you've read the chapter is a good idea, because the questions help reinforce what you've just learned. However, it's an even better idea to go back later and do all the questions in the book in one sitting. Pretend that you're taking a live exam. When you go through the questions the first time, you should mark your answers on a separate piece of paper. That way, you can run through the questions as many times as you need to until you feel comfortable with the material.

ACKNOWLEDGMENTS

We thank the many dedicated people at McGraw-Hill Professional who have been so helpful to us, proving once again that writing a book is truly a team effort. A special thank-you goes to Timothy Green, Executive Acquisitions Editor, and his great team with whom we have worked on different projects for several years. His cohorts guided us through this project. They are Meghan Riley Manfre, Associate Acquisitions Editor, and Stephanie Evans, Acquisitions Coordinator. They have all smoothed the way for us and deserve great credit for the success of this book. Meghan found a researcher for us when we desperately needed help with the work load, and Stephanie devised an incentive system for on-time work that involved YouTube videos!

We were very fortunate once again to have Chris Crayton as our technical editor. After we used up all the slack in the schedule (and more), Chris still managed to turn around tech edits in hours, catching things we had missed, and pointing out nuances to concepts that we overlooked. We could go on for pages about Chris' contribution to this book. He had our backs. But Chris, how many people are going to know Norwegian history?

We had the pleasure of working, once again, with LeeAnn Pickrell, project editor, who made extremely helpful suggestions in the final edit of the book and whose friendship and dedication to high quality we much appreciate.

All projects seem to gain weight as time passes, and about halfway through the book we realized we needed more help. That's when Dan Lachance came on board as a researcher and contributor, taking some of the weight off our shoulders.

Many other people at McGraw-Hill have contributed to the creation of this book. Although we can't list all of their names, they know who they are, and we want them to know that we truly appreciate their outstanding efforts.

How to Take a CompTIA A+ Certification Exam

This section prepares you for taking the actual examinations. It gives you a few pointers on methods for preparing for the exam, including how to study and register, what to expect, and what to do on exam day.

Importance of CompTIA A+ Certification

Earning CompTIA A+ certification means that you have the knowledge and the technical skills necessary to be a successful entry-level IT professional in today's environment. The 2012 objectives test your knowledge and skills in all the areas that today's computing environment requires. Although the tests cover a broad range of computer software and hardware, they are not vendor specific.

Both the CompTIA A+ 220-801 Exam and the CompTIA A+ 220-802 Exam are required to achieve your CompTIA A+ certification. As stated by CompTIA, together, the 220-801 and 220-802 exams "measure necessary competencies for an entry-level IT professional with the equivalent knowledge of at least 12 months of hands-on experience in the lab or field. Successful candidates will have the knowledge required to assemble components based on customer requirements, install, configure, and maintain devices, PCs and software for end users, understand the basics of networking and security/forensics, and properly and safely diagnose, resolve, and document common hardware and software issues while applying troubleshooting skills. Successful candidates will also provide appropriate customer support and understand the basics of virtualization, desktop imaging, and deployment."

Computerized Testing

The most practical way to administer tests on a global level is through a testing center, such as Pearson VUE, which provides proctored testing services for many companies, including CompTIA. In addition to administering the tests, Pearson VUE scores the exam and provides statistical feedback on each section of the exam to the companies and organizations that use their services.

On Exams 220-801 and 220-802, unanswered questions count against you. Assuming you have time left when you finish the other questions, you can return to the marked questions for further evaluation.

The standard test also marks the questions that are incomplete with a letter "I" once you've finished all the questions. You'll see the whole list of questions after you complete the last question. This screen allows you to go back and finish incomplete items, finish unmarked items, and return to questions you flagged for review.

An interesting and useful characteristic of the standard test is that questions may be marked and returned *to later. This helps you manage your time while taking the test so you don't spend too much time on any one question.*

Question Types

The CompTIA A+ exams consist of several types of question formats, as described in a YouTube video on the test experience at http://certification.comptia.org/ CandidateExperience. We strongly recommend that you take the time to watch this short video. Here is a brief overview of the question formats you may see on your exam.

Multiple Choice Questions

Many CompTIA A+ exam questions are of the multiple-choice variety. Below each question is a list of four or five possible answers. Use the available radio buttons to select the correct answer from the given choices.

Multiple Response Questions

A multiple-response question is a multiple-choice question with more than one correct answer, in which case, the number of correct answers required is clearly stated.

Graphical Questions

Some questions incorporate a graphical element or a video available via an Exhibit button to provide a visual representation of the problem or present the question itself. These questions are easy to identify because they refer to the exhibit in the question and there is an exhibit. An example of a graphical question might be to identify a component on a drawing of a motherboard. This is done in the multiple-choice format by having callouts labeled A, B, C, or D point to the selections.

Drag-and-Drop Questions

A drag-and-drop question is a form of graphical question in which you select a token, such as a graphic of a computer component, and drag and drop it to a designated area, in response to the question.

Free Response Questions

Another type of question is one that requires a free response or type-in answer. This is a fill-in-the-blank-type question where a list of possible choices is not given.

Performance-Based Questions

Performance-based questions include simulations and require the candidate to perform certain tasks based on multifaceted scenarios. When you encounter one of these questions, you will click a Simulations button and enter a simulated environment in which you must perform one or more tasks.

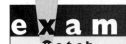

watch   *Due to the limitations*   *do not contain simulations of the drag-*
of the practice test engine software, the   *and-drop, free response, and performance-*
practice exams included on the CD-ROM   *based question types.*

Study Strategies

There are appropriate ways to study for the different types of questions you may see on CompTIA A+ certification exams. The amount of study time needed to pass the exam will vary with the candidate's level of experience. Someone with several years experience might only need a quick review of materials and terms when preparing for the exam. Others may need several hours to identify weaknesses in their knowledge and skill level and work on those areas to bring them up to par. If you know that you are weak in an area, work on it until you feel comfortable talking about it. You don't want to be surprised by a question knowing it was in your weak area.

Knowledge-Based Questions

Knowledge-based questions require that you memorize facts. These questions may not cover material that you use on a daily basis, but they do cover material that CompTIA thinks an IT professional should be able to answer. Here are some keys to memorizing facts:

■ **Repetition**   The more times you expose your brain to a fact, the more it sinks in, and your ability to remember it increases.

■ **Association**   Connecting facts within a logical framework makes them easier to remember.

■ **Motor association**   Remembering something is easier if you write it down or perform another physical act, like clicking the practice exam answers.

Performance-Based Questions

The first step in preparing for performance-based questions is to absorb as many facts relating to the exam content areas as you can. Of course, actual hands-on experience will greatly help you in this area. For example, it really helps in knowing how to install a video adapter if you have actually done the procedure at least once. Some of the questions will place you in a scenario and ask for the best solution to the problem at hand. It is in these scenarios that having a good knowledge level and some experience will help you.

CompTIA A+ Certification Exam 220-801

The CompTIA A+ Certification Exam 220-801 consists of five domains (categories). CompTIA represents the relative importance of each domain within the body of knowledge required for an entry-level IT professional taking this exam.

1.0 PC Hardware	40%
2.0 Networking	27%
3.0 Laptops	11%
4.0 Printers	11%
5.0 Operational Procedures	11%

CompTIA A+ Certification Exam 220-802

The CompTIA A+ Certification Exam 220-802 consists of four domains (categories). CompTIA represents the relative importance of each domain within the body of knowledge required for an entry-level IT professional taking this exam.

1.0 Operating Systems	33%
2.0 Security	22%
3.0 Mobile Devices	9%
4.0 Troubleshooting	36%

Taking the Exam

The best method of preparing for the exam is to create a study schedule and stick to it. Although teachers have probably told you time and time again not to cram for tests, some information just doesn't quite stick in your memory. It's this type of information you want to look at right before you take the exam so it remains fresh in your mind. You can brush up on good study techniques from any quality study book, but some things to remember when preparing and taking the test are

- Get a good night's sleep. Don't stay up all night cramming for this one. If you don't know the material by the time you go to sleep, your head won't be clear enough to remember it in the morning.
- The test center needs two forms of identification, one of which must have your picture on it (for example, your driver's license). Credit cards are also acceptable forms of identification.
- Arrive at the test center a few minutes early. You don't want to feel rushed right before taking an exam.
- Don't spend too much time on one question. If you think you're spending too much time on it, just flag it and return to it later if you have time.
- If you don't know the answer to a multiple-choice question, think about it logically. Look at the answers and eliminate the ones that you know can't possibly be the answer. This may leave you with only two possible answers. Give it your best guess if you have to, but you can resolve most of the answers to the questions by the process of elimination. Remember, unanswered questions count as incorrect whether you know the answer to them or not.

■ No books, calculators, laptop computers, or any other reference materials are allowed inside the testing center. The tests are computer based and do not require pens, pencils, or paper, although, as mentioned previously, some test centers provide scratch paper to aid you while taking the exam.

After the Exam

As soon as you complete the exam, your results will show up in the form of a bar graph on the screen. As long as your score is greater than the required score, you pass! The testing center will print and emboss a hard copy of the report to indicate that it's an official report. Don't lose this copy; it's the only hard copy of the report made. The testing center sends the results electronically to CompTIA.

The printed report will also indicate how well you did in each section. You will be able to see the percentage of questions you got right in each section, but you will not be able to tell which questions you got wrong.

After you pass both exams, you will receive a CompTIA A+ certificate by mail within a few weeks. You are then authorized to use the CompTIA A+ logo on your business cards, as long as you stay within the guidelines specified by CompTIA. Please check the CompTIA Website for a more comprehensive and up-to-date listing and explanation of CompTIA A+ benefits.

If you don't pass the exam, don't fret. Examine the areas where you didn't do so well, and work on those areas for the next time you register to take the exams.

Exam Readiness Checklists

The following two tables, one for each of the CompTIA A+ exams (Exam 801 and Exam 802), describe each of the A+ objectives with a mapping to the coverage in the Study Guide. There are also three check boxes labeled Beginner, Intermediate, and Expert. Use these to rate your beginning knowledge of each objective. This assessment will help guide you to the areas in which you need to spend more time studying for the exams.

Exam 220-80 I

Exam Readiness Checklist

Official Objective	Study Guide Coverage	Ch #	Pg #	Beginner	Intermediate	Expert
801: 1.0 PC Hardware						
1.1 Configure and apply BIOS settings.	Configuring a Motherboard	3	130			
1.2 Differentiate between motherboard components, their purposes, and properties.	Motherboard Form Factors and Components	3	108			
1.3 Compare and contrast RAM types and features.	Memory	4	156			
1.4 Install and configure expansion cards.	Expansion Cards and Built-in Adapters	4	165			
1.5 Install and configure storage devices and use appropriate media.	Storage Devices and Interfaces	4	181			
1.5 Install and configure storage devices and use appropriate media.	Installing Storage Devices	6	290			
1.6 Differentiate among various CPU types and features and select the appropriate cooling method.	CPUs	3	119			
1.7 Compare and contrast various connection interfaces and explain their purpose.	Expansion Cards and Built-in Adapters	4	165			
1.7 Compare and contrast various connection interfaces and explain their purpose.	Wireless Communications	7	342			
1.8 Install an appropriate power supply based on a given scenario.	Power Supplies	5	214			
1.9 Evaluate and select appropriate components for a custom configuration to meet customer specifications or needs.	Selecting Components for Custom PCs	6	268			
1.10 Given a scenario, evaluate types and features of display devices.	Video Adapters and Displays	5	222			
1.11 Identify connector types and associated cables.	Expansion Cards and Built-in Adapters	4	165			

Exam Readiness Checklist

Official Objective	Study Guide Coverage	Ch #	Pg #	Beginner	Intermediate	Expert
1.11 Identify connector types and associated cables.	Video Adapters and Displays	5	222			
1.12 Install and configure various peripheral devices.	Installing and Configuring Peripheral Devices	5	243			
801: 2.0 Networking						
2.1 Identify types of network cables and connectors.	Network Hardware	14	768			
2.2 Categorize characteristics of connectors and cabling.	Network Hardware	14	768			
2.3 Explain properties and characteristics of TCP/IP.	Network Software	14	752			
2.4 Explain common TCP and UDP ports, protocols, and their purpose.	Common Ports	14	766			
2.4 Explain common TCP and UDP ports, protocols, and their purpose.	Internet Services and Protocols	15	832			
2.5 Compare and contrast wireless networking standards and encryption types.	Wireless LAN (WLAN)	14	740			
2.5 Compare and contrast wireless networking standards and encryption types.	Securing a Wireless Network	15	807			
2.6 Install, configure, and deploy a SOHO wireless/wired router using appropriate settings.	Creating a Wi-Fi Network	15	800			
2.7 Compare and contrast Internet connection types and features.	Wide Area Network	14	743			
2.8 Identify various types of networks.	Network Topologies, Classifications, and Performance	14	734			
2.9 Compare and contrast network devices, their functions, and features.	Network Hardware	14	768			
2.10 Given a scenario, use appropriate networking tools.	The Hardware Toolkit	3	104			

Exam Readiness Checklist

Official Objective	Study Guide Coverage	Ch #	Pg #	Beginner	Intermediate	Expert
801: 3.0 Laptops						
3.1 Install and configure laptop hardware and components.	Installing and Upgrading Laptops	7	321			
3.2 Compare and contrast the components within the display of a laptop.	Installing and Upgrading Laptops	7	340			
3.3 Compare and contrast laptop features.	Installing and Upgrading Laptops	7	321			
801: 4.0 Printers						
4.1 Explain the differences between the various printer types and summarize the associated imaging process.	Printer Basics	21	1084			
4.2 Given a scenario, install and configure printers.	Installing and Configuring Printers	21	1094			
4.3 Given a scenario, perform printer maintenance.	Printer Maintenance	21	1110			
801: 5.0 Operational Procedures						
5.1 Given a scenario, use appropriate safety procedures.	Workplace Safety and Safe Equipment Handling	1	2			
5.2 Explain environment impacts and the purpose of environmental controls.	Environmental Concerns for IT Professionals	1	20			
5.3 Given a scenario, demonstrate proper communication and professionalism.	Professionalism and Proper Communication	1	29			
5.4 Explain the fundamentals of dealing with prohibited content/activity.	Dealing with Prohibited Content and Prohibited Activities	1	36			

Exam 220-802

Exam Readiness Checklist

Official Objective	Study Guide Coverage	Ch #	Pg #	Beginner	Intermediate	Expert
1.5 Given a scenario, use Control Panel utilities.	Configuring Internet Explorer	15	839			
1.5 Given a scenario, use Control Panel utilities.	Local User and Group Accounts	18	941			
1.5 Given a scenario, use Control Panel utilities.	Implementing a Defense Against Malware	18	957			
1.5 Given a scenario, use Control Panel utilities.	Applying Share Permissions	19	1011			
1.5 Given a scenario, use Control Panel utilities.	Installing and Configuring Printers	21	1094			
1.6 Set up and configure Windows networking on a client/desktop.	Configuring Windows Clients for File and Printer Sharing	19	992			
1.6 Set up and configure Windows networking on a client/desktop.	Installing and Configuring Networks	15	1094			
1.6 Set up and configure Windows networking on a client/desktop.	Proxy Servers	15	835			
1.7 Perform preventive maintenance procedures using appropriate tools.	Preventive Maintenance for Windows OSs	13	713			
1.8 Explain the differences among basic OS security settings.	Implementing Authentication for Digital Security	18	939			
1.8 Explain the differences among basic OS security settings.	Implementing Data Security	19	1008			
1.8 Explain the differences among basic OS security settings.	File Management	10	517			
1.9 Explain the basics of client-side virtualization.	Introduction to Virtualization	8	375			
1.9 Explain the basics of client-side virtualization.	Implementing Client-Side Desktop Virtualization	8	380			
802: 2.0 Security						
2.1 Apply and use common prevention methods.	Defense Against Threats: Physical Security	17	917			
2.1 Apply and use common prevention methods.	Implementing a Defense Against Malware	18	957			
2.1 Apply and use common prevention methods.	Implementing Authentication for Digital Security	18	939			

Exam Readiness Checklist

Official Objective	Study Guide Coverage	Ch #	Pg #	Beginner	Intermediate	Expert
2.1 Apply and use common prevention methods.	Implementing Data Security	19	1008			
2.2 Compare and contrast common security threats.	Security Threats	17	900			
2.3 Implement security best practices to secure a workstation.	Best Practices to Secure a Workstation	18	952			
2.4 Given a scenario, use the appropriate data destruction/disposal method.	Securing Physical Access to Documents	17	922			
2.4 Given a scenario, use the appropriate data destruction/disposal method.	Digital Data Wiping	19	1023			
2.5 Given a scenario, secure a SOHO wireless network.	Creating a Wi-Fi Network	15	800			
2.6 Give a scenario, secure a SOHO wired network.	Installing and Configuring Networks	15	793			
802: 3.0 Mobile Devices						
3.1 Explain the basic features of mobile operating systems.	Overview of Mobile Devices	20	1045			
3.2 Establish basic network connectivity and configure email.	Configuring Mobile Devices	20	1057			
3.3 Compare and contrast methods for securing mobile devices.	Securing Mobile Devices	20	1066			
3.4 Compare and contrast hardware differences in regard to tablets and laptops.	Overview of Mobile Devices	20	1045			
3.5 Execute and configure mobile device synchronization	Configuring Mobile Devices	20	1057			
802: 4.0 Troubleshooting						
4.1 Given a scenario, explain the troubleshooting theory.	Troubleshooting Theory	11	559			
4.2 Given a scenario, troubleshoot common problems related to motherboard, RAM, CPU, and power with appropriate tools.	Troubleshooting Motherboards, RAM, CPUs, and Power	11	566			

Exam Readiness Checklist

Official Objective	Study Guide Coverage	Ch #	Pg #	Beginner	Intermediate	Expert
4.3 Given a scenario, troubleshoot hard drives and RAID arrays with appropriate tools.	Troubleshooting Storage Devices	11	579			
4.4 Given a scenario, troubleshoot common video and display issues.	Troubleshooting I/O Devices	11	591			
4.5 Given a scenario, troubleshoot wired and wireless networks with appropriate tools.	Using Networking Tools	15	793			
4.5 Given a scenario, troubleshoot wired and wireless networks with appropriate tools.	Troubleshooting Common Network Problems	16	858			
4.6 Given a scenario, troubleshoot operating system problems with appropriate tools.	Overview of Troubleshooting Software Problems	13	662			
4.6 Given a scenario, troubleshoot operating system problems with appropriate tools.	Windows Troubleshooting Tools	13	664			
4.6 Given a scenario, troubleshoot operating system problems with appropriate tools.	Symptoms and Solutions	13	701			
4.7 Given a scenario, troubleshoot common security issues with appropriate tools and best practices.	Windows Troubleshooting Tools	13	664			
4.7 Given a scenario, troubleshoot common security issues with appropriate tools and best practices.	Security Threats	17	900			
4.7 Given a scenario, troubleshoot common security issues with appropriate tools and best practices.	Implementing a Defense Against Malware	18	957			
4.8 Given a scenario, troubleshoot and repair common laptop issues while adhering to the appropriate procedures.	Troubleshooting and Preventive Maintenance of Laptops	12	630			
4.9 Given a scenario, troubleshoot printers with appropriate tools.	Troubleshooting Printers	21	1120			

1

Operational Procedures

Operational procedures for IT professionals cover many activities. They include on-the-job safety, procedures for minimizing environmental impact, communication skills, workplace professionalism, and lastly, policies and procedures for dealing with prohibited content and/or prohibited activity. Your technical skills with computers, networks, and operating systems may be excellent, but if you do not follow proper operational procedures, you may put your job and career at risk.

CERTIFICATION OBJECTIVE

■ **801: 5.1** *Given a scenario, use appropriate safety procedures*

The A+ candidate must prove knowledge of appropriate safety procedures and how to participate in a safe work environment in which each person handles equipment safely to protect the equipment and prevent injury to people.

Workplace Safety and Safe Equipment Handling

Safety is everyone's job, even in an organization in which designated employees are assigned direct responsibility for safety compliance and implementation. Everyone in an organization must play an active role in maintaining a safe work environment, which includes having an awareness of, and acting to remove, common safety hazards, such as spilled liquids, floor clutter, electrical dangers, and atmospheric hazards. You must be proactive to avoid accidents that can harm people and equipment. Safe equipment handling begins with using the appropriate tools; taking care when moving equipment; protecting yourself and equipment from electrostatic discharge; avoiding damage to transmission links and data from electromagnetic interference; and taking appropriate precautions when working with power supplies, displays, and printers.

Cable Management

One often-overlooked hazard is the jumble of cables connecting the various pieces of equipment in an office. If someone trips on the cables, they may injure themselves and/or damage equipment. Therefore, control the chaos, even if you need to use cable management products to eliminate such clutter and hazards. You'll find a wide selection of cable management products on the Internet. The simplest are cable ties—either Velcro straps or plastic zip ties—that allow you to tie cables together to keep them out of the way, or cable sleeves that you use to enclose a group of cables. More sophisticated products include cable raceways (Figure 1-1) that you can attach to furniture or walls to conceal a bundle of cables, cable trays for containing cabling within ceilings, and patch panels that network engineers use to manage the power and network cables in utility closets or server rooms. Even with the use of channels and cable raceways, however, the cables under a single desk can quickly turn into a tangled mess. Figure 1-2 shows the cabling for a single PC, its two displays, Ethernet cable, speakers, two printers, and an uninterruptible power supply (UPS).

FIGURE 1-1

A cable raceway mounted on a desk with the cover of the near section removed

FIGURE 1-2

The cabling for a single PC and its peripherals

Using Appropriate Tools

The typical computer technician's tool kit is not extensive; we will discuss what it should include in Chapter 3. For now, just know that such a hardware tool kit will include various types and sizes of screwdrivers, a parts grabber, a flashlight, extra screws, and some other handy items.

Use appropriate tools to avoid damage to computer components and possible personal injury—and be meticulous about using each tool only for its intended purposes. For instance, attempting to use a flat-bladed screwdriver on a Phillips-head screw can damage both the screw and the screwdriver, and it does not work very well. Worse yet, using a tool that does not fit properly may cause it to slip and damage a component such as the motherboard, or perhaps even injure yourself. Figure 1-3 shows several screwdrivers designed for specific types of screw heads.

on the Job

Do not carry loose objects like screwdrivers in shirt pockets or hip pockets because they can fall into computers and other equipment when you lean over or stab you if you sit down.

Notice the differences in the blades of the four screwdrivers on the left—each only works with a specific screw head. The nut driver on the right works on one size of hex nut.

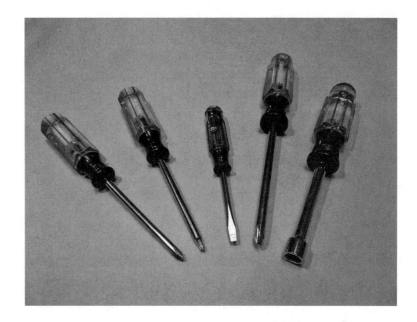

In Chapter 11, we describe methods for maintaining and cleaning computer components, and one of the tools described there is a vacuum. If you use a vacuum around open computer equipment, be sure to power down, disconnect the component, and avoid touching any power supplies with your hands or the vacuum. Further, if the vacuum does not have a filter, be sure to wear a filter mask, such as the inexpensive ones you can buy at a hardware store or pharmacy. Using a vacuum can generate static, so, if available, use an antistatic vacuum—one that has a conductive path to ground to protect against causing electrostatic discharge damage to a computer during use.

If you choose to use canned compressed air to clean dust out of components, follow the instructions in Chapter 11, and wear a mask and be sure to aim the nozzle away from you to avoid blowing particles in your face.

Fire Safety

Any workplace can experience a fire, and if a fire should start, your first concern is safety for yourself and others. If you are untrained and/or are uncertain about the fuels involved in a fire, it is better to escape a fire, trigger a fire alarm, and close doors behind you than to fight a fire. The following discussion will not fully prepare you to fight a fire, but it will educate you and make you aware of the dangers and the need for proper training.

The typical workplace has a variety of potential fire sources and fuels. Look around areas such as the break room, offices, work cubicles, the wiring closet, server room, and computer workbench and imagine how a fire could start and what would fuel the fire. When working around computers, one potential fire source is a faulty computer or peripheral power supply that can result in an electrical fire. The wiring in the wall, as well as in any equipment or appliance, could develop a short, resulting in heat that could ignite the material within the equipment and spread to nearby fuels, such as paper, solvents, furniture, and more. You need to extinguish these various types by using the appropriate fire extinguisher; they come in several classes based on the fuel feeding the fire. Clearly, it is best to extinguish a fire at the source before multiple fuels are involved. Following is a description of the most common fire extinguisher classes:

■ **Class A** Use for fires involving ordinary combustible materials, such as wood, paper, cardboard, and most plastics.

■ **Class B** Use on fires involving flammable or combustible liquids, including gasoline, kerosene, grease, and oil.

■ **Class C** Use on fires involving electrical equipment, such as wiring, circuit breakers, outlets, computers, and appliances. The material in a Class C extinguisher is nonconductive to reduce the risk of shock that could result from using a conductive material.

■ **Class D** Use on chemical fires involving magnesium, titanium, potassium, and sodium.

■ **Class K** Use on fires involving cooking oils, trans-fats, or other fats in cooking appliances. This type of extinguisher should be in commercial kitchens and restaurants.

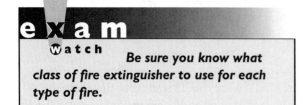

Watch *Be sure you know what class of fire extinguisher to use for each type of fire.*

Keep at least one fire extinguisher of the appropriate class or classes handy by your desk or workbench, in the wiring closet, the server room, and other locations. In some locations, you may have air-pressurized water (APW) fire extinguishers. Only use these on fires involving ordinary combustibles (See Class A in the previous list).

Some fire extinguishers contain dry chemicals, which leave a residue that reduces the chance of the fire reigniting, and some dry chemical extinguishers are rated

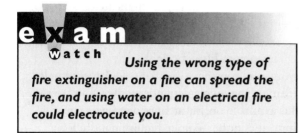

e x a m

⊕ a t c h *Using the wrong type of fire extinguisher on a fire can spread the fire, and using water on an electrical fire could electrocute you.*

for more than one class, which is very handy for a multiple-fuel fire. For instance, a BC extinguisher can be used on Class B or Class C fires, but be aware that it will leave a residue that must be cleaned immediately because it is corrosive. An ABC fire extinguisher is rated for all three fire types, but it leaves a sticky residue that can damage computers and electrical appliances.

Some Class B and C extinguishers contain carbon dioxide (CO_2), a nonflammable gas. One advantage of a CO_2 extinguisher is that it does not leave a residue, but because a CO_2 extinguisher relies on high pressure, it may shoot out bits of dry ice. Never use a CO_2 extinguisher on a Class A fire, because it may not smother the fire enough to fully extinguish it.

Lifting and Moving Equipment

In the United States, lifting is the number one cause of back injuries. Therefore, when lifting and moving computer equipment or any objects, take the time to do it safely, protecting yourself and the equipment, as described here.

Protecting Yourself

It is easy to injure your back when moving equipment. Therefore, the weight of what you lift, as well as how you lift it, are important, which means that every instance of lifting and moving is different.

Lifting Weight Limits   Ironically, as far as laws and regulations go, there are no clear limits on what an employee can lift, and the Occupational Safety and Health Administration (OSHA) has no standards written for many specific workplace lifting situations. This is because the actual circumstances differ widely, and the weight is just one consideration. Lifting hazards are very broadly addressed under the General Duty Clause of the OSH Act, specifically Section 5(a)(1). It states:

"Each employer—shall furnish to each of his employees employment and a place of employment which are free from recognized hazards that are causing or are likely to cause death or serious physical harm to his employees."

The National Institute for Occupational Safety and Health (NIOSH) publishes a lifting equation so that employers can evaluate the lifting tasks for employees and establish a recommended weight limit. This is a rather complicated equation requiring considerable effort to gather information about each situation. Then, when you factor in all the human variables of every lifting situation, you understand the difficulty of attempting to calculate a maximum lifting weight.

Government agencies and other organizations have created calculators to help employees establish guidelines for lifting. One such calculator by the Ohio Bureau of Workers' Compensation (BWC) is available online at www.ohiobwc.com. Figure 1-4 shows this calculator. This one is rather simple, requiring just a few pieces of information. When we selected "lower back disorder, with a shoulder level lift, a horizontal reach of 12," and the trunk-twisting angle during the lift of 30 degrees, the results box showed that lifting up to 20 pounds with the presented criteria resulted in a low risk level. It also showed that lifting between 20 and 25 pounds resulted in a moderate risk level. Exercise 1-1 will help you research lifting guidelines.

FIGURE 1-4

A lifting guideline tool published by the Ohio Bureau of Workers' Compensation

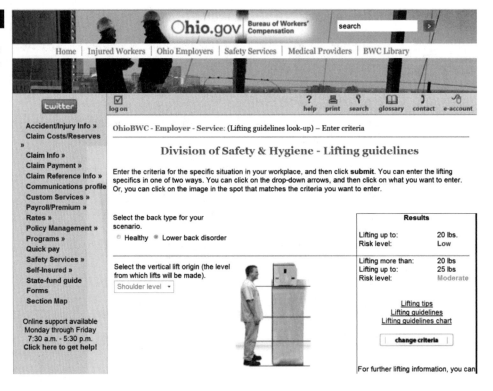

EXERCISE 1-1

Research Lifting Guidelines

It is important to protect yourself from injury while lifting, so take some time to research the guidelines:

1. Use your favorite Internet search engine to search on the keywords "workplace safety lifting guide." Search through the results to find a guide that will help you with your own situation.

2. We also recommend the Ohio Bureau of Workers' Compensation site. If you cannot reach this site through a keyword search, then go to their home page at www.ohiobwc.com. In the search box on this page enter "lifting guidelines" (without the quotes). You will need to poke around in the results until you locate the lifting guide. We found it by selecting the result labeled "OhioBWC— Employer (Safety Services)—Ergonomics," and on the resulting page we selected "Lifting guidelines" from the list of related links.

3. It you find a guide that allows you to enter criteria for a lift, such as that at the Ohio BWC site, make up a scenario, enter the data, and see the results it calculates.

Do Back Belts Help? We have all seen workers wearing *back belts*—those thick fabric belts worn snugly about the lower back, presumably to provide lumbar support while lifting. And sometimes this is a job requirement that you may not be able to avoid. However, the benefits of wearing a back belt when lifting or moving objects are questionable. In fact, several authorities say that back belts are not proven effective at preventing back injuries. In fact, the Centers for Disease Control and Prevention reports under Workplace Safety & Health Topics on their Website that studies published by NIOSH and the *Journal of the American Medical Association* state that no evidence was found that back belts reduce back injury or back pain for certain workers who lift or move objects.

Tips for Safe Lifting and Moving The best protection is common sense and very careful lifting. So, when lifting a heavy object, protect your back by following these tips:

■ Plan the move and clear the path before beginning.

- Move as close to the item as possible.
- Check the weight of the equipment to see if you need assistance in lifting and moving it.
- Keep your back straight and vertical to the floor.
- Keep your head up and look straight ahead.
- Do not stoop, but bend your knees.
- Carry the item close to your body.
- Tighten abdominal muscles to help your back.
- Use slow, smooth movements, and do not twist your back while lifting.
- Don't try to carry heavy items farther than a few feet without the aid of a utility cart, such as the one shown in Figure 1-5.

Watch Out for Sharp Edges   Whenever handling computer components, be very careful of the sharp edges on sheet metal computer cases and in some peripherals.

FIGURE 1-5

A utility cart is handy for moving computer equipment.

It is very easy to cut yourself on these. Similarly, the backs of many circuit boards contain very sharp wire ends that can cause puncture wounds. Work gloves offer protection, even if they are a bit awkward to use while handling delicate computer equipment. If you cannot wear gloves, be very cautious, checking each surface before positioning your hands.

Protecting the Equipment

While personal safety is paramount, you are also responsible for protecting the equipment you handle. Therefore, power down each piece of equipment and disconnect it from power outlets before moving it—even when moving it from one side of a desk to another. This includes laptops! Yes, they are portable devices, but if a computer has a conventional hard-disk drive, moving it around while it is actively running can harm the hard drive.

Do not just flip the power switch, but select Shut Down from the Windows Start menu. After the computer turns off, unplug the power cord. You may question always unplugging a device before moving it—even from one side of a desk to another, but we have seen too many instances in which a connected power cord caused personal injury or damage to other things. You simply are not in complete control of a device when it is still tethered to the wall.

Be very careful when moving displays—whether cathode ray tubes (CRTs) or flat panel displays. Both types are fragile, and you must take care not to drop a display or put any pressure on the front of it.

Other devices require special handling when moving them. If you are unsure of the proper way to move a computer or peripheral, check out the documentation. For instance, in order to protect fragile components, a scanner may have a transportation lock that you must engage before moving it.

Hot Components

When you open up a computer or printer, be very careful to not touch hot components or let anything else touch them because some components, such as a CPU heat sink and a printer's fusion roller, remain hot enough to burn you for several minutes after powering them down. Cautiously check for hot components by holding your hand near, but not on, computer components before you touch them.

Electrical Safety

Both high voltage and low voltage can be dangerous, so be sure to follow precautions when working around high- and low-voltage devices, and avoid contact with them.

High Voltage

Leave servicing high-voltage peripherals such as CRT monitors, laser printers, and power supplies to technicians trained in that area. Even when unplugged for an extended period, such devices can store enough voltage to cause severe injury or death from electrical shock. Never use an electrostatic discharge (ESD) wristband or other antistatic equipment (discussed later in this chapter) when working with high-voltage devices.

Low Voltage

Although high voltage is obviously dangerous, low voltage, under certain circumstances, can also cause serious injury or death. People have died from electrical injuries involving as little as 50 volts! Many variables determine the amount of damage electric shock can cause to a victim. These include (but are not limited to) the body's resistance or lack of resistance to the current, the path of the current through the body, and how long the body is in contact with the electrical current.

If the skin offers little electrical resistance (if it is wet, for instance), it may appear undamaged, although internal organs might be damaged. If the skin, due to dryness, thickness, or a combination of characteristics, offers greater resistance, it may burn badly but internal organs may not be damaged.

Remember that both high voltage and low voltage can cause serious injuries and even death. Lack of external burns on a person who has had an electric shock does not necessarily mean that the injury is minor.

Electrostatic Discharge (ESD)

One of the most prevalent threats to a computer component is *electrostatic discharge (ESD)*, also known as static electricity, or simply, static. Static is all around us, especially when both the humidity and the temperature are low. When putting on a jacket makes the hair on your arm stand up, you are encountering static electricity. When you slide your feet across a carpet and then touch a person, a doorknob, or a light switch and feel a jolt, you are experiencing a static discharge.

The Dangers of ESD

ESD happens when two objects of uneven electrical charge encounter one another. Electricity always travels from an area of higher charge to an area of lower charge, and the static shock that you feel is the result of electrons jumping from your skin to the other object. The same process can occur within a computer. If your body has a high electric potential, electrons will transfer to the first computer component that you touch.

Electrostatic discharge can cause irreparable damage to your computer's components and peripherals. Typical ESD discharges range from 600 to 25,000 volts, although at tiny amperages. Most computer components can safely withstand voltages of ±12 volts, so damage to computer components can occur at as little as 30 volts—a charge you will not even detect because, under the right conditions, your body can withstand 25,000 volts.

on the
job

Do not count on the body's ability to withstand 25,000 volts. This ability depends on the right circumstances. Learn more about this in the next section.

These very low-voltage static charges, or "hidden ESD," can come from many sources, including dust buildup inside a computer. Dust and other foreign particles can hold an electric charge that slowly bleeds into nearby components. This hidden ESD can cause serious problems because you will have no hint of trouble until damage has occurred and the component malfunctions. This damage is very difficult to pinpoint.

ESD can cause the immediate, catastrophic malfunction of a device, or it can cause a gradually worsening problem in a device—a process called degradation. As unlikely as it might seem, degradation damage can be more costly in lost work time and in troubleshooting and repair time than catastrophic damage. When a device suffers catastrophic damage, typically the result is immediate and obvious, so you will know to replace it right away. Degradation, on the other hand, can cause a component to malfunction sporadically, sometimes working and sometimes not. This makes pinpointing the cause harder, and the problem will persist for a longer period and be more disruptive to the user and to the support professional.

Additionally, a total failure of one component will typically not affect the usability of other components. However, degradation can cause a component to fail in ways that also result in the failure of other components.

exam

Watch *Most static discharges are well above 600 volts, but it takes a charge of only about 30 volts to destroy a computer component.*

Protection from ESD Damage and Injury

There are many ways to prevent ESD from damaging computer equipment. First, low humidity contributes to ESD; therefore, when possible, keep computer equipment in a room in which the humidity is between 50 and 80 percent. Avoid cold and dry (below 50 percent humidity) conditions, as that creates the ideal environment for ESD to occur. But do not allow the humidity to rise above 80 percent, or condensation could form on the equipment and cause it to short out.

To prevent damage to the system, you must equalize the electrical charge between your body and the components inside your computer. Touching a grounded portion of your computer's chassis will work to some extent, but for complete safety, use an *ESD wrist strap* with a ground wire attached to the computer frame. See Figure 1-6 showing an ESD wrist strap with an alligator clip for attaching the ground wire to a grounded object. This will drain static charges from your body to ground. If a static charge has built up in the computer equipment, it will also bleed from the computer through your body to ground. This is true of any electrical flow; therefore, you must never use an antistatic strap attached to your body when working around high-voltage devices.

> **exam**
> **⚙atch** *Remember that the ideal humidity range for a room containing computer equipment is between 50 and 80 percent.*

FIGURE 1-6

An ESD wrist strap with grounding wire and alligator clip

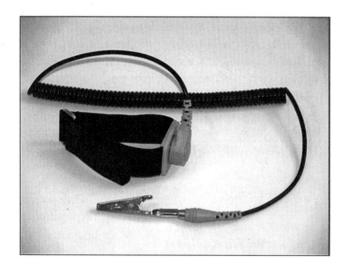

on the Job

Avoid severe electric shock caused by misuse of an ESD device. Never use one of these devices in a manner that puts your body between a power source and ground, such as when working around high-voltage devices.

Many computer assembly and repair shops use an *ESD mat* that discharges static when you stand on it. Similarly, an ESD mat on the bench table is a safe place to put expansion cards or other internal components that you have removed from the computer. An ESD mat looks like a vinyl placemat, but it has a wire lead and (usually) an alligator clip to connect it to ground.

Before you pick up a loose computer component, if you are not wearing or touching an antistatic device, discharge any static electricity on your body by touching something metal, such as a table leg or chair. Equipment placed on the mat will discharge static through it. All of these ESD devices usually have cables that you must attach to a grounded metal object. Some have a single prong that you insert into the ground socket in a regular self-grounding wall outlet. In the United States and Canada, the ground socket is the single round socket offset from the two slender blade sockets. Other cables on ESD wrist or ankle straps or on ESD mats may use alligator clips for making this attachment. Components like memory sticks and adapter cards may come in antistatic packaging, often an antistatic bag, and you should store used components in antistatic bags if their original packaging is not available. Do not remove the item from the packaging or bag until you are prepared to install it, and never place it on top of its antistatic packaging, since the outside does not offer protection.

In addition to the ESD/antistatic products mentioned in this section, there are others, including gloves, finger cots, labels, cleaners, bins, meters, and spray. Exercise 1-2 will lead you through the process of protecting your workspace and computer from ESD damage using some of these products.

EXERCISE 1-2

ESD-Proofing Your Workspace

Whether your workspace is a cubicle or desk at which you do minor repairs, or a computer workbench where you do more extensive service on computers and peripherals, follow these simple steps to ESD-proof your workspace:

1. Maintain the room's humidity between 50 percent and 80 percent.
2. Spray your clothing and the work area with antistatic spray. Never spray directly on the computer, its components, printers, or scanners.

3. Place an ESD mat on the workspace and attach its alligator clip to something stationary and metal, such as the leg of a table.

4. Remove all jewelry, including rings.

5. Put an ESD strap around your wrist, and attach the other end to a stationary metal object (if it has an alligator clip) or plug it into a wall outlet's ground socket (only if the grounding strap has an outlet prong).

Electromagnetic Interference (EMI)

Another problem related to electricity is *electromagnetic interference (EMI)*, which is the disruption of signal transmission caused by the radiation of electrical and magnetic fields. Equipment such as electric motors, high-voltage transformers, electrical panels, and fluorescent lights are sources of EMI. The EMI from these devices can temporarily interfere with the functioning of computer equipment, such as older CRT monitors. EMI interference will cause a CRT to have a jittery or distorted picture, but removing the source of the interference, or moving the monitor, will cause the picture to return to normal. The biggest problem with EMI is that it can disturb the transmission of data over copper wires, such as Ethernet cables.

Putting magnetic business cards and refrigerator magnets on a computer is highly risky. Remember, a traditional hard drive's read/write head is actually a tiny electromagnet that writes magnetic information on a magnetic surface, so erasing data by putting a magnet near it is easy. Keep magnets away from computers!

e x a m
᙭atch
Do not be confused by the similarity in the names: ESD can damage or destroy hardware, whereas EMI usually causes temporary problems and is more dangerous to data than to hardware.

Similarly, devices such as cordless phones and microwave ovens can cause radio frequency interference (RFI), described in Chapter 16), and can disrupt network communications.

Working Safely with Power Supplies

The power stored in the capacitors in a computer's high-voltage power supply is enough to cause injury or death. Simply turning off the power switch is not enough.

Even when turned off, the power supply in a computer or printer can provide electricity, and most motherboards continue to have power applied—a technology called soft power that we describe in Chapter 5. To be safe, unplug the power supply and never wear an ESD wrist strap when replacing or handling a power supply. Also, never open a power supply.

on the job

Some technicians prefer to leave the power supply plugged in while they work on the computer to allow static to bleed away from the computer into the wall outlet's ground wire. However, we do not recommend this; safer methods are available for removing static, such as placing the computer on an ESD mat.

Display Devices

Although flat-panel displays have largely replaced CRT monitors, there are still many CRTs out in the real world and you may well have to work with them. Remember—like power supplies, CRT monitors are high-voltage equipment and can store a harmful electrical charge, even when unplugged. Never open a CRT case, and never wear a wrist strap when handling a CRT. You do not want to provide a path to ground through your body for this charge.

Printers

Printers have many moving parts, so you need to follow several basic safety procedures whenever you work with or around a printer. Do not allow long hair, clothing, jewelry, or other objects near the moving parts of a printer, because of the danger of their being entangled in the moving parts, including feed or exit rollers. In particular, a necktie or scarf itself may build up a static charge that it can pass to the component if it touches it. When wearing a tie or scarf, make sure you either tuck it into your shirt or use some kind of clip or tie tack. Figure 1-7 shows an open printer and the cartridge assembly, which rapidly moves back and forth when operating.

exam

watch *Power supplies and CRT monitors are high-voltage equipment. Never open them, and never wear an antistatic strap while working with either of these components.*

Furthermore, do not try to operate a printer with the cover off. The cartridge in an inkjet printer, and the print head in a dot matrix printer, move rapidly back and forth across the page, and getting your hands or other objects caught is possible, damaging both you and the printer. The laser beam in a laser printer can cause eye damage. Fortunately, most printers do not work when their covers are open.

FIGURE 1-7

Keep loose clothing and jewelry away from open printers.

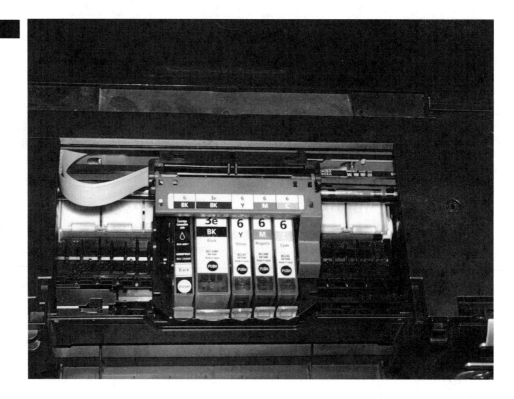

The fusion assembly and the power supply pose the two biggest dangers associated with working with a laser printer. Avoid touching the fusing roller in a laser printer because it can be hot enough to burn. Power down a laser printer and allow it to cool off before opening it. Laser printers also use both high-voltage and low-voltage/ high-current power supplies. Make sure you power off and unplug the laser printer before opening it. See Figure 1-8.

Compressed Air

You can use compressed air to clean dirt and dust out of computers, as described in Chapter 11. When using canned compressed air to blow dust out of computers and peripherals, take care to keep the can upright while spraying and avoid tilting or turning the can upside down because the liquid gas that forces the air out may spill and cause freeze burns on your skin and/or damage components. Never use compressed air from an air compressor because the pressure is too high and it can damage delicate components.

Additionally, when you use compressed air to clean anything, you should wear eye protection and even a filter mask to keep from inhaling dust and getting airborne particles in your eyes. Figure 1-9 shows these items, ready to use.

FIGURE 1-8

A laser printer with the toner cartridge removed, showing the potentially very hot fusion area deep in the back

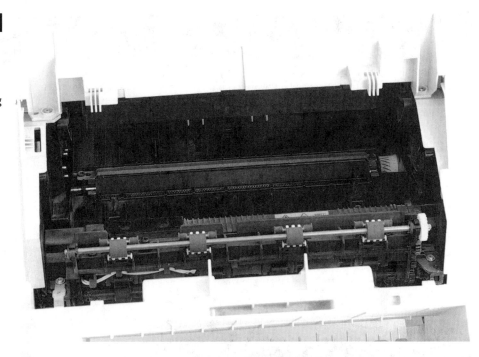

FIGURE 1-9

A can of compressed air, eye protection, and a filter mask

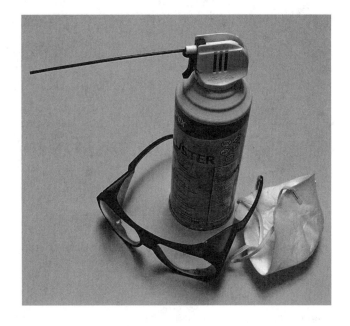

SCENARIO & SOLUTION

I need to remove a Phillips-head screw from a computer case, but I don't have a Phillips-head screwdriver that will fit. I would like to try a flat-bladed screwdriver. Should I do it?	Don't use a flat-bladed screwdriver in a Phillips-head screw unless it is an emergency. To avoid damaging the screw or the computer, wait until you can obtain the correct tool.
Since a laptop is portable, is there any reason why I should not move it from desk to desk while it is operating?	A laptop's portability does not apply when it is up and running with the hard drive spinning. Before moving any PC, even a laptop, select Shut Down within Windows. After the computer turns off, unplug the power cord.
We have excellent climate control in our computer server room and equipment closet, but the manager prefers to keep the setting very cool and with a humidity level below 50 percent. Is this OK?	Such very low humidity levels create a perfect environment for ESD. At the very least, the manager should adjust the climate controls so that the humidity is above 50 percent, and raise the temperature to a comfortable level for employees.

CERTIFICATION OBJECTIVE

■ *801: 5.2 Explain environmental impacts and the purpose of environmental controls*

The A+ candidate must prove knowledge of the dangers posed by inappropriate disposal of computer equipment and chemical solvents that contain materials hazardous to the environment. Similarly, the A+ exams will test your knowledge of how to discover proper disposal methods in your community.

Environmental Concerns for IT Professionals

As an IT professional, you will be concerned with the environment of the workplace and its effect on the health of people and equipment. Earlier, we detailed the issues of safety in the workplace, which is just one part of addressing your workplace environment. Next we will look at protecting people and equipment from the airborne particles generated by manufacturing or computer equipment, and then we will examine proper disposal of computer waste without causing a negative impact on the environment.

Working in a Harsh Environment

Computers and peripherals, as well as the people who use and support them, often operate in harsh work environments that can negatively affect both the equipment and the people. These workplaces can be too hot, too cold, dusty, dirty, and noisy. Further, some worksites do not have the reliable, consistent power computers require. Now we'll look at measures you can take to protect people and equipment from problematic work environments.

Providing the Proper Environment for Equipment

Extremes of heat, humidity, and airborne particles are damaging to computers and peripherals. To find the actual temperature and humidity extremes listed in the user or technical manual for a PC or component, look under "Operating Environment." A recommended operating environment is in the range of 50 to 90 degrees Fahrenheit (10 to 32 degrees Centigrade) with relative humidity between 50 and 80 percent. A rough guideline: if you are not comfortable, the PC is not either.

Therefore, the best operating environment for computers is a climate-controlled room with a filtration system to control these three enemies of electronics. However, since this is not always possible, consider an appropriate enclosure or case that will provide better ventilation and filtration.

Providing Good Power

Matching power requirements for equipment with power distribution is important. Therefore, ensure a power supply in a computer can handle the requirements of the components it supplies. Learn more in the discussion of power supplies, electrical terminology, and power requirements for PC components in Chapter 5, and learn about power requirements for laptops in Chapter 7.

When you consider a proper environment for computer equipment, you must also think of the power it receives. Therefore, you should never plug critical equipment into a wall outlet without some provision to protect it from the vagaries of the power grid. While sags in power below the 115 V U.S. standards can cause your computer to reboot or power off, a power surge can do significant damage. A *power surge* is a brief, potentially damaging increase in the amount of electrical power. A simple power strip offers no protection because it is nothing more than an extension cord with several power outlets. At a minimum, use a surge protector to protect all computer equipment, including modems and phone and cable lines.

Surge Protectors   At first glance, a *surge protector* (also called a *surge suppressor*) may look like an ordinary power strip, but it protects equipment from power surges. Your PC's power supply will also do this for small power fluctuations above the 115 V U.S. standard, but it will eventually fail if it is the first line of defense. Therefore, plug your PC into a surge protector that has a protection rating of more than 800 joules. (A joule is a unit of energy.) Look for a surge protector that carries the Underwriters Laboratories label showing that it complies with UL standard 1449; this is the least expensive power protection device.

on the
Job

To distinguish a surge protector from a simple power strip, look for the UL label showing a protection rating of more than 800 joules.

Beyond Surge Protectors   Do not just buy the minimum; buy the best power protection you can afford, which should include protection from power fluctuations, brownouts, and blackouts. *Power fluctuations* involve all sorts of inconsistencies in the delivery of electrical power—both too much (surges) and too little. A *brownout* is a period during which heavy demand or other problems cause a reduced flow of power, which can cause computers to behave erratically and suddenly power off. A *blackout* is a complete loss of power. The duration of a brownout or blackout depends on the cause and the ability of responsible parties, such as electrical utilities, to correct the problem. Blackouts can last hours or days, and your first concern related to a brownout or blackout is to have enough time to safely save your data and shut down your computer. The most common device that protects from power brownouts and blackouts while giving you time for these tasks is an *uninterruptible power supply (UPS)*. A UPS will also normally protect from power surges. A UPS is more expensive than a simple surge protector, but UPS prices have come down as more manufacturers have introduced consumer-level versions of these devices, such as the one shown in Figure 1-10. Notice the ports labeled Battery Backup and Surge Protection at the top and the ports labeled Surge Protection on the bottom. You would plug your computer and display into the Battery Backup ports and they will be doubly protected. Plug less critical equipment into the second type of port to protect it from surges only, not from power outages.

In order to select a UPS, first determine the power requirements in watts for each device you will connect to the UPS and add them up. Then decide how much time you would require to save your data when main power fails.

A computer or other device plugged into a UPS battery backup port is truly isolated from line power because during normal operation, the device runs directly

This type of UPS contains a battery backup that provides battery power for a limited period in the event of a power outage.

off the battery through an inverter, which takes the direct current (DC) power stored in the battery and converts it to 110 V, 60-cycle alternating current (AC) power. The battery is continually charging from line power, and when it loses line power, the battery continues to power the computer for a short period. The time the battery can power the computer is limited and varies by the capacity of the battery in the UPS and by how much power the computer draws. Unless line power comes back on quickly, you probably have a window of just minutes to save your data and to power down the computer. For this reason, a UPS device usually includes a data cable and software. Once the software is installed and the UPS senses a power outage, the software warns you to shut down. If no one is at the keyboard to respond, it will automatically save open data files, shut down the operating system, and power down the computer before the UPS itself runs out of battery power. A UPS is more expensive than a surge protector, but it gives excellent power protection.

on the job

In a real disaster, power can be off for days or weeks. If you work with mission-critical systems in certain industries, like banking and hospitals, the organization should have backup power generators that can kick in and provide power. Propane or diesel usually powers such generators.

Disposing of Computing Waste

Lead, mercury (including the mercury in laptop backlights), cadmium, chromium, brominated flame retardants, polychlorinated biphenyls (PCBs)—what do they all have in common? They are toxic to the environment and to humans if mishandled. They are widely used in electronics, including computers, printers, and monitors, so you must dispose of or recycle these items in the proper manner. You should never discard them directly into the trash where they will end up in landfills and potentially pollute the ground water.

In addition, electronics contain plastic, steel, aluminum, and precious metals—all of which are recoverable and recyclable. Provide containers in which to collect these components for proper sorting and disposal. Check with local agencies to ensure that you comply with local government regulations concerning disposal of all computer waste materials.

Manufacturers' Recycling Programs

Some computer companies, such as Dell and Hewlett-Packard (HP), and other electronics companies such as Nokia, are using more environmentally friendly components and working to recycle components from discarded computers. In fact, there is a relationship between these two activities. The more a manufacturer is involved in recycling the wastes from its products, the more changes that company makes to use more eco-friendly material. If companies don't use environmentally hazardous materials in electronic components in the first place, then the environment is in less danger. Manufacturers are a long way from eliminating hazardous materials from electronics, however, so we need to continue recycling for both hazardous and nonrenewable materials, such as gold, copper, and aluminum. In spite of efforts by several manufacturers to help users recycle computer components, estimates are that only 10 to 15 percent of electronics are recycled.

Batteries

Many batteries contain environmentally hazardous materials, such as lithium, mercury, or nickel and cadmium, so you cannot just put them in the trash where they will end up in a landfill. Many communities have special recycling depots that accept batteries so they do not introduce harmful elements into the environment; they may also periodically conduct hazardous material pickups in which you can hand over toxic materials, such as batteries and paint, for proper disposal.

Never store computer batteries for extended periods, and never leave batteries in equipment being stored for extended periods because battery casings are notorious for corroding, allowing the chemicals inside to leak or explode out. Leaking or exploding chemicals can cause a large mess within the equipment, destroy nearby components, and cause skin burns if you touch them.

Laser Printer Toner Cartridges

Laser printer toner cartridges contain the toner, which is the print medium for laser printers, and they often contain other components important to the printing process, such as the photosensitive drum. *Toner* is the medium for laser printers and is normally available packaged within a *toner cartridge*. The toner consists of very fine particles of clay combined with pigment and resin. Although the chemical makeup of laser toner may not be harmful, the super-fine powder of laser toner poses a hazard to your lungs. For this reason, be careful when cleaning up toner residue, using a damp cloth for any residue outside the printer, and a filtered vacuum (antistatic, if possible) when cleaning up spilled toner inside a printer that has been powered down and unplugged from a power source.

 o n   t h e
⊙ o b

When working with laser printers and handling toner cartridges, avoid breathing in the toner powder.

The cartridges for many laser printers also contain the cylindrical photosensitive drum, the cleaning blade, and other components that are also considered consumables, because you normally replace the entire cartridge together with its contents once the toner is gone. Therefore, you will need to dispose of many toner cartridges over the life of a laser printer.

Laser printer toner cartridges also provide a potential environmental hazard due in part to their large numbers and the space they can take up in a landfill. For this reason, you should not simply throw them away. Fortunately, most toner cartridges have reusable components. That is, many companies will buy back used toner cartridges, refill and recondition them (if necessary), and then resell them. Figure 1-11 shows a laser toner cartridge removed from a printer. Learn more about the laser printing process in Chapter 21.

Ink Cartridges

The most common color printers found in homes and offices are inkjet printers that use wet ink that comes in cartridges. These cartridges are reusable, or you can recycle them for the plastic and other materials they contain. A large number of

FIGURE I-II

A laser printer
toner cartridge

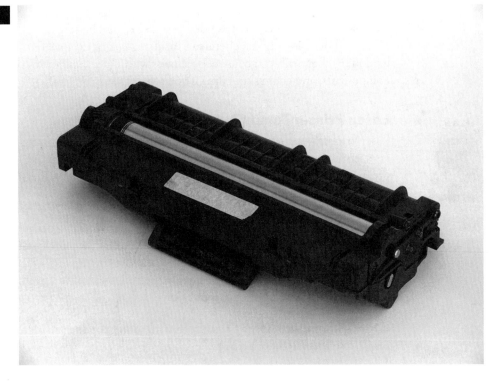

organizations accept used inkjet cartridges for recycling. Some, such as retailers, have collection containers for printer cartridges and other computer waste, and will give you credit toward new or recharged cartridges. Some organizations apply the profit from recycling the cartridges to some worthy cause. We use special preaddressed envelopers we received from a charity. Once we have enough to fill the envelope, we mail it in. It is easy to do this and it helps the environment as well as a charity of your choice. Do this with used cartridges, as well as those unused cartridges we often are left with after a printer fails and we discard it. Figure 1-12 shows print cartridges and a mailer for sending them in to a recycling center.

Display Devices

The two basic types of display devices are CRT and flat panel. CRT displays contain lead, which is toxic to the environment, but it is also a useful recyclable metal. Therefore, never throw CRTs in trash destined for a landfill. Always search for ways to recycle a CRT. Flat-panel displays, including those in laptop computers,

Used inkjet
cartridges ready
for recycling

use fluorescent lamps that contain toxic material, so these displays, too, must be recycled. Call your local waste disposal organization and arrange to drop CRTs and flat-panel displays off at its site. Many communities advertise locations and hours for these recycling services.

Chemical Solvents and Cans

All chemical solvents are potentially hazardous to the environment, so you must dispose of them properly. If you are unsure of the proper handling or disposal procedures for a chemical, look for its *material safety data sheet (MSDS)*. An MSDS is a standardized document that contains general information, ingredients, and fire and explosion warnings, as well as health, disposal, and safe transportation information about a particular product. Any manufacturer that sells a potentially hazardous product must issue an MSDS for it.

If an MSDS did not come with a particular chemical, contact the manufacturer or search for it on the Internet. A number of Websites contain large lists of MSDSs. There have been some major changes in these Websites. Therefore, if you wish to find an MSDS on a particular product or type of product, use a search engine with appropriate keywords, including MSDS and terms associated with the product.

Many communities collect solvents and paints and make them available for recycling. Residents can go to the recycling center and obtain the solvents or paints for free or at a reduced cost. Those solvents and paints deemed unsafe for recycling are disposed of properly. Look for a hazardous material pickup or depot in your area.

exam

ⓦatch   *Be sure you know the purpose of an MSDS and how to obtain one.*

Similarly, empty cans, including aerosol cans, should be disposed of in an appropriate manner. Contact your local waste disposal company for the proper handling and disposal of empty cans that once held solvents or other toxic materials. They may be as dangerous as their previous contents.

EXERCISE 1-3

Researching Recycling Centers

Research the recycling options in your community.

1. First, use the local phone book and look under the local government listings for recycling. List the center nearest your home here:_____.

2. Call the center and determine if it accepts the following items: computer monitors, chemicals, empty paint and solvent cans, circuit boards, old computers, or batteries.

3. Find out the days and times when the center accepts these items for recycling and list them here:_____.

4. Ask if the center has private home pick-up service for recycling, and ask how to arrange it.

5. Ask if the center has a business pick-up service for recycling, and ask how to arrange it.

SCENARIO & SOLUTION

You work for a new small business that is planning to create an equipment room to house their network servers, network connection devices, and cabling. Describe the temperature and humidity ranges that are generally safe for this equipment.	The recommended operating environment for computer equipment is in the range of 50 to 90 degrees Fahrenheit (10 to 32 degrees Centigrade) with relative humidity between 50 and 80 percent.
What may happen to a computer when power to it sags below the 115 V U.S. standard?	The computer may reboot or power off.
What documentation should a manufacturer provide that describes the proper disposal information for a chemical?	A material safety data sheet (MSDS) is a standardized document that contains general information, ingredients, and fire and explosion warnings, as well as health, disposal, and safe transportation information about a particular product.

CERTIFICATION OBJECTIVE

■ *801: 5.3*   *Given a scenario, demonstrate proper communication and professionalism*

CompTIA requires an A+ candidate to demonstrate knowledge of appropriate interpersonal communication skills and professionalism in the workplace. Real communication between people consists of both the verbal and nonverbal behavior that results in exchanging thoughts, messages, or information. Not only must you say the right words, but your body language must convey the same message as your words. Professionalism includes your behavior in all interactions, as well as how you treat property belonging to your employer and customers.

Professionalism and Proper Communication

You show professionalism on the job in the way you dress and behave, as well as in how you communicate with customers and colleagues. In this section, we'll explore the intertwined topics of professionalism and proper communication. In short, it isn't just what you say—it's how you say it and what you do while you are saying it.

Professionalism

Professionalism is a set of behaviors that each of us should use whether we are being observed or not. Many professions have a formal code of ethics that defines professionalism framed in the context of that profession. In this section, we will explore a general definition of professionalism for an IT worker, as it applies to behavior in dealing with others and in the treatment of property.

Professional Dress and Good Hygiene

Although not explicitly listed in the objectives for the A+ exams, good grooming, cleanliness, and proper dress are part of professional behavior. Wear freshly laundered clothes appropriate for the tasks required and that fit into your work environment. If you support computers for a group of attorneys, you may need to wear pressed slacks, shirt, and even a jacket. Tank tops are not appropriate in any office; skimpy clothes and flip flops are for picnics and the beach, not for work. Wear closed-toe shoes with nonskid soles. Even if your employer allows blue jeans, consider upgrading yourself to neatly pressed khakis to look a bit more professional.

exam Watch

Unfortunately, any job in which you provide a service involves encounters with difficult customers, so expect some scenario-based questions on the exam involving your response to such situations.

Respect toward Others—Even the Difficult Customer

Professional behavior is respectful and ethical. This includes being pleasant, reasonable, and positive in the face of the variety of events that can occur in the work environment, such as dealing with difficult customers or situations. Ethics includes how you react to a wide variety of situations.

Proper Language

Jargon is not necessarily bad—it is simply using words or acronyms, often technical and uncommon, that only people who share a common profession or interest understand. It is okay to use jargon when both parties understand it. It is not okay, or professional, to use jargon with people unfamiliar with it, such as the ordinary computer user you may encounter on the job, or nontechnical customers and coworkers. Similarly, be very careful to avoid common or vulgar slang expressions.

on the Job

Every single profession in the world has its own jargon. Because professions tend to be separate cultures, the use of jargon, abbreviations, acronyms, and slang among peers is generally acceptable, but do not let this spill over to your communications with people who are not part of your specific culture.

exam Watch

Listening without interruption may be the most important communication skill you can develop, and you should expect scenario-based questions that test how well you embrace this idea.

Listen and Do Not Interrupt

When a coworker or customer is explaining something to you—for example, when describing the symptoms of a problem, do not interrupt. Allow them to complete their statements. Do not jump to conclusions. If necessary, without interrupting, clarify customer statements by asking pertinent questions or restating your understanding in your own words. This shows that you are listening, and helps you to avoid making incorrect assumptions.

Get Acknowledgment

Frequently confirm that the customer understands what you are saying by asking questions like, "Does that make sense?" "Does that sound okay to you?" "Would you like to go through those steps while I am here?" Think of the conversation as a train, with you as the engineer. The customer is a passenger waiting on the platform; if you do not stop or slow down, the customer cannot get on the train, and you will find yourself at the destination, but the customer will still be back at the station. Slow down and confirm that he is on board before you race ahead with a technical explanation that would please your coworkers but bewilder the customer.

Deal Appropriately with Customers' Confidential Materials

Deal appropriately with customers' confidential materials using tact and discretion, two very important components of effective communication. *Tact* involves showing consideration for others. Tactful communication is more about what you do not say than what you do say. Take care to not offend, no matter what you may think of the other person or what your own situation is. Being discreet includes not revealing information about someone that would be harmful to or embarrass her.

People often see *discretion* and tact as synonyms, but there is a subtle difference between them. For instance, a tactful person avoids embarrassing or distressing another. But discretion assumes a measure of good judgment based on the situation. It doesn't matter whether your encounters with customers are face-to-face, by phone, or purely via electronic messages (e-mail, newsgroups, or messaging)—you must still use tact and discretion.

Be culturally sensitive. In today's world, you may be dealing with people from around the globe. A smart-aleck comment that may be amusing in your own culture may be very offensive to a person from another culture. Be cautious and tactful when dealing with people from other cultures.

Using Tact   Many times we have seen a customer who does not seem to understand the connection between the power switch and the computer, but still manages to figure out how to customize the Windows desktop with family photos on the background; customized pointers; and a desktop cluttered with dozens of files, folders, and shortcuts. Unless you are there specifically to help him clean up the desktop, stick to the purpose for the visit, and don't offer your opinion. This is using tact. After you have solved the technical problem, you might inquire if he has had end-user training on using the Windows desktop. If the answer is "Yes," then just drop the subject. If he lets you know that his own desktop actually bewilders him and he would like help cleaning it up and organizing his files, then you can go ahead and help him.

Using Discretion   Being discreet requires that you deal appropriately with confidential materials located on a customer's computer, desktop, printer, etc. Whatever you see on her desk or in her computer is her property, and to be discreet, you don't reveal it to anyone. Further, don't reveal unnecessary information to customers or coworkers. Gossiping about other people, company policies, or other proprietary information about the company is indiscreet. If the information would hurt or offend a third party or harm your company—keep it to yourself.

If you do not follow this advice and you divulge information you have no authority to share, you will find it difficult to build trust with other people. Even when someone seems to enjoy hearing the information, your behavior tells her that you are not trustworthy.

Be Cautious   Be careful with what you share with the customer. Sometimes technicians go too far in empathizing with the customer's plight and speak negatively about the equipment or software that the company pays you to support. The customer does not need to know that you think the printer the company bought for her is a poor one, or even that you dislike driving out to her office because of the terrible traffic conditions.

Avoid Arguing or Being Defensive   Avoid arguing with customers or coworkers, even if you feel the other person is being especially difficult. If you discover something that makes you angry, work to calm yourself before engaging about the problem. When others approach you angrily, stay calm and avoid becoming defensive. Resist falling into the payback trap of acting toward them the way they are acting toward you. These measured responses can defuse a potentially volatile situation.

Maintain a Positive Attitude   Work to maintain a positive attitude and tone of voice. A positive attitude takes practice and discipline; everyone has personal problems and challenges in their lives, along with all the job issues such as politics, personalities, work goals, and more. You need to literally compartmentalize your life. Hold an image in your mind such that when you are at work the other parts of your life are behind doors. Try to keep the doors to these other parts of your life closed when you are at work, and only open them at an appropriate time. When you become successful at this, you will find that you are more effective in all the areas of your life, because you can give each area the full attention it deserves at the appropriate time.

Do Not Minimize Others' Concerns   Never minimize another person's problems and concerns. You are minimizing when you interrupt an explanation or show through body language, such as a dismissive wave of the hand, that his concern is not important to you. Do not tell the customer about someone else who has a worse predicament—that is irrelevant to him. Imagine how you would feel if you could not get some work completed on time due to a computer problem, and while trying to explain your plight to a technician, she minimized or dismissed your concern as being unimportant.

You must also strike a balance between not minimizing and assuring the customer that you have an easy fix for the problem. An easy fix just means that you can solve the problem soon; it does not mean the customer has no reason to mourn the lost time, lost deadline, or loss of productivity.

Avoid Judgmental Behavior   Avoid being judgmental and/or insulting to anyone. Never resort to name-calling, which is damaging to any relationship and is completely unprofessional. For instance, if computer hardware and software fascinate you, you may find it difficult to be patient with those people who cannot seem to understand or even care how a computer works, and who frequently need help with hardware or software. It is just a small baby step to behaving judgmentally toward the customer.

Confidentiality and Respect for Privacy   When interacting with people, we learn things about one another; some of what we learn is personal, and we should not share it with others. Being professional includes knowing when to keep your mouth shut; this includes both company matters and someone's personal life. Being discreet shows respect for the privacy of others. Keeping such information to yourself helps you gain the trust of your coworkers and customers. Of course, being respectful of someone's privacy, you do not try to gain personal information, but sometimes you learn it inadvertently. However you learn such information, keep it to yourself.

Even if your organization does not formally provide a privacy policy, you should have your own personal policy that should be part of your personal standards of behavior.

Avoid Distractions

Distractions reduce your productivity and value as an employee. Some jobs are filled with distractions—ringing phones, conversations, music, construction noise, traffic noise, and more. Many distractions are unavoidable, but you can control some distractions, and how you control them is a measure of your professionalism. Personal calls, personal interruptions, and talking to coworkers while helping customers are distractions you must avoid because they show disrespect.

Personal Calls   Because you can only make personal calls, such as calls to your doctor or child's school during normal business hours when doctors have hours and schools are open, if your workplace permits these, don't abuse the privilege. Keep them very short. Unless your employer has a rule permitting personal long-distance phone calls, do not spend company time and resources making them.

Talking to Coworkers   A productive work environment normally involves a community of people who treat each other professionally and work as a team. Therefore, in most jobs, you will have frequent conversations with coworkers—on both personal and professional topics. Personal discussion with coworkers should not occur within earshot of customers. When you are talking to a customer, he should have your full attention. The only excuse for a side conversation is if it concerns solving the customer's problem, and you should even do that outside the customer's hearing if possible. The best rule is not to talk to coworkers while interacting with customers.

Personal Interruptions   Personal interruptions come in many forms, such as personal calls, leaving the office during working hours for personal business, a family member or friend visiting the workplace, and attending to personal business in any way during work hours. Try especially hard to avoid these while helping a customer. Avoid personal interruptions as much as possible, and when such an interruption is necessary, be sure to minimize its impact on the customer by keeping it very brief and don't extend its effect by sharing details of the interruption with the customer.

Set and Meet Expectations

Many things, both actual and perceived, influence a customer's expectations. Your company may set expectations by describing your department and/or job function and the services it will provide to customers. This expectation exists even before you answer the customer's call or walk into their office.

Beyond that, you control the expectations—either consciously or unconsciously. Be aware of ways in which you do this. If a customer makes an unreasonable demand, do not simply smile without comment. This sets the expectation that you will deliver according to his demand. If you must disappoint, do it as soon as possible, so a simple disappointment doesn't turn into the perception that you broke a commitment—perceived or otherwise.

Control expectations, beginning with the expectation that you will be on time. If delayed, be sure to contact the customer, apologize, and provide a reliable estimate of when you will arrive. Then, once you have determined what the problem is, be sure to give the customer your best and most honest estimate of the timeline for solving the problem. When possible, offer different repair or replacement options because they give the customer a sense of control of a situation.

At the conclusion of a service call or visit, provide the customer with proper documentation on the services you provided. Sit down with the customer and review all that you did. If appropriate, have her sign a receipt confirming the work you performed.

Follow up with each customer later to verify satisfaction. This is important because people don't always tell you when they are not happy, and a quick phone call or e-mail might alert you to their dissatisfaction and give you a chance to rectify the situation.

SCENARIO & SOLUTION

How can I avoid a confrontation when someone else shows anger toward me?	Try to stay calm, avoid becoming defensive, and do not reciprocate the anger.
I try to put customers' concerns into perspective for them by telling them about others who are worse off. Is this a good practice?	No, this is not a good practice because the customers will believe (rightly so) that you are minimizing their concerns.
If the company gives me a laptop to take home, do I have the right to use it for personal purposes?	No. Unless you have an unusual arrangement, you are to use the laptop given to you by the company for business purposes only. Using it for personal purposes is unprofessional.
I get very bored with talking to customers at the front counter, and I find that I can pick up my e-mail while listening to a customer's description of a problem. My boss has told me not to do this. Why is that?	This behavior is inappropriate for many reasons. Just one is that you are not showing the customer respect by letting him know that you are listening. And you may miss important information if you do not use active listening techniques.
I enjoy sharing information about office politics and unannounced changes in company policy. My boss has reprimanded me for this, but people seem to enjoy listening. Why is doing this a problem?	This behavior is inappropriate for many reasons. At the very least, revealing this information shows a lack of discretion and does not engender trust in you, even though people may seem to enjoy hearing the information.

CERTIFICATION OBJECTIVE

■ **801: 5.4** *Explain the fundamentals of dealing with prohibited content/activity*

The A+ exam will test your knowledge of the general concepts surrounding prohibited content in the workplace and how you, as an IT professional, should handle the discovery of prohibited activity.

Dealing with Prohibited Content and Prohibited Activities

Access to the Internet gives you access to the world with all its imperfections. Similarly, access to a corporate network gives you access to all types of content owned and managed by the corporation. As an IT professional, you need to be aware of issues related to the types of content available on the Internet, and, on a smaller scale, on a corporate network and local computers. In the following, we will discuss prohibited content and activities, and the government agencies and institutions that define and combat them. Then we will look at what you need to know about how you should respond on the job to discovery of prohibited content or activities.

Defining Prohibited Content and Behavior

Prohibited content is any content that an organization or government deems is harmful to the institution in general and to all persons or a class of persons for which it is responsible. An example of a class of persons is children, who can be harmed by content deemed pornographic or violent. In the case of an organization, the persons for whom this content is defined may be their employees, customers, or members. For a government, it covers their citizens and anyone who enters the country or, in the case of the Internet, communicates over the Internet.

Censorship
When any person or organization decides to define prohibited content, as well as restrict access to that content, they are employing *censorship*.

Slander and Libel

However, prohibited content does not just cover content of a sexual or violent nature. It also includes slanderous or libelous content. Both slander and libel are content that is malicious, false, and defamatory, and that can ruin the reputation of an individual or organization. By law, *slander* occurs when such statements are verbal. *Libel* occurs when such statements are in writing or printed words or pictures, and includes such published statements in any media, such as Internet sites and newspapers.

National and Corporate Secrets

Another class of prohibited content is secrets crucial to the well-being of a nation or organization. National security relies on a great deal of information that the general public cannot access. There are many laws involved in classifying secret information, protecting it, and defining punishable behavior, such as sharing this information with someone who does not have the appropriate clearance.

Similarly, corporations, by law, must protect their employees' and customers' personal information as well as a large list of categories that come under the heading of trade secrets. These include, but are not limited to, manufacturing processes, research and development of new products, and financial plans. Therefore, government agencies and corporations have guidelines, usually in the form of a policy manual that defines prohibited content and prohibited behavior.

So, no matter where you work, as an IT professional, you will need to be aware of what constitutes prohibited content and prohibited behavior in your organization, and what you are expected to do about it.

Policies Concerning Prohibited Content and Behavior

While governments have laws concerning prohibited content and behavior, most organizations have, or should have, documents defining how laws and the corporations' rules apply to employees and what they must do to comply. These may fall under a set of organizational policies and procedures, security policies, or both. Such policies vary by organization, but should cover certain areas and define prohibited behavior.

Acceptable-Use Policy

An *acceptable-use policy* is a security policy that defines what actions can be taken on data and computing resources, including—but not limited to—storing, accessing, deleting, disseminating, and sharing of that data through computers and networks.

Such policy must comply with all applicable laws as well as the policies and rules of the organization. An acceptable-use policy normally defines how acceptable use is managed, ownership of data, what acceptable use is for various types of data and computing resources, and what incidental use of computing resources (e-mail, Internet access, fax machines, printers, copiers, etc.) is allowed for employees for personal use. We'll discuss some of the topics you should expect to find in an acceptable-use policy.

Management of Acceptable Use   In defining how acceptable use is managed, the policy will define who is responsible for defining and maintaining this policy, who is responsible for training and educating employees about the acceptable-use policy, who is responsible for establishing a formal review cycle for the acceptable-use policy, and the initiatives that result from it.

Further, the acceptable-use policy will define an incident-report policy describing to whom employees should report any prohibited activity, what proof is needed to substantiate the claim, and what methods should be used to make a report.

Classification and Ownership of Data   An acceptable-use policy should define classes of data, depending on the type of organization. Confidential data is often organized into categories, such as patient medical data, patient/customer financial data, product data, research data, and many others.

An acceptable-use policy usually defines ownership of all data created and stored on the organization's computer systems as belonging to the organization. It also will state that, as part of managing acceptable use, designated employees have the right to monitor and/or log all employee use of such data and may access all such data stored at any time without employee knowledge.

Acceptable-Use Requirements and Behavior   An acceptable-use policy will also define the behavior of employees expected as part of acceptable use. This is usually a long list of requirements as well as prohibited behaviors. For instance, it will require that employees report any indication of a problem with computer security to the appropriate support staff. This includes unusual system behavior that could indicate a security threat. Employees are also required to report incidents of possible misuse or violation of the policy through the processes defined in the acceptable-use policy and to the appropriate staff. Other stipulations of an acceptable-use policy will prohibit users from sharing their user accounts (network, e-mail, and others) and related passwords, personal identification numbers (PINs), smartcards and similar

Remember that your first response to prohibited behavior should be to identify the behavior, report through proper channels, and preserve the data (logs, etc.) or devices containing evidence of the prohibited behavior.

security tokens, and other means of accessing accounts. Some organizations define a separate e-mail policy for employees, while others may combine these policies to include all user accounts.

Incidental Use   If incidental use of the organization's computer resources is allowed, the policy will define that use and most certainly will stipulate that the use must not result in any direct cost, legal action against, or embarrassment to the organization. Further, the acceptable use must not interfere with normal performance of the employee's job.

Educating Employees on Policies and Procedures

Organizations use a range of methods to educate employees on policies and procedures. These include documents, such as an employee handbook, which may serve as an introduction to policies and procedures, as well as a reference. A new employee may have to sign a receipt and acknowledgement document stating that they received the handbook and have read and understand the content.

Ongoing training is also important for educating employees about policies and procedures, especially in an organization, such as a hospital or clinic, which comes under strict laws concerning patients' confidentiality. Further, an organization may require that employees sign confidentiality and nondisclosure documents.

Additionally, some organizations will post signs reminding employees of required behavior, as well as informing customers/patients of their part in preserving their confidential data. For instance, we are all familiar with the signs in pharmacies requesting that clients line up an adequate distance from the pharmacy window to give others privacy while discussing and purchasing prescriptions.

Responding to the Discovery of Prohibited Content and/or Behavior

So, what should you do when you become aware of prohibited behavior? Perhaps you discover confidential patient information displayed on the screen of an unattended PC against company policy, or you find evidence of a coworker's access to a known pornographic Website on their work PC. The answer is, "It all depends." Let's look at the three components of a first response to the two scenarios presented here.

Once you have clearly identified prohibited behavior, your first response will depend on the actual behavior as well as the company's policies and procedures. The three parts to a first response are 1) identify the behavior as one described in policies, 2) report it to proper channels, and 3) preserve the proof in the form of the data and the device on which it is stored.

Identify the Problem

Identify the problem by asking yourself if it is truly a case of inappropriate behavior. In the case of the unattended PC with confidential patient information, this is inappropriate behavior, but you may need to determine if any harm has been done, and how you react also depends on the urgency of the situation and if harm has actually been done. Are unauthorized persons within viewing range of the computer screen? If so, then do whatever you can to change the screen content to hide such information. Is the responsible employee nearby? If so, then call it to that person's attention and have it corrected. Once you have identified that inappropriate behavior has occurred, you need to comply with company policies and procedures to determine if you are required to report the problem.

Report through Proper Channels

In the case of finding clear evidence of, or upon witnessing a coworker's access to prohibited content, you are required as an IT professional to report the incident through proper channels as defined in the organization's policies and procedures documents.

Maintain Chain of Custody

Because such reporting can result in consequences to the employee, as an IT professional you will need to preserve and track evidence of the improper or even illegal behavior and present it to the proper person. It must be clear who has had access to the evidence, even digital evidence. This record of who has access or possession of evidence is called the chain of custody, and you will need to follow the procedures described in the policies and procedures documents. Someone—maybe you—must be responsible for tracking the evidence and documenting the entire process.

Data/Device Preservation

Take steps to carefully preserve any data or device involved in the use of prohibited content; that includes capturing data that proves prohibited behavior. The steps you take will depend on the location of this data and/or device. If the data was stored on a local PC, you may need to remove the PC and store it in a secure location. If the incriminating data is stored on a network server, you may need to find a way to protect the data and leave it unaltered on the server, at the same time ensuring that no unauthorized person has access to it.

Use of Documentation and Documentation Changes

Accusing someone of breaking a law or violating company policies can have serious consequences and you should not take it lightly. Therefore, you will need to document your observations that resulted in the accusation. This may require that you write a few simple statements or it may require that you fill out forms. Whatever the case, when documenting any prohibited behavior, be sure to avoid expressing personal opinion and conjecture. Simply state what you observed.

SCENARIO & SOLUTION	
You suspect that another employee is involved in prohibited activities. What should you do?	If all you have is a suspicion, you really cannot take action. Wait until you have proof.
You are unsure what is defined as prohibited content and prohibited behavior regarding the use of computer equipment in your organization. How can you learn more?	Go to a supervisor and tell her of your concern. Most organizations have manuals defining acceptable-use policy and also offer training to all employees.
Your company has a searchable policy document defining acceptable use. What term should you search to discover what actions you must take in order to file a claim against an employee for prohibited behavior?	Search on "incident report" or similar language in order to find to whom you report, what proof is needed, and the procedures required to file a claim.

CERTIFICATION SUMMARY

This chapter explored operational procedures, first by examining appropriate safety and environmental procedures, and then by detailing the use of communication skills and professionalism in the workplace. Safety in an organization is everyone's responsibility. Always be aware of potential safety hazards and practice safe equipment handling to protect both yourself and equipment. Always dispose of computer components properly. Handle components carefully when you store them. Keep them out of hot or damp places, and keep magnetic storage devices away from EMI-emitting devices.

Candidates for an A+ certificate must understand the communication skills required for success on the job. This includes listening and communicating clearly while employing tact and discretion with all interpersonal contacts. Be conscious of your body language to ensure that your words and actions are not sending conflicting messages.

You should understand what your organization and all applicable laws define as prohibited content and prohibited activity. Know how to respond to an instance of use of prohibited content or prohibited activity, including how to report it through proper channels, how to preserve the data or devices involved, how to document it, and the proper chain of custody for the evidence.

TWO-MINUTE DRILL

Here are some of the key points covered in Chapter 1.

Workplace Safety and Safe Equipment Handling

❑ Organize cables to avoid tripping hazards, and use each appropriate repair tool only for its intended purpose.

❑ Learn about fire safety, including the types of possible fire fuels and the appropriate fire extinguisher to use for each.

❑ Protect your back when lifting and moving equipment by following published guidelines for what and how to safely lift.

❑ Turn off all equipment and disconnect the power cord before moving it, even laptops. Moving any computer while powered up could damage the hard drive(s).

❑ Avoid touching hot components, even after powering the equipment off.

❑ Do not try to service high-voltage peripherals, such as CRTs, laser printers, and power supplies.

❑ Do not use an ESD wristband when working with high-voltage devices.

❑ Both high-voltage and low-voltage devices can cause serious injury or death under certain circumstances.

❑ Electrostatic discharge (ESD) can cause damage to equipment, and low humidity contributes to ESD.

❑ Use ESD devices (ESD wrist straps, ESD mats, and antistatic bags) when working with and storing computer equipment, especially internal components.

❑ Electromagnetic interference (EMI) usually causes temporary problems and is more of a danger to data than to equipment.

❑ Once removed from a computer, a component is susceptible to damage unless it is properly stored to protect it from ESD and extremes of heat, cold, and humidity.

❑ Take extra precautions when working with a printer because long hair, loose clothing, and jewelry can catch in the moving parts or pass ESD to the printer.

❑ Do not try to operate a printer with the cover off.

Environmental Concerns for IT Professionals

❑ You need to be aware of the workplace environment and its effect on the health of people and equipment.

❑ Use a climate-controlled environment whenever possible for both people and equipment.

❑ If you cannot maintain a good working environment for equipment, consider using an appropriate enclosure or case that will provide better ventilation and filtration.

❑ The power a computer receives is also part of its working environment. Use equipment to protect crucial equipment from power fluctuations. A surge protector with a rating of 800 joules or better is the least expensive protection from power surges.

❑ An uninterruptible power supply (UPS) protects from power fluctuations, brownouts, and blackouts.

❑ Toxic metals and chemicals used in computers and peripherals include mercury, cadmium, chromium, brominated flame-retardants, and polychlorinated biphenyls (PCBs).

❑ When a computer or component reaches the end of its useful life, dispose of it appropriately for proper handling of the toxic and reusable components.

Showing Professionalism and Communicating Properly

❑ Professionalism is a set of behaviors that you should do whether you are being observed or not.

❑ Always practice tact and discretion in interactions with other people.

❑ Professional behavior is respectful and includes having a positive attitude, avoiding confrontation or having a judgmental attitude, and never minimizing others' concerns.

❑ When you are respectful, you are attentive and you respect confidentiality and privacy.

Dealing with Prohibited Content or Activities

❏ Prohibited content is any content that an organization or government deems is harmful to the institution in general and to all persons, or a certain class of persons, for which it is responsible.

❏ Censorship is the act of defining prohibited content, as well as restricting access to that content.

❏ Slander is when someone makes verbal statements that are false and defamatory about an individual or organization.

❏ National and corporate secrets are another form of prohibited content.

❏ Governments have laws about prohibited content and behavior, and many organizations have documents defining how laws and the corporations' rules apply to the employees and what employees must do to comply, published as policies and procedures and/or security policies.

SELF TEST

The following questions will help you measure your understanding of the material presented in this chapter. Read all of the choices carefully because there might be more than one correct answer. Choose all correct answers for each question.

Workplace Safety and Safe Equipment Handling

1. Which of the following is the correct fire extinguisher class for an electrical fire?
   A. A
   B. B
   C. C
   D. D

2. Which statement is a true general comparison of the effects of EMI versus ESD?
   A. ESD can damage hardware; EMI harms data.
   B. EMI can harm hardware; ESD harms data.
   C. ESD and EMI are identical.
   D. EMI can cause injury or death; ESD is less harmful to people.

3. I plan to replace the power supply in a computer. What is the most important safety measure I should take to protect myself?
   A. Wear an antistatic wristband.
   B. Do *not* ground yourself.
   C. Bend your knees when you lift it.
   D. Buy a name-brand power supply.

4. My CRT display is only a few years old and was quite expensive. It is now malfunctioning, and none of the external buttons on the monitor help, nor can I fix it using the Properties settings in Windows. What should I do?
   A. Open the CRT case and look for a loose connection.
   B. Take it to a qualified repair center.
   C. Immediately discard it.
   D. Recycle it.

5. What can I use to protect my PC from power sags?
   A. Surge protector
   B. Power supply
   C. UPS
   D. APS

6. What should you do before moving any computer equipment?

    A. Power down and disconnect the power cord.

    B. Wear work gloves.

    C. Put on a facemask.

    D. Remove the power supply.

7. What is the ideal environment for ESD to occur?

    A. Hot and humid

    B. Cold and humid

    C. Hot and dry

    D. Cold and dry

8. You are getting ready to install a new component, a memory stick that came in its own antistatic bag. What is the correct way to handle this component and the bag?

    A. Remove the component from the bag and place it on top of the bag until ready to install.

    B. Remove the component from the bag and immediately discard the bag.

    C. Leave the component in the bag until you are ready to install it.

    D. Remove the component from the bag and turn the bag inside out before placing the component on the bag.

9. My CRT display is jittery; should I replace the display?

    A. Yes, this is a fatal defect.

    B. No, look for a source of EMI and increase the distance between that source and the display.

    C. Yes, and buy a display that resists ESD.

    D. No, look for a source of ESD and move it away from the display.

Environmental Concerns for IT Professionals

10. When a computer system is no longer functioning and is not repairable, how should you dispose of it?

    A. Put it in the trash.

    B. Donate it to a charity.

    C. Send it to a recycling center.

    D. Send it to a landfill.

11. We do not know the proper handling of an old solvent previously used in our company, and now we need to discard it. How can I find out more about it?
   A. Contact the manufacturer and ask for an MSDS.
   B. Send it to a recycling center.
   C. Transfer it to a glass jar for safe storage.
   D. Call 911.

12. What should we do with the large number of used batteries we accumulate in our office?
   A. Dispose of them in the trash.
   B. Find a recycling center that will accept them.
   C. Send them back to the manufacturers.
   D. Let them accumulate and dispose of them about once a year.

13. Which of the following is a complete "online" power protection device?
   A. Power strip
   B. Surge protector
   C. Inverter
   D. UPS

Professionalism and Proper Communication

14. When you are explaining something technical to a customer, which of the following is the best technique to use to confirm the customer understands your explanation?
   A. As you explain, intersperse questions such as, "Does that make sense?"
   B. After the explanation, give the customer a quiz.
   C. Give the customer a printed explanation to read as you speak.
   D. Maintain eye contact.

15. When someone has explained something to you, how can you make sure you heard and understood what she said?
   A. Focus.
   B. Repeat it back in your own words.
   C. Imagine how you sound and appear to the other person.
   D. Nod your head frequently.

16. Which of the following is a technique you would use to show respect to a customer? Select all that apply.

    A. Be as clear as possible and correct any misunderstandings.

    B. Show the customer your company's security policy.

    C. Avoid disregarding what someone else tells you.

    D. Treat others the way you like to be treated.

17. When a customer is explaining a problem, what is the single most important thing you must do?

    A. Nod your head to show understanding.

    B. Empathize.

    C. Allow the customer to explain the problem without interruption.

    D. Show respect.

18. What behavior shows a positive and professional attitude? Select all that apply.

    A. Avoiding confrontation

    B. Avoiding judgmental behavior

    C. Showing respect

    D. Minimizing another's concerns

Dealing with Prohibited Content and Prohibited Activities

19. Which of the following is the legal term that describes malicious, false, and defamatory statements made in printed words or pictures?

    A. Libel

    B. Slander

    C. Censorship

    D. Prohibited content

20. You believe you have witnessed prohibited behavior, and you have clearly identified it by referring to company policies. What should you do next?

    A. Do not minimize problems.

    B. Report the incident through proper channels.

    C. Avoid being judgmental.

    D. Be on time.

SELF TEST ANSWERS

Workplace Safety and Safe Equipment Handling

1. ☑ **C.** Class C is the correct fire extinguisher class for an electrical fire.
   ☒ **A, B,** and **D** are incorrect because they are the classes for, respectively, ordinary combustible materials, flammable or combustible liquids, and chemical fires.

2. ☑ **A.** ESD can damage hardware; EMI harms data. This general comparison is true concerning the effects of EMI versus ESD.
   ☒ **B** is incorrect because the opposite is true. **C,** ESD and EMI are identical, is incorrect. There is a difference. **D,** EMI can cause injury or death; ESD is less harmful to people, is incorrect because ESD is potentially more harmful.

3. ☑ **B.** The most important safety measure you should take to protect yourself is to not ground yourself because you do not want to make your body a path for electricity to take to ground. Wearing an antistatic wristband, standing on a grounding mat, or touching something already grounded would do this and put you in danger.
   ☒ **A,** wear an antistatic wristband, is incorrect because this would expose you to possible electrical shock. **C,** bend your knees when you lift it, is incorrect because replacing a power supply should not require heavy lifting. **D,** buy a name-brand power supply, is incorrect because this is not a safety measure.

4. ☑ **B.** Take it to a qualified repair center.
   ☒ **A,** open the CRT case and look for a loose connection, is incorrect because it is dangerous to open a CRT, and only highly trained technicians should open a CRT case. **C,** immediately discard it, is incorrect because this is an extreme reaction until you know more about the nature of the problem and whether the CRT can be repaired. If it cannot, then recycle it, rather than "discard" it. **D,** recycle it, is also incorrect until you have more information about the problem and whether the CRT can be repaired. If you cannot get it repaired, then you will need to recycle it.

5. ☑ **C.** A UPS will protect a PC from power sags because it provides conditioned power, free from the surges, spikes, and sags coming from the power company.
   ☒ **A,** a surge protector, is incorrect because this only protects from power surges, not from power sags. **B,** power supply, is incorrect because a power supply does not protect a PC from power sags. **D,** an APS, is incorrect because this is not a standard acronym for a power protection device.

6. ☑ **A.** Power down and disconnect the power cord before moving any computer equipment.
☒ **B,** wear work gloves, is incorrect because you only need to wear gloves when you are moving something with sharp edges, and not all computer equipment has sharp edges. **C,** put on a facemask, is incorrect because a facemask is only needed if you expect to be exposed to airborne particles. **D,** remove the power supply, is incorrect because this is a very extreme and unnecessary action to take before moving computer equipment.

7. ☑ **D.** Cold and dry is the ideal environment for ESD to occur. This should be avoided because ESD can damage equipment.
☒ **A, B,** and **C** are all incorrect because none of these is as ideal an environment for ESD as is a cold and dry environment.

8. ☑ **C.** Leave the component in the bag until you are ready to install it.
☒ **A,** remove the component and place on top of the bag until ready to install, is incorrect because the outside of the bag may hold a static charge. **B,** remove the component from the bag and immediately discard the bag, is incorrect because you may want to reuse the bag if you need to store this or another component at some time. **D,** remove the component from the bag and turn the bag inside out before placing the component on the bag, is incorrect because this procedure is not recommended and could expose the component to ESD.

9. ☑ **B.** Look for a source of EMI and increase the distance between that source and the CRT display because you should not replace the display until you know more about the problem, and it sounds more like an EMI problem.
☒ **A,** yes, this is a fatal defect, is incorrect because you do not know that it is a defect at all, and it sounds like a possible EMI problem. **C,** yes, and buy a display that resists ESD, is incorrect because you do not yet know that the display should be replaced, and you have no reason to believe the problem has anything to do with ESD. **D,** no, look for a source of ESD and move it away from the display, is incorrect because the symptom is more likely to be caused by EMI.

Environmental Concerns for IT Professionals

10. ☑ **C.** Send it to a recycling center. Even a nonfunctioning computer has material in it that can and should be recycled.
☒ **A** is incorrect because something put into the trash will usually end up in a landfill (see response to **D**). **B** is incorrect because donating something that is beyond repair is not ethical, and is passing on the responsibility for disposing of the computer. **D,** send it to a landfill, is incorrect because computers contain components that can contaminate the environment and components that should be recycled.

11. ☑ **A.** Contact the manufacturer and ask for an MSDS because this document will contain instructions on safe handling and safe disposal of the chemical.
    ☒ **B,** send it to a recycling center, is incorrect, although this is what you may ultimately do. You first need to know how to safely handle the chemical. **C,** transfer it to a glass jar for safe storage, is incorrect because no information is available to lead us to believe the original container is not adequate. **D,** call 911, is incorrect because there is no emergency.

12. ☑ **B.** Find a recycling center that will accept batteries is correct.
    ☒ **A,** dispose of them in the trash, is incorrect because you should never throw batteries in the trash. They contain environmentally dangerous components and chemicals. **C,** send them back to the manufacturers, is incorrect in general. Some manufacturers may have a program for used batteries, but first locate a recycling center. **D,** let them accumulate and dispose of them about once a year, is incorrect because batteries stored for long periods can leak toxic chemicals.

13. ☑ **D.** UPS is correct. This is an online power protection device.
    ☒ **A,** power strip, is incorrect because this provides no power protection whatsoever. **B,** surge protector, is incorrect because it only protects against power surges, and is not an online power protection device in the way that a UPS is, providing full-time power from the battery, and **C,** inverter, is incorrect because an inverter takes low-voltage DC power and transforms it to 110 V 60 cycle AC output.

Professionalism and Proper Communication

14. ☑ **A.** As you explain, intersperse questions such as "does that make sense?" to confirm the customer's understanding.
    ☒ **B,** after the explanation, give the customer a quiz, is incorrect because giving a quiz is not the best technique and would probably make the customer angry. **C,** give the customer a printed explanation to read as you speak, is incorrect because this is not the best way to treat a customer. **D,** maintain eye contact, is incorrect because although this should always be part of face-to-face interactions, eye contact is not the best technique to use to confirm understanding.

15. ☑ **B.** Repeat it back in your own words. This confirms that you heard and understand.
    ☒ **A,** focus, is incorrect although focusing on the customer and the problem is an important thing to do. **C,** imagine how you sound and appear to the other person, is incorrect, although this is a good habit when you are the one doing the speaking. **D,** nod your head frequently, is incorrect because, although this tells the speaker that you are listening, nodding does not confirm that you heard and understood what she said.

16. ☑ **A, C,** and **D** are all correct techniques for showing respect.
☒ **B,** show the customer your company's security policy, is incorrect because although this is an important policy for an organization, this behavior does not directly show respect at the personal level.

17. ☑ **C.** Allow the customer to explain the problem without interruption is the most important thing you must do when a customer is explaining a problem.
☒ **A, B,** and **D** are all incorrect because although you should use all of these in your interactions with the customer, the most important thing to do in this case is to allow the customer to explain without interruption.

18. ☑ **A, B,** and **C.** These are all correct behaviors that show a positive and professional attitude.
☒ **D,** minimizing another's concerns, is incorrect because this is negative and unprofessional behavior.

Dealing with Prohibited Content and Prohibited Activities

19. ☑ **A.** Libel is the term that describes malicious, false, and defamatory statements made in printed words or pictures.
☒ **B,** slander, is incorrect because slander is when such statements are made verbally.
C, censorship, is incorrect because censorship occurs when a person or organization decides to define prohibited content and restricts access to that content. **D,** prohibited content, is incorrect because in this chapter the term describes content that a government or organization forbids its citizens or employees from using or viewing.

20. ☑ **B.** Report the incident through proper channels.
☒ **A, C,** and **D** are all incorrect. While it is always important to not minimize problems, avoid being judgmental, and be on time, these do not directly relate to responding to prohibited behavior.

2

Operating System Fundamentals

I f you lump together all the Windows versions currently in use and count them as a single operating system (OS), Windows is the most widely used PC operating system for home and business. Therefore, technicians should prepare themselves to work with recent versions of the Microsoft Windows desktop operating systems. Like many people, you may have used Windows for much of your life, and you can competently do ordinary tasks, such as navigating folders, saving files, downloading files, and running programs. With such proficiency, you may wonder why you need to study the operating system any further. It's because you need a far different set of skills and knowledge to support Windows than you need to simply use it. Those skills include understanding it enough to competently install, configure, troubleshoot, and maintain it.

On the other hand, you do not need to be a systems programmer who understands the OS's programming code. You only need a base of knowledge, a sharp mind, good powers of observation, and patience.

The coverage of Windows begins in this chapter with an overview of the versions included on the A+ exam, moves to a brief survey of important considerations you should know before installing or upgrading Windows, and finishes with a tour of the user interface.

Discussion of Windows continues in Chapters 8, 9, 10, 13, 19, and 20. Each chapter will take you through a different aspect of supporting Windows, from working with Windows client virtualization (Chapter 8), then installing and upgrading Windows—either into a virtual machine or more conventionally on a physical PC (Chapter 9), managing disks and files (Chapter 10), troubleshooting and maintaining Windows (Chapter 13), and finally, supporting Windows as a network client (Chapter 19). And most other chapters include some mention of Windows relating to the chapter topic.

CERTIFICATION OBJECTIVE

■ **802: 1.1** *Compare and contrast the features and requirements of various Microsoft operating systems*

CompTIA Exam Objective 802: 1.1 requires that you understand the differences among various editions of three versions of Windows: Windows XP, Windows Vista, and Windows 7, including the implications of using the 32-bit or 64-bit versions of each. Be sure that you know the minimum system requirements for each of these versions, their system limits, and upgrade paths. You should be able to recognize the user interface and identify such features as Sidebar, Aero, gadgets, Compatibility Mode, XP Mode, Windows Easy Transfer, Administrative Tools, Windows Defender, Windows Firewall, Security Center, and Event Viewer. Understanding file structure and paths will also help you support Windows, and you should know how to work with Windows User Account Control (UAC).

Introduction to Windows Operating Systems

In this section, you will learn the purpose of operating systems, the differences among versions of the Windows operating system, the characteristics of 32-bit versus 64-bit Windows OSs, and the importance of updates and service packs. This section also contains an overview of selected features, and an explanation of Microsoft Support Lifecycle.

The Purpose of Operating Systems

The purpose of an *operating system (OS)* is to control all of the interactions among the various system components, the human interactions with the computer, and the network operations for the computer system. An OS is actually a group of programs that accomplishes its tasks by building an increasingly complex set of software layers between the lowest level of a computer system (the hardware) and the highest levels (user interactions). An important type of software that works closely with the OS is a *device driver*—program code that allows the OS to interact with and control a particular device. Many device drivers come with Windows and you can easily add others to the OS. That is why new hardware comes packaged with a disc containing a device driver for one or more versions of Windows and other OSs.

The OS is responsible for managing the computer's files in an organized manner and allowing the user to manage data files. The OS keeps track of the functions of particular files and brings them into memory as program code or data when needed. Furthermore, the OS is responsible for maintaining file associations so data files launch in the proper applications. The OS is also responsible for managing the computer's disks, keeping track of each disk's identification, and managing disk space use.

A *user interface (UI)* is both the visual portion of the operating system and the software components that allow the user to interact with the OS for starting programs, creating data, saving files, and other user tasks. A *graphical user interface (GUI)* is a user interface that takes advantage of a computer's graphics capabilities to make it easier for the user to interact with the OS by manipulating graphic objects on the desktop to accomplish a multitude of tasks.

An operating system also works with one or more computer architectures. A *computer architecture* (sometimes called the platform) is the basic design of a computer describing the data pathways and the methods the computer's CPU uses to access other components with the computer. In physical terms, the main components are the CPU, BIOS, and chipset—all of which you will study in Chapter 3.

The Many Flavors of Windows

Windows comes in many "flavors" involving versions and editions, and updates and service packs from Microsoft occasionally modify each of these. We will clarify the differences among these terms.

Versions

Each Microsoft Windows *version* is a new level of the venerable operating system, with major changes to the core components of the operating system as well as a distinctive and unifying look to the GUI. The Windows versions included on the CompTIA A+ Exam Number 220-802 include Windows XP, Windows Vista, and Windows 7. Although the objectives do not include Windows 8 yet, we do include some coverage of that version as well. Here is a portion of the Windows history to help you see where Microsoft has been with the Windows OS.

In 1995 and 1998, respectively, Microsoft released two desktop versions, Windows 95 and Windows 98—both more or less based on the MS-DOS kernel and targeted to the consumer market, although Windows 98 was widely accepted in the corporate world. At the same time they had an entirely different line of Server OS, Windows NT, based on a much more robust kernel and with built-in security features. In 2000, both their Windows 2000 Workstation product for business desktops and Windows 2000 Server products were built on the same kernel with the same GUI. With the same GUI on the desktop as on servers, IT professionals thought that going forward life would be a bit easier for those who supported both desktop Windows and Windows Server, but that was not going to last because in 2000 Microsoft also introduced Windows Me for home users with new features and a significantly changed look. This product was not successful, and Windows XP, yet another version targeted at the desktop and with a different GUI than the server products, followed it a year later. The following is a simple summary of the versions that followed Windows Me.

Windows XP   Microsoft released Windows XP in 2001 as a desktop operating system. Windows XP has been by far the most popular version of Windows so far. This is mainly due to the shortcomings of its successor, which led many users to stay with Windows XP.

on the

Job

Windows Server 2003 was the first post-Windows XP server version of Windows, and Windows Server 2008 is the most current released version. Since then, the Windows server products have been separate from the consumer versions of Windows, much as they were in the 1990s. They do not share the same kernel with desktop Windows, have many features targeted only to servers, and have names distinct from the desktop version. Server versions, like desktop versions, come in several editions for each version.

The Windows XP default desktop was different from that of Windows 2000 in the overall look, if not in functionality (see Figure 2-1). It also had a cleaner look because the only icon on the desktop by default was the *Recycle Bin*, which pointed to the location where Windows sends deleted files. In addition, Microsoft redesigned and reorganized the Start menu to have two columns rather than just one. Learn more about the Start menu later in this chapter.

Windows Vista   Microsoft released Windows Vista in 2007. Seen more as an up-grade to the extremely popular Windows XP, it included improvements in how Windows handles graphics, files, and communications. With enhancements to the GUI, Vista is attractive (see Figure 2-2), but it was not widely adopted due to problems with slow speed and high hardware requirements. As a result, Microsoft extended the support lifecycle of Windows XP, allowing sales of new PCs with Windows XP preinstalled until October 22, 2010.

Windows 7   Released in 2009, Windows 7 includes an enhanced GUI, improved speeds in just about any way you want to measure an OS, and nearly identical hard-ware requirements as Windows Vista (see Figure 2-3). Given that computers became faster and cheaper (as they do) in the two years between the release of Windows Vista and the introduction of Windows 7, the hardware requirements for Windows 7 are not the burden on the customer that they were for Windows Vista.

FIGURE 2-1

FIGURE 2-1

The Windows XP
desktop

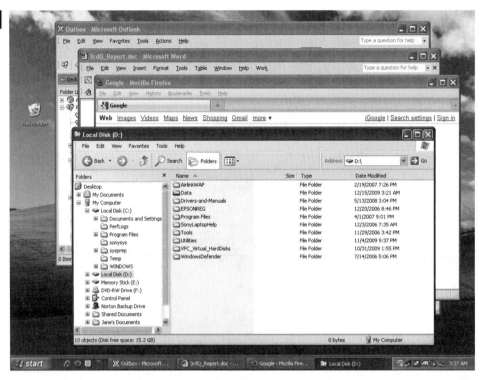

FIGURE 2-2

The Windows
Vista desktop

FIGURE 2-3

The Windows 7
desktop

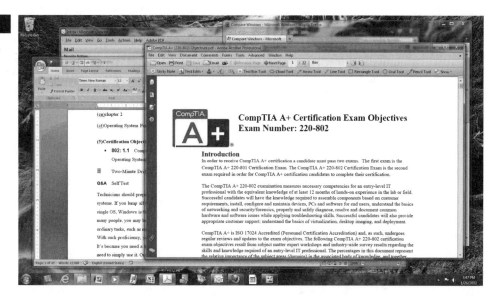

Windows 8   Windows 8 is a faster and leaner Windows OS with many improvements
over previous versions and some surprising new features. The most obvious is the
new Metro GUI, an updated version of the Metro user interface found on Microsoft
Windows Phone 7.5. The Start screen shown in Figure 2-4 contains one active tile for
every installed application, and these tiles show active content, such as news feeds,
stock quotes, slideshows, and more, depending on the application.

FIGURE 2-4

The Windows 8
Start screen

Editions Microsoft brings out an entirely new group of products for each version of Windows. What distinguishes each of these products, called an *edition*, from one another is the mix of features in each that is designed for a specific target market. Some Windows editions are available through retail channels as separate boxed or downloadable products, other editions—sometimes referred to as *original equipment manufacturer (OEM)* editions—are only available preinstalled by manufacturers on new computers. Then, there is the Enterprise edition, only available to large organizations that purchase volume licenses from Microsoft.

One thing that all the editions included on the exam have in common is that they all target desktop, laptop, and tablet PCs. Therefore, the server editions of Windows are not included on the exam.

The list in Table 2-1 contains the Windows editions included in the CompTIA A+ 220-802 exam.

TABLE 2-1	Comparison of the Windows Editions listed on the CompTIA A+ 802 Exam

Windows Version and Edition	Description
Windows XP Home	Designed for home users, it lacked many features included in the Professional edition.
Windows XP Professional	For business or power users, this edition included the ability to join a Windows Server domain, more security features, the ability to be operated by another Windows XP user remotely, and other features required in a business network environment.
Windows XP Media Center	An OEM edition preinstalled on computers with media center capabilities. Not sold separately.
Windows XP 64-bit	The first 64-bit version of Windows, it only ran on systems with the Intel Itanium CPU. They released an updated edition in 2003, but discontinued it in 2005 due to the lack of new Itanium-based computers.
Windows Vista Home Basic	Designed for home users with a limited budget, it lacked many features included in Windows Home Premium, such as the Windows Aero screen effects, and advanced media support found in other versions of Vista, but it does include Windows Photo Gallery and Windows Movie Maker. It does not support high-definition video, but Windows Vista was the first version of Windows to include a performance enhancement called *ReadyBoost*, which allows you to use flash memory devices as additional cache memory to improve system performance. It also includes security for the home user, such as Windows Firewall and parental controls.
Windows Vista Home Premium	Includes all of the features in Windows Vista Home Basic, with the addition of more advanced multimedia support of Windows XP Media Center, including HDTV, DVD authoring, and much more. Lacks features used in a Microsoft Windows Server domain.

TABLE 2-1   Comparison of the Windows Editions listed on the CompTIA A+ 802 Exam (*Continued*)

Windows Version and Edition	Description
Windows Vista Business	For business or power users, this edition includes all of the features of Home Basic, except Parental Controls, and it is missing one basic desktop theme. It has the ability to join a Windows Server domain, more security features, the ability for another Windows user to operate remotely, and other features required in a business network environment. Includes *Shadow Copy*, the ability to track and maintain backup copies of versions of user data files. It works together with *System Restore*, an automated system for creating backups of the entire Windows operating system, allowing you to roll the system back in time.
Windows Vista Enterprise	Includes all of the features of the Business edition, but with more features targeted to large enterprises. Only available through Microsoft Software Assurance (SA), a software purchasing, volume licensing, and support plan, mainly for large organizations.
Windows Vista Ultimate	Combines the features of both Home Premium and Enterprise editions, as well as a group of optional features bundled as Ultimate Extras that are free through Windows Update. Included is a utility, DreamScene, for using a video as a desktop background; tools for use with BitLocker and Encrypting File System (EFS); a poker game; sound schemes; additional language packs; and a puzzle game.
Windows 7 Starter	Available only as a 32-bit OEM version, preinstalled on low-end computers, such as a *netbook*, which is a minimally configured computer in the ultra-portable category, designed for connecting to the Internet and little else. The least capable of all the editions, it does include support for playing audio and video and for streaming audio or video to devices or other PCs running Windows 7. It does not include the ability to watch, pause, or record live TV on your PC. You cannot change the desktop backgrounds or themes. It is minimally configured for networking on a home network.
Windows 7 Home Premium	Targeted to the home market, this edition includes Windows Media Center, Windows Aero, and multi-touch support on compatible touch screen devices.
Windows 7 Professional	Designed for power users and small-business users, this edition includes all the features of Home Premium, with additional networking and security features, such as the ability to join a Microsoft Windows Server domain, support for Encrypting File System, and Windows XP Mode for running old applications in a virtual machine running Windows XP.
Windows 7 Enterprise	Similar to the Ultimate edition, but with more features targeted to large enterprises. Only available through Microsoft Software Assurance (SA), a software purchasing, volume licensing, and support plan, mainly for large organizations.
Windows 7 Ultimate	Combines the multimedia features of Home Premium with the security, networking, and compatibility features of Professional editions, including Windows XP Mode for running old applications in a virtual machine running Windows XP. It also includes the data encryption features of BitLocker Drive Encryption and BitLocker To Go and support for 35 languages.

e**x**a m

ⓦ a t c h *Several advanced Windows features are just defined here because they are part of the CompTIA A+ Exam 802 1.1 Objective, but you will learn more about* *them later in the book. For instance, learn how to work with ReadyBoost in Chapter 9, Shadow Copy in Chapter 10, and System Restore in Chapter 13.*

The Windows editions included in the exams are available through retail channels—either the Windows OS purchased alone in retail packaging (sometimes referred to

e**x**a m

ⓦ a t c h *For the exam, be prepared to differentiate among the various editions.*

as "full retail") or Windows preinstalled and bundled with a computer and known as "OEM Windows." Microsoft makes OEM Windows available at low prices to manufacturers or system builders with the agreement that they cannot sell it separately from the hardware.

32-Bit vs. 64-Bit Windows Operating Systems

Operating systems tie closely to the CPUs on which they can run. Therefore, we often use CPU terms to describe an operating system's abilities. For instance, Windows 2000 is a *32-bit operating system*. Windows XP, Windows Vista, and Windows 7 come in both 32-bit and 64-bit versions. Most of the Windows XP editions are 32-bit except for a special edition, Windows XP Professional x64 Edition.

The biggest difference between the 32-bit and 64-bit versions of Windows is in the maximum address space used by both system RAM and other RAM and ROM in your computer (see Table 2-2). Windows 64-bit does not use the maximum theoretical address space of a 64-bit CPU.

A *64-bit operating system* requires 64-bit applications, although Microsoft has offered ways to support older applications in each upgrade of Windows, described later in this chapter in "Running Old Applications in Windows." To determine if a computer is running 32-bit or 64-bit Windows 7, open Control Panel and click System and Maintenance, and then click System and look at the System Type field, which will say "32-bit Operating System" or "64-bit Operating System."

TABLE 2-2	Edition	RAM Limit in 32-bit Windows	RAM Limit in 64-bit Windows
Windows Memory Limits	Windows XP Home	4 GB	N/A
	Windows XP Professional	4 GB	N/A
	Windows XP Media Center	4 GB	N/A
	Windows XP Starter	512 MB	N/A
	Windows XP 64-Bit	N/A	128 GB
	Windows Vista Ultimate/Enterprise/Business	4 GB	128 GB
	Windows Vista Home Premium	4 GB	16 GB
	Windows Vista Home Basic	4 GB	8 GB
	Windows Vista Starter	1 GB	N/A
	Windows 7 Ultimate/Enterprise/Professional	4 GB	192 GB
	Windows 7 Home Premium	4 GB	16 GB
	Windows 7 Home Basic	4 GB	8 GB
	Windows 7 Starter	2 GB	N/A

Updates

Computer hardware technology does not stand still; therefore, operating systems must change to keep up. Each of the major operating systems is modular, so incremental updates can make some changes to the existing OS version. In Microsoft terminology, an *update* contains one or more software fixes or changes to the operating system. Some updates add abilities to the OS to support new hardware, and some resolve problems discovered with the operating system. This second type of update is often required to fix security problems. A *hotfix* or *patch* is a software fix for a single problem. Hotfix seems to be Microsoft's preferred term.

At one time, these updates, whether for functional or security problems, were issued without a predictable timetable. In recent years, Microsoft has assigned the second Tuesday of each month as the release day for updates. This day is widely called "patch Tuesday."

Service Packs

A *service pack* is a bundle of patches or updates released periodically by a software publisher. Windows service packs are major milestones in the life of a Windows version. For that reason, some devices and applications will require not simply a certain version of Windows, but also a certain service pack.

EXERCISE 2-1

Viewing the Windows Version, Edition, and Service Pack Information

Here is an easy way to determine the version, edition, and service pack level for Windows 7:

1. Open the Start menu and right-click Computer in the column on the right.
2. Select Properties.
3. Look for the version, edition, and service pack information near the top of the window, as shown in Figure 2-5.

Microsoft Support Lifecycle

Each version of Windows has a *support lifecycle*, as defined in Microsoft's Support Lifecycle Policy, first announced in 2002 and updated since then. A support lifecycle defines the length of time Microsoft will support a product, as well as the support options. It applies to most of their products that fall into two broad categories: Business and Developer products and Consumer, Hardware, and Multimedia products. All versions of Windows are included in the support lifecycle.

The lifecycle for each product moves through two phases: first is the Mainstream Support phase, followed by the Extended Support phase. Table 2-3, derived from information on Microsoft's Support Lifecycle page, illustrates the support options available during these two phases.

The lifecycle of each version also ties to the installed service pack level. Presently, Microsoft's policy is to end the support of a service pack 24 months after the next service pack releases or at the end of the product lifecycle, whichever comes first.

For instance, the last service pack for the 32-bit version of Windows XP was SP 3, and as of October 22, 2010, Microsoft no longer permits its retail partners or its original equipment manufacturers to sell Windows XP. The company ended support

This System dialog box shows that the version is Windows 7, the edition is Ultimate, and it includes Service Pack 1.

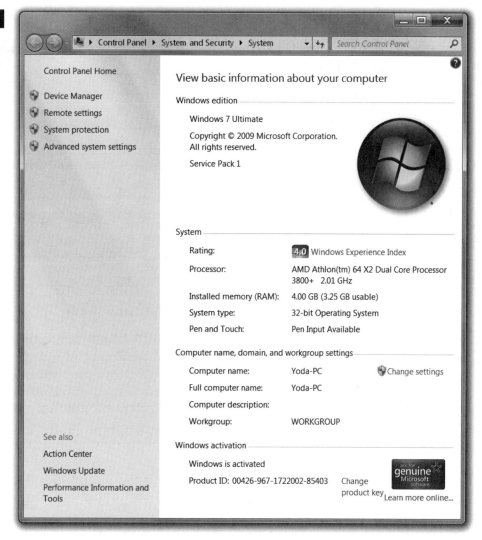

for Windows XP Service Pack 2 (all 32-bit editions) in July 2010. The 64-bit edition did not include a third service pack, and support for the 64-bit edition of XP SP 2 is scheduled to end in April 2014, when support also will end for SP 3 of the 32-bit edition.

TABLE 2-3	Available Support	Mainstream Support Phase	Extended Support Phase
	Paid support	X	X
Microsoft Support Phases *Extended Support only available with an extended hotfix agreement purchased within 90 days of the end of mainstream support.	Security update support	X	X
	Nonsecurity hotfix support (to fix a specific problem)	X	*
	No-charge incident support	X	
	Warranty claims	X	
	Design changes and feature requests	X	
	Product-specific information available in the online Microsoft Knowledge Base	X	X
	Product-specific information available by using the Support site at Microsoft Help and Support	X	X

The current lifecycle for consumer versions of Windows is ten years, as announced in February 2012. Therefore, support for Windows Vista will end April 11, 2017, and for Windows 7 the end date is January 14, 2020. So we can count on updates and security patches for these products until those dates.

To learn more about the lifecycle for a specific product, enter the keywords "Microsoft support lifecycle" into your favorite search engine and select the result that points to the Microsoft Support Lifecycle page. From there, you can do a search on a product, such as Windows 7.

Considerations for Installing or Upgrading Windows

Unless you buy or build a custom computer, when you purchase a PC from a major manufacturer, it will come with the latest version of Windows installed. But what if you wish to install the latest version on your existing PC? It turns out you need to do a bit of homework before you make that step. First, you need to see if your computer meets the recommended system requirements. Then you will want to discover if the new version will be compatible with your existing hardware and applications, and finally, you need to know the upgrade paths to the new version because, in some cases, you cannot upgrade from the installed version and need to be prepared to take the correct steps to successfully install the new version. This section will prepare you for the actual installation or upgrade of Windows as presented in Chapter 9.

System Requirements

Each revision or version of an OS has specific minimum requirements for the level of CPU, amount of memory, and amount of free hard disk space. To determine if it will run on your existing computer, check the *system requirements* listed on the package and published on Microsoft's Website. This will describe the minimum CPU, RAM, free hard disk space, and video adapter required. You can normally count on the system requirements being greater as you move from one version to another, as from Windows XP to Windows Vista.

Another system requirement is the computer platform on which a given OS will run. Windows runs on the Microsoft/Intel platform, with a range of CPUs (from Intel and makers of compatible products, such as AMD), BIOSs, and chipsets compatible with Microsoft OSs. Some call this the *Wintel* architecture. We make another distinction between x86 systems, which are Wintel computers that support 32-bit Windows, and x64 systems, which support the 64-bit Windows. To make things a bit more complicated, Windows 8 supports both 32-bit and 64-bit Wintel systems, plus (in a special version) the ARM architecture, named for the manufacturer of these ultra-small CPUs and chipsets designed for mobile devices, such as tablets and smartphones.

Table 2-4 describes the system minimums for three versions of Windows—all Wintel systems. Additionally, an optical drive is required if you want to install from the Windows CD. But these requirements are modest and far less than you will find in the most minimally configured new desktop PC.

You would be very unhappy trying to work on a PC with a minimal configuration, because the programs most people choose to run on desktop computers have grown in their hardware requirements; you will want many hundreds of GBs of hard drive space for the programs you add and the data you will create with those programs. Therefore, our recommended configuration for 64-bit Windows 7 Home Premium, Professional, or Ultimate is 2 GHz 64-bit multicore processor, 2+ GB of system memory, a 120 GB hard drive, and a DirectX 11 adapter with 256 MB graphics memory. Many of the features available with Windows require additional hardware support. For instance, Windows Media Center features need more video RAM and specialized hardware

| TABLE 2-4 | Windows System Minimums | | |

	Windows XP Professional	**Windows Vista Home Premium/Business/Ultimate**	**Windows 7**
CPU	Intel or AMD 233 MHz	800 MHz	1 GHz (32-bit or 64-bit)
RAM	64 MB	512 MB	1 GB (32-bit) or 2 GB (64-bit)
Free Hard Disk Space	1.5 GB	15 GB	16 GB (32-bit) or 20 GB (64-bit)
Video Adapter	Super VGA (800 × 600)	Support for Super VGA graphics	DirectX 9 adapter with WDDM 1.0 or higher device driver

like a TV tuner. Windows Vista's Windows XP Mode requires an additional 1 GB of RAM and an additional 15 GB of available hard disk space, as well as a processor that supports hardware virtualization.

Application and Hardware Compatibility

After Microsoft releases a new Windows version, there is a transition time during which many individuals and organizations choose to stay with the old version; some move to the new version right away; and others make the change gradually. Not everyone immediately embraces the new OS and replaces their old OS with the new one. There are many reasons for this.

System Requirements

Old hardware may be below the system requirements. Therefore, if the old operating system is functioning adequately, individual users, as well as businesses, will not simply reflexively upgrade to the new OS until they have a compelling reason to do so.

Hardware Compatibility

The BIOS in an older PC may not support critical features of the new OS, and if the manufacturer does not offer a BIOS upgrade, the computer will not support the new OS. Hardware compatibility problems extend to peripherals when manufacturers do not create new device drivers for a new OS.

Software Compatibility

Some applications are written to take advantage of certain features (or weaknesses) in older versions of Windows. Large organizations have often delayed upgrading to a new OS until they could either find a way to make the critical old applications run in the new OS or find satisfactory replacements that would work in the new OS.

Ugrade Advisor

Although the recent versions of Windows test the compatibility of the hardware and (in the case of an upgrade) software early in the installation process, you would be smart to run this test yourself before you start the installation process—even before purchasing the new OS. Microsoft provides a utility for each of its recent upgrades that lets you test your computer and hardware for compatibility. This program is Upgrade Advisor.

Upgrade Advisor comes on the Windows XP installation disc, so you can select it from the menu that appears during Autorun. The Windows Vista and Windows 7 CDs will run the Upgrade Advisor from the Internet. For those who want to run the test before purchasing a version of Windows, download Upgrade Advisor from the Internet. Check out the Microsoft Website to locate the Upgrade Advisor for a specific version of Windows.

After testing the hardware and the software, the Upgrade Advisor produces a report providing valuable information and recommendations or tasks that you need to perform before installing the next version of Windows, and it may show tasks to perform after the installation. You may find the tasks needed to make a computer meet the compatibility and minimum system requirements are too expensive to perform on an older computer and decide to postpone your move to the new version until you are ready to replace the old system.

Exercise 2-2 provides the steps for acquiring and running the Windows 7 Upgrade Advisor. Chapter 9 includes details on the practice of upgrading an installed Windows OS with a new Windows OS.

EXERCISE 2-2

Running Upgrade Advisor

You can see if your Windows computer hardware and application software will be compatible with Windows 7. You will need a broadband Internet connection to successfully complete this exercise.

1. Open your Internet browser and enter the keywords **windows upgrade advisor** into your favorite search engine.
2. From the results, select a link (within the Microsoft.com domain) for the version of the Upgrade Advisor you desire.
3. Download and save the Upgrade Advisor file to the desktop.
4. When the download completes, locate the file on the desktop and double-click it to run the Advisor.
5. When the Upgrade Advisor completes, it will display a task list similar to the one in Figure 2-6. Print this out or save it.

Once, when we ran the Upgrade Advisor, it produced a report that found only one incompatibility—an antivirus program that was only incompatible with the Setup program but was compatible with the new version of Windows. Therefore, it suggested removing the program before installing the OS, and then reinstalling it afterward. The computer in question was a test computer, so we ignored the instructions just to see what the consequences would be. After the upgrade, Windows did not run, and it would not even boot up into Windows's Safe Mode (described in Chapter 13). After several hours of trying to fix the installation, we had to wipe the hard drive clean and start from scratch.

Running Old Applications in Windows

Many individuals and organizations use older applications that will not work on newer versions of Windows. The program may fail to install in the new OS, or, if you have upgraded a system to a new version of Windows, an old application may issue an error message, such as "This program requires Windows x," where x is an older version of Windows.

Or, you may not receive such a clear message, but the program may behave erratically. If this program worked in the older version of Windows, you may need to take measures to make it happy in the new version. The official answer to this is to use Compatibility

FIGURE 2-6

A portion of the Windows 7 Upgrade Advisor task list

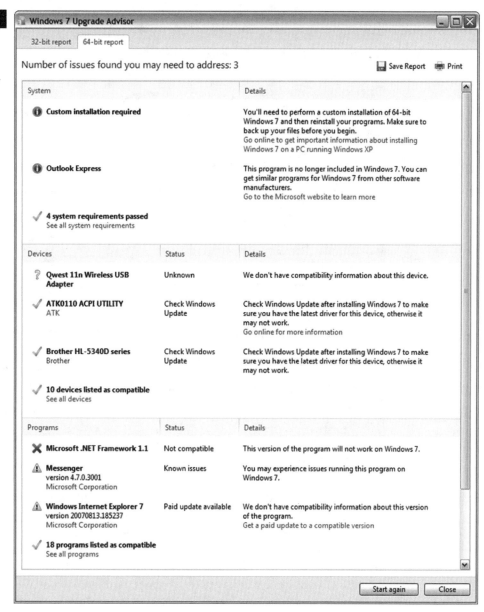

Mode in all versions of Windows discussed in this book or Windows XP Mode in Windows 7. An additional option is available for Windows XP and Windows Vista that is similar to Windows XP Mode. We'll examine these options.

Compatibility Mode

Some programs will run in a newer version of Windows if you first make temporary changes to Windows XP, Windows Vista, or Windows 7 that only affect the problem program while it is running and do not directly affect other programs. This feature is *Compatibility Mode* and you can enable and configure it using the *Program Compatibility Wizard*, also called the *Program Compatibility Troubleshooter* in Windows 7. Call up this Wizard from the Help and Support Center, and it guides you through the steps to select the application program, the older Windows OS you wish to emulate, and the display settings. The wizard saves the settings it creates in the properties of the application's shortcut or program file.

Alternatively, you can manually alter the compatibility settings for any program from the program's properties or from its shortcut.

on the

j o b

Only use Compatibility Mode for old productivity applications (word processing, spreadsheet, and so on.). Never use Compatibility Mode for antivirus programs, backup programs, or system programs (such as disk utilities and drivers) because these types of programs require more access to the disk and other resources than they will be allowed within Compatibility Mode.

Windows XP Mode and Windows Virtual PC

If Compatibility Mode does not enable an old program to run properly, and if you are running Windows 7 Professional, Enterprise, or Ultimate edition, then you can use Windows XP Mode, which is Microsoft Virtual PC with a fully licensed version of XP installed. Windows XP Mode is not designed for 3-D games and other programs with high-end graphics needs, and it may not work with certain hardware, such as TV tuners. Once again, use this for the business productivity program that you need but cannot upgrade to a compatible version. Learn more about Windows XP Mode in Chapter 8, when we explore the topic of operating system virtualization for Windows.

Clean Install versus an Upgrade

An upgrade of an operating system, also called an *in-place upgrade*, is an installation of a newer operating system directly over an existing installation. An upgrade has the benefit of saving you the trouble of reinstalling all your programs and creating all your preference settings. You would have to do all this after a clean installation, which is an installation on a blank or "clean" hard drive. Upgrades also leave you with a brand-new OS on an old computer, but that is your choice.

Upgrade Paths

You can directly upgrade to Windows XP Professional from Windows 98, Windows Me, Windows NT 4.0 Workstation SP 5, and Windows 2000 Professional. Upgrade paths to Windows Vista from Windows XP are edition-specific, as shown in Table 2-5, in which an "X" indicates in-place installation (upgrade). N/A indicates that you must do a clean installation. The upgrade path from Windows XP Professional requires a clean reinstall.

You cannot directly upgrade from Windows XP or older versions to Windows 7. Table 2-6 lists the direct upgrade paths to Windows 7, and, as in Table 2-5, N/A indicates that you must do a clean install.

Migrating Data and Settings

When preparing to move to a new version of Windows from an older version, whether you plan to do a clean install or an in-place upgrade, you will want to

TABLE 2-5 Upgrade Paths to Windows Vista

	Windows Vista Home Basic	Windows Vista Home Premium	Windows Vista Business	Windows Vista Ultimate
Windows XP Professional	N/A	N/A	X	X
Windows XP Home	X	X	X	X
Windows XP Media Center	N/A	X	N/A	X
Windows XP Tablet PC	N/A	N/A	X	X

| TABLE 2-6 | Upgrade Paths to Windows 7 |

	Windows 7 Home Basic	Windows 7 Home Premium	Windows 7 Professional	Windows 7 Enterprise	Windows 7 Ultimate
Windows Vista Business	N/A	N/A	X	X	X
Windows Vista Enterprise	N/A	N/A	N/A	N/A	X
Windows Vista Home Basic	X	X	N/A	N/A	X
Windows Vista Home Premium	N/A	X	N/A	N/A	X
Windows Vista Ultimate	N/A	N/A	N/A	N/A	X

migrate your data and settings from the old to the new. Microsoft has provided tools for doing this, including *Windows Easy Transfer (WET) Wizard*, a utility introduced in Windows Vista. Learn more about this and other data migration tools in Chapter 9.

SCENARIO & SOLUTION

Which is generally more expensive—Windows purchased as a full retail product or an OEM version purchased preinstalled on a computer?	Windows purchased as a full retail product is more expensive than an OEM version purchased preinstalled on a computer (excluding the cost of the computer).
What is "patch Tuesday?"	Patch Tuesday is the second Tuesday of the month—the day when Microsoft releases regular updates to their products.
Describe the biggest difference between 32-bit Windows and 64-bit Windows.	The biggest difference is in the address space used by both system RAM and other RAM and ROM. A 64-bit Windows OS uses a great deal more address space than the 4 GB of 32-bit Windows, with the actual maximum varying among the versions and editions, but ranging from 8 GB to 192 GB.

The Windows User Interface

This section provides an overview of the Windows user interface, including both the obvious and the less obvious GUI components, such as the Aero feature in Windows Vista and Windows 7, which affects the look of all graphical components. Learn about such objects as the taskbar, Start menu, command prompt, Sidebar, Windows Explorer, and so forth.

This section describes the functions and the ways to use the various user interface components in Windows. It also distinguishes between those utilities you use from the command prompt and Run line utilities. You learn that many of the GUI utilities used to administer Windows run in a special graphical console called an MMC. Although you will see some of these utilities in this section, you will have opportunities to work with most of them in the following chapters of this book, where appropriate.

The Windows Desktop

Windows provides a graphical user interface (GUI) that the user can navigate using a keyboard and mouse or other pointing device. The Windows GUI uses the desktop metaphor. The main Windows screen, called the "desktop," has containers for your work like when you use a physical desk. Windows organizes these containers, called "folders," in a hierarchical fashion. This organization allows for easy access to the commonly used files and programs, using a mouse or other pointing device for point-and-click operations.

The Windows desktop has a variety of graphical objects in addition to folders, including, but not limited to, the mouse pointer, icons, shortcuts, dialog boxes, windows, buttons, toolbars, menus, and the taskbar. Not all of these appear at the same time, or at least they are not on the desktop at the end of a standard Windows installation.

Icons and Shortcuts

You encounter and use these icons as you navigate in Windows using your keyboard and pointing device. An *icon* is a tiny graphic image representing applications, folders, disks, menu items, and more. A *shortcut* is an icon that represents a link to any object that an icon can represent. Activating a shortcut (by double-clicking it) is a quick way to access an object, or to start up a program from the desktop, without having to find the actual location of the object on your computer. You can represent a single object, like a program file, by more than one shortcut, and you can place a shortcut on the desktop, taskbar, and other places within the Windows GUI. Shortcut icons are often (but not always) distinguished by a small bent arrow on the lower left, and they have a title below the icon, like the Microsoft Word shortcut icon shown here.

Windows Explorer

Windows has a very important GUI component, *Windows Explorer*—the program EXPLORER.EXE. This program supports the entire Windows GUI. So, as long as the GUI is running, which means as long as you are able to work in Windows, this program is loaded into memory. Once in the Windows GUI, if you call this program, it opens a window called Windows Explorer that you use for browsing your local disks and files. You open Windows Explorer windows every time you open many Start menu shortcuts, such as My Computer/Computer, My Documents/Documents, and so forth. You can also open Windows Explorer from the Accessories menu of All Programs or by entering **explorer** in the Start | Run dialog box. Switch from the Start screen to the Windows Explorer desktop in Windows 8 by clicking or tapping (with your finger on a touch-sensitive computer) the Desktop tile. Paradoxically, entering **explorer** in the Start Search box in Windows Vista or Windows 7 will bring up Internet Explorer, but entering **explorer.exe** will bring up Windows Explorer.

Microsoft makes incremental changes to Windows Explorer in each new version of Windows. For instance, the Search box in Windows Vista and Windows 7 replaced the Search toolbar button in Windows Explorer in Windows XP. The old Search option did not begin the search until you finished typing in the search string, and then it seemed rather slow. The new Windows Explorer Search box starts searching the contents of the current windows and its folders as you enter the string and displays results as it continues the search.

Windows Aero

Aero is an enhancement to the desktop that Microsoft introduced in Windows Vista and continues in Windows 7 and in Windows 8 Explorer view. These versions of Windows support Aero in all editions except Home Basic, and require a compatible graphics adapter. Aero features include such visual effects as Glass, which makes the frames of a windows transparent (look back at Figure 2-3), and Aero Wizards, a standard design for the wizards that walk you through various functions. Aero includes windows animations, such as Windows Flip 3D, that allows you to switch between open Windows by pressing the WINDOWS key and TAB key simultaneously, as shown in Figure 2-7 . These are but a few of the many features of Aero.

Sidebar and Gadgets

The *Sidebar* was introduced in Windows Vista and removed from subsequent versions. It is a vertical bar located by default on the right side of the Vista desktop with the purpose of containing gadgets. A *gadget* is a mini-program that shows information, such as time and temperature in various locations, stock quotes, and handy tools such as a small yellow notepad or calculator. The Windows Vista Sidebar, shown in Figure 2-8, fits nicely on wide displays where you have enough real estate to keep it visible while working at your normal tasks. You can choose the various gadgets you wish to display, move gadgets off the Sidebar where some of them will automatically grow larger, or choose to eliminate the Sidebar altogether. Microsoft removed the Sidebar from Windows 7 as unnecessary, since gadgets can reside anywhere on the desktop.

To enable a gadget, simply right-click an empty spot on the desktop and click Gadgets to open the Gadget Gallery, shown along with some active gadgets in Figure 2-9. Double-click a gadget to have it appear on the desktop. Windows 8 Live Tiles are more configurable than gadgets.

Taskbar and Systray

By default, Windows displays the *taskbar* as a horizontal bar across the bottom of the desktop. You can reposition the taskbar by simply moving the pointer to an

FIGURE 2-7

Using Flip 3D in Windows 7

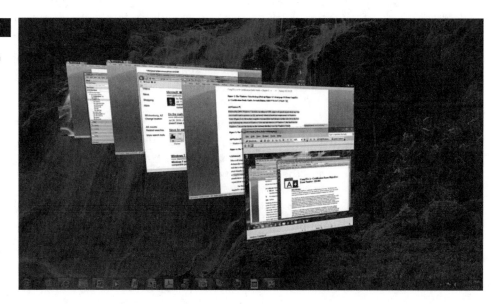

FIGURE 2-8

The Sidebar in
Windows Vista
with several
gadgets

"empty" taskbar area and dragging it to a new position, such as at the top of the desktop or vertically positioned at either side. You can also resize the taskbar by dragging just an edge of it until it is the desired size. The taskbar is also (rarely) called the *Start Bar* because it contains the Start button. The Start button has a label in Windows XP, but in Windows Vista and Windows 7, it is a simple icon with a Microsoft logo, sometimes called the *Windows orb*. The Windows XP taskbar (Figure 2-10) and the Windows Vista taskbar (Figure 2-11) are very similar. Each includes (from left to right) a Start button, the Quick Launch toolbar, buttons for currently running programs, and at the far right, the *systray*, also called the *notification area* or *system tray*. Programs and some hardware devices use the systray to display status icons. These icons may represent devices, such as a network adapter, or represent software, such as a battery meter, antivirus program, and so on. Pausing the mouse pointer over one of these icons will cause a rectangular status box to pop up, as shown in Figure 2-12. Occasionally, a message balloon will pop up over the systray for events relating to one of the icons, such as when making or disconnecting a wireless connection.

The *Quick Launch toolbar,* just to the right of the Start button, is an optional toolbar you can add to the taskbar using the properties dialog box for the taskbar. You can launch any shortcuts on the Quick Launch toolbar with a single click without having to first open the Start menu. The Windows 7 taskbar (Figure 2-13) replaced the Quick Launch toolbar with the ability to pin program icons to the taskbar—a capability previously reserved for the Start menu, and, of course, we have long had the ability to create new icons on the desktop, called shortcuts.

Configure the taskbar, control the default positioning of windows on the desktop, or open the Task Manager by right-clicking in the empty area of the taskbar and selecting the desired option from the taskbar menu, as shown in Figure 2-14. The choice labeled Properties opens the Properties dialog box for the taskbar and Start menu.

Start Menu

The Start button on the taskbar opens the *Start menu,* which has areas containing shortcuts and submenus. It is the central tool for finding and starting a variety of

FIGURE 2-9

On the left is the Windows 7 Gadget Gallery where you can select a gadget. On the right are several active gadgets.

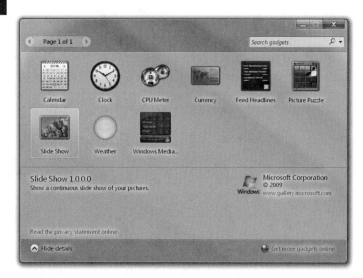

FIGURE 2-10   The Windows XP taskbar

FIGURE 2-11   The Windows Vista taskbar

FIGURE 2-12   Pause the mouse pointer over an icon in the systray to see status information.

FIGURE 2-13   The Windows 7 taskbar

Right-click the
Windows 7
taskbar to open
the taskbar menu.

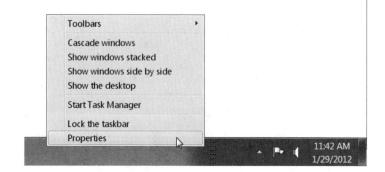

programs in Windows. Beginning in Windows XP and continuing through Windows 7, the Start menu has a two-column format. The right column contains a fairly standard set of icons that you can configure through the Start menu Properties dialog box. An arrow next to one of these icons indicates that you can expand the item to display the contents or submenus.

At the bottom of the Windows XP Start menu is a bar containing two choices: Log Off and Turn Off Computer. The Log Off option will log off the currently logged-on user, replacing the desktop with a logon screen. Selecting Turn Off Computer will open the Turn off Computer dialog box, which will give you three choices: Standby, Turn Off, or Restart. If you have enabled hibernation, the middle button will read Hibernate.

In Windows Vista, Microsoft moved the Turn Off button (without a label) to the bottom of the Start menu, as shown in Figure 2-15. Clicking this button will normally shut down the computer without displaying an additional dialog box. To the right of the Turn Off button is a lock button to lock the computer while leaving it running. We will describe the use of Lock Computer in Chapter 18. To select more options, click the arrow to the right of the Turn Off button. The standard options here are Switch User, Log Off, Lock, Restart, Sleep, and Shut Down.

FIGURE 2-15

The Windows
Vista Start menu

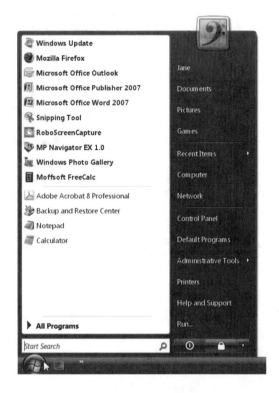

If an update has downloaded to your Windows computer but did not install, you will see an indication of this when you attempt to shut down. In Windows XP, the Turn Off Computer dialog box will display as shown in Figure 2-16, with the Microsoft Security Center icon positioned over the Turn Off button. In Windows Vista and Windows 7, the security icon will display on top of the Turn Off button on the Start menu. In either case, a message will instruct you to click Turn Off to install the updates. If you choose this, do not power off the computer because that will interrupt the update. The computer will turn off automatically after installing the updates.

Pinned Items List   A *pinned items list* is located on the top left of the Windows XP, Windows Vista, and Windows 7 Start menus. By default, the pinned items list contains shortcuts to Windows Update and programs for browsing the Internet and using e-mail. The shortcuts in the pinned items list remain there unless you choose to remove or change them. To add shortcuts to the pinned items list, right-click any shortcut and choose Pin To Start Menu. To remove an item from this list, right-click it and choose Unpin From Start Menu. In Windows 7, you can also pin items to the taskbar.

The Windows
XP Turn Off
Computer dialog
box showing the
Security Center
icon to indicate
that an update
is waiting to be
installed

Recently Used Programs List   Beginning in Windows XP, the Start menu
has a separator line that marks the end of the pinned items list and the beginning
of the *recently used programs list*, which contains shortcuts to recently run programs.
You can change the number of items maintained in this list through the Start menu
Properties dialog box.

All Programs   Beginning in Windows XP, the All Programs menu item points to
a folder containing links to programs and other folders containing programs. When
you click All Programs, it opens a pop-up menu with a list of programs and program
categories. Changed in Windows Vista and Windows 7, the list opens on top of the
pinned items and recently used programs lists, as shown in Figure 2-17, and you click
Esc (to close the entire Start menu) or Back to close this list and keep the Start menu
open. In all three versions, when you install a new application in Windows, it will
usually add a folder or program icon to this list.

Personal Folders   The Start menu contains shortcuts to your *personal folders*.
In Windows XP, My Documents, My Recent Documents, My Pictures, and My Music
point to the currently logged-on user's personal data folders. Microsoft dropped the
"My" in My Computer and My Network Places in Windows Vista. The exact folders
displayed will depend on how you have configured the Start menu using the Properties
dialog box.

The My Documents/Documents folder contains data files you create. Many
applications will, by default, save their data files in this location. In Windows XP, the
actual path to the My Documents folder is C:\Documents and Settings*username*\\
My Documents, where *username* is the user name used to log onto the computer.
In Windows Vista/7, the path to the Documents folder is C:\Users*username*\\
Documents. The other personal folders are also located in the *username* folder. My
Recent Documents/Recent Items contain shortcuts to recent data files, no matter

where you saved the files. My Music/Music contains audio files; My Videos/Videos contains video files such as movies, whereas My Pictures/Pictures is the default location for graphic files such as photo files from digital cameras. Some applications with special file types will create their own folders under My Documents/Documents. Each of these icons on the Start menu points to a folder created as part of the user's personal folders, giving the user a ready-made folder structure for organizing data files of many types.

Start Search   In Windows Vista and Windows 7, the Start Search box, mentioned earlier in this chapter, is very powerful and useful. Also called Quick Search or Instant Search, it works like the Run line for launching programs, but that is not all it does; it is much more powerful, searching your entire computer. When you search

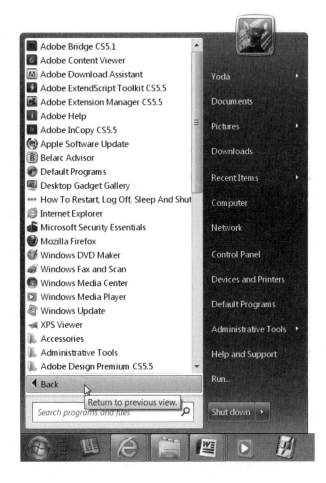

on a program it will find it by either its executable name or more common name. Then, once it is selected, press ENTER or click it to launch it. We have come to use this as a replacement for the Run line. It saves having to discover where a favorite GUI utility is located in Windows. For instance, by default, Microsoft tucked Device Manager away, requiring several mouse clicks to locate it in the GUI and then launch it. Starting it from the Run line is better, but you must carefully type in its executable name, **devmgmt.msc**. Leave off the extension and you get an error message, but using Start Search, all you need to do is enter **device manager** and voila! Device Manager blossoms on your desktop. So, forget the Run line (except for the A+ exams, of course) and use Start Search.

In Windows 8, Microsoft has again made the Search command both easier to use and more powerful. Simply start typing from the Start screen and searching will start.

on the job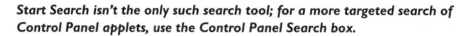

Start Search isn't the only such search tool; for a more targeted search of Control Panel applets, use the Control Panel Search box.

My Computer/Computer   My Computer resides on the Start menu in Windows XP; in Windows Vista, it is renamed Computer. Whatever the name, use it to open the My Computer or Computer folder in Windows Explorer and display file folders, hard disk drives, and removable storage on the local computer. The actual objects shown depend on the computer's configuration. In Windows XP, clicking the Folders button on the toolbar will change the view from the default view with a task pane on the left and a contents pane on the right to a two-pane view showing a folder hierarchy in the left pane and the contents of the currently selected folder on the right. In the first view, you can select an action from the task pane on the left, or open a folder or drive on the right. In Folder view, you can see the entire folder hierarchy on the left while browsing folders in the right pane. The Windows 7 Computer folder shown in Figure 2-18 has a button bar with buttons that change to match the context of whatever you selected. Use My Computer/Computer for file and folder management outside of your applications.

To work with files and folders you need to understand a few concepts. We will begin with files, folders, and other related concepts, and then move on to discuss paths.

A *file* is a container for data (whether program code or some type of user data) organized as a unit, saved on mass storage, and identified with a special name, called a filename. In Windows and other graphical OSs, a saved file appears to reside in a special container called a *folder* or *directory*, used to organize stored files. A folder can contain files and other folders. We call the folders and files as they exist on a disk, including their relationship to each other and their content, a *file structure* or *folder structure.* Each version of Windows has a default file structure. This file structure will have other folders and files added to it as you install more programs and save your data files. Figure 2-19 shows part of the default file structure for Windows 7. Among the folders displayed in the left pane, the following are default folders installed by Windows 7: PerfLogs, Program Files, Program Files (x86), Temp, Users, and Windows. The Windows folder and its subfolders contain the core Windows OS components.

A *path* is a method for describing the location of a file on storage in Windows. It includes the drive on which the file resides as well as the folder or folders within which the file sits. For instance, a file named salary rpt.docx located in the data folder on drive C: has a path of C:\data\salary rpt.docx. Notice that a backslash (\) separates the drive designation and the folder name (data), as well as the folder name and the filename. Learn more about files and folders in Chapter 10.

My Network Places/Network The Start menu icon labeled My Network Places in Windows XP, or simply Network beginning in Windows Vista, opens a folder containing shortcuts to network locations on the LAN or the Internet. If the

FIGURE 2-18

The Windows 7 Computer folder

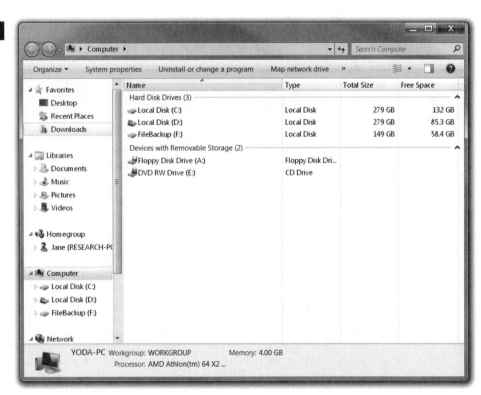

FIGURE 2-19

The Windows 7
default file
structure

task list in Windows XP is visible, it includes tasks appropriate for working with network locations, such as Add A Network Place, View Network Connections, View Workgroup Computers, and Set Up A Home Or Small Office Network. These tasks are available through the button bar beginning in Windows 7.

Administrative Tools   *Administrative Tools* is an optional Start menu item that provides shortcuts to administrative and troubleshooting tools. Click Administrative Tools to see a pop-up menu with a selection of utilities, as shown in Figure 2-20. The actual utilities shown vary among Windows versions, and even among editions of a version. Look for common tools, such as Services, Event Viewer, and Computer Management, among others.

Event Viewer is an administrative tool for logging errors, warnings, and other events that occur in Windows. If someone is having a problem with their computer and reports seeing an error in Windows but cannot recall what it said, open the Event

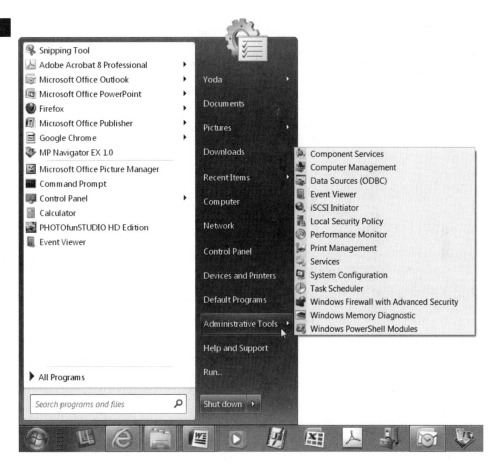

FIGURE 2-20

Administrative
Tools in
Windows 7

Viewer and search for the error. Beyond retrieving fleeting error messages, Microsoft
improved Event Viewer over the years, and it is a great tool for troubleshooting
problems, allowing you to pinpoint the source of a problem. You will learn how to use
it in Chapter 13, and we will explore other Administrative Tools in later chapters.

Control Panel   *Control Panel* is a special folder in Windows that contains icons
for several dozen small programs, called applets, which we use to make changes to the
Windows configuration. Before Windows Vista, all of the applet icons were displayed
together in the Control Panel folder. Beginning in Windows Vista, they changed
the look of this folder, as well as how the applets are organized. This new look and
organization is called *Category View*, because the many applets are organized into a
handful of categories. Figure 2-21 shows the Windows 7 Control Panel.

FIGURE 2-21

Windows 7
Control Panel in
Category View

To switch from Category View to *Classic View* in Windows 7, simply click the down arrow next to Category in the top right of the Control Panel folder. Then select Large Icons or Small Icons, either of which will change Control Panel to Classic View with individual icons for the Control Panel applets. Conversely, to switch back to Category View, simply click the down arrow by Large Icons or Small Icons and select Category. To switch between these two views in Windows Vista Control Panel (not shown here), look for the task pane to the left of the main pane and select either Control Panel Home (for Category View) or Classic View.

Security Tools

We have two entire chapters devoted to security, but the A+ 802 Objective 1.1 explicitly lists several Windows features, so we will introduce them here, explain security fundamentals in Chapter 18, and show you how to use security tools in Chapter 19.

- *User Account Control (UAC)* is a security feature introduced in Windows Vista to prevent unauthorized changes to Windows. It has been modified and improved on in later versions of Windows.

- *BitLocker drive encryption* is a drive encryption technology introduced in Windows Vista Enterprise and Ultimate editions and continues to be improved in new versions of Windows, although only available in certain editions.

- *Windows Defender* is an antispyware program, built into Windows since Windows 7, and a free download for Windows XP and Windows Vista.

- *Windows Firewall* is Microsoft's free personal firewall, which is software that guards against unauthorized network access to a single computer. First available in Service Pack 2 for Windows XP, it has been built into Windows since then.

- *Windows Security Center* is the Windows Vista page of the Control Panel that presents security status and gives access to Window's security tools, as shown in Figure 2-22.

FIGURE 2-22

The Windows Vista Security Center

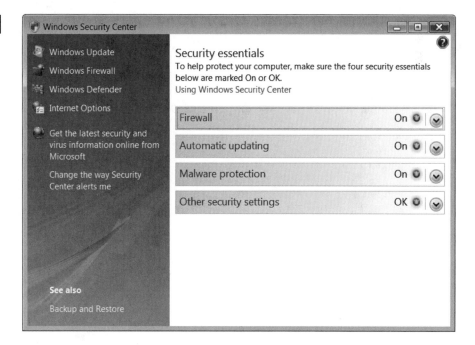

SCENARIO & SOLUTION

The pinned items list on my Start menu contains a program I no longer want in this list. How can I remove it?	Right-click the item and choose Unpin From Start Menu.
I have Windows 7. How can I store my data files in an organized folder structure to make it easy to find the files?	The folder structure for this is already set up in Windows 7. You access these folders through the Start menu Documents shortcut.
As a long-time Windows XP user, the Windows 7 Control Panel confuses me. What can I do to more easily find the applets I am familiar with?	The default view in Windows 7 Control Panel is Category View. To switch to the Windows XP view (Classic View), locate "view by" in the upper right of Control Panel, click the down arrow, and select either Large Icons or Small Icons.

CERTIFICATION SUMMARY

Before you can install and support computers, you must develop an understanding of the concepts beyond those required to simply use an OS. This begins with understanding the purpose of operating systems; knowing the differences among the major operating systems; and understanding updates, service packs, and revision levels. The versions of Windows presently included in the CompTIA A+ exams are Windows XP, Windows Vista, and Windows 7. These versions have many GUI elements in common, but with each new version, Microsoft has made changes, such as modifications to the Start menu, additions of GUI elements, and the visual enhancements of Aero that were introduced in Windows Vista, and improved upon in Windows 7.

TWO-MINUTE DRILL

Here are some of the key points covered in Chapter 2.

Introduction to Windows Operating Systems

❏ An OS controls all the interactions among the various system components, human interactions with the computer, and network operations for the computer system.

❏ Microsoft Windows comes in versions, such as Windows XP, Windows Vista, Windows 7, and Windows 8.

❏ Each Windows version also comes in editions, such as Windows 7 Starter, Windows 7 Home Premium, Windows 7 Professional, Windows 7 Ultimate, and Windows 7 Enterprise.

❏ Windows updates are software fixes to the operating system code to fix problems or enhance security. A patch is a fix for a single problem. A service pack is a bundle of patches or updates released periodically by a software publisher.

❏ Operating systems tie closely to the CPUs on which they run. Therefore, CPU terms such as 32-bit and 64-bit may also describe an OS. Windows XP, Windows Vista, Windows 7, and Windows 8 all have both 32-bit and 64-bit versions.

Considerations for Installing or Upgrading Windows

❏ Each version of an OS has a certain set of system requirements, which include the computer platform, as well as the amount of RAM and disk space.

❏ Each new OS also introduces hardware and software compatibility issues. Windows has features for managing incompatible applications, including Compatibility Mode in Windows XP, Windows Vista, and Windows 7. In addition, Windows 7 has Windows XP Mode, which uses Windows Virtual PC with an instance of a fully licensed Windows XP Professional edition.

❑ Each edition of Windows at each version level has unique upgrade paths that allow you to upgrade directly, performing an in-place installation, from certain earlier editions of Windows. In some cases, you cannot upgrade from a previous version or specific edition and must do a clean installation.

The Windows User Interface

❑ The Windows GUI includes important elements, such as the taskbar, Start menu, Windows Explorer, My Computer, Personal folders, Control Panel, command prompt, and My Network Places.

❑ The Start menu has many shortcuts—their placement and names vary somewhat among the Windows versions. There are lists of shortcuts, such as the pinned items, recently used programs, and All Programs. There are shortcuts to personal folders, such as My Documents or Documents, containing user data. There are also shortcuts to various utilities.

SELF TEST

The following questions will help you measure your understanding of the material presented in this chapter. Read all of the choices carefully because there might be more than one correct answer. Choose all correct answers for each question.

Introduction to Windows Operating Systems

1. What makes up the layers of an operating system?
   A. Hardware
   B. Software
   C. Memory
   D. Silicon

2. An operating system typically controls what interactions?
   A. Between the system and the human
   B. Between the chair and the keyboard
   C. Between the AC adapter and the wall outlet
   D. Between Windows and Linux

3. Which of the following describes responsibilities of an OS?
   A. Printer cartridges
   B. AC to DC conversion
   C. Disk and file management
   D. Inverters

4. If Windows 7 is a version, what is Windows 7 Ultimate?
   A. OEM Windows
   B. Edition
   C. Patch
   D. Update

5. Which of the following describes the OS code in all but one of the Windows XP editions?
   A. GUI
   B. Multitasking
   C. 64-bit
   D. 32-bit

6. What Microsoft policy defines the length of time Microsoft will support a product, as well as the support options for that product?

   A. Software Assurance

   B. Support Lifecycle

   C. Upgrade Advisor

   D. Compatibility Wizard

7. Which of the following is the biggest difference between 32-bit and 64-bit Windows?

   A. Memory requirements

   B. Drive space requirements

   C. Maximum address space

   D. Administrative tools

Considerations for Installing or Upgrading Windows

8. Which of the following best describes system requirements for an OS?

   A. Platform

   B. CPU, amount of RAM, hard disk space, and platform

   C. Form factor

   D. Code size

9. Which of the following cannot be directly upgraded to Windows 7 Professional?

   A. Windows Vista Ultimate

   B. Windows Vista Home Premium

   C. Windows Vista Business

   D. Windows XP Professional

10. Before you install Windows 7, download the latest version of this program to determine if your computer's hardware and software is compatible with the new OS.

   A. Setup

   B. Backup

   C. Upgrade Advisor

   D. Help | About

11. If an old app will not run in Windows 7 Professional, Enterprise, or Ultimate editions, even after trying other methods to help it run, use this free Microsoft tool, which includes a fully licensed version of XP installed in a virtual machine.

  A. Administrative Tools

  B. Windows Virtual PC

  C. Windows XP Mode

  D. Compatibility Mode

The Windows User Interface

12. The Windows GUI uses this metaphor.

  A. Mouse

  B. Desktop

  C. Taskbar

  D. Task list

13. Folders, mouse pointer, icons, shortcuts, dialog boxes, windows, buttons, etc., are all examples of these components of a GUI.

  A. Pixels

  B. Pictures

  C. Graphics

  D. Graphical objects

14. What is the horizontal bar that is usually across the bottom of the Windows desktop?

  A. Taskbar

  B. Start menu

  C. Systray

  D. Menu bar

15. What is the central tool for finding and starting programs in Windows XP, Windows Vista, and Windows 7?

  A. Taskbar

  B. Start menu

  C. Computer

  D. Menu bar

16. By default, what is the only shortcut displayed on the Windows XP desktop?

    A. Start menu

    B. Recycle Bin

    C. My Programs

    D. My Computer

17. What three buttons usually appear on the Turn off Computer dialog box in Windows XP?

    A. Shut Down, Log Off, Restart

    B. Standby, Shut Down, Restart

    C. Log Off, Turn Off, Restart

    D. Standby, Turn Off, Restart

18. What is the name for the list of items on the upper left of the Start menu beginning in Windows XP, Windows 7, and Windows 8?

    A. Recently used programs list

    B. Pinned items list

    C. Quick Launch toolbar

    D. Task list

19. This enhancement, introduced in Windows Vista, brings to the Windows desktop many new features that affect the entire Windows GUI.

    A. Sidebar

    B. Gadgets

    C. Windows Aero

    D. Systray

20. Which of the following is a feature of Windows Aero that allows you to switch among open windows?

    A. Taskbar

    B. Aero Wizards

    C. Windows Flip 3D

    D. Glass

SELF TEST ANSWERS

Introduction to Windows Operating Systems

1. ☑ **B.** Software makes up the layers of an operating system.
   ☒ **A,** hardware, is incorrect because the operating system itself is entirely software. **C,** memory, is incorrect because although the OS runs in memory, the layers running in memory are composed of software. **D,** silicon, is incorrect because this is a physical ingredient in computer hardware components, not a part of an operating system.

2. ☑ **A,** between the system and the human, is correct because these interactions are the main reason we have operating systems.
   ☒ **B,** between the chair and the keyboard, is incorrect because the human resides between the chair and keyboard, and the operating system does not control that interface. **C,** between the AC adapter and the wall outlet, is incorrect because all that resides there is a power cord. **D,** between Windows and Linux, is incorrect because this is not an interaction typically controlled by an operating system.

3. ☑ **C.** Disk and file management are responsibilities of an OS.
   ☒ **A,** printer cartridges, is incorrect because they are not responsibilities of an OS—they are hardware supplies. **B,** AC to DC conversion, is incorrect because this is the responsibility of a computer power supply. **D,** inverters, is incorrect because this is not an OS responsibility, but a hardware device.

4. ☑ **B,** edition, is correct because Windows 7 Ultimate is an edition of the Windows 7 version.
   ☒ **A,** OEM Windows, is incorrect because that describes any edition of Windows that is bundled with a computer. **C,** patch, is incorrect because a patch is a software fix for a single problem. **D,** update, is incorrect because an update is software that contains fixes to problems in Windows, often security issues.

5. ☑ **D.** 32-bit describes the OS code in all but one of the Windows XP editions.
   ☒ **A,** GUI, is incorrect because a GUI is a component of any Windows XP edition. **B,** multitasking, is incorrect because this describes the OS code of all Windows XP editions. **C,** 64-bit, is incorrect because this describes the OS code in only one edition: Windows XP x64 edition.

6. ☑ **B.** Support Lifecycle is the Microsoft policy that defines the length of time Microsoft will support a product.
☒ **A,** Software Assurance, is incorrect because this is Microsoft's software purchasing, volume licensing, and support plan for large organizations. **C,** Upgrade Advisor, is incorrect because this is a utility for determining if an existing installation of Windows can be successfully upgraded to a newer version. **D,** Compatibility Wizard, is incorrect because this is a Microsoft wizard for applying compatibility settings for the application program.

7. ☑ **C.** Maximum address space is the biggest difference between 32-bit and 64-bit Windows.
☒ **A,** memory requirements, **B,** drive space requirements, and **D,** administrative tools, are all incorrect, as none of these is the biggest difference between 32-bit and 64-bit Windows.

Considerations for Installing or Upgrading Windows

8. ☑ **B.** CPU, amount of RAM, hard disk space, and platform best describe system requirements for an OS.
☒ **A,** platform, is incorrect because this alone does not best describe the system requirements for an OS. **C,** form factor, is incorrect because this describes the dimensions of a hardware device, not the system requirements for an OS. **D,** code size, is incorrect because this just describes the size of the OS code, not the system requirements for the OS.

9. ☑ **D.** Windows XP Professional is correct because you cannot directly upgrade any version of Windows XP to any version of Windows 7.
☒ **A,** Windows Vista Ultimate, **B,** Windows Vista Home Premium, and **C,** Windows Vista Business, are all incorrect because you can upgrade all of them to Windows 7 Ultimate.

10. ☑ **C.** Upgrade Advisor is the program that will determine if your computer has hardware and software compatible with Windows XP, Windows Vista, or Windows 7.
☒ **A,** Setup, and **B,** Backup, are incorrect. Neither Setup nor Backup is the program named in this chapter for testing hardware and software compatibility. **D,** Help | About, is incorrect because this is a menu choice in My Computer (and other programs) that will provide version information, not hardware and software compatibility information.

11. ☑ **C.** Windows XP Mode is a virtual machine with a fully licensed version of XP installed that is a free feature for Windows 7, used to run incompatible older apps.
☒ **A,** Administrative Tools, is incorrect because this is simply a Start menu item that gives access to several helpful utilities. **B,** Windows Virtual PC, is incorrect, because by itself, it is only one part of Windows XP Mode. **D,** Compatibility Mode, is incorrect because this is simply a tool for tweaking the Windows environment in which an incompatible app runs; it is not Windows XP Mode, which is Microsoft Virtual PC with a fully licensed version of XP installed.

The Windows User Interface

12. ☑ **B.** Desktop is the metaphor used by the Windows GUI.
    ☒ **A,** mouse, is incorrect because this is not a metaphor for the Windows GUI, but a hardware pointing device used with the Windows GUI. **C,** taskbar, is incorrect because, although this is a Windows GUI component, it is not the metaphor used to describe the Windows GUI. **D,** task list, is incorrect because this is part of the Windows GUI, not a metaphor describing the GUI.

13. ☑ **D.** Graphical objects, such as folders, mouse pointer, icons, shortcuts, dialog boxes, windows, buttons, etc., are components of the Windows GUI.
    ☒ **A,** pixels, is incorrect because this describes a dot on a display screen, not a component of the OS GUI. **B,** pictures, is incorrect, even though you could call each of the GUI objects a picture. **C,** graphics, is incorrect, even though you could call each of the GUI objects a graphic.

14. ☑ **A.** The taskbar is usually across the bottom of the Windows desktop.
    ☒ **B,** Start menu, is incorrect because this is just a small portion on the left end of the taskbar. **C,** systray, is also incorrect because this is just a small portion of the taskbar—located on the far-right side. **D,** menu bar, is incorrect because this is a component of a window, not the horizontal bar that is usually across the bottom of the Windows desktop.

15. ☑ **B.** The Start menu is the central tool for finding and starting programs in Windows.
    ☒ **A,** taskbar, is incorrect because this is only the location of the Start menu and the place that displays buttons for pinned shortcuts (Windows 7) and open programs. **C,** Computer, is incorrect because this is a shortcut in Windows Vista and Windows 7 that opens to display file folders, hard disk drives, and removable storage on the local computer. **D,** menu bar, is incorrect because this is a component of an open window, not the central tool for finding and starting programs in Windows.

16. ☑ **B.** Recycle Bin is the only shortcut displayed by default on the Windows XP desktop.
    ☒ **A,** Start menu, is incorrect because this menu is not a desktop shortcut but is located on the taskbar. **C,** My Programs, and **D,** My Computer, are both incorrect because they are not desktop shortcuts (by default) but are located on the Start menu.

17. ☑ **D.** Standby, Turn Off, Restart are the usual three buttons on the Turn Off Computer dialog box in Windows XP.
    ☒ **A,** Shut Down, Log Off, Restart; **B,** Standby, Shut Down, Restart; and **C,** Log Off, Turn Off, Restart, are all incorrect because they are not the usual three buttons in the Turn Off Computer dialog box.

18. ☑ **B.** Pinned items list is the name for the list of items on the upper left of the Windows Start menu.

    ☒ **A,** recently used programs list, is incorrect because this is the list below the pinned items list on the Start menu. **C,** Quick Launch toolbar, is incorrect because this is an optional item on the taskbar, not a list on the Start menu. **D,** task list, is incorrect because this is not the name of the list of items on the upper left of the Windows Start menu.

19. ☑ **C.** Windows Aero is the enhancement to the Windows GUI introduced in Windows Vista.

    ☒ **A,** Sidebar, is incorrect. Although this is new in Windows Vista, it does not affect the entire Windows GUI. **B,** Gadgets, is also incorrect because a gadget is simply a small program accessed from the sidebar. **D,** systray, is incorrect because it is a portion of the taskbar.

20. ☑ **C.** Windows Flip 3D is a feature of Windows Aero that allows you to switch among open windows.

    ☒ **A,** taskbar, is incorrect. Although you can use the taskbar buttons to switch among open windows, the taskbar is not a feature of Windows Aero. **B,** Aero Wizards, and **D,** Glass, while both are features of Windows Aero, do not allow you to switch among windows.

3

Personal Computer Components— Motherboards and Processors

T ogether, this chapter and Chapters 4 and 5 introduce you to basic computer technology concepts, including categorizing, explaining, classifying, and identifying common components. Consider the contents of these three chapters to be the basic technical knowledge computer professionals need when working with PCs and laptops. Familiarity with the components, as well as a good working knowledge of their function, will allow you to work comfortably with most types of computers, in spite of different layouts or new component designs. Once you have a good sense of how the parts of a computer system work together, you will be on the road to becoming a PC technical professional. This knowledge will aid in all the technical tasks ahead of you and in passing your CompTIA A+ Certification exams. Later chapters will give you an opportunity to learn skills for installing and troubleshooting these components.

CERTIFICATION OBJECTIVE

■ **801: 2.10** *Given a scenario, use appropriate networking tools*

CompTIA A+ Exam 801 Objective 2.10 requires that you know when and how to use appropriate networking tools. Furthermore, at the very end of the published objectives for CompTIA A+ Exams 801 and 802 is a list titled "A+ Proposed Hardware and Software List." Therefore, the following hardware toolkit is composed of tools listed in the 2.10 objective, the list of tools they provided, as well as some tools we felt should be mentioned. We are presenting the entire list here, but we will revisit many of these tools in scenarios in coming chapters.

The Hardware Toolkit

Before we look at computer hardware, we should discuss the hardware toolkit. You begin with a repair toolkit that is not very extensive, perhaps a small assortment of screwdrivers and nut drivers, a small flashlight, and an assortment of screws and nuts. Then add tools as you need them. For this, you may decide to purchase a basic computer technician's toolkit, or assemble the components yourself. Figure 3-1 shows some of the most basic tools a computer technician uses on the job, and following that is a more complete list of components you should have in your kit, depending on your responsibilities. For instance, if you are not required to test

FIGURE 3-1

An assortment of
basic tools

network equipment, you will not need a toner probe, and if you never need to crimp
connectors onto lengths of cables, you will not need a crimper.

- An assortment of Phillips-head, flathead, and Torx screwdrivers, as well as
  varying sizes of nut drivers.

- Several types of small parts used on circuit boards, including various sizes of
  screws and nuts; extra jumpers (the tiny devices used to make connections
  between the pins on certain circuitry); screws; and *stand-offs*, small washer-
  type parts made of a nonconducting material, often nylon, used to ensure that
  a motherboard does not come in contact with a computer case.

- Several sizes **of *slot covers***, the metal brackets that cover the openings (slots)
  in the back of a PC for accommodating expansion cards. A slot cover serves
  to keep dust out when an expansion slot is empty and helps cooling airflow.

- A *parts grabber*, also called an *extending extractor*. This pen-sized tool has a
  plunger at one end, which, when pressed, causes small, hooked prongs to
  extend from the other end of the tool. These are useful for retrieving dropped
  objects, such as jumpers or screws, from inside a computer. Be very careful not
  to touch any circuitry when using one.

- An *extension magnet*, a long-handled tool with a magnet on the end. Use
  it like a parts grabber, only it has a magnet that attracts small objects that
  contain iron. This is handy for picking up objects that fall on the floor, but
  the potential dangers may not be worth the convenience. Never use an
  extension magnet near a computer or any peripherals that contain magnetic
  storage because the magnet can damage data.

- A flashlight for illuminating dark places.
- A small container for holding extra screws and other small parts (a pill bottle works well).
- An ESD wrist strap to use when working on any component except the power supply, monitor, and laser printers. We discussed ESD wrist straps in Chapter 1.
- An ESD mat provides a static charge with a path to ground and is designed for the desktop or floor of a workspace. While this mat may not fit in your toolkit, it is something that should be available at any PC technician's workbench.
- *Field replaceable units (FRUs)* should be included in your hardware toolkit. An FRU is any component that you can install into a system onsite. This includes such items as memory modules, heat sinks, CMOS batteries, various adapter cards, hard drives, optical drives, keyboards, mice, fans, AC adapters, spare cables and connectors, power supplies, and even spare motherboards. Of course, all of this depends on the scope of your job and how cost-effective it is to have these items on hand.
- A *multimeter* is indispensable in determining power problems from a power outlet or from the power supply. You'll use this handheld device to measure the resistance, voltage, and/or current in computer components (see Figure 3-2) using two probes (one negative, one positive) that you touch to power wires in the equipment you are testing.
- A *power supply tester* is a specialized device for testing a power supply unit, and is a bit safer to use than a multimeter for this purpose. A power supply

FIGURE 3-2

A simple multimeter

tester comes with connectors compatible with the output connectors on a standard power supply, rather than with just the simple probes of a multimeter. An LCD display or LEDs show the test results.

- A *cable tester* will detect if a cable can connect properly end to end and determine if there is a short. Several types of cable testers are available, such as those for copper Ethernet and phone cables, fiber-optic cable testers, and coaxial cable testers. A *toner probe* is a cable tester that generates a tone on one end of a cable and evaluates the signal received on the other end. We will revisit cable testers in Chapter 16.

- A *loopback plug*, a plug wired to send signals back to a specific port type (serial, parallel, USB, etc.) or device, such as an Ethernet adapter, as a test of the device. It reroutes the sending pins from the port or device to the receiving pins, thus allowing you to test the ability to send and receive without connecting to an external device or network.

- A digital camera will enable you to document the condition of a computer before you begin troubleshooting. One important way we use a digital camera is to document the cabling and connections—both external and internal—before making any changes, so that we can reconnect all components correctly. A camera is also handy for capturing low-level error messages that cannot be captured otherwise.

- Wire cutters for cutting various types of wires, but especially for Ethernet cables.

- A *punch down tool* is a hand tool with a screwdriver-type handle and one or more specialized blades used for inserting various types of wire into appropriate wiring panels. The wiring may be for electrical power or network cabling.

- A *crimper*, also called a *crimp tool*, resembles a pair of pliers, but is used to terminate a multistranded cable into a connector, clamping each wire in place in the connector so that the wires line up with the wires in the connector.

- A *cable stripper* is a cross between a pair of pliers and scissors and is designed to strip the insulation from around the wires in a cable.

- A *POST card* is an adapter card used to run a special diagnostic test on a computer as it powers up. These tests go beyond those performed by the computer's own BIOS-based testing that occurs as it starts up. We'll revisit POST cards in Chapter 11.

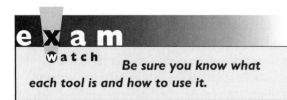

EXERCISE 3-1

What's in Your Toolkit?

1. If you are already working as a technician, gather your tools and compare them to the previously mentioned list. What would you add to the printed list? What is in the list that you would like to add to your toolkit?

2. If you are not a technician, find one who will talk to you about the tools of the trade. You may find this person at work, school, or even at a local PC repair business. Ask the technician to tell you which tools he uses the most and what he recommends you have in a basic toolkit.

CERTIFICATION OBJECTIVE

■ **801: 1.2** *Differentiate between motherboard components, their purposes, and properties*

The motherboard is the real estate on which a PC is built; all PC components are directly or indirectly connected to this large printed circuit board. This chapter introduces all of the topics of the CompTIA A+ Certification Exam Objective 801: 1.2, including motherboard sizes (ATX, Micro-ATX, and ITX), expansion slots, RAM slots, CPU sockets, chipsets, jumpers, power connections and types, fan connectors, front panel connectors, and bus speeds.

Motherboard Form Factors and Components

The average PC that resides in most offices may look like a simple device: a box connected to a display, keyboard, and mouse; but it is an extremely complicated piece of equipment that includes a vast array of technologies in its components. As a computer technician, you do not really need to be overly concerned about the actual inner workings of these components, but you must understand their general functions.

We will begin with the motherboard, the foundation of every PC. Each internal and external PC component connects, directly or indirectly, to a single circuit, the motherboard. The *motherboard*, also referred to as the *mainboard*, the *system board*, or the *planar board*, is made of fiberglass, typically brown or green, and with a meshwork of copper lines, called *traces*. Power, data, and control signals travel to all connected components through these pathways. A group of these wires assigned to a set of functions is collectively called a *bus*.

on the
(!)ob

Safety first! Hands-on experience is important for preparing for your A+ exams, and as you study you will want to install and remove components on a PC system. Therefore, you must thoroughly understand safety procedures, as detailed in Chapter 1.

In this section, we focus on types of motherboards, their typical integrated components, and the differences between the motherboard's communication busses and what components can connect to a motherboard through these various busses.

Sizes/Form Factors

A motherboard *form factor* defines the type and location of components on the motherboard, the power supply that will work with it, the size of the motherboard, and the corresponding PC case that will accommodate both. There are several motherboard form factors, each with different layouts, components, and specifications. A motherboard will use only certain CPUs and types of memory, based on the type of CPU and memory sockets installed. Therefore, if you decide to build a computer from components, you must ensure that the motherboard, power supply, CPU, memory, and case will all work together.

Personal computer motherboards have evolved over the past several decades, and continue to do so. Although motherboards can vary from manufacturer to manufacturer, Intel Corporation, a major manufacturer, has developed several form factors over the years, including the early AT (not discussed here) and NLX form factors, and the ATX, BTX, and ITX form factors. Form factor standards also have smaller variations. We will discuss their sizes, typical components, and prevalence next. The following paragraphs include brief descriptions of the form factor standards.

e x a m

w a t c h
The CompTIA A+ Certification Exam Objective 1.2 for exam 801 does not mention the term "form factor," but it does mention "sizes," under which it lists the ATX, Micro-ATX, and ITX form factors. Be sure to pay attention to
the differences among these form factors. Size is just one feature of a motherboard form factor. We discuss these form factors, as well as others that have some relevance to the exams, even if they are not listed in the objectives.

NLX

One step up from the AT form factor of the 1980s, *New Low-profile eXtended (NLX)* was an Intel standard for motherboards targeted to the low-end consumer market. It was an attempt to answer the need for motherboards with more components built in, including both sound and video, while also saving space and fitting into a smaller case. One method they used to save space was a bus slot called a riser slot, which accepted a card that created an expansion bus perpendicular to the motherboard. This *riser card*, in turn, accepted expansion cards that were oriented horizontally to the motherboard. These motherboards became obsolete very quickly, in part because they used a very old expansion bus, the *industry standard architecture (ISA)* bus, which had some severe limitations that later bus designs overcame. However, at least for a while, manufacturers needing to squeeze more expansion cards into smaller boxes used riser cards.

 on the job

If you work with experienced PC technicians, read trade publications, or visit technical Websites, you'll probably see the slang term mobo *used in place of* motherboard.

ATX

The *Advanced Technology eXtended (ATX)* motherboard standard was released by Intel Corporation in 1996 and has been updated many times over the years—both officially and through proprietary variations by manufacturers. Counting all the variations, it is the most commonly used form in PCs. The original ATX motherboard measures approximately 12" wide by 9.6" from front to back (305mm × 244mm) keeping it from interfering with the drive bays, which was a problem with the now-ancient AT motherboards. The processor socket is located near the power supply, so it will not interfere with full-length expansion boards. Finally, the hard- and floppy-drive connectors are located near the drive bays. Figure 3-3 shows a motherboard with the CPU next to the power supply along with various cables connected between the power supply and motherboard.

When first introduced, the ATX motherboard included integrated parallel and serial ports (I/O ports) and a mini-DIN-6 keyboard connector. Depending on the manufacturer and the intended market, an ATX motherboard will contain memory slots for the latest RAM types, support for BIOS-controlled power management, multimedia, Intel or AMD CPU sockets, both PATA and SATA drive controllers, and support for USB and IEEE 1394.

FIGURE 3-3

An ATX
motherboard
installed in a case
with the CPU
and some cables
visible

There are at least three additional size variations in the ATX form factor. See
Table 3-1 for the sizes of the Micro-ATX, Flex-ATX, and Mini-ATX form factors.

BTX

Introduced in 2003 by Intel Corporation, the *Balanced Technology eXtended (BTX)*
motherboard form factor was intended to be the successor to the ATX standard, but
the ATX never really went away. BTX was a major departure from ATX and offered

TABLE 3-1

Motherboard
Approximate Size
Comparison

Form Factor	Approximate Size
ATX	12" × 9.6" (305mm × 244mm)
Micro-ATX	9.6" × 9.6" (244mm × 244mm)
Flex-ATX	9" × 7.5" (228.6mm × 190.5mm)
Mini-ATX	5.9" × 5.9" (150mm × 150mm)
ITX	8.5" × 7.5" (215mm × 191mm)
Mini-ITX	6.7" × 6.7" (170mm × 170mm)
Nano-ITX	4.7" × 4.7" (120mm × 120mm)
Pico-ITX	3.9" × 2.8" (100mm × 72mm)
Mobile-ITX	2.9" × 1.77" (75mm × 45mm)

improved cooling efficiency and a quieter computer through careful placement of the components for better airflow. However, by 2006, manufacturers suspended production of this form factor due to the improved cooling of individual components and BTX's incompatibility with newer chipsets and processors. Manufacturers continue to use variations of the ATX form factor.

ITX

ITX, originally named EPIA, was developed by chipset-company VIA in 2001 for use in low-power CPUs and chipsets in low-cost PCs, but was never used in production. Subsequent designs—the Mini-ITX, Nano-ITX, Pico-ITX, and Mobile-ITX—have been progressively smaller and targeted to embedded systems. See Table 3-1.

EXERCISE 3-2

Compare Motherboards

1. From a computer with an Internet connection, use your browser to search on the ATX and ITX form factors and their smaller variations.

2. Notice the locations of the CPU, expansion bus, and memory slots.

3. If possible, open a PC, following the safety guidelines outlined in Chapter 1, and determine the form factor of the motherboard. Do not disconnect or remove any components within the case.

4. Keep the computer open while you complete this chapter, locating as many of the components described as you can.

5. When you are finished, close the computer case, reconnect the computer, and make sure that it works as well as it did before you opened it.

Motherboard Components

The components built into a motherboard include sockets for various PC components, including the CPU and memory, and built-in components such as video and sound adapters, hard drive controllers, support for various port types (parallel, serial, USB, and IEEE 1394), and the chipset. Following is an explanation of all of these, with the exception of hard drive controllers, which we will describe in Chapter 4 during the discussion of storage type.

RAM Slots

A motherboard has slots, or sockets, for system memory. Depending on the vintage and the manufacturer of a motherboard, special sockets accept one of the various types of RAM chips attached to small circuit boards called *memory modules* or, less formally, *memory sticks*. These modules are *Single Inline Memory Module (SIMM)*, *Dual Inline Memory Module (DIMM)*, and *RAMBUS Inline Memory Module (RIMM)*. SIMM is the oldest technology, and you will not see these sockets in new PCs. Both of these physical memory slot types move data 64 bits or 128 bits at a time.

DIMM sockets are the most common RAM slots today on PCs, and those for desktop or tower PCs may have 168 pins, 184 pins, or 240 pins. RIMM sockets for desktop or tower PCs have 184 pins. The current standard is DIMM, and you will only find RIMM on very old computers.

DIMM and RIMM sockets for portable computers are yet another story. Laptop motherboards have special sockets to accommodate smaller memory sticks, such as SODIMM or SORIMM. Learn more about memory for laptops in Chapter 7.

This is only part of the RAM story. In Chapter 4, you will learn about the many characteristics of modern RAM and how to select the correct RAM modules for your motherboard based on the characteristics the motherboard supports.

on the
job

Read a good (motherboard) book. How do you find out what memory modules will work on a specific motherboard? You read the motherboard user guide. If you cannot find one for your computer, find the manufacturer's name and the model of the motherboard (or computer system) and query your favorite Internet search engine. You will often find the right book in PDF format.

External Cache Memory

The motherboard may have sockets for external cache memory used by the CPU. See the discussion of cache memory later in this chapter under the topic CPUs.

Bus Architecture

The term bus refers to pathways that power, data, or control signals use to travel from one component to another in the computer. Standards determine how the various bus designs use the wires. There are many types of busses on the motherboard, including the *memory bus* used by the processor to access memory. In addition, each PC has an *expansion bus* of one or more types. The most common types of expansion bus architectures are PCI, PCI-X, PCIe, miniPCI, and AGP, and we discuss these next, as well as the less common CNR. The following bus types are those that you can expect to see in PCs today.

on the

() o b

The terms *bus, system bus, and* expansion bus **are interchangeable. A bus refers to either a system bus or an expansion bus attached to the CPU.**

PCI   *Peripheral Component Interconnect (PCI)* is an expansion bus architecture released in 1993 but was replaced by newer bus types. The PCI bus transfers data in parallel over a data bus that is either 32- or 64-bits wide. Over the years several variants of the PCI standard were developed, and data transfer speeds vary, depending on the variant and the bus width. The original 32-bit PCI bus ran at 33.33 MHz (megahertz) with a transfer rate of up to 133 megabytes per second (MBps). PCI is a *local bus*, meaning that it moves data at speeds nearer the processor speeds.

The variants on the original PCI bus include PCI 2.2, PCI 2.3, PCI 3.0, PCI-X, Mini PCI, CardBus, Compact PCI, and PC/104-Plus. These vary in signaling speed, voltage requirements, and data transfer speed. Introduced in 1998 as an improvement to PCI, *PCI-eXtended (PCI-X)* was still 32-bits wide; it ran at speeds up to four times PCI and PCIe replaced it.

PCI slots are 3" long and are typically white. PCI cards and slots are not compatible with those of other bus architectures. Although initially developed for video cards, PCI cards are also available for networking, SCSI controllers, and a large variety of peripherals.

MiniPCI and CardBus brought PCI to laptops, requiring entirely different connectors to save space. Read more on these two busses in Chapter 7.

PCIe   *Peripheral Component Interconnect Express (PCIe)* differs from PCI in that it uses serial communications rather than parallel communications as well as different bus connectors. Also called PCI Express and PCI-E, it has, for the most part, replaced PCI and is incompatible with PCI adapter cards. Although PCIe programming is similar to PCI, the newer standard is not a true bus that transfers data in parallel, but rather a group of serial channels. The PCIe connector's naming scheme describes the number of serial channels each handles, with the designations x1, x4, and x16 indicating 1, 4, and 16 channels, respectively. On the motherboard, a PCIe x1 connector is approximately 1½" long, whereas PCIe x4 is about 2" long, and PCIe x16 is close to 4" long. Figure 3-4 shows a black PCIe x16 connector at the top and three white PCI connectors below it on the motherboard.

FIGURE 3-4

Comparison of
PCIe x16 (the
dark slot) and
the older, light-
colored PCI bus
connectors

The PCIe transfer rate depends on which version of the standard the bus installation supports. For instance, PCIe 1.0 supports data transfers at 250 MBps per channel, with a maximum of 16 channels. Therefore, the maximum transfer rate for 16-channel PCIe 1.0 is 4 GB per second. PCIe 2.0, released in late 2007, added a signaling mode that doubled the rate to 500 MBps per channel. This rate was redoubled to 1 GBps per channel with the PCIe 3.0 standard, expected to support a signaling mode of 1 GBps per channel but be downward compatible with existing PCIe products.

e**x**a m
🕅**a t c h**   For the A+ exams, you
don't need to know the full specifications
of standards, such as PCI and PCIe, but
you should understand the basics of each
standard. For instance, know that PCI and
PCIe are both expansion bus interfaces;
remember that PCIe is the newer of the
standards and is serial versus PCI, which
was parallel. Be sure you can identify their
physical differences on a motherboard.

AGP   *Accelerated Graphics Port (AGP)* is a local bus designed for video only that you may see in older motherboards; however, PCIe has, for the most part, replaced it. Because this architecture provides a direct link between the processor and the video card, and gives the graphics adapter direct access to main memory, it is a "port"

An AGP connector (the dark one) above two white PCI connectors

rather than a bus. It runs at the speed of the processor's memory bus. AGP is available in 32-bit and 64-bit versions. Figure 3-5 shows a motherboard with a dark AGP connector above two white PCI connectors.

To use AGP, the system's chipset and motherboard must support it. If a motherboard has an AGP slot, there is normally only one AGP, and it looks very similar to a PCI slot, but it is not compatible with PCI cards. The AGP architecture also includes an AGP controller, which is typically a small, green chip on the motherboard. AGP cards typically run four to eight times faster than PCI and are rated as 2X, 4X, or 8X. A 64-bit 8X AGP transfers data to the display at up to 2 GB per second. Fast cards can run in slow AGP slots; however, they will only run at the speed of the AGP port. AGP Pro is a name given to various modified AGP cards with performance enhancements targeted to the very-high-performance market.

CNR *Communications and Networking Riser (CNR)* is an expansion slot that accepts multifunction adapter cards that include networking and communications functions. Manufacturers now integrate these functions into the motherboard, so you are not likely to see these slots in computers built in the last decade.

Motherboard Power Connectors

If you carefully examine a motherboard, you will see many connectors that range from tiny 3-pin connectors to long 24-pin connectors. These range from power connectors to connectors for onboard components, such as audio, I/O interfaces, and more. These will normally be labeled and well documented in the motherboard user's manual. We'll consider the power connectors you should expect to find.

A motherboard will have several 12-volt power connections for various cables coming from the power supply. The main power connector for the motherboard is a 24-pin connector with a label, such as ATXPWR1. In addition, look for a 4-pin connector for the motherboard, perhaps labeled ATX12v1. Then look for a 4-pin power connector for additional power to the expansion bus, located near it, with a label such as ATX4P1. The CPU fan, a system fan, and auxiliary fans will have 3-pin connectors, which the manufacturer will usually clearly label so that you can identify them. These labels may be CPUFAN1, SYSFAN1, AUXFAN1, and AUXFAN2.

Firmware

Firmware refers to software instructions, usually stored on *read-only memory (ROM)* chips—special memory chips that retain their contents when the computer is powered off. Most PC components, such as video adapters, hard drives, network adapters, and printers, contain firmware. Firmware built into the motherboard controls the basic functions, capabilities, and configurability of a computer system. Firmware on the motherboard includes the chipset and system BIOS.

A critical component of the motherboard firmware is the *chipset*. When technicians talk about the chipset, they are usually referring to one or more chips designed to work hand in glove with the CPU. See Figure 3-6. A specialized chipset component, called the *DMA controller*, manages the use of the *direct memory access (DMA) channels*, which are system resources that certain devices, such as sound cards and hard drives, can use to move data between the device and system RAM without involving the processor.

One part of this chipset, referred to as the *Northbridge*, controls communications between the CPU and high-speed motherboard components, such as system RAM and video adapter. The Northbridge may also be referred to as a *memory controller chip (MCC)*, and it connects directly to the CPU's front side bus (FSB). Another portion of the chipset, the *Southbridge*, manages communications between the CPU via the Northbridge and such I/O busses as the ATA PS2, SATA, USB, and the BIOS.

Chipset manufacturers include Intel, AMD, VIA Technologies, and NVIDIA Corporation, among many others. Manufacturers may vary the functions of the chipset, based on the capabilities of the CPUs with which the chipset is paired.

Another important firmware component is the system BIOS, which we will discuss later in this chapter when we look at configuring a motherboard. But first we explore the topic of CPUs.

FIGURE 3-6

The chipset is between the CPU and the computer's other resources

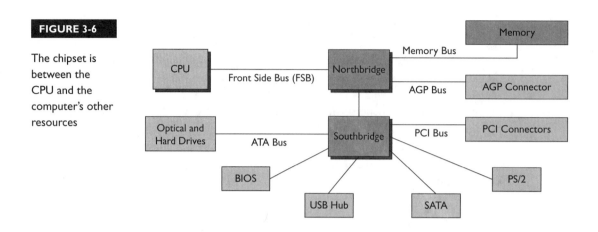

SCENARIO & SOLUTION

What are the most common bus architectures in use today?	PCI and PCIe
What standard, also used by other expansion cards, replaced AGP for video?	PCIe
You have opened a PC, looking for the PCIe slots, and you see two sets of long slots in the expansion area; some are light in color, and others are dark in color and slightly longer than the others. Which is more likely to be a PCIe x16 slot?	The longer dark-colored slots are more likely to be PCIe x16.

CERTIFICATION OBJECTIVE

■ **801: 1.6** *Differentiate among various CPU types and features, and select the appropriate cooling method*

The CompTIA A+ Exam Objective 801: 1.6 includes the following subtopics: socket types, characteristics, and cooling. It does not require that you memorize the hundreds, or perhaps thousands, of CPU models you will encounter on the job.

CPUs

A personal computer is more than the sum of its parts. However, the most important part, without which it is not a computer, or even a useful tool, is the *central processing unit (CPU)*, also called the *processor*. But a CPU may not be the only processor in a PC. Other components may include a processor for performing the intense work of the component. The most common example of this is the *graphics processing unit (GPU)* found on modern video adapters, used to render the graphics images for the display. GPUs were integrated onto system boards along with the video adapter, and now there is a trend of integrating the GPU into some CPUs. Wherever it is located, the GPU saves the CPU for other system-wide functions and improves system performance. The following is an overview of CPUs, their purposes and characteristics, manufacturers and models, and technologies.

CPU Purposes

In a PC, the central processing unit (CPU) is the primary control device for the entire computer system. The CPU is simply a chip containing a set of components that manages all the activities and does much of the "heavy lifting" in a computer system. The CPU interfaces with, or connects to, all of the components such as memory, storage, and input/output (I/O) through busses. The CPU performs a number of individual or discrete functions that must work in harmony in order for the system to function.

Additionally, the CPU is responsible for managing the activities of the entire system. The CPU takes direction from internal commands stored within it, as well as external commands that come from the operating system and other programs. Figure 3-7 shows a very simplified view of the functions internal to the CPU.

FIGURE 3-7

Simple functional diagram of a CPU

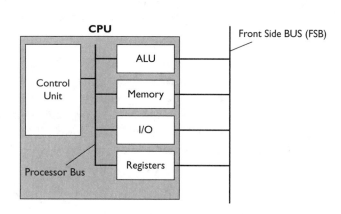

CPU Technologies and Characteristics

There are a number of technologies employed in a CPU, based on both standards and proprietary designs, which are constantly changing. The following describes common CPU technologies and characteristics.

Multicore CPUs

The most visible change in CPUs in recent years has been the introduction of *multicore CPUs* with more than one core on the same integrated circuit. Each *core* is essentially a CPU with its own cache, controller, and other CPU components. The first of these were *dual-core* CPUs containing two CPU cores. Quad-core CPUs are commonly available, and manufacturers offer 6-core, and more—even 128-core Superchip CPUs.

What is the advantage of these multicore CPUs? Server computers have long been available with multiple CPUs, so why not simply install two or more single-core CPUs on the same motherboard? The answer to both questions is that two cores on the same chip can communicate and cooperate much faster than two single-core processors. A dual-core CPU can simultaneously process two threads in true parallel execution, and each core has its own L1 cache; triple-core CPUs can simultaneously process three threads, and so on. On top of the advantage of using multiple cores, the manufacturers have made other changes to the CPU architecture to make them faster and more energy efficient.

Control Unit

The *control unit* shown in Figure 3-7 is primarily responsible for directing all the activities of the computer. It also manages interactions between the other components in the computer system. In addition, the control unit contains both hardwired instructions and programmed instructions called microcode. See the explanation later in this chapter on microcode.

Busses

Notice in Figure 3-7 that there are several pathways among components in the CPU. These are busses, used for special purposes such as moving data from internal memory to the control unit. The *processor bus*, also called an *internal bus*, is the bus located within a CPU that is usually much faster than the external busses. The *front side bus (FSB)* connects the CPU to the Northbridge, described earlier. These busses do not usually connect directly to external busses, such as PCI, except through the chipset via the Northbridge and Southbridge, which function as *controllers* that manage the communications for a bus or type of device.

Although certain Intel CPU models contained a 36-bit front side or address bus, computer manufacturers generally did not use the additional wires in the address bus to address memory. Therefore, many computers that included these CPUs supported only 32-bit addressing and could use only up to 4 GB of system RAM memory. As the need for more memory grew, so did the address bus. Some implementations used the 36-bit address bus, allowing up to 64 GB of addressable memory, and a CPU with a 64-bit address bus will address up to 1 terabyte (TB) of memory. This also depends on motherboard support, as well as an operating system and application programs that can handle the 64-bit processing. Chapter 2 described 32-bit and 64-bit operating systems.

ALU

The *arithmetic logic unit (ALU)* is responsible for all logical and mathematical operations in the system. The ALU receives instructions from the control unit. The ALU can take information from memory, perform computations and comparisons, and then store the results in memory locations as directed by the control unit. An additional type of ALU, called a *floating-point unit (FPU)* or *math coprocessor*, is frequently used to perform specialized functions such as division and large decimal-number operations. Most modern microprocessors include an FPU processor as part of the microprocessor. This includes both those used as the central processor on PC motherboards, and the GPUs used on modern video adapters.

Registers

The ALU and control unit communicate with each other and perform operations in memory locations called registers. A *register* is a memory location, internal to the CPU, used as a scratch pad for calculations. There are two types of registers used in modern systems: dedicated registers and general-purpose registers. Dedicated registers are usually for specific functions such as maintaining status or system-controlled counting operations. General-purpose registers are for multiple purposes, typically when mathematical and comparison operations occur.

Memory

Computer memory provides the primary storage for a computer system. The CPU will typically have internal memory (embedded in the CPU), used for operations, and external memory, which is located on the motherboard. The important consideration about memory is that the control unit is responsible for controlling usage of all memory. You will find a more detailed discussion about memory in Chapter 4.

Cache Memory

Cache memory in a computer is usually a relatively small amount of expensive, very fast memory used to compensate for speed differences between components. The cache memory you hear about the most is between the CPU and the main memory.

A CPU moves data to and from memory faster than the system RAM can respond. You might think that the solution is to install fast RAM as system RAM, but this would make a PC too expensive. Therefore, main system memory is most often a type of RAM known as DRAM, and cache memory is the faster and more expensive SRAM. Only a relatively small amount of memory is required for cache as compared to system memory. You will learn more about these types of RAM in Chapter 4.

ex**a**m

watch   *It is important to remember the locations and general purpose of cache memory, especially L1, L2, and L3, for the exam. In general, you won't be asked the sizes, though the concepts of large and small amounts of memory are important.*

Cache memory runs faster than typical RAM, and the small programs in a component, called the *cache controller*, have the intelligence to "guess" which instructions the processor is likely to need and retrieve those instructions from RAM or the hard drive in advance. Cache memory can also hold preprocessed data, such as out-of-order processing or data used by a game or an applications program. Typical applications may require frequent processing of the same instructions. For example, a game may repeatedly call video instructions processed by the video adapter's GPU. Newer processors can even create a "decision tree" of possible future instructions and store these in the cache, allowing rapid access to information or instructions by the CPU. Even when generating the tree, some instructions are preprocessed and stored in case the specific branch of logic is followed, and those instructions do not have to be reprocessed. Intel has this down to an art, and the processors are generally correct in the tree they create.

Internal cache memory, more commonly called *L1 cache* or *Level 1 cache*, resides within the processor itself, also referred to as "on-chip cache." *External cache memory*, called *Level 2 (L2) cache*, resides external to a CPU's core. At one time, external cache memory was only on the motherboard, but today's processors usually have L2 cache installed on the same chip as the processor, but electronically separated from the inner workings of the process. This is another example of "on-chip cache." Beginning with the Itanium CPU, Intel offered a new level of external cache memory residing on the motherboard called *Level 3 (L3) cache*. It measures in megabytes, whereas L1 and L2 cache most often measure in kilobytes. The use of cache memory with CPUs has greatly increased system performance.

Hyperthreading

A *thread*, or thread of execution, is a portion of a program that can run separately from other portions of the program. A thread can also run concurrently with other threads. *Hyperthreading*, also known as *simultaneous multithreading (SMT)*, is a CPU technology that allows two threads to execute at the same time within a single execution core. This is considered partially parallel execution. Intel introduced hyperthreading in the Pentium 4 Xeon CPU, referring to it as Hyper-Threading Technology (HT Technology).

CPU Clock Speed

The *clock speed* of a CPU is the speed at which it can potentially execute instructions. Older CPUs measured this in millions of cycles per second, or megahertz (MHz); more recent CPUs have become so fast that they are measured in billions of cycles per second, or gigahertz (GHz). A CPU of a certain type and model may be available in a range of clock speeds. All other features being equal, the CPU with the faster clock speed will be more expensive.

However, when comparing different models of CPUs, the faster clock speed alone will not determine the fastest CPU. Manufacturers use many technologies to speed up CPUs. For example, the number of clock cycles required for completing the same operation can vary among CPU models. To the end user, the perceived speed of a PC, or lack of it, may involve other aspects of the computer's total design, such as the cache size, the amount and speed of the RAM, the speed of the busses, and the speed of the hard drive. Some experts give the "actual" speed of a CPU as the speed determined by the manufacturer through testing each CPU. This speed then becomes part of the rating for that CPU. There are software tools for measuring the speed of the CPU while performing certain operations, the results of which you could consider the "real" speed.

Overclocking

Overclocking is the practice of forcing a CPU or other computer component to run at a higher clock rate than the manufacturer intended. PC hobbyists and gamers often overclock their systems to get more performance out of CPUs, video cards, chipsets, and RAM. The downside to this practice is that overclocking produces more heat and can cause damage to the motherboard, CPU, and other chips, which may explode and/or burst into flames.

Microcode

Microcode (also called a *microprogram*) is one of many low-level instructions built into the CPU's control unit. An example of an instruction might be the command to fetch information from memory. People often call microcode "hardwired" because you cannot change it.

VRM

A *voltage regulator module (VRM)* is a chip or tiny circuit card used to condition the power to the CPU and reduce it from the 5 volts of the motherboard to the lower voltage (3.3 volts or less) of the CPU. Modern CPUs in PCs inform the motherboard of the voltage they require and, therefore, may not require a VRM.

Virtualization Support

Virtualization is a big topic that we will discuss more in Chapter 8. For now, understand that many modern CPUs include virtualization support that is enabled through BIOS settings. In Intel CPUs, the name of the group of technologies involved is *Virtualization Technology (VT)*, which may have an additional symbol or letter associated with a particular CPU model. AMD's virtualization technology is *AMD-V*.

Manufacturers and Models

There are many CPU manufacturers, but the prevailing ones in the PC market today are *Intel Corporation* and *Advanced Micro Devices, Inc. (AMD)*. Intel received a huge boost when IBM selected their 8088 processor for the original IBM-PC in 1981. For over a decade, AMD produced "clones" of Intel CPUs under a licensing agreement granted to them at a time when Intel's manufacturing capacity could not keep up with the demand for CPUs. Since 1995, AMD has designed and produced its own CPUs. Both companies manufacture more than CPUs, but their competition in the CPU market gets more attention in the trade and business press since AMD emerged as Intel's major competitor.

The world has gotten a bit more complicated for those supporting PCs, laptops, and tablet PCs, because beginning with Windows 8, Microsoft has included an additional supported architecture built around the ARM CPU by ARM Holdings. This architecture is designed for very small devices like tablet PCs and smartphones that need tiny, but powerful chips with low power needs. Windows 8 comes in separate editions for the Wintel 32- or 64-bit architectures, as well as ARM. Because only Intel and AMD are listed in the objectives, the following discussion includes a sampling of CPU models from these two manufacturers.

Intel

Over time, Intel Corporation has released a number of CPU models ranging from the Intel 8086 in 1978 to the latest generation of processors, which come with a variety of model names. Some of these model names carry on the Intel Pentium, Celeron, Xeon, Itanium, and Atom brands. As for CPU branding, the word "Core" is now used in the flagship brand, and Intel is moving away from such terms as "Solo," "Core 2 Duo," and "Core 2 Quad." The newer identifiers for the Core brands are Core i3, Core i5, and Core i7.

Further, the old brand names (Pentium, Celeron, and Atom) are assigned to lower-performance CPUs. Of course, all this is subject to change.

What is important for a tech to understand is that each of the CPU brands includes many—even dozens—of individual models and the various models are categorized by the purposes for which they were designed, such as desktop, server, workstation, notebooks, and Internet devices. Additionally, they designed an entire category of CPUs for the embedded and communication devices markets.

AMD

Advanced Micro Devices, Inc. (AMD) is Intel's greatest competitor in the CPU arena. They manufacture a large variety of products based on integrated circuits. Like Intel, they categorize their CPUs by their design purposes, such as desktop, server, workstation, notebooks, and embedded devices. They also stay competitive with Intel by offering each brand in a variety of multicore configurations. They target the AMD Opteron CPU brand for use in servers, whereas the AMD FX brand is used in high-end desktops and graphics workstations. Several AMD brands target different levels of laptop uses. For instance, you'll find the A-Series CPUs with integrated GPU on laptops targeted for the home market. AMD targets some Athlon and Sempron CPU models to desktop computers. As with Intel, this is all subject to change, but look for more simplification in the product lines from both manufacturers, even as they continue to bring out dozens of CPU models each year.

CPU Sockets

The two major CPU manufacturers, Intel and AMD, each offer, at any given time, only a few current processor lines, but numerous, even hundreds, of processor models within each line. One of the many differences among the individual processor models is how the CPU attaches to the motherboard. The connection on a motherboard for a CPU is referred to as the *CPU socket*. Every motherboard contains at least one CPU socket, and the location varies from one motherboard standard to another. A common CPU socket type is a *zero insertion force (ZIF)* socket, which is square, has a retention lever that holds the CPU securely when it is closed, and makes it easy to put a CPU in the socket when it is open.

For many years both manufacturers used some variation of *pin grid array (PGA)* CPU packaging, meaning that a processor has a rectangular array of pins (numbered in the many hundreds) that insert into a matching socket on the motherboard. One variation is *pin grid array 2 (PGA2)*, which was used with Intel Pentium processors, and later the *staggered pin grid array (SPGA)* came along, in which the pin rows are staggered to allow for a higher pin density than PGA.

More recently, Intel has moved to the *land-grid array (LGA)* socket. An LGA CPU has pads rather than pins. These pads on the processor contact pins in the socket on the motherboard and permit a higher density than possible with PGA. In many cases, with both PGA and LGA processors, a number that indicates the number of pins or pads in the array follows the word "socket." For instance, an Intel LGA CPU with 775 pads is referred to as using Socket 775, but Intel also has alternative names for the sockets, as shown in Table 3-2, which lists the Intel socket types named in Objective 1.6 of the CompTIA A+ Exam, along with the year Intel introduced each of them.

While AMD has used LGA, a survey of their recent models shows that they are still using some form of PGA. Table 3-3 lists the AMD sockets named in Objective 1.6 of the CompTIA A+ Exam, along with the number of pins and the year AMD introduced each of them.

Read the motherboard and CPU documentation very carefully to be sure the CPU and socket match, because there are many versions of PGA and LGA sockets. Learn how to install a processor on a motherboard in Chapter 6.

TABLE 3-2
Intel LGA CPU Sockets

Socket Name/Pins	Year Introduced
Socket T/775	2004
Socket B/1366	2008
Socket H/1156	2009
Socket H2/1155	2011/First Quarter
Socket R/2011	2011/Third Quarter

TABLE 3-3	Socket Name/Pins	Socket Type	Introduced
AMD CPU Sockets	940/940	PGA	2003
	AM2/940	PGA	2006
	F/1207	LGA	2006
	AM2+/940	PGA	2007
	AM3/940 or 941	PGA	2009
	AM3+/942	PGA	2011
	FM1/905	PGA	2011

Cooling Systems

The more powerful PCs become, the more heat they generate within the case. Heat is your PC's enemy, and it should be yours, too. An overheated CPU will fail. Rather than allow heat to cause damage, several techniques—both passive and active—are used to maintain an optimum operating temperature. Some components will even slow down so they produce less heat before any damage occurs. Manufacturers have struggled to keep ahead of the heat curve and provide sufficient cooling for the entire system. These methods involve fans, heat sinks, thermal compounds, and even liquid cooling systems.

CPU and Case Fans

Early PCs relied on the design of the PC case and the power supply fan to provide all the cooling for the computer's interior. During this era, the typical PC had vents in the front through which the power supply fan pulled cool air and in the back through which the heated air was exhausted. Today, we usually employ additional methods, but the power supply fan still plays an important part in cooling the PC. It is very common to see a fan mounted directly over the CPU, as shown in Figure 3-8, in which the *CPU fan* is clearly visible in the center of the photo.

One or more case fans may also supplement a power supply fan. A *case fan* is a fan mounted directly on the case, as opposed to a power supply fan, which is inside the power supply. Figure 3-8 also shows a black case fan on the far left, just below the power supply. Systems that do not come with a case fan may have mounting brackets for adding one or more case fans.

An open PC
with the CPU
fan visible in the
center and the
power supply at
the top left

Heat Sinks

Another device that works to cool hot components is a *heat sink*. This is usually a passive metal object with a flat surface attached to a component, a chip, for instance. The exposed side of a heat sink has an array of fins used to dissipate the heat. Look for the light-gray heat sink that is partially visible at the bottom of Figure 3-8, just below the CPU fan. A combined heat sink and fan may even attach directly to a chip.

Thermal Compounds

A special substance, called *thermal compound, thermal paste*, or *heat sink compound*, increases the heat conductivity between a fan or heat sink and a chip. The most common is a white, silicone-based paste, but there are also ceramic-based and metal-based thermal compounds that create a bond between the chip and the fan or heat sink, increasing the flow of heat from the chip.

Liquid Cooling Systems

Many of today's motherboards for sale on the Internet or at large electronics stores feature one or more *liquid cooling systems*, which range from sealed liquid cooling systems that transfer heat by conduction from several components to active systems that use tiny refrigeration units.

Case Design

The design of each case allows for maximum airflow over the components. Part of this design is the placement of vents, positioned to either bring in fresh air or to exhaust air. If this airflow is disturbed, even by additional openings, the system may overheat. Therefore, be sure that all the expansion slot openings on the back of the PC are covered. The expansion card's bracket covers each opening that lines up with an occupied expansion slot. A metal slot cover covers an empty slot in order to preserve the correct airflow.

EXERCISE 3-3

Check Out Your Cooling System

If you have access to a PC with the conventional case fan cooling system, check it out now.

1. Without opening the computer case, look for vents in the case.

2. If the computer is running, and if it is of a conventional design, you should hear a fan running in the power supply and see the vent from the power supply. You may hear another fan running and see a set of vents for that fan.

3. Are there vents that do not appear to have a case fan behind them?

4. Hold your hand by the vents you located and determine if air flow is going into or out of the computer case. Is the power supply fan blowing in or out? If you located a case fan, is it blowing in or out?

5. Make note of your findings and discuss with your classmates or coworkers.

SCENARIO & SOLUTION

Briefly describe hyperthreading.	Hyperthreading is a CPU technology that allows two threads to execute at the same time within a single execution core.
Define CPU-based microcode.	Microcode is one of many low-level instructions built into the CPU's control unit. An example of an instruction might be the command to fetch information from memory.
You are planning to build a custom PC and want to use the most standard CPUs, so you plan to use one of the two major manufacturers of CPUs. Who are they?	The two major manufacturers of CPUs are Intel Corporation and Advanced Micro Devices, Inc., better known as AMD.

CERTIFICATION OBJECTIVE

■ **801: 1.1** *Configure and apply BIOS settings*

CompTIA Certification Objective 801: 1.1 requires that you understand how a BIOS is upgraded through flash BIOS, what information you can glean from the BIOS-setting program, how to make important configuration settings to the BIOS using the built-in BIOS, and what BIOS settings will monitor the health of a computer.

Configuring a Motherboard

Once we physically attach components to a motherboard, there are three ways that we configure the motherboard and enable the features of both built-in and added components. One way is through some primitive-seeming hardware settings, the second is done through firmware settings in the system BIOS, and the third is via software drivers you install after you have installed an operating system on the computer. In this section, we'll examine these methods in the order in which they would be applied: first the hardware settings, then we'll examine BIOS and its purpose and how to configure system BIOS settings, and finally the motherboard drivers a technician installs after the OS is installed.

Hardware Configuration

Motherboards and other circuit boards commonly have jumpers and switches used to configure, enable, or disable a feature. A *jumper* is a small connector that slides down on a pair of pins jutting up from a circuit board. There are often a number of pins side by side on the board. A hardware switch may be in the form of a *DIP switch*, a very tiny slide that indicates one of two states. If two or more switches are together, they can both be used to represent binary values of settings. Each possible jumper or switch configuration is interpreted by the system firmware as a setting. Check the user manual that came with the motherboard or other circuit board to discover how to configure the settings you desire.

 o n t h e
ⓙo b

*DIP **stands for** dual inline package, **referring to a type of now-obsolete packaging for connecting integrated circuit chips to motherboards. Old timers may recall when the early CPUs, such as the Intel 8088 in the IBM PC, used DIP packaging.***

Understanding BIOS

While the chipset can manage communications between the CPU and components, it really doesn't understand those components, or know what each needs, but the *basic input/output system (BIOS)* does. Well, the right BIOS does. Every device needs BIOS code, and the first BIOS accessed by the computer is the system BIOS on the motherboard. The system BIOS is responsible for performing a test during startup and informing the processor of the devices present and how to communicate with them. Whenever the processor makes a request of a component, the BIOS steps in and translates the request into instructions that the component can understand. That was true for many years and is true today, up to the point when an operating system loads, whereupon drivers loaded by the OS take over most of the BIOS functions. But we get ahead of ourselves. Let's first look at how we arrived at today's BIOS or BIOS replacement because the CompTIA A+ 801 exam requires that you understand many terms anchored in the past. That includes the term BIOS, since the traditional BIOS is being either supplemented or replaced by firmware complying with a new specification that allows the OS to interact more closely with modern computer components. This specification is the *Unified Extensible Firmware Interface (UEFI)*.

An early 1980s vintage PC contained true read-only BIOS, stored on ROM, that was not alterable. This meant that one could not add new types of components to the computer since the BIOS would not know how to communicate with them. Because this seriously limited users' ability to install a new type of device not recognized by the older BIOS, *flash BIOS* was developed. Arguably, the correct term is *flash ROM*, since we are able to replace the BIOS with a new version only because the ROM is of a newer technology that is not read-only, but writable using the correct method. Now you can electronically upgrade (or flash) the BIOS, updating it so that it can recognize and communicate with a new device type.

Usually you can obtain the flash program from the Website of the motherboard manufacturer. The upgrade process typically requires you to copy the flash program to either a Windows program or a bootable device and follow the detailed instructions included in the download to flash the BIOS.

Furthermore, modern motherboards include a great many more devices and capabilities than older motherboards—often more than can be adequately supported by BIOS-based programs. Therefore, when you purchase a motherboard, you will also have a driver disc. You will learn about installing and configuring motherboards and using the driver disc in Chapter 6. Companies such as Phoenix Technologies and AMI specialize in manufacturing BIOSs for PC manufacturers, and many PC and/or motherboard manufacturers make their own BIOSs.

It is very important that you follow the directions given by the manufacturer when performing a flash upgrade. If done incorrectly, the system can become inoperable and require a replacement BIOS chip from the manufacturer.

CMOS

Another important type of firmware is *complementary metal-oxide semiconductor (CMOS)*. The CMOS chip retains BIOS settings such as the date and time tracked by an onboard *real-time clock (RTC)* chip, keyboard settings, and boot sequence. CMOS also stores interrupt request line (IRQ) and input/output (I/O) resources that the BIOS uses when communicating with the computer's devices. Learn about IRQs and I/O resources in Chapter 11. The CMOS chip is able to keep these settings in the absence of computer power because of a small battery, which usually lasts from two to ten years.

BIOS Configuration

The most common way to optimize a motherboard is to modify the BIOS setup configuration, also called the *BIOS settings* or *CMOS settings*. Literally hundreds of settings are available in different computers; we discuss the most common basic and advanced BIOS settings here. The choices available, and the methods for selecting them, may vary from one BIOS manufacturer to another. The best reference for using the BIOS setup menus is the motherboard manual.

on the **job**

*Interestingly, the term CMOS settings **is a bit of a misnomer. When people talk about the computer's CMOS or its settings, they are usually referring to the things just described, but CMOS is really simply a type of physical chip. CMOS chips do a variety of things other than retaining BIOS settings. In fact, many processors are actually CMOS chips.***

Accessing BIOS Settings

To access the computer's BIOS settings, closely watch the computer screen at startup. Following the system hardware test, a message appears indicating the proper key sequence you should use to enter the BIOS settings program. It may simply say "Setup" followed by a key or key sequence name. This key or key combination varies among computers but is typically F2, DELETE, or CTRL-ALT-ESC. In most systems, the message will appear for only three to five seconds, and you must use the indicated key combination within that allotted time.

BIOS-setting programs differ from each other. Some allow you to use the mouse, and some only the keyboard. Furthermore, the names of the settings might also vary slightly. Use the program's Help feature for information about how to navigate through the program and save or discard your changes. Next we'll talk about backing up existing settings and then take a tour of possible BIOS settings.

EXERCISE 3-4

Viewing the BIOS Settings

1. Restart the computer and watch the screen closely for the correct key or keys to press.
2. Enter the BIOS-setting program using the specified key combination.
3. Do not make any changes to the settings.
4. Look at the bottom of the screen for navigation instructions, as well as how to access the Help utility (normally the F1 key).

5. Page through the screens carefully, and if you have a digital camera handy, take a picture of each screen.

6. Locate the settings described in the following paragraphs.

7. When you have finished, use the indicated key combination to exit *without* saving any changes.

Backing Up BIOS Settings

Make notes about the current BIOS settings before you change them, in case you need to change them back. We prefer to do this using a digital camera, taking a picture of each screen without making any changes. Also, look for a BIOS-settings backup utility in the BIOS menus, sometimes located on a Tools menu, or check out the BIOS manufacturer's Website for BIOS backup instructions. Alternatively, look for a third-party BIOS backup program.

Main Settings

A main settings screen will be mostly informational. Only such settings as System Time and System Date will be configurable from this screen, and you don't have to go into the BIOS settings to change the date and time on your computer. In Windows, you simply click the real-time clock display on the right side of the taskbar, click Change Date And Time Settings, and make the changes.

Aside from date and time, this screen has a great deal of information about your computer. For instance, on my Dell XPS laptop, this screen displays the component information shown in Table 3-4.

Watch *Although there are easier methods for seeing at least most of this system information from within Windows, The CompTIA A+ Exam 801 Objective 1.1 requires that you understand where and how to find this information in system setup and where to set configuration options in the BIOS.*

Notice the information in this screen, such as the amount of RAM installed (System Memory and Extended Memory taken together makes 8 GB in this case), the size and model of the hard drive (Fixed HDD), and the model and type of optical drive installed (SATA ODD), as well as the model of the CPU and its speed and the size and types of CPU cache. While it does not explicitly state this fact, the model name, Intel Core i7-2670QM, indicates that this CPU has four cores. Next we'll take a tour of the configuration settings found in our computer.

TABLE 3-4	Setting Name	Actual Configuration	
	BIOS Version	A06	
The Main Screen	Product Name	XPS L502X	
of a BIOS Setting	CPU Type	Intel Core i7-2670QM CPU @ 2.20GHz	
Menu	CPU Speed	2.20GHz	

	CPU Cache
	   L1 Cache
	   L2 Cache
	   L3 Cache
		
		64 KB
		256 KB
		6,144 KB	

	Fixed HDD	WDC WD7500BPKT–75PK4T0	–(S0) 750GB
	SATA ODD	HL-DT-ST DVDRW/BDROM CT30N	–(S1) ATAPI
	eSATA Device	None	
	AC Adapter Type	130 W	
	System Memory	630 KB	
	Extended Memory	8,191 KB	
	Memory Speed	1,333 MHzpeed MH displayed in the main screen, which includes RAM.	

Advanced Settings

Continuing to use the Dell Laptop system BIOS as our model, we find an advanced menu with plenty of items we can configure. Table 3-5 lists some of these items, along with a brief explanation. Notice the virtualization setting that enables hardware-level support for running virtualization software on your computer. This is important to know for the exam, and you will learn more about virtualization in Chapter 8.

Security Settings

System BIOS also has security settings that include one or more passwords. We do not generally recommend setting BIOS-level passwords, unless your computer is exposed to the risk of physical theft, as is the case when you travel with a laptop. BIOS-based passwords could then keep thieves from using the computer or stealing the data on it.

Let's look at how BIOS-level passwords work on the computer we are using as an example. Here, we have the option to configure three passwords: Supervisor, User, and Hard Disk Drive. Some systems (typically newer ones) include both password options;

TABLE 3-5   The Advanced Screen of a BIOS Setting Menu

Setting Name	Setting State	Description
Intel SpeedStep	Enabled	Turns on a feature of the CPU that "steps" the CPU up when more power is needed, and steps it down when it is not needed so as to conserve power usage.
Virtualization	Enabled	Enables Intel Virtualization Technology (VT-x).
Integrated NIC	Enabled	Enables or disables the onboard network interface card (NIC).
USB Emulation	Enabled	Determines whether the system basic input/output system (BIOS) controls Universal Serial Bus (USB) keyboards and mice. When enabled, the system BIOS controls USB keyboards and mice until a USB driver is loaded by the operating system.
USB Wake Support	Disabled	Enables or disables a USB mouse or keyboard to wake a computer from sleep.
SATA Operation	AHCI	AHCI enables full capabilities of SATA. Choose AHCI when using a recent version of Windows that works with SATA. Choose ATA, which will emulate the old PATA interface for an older OS.
Adapter Warnings	Enabled	When enabled, the system will warn you if you attempt to use a power adapter with too little capacity.
Function Key Behavior	Function Key	When "Function Key" is selected, the FN key must be pressed before pressing one of the alternate functions on the laptop's function keys. If "Multimedia Key" is selected, only the function key (F1, F2, etc.) with the alternate function needs to be pressed. Disabled during startup so that you can call up the System menu with the F2 key.
Charger Behavior	Enabled	When enabled, the battery will be charged when the laptop is connected to external power. If disabled, the laptop will be powered but the battery will not be charged.

Miscellaneous Devices
    External USB Ports
    eSATA Ports
	Enabled
	Enabled
		When enabled, the external ports are enabled and visible to the OS. When disabled, the external ports are disabled and not visible to the OS.

much older systems typically include only supervisor-type passwords, required both to boot the system and to enter the BIOS-settings program. These are all disabled by default.

You can set a User password to allow or restrict booting the system. A Supervisor password can be set to allow or restrict access to the BIOS-settings program itself or to change user passwords. Our computer requires that you first set a supervisor password before it allows you to set a user password. The hard disk drive (HDD) password is separate in this case, and if enabled must be entered before a user can access the hard drive.

Additionally, our computer has an option that allows you to enable the BIOS interface to connect to a for-pay antitheft service. Disabled by default on our computer, enabling it involves signing up for the service over the Internet at which point it downloads additional software. Once you have enabled and subscribed to the service and connected the computer to the Internet, the software installed into your OS will contact the service's servers and check for a theft report, as well as transmitting the system and GPS tracking information concerning the location of the computer. This service may have a product name attached to it, such as Computrace or LoJack. The name LoJack may be familiar for their auto-theft prevention products.

<table>
<tr><td>

e x a m

ⓦ a t c h   *CompTIA A+ Certification Exam Objective 801: 1.1 uses the spelling "lo-jack" which is incorrect. However, if you see that spelling on the exam, assume it to mean "LoJack."*

</td><td>

Even formatting or replacing the existing hard drive will not bypass this security because it takes advantage of the built-in *Trusted Platform Module* (TPM), an embedded security chip that stores encrypted passwords, keys, and digital certificates. Various services can use the TPM chip. Even without a for-pay location service, when you combine the use of TPM with a BIOS-level Administrator password and a User password required at power-on, the

</td></tr>
</table>

computer is virtually useless to a thief. Learn more about other security measures in Chapters 17 and 18.

on the

ⓙ o b   *Considering how often users forget passwords, using the combination of TPM, Administrator password, and require-User password at power-on may make a computer useless to the user! Use these security measures only where and when required, such as protecting mobile computers that contain sensitive information.*

A less common BIOS security feature found on some models is a chassis *Intrusion Detection System* (IDS). When turned on, if this feature detects that someone opened the case then on the next reboot, it will display a message such as "Alert! Cover was previously removed." This is useful in a situation in which someone steals computer components out of computers, but, with the trend toward integrating more and more components on the motherboard, it may be more sensible to secure the building against the theft of the entire computer system.

Boot Sequence

Your system BIOS will no doubt have a setting for selecting the order in which the BIOS will search devices for an OS. You can normally select from among a variety of possible boot devices, including A: or Floppy, C: or Hard Disk, CD/DVD drive, removable drive, USB devices, and even the network. In the last case, the BIOS will perform a PXE boot via your network interface card (NIC). All modern network cards support the ability to start a computer over the network, without relying on a disk-based OS, using an Intel standard called Preboot eXecution Environment (PXE).

If we plan to install a new OS on a system using a bootable optical disc, we go into the setup menus and set the boot order so that the optical drive precedes the hard drive. With this turned on, every time the system restarts, you briefly see a message to press any key to boot from the optical disc. After installing a new OS, we may change the boot order to start from the hard drive first. Then it only searches other drives at bootup if it does not find an OS on the hard drive.

Installing Motherboard Drivers

Every motherboard, at least when purchased separately, comes with a driver disc for all the onboard components, such as the chipset and video adapter. This disc contains drivers compatible with the latest operating systems. If you do not install the motherboard drivers you may not be happy with some aspects of the system and may not be able to access all features. For instance, without the video driver it may not fully support the optimum mode of the video adapter.

To install the motherboard drivers, once the entire system is assembled, start the computer and install the operating system. During the OS installation you can either accept the default drivers (our preference) or, when prompted, supply the driver disc for onboard components

Replacing or Upgrading BIOS

The function of the BIOS is to translate communications among devices in the computer. The BIOS is able to do this because it contains the basic instruction set for those device types. This is required only for certain system devices, such as hard disk drives, floppy disk drives, memory, I/O ports, and so on. You do not need to upgrade the BIOS to use a new mouse or printer. It is important to understand that this is not necessary for a new device, but only for an entirely new device type, and that it requires communications with the computer at a low level even before operating-system-level drivers install. Look for instructions in the motherboard manual or at the manufacturer's Website.

BIOS-based Diagnostics and Monitoring

In addition to the configuration settings program, the typical BIOS includes built-in diagnostics and a variety of monitoring features, depending on the manufacturer and the type of system to which it is targeted, such as desktop, laptop, or tablet. We'll discuss these now.

Power-on-Self-Test

The *power-on self-test (POST)* is actually a group of tests stored in the BIOS and performed every time a PC boots up. These tests check for the presence and status of recognized components. A visual (text) error message on the screen, or a series of beeps, typically indicates errors found during the POST.

Optional Tests

Further, a BIOS may also include additional tests that you can initiate through the BIOS setup menus to perform more advanced tests on components. These were not available in our sample BIOS, but if you poke around in a BIOS setup program you may discover diagnostic tests for the motherboard components and memory. Some manufacturers install special diagnostic software for their hardware when they preinstall Windows on a system. Browse through the Start menu for clues to such a program.

BIOS-based Monitoring and Alerts

Some BIOSs include the ability to monitor the health of a computer, including such indicators of possible problems as CPU and system temperatures, CPU and case fan speeds, CPU core voltage, and voltages supplied to the motherboard. A couple older systems we support have this feature, and in those instances, the monitoring is always happening, but you can optionally choose a BIOS setting to turn on alarms and even shut down the computer for some of the more critical indicators, such as fan failure and CPU temperature.

SCENARIO & SOLUTION

You need to access a PC's BIOS setup program; in general terms, how will you do that?	Restart the computer and watch carefully for a brief message that may say "Setup" followed by a key or key combination name. Press that key or combination to enter BIOS.
You need to boot a computer from an optical disc, but every time you try, it immediately boots from the hard drive and loads Windows. What can you do?	Go into the BIOS setup and add the optical disc to the boot order, making sure it precedes the hard drive.
You want to change the system time and date on your PC. What is the easiest way to do this?	Although this is a BIOS setting, the easiest way to do this is from the OS.

The PC Case

The typical PC user only knows his or her computer by its most visible components— the display, the keyboard, the mouse, and the box that houses the main system, called the *case*. Let's explore the need for cases and the types of cases, including the popular trend that does away with separate cases.

on the **Job**

Computer case knowledge is not included in the CompTIA A+ exams. It is included in this book as useful on-the-job information.

Just as you should not judge a book by its cover, you should not judge a computer by its case. A simple case may hide a very powerful computer, and a well-designed case, built with heavier-than-usual materials, insulation, and quieter fans, can provide noise reduction, a valuable feature to many people. Within the computer gaming community, creating highly personalized cases, a practice called case *modding* (modifying), is very popular. These cases may have internal lighting, colorful cable covers, and transparent sides. There are many computer case manufacturers—some who specialize in gaming cases.

Purpose and Features

The purpose of a PC case is to hold all the basic components, to protect those components from dust and dirt, to cool the components, and to provide noise reduction. This last is not a high priority with most common cases, but cases are available that provide noise dampening using heavier materials, insulation, quieter power supplies, and quieter cooling fans.

A case typically comes with a power supply, cable management systems, and mounting locations for the motherboard, drives, and other internal components. A case will also provide a panel on the back containing connectors for USB, IEEE 1394, power, audio, and microphone, as shown in Figure 3-9. (Learn more about the standards for USB and IEEE 1394 in Chapter 4.) Most cases will also have a panel on the front with similar connectors, as well as the power button, a reset button, a power light, and a drive activity light.

A high-quality case comes with premium features such as a large-capacity, quiet power supply; easy-to-remove exterior body panels; and easy-to-use hard drive bays with features such as shock absorption. Similarly, better models will have features that make the job of installing a motherboard easier, such as a removable tray to hold it.

Case Form Factors

PC cases come in form factors to match motherboard form factors, such as ATX, MicroATX, and Mini-ITX. A case form factor must take into consideration the location of the motherboard-based components so you can access them. For instance,

FIGURE 3-9

A PC case from the back showing a panel of ports and expansion slots

the case needs to have exterior openings for the adapter cards and port connectors built into the motherboard. It must also position drive bays so they will not interfere with any motherboard components. A case also accommodates the standard power supply formats, described in Chapter 5. A case, motherboard, and power supply must match, or the motherboard and power supply may not even fit in the case.

Case Categories

Most PC cases fall into one of two categories: tower and desktop. A tower is designed to stand on a desk or floor with its largest dimension oriented vertically. A desktop case is designed to sit on a desk with its largest dimension oriented horizontally. In a tower, the motherboard is normally mounted vertically, and in a desktop, the motherboard is mounted horizontally.

Case Sizes

Case sizes are not standardized, nor are the names manufacturers give the various sizes. Quality and features vary, so bigger is not always better. When quality is comparable, then, as size and features expand, so will the prices for PC cases. Common names used to describe case sizes include (from largest to smallest) full-tower, mid-tower, mini-tower, desktop, and low-profile. Mini-tower is the case size of most brand-name PCs. However, the current trend is moving away from separate PC cases, which we'll explore next.

All-in-Ones: The Anti-Case

Most major manufacturers offer at least a few desktop models that integrate everything but the mouse and keyboard into the display case. This is an *all-in-one computer*, and it typically contains the motherboard, hard drive, and optical drive within the case, with an opening for the optical drive on the side and all I/O ports on the sides and/or back of the display case. The Apple iMac line may be the most famous, and maybe the most elegant, but several major PC manufacturers have all-in-one PCs. You cannot open these cases unless you are willing to void the warranty, although they usually have a small access panel for adding RAM. Otherwise, you can only add components to one of these systems via the external connectors, but expect to find at least one video connector, two or more USB connectors, eSATA, FireWire, and multimedia connectors.

CERTIFICATION SUMMARY

Common computer components include the processor, memory, storage devices, and input and output devices. All of these devices have specific functions, and your familiarity with them will help you to determine when to upgrade or replace a component.

This chapter described general characteristics of motherboards, installed motherboard components and form factors, and CPU technologies. You must use a motherboard that supports the selected CPU and RAM. Motherboards have many integrated functions. This chapter introduced several of the technologies that the A+ exams may test you on. A good knowledge of these concepts is also important when you are repairing or upgrading a computer system. Chapters 4 and 5 will continue with explanations of other important PC components, and Chapter 6 will describe how to install and upgrade PC components.

TWO-MINUTE DRILL

Here are some of the key points covered in Chapter 3.

The Hardware Toolkit

❑ Start out with a basic toolkit of an assortment of screwdrivers and nut drivers, a small flashlight, and an assortment of screws and nuts.

❑ A motherboard form factor defines the type and location of the components on the motherboard, the power supply that will work with that motherboard, and the PC case the components will fit into.

❑ In addition to a variety of tools and replacement parts, consider keeping a digital camera handy to document the physical condition of a computer before you begin troubleshooting, and to capture low-level error messages that you cannot capture otherwise.

Motherboard Form Factors and Components

❑ All components, including external peripherals, connect directly or indirectly to the motherboard.

❑ A motherboard form factor defines the type and location of the components on the motherboard, the power supply that will work with that motherboard, and the PC case the components will fit into.

❑ ATX remains the standard for motherboards, in spite of the introduction of the no-longer-in-production BTX standard in 2003 by Intel Corporation.

❑ The ATX and ITX form factors come in a variety of sizes, beginning with the standard ATX at 12" × 9.6", the Micro-ATX at 9.6" × 9.6", and down to the Mobile-ITX, which easily fits in the palm of your hand.

❑ Motherboard components include sockets for various PC components, including the CPU and memory, built-in components such as video and sound adapters, hard drive controllers (PATA and SATA), support for various port types, and the chipset.

❑ Memory sockets can include DIMM or RIMM on motherboards for desktop systems, and SODIMM or SORIMM on laptop motherboards.

❑ A motherboard may have sockets for external cache memory used by the CPU.

❑ Every motherboard contains at least one CPU socket, and the location varies, based on the form factor.

❑ The most common types of bus architectures are PCI (now obsolete), the nearly obsolete AGP, and the current standards: PCIe, and PCI-X.

❑ PCI, PCIe, AGP, and PCI-X bus architectures are "local" because they connect more directly with the processor.

❑ The chipset is now one to three separate chips on the motherboard that handle very low-level functions relating to the interactions between the CPU and other components.

CPUs

❑ The CPU chip is the primary control device for a PC. A GPU is a processor on a video adapter, dedicated to the rendering of display images.

❑ The CPU connects to all of the components, such as memory, storage, and input/output, through communication channels called busses.

❑ CPU (and GPU) components include the control unit, busses, the arithmetic logic unit (ALU), memory, controllers, and cache memory.

❑ Hyperthreading is a technology that allows a CPU to execute two threads at the same time.

❑ A multicore processor contains two or more processing cores and can process multiple threads simultaneously, performing true parallel execution.

❑ Intel Corporation and AMD (Advanced Micro Devices, Inc.) are the two top manufacturers of PC CPUs.

❑ Intel has many models under a variety of brand names, such as Pentium, Celeron, Xeon, Itanium, Atom, Centrino, and Core. This last is the latest brand of the newest technology, whereas the older brand names identify lower-end products.

❑ AMD also has many CPU lines under many names. Just a few are Athlon, Opteron, Sempron, and the FX and A-Series.

Configuring a Motherboard

❑ Beyond installing components, configure a motherboard with hardware (jumpers and switches) through BIOS settings and through motherboard drivers installed into an operating system.

❑ The basic input/output system, or BIOS, is firmware that informs the processor of the hardware that is present and contains low-level software routines for communicating with and controlling the hardware. Configured through a BIOS setup program, you may also need to upgrade, or flash, an older BIOS.

❑ The CMOS chip is nonvolatile RAM, supported by a battery. CMOS stores basic hardware configuration settings (BIOS settings).

❑ The power-on self-test (POST) is a group of tests stored in BIOS and performed every time a PC boots up. It issues error messages on the screen or a series of beeps when it discovers errors.

❑ Additional monitoring options and diagnostics tests are available with some BIOSs.

The PC Case

❑ The computer case is the container that houses and protects the PC motherboard, power supply, and other components.

❑ A computer case is constructed of metal, plastic, and even acrylic.

❑ Cases come in a variety of sizes that are not always standardized, but each fits a certain motherboard form factor and usually comes with a power supply. They include full-tower, mid-tower, mini-tower, desktop, and low-profile. Many computer manufacturers also offer all-in-one computers that contain everything but the keyboard and mouse within the display case.

SELF TEST

The following questions will help you measure your understanding of the material presented in this chapter. Read all of the choices carefully because there might be more than one correct answer. Choose all correct answers for each question.

The Hardware Toolkit

1. Use this tool to detect if a cable can connect properly end-to-end and determine if there is a short.

    A. Stand-off

    B. FRU

    C. Cable tester

    D. POST card

2. What would you use to measure the resistance, voltage, and/or current in computer components using two probes?

    A. Multimeter

    B. FRU

    C. Cable tester

    D. Punch down tool

Motherboard Form Factors and Components

3. Which is the most common type of RAM slot on desktop motherboards?

    A. RIMM

    B. SIMM

    C. SODIMM

    D. DIMM

4. Which of the following statements is true?

    A. The motherboard must always be in a horizontal position.

    B. Each internal and external PC component connects to the motherboard, directly or indirectly.

    C. The "lines" on the motherboard provide cooling.

    D. A system board is an unusual motherboard variant.

5. Which of the following describes a motherboard form factor?
    A. The size and color of a motherboard
    B. The processor the motherboard supports
    C. The type and location of components and the power supply that will work with the mother-board, plus the dimensions of the motherboard
    D. Mid-tower

6. This variant of the most enduring and popular motherboard form factor measures 9.6" on each side.
    A. Mini-ATX
    B. ATX
    C. Mobile-ITX
    D. Micro-ATX

7. Which statement is correct of Northbridge?
    A. A chipset component that connects directly to the CPU's front side bus
    B. A chipset component that controls communications between the CPU and I/O busses
    C. A component that saves configuration settings
    D. The system setup program itself

8. Which of the following describes a difference between PCI and PCIe?
    A. PCIe is only used for graphics adapters; PCI is used by a variety of adapters.
    B. PCI uses parallel data communications; PCIe uses serial communications.
    C. PCIe uses parallel data communications; PCI uses serial communications.
    D. PCIe is used by a variety of adapters; PCI is only used by video adapters.

9. What type of local bus connector designed for video adapters was phased out in favor of PCIe?
    A. PCI
    B. NIC
    C. AGP
    D. USB

CPUs

10. What is the maximum address space of a CPU with a 64-bit address bus?
    A. 4GB
    B. 8GB
    C. 1TB
    D. 128GB

11. Which of the following most accurately describes a function of the CPU's cache memory?

    A. To store instructions used by currently running applications

    B. To provide temporary storage of data that is required to complete a task

    C. To anticipate the CPU's data requests and make that data available for fast retrieval

    D. To store a device's most basic operating instructions

12. What component in a CPU is responsible for all logical and mathematical operations?

    A. ALU

    B. Processor

    C. Control unit

    D. Processor bus

13. What CPU component contains microcode?

    A. ALU

    B. Processor

    C. Control unit

    D. Bus

14. What Intel CPU technology allows two threads to execute at the same time within a single execution core?

    A. Hyperthreading

    B. Core

    C. Cache memory

    D. Microcode

15. What type of memory is very fast and too expensive to use as system RAM, but is used as cache memory?

    A. DIMM

    B. RIMM

    C. DRAM

    D. SRAM

Configuring a Motherboard

16. Which statement most accurately describes the relationship between the computer's BIOS and CMOS?
    A. The CMOS uses information stored in the BIOS to set computer configurations, such as the boot sequence, keyboard status, and hard drive settings.
    B. The BIOS configuration settings are stored on the battery-supported CMOS chip so they are not lost when you turn off the computer.
    C. The CMOS uses information stored in the BIOS to communicate with the computer's components.
    D. They perform the same functions, but the BIOS is found only in newer computers.

17. Which of the following are hardware devices used to configure a motherboard?
    A. Slot covers
    B. Jumpers and DIP switches
    C. Stand-offs
    D. POST cards

18. After installing a motherboard and assembling the entire computer system and installing the operating system, what should you do next in order to access all the features of a motherboard?
    A. Flash the BIOS
    B. Install jumpers
    C. Install motherboard drivers
    D. Install a POST card

The PC Case

19. Which statement is true?
    A. A case, motherboard, and power supply must match, or the motherboard or power supply will not fit in the case.
    B. Any power supplies will fit into any case.
    C. Any motherboards will fit into any case.
    D. The relative position of drive bays to the motherboard is not a consideration because the motherboard is flat.

20. How can you add components other than RAM to an all-in-one computer?
    A. Small access panel
    B. Jumpers
    C. Registers
    D. External connectors

SELF TEST ANSWERS

The Hardware Toolkit

1. ☑ **C.** Cable tester is the tool to use to detect if a cable can connect properly end-to-end and determine if there is a short

   ☒ **A,** stand-off, is incorrect, because stand-offs are small washer-type parts used to ensure that a motherboard does not come in contact with a computer case. **B,** FRU, is incorrect, because FRU stands for field replaceable units: any computer component that you can install into a system onsite. **D,** POST card, is incorrect because a POST card is an adapter card used to run a special diagnostic test on a computer as it is powering up.

2. ☑ **A.** Multimeter is the device you would use to measure the resistance, voltage, and/or current in computer components using two probes.

   ☒ **B,** FRU, is incorrect because an FRU is a field replaceable unit, or any component that you can install into a system onsite. **C,** cable tester, is incorrect because a cable tester is usually used for network cables to test if a cable can connect properly end-to-end. **D,** punch down tool, is incorrect because it is a hand tool used for inserting various types of wire into appropriate wiring panels.

Motherboard Form Factors and Components

3. ☑ **D.** DIMM RAM slots are the most common type of RAM slots on desktop motherboards.

   ☒ **A,** RIMM, and **B,** SIMM, are both incorrect because they are old technologies not likely to be found on new desktop motherboards. **C,** SODIMM, is incorrect because this type of RAM slot is usually found on laptops.

4. ☑ **B.** Each internal and external PC component connects to the motherboard, directly or indirectly. This statement is true.

   ☒ **A** is not true because the motherboard can be oriented in whatever position the case requires. **C** is not true because the lines on the motherboard do not provide cooling but carry signals and are part of various busses installed on the motherboard. **D** is not true; system board is simply another name for motherboard.

5. ☑ **C.** A motherboard form factor is the type and location of components and the power supply that will work with the motherboard, plus the dimensions of the motherboard. This statement is true.

   ☒ **A** is not correct because, while size may be part of a form factor, color has nothing to do with the form factor. **B** is incorrect because the processor the motherboard supports is not, by itself, a description of a form factor. **D** is incorrect because mid-tower is a case size, not a motherboard form factor.

6. ☑ **D.** Micro-ATX. This variant of the ATX form factor measures 9.6" × 9.6".
   ☒ **A** is incorrect because mini-ATX measures 5.9" × 5.9". **B,** ATX, is incorrect because it measures 12" × 9.6". **C,** Mobile-ITX, is incorrect because it measures just 2.9" × 1.77".

7. ☑ **A.** A chipset component that connects directly to the CPU's front side bus.
   ☒ **B** is incorrect because it describes the Southbridge (a chipset component that controls communications between the CPU and I/O busses). **C** is incorrect because it describes CMOS memory. **D,** the system setup program itself, is incorrect because this program is found in the system BIOS.

8. ☑ **B.** PCI uses parallel data communications; PCIe uses serial communications.
   ☒ **A** and **D** are both incorrect because both PCIe and PCI are used by a variety of expansion cards. **C** is incorrect because the very opposite is true. PCIe uses serial data communications, and PCI uses parallel data communications.

9. ☑ **C.** AGP is correct because manufacturers have replaced this video-only local bus connector with PCIe.
   ☒ **A** is incorrect because, although PCI is also being phased out and replaced by PCIe, it is not only for video adapters. **B,** NIC, is incorrect because this stands for a type of expansion card, a network interface card, not a bus connector. **D,** USB, is incorrect because this is a peripheral bus, not a bus connector on the motherboard in which an expansion card is installed.

CPUs

10. ☑ **C.** The maximum address space of a CPU with a 64-bit address bus is 1TB.
    ☒ **A,** 4GB, **B,** 8GB, and **D,** 128GB, are all incorrect.

11. ☑ **C.** A function of a CPU's cache is to anticipate the processor's data requests and make that data available for fast retrieval.
    ☒ **A,** to store instructions used by currently running applications, and **B,** to provide temporary storage of data that is required to complete a task, are incorrect because these are both functions of RAM memory. **D,** to store a device's most basic operating instructions, is incorrect because this is a function of a device's ROM memory.

12. ☑ **A.** The ALU is the CPU component that is responsible for all logical and mathematical operations.
    ☒ **B,** processor, is incorrect because this is just a synonym for CPU. **C,** control unit is incorrect because this is the component responsible for directing activities in the computer and managing interactions between the other components and the CPU. **D,** processor bus, is incorrect because this is just a pathway among components in the CPU.

13. ☑ **C.** The control unit is correct because it contains microcode.

☒ **A,** ALU, is incorrect because it does not contain microcode but receives instructions from the control unit. **B,** processor, is incorrect because this is just another name for CPU. **D,** bus, is incorrect because this is just a group of wires used to carry signals.

14. ☑ **A.** Hyperthreading is the CPU technology that allows two threads to execute at the same time within a single execution core.

☒ **B** is incorrect because a core is a CPU with its own cache, controller, and other CPU components. **C,** cache memory, is incorrect because it is usually a relatively small amount of expensive, very fast memory used to compensate for speed differences between components. **D,** microcode, is incorrect because it is the name for the low-level instructions built into a CPU.

15. ☑ **D.** SRAM is correct. Static RAM is fast and expensive. It is used as cache memory because relatively small amounts are required.

☒ **A,** DIMM, and **B,** RIMM, are both incorrect because they are each a type of slot and a type of packaging for sticks of DRAM. **C,** DRAM, is incorrect because it is dynamic RAM, which is much slower and cheaper than SRAM.

16. ☑ **B.** The BIOS configuration settings are stored on the battery-supported CMOS chip so they are not lost when you turn the computer off. This is the correct answer.

☒ **A** is incorrect because it is the CMOS, not the BIOS, that stores computer configurations. **C,** that CMOS uses information stored in the BIOS to communicate with the computer's components, is incorrect because this is the opposite of the actual relationship between the BIOS and CMOS. **D** is incorrect. The CMOS and BIOS do not perform the same functions, and both are found in all PCs, old and new.

17. ☑ **B.** Jumpers and DIP are hardware devices used to configure a motherboard.

☒ **A,** slot covers, is incorrect because a slot cover is used to cover the opening behind an empty expansion slot. **C,** stand-offs, is incorrect because stand-offs are small washer-type parts used to ensure that a motherboard does not come in contact with a computer case. **D,** POST cards, is incorrect because a POST card is an adapter card used to run a special diagnostic test on a computer as it is powering up.

18. ☑ **C.** In order to access all the features of a motherboard you should install motherboard drivers after installing a motherboard, assembling the entire computer system, and installing the operating system.

☒ **A,** flashing BIOS, is incorrect because you should only need to flash the BIOS if you discover it needs updating to support newer hardware. **B** is incorrect because if jumpers were necessary, based on the motherboard manual, you would have installed them while assembling the computer hardware. **D** is incorrect because you only need a POST card when doing diagnostics.

The PC Case

19. ☑ **A.** A case, motherboard, and power supply must match, or the motherboard or power supply will not fit in the case.

    ☒ **B** and **C** are both incorrect because each case is designed to fit certain power supplies and motherboards. **D** is incorrect because even though the motherboard itself is flat, the components on the motherboard take up varying amounts of vertical space, and therefore, the position of drive bays is a consideration.

20. ☑ **D.** External connectors are how you add components other than RAM to an all-in-one computer.

    ☒ **A,** small access panel, is incorrect because this is not how you add components other than RAM. If available, an access panel may be how you do add RAM. **B,** jumper, is incorrect because this is not how you add components to an all-in-one computer; it is a tiny device used to make connections between the pins on certain circuitry. **C,** a register, is a component of a CPU.

4

Personal Computer Components— Memory, Adapters, and Storage

This chapter is a continuation of the survey of PC concepts and components begun in Chapter 3, which provided the purposes and technologies of PC motherboards, CPUs, and cases. In this chapter, you will continue along the same vein and explore RAM memory, adapter cards, and storage devices. Further, we'll define the connection interfaces, connectors, and ports associated with the expansion cards and storage devices. Chapter 5 will continue this survey of PC concepts and components, and then in Chapter 6 we'll put it all together by installing components in a PC.

CERTIFICATION OBJECTIVE

■ **801: 1.3** *Compare and contrast RAM types and features*

This section introduces all of the topics of the CompTIA A+ 801 Exam Objective 1.3, including types of RAM, parity versus nonparity, ECC versus non-ECC, single-sided versus double-sided, and single channel versus dual channel versus triple channel. You will also learn about the various speeds of RAM found in PCs today. RAM types for laptops will be discussed in Chapter 7.

Memory

In Chapter 3, you learned about a type of memory chip called read-only memory (ROM) and about the programs, called firmware, stored on those chips. Recall that system ROM is used to store low-level drivers and programs, as well as the system setup program. Typically, when people discuss computer *memory*, they are referring to *random access memory (RAM)*, so called because data and programs stored in RAM are accessible in any (random) order. Most of the memory in a PC is volatile RAM, meaning that when the computer is off and the RAM no longer receives power, the contents of this memory are lost. Computers use several types of RAM, each with a different function and different physical form. Chapter 3 described the various types of RAM memory slots used to connect RAM modules to motherboards, and we will complete that discussion in this chapter by describing how RAM and ROM are used, and features and configurations of RAM chips and modules. But first we will define how we measure data quantities and the speeds of electronic components.

From Bits to Exabytes

When we talk about storing data—whether it is in RAM or ROM memory or on storage devices—we casually throw out terms describing the amount of data, or the amount of memory or storage capacity. These terms begin with the lowly *binary digit* (*bit*). Think of a single bit as being like a light switch: it can represent two states—either on or off. In computer storage, when a switch is on, it represents a one (1); when it is off, it represents a zero (0). This is the basis for binary numeric notation, and binary works well with computers because RAM, ROM, and storage devices all use binary, two-state methods of storing data. We won't go into just how they do this, just understand that they do.

e x a m

ⓦatch *Be sure you understand the acronyms KB, MB, GB, and TB, as they are all included in the CompTIA A+ Acronyms list at the end of the objectives for both CompTIA A+ exams.*

In computing, we combine bits into groups to create a code or define memory or storage capacity. We call each group of bits a *byte*. Although a byte can be other sizes, it is usually a number divisible by eight. A single 8-bit byte may represent a character, like the letter A in a word processing document, or a very simple command, like the command to move down one line in a document. When we talk about memory and storage capacity, it is most commonly in terms of 8-bit bytes, and when you have 1024 bytes, you have 1 kilobyte (2 to the 10th power—"kilo" means one thousand). Other terms we use represent larger quantities, which Table 4-1 shows. We tend to think about these values in round numbers, so a kilobyte is about a thousand, a megabyte is about a million, a gigabyte is about a billion, a terabyte is about a trillion, and so forth. However, this type of rounding can be deceptive, as you can see that a gigabyte is actually almost 74 million bytes larger than you may expect it to be.

TABLE 4-1		Calculation	Result in bytes
	One *kilobyte (KB)*	2^{10}	1024
Common Values	One *megabyte (MB)*	2^{20}	1,048,576
Used to Measure	One *gigabyte (GB)*	2^{30}	1,073,741,824
Data	One *terabyte (TB)*	2^{40}	1,099,511,627,776
	One *petabyte (PB)*	2^{50}	1,125,899,906,842,624
	One *exabyte (EB)*	2^{60}	1,152,921,504,606,846,976

Hertz to Gigahertz

When we talk about the speed of electronics, such as RAM memory modules, we use the word *hertz (Hz)*, a unit of measurement representing the number of electrical cycles or vibrations per second. One hertz is one cycle per second. Then, a *kilohertz (KHz)* is one thousand cycles per second, a *megahertz (MHz)* is one million cycles per second, and a *gigahertz (GHz)* is one billion cycles per second. Watch for these terms a little later when we discuss memory speeds.

Overview of RAM and ROM

When a user makes a request, the CPU intercepts it and organizes the request into component-specific tasks. Many of these tasks must occur in a specific order, with each component reporting its results back to the processor before it can go on to complete the next task. The processor uses RAM to store these results until they can be compiled into the final results.

RAM also stores instructions about currently running applications. For example, when you start a computer game, a large set of the game's instructions (including how it works, how the screen should look, and which sounds must be generated) is loaded into memory. The processor can retrieve these instructions much faster from RAM than it can from the hard drive, where the game normally resides until you start to use it. Within certain limits, the more information stored in memory, the faster the computer will run. In fact, one of the most common computer upgrades is to increase the amount of RAM. The computer continually reads, changes, and removes the information in RAM, which is *volatile*, meaning that it cannot work without a steady supply of power, so when you turn your computer off, the information in RAM disappears.

Unlike RAM, ROM is read-only, meaning the processor can read the instructions it contains, but cannot store new information in ROM. As described in Chapter 3, firmware is stored on ROM chips on the motherboard as well as on adapter cards. ROM has an important function; it is rarely changed or upgraded, and even then, instead of being physically replaced, it is more often "flashed," as described in Chapter 3, to change the information. So ROM typically warrants less attention by most computer users.

Features and Configurations of RAM Chips and Modules

When shopping for RAM, you need to understand the features and configurations of RAM chips and modules, such as the error-checking methods, single-sided versus double-sided, and single-channel versus multichannel. You should also understand the types of RAM and how to select among the various generations of DDR SDRAM, depending on the requirements and capabilities of a motherboard, which are described in a motherboard manual.

Memory Error Checking

Earlier you learned that RAM memory is volatile, so you should realize that memory can be error-prone. The fact is that modern memory modules are very reliable, but there are methods and technologies that you can build into RAM modules to check for errors. We'll look at two of these methods: parity and error-correcting code (ECC).

Parity   In one type of memory error checking, called *parity*, every eight-bit byte of data is accompanied by a ninth bit (the parity bit), which is used to determine the presence of errors in the data. Of course, *nonparity* RAM does not use parity. There are two types of parity: odd and even.

In *odd parity*, the parity bit is used to ensure that the total number of ones in the data stream is odd. For example, suppose a byte consists of the following data: 11010010. The number of ones in this data is four, an even number. The ninth bit will then be a one to ensure that the total number of ones is odd: 110100101.

Even parity is the opposite of odd parity; it ensures that the total number of ones is even. For example, suppose a byte consists of the following data: 11001011. The ninth bit would then be a one to ensure that the total number of ones is six, an even number.

Parity is not failure-proof. Suppose the preceding data stream contained two errors: 101100101. If the computer was using odd parity, the error would slip through (try it; count the ones). However, creating parity is quick and does not inhibit memory access time the way a more sophisticated error-checking routine would.

A DIMM is 64-bits wide, but a parity-checking DIMM has 8 extra bits (1 parity bit for every 8-bit byte). Therefore, a DIMM with parity is 64 + 8 = 72 bits wide. Although parity is not often used in memory modules, there is an easy way to determine if a memory module is using parity—it will have an odd number of chips. A nonparity memory module will have an even number of chips. This is true even if the module only has two or three chips total.

If your system supports parity, you must use parity memory modules. You cannot use memory with parity if your system does not support it. The motherboard manual will define the memory requirements.

on the **Job**

Be aware that the majority of today's motherboards do not support memory that uses parity. Other computing devices use parity, however. One example of parity use is in some special drive arrays, called RAID 5, mostly found in servers. Therefore, understanding the basics of parity is useful.

ECC   *Error-correcting code (ECC)* is a more sophisticated method of error checking than parity, although it also adds an extra bit per byte to a stick of RAM. Software in the system memory controller chip uses the extra bits to both detect and correct errors. Several algorithms are used in ECC. We call RAM that does not use this error checking and correcting method *non-ECC RAM*.

Single-Sided vs. Double-Sided Modules

The DIMM modules discussed in this chapter come in both single-sided and double-sided versions. *Single-sided modules* have chips mounted on just one side of the memory circuit card, while *double-sided modules* have chips mounted on both sides. Most memory sticks are single-sided because there are incompatibility problems—mainly involving space—with the double-sided modules and motherboards.

SRAM

Static RAM (SRAM) (pronounced "ess-ram") was the first type of RAM available. SRAM is accessible within approximately 10 nanoseconds (ns), meaning it takes only about 10 ns for the processor to receive requested information from SRAM. Although SRAM is very fast compared with DRAM, it is also very expensive. For this reason, PC manufacturers typically use SRAM only for system cache. As you learned in Chapter 3, cache memory stores frequently accessed instructions or data for the CPU's use.

DRAM

Dynamic RAM (DRAM) (pronounced "dee-ram") was developed to combat the restrictive expense of SRAM. Although DRAM chips provide much slower access than SRAM chips, they are still much faster than accessing data from a hard drive. They can store several megabytes of data on a single chip (or hundreds of megabytes, and even gigabytes, when packaged together on a "stick"). Every "cell" in a DRAM chip contains one transistor and one capacitor to store a single bit of information. This design makes it necessary for the DRAM chip to receive a constant power refresh from the computer to prevent the capacitors from losing their charge. This constant refresh makes DRAM slower than SRAM and causes a DRAM chip to draw more power from the computer than SRAM does.

Because of its low cost and high capacity, manufacturers use DRAM as "main" memory (system memory) in the computer. The term "DRAM" typically describes any type of memory that uses the technology just described. However, the first DRAM chips were very slow (~80 to 90 ns), so faster variants have been developed.

The list of DRAM technologies is quite large and continues to grow. We will limit the discussion to RDRAM, SDRAM, and the major implementations of DDR SDRAM.

RDRAM As processors in the early 2000s came out with faster front-side busses than previous processors, manufacturers needed to create faster RAM. One answer to this need was *Rambus Dynamic RAM (RDRAM)*, which gets its name from the company that developed it—Rambus, Inc. The first Rambus *channel*, which is the communication pathway between each memory module and the memory control chip (MCC), transferred data at 800 MHz. Then they doubled the speed with a *dual-channel architecture*, in which the RDRAM MCC, or Northbridge, alternated between two memory modules. This resulted in a 1.6 GHz data transfer, and effectively a 128-bit bus. Previous DRAM modules used *single-channel architecture* in which the MCC did not alternate between memory modules and, therefore, the speed tied to the memory refresh rate. Don't look for RDRAM in computers manufactured after 2003, the year Intel stopped making motherboards that supported RDRAM. But that wasn't the end of multichannel architecture. Read on to learn more.

SDRAM *Synchronous Dynamic RAM (SDRAM)* runs either at the speed of the system clock or at a multiple of that speed. SDRAM is the dominant RAM technology in PCs today, and there are many different sticks of SDRAM, in its many physical variations, such as DDR1, DDR2, DDR3, and the up and coming DDR4. They all use dual-channel architecture (at least).

DDR1 SDRAM People often call any version of *double-data rate SDRAM (DDR SDRAM)* simply "DDR RAM," but there are several versions. The first version, now called *DDR1 SDRAM*, doubled the speed at which standard SDRAM processed data by accessing the module twice per clock cycle. In addition, when you combine DDR memory with multichannel architecture you get even faster memory access, which means that you need a motherboard and chipset configured for multi-channel memory access. While Rambus was the first manufacturer to do this, others soon developed the capability, and DDR SDRAM modules in multichannel configurations became the norm.

The JEDEC Solid State Technology Association (once known as the Joint Electron Device Engineering Council, or JEDEC) defines the standards for DDR SDRAM. There are two sets of standards involved here—one for the module (the "stick") and another for the chips that populate the module. The module specifications include PC1600, PC2100, PC2700, and PC3200. This labeling refers to the total bandwidth of the memory, as opposed to the old standard, which listed the speed rating (in MHz) of the SDRAM memory—in that case, PC66, PC100, and PC133. The numeric value in the PC66, PC100, and PC133 refers to the MHz speed at which the memory operates, which should match the computer's clock speed. Each module specification pairs the stick with chips of a certain chip specification.

A stick of DDR SDRAM memory is an 184-pin DIMM module with a notch on one end so it can only fit into the appropriate DIMM socket on a motherboard. It requires only a 2.5 V power supply, compared to the previous 3.3 V requirement for SDRAM.

DDR2 SDRAM   *Double-data-rate two SDRAM (DDR2 SDRAM)* replaced the original DDR standards, now referred to as DDR1. DDR2 can handle faster clock rates than DDR1 can, beginning at 400 MHz. This is mainly due to the adoption of an RDRAM-style dual-channel architecture in which the MCC that manages memory for the CPU switches between two 64-bit-wide memory modules, effectively doubling the speed of the memory. To take advantage of the dual-channel architecture, you must install DDR2 SDRAM sticks in pairs.

As with DDR1, there are specifications for the chips, as well as for the modules. Table 4-2 shows the JEDEC speed standards for DDR2 SDRAM chip and module combinations.

TABLE 4-2	**DDR2 Chip Specification**	**Chip Operating Speed**	**I/O Clock Speed**	**DDR2 Module Specification**
JEDEC Speed Standards for DDR2 SDRAM Chip and Module Combinations	DDR2-400	100 MHz	200 MHz	PC2-3200
	DDR2-533	133 MHz	266 MHz	PC2-4200
	DDR2-667	166 MHz	333 MHz	PC2-5300
	DDR2-800	200 MHz	400 MHz	PC2-6400
	DDR2-1000	250 MHz	500 MHz	PC2-8000
	DDR2-1066	266 MHz	533 MHz	PC2-8500

DDR2 sticks are only compatible with motherboards that use a special 240-pin DIMM socket. The DDR2 DIMM stick notches are different from those in a DDR1 DIMM. A DDR2 DIMM only requires 1.8 V compared to 2.5 V for DDR1. Manufacturers of motherboards and processors were slow to switch to support for DDR2, mainly due to problems with excessive heat. Once manufacturers solved the problems, they brought out compatible motherboards, chipsets, and CPUs for DDR2.

DDR3 SDRAM   First appearing on new motherboards in 2007, *double-data-rate three SDRAM (DDR3 SDRAM)* chips use far less power than the previous SDRAM chips—1.5 V versus DDR2's 1.8 V—while providing almost twice the bandwidth, thanks to several technology improvements on the chips and modules. As with DDR2, the DDR3 DIMMs have 240 pins and they are the same size. However, they are electrically incompatible and come with a different key notch to prevent you from inserting the wrong modules into DDR3 sockets. DDR3 modules can take advantage of dual-channel architecture, and you will often see a pair of modules sold as a dual-channel kit. And it gets better—MCCs that support a triple-channel architecture (switching between three modules) are available, and DDR3 memory modules are sold in a set of three as a triple-channel set. DDR3 SDRAM is quickly replacing DDR2 SDRAM.

As with DDR1 and DDR2, there are specifications for the chips, as well as for the modules. Table 4-3 shows the JEDEC speed standards for the DDR3 SDRAM chip and module combinations.

DDR4 SDRAM   We expect the long-delayed *double-data-rate four SDRAM (DDR4 SDRAM)* specification within a year or so of publication of this book. It will be faster yet, and use less power. One big difference is that DDR4 changes how the

TABLE 4-3 Some JEDEC Speed Standards for DDR3 SDRAM Chip and Module Combinations	DDR3 Chip Specification	Chip Operating Speed	I/O Clock Speed	DDR3 Module Specification
	DDR3-800	100 MHz	400 MHz	PC3-6400
	DDR3-1066	133 MHz	533 MHz	PC3-8500
	DDR3-1333	166 MHz	667 MHz	PC3-10600
	DDR3-1600	200 MHz	800 MHz	PC3-12800
	DDR3-1866	233.33 MHz	933.33 MHz	PC3-14900
	DDR3-2133	266.66 MHz	1,066.66 MHz	PC3-17000

channels are accessed, using a point-to-point architecture whereby each channel connects to a single module. This is a departure from the multi-channel architectures of DDR1, DDR2, and DDR3.

exam
ⓦatch

The CompTIA A+ Acronyms, listed at the end of both sets of exam objectives, includes many useful acronyms that you should be sure to understand. However, several of the listed acronyms are for outdated technologies. For instance,

FPM is an acronym for fast page mode, a memory technology that is faster than the original DRAM, but far behind the curve when compared to newer RAM technologies.

VRAM

Video RAM (VRAM) is a specialized type of memory used only with video adapters. The video adapter is one of the computer's busiest components, so to keep up with certain applications' video requirements, many adapters have an onboard graphical processing unit (GPU) and special video RAM. The adapter can process requests independent of the CPU, and then store its results in the VRAM until the CPU retrieves it. VRAM is fast, and the computer can simultaneously read from it and write to it. The result is better and faster video performance. In the generic sense, *synchronous graphics RAM (SGRAM)* was a relatively inexpensive early type of VRAM. In Chapter 5, you will learn about other techniques for improving video performance.

RAM Compatibility

Before purchasing RAM modules for a computer, you should read the motherboard manual or other documentation from the manufacturer to determine what RAM is compatible with the motherboard. Normally, all RAM modules must match the features supported by the motherboard and chipset, including the features described in the following sections, as well as speed. The manual will describe any acceptable exceptions to this "perfect match" rule. Keep in mind that even if the motherboard and chipset support differences in RAM modules, such as different speeds, this will not be the optimum configuration and it is fraught with potential for problems. It is best to have identical modules.

SCENARIO & SOLUTION

Which type of memory is responsible for...?	Solution
Storing low-level drivers and programs, as well as the system setup program	System ROM
Providing temporary storage for application files	RAM
Storing frequently accessed instructions or data for the CPU's use	Cache

CERTIFICATION OBJECTIVES

■ **801: 1.4** *Install and configure expansion cards*

■ **801: 1.7** *Compare and contrast various connection interfaces and explain their purpose*

■ **801: 1.11** *Identify connectors and associated cables*

This section introduces the various types of adapter cards listed under CompTIA A+ Exam Objective 801: 1.4, including sound, video, network, various I/O cards, modem cards, TV tuner cards, video capture cards, and riser cards, but the discussion of storage cards is later in the chapter under "Storage Devices and Interfaces." In this section, we also examine various connection interfaces, including all the interfaces listed in Objective 1.7, except VGA, and DVI, HDMI, which we include in Chapter 5. We will also delay the discussion of various wireless devices for Chapter 7.

This section explores those connectors listed in Objective 1.11 that you should expect to see on the adapter cards described here, and at the end of this section is a very brief overview of cable types. We'll describe connectors on storage interfaces in the following section and other connectors in the appropriate chapter for the connector type. We will save the actual installation of, and configuration of, the components described in this section for Chapter 6.

Expansion Cards and Built-in Adapters

Traditionally, an *expansion card* or *adapter card* is a printed circuit board installed into a PC's expansion bus to add functionality. An expansion card is actually a controller containing the sophisticated circuitry of an entire device, but many such devices do not fit the traditional description because they are external, connecting to a computer via a USB, FireWire, or eSATA port.

Examples of common adapter cards include those for controlling video, multimedia, I/O interfaces, networking, and modem communications. As you read about these types of devices, keep in mind that PC motherboards contain increasing numbers of these functions so they no longer need an adapter card added to the system. Therefore, although the CompTIA 801 exam 1.4 Objective lists each of these as cards, we will refer to them as adapters, which is what they are whether the device is on a separate circuit card or built into the motherboard. The functions, however, remain as described in the following sections that describe each of the most common adapters. The difference, of course, is in the necessity of physically installing expansion cards.

on the **ⓙob** *The term "adapter" is somewhat confusing, because it also applies to a plug-like device that contains a simple circuit for changing one set of signals to another, like a serial-to-USB adapter.*

Video Adapter

A *video adapter* controls the output to the display device. This function may either be built into the motherboard of a PC or provided through an expansion card installed into the PCI expansion bus, an Accelerated graphics port (AGP) connector, or a PCIe connector. Learn more about video adapters in Chapter 5 when we look at the various video technologies along with displays that connect to the video adapters and the various connectors for attaching displays to video adapters.

Multimedia Adapters

In the early 1990s, the term "multimedia PC" described a PC with a stereo sound card and a CD-ROM drive. Today this is less than the minimum configuration for the most basic consumer PC from a major manufacturer. Today's multimedia PC brings not just music and photos to the user, but also support for sophisticated games and integration with home electronics. A typical user may connect a PC to a digital still or video camera, a television, or much more. The latest versions of Microsoft Windows come in editions that include Windows Media Center and that aim at this more advanced multimedia PC and the consumers who desire these features.

PC manufacturers have created multimedia PCs to meet this need. They often have the words "Media Center" in their product name or description. Multimedia capabilities in PCs can now include enhancements to allow users to store and edit media data such as photos, music, and videos, and to watch and record TV thanks to a tuner integrated into the PC.

The PC now includes these multimedia capabilities through specialized components, either installed on separate adapter cards or integrated into the motherboard with appropriate connectors on the front or back of the case. The following sections give an overview of sound cards, TV tuner cards, and capture cards.

Sound Adapters and Connectors

A modern sound adapter processes multiple sound formats, including a variety of recorded sound formats, and computer-generated Musical Instrument Digital Interface sound. The *Musical Instrument Digital Interface (MIDI)* is a standard for connecting electronic musical instruments, such as a synthesizer keyboard, to computers or among themselves. This allows musicians—experienced and budding alike—to input their music for mixing and to convert it to musical notation. MIDI has been around almost as long as the PC. A MIDI device also requires an additional piece of equipment in the form of a box connecting the PC and MIDI device.

Newer MIDI devices may have USB connectors and connect to a USB port on a PC, but the classic MIDI device has at least two MIDI ports, each with a mini-DIN keyboard connector (described in Chapter 5), and labeled "In" or "Out." There may be more than one "Out" port. On an older PC, look for a special MIDI port on the back of the sound card. The MIDI port is often called the *gameport*, because you can attach a joystick for use with games. The classic MIDI port on the computer side uses a female DB-15 connector that has only two rows of pins, as opposed to the DB-15 connector used for analog video. This type of MIDI cable is coaxial.

Even the most basic sound adapter includes support and ports for a joystick, a MIDI musical device, a microphone, and at least two speakers (a pair of stereo speakers plugged into one port). Sound adapters come in a full range of prices, based on the quality of the components and the number of features. For instance, many support five speakers, including a woofer, to give realistic sound. Some support high-quality recording.

A typical configuration of sound connectors consists of three color-coded audio ports, or "jacks." Pink identifies a microphone input port, green identifies a speaker output port, and blue is the auxiliary port. Additional audio ports may be present for additional audio channels, identified by white for left speaker, red for right speaker, and yellow for composite video (described in Chapter 5). All of these use 1/8" single-pin *mini-audio connectors*, a few generations removed from the larger single-pin RCA phone (as in earphone) connector. Some handheld devices use the 3/32" *sub-mini audio connector*. All of these single-pin plugs come in mono versions

FIGURE 4-1

Headphone and microphone ports on a laptop

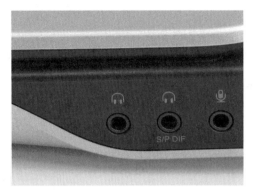

and stereo versions. Look for a single black ring around the front end of a mono plug and two black rings around a stereo plug. The consumer version of *Sony/Philips Digital Interface (S/P DIF)* uses a single-pin RCA phone jack for transferring digital audio from CD and DVD players to amplifiers and speakers, as seen in Figure 4-1, which shows (from left) one headphone port, a combination headphone S/P DIF port, and a microphone port on the side of a laptop.

ⓦatch *The CompTIA Acronym list for both sets of A+ objectives uses the acronym "SPDIF," but it is normally shown as S/P DIF.*

Capture

A *video capture card* is a category of adapter card that accepts and records video signals to a PC's hard drive in digital form, storing both the digital image and sound. One type of capture card, called a *TV tuner card*, brings a TV signal into a computer in order to record TV programs onto a hard drive, thus turning your computer into a digital video recorder (DVR). Some capture cards simply capture video from a VHS tape or other video format, while others are for editing video files, regardless of how they were obtained.

I/O Adapters

PCs have evolved, and, with the invention of more and more I/O devices, manufacturers have continued to integrate these new capabilities into the motherboard. While your PC has various I/O technologies built in, you may still wish to add an expansion card to give you additional ports. Typically, the term *connector* refers to the plug at the end of a cable, and *port* refers to the socket where the cable attaches to the device or computer. Even though we refer to connectors and ports, remember the port is also a connector. The following sections contain descriptions of some common I/O interfaces and the connector types related to each, including serial, parallel, USB, IEEE 1394, and SCSI.

Serial: RS-232-C

Although many of the peripheral interfaces described in this book use serial communications, they are newer and much faster than the classic serial port for a PC; the *RS-232-C port* complies with the Recommended Standard-232 Revision C (RS-232-C) in its circuitry, cabling, and connector design. Like all serial communications, RS-232-C transfers data serially, one bit at a time. The circuitry behind the physical connector is the *universal asynchronous receiver/transmitter (UART)* chip, which does the parallel-to-serial and serial-to-parallel data conversion required between the parallel bus of the PC and the serial port and its devices.

In the early 1980s, serial input/output (I/O) cards had to be added to the expansion bus because this basic I/O interface was not integrated into the motherboard. Today, serial interface is often actually built into the motherboard, but due to decreased use of this old technology, it is often disabled and does not have external connectors. It is disappearing from PCs, and you rarely will encounter serial cards unless you need to connect a very old serial device to a PC.

RS-232-C serial communication has a maximum speed of 115 kilobits per second (Kbps). In early PCs, the RS-232 port used a 25-pin male D-Shell connector (or DB-type connector), but because it did not use all the pins, the 9-pin male D-Shell connector with 9 pins in two rows (5 in one row and 4 in the other) replaced it. Also called a *DB-9* connector, all D-Shell connectors have this same trapezoidal shape (see Figure 4-2). Although the connector on the computer had only 9 pins, the connector on the device, such as a serial modem, was a female 25-pin *DB-25* D-Shell connector. The serial RS-232 interface was most commonly used for

A female DB-25 connector (top) and two male DB-9 connectors (bottom)

serial devices such as mice and external modems, but it has been replaced by faster interfaces with much smaller connectors and cables, mainly USB.

Parallel

In parallel communications, multiple wires simultaneously transmit one bit per wire, in parallel. All other things being equal, this results in faster data transfers for large packets. The parallel interface for peripherals used on PCs in the 1980s was unidirectional at 150 kilobytes per second (KBps), so a computer could send data to a device, such as a printer, but the device could not send information back to the computer.

In 1991, the *IEEE 1284* standard, which supports bidirectional communication and transfer rates of up to 2 MBps, corrected the shortcomings of the old parallel interface. If you buy a parallel cable today you will see this standard prominently displayed on its packaging. Modern parallel interfaces in PCs and parallel devices follow this standard but also support the previous implementations. If a PC has a built-in *parallel port* now, it has several modes of operation, configurable through the system BIOS Settings menu.

At one time, external drives and other devices used the parallel interface, and it was the "gold standard" for PC printers. Today, most of the newer external peripherals use USB, FireWire (IEEE 1394), or eSATA because all achieve faster speeds, are *plug and play (PnP)*, and use slender cables and small connectors as opposed to bulky parallel cables and connectors.

exam

ⓦatch   *Plug and play (PnP) is a standard by which the computer BIOS and operating system recognize a device, and the operating system automatically installs* *and configures a device driver. Very old technologies like RS-232-C described above and parallel ports discussed here are not plug and play.*

The parallel port connector is a D-Shell connector with 25 pins or sockets—13 in one row and 12 in the other. Until several years ago, most computers included one female DB-25 parallel connector. You can see an example of a DB-25 connector back in Figure 4-2. On the device end is a 36-pin connector, sometimes referred to as a *Centronics* connector. This required a heavy cable—over half an inch thick, with large connectors to match the DB-25 and Centronics ports on the computer and device.

USB

The *Universal Serial Bus (USB)* interface has become the interface of choice for PCs, making both parallel and serial ports obsolete and even replacing SCSI and FireWire/IEEE 1394 (discussed later in this chapter). PCs manufactured in the last several years have at least one USB port, and many PCs literally bristle with USB connectors located conveniently on the front, as well as the back, of a desktop PC case, and on the sides and back of a laptop. So, you are not likely to need to add a USB expansion card to a system. If you do need more USB ports, you can add a USB hub, multiport connecting device for USB devices.

USB is an external bus that connects into the PC's PCI bus. With USB, you can theoretically connect up to 127 devices to your computer. There have been several versions of the USB standard; most notable are 1.0, 1.1, 2.0, and 3.0.

USB 1.0, 1.1   The low-speed 1.0 and 1.1 versions transmit data up to 1.5 Mbps, whereas the full-speed 1.1 standard is rated at 12 Mbps. Communications are controlled by the host system and can flow in both directions, but not simultaneously. This one-way-at-a-time transmission is called *half-duplex communication*.

Hi-Speed USB 2.0   *Hi-Speed USB 2.0* transmits data at speeds up to 480 Mbps, which equals 60 MBps in half duplex. You can attach a low-speed device like a mouse to a Hi-Speed port, but devices designed for Hi-Speed require, or run best, when attached to a USB port that is up to the 2.0 standard. USB hubs and peripherals are downward compatible with hardware using the older standard, but when you plug an older device into a Hi-Speed USB port, or connect a Hi-Speed USB device to a full-speed USB 1.1 port, the resulting speed will be at the lower rate, a maximum of 12 Mbps.

SuperSpeed USB 3.0   The *SuperSpeed USB 3.0* standard was introduced in the third quarter of 2008, and is now common on new PCs and laptops. USB 3.0 operates at up to 5 Gbps (625 MBps), which is ten times the speed of USB 2.0 and faster than the present 300 MBps eSATA speed (more about eSATA later in this chapter). USB 3.0 also supports *full-duplex communication*, the ability to communicate in both directions at once. Figure 4-3 shows a SuperSpeed USB 3.0 port on a laptop with the familiar forked USB symbol and the letters "SS" indicating SuperSpeed. Look for this symbol identifying a SuperSpeed USB 3.0 port. Manufacturers now integrate USB 3.0 into chipsets, so look for these fast ports on recently manufactured computers. Aside from physical marking on a USB 3.0 port, if you open the Universal Serial

Bus node in Device Manager it may identify the USB level for the USB Host Controller and Root Hub as 2.0 or 3.0. This is true on our recent laptop running Windows 7, although we have never seen previous versions of USB identified so clearly.

Power for USB Devices   Until USB 3.0, only low-power devices, such as flash drives, could receive power through the USB bus, and some rechargeable devices could recharge via a USB 2.0 port. However, USB 2.0 could only output 500 milliamps. USB 3.0 outputs 900 milliamps, which permits faster charging. Additionally, USB 3.0 is actually more efficient in its use of power compared to USB 2.0.

USB Ports, Connectors, and Cables   A standard USB port on a computer is rectangular and acts as a receiver for a USB type-A connector measuring 1/2" by 1/8" (look back at Figure 4-3). Most computers and devices clearly identify USB ports with a trident, or fork-shaped symbol. A plastic device in the port holds the four wires for USB 1.x or 2.0, and USB 3.0 has an additional five wires positioned behind the first four so that the connectors and ports from 3.0 are downward com-patible with older ports and connectors. This, together with a similar plastic device in the connector, polarizes the connectors, which keeps the two from connecting incorrectly.

The connector on the device end of a USB cable is a type-B connector, but there are several sizes of B connectors. Figure 4-4 shows a USB cable with a 2.0 A connector on the right and a full-size, nearly square 2.0 B connector on the left.

Notice that the two corners of the B connector are beveled so that it cannot be inserted incorrectly. A USB 3.0 B connector has a smaller connector containing the additional five wires, mounted on top of what looks like a 2.0 B connector.

There are also variations of small USB A-type and B-type connectors found on portable devices. The micro USB B-type connector measures about ¼" × 1/16". The mini USB B-type connector is the same width as the micro USB B-type connector, but it is twice as thick, measuring about ¼" × 1/8". Figure 4-5 shows an example of a micro USB B connector and a mini USB B connector.

USB cables have a maximum length based on the version. For instance, USB 2.0 has a cable length limit of five meters, while USB 1.0 had a limit of three meters. The USB 3.0 specification does not give a maximum cable length, so it depends on the quality of the cable needed to maintain the speed of USB 3.0, which could limit the cable to as little as three meters. Further, a USB type A connector has an additional pair of wires, but this type A connector can still connect to a USB type A port.

USB 3.0 is downward compatible with USB 2.0, meaning that you can plug a USB 2.0 device and cable into a USB 3.0 port. You can also plug a USB 3.0 type A connector to a USB 2.0 type A computer port, even though the USB 3.0 type A connector has an additional pair of wires. The USB 3.0 device at the other end of this cable will only run at USB 2.0 speed. Further, you cannot use a USB 3.0 cable with an older USB device, and a USB 3.0 device cannot use a USB 2.0 cable. This is because the USB 3.0 type B connector that plugs into a device does not fit into the USB 2.0 B port on a device.

USB hubs take you beyond these limits, but the connecting cables still must be within the prescribed limits. You can also find a USB cable that has a hub built in to extend the length, but this only works to connect one device to a computer.

FIGURE 4-5

Connectors on two separate cables: the one on the left has a USB mini type B, and next to it is a USB micro type B

Another type of USB cable is a simple extension cable that has a type A connector on one end and a receiving USB port connector on the other end. These come in varying lengths, and we keep several on hand. You never know when you might want to connect to a USB port on the back of a computer or on the front of a computer that is out of reach, such as under a table or in a cabinet. Plug in the extension cable and run it to your desk, where it is handy for plugging in your flash drives or other devices. Short extension cables also have their use. Many USB devices described in this book are very small and come without a cable. You simply connect the device to a USB port and it juts out from the computer, barely visible, but vulnerable. One wrong move and you can ruin the device or the port into which it is plugged. Our solution is to purchase and keep handy a couple of short (about 9") USB extension cables. Then the device sits on the desk, tethered to the port, and bumping it won't damage the device or the port.

on the
O o b
Keep USB extension cables on hand for connecting devices to hard-to-reach ports or to protect a device.

EXERCISE 4-1

Research USB Connectors

There are many variations of USB connectors. If you have a computer with an Internet connection, research USB connectors.

1. Open your favorite Internet search engine, such as Google at google.com or Bing at bing.com.
2. Search on the keywords "usb connectors" without the quotes.
3. Search the results for a site that gives you a range of connectors, as well as photos of each type.
4. Keep track of the number of variations you find, looking for the differences in the USB 2.0 and USB 3.0 connectors.

USB Plug and Play   USB supports plug and play, meaning the computer BIOS and operating system recognize a USB device, and the operating system automatically installs and configures a device driver (if available). Always check the documentation for a USB device, because many require that you install a device driver before you connect the device. USB ports also support *hot swapping,* which is the act of safely disconnecting and connecting devices while the computer is running, giving you instantly recognized and usable devices.

Adding More USB Hubs   If a PC has too few USB ports for the number of USB devices a user wishes to connect, the easiest fix is to purchase an external USB hub and connect it to one of the PC's USB connectors. In fact, you can add other hubs and devices in this way. Although the USB standard allows for daisy-chaining of devices, manufacturers do not support this capability because they prefer to use hubs connected directly to the USB controller, which includes the root hub, in the computer. There is a limit of five levels of hubs, counting the root hub. Each hub can accommodate several USB devices, possibly creating a lopsided tree. USB supports different speeds on each branch, so you can use devices of varying speeds. Figure 4-6 shows a PC with an internal root hub. Connected to this hub are a USB keyboard and another USB hub. Several devices connect to the first USB hub, including yet another hub, which in turn has several devices connected to it.

FIGURE 4-6

USB hubs can add more USB ports to a PC.

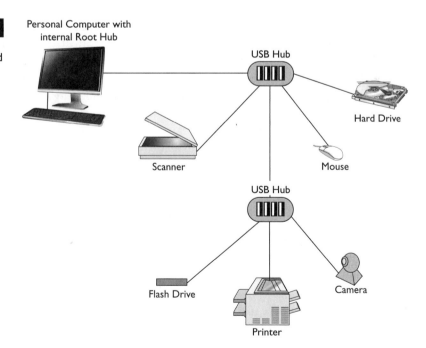

Personal Computer with internal Root Hub

USB Hub

Hard Drive

Scanner

Mouse

USB Hub

Flash Drive

Printer

Camera

IEEE 1394/FireWire

The *Institute of Electrical and Electronics Engineers (IEEE)* is an international nonprofit organization that sets standards as part of its charter. You will encounter many IEEE standards, represented by "IEEE" followed by a number assigned to that standard. Like USB, the *IEEE 1394* standard describes an external serial bus that connects to the internal PCI bus. The CompTIA A+ 801 exam uses the term *FireWire*, which is Apple's trademarked name, but it is also the commonly used name. But Sony calls their implementation of it i.LINK, and Texas Instruments uses the name Lynx.

PC motherboards often have FireWire support built in with an external FireWire port. Each FireWire device can be part of a daisy chain to more devices. A single FireWire port can support up to 63 daisy-chained devices. Therefore, adding ports to the computer itself is not usually necessary, although you may add them by installing an expansion card.

FIGURE 4-7

At top, FireWire port with an identifying label. Below it are two USB ports.

The original standard, now called *IEEE 1394a*, supports speeds up to 400 Mbps with maximum individual cable length of 4.5 meters. Many in IT call this *FireWire 400*. A standard 1394a six-pin FireWire port is about half an inch long, with one squared end and one three-sided end to guarantee the cable connector is connected correctly. As with USB, the wires connect to a plastic device. Alternatively, you will find smaller four-wire ports, especially on laptops. Most computers and devices clearly identify FireWire ports and cable connectors with a Y-shaped symbol. Figure 4-7 shows a FireWire port on a computer, while Figure 4-8 shows two connectors on a FireWire cable.

In 2003, the IEEE released the *IEEE 1394b* specification, with cable distances of up to 100 meters and top speeds of 800 Mbps (also known as *FireWire 800*), 1600 Mbps, and 3.2 Gbps. A significant limit is that one 1394a device in a chain will cause any 1394b devices to operate at the lower speed. In addition, although 1394b is generally downward compatible with 1394a, 3.2 Gbps is only available with special hardware that is not downward compatible with 1394a devices, and the IEEE 1394b cable terminates with a connector that resembles an Ethernet RJ-45 connector, but uses nine wires.

e x a m

⦿ a t c h *Be sure you understand the differences between USB and FireWire and are able to describe the ports and connectors, as well as how multiple devices are normally connected.*

FIGURE 4-8

A FireWire cable
with two 6-pin
connectors

A subsequent standard, *IEEE 1394c-2006*, came out in 2007 and is a major departure from the old standards in that it uses Category 5e twisted-pair cable with RJ-45 connectors, combining Ethernet and FireWire, meaning that it can connect to either an Ethernet network interface card or a FireWire device. In 2008 these updates combined into *IEEE 1394-2008*.

Communication Adapters

We have used the term "communication" many times in this and the preceding chapter, mostly in talking about communication between components within the PC. Now we will talk about the communication devices that connect a PC to a network, whether it is a local area network (LAN) or the Internet. Once again, the motherboards of most PCs now have these functions built in, and it is not usually necessary to add an adapter card to a computer for communications.

Network Adapters

A network adapter (or network card), often called a *network interface card (NIC)*, connects a PC or other device to a type of network, such as a wired Ethernet network or a wireless Wi-Fi or cellular network. Most PCs and laptops contain an Ethernet NIC because most PC users require network communications and can usually connect to the Internet—directly or indirectly—through an Ethernet network. Many computers also include a wireless NIC—either Wi-Fi (the most common) or another wireless type, such as cellular.

On the job, a typical desktop PC is connected to a LAN, which in turn may be connected to a larger private network and, ultimately, to the Internet. At home, you may connect two or more PCs via a LAN connection to share a DSL or cable modem Internet connection. The network adapter in the PC may be an Ethernet wired network adapter or a wireless adapter, depending on whether you wish to connect to a wired Ethernet LAN or a wireless LAN. We will save the larger

FIGURE 4-9

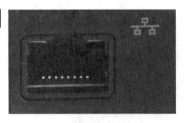

The RJ-45 Ethernet port on this laptop is labeled with a symbol resembling three computers connected to a network.

discussion of networking for Chapters 14, 15, and 16, and in Chapter 7 we will describe the various types of wireless adapters found in laptops.

The most common connector for Ethernet NICs is RJ-45. A *registered jack (RJ)* connector is rectangular in shape and has a locking clip on one side. The number designation of an RJ connector refers to its size rather than to the number of wire connections within it. RJ-45 contains eight wires and most commonly attaches twisted-pair cables to Ethernet network cards. Figure 4-9 shows an RJ-45 port with the small notch to accommodate the locking clip on a cable connector labeled with a symbol representing a network.

Modem Adapters

A *modem*, so named for its combined functions of *modulator/demodulator*, allows computers to communicate with one another over existing phone lines, a type of communication called dial-up that will be described in Chapter 14 when we look at how to connect to networks. A modem may be internal in the motherboard, or it may be an adapter card in the expansion bus. An external modem connects to a port on the computer, either serial or USB. Whether internal or external, a modem connects to a regular telephone wall jack using the same connector as a phone.

This type of modem is an *analog modem* as opposed to the data communication devices used to connect to a cable network or to phone lines for DSL service. "Modem" is actually a misnomer for the devices used on cable or DSL networks because the signals involved are all digital signals, and, therefore, there is no modulating or demodulating of the signal. However, because they are physically between the computer and the network, much like a modem is, manufacturers use the term "modem."

Be prepared to demonstrate that you understand the differences between RJ-11 and RJ-45 connectors. Remember their uses and the number of wires in each.

An RJ-11 port is where you attach a phone cable to a modem (analog or other) and to a wall-mounted phone jack. It is similar to an RJ-45 port—only slightly smaller, and it contains either two or four wires. Figure 4-10 shows two RJ-11 connectors on a modem adapter: one that connects to the wall jack, and the other that attaches to a phone set. A cable with an RJ-11 connector attached is resting on top of the card.

FIGURE 4-10

An analog modem adapter card with two RJ-11 connectors on the left side and a cable with an RJ-11 plug attached resting on top of the card

Riser Cards

There are two types of riser cards. The first type, also called a *daughter card,* is a specially designed circuit board that connects directly into a motherboard and adds no functionality on its own. Rather, it extends the expansion bus and allows you to add expansion cards in a different physical orientation. The riser card is installed perpendicular to the motherboard and may include several expansion slots. An expansion card inserted into a riser card is then on the same plane as the motherboard. Riser cards are available for the standard bus architectures, such as AGP, PCI, and PCIe. Ironically, you will find riser cards both in the largest network servers and in the smallest of low-profile desktop computer cases. In the case of network servers, the use of a riser card allows the addition of more cards than the standard motherboard allows.

The second type of riser card is a small expansion card containing multiple functions. The two standards for this type of riser card are AMR and CNR. The *Audio Modem Riser (AMR),* introduced in the late 1990s, allows for the creation of lower-cost sound and modem solutions. The first Communications Network Riser (CNR) card was introduced in 2000. Similar to the AMR except that it supported plug and play, CNR included support for a NIC in addition to audio, modem, and multimedia systems. Both of these standards have become obsolete since manufacturers now build the functions found on these cards into the chips on the motherboard.

SCENARIO & SOLUTION

What term is most proper to use for a communications device that allows a computer to make a dial-up connection?	Modem
What type of device would you install in a PC if you wanted to record TV programs onto a hard drive?	TV tuner card
Which three external serial bus standards are available on PCs today?	USB, IEEE 1394, and eSATA

EXERCISE 4-2

CertCam

View Adapter Cards in Device Manager

Look at the list of adapter cards in Device Manager in Windows 7.

1. Select Control Panel | Device Manager.

2. In the list of devices in the Device Manager window, note those for adapters named in the previous section. This list will include, but not be limited to, display adapters, network adapters, and various controllers.

3. Close the Device Manager window.

CERTIFICATION OBJECTIVE

■ **801: 1.5** *Install and configure storage devices and use appropriate media*

This section introduces the storage types listed in CompTIA A+ 801 Exam Objective 1.5, including floppy disk drives (FDDs), hard disk drives (HDDs), optical drives, and solid-state drives (SSDs). We'll also define special configurations of drives, called RAID, and the various media type and capacities of storage devices. However, the actual installation and configuration of storage devices is in Chapter 6, including IDE configuration and setup (master, slave, and cable select) and using SCSI IDs.

Storage Devices and Interfaces

In computing, the function of a *mass storage device* is to hold, or store, a large amount of information, even when the computer's power is off. Unlike information in system RAM, files kept on a mass storage device remain there unless the user or the computer removes or alters them. In this section, we will first explore the types of interfaces for connecting storage devices to computers, and then we'll explore various types of storage devices in use today.

Drive Interfaces

In Chapter 3, we described I/O bus architectures for attaching video and other expansion cards to the computer. Then, in the previous section of this chapter, we explored various I/O technologies, from the old serial and parallel interfaces, to USB and FireWire. USB and FireWire are among the many options today for connecting storage devices to computers. Next we will look at the more traditional mass storage interface options that have evolved from the ATA drive interface standards for connecting hard drives and optical drives internally and externally to computers. Finally, we will look at the SCSI standards used for storage and other types of devices.

ATA Drive Interface Standards

The standards for the traditional drive interface are descendants of the *Advanced Technology Attachment (ATA)* standard, developed decades ago. They include a parallel interface, PATA, and a newer serial interface, SATA. The drive and the interface must comply with the same ATA standard in order to benefit from the features of that version. We will clarify where the terms IDE and EIDE fit into this picture, define the PATA and SATA interfaces, and then look at other drive interface technologies that are part of the ATA standards.

e x a m

ⓦ a t c h   *The Acronym list at the end of the published objectives for both the CompTIA 801 and 802 exams includes an acronym from the early days of ATA standards. It is logical block address (LBA), a method for allowing early BIOSs to access disks up to 8.3 GB.*

IDE and EIDE   Since the early years of PCs, the terms *Integrated Drive Electronics (IDE)* and, later, *Enhanced IDE (EIDE)* have been used to describe any drive that has the controller circuitry mounted on the drive itself—true of virtually every hard drive and optical drive.

Strictly speaking, this is separate from the ATA interface that connects to one of these drives.

PATA   The first ATA standards defined an interface in which the data signals traveled over a parallel bus. Originally simply called ATA (when it wasn't erroneously called IDE or EIDE), this interface is now called *Parallel AT Attachment (PATA)* to distinguish it from the Serial ATA standard introduced in 2003. Naming of early versions of the ATA standards were successively ATA-1, ATA-2, and so forth. Important milestones in the evolution of ATA include ATA-4, which added support for nonhard disks, such as optical drives, tape drives, and some special large-capacity floppy drives via a protocol that allows the ATA interface to carry commands from these devices. This protocol is the *ATA Packet Interface (ATAPI)*. In Figure 4-11, notice the large ribbon cable on the right. It is connected to (and partially obscuring) the connector labeled IDE 2; the open connector is labeled IDE 1. In this computer, this cable connects to a DVD drive using the ATAPI standard.

When you open a PC and see wide ribbon cables, they usually connect EIDE or optical drives to the PATA interface. Following one of these ribbon cables from a hard or optical drive to the motherboard may lead to a connector labeled "EIDE controller 01" or "EIDE controller 02" or "IDE 1" or "IDE 2." Never mind that EIDE and IDE are about the drives and PATA is about the interface for these drives. Figure 4-11 shows the long PATA connector on the right, labeled "IDE 1," sitting next to four SATA drive interface connectors. SATA is the standard replacing PATA, and we will discuss SATA shortly.

FIGURE 4-11

The long, vertically oriented connector on the right (partially hidden by a ribbon cable) is a PATA connector labeled IDE 1. It is next to four SATA connectors (one has a cable attached).

Technicians have long detested the wide ribbon cabling used for PATA connectors because it blocks airflow, and it can sometimes be difficult to get unwieldy ribbon connectors tucked into a case without crimping them when closing the case. Space-saving round cables are available for PATA, but we still see mostly ribbon cables. PATA cables cannot be more than 18 inches in length. PATA does not support hot swapping, so to replace a drive on a PATA interface you must shut down the computer. While EIDE drives may advertise transfer rates above 80 megabytes per second, in reality, the PATA interface limits the speed due to both protocol overhead and because PATA shares the PCI bus with all other PCI devices.

SATA   The ATA-7 standard introduced *Serial ATA (SATA)*, a faster serial drive interface that has replaced PATA. Although some converters will allow older drives with PATA connectors to connect through this interface, today's drives use the SATA interface.

Most PCs now come with small SATA connectors on the motherboard, as shown back in Figure 4-11. To the end user, the speed of SATA devices is the most attractive feature, but for the technician, another advantage of SATA is that it uses thinner cabling that can be up to 39.4 inches long and has smaller connectors that fit better on smaller devices. Because each SATA device has a direct connection to the SATA controller, it does not have to share a bus with other devices, and therefore it provides greater throughput. Unlike PATA, SATA also supports hot swapping.

Even the first two SATA standards, SATA 1.5 Gbps (150 MBps) and SATA 3 Gbps (300 MBps), far exceeded the PATA speeds. The SATA 3.0 standard, or SATA 6 Gbps, released in May 2009, is fast enough for SSDs. SATA 3.1 includes support for SSDs in mobile devices, or *mSATA* (also called *MiniSATA*) defining a scaled-down form factor. Figure 4-12 shows the SATA ports on the back of an internal hard drive. The power port on the right has 15 contacts, while the SATA data port to the left of it has 7 contacts. Figure 4-13 shows the corresponding connectors on a power cable and a SATA data cable. SATA connectors are "L" shaped.

FIGURE 4-12

The SATA power
and data ports
on a hard drive.
The power port
is the long one
on the right, and
the data port is
immediately to
its left.

eSATA *External Serial ATA (eSATA)* is an extension of the SATA standard for
external SATA devices, with the same speeds as the SATA standard it supports,
which at present is 300 MBps. Internal eSATA connectors are included in newer
motherboards, in which case, cabling is required to connect them to an eSATA port
on the PC case. Use eSATA adapter cards to add eSATA to older motherboards
without built-in support. eSATA is replacing FireWire and at least competing with
USB. Figure 4-14 shows an eSATA port on an external hard drive enclosure, and
Figure 4-15 shows the connectors on either end of an eSATA cable. Notice that
the eSATA connectors do not have the "L" shape of the SATA connectors you saw
earlier in Figures 4-13 and 4-14.

FIGURE 4-13

The power
cable on the left
connects to the
power connector
on a SATA drive,
while the SATA
data cable with its
smaller connector
is next to it.

FIGURE 4-14

An eSATA port
on an external
hard drive
enclosure

Ultra DMA   In any PC, a hard drive is potentially a bottleneck because it
depends on moving parts. Therefore, various schemes developed over the years for
speeding up the flow of data to and from a hard drive, as well as the actual writing
and reading from the hard drive platters. Several methods for speeding up the movement of data between a hard drive system and memory come under the heading of
Ultra DMA (UDMA), which uses direct memory accessing (DMA) between the
device and the CPU. These methods, called modes, worked with hard-drive PATA
interfaces. One of the last modes was Ultra DMA mode 5, introduced with ATA-6,
which boosted the data transfer rate to 100 MBps, giving it the popular name of
ATA/100. The last of the parallel ATA modes was Ultra DMA mode 6, known as
ATA-7 or ATA/133 for the speed (133 MBps). Recall that ATA-7 is the same standard that also introduced SATA.

FIGURE 4-15

The eSATA
connectors on
either end of an
eSATA cable

SCSI

Small Computer System Interface (SCSI) is a set of standards for interfacing computers and internal and external peripherals. SCSI, pronounced "scuzzy," is maintained by the T10 SCSI committee of the *InterNational Committee on Information Technology Standards (INCITS)*, pronounced "insights." Another technical standards organization, the *American National Standards Institute (ANSI)*, accredits INCITS. The original standard dates back over 40 years, but has been updated many times. Information on the current standards and revisions of SCSI are available at www.t10.org. We describe installation and configuration of host adapters and SCSI devices in Chapter 6.

For several years, SCSI was popular for high-end devices, such as hard drives, optical drives, and scanners; it was the disk controller of choice for many high-end servers. However, it had stiff competition from technologies that improved on the original PATA standard, and today SATA technology has pretty much replaced SCSI.

e x a m

ⓦ**a t c h**

The objectives for each of the two CompTIA A+ exams include an Acronym list with which you should be familiar. One item in that list, **low-voltage differential (LVD),** *or low-voltage differential signaling (LVDS),* **is a technology for transferring serial data at high speed. Many interfaces use it, including FireWire, the graphics adapter-to-LCD link in a laptop and in later implementations of SCSI.**

SCSI has several implementations with a variety of speeds. Until recently, SCSI systems all used a parallel interface to the computer. For the traditional parallel SCSI interface, there are four different connectors, including 50-pin Centronics (it resembles the device end of a parallel cable), 50-pin HD D-type, 68-pin HD D-type, and a 25-pin D-Shell identical in appearance to a parallel port. More recently, a serial interface has been used with SCSI—a marriage of SCSI and Serial ATA called *Serial Attached SCSI (SAS)*. There are many types of SAS connectors, and they are much smaller than previous SCSI connectors—some are similar in size to USB and mini USB connectors—and the number of pins ranges from 26 to 36. Currently, we find SAS mainly on high-end systems, such as servers.

The rapid adoption of SATA technology by manufacturers means they are replacing SCSI on desktop and laptop computers—to a large extent due to availability and low cost. SCSI is still found in some high-performance workstations and servers and in server RAID arrays, although SATA is making inroads there, too.

Mass Storage Devices

Many types of mass storage devices are available, including those that store data on magnetic media, devices that use optical technologies, and devices based on solid-state technology. Note that this list includes both removable and fixed (nonremovable) devices. Further, certain of these, depending on their interfaces, are hot-swappable devices, and many are considered backup media. Let's explore all these dimensions.

Magnetic Mass Storage

Magnetic mass storage devices used with computers store digital data on magnetized media, such as floppy disks, the metal platters in hard disk drives, and magnetic tape media used in tape drives. Unlike RAM memory, which disappears when power to the device is off, this type of storage is nonvolatile. Read/write heads create magnetic patterns on the media that stay there until altered. Following are descriptions of three types of devices that can save data onto magnetic media: floppy disk drives, hard disk drives, and tape drives. Note that the terminology differs slightly: magnetic media on metal or plastic platters are called "disks," whereas optical media are called "discs." Don't let it confuse you; they are both devices that spin disks/discs and write and read data.

Floppy Disk Drives   A 3.5-inch *floppy disk drive (FDD)* reads data from a removable floppy disk and provides a now-primitive method for transferring data from one machine to another. A *floppy disk* contains a thin internal plastic disk with a thin magnetic coating. A hard plastic and metal protective casing, part of which retracts to reveal the storage medium inside, surrounds the disk. The back of the disk has a coin-sized metal circle that the drive can grasp to spin the disk. Inserting a floppy disk into a computer's floppy disk drive causes the drive to spin the internal disk and retract the protective cover. An articulated arm moves the drive's two *read/write heads* back and forth along the exposed area, reading data from and writing data to the disk. Each head reads and writes to one side of the disk. Read/write heads are used in floppy drives, hard drives, and optical drives, although in optical drives the heads use different methods for reading and writing.

Floppy drives have all but disappeared from PCs. Most new consumer models do not have built-in floppy drives. If you need one, consider buying an inexpensive external USB floppy drive, like that pictured in Figure 4-16.

A 3.5-inch floppy disk can hold 1.44 MB (high density) or 2.88 MB (extra high density) of information. The most commonly used such disk is the 1.44 MB capacity disk.

FIGURE 4-16

An external
floppy disk drive
with its USB
interface

Hard Disk Drives   A *hard disk drive (HDD)* stores data in a fashion similar to a floppy drive, but it typically is not removable and has a different physical structure (see Figure 4-17). A hard drive consists of one or more hard platters, stacked on top of, but not touching, one another. The stack of platters attaches through its center to a rotating pole, called a *spindle*. Each side of each platter can hold data and has its own read/write head. The read/write heads all move as a single unit back and forth across the stack. All of these components are within a sealed protective metal case.

Hard drives designed for installation within a computer have controlling circuitry on a board mounted on the exterior of the case and receive power through a cabled connection to the computer's power supply. Most desktop PCs have a single hard disk

FIGURE 4-17

The internal
structure of a
hard disk

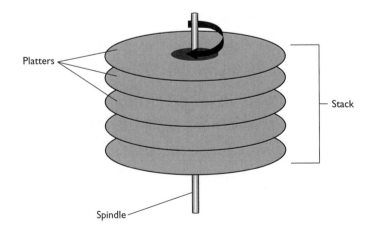

drive inside the computer case in a drive bay without external access. Figure 4-18 shows a 2 TB hard disk system designed for internal installation. Hard drives designed for external use have a protective case around both the hard drive and its circuit board, and usually have a built-in power supply or connection for a power adapter, all of which makes an external hard drive more expensive than a comparable internal hard drive. Hard drives are available in a wide range of capacities, and new hard drives now have a capacity between several hundred gigabytes and several terabytes.

When buying a new computer or additional hard drive, we now look for the preferred interface (SATA or eSATA), the capacity, and the speed of the drive, and try to buy the largest, fastest drive we can afford. The most common way to measure drive speed is the rate at which the platters spin—called *spindle speed*—measured in *revolutions per minute (rpm)*. Commonly available speeds in existing and new hard drives include 5400 rpm, 7200 rpm, 10,000 rpm, and 15,000 rpm. Data transfer rates tend to favor the higher rpms; prices vary accordingly.

Tape Drives   A *tape drive* is a mass storage device primarily used for backing up data from computers. It uses special removable magnetic data tape cartridges. People often choose tape drives for archiving data and backups because the media is relatively inexpensive and long lasting. Because data must be stored sequentially on tape, the access time for restoring individual files is slow. However, some high-end tape drives can write data to tape at transfer rates that compare well to hard drive speeds.

Normally, tape drives read and write just one tape size and format, such as the venerable *Digital Linear Tape (DLT)* technology. Developed in the 1980s, this technology was improved upon over the years as the *Super DLT (SDLT)* technology, and variations of this standard are still in use today. Both DLT and SDLT are one-half inch (12.7 mm)

An internal hard
drive system

wide and contained within a cartridge that you insert into a tape drive without touching the tape itself. These data tapes are guaranteed to store data reliably for up to 80 years, under controlled conditions.

Optical Disc Drives

Optical disc drives have come a long way since the 1980s. There are now three general *optical drive* categories and the media (discs) they use—CD, DVD, and a high-definition optical drive technology called Blu-ray. In addition, although some drives can only read one or two of these disc types, other drives can both read and write to one, two, or all three of these disc types. We call a drive that can write to an optical disc a *burner* and a drive that can read and/or write to multiple disc formats a *combo drive*. There are combo drives that read and write most, or all, optical disc formats (CD, DVD, and Blu-ray). Are you confused yet? When it comes to understanding these drives, it is best to start with the discs they use, and then look at the drives.

A typical optical disc of any type is, well, disk-shaped and made of polycarbonate. The standard disc is approximately 4.75 inches (12 cm) in diameter, but there are minidiscs that measure about 3.125 inches (8 cm). The surface is smooth and shiny with one labeled side and one plain side (there are exceptions to this single-sided form). The data, music, or video is stored on the disc using microscopic depressed and raised areas called *pits* and *lands,* respectively, which are covered by a protective transparent layer. A laser beam reads the data from the disc. You can access data much faster from a hard drive than from an optical disc, but optical storage is more permanent and more portable. Optical disc capacity is generally much smaller than commonly available hard drives.

Now that you know what they have in common, we will drop the phrase "optical drive" and "optical disc" and talk about the various types, mainly CD, DVD, and Blu-ray, and the variations of each.

CD-ROM, CD-R, CD-RW   The original optical drives used *compact discs (CDs)* and at first there were CD music players and eventually CD drives for computers. CDs sold at retail stores that contain music (audio CDs) or software (data CDs) are *Compact Disc–Read-Only Memory (CD-ROM)* discs, meaning they are only readable; you cannot change the contents. There are other CD media and drive types, a few differences in capacities, and, as the technology has matured, various speeds.

CD Drives and Media   CD music players can usually only play music discs. A CD drive in a computer that can play music CDs and read data CDs, but cannot write to a CD, is a CD-ROM drive. The next level up includes CD drives that can

write to, as well as read from, CDs. A *CD-Record (CD-R)* drive can write once to each specially designed blank CD-R disc. There are two types of CD-R discs. One type holds 650 MB of data or 74 minutes of audio, whereas the other holds 700 MB of data or 80 minutes of audio. The oldest CD-R drives only support the first format, whereas the next-generation CD-R drives support both formats. All but the earliest CD-R drives are multisession, meaning you can add data to a CD-R disc until you run out of space, but you cannot rewrite to occupied space on the disc. CD-R drives can read CD-ROMs and CDs created on a CD-R drive.

Today, CD-R drives are obsolete due to the many more capable drives that are normally downward compatible, beginning with *CD-Rewritable (CD-RW)* drives, which can write either to CD-R discs (once only) or to specially designed CD-RW discs. What made CD-RW drives such an improvement over CD-R drives is that they can write more than once to the same portion of disc, overwriting old data. This is not possible with CD-R drives.

CD-ROM, CD-R, and CD-RW drives can play or read from all three types of discs, with the exception of very old CD-ROM drives that have problems reading some newer CD discs.

CD Drive Speeds   The first CD drives transferred (read) data at 150 KBps, a speed now called 1x. CD drives are now rated at speeds that are multiples of this and have progressed up through 72x, which is 10,800 KBps. The appropriate name, such as CD-ROM, CD-R, and CD-RW, will describe a CD drive, and it may be followed by the speed rating, which may be a single number, in the case of a CD-ROM or, in the case of a CD-RW, will be three numbers, such as 52x24x16x. In this case, the drive is rated at 52x for reads, 24x for writes, and 16x for rewrites.

DVD Drives   Originally created for video storage in 1995, *digital video discs* have evolved into *digital versatile discs (DVDs)* used extensively on PCs for all types of data storage. Following are the various types of DVD drives and media.

DVD Drive Speeds   DVD drive speeds are expressed in terms similar to those of CD drives, although the spin speed of a 1x DVD drive is three times that of a CD 1x. In fact, a 1x DVD drive transfers data at 1352.54 KB/second, which is faster than a 9x CD drive. When looking at advertisements for DVD drives or PCs that include DVD drives, you will see the combined drive types followed by a combination of drive speeds, depending on the drive's operating modes. For instance: "DVD+R/RW 40x24x40x" indicates the three speeds of this drive for reading, writing, and rewriting because each drive has a different potential speed for each type of operation.

However, you need to read the manufacturer's documentation to know the order. As a general rule on DVD drives, reads are fastest, writes may be as fast as or a bit slower than reads, and rewrites are the slowest. Table 4-5 shows the read/write transfer rates of a selection of DVD drive speeds along with the equivalent CD drive speeds. Notice that DVD drives leave CD drives behind at the DVD 8x speed.

DVD Media   DVD discs are the same physical size as CD discs but have a higher storage capacity and several other differences. Whereas CDs only store data on a single side, DVDs come in both a conventional *single-sided DVD (SS DVD)* and a *dual-sided DVD (DS DVD)* variant that stores data on both sides, requiring that you turn the DVD over to read the second side.

In addition, the format on each side may be *single-layer (SL)* or *dual-layer (DL)*, indicated as SL DVD or DL DVD. Although the SL format is similar to the CD format in that there is only a single layer of pits, the DL format uses two pitted layers on each data side, with each layer having a different reflectivity index. The DVD package label shows the various combined features as *DVD-5, DVD-9, DVD-10*, and *DVD-18*. Therefore, when purchasing DVD discs, understanding the labeling is very important so you know the capacity of the discs you're buying. Table 4-6 shows DVD capacities based on the number of data sides and the number of layers per side.

Regardless of the actual format, we use the term "DVD." However, the original DVD encoding format for video used for movies is *DVD-Video*. DVD music discs sold at retail stores are *DVD-Audio* discs. An encoding format designed for data is

TABLE 4-4	DVD Drive Speed	Data Transfer Rate, MB/second	Equivalent CD Transfer Rate
	1x	1.35	9x
DVD Drive Speeds and Data Transfer Rates Compared to CD Drive Speeds	6x	8.1	54x
	8x	10.8	NA
	10x	13.5	NA
	12x	16.2	NA
	16x	21.6	NA
	18x	24.3	NA
	20x	27	NA
	22x	29.7	NA
	24x	32.4	NA

TABLE 4-5	DVD Type	Capacity
	DVD-5 (12 cm, SS/SL)	4.7 GB of data, or over two hours of video
DVD Capacities	DVD-9 (12 cm, SS/DL)	8.54 GB of data, or over four hours of video
	DVD-10 (12 cm, DS/SL)	9.4 GB of data, or over four and a half hours of video
	DVD-18 (12 cm, DS/DL)	17.08 GB of data, or over eight hours of video

DVD-RAM. Most discs that are not, strictly speaking, DVD-Video or DVD-RAM are all lumped together as *DVD-Data discs*, even if they contain video.

When it comes to selecting DVD data discs based on the ability to write to them, you have a selection equivalent to CD discs. The DVD discs sold at retail stores containing video or software are *DVD-ROM* discs, meaning they are only readable; you cannot change the contents. DVD-ROM has a maximum capacity of 15.9 GB of data. Logically, DVD drives that cannot write to, but can only read from, DVDs are also labeled DVD-ROM.

There are six standards of recordable DVD media. The use of the "minus" (–) or "plus" (+) has special significance. The minus, used in the first DVD recordable format and written as DVD-R and DVD-RW, indicates an older standard than those with the plus. *DVD-R* and *DVD-RW* are generally compatible with older players. *DVD-R* and *DVD+R* media are writable much like CD-Rs. DVD-RAM, DVD-RW, and *DVD+RW* are writable and rewritable much like CD-RW. When shopping for a DVD drive, or a PC that includes a DVD drive, you will see the previously described types combined as DVD+R/RW, DVD-R/RW, and simply DVD-RAM. Drives may also be labeled with the combined + and –, showing that all types of DVD discs can be used.

on the **Job** *Because CDs and DVDs have no protective covering, handling them with care is important. Scratches, dust, or other material on the CD surface can prevent data from reading correctly. Because data is located on the bottom side of the CD, always lay the CD label-side down.*

Blu-ray   The introduction of *high-definition television (HDTV)* to the consumer market in the late 1990s created the need for a standard for recording high-definition content. The response to this demand included two competing high-definition optical disc formatting standards: the *HD-DVD* standard, supported by Toshiba, and the *Blu-ray Disc (BD)* standard, developed by the Blu-ray Disc Association (originally named Blu-ray Disc Founders). A drive that complies with this standard is *Blu-ray drive*. Just a few of the member companies of this organization are Sony

Corporation, 20th Century Fox, Dell, Hewlett Packard, Hitachi, Pioneer, Sharp, and TDK. Sony Corporation is the name most frequently attached to this standard.

The battles fought in the marketplace were won by Blu-ray Disc, with the war officially ending in February 2008. Going forward, mass production of optical discs and drives for high-definition video will only use the winning Blu-ray standard. Further, the standard avoids using the term "DVD" for Blu-ray Disc products, preferring to simply use "Blu-ray Disc" or "BD." Following the CD and DVD precedence, different types of Blu-ray discs are *BD-ROM* (read-only) and *BD-R* (write once), with a third designation, *BD-RE*, that describes the rewritable Blu-ray disc. Blu-ray discs are the same physical size as CD and DVD discs but have a much higher storage capacity. And, like the CD and DVD technologies, the new Blu-ray disc drives can read from and write to the older CD and DVD discs.

Blu-ray drives use a blue-violet laser to read the discs, compared to the standard DVD, which uses a red laser. The blue laser, combined with a special lens, allows for a more focused laser, which results in higher density data storage.

Recall the discussion of layers when describing DVDs, because Blu-ray discs come in single-, double-, triple, and quadruple-layer versions. Single-layer Blu-ray discs hold 25 GB, double-layer discs hold 50 GB, triple-layer discs hold 100 GB, and quadruple-layer discs hold 128 GB. Movie titles available in Blu-ray format were on 25 GB discs until November 2007, when the first title appeared on 50 GB discs. Blu-ray disc isn't just for video. Like DVD, you can use Blu-ray to store any type of data. Table 4-6 compares selected features of Blu-ray versus DVD.

Solid-State Storage

Up to now, the storage devices we have looked at use magnetic or optical technologies. However, a growing category of storage devices uses integrated circuits, which are much faster than these other technologies. Generically called *solid-state storage*, *solid-state drives (SSDs)*, or *flash memory*, this technology has no moving parts and uses large-capacity, *nonvolatile memory*, meaning it does not require power to keep

TABLE 4-6	Feature	Blu-ray	DVD
	Disc diameter	12 cm	12 cm
Comparison of Blu-ray and DVD Features	Data read rate	36 Mbps (1x)	11.08 Mbps (1x)
	Video/audio data transfer rate	54 Mbps (1.5x)	10.08 Mbps (<1x)
	Maximum video resolution	1920×1080 (1,080p)	720×480/720×576 (480i/576i)
	Maximum video bit rate	40 Mbps	9.8 Mbps

the stored data intact. These devices are more expensive on a per-gigabyte basis than conventional hard drives, but there are many uses for these very lightweight devices. They have many names, in addition to the generic names listed earlier, and some are trademarked. SSDs come in a range of form factors. There are external SSDs and internal SSDs. There are 1 inch, 1.8 inch, 2.5 inch, 3.5 inch, and other sizes. They are very easy to install, with a variety of interfaces and several storage technologies used. There are SSDs designed to withstand harsh usage, such as internal SSDs installed in *embedded systems*—special-purpose computers used for certain tasks and installed within a device. Embedded systems exist within mobile phones, sophisticated network devices, home appliances, GPSs, climate control systems, automobiles, and just about every device you encounter from day to day.

On rare occasions, nontechnical PC users embrace a new computer device as quickly as the technically minded users do. One such device is the external SSD called a *thumb drive, jump drive,* or *flash drive.* This type of drive is very lightweight and small—it really is about the size of a small (flattened) thumb—most often has a USB interface, and can hold several hundred gigabytes of data. When plugged into your computer, it appears as an ordinary drive with a drive letter assigned to it (see Figure 4-19).

Internal flash memory cards are commonly used in a variety of devices, such as in digital cameras to store photos. A prolific photographer will carry several of these devices, swapping out full cards for empty ones. Although many cameras come with software and cables for transferring the photos from the camera's memory card to a

FIGURE 4-19

A USB flash drive

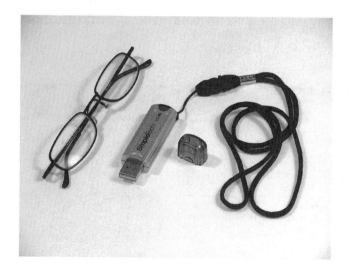

FIGURE 4-20

A 128 MB
CompactFlash
card

computer and/or printer, another method does not require either cable or software. In this method, you remove the card from the camera and insert it into a special slot on the PC or printer. Whether the card is in a camera or inserted directly into the computer's card reader, it is treated like a drive. There are many types of flash memory cards using various solid-state technologies, some with trademarked names.

CompactFlash (CF), by SanDisk, first appeared on the scene in 1994, making it a very early SSD, but it is still popular in its updated variations, now standardized through the CompactFlash Association. Dozens of manufacturers have produced CF cards. Figure 4-20 shows a 128 MB CF card measuring about one inch square.

The xD-Picture Card, by Olympus and Fujifilm, was used in digital cameras in the early and mid-2000s and had a capacity up to 2 GB, but is no longer used in new cameras. The xD-Picture Card is smaller than the standard SD card (discussed next), but larger than mini and micro SD form factors.

Secure Digital (SD) Cards are high capacity yet tiny and support high-speed data transfer. SD cards are used in portable devices, such as digital video recorders, digital cameras, handheld computers, audio players, and cell phones. (See Figure 4-21.)

SD cards come in several capacities and three major form factors. The standard form factor measures 32 mm × 24 mm × 2.1 mm, while the mini form factor measures 21.5 mm × 20 mm × 1.4 mm, and the micro form factor measures 15 mm × 11 mm × 1.0 mm. Table 4-7 shows the major capacities and form factors for SD cards. Figure 4-21 shows a Secure Digital High Capacity SD (SDHC) card.

TABLE 4-7

Capacities and
Form Factors for
SD Cards

	Maximum Capacity	Form Factors
Standard-capacity SD (SDSC or SD)	2 GB	Standard, miniSD, microSD
Secure Digital High Capacity (SDHC)	32 GB	Standard, miniSDHC, microSDHC
Secure Digital eXtended Capacity (SDXC)	2 TB	Standard, miniSDXC, microSDXC

The *Memory Stick (MS)* is a Sony flash memory card format measuring roughly 5/8" × 1¾" in its original form factor. It was available in capacities between 4 MB and 128 MB, and was followed by the *Memory Stick Pro (MSP)*, which held up to 1 GB. Then came the physically smaller *Memory Stick Duo (MSD)*, with a capacity of a mere 128 MB. The improved *Memory Stick PRO DUO (MSPD)* followed with at first a 16 GB maximum, followed soon after with a version with a 32 GB maximum. Inevitably, Sony, together with Sandisk, improved on this standard with the verbosely named *Memory Stick PRO Format for Extended High Capacity* with a maximum capacity of 2 TB.

A slot that can read an SD card may also be able to read a *MultiMediaCard (MMC)*, which has a form factor similar to the standard SD card. At 24 mm × 32 mm × 1.4 mm, MMC is just slightly thinner, but pin-compatible. This is why you will see labels on card readers. Figure 4-22 shows the front panel of a PC with a variety of flash memory slots, including one labeled MMC/SD. If a card reader is not built into your PC, and you require one, you can buy a bus card or an external USB card reader to add one to your PC.

EXERCISE 4-3

Identify Your Storage Devices

Use Windows to view your connected storage devices.

1. Open Computer (Windows Vista or Windows 7) or My Computer (Windows XP). This will show you all the attached disk drives.

2. Is there a drive labeled "Floppy Disk Drive (A:)" or "Floppy (A:)"? Don't be surprised if your computer does not have a floppy drive.

3. Identify the other drive or drives displayed in the Computer or My Computer folder.

Hot-Swappable Drives

A *hot-swappable drive* can be connected or disconnected without shutting down the system. Some hard drive systems are hot swappable, depending, in large part, on the interface. Until USB, FireWire, and SATA/eSATA were developed, hot-swappable drives were specially designed drive systems used on servers—often with their own separate case containing two or more drives and using the SCSI interface. They were expensive, but the ability to keep a server up and running after a single drive died offset the cost. You may wonder what happened to the data and programs held on the drive while all this occurred. The answer is that these hard drive systems were not just hot-swappable, but they also were configured as RAID arrays, which are discussed in the following section of this chapter, "RAID Arrays."

Hard drives with USB, FireWire, SATA, and eSATA interfaces are usually hot-swappable, but the system they are installed in must also support hot swapping, so always check the documentation. This doesn't mean you can just "pull the plug," so to speak, any old time. In order to avoid losing data, you need to ensure the disk is not in use before disconnecting it. Close any applications or windows that may be using the drive, and then take the steps necessary, depending on your operating system. In Windows, use the Safely Remove Hardware applet found in the status area on the right end of the taskbar.

RAID Arrays

Redundant array of independent disks (RAID) is a group of schemes designed to provide either better performance or fault-tolerant protection for data through the use of multiple hard drives. Often (but not always) RAID uses specialized hardware called a *RAID controller*. RAID can also be achieved using specialized software, but it always requires multiple drives configured to work together to use one of the RAID schemes. We call this set of disks collectively a *RAID array*. The drives should be of equal size, or you will waste space. We identify each RAID scheme by the word "RAID" followed by a number. Figure 4-23 shows a small RAID array for a home or small office.

Fault tolerance is the ability to survive a failure of a part of a system. When speaking of RAID arrays, fault tolerance is the ability to protect data from a failure. This is done through data redundancy or through a special algorithm. Only RAID 1 and RAID 10 provide fault tolerance through data redundancy, and RAID 5 provides fault tolerance through the use of an algorithm. Learn how these different RAID levels work.

RAID 0 *RAID 0* defines a simple striped set without parity. It gives improved drive read and write speeds. The operating system sees the separate physical drives in the array as a single hard drive, and each time data must be written to the drive

FIGURE 4-23

A small RAID array

array, the controller writes a portion of the data to each drive in the drive array, which is called a stripe. RAID 0 uses the total disk space in the array for data storage, without any fault-tolerant protection of the data from drive failure. If one of the drives in a RAID 0 array fails, all the data is lost.

RAID 1   *RAID 1*, also called *mirroring*, provides fault tolerance by writing all data simultaneously to the two drives in the *mirrored set*. If one of the drives should fail, the data still exists on the surviving drive. You may experience some improved performance on reads with RAID 1, depending on the operating system.

RAID 5   *RAID 5*, also called *striping with distributed parity* or *striping with interleaved parity*, requires at least three physical drives. As data is written to the striped set, it is written in blocks on each drive. In each stripe, the block written on just one of the drives (different with each write) is not the actual data, but the result of an algorithm performed on the data contained in the other blocks in the stripe. A single drive in a RAID 5 striped set can fail without a loss of data, because until the drive is replaced, the blocks in each stripe on the surviving drives are either the data itself (if the parity block was on the failed drive) or a parity block. Therefore, the controller uses the surviving data block and parity block in each set to reconstruct the data.

Once the missing drive is replaced, the RAID controller will automatically rebuild the data as it existed on the failed drive, using the existing data and parity blocks. Also, until you replace the missing member of the set, the reads from the striped set are slower, due to the need to run the algorithm in order to produce the data.

RAID 10   A *RAID 10* array is a stripe of mirrors, requiring a minimum of four identical disks paired into two mirrored sets. Data is written in a stripe across the two mirrored sets as if they were simply two disks in a RAID 0 array. This gives you the fault tolerance of a mirror and the performance of RAID 0.

on the job

In most organizations, RAID is valued for the protection of data through redundancy, available with RAID levels 1 and 5. Therefore, expect to encounter these types of RAID on the job, especially on servers. Outside IT departments, gamers are very savvy about RAID, but they lean toward RAID level 0, which gives performance gains without redundancy protection.

RAID for Everybody   RAID isn't just for expensive server systems anymore. Built-in drive controllers on modern motherboards are often RAID controllers because they include the ability to support one or more levels of RAID. Similarly, when you shop for a separate drive controller to install in a PC, you will find many that include RAID support.

RAID created using specialized RAID controllers is invisible to the operating system. This is a good thing, because managing a RAID array is a job that your operating system shouldn't see, and a RAID controller will do that for you. Many operating systems support software RAID, only requiring the correct number of drives, not a special RAID controller.

What is possible is not always advisable. That is true of software RAID. RAID controllers are now much less expensive and widely available. One may exist in your own desktop computer. Therefore, if you want to install a RAID array in a computer, use a hardware RAID controller and configure it per the controller's documentation. Normally, configuring a RAID controller is much like configuring system BIOS settings, with the addition of a utility for configuring the desired

exam ⓦatch   *Although there are many RAID levels, only RAID 0, 1, 5, and 10 are listed under CompTIA A+ Exam 801: Objective 1.5, so be sure you understand these four RAID levels.*

RAID level. Doing software RAID is interesting, and something many of us did more as a lab exercise years ago when it was cheaper to simply install multiple hard drives and use software RAID just for the experience of working with RAID than to purchase an expensive RAID controller. That was then, and things are much different now.

Removable Storage

Many storage devices include removable media, meaning the drive stays in place while the media (disk, disc, or tape) is removed and then replaced with another disk, disc, or tape. Traditionally, *removable storage* includes floppy disks, all types of optical discs, tape, and many of the SSDs discussed earlier.

Removable hard disk drives, primarily but not exclusively external devices, are the exception to the rule that the media is removed, not the drive. Removable hard drives come in two types. The most common for everyday users is external hard drives, which usually have their own power supplies, come with their own case, and require an interface cable such as USB, FireWire, or eSATA. Another type of removable hard disk drive is merely an internal hard drive, installed into a special carrier that in turn plugs into a companion cage installed in a PC.

Backup Media

At one time, only professional IT staff did serious data backup on corporate servers. PCs have become commonplace, not just in corporations and small businesses, but also in homes, and the amount of business and personal data stored on those PCs is huge. Aside from business data, many of us keep financial documents, family photos, and other valuable documents on our PC hard drives. When you consider the software and multimedia files stored on these systems, we all need to back up our data to avoid disasters.

For many years, tape drives were the media of choice for backing up large server systems, using expensive specialized equipment that combined tape drives with autoloaders that selected tapes for use and stored filled tapes in tape libraries. High-end tapes can store hundreds of gigabytes per tape.

Today, the average consumer has many options to select for their backups, and backup media can be any writable mass storage device—removable or fixed in place. Hard drive manufacturers offer a large variety of external drives, with a variety of interfaces, such as USB, FireWire, and the most popular new interface: eSATA. They have replaced tape drives for most consumers and small businesses.

Consumers can also choose from a huge selection of backup software, ranging from that included with your operating system to individual programs or software bundled with new external hard drives. Internet-based backup storage is available from

SCENARIO & SOLUTION

What type of drive is required to play the latest standard for high-definition video?	Blu-ray disc drive
You are asked to recommend a computer to be a file and print server for a small business. What drive configuration should you recommend to the small business owner to add data redundancy to the system?	RAID level 1; consider mirroring to give the server redundancy.
What drive interface standard replaced PATA for hard drives?	SATA
You sometimes use the lab computers at school to write your papers and need a very small, inexpensive, portable device to take back and forth. The files you expect to save are not terribly large, even with a few graphics files added. What type of device should you consider?	A solid-state drive, commonly known as a thumb drive, would fit the criteria.

many sources—even from security software vendors. Also, many online data backup services allow you to store your data in the Internet "cloud." These services are often free for small amounts of data. The theory is that you will try the free service, and then pay a subscription fee to back up larger amounts of data to their servers.

Medium to large businesses and government agencies have traditionally used elaborate tape backup systems, but many are transitioning from tape systems to other backup options, such as a *storage area network (SAN)*, which is made up of a variety of mass storage devices on a dedicated high-speed network, used to back up data from networked computers.

CERTIFICATION SUMMARY

Identifying personal computer components and their functions is the first step in becoming a computer professional. While PC component technologies are ever-changing, understanding the basics of the components and their functions today will help you to understand newer technologies as they are introduced. This chapter described the important features of memory, expansion cards, and storage. It isn't enough to understand the technologies of these important components; you also need to understand the various connection interfaces related to them and the connectors and related cables, which were included in this chapter.

TWO-MINUTE DRILL

Here are some of the key points covered in Chapter 4.

Memory

- ❑ Data storage capacity is described in terms of bits, bytes, kilobytes, megabytes, and terabytes.

- ❑ The speed of electronics, such as RAM, is often described in terms of hertz (Hz), kilohertz (KHz), megahertz (MHz), and gigahertz (GHz).

- ❑ RAM is volatile, and used to store active programs and data. ROM is nonvolatile, and used to store firmware on motherboards and adapters.

- ❑ Most memory modules do not perform error checking. Some older memory modules use an error-checking method called parity, and others may use a more complex method called ECC.

- ❑ DIMM modules come in both single-sided and double-sided versions.

- ❑ SRAM is very fast and very expensive, and is used for system cache in most systems.

- ❑ DRAM is slower than SRAM. It is less expensive, has a higher capacity, and is the main memory in the computer.

- ❑ DRAM technologies include RDRAM, SDRAM, DDR1 SDRAM, DDR2 SDRAM, and DDR3 SDRAM. DDR4 will be the next specification for SDRAM.

- ❑ Specialized RAM for video adapters is called VRAM.

- ❑ To avoid compatibility problems, read the motherboard manual before buying and installing additional RAM modules in a computer.

Expansion Cards and Built-in Adapters

- ❑ Common expansion cards (adapters) include video adapters, a variety of multimedia devices, communications, and I/O adapters for the legacy parallel and serial (RS-232-C) interfaces, as well as the newer versions of USB, FireWire, and eSATA.

- ❑ The need for expansion cards has diminished as PC motherboards contain more functions.

❑ Riser cards come in two types: (1) a card used to expand a computer's bus and allow insertion of other cards into the riser card—usually in a different orientation in order to fit into a small computer case, and (2) a small expansion card, such as an AMR or CNR card, containing multiple functions.

Mass Storage Devices and Backup Media

❑ The long-reigning drive interface standards based on the EIDE/PATA technology gave way to the SATA interface for internal mass storage and to eSATA for external devices.

❑ A mass storage device holds large amounts of information, even when the power is off.

❑ Mass storage devices come in three general categories: magnetic, optical, and solid-state storage.

❑ Floppy disk drives, hard disk drives, and tape drives are examples of magnetic mass storage devices that store digital data on magnetized media.

❑ Optical drives include CD, DVD, and Blu-ray drives, each of which has a variety of capacities and speeds.

❑ Solid-state storage, or solid-state drives (SSDs), have no moving parts and use large-capacity, nonvolatile memory, commonly called flash memory.

❑ Hot-swappable drives can be connected or disconnected without shutting down the system. Some hard drive systems are hot-swappable, depending, in large part, on the interface.

❑ Hard drives with USB, FireWire, SATA, or eSATA interfaces are usually hot-swappable, as is nearly any USB or FireWire device.

❑ RAID, which stands for redundant array of independent (or inexpensive) disks, is a group of schemes designed to provide either better performance or improved data reliability through redundancy.

❑ RAID 0 defines a striped set without parity. It gives improved drive read and write speeds.

❑ RAID 1, also called mirroring, provides fault tolerance because all the data is written identically to the two drives in the mirrored set.

❑ RAID 5, also called striping with distributed parity or striping with interleave parity, requires at least three physical drives.

❑ RAID 10 is a stripe of mirrors, requiring a minimum of four identical disks, paired into two mirrored sets, with data written in a stripe across the two mirrored sets.

❑ Many storage devices include removable media, meaning that the drive stays in place, while the media (disk, disc, or tape) is removed and replaced with another disk, disc, or tape.

❑ Tape has long been a reliable backup medium, but consumers have other options, such as hard drives and online backup services. Medium to large organizations may still use sophisticated tape systems, but many are moving to other options, such as storage area networks.

SELF TEST

The following questions will help you measure your understanding of the material presented in this chapter. Read all of the choices carefully because there might be more than one correct answer. Choose all correct answers for each question.

Memory

1. This type of memory is volatile, used as temporary workspace by the CPU, and loses its contents every time a computer is powered down.
   A. ROM
   B. RAM
   C. CMOS
   D. Solid state

2. Cache memory uses which type of RAM chip because of its speed?
   A. DRAM
   B. VRAM
   C. DIMM
   D. SRAM

3. This type of SDRAM doubled the speed at which standard SDRAM processed data by accessing the module twice per clock cycle.
   A. Dual-channel
   B. Multichannel
   C. Double-sided
   D. DDR1

4. This type of RAM module uses a special 240-pin DIMM socket and requires far less power than the previous modules, while providing almost twice the bandwidth.
   A. DDR1 SDRAM
   B. DDR2 SDRAM
   C. DDR3 SDRAM
   D. VRAM

5. This specialized type of RAM memory chip is for use on video adapters.
   A. SRAM
   B. SDRAM
   C. DRAM
   D. VRAM

6. This type of SDRAM module has memory chips mounted on both sides.
   A. Single-sided
   B. Double-sided
   C. ECC
   D. Dual channel

7. This chip manages the main memory on a motherboard.
   A. CMOS
   B. VRAM
   C. MCC
   D. DDR3

Expansion Cards and Built-in Adapters

8. Which of the following is not an I/O technology?
   A. RS-232-C
   B. USB
   C. IEEE 1394
   D. DB-9

9. Name a common communications adapter card used to connect PCs to a LAN or to take advantage of a DSL or cable modem Internet connection.
   A. NIC
   B. Modem
   C. USB
   D. Serial

10. This category of adapter card accepts and records video signals to a PC's hard drive.
   A. Network adapter
   B. Modem
   C. Capture card
   D. Video adapter

Mass Storage Devices and Backup Media

11. This is a component in a hard drive system that reads and writes data.
   A. Spindle
   B. Head
   C. Platter
   D. Cable

12. Name the rotating shaft to which a hard drive's platters attach.
   A. Head
   B. Cable
   C. Pin
   D. Spindle

13. Which of the following is *not* an example of a magnetic mass storage device?
   A. FDD
   B. DVD drive
   C. HDD
   D. Tape drive

14. Name two common interfaces for external hard drives.
   A. IDE and SATA
   B. Serial and parallel
   C. USB and eSATA
   D. Modems and hubs

15. This DVD type stores 17.08 GB of data, or over eight hours of video.
   A. DVD-18
   B. DVD-9
   C. DVD-10
   D. DVD-5

16. This type of optical mass storage device was developed to read and write high-definition video.
   A. DVD-18
   B. CD-RW
   C. Blu-ray disc
   D. DVD-RW

17. This type of mass storage device, once found in nearly every PC, is now rarely installed in a new PC.
   A. Tape drive
   B. Floppy disc drive
   C. Hard disk drive
   D. Optical disc drive

18. This feature indicates that a drive can be connected or disconnected without shutting down the system.

   A. External

   B. RAID

   C. USB

   D. Hot-swappable

19. This magnetic mass storage device type stores data sequentially and has been primarily used as backup storage for servers.

   A. FDD

   B. Tape drive

   C. Optical drive

   D. HDD

20. This is a group of standards defining several schemes for using multiple identical hard drives, working together in an array with the goal of achieving either better performance or redundancy.

   A. RAID

   B. eSATA

   C. USB

   D. Serial

SELF TEST ANSWERS

Memory

1. ☑ **B.** RAM is the type of volatile memory used by the CPU as workspace.
   ☒ **A,** ROM, is incorrect because this type of memory is not volatile; its contents are not lost every time the PC is powered off. **C,** CMOS, is incorrect because it is special battery-powered support memory that holds basic system configuration information used by the computer as it powers up. **D,** solid state, is incorrect because this is a type of storage device that is nonvolatile and is not used by the processor in the manner described.

2. ☑ **D.** SRAM is the type of RAM used for cache memory because of its speed.
   ☒ **A,** DRAM, is incorrect because this is slower than SRAM. **B,** VRAM, is incorrect because although it is fast, this type of RAM is used on video adapters. **C,** DIMM, is incorrect, as it is a RAM connector/slot type, not a type of RAM chip.

3. ☑ **D.** DDR1 SDRAM doubled the speed at which standard SDRAM processed data by accessing the module twice per clock cycle.
   ☒ **A,** dual-channel, and **B,** multichannel, are both incorrect. Both are used to describe an architecture that speeds up memory access by having the MCC access each module on a different channel. **C,** double-sided, describes a RAM module with chips populating both sides.

4. ☑ **C.** DDR3 SDRAM is the type of RAM module that uses a special 240-pin DIMM socket and requires far less power than the previous modules, while providing almost twice the bandwidth.
   ☒ **A,** DDR1 SDRAM, is incorrect because it uses a 184-pin DIMM socket, not a 240-pin DIMM socket. **B,** DDR2 SDRAM, is incorrect because although it also uses a (different) 240-pin DIMM socket, it requires more power than the previous RAM module type (DDR1 SDRAM). **D,** VRAM, is incorrect because it is a chip type that mounts on a video adapter, not on a DIMM module.

5. ☑ **D.** VRAM is correct, as this type of memory chip is for use on video adapters.
   ☒ **A,** SRAM, **B,** SDRAM, and **C,** DRAM, are all incorrect because none of these memory chip types are used on video adapters.

6. ☑ **B.** Double-sided is correct because this type of RAM module has memory chips mounted on both sides.
   ☒ **A,** single-sided, is incorrect because a single-sided memory module only has chips mounted on one side. **C,** ECC, is incorrect because this stands for error-correcting code, which is an error detecting and correcting mechanism used by some memory modules. **D,** dual channel, is incorrect because this refers to a technique for speeding up memory access in which the MCC switches between two memory modules, effectively doubling the memory speed.

7.   ☑   **C.** MCC, or memory controller chip, is correct because this chip controls the main memory on a motherboard.
☒   **A,** CMOS, is incorrect because the CMOS chip is a special battery-supported chip that retains the system settings. **B,** VRAM, is incorrect because this is a type of RAM used on video adapters. **D,** DDR3, is incorrect because this is a type of SDRAM, not a controller chip.

Expansion Cards and Built-in Adapters

8.   ☑   **D.** DB-9 is not an I/O technology, but a type of connector with a trapezoidal shape and nine pins.
☒   **A,** RS-232-C, **B,** USB, and **C,** IEEE 1394, are incorrect because they are I/O technologies.

9.   ☑   **A.** A network interface card (NIC) is a common communications adapter card used to connect PCs to a LAN or to take advantage of a DSL or cable modem Internet connection.
☒   **B,** modem, is incorrect because, although it is a communications adapter card, it is used for a dial-up connection, not for a LAN connection. **C,** USB, is incorrect because it is an I/O interface, not a communications adapter. **D,** serial, is incorrect because it is an I/O interface, not a communications adapter, although some external modems can connect to a serial port.

10.   ☑   **C.** A capture card is a type of adapter used to record video signals to a PC's hard drive.
☒   **A,** network adapter, is incorrect because this type of adapter is used for network communications. **B,** modem, is incorrect because it is used for a dial-up connection, not for recording video signals. **D,** video adapter, is incorrect because it is used to drive a display device, not to capture video signals.

Mass Storage Devices and Backup Media

11.   ☑   **B.** The head is the component in a hard drive system that reads and writes data. There is one head for each platter side.
☒   **A,** spindle, is incorrect because this rotating pole holds the platters in a hard drive. **C,** platter, is incorrect because this component holds the data. **D,** cable, is incorrect because a cable connects a device to a computer but does not read data from a hard drive.

12.   ☑   **D.** The spindle is the rotating shaft to which a hard drive's platters are attached.
☒   **A,** head, is incorrect because this component reads and writes data. **B,** cable, is incorrect because a cable connects a device to a computer and is not a rotating shaft. **C,** pin, is incorrect because it is a component of a cable plug, not the rotating shaft in a hard drive.

13.   ☑   **B.** A DVD drive is *not* an example of a magnetic mass storage device; DVD drives use optical technology.
☒   **A,** FDD, **C,** HDD, and **D,** tape drive, are all incorrect because they are all examples of magnetic mass storage devices.

14. ☑ **C.** USB and eSATA are two common interfaces for external hard drives.
    ☒ **A,** IDE and SATA, is incorrect because these are common interfaces for internal hard drives, not for external hard drives. **B,** serial and parallel, is incorrect because these are not common interfaces for external hard drives. **D,** modems and hubs, is not correct because these are not common interfaces for external hard drives.

15. ☑ **A.** DVD-18 stores 17.08 GB of data, or over eight hours of video.
    ☒ **B,** DVD-9, is incorrect because it only holds 8.54 GB of data, or over four hours of video. **C,** DVD-10, is incorrect because it only holds 9.4 GB of data, or over four and a half hours of video. **D,** DVD-5, is incorrect because it only holds 4.7 GB of data, or over two hours of video.

16. ☑ **C.** Blu-ray disc was developed to read and write high-definition video.
    ☒ **A,** DVD-18, **B,** CD-RW, and **D,** DVD-RW, are all incorrect because, although they are all optical mass storage devices, none of them can handle high-definition video formats.

17. ☑ **B.** Although a floppy disc drive was once standard equipment, you now rarely see this type of drive installed in a new PC.
    ☒ **A,** tape drive, is incorrect because tape drives were never common in PCs. And it is even less likely that you will ever see one in a new PC. **C,** hard disk drive, is incorrect because hard disk drives are almost always installed in every new PC. **D,** optical disc drive, is incorrect because they frequently are installed in new PCs.

18. ☑ **D.** Hot-swappable is a feature that indicates that a drive can be connected or disconnected without shutting down the system.
    ☒ **A,** external, is incorrect because while some external drives are also hot-swappable, the term "external" itself does not indicate that a drive has this feature. **B,** RAID, is incorrect because although drives that are part of a RAID array may be hot-swappable, the term "RAID" itself does not indicate that a drive has this feature. **C,** USB, is incorrect because, although some hot-swappable drives use the USB interface, the term "USB" itself does not indicate that a drive has this feature.

19. ☑ **B.** A tape drive is a magnetic mass storage device type that stores data sequentially, and it has been primarily used as backup storage for servers.
    ☒ **A,** FDD, and **D,** HDD, are incorrect because, although both are magnetic mass storage device types, neither has been primarily used as backup storage for servers. **C,** optical drive, is incorrect because it is not a magnetic mass storage device type, and it has never been primarily used as backup storage for servers.

20. ☑ **A.** RAID is the acronym for redundant array of independent (or inexpensive) disks, a group of schemes designed to provide either better performance or improved data reliability through redundancy.
    ☒ **B,** eSATA, is incorrect because this is a standard for an external version of the serial ATA interface. **C,** USB, is incorrect because this is the Universal Serial Bus standard. **D,** serial, is incorrect because this is another interface, not a standard for disk arrays.

5

Power Supplies, Display Devices, and Peripherals

T his chapter explores power supplies, display devices (both video adapters and displays), and peripheral devices, identifying the connector types and cables associated with these computer components. Also included are instructions for installing and configuring each type of device, with the exception of the physical installation of video adapter cards, which will be described in Chapter 6 as part of the how-to instructions for installing any expansion card.

CERTIFICATION OBJECTIVE

■ *801: 1.8   Install an appropriate power supply based on a given scenario*

This section describes power supply types and characteristics. You will learn about voltage, wattage, capacity, power supply fans, and form factors. Also included are descriptions of power cables and connectors. This section prepares you to select an appropriate power supply, remove an older power supply, and install a new one.

Power Supplies

A *power supply*, or *power supply unit (PSU)*, is the device that provides power for all other components on the motherboard and is internal to the PC case. Every PC has an easily identified power supply; it is typically located inside the computer case at the back, and parts of it are visible from the outside when looking at the back of the PC. On a desktop computer (PC or iMac), you will see the three-prong power socket. Most PCs also have a label, and sometimes a tiny switch. Figure 5-1 shows the interior of a PC with a power supply on the upper left. Notice the bundle of cables coming out of the power supply. These cables supply power to the motherboard and all other internal components. Each component must receive the appropriate type and amount of power it requires, and the power supply itself has its requirements. Therefore, you should understand some basic electrical terminology and apply it to the power supply's functions.

Electrical Terminology

Electricity is the flow of electrons (*current*) through a conductor, such as copper wire, and we use it in two forms: *direct current (DC)* and *alternating current (AC)*. In DC, the type of electrical current generated by a battery, the flow of negative electrons,

The power supply, shown in the upper left, is usually located in the back of the computer case, with a three-prong power socket visible on the exterior of the PC.

is in one direction around the closed loop of an electrical circuit. In AC, the flow of electrons around the electrical circuit reverses periodically and has alternating positive and negative values. AC is the kind of electricity that comes from a wall outlet.

A *volt* (V) is the unit of measurement of the pressure of electrons on a wire, or the electromotive force. A *watt* (W) is a unit of measurement of actual delivered power. An *ampere* (A *or amp*) is a unit of measurement for electrical current, or rate of flow of electrons, through a wire. When you know the wattage and amps needed or used, you calculate volts using the formula volts = watts / amps. When you know the voltage and amps, you can calculate wattage used or required with the formula watts = volts × amps. And if you need to know the amps but only know the wattage and voltage, use the formula amps = watts / volts. All these calculations are versions of Ohm's Law, which represents the fundamental relationship among current, voltage, and resistance.

Voltage

The power supply is responsible for converting the AC voltage from wall outlets into the DC voltage that the computer requires: ±12 VDC, ±5 VDC, or ±3.3 VDC (volts DC). The PC power supply accomplishes this task through a series of switching transistors, which gives rise to the term *switching-mode power supply*.

A device, such as a laser printer or a cathode-ray tube (CRT), that requires high voltage has its own *high-voltage power supply (HVPS)*.

Typical North American wall outlets provide about 110 to 120 volts AC (VAC) at a frequency of 60 Hertz (Hz–cycles per second), which is also expressed as ~115 VAC at 60 Hz. The *frequency* is the number of times per second that alternating current reverses direction. Elsewhere in the world, standard power is 220 to 240 VAC at 50 Hz.

Power supplies manufactured for sale throughout the world are dual voltage, providing either the U.S. standard or the international standard. Dual-voltage options in power supplies come in two categories: power supplies that automatically switch and those that must be manually switched. An *auto-switching power supply* can detect the incoming voltage and switch to accept either 120 or 240 VAC, but a *fixed-input* power supply will have a switch on the back for selecting the correct input voltage setting. Figure 5-2 shows the back of a power supply with the *voltage selector switch* for selecting 115 VAC or 240 VAC. It is the tiny slide switch positioned below the power connector.

Wattage and Size

How big a power supply do you need? First, we are not talking about physical size, but the capacity or wattage a power supply can handle. Figure 5-3 shows the label on a power supply. Notice that this is a 300-watt power supply. Notice also that the label specifies this power supply will run on either 120 VAC or 240 VAC and at

The back of a power supply, power connector socket, and the voltage selection switch below it

FIGURE 5-3

The maximum
wattage supported
by a power supply
appears on the
left side of this
label, under the
word "output."

either 50/60 Hz, which means it will run in almost any country. Just a few years ago power supplies ranging from 230 to 250 watts were considered more than adequate for PCs; today you will find many modestly priced PCs with 300-watt or greater power supplies. Higher-end computers use 500- to 1200-watt power supplies. Therefore, to answer the question, you need a power supply with a capacity that exceeds the total watts required by all the internal components, such as the motherboard, memory, drives, and various adapters.

on the job

If a device label does not state the number of watts required, simple math will give you the answer. All you need is the volts and amps, which you should find printed on the device somewhere. Once you have these two numbers, multiply them together (watts = volts × amps) and you will have the wattage of the device.

EXERCISE 5-1

Check Out the Wattage on PCs and Other Devices

1. Look at the back of a PC and find the power supply label. Record the wattage information. If wattage is not shown but the volts and amps are, multiply those two numbers to calculate the wattage.

2. Do the same on computer peripherals that are available to you, such as displays, printers, and scanners.

3. Similarly, check out the wattage on noncomputer devices in the classroom or at home.

Fans

Another function of a power supply is to dissipate the heat it and other PC components generate. Heat buildup can cause computer components (including the power supply) to fail. Therefore, power supplies have a built-in exhaust fan that draws air through the computer case and cools the components inside. For more information on cooling, flip back and review the section on cooling systems in Chapter 3.

AC Adapters

Another form of power supply is an AC adapter used with portable computers and external peripherals. An AC *adapter* converts AC power to the voltage needed for a device. Like the power supply in a desktop PC, it converts AC power to DC power. The connector between the AC adapter and the laptop or device may be one of several types. The traditional connectors are various sizes of coaxial connectors, but AC adapters also come with one of several types of Universal Serial Bus (USB) connectors. Figure 5-4 shows an AC adapter for a laptop with a coaxial connector on the right. On the far left is the cable that connects the adapter to a wall socket via a grounded plug. Notice the smaller three-prong plug that connects to the matching socket on the AC adapter.

If you must replace an external adapter, simply unplug it and attach a new one that matches the specifications and plug configuration of the adapter it is replacing. Since AC adapters have different output voltages, only use an AC adapter with output voltage that exactly matches the input voltage for the laptop. Previously, laptop power supplies were *fixed-input power supplies* set to accept only one input power voltage. Now, many laptop AC adapters act as *auto-switching power supplies*, detecting the incoming voltage and switching to accept either 120 or 240 VAC.

FIGURE 5-4

An AC adapter
for a laptop

Power Supply Form Factors and Connectors

When building a new computer, a power supply may come with the computer case, or you can purchase one separately, but you need to consider both power needs and form factor. Like motherboards and cases, computer power supplies come in a variety of form factors to match both the motherboard and case. The most common power supply form factor for desktop PCs is referred to as the *ATX power supply*, used in most case sizes, except the smallest low-profile power supplies and the largest, jumbo-sized full-tower cases. A smaller version of the ATX power supply is the *micro-ATX power supply*, which works in many of the smaller cases with the micro-ATX and similar motherboard form factors. There are many other form factors that are variations on the ATX PSU form factor. Whenever you need to match a power supply with a computer, start with the motherboard manual, and pay close attention to all the features required by the motherboard. Then consider the case and what will fit in it. In fact, when putting together a custom computer, a PSU will often come with the case.

In response to the demands of PC-based servers and gamers, power supply manufacturers have added proprietary features beyond those in any standards. You can find power supplies that offer special support for the newest Intel and AMD CPU requirements and greater efficiency, which saves on power usage and reduces heat output.

The form factor of the power supply determines the motherboard it works with and the type of connector used to supply power to the motherboard, but most motherboards use 20- or 24-pin connectors, called *P1 power connectors*. The ATX power supply connector for older ATX motherboards is a one-piece 20-pin keyed connector. There is some confusion caused by the various 24-pin power supply connectors.

If a motherboard requires additional power, a separate cable will connect to the motherboard with a 4-, 6-, or 8-pin connector. Under the *ATX 12V* standard, a 4-pin, *P4 connector*, also called a *P4 12V connector*, supplies 12 volts in addition to that provided by the P1 connector, or, based on the *ATX 12V 2.0* standard, a 24-pin main connector and a 4-pin secondary connector. Some motherboards require EPS12V connectors, which include a 24-pin main connector, an 8-pin secondary connector, and an optional 4-pin tertiary connector.

There are several types of 6-pin and 8-pin connectors. A now-obsolete 6-pin connector, called the *AUX power connector*, added 3.3 volts or 5.0 volts to AMD dual-processor motherboards. A newer type of connector is the *PCI Express (PCI-e) power connector*, which comes in 6-pin or 8-pin configurations. A PCIe power connector attaches to a connector on a motherboard (if available) or to a connector on a specialized expansion card.

Some high-end non-ATX motherboards used in network servers and high-end workstations include a 4-pin or 8-pin connector to provide additional power to the CPU, which also derives power through its own motherboard socket.

ATX and other power supplies and motherboards work together to provide a feature called *soft power*. Soft power allows software to turn off a computer rather than only using a physical switch. Most PCs have soft power. A computer with soft power enabled has a pair of small wires leading from the physical switch on the case to the motherboard. Usually, there is a system setting that controls just how this feature is used. For safety's sake, you should always consider soft power as being on, because when you have enabled soft power, turning the power switch off means that although the computer appears to be off, the power supply is still supplying ±5 volts to the motherboard. This means you can never trust the on-off switch. Some PCs come equipped with two power switches. One is in the front, and you can consider it the "soft" off switch. The other is on the back of the case, in the power supply itself, and this is the "real" off switch. Even so, the safest thing to do is to unplug the power cable from the wall outlet to ensure no power is coming to the motherboard.

on the job

A motherboard with soft power is never off, even when the switch on the front of the PC is in the "Off" position. There is always a ±5 V charge to the motherboard from the power supply. The only way to ensure that there is no power is to unplug the power supply from the power source. Always do this before opening a PC case.

Connecting Power to Peripherals

In addition to providing power to the motherboard, power supplies have ports and connectors for providing power to internally installed peripherals—mainly various drives, but sometimes to expansion cards. Power supplies often have cables that are permanently connected to the PSU, and they may have additional ports to which you connect additional cables, allowing for expansion. The cable connections on the peripheral end vary based on the type of device and power requirements.

Two traditional peripheral connectors are the 4-pin *Molex connector*, measuring about 7/8" wide and the much smaller 4-pin *miniconnector*. The Molex and miniconnector each provide 5 or 12 volts to peripherals. Molex connectors traditionally connected to most internal devices, while the miniconnector mainly connected to floppy drives. Figure 5-5 shows a power splitter cable with a single Molex connector on one end and two miniconnectors on the other.

A power splitter cable with a single Molex connector and two miniconnectors

To connect a SATA device to a power supply, look for a SATA power cable coming off the power supply with a 15-pin L-shaped connector for connecting to most optical or hard drives. If an older power supply does not have this cable, use a Molex-to-SATA power connector adapter to connect the SATA power cable to a Molex connector from the power supply. Small SATA storage devices have a tiny 15-pin micro SATA power connector. The pins in a SATA power connector supply different voltages for SATA devices, including 3.3 V, 5 V, and 12 V; and they support hot-swapping SATA devices.

Energy Efficiency

Although not directly a power supply issue, energy efficiency in all PC components has become a very important feature and affects the selection of a power supply. We seem to need bigger and bigger power supplies to accommodate the increasing number and types of components we include in our PCs: more memory, larger hard drives, more powerful video adapters, and so on. The good news is that the power requirements have not grown proportionally with the performance improvements of these components, which are more energy efficient and have features that reduce their power consumption during idle times. Learn more about managing these energy-saving features in laptops in Chapter 7.

Removing a Power Supply/Installing a Power Supply

Whether you are purchasing a power supply for a new system or replacing an old one, you have the same set of concerns when selecting, installing, or removing a power supply. Power supplies in existing computers do fail from time to time, and you can replace them using the procedure outlined in Exercise 5-2, which provides basic steps for removing an old power supply and replacing a new one.

Recall that power supplies can still hold a charge when turned off, especially if you use only the soft power switch. Before removing any power supply, even a failed one, be sure to unplug it from the wall outlet. To avoid the danger of electric shock, do not wear an antistatic wristband while working with power supplies.

EXERCISE 5-2

Replacing a Power Supply

1. Turn off the power and remove the power connector from the wall socket.
2. Remove the power connector(s) from the motherboard, grasping the plastic connector, not the wires.
3. Remove the power connectors from all other components, including hard, floppy, and optical drives.
4. Using an appropriately sized screwdriver, remove the screws that hold the power supply to the PC case. Do not remove the screws holding the power supply case together!
5. Slide or lift the power supply away from the computer.
6. Reverse these steps to install a new power supply.

CERTIFICATION OBJECTIVES

■ **801: 1.10** *Given a scenario, evaluate types and features of display devices*

■ **801: 1.11** *Identify connector types and associated cables*

■ **802: 1.5** *Given a scenario, use Control Panel utilities*

This section introduces all of the topics covered by the CompTIA A+ Exam 801 Objective 1.10, including the various types of display devices (projectors, CRTs, LEDs, OLEDs, plasma, and LCDs), display technologies, and display settings. Control Panel Display resolution settings are described here, per Objective 802: 1.5. Also included here are two areas of Exam 801 Objective 1.11: connector types for display devices and display cable types. Connectors and cables used in networking are explored in Chapter 14.

Video Adapters and Displays

The quality of the image you see on a PC display depends on both the capabilities and configuration of the two most important video components: the video adapter and the display device (also called a monitor). The technologies used in video adapters and displays have become a more complex topic as we transitioned from the old analog technologies to the digital technologies in use today. We will explore that transition in this section, as well as important display settings and how they affect output to a display.

Analog vs. Digital

Video adapters, as part of inherently digital computing systems, have long been digital devices, meaning that a video adapter uses a *digital signal* composed of discrete on-off signals or pulses representing digits to compose the video image before sending it to a display. However, these adapters were connected to *analog displays* that accepted only an *analog signal*, meaning that it was a continuously variable signal. Therefore, the adapter had to translate the digital data to an analog signal. The upside to analog displays was that they could display continuously varied colors. A digital display, on the other hand, accepts digital signals, and although it does not display continuously variable colors, the typical digital display shows more complex colors and intensities not possible on an analog display. In the days when analog displays prevailed, the video adapter translated that image to an analog signal before sending it to the display. In the following discussion of video interface modes, we begin with the analog video technologies based on the old VGA standard and end with the several digital standards in use today.

Video Adapters

The video adapter controls the output from the PC to the display device. Although the video adapter contains all the logic and does most of the work, the quality of the resulting image depends on the modes supported by both the adapter and the display. If the adapter is capable of higher-quality output than the display, the display limits the result—and vice versa. In this section, we will explore video interface modes, screen resolution and color density, the computer interfaces used by video adapters, and the connectors used to connect a display to the video adapter.

Computer Interfaces

When purchasing a video adapter card, pay attention to the interface between the video adapter and the computer so that you select one you can install into your PC. If the motherboard contains a video adapter, it still accesses one of the standard busses in the computer. If the video adapter is a separate expansion card, it installs into one of three types of bus connectors: PCI, PCIe, or AGP. We discussed these bus types in Chapter 3. You will find the current version of the video standards mentioned here available with any of these interfaces.

Video Modes and Technologies

In order to be compatible with older displays and software, even the latest video adapter supports many of the less-capable modes that preceded it. Therefore, the following is a survey of these modes.

The most basic of video modes are text and graphics. As a PC boots, and before the operating system takes control, the video is in text mode and can only display the limited ASCII character set. Once the operating system is in control, it loads drivers for the video adapter and display, and it uses a graphics mode that can display bitmapped graphics. Today these graphics modes—commonly called video modes—support millions of colors. Many video modes have been introduced since the first IBM PC in 1981. However, we will only discuss the video modes you can expect to encounter on the A+ exam, as well as in businesses and homes today. Along with each new mode comes the supporting technology, along with a specific type of connection between the video adapter and the display. These connectors will be identified in the following discussion of video modes and technologies.

e x a m

⚙ a t c h *Be able to identify on sight the various types of connectors and the video mode or technology associated with them.*

VGA   *Video graphics array (VGA)* is a video adapter standard introduced with the IBM PS/2 computers in the late 1980s. VGA sends analog signals to the display, producing a wide range of colors. VGA is an old technology today because we have gone far beyond it in capabilities, but some software packages still list it as a minimum requirement for installing the software, and the connector used on VGA adapters is in use today on many video adapters that also support more advanced video modes—although newer connectors are also available, often on the same adapter. VGA mode most often consists of a combination of 640 × 480 *pixels*

FIGURE 5-6

DVI-I Dual Link,
S-Video, and
DB-15 connectors
on a video
adapter card

(a contraction of picture elements), the tiny dots used to create an image, and 16 colors. In text mode, VGA has a maximum resolution of 720 × 400 and can produce around 16 million different colors, but can only display up to 256 different colors at a time, a VGA color setting known as 8-bit high color ($2^8 = 256$).

For nearly two decades, technicians only needed to work with one video display connector—the DB-15. Now other options are available that go with newer technologies. As you study the various video technologies, you will learn about common display connectors. Figure 5-6 shows the back of a video adapter with three connectors: (from left to right) DVI Dual Link, a 9-pin S-Video, and DB-15. The last is often labeled "VGA."

The DB-15 connector, also called a 15-pin D-Sub connector, used on video adapters for connecting to both traditional CRT monitors and many flat-panel displays, has three rows of five pins each, slightly staggered. This connector is also commonly called a VGA connector, or *Video Electronics Standards Association (VESA)*, for the standards organization that developed this standard, as well as many others. This name does not reflect the ability of the video adapter, but only the fact that the earliest VGA video adapters used it. The connector on the monitor cable is male, whereas the connector on the video adapter (the computer end) is female. A male port or connector has pins, and a female port or connector is a receiver with sockets for the pins of the male connector.

Liquid crystal display (LCD) displays use a digital signal. Although video adapters actually store information digitally in video RAM, they have long been able to convert the digital signal to analog for CRT displays. Therefore, LCD displays that connect to these traditional video adapters (as distinguished by the DB-15 connector on the LCD's interface cable) must include the ability to reconvert the analog signal back to digital! We call such a display an *analog LCD display* (in spite of its digital nature).

SVGA   In the past two decades, video standards have advanced nearly as fast as CPU standards. *Super video graphics array (SVGA)* is a term that was first used for any video adapter or monitor that exceeded the VGA standard in resolution and color depth. But improvements to SVGA's early 800 × 600–pixel resolution led to resolutions of 1024 × 768, 1280 × 1024, 1600 × 1200, and 1680 × 1250. Although SVGA also supports a palette of 16 million colors, the amount of video memory present limits the number of colors SVGA can simultaneously display. This is also true of the newer digital video standards, which are designed to work with flat-panel LCD and other digital display devices, including Digital Visual Interface (DVI), High-Definition Multimedia Interface (HDMI), and DisplayPort.

DVI   Of the three newer video technologies, only *DVI* offers downward compatibility with analog displays via its analog mode, DVI-A. A *DVI-A* connector supports analog signals, with four pins positioned around the blade to the side of the main pin grid area. It has two other groupings of pins: the first contains eight pins in a 3 × 3 grid (the ninth position is empty); the second group contains two sets of two pins with space between them.

The digital mode of DVI, *DVI-D*, is partially compatible with HDMI (described later). *DVI-I*, or DVI-Integrated, supports both DVI-D and DVI-A signals and can control both digital and analog displays. A DVI-D connector is digital only and comes in two varieties called Single Link and Dual Link. The DVI-D Single Link connector has two 3 × 3 grids of nine pins each, whereas the DVI-D Dual Link has a single 24-pin 3 × 8 grid.

The current version of the DVI standard is version 1.4. Depending on the exact implementation of DVI, it supports several screen resolutions and color densities. Common resolutions include 1920 × 1200 *Wide UXGA (WUXGA)* running at 60 Hz, 1280 × 1024 *Super SXGA* running at 85 Hz, and 2560 × 1600 *Wide Quad XGA (WQXGA)* running at 60 Hz. There are several connector types to support these modes.

Now that LCD displays have replaced CRTs, you will find displays that do not perform the digital-to-analog conversion or that, alternatively, accept both digital and analog signals—the latter requiring the old conversion. Such a display has a connector that accepts the digital signal. You have to match this type of display with an adapter card with the appropriate connector. In the case of DVI, you will also need to match the pins, because several different configurations of DVI connectors look alike until you compare them (see Figure 5-7). The typical DVI cable is thick and heavy and requires screws to hold it firmly in place.

As a technician, you must pay close attention to DVI pin compatibility because there are five standard DVI connector configurations, distinguished by the type or types of signals they can transmit. All standard DVI type connectors

FIGURE 5-7

DVI connector
pin layouts for
DVI-I, DVI-D,
and DVI-A

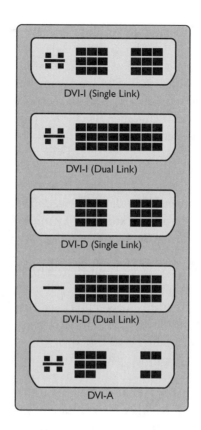

measure 1" by 3/8" with a variety of pin configurations, including one or two grids of pins and a flat blade off to the side of the pin grid area.

DVI-I is interchangeable, supporting either analog or digital signals. It also comes in single-link and dual-link versions. Both versions resemble their DVI-D counterparts, with the addition of the four pins around the blade to support analog mode.

Apple briefly used a smaller version of the DVI connector called a Mini-DVI, which they are phasing out. The Mini-DVI connector is about the same width as a standard USB connector, but is twice as thick, containing four rows of eight pins. Yet another miniaturized version, the Micro-DVI connector, is used by ASUS and Apple. This DVI-D-compatible connector is almost the exact size of a USB connector. This connector was also briefly supported by Apple as they moved from DVI to DisplayPort and Mini DisplayPort.

HDMI   *HDMI* is a recent interface standard for use with devices that output high-definition digital video signals, such as DVD/Blu-ray players, *digital television*

(DTV) players, set-top cable or satellite service boxes, camcorders, digital cameras, and other devices. It combines audio and video signals into an uncompressed signal and has a bandwidth of up to 10.2 Gbps. HDMI is integrated into many media center PCs, replacing DVI, and many home theater PCs (HTPCs) use this interface. Further, it supports a *digital rights management (DRM)* feature called *High-Bandwidth Digital Content Protection (HDCP)* to prevent illegal copying of Blu-ray discs. Version 1.4 of this specification was released in May 2009, and it was followed by updates 1.4a and 1.4b. HDMI has added support for 3D video, as well as high-speed Ethernet communications.

on the
(j)ob

There is normally a delay between the release of a new standard and acceptance of that standard by manufacturers, delaying the appearance of products using the new technology by months and sometimes years.

HDMI is backward-compatible with the DVI standard as implemented in PC video adapters and displays. Therefore, a DVI video adapter can control an HDMI monitor, provided an appropriate cable and converter are used. The audio and remote control features of HDMI, however, will not be available via a DVI video adapter, nor will 3D and Ethernet. One specially designed cable with an HDMI connector is all you need now between a compatible video device and the TV. Previously, several cables were required.

Five types of HDMI connectors are available: A, B, C, D, and E. Type A and B were part of the original specification, whereas Type C is defined in the 1.3 version of the specification, and Type D was defined in the 1.4 version. Type A is electrically compatible with DVI-D Single Link. Type B includes the same support as Type A, plus it supports very-high-resolution displays, such as WQUXGA (3840 × 2400). It is electrically compatible with DVI-D Dual Link.

Two types of HDMI connectors are designed for use in laptops and other small devices. The first is the Type C Mini-HDMI connector, defined by the version 1.3 standard. It has the same 19 pins as a Type A connector but some changes in assignments. Figure 5-8 shows an HDMI socket for a Type C Mini-HDMI connector, and Figure 5-9 shows Type C Mini-HDMI connectors on a cable. The second connector for small devices is the Type D Micro-HDMI connector, introduced in the HDMI 1.4 specification. HDMI also introduced the Type E Automotive Connection System for use in video systems installed in cars.

FIGURE 5-8

An HDMI socket on a computer

The Type E Automotive Connection system is both a cable and connector designed for the stresses placed on equipment installed in cars. The connector has a special locking mechanism to prevent it from working loose, but

FIGURE 5-9

Two Type C Mini-
HDMI connectors
on a cable

you will not see this connector on PCs, laptops, and other portable devices. Table 5-1 describes the HDMI Type A through D pins and plug dimensions.

Before any HDMI device or cable can display the HDMI logo, it must be licensed by HDMI Licensing, LLC, the licensing agent for the HDMI Founders. Look for this logo on any HDMI products. There are five HDMI cable types to match the various HDMI standards. Those standards include HDMI Standard, HDMI Standard with Ethernet, HDMI Standard Automotive, HDMI High Speed, and HDMI High Speed with Ethernet. Cables terminated with all but the B connector type have 19 wires, while those with B connectors have 29 wires. Most HDMI cables that you will encounter for computers and HDTV, the standard for digital high-definition TV, are rounded and about ¼" thick.

DisplayPort   *DisplayPort,* a digital display interface standard developed by VESA, is the newest of the standards discussed here. Like HDMI, it supports both video and audio signals and contains HDCP copy protection. It is unique in that it is royalty-free to manufacturers and has some important proponents, such as Apple, Hewlett-Packard, AMD, Intel, and Dell. At first, industry experts observed that we did not need this standard after the wide acceptance of HDMI, but that changed after DisplayPort received a huge boost in the fall of 2008 when Apple introduced new MacBooks with DisplayPort replacing DVI. DisplayPort neither supports all the color options supported by HDMI, nor is it electrically compatible with DVI, whereas HDMI is backward compatible with DVI. DisplayPort also includes copy

TABLE 5-1

HDMI
Connectors

Connector Type	Number of Pins	Plug Dimensions
A	19	13.9 mm × 4.45 mm approximately .5" × .18"
B	29	21.2 mm × 4.45 mm approximately .8" × .18
C (Mini-HDMI)	19	10.2 mm × 2.42 mm approximately .4" × .1"
D (Micro-HDMI)	19	6.4 mm × 2.8 mm approximately .1" × .25"

FIGURE 5-10

A Mini-DisplayPort socket

FIGURE 5-11

A Mini-DisplayPort connector on a cable

protection for DVDs in the form of DisplayPort Content Protection (DPCP). At this writing, the current version of DisplayPort is 1.2.

At less than ¼" thick, a DisplayPort cable is slimmer than those of its predecessor, and the connectors are much smaller and do not require thumbscrews like those on DVI plugs. Some manufacturers include both DisplayPort and HDMI in the same devices, evidenced by the presence of both connectors. DisplayPort comes in two sizes: standard and Mini-DisplayPort. Figure 5-10 shows a Mini-DisplayPort socket on a computer. The Ethernet port accepts an RJ-45 connector. Notice the symbols identifying each port. Figure 5-11 shows a Mini-DisplayPort connector on a cable end.

Composite Video   The next time you watch television, take a close look at the image. You will notice variations in both brightness and color (unless you are watching a black and white TV!). The traditional transmission system for television video signals, called *composite video*, combines the color and brightness information with the synchronization data into one signal. While television sets have long used separate signals, called *luminance* —brightness, measured in units called *lumens*— and *chrominance* (color), they receive composite signals and have to separate out the luminance and chrominance information. Errors in separating the two signals from the composite signal result in on-screen problems, especially with complex images.

Component Video Signals   *Component video* is a video-signaling method in which analog video information is transmitted as two or more discrete signals. Two types of component video are RGB Video and S-Video. A typical component cable is actually a bundle of thin cables terminating with a single DB-15 connector on one end and three RCA connectors (each carrying one of the red, blue, or green signals). It may also have a fourth S-Video connector. DVI, HDMI, and DisplayPort are replacing these component-signaling interfaces, but you will see them on older systems.

■ *RGB video* is a simple type of component video signal that sends three separate signals: red, green, and blue, using three coaxial cables. Variations on RGB component signaling are based on how the synchronization signal is handled. The SVGA RGB signaling method was widely used for PC displays before DVI and HDMI came along.

■ *Super-Video (S-Video)* refers to the transmission of a video signal using two signals. These two signals are luminance, represented by "Y," and chrominance, represented by "C." The luminance signal carries the black-and-white portion of video, or brightness. The chrominance signal carries the RGB color information, including saturation and hue. Further, the chrominance signal can be broken into multiple channels for improved speed and more precise color. S-Video ports are round to accommodate a round plug, and the standard S-Video connector has four pins, but proprietary S-Video connectors on computers may have seven or nine pins. Flip back to Figure 5-6 to see a 9-pin S-Video port on a video adapter card.

Screen Resolution and Color Density

And so it goes; as fast as new standards are developed and adopted by manufacturers, they are modified and improved upon. Table 5-2 gives a summary of screen resolution and color density typical of the listed video standards. There are additional standards

TABLE 5-2   A Selection of Video Standards and Their Resolution, Color Palette, and Color Density

Name	Maximum Graphics Resolution	Number of Colors in Palette	Number of Colors Displayed Simultaneously in Standard Color Density
Video graphics array (VGA)	640 × 480	Over 16 million	16
eXtended Graphics Array, (XGA), an IBM standard	1024 × 768	Over 16 million	256 or 65,536
Extended Video Graphics Array (EVGA), a VESA standard	1024 × 768	Over 16 million	256 or 65,536
Super video graphics array (SVGA)	1600 × 1200	Over 16 million	Over 16 million*
Super XGA (SXGA)	1280 × 1024	Over 16 million	Over 16 million*
Super XGA Plus (SXGA+)	1400 × 1050	Over 16 million	Over 16 million*
Ultra XGA (UXGA)	1600 × 1200	Over 16 million	Over 16 million*
Wide UXGA (WUXGA)	1920 × 1200 (widescreen)	Over 16 million	Over 16 million*
Wide Quad XGA (WQXGA)	2560 × 1600 (widescreen)	Over 16 million	Over 16 million
Wide Quad UXGA (WQUXGA)	3840 × 2400 (widescreen)	Over 16 million	Over 16 million

*The actual number of simultaneous colors depends on the video adapter and the amount of video memory installed.

available, particularly those starting with "W," which apply to widescreen monitors. Keep in mind the best resolution and color density you will see on your display depends on the capabilities of both the video adapter and display and, increasingly, the aspect ratio of the screen. Widescreen monitors have different resolutions, which are expressed in columns and rows, as in 1920 columns by 1200 rows. We will discuss aspect ratio, refresh rates, and other display features later in this chapter in the sections, "Display Types" and "Display Settings."

Miscellaneous Connectors and Cables

In this section, we'll describe several connector types listed under Objective 1.11 of Exam 801 that are not associated with the technologies detailed so far. Then we'll look at some basic cable types that you will encounter when working with computers.

RCA *RCA connectors* have been around for a long time. They consist of a coaxial plug with an outer shield. The center plug goes into the socket, while the shield

slides around the outside of the socket completing the connection. Figure 5-12 shows an RCA Y-adapter. Used to connect audio components for decades, they have connected video components for many years as well. They are inexpensive, and you can buy them anywhere. Better quality ones are gold plated.

BNC The acronym BNC used for this connector is the subject of some debate. It may stand for "Bayonet-Neill-Concelman" or "British Naval Connector." *BNC connectors* attach coaxial cables to BNC ports. The cable connector is round and has a twist-lock mechanism to keep the cable in place. BNC connectors have a protruding pin that corresponds to a receiver socket in the port.

DIN Connectors *DIN connectors* get their name from Deutsche Industrie Norm, Germany's standards organization. Most (but not all) DIN connectors are round with a circle or semicircle of pins. The mini-DIN connector, or more accurately, the *mini-DIN-6* connector, gets its name from the fact that it is smaller than the *DIN-6* keyboard connector found on early PCs. Mini-DIN connectors most commonly connect mice and keyboards. Because these connectors first appeared on IBM's Personal System/2 (PS/2) computers in the 1980s, mini-DIN connectors are also known as PS/2 connectors. Figure 5-13 shows two mini-DIN-6 connectors at the top of the back panel of a PC, one for a keyboard and another for a mouse. These are disappearing from computers, as more mice and keyboards come with USB connectors.

FIGURE 5-13

The back panel
of a PC showing
two mini-DIN-6
connectors at
the top

Cable Basics: What's Inside a Cable?   A wide variety of cables physically
connect computer components and networks. These cables carry electronic signals
for power, control of devices, and data. But what's inside these cables? The basic cable
types you will encounter are straight pair, twisted pair, fiber-optic, multicore twisted
pair, and coaxial. A *straight-pair cable* consists of one or more metal wires surrounded
by a plastic insulating sheath. A *twisted-pair cable* consists of two sheathed metal wires
twisted around each other along the entire length of the cable to avoid electrical
interference, with a plastic covering sheath surrounding it. A *multicore twisted-pair
cable* has multiple pairs of twisted wires, but in practice even the multicore twisted
pair is simply called "twisted pair." A *fiber-optic cable* has a core made of one or more
optical fiber strands surrounded by a protective cladding, which is in turn reinforced
by strength fibers; all of this is enclosed in an outer jacket. Fiber-optic cable carries
light pulses rather than electrical signals, so it is not susceptible to electromagnetic
interference (EMI). A *coaxial cable* contains a single copper wire, surrounded by
at least one insulating layer, a woven wire shield that provides both physical and
electrical protection, and an outer jacket. Figure 5-14 displays these five basic cable
types. We will revisit the use of various cables in future chapters.

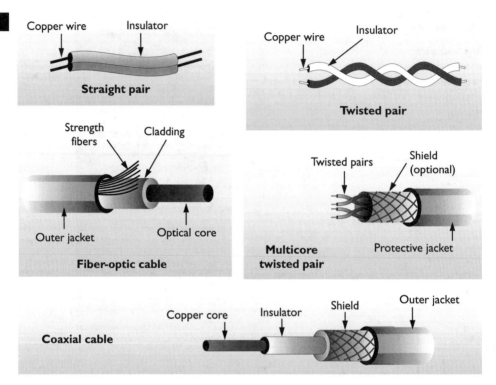

FIGURE 5-14

Common cable types used to connect computer components and networks

Multiple Displays

For some years, people who work with simultaneously open multiple documents or who have large spreadsheet or image requirements have used *multi-monitor PC* configurations that extend the desktop to two or more displays. People in certain jobs, such as engineering, stock day trading, and software development, use multiple monitors on one computer. Multi-monitors previously required expensive hardware and special software, but today it is easy to have two or more monitors. These days a "dual-headed" video adapter won't break most budgets, and with the correct drivers, a modern operating system manages the image placement. Today's video adapters, which have large amounts of dedicated RAM available, manage these tasks without taking a big performance hit. Monitors can be CRTs or flat-panel displays, and analog, digital, or both, depending on the video adapter. Laptops have long supported two monitors, but for many years the second monitor was a replacement for the laptop display—something a user attached to a laptop while in the office. Once operating systems supported multiple displays, people caught on to using the desktop monitor, not as a replacement, but as an extension of the desktop.

Multi-monitor is also known as dual-monitor (if only two), multi-display, and even multi-head.

Multiple Video Adapters for One Monitor

The opposing model to multi-monitor is the use of two or more video adapters to drive one display to improve video graphics performance. This is generically called a *multi-GPU solution,* because the graphics processing unit is one of the most important components of the video adapter. Two manufacturers stand out for their proprietary multi-GPU systems: ATI and NVIDIA.

Although each manufacturer has several possible configurations for their multi-GPU solutions, both now offer a direct connection between the video adapters that are working together in a PC. This direct connection bypasses the PCIe bus for communications between the adapters, thus avoiding an additional load on the shared bus. The ATI solution is commonly called *CrossFire,* and the third-generation products carry the ATI CrossFireX or AMD CrossFireX brand name. The NVIDIA multi-GPU solution is branded *Scalable Link Interface (SLI).* In addition to specific video adapter models, both manufacturers require motherboards with chipsets that support their solution. Expect to encounter multi-GPU solutions in systems that must render high-performance graphics.

Display Types

The function of a PC video *display* device is to produce visual responses to user requests. Often called simply a display or *monitor,* it receives computer output from the video adapter, which controls its functioning. The display technology—which you have already learned about—must match the technology of the video card to which it attaches, so in this section we will explore types of displays and display settings. Until a few years ago, most desktop computers used CRT monitors, but today flat-panel displays (FPDs) are inexpensive and universally available. This is true both for computer displays and for televisions.

CRTs

A *CRT monitor* is bulky because of the large cathode ray tube it contains. A CRT uses an electron gun to activate phosphors behind the screen. Each pixel on the monitor has the ability to generate red, green, or blue, depending on the signals it receives. This combination of colors results in the display you see on the monitor.

CRT monitors are rapidly phasing out in favor of flat-panel displays, but there are many still in use. CRTs have extremely-high-voltage components inside, so be careful when working on them.

Flat Panel Displays

An *FPD* is a computer display that has a form that is very thin—many are thinner than ½" and take up far less desk space (at least front to back) than the traditional CRT displays. Some of the newer FPDs go beyond the standard two-dimensional images, offering *three-dimensional (3D)* images with realistic depth that require HDMI video adapters that can output the 3D video signals. Let's look at FPD technologies, which are common to both computer displays and TVs.

LCD Displays   An *LCD* and a *light-emitting diode (LED) display* are both actually types of LCDs because each has a layer of liquid crystal molecules, called subpixels, sandwiched between polarizing filters, that are backlit when the display is powered on. The biggest difference between LCD and LED displays is the backlight source. In an LCD display, the source is one or more *cold cathode fluorescent lamps (CCFLs)*, a type of lamp that provides a bright light, but is energy efficient and long-lasting. On the other hand, the light source in an LED panel is a grid of many tiny light bulbs called *light-emitting diodes*, positioned behind the glass enclosing the liquid crystals. When power is applied to the diodes, the bulbs glow. In the following discussion, references to LCD will apply to both backlighting methods, unless we specify one or the other. When necessary to make the distinction, an LED back-lit display will be referred to as an *LED-lit LCD*.

In a color LCD display, the individual molecules of liquid crystal are called *subpixels*. A see-through film in front of the crystal liquid consists of areas colored red, green, and blue. Each cluster of this trio of colors makes up a *physical pixel*. Images and colors are created by charging subpixels within the physical pixels.

The first LCD panels, called *passive matrix displays*, charged the pixels using a grid of horizontal and vertical wires. At one end of each wire was a transistor, which received display signals from the computer. When the two transistors (one at the x-axis and one at the y-axis) sent voltage along their wires, the pixel at the intersection of the two wires lit up.

Active matrix displays are newer and use different technology, called *thin-film transistor (TFT)* technology. Active matrix displays contain transistors at each pixel, resulting in more colors, better resolution, a better ability to display moving objects, and the ability to view it at greater angles. However, active matrix displays use more power than passive matrix displays. Modern LCD displays are also called *digital LCD displays* because they accept digital signals, whereas early LCD displays accepted only analog signals and converted them to digital internally.

An LCD display requires less than half the wattage of a comparably sized CRT. Add to this the power-saving features built into displays, such as the features defined by the *display power-management signaling (DPMS)* standard of the VESA. Rather than needing to turn off a display manually when you leave your desk or are not using the computer, DPMS-compliant displays automatically go into a lower power mode after a preconfigured amount of time without any activity.

LCD Contrast Ratio   *Contrast ratio*, the difference in value between a display's brightest white and darkest black, is an area in which the early LCD displays could not compete with CRTs. Today, however, even inexpensive LCD and LED displays offer a dynamic contrast ratio of 3000:1 or a static contrast ratio of 800:1 or greater, which is excellent.

Display Aspect Ratio   The *aspect ratio* is the proportion of the width to the height. For instance, a traditional CRT monitor has a width-to-height aspect ratio of 4:3. LCD panels come in the traditional 4:3 aspect ratio as well as in wider formats, of which the most common is 16:9, which allows you to view wide-format movies. When viewing a widescreen movie video on a 4:3 display, it shows in a *letterbox*, meaning the image size reduces until the entire width of the image fits on the screen. The remaining portions of the screen are black, creating a box effect. Figure 5-15 shows an LCD display with a 16:9 aspect ratio.

FIGURE 5-15

An LCD display with a 16:9 aspect ratio

OLED   Yet another type of thin display technology uses *organic light-emitting diode (OLED)*, which does not require backlighting. OLED diodes use organic compounds for the electroluminescence. There are *passive-matrix OLED (PMOLED)* displays and *active-matrix OLED (AMOLED)* displays. A PMOLED display panel relies strictly on the electroluminescent layer to light the screen and does not use a TFT backplane, as does an AMOLED. OLED screens are found in a wide range of devices from smart phones and tablets to computer displays and TVs. Samsung calls their version of AMOLED technology *Super AMOLED Plus*, and uses this in the display on many products including the Galaxy Tab, which has a high-resolution 1280 × 800, 7.7-inch screen. Presently, the organic materials in OLED displays degrade over time, making this technology more appropriate for devices that are not powered on for several hours a day, but intermittently turned on, as with a smart phone or tablet.

Plasma Displays   *Plasma display* technology is offered mostly for HDTVs, although today a TV usually can double as a computer display by simply cabling the computer and TV. Plasma HDTV sizes begin at about 32" due to the large pixel size.

Much like the difference between LCD and LED displays, plasma displays have yet another method for lighting the screen: they use phosphorous cells in place of liquid crystals, and the phosphors do not require backlighting. Plasma displays are also less expensive than LED displays. The downside to plasma displays is that they are generally thicker and require more power to run. Previously, plasma displays had better image quality when subjected to careful testing, but tests on recent LED-lit LCDs, especially in HDTVs, have shown better image quality compared to plasma displays. Plasma displays have a wide viewing angle.

Projectors

A *projector* takes video output and projects it onto a screen for viewing by a larger audience. Most digital projectors pass the light from a high-intensity bulb through an LCD panel to project an image on a screen. There are also projectors that use *digital light processing (DLP)* chips that yield a larger, brighter image, and small projectors that use LEDs or lasers. DLP projectors are also used in rear-projection televisions.

Digital projectors have been available for years, but they were bulky and expensive. Today the prices of projectors have dropped to the point where they are usable as TVs because they can use video as well as digital sources. Their physical size has dropped as well, and now some tiny digital projectors fit in the palm of your hand and can be used with a laptop computer for presentations to small groups. They are available in many video modes, including XGA, SVGA, WXGA, and SXGA, among others. Add to this built-in support in Windows operating systems and the ability to network these devices by name or IP, and you have a very popular device.

Touch Screens

A *touch screen* is a video display that allows you to select and maneuver screen objects by touching, tapping, and sliding your finger or a stylus on the screen, making a touch screen an input device, as well as an output device. Touch-screen technology was developed in the late 1960s, appeared on special-use systems as early as the 1970s, and continued to be popular for use in kiosk-based computer systems. Touch screens for personal computers have been around almost as long as personal computers, but have never enjoyed a great deal of popularity for general use. Today's touch screens are so improved over those of 20 years ago that there is very little resemblance. They are now found on many handheld devices, such as smart phones like the Blackberry and the Apple iPhone, personal digital assistants (PDAs), global positioning system (GPS) navigation systems, electronic reading devices, and the increasingly popular tablets, such as the Apple iPad and Samsung Galaxy models. New touch-screen devices accept many more subtle gestures than previously.

Screen Filters (Privacy and Antiglare)

There are several types of screen filters, all of which are translucent and often made of a plastic film placed over a display screen. An *antiglare filter* reduces the glare created by light coming from the display backlight, while an *antireflective filter* blocks ambient light that would bounce off the screen. A *privacy screen filter* provides privacy from onlookers attempting to see your confidential information by viewing it over your shoulder by reducing the viewable angle for the display. On a TV a wide viewing angle is a desirable feature, but you may not want people to be able to see your screen while you are entering a password or working on a confidential document while sitting in a coffee shop or airport. Some screen filters fulfill more than one purpose, and manufacturers such as 3M have screen filters to fit almost any screen—desktop, laptop, or handheld.

Display Settings

You can adjust a variety of display settings—some of these settings, such as vertical hold, horizontal hold, and refresh rate, are only on a CRT display, whereas others, such as resolution, apply to both CRT and LCD displays. Other settings are specific to LCD displays. Some settings are only available from a special menu built into

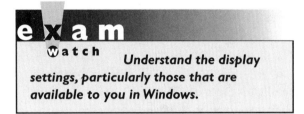

your display. This menu is independent of your operating system, and you access it through buttons mounted on the monitor, as long as the monitor is powered up, regardless of the presence or absence of a PC. Other settings are accessible from within the Display settings in Windows. You will want to locate this in your version of Windows and search for these settings as you read through the following sections. In Windows XP, open the Display applet from Control Panel, and in Windows 7, simply open the Start menu, type **display** in the Search box, and then press the ENTER key. You will then have to search for the individual settings.

V-Hold/H-Hold

The *v-hold* setting, also known as *vertical hold,* is a CRT display setting found on the menu built into a CRT. Like CRT televisions, this setting stabilizes the image vertically on the screen. If this setting is only slightly out of adjustment, the screen image will be stationary but out of position vertically. If this setting is badly out of adjustment, the image will dynamically roll vertically. Similarly, *h-hold,* or *horizontal hold,* is a CRT-only setting that stabilizes the image horizontally.

Vertical Position/Horizontal Position

The built-in menu on an LCD display will have the *vertical position* setting, which adjusts the viewable area of the display vertically, whereas the *horizontal position* setting adjusts the viewable area of the display horizontally.

CRT Refresh Rate

The *refresh rate* of a display is a significant setting for a CRT display. On a CRT, this refers to the *vertical refresh rate*, which is the rate per second at which an image appears on the tube. The video adapter drives this setting. If you are running Windows, you can see the refresh rate of your display under the Advanced Settings in the Display applet. In order to avoid eyestrain, a CRT display should refresh at a rate of 60 Hertz or above. On some CRTs, you may need to reduce the resolution to achieve an adequate refresh rate. Do not confuse refresh rate with the number of images (frames) per second. A traditional movie projector runs at 32 frames per second. A human eye can detect flicker in a movie if it runs at a rate close to or less than 20 frames per second.

o n   t h e
j o b

Selecting a refresh rate higher than a CRT can support can cause damage to the display.

LCD Response Time

Although you will find a refresh rate setting in Windows for an LCD display, it is still a video adapter setting. On LCD displays, the closest equivalent to a CRT's refresh rate is *response time*, the time it takes for a single pixel to go from the active (black) to inactive (white) state and back again. This is measured in milliseconds (ms); a *millisecond (ms)* is a thousandth of a second. This setting is a feature that a manufacturer will list with the other specifications for the model, and it is not adjustable. The response time, now commonly in the single digits, is a best-case scenario under controlled testing. A low number is desirable because the lower the number, the faster the response time. If your LCD display occasionally seems to blur moving images, the display has a slow response time (high number).

Display Resolution

Display resolution is the displayable number of pixels. A CRT display may easily support several different display resolutions, so if you have a CRT, you can play with this setting, along with others, until you have the most comfortable combination of resolution, color density, and refresh rate. On an LCD display, however, you should keep this setting at the *native resolution* of the display, which is the number of physical pixels, horizontally and vertically, such as 1920 × 1080, beyond which it cannot operate. In addition, if you set a display at a lower resolution, the image degrades. For this reason, always set an LCD display at its native resolution, as stated on the box and in the display documentation. It is usually the highest available resolution in the Windows Display applet and is labeled "recommended," as shown in Figure 5-16. Also, notice that this is a dual-display system, and the resolution shown is for the display on the left.

o n   t h e
j o b

The 1920 × 1080 pixel screen resolution is the screen resolution of an HDTV. It is also shown as 1080p.

Color Quality

The Color Quality setting in the Windows XP Display applet allows you to adjust the number of colors used by the display. Also called *color depth,* this setting may be expressed in terms of 16 bits or 32 bits. In newer versions of Windows, you need to dig a little deeper to find the color quality setting. Exercise 5-3 will walk you through the steps for locating the color quality setting for Windows 7.

FIGURE 5-16

The Screen
Resolution page
of the Windows 7
Display applet

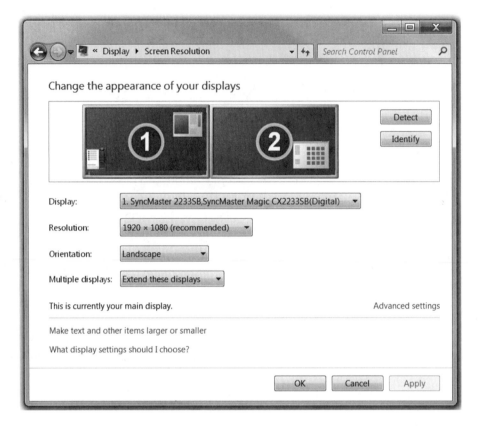

EXERCISE 5-3

Check Out the Color Quality Setting in Windows 7

1. Open the Start menu, type **display** in the Search box, select the Display
   result, and press the ENTER key.
2. Click Adjust Resolution to open the Screen Resolution page.
3. Locate the Advanced Settings link near the lower right, and click this link.
4. Click the Monitor tab.
5. At the bottom of the Monitor tab page, notice the spin box labeled Colors
   and click to see the selections.
6. You can experiment with changing the color setting, but be sure to set it back
   to your preferred setting.

SCENARIO & SOLUTION

A video adapter will have a connector for one of these three busses.	PCI, AGP, or PCIe
What aspect ratio is desirable on a flat-panel display intended for viewing wide-format videos?	16:9
What resolution should you always use on an LCD display?	The native resolution

CERTIFICATION OBJECTIVE

■ *801: 1.12*   *Install and configure various peripheral devices*

This section defines the types of peripheral devices listed in Objective 801: 1.12.

Installing and Configuring Peripheral Devices

Although the processor is the central component of a PC, it would not have anything to process without input, and that processing doesn't do any good unless you can get it out of the computer some way—output. Therefore, it is fair to say that computers are all about input and output—both within the system box and between the system box and a variety of external devices. The term *input/output (I/O)* covers both types of these interactions and the various devices that must connect to a computer for the users' interaction.

Examples of common input devices include the keyboard and any pointing device (mouse, trackball, pen, etc.). Data can also be input from devices that also take output, such as storage devices and network cards. The most common output devices are the display, sound card, and printer. Less common I/O devices include bar code readers, biometric devices, touch screens, and KVM switches. Today's computers come with a variety of connectors to internal interfaces to accommodate a huge selection of peripheral devices.

You have already learned about display interfaces and connectors, so we will begin with installing displays. Then, we'll describe how to install the most common input devices as well as the various classic multimedia devices and the interfaces used for I/O peripherals. You will learn about installing printers in Chapter 21.

Installing Displays

An easy and satisfying PC upgrade is a new, larger, and better-quality display. In most cases, this will not require replacing the video adapter, since even the most standard video adapter in recently manufactured PCs provides excellent output. In addition, many PC tasks are so much easier with two displays. Therefore, you might not be replacing a display, but augmenting it with a second display so that you can spread your on-screen work across the real estate of two displays.

Removing a Display

In order to remove a display, power down the computer and the display, unplug the display from the power outlet, and disconnect the display data cable from the computer.

Installing a Single Display

In order to install a display, simply attach the display's cable to the proper connector on the computer and plug in the power cord. Then power up both the display and the computer. Windows will normally recognize a display and install an appropriate driver; optionally, you may need to install a driver to access advanced features of a display. Once the display is connected and the driver installed, take a look at the display settings discussed earlier in this chapter, and check out the resolution and color quality.

Installing Multiple Displays on a Single PC

As for a multi-monitor configuration, most laptops come with the ability to support both the built-in screen and an external display, but a PC normally has a video adapter for just a single display. Therefore, to add a second display (or more) to a PC, you will need to install a video adapter. For better performance, we recommend replacing the PC's single-output video adapter with a multiheaded video adapter. Consult the computer's documentation. If the computer has an inboard video adapter, you may choose simply to add a single-headed bus video adapter, but you must be certain that the computer will support this configuration. We have found installing a dual-headed adapter to be the best solution.

Once the adapter is installed, connect to each of the two displays exactly as you would connect to one, and power up after everything has been connected. Then, using the disc that came with the video adapter, run the setup program. After that you will need to go into the Windows Display utility and configure one of the monitors to be the main monitor and the other one (or more) to have the desktop extend onto it. If you don't select this setting, the two monitors will simply display the exact same thing. Once you extend the desktop, the main monitor will contain the taskbar and desktop icons, while the other will contain any windows or objects you wish to place there. Figure 5-16 shows a dual display configuration in the Screen Resolution page of the Windows 7 Display applet. Figure 5-17 shows a screenshot of the Windows desktop on a dual-display system. Of course, two separate physical displays are not as seamless as this screenshot shows, but it illustrates how much space you have when working with two displays.

o n t h e
Ⓙ o b   *The authors have used dual displays for years, even using displays of two different sizes when we added an external monitor to a laptop. This was very workable, but we find it much more pleasant to use monitors of identical size and resolution.*

Installing Touch Screen Displays

A touch screen will take just a few more steps to connect and install on a PC. First, we are assuming you have a free-standing PC and wish to install a retail touch screen display, rather than convert a conventional display to a touch screen display. Most touch screen monitors will have two interfaces—a standard video connector for the video output to the screen, and a USB connector for the input from the touch screen component of the monitor. Before you purchase a touch screen, be sure the interfaces will work with the computers to which you will connect them. Connect the cables, power up the display and computer, and then install the device drivers.

Some models of touch screen displays require a reboot after installing the drivers. With a conventional display, your job would be done at this point, but with a touch screen display, you still need to calibrate it. Run the calibration program that comes with the display. It will require that you perform several tasks, touching the screen at specific spots, to enable the touch screen interface to line itself up with the images

FIGURE 5-17

A screenshot from a dual-display Windows 7 system

on the screen. After calibration, test the programs you wish to use on this computer. If you are not happy with the results, run the calibration program again. If it still is not satisfactory, you may need to contact the manufacturer to see if a driver upgrade is available.

Selecting Input Devices

An input device sends signals into a computer. The two most common input devices are the keyboard and a pointing device, such as a mouse. In retail settings, and any other venue in which it is important to control inventory, specialized scanners called bar code readers are a very common input device. Devices used where a retail sale occurs, such as at a checkout stand, are often categorized as *point of sale (PoS)* devices. And multimedia devices, which were once optional for desktop and laptop computers, are now ubiquitous on consumer-grade computers. An output device, such as a display, printer, and even speakers, receives outgoing data from a computer. Most of the devices detailed here are input devices, with the exception of audio devices.

Keyboards

For the vast majority of PC users, the *keyboard* is their primary input device for entering numbers, letters, and symbols. There are several types of keyboards, including 84- and 101-key designs. Newer keyboards might include a variety of additional keys for accessing the Internet, using Microsoft Windows, and performing other common functions. Some keyboards even include a pointing device, such as a mouse or touch pad.

There are also several keyboard layouts. The keyset on an ergonomic keyboard's physical form factor (see Figure 5-18) is split in half and each half slants outward to provide a more relaxed, natural hand position. The layout of the keys themselves can also vary, regardless of the form factor. Typical English-language keyboards (even ergonomic keyboards) have a QWERTY layout (see Figure 5-19), named after the first six letters on the second row of the keyboard. The Dvorak keyboard has an entirely different key layout (also shown in Figure 5-19), and allows for faster typing speeds. Unfortunately, the Dvorak keyboard has not been widely adopted. Accurately learning and using both layouts is exceptionally difficult, so most people stick to the old QWERTY standby that they learned in school.

FIGURE 5-18

An ergonomic keyboard has a different structure from a conventional keyboard.

FIGURE 5-19

QWERTY and Dvorak keyboard layouts

QWERTY

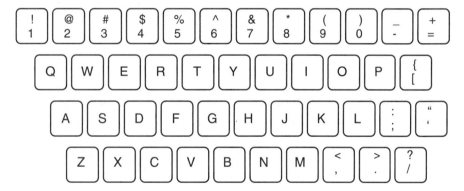

Dvorak

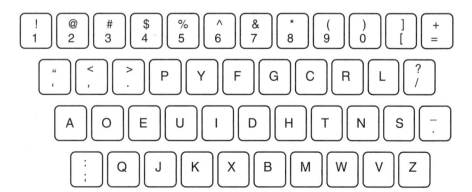

Pointing Devices

A *pointing device* is used to manipulate a pointer and other items on the computer display for input. The *mouse* is by far the most popular pointing device. Users learn mouse operations quickly; the movement of a mouse over a surface translates into the movement of the pointer across the screen. Two or more buttons on the mouse allow the user to perform various operations such as selecting items and running programs. Another popular pointing device is the trackball, a device that is generally larger than a mouse but remains stationary, so it requires less desk space. The user moves the pointer by rolling a ball mounted in the trackball device. A trackball will also have buttons that you use like the buttons on a mouse.

Installing Keyboards and Pointing Devices

Older keyboards and mice come with mini-DIN-6 connectors, while newer ones usually come with USB connectors. Most keyboards and mice will work without the need for add-on device drivers. The standard mouse and keyboard drivers installed with the operating system will be sufficient. To access nonstandard keyboard and mouse features, or to use one of many other types of pointing devices, you will need to install and configure a device driver in Windows and sometimes in a special application. See the section titled "Installing USB Devices" for instructions on installing a USB keyboard or mouse.

Some keyboards and mice come with one of the short-range wireless radio frequency (RF) interfaces that we will describe in Chapter 14. The most common is Bluetooth, and a less common one today is infrared (IR). Bluetooth and infrared require a transceiver device attached to the computer—usually via USB—unless it is built in, which is often the case with laptops and tablets. An important difference between using a Bluetooth device and an infrared device is that with Bluetooth, you are primarily concerned about keeping the device and receiver within the appropriate distance for the signal. With infrared, line-of-sight is as important as proximity because the infrared signal must not be blocked by anything in its way.

Joysticks

A *joystick* is an input device that has a slender gimbaled stick that can move around a single axis in two dimensions, allowing the user to move a computer's cursor or other graphical objects around the screen. As input devices for computer games go, the joystick is the oldest, showing up on the old commercial game consoles, such as *Pac-Man* and others seen in bars and game rooms, before the PC appeared in our homes and offices. The joystick also owes both its functional movements and name to aviation, since that was the name given to an airplane's control stick decades before it showed up on game consoles. A joystick is the basic accessory for using Microsoft's venerable *Flight Simulator*. A modern computer joystick will have several controls on it, including a trigger, switches, and various configurable buttons.

A joystick will connect to a PC either via USB or wirelessly. Read the manufacturer's instruction before installing either type. The section in this chapter titled "Installing USB Devices" gives general directions. For a wireless device—either Bluetooth or infrared—you will need to install a receiver that will usually connect to the computer via USB. Again, follow the manufacturer's instructions for installing the receiver. Then you will need to install the software for controlling the device and configure any programmable buttons—either through the joystick's software or through the gaming software.

Game Pads

A *game pad* is a much more elaborate computer game control device than a joystick, although one or more joysticks will usually be included in the gamepad, along with programmable buttons and directional pads. Many gamepads also provide feedback in the form of vibration. Connecting a gamepad is much like connecting and configuring a joystick.

Digitizers

A *digitizer* (also known as a drawing tablet or *digitizing tablet*) is a touch-sensitive input device that uses a finger, stylus, light pen, or other pointing device that you drag across the surface. The tiny touchpad on a laptop is a form of digitizer, and recent laptop touchpads accept the many gestures of the latest touch screens. But when we speak of a digitizer we usually are referring to the type of digitizer used by engineers, artists, and designers to create elaborate drawings and schematics. It is usually an external device that connects to a computer via USB or Bluetooth, and it converts analog data to digital data, the analog data being the lines traced across the surface of the tablet with a pointing device. A digitizer tablet may be pressure sensitive to thousands of levels and sense the tilt angle of a pen or stylus, produce high-resolution drawings, and may come with several interchangeable nibs for the stylus. Digitizers come in formats measuring from several inches square to very large formats such as 2' × 3' and 3' × 4'. Figure 5-20 shows a Wacom digitizer, called a pen tablet, with an overall size of approximately 12" × 8" and with a tablet surface measuring 7" × 5". This one also has ten spare nibs that allow you to produce different drawing effects.

FIGURE 5-20

A small digitizer
with stylus and
spare nibs

After installing the drivers for a digitizer and connecting it, you will need to calibrate it, much as you calibrate a touch screen. The installation program will take you through the calibration process.

Bar Code Readers

On nearly every item you buy, every package you ship, and the membership cards you carry, there is a small rectangular image with a unique pattern of black bars and white space. This is a *bar code,* which contains information appropriate to the type of use and can be optically scanned and interpreted by computer software. On product packaging, a bar code will contain vendor, inventory, and pricing information. On your library card, it will identify you as a dues-paying member. A *bar code reader* is a device used to optically scan the bar code. The design of the reader must match the type of code on the item it scans in order to interpret it. The bar code reader uses a laser beam to measure the thicknesses of the lines and spaces. This information is converted to digital data and transferred to a computer. At the grocery store, the computer is in the cash register, which tallies up your total and sends inventory information to a central computer.

There are various types of bar code readers, so select the reader that best meets your needs. The most common readers that you will encounter for PCs are handheld scanners and stationary scanners, such as those you see in retail stores.

Once you select an appropriate bar code reader, your next concern is the interface. Traditionally, bar code readers used an RS-232-C serial interface; later ones used a mini-DIN-6 keyboard connector, but newer bar code readers use USB. Those that used a mini-DIN-6 keyboard interface used a special "Y" connector so a keyboard could also be connected. Read the instructions that come with the device before installing it. To install a USB bar code scanner, follow the instructions later on for installing a USB device.

Scanners

A *scanner* is a device that can optically examine a piece of paper and create a bitmap image of what it sees in full color or in black and white. In some small scanners you pass the scanner over the paper slowly to get an image, but most scanners are able to scan an entire page of text. The form factor of flatbed scanners lets you lay the paper to scan on the glass plate, close the cover (usually called a platen) on the paper, and press the scan button. Some flatbed scanners open up so you can scan a thick object such as a book. Multifunction devices generally include a scanner with a document feeder, a printer, and a fax machine in one box. Many multifunction devices are able to scan one side of the paper and then automatically turn the paper over to scan the other side. The latest scanners are able to simultaneously scan both sides of a page very rapidly, up to 20 pages a minute, or three seconds per page, and their document feeders let you insert many pages at a time, even ones of different sizes, for automatic scanning.

Install a scanner per the manufacturer's instructions, paying close attention to whether the driver must be installed before or after connecting and powering up the scanner. The scanner's driver will likely conform to the *TWAIN* set of standards (this is not an acronym) for scanners and cameras, and is often called a "TWAIN driver." It manages the scanning process. Other software, such as *optical character recognition (OCR)* software, should also be TWAIN-compliant. OCR software is important. Your computer sees a scanned image as a graphic bitmap image, which is fine for a photo or other image, but when the scanned image is of a printed page and you want to be able to edit the document, you will need OCR software to interpret the pattern of dots in the image as alphanumeric characters. There are several very good OCR software programs to convert a scanned bitmap image to editable text.

Multimedia

A variety of multimedia input devices are available for PCs. The short list includes Web video cameras, digital still cameras, MIDI devices, and microphones.

Cameras

The most common type of camera attached to a PC is a *Web camera*, or *Webcam*. This type of digital video camera broadcasts video images (usually live) over the Internet. A Webcam is an inexpensive and easy-to-use addition to a PC that provides a visual component for meetings and other business communications, as well as entertainment and security functions.

A handheld *digital video camera,* as opposed to a Webcam, does not spend its useful life tethered to a computer, but only connects to a computer to transfer its digital video files to the PC for review, editing, and distribution by the user.

A *digital camera* is a camera type that has taken the world by storm, replacing film-based cameras for amateur photographers, as well as for many professional photographers. Today, most digital cameras have some limited video capability. Like the digital video camera, a digital still camera spends much of its time detached from a PC, connecting only to upload digital photographs or movies to the computer to be reviewed, modified, and printed.

MIDI

The Musical Instrument Digital Interface (MIDI) is a standard for connecting electronic musical instruments, such as a synthesizer keyboard, to computers or among themselves. This allows musicians to input their music for mixing and to convert it to musical notation. Modern MIDI devices have USB connectors, and therefore, you will normally need to install the driver before connecting the MIDI device to a USB port on the computer.

Sound Output

Sound is generated by a *sound card* and output to a sound device, such as a set of speakers or a pair of headphones. Sound cards normally have connectors for both types of devices. The classic connector for these devices is the 1/8" single-pin mini-audio connector, but some handheld devices use the 3/32" single-pin submini audio connector. They come in both mono and stereo versions. The mono version will have a single black ring around the front end of the pin, and the stereo version will have two black rings. If you are connecting a CD or DVD player to an amplifier or speaker, you will need the consumer version of the Sony/Philips Digital Interface (S/P DIF), as described in Chapter 4. Simply insert the correct connector firmly into the socket.

Microphones

As a PC input peripheral, a microphone gives a remote meeting attendee a voice at the meeting, and the latest voice recognition programs allow a user to dictate entire documents with a very low error rate. A microphone typically connects to a PC's sound card using a mini-audio connector.

Installing Multimedia Devices

Most multimedia devices are fairly simple to connect and use. Many multimedia devices, such as Webcams, digital cameras, and MIDI, often use a USB interface, which usually requires that you install the device driver before attaching the device to a USB port, as described later in the section "Installing USB Devices." Microphones or headsets only need to be connected to the correct port(s) and do not usually require a special device driver.

Video capture cards can take a bit more work to install. These cards are available as bus cards (PCI or PCIe) and as USB devices. However, the bus cards are generally less expensive and have more features than the USB devices. If you decide on a bus card, you will install it like most other adapter cards. Either interface will require a special driver and software. Follow the instructions that come with the card. For a bus card, you will normally install the drivers and software after the physical installation. The software that comes with the device may install as part of the driver installation, or you may need to initiate that install. Common software includes Nero for capturing video and burning DVDs, and Beyond TV, which includes *digital video recorder (DVR)* capabilities for recording video to disk. Once the software is installed, shut down the computer and connect the device to the appropriate TV input, whether cable TV, satellite TV, or broadcast TV. The types of cables you will need depend on the input. For instance, coaxial cable is used for cable TV, while S-Video, composite, or component cables are used for other inputs.

Biometric Devices

A *biometric* device uses a measurement of a body part, such as a fingerprint or retina scan, to provide greater authentication security than simply supplying a user name and password.

You must install a biometric device as an I/O device, as well as a security device. We will save the detailed discussion of security devices for Chapter 17, and only concern ourselves at this point with the local installation of a fingerprint scanner as a representative biometric device. Some laptops come with a fingerprint scanner physically installed. When adding one to a computer, read the instructions and install the scanner as you would any device, installing the drivers at the appropriate time. The software that comes with a fingerprint scanner requires a fingerprint to compare with the scanned print. It may store the fingerprint locally, or it may store it in a central database. We will discuss the latter scenario in Chapter 17. In the case of a locally stored fingerprint, typically done when using a portable device, you will run a special program after installing the device. This program will take a baseline scan of your fingerprint and store it locally. After that, you simply follow the instructions for the placement of your finger in order to gain access to the computer.

KVM Switches

A *KVM switch* is a device traditionally found in server rooms to control multiple computers with one keyboard, mouse, and monitor. The acronym KVM stands for keyboard, video, and mouse. A KVM switch is a box to which you connect one local monitor, keyboard, and mouse. Ports on the switch provide a number of keyboard, mouse, and video connectors for cables to each of the computers being controlled. KVM switches are now divided into two broad categories: local KVM and remote KVM.

Local KVM Switches

The *local KVM switch* category is still the norm in server rooms, where it creates a one-to-many connection that allows you to control any one of the servers connected through the switch. Some local KVM switches have USB ports for the shared devices and may share additional types of devices, such as speakers. Other KVM switches reverse this model, connecting two or more sets of keyboards, displays, and mice to one computer. This model is commonly used in a kiosk scenario where the public has access through one set of peripherals, and an administrator has access via another set. In either situation, control is switched through the KVM switch using software and special keyboard commands, and such a KVM switch is called an *active KVM switch* or *electronic KVM switch*. You control an *inactive KVM switch*, the least expensive type of KVM switch, through a mechanical switch on the box itself. Inactive switches have many limitations and problems; you are unlikely to encounter them, so we will describe how to install a local active switch.

Before installing a local active KVM switch, read the installation instructions and assemble the cabling, devices, and computers you wish to connect. Memorize the keystrokes required to switch control from one computer to another. Check for the needed drivers. In our experience, these are not necessary because the KVM switch itself captures the keystrokes and changes the focus from computer to computer based on your keyboard commands.

Installing a local active KVM switch is just a bit more complicated than connecting a keyboard, display, and mouse to a computer. In fact, the first thing you do is connect your keyboard, display, and mouse to the appropriate connectors on the KVM switch. You will find them grouped together, and there may even be more than one type of connector for the mouse or keyboard and it may have speaker ports. Once the devices are connected to the switch, you can connect the KVM switch to the computers you wish to control. This requires special cables that are usually bundled together with the connectors split out on each end. This bundling ensures that you won't mistakenly connect a cable from one set to two different computers. If you do not have bundled cables, bundle them yourself.

Once all the computers are connected to the KVM switch, power up the switch and then power up each PC. During bootup, the PC should recognize the KVM switch as the keyboard, video, and mouse devices.

Remote KVM Switches

The *remote KVM switch* category is further divided into two types: local remote KVM and KVM over IP. A *local remote KVM switch* uses either Ethernet cable or USB cabling. A local remote KVM switch using Ethernet cabling can be used to control computers over a distance of up to 300 meters, using a proprietary protocol (not IP) and special hardware. A remote KVM switch using USB cabling has a distance limit of up to five meters.

A *KVM over IP switch* uses specialized hardware to capture the keyboard, video, and mouse signals; encodes them into IP packets; and sends them over an IP network. They can connect a keyboard, video display, and mouse to a special remote console application that allows the user to control multiple computers across a LAN or WAN. They are also used in one-to-one situations; for example, in hospitals or clinics with a centralized records system and consoles in the locations where they do not want system units (for a variety of reasons, including sanitary). The console consists of a keyboard, video display, and pointing device—all connected to a KVM device, such as a KVM port extender. There are many possible configurations, but in medical installations, the console may connect to the central system (directly or indirectly) to access and update patient records.

The physical connection of a KVM over IP switch is much like connecting a computer to a network, which you will learn about in Chapter 15. Once the device connects to the network, follow the manufacturer's instructions for installing the software. You will need guidance from your network administrator in order to log in and access the remote data.

Installing USB Devices

Today, most input devices come with a USB interface and are plug and play. Even some devices that traditionally had a dedicated interface, such as keyboards and mice, now usually come with a USB interface. In spite of the variety of devices using

USB, installation and removal are simple because of the plug-and-play interface. As always, we remind you to read the manual before installing any device, but the general rule for a USB device is to install the driver before connecting the device. Then, as with most connectors, you simply plug the device's USB connector into a USB socket on the computer. With several types of USB connectors, be sure that your USB cable has the appropriate connectors for both the device's end and the computer port. One caution: With the newer and faster USB interfaces, be sure that any high-speed device is matched to a high-speed connection, especially when connecting a newer device to an older PC. The speed of the connection will be limited by the slower component. Refer to Chapter 4 where we discussed the various USB speeds and connectors.

CERTIFICATION SUMMARY

This chapter wraps up the discussion of PC components begun in Chapter 3 and continued in Chapter 4, describing power supplies, display devices, and peripheral devices, and how to install them.

Because power supplies provide the DC voltages required by various other components, they produce heat. Therefore, a typical power supply has a fan that dissipates the heat the power supply creates, as well as contributes to cooling the entire system. In most PCs, this is not sufficient, so additional methods are used to keep PCs cool enough for the components to function safely.

Display technologies have changed a great deal. The most recent developments include support for both video and audio through a single interface, connection, and cable. The physical form of the cable, and the connectors and ports used with a cable, depend on the purpose and design of the interface used and the device or devices that use the cable.

There are many types of interfaces for connecting peripherals, but, excluding display devices, most peripherals today connect to a PC using a USB connection, although some use wireless Bluetooth or infrared connections. Always read the documentation that comes with a device and follow the instructions for connecting and installing the drivers and other software.

✓ TWO-MINUTE DRILL

Here are some of the key points covered in Chapter 5.

Power Supplies

- ❏ A power supply provides power for all components on the motherboard and those internal to the PC case.
- ❏ A volt is the unit of measurement of the pressure of electrons. A watt is a unit of measurement of actual delivered power. An ampere (amp) is a unit of measurement for electrical current or rate of flow of electrons through a wire.
- ❏ A power supply converts alternating current (AC) voltage into the direct current (DC) voltage required by the computer.
- ❏ Power supply capacity is measured in watts, with power supplies for desktop computers ranging up to about 1200 watts.
- ❏ An AC adapter is a form of power supply used with portable computers and external peripherals.
- ❏ Select a power supply that is of the correct form factor for both the motherboard and the case, and select one that has sufficient wattage for the internal components you expect to have.
- ❏ Older ATX motherboards used a 20-pin ATX (P1) connector to provide power. Some recent motherboards require two ATX12V 2.0 connectors—one is a 24-pin main connector, and the other is a 4-pin secondary connector. Other newer motherboards require EPS12V connectors, which include a 24-pin main connector, an 8-pin secondary connector, and an optional 4-pin tertiary connector.

Video Adapters and Displays

- ❏ The video adapter controls the output from the PC to the display device. Display adapters support a variety of display modes and technologies, including VGA, SVGA, DVI, HDMI, and DisplayPort.
- ❏ A video adapter may be built into the motherboard or may be a separate circuit board that plugs into a PCI, AGP, or PCIe connector.
- ❏ Display connectors include DB-15 (VGA), DVI, HDMI, DisplayPort, Composite Video, and Component Video.
- ❏ Classic multimedia interfaces include MIDI and a variety of audio ports using the 1/8" single-pin mini-audio connector.

❏ Classic connectors and ports include BNC and mini-DIN-6 (PS/2).

❏ Common electronic cables used with PCs include straight pair, twisted pair, and coaxial.

❏ Multi-monitor systems have two or more displays on a single computer.

❏ The two general PC display types are CRT and FPDs. FPDs have largely replaced CRT displays. Most FPDs use a form of LCD, LED, or plasma technology, with tablet PCs using OLED or AMOLED.

❏ Projectors take video output and project it onto a screen for viewing by a larger audience. A touch screen is a video display element that allows you to select and maneuver screen objects by touching, tapping, and sliding your finger or stylus on the screen.

❏ To install a display, connect it to the PC and then to a power outlet. A touch screen display requires an extra step to calibrate the touch screen with the images on the computer desktop.

❏ Some display settings, such as v-hold/h-hold (for CRTs) and vertical position/ horizontal position (for LCDs) are only available through a menu on the display itself.

❏ Response time is an LCD feature that is not controllable through any menu settings.

❏ Display resolution is a setting that you can control through Windows.

Installing and Configuring Peripheral Devices

❏ Displays, printers, and sound cards are the most common output devices. Keyboards, pointing devices, bar code readers, and many multimedia devices are input devices. A special category of device, a KVM switch, is used in a variety of scenarios, but most commonly to allow a single person using one keyboard, video display, and pointing device to control many computers.

❏ A biometric device must be installed as an I/O device and also configured as a security device.

❏ To install a KVM switch for the purpose of controlling two or more computers using one keyboard, video display, and mouse, first connect the keyboard, display, and mouse to the device in the properly marked connectors. Then connect each computer to the appropriate connectors on the switch.

❏ The installation and configuration of an I/O device depends on the interface. Always read the documentation for the device before installing.

SELF TEST

The following questions will help you measure your understanding of the material presented in this chapter. Read all of the choices carefully because there might be more than one correct answer. Choose all correct answers for each question.

Power Supplies

1. Which statement is true?
- A. A PC power supply converts wattage to voltage.
- B. A PC power supply converts voltage to wattage.
- C. A PC power supply converts AC to DC.
- D. A PC power supply converts DC to AC.

2. What is the name of the main power connector that goes between an ATX power supply and an ATX motherboard?
- A. P3
- B. P1
- C. P2
- D. P4

3. The capacity of a power supply is normally stated in these units.
- A. Volts
- B. Watts
- C. Amperes
- D. Ohms

4. What type of current is required by internal PC components?
- A. Alternating current (AC)
- B. Direct current (DC)
- C. IEC-320
- D. PSU

5. Which of the following calculations would you use to determine the capacity you require in a power supply?
- A. Add the voltage for all internal components.
- B. Add the wattage for all internal components.
- C. Add the voltage for all external components.
- D. Add the wattage for all external components.

6. This component of a typical power supply dissipates heat.
   A. Heat sink
   B. P1 connector
   C. Fan
   D. IEC-320

7. What is a common term for a laptop power supply?
   A. PSU
   B. Heat sink
   C. AC adapter
   D. Thermal compound

8. Select all the items that should be considered when selecting a new power supply.
   A. Wattage
   B. CPU
   C. Form factor
   D. Power connectors

9. What equipment should you never use when working with a power supply?
   A. Screwdriver
   B. Connectors
   C. Motherboard
   D. Antistatic wrist strap

Video Adapters and Displays

10. This venerable video interface standard was introduced with the IBM PS/2 computer in the 1980s.
    A. DisplayPort
    B. HDMI
    C. DVI
    D. VGA

11. Which of the following video interface standards supports both analog and digital signals?
    A. DisplayPort
    B. HDMI
    C. DVI
    D. VGA

12. This video standard supports both digital video and audio and has the thinnest cable and the smallest connectors.

 A. DisplayPort

 B. HDMI

 C. DVI

 D. VGA

13. This type of display uses an electron gun to activate phosphors behind the screen.

 A. CRT

 B. FPD

 C. LCD

 D. Plasma

14. This type of display device takes up less desk space and replaces an older technology that uses more power.

 A. CRT

 B. FPD

 C. ATX

 D. USB

15. Which of the following connectors is *not* used to connect a display to a digital video interface?

 A. DVI

 B. DB-15

 C. HDMI

 D. DisplayPort

16. Which of the following is *not* a DVI connector type?

 A. DVI-A

 B. DVI-B

 C. DVI-I

 D. DVI-D

17. After physically connecting a touch screen and installing necessary device drivers, what important configuration task must you perform?

 A. Record a fingerprint scan.

 B. Calibrate.

 C. Upgrade Windows.

 D. Wash the screen.

Installing and Configuring Peripheral Devices

18. This type of input device is ideal for the more elaborate computer games.

  A. Joystick

  B. Digitizer

  C. Bar code reader

  D. Game pad

19. When adding this type of device to a PC, you will normally have two cables for two separate connections between the device and the PC.

  A. Printer

  B. Touch screen

  C. Touch pad

  D. Joystick

20. The local version of this type of device is found in server rooms, connecting multiple servers to a single set of I/O devices (mouse, display, and keyboard).

  A. Scanner

  B. Biometric

  C. KVM Switch

  D. Multimedia

SELF TEST ANSWERS

Power Supplies

1. ☑ **C.** A PC power supply converts AC to DC.
☒ **A,** a PC power supply converts wattage to voltage, is incorrect. **B,** a PC power supply converts voltage to wattage, is incorrect. **D,** a PC power supply converts DC to AC, is incorrect. It does just the opposite.

2. ☑ **B.** P1 is the main power connector used between an ATX power supply and an ATX motherboard.
☒ **A,** P3, is incorrect because the chapter mentioned no such connector. **C,** P2, is incorrect because the chapter mentioned no such connector. **D,** P4, is incorrect because this is a four-wire 12 V connector used in addition to the P1 connector.

3. ☑ **B.** The capacity of a power supply is stated in watts.
☒ **A,** volts, is incorrect because it is a measurement of electrical potential. **C,** amperes, is incorrect because it is a measurement of electrical current, or rate of flow of electrons through a wire. **D,** ohms, is incorrect because ohms is a measurement of resistance.

4. ☑ **B.** Direct current (DC) is the type of current required by internal PC components.
☒ **A,** alternating current (AC), is incorrect because this is the type of current that is provided through the typical wall outlet. **C,** IEC-320, is incorrect because this is a type of switch found on many power supplies to select the correct power setting. **D,** PSU, is incorrect. This is an acronym for "power supply unit."

5. ☑ **B.** Add the wattage for all internal components to determine what capacity you require in a power supply.
☒ **A,** add the voltage for all internal components, is incorrect because this is not the correct measurement required. **C,** add the voltage for all external components, and **D,** add the wattage for all external components, are both incorrect because external components normally have their own power supplies and do not need to draw power from the computer's power supply.

6. ☑ **C.** The fan is the component in a typical power supply that dissipates heat.
☒ **A,** heat sink, is incorrect because a heat sink is something that draws heat off something and dissipates it in some passive manner, such as via metal fins. **B,** P1 connector, is incorrect because this is a power supply connector, not a part of a power supply that dissipates heat. **D,** IEC-320, is incorrect because this is a type of switch found on many power supplies to select the correct power setting.

7. ☑ **C.** AC adapter is the common term for a laptop power supply.

    ☒ **A,** PSU, is incorrect because this is an acronym for "power supply unit." **B,** heat sink, is incorrect because heat sinks dissipate heat. **D,** thermal compound, is incorrect because thermal compound is used to increase the heat conductivity among components.

8. ☑ **A, C,** and **D.** You should consider wattage, form factor, and power connectors when selecting a new power supply.

    ☒ **B,** CPU, is incorrect because although its wattage requirements are important, the CPU itself is not an issue when selecting a power supply.

9. ☑ **D.** You should never use an antistatic wrist strap when working with a power supply.

    ☒ **A,** a screwdriver, is incorrect because it may be necessary to remove the screws holding a power supply to the case. **B,** connectors, is incorrect because you must work with the connectors from the power supply to the motherboard and other components. **C,** motherboard, is incorrect because you may need to work with the power supply connectors on the motherboard.

Video Adapters and Displays

10. ☑ **D.** VGA is the video interface standard introduced with the IBM PS/2 computer in the 1980s.

    ☒ **A, B,** and **C.** DisplayPort, HDMI, and DVI are all incorrect because they are recent standards.

11. ☑ **C.** DVI is the video interface standard that supports both analog and digital signals.

    ☒ **A,** DisplayPort, and **B,** HDMI, are incorrect because they only support digital signals. **D,** VGA, is incorrect because it is an analog video interface standard.

12. ☑ **A.** DisplayPort supports both digital video and audio and has the thinnest cable and the smallest connectors.

    ☒ **B,** HDMI, is incorrect because, although it supports both video and audio, it does not have the thinnest cable and smallest connectors. **C,** DVI, is incorrect because it does not support both digital video and audio. **D,** VGA, is incorrect because it only supports analog video.

13. ☑ **A.** CRT is the type of display that uses an electron gun.

    ☒ **B, C,** and **D** are all incorrect because none of these displays types (FPD, LCD, and plasma) use electron guns.

14. ☑ **B.** An FPD display takes up less desk space and replaces an older (CRT) technology that uses more power.

    ☒ **A,** CRT, is incorrect because it takes up more desk space than an LCD display and uses more power. **C,** ATX, is incorrect because it is a motherboard and power supply form factor, not a type of display. **D,** USB, is incorrect because it is an I/O interface.

15.   ☑   **B.** A DB-15 connector is not used to connect a display to a digital video interface.
☒   **A,** DVI, **C,** HDMI, and **D,** DisplayPort, are all incorrect because these connectors are all used to connect a display to a digital video interface (of the same name).

16.   ☑   **B.** DVI-B is not a DVI connector type.
☒   **A, C,** and **D** are all incorrect because DVI-A, DVI-I, and DVI-D are all DVI connector types.

17.   ☑   **B.** Calibrate is correct because this will allow the touch screen interface to line itself up with the images on the screen.
☒   **A,** record a fingerprint scan, is incorrect because a touch screen is not intended to scan fingerprints. **C,** upgrade Windows, is incorrect because screen calibration is the task required by a touch screen display. **D,** wash the screen, is incorrect because, although you will want to do this from time to time for any screen (using the correct method), this is not a configuration task.

Installing and Configuring Peripheral Devices

18.   ☑   **D.** A game pad is a type of input device that is ideal for the more elaborate computer games because it typically comes with programmable buttons and directional pads and one or more joysticks.
☒   **A,** joystick, is incorrect because a joystick is a rather primitive input device when compared to a game pad. **B,** digitizer, is incorrect because this is not an appropriate input device for a game, but more appropriate for working with drawings and schematics, converting the analog data (lines) to digital data. **C,** bar code reader, is incorrect because this is a device that optically scans a unique pattern of bars and white space that is interpreted by computer software.

19.   ☑   **B.** A touch screen that you add to a PC will normally have two cables between the device and the PC: one for video signals and the other for input from the touch screen component of the monitor.
☒   **A,** printer, and **D,** joystick, are incorrect because they normally have one cable between the device and the PC. **C,** touch pad, is incorrect because it normally is part of a laptop or keyboard, and, as such, doesn't have a cable to connect to the PC. An external touch pad will have a single cable.

20.   ☑   **C.** KVM switch is correct. A local KVM switch connects multiple computers to a single keyboard, video display, and mouse.
☒   **A,** scanner, is incorrect because a scanner optically scans an image; it is not used as described in the question. **B,** biometric, is incorrect because a biometric device uses a measurement of a body part, such as a fingerprint or retina, to use in authentication. **D,** multimedia, is incorrect because a multimedia device cannot be used to connect multiple computers to a single set of I/O devices.

6

Installing and Upgrading PC Components

T his chapter begins with examples of custom computer configurations for various needs and then it moves on to describe and demonstrate how to install and replace common PC components. With a little practice, you will be capable of performing these tasks on most personal computers, in spite of different layouts or new component designs.

CERTIFICATION OBJECTIVE

■ **801: 1.9** *Evaluate and select appropriate components for a custom configuration to meet customer specifications or needs*

This certification objective requires that you understand how to select the right components for building or ordering a custom computer for a specific job. The custom computers listed under this objective are a graphic/computer-aided design (CAD)/computer-aided manufacturing (CAM) design workstation, an audio/video editing workstation, a virtualization workstation, a gaming PC, a home theater PC, a standard thick client, a thin client, and a home server PC. The past three chapters have prepared you to understand the decisions you need to make for each configuration.

Selecting Components for Custom PCs

In Chapter 3, you learned about motherboards, CPUs, and cases; in Chapter 4, you learned about storage devices, memory, and adapter cards; and Chapter 5 detailed the features of power supplies, cooling systems, and peripherals. This section draws on the knowledge you gained in those three chapters by giving examples of the components you would select when building a custom PC to meet specific needs.

First, notice that some of the configurations described next are called "workstations" while others are called "PCs." What is the difference? While these terms are often used interchangeably, when a distinction is made, a *personal computer (PC)* is a computer intended for home or standard office productivity work and intended for the use of a single user, while a *workstation* is a computer that is more powerful than the average office or home desktop PC, with more expensive, higher-performance components, although it also may be dedicated to a single user. Despite the distinction, the latter is most often still a PC, though a powerful PC targeted for a specific use.

When selecting a motherboard, you cannot tell which components it supports solely by knowing the form factor of the motherboard. Therefore, you must always check the manufacturer's documentation before you select a motherboard and the components you wish to install on it. To do this, check the manufacturer's Website for the specifications for each model with a list of installed and supported components, such as chipset, CPUs (models, speeds, and number of CPUs), and memory (type, speed, data width, and maximum amount of memory the motherboard will support), as well as the speed of the motherboard's front side bus (FSB).

A benefit of an open platform like a PC is that they are easy to customize. You can design modifications to a basic PC computer that will allow it to fulfill specific requirements.

What kind of requirements are we talking about? They range from a thin client machine that really only requires enough CPU power, random access memory (RAM), and communication ability to handle basic applications and function as a terminal, up through a gaming PC that needs a powerful processor, a high-end video or specialized graphics processing unit (GPU), a better sound card, and high-end cooling capability, to a graphics/CAD/CAM design workstation with even higher requirements.

Today's computers are so powerful that an appropriately configured laptop, such as one with a multicore central processing unit (CPU), 4+ GB of RAM, and a 1+ TB hard drive can serve in several of these configurations. Let's look at seven custom configurations.

Graphics/CAD/CAM Design Workstation

Designers, engineers, and architects need computer systems capable of creating very complex graphics. The software they use must do complex graphics rendering for design and manufacturing.

One category of software used by engineers and architects is *computer-aided design (CAD)*, which allows them to design a wide variety of objects from machine parts to extremely complex products such as aircraft, cars, or boats. CAD software allows you to view the design in 2-D or 3-D from all angles and from different distances. Another type of software sometimes combined with CAD is *computer-aided manufacturing (CAM)*. A CAM system can control the machines used to manufacture an object. A *combined computer-aided design/computer-aided manufacturing (CAD/CAM)* system allows the engineer to go from design directly to manufacturing. The software's graphics product is usually a vector graphic, which defines images using algorithms for defining lines and shapes, rather than explicitly describing an image as a map of dots (a bitmap).

A design workstation requires a powerful processor to handle all the required computation, a high-end video card driving a high-quality industry-certified graphics display, a lot of disk space, and a lot of RAM. How much RAM? Sixteen GB is good; 32 GB is better. On the extreme high end 128 GB is great. The CPU could be a 64-bit four-, six-, or eight-core processor or two four-core processors. You'll need fault-tolerant RAID 1, 5, or 10 capability so as to not risk losing valuable design data.

Furthermore, a designer, engineer, or architect working at a graphics workstation will usually want a pointing device such as a light pen or digitizing tablet that has finer control than you have with an ordinary mouse. You will also need to select an appropriate printer for rendering images and specifications, such as a large format printer or plotter—both of which are more expensive than your average office printer. A plotter is a specialized high-precision device used by engineers and architects that creates images in black and white or color using special pens rather than ink cartridges. They can print on paper up to 44" wide and of any reasonable length.

e x a m
w a t c h
Remember that the most important components of a graphics/CAD/CAM design workstation are a powerful CPU, high-end video, and maximum memory.

Audio/Video Editing Workstation

An audio/video editing workstation requires a specialized audio and video card for the highest fidelity possible while editing. A large monitor, preferably two, is required, and you need large and very fast Serial Advanced Technology Advancement (SATA) or Serial Attached SCSI (SAS) hard drive(s). An effective configuration is three hard drives: one for system and application programs, one for video streaming while rendering, and one for storing the edited video. A bottleneck for an editing workstation is the vast amount of data it moves on and off disks, so these drives should be very fast; standard 7200 rpm drives are good; 10,000 rpm drives work better. You need a larger power supply to feed all this equipment too. You can add specialized equipment such as stereo 3-D capture and editing capability and real-time effects.

e x a m
w a t c h
Remember that the most important components of an audio/video editing workstation are specialized audio and video cards; a large, fast hard drive; and dual displays.

Virtualization Workstation

A *virtualization workstation* is a computer used to support the on-screen simulation of a computing environment. It can be a simulation of a complete computer including hardware, desktop or server operating system, and running applications. Or it may be virtualization of an application and all the supporting software, but not an entire operating system and desktop, allowing you to run an incompatible application on a computer isolated from the OS and hardware of the computer. A single instance of such a simulation is a *virtual machine,* and there can be multiple virtual machines running on the same workstation, as long as there is sufficient computing power, memory, and diskspace to support them.

A virtualization workstation needs a very fast multicore CPU, and both the CPU and BIOS must physically support virtualization. In Intel CPUs and chipsets, look for the term Virtualization Technology (VT), and in AMD CPUs and chipsets, look for the term AMD-V. The technologies were introduced in Chapter 3, but virtualization will be further detailed in Chapter 8.

A virtualization workstation must also have lots of RAM in order to handle not only the virtualization process but also to allow for the real work the virtual programs are doing. Of course, the scale of virtualization you intend to do is also important and affects how much RAM and hard drive space you need, and even how many cores or even additional CPUs you will use. If you only wish to run a single virtual machine in order to test a new version of Windows, a dual-core or quad-core CPU, 4 to 8 GB of RAM, and about 20 GB of additional space for the virtual machine may be all you need. If this workstation is going to run many virtual machines, you will want more CPU power, more RAM, and more disk space. High-speed data busses help too. If you intend to do server virtualization, then you need fast network interface cards (NICs) connected to a high-speed network.

Gaming PC

Gamers require a very powerful processor to handle all the graphics calculations. You'll want at least 8 GB of RAM installed, a motherboard that enables SATA3, a 1 TB or 2 TB 7200 rpm or faster hard drive, and a high-end video GPU card with

e x a m

ⓦatch   *Remember that the most important components of a gaming PC are a powerful CPU, high-end video with a specialized GPU, a high-quality sound card, and high-end cooling.*

1 GB of RAM in it. You'll want a high-end sound card as well. Gamers often overclock the CPU, which increases the heat output considerably, so you'll want to install high-end cooling capability, perhaps even going to liquid cooling if necessary. In addition to a keyboard and mouse, a gamer will want the appropriate peripherals, such as gamepads or gameboards, joysticks, and wheels, which are used in certain types of games. Multichannel sound, up to 7.1 channel high-definition (HD) surround sound, which provides a subwoofer and six surround speakers, helps with the realism.

Home Theater PC

A *home theater PC (HTPC)* is a computer that houses components for a home theater system. It often comes in a smaller format that can fit inside your entertainment console. The HTPC should contain a medium-speed CPU and 4 GB or 8 GB of RAM with multiple large hard drives in a RAID 1, 5, or 10 configuration because it stores movies and music that you don't want to lose. You'll need a TV tuner card that lets you access cable TV, broadcast, Internet, or other signal sources. A popular option is to install digital video recorder (DVR) software that takes video input from the TV tuner and records it.

A single HTPC box can replace several boxes, but, of course, you need to connect it to a high-definition TV (HDTV), using High Definition Multimedia Interface (HDMI) or Digital Visual Interface (DVI) cables. And don't forget to install a high-end sound adapter card that outputs 7.1 channel (or higher) HD surround sound to great speakers. Further, install the latest Blu-ray combo drive for playing and burning DVDs and Blu-ray discs, and connect your HTPC to a high-speed local area network (LAN), preferably one supporting Gigabit Ethernet or Wi-Fi to stream video to other computers or TVs in the house.

e x a m

ⓦatch   *Remember that the most important components of a home theater PC are a surround-sound audio system, HDMI output (required by high-quality HDTVs), the HTPC compact form factor so that the box fits in the entertainment cabinet, and a TV tuner.*

Standard Thick Client

A *client* is software that connects over a network to related server software, such as a file and print client that accesses a file and print server for saving, retrieving, and printing files. Or an email client that connects to an email server. The operating system running under these clients may also be referred to as the client, as is true of Windows versions that are not explicitly server versions. In fact, the file and print client is part of Windows. In a broader sense, we may speak of the computer underneath all that as a client. A *thick client* is just another name for a typical network-connected desktop PC with various applications installed—one that you would see on most desktops at work, school, and the home office. The word "client" implies that the computer connects to a network as a client to various services for email, network browsing, file sharing, and more that you will learn about in Chapter 19. A thick client meets the recommended requirements for CPU, memory, and disk storage for Windows and all installed desktop applications. A reasonably fast Internet connection is desired, and the desktop applications are usually Microsoft Office, or an equivalent productivity suite, along with one or more Internet browsers and other applications required or desired by the user.

e x a m
ⓦ a t c h   *Remember that the most important components of a standard thick client are desktop applications and a system that meets the recommended requirements for running Windows.*

Thin Client

A *thin client* is a low-cost, scaled-down PC used primarily for Internet access and not requiring a full suite of local applications. Therefore, a PC configured as a thin client only needs to meet the minimum requirements of the Windows version installed, because it is assumed that all work is done and saved out on the network (private or Internet) somewhere. However, a fast Internet connection would be very important for the user. Basic applications would include an Internet browser, an e-mail client (unless the user accesses email solely via the Internet browser), and something for some basic word processing, although this may not be required.

e x a m
ⓦ a t c h   *Remember that the most important components of a thin client are just basic applications and a system that meets the minimum requirements for running Windows.*

Home Server PC

Depending on your needs, we see a home server PC as a combination of the HTPC described earlier and a home office file-sharing PC. The HTPC aspects should include media streaming capabilities and any of the other HTPC components desired. All of this would require a high-speed LAN, preferably Gigabit Ethernet using a Gigabit Ethernet NIC, and the system must have a high-speed Internet connection.

As a home office file-sharing computer, it should include a Windows OS that supports media streaming as well as file and print sharing. And because you will store your personal and maybe business data on this system, consider configuring multiple drives as a fault-tolerant RAID 1, 5, or 10 array.

e x a m

watch   *Remember that the most important components of a home server PC are support for media streaming, file sharing, and print sharing. The computer should also have a Gigabit Ethernet NIC and a RAID array.*

CERTIFICATION OBJECTIVES

- **801: 1.2** *Differentiate between motherboard components, their purposes, and properties*

- **801: 1.3** *Compare and contrast RAM types and features*

- **801: 1.6** *Differentiate among various CPU types and features and select the appropriate cooling method*

Strictly speaking, the requirements for Objectives 1.2, 1.3, and 1.6 of the CompTIA 801 exam have been satisfied in Chapters 3 and 4 where you explored these computer components. However, what is the sense of understanding motherboards and their components, RAM, and CPUs if you don't know how to physically work with them? Therefore, in this section, you will look at how to install these components. Then, an important task required after you install a new motherboard and components is to configure the motherboard via any hardware switches, by applying BIOS settings, and by installing motherboard device drivers. We described these motherboard configuration steps in Chapter 3.

Installing and Upgrading Motherboards and Onboard Components

Installing and upgrading a motherboard requires that you understand the CPU models that will work with the motherboard, as well as the appropriate type of memory compatible with both the CPU and motherboard and the amount of memory they can handle. Your best source for this information is the motherboard manual.

on the
job

Whenever you install or replace a computer component that involves opening the case, you must turn the computer's power off and ensure that you follow the electrostatic discharge (ESD) procedures discussed in Chapter 1. All the exercises described in this book assume that you have taken steps to protect yourself, and the computer, from harm.

Replacing a Motherboard

Replacing a motherboard is not a common occurrence. For one thing, if a motherboard fails while a computer is under warranty, it will be replaced as part of that coverage. Therefore, only if you work for a company that does such warranty work will motherboard replacement be a big part of your job. Second, if a motherboard fails after the warranty period, you will need to decide if a suitable replacement is available and if you will be able to use all your old components in a newer motherboard. Because most components attach physically to the motherboard, replacing it can be one of the most time-consuming tasks. If you are replacing one motherboard with another of exactly the same brand and version, you should make notes about any BIOS settings and jumper and switch positions (described in Chapter 3) for the old motherboard in case you need to change them on the new board. You will use the BIOS settings the first time you start up the computer after the installation, but make the physical jumper and switch changes before securing the new motherboard in the case. They may not be as easy to reach after the motherboard is installed, especially if you don't do it until after you install other components. Once you have done this, you are ready for the real work.

When it comes to replacing a motherboard versus building an entirely new system from scratch, doing the latter may be easier, because you can buy all the pieces at once from one source and request their help and guarantee that all the components will play nicely together.

Installing a Motherboard

When installing or replacing a motherboard, you should follow the instructions in the motherboard manual, your most important tool. In addition to listing the components supported, the typical motherboard manual includes instructions on installing the motherboard in a case and installing components, such as the CPU, memory, and power supply. The manual will explain how to set appropriate switches and jumpers on the motherboard and how to attach all the various power and data cables. These include all the drive interface cables and connections to both front and back panel connectors for the various interfaces, such as parallel, serial, Universal Serial Bus (USB), FireWire, External SATA (eSATA), and even video, if the video adapter is on board the motherboard.

Exercise 6-1 will guide you through the task of removing an old motherboard.

Before you open a computer case, be sure to unplug any power cords and turn off the power supply. Then, to prevent damage to the system, equalize the electrical charge between your body and the components inside your computer. If nothing else, touch a grounded portion of your computer's chassis. A better option is to place the computer on a grounded mat, which you touch before working on the PC. You could also wear an antistatic wrist strap. Warning: Do not use an antistatic wrist strap when working with high-voltage devices, such as power supplies, cathode ray tube (CRT) monitors, and laser printers.

EXERCISE 6-1

Removing an Old Motherboard

If possible, use a digital camera to record the steps, beginning with pictures of the unopened PC from all sides, then at each point before and after you make a change, such as opening the case and removing components. This can serve as your documentation for reassembling the computer.

1. If you haven't done this already, power down and unplug the PC's power cord.
2. Remove all expansion cards and cables from the motherboard.

3. If the drives and/or the drive bays interfere with access to the motherboard, remove them.

4. Remove any screws or fasteners attaching the motherboard to the case, lift the board out of the case, and put it aside. Be sure to carefully save any screws you remove.

The first three steps of Exercise 6-2 describe a recommended procedure for handling a motherboard, which applies to any circuit board. The remainder of Exercise 6-2 includes general steps for installing a motherboard. It assumes that the BIOS, complementary metal oxide semiconductor (CMOS), CMOS battery, and chipset have come preinstalled on the motherboard (as is customary). Always check the instructions included with the motherboard or other component.

EXERCISE 6-2

Properly Handling and Installing a Motherboard

1. Before unpacking a new motherboard, ensure that you have grounded your body properly. One method is to wear a static safety wrist strap, as described in Chapter 1. Your work area should include a grounded antistatic mat.

2. Hold the board by its edges and avoid touching any contacts, integrated circuit (IC) chips, or other components on the surface.

3. Place the board on a grounded antistatic mat (described in Chapter 1).

4. Install the CPU and memory on the motherboard, per manufacturer's instructions.

5. Follow the motherboard manual's instructions for setting any switches on the motherboard and pay attention to instructions for how to attach screws and stand-offs, which keep the motherboard from touching the metal floor or wall of the case. Now you are ready to install the board.

6. To place the new motherboard in the computer, line it up properly on the chassis screw holes, and fix it into place.

7. Attach the power and drive connectors, as well as connectors to the correct ports on the case (both front panels and back panels).

Upgrading a CPU

Upgrading a CPU is a major undertaking, but may not be impossible if you believe that your processor is the only thing holding back performance on your computer. It all depends on the motherboard. In fact, with a little research, you may find that all you need to do is change the motherboard's speed, because most motherboards support more than one speed for a particular CPU.

If you find that a new CPU is both necessary and possible, be sure to consult the manufacturer's documentation for your motherboard to determine which processor and speeds it supports. In most cases, you will need to configure the board for the new speed or model using a set of jumpers, but many BIOSs allow you to make such changes through BIOS system setup. You can run a software test to see just what CPU is installed. For instance, the free program CPU-Z will scan your computer and report on many onboard components, including the CPU, caches, the motherboard, memory, memory speed, and graphics.

on the
job

Nothing is free. Therefore, only download and install software from sources that you trust or that are recommended to you by someone you trust. When we mention free software in this book, we are only using it as an example. If you should download and install such software, note that most of the Websites offering free software also show links to download other software—sometimes those links are positioned so that you might inadvertently download a program other than the one you intend. The installation program of the software you desire may also include installing add-ons to your browser. Watch for these, and do not install anything you do not explicitly want.

Removing a CPU

How you remove an installed CPU depends on the type of socket. Computers manufactured since 2010 will have land-grid array (LGA) sockets, but you may encounter some CPUs in zero insertion force (ZIF) sockets in older computers, and as time goes by, it will become harder to replace the older CPUs. Once again, read any manuals available for your motherboard or computer. You may need to consult the manufacturer for more information. No doubt the processor will have a heat sink and/or fan attached to it. If possible, remove the processor without removing these attachments. However, if they interfere with the mechanism for releasing the processor, you may need to remove them.

The main difference you will see between CPUs with ZIF sockets and those with LGA sockets is that the latter have a cover in addition to the lever. The cover holds the CPU firmly in place, while only the lever and the fit of the pins in the holes, and maybe a bit of solder, hold a CPU in a ZIF socket. The steps for removing CPUs from both types of sockets are similar, with one important difference, as shown in Exercises 6-3 and 6-4.

on the job

The processor will be very hot when you first turn off a PC. You can lose skin if you touch a hot CPU chip, and it will hurt! Always allow at least five minutes for the chip to cool before you remove it.

EXERCISE 6-3

Removing a PGA Processor from a ZIF Socket

1. First, ensure that you have an antistatic bag at hand.
2. Lift the socket lever. You might have to move it slightly to the side to clear it from a retaining tab.
3. Pull out the processor. Because this is a ZIF socket, you should encounter no resistance when you remove the CPU.
4. Place the CPU in an antistatic bag.

EXERCISE 6-4

Removing a Processor from an LGA Socket

1. First, ensure that you have an antistatic bag at hand.
2. Lift the socket lever and cover.
3. Lift out the processor.
4. Place the CPU in an antistatic bag.

Installing a CPU

The CPU socket on the motherboard will usually have a mechanism to make it easier to install the CPU without damaging any pins. As described earlier, CPUs designed for the older ZIF sockets and those requiring the newer LGA sockets have levers, but the LGA sockets also have a cover.

When installing a CPU into a ZIF, raise the lever and position the CPU with all pins inserted in the matching socket holes. Then close the lever, which lets the socket contact each of the CPU's pins. Exercise 6-5 describes how to install a CPU in an LGA socket. In all cases, do not count on these simple instructions alone, but follow those provided in the manuals that come with the motherboard and CPU.

EXERCISE 6-5

Installing a Processor in an Empty LGA Socket

1. First, open the antistatic packaging containing the CPU, including any packing securing the CPU, but keep it within the packaging until you are ready to install it in the socket. Do not place the CPU on top of the packaging because that will expose it to static.

2. Lift the socket lever and cover.

3. Align the CPU over the socket.

4. Position the cover over the CPU.

5. Press the lever down.

on the
Job
When handling a CPU grasp it by the sides—never touch the pins of a CPU.

Removing and Installing Cooling Systems

As a rule, the typical PC comes with a cooling system that is adequate for the standard components delivered with the PC. Once you start adding hard drives, memory, and additional expansion cards, you should give some thought to supplementing the existing cooling system. How far you go with this depends on just how much you add to the PC.

An overheated computer will slow down, thanks to built-in technology that senses the temperature of the motherboard and slows down the processor when the temperature exceeds a certain limit. This reduces the heat the processor puts out. In the extreme, overheating can damage PC components. The other side of this is that modern cooling systems also use heat sensors, and as temperatures rise they will adjust their performance to keep the system cool. Newer power supply and case fans will change speed to match the temperature.

Common Sense First

Before you consider spending money on a new cooling system, make sure you are not impairing the installed cooling systems. Begin by ensuring that the PC case is closed during operation, that all slot covers are in place, that airflow around the case is not obstructed, and that the computer system is not installed in an unventilated space, such as an enclosed cabinet. Also, check to see if ribbon cables are blocking air flow inside the case. Use plastic ties to secure cables out of the way. Correct these problems before spending money supplementing the cooling system.

In addition, open the case and give the interior of the PC a good vacuuming before you spend money on upgrading the cooling system. Excessive dust and dirt on components will act as an insulator, keeping the heat from dissipating and causing a computer to overheat, which in turn can cause it to slow down, stop operating, or be permanently damaged. Learn more about vacuuming a PC and other maintenance tasks in Chapter 11.

Case Fan

New PCs often come with both a power supply fan and a separate case fan. Perhaps you can simply upgrade the present case fan. Also, check to see if the PC has an empty bay or bracket for a case fan. A case fan is a very inexpensive upgrade, cheaper than a latte and muffin at your favorite coffee shop. The only requirement is a bracket or bay in the case that will accommodate a case fan, and the appropriate power connector.

When shopping for a case fan, you will need the dimensions of the fan bay (usually stated in millimeters), rated voltage, and power input. Features to compare are fan speed in revolutions per minute (RPM), airflow in cubic feet per minute (CFM), and noise level in decibels. A *decibel (dbA)* is a commonly used measurement of sound. The fan speed and airflow reflect the fan's effectiveness for cooling. The noise level is an important consideration because fans and drives are the only moving parts in a PC and generate the most noise. Look for fans with a noise decibel rating in the 20s or below. In addition, check out the power connector on new case fans. Many come with a Molex connector that can connect directly to the power supply, and some have a special connector that must connect directly to the motherboard. Figure 6-1 shows a 100-mm-wide case fan with a Molex connector.

CPU Fans and Heat Sink

If you are installing a CPU, then you will also need to install a cooling system for it. Today's processors may require a fan/heat sink combination. Often, the

A case fan

cooling system and the CPU are packaged together, making the choice for you. Pay attention to the power connector for the fan, and locate the socket for this connector on the motherboard ahead of time. It is unlikely that you will replace an existing CPU fan and/or heat sink unless the CPU fan has failed. Even then, considering the complexity of it and the danger of damaging the CPU, it may be easier to replace the entire CPU if the same or similar model is available.

Liquid Cooling Systems

Liquid cooling systems are not just for gamers anymore. Like most technologies, as manufacturers improve liquid cooling systems, more people adopt them, and the prices for the improved systems drop. If you decide to look into this option, do your homework because these systems have several issues. For one, they require special skills to install, and they take up considerable space inside a computer because they require specific tubing, reservoirs, fans, and power supplies to work effectively.

Removing a Cooling System   If a cooling system fails or is inadequate, you will need to remove it from the PC. In that case, turn the computer's power off and ensure that you follow the ESD procedures. Then reverse the steps for installing the component, unplugging power and motherboard connectors, unscrewing mounting screws, and lifting it out of the case.

Installing and Configuring a Cooling System   When installing a new cooling system, be sure to read the documentation for the new components as well as for the motherboard, if appropriate. Assemble the components required, and follow good practices to avoid damaging the computer or injuring yourself. Turn the computer's power off, disconnect the power cord, and ensure that you follow the ESD procedures discussed in Chapter 1.

When installing a new case fan, affix the fan to the case in the appropriate bracket or bay, using the screws that came with either the case or the fan. Connect the power connector and any required motherboard connectors.

When installing a heat sink and/or fan on a CPU, be sure to apply thermal compound according to the instructions, and carefully connect the heat sink or fan using the clip provided. Plug the fan into the appropriate power socket on the motherboard.

SCENARIO & SOLUTION

I would like to build a PC. Is it best to shop for the best price on each component (motherboard, CPU, memory, etc.) from several sources?	No. The best strategy, especially if you are new to this, is to buy all the components from one source and get a guarantee that they will work together.
I read that I might have to upgrade my BIOS before installing the next Windows operating system? Does this mean I have to replace the physical BIOS chip?	You probably will not have to do something this drastic. Most BIOSs today are actually flash BIOS chips that can be electronically upgraded using software from the BIOS manufacturer.
The PC I want to build will be used mostly for running standard office productivity software. Should I consider a water-cooled system?	Generally, a water-cooled system would be overkill in a PC running standard office productivity software, but some new motherboards have built-in sealed (passive) liquid cooling systems.

Optimizing a System with RAM

One function of RAM is to provide the processor with faster access to the information it needs. Within limits, the more memory a computer has, the faster it will run. One of the most common and effective computer upgrades is the installation of more system RAM, usually into Dual Inline Memory Module (DIMM) sockets. A rare upgrade is to add cache memory. Depending on the vintage and configuration of the motherboard and CPU, special sockets may be available for adding more L2 or L3 cache, but both types of caches are now found on newer CPUs, not on the motherboard. Again, check the documentation!

The optimum amount of memory to install is best determined by considering the requirements of the operating system you are installing and how you will use the computer. On an existing system, you can run a software test that will scan your memory, report on what it finds (including the type and quantity of installed memory), the number of memory slots, and the number of available (empty) memory slots. It will then recommend upgrade requirements right down to the specifications you will need to select and purchase the correct RAM modules. One such software test is available at www.crucial.com. Exercise 6-6 will walk you through running the Crucial® System Scanner.

on the job

Recall the earlier warning about downloading and installing free software. If you choose to use the Crucial System Scanner, be sure that you only download the scanner, and that you do not agree to make any changes, such as an add-in to your Web browser.

EXERCISE 6-6

Running a Memory Scanner

For this exercise, you will need a computer with Internet access. The instructions are for using the Firefox Web browser in Windows 7.

1. Enter the URL **www.crucial.com/systemscanner** into the address box of your Web browser.
2. Download the Crucial System Scanner. If you are running a Mac OS, you will be automatically redirected to a page from which you can download the Crucial Mac System Scanner.
3. On the page with the download button read the terms and conditions, and if you agree, place a check in the box that indicates your agreement.
4. Click the button labeled Download The Scanner.
5. In the dialog box titled Do You Want To Run Or Save CrucialScan.exe, click the Save File button.
6. In Downloads, locate and click CRUCIALSCAN.EXE.
7. In the User Account Control dialog box, click the Yes button (if you are logged on as an administrator) or enter the administrator password if you are not logged on as an administrator.
8. A Scan In Progress message will appear followed by a page of results.
9. Review the results.

A recent scan of an older system showed four 1 GB double data rate (DDR1) memory modules installed in four slots, with no slots available. To upgrade this computer we would need to replace at least two of the modules with two denser (more memory per module) modules that match each other in size. This was an interesting test, but we will not add memory to this older computer because it has a 32-bit version of Windows 7 and cannot use more memory. A scan of a new computer running a 64-bit version of Windows 7 Home Premium also shows that all slots were occupied, but if we replaced the existing modules we could upgrade the amount of memory in the system. If you flip back to Chapter 2 and locate Table 2-2, you will see that 64-bit Windows 7 Home Premium can use up to 16 MB of RAM.

Installing and Removing Memory

Installing or removing memory modules is similar for Single Inline Memory Modules (SIMMs), DIMMs, and RAMBUS Inline Memory Modules (RIMMs), but you are most likely to work with DIMMs. The following sections describe the specifics of each type of socket. Before you begin, take steps to protect against static electricity damage to the memory modules and motherboard, as described in Chapter 1.

w a t c h *Recall the descriptions of the various memory slots in Chapter 3 and memory sticks in Chapter 4. Be sure*	*you remember that although the various memory sockets may seem similar, they are all keyed differently.*

DIMM and RIMM Modules

Dual Inline Memory Module (DIMM) sockets are often dark in color with plastic clips at each end. DIMM sockets for PCs come in two sizes and three configurations: 184-pin for DDR1 synchronous dynamic random access memory (SDRAM) and 240-pin for both DDR2 SDRAM and DDR3 SDRAM sticks. They are all keyed differently to fit into slots that support just that type of DDR RAM, and they are not interchangeable. You do not have to install DIMMs in pairs. If a motherboard has two types of memory slots, such as four DIMM slots supporting DDR2 and two DIMM slots supporting DDR3, it is an either/or situation: you can install one or the other type of memory. If you install both, the system will not boot up.

RAMBUS dynamic random access memory (RDRAM) RIMM modules have not been manufactured for several years, but if you should encounter an old computer that requires an upgrade, first determine if it is worth the effort. If you decide that it is, you will need to know these basics. RDRAM RIMM sticks for desktops have 184, 232, or 326 pins. The smaller RIMM form factors for laptops are called small outline RIMMs (SORIMMs) and have 160 pins. When you install RDRAM, they must be installed in pairs of equal capacity and speed. Because RDRAM has a dual-channel architecture, you cannot leave any RIMM sockets unoccupied, but must install a special terminating stick called a *continuity RIMM (CRIMM)* into the open sockets.

The technique for installing both DIMM and RIMM modules is the same, as described in Exercise 6-7. A notch in each type of module is positioned to only fit in the appropriate type of memory socket, where a matching socket key will prevent you from installing the wrong type of module. So even if the number of pins is the same, you will not be able to install one type of module in the socket for another. This is true of RIMM versus DIMM, and also of DDR1 DIMM versus DDR2 DIMM versus DDR3 DIMM. When installing a memory module, pay attention to the location of the key on both the module and in the socket, and orient the module notch to line up with the socket key. Then open the retention clips on the socket and align the module vertically with the socket holding the module upright. Chapter 7 will detail how to install small outline DIMM (SODIMM) modules in laptops.

EXERCISE 6-7

Installing and Removing a DIMM Module

1. Open the retention clips on the socket and align the module with the slot, keeping it upright so the notches in the module line up with the tabs in the slot.

2. Gently press down on the module. The retention clips on the side should rotate into the locked position. You might need to guide them into place with your fingers.

3. To remove a DIMM module, press the retention clips outward, as shown in Figure 6-2, which lifts the module slightly, and then grasp the module and lift it straight up.

FIGURE 6-2

Removing a DIMM

■ *801: 1.4*   *Install and configure expansion cards*

Chapter 4 described features and characteristics of the expansion cards listed in Objective 1.4 of CompTIA's 801 A+ Exam. In this section, we will expand that discussion to describe the installation and configuration of expansion cards.

Installing Adapter Cards

Even with the large number of features built into PCs, technicians need to know how to add new adapter cards to PCs in order to add new functionality. Installing an adapter card is a nontrivial task, requiring that you open up the case and install the card in an available expansion port. For this reason, give careful thought to your decision. What function do you need to add? Must you use an adapter card to add this function, or is this something you can add by purchasing a device with a USB, eSATA, or IEEE-1394 connection? These options are much more desirable than installing an adapter card, if you have a choice. Sometimes, however, an expansion card will provide better bandwidth, as in a network adapter, or performance, as in a video or sound card.

Do you simply need more USB or IEEE-1394 ports? Then, in the case of USB, simply plug one or more USB hubs into your existing USB ports. IEEE-1394 devices usually come with ports that allow the device to participate in a daisy chain. Therefore, if you have an IEEE-1394 connector on the computer, you may simply daisy-chain devices to this port. On the other hand, does your computer not have one of these types of ports, or are the ports it has outdated? Some USB devices refuse to work on older USB ports or are forced to transfer data slower due to an older port. In that case, you will need to add a new USB adapter card to upgrade to the new version.

Are you replacing the onboard video adapter with an enhanced video adapter? Are you adding an adapter that will support two monitors, often called dual-headed video adapters? There is no way to avoid installing an adapter to solve these problems. As new or better technology comes available, you will need experience installing adapters in a PC.

Removing an Adapter Card

Before removing an adapter card, be sure you have an antistatic bag in which to store the removed adapter card. Exercise 6-8 describes the general steps for removing an adapter card.

EXERCISE 6-8

Removing an Adapter Card

1. Turn off the computer, unplug it, and ensure that you carry out proper ESD procedures, as described in Chapter 1.
2. Use a nut driver or screwdriver to remove the screw fastening the card to the slot in the back of the computer case.
3. Grasp the adapter card with both hands and pull straight up to remove it from the socket.
4. Place the card in an antistatic bag.

Installing and Configuring an Adapter Card

Once you have selected the adapter card that meets your needs, you will need to install it in the PC. Exercise 6-9 provides general steps for installing an adapter card. Although installing and configuring most adapter cards is straightforward, you must understand the card's purpose. Before you begin, check the documentation for both the adapter card and the motherboard, and note any variations from this general procedure. Check if the adapter card has any physical switches for jumpers that you need to position. As with a motherboard, these should be set to the desired positions before installing the adapter card. Be sure to have any device driver disc handy so that you can install the device driver and any related software after you install the adapter card; also, test the card after installing the driver and before securing the case cover, as described in the exercise.

EXERCISE 6-9

Installing an Adapter Card

1. Set any switches or jumpers identified in the documentation for the card.
2. Turn off the computer, unplug it, and ensure that you carry out proper ESD procedures, as described in Chapter 1.
3. Remove the slot cover for the appropriate expansion slot, removing whatever hardware is holding the slot cover in place.
4. Position the adapter card upright over the empty slot, aligning the card's slot cover with the opening behind that expansion slot. (See Figure 6-3.)
5. Place your thumbs along the top edge of the card and push straight down.
6. Secure the card to the case using the existing screw holes.
7. After the board is installed but the case is still open, connect all necessary cables and start up the computer.
8. After the operating system starts up, install the device driver and test the device. (Learn more about installing drivers in Windows in Chapter 9.) Once the device is working, turn the computer off and secure the case cover.
9. Restart the computer again to ensure that replacing the case cover did not disturb any cables and connectors.

Installing an
adapter card

CERTIFICATION OBJECTIVE

■ *801: 1.5* *Install and configure storage devices and use appropriate media*

Chapter 4 introduced the various PC storage devices and media that are listed in
CompTIA A+ Exam 801 Objective 1.5, but we delayed coverage of the installation
and configuration of these devices for this chapter.

Installing Storage Devices

Replacing storage devices is a common task because those storage devices with
moving parts tend to fail more than other components. Adding more storage space is
also a common upgrade. Fortunately, because most drives are standardized, they can
be recognized by any PC and don't need special configuration.

Removing an Internal Storage Device

To remove an internal storage device of any type, check the documentation for the device. Exercise 6-10 provides general steps that will work for all types of internal storage devices.

Removing a Drive

1. Remove the power supply and data cables from the back of the drive. Ensure that you grasp the plastic connector, not the wires themselves. If the connector doesn't come out easily, try gently rocking it lengthwise parallel to the socket from end to end (never side to side) while you pull it out.

2. Remove the screws that attach the drive to the drive bay. These are usually located on the sides of the drive. Be sure to carefully save any screws you remove.

3. Slide the drive out of the computer.

Installing Drives on PATA Channels

Older PC motherboards typically have two parallel advanced technology attachment (PATA) hard-drive controller channels. That is, the motherboard has connectors for two ribbon cables. Each PATA channel supports two drives, so you can install four drives, in total, on the standard two PATA channels. One of the motherboard connectors is the primary connector, and the other is the secondary connector. Unfortunately, manufacturers use several conventions for labeling them on the motherboard, such as primary and secondary (see Figure 6-4), IDE1 and IDE2, or EIDE1 and EIDE2. If only one drive is present, it must connect to the primary channel.

The onboard drive controller of an enhanced integrated drive electronics (EIDE) hard drive receives commands to the drive and controls the action of the drive itself. The technology incorporated in EIDE and ATA devices allows one controller to take over the function of an additional drive. The controlling drive is the *master drive*, while the second drive it controls is the *slave drive*. PATA channels support one master and one slave drive on each channel.

FIGURE 6-4

The primary
and secondary
PATA controller
connectors on
the motherboard

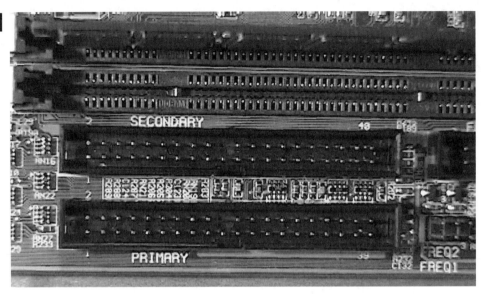

If only one drive is present on a channel, it must be a master drive. The master drive on the first channel is the *primary master*. The slave drive on the first channel is the *primary slave*. Similarly, the master drive on the second channel is the *secondary master,* and the slave drive on the second channel is the *secondary slave*.

In most cases, although a master can function without a slave drive present, a slave drive will work only if a master drive is present. Before you install an EIDE drive on a PATA channel, you will need to configure it for its master or slave role. Do this by setting jumpers on the back of the drive. Most EIDE/PATA drives have a label that shows the master and slave jumper settings. Figure 6-5 shows a drive with two white jumpers over two pairs of pins. This position, according to the drive's label, indicates that it is the master drive. Moving these two jumpers to the two rightmost pairs of pins would configure the drive for the slave role.

In many cases, it doesn't matter which is which. That is, there is no real performance difference between master and slave drives. However, as with most computer configurations, there are some exceptions. When using a mixture of old and newer hard drives within the same system, set the newer drive as the master and the older drive as the slave because newer drives can recognize and communicate with older drives, but the reverse isn't true. An older drive's controller will typically be unable to control the newer drive.

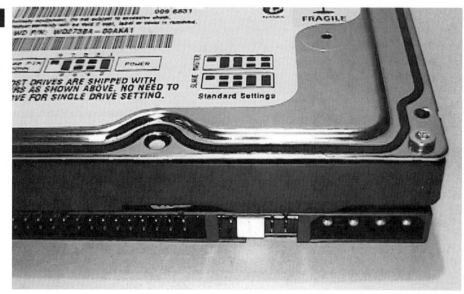

FIGURE 6-5

The back of an EIDE/PATA drive, showing two white jumpers over two pairs of pins

It is important to note here that PATA channels can support a mixture of EIDE and advanced technology attachment packet interface (ATAPI) (optical) drives. How do you determine which drive should be the master and which should be the slave?

When using a hard drive and CD-ROM optical drive together in a master/slave configuration, always set the hard drive as the master and the CD-ROM as the slave, because the CD-ROM's controller is unable to control the hard drive. In addition, some (but not most) older optical drives work only as slaves, and you simply cannot configure them as master drives. To create a master/slave configuration, follow the steps in Exercise 6-11.

PATA uses flat ribbon cables or (rarely) round cables. There are two important differences between the flat ribbon and the round cables—price and cooling. The round cables are currently more expensive, but they are superior to the 2" wide flat cables because they allow better airflow. Both types of PATA cables normally come with three 40-pin connectors—one on each end and one in the middle. One end connects to the PATA channel connector on the motherboard, while the other two connectors plug into the drives. If the system has only one hard drive, attach it to the end of the ribbon cable. The red stripe along the length of the cable represents pin 1. Make sure this stripe aligns with pin 1 on both the hard drive and on the channel connector on the motherboard.

Early PATA cables had just 40 wires, but newer cables have 80 wires, although they still have the same 40-pin connectors. The extra wires ensure better signal quality through grounding that shields against interference.

Some drives have a jumper setting called *cable select*. If this setting is used, the position of the drive on the cable will automatically determine the drive's role. If the drive is on the end of the cable, it is the master drive, and if it is on the middle of the cable, it is the slave drive.

EXERCISE 6-11

Choosing a Master

1. Determine which drive will be the master.
2. Locate the master/slave jumper pins and jumpers using the information on the drive label to determine which jumper settings to use for a master or slave (or cable select) configuration.
3. Use the jumper(s) to set this drive as a master (or cable select).
4. Secure the drive to an available drive bay.
5. Align the red stripe on the cable with pin 1 on the primary channel connector of the motherboard; attach the cable. Then attach the connector on the far end of the cable to the master drive, also ensuring that the red stripe on the cable aligns with pin 1 on the drive.
6. Locate an available Molex connector at the end of a cable coming from the power supply, and connect it to the drive.
7. To install a second drive on the same channel, follow the instructions in the previous steps, but set the drive's jumpers to the slave setting. Figure 6-6 shows the completed installation of two drives on one channel. Notice that both drives connect to the same ribbon cable.

Installing Optical Drives

Physically installing and removing an internal CD or DVD drive is the same as installing and removing hard and floppy drives, except that the CD or DVD drive must be installed into a bay with a front panel that allows access to the drive for inserting and removing discs. The optical drive also requires the connection of a sound cable to the sound card.

FIGURE 6-6

The finished installation of two hard drives on the same PATA channel

In addition, a DVD drive may need to connect to a decoder card using separate cables. Normally, the BIOS will automatically recognize the CD or DVD drive, but it may be necessary to enable the device in the BIOS settings. If the computer doesn't recognize, or can't communicate with, the new drive, you need to load a driver for it. Learn about installing device drivers in Chapter 9.

If you are installing two optical drives (of any type) using a PATA interface with the intention of copying from one to the other, for best performance, make sure the rewritable (RW) drive you plan to copy to is primary on the channel to which it is installed.

Blu-ray drives are presently a common option when customizing a new system. Today they are inexpensive and can hold an enormous amount of data. When selecting a drive, carefully consider the reason for the upgrade. Will it only be used for storing nonvideo data, or will it be used to run Blu-ray movies? You can add a Blu-ray drive for storing nonvideo data to a system without upgrading the video system, but in order to run Blu-ray movies, the video system must support HD resolutions, usually stated as 720 pixels, 1080i, or 1080p over a digital connection. Further, it must also support High-Definition Content Protection (HDCP) at the graphics chipset level and display level. Part of this is the requirement that the digital connection between the video adapter and display support be either DisplayPort or HDMI to support the HDCP signal. This extends to an HDCP-compliant graphics driver and disc-playback software.

Finally, before installing an optical drive to support the running of high-definition video content, be sure you have a multicore CPU and at least 2 GB of RAM under either Vista or Windows 7, or 1 GB of RAM for a Windows XP PC.

on the job

You can usually install hard drives and other devices on their sides with no impact on operation or performance. Never install a hard drive upside down.

Installing Solid-State Storage

Solid-state storage is available for nearly every storage need. At the low end of the price scale, thumb drives provide a solution for someone needing ease of use and portability when transferring data among computers. Similarly, we use a variety of storage devices in smart phones and cameras, often connecting these devices, or their solid-state cards, to our PCs to transfer data. And solid-state drives are offered as a lighter-weight option compared to conventional hard drives in laptops because they add very little weight. At the high end, solid-state drives are available for large server systems at a higher price than comparably sized hard-drive systems, but they offer better reliability and power savings over conventional hard drives. Low-end solid-state storage will plug into a PC's bus through a media reader, whereas high-end solid-state storage is more likely to come with the SATA interface.

Installing Drives on SATA Channels

SATA replaced PATA; as with many replacement technologies, it is faster, but also easier to install. Each SATA device has its own dedicated channel and does not require setting jumpers as you would for most devices on a PATA channel. Simply connect one end of the SATA data cable to a SATA channel and connect the other end to the drive's data connector. In addition, SATA devices may come with two power connectors on the drive. If so, one accepts a standard 4-pin Molex connector from the power supply, while the other accepts a special 15-pin SATA power connector. This is an "either-or" situation. Only connect to one of these power connectors—if both are used the drive will be damaged. Exercise 6-12 provides general instructions for installing an internal SATA drive. Be sure to follow the instructions in the manual for your motherboard and drive when installing a SATA drive. Figure 6-7 shows a SATA data cable alongside a SATA power cable.

FIGURE 6-7

A SATA data cable connector (left) next to a SATA power connector (right)

EXERCISE 6-12

Installing a SATA Drive

1. Secure the drive to an available drive bay.

2. Locate an available SATA connector on the motherboard or on a SATA expansion card. Plug one end of the SATA cable into the motherboard and the other end to the drive. (The plugs on the ends of the cable are different so you will have no trouble plugging the cable in correctly.)

3. Locate a power connector coming from the power supply that matches the power connector on the SATA drive and connect it to the drive. Figure 6-8 shows an installed SATA drive connected to a SATA channel on the motherboard. Notice the three open SATA channel connectors at the bottom left.

Installing RAID Arrays

Not too many years ago, if you wanted RAID, you had to add a special RAID controller adapter card to your computer. Today, many motherboards come with a RAID controller built in. Therefore, if you need to create a RAID array on a recently manufactured computer, you will probably only need to add the appropriate

Installed SATA drive (top) connected to SATA channel on motherboard (bottom left)

number of hard drives. If this is not true of the computer you wish to add RAID to, then you will need to purchase an adapter and install it.

The physical installation of a RAID adapter is identical to installation of any other bus adapter. After installing it, you will need to install and connect each drive in the array to the controller, and then start the computer and run the RAID controller setup program.

The setup program will be similar whether the controller was integrated on the motherboard or on a separate controller card. You access it while starting up the machine. In the case of an integrated controller, the RAID setup program may be on the system BIOS Setup menu, normally on an advanced menu. In the case of a separate RAID controller, watch during bootup for a prompt to press a key to enter the RAID setup. From there, you simply follow the menus and select the RAID level you desire.

Installing Internal Floppy Disk Drives

Floppy drives have gone from being a necessity in the early IBM PC to being considered as useless as rotary-dial phones. For this reason, you will rarely see a floppy drive in a new PC, and they vanished from most laptops years ago.

Installing an Internal Floppy Disk Drive

Many modern motherboards still have an integrated floppy drive controller. Therefore, if you desire to add an internally installed floppy drive to a new computer, you just need to obtain a floppy drive and the cabling. Before installing the drive, be sure to turn off the PC and disconnect the power cord.

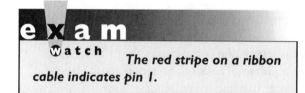

Internally mounted floppy drives are installed in a fashion similar to hard drives, and as with optical drives, you must install the floppy drive into a bay with a front panel that allows access for inserting and removing floppy disks. Some PC cases still come with this bay. Locate the bay, slide the drive into the drive bay, and fasten it with the retaining screws.

e x a m

ⓦ a t c h *The red stripe on a ribbon cable indicates pin 1.*

A floppy drive uses a flat ribbon cable that measures $1^1/_8$ inches wide with a 34-pin connector on each end. This cable is keyed to only insert one way, with the red edge lined up with pin 1 of the floppy connector on the motherboard and with pin 1 on the drive's connector. Attach the floppy drive to the end of the ribbon cable; this drive will be assigned drive letter A.

As it is highly unlikely that you will need to install even one floppy drive in a computer, it is even less likely that you will install a second one. However, in that very unlikely situation, you would need a 34-pin ribbon cable with three connectors, and then the floppy drive connected to the middle connector is assigned the drive letter B.

Once the drive is in place and the ribbon cable connected, locate a power cable coming from the power supply that has a plug that fits the floppy drive. This is usually a 4-pin miniconnector.

Removing a Floppy Disk Drive

To remove a floppy drive, disconnect the power and ribbon cables, unfasten the retaining screws, and then slide the drive out of the bay.

Installing and Configuring SCSI Devices

Small Computer System Interface (SCSI) systems allow you to attach more devices to the computer than the common EIDE/PATA or SATA systems do, but fewer than USB or IEEE 1394. Like many other computer standards, SCSI systems have evolved and improved over time. Most motherboards do not come with integrated support for SCSI, but by installing a *SCSI host adapter* (also called a *SCSI controller*), you can attach 7, 15, 31, or more additional devices to the computer, depending on the type of SCSI host adapter you are using. SCSI adapters that conform to newer standards, such as SCSI SAS, FC-AL, and SSA, can support more than 31 devices. SCSI systems have the disadvantage of being more expensive than PATA systems and more difficult to configure. When cost and easy installation are factors, PATA, USB, IEEE 1394, SATA, or eSATA systems are generally preferred.

Devices attach to the SCSI controller in a daisy-chain configuration, meaning that each SCSI device participates in moving data, as it typically comes with both input and output connectors so another device can connect to the SCSI bus through the previous device. Figure 6-9 shows three external devices on a SCSI chain.

Each external SCSI device has two ports: one port receives the cable from the device before it in the chain and one port attaches to the next device in the chain. An internal SCSI device may have only one port and it requires a special cable for daisy-chaining other internal devices.

Configuring SCSI

Configuring the SCSI host adapter, and each device on a SCSI chain, requires paying attention to a special address for each called a *SCSI ID*. In addition, each SCSI chain must physically terminate, or the entire chain will not function. The following describes the proper procedures for addressing and terminating SCSI devices so conflicts do not occur. The normal order of steps is to first attach the device to the chain, terminate the SCSI chain, set the SCSI ID, and load the device driver (if applicable).

Addressing SCSI Devices　You must allocate a SCSI ID to each SCSI device in a chain so it can communicate with the controller but not interfere with other SCSI devices in the system. If two devices share an ID, an address conflict will occur.

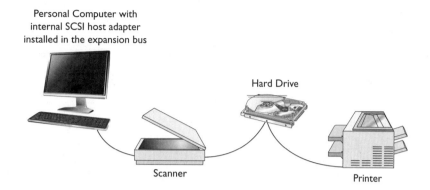

FIGURE 6-9

Three devices on
a SCSI chain

Personal Computer with
internal SCSI host adapter
installed in the expansion bus

Hard Drive

Scanner

Printer

The controller will not be able to distinguish the conflicting devices, and it is likely
that neither device will work.

Some SCSI devices are hard-wired to use one of only two or three IDs; others might
use any available ID. If the device supports plug and play, the system will automatically
assign it an available ID address, whereas other devices require configuring the address
manually. On some devices, this configuration is via jumpers on the device, and others
depend on a setup program residing on the device's ROM chip. Some SCSI devices
that require address assignment through jumpers will indicate through a label on the
device which setting to use.

The priority of ID addresses is important. The SCSI controller itself usually has
ID 7 assigned to it; addresses increase in priority within each octet, and each
successive octet has a lower overall priority than the one before it (see Figure 6-10).
That is, IDs 8–15 have a lower priority than 0–7. In a 32-bit system, 7 has the
highest priority, and 24 has the lowest.

If two SCSI devices try to send data at the same time, permission to transmit will
go to the device with the highest-priority ID, and the other device will have to wait.
Incidentally, "at the same time" means within 0.24 microseconds!

SCSI System Termination   Equally important is terminating the SCSI system
properly. Improper termination can result in the total or intermittent failure of
all devices in the SCSI chain. Special terminators, or terminating resistors, must
be present to ensure that signals at the end of the chain are absorbed rather than
bounced back along the chain. In some cases, the resistor fits into the unused second
port on the last SCSI device in the chain. In other cases, the SCSI device will include
an onboard terminator, made active by using the appropriate jumper setting.

FIGURE 6-10

SCSI ID priorities

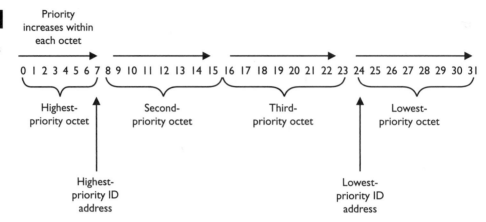

Whether the SCSI chain is strictly internal or strictly external, the last device and the controller must have terminators. Finally, if the SCSI chain is a mixture of both internal and external devices (which is not recommended), both the last external and last internal devices on the chain are terminated.

SCSI Cabling

SCSI systems employ a variety of cable types. The specific cable type depends on the SCSI type, the device type, and whether the device is internal or external. Furthermore, each cable type might have a different connector. Until recently, SCSI systems all used a parallel interface to the computer. Although new SCSI specifications no longer support 32-bit systems, you might be required to work on an older one. All 32-bit systems use a 68-pin P-cable and a 68-pin Q-cable or one 110-pin L-cable.

Connecting an External SCSI Device

Read the documentation for each external device carefully before connecting it, because procedures differ from one manufacturer to another. Most follow the basic steps described previously.

Serial Attached SCSI

Serial Attached SCSI (SAS), described in Chapter 4, targets the server market, not the desktop PC market. However, like many such technologies, it will probably filter down to the desktop, but it will take time before this happens. Currently, although most new motherboards for PCs have SATA connectors built in, they do not have SAS, so before a SAS device can be added to a PC, a special SAS host adapter card must be installed.

Removing and Installing an External Storage Device

External storage devices come in many types and sizes. This was not true ten years ago, when external storage was limited to optical drives or conventional hard drives using SCSI or parallel interfaces. These drives were expensive and cumbersome.

Today, the market is practically flooded with inexpensive external storage devices of all types and sizes. In addition, back then external optical drives were popular because they did not come standard in PCs and especially not in laptops. Today, with one or two optical drives standard in new PCs, the demand for external optical drives is down, but the need for external hard drives and solid-state drives has grown, and so have the choices.

Most flash memory drives come with a USB interface, and external hard drives have USB, IEEE-1394, or eSATA interfaces. Newer computers come with eSATA ports for attaching external eSATA devices. An eSATA port connects to the motherboard's SATA bus. If you wish to connect an eSATA device to a computer without SATA support, you will need to add an adapter card.

Traditional external hard disk drives also come in a full range of sizes from the low gigabytes to hundreds of gigabytes and even terabytes. The tiny two-inch format drives, like the thumb drives, do not need power supplies because they draw their power from the USB interface. The more conventionally sized drives require their own power supplies that will need to plug into the wall outlet. Besides that one issue, all of these drives are so simple to use that they hardly need instructions. Plug one in, and your Windows OS (unless it is very old) will recognize the drive, assign it a drive letter, and include it in the drive list in My Computer. You can then browse the contents of the drive and manage data on the drive using the Windows interface.

You do need to take care when removing a USB- or IEEE-1394-connected storage device. Many people simply unplug their thumb drive when they finish with it, but they risk losing their data or damaging the thumb drive. Windows requires an important step before the drive is disconnected: Click the Safely Remove Hardware icon in the tray area of the taskbar, and select the external storage device from the list that pops up. This will notify the operating system that the device is about to be removed so the operating system "stops" the device. If files are open, Windows may issue a message that the device cannot be stopped. Wait until the status message declares that it is safe to remove the device (Windows will turn off the light-emitting diode [LED] on a thumb drive) before unplugging it from the USB or IEEE-1394 port.

Preparing a Storage Device for Use

Fresh from the factory, a hard disk comes with its disk space divided into concentric tracks, each of which is divided into equal-sized 512-byte sectors. This is the physical format of the disk. The first physical sector on a hard disk is the *master boot record (MBR)*. Next we will look at the tasks that make a disk usable: partitioning and formatting.

on the
Ø o b
Other types of mass storage are not divided into multiple partitions. For instance, an optical disk is a single volume with a drive letter assigned, as is a floppy disk, should you ever encounter a floppy disk.

Partitioning a Hard Disk Drive

When you *partition* a disk, a partition table, defining the boundaries of the partitions on that disk, is written in the MBR. A *partition* is a portion of a hard disk that can contain one or more volumes. A physical hard disk must have at least one partition. On a hard disk, a *volume* is all or a part of a partition that can be formatted to contain a file system, and most often is represented in Windows by a drive letter. In most cases, a volume is an entire partition. In special circumstances, a volume can span multiple drives. The volume must be formatted (a different format from the physical format) to place the logical structure of a file system on the volume.

New hard drives, especially external hard drives, come prepartitioned and preformatted. Most operating systems include the partitioning step in a menu-driven process of the installation program, so anyone who can answer a few simple questions can at least succeed in creating a partition on which to install the OS. In addition, each operating system comes with a partitioning program you can use after installing the operating system on a PC. This program allows you to partition any additional drives you add to the computer. Figure 6-11 shows the Windows 7 Computer Management console open to the Disk Management node. A newly installed hard drive shows as Disk 2. The OS has recognized it but has not yet partitioned it; therefore, the space is shown as "unallocated." Tools in Disk Management allow you to partition and format drives. In Chapter 10, you will learn the options and the steps for partitioning hard drives.

| FIGURE 6-11 | The Windows 7 Disk Management program, showing a newly installed unpartitioned hard drive |

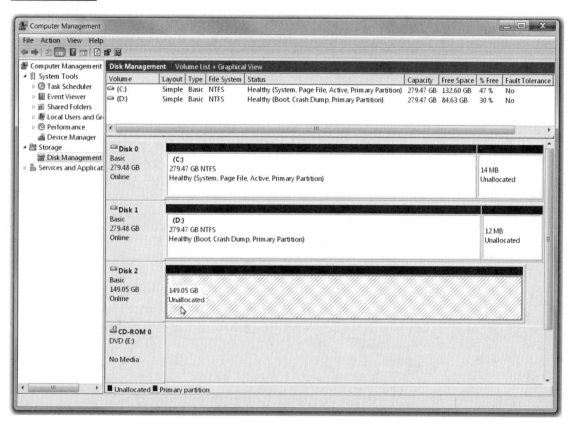

Formatting a Hard Disk Drive

You can format each partition with the logical structure required by a file system. File systems and their logical structures are described in Chapter 10. This logical format is often simply called the *format*. Once you have created the partition, use the appropriate utility to format the drive, which, in most operating systems today, requires selecting the file system. This is because Windows and other operating systems support more than one file system. Chapter 10 will go into detail on the types of file systems available in Windows and how to organize files within this logical structure.

CERTIFICATION SUMMARY

This chapter led you through the processes required to install, upgrade, and configure PC components. You also learned the important issues for selecting each type of component, because whether you are building a system from scratch or just upgrading one or more components, you need to go through a selection process to ensure that the components will function well together. For this, use the knowledge gained in Chapters 3, 4, and 5 about the basic technologies and features of the components. Then, follow the appropriate step-by-step instructions from the manufacturer for the component you are installing. Never fail to read all the appropriate documentation for both a component and the PC or, specifically, the motherboard.

TWO-MINUTE DRILL

Here are some of the key points covered in Chapter 6.

Selecting Components for Custom PCs

❑ The most important components of a graphics/CAD/CAM design workstation are a powerful CPU, high-end video, and maximum memory.

❑ The most important components of an audio/video editing workstation are specialized audio and video cards, a large, fast hard drive, and dual displays.

❑ According to CompTIA Exam 801 Objective 1.9, the most important components of a virtualization workstation are maximum RAM and a powerful CPU. In addition, there is yet another crucial requirement: Both the CPU and BIOS must support virtualization.

❑ The most important components of a gaming PC are a powerful CPU, high-end video with a specialized GPU, a high-quality sound card, and high-end cooling.

❑ The most important components of a home theater PC are a surround-sound audio system, HDMI output (required by high-quality HDTVs), the HTPC compact form factor so that the box fits in the entertainment cabinet, and a TV tuner.

❑ The most important components of standard thick clients are desktop applications and a system that meets the recommended minimums for running Windows.

❑ The most important components of a thin client are just basic applications and a system that meets the minimum requirements for running Windows.

❑ Remember that the most important components of a home server PC are support for media streaming, file sharing, and print sharing. The computer should also have a Gigabit Ethernet NIC and a RAID array.

Installing and Upgrading Motherboards and Onboard Components

❑ Select motherboard, CPU, and memory modules that are compatible with each other by researching the specifications of each.

❑ When installing a motherboard, follow the instructions in the motherboard manual.

❑ The ability to upgrade an existing CPU depends on the limits of the motherboard.

❑ One of the most common and most effective PC upgrades is the installation of more RAM.

❑ An overheated PC will slow down, stop functioning altogether, or become damaged.

❑ The typical PC comes with a cooling system adequate for the standard components delivered with it.

❑ Supplement the cooling system when adding hard drives, memory, and additional expansion cards or if the PC must function in a hot environment.

Installing Adapter Cards

❑ Select an adapter card that will add the functionality you need and that also fits an available expansion port on the motherboard.

❑ Read the documentation for the adapter card and the motherboard before installing the card.

❑ Physically install an adapter card; then restart the computer and install any necessary device driver and related software, and then test the adapter.

Installing Storage Devices

❑ Most older computers have two PATA channels that can each support two EIDE or ATAPI drives.

❑ Each PATA channel can have one master device, or one master and one slave device, and you must configure each device on a PATA channel for its role on the channel.

❑ Only one SATA device connects to each SATA channel, so there are no configuration issues.

❑ Newer PC BIOSs often support at least one or two types of RAID arrays. Install the correct number of drives for the type of array, and configure the array through BIOS setup.

❑ Most new PCs do not come with floppy drives, but many motherboards have an integrated floppy drive controller.

❏ Normally, manufacturers do not build SCSI systems into the typical PC. If you want to add SCSI devices to a PC, you need to install a SCSI host adapter.

❏ Various external storage devices, such as those with USB or IEEE-1394 connectors, are available today. These devices are truly plug and play, and once one is plugged in, the system recognizes it and assigns it a drive letter.

❏ To disconnect an external storage device, use the Safely Remove Hardware icon on the tray area of the Windows taskbar to stop the device, and only after it is stopped, unplug it.

❏ To prepare a hard drive for use, you must first partition it and then format it for a specific file system.

SELF TEST

The following questions will help you measure your understanding of the material presented in this chapter. Read all of the choices carefully because there might be more than one correct answer. Choose all correct answers for each question.

Selecting Components for Custom PCs

1. What category of software is used by engineers to design complex products, allowing you to view a design in 2-D or 3-D?
   A. CAM
   B. CAD
   C. Device driver
   D. Graphics

2. This type of custom computer configuration often uses a special small-format case in order to fit into an entertainment console.
   A. Audio/video editing workstation
   B. Graphics workstation
   C. Home theater PC
   D. Standard thin client

3. Which of the following is an appropriate set of components for a custom audio/video editing workstation?
   A. Basic applications and minimum requirements for running Windows
   B. Powerful processor, high-end video/specialized GPU, better sound card, and high-end cooling
   C. Maximum RAM and CPU cores and hardware support for virtualization
   D. Specialized audio and video card; large, fast hard drive; and dual monitors

4. What is the generic term for a single instance of an on-screen simulation of a complete computer?
   A. CAD
   B. CAM
   C. Virtual PC
   D. Virtual machine

Installing and Upgrading Motherboards and Onboard Components

5. How can you determine which CPU and memory modules to use with a certain motherboard?

   A. No problem. All ATX motherboards accept all Intel and AMD CPUs and DIMM memory modules.

   B. Each motherboard is unique; check the manual.

   C. Check the CPU documentation.

   D. Check the RAM module documentation.

6. What's a common name for a CPU socket that uses a lever for aligning the contacts and a cover for firmly securing a CPU?

   A. ZIF

   B. LGA

   C. HTPC

   D. CRIMM

7. How should you handle a motherboard?

   A. Grasp the largest component on the board.

   B. Grasp the handle.

   C. Hold it by the edges.

   D. Use a parts grabber.

8. Which of the following must you do when installing a DIMM module?

   A. Open the retention clips on the socket and tilt the DIMM at a 45-degree angle to the socket.

   B. Open the retention clips on the socket and align the DIMM module vertically with the socket.

   C. Close the retention clips on the socket and tilt the DIMM at a 45-degree angle to the socket.

   D. Close the retention clips on the socket and align the DIMM module without tilting.

9. What prevents you from installing a DDR2 module into a DDR3 socket?

   A. DDR3 installs at a 45-degree angle; DDR2 installs vertically.

   B. Socket key

   C. Socket notch

   D. DDR2 and DDR3 have a different number of pins.

10. What do modern PC cooling systems use to detect when to adjust the performance of the cooling system to keep the system cool?

    A. CAM

    B. Heat sensors

    C. Case fan

    D. Liquid cooling

11. Which of the following could impair the functioning of the installed cooling system? Select all that are correct.

    A. Keeping the case open during PC operation

    B. Removing slot covers behind empty expansion slots

    C. Vacuuming the interior

    D. Dirt and dust

12. Adding this cooling component is an easy and cheap cooling system upgrade.

    A. Liquid cooling system

    B. Case fan

    C. CPU heat sink

    D. CPU fan

Installing Adapter Cards

13. You have just purchased a new device that requires the latest version of USB, but your USB ports are only at USB 1.1. What is a good solution?

    A. Buy a new computer.

    B. Buy a converter for the device so it can use a parallel port.

    C. Install a USB adapter card with the latest version of the USB standard.

    D. Exchange the device for one with a parallel interface.

14. Before installing an adapter card in a computer, check the documentation and do one of the following, if necessary.

    A. Set switches or jumpers

    B. Install the driver

    C. Upgrade the card's BIOS

    D. Partition the card

Installing Storage Devices

15. Which one of the following statements about EIDE/PATA hard drive configurations is true?

    A. Before a master drive will function properly, a secondary drive must be present on the cable.

    B. The master drive must attach to the ribbon cable using the connector closest to the motherboard.

    C. The term for any hard drive on the secondary controller is slave.

    D. A slave drive cannot work in the absence of a master drive.

16. You are planning to install a hard drive and an optical drive using the PATA interface in a new system as the only drives. Which of the following is typically a valid drive configuration for you to use?

    A. Install the hard drive as a primary master and install the optical drive as a secondary master.

    B. Install the optical drive as a primary master and the hard drive as a primary slave.

    C. Install the optical drive as either a primary master or a secondary slave.

    D. Install the optical drive anywhere, as long as the hard drive is a secondary master.

17. What makes the installation and configuration of a drive with a SATA interface easier than on a PATA interface?

    A. Master/slave is easier to configure with SATA.

    B. The SATA cables are much thinner than PATA.

    C. No need to configure jumpers because each drive has its own channel.

    D. SATA drives are physically smaller.

18. What should you do when a SATA drive has two types of power connectors?

    A. Insert a CRIMM in the connector you are not using.

    B. Connect a P1 connector to the larger power connector.

    C. Set a jumper to activate one of the connectors.

    D. Only attach power to one connector.

19. Which of the following SCSI IDs has the highest priority on a single SCSI chain?

    A. 1

    B. 7

    C. 15

    D. 24

20. What creates the logical structure required by a file system?

    A. Sectoring

    B. Formatting

    C. Recording

    D. Partitioning

SELF TEST ANSWERS

Selecting Components for Custom PCs

1. ☑ **B.** CAD (computer-aided design) software is used by engineers to design complex products, allowing you to view a design in 2-D or 3-D.

   ☒ **A,** CAM (computer-aided manufacturing), integrates with manufacturing equipment; it does not, by itself, include design. **C,** device driver, is incorrect because a device driver is simply the software that allows the OS to control a device. **D,** graphics, is incorrect because although CAD software allows you to work with graphics, it is a specialized type of software, allowing for designing and viewing in both 2-D and 3-D.

2. ☑ **C.** A home theater PC often uses a special small-format case in order to fit into an entertainment console.

   ☒ **A,** audio/video editing workstation, **B,** graphics workstation, and **D,** standard thin client, are incorrect because none of these systems is likely to be installed in an entertainment console.

3. ☑ **D.** Specialized audio and video card; large, fast hard drive; and dual monitors is an appropriate set of components for a custom audio/video editing workstation.

   ☒ **A** is incorrect because basic applications and minimum requirements for running Windows is appropriate for a thin client. **B** is incorrect because powerful processor, high-end video/specialized GPU, better sound card, and high-end cooling are appropriate for a gaming PC. **C** is incorrect because maximum RAM and CPU cores and hardware support for virtualization are appropriate for a virtualization workstation.

4. ☑ **D.** Virtual machine is the term for an on-screen simulation of a complete computer.

   ☒ **A,** CAD, is incorrect because CAD is an acronym for computer-aided design, a type of software. **B,** CAM, is incorrect because CAM is an acronym for computer-aided manufacturing, a type of software. **C,** virtual PC, is incorrect because virtual PC is not the generic term used for on-screen simulation of a complete computer.

Installing and Upgrading Motherboards and Onboard Components

5. ☑ **B** is correct. Each motherboard is unique; check the manual.

   ☒ **A** is incorrect because it states that all ATX motherboards accept all Intel and AMD CPUs and DIMM modules. Each motherboard is unique in the components it will support. **C** is incorrect because checking the CPU documentation will not tell you if the motherboard itself will support this CPU. **D,** check the RAM module documentation, is incorrect because this will not tell you if the motherboard itself will support this RAM module.

6. ☑ **B.** LGA (land-grid array) is correct because this type of socket uses both a lever for aligning the contacts and a cover for firmly securing a CPU.

☒ **A,** ZIF (zero insertion force), is incorrect, because while ZIF uses a lever, it does not use a cover. **C,** HTPC, is incorrect because this is the acronym for home theater PC. **D,** CRIMM, is incorrect because this is the acronym for continuity RIMM.

7. ☑ **C.** Hold it by the edges is correct.

☒ **A,** grasp the largest component on the board, is incorrect because you should never touch any components on the board. **B,** grasp the handle, is incorrect because circuit boards do not have handles. **D,** use a parts grabber, is incorrect because you will not be able to remove or install a circuit board with a parts grabber.

8. ☑ **B.** Open the retention clips on the socket and align the DIMM module vertically with the socket.

☒ **A** is incorrect because you must install DIMMs in an upright position. **C,** close the retention clips on the socket and tilt the DIMM at a 45-degree angle to the socket, is incorrect because you cannot insert a module if the clips are closed, and you do not insert a DIMM at an angle to the socket. **D,** close the retention clips on the socket and align the DIMM module without tilting, is incorrect, only because you must open the clips first.

9. ☑ **B.** The socket key in the DDR3 socket will only allow for the notch in a DDR3 RAM module.

☒ **A,** DDR3 installs at a 45-degree angle; DDR2 installs vertically, is incorrect. They both install vertically, aligned with the socket. **C,** socket notch, is incorrect because a socket has a key that fits the notch in the correct type of module. **D,** DDR2 and DDR3 have a different number of pins, is incorrect, because they both have 240 pins.

10. ☑ **B.** Heat sensors are used by modern cooling systems to detect when to adjust the performance of the cooling system to keep the system cool.

☒ **A,** CAM, is incorrect because CAM is an acronym for computer-aided manufacturing. **C,** case fan, is incorrect because this is a part of a cooling system, not something that would be used to detect a temperature problem. **D,** liquid cooling, is incorrect because this is a type of cooling system, not something that would be used to detect a temperature problem.

I I. ☑ **A, B,** and **D** are all actions that would impair the functioning of the cooling system. **A** and **B,** keeping the case open during PC operations and removing slot covers, disturb the airflow design for the case. **D,** dirt and dust, act as insulation and reduce the cooling ability.

☒ **C,** vacuuming the interior, is incorrect because this will remove dirt and dust from components, improving the efficiency of cooling and not impairing it.

12. ☑ **B.** Case fan is correct, as this is an easy and cheap cooling system upgrade, as long as there is a place to mount the fan in the case and power is available.

☒ **A,** liquid cooling system, is incorrect because this is the most difficult and most expensive cooling system upgrade. **C,** CPU heat sink, is incorrect because it would not be easy, although it may be cheap, unless the CPU is damaged in the process. **D,** CPU fan, is incorrect because it would not be easy, although it may be cheap, unless the CPU is damaged in the process.

Installing Adapter Cards

13. ☑ **C.** Install a USB adapter card with the latest version of the USB standard is correct.

☒ **A** is incorrect because buying a new computer is not necessarily the solution to a single outdated component on a PC. **B,** buy a converter for the device so it can use a parallel port, is incorrect because you do not know that this is even possible with the device or that the PC has a parallel port. **D,** exchange the device for one with a parallel interface, is incorrect because most devices have a USB interface, not parallel, and many PCs do not have parallel ports.

14. ☑ **A.** Set switches or jumpers, if necessary.

☒ **B,** install the driver, is incorrect because you will do that the first time you start the computer after installing the card. **C,** upgrade the card's BIOS, is incorrect. **D,** partition the card, is incorrect because this is not something you do to an adapter card.

Installing Storage Devices

15. ☑ **D.** A slave drive cannot work in the absence of a master drive. If a drive is a slave and there is no master present, the slave drive will not be able to communicate.

☒ **A** is incorrect because a master drive can be alone on a PATA channel, and "secondary drive" is not a correct term, although "secondary channel" is a correct term. **B** is incorrect because it states that the master drive must attach to the ribbon cable using the connector closest to the motherboard. The opposite is true. The master drive must be installed at the end of the ribbon cable. **C,** the term for a hard drive on a secondary controller is slave, is also incorrect. The primary controller and the secondary controller can each have a slave drive, as long as there is a master drive on each controller.

16. ☑ **A.** Install the hard drive as a primary master and install the optical drive as a secondary master. This is most common, although you could also install the hard drive as a primary master and the optical drive as a primary slave.

☒ **B** and **C** are incorrect because they suggest installing the optical drive as a primary master and hard drives cannot be slaves to optical drives. **C** is also incorrect because it suggests installing the optical drive as the secondary slave, but slave drives must be accompanied by a master drive on the same channel. **D** is incorrect because only the hard drive must be a primary master.

17. ☑ **C.** There is no need to set jumpers (for master/slave), because each drive has its own channel.
☒ **A** is incorrect because there is simply no notion of the master and slave roles with SATA since each device has its own channel. **B** is incorrect because, although it is true that the SATA cables are thinner, this is not what makes them easy to install and configure. **D** is incorrect because it is not true that SATA drives are smaller than PATA drives, and even if it were true, smaller drives would not necessarily be easier to install and configure.

18. ☑ **D.** Only attach power to one connector. It is an either/or situation.
☒ **A,** insert a CRIMM in the connector you are not using, is incorrect because a CRIMM has nothing to do with selecting a power connector. **B,** connect a P1 connector to the larger power connector, is incorrect because a P1 connector plugs into a motherboard. **C,** set a jumper to activate one of the connectors, is incorrect because you only need to connect a power cable to one of the connectors to use it.

19. ☑ **B.** The SCSI ID with the highest priority on a single SCSI chain is 7.
☒ **A** is incorrect because 1 would come after 7, 6, 5, 4, 3, and 2. **C** is incorrect because 15 would come after 7, 6, 5, 4, 3, 2, and 1. **D** is incorrect because 24 would have the very lowest priority on a 32-bit SCSI system.

20. ☑ **B.** Format creates the logical structure required by a file system.
☒ **A,** sectoring, is incorrect because while there are sectors on a disk, sectoring is not the action that creates the logical structure. **C,** recording, is not the correct term for creating the logical structure. **D,** partition, is incorrect because partitioning defines the boundaries on a disk within which a logical drive can reside.

7

Installing and Configuring Laptops

everal years ago, industry analysts predicted that by 2008, laptop sales would surpass desktop sales. That prediction didn't quite hit the mark, because they reached that milestone three years earlier, in 2005, not counting large sales to corporations or direct sales from computer companies. By 2008, laptops accounted for 80 percent of personal computer sales. Why is this? Price and performance. While laptops once commanded premium prices, by 2005, they offered higher performance without the high price tags (for the most part), although desktops continue to be a better value in computing power and have larger screens. But you cannot ignore the mobility issue. And mobility is the issue, especially as more and more Wi-Fi hotspots appear in public places (and in some of our mobile devices) and cellular networks are now fast enough for high-speed Internet access. Because these factors make working away from an office more convenient for certain professions, PC technicians need to understand laptop-specific technologies.

However, the explosion in high-end tablet computers, such as the Apple iPad and Samsung Galaxy models, means that a laptop is only one option for mobile computing. In fact, industry analysts predict that tablet computer sales will exceed laptop sales by 2015. The whole topic is too big to contain in a single chapter. Therefore, we will limit the discussion in this chapter to the installing and configuring laptops objectives of the CompTIA A+ 801 Exam domain 3.0, features of wireless technologies required by just a portion of Exam 801 Objective 1.7, and a subset of the objectives listed in troubleshooting laptops per Exam 802 Objective 4.8. Chapter 20 will explore the objectives in the 3.0 Mobile Devices domain in the CompTIA A+ 802 Exam. The final topic in this chapter explores Windows Power Options for Exam 802 Objective 1.5.

CERTIFICATION OBJECTIVES

- **801: 1.7** *Compare and contrast various connection interfaces and explain their purpose*

- **801: 3.1** *Install and configure laptop hardware and components*

- **801: 3.2** *Compare and contrast the components within the display of a laptop*

- **801: 3.3** *Compare and contrast laptop features*

- **802: 4.8** *Given a scenario, troubleshoot and repair common laptop issues while adhering to the appropriate procedures*

This section begins with coverage of a portion of CompTIA A+ Exam 802 Objective 4.8 in describing the disassembly processes for proper reassembly of a laptop. Then for CompTIA A+ Exam 801 Objective 3.1, we describe how to install and configure laptop components, demonstrating knowledge of laptop-specific expansion slots, laptop devices, and how to replace them, including keyboards, hard drives, memory, optical drives, wireless cards, screens, direct current (DC) jack, battery, touchpad, plastics, speaker, system board, and central processing unit (CPU). To prepare for CompTIA A+ Exam 801 Objective 3.2, be sure that you understand the components of a laptop display, and then for CompTIA A+ Exam 801 Objective 3.3, compare and contrast all laptop features described in this section. Features of wireless technologies used in laptops are detailed, as required by a portion of Exam 801 Objective 1.7.

Installing and Upgrading Laptops

This section defines laptop computers, as distinguished from other portable computers, and then provides an overview of opening up a laptop and the proper procedure for disassembly and reassembly of a laptop. Finally, it introduces you to some laptop-specific components and peripherals, describing installation and upgrading procedures where applicable. In all cases, when you consider installing a new component or replacing an old one, you should first check with the manufacturer for any Basic Input-Output System (BIOS) upgrades. If one is available, install it before you proceed.

What Is a Laptop?

A *portable computer* is any type of computer that you can easily transport and that has an all-in-one component layout. In addition to the size difference, portable computers differ from desktop computers in their physical layout and their use of battery power when not plugged into an alternating current (AC) outlet. Portable computers fall into two broad categories: laptops (by several different names) and handhelds, but they all are integral to mobile computing.

A *laptop* (also called a *notebook*, *netbook*, or *ultrabook*) generally weighs less than seven pounds, fits easily into a tote bag or briefcase, and has roughly the same dimensions as a one- to two-inch-thick stack of magazines. The top contains the display, and the bottom contains the keyboard and the rest of the computer's internal components. A typical laptop uses a liquid crystal display (LCD) and requires small circuit cards that comply with modified versions of the bus standards found in full-size PCs. A laptop, as seen in Figure 7-1, opens in the same manner as a briefcase.

A typical laptop

Initially, people called most portable computers "laptops" because they could fit on the user's lap, although early laptops were a little heavy to do this comfortably. As technology improved, laptops became smaller and lighter, and the term "notebook" came into use to reflect this smaller size.

As circuitry shrinks, we discover smaller and smaller portable computers and newer terms, such as *ultra-portable* or *mini-notebook* for a laptop that weighs less than three pounds and gives up features to keep the weight down and maintain the highest battery life. Netbook is a recent term for scaled-down laptops in the ultra-portable category, designed mainly for Internet access, and costing about $300 a system. People purchase netbooks as a second (or even third) computer for traveling, as a teaching aid for schoolchildren, and as a first computer for people in developing countries. At the other extreme, many purchase laptops as full-featured desktop replacements in which performance is more important than battery life. These have large screens and weigh in at the top of the range. As we are writing this book, a new breed of laptop, called ultra-books, is entering the market. A number of manufacturers have announced products in this category. An ultra-book is very thin and light but contains very powerful components. They are particularly attractive devices, but tend to be much more expensive than other laptops. Regardless of the size and type of portable computer, throughout this book we will use the term "laptop" to encompass all of these types.

Laptops based on the Wintel platform can run the same operating systems as desktop PCs. Most laptops come with a version of Microsoft Windows installed, but you can also find laptops with Linux installed, or you can install it yourself. In addition, Apple computers use an Intel platform for their iMac and MacBook products running the OS X operating system, although it is not strictly a Wintel platform.

Opening a Laptop Case

Before opening a laptop case, follow all the safety precautions described in Chapter 1. Before you begin, locate the manufacturer's documentation for the laptop and for any component you are adding or replacing. You may find a service manual for the laptop on the manufacturer's Website that you can use to learn how to access the components you wish to replace and plan the actual steps you will take. Let the manufacturer's documentation be your guide. With that in mind, follow the processes described here when preparing for and performing the disassembly and reassembly of a laptop.

A laptop has two sources of power: the AC adapter and the battery. Therefore, for your own safety, ensure that there is no power to components. Always unplug the AC adapter and remove the battery before opening the case in any way. For instance, to replace some internal laptop components, you may only need to remove an access panel on the bottom, but you should still remove all sources of power. These panels usually have one to three screws to remove. Other components may require that you disassemble the laptop, removing the keyboard, drives, or video adapter, and even the entire display assembly (in the worst case). The keyboard may attach with screws or latches.

o n t h e
0 o b

Search the Internet for technical manuals, tutorials, and videos on how to replace laptop components. These tutorials are often specific to certain models, but they offer lots of useful tips. Use your own judgment and the manufacturer's documentation when doing this type of work.

Use Appropriate Hand Tools

After reading the manufacturer's documentation, and before beginning, assemble all the hand tools you expect to use. Please refer to Chapter 3 for a list of tools.

Organize Parts

Have containers ready to temporarily hold the screws and other parts that you will remove (small pill bottles work well), and have antistatic bags handy for any circuit boards you remove. After you reassemble the laptop, you should not have any extra parts except for those that you replaced.

Document and Label Cable and Screw Locations

This most important step is also the one most people would rather skip. For internal component replacements, you will begin by removing screws from the body of the laptop. Before you open the laptop compartment, take photos with a digital camera or make a rough sketch of the exterior portion involved, and label cable and screw locations. You don't have to be an artist to do this—simple lines and shapes, carefully labeled, will suffice. Once you have removed any panels, photograph or sketch the inside, labeling any components and their cables so you will be able to reassemble the laptop after replacing or adding a part.

Laptop Components

Laptop components that distinguish one manufacturer's models from all the others are at least partially proprietary, but most manufacturers use at least some generic components, such as the CPU, memory, and hard drives. Therefore, if a laptop component fails, a carefully worded query in an Internet search engine should reveal sources for an appropriate replacement part or the name of a company that will replace the part for you. Both interior and exterior replacement parts are available, even plastic exterior components, such as the case, LCD lid, LCD bezels, palm rest, button panels, doors, and compartment covers for some popular laptop models. Always research whether replacing the part is more cost effective than replacing the entire laptop.

Plastics

The nature of a laptop—its portability—and the tendency of a laptop owner to take for granted that a laptop can survive the rigors of travel—means a laptop will typically experience rough treatment during its short lifetime. Although designed for portability, manufacturers do not design most laptops to survive harsh treatment. Those purposely designed for rough treatment, such as the Panasonic Toughbook line of laptops that can withstand water, dust, temperature extremes, and impact, sell for a premium price that most users cannot justify.

Unless you work for an organization that requires the use of laptops under extreme conditions, you will work on the more vulnerable commonplace laptops, so you need to know what to do in case the plastic that makes up the laptop case falls victim to a mishap that doesn't damage the internals. Cracked or broken laptop case corners can happen. If the laptop is out of warranty but new enough to be valuable to the owner, you need to research replacing the laptop case or some part of it. You could attempt a repair, using epoxy glue for cracks and epoxy putty to fill voids, but if you do this, be very careful not to drip the glue or putty into the interior.

Motherboard

Although laptops run standard PC operating systems and applications, laptop motherboards have different form factors than PCs because of the miniaturization required. A laptop motherboard contains specialized versions of the components you would expect to find in a desktop PC, such as the CPU, chipset, random access memory (RAM), video adapter (built in), and expansion bus ports.

If you find that a motherboard has failed, and your research and evaluation shows that a replacement is available and cost effective, be sure the replacement exactly matches the form factor and all electrical connections. This type of repair is fraught with failure potential, so you risk going to the expense and trouble of replacing a motherboard but botching the repair. Then you face the expense of the repair plus the cost of replacing the failed laptop.

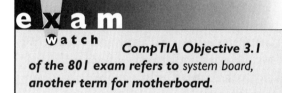

CompTIA Objective 3.1 of the 801 exam refers to system board, another term for motherboard.

CPU

Both Intel and AMD have a number of CPUs designed especially for laptops that include mobile computer technologies such as power-saving and heat-reducing features and throttling that lowers the clock speed and input voltage when the CPU is idle. Different models of mobile processors are available, including high-performance models requiring more power that are appropriate for desktop replacement laptops, and CPUs that run at lower voltage and reduced clock speeds to give the best battery life. Many mobile CPUs support Wi-Fi networking. Learn about wireless networking in Chapters 14 and 15.

If a laptop CPU fails, or if you wish to replace it in the hopes of obtaining better performance, contact the manufacturer for specifications for a replacement CPU. You may discover the CPU is not replaceable because they soldered it to the motherboard. Manufacturers will not usually sell you a replacement CPU, so if you find the CPU is replaceable, use the specifications to find a compatible CPU. Or, if the CPU is still functioning, you can download a utility program from either the Intel or AMD Web-sites that will give you the specs of the currently installed CPU. Note the information from the utility program, especially the voltage and power draw, and then look for a chip that matches the specs. Power-wise, you want a chip with the same voltage and a power draw that is equal to or less than the one you are replacing.

To replace the CPU, you will need to open up the area inside the case that houses it. Refer to the earlier section "Opening a Laptop Case." No doubt you will need to remove a heat sink from the installed CPU; set this aside. Once the

CPU is exposed, you will need to release it by loosening a screw or other locking mechanism and lifting it out. Remove the old thermal compound from the heat sink with isopropyl alcohol and a lint-free rag. When the heat sink is dry, apply a very thin layer of thermal paste to the top of the new CPU. Attach the heat sink to the new CPU and install it into the laptop socket, being sure to lock it in place again. Reassemble the system and start it up, taking care to go into the BIOS setup program to check that it recognizes the CPU.

External Expansion Slots

Until a few years ago, the typical laptop came with two specialized small-form-factor external expansion slots. The most common expansion slots were those based on standards developed by the *Personal Computer Memory Card International Association (PCMCIA)*, an organization that created standards for laptop computer peripheral devices. Although the original organization is no longer in existence, the Implementer's Forum at www.usb.org manages the former PCMCIA organization's activities.

We will discuss these standards that support hot swapping, meaning you can connect and disconnect devices while the computer is running. The early cards, PC Card or CardBus, depend on a service called *socket services*, running in the laptop's operating system, to detect when you have inserted a card. After socket services has detected a card, another service, called *card services*, assigns the proper resources to the device. The ExpressCards, manufactured to more recent standards, have either a Peripheral Component Interconnect Express (PCIe) or Universal Serial Bus (USB) bus.

PC Card/CardBus   At first, people referred to the early standard developed by PCMCIA simply as the "PCMCIA" interface. They also called the credit card–sized cards that fit into this interface, which slid in from slots on the side of a laptop, "PCMCIA cards," but eventually the name changed to *PC Card*. The earliest inter-faces and cards used a 16-bit interface. Eventually, PCMCIA modified the standard to use a 32-bit parallel PCI bus, known as *CardBus*. Although the CardBus allows 32-bit burst-mode transfers, it still only allows 16-bit memory transfers (for memory devices) and 16-bit I/O transfers for network cards, modems, and other I/O devices.

The cards that fit into the PC Card interface, including both PC Card and CardBus cards, measure 85.6 mm long by 54 mm wide. The three types vary in thickness: *Type I* measures 3.3 mm thick, *Type II* (seen in Figure 7-2) measures 5.0 mm thick, and *Type III* measures 10.5 mm thick.

The PC Card slots are downward compatible. A Type III card can only fit in a Type III slot, whereas a Type II card can fit in either a Type II or a Type III slot, and a Type I card can fit in all three. They all have 68 pins, fit into the PC Card sockets,

FIGURE 7-2

A Type II PC Card
with a dongle
to attach to a
network

and only vary in thickness. The thickness and the circuitry that fits into each size
slot dictate the type of device that will use each PC Card type. Table 7-1 lists the PC
Card types and the devices that would use each type.

In addition, there is a physical distinction between the older 16-bit PC Card and
a CardBus PC Card. When comparing the two types of cards, look at the area above
the connector. On a 16-bit card, this area is smooth, whereas on the newer CardBus
PC Card, a gold grounding strip appears that usually has eight bumps. You can insert
a 16-bit PC card into a 16-bit slot or a CardBus slot, but you can only insert the
CardBus PC Card into a CardBus slot.

ExpressCard   The immediate successor to PC Card was the first *ExpressCard*
standard, which came in two interfaces: the PCIe (PCI Express) interface, at 2.5
gigabits per second, and the USB 2.0 interface, at up to 480 megabits per second.
The more recent ExpressCard 2.0 standard continues to support the latest PCIe

TABLE 7-1

The Devices That
Use Each Type of
PC Card

Type	Device
I	Solid-state memory cards
II	I/O devices: modems and network interface cards
III	Rotating mass storage hard drives

standard as well as USB 3.0 with transfer rates of up to 5 Gbps. Plus, ExpressCard 2.0 cards are downward compatible and fit in slots designed for the 1.0 standard.

ExpressCard is incompatible with either PC Card standard. To begin with, ExpressCard uses multiple serial pathways, while its predecessors used parallel. Further, the ExpressCard interface does not have actual pins, but instead has 26 contacts in a form referred to as a *beam-on-blade connector*. Although all ExpressCard modules have the same number of contacts (also called "pins"), there are currently two sizes of modules: both are 75 mm long and 5 mm high, but they vary in width. The form factor known as *ExpressCard/34* is 34 mm wide, whereas *ExpressCard/54* is 54 mm wide. ExpressCard/34 modules will fit into ExpressCard/54 slots, but the opposite is not true.

ExpressCard supports a variety of device types, including local area network (LAN) and wide area network (WAN) adapters, FireWire, Serial Advanced Technology Attachment (SATA), solid-state drives (SSDs), USB hubs, micro hard drives, and much more. ExpressCard technology is not simply for laptops. The ExpressCard interface is also available as standard bus cards for desktops. However, most new laptops do not come with ExpressCard slots, and we expect to see these disappear within a few years.

Installing Cards into External Expansion Slots   The various small devices that install in the PC Card, CardBus, or ExpressCard slots are all plug and play, and you can install them without opening up the computer. You simply slide the card into the appropriate slot, pushing it in until it feels firmly seated. Recall that PC Cards and CardBus cards have pin and socket connectors, whereas the ExpressCards have contacts in a beam-on-blade configuration. Once properly installed, the card should not wiggle when gently tapped. When removing a PC Card or CardBus card, look for a small button next to each card that releases it from the socket. Press the button to eject the card. An ExpressCard slot on a laptop usually comes with a blank inserted to protect it. To remove either the blank or an ExpressCard, gently press the button into the slot. A spring will then partially eject the blank or card, and you can remove it. To install an ExpressCard, insert it into the empty slot and gently push it until you hear and feel it engage.

Internal Expansion Slots

Some laptops also have one or more special mini-expansion slots inside the case. Two, based on the full-sized PCI and PCIe expansion bus found in a desktop PC, are Mini PCI and Mini PCIe. Another is mSATA, a physically smaller form of the SATA interface. We described PCI, PCIe, and SATA in Chapter 4.

Mini PCI   Mini PCI is a standard based on PCI (see Chapter 3). The biggest difference (although there are others) is that Mini PCI is much smaller than PCI—both the card and the slot. Mini PCI has a 32-bit data bus. If a laptop has an installed Mini PCI slot, it is usually accessible via a small removable panel on the bottom of the case. Mini PCI cards also come in three form factors: Type I, Type II, and Type III. Types I and II each have 100 pins in a stacking connector, whereas Type III cards have 124 pins on an edge connector. Each type is further broken down into A and B subtypes, as Table 7-2 shows.

exam

watch   *Remember, PC Card, CardBus, and ExpressCard all have slots you can access without opening the laptop. Mini PCI and Mini PCIe use bus connectors that you must access by opening the case—usually via a small cover over the card and its connector.*

Mini PCIe   A newer standard for Mini Cards has replaced the Mini PCI standard on laptop motherboards. That is the *Mini PCIe Card* (depending on the manufacturer, this is also called *PCI Express Mini Card, Mini PCI Express, Mini PCI-E, or simply MiniCard*). This specification provides much faster throughput with a 64-bit data bus. At 30 mm × 26.8 mm, it is much smaller than a Mini PCI card and has a 52-pin edge connector.

mSATA   Today's laptops and other mobile devices may use a mass-storage interface designed for mobile devices called mSATA (or MiniSATA), as described in Chapter 4. Introduced in 2009, the SATA 3.1 standard is a scaled-down form factor of the SATA mass storage interface with added support for SSDs in mobile devices.

Memory

Laptop memory modules come in small form factors. The most commonly used is *Small Outline DIMM (SODIMM)*, which measure about $2\frac{5}{8}$ ", or about half the

TABLE 7-2	Card Type	Dimensions in mm (depth × length × width)
Dimensions of the Various Types of Mini PCI Cards	IA	7.5 × 70 × 45
	IB	5.5 × 70 × 45
	IIA	17.44 × 70 × 45
	IIB	5.5 × 78 × 45
	IIIA	2.4 × 59.6 × 50.95
	IIIB	2.4 × 59.6 × 44.6

size of a Dual Inline Memory Module (DIMM) module. First-generation SODIMM modules had 30 pins, and the next generation had 72 pins. These had a data bus width per module of 8 bits and 32 bits, respectively. Next came the 100-pin, 32-bit SODIMMs. Expect to encounter the more current 64-bit SODIMMs with 144, 200, or 204 pins. Look for the 144-pin and 200-pin SODIMMs in older laptops. Recent laptops will have the 204-pin SODIMMs.

As with DIMM modules, SODIMM modules have notches in them so that they only fit into the properly keyed SODIMM slots. The 144-pin SODIMM modules have a single notch just off center. However, 200-pin SODIMMs have at least three different locations for the notch, depending on the DDR level, as described in Chapter 4. At this time, you can find 200-pin DDR1, DDR2, and DDR3 SODIMM modules, although the latter are more common in new laptops. All have a single notch that is off center and in a different location for each type (DDR1, DDR2, and DDR3). Figure 7-3 shows a 200-pin DDR1 SODIMM. The 204-pin SODIMMs are available with DDR3 RAM and have a notch that is just off center. Figure 7-4 shows a laptop with the battery removed and the access panel open to expose two 204-pin DDR3 SODIMM modules, each populated with 4 GB of RAM. The top one (at bottom) has eight chips on it, and it covers up half of the module under it, showing only its top four chips. Visible near the are 102 of the top module's 204 pins, as well as the module notch. Also visible on the sides of each module are the clips used to secure them in place.

FIGURE 7-3

A 200-pin
SODIMM module

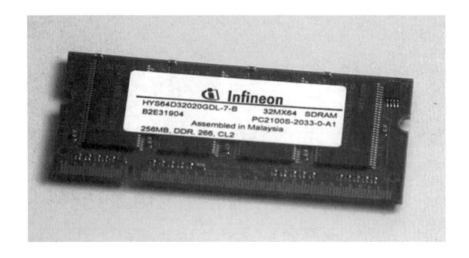

FIGURE 7-4

A laptop with
access panel
removed to
expose the two
DDR3 SODIMM
modules

MicroDIMM, a RAM module designed for subcompact and laptop computers, is half the size of a SODIMM module and allows for higher-density storage.

You can add RAM to most laptops if there is a RAM slot available. If none is available, you must swap the existing RAM module or modules out for denser modules. Some systems include extra RAM slots within the chassis, which requires either opening the computer's case or removing the compartment cover and inserting the RAM module in an available slot. Exercise 7-1 describes the steps for installing memory in a laptop and for verifying that the system recognizes it.

EXERCISE 7-1

Installing SODIMM Memory

For this exercise, you will need a way to ground yourself and/or your work area. You will also need a new module of SODIMM memory appropriate for your laptop in an antistatic bag, the user's manual, a spare antistatic bag, and a small nonmagnetic screwdriver for opening the case. If you do not have a new module, simply remove an already installed module and reinstall it. In this case, you will just need an antistatic bag in which to place the module should you need to set it down.

1. Ground yourself using one of the methods described in Chapter 1.
2. Turn off the computer and all external devices.
3. Unplug the computer and disconnect all exterior cables and devices. Remove the laptop battery.

4. Following the instructions in the laptop user manual, open the compartment containing the SODIMM slots. Be careful, since the cover may have retaining tabs that break off easily.

5. Your laptop may have one or two memory slots. Look for numbers near any open slots and fill the lowest numbered slot first.

6. If you are replacing memory, remove the module or modules you are replacing. To remove a module, press down on the retaining clips located on the sides, lift the edge of the module to a 45-degree angle, and gently pull it out of the slot, being careful to hold it by its edges without touching the contacts or chips.

7. Place the old module in an antistatic bag. Remove the new module from its antistatic bag, being careful to hold it by its edges without touching the contacts or chips.

8. Align the notch of the new memory module with that of the memory slot, as shown here, and gently insert the module into the slot at a 45-degree angle. Carefully rotate the module down flat until the clamps lock it in place.

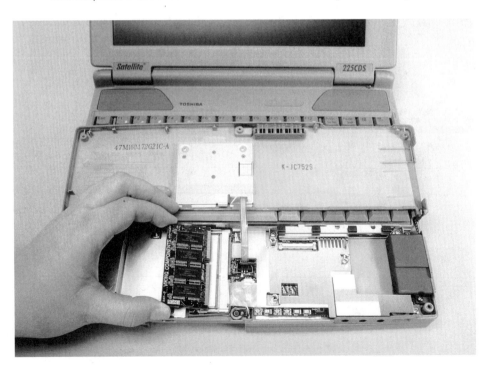

9. Close the memory compartment, reinstall the battery, and reconnect the power cable.

10. Power up the computer, and, if necessary (according to the user manual), configure memory in BIOS setup, although this is not normally required.

11. Perform a normal startup in Windows, and check the System Properties applet in the Control Panel to see if it recognized the new memory.

Another way to add more RAM to your laptop is to use a memory card of the correct form for your laptop. The choices are PC Card, CardBus PC Card, or ExpressCard, all of which we described in the section titled "External Expansion Slots."

No matter how you add memory to your laptop, you may notice the memory count during bootup does not quite add up to the total memory installed, which means your laptop may be using some of your system RAM for the video adapter, which often is the case with integrated video adapters if they do not have their own volatile random access memory (VRAM). Main RAM memory used in this way is *shared video memory* and is not available to the operating system.

Memory Card Reader

A laptop today will often come with a built-in, solid-state card reader. While we often lump all of these devices together as flash memory, they have several formats (see Chapter 4). Therefore, be sure your laptop supports the format you use, such as CompactFlash (CF), miniSD, MultiMedia Card (MMC), Smart Media (SM), and Memory Stick (MS).

Fans

Before considering replacing a seemingly failed laptop fan, open the laptop and clean the fan blades. If the fan still does not work, attempt to replace the fan. This process will require the usual search for a suitable fan. Once you locate one and determine that the cost is worth the effort, follow the manufacturer's instructions to replace the failed fan, being careful to remove and replace the *heat pipe,* a tubular device that works with the fan to draw heat away from the interior of the laptop. If the installation is successful, you should hear the fan when you power up the laptop.

Storage Devices

For years, laptops came with two mass storage devices: a hard drive and an optical drive. Today you will still find an optical drive in most laptops, but in high-end and/or very light weight laptops an SSD may replace the hard drive. As the price of SSDs comes down, this will become more common. Recall the discussion of SSDs in Chapter 4.

Although the optical drives in laptops are low profile, they still must accommodate 4.75" optical discs. Laptops typically use 2.5" hard drives versus the 3.5" hard drives used in desktop PCs. There are also hard drives that you can install into the PC Card expansion bays. The biggest change in laptop mass storage, however, is large-capacity SSDs replacing hard drives at all price points of the newer ultra-portable models. An SSD drive will typically have a SATA interface, which is the most common storage interface today. SSDs in laptops are desirable because they are faster than hard drives, lighter, and less vulnerable to damage from impacts or excess motion. While some low-priced netbooks do contain these drives, they are of modest size; high-end laptops have relatively larger SSD drives, around 500 GB. These larger drives use newer technology that allows for denser storage and, therefore, higher capacity. One such technology is Secure Digital High Capacity (SDHC) cards, described in Chapter 4.

Replace a hard drive only with another of the same type from the same manufacturer. After you power down the computer, use the same precautions you would use with a PC case before proceeding. Accessing an internal storage device may be as simple as removing a plastic access cover on the bottom or side of the laptop, as seen in Figure 7-5. In which case, simply slide the drive out, and then replace it with a new drive and replace the cover. Replacing a storage device may involve removing the keyboard or the entire bottom of the case, in which case, it is not a user-serviceable component, and you may void the warranty simply by opening the case.

In some cases, you may be able to replace an existing hard drive with an SSD, but it all depends on the SSD using the same interface (often SATA) and fitting into the drive bay. A search of the Website of SSD manufacturer SanDisk shows instructions for replacing a hard drive with a SSD drive in certain laptop models, but the instructions lack important steps and details.

Video Adapter

As in a desktop PC, a video adapter controls a laptop's video output, but laptop manufacturers typically integrate the video adapter into the motherboard, or on a separate, scaled-down proprietary card connected to a type of riser card that holds the video adapter just above the motherboard, oriented on the same plane. An integrated card is not upgradeable, and, in most cases, a faulty video adapter requires that you replace the motherboard. You might be able to replace a separate video adapter if you can find a compatible replacement for it that will fit. To replace

FIGURE 7-5

Removing a hard drive from a laptop computer

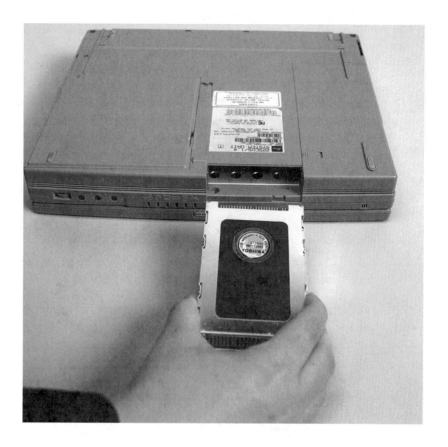

a video adapter, open the case and locate the component, as discussed earlier in "Opening a Laptop Case." This is a bit simpler than replacing a CPU, but it is still a very delicate operation. You will remove the old video adapter and replace it with a new one. As when replacing the CPU, after you close up the case, plug it in and restart the system, running system BIOS setup. Of course, if you can even see the Power On Self Test (POST) information and access the BIOS screen, you've won half the battle. The rest will depend on whether the operating system drivers support the adapter or whether you can access all of its functionality.

I/O Devices

As with a PC, the primary input devices for a laptop are the keyboard and a pointing device. The primary output device is the display. We will now look closer at the display, keyboards, and other I/O devices designed for portability.

Keyboards   Due to size constraints, the built-in keyboard in a laptop has thinner keys that do not have the vertical travel that those on traditional keyboards do, so they do not give the same tactile feedback. If you often work in low-light environments, you may want a laptop with a *keyboard backlight*, a feature that gently lights the keyboard for ease of use. Just a few years ago, this feature was in only a few premium laptops, such as the MacBook Pro, but in the last few years manufacturers have created more models with this feature, or offer it as an upgrade option, but it is still not common. If you choose a laptop with a backlit keyboard, accept the fact that using it will be yet another draw on the battery. You can also purchase an external keyboard with this feature.

A laptop keyboard, as shown in Figure 7-6, has the alphanumeric, ENTER keys, function keys (F1, F2, ... F12), and some of the modifier keys (SHIFT, CTRL, ALT, and CAPS LOCK) in the same orientation to one another as on a full-sized keyboard. But many of the special keys—the directional arrow keys and the INSERT, DELETE, PAGE UP, and PAGE DOWN keys—are in different locations.

The separate numeric keypad disappeared a long time ago from laptops. Rather, the keypad is completely absent or the function integrates into the alphanumeric keys, and small numbers on the sides of keys or in a different color on the top of each key indicate what number they are. Each alphanumeric key normally produces two characters—one when pressing the key alone and another when NUM LOCK is toggled on to enable the keypad. Or this may be controlled by pressing the function-modifying *FN key* while pressing certain marked keys. This special modifier key enables the alternate functions for a laptop keyboard. Look for special symbols on several laptop keys. For instance, one of the standard function keys across the

FIGURE 7-6

A laptop
keyboard

top of the keyboard may have the symbol of a display screen on it. Pressing the FN key and this key together toggles the video output among the display modes, as described in the discussion that follows on displays. Another specially marked key on the keyboard works with the FN key to enable or disable the speaker. Figure 7-7 shows the symbol that appears on the screen of our laptop when the FN-F12 key combination is pressed to turn the speaker volume up. Pressing the FN-F11 key combination on this laptop will lower the speaker volume. The FN-F4 key combination dims the display, while FN-F5 turns up the display brightness. Yet another combination toggles the Wi-Fi and Bluetooth radio transmissions on and off, displaying the symbol shown in Figure 7-8 on the screen. While they may differ from one manufacturer to another, if you look you will see these marked keys.

Laptop keyboards have greatly improved over the last two decades, but, for a variety of reasons, users often wish to use an external keyboard. A user who employs the numeric keypad may add an external keyboard or a separate numeric keypad. Some people simply prefer the tactile feel of certain external keyboards and will add the external keyboard when they are at home or in the office—sometimes just because an external keyboard lets you sit farther from the screen.

Like other laptop components, you can replace the built-in laptop keyboard if you can find a suitable replacement. So if a laptop keyboard became damaged and you decide that you must replace it and you have determined that it is cost effective to do so, follow the manufacturer's instructions. Alternatively, you might just decide to use an external keyboard—a very inexpensive alternative since you simply plug it in. The only trick is to buy a keyboard with the correct connector. Most new laptops have done away with the mini-DIN keyboard connector, and they all now have USB ports—the newer the laptop, the more USB ports it will have. In some portables, plugging in an external keyboard disables the onboard keyboard while in others it stays fully functional with an external keyboard plugged in. You can manually disable it per the manufacturer's instructions.

FIGURE 7-7

This icon on the screen displays briefly while you use the key combination to increase the speaker volume.

FIGURE 7-8

This symbol displays on the screen when you use the keyboard to turn off Wi-Fi and Bluetooth.

on the **!** **ⓘ** o b

With the availability of USB devices, it is convenient to add a USB mouse and full-sized keyboard to your laptop, and you can add or remove it as needed. This allows the use of a full-sized keyboard when you are not traveling. Or, if you do a great deal of number-entry work while traveling and feel more comfortable using a traditional numeric keypad, consider buying a separate numeric keypad (without the keyboard) and attaching it to the laptop or desktop PC.

Pointing Devices When shopping for a new laptop, you can expect to find a built-in pointing device on all the popular models. After experimenting with a variety of such devices, most manufacturers have settled on the *touchpad* (or *touch pad*), a smooth, rectangular, touch-sensitive panel sitting in front of the keyboard, as shown in Figure 7-9. Moving your finger across the surface of the touchpad moves the pointer on the display, and you use the buttons next to the touchpad as you would use those on a mouse or trackball. Alternatively, you can tap the touchpad in place of clicking a button.

Other pointing devices you may encounter on laptops are variations of a *pointing stick* (or *point stick*)—a very tiny, joystick-type device that usually sits in the center of the keyboard, sometimes between the G, H, and B keys. Barely protruding above the level of the keys, this device usually has a replaceable plastic cap for traction and two buttons located in the front of the keyboard. You operate a pointing stick by pushing it in the direction you want to drive the on-screen pointer. Lenovo's version

FIGURE 7-9

A laptop
touchpad

of the pointing stick is *TrackPoint* and you can see the red-tipped TrackPoint on their laptops. In fact, the entire keyboard on the ThinkPad line is called the TrackPoint keyboard. Many techs use this term generically as *track point*.

Because these devices are small and can be difficult to use, people often attach an external desktop mouse with a PS/2 mini-DIN or USB connector. If connecting a mouse to a PS/2 mini-DIN connector, you need to restart the computer to have it be recognized. It is not necessary to turn the system off first if the mouse connects to a USB port. Check for a small switch on or near the touchpad that acts as a toggle to turn it on or off. Or look for a function key combination to do this. Figure 7-10 shows the notification that briefly appeared when we disabled the touchpad. Some portables will automatically disable the on-board pointing device when an external pointing device is connected.

If the installed pointing device, such as a touchpad, fails, replacing it is much like replacing the keyboard because you need to locate a suitable replacement and then open the computer and install it. If your touchpad fails and the laptop is not still under warranty, consider using an external pointing device.

Displays   A laptop has a flat-panel display integrated into the "lid" of the case and connected to the integrated video adapter. A laptop display is usually some form of LCD display as described in Chapter 5—most often lit with *light-emitting diodes (LEDs)*. Some small-screen laptops or touchscreen tablets have organic light-emitting diode (OLED), active matrix organic light-emitting diode (AMOLED), or Super AMOLED screens, also described in Chapter 5. Some high-end laptop displays support 3-D, which also requires a built-in High Definition Multimedia Interface (HDMI) video adapter. An LCD screen requires an internal *inverter* to convert the DC current from the power adapter or battery to the AC current the display requires.

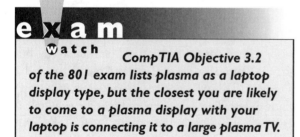

FIGURE 7-10

This notification appears when you disable the touchpad.

Most laptop video adapters can drive two displays—the integrated flat-panel display and an external display. You can use the external display as a replacement for the integrated display, display the same desktop on both simultaneously, or use the external display in addition to the built-in display in a multi-monitor configuration, as described in Chapter 5. Use the laptop's FN key that doubles as the DISPLAY MODE toggle key to switch the video output among the display modes: laptop display only, external display only, or both displays. On our laptop the F1 key is the DISPLAY MODE toggle key. Pressing this brings up the options bar shown in Figure 7-11, from which you can quickly select among four display modes. We often use this laptop with a projector, so this gives us a quick way to switch to the project. When we do that, we prefer to use the Extend option, so that we have the PowerPoint program open on the laptop display, while we direct the slideshow to the projector.

The three main components of the video system in a laptop include the LCD screen, the inverter, and the built-in video adapter.

The video display is one of the most expensive laptop components, and one of the most difficult to replace. If you have a failed laptop display and manage to find a suitable replacement, follow the manufacturer's instructions for removing the old display and installing the replacement.

Media/Accessory Bay

To save space, a laptop may contain a *media bay*, a compartment that holds a single media device that you can switch with another. For instance, you may switch an optical drive, a secondary hard drive, or a floppy drive into and out of a single bay, but you can use only one device in the bay at a time. Figure 7-12 shows a media bay and two drives that you can alternate in the bay. This type of bay, also called an *accessory bay*, is now less common, since so many external accessories and drives are available with USB, FireWire, or External Serial Advanced Technology Attachment (eSATA) interfaces, including external media bays that hold optical drives or hard drives.

FIGURE 7-11

The Display Mode toggle key on our laptop lets us quickly choose a mode.

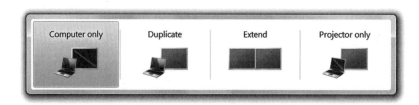

FIGURE 7-12

A media bay in a laptop, with two drives that you can swap into this bay

Wireless Communications

Wireless devices use radio waves or infrared light waves. The major wireless technologies support a range of distances from one meter to many miles. Those wireless devices that communicate over the shortest distances create a personal area network (PAN). Infrared and Bluetooth are two standards for such short-distance networking. Other types of wireless devices have a range in the hundreds of feet and work in a wireless local area network (WLAN). A group of wireless network standards we lump together as Wi-Fi are used in WLANs. When you need to communicate wirelessly through your laptop over a distance of miles, you need a cellular wireless device; another term for this type of network is a wireless wide area network (WWAN). We will define these three types of networks more specifically in Chapter 14. For now, we'll look at wireless network devices for laptops.

Infrared   One technology that allows you to create a personal area network for your devices to communicate with your laptop is *infrared (IR)*. These devices use light waves in the infrared spectrum (normally invisible to the human eye) to communicate with each other through infrared transceiver ports. The ports must comply with the *Infrared Data Association's (IrDA)* data transmission standards. IrDA is an organization that creates specifications for infrared wireless communication. Microsoft Windows supports plug and play for IrDA infrared devices. IrDA infrared devices support a maximum transmission speed of 4 Mbps. You can add IrDA devices to a system by installing an infrared adapter. They come in a variety of interfaces, but USB is the most common. Any two IrDA-enabled devices can communicate with each other. The drawback to this type of communication is the very short distance supported (one meter) and the fact that it requires line-of-sight, so the ports on the communicating devices must be directly facing one another with nothing in the way.

Bluetooth   *Bluetooth* is another wireless standard. Bluetooth devices use radio waves to communicate with each other. Some laptops come with a Bluetooth adapter built in. If not, you can purchase one—often along with one or more wireless devices that use the Bluetooth standard. A popular peripheral package is a Bluetooth keyboard and mouse bundled with a Bluetooth transmitter adapter using a USB interface. Many cell phones have Bluetooth built in for use with wireless headsets and for communicating with a Bluetooth-enabled computer to share the phonebook and other data stored in the phone.

Although one thinks of Bluetooth as mainly a very-short-distance communications standard, there are actually three classes of Bluetooth, each with its own power requirements, and each with a power-dependent distance. Class 1 Bluetooth devices have a distance limit of about 100 meters, whereas Class 2 devices are limited to about 10 meters, and Class 3 are limited to 1 meter. The class we describe in this chapter is Class 3. Microsoft Windows operating systems have included support for the Bluetooth standard since Windows XP. On laptops with an integrated Bluetooth adapter, you use a switch on the case or a key combination to enable or disable the adapter. This may be the same mechanism used to enable or disable a Wi-Fi adapter, if both are integrated.

ex**a**m

ⓦ**a t c h**   *When you have your laptop with you on a commercial airliner, you are asked before takeoff to turn off all wireless radio devices. Use the switch or special key combination on your laptop to turn off built-in Bluetooth and Wi-Fi adapters.*

Wi-Fi   Most new laptops today come with a Wi-Fi radio frequency networking adapter built in. For those laptops without built-in Wi-Fi, a variety of Wi-Fi adapters is available in some form of PC Card, Mini PCIe, or as an external USB device. We will describe Wi-Fi in more detail in Chapter 14 and talk about configuring a Wi-Fi adapter in Chapter 15. The built-in Wi-Fi adapter will usually have a hidden antenna integrated into the screen lid and a separate switch on the case that enables and disables the adapter. Or it will have a key combination (such as FN-F2) with that function. Either way, the wireless adapter can be accidently disabled. Therefore, any time someone using a laptop complains about the loss of wireless communications, try the switch or key combination to see if that corrects the problem.

Figure 7-13 shows a Wi-Fi wireless LAN adapter installed in a Mini PCIe slot. This particular adapter is actually two in one, as it is both a Wi-Fi adapter and a Bluetooth adapter. The antennas for this card run through the small black cable visible on the upper right of the card and running to the upper left. It leads up through the lid hinge into the lid behind the screen. If the antenna fails, it requires dismantling the screen of the laptop.

on the job

The switch to enable or disable a wireless adapter is often very easy to accidently trigger, causing the wireless to turn off. If you support laptop users, educate yourself on the method used on each laptop so that you can help a client who accidently disables the wireless adapter.

Cellular WAN As stated earlier, a cellular network is a WWAN, or *cellular WAN*. Participation in a cellular network requires some type of subscription plan with the cellular provider. The major cellular telecommunications providers now offer a variety of options for data communications over the cellular networks, but unlike Wi-Fi, laptop manufacturers do not usually build cellular adapters into their systems, although several providers bundle their adapter and a contract plan with

FIGURE 7-13

A Mini PCIe WLAN card installed in a laptop

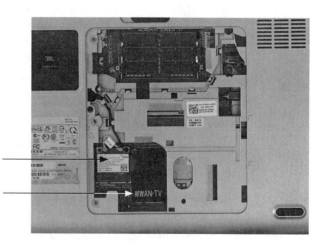

A wireless LAN (WLAN) adapter

An empty bus connector for either a WWAN or a TV tuner card

certain e-books and tablets. And more and more, laptops have a slot available for an optional WWAN adapter. Although this is not usually considered something a user should add, it makes it easy for the manufacturer or supplier to add a WWAN card as an option when you order your laptop. Notice in Figure 7-13 the Mini PCIe slot is reserved for either a WWAN adapter or a TV tuner card.

If there is no cellular adapter installed, or an appropriate internal slot is not available, you need to contact a cell provider, sign up for the service, and buy a cellular adapter from that provider. You must be sure the card they offer is of a type (PC Card, CardBus, ExpressCard, Mini PCIe, etc.) that will work in your laptop. Then install it as you would any device in that format.

Wired Communications

When it comes to wired communications, the choices are the same as those for a desktop PC—dial-up modem or Ethernet. Chapter 14 offers the basics of these networking technologies and Chapter 15 tells you how to install and configure them.

Modem   The need for using a dial-up connection to connect to the Internet or to a business network was once so common that you simply expected a laptop to have an integrated modem. That is no longer the case, and if you are ordering a new laptop and require a modem, you will need to order it as an option, in which case it may be built in or may be an add-on. If it's an add-on, consider buying a USB modem, which is the size of a flash drive. We recommend either buying a USB modem with its own cable or purchasing an extension cable so that the modem isn't sticking straight out from the USB port where you can easily bump or damage the port itself.

Whether the modem is built in or external, it has an RJ-11 connector (described in Chapter 4). To connect to the Internet all you need is the services of an Internet service provider (ISP) that still offers dial-up, and then connect a cable between the modem and a land-based phone line. You will use a phone number and instructions provided by the ISP. Learn how to configure a dial-up connection in Chapter 15.

If a built-in modem fails, you should determine if a replacement modem is available from the manufacturer. You will probably find it is more cost effective to buy a replacement modem with a USB interface, although this adds the inconvenience of more equipment to pack when traveling and the need to locate the modem and connect it to your laptop.

Ethernet   Most, if not all, laptops now come with a built-in Ethernet adapter for connecting to a wired network. The only part of a built-in Ethernet adapter visible on the outside of the case is an RJ-45 connector (described in Chapter 4). As with a built-in modem, if your built-in Ethernet adapter fails, you will need to research the replacement options, and you will face the same choice between the higher cost but convenience of an internal replacement versus the lower cost and inconvenience of an external Ethernet adapter—also now the size of a flash drive. Either buy one that comes on its own USB cable or purchase an extension cable so that the device isn't vulnerable to damage from jostling. Recall our On the Job tip in Chapter 4, in which we recommended using USB extension cables.

Power and Electrical Input Devices

Laptops come with two sources of electrical input: an AC adapter for when AC power is available and a built-in battery for when external power is not available. Laptops also have a special power component called the DC controller and a battery to support the complementary metal-oxide semiconductor (CMOS) chip.

Laptop Batteries   When not plugged into a wall outlet, a laptop computer gets its power from a special rechargeable battery. The typical laptop today has a *lithium ion (Li-Ion) battery*. You may also run into *nickel metal hydride (NiMH)* batteries in older laptops, or a very old laptop may have a heavy, inefficient, and obsolete *nickel-cadmium (NiCD)* battery. A Li-Ion battery is smaller and lighter than its predecessors and produces more power. These rechargeable batteries have a battery life between recharges in the range of five to eight hours at best.

Laptop batteries have only a few years of life, so expect to replace a laptop battery as it approaches two years of age. Purchase replacement batteries from the laptop manufacturer or other sources that specialize in laptop parts or batteries. Laptops allow easy access to the battery to change it. In many cases, the battery fits into a compartment on the bottom or on the side of the computer. Look for a release mechanism, such as a slide, to remove the battery. Figure 7-14 shows a Li-Ion laptop battery removed from a laptop, turned upside down, and resting on the case.

The AC adapter recharges the battery, but if you are not near a wall outlet when the battery's power fades, you will not be able to work until you replace the battery with a fully charged one or until AC power is available again.

Fortunately, most portable systems give you plenty of notice before the battery goes completely dead. Many systems include a power-level meter in the notification area of the Windows desktop that allows you to see the battery's charge level at all times, whereas others simply give you a pop-up warning when the battery's power dips below a certain level. Also, check for a battery indicator light on the laptop case that will flash when the battery is low. Figure 7-15 shows a simple battery tester on a laptop battery. Pressing the button on the left causes the LEDs to light up. In this

FIGURE 7-14

A Li-Ion laptop battery removed from the case

case, all five are lit, showing that the battery is fully charged; fewer lights indicate a depleted battery. While this is not a very precise measurement, it gives you a rough idea of how long you can use your laptop before recharging it.

DC Controller   Most laptops include a *DC controller* that monitors and regulates power usage, providing just the correct amount of DC voltage to each internal component. The other features of DC controllers vary by manufacturer, but typically, they provide short-circuit protection, give "low battery" warnings, and can be configured to shut down the computer automatically when the power is low.

AC Adapter   As described in Chapter 5, the AC adapter is your laptop's external power supply that you plug into an AC power source. Like the power supply in a desktop PC, it converts AC power to DC power. If you must replace an external adapter, simply unplug it and attach a new one that matches the specifications and

FIGURE 7-15

Pressing the button on this battery tester turns on lights that show how much charge is remaining.

plug configuration of the adapter it is replacing. Furthermore, since AC adapters have different output voltages, never use one with any laptop other than the one it was made for.

DC Jack   A *DC jack* is the connector on a laptop to which an AC adapter connects. The actual socket in the jack will vary, as described in Chapter 5. If a DC jack becomes damaged and must be replaced, you may be able to find one from the manufacturer or another source. The entire DC jack assembly is usually no bigger than a single die from a gaming dice. To install it, you must disconnect the power cord, remove the battery, and open the case. Then remove the old DC jack assembly and install the replacement.

CMOS Battery

Like a PC, a laptop has a battery on the motherboard that supports the CMOS chip that holds the system's BIOS settings. If a laptop shows signs of a failing CMOS battery—namely, losing the date and time when the computer is off and also out of main battery power—you will need to investigate the type and location of the battery in the laptop and purchase a replacement only if the laptop's documentation describes how to open it to replace the CMOS battery. While some laptop components are accessible under easy-to-remove panels, the CMOS battery usually requires that you dissemble the case. For instance, our Dell XPS L502X hides the battery under the palmrest—the area in front of the keyboard that contains the touchpad. Further, a laptop CMOS battery may resemble the typical lithium battery, also called a coin-cell battery, or it may be an entire battery pack of coin-sized batteries shrink-wrapped in plastic with a special connector on one end.

Speakers   Laptops often come with very small speakers that provide marginally adequate sound. If these speakers fail, you may be able to find suitable replacements, but a better alternative is to plug external speakers into the laptop using either the earphone jack, if that is all that is available, or other audio-out jacks. Replacing internal laptop speakers is nearly as involved as replacing a video adapter, along with all the inherent dangers of opening the laptop, but plugging in external speakers is risk-free, takes only a few seconds, and will improve the sound output. Be sure to test the speakers after replacing or adding them.

Some built-in laptop speakers are more than adequate for a multimedia laptop, such as the Dell XPS L502X, which comes with very capable 20-watt stereo speakers and a subwoofer, and external speakers may not be necessary unless you want to project sound to a large group of people. Flip back to Figure 7-6, which shows a laptop keyboard, and notice the screens that cover the stereo speakers visible on either side of the keyboard. Figure 7-16 shows the subwoofer (measuring about 2" × 3") on the bottom of that same laptop.

Miscellaneous Accessories

There are perhaps more accessories for laptops than for desktop PCs. Two categories worth noting are first, port replicators and docking stations, and second, physical security devices.

Port Replicators and Docking Stations

The laptop owner who uses a laptop while traveling, but also as a desktop replacement, usually has a "base of operations" office. This office is where the owner will use external devices such as a keyboard, printer, display, mouse, and external hard drive storage. The user must connect and disconnect the laptop from these components every time he or she returns to or leaves the office with the laptop. The solution to that inconvenience is a port replicator or docking station.

A *port replicator*, a device that remains on the desktop with external devices connected to its ports, can make this task less time-consuming by providing a single connection to the laptop and permanent connection to these external devices.

A more advanced (and more expensive) alternative to the port replicator is a *docking station*. In addition to the ports normally found on a port replicator, a docking station may include full-size expansion slots and various drives. In the past, port replicators and docking stations were always proprietary—often only fitting one model of laptop. If the manufacturer did not make one of these devices to fit your laptop, you had no options. Now you can easily find an inexpensive "universal" port replicator or docking station that interfaces with a laptop via a USB port. Whether you have a proprietary device that fits your laptop or one that uses a USB connector, be sure to read the documentation that comes with the docking station or port replicator and follow the instructions for connecting and disconnecting the device.

FIGURE 7-16

A subwoofer speaker on the bottom of a laptop

Physical Security Devices   Most laptops have a security slot, usually on the rear-left corner of the case, which is easy to overlook at approximately ¼" × ⅛". This slot accepts a lock head from a laptop security device—usually a cable lock resembling a bicycle cable lock. The cable is usually made of high-quality woven wire—sometimes combined with other materials for added strength, and usually covered with a plastic sleeve. To secure a computer with a cable lock, first wrap the cable around a strong stationary object and then pass the lock head through the loop on the opposite end of the cable before inserting it into the security slot. Engage the lock to secure it within the slot. These locks are available from several manufacturers and come with a variety of locking mechanisms, such as key or combination lock.

A less common physical security device for a laptop is what one manufacturer, TryTen, calls a Laptop Locker. This steel box, about the size of a briefcase, encloses a laptop, but has openings for cables and ventilation so that a locked-up laptop can be used but not removed from the locked case. This requires an external display, keyboard, and pointing device.

SCENARIO & SOLUTION

I plug my laptop into an external display, printer, and keyboard every time I return to the office. Is there an easier way to do this?	Yes. Plug each of these devices into a port replicator and leave them there. To access the devices, simply attach your laptop to the port replicator.
What important step in the disassembly of a laptop will help you the most when you attempt to reassemble it?	Document and label cable and screw locations.
What laptop component allocates just the right amount of DC power to each internal component?	The DC controller.

CERTIFICATION OBJECTIVE

■ **802: 1.5**   *Given a scenario, use Control Panel utilities*

CompTIA A+ Exam 802 Objective 1.5 contains a long list of Windows Control Panel utilities with a wide range of functionality. We will discuss most of these in later chapters, as appropriate, but here we will address an important subset for use on laptops, the power options. In this section you'll learn about Windows power management features that power down the screen and hard drive when it detects no activity, and power-saving modes called Hibernate, Sleep, Standby, and Suspend. You'll also learn about various power options as well as when and under what circumstances these various power plans are used.

Power Options

Nearly every component in a modern laptop has some sort of *power management* feature, a group of options in the hardware and the operating system that allows you to minimize the use of power—especially, but not exclusively—to conserve a laptop's battery life. In fact, even desktop computers come with power-saving features. Many devices, like the hard drive, will power down when not in use; and CPUs and other circuitry will draw less power when they have less demand for their services. Displays will power down after a configurable period of time during which there was no activity from the mouse or keyboard. If a component is not drawing power, it is not creating heat, so power management and cooling go hand-in-hand.

Power Management Standards

Supporting the power management features in laptop hardware requires that the system BIOS, the chipset, the operating system, and device drivers be aware of these features and be able to control and manage them. Several standards and practices have come together for power management to work at both the hardware and operating system level. They include SMM, APM, and ACPI, described next.

System Management Mode

For over two decades, Intel CPUs have included a group of features called *System Management Mode (SMM)*, and other CPU manufacturers have followed suit. SMM allows a CPU to reduce its speed without losing its place, so to speak, so it does not stop working altogether. In addition, a CPU using SMM mode triggers power savings in other components. System BIOSs and operating systems take advantage of SMM. Intel took the first two steps for involving the BIOS and operating system in power management when they developed two standards, APM and ACPI.

Advanced Power Management

Advanced Power Management (APM) defines four power-usage operating levels: Full On, APM Enabled, APM Standby, and APM Suspend. Details of these operating levels are not important, as they are now a subset of the next standard, ACPI.

Advanced Configuration and Power Interface

Advanced Configuration and Power Interface (ACPI) includes all the power-usage levels of APM, plus two more. It also supports the soft-power feature described in Chapter 5. ACPI defines how to configure the power management feature in the BIOS settings and has seven power-usage levels, called *power states*. These range from a power state in which the computer is fully on and all devices are functional, through several sleeping states to two power-off states. The details of ACPI are not important, as long as you know how to configure power management in Windows.

Active State Power Management

Active State Power Management (ASPM) is a standard for PCI Express that allows power to be incrementally reduced to individual PCIe serial links (paths). Windows enables or disables a link based on several parameters, including the system power plan, PCIe capabilities, and more. In the Windows graphical user interface (GUI), this is called *Link State Power Management*.

Configuring Power Management in Windows

Getting the most out of your laptop battery depends on how you manage the use of the battery's power. Using the Power Options Control Panel utility in Windows, you can configure the power management settings to minimize the power usage of laptop components. While this utility is available in Windows on all computers, you will find some differences in it when you compare Windows installations on desktops versus laptops and when you compare Windows 7 with Windows 8. Figure 7-17 shows the Windows 7 Power Options utility on a Dell laptop on which Windows 7 was preinstalled. Notice the references to the Dell Battery Meter and the Dell plan. Also notice the screen brightness control at the bottom. Dimming the screen helps conserve power use, and many find dimming the screen in low-light environments is a bit easier on their eyes. There is also a setting in the left pane for choosing what closing the lid does—a very laptop-centric setting. This option is not shown in Figure 7-18, in the retail version of Windows 7, installed on a desktop PC. Missing also is any branded information, such as the Dell Battery Meter and Dell power plan. Power Options on a PC does not include a battery meter, because the desktop computer would never need to run on battery.

on the **j o b**

The initial Windows 8 Power Options is identical to the one in Windows 7, with some new twists in the more advanced options.

FIGURE 7-17

Windows 7
Power Options
on a Dell laptop
computer

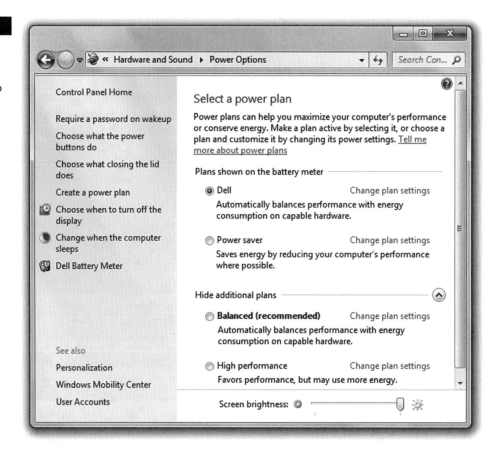

Now check out the Power Options utility in Windows 8, shown in Figure 7-19. This was installed on the same Dell laptop, but since it was not preinstalled by Dell and was not installed as an upgrade, it installed as a more generic version. When the laptop hardware was detected during installation, Windows automatically installed support for the laptop hardware. This is evidenced by the setting for what closing the lid does, as well as the screen brightness control. While it lacks the battery meter option seen in the Dell factory installation, Windows 8 does have a battery meter in the notification area of the taskbar in Windows desktop view.

FIGURE 7-18

Windows 7
Power Options
on a generic
desktop PC

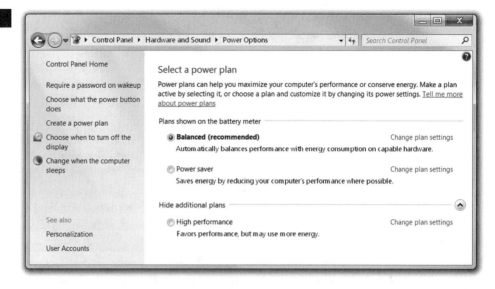

FIGURE 7-19

Windows 8
Power Options
folder on a Dell
laptop computer

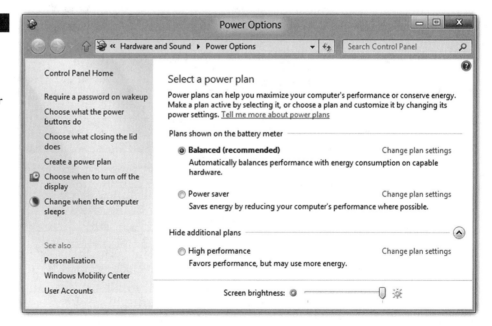

Using Power-Saving Modes

Imagine you are a business traveler waiting to board a commercial jet. You arrive at the airport and find yourself at the departure gate with 90 minutes to spare. Is this wasted time? No. You open your laptop, complete a report on your trip, and begin to create an expense request. You are not quite finished with it when it is time to board. Rather than completely shutting down your computer, you put it into a sleep mode that will preserve your open files just as they are, slip the machine into your carry-on case, and board the plane. Once settled in your seat, you open your laptop and within seconds you are back where you left off. The actual sleep mode you select and what it does depends on the version of Windows you are running. You can also set the time period for mouse and keyboard inactivity that must pass before the computer goes into power-saving mode. We will look at where and how you make these settings, but first we'll define power-saving sleep modes: Sleep, Suspend, Standby, and Hibernate.

Standby, Sleep, and Suspend   In Windows XP you would select *Standby*, a power management sleep state that would save your desktop and all open files in RAM memory in a working state. In this state, the computer appears to be off, and when you wish to resume, you simply press the power button. Your desktop either appears immediately, or after you log on if your computer is configured to require a logon. Standby requires a power source to be available, so when the laptop is running on a battery and the battery runs out of power, any data saved for Standby mode but not saved to disk will be lost. Once configured, the system will go into Standby after the time period defined by the sleep timer or when you select Standby from the Windows XP Shutdown menu.

Standby underwent a name change to *Sleep* beginning with Windows Vista. Plus, Microsoft added a new sleep state called Hybrid Sleep that combines the Sleep state with Hibernate (see the next section on Hibernate), saving contents of memory into RAM as well as to disk. Hybrid Sleep is turned on by default in Windows on desktop PCs, but off by default on laptops.

Suspend is the term used in Windows 95 to describe any of these actions, since they all suspend your work. Suspend-to-disk is what we now call Hibernate. Suspend-to-RAM is standby or sleep. The term Suspend was tied to the earlier power management standard, APM, but went out of use when Windows and more hardware manufacturers adopted the newer ACPI power management standard. Suspend is an obsolete term and it is mentioned here only because it is listed in Exam 802 Objective 1.5.

Hibernate   The *Hibernate* power-saving mode uses hard drive space to save all the programs and data that are in memory at the time you choose this mode. The computer then completely shuts down, using no power while it is hibernating. Like Standby, Hibernate lets you stop work on your computer but quickly pick up where you left off. It takes slightly longer to go into and out of hibernation. Hibernate is a safer option as it does not require any power since everything is saved to disk.

Windows 8 adds another twist to the Hibernate feature. When you shut down a Windows 8 computer, Windows actually uses a form of hibernation—not the entire saving-all-your-programs-and-data-to-disk hibernation, but a saving to disk of the Windows OS kernel as it appears in memory at the moment you shut down. As a result, Windows 8 startup is very fast because it brings the Windows kernel out of hibernation, fully configured and ready to run. This startup using the hibernated kernel is called *Hybrid Boot*, and it is enabled by default in Windows 8.

Configuring Low Battery Options

On a laptop, the Windows notification area of the taskbar displays a tiny battery icon that serves as an indicator of battery charge level. Hover the mouse pointer over this icon to see battery charge status, as shown in Figure 7-20. Click the icon to display a pop-up menu (Figure 7-21) that will allow you to switch power plans, adjust the screen brightness, or open Power Options for even more choices. To quickly change power plans from here, click the radio button next to the plan you wish to select. To view and change plan settings, click the battery icon, and then click More Power Options.

Exploring Power Plans/Power Schemes

Windows has preconfigured power settings. Each group of settings was called a Power Scheme in Windows XP, and is called a Power Plan in Windows Vista, Windows 7, and Windows 8. Of the preconfigured plans, the Balanced Power Plan is a good bet for most laptop users because it balances power savings with performance. However,

The battery
charge status

FIGURE 7-21

Click the battery
icon to access a
pop-up menu.

if better performance is more important to you than battery life, select the High
Performance power plan. If you need every minute of battery power you can squeeze
out of your laptop while away from the office, then you should select the Power
Saver power plan.

Exercise 7-2 will guide you as you create a new plan in Windows 7. If you have
Windows Vista, the screens you will see are similar to those in Windows 7. If you
are working in Windows XP, you will see different screens, but you should be able
to find your way around if you carefully read the descriptions and press F1 to call up
context-sensitive help at any point.

EXERCISE 7-2

Exploring Power Options on a Laptop

For this exercise, you will need a computer with Windows 7 installed. It is not
necessary to have a laptop for this, although there will be some differences. For
instance, the screen brightness and lid-closing settings will not be available.

1. Open the Start menu and in the Search box, type **power options**.

2. In the search result list, click Power Options.

3. In the Power Options folder, notice which plan is selected.

4. In the left pane, click to select Create A Power Plan.

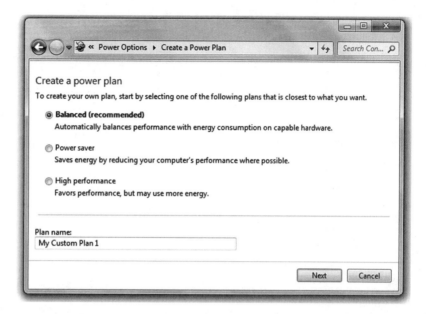

5. In the Create A Power Plan folder, select one of the plans and click Next.

6. Notice the two groups of settings—one for when you're on battery and one for when the laptop is plugged in.

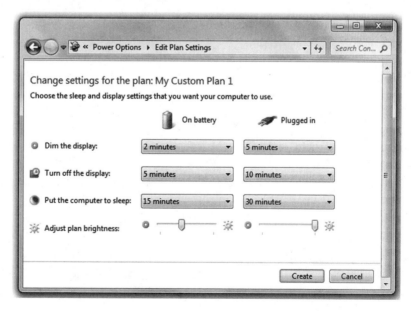

7. Now make changes to the settings.

8. Click Create to save the new plan.

9. The new plan is now listed in Power Options.

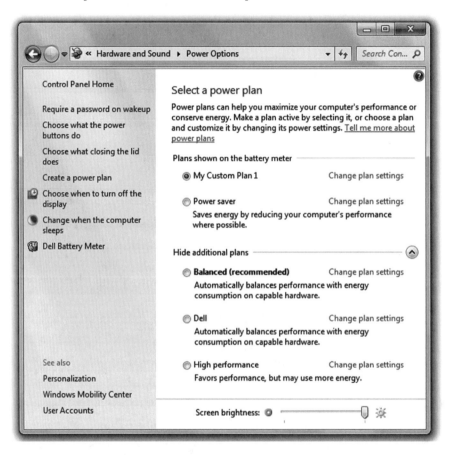

Changing Power Settings

To dig even deeper into power settings, open Power Options, and click Change Plan Settings for the current power plan. Then, in the Edit Plan Setting folder, click Change Advanced Power Settings. This will display the Advanced settings shown in Figure 7-22 where you can scroll through a long list of settings, each of which varies based on whether the computer is on battery or plugged in and, with the exception

FIGURE 7-22

In the Edit Plan Settings folder, select Change Advanced Power Settings; then use the scrollbar to view and/or change various power settings.

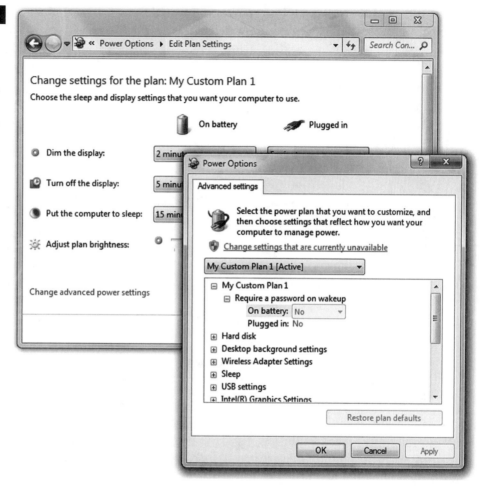

of the Require A Password On Wakeup setting, controls the power management for an individual component. The actual items in this list may vary, based on what hardware is present (note the Intel Graphics Settings). Following is a sample list of settings found in both Windows 7 and Windows 8:

■ **Require a password on wakeup**   Select Yes if you want to lock the screen and require a password to unlock the computer when it wakes from Sleep.

■ **Hard disk**   Control how long the system waits after no activity before turning off the hard disk.

- **Desktop background settings**   If the desktop background is a slideshow, this setting will control whether it is available or paused.
- **Wireless adapter settings**   Save power by enabling the power-saving mode for the wireless adapter.
- **Sleep**   Several settings control what length of inactive time will trigger sleep and which sleep mode is used (Sleep, Hybrid Sleep, or Hibernate). Also configure wake timers.
- **USB**   Enable or disable USB selective suspend, a USB feature whereby a device driver can send a message to Windows requesting that the OS put the device into an idle (suspended) state. If this is disabled, Windows puts the device into suspend when the rest of the OS is suspended.
- **Intel Graphics Settings**   Select an Intel power plan for the Intel graphics adapter.
- **Power buttons and lid**   Select what action will occur when (1) the lid is closed, (2) the power button is pressed, and (3) the sleep button (if physically present) is pressed.
- **PCI Express**   Enable or disable Link State Power Management implementation of ASPM power plans.
- **Processor power management**   Configure several power management settings for the system CPU.
- **Display**   Configure power management settings for the display to control when the display is dimmed and by how much. Also enable or disable automatic (adaptive) brightness on systems with ambient light sensors.
- **Multimedia settings**   Control power management under two sets of circumstances: (1) when an external device is playing media shared from this computer, and (2) when this computer is playing video.
- **Internet Explorer**   Select power management settings for when JavaScript is running in Internet Explorer.
- **Battery**   Define what constitutes critical and low battery levels, the actions taken when the critical level is reached, and the notification settings for when low-battery level exists. Also, set the level at which the battery will go into reserve power mode. A smart configuration will issue a warning sound for both low and critical, and place the computer into Sleep or Hibernate (better choice) when the critical level is reached.

on the **Job**

Power management isn't just for laptops, although some features, such as battery management, only apply to laptops. However, minimizing power usage of desktop computers is important to both individuals and big organizations. Therefore, you will want to apply what you learn here to the desktop computers that you support.

SCENARIO & SOLUTION

I use my laptop at work, carrying it with me from meeting to meeting in order to take notes. How can I avoid the hassle of waiting for it to power up at the beginning of each meeting?	Select Sleep when you power down.
When traveling, I would like to save all my work and the desktop when I shut down, and have the laptop start up with my work state exactly as it was when I stopped. How do I achieve this, plus conserve as much battery life as possible?	Enable Hibernate in the Power Options applet in Control Panel, and then, when you are ready, select Hibernate from the Turn Off Computer dialog box.
How do I configure a different set of behaviors for when my laptop is on battery as opposed to when it is plugged in?	Open the Power Options applet, select Change Plan Settings for the current plan. In the Edit Plan Settings dialog box, you can configure one group of settings for when the laptop is on battery and another set for when it is plugged in.

CERTIFICATION SUMMARY

Most PC technicians will need to understand laptop technologies and how to replace components in them since use of these portable computers remains widespread in both the workplace and the home—even as the sales of newer tablet computers cut into the number of laptops sold each year. Laptops come in many sizes, from the very lightweight ultra-portables or netbooks to desktop replacements and ultra-books.

Although laptops are basically compatible with the Wintel architecture, they use smaller integrated components that, for the most part, do not conform in either form or size with the standard PC components.

A technician should know how to conserve battery usage, and the best Windows tool for doing that is Power Options.

✓ TWO-MINUTE DRILL

Here are some of the key points covered in Chapter 7.

Installing and Upgrading Laptops

❑ A portable computer is any type of computer you can easily transport and that has an all-in-one component layout.

❑ A laptop is a portable computer that can run the same operating systems as a desktop PC, with a keyboard in the base and a display in a hinged top.

❑ Internal and integrated laptop hardware, such as the display, keyboard, pointing device, motherboard, memory, hard drives, and expansion bus, has special scaled-down form factors, but a laptop can use most standard external PC peripherals.

❑ Your laptop disassembly and reassembly processes should include consulting the manufacturer's documentation, using appropriate hand tools, organizing parts, and documenting and labeling cable and screw locations.

❑ Although laptop components are at least partially proprietary, you can find replacement parts from the original manufacturer or from other sources. Always research the cost-effectiveness of replacing parts rather than replacing the entire laptop.

❑ You add memory to a laptop in the form of SODIMM modules installed into slots inside the case. You can also add it in the form of a PC Card, CardBus, or ExpressCard, if slots are available.

❑ PC Card, CardBus, or ExpressCard cards are all PCMCIA standards for external expansion slots and cards, but even the most recent, ExpressCard, has lost favor with manufacturers and is rarely seen on new laptops.

❑ Internal expansion slots include Mini PCI, Mini PCIe, and mSATA.

❑ Laptops often come with built-in communications adapters—including Wi-Fi and Ethernet for LAN connections, IrDA infrared and Bluetooth for short-distance wireless communications, analog modems for dial-up connections, and cellular adapters for connecting to cellular networks.

❑ A laptop comes with two sources of electrical power: a rechargeable battery and an AC adapter.

❑ Laptops allow you to change the battery easily.

❑ Most standard peripherals connect to a laptop using the same techniques for desktop PCs.

❑ Some laptops have a media/accessory bay holding a single device that you can switch with another device that fits in the bay.

❑ Port replicators and docking stations provide permanent connections for external devices used in the laptop user's office. Universal docking stations and port replicators have USB interfaces and, therefore, connect in the same manner as other USB devices.

Power Options

❑ You can use the Windows Power Options utility to configure power management settings in laptops that comply with power management standards through the operating system to shut down the display, the hard drive, and even the entire system after a period of inactivity and/or when the battery is low.

❑ Hibernate is a Windows sleep state that uses hard drive space to save all the programs and data that are in memory at the time you choose this mode. The computer then completely shuts down and requires no power while it is hibernating.

❑ In Windows XP, Standby is a sleep state that conserves power while saving your desktop in RAM memory in a work state; it requires a minimum amount of power. Beginning in Windows Vista, this mode is called Sleep, and there is also a third sleep state that is a hybrid of Sleep and Hibernate, called Hybrid Sleep.

❑ Windows 95 complied with an older power management standard and used the term Suspend for both states that we now call Sleep and Hibernate.

SELF TEST

The following questions will help you measure your understanding of the material presented in this chapter. Read all of the choices carefully because there might be more than one correct answer. Choose all correct answers for each question.

Installing and Upgrading Laptops

1. How many pins are on the latest version of SODIMMs mentioned in this chapter?
   A. 256
   B. 204
   C. 200
   D. 144

2. What is the name for system memory used by the video adapter and, therefore, unavailable to the operating system?
   A. VRAM memory
   B. SODIMM memory
   C. Shared video memory
   D. SRAM memory

3. What built-in component allows laptop use for short periods (hours) without an outside power source?
   A. Keyboard
   B. Touchpad
   C. Pointing stick
   D. Battery

4. A replacement motherboard must match the form factor of the one being replaced and which of the following?
   A. Weight
   B. Manufacturer
   C. Serial number
   D. Electrical connections

5. CPUs for laptops have special power-saving and heat-reducing features, and some have support for which of the following?

 A. Wi-Fi

 B. Video

 C. Audio

 D. Ethernet

6. Which of the following is a laptop component used to convert the DC power from the power adapter or battery to the AC power required by the LCD display?

 A. Inverter

 B. Converter

 C. Power switch

 D. Generator

7. What is the most common laptop memory module?

 A. SORIMM

 B. MicroDIMM

 C. SODIMM

 D. DIMM

8. Which is a common size for a laptop hard drive?

 A. 2.5"

 B. 5"

 C. 3.5"

 D. 1"

9. Which of the following allows you to attach nearly any type of desktop component to a laptop?

 A. Port replicator

 B. Enhanced port replicator

 C. Extended port replicator

 D. Docking station

10. Select the two names for a compartment in some laptops that can hold a media device (secondary hard drive, optical drive, floppy drive, etc.) that you can swap with another device.

 A. Slot

 B. Media bay

 C. USB port

 D. Accessory bay

11. Which of the following is a high-speed serial interface standard that supports PCIe as well as USB 3.0 with transfer rates of up to 5 Gbps?

    A. PC Card

    B. CardBus

    C. ExpressCard

    D. ExpressCard 2.0

12. What two card standards come in types labeled Type I, Type II, and Type III?

    A. PC Card

    B. CardBus

    C. ExpressCard

    D. Mini PCIe

13. Which two wireless communications standards are used between a laptop and nearby devices that are within one meter of the computer? (Select two.)

    A. Cellular

    B. Wi-Fi

    C. Bluetooth

    D. Infrared

14. What is a battery type commonly used in recently built laptops?

    A. Lithium ion

    B. AC adapter

    C. DC controller

    D. Nickel metal hydride

15. This group of keys, usually in a separate area of a desktop keyboard, is often integrated into the main group of alphanumeric keys on a laptop keyboard.

    A. Function keys

    B. Directional arrow keys

    C. Numeric keys

    D. Numeric keypad

16. What are two types of built-in pointing devices often found on laptops?

    A. Trackball

    B. Pointing stick

    C. Keyboard

    D. Touchpad

Power Options

17. What Windows utility can you use to configure low battery options for a laptop?

    A. Power Options

    B. System Properties

    C. Battery Options

    D. BIOS setup

18. Which of the following is the acronym for a standard for incrementally reducing power to individual PCIe serial links?

    A. ACPI

    B. ASPM

    C. APM

    D. SMM

19. What is the name for the power-saving mode supported by Windows Vista, Windows 7, and Windows 8 whereby the contents of memory are saved into RAM as well as to disk?

    A. Hybrid Boot

    B. Suspend

    C. Hybrid Sleep

    D. Fast Start

20. What Windows utility allows you to turn on the option to require a password on wakeup?

    A. Inverter

    B. Display Mode

    C. Power Options

    D. Soft power

SELF TEST ANSWERS

Installing and Upgrading Laptops

1. ☑ **B.** The number of pins on the latest version of SODIMMs mentioned in this chapter is 204.
   ☒ **A,** 256, is not, at this writing, a valid number for pins on any SODIMM. **C,** 200, is the number of pins found in older SODIMMs. **D,** 144, is the number of pins found in some older SODIMMs.

2. ☑ **C.** Shared video memory is the name for system memory used by the video adapter and, therefore, is unavailable to the operating system.
   ☒ **A,** VRAM memory, is incorrect because this type of memory is on a video adapter (Chapter 4). A video adapter with VRAM installed does not need to use system memory. **B,** SODIMM memory, is incorrect because, although this is the physical memory module used in most laptops, the name for the portion of this memory used by the video adapter is what we are looking for. **D,** SRAM memory, is incorrect because SRAM (static RAM) is simply a type of very high-speed RAM.

3. ☑ **D,** battery, is correct because it provides power to the laptop when not plugged into AC power.
   ☒ **A,** keyboard, **B,** touchpad, and **C,** pointing stick, are all incorrect because although they may be built into a laptop, they do not make it possible for a laptop to be used for short periods without an outside power source.

4. ☑ **D.** Electrical connections must match when replacing a laptop motherboard.
   ☒ **A,** weight, is incorrect because weight is irrelevant in selecting a replacement motherboard. **B,** manufacturer, is incorrect because replacement motherboards are available from many manufacturers. **C,** serial number, is incorrect because even the exact model motherboard from the same manufacturer will have a unique serial number.

5. ☑ **A** is correct, as some mobile CPUs have support for Wi-Fi.
   ☒ **B,** video, **C,** audio, and **D,** Ethernet, are all incorrect because they are not integrated into CPUs, but are included in other components.

6. ☑ **A.** Inverter is correct. This component converts DC power to the AC power required by an LCD panel.
   ☒ **B,** converter, is incorrect because a converter does just the opposite, converting AC power to DC power. **C,** power switch, is incorrect because the power switch simply turns the main power to the laptop on and off. **D,** generator, is incorrect because this is not a component of a laptop. A generator generates power using an engine powered by fuel such as gasoline or diesel.

7. ☑ **C.** SODIMM is correct because this is the most common memory module. SODIMM is a scaled-down version of the DIMM memory module.

☒ **A,** SORIMM, is incorrect because this is a now-obsolete memory module form not discussed in the book. **B,** MicroDIMM, is incorrect because this module is half the size of SODIMM and is used in handheld computers and less often in laptops. **D,** DIMM, is incorrect because this is a full-sized memory module for desktop PCs.

8. ☑ **A.** 2.5" is correct because this is the most common size of a laptop hard drive.

☒ **B,** 5", is incorrect because this very large size is not used in laptops. **C,** 3.5", is incorrect because this is also a large size that is not used in laptops but is common in desktop PCs. **D,** 1", is incorrect (at this writing) because it is not a size commonly used in laptops.

9. ☑ **D.** A docking station allows you to attach nearly any type of desktop component to a laptop. The docking station can remain on the desk with all the desired devices installed or connected to it. To access these devices, simply plug the laptop into the docking station.

☒ **A,** port replicator, and **B,** enhanced port replicator, are incorrect because they do not allow access to the number and variety of devices that a docking station does. **C,** extended port replicator, is incorrect because this is not a real type of portable system component.

10. ☑ **B and D.** Media bay and accessory bay are the correct names for the compartment some laptops have for swapping between one device and another.

☒ **A,** slot, is incorrect because that is the socket a circuit card plugs into. **C,** USB port, is incorrect because it is what a USB cable plugs into.

11. ☑ **D.** ExpressCard 2.0 is a high-speed serial interface standard using multiple serial pathways to achieve transfer rates of up to 5 Gbps.

☒ **A,** PC Card, and **B,** CardBus, are incorrect because both are standards for parallel interfaces. **C,** ExpressCard, is incorrect because it can refer to the first ExpressCard standard, which ran at speeds of up to 480 megabits per second.

12. ☑ **A and B.** PC Card and CardBus are the two card standards that come in types labeled Type I, Type II, and Type III.

☒ **C,** ExpressCard, and **D,** Mini PCIe, are incorrect because they are entirely different form factors from the cards that are labeled Type I, Type II, and Type III.

13. ☑ **C and D.** Bluetooth and infrared are two wireless communications standards used between a laptop and nearby devices that are within one meter of the computer.

☒ **A,** cellular, is incorrect because this is technology that can be used to connect a laptop to the Internet. **B,** Wi-Fi, is incorrect because this technology connects a laptop to a wireless local area network (WLAN).

14. ☑ **A.** Lithium ion (Li-Ion) is the battery type commonly used in recently built laptops.
    ☒ **B,** AC adapter, is incorrect because this is the laptop's power supply that plugs into an AC power source. **C,** DC controller, is incorrect because this is not a battery type, but a laptop component that monitors and regulates power usage. **D,** nickel metal hydride, is incorrect because this type of battery is more common in older laptops.

15. ☑ **D.** Numeric keypad is correct because this group of keys often integrates into the alphanumeric keys in order to save space.
    ☒ **A,** function keys, is incorrect because these are usually in their normal position across the top of the keyboard. **B,** directional arrow keys, is incorrect because these are often (but not always) separate on the laptop keyboard. **C,** numeric keys, is incorrect because these are usually in their normal position in the row immediately below the function keys.

16. ☑ **B and D.** Pointing stick and touchpad are two types of built-in pointing devices often found on laptops.
    ☒ **A,** trackball, is incorrect because although it is sometimes built into a laptop, the pointing stick and touchpad are used more often. **C,** keyboard, is incorrect because although this is an input device, it is not a pointing device.

Power Options

17. ☑ **A.** Power Options is the utility where you can configure a low-battery alarm for a laptop.
    ☒ **B,** System Properties, is incorrect because you cannot configure a low-battery alarm here. **C,** Battery Options, is incorrect because there is no such utility in standard Windows. **D,** BIOS setup, is incorrect because BIOS setup is not in Windows, but at the system level of the computer.

18. ☑ **B.** ASPM is correct, as this is the acronym for Active State Power Management, a standard for incrementally reducing power to individual PCIe serial links.
    ☒ **A,** ACPI, the acronym for Advanced Configuration and Power Interface, is not the standard for incrementally reducing power to PCIe serial links. **C,** APM, or Advanced Power Management, is incorrect because this is a standard for four power-usage operating levels in a computer. **D,** SMM, or System Management Mode, is incorrect because it is a group of power-saving features in Intel CPUs.

19. ☑ **C.** Hybrid Sleep is the name for the power-saving mode supported by Windows Vista, Windows 7, and Windows 8 whereby the contents of memory are saved into RAM, as well as to disk.
    ☒ **A,** Hybrid Boot, is incorrect because this is the method used by Windows 8 at startup in which the hibernated kernel from the last shutdown is quickly brought into memory to speed up startup. **B,** Suspend, is incorrect because this is simply an old term for power management features, such as Standby, Sleep, and Hibernate. **D,** Fast Start, is incorrect because it is not even a term discussed in this book.

20. ☑ **C.** Power Options is the utility allows you to turn on the option to require a password on wakeup.

☒ **A,** inverter, is incorrect because this is a device that converts DC power to AC power. **B,** Display Mode, is not a Windows utility, but can refer to actual video modes described in Chapter 5, or the video output options available on a laptop, such as laptop display only, external display only, or both displays. **D,** soft power, is incorrect because this is a power supply and motherboard feature, not a Windows utility.

8

Client-Side Virtualization

I T professionals who support desktop or server systems need to keep up-to-date on the newest operating systems and applications. This can become expensive if they use dedicated computers for testing new software. But many do not. They use virtualization software to run the desktop or server OSs in a test environment, isolated from their organization's network. You can too, once you learn how to work with the latest technologies in virtualization.

In Chapter 6, when we described components for a virtualization workstation, we defined a few terms associated with virtualization, saving the bulk of the information for this chapter. Those terms defined in Chapter 6 include virtualization workstation and virtual machine. In this chapter we give the big picture of virtualization with examples of the different types. Then we will compare server-side virtualization with client-side virtualization, and provide more details on client-side virtualization to guide you through the hands-on experience of installing and configuring the software that supports desktop virtualization as an example of client-side virtualization.

CERTIFICATION OBJECTIVE

■ **802: 1.9** *Explain the basics of client-side virtualization*

As you prepare for the CompTIA A+ certification exams, be ready to answer questions about the basics of client-side virtualization, including being able to define a hypervisor and install and use one. You should understand the purpose of virtual machines and be able to describe resource requirements for client-side virtualization, emulators, and networks, as well as the security requirements. In this chapter we go somewhat beyond the actual CompTIA A+ exam objectives to give you a broader understanding of client-side virtualization because, for over a decade, we have found it to be a very useful tool, and feel almost evangelical about bringing this knowledge to new IT workers. To that end, this chapter begins with an overview of virtualization, introducing the many purposes of virtualization and the part that hypervisors play in virtualization of operating systems. Then we will look at the specifics of Windows client virtualization, beginning with your choices for doing it, the hardware requirements, and the types of virtual machines, and ultimately we home in on client-side virtualization and give you an opportunity for hands-on experience. When you complete this chapter, you will have installed a hypervisor and created a virtual machine for a Windows operating system. Then, in Chapter 9 you can choose to install Windows into the virtual machine you create in this chapter.

Introduction to Virtualization

In this section, we expand on the limited definition of virtualization provided in Chapter 6 to detail the many purposes of virtualization and to compare server-side virtualization versus client-side virtualization. Finally, we will explore the types of client-side virtualization in preparation for the section that follows in which you will implement client-side virtualization.

Purposes of Virtualization

Virtualization is the creation of an environment that seems real but isn't, and today it seems like virtualization is everywhere, and there are many types. You can explore a *virtual world*, such as Second Life or one of many massively multiplayer online games. Each of these virtual worlds contains a simulated environment within which participants create an online community. Within a virtual world a user often selects an *avatar*, an animated computer-generated human or animal image, to represent him or her. Virtual worlds are used in online training, in marketing of products, and in games because virtual worlds usually allow your avatar to interact with those of other people.

A *virtual classroom* is an eLearning tool for distance learning, usually provided as a service from an Internet-based source, such as eLecta Live (www.e-lecta.com) or iLinc (www.ilinc.com). If you have taken online classes you have probably experienced virtual classrooms, used by instructors for presenting interactive lectures, and even completion of coursework. The screen for a virtual classroom session has several panes. The largest pane is for the main presentation, which may include a virtual whiteboard where the presenter (and attendees, when permitted) writes in digital tools, a pane for PowerPoint slides, videos, various types of documents, or shared Web pages. A small pane will track the attendees, another will allow for text chat among the participants, and there are other tools for encouraging attendee interaction and feedback, such as virtual breakout rooms, polling tools, and more, depending on the vendor. Of course, don't forget sound—you need a headset with a microphone. A Webcam is nice to have to fully participate in a virtual classroom, and that will necessitate more panes. And none of this is any fun without a very fast Internet connection. Virtual classrooms may not be as exciting as virtual worlds, but they are great for distance learning. Figure 8-1 shows a virtual classroom in which the presenter is sharing a Web page with a student.

Many organizations use *storage virtualization* in which client computers can utilize many networked hard drives as though they are one drive or location. Network

FIGURE 8-1

The eLecta Live virtual classroom

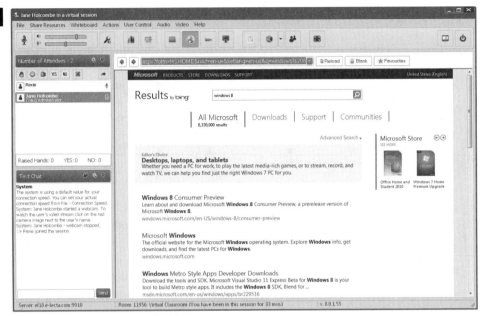

engineers work with *network virtualization* in which they create a network address space that exists within one or more physical networks. It is logically independent of the physical network structure, and users on computers accessing this virtual network are not aware of the underlying network. A *virtual network* can exist over a physical network, or one can be fully virtualized within a host computer.

Then there is *server virtualization*, in which a single computer hosts one or more server operating systems, each in a virtual machine and each performing tasks independently from the other virtual machines and from the host. Companies that provide low-cost Web hosting services can create a separate virtual Web server for each customer. Many organizations use server virtualization for a large number of reasons, including but not limited to, the ease of centrally managing servers, efficient use of server hardware, improved server availability, as a disaster recovery tool, for testing and development, and, of course, to reduce costs.

With only a small leap from server virtualization, we come to *desktop virtualization*. This is virtualization of a desktop computer, into which you can install a desktop operating system, its unique configuration, and all the applications and data used by (normally) a single person. Each simulation of a machine is a virtual machine— whether you install a desktop or server OS. We have used desktop virtualization

for over a decade for testing beta versions of software and various configurations. Desktop virtualization has also been a great tool for acquiring screenshots of things you cannot normally capture, such as the early stages of an OS installation or the startup of a computer.

Today, desktop operating systems and their installed apps are clients to numerous services on private and public networks. The typical computer user seamlessly connects to a home network, corporate network, or the Internet to access services such as file and print sharing, email, media streaming, social networking, and much more. For that reason, we often refer to desktop operating systems as clients, and it follows that when you create a virtual machine for, say, Windows 7, we may also use the term Windows client virtualization. As an IT professional, your professional life will be touched by some form of virtualization. Consider the February 2012 article by Joseph Marks of Nextgov (www.nextgov.com) in which he states, "More than 80 percent of federal information technology leaders say their agencies have implemented some manner of server virtualization and, overall, the government is saving nearly 20 percent of its IT budget through virtualization, according to a recent survey." Private and government organizations are increasingly using all types of computer virtualization.

Server-Side Virtualization vs. Client-Side Virtualization

In Chapter 6 we described a client as software that connects over a network to related server software. The client can also mean the operating system, or the entire computer beneath that client. Therefore, *client-side virtualization* is any virtualization that happens on the client side of a client-server relationship. And usually, but not always, it means the physical client side of things. For instance, in desktop virtualization, you can host the virtual desktops on either the client side or the server side. Quite often they are hosted on the server side in specialized servers. This is *server-side virtualization*. The desktop environment—in most cases, a version of Windows—displays on the user's screen as if the operating system was local. The value of this approach is that the local computer can be an older, less powerful computer (a thin client) because it only needs to run software to connect to the server, transfer video downstream to the thin client, and send mouse and keystrokes upstream to the app on the server. This hosting of the desktop environments and applications on servers centralizes all support tasks, simplifying the upgrading and

Windows 8 running in a virtual machine in Mac OS X on an iMac

patching of the operating system and applications in the virtual machines within the server or servers. This same centralization gives IT more control over the security of the desktop.

The term used today for hosting and managing multiple virtual desktops (often thousands) over a network is *virtual desktop infrastructure (VDI)*. The term is attributed to VMware in distinguishing its virtual desktop server products from the products offered by competitors, specifically Citrix and Microsoft. Today VDI applies to any server product that provides full virtual desktop support.

You can host one or more virtual machines on your PC if it meets the requirements for both the hypervisor and for each guest OS. Common examples of client-side virtualization of desktop environments include hypervisors that allows you to run Windows, Linux, Unix, and even DOS guest OSs in virtual machines on Windows, Linux, Unix, or Mac OS X host OSs. Figure 8-2 shows a Mac OS X desktop with a window open to a virtual machine that is running Windows 8. The hypervisor in this case is Oracle VirtualBox, a free and very capable hypervisor.

Types of Client-Side Virtualization

While we will use desktop virtualization in our working examples, client-side virtualization is not just about desktops. In recent Webcasts from Microsoft, they featured three types of client-side virtualization: desktop virtualization, application virtualization, and presentation virtualization. We have already defined desktop virtualization, and will soon move into more details about that type. Here we will describe presentation virtualization and application virtualization.

In *presentation virtualization*, a user connects to a server from their desktop or laptop and accesses an application rather than an entire desktop environment. The application user interface (window) is "presented" on the user's desktop as if it were running locally, but it is actually running on the server. This allows the user to use an application that is incompatible with their local operating system or that cannot run on the local computer because the computer hardware is old or underpowered. Microsoft currently uses Windows Server 2008 R2 running Windows Terminal Services for presentation virtualization. Notice that this is client-side virtualization, but it physically occurs on the server side and is presented on the client side, as shown in Figure 8-3. Specialized software sends the screens to the client computer and returns all input to the application on the server.

FIGURE 8-3

Presentation virtualization

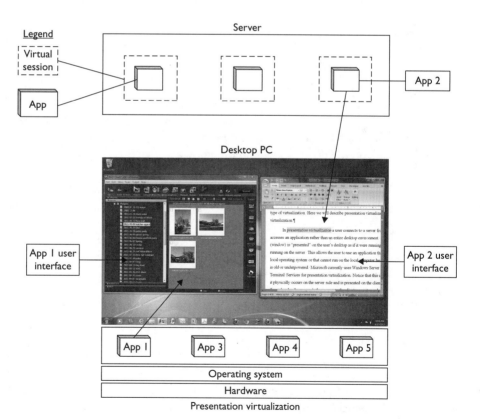

Presentation virtualization

FIGURE 8-4

Application
virtualization

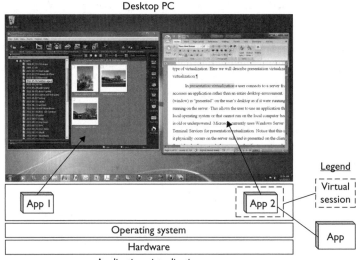

Application virtualization

Another type of client-side virtualization is *application virtualization* in which the application runs in a virtualized application environment on the local computer. The application is isolated from the surrounding system, interacting with the hardware (and user) through application virtualization software, a virtual machine with only the support required by the app. See Figure 8-4. This isolation of the application on the desktop computer requires a sufficiently powerful computer, but it has the advantage of being a compatibility solution when older, critical apps will not run on newer hardware or software. Another benefit is that a virtualized app is under IT control because they can install or update it over a network as a complete application without concern for the underlying system beyond the application virtualization software. Microsoft's current implementation of application virtualization is *Microsoft Application Virtualization (App-V)*.

Implementing Client-Side Desktop Virtualization

In this section we begin by describing hypervisors, the software that supports desktop virtualization. Then we will look at specific hypervisors and their resource and network requirements. Finally, we guide you through the process of selecting and installing a hypervisor on a desktop computer and creating one or more virtual machines in preparation for installing an OS into that virtual machine.

Hypervisors

To do desktop or server virtualization, you first need a hypervisor. A *hypervisor*, also called a *virtual machine monitor (VMM)*, is the software that creates a virtual machine, providing access to the necessary hardware on the host machine in isolation from other virtual machines and the host operating system, if present. This allows multiple operating systems to run simultaneously on a single physical computer, such as a network server or desktop computer. A hypervisor must create a virtual CPU compatible with that of the underlying machine—mainly either an Intel or an AMD CPU. This means that the installed OS must be capable of installing directly on the underlying computer. Also, today's hypervisors require, or

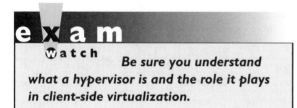

w a t c h   *Be sure you understand what a hypervisor is and the role it plays in client-side virtualization.*

at least work best on, computers with *Hardware-Assisted Virtualization (HAV)* features, either Intel Virtualization Technology for x86 (Intel VT-x) or AMD Virtualization (AMD-V). HAV supports and improves the performance of virtual machines on the host. Both Intel and AMD CPUs have supported HAV since 2006.

Virtualization versus Emulation

You may have heard the term emulation or mention of something called an emulator. At first glance, emulation and virtualization seem synonymous, but in computing these terms are very different. Emulation differs very much from the virtualization of servers or desktops we discuss here. The key is compatibility. When we use a virtual machine, the hypervisor that creates and manages it must create a virtual machine compatible with the underlying virtual machine, even while isolating the virtual machine from the underlying hardware.

An *emulator*, on the other hand, is software that allows you to run an OS or device on hardware with which it is completely incompatible. This is done in order to run a critical application designed for an old type of computer system that is no longer available. In fact, in the early days of PCs many organizations used special adapter cards and software on PCs to emulate the old dumb terminals that connected to their large mini- or mainframe computer systems. Now we do this with terminal emulation software, such as the VT Series terminal emulators from Ericom (www.ericom.com) used to emulate physical terminal hardware systems by DEC, Compaq, and Hewlett-Packard. Vendors like Ericom offer versions of their terminal emulation software that will run on Windows, Mac OS X, or Linux operating systems. Today developers wanting to write apps for phones running the Android

OS can use software that will emulate the underlying CPU and other hardware of an Android phone and run an Android OS—all on their desktop computer.

All things being equal, an emulator requires more computing resources (processing power and RAM) than a hypervisor needs for a virtual machine, and the OS or applications generally run much slower in the emulator than they would on the original hardware due to the translation and redirection of commands from within the emulator to the underlying computer. On the other hand, apps running in a virtual machine with no need for emulation will often run nearly as fast as they would on the physical machine.

Having made the distinction between virtualization and emulation, we acknowledge that people still use the term "emulate" for what a hypervisor does in creating a virtual machine, saying that the virtual machine is an emulation of the underlying hardware. Sometimes they are correct. In some instances, the hypervisor must do emulation. While virtualization requires that the virtual machine must have a virtual CPU that is compatible with that of the underlying computer, if the chipset in the computer is incompatible with the OS to be installed in the virtual machine, the hypervisor can emulate the compatible chipset within the virtual machine and translate or redirect instructions from the OS installed in the virtual machine to the underlying chipset. Think of this as partial emulation, but as with any emulation, there is a performance cost for this. If the chipset were compatible, these instructions would only need the hypervisor to pass them on to the chipset, with little effect on performance, but when the hypervisor must redirect and translate these instructions, things slow down. So, when necessary, modern hypervisors do some emulation as well as virtualization. One example of this is when we use a hypervisor on an Apple computer running Mac OS X to create a virtual machine for running Windows. A modern Apple computer running Mac OS X has an Intel CPU, but a different chipset than a Wintel computer for which Windows is written.

e x a m

w a t c h

Be sure that you understand that an emulator generally requires more processing power and RAM than a hypervisor requires for a virtual machine and that the operating systems and applications generally run much slower in the emulator than they would on the original hardware due to the translation and redirection of commands from within the emulator to the underlying computer.

Types of Hypervisors

There are two types of hypervisors, Type I and Type II, as Figure 8-5 shows. A *Type I hypervisor*—sometimes called a *bare-metal hypervisor*—can run directly on a computer without an underlying host operating system and then manage one or more virtual machines. A *Type II hypervisor* requires a host operating system, such as Windows, Mac OS, or Linux. The Type II hypervisor actually runs as an app in that host operating system, putting more software layers between each virtual machine and the hardware.

Type I Hypervisors   Type I hypervisors first appeared on high-powered servers running server OSs in virtual machines. Examples of current Type I server hypervisors include VMware ESXI, Citrix XenServer, and Microsoft Hyper-V. Type I hypervisors are very appealing because, when compared to an equivalent Type II hypervisor, a Type I hypervisor has a smaller layer of software between each *guest* OS running in a virtual machine and the underlying hardware. Therefore, in recent years, specialized software vendors, such as Citrix, MokaFive, Virtual Bridges, and Virtual Computer, have brought out Type I client hypervisors.

Type I client hypervisors are a solution to the problem of centrally distributing images of Type I hypervisors with client operating systems, fully configured with installed apps, to large numbers of desktops and laptops. You may say that you can already do that by centrally distributing more conventional images to the desktop without having a hypervisor and virtual machine as part of the image. However, consider an image that includes a Type I client hypervisor with two virtual machines— one with security locked down for the user to use at work or when traveling, and another that grants the user a much higher level of privilege for their personal use— and the user can easily switch between the two virtual machines as needed.

FIGURE 8-5

Comparison of Type I and Type II hypervisors

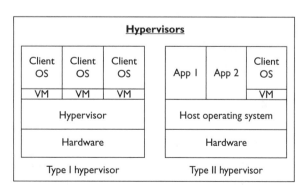

If a user loses a laptop and needs the same image installed on a new one, the image can be sent to the new computer over the network, taking only minutes before the user is up and working again. In fact, some Type I client hypervisor products are targeted specifically at laptops, and the distribution service for the hypervisor may have a feature that allows a central administrator to issue a kill command to remotely wipe out a stolen laptop when the thief connects it to the Internet.

This targeting of specific hardware can be one of the drawbacks, since each Type I hypervisor may support only certain computer (usually laptop) models because of their close relationship to the hardware. Although some Type I hypervisors run on a large number of PC and laptop models, some will run on any computer with a CPU that supports Intel's VT-x technology, which includes the majority of new PCs and laptops.

Type II Hypervisors   The hypervisors we use in our examples and exercises in this chapter are all Type II hypervisors requiring an underlying operating system, the *host* OS, which is the operating system installed directly on the computer, and one or more guest OSs, which are the operating systems running within virtual machines.

You have several choices for Type II hypervisors for desktops. The major sources of hypervisors are VMware, Parallels, Microsoft, and Oracle. There are many other players in the field, with virtualization topics appearing in the technical press every week. You can install a Type II hypervisor on your Linux, Windows, or Mac OS X desktop and test another operating system without the expense of a separate computer.

Implementing Desktop Virtualization

To implement desktop virtualization, you must first determine what desktop OS you will use as a guest OS. When it comes to selecting and installing a hypervisor, the general considerations and steps remain the same, whether you are planning server virtualization or desktop virtualization. For our purposes, we will focus on selecting and installing a Type II client hypervisor on a desktop computer for testing Windows and Linux operating systems. In this case, the available computer may drive your choice of hypervisor, so we will first select a computer and then a hypervisor. We'll then prepare the computer for installation of the hypervisor, install the hypervisor, and create one or more virtual machines based on the operating system or systems we plan to install.

Security for Virtual Machines

We cannot emphasize enough that you must keep your guest OS as secure as the host OS. At minimum, you should create a strong password for the account used to log in to the guest OS and install security software in your guest OS. Chapters 17 and 18 give the bigger story of computer security, and you can flip forward to those chapters for details. However, there are many excellent free security suites from third parties and Microsoft has free solutions. So, for a Windows guest OS other than Windows 8, consider connecting to the Microsoft site and downloading and installing the free Windows Security Essentials. Windows 8 has security software preinstalled.

e x a m

ⓦ a t c h

For the exam, remember that you must treat a virtual machine as you would a physical machine and take the same security precautions, such as creating   *a strong password for the account used to log in to the guest OS and installing security software in your guest OS.*

Networking Requirements

While it is possible to do desktop virtualization on a computer without an Internet connection, it would be very awkward for several reasons. First, the easiest way to obtain a hypervisor is over the Internet, and updates to the hypervisor, host OS, and guest OS are easily available with an Internet connection. Furthermore, if you create a virtual machine to test an operating system or other software for use in a normal environment, then you certainly should include testing how it works on a network. Therefore, the hypervisors we use simulate a network card within each virtual machine, as well as a network on the host, so that multiple virtual machines can communicate with each other and the underlying host. Then, through a virtual connection to the host computer's physical network adapter, each VM has access to an external network, and through that to the Internet, if available. Of course, you can turn off these and other features for a VM, if you desire.

e x a m

ⓦ a t c h

Recall that while a network may not be required for a virtual machine, it is essential to have network access in order to easily update all the software   *and to create a real-world environment in which a computer is connected to a network.*

Selecting a Guest OS for Desktop Virtualization

The selection of a guest OS for virtualization may be less selection and more necessity. Perhaps you need to learn Linux for a class you are taking, but you do not have a spare computer. Or maybe you would like to look at the next version of Windows without installing it over your present OS. Or maybe, you just need to select an OS so that you can experiment with desktop virtualization. Whatever the reason, you will need a legal license to install it, just as you do on any computer. If you plan to install Linux, you will find many free versions online, and if you are testing a pre-release version of Windows, simply download it and save it as an ISO file, something we will talk about in Chapter 9 when we install Windows on our real or virtual machines. If you are looking for an OS to install just for learning to work with virtualization, consider using an older version of Windows, if you happen to have an old disc around along with the product key. A *product key* is a string of alphanumeric characters, usually five groups of five each, printed on the packaging for retail editions of Microsoft software. You must provide this product key during the installation, or within 30 days, or the software will be disabled. This is Microsoft's protection against piracy.

While we will talk about installing a hypervisor and creating a virtual machine in preparation for installing an OS, we will save the details of installing the Windows OS for the next chapter.

Selecting a Host OS for Desktop Virtualization

Deciding on the host OS and a host computer for desktop virtualization seems like the chicken and egg situation—which comes first? First, it depends on what is available to you. However, since the CompTIA A+ exams focus mainly on the Windows OS, we will use the Windows OS as our host OS in the following exercises. But if you have a Linux system, there are hypervisors for Linux hosts. Over the years, we have mainly used various versions of Windows as the host OS, but we have had equally good experiences in the last year using an Apple iMac with Mac OS X as the host OS.

Selecting a Host Computer for Desktop Virtualization

We have occasionally installed a hypervisor on a primary desktop without incident. However, we do not recommend this if you have any other option, because there is some risk in installing any app, and a hypervisor is a bit more powerful than just any app. For our most recent work, we use our two newest, but not primary, computers: a Dell laptop and an iMac, both of which have HAV support.

How can you discover if your computer supports HAV? You may already know if you completed Exercise 3-4 in Chapter 3. One of the BIOS settings on a computer with HAV support will be virtualization and the ability to enable or disable it. If you are uncertain, rerun that exercise and make sure virtualization is present. Alternatively, you can run a software test. If your computer is running Windows, use Microsoft's Hardware-Assisted Virtualization Detection Tool. Exercise 8-1 describes the test for locating, downloading, and running this test on your Windows computer.

You can run the Hardware-Assisted Virtualization Detection Tool if you have one of the following versions of Windows:

- Windows Vista Home Basic, Home Premium, Business, Enterprise, or Ultimate (Service Pack 1 or 2)
- Windows XP Professional Service Pack 2 or 3
- Windows 7 Home Basic, Home Premium, Professional, Enterprise, or Ultimate

EXERCISE 8-1

Testing a Computer for HAV Support

If you have one of the compatible versions of Windows listed earlier, you can download and run the Windows utility to test for HAV.

1. Use an Internet search engine such as Google or Bing to search on the keywords "virtual detection tool." (You do not have to type "virtualization"— typing "virtual" will give you usable results.)

2. From the search results, locate and select the result titled "Windows Virtual PC: Configure BIOS." It should point to a page at Microsoft.com.

3. Read the short article "How to confirm your PC supports hardware virtualization."

4. Follow the instruction in Step 1 of the article to download and run the Hardware-Assisted Virtualization Detection Tool. You may need to respond to a User Account Control dialog box, and you will need to accept the license terms before the utility will run.

5. If the tool finds that your computer has HAV and it is enabled, you will see the message shown here and you can click OK.

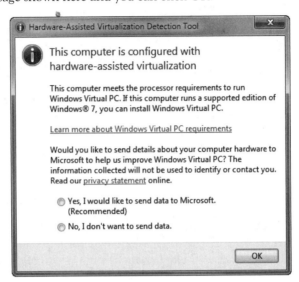

6. If you run the tool and see the message shown here, change your BIOS settings to enable HAV. Notice that the Web page gives example instructions for specific PC models.

7. If your computer does not support HAV, you will need to use a hypervisor that does not require HAV—we will discuss this later.

Selecting a Type II Client Hypervisor

You have several options—both commercial and free—for running Linux, DOS, or Windows on a Windows desktop computer. At this writing, you cannot run any version of Mac OS X in a VM on a PC, due more to licensing issues rather than technical issues. The hypervisors we use in our exercises are free. Two are from Microsoft and one is from Oracle.

The Microsoft hypervisors, Microsoft Virtual PC 2007 and Windows Virtual PC (both with and without Windows XP Mode), that we will demonstrate will only install in a verified legal copy of Windows. We selected Microsoft Virtual PC 2007 as a choice for computers with or without HAV that are running Windows XP or Windows Vista because Windows Virtual PC only runs on Windows 7.

Microsoft does not require that you register with them in order to acquire these free Microsoft hypervisors for the Windows desktop, nor does it require that you use any type of key to make it work. However, the installation program will verify that your host OS is a legitimate version of Windows before the Microsoft virtualization products will install.

The hypervisor included with Windows 8, Hyper-V, is not presently on the exam, but you should be aware of it. It only runs in the 64-bit version of Windows 8, and you enable it through Programs and Features in Control Panel; then you can launch the Hyper-V Manager from the Start screen by simply typing the search string **"hyper"** and clicking or tapping the Hyper-V Manager. Now, it is much like the other hypervisors you will work with here, in how you create a virtual machine and install a guest OS into it. Although it lacks the XP Mode of Windows Virtual PC, Hyper-V will run 32-bit or 64-bit clients and easily supports multiple virtual machines running simultaneously.

Of the non-Microsoft hypervisors, we selected Oracle VirtualBox because it works on both platforms (Mac OS X and Windows) that we have in our office (plus others), and it simply works well for us. There are other free hypervisors, most notably VMware Player, which doesn't have a version for Mac OS X. The free VMware Player also has fewer features than VMware Workstation ($199 retail), which also does not come in a version for Mac OS X hosting. Both VMware products come in versions for Linux and Windows hosts. However, the entire suite of VMware products is very popular in organizations, so you may want to download and install VMware player on your own to become familiar with the VMware virtualization look and feel. All of these hypervisors are downloadable from the

Internet and they all work in a similar way, so working with one will teach you the basics of working with desktop virtualization.

This chapter would not be complete without some mention of Parallels, a very popular hypervisor for Mac OS X hosts. It does not come in a free version, only a 14-day trial, which you may want to download from their Website (www.parallels.com). While Parallels has versions for Windows and Linux hosts, their main efforts go to their product for Mac OS X hosts, and the other versions are not kept as up-to-date. Therefore, since we work on both Windows and Mac OS X hosts, at this time we prefer to use Oracle VirtualBox on both platforms.

Microsoft Virtual PC 2007   Microsoft Virtual PC 2007 will run on any computer running most editions of Windows beginning with Windows XP. You can create VMs and install other versions of Windows, Linux, and DOS as clients, although Microsoft does not provide support in the form of client additions/drivers for older Windows clients and for other non-Windows OSs. Two important distinctions between Microsoft Virtual PC 2007 and its successor, Windows Virtual PC (discussed next), are the following: first, Windows Virtual PC only runs on Windows 7 and requires HAV, unless you install an update to Windows Virtual PC; and second, Virtual PC 2007 does not require HAV, but supports HAV if it is present. Therefore, even though Windows Virtual PC is the newer version, introduced with Windows 7, you may decide to use the older Microsoft Virtual PC 2007 if your computer does not support HAV and/or your host OS is not Windows 7.

The system requirements for Microsoft Virtual PC 2007 are as follows:

- 400 MHz Pentium-compatible 32-bit/64-bit CPU (1.0 GHz or faster recommended)
- 2 GB RAM or higher (add RAM required for host OS to that for each guest OS to determine if more than 2 GB is required)
- 35 MB hard disk space
- **Host OS**   Windows Vista Business, Enterprise, and Ultimate, all with Service Pack 1 (SP 1); Windows XP Professional, Windows XP Tablet PC Edition, all with Service Pack 3 (SP3)

■ **Guest OS**   Windows 98, Windows NT Workstation, Windows 2000, Windows XP, OS/2, Windows Vista, Windows 2000 Server, and Windows Server 2003. Current and previous versions of Microsoft OSs will run, but not all are supported with special client software from Microsoft. If Microsoft no longer supports the OS, it is not officially supported, but may be installed into Virtual PC 2007. It just may not be optimized with the client support. Note: We have successfully run DOS and Linux as well as older Windows OSs as clients.

You can download Virtual PC 2007 from the Microsoft site. This requires a high-speed broadband connection, but the 30 MB file should take only a minute or two to download. There are separate downloads for the 32-bit or 64-bit host OSs. After you download, you are ready to install it on your computer. Do not install this if you have another hypervisor already installed. You will need to uninstall it first.

EXERCISE 8-2

Installing Microsoft Virtual PC 2007

Using the file you downloaded, install Microsoft Virtual PC 2007 on your Windows computer. For our example, we will use Windows Vista in the screenshots, but the instructions also work for Windows XP and Windows 7. To complete this exercise, you will need the following:

■ A computer running Windows XP, or a more recent version, with the minimum hardware requirements listed earlier

■ The user name and password of an administrator account for this computer

■ A broadband Internet connection

   1. Locate and double-click the installation program. This will start the Microsoft Virtual PC 2007 Wizard.

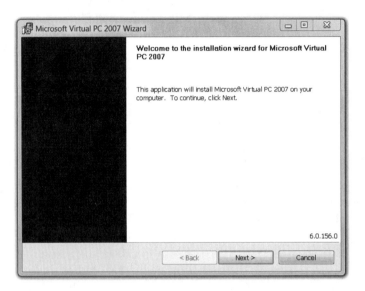

   2. Click Next on the Welcome page and follow the instructions. You will need to accept the license agreement.

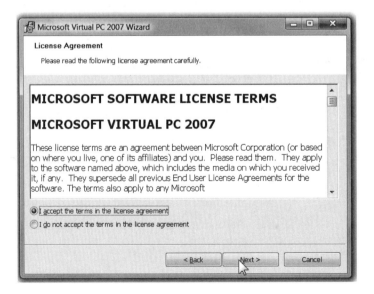

3. Enter the user name (this does not need to match your user account name) and organization information in the Customer Information page. Notice that Microsoft automatically entered the product key on this page and grayed it out, so you can't enter it or change it.

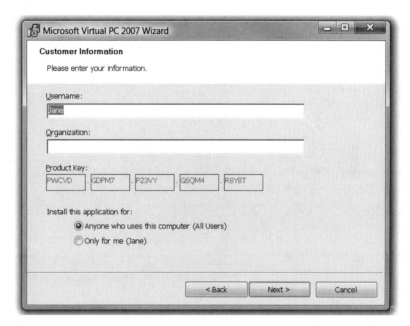

4. Click Next on the Customer Information page and on the Ready To Install The Program page. Notice the location in which the program will install. You will normally allow it to install in the default location, but if you need to change this, click the Change button and browse to another

location. When you are ready to have the installation begin, click the Install button.

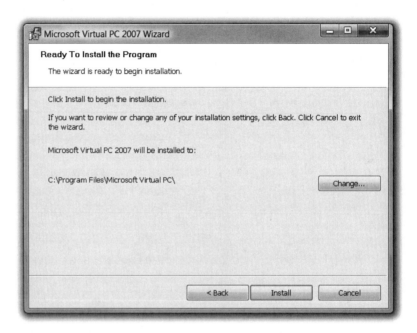

5. The Installing Microsoft Virtual PC 2007 page shows the status of the installation with a progress bar. When the installation is complete, the Next button will become active; click it to proceed to the Installation Complete page, and on the Installation Complete page, click Finish.

6. Verify that Virtual PC installed by locating it on the Start menu where it should be highlighted as a new program.

As with any hypervisor, once you have installed Virtual PC 2007, the next step is to create a virtual machine appropriate for the first operating system you wish to install. Begin by launching Virtual PC 2007 from the Start menu. This launches the New Virtual Machine Wizard. On the Welcome page, click the Next button. On the Options page, there are three choices, as Figure 8-6 shows. The first choice lets you create a virtual machine, allowing you to customize the configuration beyond the bare minimum for the operating system you will install. This includes both the virtual machine (saved in a .vmc file) and the virtual hard disk (saved in a .vhd file).

FIGURE 8-6

Select the correct option.

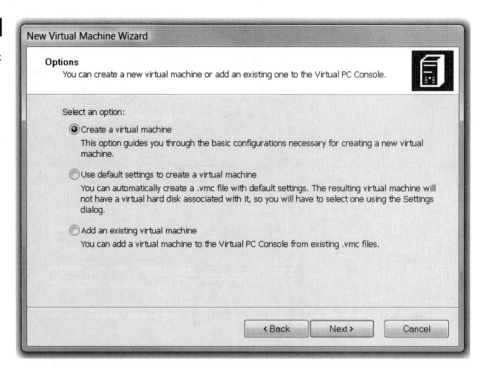

We prefer to use this when creating a virtual machine. The second option is quicker, but creates a virtual machine with the default settings but no virtual hard disk. You would choose this if you wanted only a minimally configured virtual machine and wanted to use a previously created virtual hard disk. The third option lets you add a preexisting virtual machine, which means you need an existing .vmc file.

Select the first option to create a virtual machine and click Next. The Virtual Machine Name And Location page appears. Enter a meaningful name—such as the name of the OS you plan to install, as Figure 8-7 shows. Use the Browse button only if you want to specify a location other than the default location. Click Next, and on the Operating System page, select the operating system you plan to install. Figure 8-8 shows this page with the drop-down box open and displaying the list of supported guest OSs. Select Other if you wish to install DOS or Linux.

Select Next to proceed to the Memory page. On this page, you may either keep the default setting for the selected OS or choose to adjust the amount of RAM the virtual machine can use; click Next to move to the Virtual Hard Disk Options page. Select the option to create a new virtual hard disk and click Next. On the Virtual

FIGURE 8-7

Enter a name
for the virtual
machine.

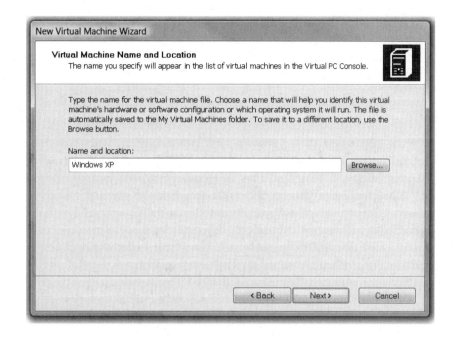

FIGURE 8-8

Select the
operating system
you wish to
install.

Hard Disk Location page, keep the default disk location, unless you wish to move it to a drive with more space. Then click Next to continue. The Completing The New Virtual Machine Wizard page displays a summary of the choices you made. Double-check the choices, and if they are okay, click Finish. You can configure several virtual machines—even before you begin installing the guest operating systems. If you do, the Virtual PC Console will list all the virtual machines, as shown in Figure 8-9.

Once you have configured a virtual machine, you have the equivalent of a new computer with an empty hard drive, and you are ready to install an OS into it. You will need the distribution disc for the OS you wish to install. You can also provide the file in ISO form. Let's assume you have the disc. Before beginning, place this disc in the host computer's optical drive. To start an OS installation, open Virtual PC from the Start menu; this opens the Virtual PC Console. Select the virtual machine for your OS and then click the Start button. This is the equivalent of turning on your PC. A window will open, and at first the background will be black while it loads the virtual system BIOS. This generally happens so fast that you cannot even read what displays there. It will then boot from your disc, starting the OS installation. From there, you install the OS just as you would on a physical machine, following the instructions in the setup program. We will provide instructions for installing Windows XP, Windows Vista, Windows 7, and Linux in the following chapters. You can install each of these into a virtual machine. You will also receive instructions for installing Mac OS X, but we will not be installing that on a virtual machine.

FIGURE 8-9

The Virtual PC Console with four virtual machines listed

Windows XP Mode and Windows Virtual PC Do you have old apps written for an older version of Windows that refused to run or that run poorly in Windows 7? If so, you should first consider using Compatibility Mode, which we described in Chapter 2. Then if your app still does not run correctly, consider two virtualization options from Microsoft: Windows XP Mode and Windows Virtual PC. However, Compatibility Mode requires less disk space and memory than virtualization does.

For scenarios in which you need to run legacy Windows XP applications that will not run well in Windows 7, Microsoft provides Windows XP Mode, which is Windows Virtual PC preconfigured with one virtual machine, with a legally licensed (for this purpose) instance of Windows XP preinstalled. However, you can also create VMs to run other guest systems, including Windows Vista, Windows 2000, Windows 8, and some versions of Linux. When you install XP Mode, you are actually installing two components: Windows Virtual PC and the VM image for XP Mode.

Once installed, it is so well integrated into Windows 7 that you can start programs installed in the Windows Virtual PC VM from Start menu shortcuts of the host OS. Beyond that, if you have a certain data file type that you prefer to run in a program that is in the VM, you can assign that file type to the program in the host. Then, double-clicking such a data file will launch the VM and the program within it. These capabilities are part of the Windows Virtual PC Virtual Applications feature.

All editions of Windows 7 support Windows Virtual PC, but you cannot install Windows XP Mode in the Home editions. If your host OS is the Basic or Home Premium edition, you need to install Windows Virtual PC, create your own virtual machine for Windows XP, and then install Windows XP using a valid, licensed setup disc or downloaded Windows XP installation files.

The system requirements for Windows Virtual PC are as follows:

- 1 GHz 32-bit/64-bit CPU
- 2 GB RAM or higher
- 15 GB hard disk space per virtual machine
- **Host OS** Windows 7 Home Basic, Home Premium, Enterprise, Professional, and Ultimate
- **Guest OS**
    - Windows XP: The Virtual Applications feature is only supported in Windows XP Professional with Service Pack 3 (SP3).
    - Windows Vista: The Virtual Applications feature is only supported in Windows Vista Enterprise and Ultimate editions.
    - Windows 7: The Virtual Applications feature is only supported in Windows 7 Enterprise and Ultimate editions.

e x a m

ⓦ a t c h   *Windows Virtual PC requires HAV unless you run an update from Microsoft. Its minimum hardware requirements are a GHz-32-bit/64-bit CPU, 2 GB RAM or higher, 15 GB hard disk space per virtual machine. It only supports Windows 7 as a host OS.*

Windows XP Mode and Windows Virtual PC require hardware-assisted virtualization technology, unless you run an update, available from the Microsoft site, to remove this requirement.

You can download Windows XP Mode for Windows 7 at the Windows Virtual PC home page. Because URLs change, we recommend that you enter the search string **"windows virtual pc"** into your favorite search engine and then select the result that points to the Virtual PC home page at Microsoft.com. Exercise 8-3 describes the steps to download and install Windows XP Mode and Windows Virtual PC on a computer that supports HAV.

EXERCISE 8-3

Installing Windows XP Mode and Windows Virtual PC

To complete this exercise, you will need an Internet-connected, HAV-enabled computer running any edition of Windows 7 except Windows 7 Home editions. If your computer has Windows 7 Home Basic or Home Premium edition, you can install Windows Virtual PC, but not Windows XP Mode. Your screens may be different if Microsoft changes the Web pages or programs shown.

1. Connect to the Windows Virtual PC home page and click the button/link labeled Get Windows XP Mode And Windows Virtual PC. Select your edition of Windows 7 and select your language. If you do not know what edition you have, click the blue help button next to the box and follow the instructions.

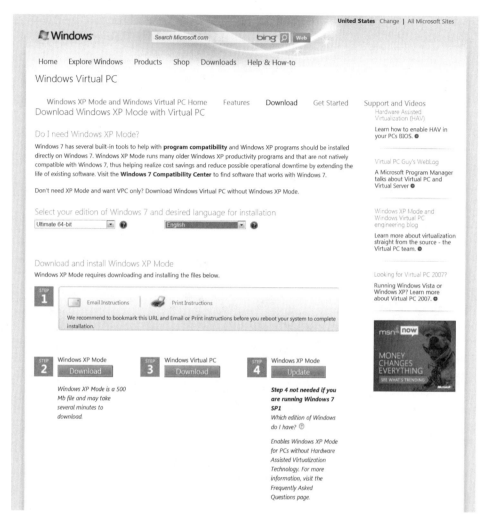

2. Bookmark the page. Do not bother emailing or printing the instructions because they are very simple:

Step 1: Download Windows XP Mode.
Step 2: Download Windows Virtual PC.
Step 3: Update Windows XP Mode.

3. Unfortunately, these instructions are a bit out of sync with the Web page, so pay attention: Do *not* do Step 3, which is Step 4 on the Web page, unless you are running Windows 7 without Service Pack 1.

4. For now, click the button to download Windows XP Mode.

5. There will be a delay while it checks your Windows installation to verify that it is legal. Click Continue when you see the message that validation was successful.

6. Then respond to the prompt (at the bottom of the screen in Internet Explorer version 9) by clicking Run. The 500 MB file may take several minutes to download, depending on the speed of your Internet connection.

7. If you chose Run, after the program downloads, it will open the Windows XP Mode Setup Wizard.

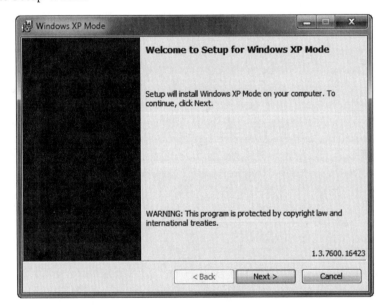

8. Click Next to begin the Windows XP Mode setup.

9. On the following page, keep the default location and click Next.

10. A progress bar will display as it copies files and creates a virtual hard disk for Windows XP Mode. When the Setup Completed page appears, click Finish.

11. Now return to the Windows XP Mode download page and click the Download button in Step 3 (under Windows Virtual PC).

12. Then respond to the prompt (at the bottom of the screen in Internet Explorer version 9) by clicking Open. This file is much smaller than the previous one, so it will download more quickly.

13. If prompted, click Yes to install the Windows software updates and accept any license terms. It will take a few minutes to install the updates.

14. Once the updates are installed, click the Restart Now button to restart your computer. Log in, and when the desktop is available, click the Start button to open the Start menu. Click All Programs and scroll down to the Windows Virtual PC folder. Click it to open it, and then click Windows XP Mode.

15. The first time you launch it, you will need to accept the terms of the Windows XP Mode license agreement by clicking the box labeled I Accept The License Terms and then clicking Next.

16. In the Windows XP Mode Setup box, notice that the user name is XPMUser and is not changeable. Enter a password twice, being careful to remember the password. Click Next to continue.

17. On the next page turn on Automatic Updates by clicking the first choice. Then click Next.

18. The next page informs you that Windows XP Mode Setup will turn on sharing of the drives (on the host computer) with Windows XP Mode. This is the default, and we suggest you turn it on, as long as you follow the cautions suggested in the message and install security software after setup is complete. Click Start Setup.

19. It will take several minutes to set up Windows XP Mode. During that time the Windows XP Mode – Windows Virtual PC window displays messages and a progress bar. After it installs, Windows XP will display in a Windows Virtual PC window.

The first time Windows XP Mode runs you should install security software. In fact, you will see a status message on this, as shown in Figure 8-10. Click the balloon to open the Security Center, shown in Figure 8-11. While the Recommendations button would eventually help you find security software, we recommend that you close the Security Center now and start Internet Explorer (IE) from the shortcut on the desktop. Since this is the first time using IE in this installation, you may notice

FIGURE 8-10

Windows XP
Mode with a
warning message

FIGURE 8-11

Windows XP
Security Center

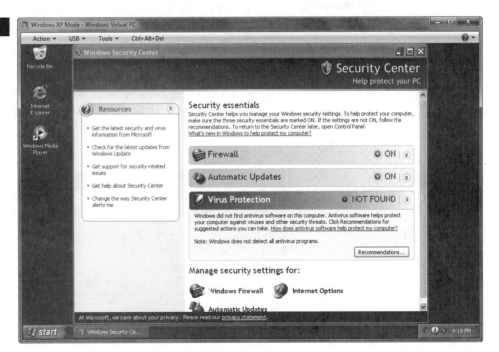

that it looks a bit dated compared to IE on your Windows 7 host. IE version 6 is installed in Windows XP Mode. Do not upgrade this right away, because this version of IE may be more compatible with some Windows XP apps.

We recommend that you install the free Microsoft Security Essentials (MSE). Therefore, when IE comes up, enter **microsoft security essentials** in the Bing Search box. You will need to respond to prompts from IE, such as the privacy message shown in Figure 8-12. Click OK to close the box.

In the results list, locate Microsoft's download page for Microsoft Security Essentials. Do not be confused by any other page that is not part of Microsoft.com. Click the link to the download page and, on the page, scroll down and ensure that the correct language is selected, and then locate (but do not click) the two Download buttons (Figure 8-13). The first is for the 64-bit version of the software. You *do not* want this version. The second is for the 32-bit version, which is identified by "x86" in the name. The English version is enus\x86\mseinstall.exe. Click the Download button to download this version. In the File Download Security Warning box, click Run. You will also see an Internet Explorer Security Warning, and you can click Run in this box too.

When the Microsoft Security Essentials Installation Wizard opens, click Next to start it (Figure 8-14). Respond to each page in turn, accepting the license terms, deciding whether or not you want to participate in Microsoft's Customer Experience Improvement Program, and letting Security Essentials turn on Windows Firewall if no other firewall is installed.

Then the real installation begins when you click the Install button on the Ready To Install page. This will take several minutes. On the last page, leave the box checked that allows MSE to scan your (virtual) computer after getting the latest updates, and then click Finish. MSE will open and immediately download the latest updates (Figure 8-15) and scan Windows XP Mode for malware, which will take several minutes.

FIGURE 8-12

Click OK to close the privacy message.

FIGURE 8-13

Scroll down on the Microsoft Security Essentials download page to select the language and the correct version of the app.

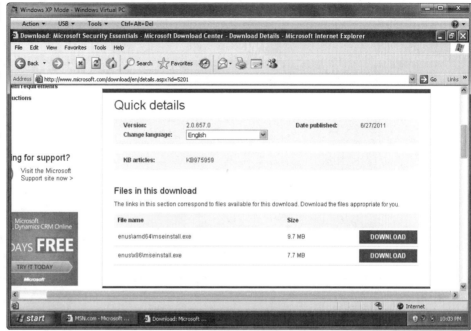

FIGURE 8-14

The Microsoft Security Essentials Installation Wizard

FIGURE 8-15

Microsoft
Security
Essentials
downloading
updates

Windows Virtual PC is installed along with Windows XP Mode. If you decide that you do not need Windows XP Mode, you can easily uninstall it without uninstalling Windows Virtual PC. Simply open Programs and Features in Control Panel and click the task in the list on the left labeled Turn Windows Features On Or Off—when the Windows Features window opens, scroll down until you see Windows XP Mode. Remove the check from the box by this feature. If you also wish to remove Windows Virtual PC, remove its check too, but you can leave it in place when removing Windows XP. Click OK to close the box, and you will see a message box with a progress bar while Windows removes the feature. When prompted, click Restart Now to restart your computer and finish the removal of Windows XP Mode.

Windows Virtual PC Without XP Mode　You can create additional virtual machines by opening Windows Virtual PC from the Start menu. Then, in the Virtual Machines console, if the Create Virtual Machine button is on the button bar, click it; if it is not visible, click the chevrons (>>) to open the drop-down menu shown in Figure 8-16 and select Create Virtual Machine. Follow the instructions on each screen, keeping the default settings until you are more comfortable working with virtual machines. You will need to provide a name for the virtual hard disk, which will be the name for the virtual machine. When you are finished, you should have a new virtual machine listed, as shown in Figure 8-17, ready for you to install a new guest OS.

Oracle VirtualBox Oracle VirtualBox will run on a variety of host operating systems, including Windows, Linux, Solaris, and Mac OS X. It is free open-source software under the terms of the GNU General Public License (GPL) version 2. It will also run on hardware that does not support virtualization, but we strongly recommend you use a system with HAV when possible for the best performance.

The minimum requirements for VirtualBox include the following:

- **CPU** Any recent Intel or AMD CPU, but the more powerful, the better.
- **Disk space** It all depends on the VirtualBox features you select, but we recommend about 1 GB of disk space just for the VirtualBox software, plus several GB per virtual machine. The exact VM requirements depend on the guest OS and the programs and data you will add to the VM.
- **Memory** Memory depends on the guest OS, but at least 512 MB and at least 1 GB for Windows XP and 2 GB for Windows 7 or Windows 8.
- **Host operating system** Windows, Linux, Solaris, or Mac OS X.
- **Guest OS** Versions of Windows, Linux, Solaris, Open Solaris, OS/2, Open BSD, or DOS.

FIGURE 8-16

Create a virtual machine in Windows Virtual PC.

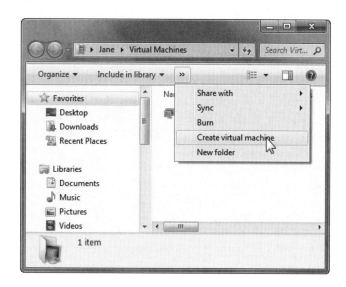

Learn more about VirtualBox at the VirtualBox Website (www.virtualbox.org) where you will find the online user manual and a link to download the software. To complete Exercise 8-4, you will need to download VirtualBox. To do that, click the Downloads link on the home page. In the Download VirtualBox page, shown in Figure 8-18, locate the version for the host OS you plan to use and select it for download. In our case, we clicked the link for VirtualBox for Windows hosts. Once it completes downloading, you are ready to install it on your system. The instructions in Exercise 8-4 are for installing VirtualBox on a Windows 7 system. The screens and steps will vary depending on the version of VirtualBox and the host OS you use. For instance, the file downloaded to a Mac OS X host (described on the VirtualBox download page as simply "OS X") will have a .dmg extension.

Before you begin Exercise 8-4, ensure that you do not have another hypervisor installed on your computer. If you do, you will need to uninstall the hypervisor in order to install VirtualBox.

FIGURE 8-18   Select the correct download for your host OS.

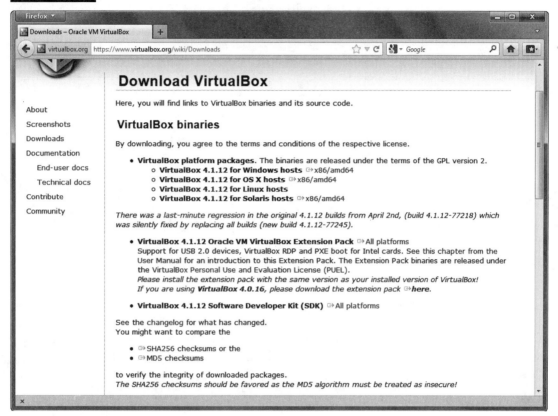

EXERCISE 8-4

Installing Oracle VirtualBox on a Windows 7 Host

Using the file you downloaded, run the VirtualBox installation wizard to install it on your Windows 7 computer. To complete this exercise, you will need a system that meets the hardware and host OS requirements listed earlier, and we recommend at least 2 GB of memory if you hope to install Windows as a guest OS when we install Windows 7 in Chapter 9. In addition, you will need the following:

■   The user name and password of an administrator account for this computer

■   A broadband Internet connection

   1.   Locate and double-click the installation program. Your version will be newer than the one we used, called "VirtualBox-4.1.12-77245-Win.exe."

2. In the Security Warning box, confirm that the name of the file is the one you intended to launch and then click Run.

3. Click Next on the Welcome page and follow the instructions. If prompted, you will need to accept the license agreement.

4. In the Custom Setup box (the first of several you will see labeled "Custom Setup"), do not make any changes and leave all the features selected, unless your disk space is limited. If you are unsure if you have enough space, click Disk Usage, which will open a box showing the available space on each of your disk volumes and highlight the volumes with too little space.

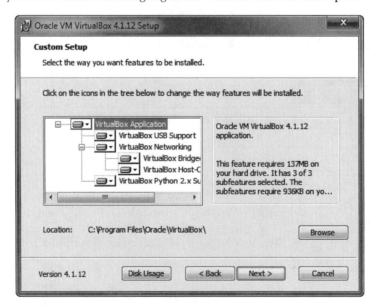

5. If you used the Disk Usage button to open the Disk Space Requirements box, click OK to return to the Custom Setup box. Click Next to continue.

6. In the next Custom Setup box, leave the options as selected and click Next.

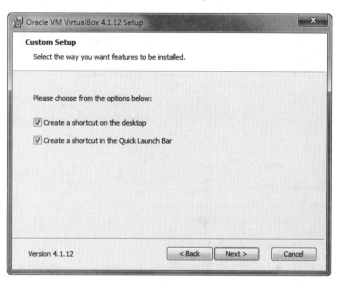

7. If, back in Step 4, you allowed selection of all the features, including Networking, you will see the warning shown here. Click Yes to continue.

8. When the box labeled Ready To Install displays, click the Install button.

9. If a User Account Control prompt displays, click the Yes button or supply an administrator password to allow the software to install.

10. A progress bar will display while VirtualBox installs.

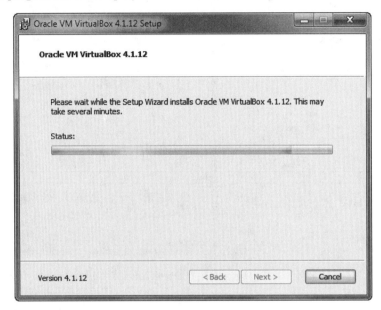

11. On the final page of the installation wizard, ensure that the box to start VirtualBox has a check mark in it and then click Finish.

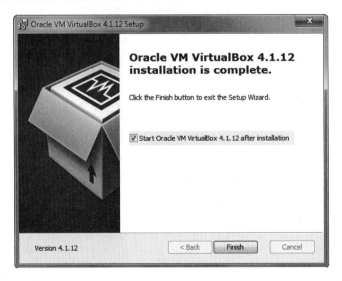

12. The VirtualBox Manager will open. This is where you create and manage virtual machines. Click New to open the Create New Virtual Machine Wizard.

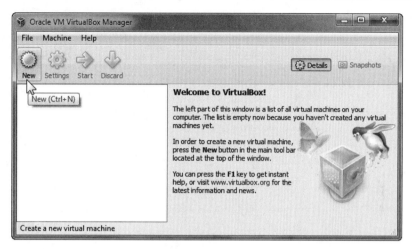

13. Click Next on the wizard's welcome page. Then on the VM Name And OS Type page, enter a name for the virtual machine. We use a name that is both unique on our network and that will easily identify the VM to us when seen over the network. For instance, W7-64-VM easily identifies this as a VM running Windows 7 64-bit. Then you must select the operating system and version under OS Type.

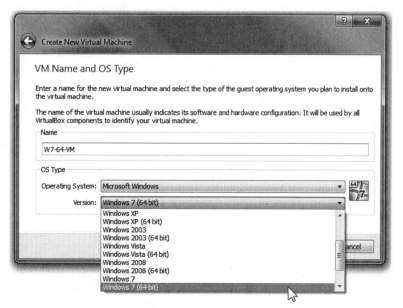

14. On the Memory page, move the slider or enter an amount in the box to the right to select at least 1 GB of memory for Windows 7.

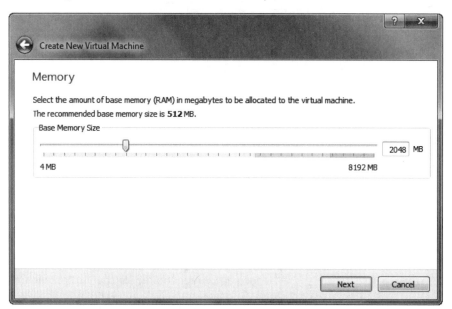

15. On the Virtual Hard Disk page, leave the defaults and click Next.

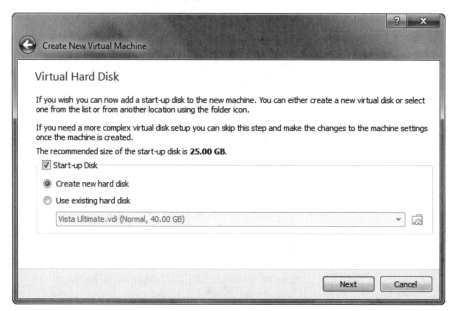

16. On the next page, leave the default for file type and click Next.

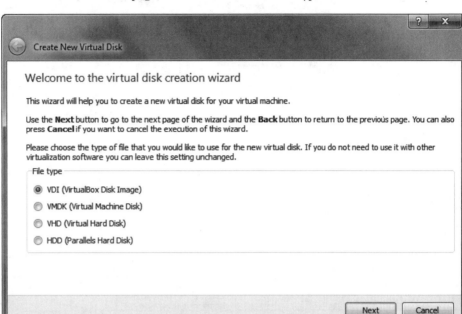

17. On the next page, ensure that Dynamically Allocated is selected and click Next.

18. On the Virtual Disk File Location And Size page, leave the default name, which matches the virtual machine name you created earlier, and the default virtual disk size as is and click Next.

19. On the summary page, read over the list of parameters you selected, and if you are satisfied, click Create. The wizard will disappear and the Virtual Box Manager will list the new virtual machine.

If you completed Exercise 8-4, Oracle VM VirtualBox Manager will resemble Figure 8-19, and the virtual machine you created is the equivalent of a brand-new computer with an empty hard drive. You are now ready to install an OS into this virtual machine. In Chapter 9 we will describe how to install Windows, and at that time you may choose to install an OS into this virtual machine or onto a physical computer.

FIGURE 8-19

Oracle VM
VirtualBox
Manager with one
virtual machine

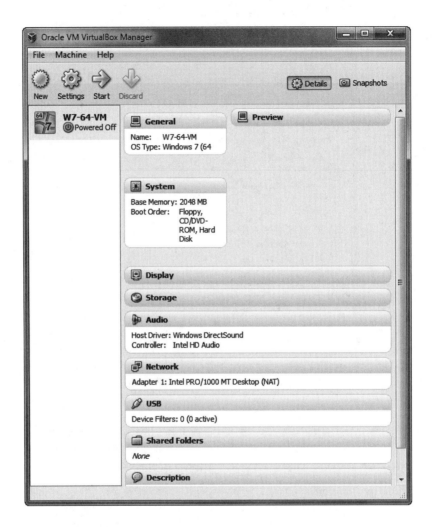

Capturing the Mouse and Keyboard in a Guest OS

Once you have a guest OS installed into a virtual machine, the guest OS and host OS are sharing the same physical hardware, but each physical device can serve only one master at a time. Most of this goes on behind the scenes without you, the user, being concerned. The keyboard and mouse are exceptions to this dynamic. You must control which OS has the focus of these input devices, and you do it with a *host key*.

Here is how it works. When your mouse is active outside the virtual machine, you simply move the mouse inside the window containing the VM and click. Then, to give control back to the host OS, you press the host key and move the mouse outside the VM window. This transfers control of both the mouse and keyboard back to the host OS. The hypervisor assigns a host key. For instance, VirtualBox on a Windows computer uses the right CTRL key as the host key. VirtualBox on a Mac OS X system uses the left COMMAND key, while Virtual PC uses the right ALT key. You should practice using the host key as soon as you have your guest OS up and running!

Improving Guest OS Performance

After you install a guest OS into a guest VM, no matter which hypervisor you use, you may find that the screen and performance are not quite up to par, with only a low resolution available to you. Hypervisors usually have special software that you can install into the guest OS. For instance, VirtualBox has special drivers and other software called collectively Guest Additions, and you install them after you install a guest OS. To do this, you start up your guest OS, and then access the VirtualBox menu on the window containing your guest OS, and click the Devices menu, as shown in Figure 8-20. Click Install Guest Additions and follow the instructions to run the

FIGURE 8-20

Oracle VM
VirtualBox
Manager with
Windows Vista
as the guest OS

program, which is presently named VBoxWindowsAdditions.exe (for a Windows guest OS). You will need to respond to a User Account Control prompt and at another point click Install in a Windows Security prompt. Notice that it installs dozens of files over several minutes. The result should be better performance overall, and you may find that Windows will have more resolution options for configuring your display.

When the Guest Additions are installed, you will be prompted to reboot the virtual machine. This is necessary before the changes take effect. Oracle VirtualBox configures your guest client to check for updates to the Guest Additions, so after you reboot the VM, if you are connected to the Internet through the host OS, you may see a message stating that there are updates—even if, as we did, you downloaded and installed VirtualBox on the same day. In the case of the Windows Vista guest client we used in this example, we could have initiated the Guest Additions installation from the Devices menu of the virtual machine, but as soon as it rebooted, a status message from Windows Problem Reports and Solutions appeared over the taskbar and we clicked it to see the window shown in Figure 8-21.

<table>
<tr><td>

FIGURE 8-21

Windows
Problem Reports
and Solutions
suggesting a
VirtualBox update

</td><td>

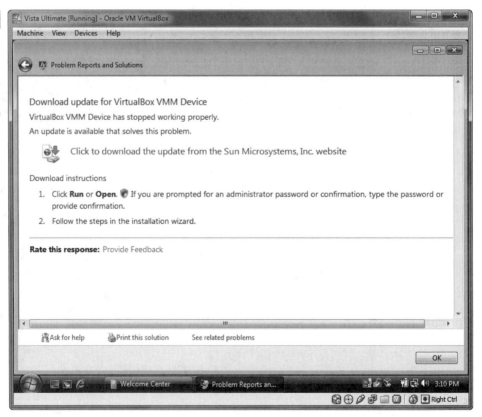

</td></tr>
</table>

We followed the instructions to download the update from the Sun Microsystems, Inc., Website. If you do this, do not be confused by any reference to Sun Microsystems. Oracle acquired Sun, who owned VirtualBox several years ago, and some of the associated screens and messages still use the old name. Follow the on-screen instructions to save and install the updates. There will be many prompts, and you will need to follow the instructions to complete the installation of the additions, accepting the defaults for file locations and shortcut placement.

Each hypervisor has its own set of drivers and other programs to improve the virtual machine performance, but they are all guest-OS-specific, and each vendor gives their group of guest OS drivers and programs a different name.

CERTIFICATION SUMMARY

A technician should understand the basics of client-side virtualization, the purpose of virtual machines, and the various requirements, including resources on the host computer, emulator needs, security, and network. Also important is understanding what a hypervisor is and the types of hypervisors available.

TWO-MINUTE DRILL

Here are some of the key points covered in Chapter 8.

Introduction to Virtualization

❏ Virtualization is the creation of an environment that seems real, but isn't.

❏ Virtualization is for many purposes, such as a virtual world, virtual classroom, storage virtualization, network virtualization, server virtualization, and desktop virtualization.

❏ Client-side virtualization occurs on the client side of a client-server arrangement.

❏ Server-side virtualization occurs on the server side of a client-server relationship.

❏ Virtual desktop infrastructure (VDI) is the hosting and managing of multiple virtual desktops on network servers.

❏ Examples of desktop virtualization include Windows, Unix, or Linux virtual machines running on Windows, Mac OS X, or Linux systems.

❏ Examples of client-side virtualization include presentation virtualization, application virtualization, and desktop virtualization.

Implementing Client-Side Desktop Virtualization

❏ A hypervisor, also called a virtual machine monitor (VMM), is the software that creates a virtual machine, providing access to the necessary hardware on the host machine in isolation from other virtual machines, and from a host operating system, if present.

❏ Most hypervisors require or, at least work better, with hardware-assisted virtualization (HAV), features of Intel Virtualization Technology for X86 (Intel VT-x) or AMD Virtualization (AMD-V).

❏ In virtualization, the hypervisor must create a virtual machine compatible with that of the underlying machine, whereas emulation allows you to run an OS or device on hardware with which it is completely incompatible. Sometimes a virtual machine may emulate some piece of hardware in the virtual machine that is either not present or not compatible in the underlying hardware.

❑ Emulators usually require more computing resources than hypervisors require for virtual machines.

❑ Internet access is important for working with virtual machines and keeping the hypervisor and its guest OSs up-to-date. A hypervisor will provide virtual network adapters, as well as a virtual network, on the host computer.

❑ The security requirements for a guest OS are the same as those for the host system. Therefore, immediately after installing a guest OS, install a security suite.

SELF TEST

The following questions will help you measure your understanding of the material presented in this chapter. Read all of the choices carefully because there might be more than one correct answer. Choose all correct answers for each question.

Introduction to Virtualization

1. You may use one of these animated graphic objects to represent you in a virtual world.
   A. Gadget
   B. Guest
   C. Avatar
   D. Orb

2. What type of virtualization is used in distance learning for interactive presentations by instructors?
   A. Server-side virtualization
   B. Virtual classroom
   C. Client-side virtualization
   D. Application virtualization

3. This type of virtualization only provides support for an app's user interface, and the user interface itself exists on a client computer, while the app runs on a server.
   A. Application virtualization
   B. Storage virtualization
   C. Presentation virtualization
   D. Server virtualization

4. In network virtualization, what portion of a network exists within one or more physical networks, creating a virtual network?
   A. Network adapters
   B. Network address space
   C. Switch
   D. Router

5. What acronym represents the term for hosting and managing of multiple virtual desktops on a network?

   A. VMM

   B. HAV

   C. VDI

   D. App-V

6. In this type of client-side virtualization, a user runs an application in a virtualized application environment on the local computer, isolating the application.

   A. Storage virtualization

   B. Application virtualization

   C. Virtual world

   D. Thin client

Implementing Client-Side Desktop Virtualization

7. Which acronym is a generic term for virtualization support found in modern CPUs?

   A. VMM

   B. VDI

   C. HAV

   D. App-V

8. Which of the following terms is used in computers to describe the use of software that allows you to run an OS or device on hardware with which it is completely incompatible?

   A. Virtualization

   B. Hardware-Assisted Virtualization

   C. Emulation

   D. Linux

9. Which of the following is a free hypervisor by Oracle with versions for Linux, Windows, and Mac OS X hosts?

   A. VirtualBox

   B. Parallels

   C. Player

   D. Virtual PC

10. Which of the following does not require a host OS?
    A. Type II hypervisor
    B. Type I hypervisor
    C. Virtual PC 2007
    D. Windows Virtual PC

11. Which of the following terms is synonymous with hypervisor?
    A. Type I
    B. Virtual machine manager (VMM)
    C. Type II
    D. Virtual PC 2007

12. Which free hypervisor used in an exercise in this chapter has versions that run on Windows, Mac OS X, and Linux hosts?
    A. Windows XP Mode
    B. Virtual PC 2007
    C. Windows Virtual PC
    D. VirtualBox

13. What legal issue must you consider when installing a guest OS in a virtual machine?
    A. Security
    B. Licensing
    C. Copyright
    D. Credentials

14. Which of the following will release the mouse and keyboard from control of a virtual machine?
    A. Host key
    B. Guest key
    C. Windows key
    D. Product key

15. Two critical apps written for Windows XP will not run on your new Windows 7 computer, and Compatibility Mode only solved the problem for one app. Which of the following is the least expensive choice for running the old app on the new computer?
    A. Windows XP Mode
    B. Microsoft Virtual PC 2007
    C. VMware Workstation
    D. Oracle VirtualBox

16. You must enter this within 30 days of installing a retail edition of Microsoft software.
   - **A.** Host key
   - **B.** Guest key
   - **C.** Windows key
   - **D.** Product key

17. Put the following steps in order: (1) Install Guest OS; (2) Install hypervisor; (3) Create virtual machine; (4) Install security software.
   - **A.** 1, 2, 3, 4
   - **B.** 1, 4, 3, 2
   - **C.** 2, 3, 1, 4
   - **D.** 4, 1, 3, 2

18. Which of the following is true?
   - **A.** No emulation is possible by the hypervisors studied in this chapter.
   - **B.** No emulation is possible by the hypervisors studied in this chapter unless the client OS is Mac OS X.
   - **C.** Some emulation of incompatible hardware is possible by the hypervisors studied in this chapter, as long as the CPU is compatible.
   - **D.** Some emulation of incompatible hardware is possible by the hypervisors studied in this chapter, as long as the CPU is incompatible.

19. Which of the following identifies Intel's CPUs with Hardware-Assisted Virtualization technology?
   - **A.** HAV
   - **B.** App-V
   - **C.** VMM
   - **D.** VT-x

20. Which of the following describes a Type I hypervisor?
   - **A.** App-V
   - **B.** Guest OS
   - **C.** VDI
   - **D.** Bare-metal hypervisor

SELF TEST ANSWERS

Introduction to Virtualization

1. ☑ **C.** Avatar is an animated, computer-generated human or animal image that represents a computer user in a virtual world.

   ☒ **A,** gadget, is incorrect, as a gadget is a small program. **B,** guest, is incorrect because the only use of guest in this chapter has been "guest OS," the OS running within a VM. **D,** orb, is incorrect. The word orb was introduced in Chapter 2 for the Windows Orb, the round Start menu button as seen in Windows Vista and Windows 7.

2. ☑ **B.** Virtual classroom is a type of virtualization used in distance learning for interactive presentations by instructors.

   ☒ **A,** server-side virtualization, and **C,** client-side virtualization, are both incorrect because these are simply terms for the hosting location of virtualization. **D,** application virtualization, is incorrect because this is a type of client-side virtualization.

3. ☑ **C.** Presentation virtualization is a type of virtualization in which only support for an app's user interface, and the user interface itself, exist on a client computer, while the app itself runs on a server.

   ☒ **A,** application virtualization, is incorrect because in this type of virtualization the entire app is virtualized and the user interface is not separated from the app, but is isolated in a VM. **B,** storage virtualization, is incorrect because this type of virtualization allows client computers to utilize many networked hard drives as though they are one drive or location. **D,** server virtualization, is incorrect because in server virtualization a single machine hosts one or more server operating systems, each in a virtual machine and each performing tasks independently from the other virtual machines and from the host.

4. ☑ **B.** Network address space exists within one or more physical networks, creating a virtual network.

   ☒ **A,** network adapters, is incorrect, as it is the address space that is virtualized in network virtualization. **C,** switch, and **D,** router are incorrect, as these are both types of network hardware not described in this chapter, and are not used to create a virtual network.

5. ☑ **C.** VDI, virtual desktop infrastructure, describes the hosting and managing of multiple virtual desktops over a network.

   ☒ **A,** VMM (virtual machine monitor), is incorrect because this is another term for hypervisor. **B,** HAV (hardware-assisted virtualization), is incorrect because this is hardware-level support for virtualization found in Intel and AMD CPUs. **D,** App-V (Application Virtualization), is incorrect because it is the term for Microsoft's application virtualization software.

6. ☑ **B.** Application virtualization is the type of client-side virtualization in which a user runs an application in a virtualized application environment on the local computer, isolating the application.

   ☒ **A,** storage virtualization, is incorrect because this type of virtualization allows client computers to utilize many networked hard drives as though they are one. **C,** virtual world, is incorrect because it is an artificial environment that users can explore, often using an avatar. **D,** thin client, is incorrect because it is a low-cost PC that runs software to connect to a server, transfer video downstream to the thin client, and send mouse and keystrokes upstream to the application on the server.

Implementing Client-Side Desktop Virtualization

7. ☑ **C.** HAV (Hardware-Assisted Virtualization) is the generic term for virtualization support found in modern CPUs.

   ☒ **A,** VMM (virtual machine manager), is incorrect because this is simply another term for a hypervisor. **B,** VDI (virtual desktop infrastructure), is incorrect because this is a term for the creation and management of multiple virtual desktops. **D.** App-V (Application Virtualization) is a Microsoft term for their application virtualization software.

8. ☑ **C.** Emulation is the use of software that allows you to run an OS or device on hardware with which it is completely incompatible.

   ☒ **A,** virtualization, is incorrect, as this is the creation of an environment that seems real, but is not. While that is close to emulation, in the context of virtualization on computers, these terms are often kept separate. **B,** Hardware-Assisted Virtualization, is incorrect because this is simply hardware support for virtualization built into modern CPUs. **D,** Linux, is incorrect because this is simply an operating system.

9. ☑ **A.** VirtualBox is the free hypervisor by Oracle with versions for Linux, Windows, and Mac OS X hosts.

   ☒ **B,** Parallels, is incorrect because it is not by Oracle and is not free. **C,** Player, is incorrect because it is by VMware not Oracle, and it does not come in a version for Mac OS X hosts. **D,** Virtual PC, is incorrect because it is by Microsoft, not Oracle, and it does not come in a version for Mac OS X hosts.

10. ☑ **B.** Type I hypervisor is correct because it does not require a host OS.

    ☒ **A,** Type II hypervisor, is incorrect because it does require a host OS. **C,** Virtual PC 2007, and **D,** Windows Virtual PC, are both incorrect because they are both Type II hypervisors that require a host OS.

11. ☑ **B.** Virtual machine manager (VMM) is synonymous with hypervisor.
    ☒ **A,** Type I, and **C,** Type II, while types of hypervisors, are not synonymous with hypervisor. **D,** Virtual PC 2007, while one of many hypervisors, is not synonymous with hypervisor.

12. ☑ **D.** VirtualBox has versions that run on Windows, Mac OS X, and Linux hosts.
    ☒ **A,** Windows XP Mode, is not, by itself, a hypervisor, and it does not run on Mac OS X or Linux hosts. **B,** Virtual PC 2007, and **C,** Windows Virtual PC, while both are hypervisors, do not have versions that run on Mac OS X.

13. ☑ **B.** Licensing of the guest OS is very important.
    ☒ **A,** security, while very important for both the guest and host OSs, is not strictly speaking a legal issue. **C,** copyright, is not a legal issue with a guest OS. **D,** credentials (user name and password), are also not the legal issue described in this chapter for a guest OS.

14. ☑ **A.** Host key is a special key or key combination that will release the mouse and keyboard from control of a virtual machine.
    ☒ **B,** guest key, is incorrect because it is not the key or key combination that will release the mouse and keyboard from control of a virtual machine. **C,** Windows key, is incorrect because this special key works within Microsoft software on its own and in combination with other keys, and is many things other than a host key. **D,** product key, is incorrect, as this is not an actual key on the keyboard, but a string of characters used by Microsoft for piracy protection.

15. ☑ **A.** Windows XP Mode is the least expensive option because it provides for free both a hypervisor and a fully licensed version of Windows XP.
    ☒ **B** is incorrect. While Microsoft Virtual PC 2007 is free, and it would work, it does not include Windows XP, so you would have to provide that client OS at your expense. Also, Virtual PC 2007 does not support HAV, so it would run slower on the computer with HAV support. **C,** VMware Workstation, is incorrect because it is not free, and it does not include a free license for Windows XP. **D,** Oracle VirtualBox, is incorrect because while it is free, you would still need to provide a licensed version of Windows XP as the client.

16. ☑ **D.** A product key, a string of alphanumeric characters that comes on the packaging for Microsoft software, must be entered within 30 days of installing the software or the software will be disabled.
    ☒ **A,** host key, is incorrect because this is a key used to release the keyboard and mouse from a virtual machine. **B,** guest key, is incorrect. This is not what you must enter within 30 days, and guest key is not a term found in this chapter. **C,** Windows key, is incorrect because this is a key on a PC keyboard, not something you would enter at the keyboard.

17. ☑ **C.** (2) Install hypervisor; (3) Create virtual machine; (1) Install guest OS; (4) Install security software.
    ☒ **A, B,** and **D** are not in the proper order as described in this chapter.

18.   ☑   **C.** Some emulation of incompatible hardware is possible by the hypervisors studied in this chapter, as long as the CPU is compatible.
    ☒   **A, B,** and **D** are all incorrect statements.

19.   ☑   **D.** VT-x identifies Intel's CPUs with Hardware-Assisted Virtualization technology.
    ☒   **A,** HAV, is incorrect because this is simply the acronym for the generic term. **B,** App-V, is incorrect because this is the acronym for Microsoft Application Virtualization. **C,** VMM, is incorrect because this is the acronym for virtual machine manager, another term for hypervisor.

20.   ☑   **D.** Bare-metal hypervisor describes a Type I hypervisor because it does not require a host OS between it and the hardware.
    ☒   **A,** App-V, is incorrect because this is Microsoft's application virtualization technology. **B,** guest OS, is incorrect because this is the OS running within a virtual machine. **C,** VDI, is incorrect because virtual desktop infrastructure describes hosting and managing multiple virtual desktops (often thousands) over a network.

9

Upgrading, Installing, and Configuring Windows

I n this chapter, we will examine the successful installation and configuration of Windows. Whether you are upgrading from an older version of Windows or installing from scratch (a clean install), you must follow certain guidelines and procedures, including basic preparation and installation steps and post-installation tasks. Configuring Windows involves many components, including network connections, registration and activation, updating, applications and Windows components, devices, power management, and, occasionally, virtual memory. They are all included in this chapter.

CERTIFICATION OBJECTIVE

■ **802: 1.2** *Given a scenario, install and configure the operating system using the most appropriate method*

CompTIA Exam Objective 802: 1.2 for installing and configuring Windows involves understanding a variety of scenarios for each of these areas. This section includes what you need to know to successfully upgrade Windows, a small portion of this objective. You should be familiar with upgrade paths, described in Chapter 2, and how the traditional in-place upgrade differs from the Anytime Upgrade previously available for Windows Vista and presently available for Windows 7, which are detailed in this section. To best prepare for the exam, give yourself hands-on experience by performing upgrade installations.

Upgrading Windows

In this section, we will look at why you would upgrade Windows rather than do a clean install, what tasks you should perform before an upgrade, and how to do an upgrade. The next section will detail how to do a clean install.

Why Upgrade?

An in-place upgrade installation of Windows involves installing the new version of Windows directly on top of an existing installation. During an in-place upgrade, Windows reads all the previous settings from the old *registry*, a database of all configuration settings in Windows; adapts them for the new registry; and transfers all hardware and software configuration information, thus saving you the trouble of reinstalling applications and reconfiguring your desktop the way you like it. Although you can upgrade Windows using the full retail disc of the latest version, you can also buy a special Upgrade version of Windows that is much less expensive. The drawback to this version is that it will only install on a computer with a previous legally licensed version of Windows preinstalled.

Pre-Upgrade Tasks

Before purchasing the Windows OS for an upgrade, check to be sure there is an upgrade path from the installed version to the new one. Then you are ready for the pre-upgrade tasks.

Checking Requirements and Compatibility

When upgrading Windows, pay close attention to compatibility issues, run the Upgrade Advisor, as described in Chapter 2, and be ready to resolve any problems you find. For example, if it shows that the new operating system does not have a driver for your network adapter and you proceed with the upgrade, you will not be able to access the network through the existing adapter. If the Upgrade Advisor found incompatible hardware or software, take steps to resolve these problems before you upgrade.

Resolving Software Incompatibility

If an upgrade is available for an incompatible application program, obtain it and check with the manufacturer. Upgrade the application before upgrading the OS, unless advised otherwise by the manufacturer.

Remove any programs that will not run in the new OS from the computer before upgrading. There are also programs that interfere with the Windows Setup program but are compatible with the new Windows version after installation. This is often true of antivirus software. The Upgrade Advisor report will list these, in which case follow the instructions under Details in the Upgrade Advisor report. You may need to uninstall the program before the upgrade and reinstall it after the new version of Windows runs successfully.

If you have a critical app that is incompatible but you must use it in the new version of Windows, then use whatever compatibility options are available in the Windows upgrade after it is installed. Recall the Windows 7 Compatibility Wizard described in Chapter 2, or Windows XP Mode for Windows 7 described in Chapter 8.

Resolving Hardware Incompatibility

When it comes to hardware incompatibility, usually the device driver, not the hardware, is the source of incompatibility with an operating system. Therefore, before upgrading, be sure to run the Upgrade Advisor, as described in Chapter 2, and if it finds incompatibilities with your hardware, contact the manufacturer to see if they have an updated driver that will work. If so, obtain the driver beforehand, and follow the manufacturer's instructions. You may need to wait to upgrade the device driver until after the Windows installation is completed.

If your research shows that a hardware incompatibility cannot be resolved, remove the hardware in question, and replace it with a component that has a driver that works with the new OS.

Cleaning Up the Hard Drive

Before upgrading your computer to a new version of Windows, clean up the hard drive, especially the C: volume. This cleanup should include removing both unwanted programs and unnecessary files.

Removing Unwanted Programs   The programs you should consider removing are those nifty programs you installed on a whim and now find you either dislike or never use. They are all taking up space on the hard drive. Many (but not all) have an uninstall shortcut on the same menu with the shortcut that launches the program. Select the uninstall shortcut to remove the program.

For programs that do not have an uninstall shortcut, open Control Panel and find the appropriate program removal tool for your version of Windows. This would be Add Or Remove Programs in Windows XP or Programs And Features in Windows Vista, Windows 7, and Windows 8. Scroll through the list looking for programs you are sure you will never use. When you complete this task, leave this applet open while you remove unwanted Windows components, as described next.

Removing Unwanted Windows Components   As you prepare to upgrade to a new version of Windows, you should also consider removing unwanted Windows components. To do this, open the applet you used to remove programs. In Windows XP, click the Add/Remove Windows Components button on the left. In Windows Vista and Windows 7, select the Turn Windows Features On Or Off task in the Uninstall Or Change A Program page of Programs And Features. In Windows XP, this will open the Windows Components Wizard. In Windows Vista, Windows 7, or Windows 8 it will open the Windows Features dialog, shown in Figure 9-1. Browse through the list and remove any unnecessary components.

FIGURE 9-1

In Windows
Features, select
the components
you no longer use.

Removing Unnecessary Files   It's amazing how fast hard drive space fills up.
One way it fills up is with large data files, especially music, video, and picture files.
Another, less obvious way hard drive space fills up is with temporary files, especially
temporary Internet files that accumulate on the local hard drive while you are browsing
the Internet. Windows has a nifty utility for cleaning up these files—Disk Cleanup.

To launch this utility, select Start | All Programs (or Programs) | Accessories |
System Tools | Disk Cleanup, or simply use the Start Search feature. It will walk
you through the process. In Windows XP, Windows 7, and Windows 8, you begin by
selecting a drive; in Windows Vista, you begin by choosing to clean up those files
associated with you, or the files for all users on your computer, and then choose the
drive. In all versions, Disk Cleanup then spends a few minutes analyzing your files
and calculating the space you can potentially free up. When finished it displays a
dialog box, shown in Figure 9-2. You may see a different selection of file types when
you run this on your system. Each type of file will have a check box; click to place a
check mark next to any items you want deleted and watch the total amount of disk
space you gain change based on your selections. Click OK and Disk Cleanup will
remove all the selected files. A progress bar will display while the utility works.

on the
job

*If you select the Recycle Bin, Disk Cleanup will only delete the contents, not
the Recycle Bin folder itself. The Recycle Bin is a special folder created by the
Recycle Bin function in Windows.*

FIGURE 9-2

Disk Cleanup

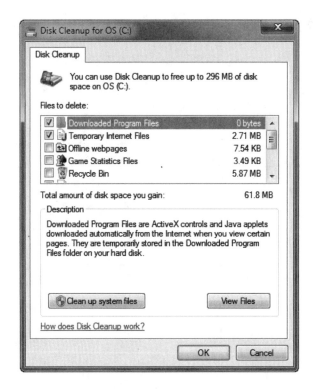

Backing Up Data

Back up any data from the local hard drive. Installing a new OS should not put your data in danger, but you just never know. Upgrading makes many changes to your computer, replacing critical system files with those of the new OS. If your computer loses power at an inopportune time, it could become unusable. This is a rare but real danger, especially if the computer is very old. Besides, surely you need to back up your hard drive. Backing up can be as simple as copying the contents of your My Documents (Windows XP) or Documents (Windows Vista/7) folder onto an external hard drive or flash drive, or using the built-in Windows Backup program. Learn more about the Windows Backup program in Chapter 10.

Defragmenting the Hard Drive

Over time, Windows develops a problem on its hard drives called "fragmented files." Fragmentation will slow the system down when reading files into memory. The solution is defragmenting, and you should do it any time you remove programs and/or delete a large number of files. The tool you will use is the Disk Defragmenter utility found in Windows Vista and Windows 7 on the same System Tools menu with Disk Cleanup (described in the previous section). In Windows 8, search in Settings for "defragment" and select Defragment Your Hard Drive from the results. When you open this, the dialog box is actually titled Optimize Drives, but it is nearly identical to the Windows 7 utility. You can choose to defrag one or more volumes immediately or to schedule it for later. The default settings in Windows Vista, Windows 7, and Windows 8 is to run on a weekly schedule, defragmenting all drives, as shown in the Disk Defragmenter dialog box in Figure 9-3.

Running an Upgrade from Older Versions to Newer Versions

The title of this section might be a bit confusing, but there is a difference between running an upgrade from earlier versions to new versions of Windows and running an upgrade from a less capable edition of Windows 7 to a more capable edition

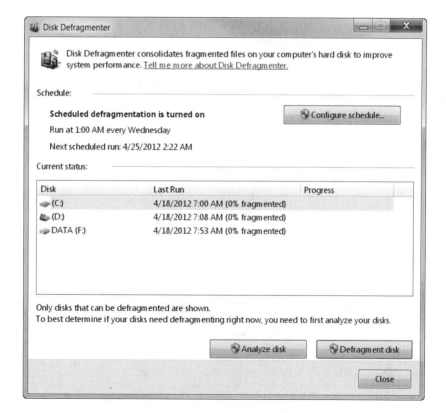

FIGURE 9-3

Windows 7 Disk Defragmenter

of Windows 7. Therefore, in this section, we will describe an older-version-to-newer-version upgrade, and in the next section, we will discuss upgrading from Window 7 editions.

For any installation, you have to decide if the installation will be unattended (run from a script) or attended. Unattended installations are usually done in large organizations to distribute software to many computers. We will discuss unattended installation later in this chapter. An *attended installation*, also called a *manual installation*, is an installation of Windows that is not automated, but requires someone present to initiate it and respond to the prompts from the Setup program. And then we have attended clean installations (described later) and attended upgrades, described here.

To start an attended upgrade from earlier versions of Windows to Windows XP, Windows Vista, or Windows 7, start the existing version of Windows and place the distribution disc into the drive. Wait several seconds to see if the Setup program starts

on its own. If it does not start, use My Computer or Computer to browse to the CD and launch the Setup program. The Setup program will then detect the existing version of Windows. If it is a version that you can directly upgrade, Windows XP Setup will show Upgrade in the Installation Type box, and Windows Vista and Windows 7 will include Upgrade as an active option in the screen shown in Figure 9-4.

Recall the upgrade paths to Windows XP, Windows Vista, and Windows 7 described in Chapter 2.

If the OS cannot be upgraded, this option will be grayed out in these newer Windows Setup programs. Click Next to continue with an upgrade, and Setup will continue in a manner similar to a clean installation, only with fewer interruptions for information, and you will not be prompted to create a new partition for the OS (something we'll look at later in this chapter) since that would wipe out the installed OS and programs. You will need to provide a product key for any retail version, full or upgrade.

Windows Anytime Upgrade

Windows 7 comes in several editions. If you have a computer with a less capable edition of Windows 7, such as Windows 7 Home Premium, and you discover it is lacking a feature you require, such as the ability to join your employer's corporate

FIGURE 9-4

Choose Upgrade in Windows Vista or Windows 7 Setup.

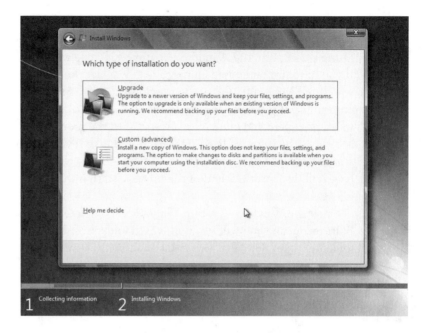

Microsoft domain, you can very easily upgrade. And while Windows 8 does not have as many editions, it does have the Anytime Upgrade feature, renamed and available through the Control Panel as Add Features To Windows 8. The lesser editions of Windows actually have the files for the higher-level versions installed; they just need to be unlocked, and Windows Anytime Upgrade is your quick path to upgrading from Home Premium or Professional to Ultimate in Windows 7. What you need to do is go online or to a retail store and purchase an upgrade key (a string of characters you enter to activate a product). Then, to start the upgrade, open the Start menu and type **anytime upgrade** in the Search box. From the list of results, click Windows Anytime Upgrade.

on the *Windows Vista also had the Anytime Upgrade option, but that was discontinued.*
job *If you want to upgrade from a lesser edition to a more capable edition of Windows Vista, you simply do a standard upgrade installation.*

Even if you try to upgrade using a retail disc of the more capable edition, Windows 7 Setup will launch Anytime Upgrade. This is a good thing because it will save you time. Using either path, the Windows Anytime Upgrade wizard will open (see Figure 9-5). If you have not purchased an upgrade key, select the first option, which will take you to the Microsoft Website to purchase a key and return you to the page for entering it. If you have an upgrade key, click the second option. Enter the key when prompted and click Next. Respond to the prompts on each page, including accepting the software license terms. It will take several minutes, during which time a page displays a progress bar, and Windows Setup will restart your computer. A page will display at the end of the process, stating that the upgrade was successful. Close this window.

After the Windows Anytime Upgrade is complete, open All Programs from the Start menu, and you will see highlighted folders, as shown in Figure 9-6. These folders contain new Windows components that were installed during the upgrade.

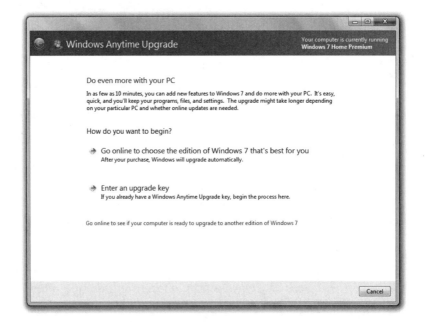

FIGURE 9-5

The Windows Anytime Upgrade screen

FIGURE 9-6

The All Programs list showing folders with new components installed during the upgrade

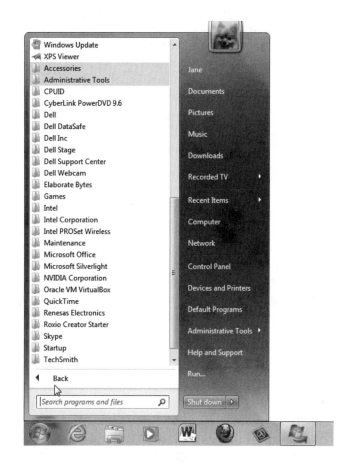

CERTIFICATION OBJECTIVES

■ **802: 1.2** *Given a scenario, install and configure the operating system using the most appropriate method*

■ **802: 1.4** *Given a scenario, use appropriate operating features and tools*

■ **802: 1.5** *Given a scenario, use Control Panel utilities (the items are organized by "classic view/large icons" in Windows)*

In this section we continue the coverage of CompTIA Exam Objective 802: 1.2 with coverage of clean installations to individual computers and other installation options and types, such as installing from an image, from a recovery CD, and from a factory recovery partition. CompTIA Exam Objective 802: 1.4 covers a broad range of operating system features and tools, but just two items in that extensive list are part of this chapter, and they are the User Data Migration Tool (UDMT), which is actually an obsolete term, and the User State Migration Tool (USMT). Similarly, CompTIA Exam Objective 802: 1.5 includes a large list of Control Panel utilities, and this section covers just one: virtual memory.

Installing Windows

Performing a clean install of a new operating system is not a one-step process—in fact, it occurs in three stages. In the first stage, you perform necessary tasks to prepare for the installation; in the second stage, you actually install the operating system; and in the third stage, you implement follow-up tasks. In this section, you will learn the necessary tasks for the first two stages when performing a clean installation of Windows.

Preparing to Install Windows

Prepare to install Windows by first ensuring a computer meets the minimum requirements. You should then verify hardware and software compatibility, understand the basics of disk preparation for installation as well as the choice of file systems (where appropriate), and finally, take steps to migrate data from a previous Windows installation to a new installation.

Hardware Requirements

In Chapter 2 you learned about the hardware requirements for Windows XP, Windows Vista, and Windows 7, and they are listed in that chapter in Table 2-4. Recall that system minimums are just that: minimum requirements for running the OS—the lowest level of CPU, the minimum amount of RAM, and the minimum free hard disk space needed to install an OS. You will need a more powerful computer, in terms of hard drive space and RAM, to run a suite of office productivity tools. The good news is that a basic consumer-grade computer today far surpasses

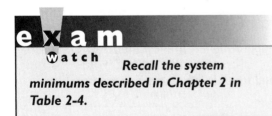

exam

ⓦatch *Recall the system minimums described in Chapter 2 in Table 2-4.*

the system minimums for all current versions of Windows, with the exception of Windows 8. It requires a screen resolution of 1024 × 768 as a bare minimum to run Windows 8 apps, but to take advantage of all of the features of Windows 8, you need a resolution of 1366 × 768.

Verifying Hardware and Software Compatibility

With each new version of Windows, Microsoft changes where we should check for compatibility before purchasing and/or installing a new version:

- *Hardware Compatibility List (HCL)*   In Windows XP, this was a simple list of compatible hardware, by vendor, that came on disc, but was also available in a more updated version online.

- *Windows Logo'd Product List*   Windows Vista introduced an online list that was found at winqual.microsoft.com/hcl/. Notice the "hcl" at the end of the Uniform Resource Locator (URL). When it was active, it listed all the vendors who participated in Microsoft's Windows Logo'd Product program. It has been replaced by the Windows 7 Compatibility Center.

- *Windows 7 Compatibility Center*   This Website maintains a list of compatible apps and hardware for Windows 7. Enter **windows 7 compatibility** into your search engine and select the result with Microsoft.com in the URL. See Figure 9-7.

- *Microsoft Store*   This is the Website that started out as a searchable list of hardware and software known to work with Windows, at first called the Windows Catalog, and later the Windows Marketplace, which functioned as an online store. If you enter the former URL for the Windows Marketplace, your browser will be redirected to the Microsoft Store.

- *Windows Store*   In Windows 8, the Store tile will open the Windows Store, Microsoft's online store for products certified by Microsoft for Windows 8.

watch

In spite of the fact that Microsoft has replaced the original Hardware Compatibility List with Websites that list both hardware and software, the CompTIA   *Exam 801 and 802 Objectives both refer to HCL in the CompTIA A+ Acronyms list, so you may see a question concerning it.*

FIGURE 9-7

The Windows 7 Compatibility Center

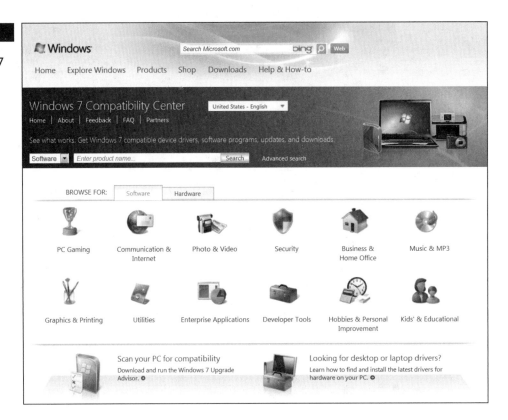

As described in Chapter 2, you can run the Upgrade Advisor specific to Windows XP, Windows Vista, or Windows 7 before purchasing the OS in order to determine if your existing computer hardware and software are compatible with the new OS. For instance, if upgrading to Windows 7, download and run the Windows 7 Upgrade Advisor from the Microsoft site on the older computer. In addition, the Setup programs for all the versions of Windows covered by the CompTIA A+ Exams perform a compatibility test of your hardware (clean installation) or hardware and software (upgrade installation). The Windows 7 and Windows 8 setup wizard will display a button labeled Check Compatibility Online. Click this button to have it connect and run the compatibility test. Or click Install Now to proceed without running the test.

Don't forget about the issues of 32-bit versus 64-bit Windows and hardware and software compatibility. Most computer manufacturers today only ship computers with 64-bit Windows preinstalled, now that more applications are available that take advantage of the larger memory space of 64-bit Windows. If you are planning to install 64-bit Windows on an older computer, you should do your homework and ensure that it will work with your computer system and peripherals. Of course, compatibility is important even when installing on a new computer.

Preparing a Storage Device

CompTIA Exam Objective 802: 1.2 lists dynamic, basic, primary, extended, and logical under the Partitioning topic. These are actually an apples-and-oranges mix. For instance, dynamic and basic are disk storage types as defined by Microsoft, while primary and extended are partition types only found on basic storage, and logical is often applied to the letter we apply to drives. Although you can also think of logical as anything that is not physical, when talking about storage, it is used—rather loosely—to describe something that is software-based rather than physical. You have a physical hard drive in a computer, versus a logical drive we create from the space on one or more hard drives. A logical drive is seen in Windows Explorer with a letter that was assigned to it by the OS.

If you install Windows on an unpartitioned hard disk, the Setup program will automatically prompt you to create a partition, assign a drive letter, and format the partition. If you accept the defaults, it will create a partition of the maximum size available on the primary hard drive, assign the drive letter C: to the partition, and format it with the New Technology File System (NTFS) file system. After that, the actual installation of Windows will proceed.

We will take a few minutes to define storage types (basic versus dynamic), partition types (primary versus extended), and file systems here, and in Chapter 10 you will work with Disk Management, the utility you use after Windows is installed to manage and maintain your storage devices.

Disk Storage Types　Microsoft introduced the concept of storage type—dynamic and basic—in Windows 2000, and they continue to use these types in the newer versions of Windows. The storage type applies to the entire disk, but it is not a physical characteristic of a disk. It is a logical characteristic that has to do with how it allocates and manages space.

The *basic storage* type was the only storage type for hard disks from the days of Microsoft DOS (MS DOS) until Windows 2000. In fact, it has only been since Windows 2000 that the term basic storage has been used, and a disk using basic storage, a *basic disk,* is somewhat limited. On a basic disk, you have two types of partitions to choose from, which we will describe in the next section when we describe partition types. What defines a basic disk is the use of the partition table, saved on disk in the first physical sector and called the master boot record (MBR).

Dynamic storage uses another location and method for storing disk configuration information. Basic storage is the default storage type when you install Windows. Techs may call a basic disk an MBR disk.

Because the dynamic storage type was created with the storage needs of network servers in mind, until recently you were more likely to use the basic storage type in Windows on desktop computers. However, MBR disks cannot support partitions larger than 2.2 TB, so you will see dynamic disks on PCs with very large hard disk drives. As time goes on, these newer PCs will also have the Unified Extensible Firmware Interface (UEFI) firmware replacement for BIOS, described in Chapter 3. UEFI provides even more support for non-MBR volumes, as it supports a replacement for the old partition table in the MBR. This replacement is called the *GUID Partition Table (GPT)*. Here is an overview of dynamic storage types.

Dynamic storage is a newer way to allocate disk space and manage hard disks. Support for dynamic storage began with Windows 2000 and continues in today's Windows versions. When a disk storage type is changed from basic to dynamic, it is then a *dynamic disk,* and does not have the limits imposed on basic disks (which we will describe when we talk about partitioning). The following statements are true of dynamic disks:

■ When you work with dynamic disks, the term "partitions" goes away, and what resembles a basic disk partition is a volume.

■ The number of volumes on a dynamic disk is not limited.

■ A volume can extend to include available space on any hard disk in the computer, and therefore, dynamic disk can support Redundant Array of Independent Disks (RAID) fault-tolerance levels described in Chapter 4.

■ Configuration information for a dynamic disk, the *dynamic disk database*, can be rather complex, as compared to basic disks, and this information is stored on the disk space beyond the first physical sector outside of any volume on the hard disk. This is set aside and not visible when you use Windows Explorer to view your disks, folders, and files. If a disk was previously configured, the conversions to dynamic disk may need to make room for this database and remove an older partition.

Once the operating system is up and running, you may choose to convert a basic disk to a dynamic disk, but the benefits of dynamic disks really aim at the needs of network servers or high-end workstations, not the needs of most desktop computers. In fact, only one RAID type, disk mirroring, is available in Windows XP, Windows Vista, and Windows 7. Other more advanced features are available only in the Windows Server products.

Basic Disk Partition Types   When we talk about partition types, we are, once again, talking about basic disks. Before a basic disk is able to save data, you must partition and format it. Partitioning a disk means dividing the disk into one or more areas that you can treat as separate logical drives, and each may, therefore, get its own individual drive letter. You must format each logical drive with a file system, and each can have a different file system. This is possible, but not usually practical, unless you have a multiboot system with operating systems that support different file systems isolated on different partitions.

Normally, you don't want to divide a hard disk into multiple logical drives, so you create a single partition that uses the entire drive. On basic disks, a partition table within the MBR holds a record of the partition boundaries on a disk, but there are limits to the old type of partition tables that apply to basic disks. A basic disk is compatible with older operating systems, and it can have up to four partitions.

Two partition types are used on basic disks in Windows: primary and extended, of which there can be a maximum of four primary partitions, or three primaries and one extended partition (see Figure 9-8).

Primary Partitions   Each *primary partition* can have only one logical drive assigned to it encompassing the entire partition. Because a computer can only boot from a primary partition that is also marked as active, a Windows PC with basic disks must have at least one primary partition.

Extended Partitions   An *extended partition* can have one or more logical drives (each with a drive letter). Older operating systems such as MS-DOS, Windows 3.*x*, or Windows 9*x* (including Windows Millennium Edition) could only create two partitions. The extended partition type was, in a real sense, a fix for the limits of these OSs. Because they could not work with more than two entries in the partition table, Microsoft created the extended partition type. An extended partition is divisible into one or more logical drives, each of which has a drive letter assigned to it. This feature allows these OSs to work with more than two logical drives on a single hard disk system. Furthermore, the older operating systems cannot work with more than one primary partition per physical hard drive. If a hard drive has two partitions, under one of these operating systems, one must be primary and the other must be an extended partition.

Things have changed. Although Windows XP computers often came configured with one primary and one extended partition, this was unnecessary, and the second partition should really have been a primary partition because Windows XP supported this, and it actually takes longer to access data on a logical drive within an extended partition. This practice has gone away with Windows Vista and Windows 7.

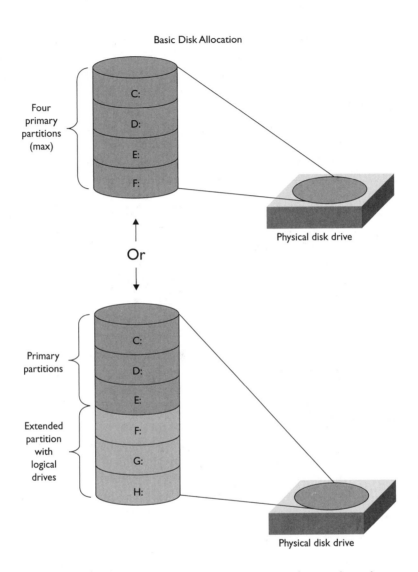

FIGURE 9-8

Basic disk allocation allows for a maximum of four partitions.

Basic Disk Allocation

Four primary partitions (max)

C:

D:

E:

F:

Physical disk drive

Or

Primary partitions

C:

D:

E:

Extended partition with logical drives

F:

G:

H:

Physical disk drive

Designating the Active Partition   In order for Windows to boot from a partition, that partition must be a primary partition marked as active. This is because the startup procedure common to all PCs looks for an *active partition* on the first physical drive from which to start an OS. Installing Windows on a new unpartitioned hard drive creates a primary active partition.

Partition Size Limits   When you partition a drive, the maximum partition size is the lesser of two values: the maximum partition size supported by the hardware or the maximum partition size supported by the file system. The older file systems that predated NTFS will be the limiting factors if you plan to format a partition with one of them. For instance, the File Allocation Table (FAT16) file system has a 4 GB partition size limit in Windows 2000 and Windows XP, and a 2 GB partition size limit in Windows 9x and DOS. The FAT32 file system has a partition size limit of 2 terabytes (2 trillion bytes).

If you use NTFS, which is the default file system when you install Windows, the hardware will be the limiting factor. In the versions of Windows included on the CompTIA A+ Exams, the NTFS file system has a partition size limit of 16 exabytes (an exabyte is one billion billion bytes). Now, this is obviously theoretical, because the hardware limit on a computer with BIOS versus UEFI is much smaller. Most modern BIOSs have a 2.2 TB limit. If you are working with a computer that has an old BIOS, you may run into the old 137 GB limit, but modern machines built in the last few years support much larger hard drives.

Selecting a File System   A *file system* is the means an operating system uses to organize information on disks. When you format a disk, you place the file system on the disk. That is, the format program creates the supporting logical structure on the disk, which is the most important component of a file system. Windows can format a hard disk with one of several file systems, including FAT16, FAT32, and NTFS. Unless you have a special reason for selecting one of the older file systems, you should choose the NTFS file system during installation.

When you format a disk previously formatted in the same file system (FAT32 on FAT32, NTFS on NTFS), you can do a quick format that only refreshes the file system components on the disk, zeroing out all directory entries so that the disk appears empty. In reality, the old data is still written to disk after a quick format, but is difficult (but not impossible) to retrieve, whereas a full format does all that a quick format does, plus it overwrites the data space. Learn more about file systems and how to manage them in Chapter 10.

exam

watch   *CompTIA Exam Objective*
802: 1.2 includes CDFS under File Systems.
Compact Disc File System (CDFS) is an ISO
9660–compliant file system used by
Windows to read CDs, DVDs, and

CD-ROMs. It does not have a great deal
of relevance to installing and upgrading
Windows, other than the fact that the
retail packaged editions of Windows come
on optical disc.

Preparing for a Multiboot Installation

It is possible to configure a computer to boot into multiple operating systems, meaning that at startup you select the OS you wish to boot. This is called *multiboot* or, in the case of multibooting between just two OSs, we simply call it a *dual boot*. This is one way to try out a new version of Windows without replacing your old Windows installation. This book was written on a computer that still multiboots between Windows Vista and Windows 7, but we haven't booted it up to Vista in months, except to grab screenshots for our writing projects. And we have a laptop that we multiboot between Windows 7 and Windows 8.

When we start up one of these computers, a menu displays for several seconds. During that time, we can select the OS; if we do not make a selection, the default OS will be started.

So, how do you prepare to multiboot? First, you should dedicate a partition to each OS. While in the distant past we have dual-booted between two different OSs installed on the same partition, that is not the most desirable configuration, nor is it always possible. The computer that dual-boots between Vista and Windows 7 has two physical hard drives, so each OS has its own hard drive. The computer that dual-boots between Windows 7 and Windows 8 came with Windows 7 preinstalled on a 600 GB hard drive. To prepare the computer to dual-boot, we opened the Disk Management utility and used the Shrink Volume option to shrink the volume (really a partition, since this is a basic disk) by 60 GB. Then, in the space we freed up, we created a new partition, formatted it, and were ready to boot into the Windows 8 setup. We installed Windows 8 into the newly created partition, and when it detected the other installation of Windows, it installed the appropriate files and configuration so that now when we boot up we see an OS Selection menu. We have configured multiboot systems for many years, and the rule we use is "oldest to newest," meaning that you install the oldest OS first and the newest OS last.

Using Data Migration Tools

The most valuable files on a PC are not the OS and applications, but the user's data. Therefore, when upgrading the OS or moving the user to a new computer, you must plan for a successful *data migration*—the moving of data from one storage device to another. When you do an in-place upgrade, you retain all the user settings and data, so data migration is a nonissue. However, when you do a clean installation on a computer that has an older version of Windows, you often need to ensure that the settings and/or data from the old installation migrate to the new installation. Or, when you purchase a new computer with a new version of Windows, you face migrating settings and/or data files from an older computer. Windows XP, Windows Vista, and Windows 7 all have ways of handling this for you, and you can use a Microsoft data migration tool, a third-party tool.

Alternatively, you can migrate your data (but not your settings) the old-fashioned way with a backup on the old system and a restore to the new system. In that case, you can use the Windows backup utility in the old version, back up to an external hard drive or optical discs, and then after the installation is complete, restore to the new OS using the Windows backup utility in the new version. This works just fine.

However, if you use a third-party backup utility to back up the old data, you may need to ensure that you will be able to restore it into the new Windows installation—by installing the third-party backup utility into the new system or using Windows backup if it can work with the third-party program's backup format.

Migration programs from Microsoft and other vendors make the migration of data from one PC to another easier, as required when you must move data from an old computer to a new computer. Microsoft provides the *Files and Settings Transfer Wizard* in Windows XP and the Windows Easy Transfer (WET) Wizard for Windows Vista and Windows 7. Both wizards bring over your data and place it in the correct locations on your hard drive to fulfill the basic task of data migration. They go further by also migrating the settings for Windows and certain Windows applications, including desktop preferences and preferences for Internet Explorer and all Microsoft applications installed on both the old and the new computers. The wizards do not install any applications on the new PC, however, so you must install your applications on the new PC before migrating the data and settings from the old PC.

exam

w a t c h   *CompTIA 802 Exam Objective 1.1 lists "easy transfer" under operating system features, giving it a more generic twist. Expect to see it on the exam as easy transfer, Files and Settings Transfer Wizard, or Windows Easy Transfer (WET) Wizard.*

Windows XP Files and Settings Transfer Wizard   You must run the Windows XP Files and Settings Transfer Wizard on both the old and new computer. You start it from Start | All Programs | Accessories | System Tools on a Windows XP computer, or from the main menu of the Windows XP CD on an old computer running Windows 2000 or Windows XP. Choose the local computer's role in the transfer. When the wizard runs on any version of Windows other than Windows XP, the only role available is that of Old Computer.

When you select Old Computer, the wizard collects files and settings and places them in the location you define. This location can be any local hard drive, flash drive, or network share. You can specify a floppy disk, but the data is normally too large for a single floppy disk, and most newer PCs do not come with a floppy drive. Another rarely used option is a direct cable attached to serial ports, but serial ports have all but disappeared from new PCs as well.

Once you have collected the data, run the wizard on the new computer, point to the data's location, and the wizard will complete the transfer. This replacement process greatly simplifies the time it once took to move your data and configure a new PC with your preferences.

Windows Easy Transfer for Windows Vista and Windows 7

The WET utility was described briefly in Chapter 2. It comes with Windows Vista and Windows 7. Use it when doing a single transfer of data and settings to a new Windows computer from an older Windows computer. It is not practical to use this utility for multiple computers because it only works on a one-to-one basis with each old and new pair. You can run the WET Wizard, shown in Figure 9-9, choosing the types of files you want to transfer and the method for transferring them to the new Windows computer.

The three transfer methods are via an Easy Transfer cable (a special USB cable available from many sources), via network, or via an external hard disk or USB flash drive. Two of these methods, the cable and network, require two separate computers, while the third method can also be used when you are planning to replace (not upgrade) the current Windows installation with a new, clean installation.

Depending on the transfer method you use, the wizard will guide you through the process of installing the WET utility into the older version of Windows and gathering the files.

User State Migration Tool   The *User State Migration Tool (USMT)* is an advanced tool that only works in a Windows server–based domain network. This is the tool for network administrators in such a network who either need to migrate data from many computers or need to perform what Microsoft calls a "wipe-and-load migration" from and to the same computer. USMT has been available for Windows XP, Vista, and Windows 7. It takes longer to prepare, involving creating custom scripts, but it results in an automated process that occurs in two stages. The first stage collects files and settings, and the second stage installs the files and settings on the target computer. As with WET, you can use a variety of media locations for USMT.

FIGURE 9-9

Windows Easy
Transfer

When installing Windows on a new computer that does not have an OS on the hard

---

CompTIA Exam Objective 802: 1.4 lists both User State Migration Tool (USMT) and User State Data Tool (UDMT). However, the last time we saw UDMT as a name for a Microsoft data migration utility was for Windows NT, and that was in the 1990s.

Selecting Boot Media and Methods

When installing Windows on a new computer that does not have an OS on the hard drive, you will need to boot into the Setup program. How you do this depends on the computer, but your choices today include optical drive, USB device, External

Serial Advanced Technology Attachment (eSATA) device, or Preboot eXecution Environment (PXE) boot (for an over-the-network installation). Older versions of Windows Setup booted up from floppy disk, but that is ancient history, and not even an option in Windows Vista or Windows 7. The most common method for starting Windows Setup for the standard retail version is to boot up from the optical disc media, and most computers will do that by default.

Modifying the Boot Order

But what if you want or need to use one of the other options? What if you have the Windows installation files on a USB or eSATA device? What if the installation files are on a network server and you need to boot up the new computer on the network and have it connect to the installation share on the server and run the setup? The answer is in your BIOS settings.

Recall the BIOS configuration discussion in Chapter 3 when you learned that one important configuration setting is Boot Sequence, which may have another name in your BIOS such as Boot Priority Order. If you locate this setting on a modern PC or laptop, you will normally see the following options or equivalent language:

- CD/DVD/CD-RW Drive
- Hard Drive
- Removable Drive
- USB Storage Device
- eSATA
- Network

In the BIOS we are using as our example, the order in which they are listed is the order in which the computer BIOS will look for an operating system every time you boot up. For instance, every time we boot up the example computer, the BIOS bootstrap program first looks for an optical disc. If it finds one in the drive, it will typically prompt you to press a key to boot from disc. The program waits a preconfigured amount of time (normally about ten seconds) and then searches the next item in the list, which is the hard drive. If it finds the boot files for an OS, it stops its search and loads the OS. This is why even with a bootable OS on your hard drive, you can boot into a bootable disc (like the Windows Setup disc). It is conceivable that you have the Windows Setup program on an eSATA device, and as long as a bootable OS does not exist in the locations that precede eSATA, the BIOS will find the boot files for Windows Setup and boot from the eSATA device.

Before you begin a clean installation requiring that you boot into the Windows Setup program, go into your BIOS settings, as described in Chapter 3, and ensure that the device you need to boot from is either first in the list or not preceded by a bootable device. Then, for most of these options, you simply reboot and Windows Setup begins.

Booting from the Network (PXE Boot)

The Network option shown in the previous bulleted list takes a little more explanation. All modern network cards support the ability to start a computer over the network, without relying on a disk-based OS, using an Intel standard called *Preboot eXecution Environment (PXE)*, or more simply *PXE Boot*. On our example computer, the Network option can be expanded to show the name of the network card, which is Realtek PXE, showing that it complies with the standard. Therefore, if this is selected, the network card will initiate the startup of the computer, downloading the initial bootup files from a network server, and then it is ready to perform a task, such as installing the new OS over the network or running centralized maintenance tests on the computer. However, someone has to do the prep work of preparing a server running the Microsoft *Remote Installation Services (RIS)*. This service responds to PXE Boot requests from network clients and supplies the boot environment needed to boot up. Then, usually through a script, the client computer is directed to connect to the network share containing the Windows installation files and run the Setup program over the network.

Over-the-Network Installation

A network installation can involve an image installation, an attended installation, or an unattended installation. Any of these network installation methods requires quite a bit of prep work, but what they have in common is the basic steps for preparing for the installation. Here, we will describe the steps required for either an attended or unattended network installation. Later, we will address an over-the-network image installation.

To prepare for an attended or unattended network installation, first, copy the Windows source files into a shared folder on the server; second, configure the client computer to boot up and connect to the server; and third, start

exam

ⓦatch   *The CompTIA Exam Objective 802: 1.2 only requires that you understand the differences among the various installation methods. You do not need in-depth, hands-on experience with the unattended or drive-imaging methods.*

the Setup program itself. The actual steps for doing this are extensive, often requiring trained personnel and testing of the procedure.

Installing from a Recovery Disc

Many manufacturers ship computers with original equipment manufacturer (OEM) Windows installed (whatever version), but most of them do not ship an OEM Windows disc with the computer. They may ship what they call a recovery disc, or they give you the option of creating a recovery disc yourself from a utility installed with Windows. In this case, don't skip creating this disc. However you acquire it, be sure to keep it in a safe place. Without the OEM Windows disc, the recovery disc is your only source of your legally licensed Windows. If you need to reinstall Windows from a recovery disc, all you need to do is boot up the disc and the recovery program will run. The sad part is that it returns your computer to the state it was in the day you unpacked it and first turned it on. It wipes out all your installed programs and data, and you will have to reinstall the programs and then restore your data from backups. Sometimes installing from a recovery CD is your only option, but not always. In Chapter 13, we will look at how to diagnose operating system failures and how to recover from certain types of failures without reinstalling Windows.

Installing from a Factory Recovery Partition

If a manufacturer does not ship a recovery disc with a Windows computer or include a utility for creating this disc, they may offer another option, which is a factory recovery partition containing an image of the drive partition on which Windows is installed. The recovery partition itself is hidden and only accessible by a method the manufacturer provides for restoring the system to its fresh-from-the-factory state. Check the manufacturer's documentation long before you need to resort to installing from a factory recovery partition. In many cases, you enter the factory recovery partition utility by pressing a function key as the system starts up. If you install a new version of Windows on a computer with a recovery partition, the new OS may overwrite a critical part of the Windows partition containing information for calling up the recovery program, so check with the manufacturer before upgrading.

Attended Clean Windows Installation

There are two main installation methods: attended and unattended. Installing Windows requires inputting certain unique information for each computer. During an attended installation of Windows, also called a manual installation, you must pay attention throughout the entire process to provide information and to respond to messages.

The Windows Setup Wizard guides you through every step of the process. The on-screen directions are correct and clear, and you will need to make very few decisions. If you are in doubt about a setting, pressing ENTER will likely perform the correct action by selecting a default setting.

Overall, the installation process takes about an hour, and you spend most of that time watching the screen. Feel free to walk away as the installation is taking place, because, if it needs input, the installation program will stop and wait until you click the correct buttons.

on the
() o b

If you get distracted or walk away and are not available to respond to a prompt on the screen during an attended installation, it will only delay completion. Microsoft has improved the Windows installation process with each version of Windows, and it requires input mainly at the very beginning and at the very end of the process.

The following description is of a clean install, meaning the partitioning and formatting of the hard disk will occur during the installation. You would perform this type of installation on a new computer, or on an old computer when you want a complete new start. A clean install avoids the potential problems of upgrading, which we will describe later in "Updating Windows."

Gathering Information

Before you begin an attended installation from a retail version of Windows, gather the specific information you need, which depends on whether you are installing a PC at home or in a business network. Either way, gather the appropriate information, including the following:

- The product ID code from the envelope or jewel case of the Windows CD or DVD
- A 15-character (or less) name, unique on your network, for your computer
- The name of the workgroup or domain the computer will join. You may need to get this information from a network administrator. Anyone can create and join a workgroup, but to join a domain, an administrator must create accounts in the domain for both you and your computer.
- A password for the account created for you as you install Windows. No matter what you name this account, the first account has administrator rights to just the computer.

■ The necessary network configuration information—ask your network administrator for this information, but the Windows default will configure the computer to receive an address automatically, which should work for you in a corporate setting, at home, and at school. Learn more about how a computer receives network addresses in Chapter 14.

In addition, gather any device driver disks or discs for the computer and its installed peripherals. You may need to download device drivers from manufacturers' Websites. Having these on hand before you start the installation is helpful. Windows may have appropriate drivers for all your devices, but if it does not, Windows Setup may prompt you to provide them. You can do that during installation or let Windows install minimal generic drivers during Setup, and wait until after the final reboot at the end to install the correct drivers according to the manufacturers' instructions.

Installing Interactively

Begin the attended Windows installation by booting into the Window Setup program from one of the sources described earlier. In most cases, when installing to a single computer you will begin by inserting the Windows distribution CD or DVD and booting the computer. Beyond that, there are some differences in how Setup runs for the various versions of Windows. All the versions examine your hardware configuration early on. Before Windows Vista, the early portion of Windows Setup ran in character mode until it had copied files to your computer to support the graphical user interface (GUI) mode portion of Setup. These screens for older Windows versions looked like the Windows XP Setup screen shown in Figure 9-10. Notice that you can choose to continue the setup or repair a Windows XP installation. All versions of Windows that we are studying here include an option to repair an existing installation that appears very early in the Setup process.

When you start up Windows Vista, Windows 7, or Windows 8 from the disc or other media with the setup files, the *Windows Preinstallation Environment (Windows PE)* starts. This is a scaled-down Windows operating system with limited drivers for basic hardware and support for the NTFS file system, TCP/IP, certain chipsets, mass storage devices, and 32-bit and 64-bit programs. Windows PE supports the Windows Setup GUI, collecting configuration information. The setup programs for these newer versions of Windows require very little user input near the beginning and the end of the process. Windows Vista, Windows 7, and Windows 8 Setup screens are nearly identical. They begin by briefly showing a black character mode screen; then the entire Setup program runs in GUI mode, showing a progress screen with

The Windows
XP text-mode
Welcome To
Setup page.

```
Windows XP Professional Setup

  Welcome to Setup.

  This portion of the Setup program prepares Microsoft(R)
  Windows(R) XP to run on your computer.

      •  To set up Windows XP now, press ENTER.

      •  To repair a Windows XP installation using
         Recovery Console, press R.

      •  To quit Setup without installing Windows XP, press F3.




  ENTER=Continue   R=Repair   F3=Quit
```

a check-off list of the tasks Setup is performing. These include copying Windows files, expanding Windows files, installing features, installing updates, and completing installation. New with Windows Vista, and included with Windows 7 and Windows 8, is a screen to select the language and other *regional settings*, such as date, time, and currency formats, and keyboard or input method. See Figure 9-11. Previously, Windows installed in English, and if you wanted a different language for the user interface, you had to add a language pack on top of English. Beginning with Windows Vista, the language component is separate from the rest of the OS code, a feature called the *Multilingual User Interface (MUI)*, which allows you to install a language other than English as the only language. You can also install multiple languages without first installing English. Except for the logo and color, this screen is identical in Windows Vista and Windows 7, as are many others.

In all versions, when prompted, enter your *product key*. This is mandatory. You cannot proceed without doing this. Windows will use the product key when activating after Setup completes. When the End User License Agreement (EULA) appears, read it and follow the instructions to acknowledge acceptance of the agreement and to continue. This is mandatory, as it is your agreement to comply with your license to use Windows that allows you to install Windows on one computer for each license that you own.

Windows Setup will display a list of existing partitions and unpartitioned space. On most systems, this page will show a single disk, and you will simply click Next.

Select a language
on this Windows
7 Setup page.

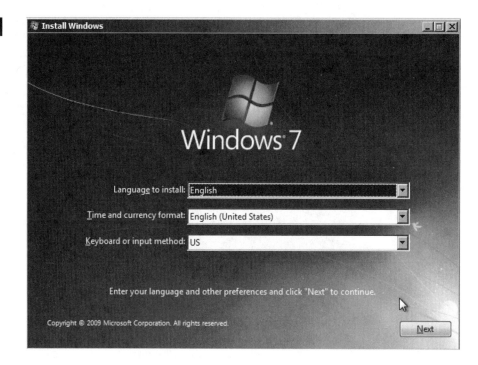

Figure 9-12 shows this page. Although it is not obvious, in this case the disk is a virtual hard drive in a virtual machine, and the virtual hard drive is smaller than we would normally choose for a typical desktop, but otherwise, this is what you would expect to see. If you click Next, the disk will be partitioned using all available space, and it will be formatted with NTFS (Windows XP would give you the option of choosing FAT or NTFS). If you need to load a third-party driver for the hard disk, click Load Driver. If you want to do anything different than the default, click Drive Options (Advanced). For instance, if the disk has enough space, you might want to create more than one partition, or install Windows into a folder other than the default. We don't recommend straying from the defaults for the majority of situations.

Setup copies files to the location you indicated or to the newly formatted partition. Unless you specify another location, Setup creates a folder named Windows in C:\, into which it installs the OS, creating appropriate subfolders below it. After it finishes

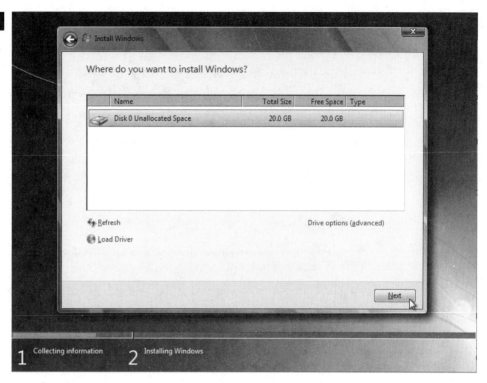

FIGURE 9-12

You will normally accept the defaults on this screen.

copying the base set of files to this location, your computer reboots. At this point in Windows XP Setup, graphical mode begins. At that same point in later versions of Windows Setup, it also reboots and returns to the graphical mode, usually at a higher screen resolution than before the restart because it is now using the newly installed drivers rather than the drivers used by PE. All versions of Windows Setup will restart, but the newer ones have fewer restarts, while it installs components and updates Windows. Follow the instructions on the screen, accepting the defaults when you are unsure.

If Setup detects a network card, the network components will install and configure with default settings. All versions will give you a chance to personalize Windows by user name and password, computer name, and information for joining a Windows workgroup or for connecting to a Windows Domain (if applicable).

As a summary of this previous explanation of an attended installation, Exercise 9-1 will walk you through the steps for performing a clean installation of Windows 7.

EXERCISE 9-1

Installing Windows 7

In this exercise, you will do a clean installation of Windows 7. To complete this exercise, you will need the Windows 7 installation disc and the information listed earlier under "Gathering Information."

1. Insert the Windows disc and boot the computer. Watch the screen for instructions to boot from the optical drive. A plain black screen will briefly flash, followed by a black screen with the message "Windows is loading files..." while Windows PE is loaded and started. The Starting Windows screen signals that Windows PE is starting and will soon load the GUI for Windows 7 Setup.

2. On the first Install Windows page, select a language, time, currency format, and keyboard input methods and select Next.

3. The most prominent feature of the next screen is the Install Now button, but you should notice two important links. One is labeled What To Know Before Installing Windows; click it to see if you have overlooked a preparation step. The second link, labeled Repair Your Computer, is an important one to re-member. If at any time after you install Windows 7 your system will not start, and if it also will not start in Safe Mode, pull out your Windows 7 disc, boot from it, and select Repair Your Computer.

4. On the license page, read the Microsoft Software License Terms, click to place a check in the box labeled I Accept The License Terms, and click the Next button.

5. On the next page, you are asked which type of installation you want. Select Custom to perform a clean installation.

6. On the next page, you need to select the target drive for the installation (see Figure 9-12).

7. Windows 7 Setup goes through the phases of the installation, restarting several times, and returning to a page that displays the progress with a green check mark by each completed phase.

8. At the completing installation phase, the message "Setup will continue after restarting your computer" displays. After this, as Windows 7 restarts, the mes-sage "Setup is checking video performance" displays. Then you will need to enter a user name for the first user and a name for the computer.

9. Next create the password for the first user account, entering it twice, and type a password hint that will help you to recall the password but not reveal it to others. The password hint will display any time you enter an incorrect password when logging on.

10. On the next page, you will need to enter the 20-character product key and check the box labeled Automatically Activate Windows When I'm Online." Already checked by default, this means it will activate automatically if your computer connects to the Internet. You must activate Windows within 30 days of installation. After that it will stop functioning. Click Next to continue the final configuration steps.

11. On the next page, configure the Automatic Update Settings. You would normally click the first option: Use Recommended Settings. Windows Setup will then continue.

12. On the next page, select your time and date settings, and click Next. Now select your computer's current location. If you are at home, select Home Network; if you are at school or work, select Work Network; if your computer has mobile broadband or you are using a public Wi-Fi network, select Public Network. There will be a short delay while Windows connects to the network and applies settings.

13. The Welcome page displays, followed by a message "Preparing your desktop…" Soon after the desktop will display and, depending on the setting you selected for updating and if you have an Internet connection, you will see a message that Windows is downloading and installing updates. Some updates require restarting Windows to complete installing the update.

After Setup is complete, your job is not finished. You will now need to configure Windows to personalize it for the user. We'll talk more about that topic after we look at unattended installations.

Unattended Installation

An *unattended installation* is one in which the installation process is automated. There are two general types of unattended installations:

- A scripted installation using *answer files* and *Uniqueness Database Files (UDFs)*, which provide the data normally provided by a user during an attended installation

- An image installation, using either Microsoft software tools or a third-party tool

Scripting for Unattended Installations

A scripted installation uses scripts that someone has prepared ahead of time. Organizations with large numbers of desktop computers needing identical applications and desktop configurations use this. This type of installation normally requires trained people who plan and implement the installation using a variety of automation methods, including scripts and access to the Windows source files on a *distribution server*. A typical scripted installation scenario involves placing the Windows source files from the distribution disc onto a file share on a server, which is then called a *distribution share*. This assumes sufficient licenses for the number of installations from these source files. Then, each desktop computer boots up, either from the local hard drive or from another source, and runs a script that connects to the distribution server to begin the installation. Although we place scripted installations under unattended installations here, the amount of interaction required ranges from none to as much as is required for an attended installation. In fact, certain software on the server side, such as Microsoft's Systems Management Server (SMS) can, with proper configuration of each client computer, push an installation down from the server with no one sitting at each desktop. This can include an automated installation of user applications on top of the newly installed Windows OS.

Drive Imaging

In organizations that want to install the same OS and all the same application software on many desktop PCs, drive imaging is often used. A *drive image,* or *disk image,* is an exact duplicate of an entire hard drive's contents, including the OS and all installed software, applied to one or more identically configured computers. This is a little tricky since each Windows installation must have a unique license and a unique computer name. Tools are available for creating drive images that solve this problem. Before Windows Vista, Microsoft had tools for preparing a computer for imaging, but it did not have imaging software. Since then, Microsoft has created a complete set of tools for preparing the image, creating the image, and distributing the image. Next, we will briefly describe working with the Microsoft tools prior to Windows Vista, and then we will provide an overview of how to do this with newer Microsoft tools.

Imaging with Pre-Windows Vista Microsoft Tools
Before Windows Vista, the Microsoft tools to perform the various functions for preparing, creating, and distributing an image used a variety of utilities that did not interact well together. A third-party program had to perform the actual imaging. Automation and customi-

zation depended on creating scripts, which required considerable knowledge and experience. The entire process was very expensive and time-consuming, so to be cost-effective, this was done only when an organization needed to roll out the images to a large number of desktops.

Imaging with Post-Vista Microsoft Tools   Microsoft has developed an entire suite of tools for deploying Windows to large numbers of desktop computers. These tools and sets of recommended procedures cover the planning, building (of the images), and deployment phases. Even an overview of these tools would take a great deal of time and space, and the CompTIA Exam Objective 802: 1.2 only requires that you understand the basics of image installations. Therefore, we will simply list and briefly describe the tools for the build and deployment phases. The acronym BDD in some of the following tools stands for Business Desktop Deployment.

- **BDD Workbench**   A technician uses this tool to create and manage both the distribution share and the various images. Plus, this tool will configure several deployment sources, including a single server, a deployment share, a DVD ISO image, or a directory that contains all the files needed for a customized deployment from a server running Microsoft's SMS Server software.
- **Windows System Image Manager**   This tool allows a technician to create the components for automating custom installs using custom scripts.
- **ImageX**   Use this tool to create the disk images.
- **Microsoft Windows Preinstallation Environment (Windows PE)**   PE is a bootable environment that gives operating system support during three types of operations: installing Windows, troubleshooting, and recovery.
- **User State Migration Tool (USMT)**   Technicians use this tool for migrating files and settings to many desktop computers. It does not migrate programs, however, just data files, operating system settings, and settings from Microsoft applications.

Microsoft is not the only source for such tools: many third-party vendors offer an array of imaging and deployment tools. Learn more about these tools by searching on the Internet.

Configuring Windows

After installing Windows, you have a few post-installation and configuration tasks. They include verifying network access (assuming connection to a network exists), registration, activation, and update installation. You should complete these tasks before moving on to customizing the desktop for yourself or another user and performing other desktop management tasks, such as installing new devices, installing applications, and configuring virtual memory.

Network Configuration

Once you have completed the installation, if the computer is on a network, verify that it can communicate with other computers on the network. If it cannot, you may need to add a device driver for the network adapter and/or configure the network components. Network connectivity is important because this is the best way to download updates to your newly installed operating system—a task you must do as soon as you have Internet access.

Checking Network Connectivity

Use My Network Places (Windows XP) to determine if you can see any computers on the network besides your own. In Windows Vista and Windows 7, look for a shortcut named Network on the Start menu. Only computers with the Server service turned on are visible. This service supports file and print sharing and is turned on by default, so you should see your computer and others on the network.

Adding a Network Adapter Device Driver

If Windows Setup does not recognize your network adapter, it may not install a driver; alternatively, it may recognize the network adapter but may not have the appropriate driver in the source directory. In this case, a prompt to provide a new device driver may appear, but we find it is best to wait until after Setup completes to install new drivers.

If you are installing network drivers or other drivers after the installation, wait until after the final reboot, and then follow the manufacturer's instructions for installing the device driver(s). Learn more about installing and configuring network components in Chapter 15.

Registration and Activation

During the installation of Windows XP, you are prompted to register Windows and to activate it; Windows Vista and Windows 7 provide a check box to allow activation to occur once installation is complete. Many people confuse registration and activation. These are two separate operations. *Registration* informs the software manufacturer who the owner or user of the product is, and provides contact information such as name, address, company, phone number, email address, and so on about them. Registration of a Microsoft product is still entirely optional.

Activation, more formally called *Microsoft Product Activation (MPA)*, is a method designed to combat software piracy, meaning that Microsoft wishes to ensure that only a single computer uses each license for Windows. This requirement extends to all versions of Windows since Windows XP. Here you'll learn more about activation.

Mandatory Activation Within 30 Days of Installation

Activation is mandatory, but you may skip this step during installation. You will have 30 days in which to activate Windows, during which time it will work normally. If you don't activate it within that time frame, Windows will automatically disable itself at the end of the 30 days. Don't worry about forgetting, because once installed, Windows frequently reminds you to activate it with a balloon message over the tray area of the taskbar. The messages even tell you how many days you have left.

on the *job* ***Understanding activation is important because all Microsoft products since Windows XP require it, and Microsoft is not the only software vendor using an activation process. Software purchased with a volume license agreement does not require product activation.***

Activation Mechanics

When you choose to activate, the product ID, generated from the product key code that you entered during installation, combines with a 50-digit value that identifies your key hardware components to create an installation ID code. This code must go to Microsoft, either automatically if you have an Internet connection, or verbally via a phone call to Microsoft, which then gives you a 42-digit product activation code.

MPA does not scan the contents of the hard disk, search for personal information, or gather information on the make, model, or manufacturer of the computer or its components. Nor does it gather personal information about you as part of the activation process.

Reactivation

Sometimes reactivation is required after major changes to a computer. To understand why, you need to understand how MPA creates the 50-digit value that identifies your hardware. MPA generates this hardware identifier value used during activation, called the "hardware hash," by applying a special mathematical algorithm to values assigned to the following hardware:

Display adapter
Small Computer System Interface (SCSI) adapter
Integrated Development Environment (IDE) adapter
Network adapter Media Access Control (MAC) address
RAM amount range
Processor type
Processor serial number
Hard disk device
Hard disk volume serial number
Optical drive

MPA will occasionally recalculate the hardware hash and compare it to the one created during activation. When it detects a significant difference in the hardware hash, you will be required to *reactivate*, and you may need to contact Microsoft and explain the reason for the reactivation. This is Microsoft's way of ensuring that you did not install the product on another computer.

Adding new hardware will not necessarily require reactivation, but replacing any components in the preceding list, or repartitioning and reformatting a drive, will affect the hardware hash. We have had to reactivate after making a number of changes to a computer and again when we decommissioned a computer and installed the licensed retail version of Windows on a different computer. In both instances, we had to do this over the phone because we had to explain the circumstances to the representative.

Updating Windows

The newer versions of Windows will automatically begin updating as part of setup. Windows XP will not. Therefore, as soon as possible after installing XP when you have confirmed network connectivity, connect to the Windows Update site and update Windows XP. This task is important for the sake of stability and improved security.

Windows Update is both a Windows Control Panel applet and the Microsoft Website that this applet connects to for updating your Windows installation. At one time, Microsoft had separate update pages for Windows and Microsoft Office. The Windows Update Website only checked for and downloaded updates for Windows, and the Microsoft Office Update page only checked for and downloaded updates for Microsoft Office. It does little good to have your OS fully updated but not your Microsoft Office programs.

Now they have combined Windows Update and Microsoft Office Update into one site, and the Windows Update applet checks for any Microsoft software updates. You can manually run Windows Update, but be sure it is configured to automatically download and install updates (the default) to keep your computer up-to-date. They call this feature Automatic Update, although you won't see that term in Windows Vista, Windows 7, or Windows 8. In Windows XP, Automatic Update was a separate tab on the System Properties dialog box, and you would turn on and configure Automatic Updates on this tab.

While Windows Update in Windows Vista, Windows 7, and Windows 8 is configured to automatically download and install updates, you can change these settings by opening Windows Update and selecting Change Settings from the Task pane on the left. Then you can configure updates to occur at a regular interval. Figure 9-13 shows the Change Settings page in Windows 7, which is nearly identical to that in Windows Vista and Windows 8.

In spite of these easy options for updating Windows over the Internet, how you actually obtain updates will depend on the organization (school or business). Many will disable automatic updates, waiting until they have conducted their own internal tests before distributing them to users' desktops and laptops. This is especially true of service packs. In some organizations, the IT department may distribute updates intended for new installations on optical disc in order to install them before a computer ever connects to a network. Other organizations may make them available on a shared folder on the network, but many large organizations use a central management system for distributing and installing all desktop software—from the operating systems to applications and updates.

w a t c h *The acronyms SP1, SP2, SP3, and SP4 stand for service pack 1, service pack 2, service pack 3, and service pack 4, respectively.*

Updates can bring their own problems. Therefore, many organizations with IT support staff will test all updates before distributing them to the user desktops. For individuals and small organizations, it is too time-consuming to set up a test computer on which to install updates to test them before updating production PCs. Therefore, they rely on the ability to uninstall an update using the Add Or Remove

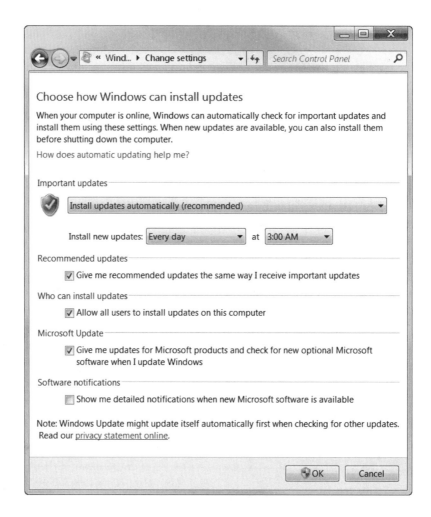

Programs applet in Control Panel in Windows XP or the Programs And Features applet in Windows Vista, Windows 7, and Windows 8.

Installing Applications and Additional Windows Components

After installing Windows and updating it, install and configure any security software, and then install the applications the user requires, including a third-party backup utility, if so desired. For the majority of applications—those that are proven compatible with the new version of Windows—you will simply follow the manufacturer's instructions for installing and configuring the program. Applications will install into a folder named Program Files, located in the root of the disk volume where you installed Windows. After installing each program, be sure to update it and to configure automatic updates for the application, if available. Microsoft knows that sometimes it's absolutely necessary to run a very old, incompatible application in a new version of Windows, so they have provided at least one solution for you. In all versions of Windows studied here, you can run the Compatibility Wizard to configure Compatibility Mode for the application. If Compatibility Mode in Windows 7 doesn't work for the application, you can run the application in Windows XP Mode, as described in Chapter 8.

Also, if you plan to use a third-party backup utility to restore data files backed up from a previous installation of Windows, install it now.

Migrating Data

At this point, restore any data and/or settings you migrated from an old Windows installation. If you used a migration tool on the settings and data on the old system, run the migration tool on the new system and provide the location of the migrated data—either a network location or media, such as discs, solid-state drive (SSDs), or external hard drive. Similarly, if you used a backup utility to back up your data on the old system, run the restore option of the Windows or third-party backup utility.

Installing New Devices

Installing a new plug and play device involves attaching the device and waiting while Windows recognizes it and installs the appropriate device driver. If Windows does not have a driver, it will prompt you to supply a location (disc drive, hard drive, or network) or connect to the Internet and search for it. A few devices may require that you run the device installation program before connecting the device; this has been true of printers in the past.

As defined in Chapter 2, a device driver is program code that allows an operating system to control the use of a physical device. Device manufacturers create device drivers for common operating systems and make the drivers available with the device.

Adequate Permissions

In order to install or uninstall device drivers, you must log on as the administrator or a member of the Administrators group. We discuss user accounts in Chapter 18 and permissions in Chapter 19. If you attempt to install a device driver while logged on with a nonadministrator account, you will see a message stating that you have insufficient security privileges to install or uninstall a device. However, once installed, an ordinary user may disconnect and reconnect the device without restriction.

Attaching Devices

You can attach most plug and play devices while the computer and the operating system are running. Because most devices today are plug and play, this is almost the rule rather than the exception—but always read the documentation.

Vendor-Supplied Installation Programs

Most devices come with a vendor-supplied installation program. If the documentation tells you to connect or install the device first, do so before installing the software. In this case, the Found New Hardware balloon will appear over the systray, from which you may launch the Add Hardware Wizard, which should then configure the device, often prompting you for information. If the documentation instructs you to install the software first, do so; then, after attaching the device, the Found New Hardware balloon will appear.

Driver Signing

A device driver becomes a part of the operating system with access to the core operating system code. Therefore, a poorly written device driver can cause problems—even system crashes. Drivers have long been a major cause of operating system instability. To prevent this problem, Microsoft works with manufacturers to ensure that driver code is safe to use.

Approved driver files have a *digital signature*, which is encrypted data placed in a file. The all-encompassing term for this is *code signing*, and when applied to device drivers, it is called *driver signing*. Microsoft began signing all of the operating system code starting with Windows 2000.

When you attempt to install a file, Windows looks for a digital signature. If it finds one, it uses a process called *file signature verification* to unencrypt the signature data and use the information to verify that the program code in the file was not modified since the signature was added. If it sees tampering, you will receive a warning and can stop the installation.

This certainly does not mean that all unsigned device drivers are bad. If you trust the source of a device driver, you can let it install on your computer. You will see a warning similar to that shown here. If you trust the source of the driver, select Continue Anyway.

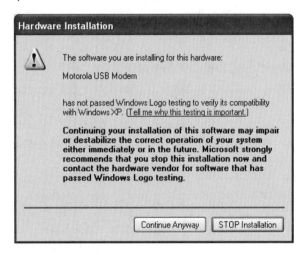

We strongly recommend that if you install an unsigned driver, you first back up all your data. When you install an unsigned driver, Windows will automatically create a restore point before making any changes.

If you suspect a problem with the device driver, restore the operating system to the restore point by opening the System Restore utility by choosing Start | All Programs | Accessories | System Restore and selecting Restore My Computer To An Earlier Time. Click Next, and then select the restore point created at the time you started the device driver installation.

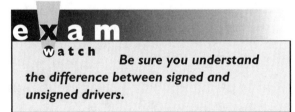

Be sure you understand the difference between signed and unsigned drivers.

Windows will not always allow you to install an unsigned driver. For instance, 64-bit Windows Vista/7 will not load unsigned drivers.

Automated vs. Manual Driver Installation

Most PCs and peripheral devices are fully plug and play, as are the Windows operating systems. Therefore, when Windows detects a newly installed device, the operating system does an automated search for an appropriate device driver. If it finds one, it installs it and configures the device. You may have to answer a few questions during the configuration process.

The driver it finds during this automated search may be one that came with Windows or one that you preinstalled before installing the device. If Windows cannot find a driver during this automated search, it will prompt you to insert media or browse to the folder containing the driver.

Verifying Driver Installation

After installing a device and its driver and associated utility program, verify the success of the installation. Do this by checking Device Manager and by testing the functionality of the new device. If a device does not work, check the documentation. You may have skipped a configuration step or need to supply more information before it is fully configured.

Device Manager   Immediately after installing a new device, open Device Manager and look for the device you just installed by browsing for it. If the device is in the list and does not have a yellow circle with an exclamation mark over its icon, the system considers it to be functioning properly.

Functionality   You should also test the functionality of the new device, because sometimes Device Manager does not detect a problem, but when you try to use the device, it does not function properly. This is usually due to a configuration option that does not show up as a problem in Device Manager. An example of this is a network adapter that is functioning okay from Device Manager's point of view but will not allow you to access the network. There are higher-level configuration options for a network adapter that must be correct before it will work. Learn more about configuring network adapters in Chapter 15.

Optimizing Windows

The most current three versions of Windows perform self-optimizing tasks such as defragmenting the hard drive and managing virtual memory. Normally, you should allow Windows to manage such tasks. In this section, we'll look at the virtual memory settings for a Windows computer and a new optimization feature for virtual memory called ReadyBoost.

Virtual Memory

Windows allows you to have several programs open in memory at the same time. Called multitasking, this feature, combined with large program and data files, means that it is possible to run out of physical RAM in which to keep all the open programs. When a Windows computer is running low on memory available for the operating system and any loaded applications, it will use and manage a portion of disk space as if it were RAM.

Virtual memory is the use of a portion of hard disk as memory. Windows uses a special *paging file*, *PAGEFILE.SYS*, to allocate disk space for virtual memory. By default, Windows creates this file in the root of C:. "Swapping" is the act of moving data and code between this file and RAM, and therefore we also call the paging file the *swap file*.

Because of virtual memory, things do not come to a screeching halt whenever we run out of memory for the operating system and for all the applications we have open. Much of the data and program code not needed in the current application will move into the swap file. The user is generally unaware of this process. When you switch to a program that has code or data in the swap file, you may experience a slight delay while the OS brings it back into memory after moving other data to the virtual memory space on disk.

As a rule, Windows manages virtual memory just fine without intervention. We recommend that, with few exceptions, you should not modify the default settings on your computer. Windows XP sets the size of the paging file, PAGEFILE.SYS, to 1.5 times the size of the installed physical RAM, which is an optimum setting for Windows XP. Our experience with newer versions of Windows shows that Windows Vista and Windows 7 also recommend 1.5 times the size of installed RAM, but Windows 8 on a system with 8 GB of installed RAM only recommends 4.5 GB and, when you allow the system to automatically manage this, the allocated amount at any given time may be much less than the recommended amount, since the system dynamically reallocates more or less virtual memory as the need arises.

There are some exceptions to this size. Sometimes the virtual memory settings need to change to improve performance. As an example, some applications (very few) recommend resizing the paging file (swap file) for better performance. It is also possible that such software would include resizing in its installation process.

If you must change the page file size, Exercise 9-2 will guide you to the virtual memory settings. These settings include the size and location of the page file and the number of page files used. If the present size is less than 1.5 times the size of the installed RAM, select the System Managed Size option and click Set, followed by OK. The next time you reboot, it will resize the paging file to 1.5 times the size of the physical RAM.

In Exercise 9-2, you will view the virtual memory settings on your computer. The default location of the paging file is on drive C:. If you are running out of free disk space on drive C:—and if you have other internal hard drive volumes—consider moving the paging file to another drive that has more free space. You can also have more than one paging file, but this is not normally necessary on a desktop or laptop computer. Never place the paging file on an external hard drive, because it may not be available during startup and this could prevent Windows from launching.

EXERCISE 9-2

Viewing the Virtual Memory Settings

You can easily view the present virtual memory settings for your computer.

1. In Windows OSs prior to Windows 8, right-click My Computer or Computer, and select Properties. If you are running Windows XP, skip to Step 3. If you are running Windows 8, enter **system** in the Settings Search box and select System.

2. In Windows Vista, Windows 7, or Windows 8, select Advanced System Settings from the task list. This will bring up the System Properties dialog box.

3. In the System Properties dialog box, select the Advanced tab.

4. Under Performance on the Advanced tab page, click Settings.

5. In the Performance Options dialog box, select the Advanced tab.

6. Under Virtual Memory, click Change to view the virtual memory settings for all the hard drives on your computer (see Figure 9-14).

7. If you made no changes, click Cancel three times to close the three dialog boxes: Virtual Memory, Performance Options, and System Properties.

ReadyBoost

ReadyBoost was mentioned in Chapter 2. This performance feature, introduced in Windows Vista and improved in Windows 7 and Windows 8, further blurs the line between RAM memory and storage, allowing you to use the memory on USB flash

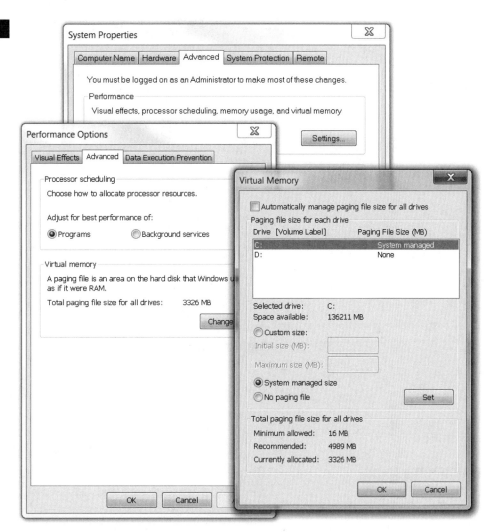

FIGURE 9-14

The Virtual
Memory dialog
box

cards and other SSD devices as cache memory to replace or supplement the use of
the hard drive for virtual memory.

If the system disk on a computer is an SSD, ReadyBoost may be automatically
disabled as unnecessary, since the speed of the SSD would make it a good location
for the swap file and it would not be improved by using a separate device as
additional cache memory.

FIGURE 9-15

The ReadyBoost
page for a
compatible flash
drive

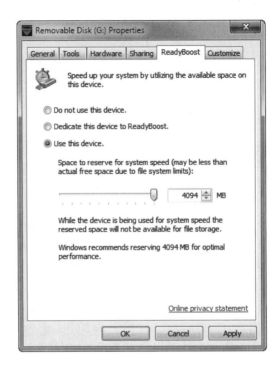

So how do you take advantage of ReadyBoost? You need to connect a compatible device and make changes on the ReadyBoost folder in the device's Properties dialog box. See Figure 9-15. Exercise 9-3 describes the steps to do this.

EXERCISE 9-3

Enabling ReadyBoost for a Flash Drive

If your computer is running low on memory, you can easily speed things up by allowing Windows Vista, Windows 7, or Windows 8 to use a flash drive. Follow these simple steps:

1. Connect a USB flash drive with at least 1 GB of available space.
2. When the AutoPlay dialog opens, locate (you may need to scroll down) and select Speed Up My System Using Windows ReadyBoost.

3. When the Properties dialog for the device opens to the ReadyBoost folder, select Dedicate This Device To ReadyBoost (this will automatically use the maximum space) or select Use This Device (this allows you to select a lesser amount) and click OK.

4. ReadyBoost will configure the device, and whenever it is connected to your computer, it will be used for system memory.

Power Management

Another configuration task to consider is power management. In Chapter 7, you learned about the power management features in Windows, how to configure the features that are especially important to a laptop (Hibernate and Standby/Sleep), and how to set the sleep timers for your settings. Power management is available on all Windows computers and is very important for saving power under all circumstances, not just for laptops. Therefore, after you install a new version of Windows, open the Power Options applet from Control Panel and explore the options.

SCENARIO & SOLUTION

How do I boot into the Windows Setup program on a computer with an unpartitioned hard disk?	If the computer can boot from the optical drive (as most can), place the Windows distribution disc into the drive, and start the computer.
Windows is prompting me to activate my upgrade of Windows, but I do not want to send personal information to Microsoft. Should I activate Windows?	This is not a problem. Although the activation process is mandatory, it does not send personal information to Microsoft.
I have Windows XP Professional running on my computer and would like to upgrade to Windows 7 Professional, but the retail version is too expensive. What should I do?	Buy the Upgrade version of Windows 7 Professional; it will be much less expensive, and it will install as an upgrade clean installation (as opposed to an in-place upgrade) to Windows XP Professional because there is no in-place upgrade path from Windows XP to Windows 7.

CERTIFICATION SUMMARY

You have many decisions to make before installing a new version of Windows. Will this be a clean installation or an upgrade? Will it be an attended or a fully automated unattended installation? What tasks should you perform before installing or upgrading? What tasks should you perform after installing Windows? Finally, what will improve the startup and running performance of Windows?

The answers to all of these questions are important to understand for passing your CompTIA A+ Exams, and for doing your job.

TWO-MINUTE DRILL

Here are some of the key points covered in Chapter 9.

Upgrading Windows

❑ An upgrade installs the new version of Windows directly on top of an existing installation, transferring all the settings from the old installation into the new one.

❑ An upgrade version of Windows is less expensive than a full retail version, but will only install into a previous legal installation of Windows.

❑ Before upgrading, test for incompatible software and hardware, and then resolve any incompatibilities.

❑ Before upgrading, back up all data, clean up the hard drive, and then defragment it.

Installing Windows

❑ Installing Windows involves three stages: preparation, installation, and follow-up tasks.

❑ Preparation tasks include verifying the target computer meets the physical hardware requirements, as well as the hardware and software compatibility requirements.

❑ It is important to plan how to start setup and the location of the source files.

❑ An attended installation requires the presence of a person who can respond to occasional prompts for information.

❑ Scripts that answer the Setup program's questions automate an unattended installation.

❑ A drive or disk image is an exact duplicate of an entire hard drive's contents, including the OS and all installed software.

Configuring Windows

❑ After installation, test network connectivity and, if necessary, add and configure a network adapter driver.

❑ Activating Windows is mandatory, but registration is optional.

❑ As long as you have an Internet connection, you should consider having Windows update automatically. Windows Vista and Windows 7 have Automatic Updates turned on by default.

❑ After completing a Windows installation and performing the most urgent configuration tasks, you should install and configure security programs and then install and configure other applications.

❑ If you must install an old application that is not compatible with the newly installed version of Windows, first attempt to get the program to run by configuring Compatibility Mode. If that does not work, and if you are trying to get a Windows XP application to run in Windows 7, use Windows XP Mode.

❑ Install any device drivers not installed during setup.

❑ Sometimes the virtual memory settings need to change to improve performance.

❑ Check the Power Options applet in Control Panel to see if you should make any changes to improve power management.

SELF TEST

The following questions will help you measure your understanding of the material presented in this chapter. Read all of the choices carefully, because there might be more than one correct answer. Choose all correct answers for each question.

Upgrading Windows

1. Which one of the following statements is not true?

A. You can upgrade with a full retail upgrade Windows disc.

B. You can install the upgrade version of Windows onto an unpartitioned hard drive.

C. You can upgrade from an upgrade Windows disc.

D. You can do a clean install from a retail version of Windows.

2. What should you do before an upgrade if you discover incompatible software or hardware?

A. Nothing. The incompatibility will be resolved during the upgrade.

B. Buy a special version of Windows for incompatibility problems.

C. Resolve the incompatibility before beginning the upgrade.

D. Repartition and format the hard drive.

Installing Windows

3. Which of the following refers to the lowest level of CPU, the minimum amount of RAM, and the free hard disk space needed to install an OS?

A. Hardware compatibility

B. Software compatibility

C. Hardware requirements

D. Hardware optimizing

4. What is the task order when preparing a new hard drive for a new OS installation?

A. Format, then partition, then install the OS

B. Partition, then install OS, then format

C. Format, then install OS, then partition

D. Partition, then format, then install OS

5. What is the preferred file system for Windows?

   A.   NTFS

   B.   FAT16

   C.   FAT32

   D.   FAT

6. Which of the following boot sources for Windows Setup is designed to initiate an over-the-network installation?

   A.   eSATA

   B.   PXE Boot

   C.   Optical drive

   D.   USB device

7. What type of installation requires a person's real-time response to prompts?

   A.   Unattended

   B.   Image

   C.   Scripted

   D.   Attended

8. What installation method places an exact copy of a hard drive containing a previously installed operating system and applications (from a reference computer) onto the hard drive of another computer?

   A.   Attended

   B.   Scripted

   C.   Image

   D.   Unattended

9. What are the two general types of unattended installations? Select all that apply.

   A.   Drive image

   B.   Scripted

   C.   Upgrade

   D.   USMT

10. No discs came with my computer purchased with Windows 7 preinstalled. What source can I use to reinstall the OS without spending more money? This is an either-or situation. Select the two best answers.

   A. Windows 7 full retail DVD

   B. Windows 7 Recovery DVD

   C. Factory recovery partition

   D. Windows 7 Upgrade

11. What feature, new in Windows Vista, allows you to install a language other than English as the first language?

   A. USMT

   B. MUI

   C. Aero

   D. Windows PE

12. Which of the following statements is true of the Windows 7 Setup?

   A. It runs entirely in GUI mode.

   B. The first half is character mode.

   C. It looks just like Windows XP Setup.

   D. You must install English as your first language.

13. What bootable environment gives operating system support during three types of operations: installing Windows, troubleshooting, and recovery?

   A. USMT

   B. MUI

   C. Aero

   D. Windows PE

Configuring Windows

14. What purpose does Microsoft Product Activation (MPA) serve?

   A. Product compatibility

   B. Prevention of software piracy

   C. Product registration

   D. Disabling the OS

15. What is the most immediate consequence of not completing the activation process for Windows within the required time period?
    A. There is no consequence.
    B. You will not receive updates.
    C. Windows is disabled.
    D. You will not receive emails about new products.

16. What task should you do as soon as possible after installation for the sake of stability and improved security?
    A. Upgrade
    B. Activate
    C. Update
    D. Partition

17. What may MPA require if you make too many hardware changes to a Windows computer?
    A. Reinstallation
    B. Removal of Windows
    C. Reactivation
    D. Update

18. To what site does Windows Update connect by default?
    A. The local workgroup
    B. Microsoft Update
    C. Windows Update
    D. Microsoft Office Update

19. What update service does Microsoft offer that will update both your Windows OS and certain Microsoft applications?
    A. Windows Update
    B. USMT
    C. Microsoft Update
    D. MUI

20. What is the term that describes disk space used by the operating system when it runs out of physical memory?
    A. Virtual memory
    B. RAM memory
    C. ROM memory
    D. Flash memory

SELF TEST ANSWERS

Upgrading Windows

1. ☑ **B.** You can install the upgrade version of Windows onto an unpartitioned hard drive is not true and is, therefore, the correct answer. The upgrade version will only install onto a computer with a previous version of Windows already installed.

☒ **A,** you can upgrade with a full retail upgrade Windows disc; **C,** you can upgrade from an upgrade Windows disc; and **D,** you can do a clean install from a retail version of Windows, are all true and, therefore, are not correct answers.

2. ☑ **C.** Resolve the incompatibility before beginning the upgrade is the correct action to take before an upgrade if you discover incompatible software or hardware.

☒ **A,** nothing, is incorrect because the incompatibility will not be resolved during the upgrade. **B,** buy a special version of Windows for incompatibility problems, is incorrect because there is no such version. **D,** repartition and format the hard drive, is incorrect because this will not solve the problem; it is extreme and will void the ability to install an upgrade.

Installing Windows

3. ☑ **C.** Hardware requirements are the CPU, minimum amount of RAM, and free hard disk space needed to install an OS.

☒ **A,** hardware compatibility, is incorrect because this refers to the actual make and model of the hardware, not the level of CPU and quantity of RAM and free hard disk space. **B,** software compatibility, is incorrect because it does not refer to the CPU, RAM, and free hard disk space. **D,** hardware optimizing, is incorrect because this does not refer to the level of CPU and quantity of RAM and free hard disk space.

4. ☑ **D,** partition, then format, then install OS, is the correct order for preparing a new hard drive.

☒ **A, B,** and **C** are all incorrect because the steps are out of order and actually impossible to complete.

5. ☑ **A.** NTFS is the preferred file system for Windows.

☒ **B, C,** and **D** are all incorrect because none of them is the preferred file system for Windows.

6. ☑ **B.** PXE Boot is correct. This boot method uses a feature of a network card that will initiate the startup of the computer, download the initial bootup files from a network server, and then it is ready to perform a task, such as installing the new OS over the network or running centralized maintenance tests on the computer.

☒ **A, C,** and **D** are all incorrect because while they are valid sources for starting an OS and going into Windows Setup, none of them was specifically designed for an over-the-network installation.

7. ☑ **D.** Attended installation is the type that requires a person's real-time response to prompts.
    ☒ **A,** unattended installation, is incorrect because this type of installation does not require a person's real-time response to prompts. **B,** image, is incorrect because this method replaces Setup altogether. **C,** scripted, is incorrect because you could use this term to describe an unattended installation.

8. ☑ **C.** Image installation places an exact copy of the operating system and applications (from a reference computer) onto the hard drive of another computer.
    ☒ **A,** attended installation, is incorrect because this does not place an exact copy of a hard drive onto another computer. **B,** scripted, is incorrect because scripting is just part of an installation, not a method of installation. **D,** unattended, is incorrect because this method may or may not include an image.

9. ☑ **A,** drive image, and **B,** scripted, are the two general types of unattended installations.
    ☒ **C,** upgrade, is incorrect because you can do this as either an attended or unattended installation. **D,** USMT, is incorrect because this is a tool for migrating user settings and data.

10. ☑ **B,** Windows 7 Recovery DVD, and **C,** factory recovery partition, are the correct answers, as the manufacturer will normally give you one of these options. If the Recovery DVD did not come with the computer, then you would have had to generate this from a utility on the computer.
    ☒ **A,** Windows 7 full retail DVD, is incorrect because, although this would work, it requires spending more money. **D,** Windows 7 Upgrade, is incorrect because this would cost money. It will also only work if your original Windows 7 OS is still working.

11. ☑ **B.** MUI, or Multilingual User Interface, allows you to install a language other than English as the first language.
    ☒ **A,** USMT, is incorrect because this is a tool for migrating files and settings to many desktop computers. **C,** Aero, is incorrect because this is a feature of the Windows GUI. **D,** Windows PE, is incorrect because Windows Preinstallation Environment is a scaled-down Windows operating system that runs at the beginning of Windows Setup.

12. ☑ **A.** It runs entirely in GUI mode is a true statement about the Windows 7 Setup.
    ☒ **B, C,** and **D** are all incorrect because these statements are false.

13. ☑ **D.** Windows PE (Windows Preinstallation Environment) is a bootable environment that gives operating system support during three types of operations: installing Windows, troubleshooting, and recovery.
    ☒ **A,** USMT (User State Migration Tool), is incorrect because it is an advanced tool that only works in a Windows server–based domain network. **B,** MUI (Multilingual User Interface), is incorrect because MUI is a feature that allows you to install a language other than English as the only language memory in Windows. **C,** Aero, is incorrect because this is a feature of the Windows GUI.

Configuring Windows

14. ☑ **B,** prevention of software piracy, is correct because this is the purpose of Microsoft Product Activation.
   ☒ **A, C,** and **D** are all incorrect because none of these is the purpose of MPA.

15. ☑ **C,** Windows is disabled, is the immediate consequence of not completing the activation process for Windows within the required time.
   ☒ **A,** no consequence, is incorrect because there is a consequence. **B,** you will not receive updates, is incorrect because you will receive updates until Windows is disabled when the required time is reached. **D,** you will not receive emails about new products, is incorrect because this may be a consequence of not registering.

16. ☑ **C,** update, is correct because you should do this task as soon as possible for the sake of stability and security.
   ☒ **A,** upgrade, is incorrect because this is not a task you should do for the sake of stability and improved security. **B,** activate, is incorrect because this is not a task you should do for the sake of stability and improved security. **D,** partition, is incorrect because this is a task for preparing a hard drive for use.

17. ☑ **C,** reactivation, is correct because MPA may require that you reactivate if you make too many hardware changes to a Windows computer.
   ☒ **A,** reinstallation, is incorrect because MPA will not require reinstallation if you make too many hardware changes. **B,** removal of Windows, is incorrect because MPA doesn't care if you remove Windows. **D,** upgrade, is incorrect; MPA will only require reactivation, not upgrading, if you make too many hardware changes.

18. ☑ **C.** Windows Update is the site to which Windows Update connects by default.
   ☒ **A,** the local workgroup, is incorrect because this is not something Windows Update connects to. **B,** Microsoft Update, is incorrect because this is not where Windows Update connects to by default. It will connect here after you connect to Windows Update and agree to install Microsoft Update. **D,** Microsoft Office Update, is incorrect because this is not where Windows Update connects by default.

19. ☑ **C.** Microsoft Update is the service that will update both your Windows OS and certain Microsoft applications.
   ☒ **A,** Windows Update, is incorrect because it will only update your Windows OS. **B,** USMT, is incorrect because this is not related to updating your software. **D,** MUI, is incorrect because this also is not related to updating your software.

20. ☑ **A.** Virtual memory is the term that describes disk space used by the operating system when it runs out of physical memory.
   ☒ **B, C, D** are all incorrect.

10

Disk and File Management

The Windows OSs have changed very little in their file management from version to version, but they changed disk management beginning in Windows 2000, and continuing through today's versions, with the notion of storage types, described in Chapter 9. In that chapter we focused on disk preparation before or during Windows installation. In this chapter, we detail how to manage disks, files, and folders from within Windows, using graphical user interface (GUI) and non-GUI tools—some for the everyday user, and some for the IT professional. Something for everyone!

CERTIFICATION OBJECTIVES

■ **802: 1.2**   *Given a scenario, install and configure the operating system using the most appropriate method*

■ **802: 1.4**   *Given a scenario, use appropriate operating system features and tools*

In this section, learn more about some of the topics of the CompTIA Exam Objective 802: 1.2 that were only defined in Chapter 9. They include the storage types (dynamic disk and basic disk) and primary and extended partitions, which are very old types of partitions. Also learn the difference between a quick format and a full format. In addition, learn how to use the Windows Disk Management tool, one of the topics in CompTIA Exam Objective 802: 1.4.

Disk Management

Disk management topics in this section include basic disks, dynamic disks, partitioning, and formatting. PC technicians need to understand how to prepare a disk for use, a topic introduced in Chapter 9, which focused on preparing a hard disk system for use and introduced the new storage types: dynamic disks and basic disks. In this section we will expand on that topic by first detailing issues related to the ongoing management of dynamic and basic disks. Since basic disks are the most common type used on Windows computers, the coverage of dynamic disks will only include those topics that are part of the objectives for the A+ exams and what only applies to dynamic disks. The coverage of basic disks includes some characteristics that are common for both storage types, such as drive letter assignments, mount points, and drive paths.

Managing Disks

The main tool for managing disks in Windows is the Disk Management console, which lets you see disk drives as more than the drive letters, folders, and files you see in Windows Explorer. As with many Windows programs and features, there are several ways to launch Disk Management. For instance, it is a part of the Computer Management console, which you will find in Administrative Tools. However, we like to open the separate Disk Management console from the Run/Search box by typing the filename: **diskmgmt.msc**. In this section we will use two scenarios. In the first we will use Disk Management to view the only disk in a computer and use this example to talk about the basic disk storage type. Then we will move on to a system in which we already have two physical disk drives and wish to add a third disk, exploring options including both basic disks and dynamic disks and what can be done with each storage type.

Viewing a Basic Disk

A basic disk, as described in Chapter 9, uses the traditional method for creating partitions, including use of a single partition table per disk that resides in the first physical sector of a hard disk. The partition table occupies a mere 64 bytes of the 512 bytes in the sector. This sector, called the master boot record (MBR), also contains the initial boot program loaded by BIOS during startup. This program, and the partition table, are created or modified in this sector when someone partitions the disk.

Figure 10-1 shows Disk Management on a computer with a single physical hard disk drive that came with Windows preinstalled with three volumes (we later created the fourth volume). Notice the volume information in the top pane displayed in labeled columns. The Status column shows the status for each volume. This same information is displayed in the rectangle representing each volume in the graphical pane below the volume information. Information on the status of the physical disk (Disk 0) and the DVD drive (labeled CD-ROM 0) is on the left. The status for the hard disk is Online, and the status for the DVD drive is No Media.

Each volume of the basic disk in Figure 10-1 is shown with the layout designation, *simple volume*, also called a primary partition in old MBR language. A basic disk has a four-volume-per-disk limit. A simple volume can reside on either a basic disk or dynamic disk. In our example, the original volumes were probably created as an image by the manufacturer. The first volume is unallocated, and it allows space to hold the dynamic disk database should we convert the disk to dynamic. The second is a recovery

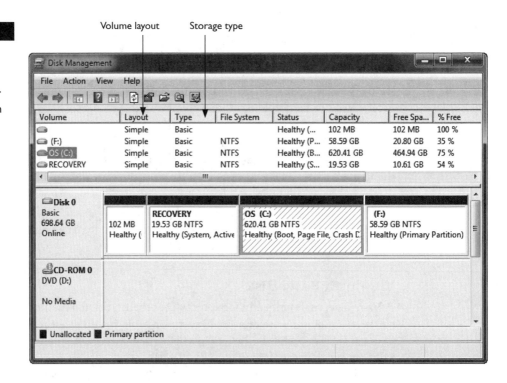

FIGURE 10-1

Disk Management showing information for the volumes on Disk 0

volume created by Dell to allow us to revert the disk to the factory-installed state. The third is the system volume, Drive C, where Windows 7 was installed at the factory.

The fourth volume takes a little explaining. Soon after we acquired the computer, we opened Disk Management, right-clicked the graphical representation of Drive C, and selected *Shrink Volume* from the menu, shown in Figure 10-2. This option is

FIGURE 10-2

Shrinking a volume in Disk Management

referred to as "splitting partitions" in the Disk Management topic of CompTIA Exam Objective 802: 1.4. We shrunk the volume holding logical drive C so that we could create another volume into which we installed Windows 8. This created a dual-boot system with Windows 7 on Drive C, and Windows 8 on Drive F.

While you can extend or shrink a volume on a basic disk, in this scenario, one consequence of shrinking the volume and creating an additional volume is that the physical disk now has four volumes—the maximum number of volumes allowed on a basic disk. In the old parlance, these are partitions. This term is still used, but the new term is volumes. If we wanted to shrink the volume again and create yet another smaller volume, that would require a fifth volume, which is not allowed on a basic disk type. At that point, you would be prompted to change the storage type to dynamic to accommodate more than four volumes—just one of the capabilities of dynamic disks.

If you have a Windows computer handy, open Disk Management and keep it open as you read through this section. Exercise 10-1 will walk you through opening this and checking out the storage type.

EXERCISE 10-1

Viewing the Disk Storage Type

You can view the disk storage type on your Windows computer by following these steps.

1. Open the Run line by pressing the WINDOWS KEY + R.

2. In the Run line, type **diskmgmt.msc** and press ENTER. There will be a short delay while Disk Management reads the disk configuration information.

3. In Disk Management, look for Disk 0. Disk 0 is normally your first internal hard disk drive, and usually the one from which Windows boots. Just below the words "Disk 0," you will see the storage type.

4. Is it a basic disk or a dynamic disk?

5. How many volumes are on Disk 0?

6. How many physical disks are in your computer?

7. Leave Disk Management open as you continue through the following section on adding a physical drive.

Adding a Physical Drive in Windows

Let's say you have added a hard disk drive to your Windows desktop computer. What storage type should it be? For most everyday desktop PCs, the basic storage type is more than adequate, and new drives actually start out their lives as MBR/basic drives. Dynamic storage is only used and understood by Windows, and not by other operating systems. Only convert to dynamic storage if you need more than four volumes on a disk or want to create a spanned, striped, or mirrored volume. But there are drawbacks. Letting Windows manage one of these multiple-disk configurations adds to the operating system's workload. Redundant Array of Independent Disks (RAID) configurations are best done at the hardware level, with the RAID controller managing the disks and presenting multiple disks to the operating system as a single volume.

To manage dynamic disks, Windows stores a special configuration database on each dynamic disk outside the area occupied by volumes. This provides the flexibility of allowing you to move the drive or array from one Windows computer to another, as long as the version of Windows understands dynamic disks. That means the Windows version must be Windows 2000 or later, and it is best to do this between computers with the same version of Windows. Older versions of Windows, such as Windows XP, cannot read dynamic disk volumes.

e x a m

ⓦatch *Dynamic disks store a special configuration database on the disk outside the area used by volumes.*

After installing an internal disk drive or connecting an external drive, open Disk Management and locate the new physical drive. Figure 10-3 shows that portion of Disk Management displaying a graph of three physical disks: Disk 0, Disk 1, and Disk 2. The last one was recently added and the space is unallocated, so it does not have a volume listed in the top pane.

Now, for full disclosure: A new disk drive, especially an external drive, will come with space allocated into a volume and that volume will be preformatted with a file system, usually FAT32. In our case, we attached an old external drive and deleted the existing volume before taking the screen shot shown in Figure 10-3.

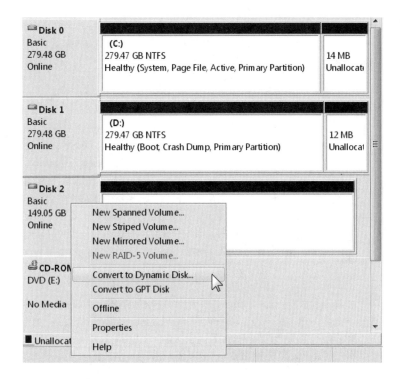

FIGURE 10-3

The pop-up menu on Disk 2 shows the available options.

All three physical disks in Figure 10-3 are basic disks, and by right-clicking Disk 2, the pop-up menu shows the actions we can take. Keep in mind that a spanned volume, striped volume, mirrored volume, and RAID 5 volume are all forms of *disk arrays* in that each volume type uses multiple physical disks in a single volume. Of all of the choices shown, only a mirrored volume and a RAID 5 volume are fault tolerant, and RAID 5 is actually not supported in desktop versions of Windows—only in Windows Server editions. If you wish to add an array to your computer, simply add the drives required; then in Windows open Disk Management and select the drives and the type of array you wish to create. In the following section we describe disk configuration options in the order in which they appear in the menu in Figure 10-3.

on the job

If you wish to create a disk array of any type, we strongly recommend that you explore doing it at the hardware level, rather than with Windows. Many computers today have BIOSs/UEFIs and disk controllers that control this at the hardware level. In that case, the multiple disks would be hidden from Windows and in Disk Management—you would see a single volume for each array. Then, the hard work of managing the array is left to the hardware and its firmware, not to the operating system, which already has plenty to do.

New Spanned Volume – Dynamic Disk A *spanned volume* combines areas of unallocated space from multiple physical disks into one volume and can only exist on dynamic disks. If you choose this option, the volumes do not need to be the same size, but a spanned volume cannot include a system volume; therefore, you cannot include the volume containing the Windows operating system files. Data written to a spanned volume is not written across the physical drives, as it is in a striped volume, but fills up the available space as if the volume were one physical drive. Think of a fountain that flows into cascading containers. The top container fills up with water until it runs out of space, and then the next container fills up, and so forth.

A spanned volume is not fault tolerant because if one of the physical disks fails, you lose the data from the entire spanned volume. The reason for creating a spanned volume is to increase the space available in a single volume when there is no more space on the physical drive where that volume resides. If you have ever heard the term *Just a Bunch of Disks (JBOD)*, it usually refers to what Microsoft calls a spanned volume.

New Striped Volume – Dynamic Disk A *striped volume* includes at least two physical disks, and the data is saved across the disks in a stripe, meaning that every time data is written to the volume, a portion is written on the first disk, then on the second disk, and so forth. A striped volume is the equivalent of a RAID 0 array, it is not fault tolerant. If you lose one disk in the array, you lose all your data, unless you have a backup on other media. On the plus side, disk access is faster with multiple accesses occurring simultaneously across all drives in the striped volume.

New Mirrored Volume – Dynamic Disk A *mirrored volume* consists of identically sized volumes on two physical disks—both dynamic disks—that are created as identical twins, with all disk activity occurring on both disks as a mirrored set. A mirrored volume is the equivalent of a RAID 1 array, and it is fault tolerant, because if one fails, the other is a complete duplicate and no data that was completely written to disk before the failure is lost. The single disk will continue to function. When ready to add a disk, you install it, then go into Disk Management and create a new mirrored volume.

New RAID 5 Volume – Not Available While New RAID 5 Volume is an option in Disk Management, it is not available in the consumer versions of Windows. You cannot convert a disk to dynamic storage if it connects via Universal Serial Bus (USB). If you select Convert To Dynamic Disk for a USB-connected drive, Windows will display the error message "The operation is not supported by the object." You can convert to dynamic drives connected through Parallel Advanced Technology

Attachment (PATA), Serial Advanced Technology Attachment (SATA), and
External Serial Advanced Technology Attachment (eSATA) interfaces.

The Professional, Enterprise, and Ultimate editions of Windows support the following dynamic disk volumes: simple, spanned, striped (RAID 0), and mirrored (RAID 1), except that Windows	**Vista does not support mirrored volumes. Although RAID 5 is shown as an option, it is only supported in Windows Server editions.**

Convert to Dynamic Disk   This option will convert a basic disk to a dynamic
disk. Only do this if you need to create more than four volumes on a disk or if you
need to create a spanned, striped, or mirrored volume.

Convert to GPT Disk   In Chapter 9 you learned about the GUID Partition
Table (GPT) that replaces the partition table of the old MBR for use with Unified
Extensible Firmware Interface (UEFI) firmware that is replacing the decades-old
Basic Input/Output System (BIOS). A *GPT disk* is one that uses a GPT rather than
an MBR. Disk Management has an option for converting a disk to use GPT, as
shown back in Figure 10-3.

Offline   If you select Offline, Disk Management will change the disk status to
offline, making it unavailable for use so that you can remove it.

Volume Layout and Formatting

Returning to Figure 10-3, whether you leave the disk as basic or convert it to dynamic,
it will not appear in the volume list until you create a volume by selecting a volume
layout and then formatting the new volume. The most common volume layout you
would create is a simple volume. In Disk Management, right-click the empty square
representing the unallocated space to bring up a menu that now includes Create
Simple Volume.

Now suppose this is a typical scenario, and your selected disk is a basic disk, and
you want to create a simple volume. Select New Simple Volume from the menu,
and the New Simple Volume Wizard will guide you through the process. After the
Welcome page, you will have a chance to specify the volume size. Once again, you

normally will select the maximum size available and click Next. On the Assign Drive Letter Or Path page, keep the default drive letter assignment and click Next. In the Format Partition page, shown in Figure 10-4, keep the defaults, but take note of two options. The first option is the Volume Label option, which we like to use to give a disk a unique name, especially if we have several disks connected. The second option to notice is Perform A Quick Format. This is the default, and is usually appropriate. A *quick format* does not actually overwrite the entire volume, but simply puts the file system components on the disk, refreshing the directory and allocation information so that the disk appears empty, whether it is or not. However, if the disk is a used disk and you are only formatting it to delete all the data to protect your privacy, you are out of luck, because the actual data is still sitting on the drive; the quick format simply makes it harder to access, and a determined person can use special software to recover the data. Therefore, if you are repurposing a used hard drive, do a full format, which only requires that you deselect the Quick Format option. Then Windows will do a *full format*, overwriting all the data space, as well as the directory information. A full format has the second benefit of finding bad physical space, which the format program will mark as such and the file system will not use again. Of course, if you do a full format and see many messages about bad space, you might want to dispose of the drive, rather than risk your data on it.

FIGURE 10-4

To do a full format, clear the Perform A Quick Format box.

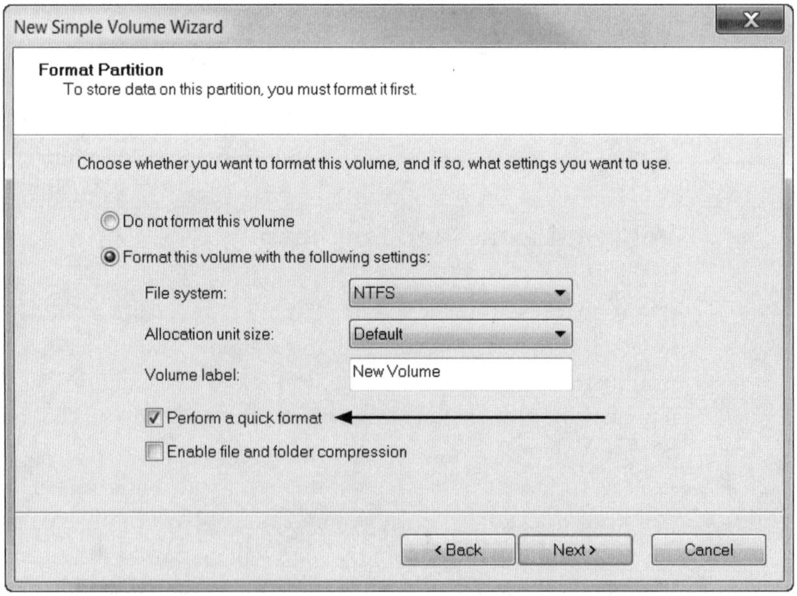

Logical Drives, Drive Paths, and Mounted Volumes

When it comes to assigning drive letters to volumes, you can select from the 26 letters of the alphabet, with the first two letters, A and B, normally reserved by Windows for floppy disk drives, but with floppy drives not present, you can also use these letters. Windows assigns drive letters automatically in a specific order. During an upgrade installation, it will preserve the drive letter assignments that existed under the previous version of Windows. The drive letter assignments are saved in the Windows registry in a location called MountMgr.

During a fresh install of Windows, the Setup program will, by default, assign letter C to the first volume it detects, marking it as active. It will then assign drive letters (D, E, etc.) to any other formatted volumes it detects. Once assigned, these drive letters are persistent until changed from the Disk Management console.

Windows also has a pair of features called drive paths and mounted drives that allow you to avoid using drive letters in some special cases. These features are available on both basic and dynamic disks. A *mounted drive* is a volume that is mapped to an empty folder on a New Technology File System (NTFS) volume. It does not need to have a drive letter assigned at all, but instead can be "connected" to an empty folder on another logical drive. This connection point to a folder is a *mount point*; and the path to the volume is a *drive path*, which requires the NTFS file system on the volume hosting the drive path. A volume can have both a drive letter and one or more drive paths. In My Computer/Computer or Windows Explorer, the mount point is listed along with local folders, but with a drive icon, as shown in Figure 10-5 where a mount point is labeled "Q1-2006," the contents of the mounted volume appear in the right-hand pane.

FIGURE 10-5

Notice the drive icon by the mount point Q1-2006.

Disk Management at the Command Prompt

It wasn't too many years ago that Windows did not come with a GUI disk management program. It came with a command-prompt tool called FDISK, which was adequate for creating and deleting MBR partitions, but it is not appropriate for use with today's hard drives and newer versions of Windows. All versions of Windows covered on the test have Disk Management, and that is where you will go to manage disks unless your system has a major problem. Then you may need to use a non-GUI disk management tool in the Windows Recovery Console, the Windows Recovery Environment, or Windows Safe Mode with Command Prompt. You will learn about these in Chapter 13.

DISKPART is an advanced utility for disk management that understands basic and dynamic storage types. You can run it at the Command Prompt or use it in automated scripts. If you enter the command `diskpart` at the Command Prompt, it actually loads its own command interpreter with a prompt that looks like this: `diskpart>`. At this prompt, you enter a command that DISKPART accepts with the correct syntax, and you must type `exit` to exit from DISKPART. Typing the command `diskpart /?` at the command line is not very helpful, and we recommend that you carefully research and test the use of this command. The information you will find through Windows Help and Support is not as helpful as the DiskPart Command-Line Options page at technet.microsoft.com.

Understanding Windows Startup

To fully understand and support Windows operating systems, you need to understand how Windows starts up, and you should learn this before we go any further in our discussion of disk and file management. The reason for this is that the critical operating system files reside on disk, and they must be found during Windows startup. While Windows has many safeguards protecting these critical files, occasionally bad things happen to them, and when they do Windows will fail to start or will start up with limited functionality. Understanding where the files are (or should be) and what role each plays in the normal Windows startup sequence will help you interpret Windows operating system startup failure symptoms, and you can determine at what point Windows startup fails. In Chapter 13 we will examine many of those symptoms and learn to use the appropriate tools to repair startup problems. In this section you will first learn about the Windows startup phases and the locations of the files.

Windows Startup Phases

The Windows startup process on PCs, laptops, netbooks, ultrabooks, and servers has several phases:

- Power-on self-test
- Initial startup
- Boot loader
- Detect and configure hardware
- Kernel loading
- Logon and plug and play device detection

In the first two phases, the hardware "wakes up" and BIOS searches for an operating system. Through the remaining phases, the operating system builds itself, much like a building, from the ground up, with more levels and complexity added at each phase. You will learn about these phases in the order in which they occur.

Power-On Self-Test

The power-on self-test phase is common to all PCs. It starts when you turn on or restart a computer. The CPU loads the BIOS programs or UEFI code from a special read-only memory (ROM) chip. The first of these programs includes the power-on self-test (POST). The POST tests system hardware, determines the amount of memory present, verifies that devices required for OS startup are working, and loads configuration settings from complementary metal-oxide semiconductor (CMOS) memory into main system memory. During the POST, it briefly displays information on the screen as it tests memory and devices.

Initial Startup

The initial startup phase is also common to all PCs. Therefore, it is not really just part of the Windows startup, but the beginning of the startup of any OS on a PC. In this phase, the BIOS startup program (or UEFI boot manager) uses CMOS system settings to determine what devices can start an OS and the order in which the system will search these devices while attempting to begin the OS startup process. One common order is A, then a CD drive, then C, in which case, the system will first look for a bootable floppy disk in drive A:. If one is not there, it will try to boot from a bootable optical disc (if present). If a bootable optical disc is not present, then the startup code will try to boot from the hard disk and load the MBR—the first sector on a hard disk—into memory for a BIOS boot, or the GUID Partition Table (GPT) in the case of a UEFI boot.

Next, the executable code from the MBR or GPT is loaded, taking control of the system and using partitioning information to find the boot sector—the first sector of the active partition—called the boot code—which is then loaded into memory. The job of the Windows boot code is to identify the file system on the active partition, find the boot loader file, and load it into memory.

Boot Loader

The actual boot loader depends on the version of Windows.

Up to this point, in the case of a BIOS-based system, the CPU is in a very limited mode called "real mode." This was the mode of the early Intel CPUs in the early PCs. Only when the CPU switches to protected mode can it access memory above 1 MB and support both multitasking and virtual memory. Protected mode refers to the fact that each application's memory space is protected from use by other applications. A UEFI-based system does not have this memory limit.

NTLDR: The Windows XP Boot Loader   The boot loader in Windows XP is *NTLDR*. During the boot loader phase, NTLDR takes control of the system, switches the CPU to protected mode, starts the file system (the in-memory code that can read and write an NTFS or FAT volume), and reads the BOOT.INI file. If the computer is configured for multiboot, an OS Selection menu will appear briefly, allowing you to select between the two versions of Windows. If you do not make a decision in the configured time (the default is 30 seconds), it will load the default version, which is normally the last one installed.

In Windows XP, NTLDR moves to the next phase in the Windows startup process. But before we move to that step, let's look at how versions of Windows beginning with Windows Vista handle things up to this point.

BOOTMGR: The Windows Vista, Windows 7, and Windows 8 Boot Loader   The boot loader for Windows Vista, Windows 7, and Windows 8 is *BOOTMGR*, which loads the Boot Configuration Database (BCD), an extensible database that replaces the old BOOT.INI file. BCD then loads WINLOAD.EXE, the OS loader boot program. Together, BOOTMGR and WINLOAD.EXE replace the major functions of NTLDR and complete the startup phases for Windows Vista,

Windows 7, and Windows 8. These OSs do not need the files NTLDR, BOOT.INI, and NTDETECT.COM, but BOOT.INI and NTDETECT.COM will be present on a computer configured for multiboot that needs to start up an older version of Windows requiring these files. Unless the computer is configured for dual boot, it will quickly move onto the next Windows startup phase; if it is configured to multiboot, it will pause for several seconds and display a Boot Manager menu, as shown in Figure 10-6, which gives you the choice to boot either Windows 7 or Windows 8. At this point, you will choose an OS to start, or if the preconfigured amount of time passes, the default OS will be selected, and the next phase, Detect and Configure Hardware, will begin.

Detect and Configure Hardware

The detect and configure hardware phase includes a scan of the computer's hardware and creation of a hardware list for later inclusion in the registry. Recall from Chapter 9 that the registry is a database of all configuration settings for Windows.

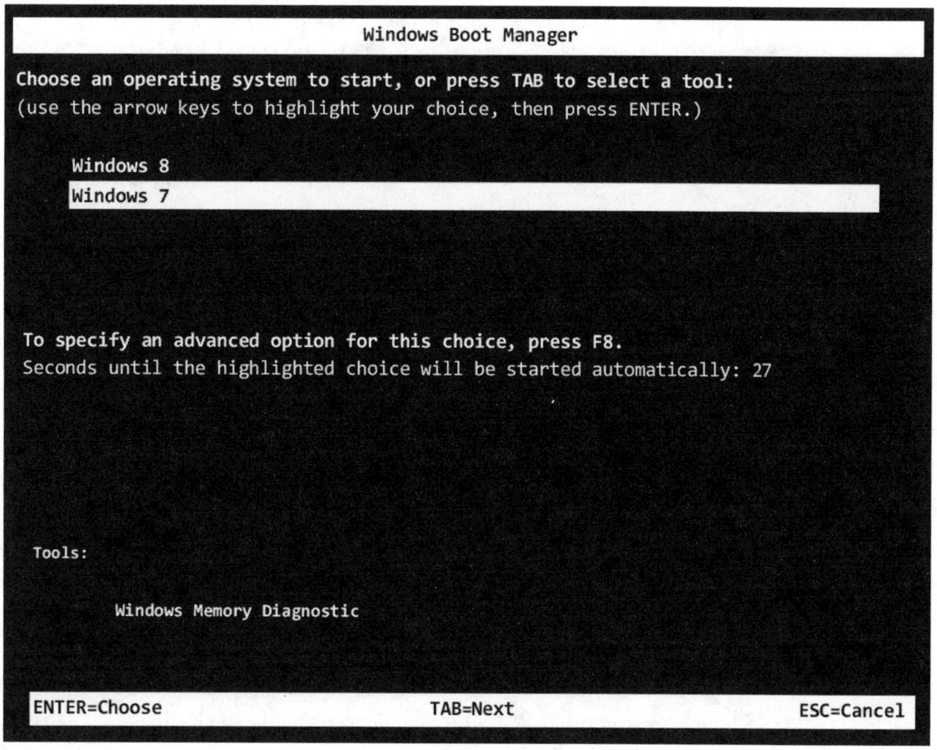

FIGURE 10-6

The Boot Manager menu for dual-booting between Windows 7 and Windows 8

```
                              Windows Boot Manager
Choose an operating system to start, or press TAB to select a tool:
(use the arrow keys to highlight your choice, then press ENTER.)

        Windows 8
        Windows 7

To specify an advanced option for this choice, press F8.
Seconds until the highlighted choice will be started automatically: 27

Tools:

        Windows Memory Diagnostic

ENTER=Choose                    TAB=Next                    ESC=Cancel
```

Kernel Loading

During the kernel loading phase, the Windows kernel, NTOSKRNL.EXE (on both old and new Windows systems), loads into memory from the location indicated in either the BOOT.INI file (Windows XP) or the BCD. During kernel loading, the Windows logo will display, as well as a progress bar.

Hardware information passes on to the kernel, and the *hardware abstraction layer (HAL)* file for the system loads into memory, too. The System portion of the registry loads, and the drivers that are configured (through registry settings) to load at startup are now loaded. All of this code is loaded into memory, but not immediately initialized (made active).

> **e x a m**
>
> **ⓦatch** **Be sure to remember that the main files required for starting up Windows XP are NTLDR, BOOT.INI, NTDETECT.COM, and NTOSKRNL.EXE. For Windows Vista and newer versions, these files are BOOTMGR, WINLOAD. EXE, and NTOSKRNL.EXE.**

Once all startup components are in memory, the kernel takes over the startup process and initializes the components (services and drivers) required for startup. Then the kernel scans the registry for other components that were not required during startup but that are part of the configuration, and it then loads and initializes them. The kernel also starts the session manager, which creates the system environment variables and loads the kernel-mode Windows subsystem code that switches Windows from text mode to graphics mode.

The session manager then starts the user-mode Windows subsystem code (CSRSS.EXE). Just a few of session manager's other tasks include creating the virtual memory paging file (PAGEFILE.SYS) and starting the Windows logon service (WINLOGON.EXE), which leads us to the next phase.

Logon

The key player in this phase is the Windows Logon service, which supports logging on and logging off, and starts the service control manager (SERVICES.EXE) and the local security authority (LSASS.EXE). In addition to the actual logon (the Windows 8 term is sign in), programs are started and plug and play detection occurs, but while that is happening under the hood, the Lock screen displays in Windows 8, and in previous versions, the Log On To Windows message may appear. Depending on how your computer was configured, you may first see the Welcome To Windows screen, requiring that the user press CTRL-ALT-DELETE before the Log On To Windows dialog box or screen appears. A user then enters a user name and password, which the local security authority uses to authenticate the user in the local security accounts database. Figure 10-7 shows just one possible logon screen that you may see in Windows 7.

FIGURE 10-7   Logging on to Windows 7

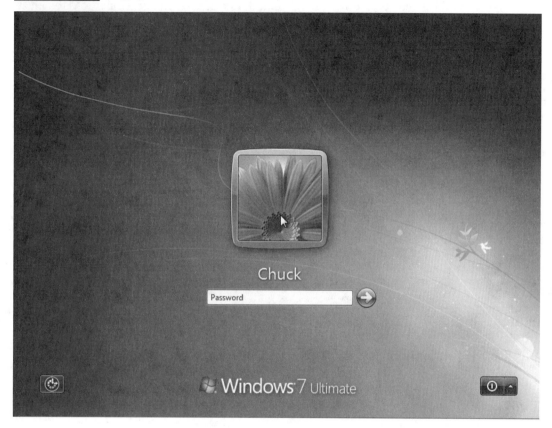

The actual screen or dialog box that appears before you log on varies with the configuration of your computer. You may not have to enter a user name and password, or you may only need to select a user name from a list. Learn more about logon authentication and its role in security in Chapter 18.

Program Startup   A lot of other things happen during the logon phase. Logon scripts run (if they exist), programs configured to start up as Windows starts up now run, and noncritical services start (critical services were started previously). Windows checks the registry to find instructions to locate and run these programs and services.

Plug and Play Detection   During the logon phase, Windows performs plug and play (PnP) detection, using BIOS/UEFI, device drivers, and other methods to detect new plug and play devices. If it detects a new device, Windows allocates system resources and installs appropriate device drivers.

Windows Startup File Locations

The Windows startup files are placed in specific locations when Windows is installed. The key files described earlier are especially critical to starting up Windows. The Windows XP NTLDR, BOOT.INI, and NTDETECT.COM files are located in the root of drive C:. On a Windows Vista, Windows 7, or Windows 8 system, the BOOTMGR file is located in the root of drive C:. These files are hidden so that they are not visible by default when you try to view them in Windows Explorer. To make them visible, simply open a Windows Explorer window, press the ALT key to make the menu bar visible, select Tools (shown in Figure 10-8), and then select Folder Options to open

FIGURE 10-8

Select Folder Options from the Tools menu to open the Folder Options Control Panel applet.

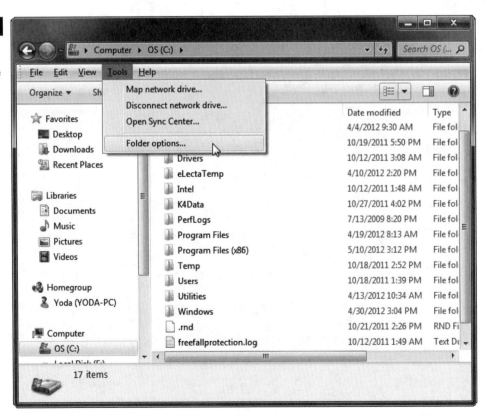

select Folder Options to open a Control Panel applet. Select the View page, and under Hidden Files And Folders, select Show Hidden Files, Folders, And Drives. If necessary, clear the check box labeled Hide Extensions For Known File Types. See Figure 10-9. Click OK, and return to Windows Explorer to view these files.

The NTOSKRNL.EXE file for Windows XP is normally located in the C:\WINDOWS\system32 folder, while the WINLOAD.EXE and NTOSKRNL.EXE files used by the newer versions of Windows are in the location specified in BCD, which on our test system is C:\WINDOWS\system32.

System Startup Settings

The location of the Windows startup settings depends on the version of Windows. Although they all store this information in the registry, the registry is not available during the computer's initial startup, so Windows places these settings in a location that is available before the OS is fully loaded. In Windows XP, that location is the BOOT.INI file, and in Windows Vista and later versions, it is the BCD file.

FIGURE 10-9

On the View page, enable Show Hidden Files, Folders, And Drives. Clear the check box for Hide Extensions For Known File Types.

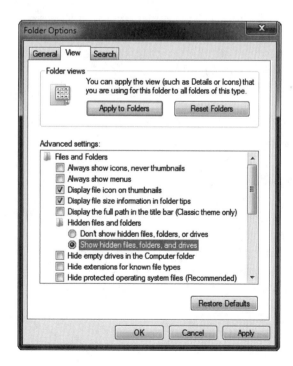

Inside BOOT.INI

The Windows XP **BOOT.INI** file is a simple text file that holds important information used by NTLDR to locate the operating system and, in the case of a dual-boot configuration, to display the OS Selection menu. Settings in the BOOT.INI file indicate where the operating system is located using the now-arcane Advanced RISC Computing (ARC) syntax.

Following is a typical BOOT.INI for a Windows XP installation:

```
[boot loader]
timeout=30
default=multi(0)disk(0)rdisk(0)partition(1)\WINDOWS
[operating systems]
multi(0)disk(0)rdisk(0)partition(1)\WINDOWS=
"Windows XP Professional" /fastdetect
```

The lines beginning with `multi` provide NTLDR with the location information in a format called an ARC path: `multi(0)disk(0)rdisk(0)partition(1)\WINDOWS`. In brief, this identifies the disk controller, the hard disk on that controller, the partition on that hard disk, and finally, the folder in that partition in which the OS is located. The words that appear in quotes on the lines under the [operating systems] section are displayed on the OS Selection menu, if it displays. Anything after the quotes is a switch that affects how Windows starts up. For instance, the /fastdetect switch is the default switch used with Windows XP. It causes NTDETECT to skip parallel and serial device enumeration. This is a good thing, now that these two types of ports have all but disappeared from PCs. While many other BOOT.INI switches exist, you should not normally need to manually add any to your desktop installation of Windows.

Inside BCD

The Boot Configuration Database is actually a hidden part of the registry, stored in a registry file named BCD, located in C:\BOOT. If you have administrator-level privileges, you can view and modify the contents using the *BCDEdit* program, a command-prompt utility. The basic information stored in BCD provides locale information, the location of the boot disk and the Windows files, and other information required for the startup process. Figure 10-10 shows the result of running BCDEdit on a computer that dual-boots between Windows 7 and Windows 8. Window 7 is installed

on drive C: and Windows 8 on drive F:. If this computer booted only from one OS, you
would see just two sections: Windows Boot Manager and one of the Windows Boot
Loader sections. Exercise 10-2 walks you through the use of BCDEdit to view BCD on
a computer with Windows Vista, Windows 7, or Windows 8.

on the
job *BCDEdit is an advanced Command Prompt utility you can use to manage,
create, and modify the BCD database in versions of Windows beginning with
Windows Vista.*

EXERCISE 10-2

Viewing the Contents of BCD in Windows Vista, Windows 7, and Windows 8

1. **In Windows Vista or Windows 7**: From the Start menu open Accessories, right-click the shortcut for the Command Prompt, and select Run As Administrator. Respond to the User Account Control dialog box by clicking Yes or by entering an administrator password, if requested.

2. **In Windows 8**: From the Start screen initiate a search by entering **com**. When the Command Prompt appears in the results list, right-click it and from the Apps bar select Run As Administrator. Respond to the User Account Control dialog box by clicking Yes or by entering an administrator password, if requested.

3. **In all versions:** In the Command Prompt window, enter the command **bcdedit**.

4. The contents of BCD will display and will resemble Figure 10-10.

5. When you are done, close the Command Prompt window.

As a command-line utility, BCDEdit is as cryptic as they come, but available on all Windows Vista or newer systems. To learn how to work with it, enter the following into the Command Prompt and press ENTER : **bcdedit /? | more**. This will display the help information for this command. As a rule, you should not directly edit the BOOT.INI or the BCD using this or a similar tool.

on the
()ob

Directly editing the BCD or the BOOT.INI file can result in a system that will not start up if you inadvertently enter the wrong settings.

SCENARIO & SOLUTION	
What is the function of NTLDR?	It controls the Windows XP boot process until the kernel is loaded.
What is the preferred file system for Windows?	NTFS is the preferred Windows file system.
You would like to divide the space of a single basic disk into four logical drives. What partitions would you create?	Create four primary partitions on a basic disk.

CERTIFICATION OBJECTIVES

■ **802: 1.1**   *Compare and contrast the features and requirements of various Microsoft operating systems*

■ **802: 1.2**   *Given a scenario, install and configure the operating system using the most appropriate method*

■ **802: 1.3**   *Given a scenario, use appropriate command-line tools*

■ **802: 1.8**   *Explain the differences among basic OS security settings*

> This section explores the few details of CompTIA Exam Objective 802: 1.1 not addressed in Chapter 2. These include an examination of file structure and paths by defining the default locations where each of the listed Windows versions stores certain files and folders, including critical Windows OS system files, fonts, temporary files, and application program files. This section also explores in more detail portions of CompTIA Exam Objective 802: 1.2 relating to disk and file management. They include file systems (FAT, FAT32, NTFS, CDFS), directory structures, and files (creation, extensions, attributes, and permissions). We also address a small portion of CompTIA Exam Objective 802: 1.8 by describing standard file attributes, leaving the much larger discussion of file and folder-level security for Chapter 19. Finally, this section addresses the use of several of the command-line tools listed in CompTIA Objective 802: 1.3.

File Management

A file, as described in Chapter 2, is a container for data or program code organized as a unit, saved on mass storage, and identified with a special name called a filename. The author/creator of a file determines just how much information to save in a single file. For instance, the chapter you are reading right now is a single file. We could have chosen to save all of the chapters of this book in a single file, but instead, we chose to save them in individual files because it breaks the information up into more workable "chunks" for us. That's the key to working with information in general—using chunks that you can manage well.

   File management begins with understanding the underlying file system that supports the saving, retrieving, deleting, and other management tasks for files.

Windows has several file systems that it supports, so we will compare those file systems. Although most file management tasks remain the same across all the file systems supported by Windows, you will learn about features that are not available in all of these file systems. We will move on to the creation of files, organization of files, and how to manage files from within the GUI and from the Command Prompt.

File Systems

Windows XP, Windows Vista, Windows 7, and Windows 8 fully support several file systems: NTFS, FAT16 (often simply called File Allocation Table, or FAT, or the FAT file system), and FAT32. All file systems have on-disk components and program code in the operating system. In other words, the operating system must have some code in memory that allows it to manage the on-disk components of the file system.

An operating system installs the on-disk components when it formats a disk with a file system. You can only format a disk partition with a single file system at a time. The General tab of a drive's Properties dialog box will show which file system is on a drive.

Windows can use the FAT and NTFS file systems on either disk type—basic or dynamic—and on any volume type. Once you partition a basic disk, you may format it with any of these file systems. This is also true of dynamic disk volumes.

on the
job
Don't confuse disk type with file system. Disk type affects the entire disk underlying the partitions or volumes on the drives. The boundaries of a file system lie within the partition or volume in which it resides.

FAT

The *FAT file system* has been around for several decades and was the file system implemented by Microsoft in the MS-DOS operating system. We have long been tempted to declare this file system dead or irrelevant, but it is still around, supported by almost any operating system you may encounter. It is also used on small storage devices because it is a file system that takes up very little space on disk for its own use, as compared to the NTFS file system, which takes up a great deal of space (overhead), even while providing many benefits in exchange. We also include this discussion because FAT and FAT32 are listed in CompTIA Exam Objective 802: 1.2 and in the Acronyms list for both the 801 and 802 exams.

We acknowledge that you can find many, many variations of the FAT file system beyond Microsoft Windows, but we will limit this overview to the FAT file system variations available in versions of Windows featured in this book. We begin with a description of the FAT file system components, and then discuss the FAT12, FAT16, VFAT, and FAT32 implementations of this file system.

FAT File System Components   When Windows formats a disk with the FAT file system, it places the FAT file system's three primary components on the disk. These components are the boot record, the FAT table, and the root directory. They reside at the very beginning of the disk, in an area called the system area. The space beyond the system area is the data area, which can hold files and subdirectories.

- **Boot record**   The *boot record* or *boot sector* is the first physical sector on a floppy disk or the first sector on a FAT-formatted hard drive partition (recall that on a hard drive the first physical sector contains the master boot record). The boot record contains information about the OS used to format the disk and other file system information. It also contains the boot code involved in the boot process, as described earlier. The boot record also exists in other file systems.

- **FAT table**   The *File Allocation Table (FAT)* is the file system component in which the OS creates a table that serves as a map of where files reside on disk.

- **Root directory**   A directory is a place where an operating system stores information about files, including a reference to the FAT table, so it knows where to find the file's contents on disk. The *root directory* is the top-level directory on the FAT file system and the only one created during formatting. The root directory also exists in other file systems. The entries in a directory point to files and to the next level of directories.

All space beyond the system area holds files and subdirectories. Let's consider how these components are organized and how Windows uses them. When Windows formats a disk with the FAT file system, it divides the entire disk space for one volume (A, C, and so on) into equal-sized allocation units called clusters. A *cluster* is the minimum disk space that a file can use. Therefore, if a file contains only a few bytes, but the cluster size is 32,768 bytes, the file owns the entire cluster space of 32,768 bytes and a lot of space is wasted.

When saving a file to disk, Windows checks the FAT table to find available space and then updates the FAT table entries for the clusters used for the file. When reading a file from disk, it reads the FAT table to determine where all the pieces of the file are located. While we use the term "FAT file system" to refer to any of the variations of the file system, those available in Windows have numeric suffixes that describe the size of each entry in its FAT table in binary. There, the FAT12 file system has 12-bit entries, FAT 16 has 16-bit entries, and FAT32 has 32-bit entries. The length of the entry limits the number of entries the FAT table can hold, and thus the maximum number of clusters that may be used on a disk. The data space on each disk volume divides into the number of clusters the FAT table can handle.

FAT12 *FAT12* is for floppy disks and very small hard drives—too small to worry about today. When you format a floppy disk in Windows, it automatically formats it with the FAT12 file system.

FAT16 The *FAT16* file system, as implemented in the versions of Windows included in this book, is limited to 65,525 clusters. The size of a cluster must be a power of 2 and a maximum size of 65,536 bytes (64 KB). Multiplying the maximum number of clusters (65,525) by the maximum cluster size limits the partition size for a FAT16-formatted disk to 4 GB.

FAT32 Windows supports the *FAT32* file system, introduced by Microsoft in a special release of Windows 95. This improved version of the FAT file system can format larger hard disk partitions (up to two terabytes) and allocates disk space more efficiently. A FAT32-formatted partition will have a FAT table and root directory, but the FAT table holds 32-bit entries, and there are changes in how it positions the root directory. The root directory on both FAT12 and FAT16 was a single point of failure, since it could only reside in the system area. The FAT32 file system allows the OS to back up the root directory to the data portion of the disk and to use this backup in case the first copy fails.

FAT32 creates 4 KB clusters for partitions up to 8 GB. Because it uses a 32-bit FAT table entry size, FAT32 theoretically supports a partition size of two terabytes (2 TB).

NTFS

Windows XP, Windows Vista, Windows 7, and Windows 8 all support an improved version of a file system introduced in Windows NT. This is the New Technology File

System (NTFS). From its beginnings, NTFS has been a much more advanced file system than any form of the FAT file system.

Master File Table In contrast to the FAT file system, NTFS has a far more sophisticated structure, using an expandable *master file table (MFT)*. This makes the file system adaptable to future changes. NTFS uses the MFT to store a transaction-based database, with all file accesses treated as transactions, and if a transaction is not complete, NTFS will roll back to the last successful transaction, making the file system more stable.

Fault Tolerance In another improved feature, NTFS also avoids saving files to damaged portions of a disk, called bad sectors. This is a form of fault tolerance.

NTFS on Small-capacity Media Windows will not allow you to format a floppy disk with NTFS, because it requires much more space on a disk for its structure than FAT does. This extra space is the file system's overhead. You may format a small hard disk partition with NTFS, but because of the overhead space requirements, the smallest recommended size is 10 MB. That's megabytes, not terabytes, so it is pretty much a nonissue today.

While a USB flash drive normally comes formatted with FAT32 (and is readable by your Windows OS), you can format one with NTFS. However, once you do this, you must use the Safely Remove Hardware applet before removing the drive to prevent damaging data on the drive. Although we recommend using this applet for any USB drive, you are more likely to damage data on an NTFS-formatted flash drive if you remove it without using this applet to stop all processes that are accessing the drive.

on the
ⓙob *As much as we favor NTFS for all its advanced features, it is very much a Microsoft-only file system. FAT32, however, is supported by many file systems, including Apple's Mac OS X and variations of Unix and Linux. When we want to use an external hard drive or USB flash drive on our PC as well as on our Apple iMac, we make sure to format it with FAT32.*

NTFS Indexing The indexing service is part of Windows and speeds up file searches on NTFS volumes. If this service is on, indexing of any folder that has the index attribute turned on will occur so that future searches of that folder will be faster.

NTFS Compression NTFS supports *file and folder compression* to save disk space, using an algorithm to reduce the size of a file as it writes it to disk. You can turn it on for an individual file or for the entire contents of a folder, and this is a very nice feature if you are running low on disk space. However, the tradeoff is that it takes Windows more time to write a file to disk when it has to compress it, and also more time to expand a compressed file as it brings it into memory when you open the file.

NTFS Security Features With the exception of the earlier editions, the NTFS file system in all the versions of Windows studied here offers encryption at the file and folder level in a feature called *Encrypting File System (EFS)*. *Encryption* is the conversion of data into a special format that cannot be read by anyone unless they have a software key to convert it back into its usable form. The encryption key for EFS is the user's authentication. Therefore, once a user encrypts a file or folder, only someone logged on with the same user account can access it.

In addition, on NTFS volumes you can apply permissions to folders and files for added security. A *permission* is the authorization of a person or group to access a resource—in this case, a file or folder—and take certain actions, such as reading, changing, or deleting. This is one of the most important differences between NTFS and FAT file systems.

The Properties dialog box of each folder and file on a drive formatted with NTFS will have a Security tab showing the permissions assigned to that folder or file. Learn more about file and folder permissions in Chapter 19.

on the *While Windows uses the term "folder" and shows a folder icon in the GUI,*
job *many of the dialog boxes and messages continue to use the old term "directory" for what we now know as a disk folder. People frequently use these two terms interchangeably. In this book, we generally use "folder" when working in the GUI and "directory" when working from the Command Prompt.*

exFAT

Extended File Allocation Table (exFAT) is a file system Microsoft introduced in Service Pack 1 for Windows Vista. Since then, all versions of Windows support this file system, which was not intended for use on hard drives, but as a replacement for FAT32 on solid-state storage. Microsoft still recommends NTFS over other file systems for hard drives. The exFAT file system is therefore intended for all types of solid-state storage, whether in a thumb drive or solid-state drive (SSD) card connected directly to a PC or within one of the many mobile devices in use, and Microsoft licenses exFAT to other manufacturers.

If you right-click a hard drive volume in Windows Explorer and select Format, the drop-down menu under File System will not show the exFAT file system as an option. Do the same thing with a thumb drive or other solid-state storage, and you will see three file systems, as shown in Figure 10-11. The exFAT file system includes the following advantages over FAT32:

■ 256 TB maximum volume size.

■ A single folder/directory can hold up to 100 high-definition movies, 60 hours of high-definition audio, or 4000 RAW images. A *RAW image* file contains unprocessed image data from a digital camera, image scanner, or digital movie scanner.

■ Faster file saves, so that solid-state devices can save at their full speed.

■ Cross-platform interoperation with many operating systems; Apple added exFAT support to Mac OS X beginning with Snow Leopard (10.6.5).

■ The file system is extensible, meaning that manufacturers can customize it for new device characteristics.

FIGURE 10-11

When a solid-state device is selected, exFAT is available in the Format dialog box.

Resilient File System

Resilient file system (ReFS) is a new file system expected to replace the NTFS file system on Windows Server. It retains many of the features of the NTFS file system, but discards some features and adds many others for servers to support really large hard drives and RAID style systems with very advanced performance and fault tolerance support.

on the **j** o b
You will not see questions concerning the resilient file system on the CompTIA A+ 801 or 802 exam. In fact, you will not see this file system on desktop computers for a long while, since it was introduced exclusively on Microsoft's Windows 8 Server product, not on the Windows 8 consumer products we describe in this book. However, what appears on Microsoft Server products eventually trickles down to the desktop products, so you will eventually see it on the job.

Other File Systems

Although NTFS is the most important file system for anyone supporting Windows PCs, several other file systems exist, and we will briefly examine them. These include CDFS, UDF, and DFS.

CDFS   Compact Disc File System (CDFS) is an ISO 9660–compliant file system used by Windows to read CDs, DVDs, and CD-ROMs. While UDF has replaced CDFS, Windows still supports CDFS to use with optical discs that do not support UDF.

UDF   UDF is an acronym with multiple identities. In Chapter 9, it made an appearance as "Uniqueness Database Files," files used in a scripted installation of Windows, and now we have another use for this acronym: *Universal Data Format (UDF)*, a file format used for optical discs. This format is for movie DVDs. Windows Vista was the first Windows version to support writing the UDF format, so prior to Windows Vista, if you wanted to write to disc using UDF format, you needed a third-party program like Roxio. In addition, some versions of Windows could read UDF-formatted discs, but could not write to them.

DFS   *Distributed File System (DFS)* is a service implemented on Windows Servers that hides the complexity of the network from end users, in that it makes files that are distributed across multiple servers appear as if they are in one place. Unless you are managing Microsoft Servers, you will not come in close contact with DFS, but it is included in the CompTIA A+ Acronyms list for the 801 and 802 exams.

Files

You save a file into a special file on disk called a folder. That isn't exactly true, but that is what you see in the GUI. Actually, a folder is just a listing of files and their actual location on disk. When you are working in an application, such as a word processor, it will usually have a default folder into which it saves your files, but you can choose to save any file in other folders—you can even create additional folders. You have choices like these when you are working with data files.

As part of managing your files, you'll perform different actions—such as opening, closing, copying, and moving files and folders. File management in the Windows GUI is easy and relatively safe, because you can see exactly what files and folders you have selected for a file management operation.

Naming Rules

MS-DOS and early versions of Windows into the 1990s used the 8.3 naming rules, in which the filename could be a maximum of eight characters long and the file extension was a maximum of three characters long. A *long filename (LFN)* is any file or folder name that breaks the 8.3 file-naming convention. Windows now supports LFNs on all file systems on all media, including hard drives, flash drives, optical discs, and even floppy disks. The support for long filenames in Microsoft's FAT file systems (FAT12, FAT16, and FAT32) is provided by a technology Microsoft called the *virtual file allocation table (VFAT)*.

Using VFAT, all versions of Microsoft Windows since Windows 95 can create filenames beyond the 8.3 limit by simply using multiple directory entries. For each file or directory with a long filename, VFAT stores a long file up to 255 characters, including spaces, which were not allowed in 8.3 filenames. In addition, it creates a legacy 8.3 filename for each long filename entry.

File Attributes

A *file attribute* is a component of a file or directory entry that determines how an operating system handles the file or directory. In all the variations of the FAT, FAT32, and NTFS file systems, the standard file attributes are read-only, archive, system, and hidden. Two special attributes, also in all Windows file systems, are volume label, which allows you to give a name to the volume (recall the Volume Label option in the New Simple Volume Wizard in Figure 10-4), and directory, which identifies an entry as a directory. The operating system modifies these attributes, as do certain programs such as file backup utilities. NTFS supports many more types of file attributes beyond these six.

The following are explanations of each of the four standard file attributes.

Read-only Attribute   The read-only attribute was designed to ensure that a file or folder will not be modified, renamed, or deleted accidentally—with emphasis on accidentally. In Windows, if you try to modify, rename, or delete a read-only file, you will receive a warning message requiring confirmation, but you can still proceed with the action.

Archive Attribute   By default, Windows turns on the archive attribute for all files when they are created or modified. This attribute, when turned "on," marks a file as one that needs backing up. Most backup utilities provide the option to back up only files that have been created or modified since the last backup. One way this is tracked is by looking for the archive attribute. A backup program can turn off the archive attribute as it backs up a file, allowing the backup program to do subsequent backups that only back up files with the archive attribute turned on, thus backing up only those files created or modified since the last backup.

System Attribute   The OS or an application gives certain folders and files the system attribute automatically to identify it as a system file. Most system files also get the hidden attribute to keep users from viewing them. From Windows Explorer (File Explorer in Windows 8), you can neither see the system attribute nor turn it on or off.

Hidden Attribute   A file or folder with the hidden attribute turned on will not show in My Computer/Computer or Windows Explorer unless the View settings allow it to be shown.

Additional Windows File Attributes   The NTFS file system has these original file attributes, as well as additional file attributes. In fact, NTFS saves a file's actual contents as one or more file attributes. NTFS allows for future expansion of attributes—making this file system more expandable.

The General tab of the Properties dialog box for a file or folder will show two of the traditional attributes: read-only and hidden. On an NTFS file or folder, the Advanced button will display the status of four attributes: archive, index, compress, and encrypt (see Figure 10-12). Index, compress, and encrypt are special NTFS file attributes. Turning on the Index attribute will make file searches much faster, as the file contents and properties will be indexed by the *Windows Indexing Service*. Use the compress attribute on a folder to compress the contents, and use the encrypt

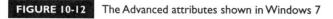

FIGURE 10-12   The Advanced attributes shown in Windows 7

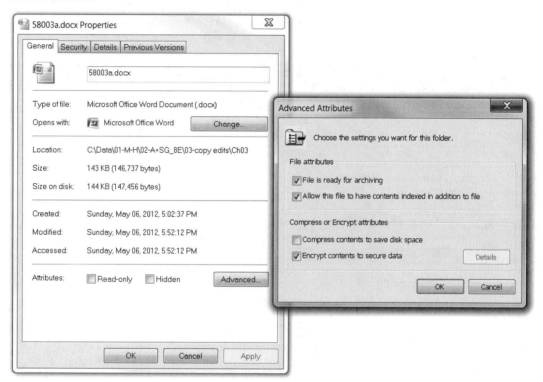

attribute to encrypt the contents of a folder using the Encrypting File System (EFS). These two attributes are mutually exclusive. You cannot both compress and encrypt, but you can apply one or the other of these attributes to a file or folder.

File Types

Windows computers use several file types, including, in broad terms, data files and program files. Data files contain the data you create with application programs. Program files (also called "binary files") contain programming code (instructions read by the OS or special interpreters). Program files include those that you can directly run, such as files with the COM or EXE extension (called "executables"), and those that are called up by other programs, such as files with the DLL extension.

Data Files When it comes to file management, you should only manage data files. Leave management of program files to the operating system. There are a large number of data file types. A short list of the file types and associated extensions is shown in the table.

File Type	Associated Extension
Compressed files	ZIP: (zigzag inline package) files
Database files	ACCDB: Microsoft Access 2007 or later MDB: Versions of Microsoft Access prior to Access 2007
Graphic files	BMP, DIB, GIF, JPG, TIF, PNG, and others
Microsoft Management Console files (Computer Management, Disk Management, etc.)	MMC
Presentation files	PPTX: Microsoft PowerPoint 2007 or later PPT: for Versions of Microsoft PowerPoint prior to PowerPoint 2007
Spreadsheet files	XLSX: Microsoft Excel 2007 or later XLS: Versions of Microsoft Excel prior to Excel 2007
Text files	TXT
Video files	Several file formats defined by the *Moving Picture Experts Group* (MPEG), including MPG, MP3, and MP4
Word-processing document files	DOCX: Microsoft Word 2007 or later DOCm: Microsoft Word 2007 or later document file with macros enabled DOC: Versions of Microsoft Word prior to Word 2007 and some other word processors

System and Program Files System files are program files and some special data files that are part of the OS, and they are very important to the proper operation of Windows. Some are located in the root of drive C:, whereas others are located in the folder in which Windows is installed. The default name for this folder is WINDOWS in all versions studied here. This folder, in turn, contains many additional folders containing important operating system files. In Windows, the default settings for My Computer/Computer will hide the contents of a folder in which system files and other important files are stored.

These files are hidden.

This folder contains files that keep your system working properly. You should not modify its contents.

Show the contents of this folder

e x a m

By default, Windows XP and later versions hide the contents of both the root folder and the Windows installation. If you decide to make them visible, do not make manual changes to these folders or their contents. Other changes you make to Windows through Control Panel applets and setup programs will alter the contents of these folders.

Some, but not all, files in these folders have the hidden attribute turned on so that Windows hides them, even when you view the folder contents. But when you are studying or troubleshooting an OS, you may want to change this default so you can see the hidden files.

Default File Locations   Let's take a brief look at the folder structure created by Windows for data and the program files belonging to the operating system, add-on components, and applications. They include:

- **Documents And Settings**   In Windows XP, this folder, located in the root folder of the boot volume, contains the personal folders for all users who log on.

- **Users**   Located in the root folder of the boot volume, this is where Windows Vista and Windows 7 create each user's personal folder.

- **Windows**   This folder, located in the root folder of the boot volume, is where the Windows operating system is stored. Note that you can create a custom installation in which you give the Setup program an alternative location for the operating system files, but we strongly suggest you resist any urge to do this!

- **Program Files**   This folder contains subfolders, where your application programs are typically installed. Under 64-bit Windows, this folder contains 64-bit Windows programs.

- **Program Files (x86)**   In 64-bit Windows, this folder contains 32-bit programs.

- **Program Data**   Located in the root folder of the boot volume in Windows Vista and Windows 7, this folder contains subdirectories for each installed program, along with each program's settings that apply to all users.

- **Fonts**   Here you will find the various fonts installed on the PC. This folder is a subfolder of the Windows folder.

- **System, System32**   These subfolders of the Windows folder are used to store dynamic link libraries (DLLs) and other necessary support files. Files in the System folder contain 16-bit code, whereas files in the System32 folder contain 32-bit code.
- **SysWOW64**   This subfolder of the Windows folder exists in 64-bit Windows installations and is where the 64-bit support files reside.
- **Temp**   This folder is used to store files temporarily, such as those files used during the installation of new application programs and those temporary files a program creates while it is working. This folder often contains out-of-date files left over from an installation operation.

on the Job

The rule for the Temp folder is that any program writing files to it should delete those files when the program is closed. If a program ends abnormally (you tripped over the power cord or the OS hung up), it can't do this important chore. Therefore, deleting files from the Temp folder that have not been used in over a week is generally safe. In practice, we delete all temporary files dated before the last restart.

Offline Files and Folders   A Windows computer that logs onto a Microsoft server domain will often be configured to save the user profile folders on a server. Therefore, all user data and user preference settings for local applications are saved on the server. If your computer does not always have access to the network, you can configure Windows to save those files to local storage so that when your computer is disconnected from the network, you can continue to work on the files. Changes you make in one location (on the server or in the offline files) will be changed in the other location the next time your computer connects to the network. The actual location of offline files and folders is in a hidden directory named CSC (for client-side cache) located in SystemRoot.

Enable or disable the offline attribute in the Offline Files dialog box, which you can open by entering **offline files** in the Start Search box and selecting Manage Offline Files from the results. Figure 10-13 shows this dialog box with offline files enabled. The Offline Files option is only available if your computer logs into a network server—either a Microsoft Domain server (corporate-type of network) or a Microsoft Home Server. Beginning in Windows Vista and continuing through Windows 8, Microsoft provides a Control Panel utility called *Sync Center* that you can use to manage file synchronization. A quick way to open Sync Center is right from the Offline Files dialog box, using the Open Sync Center button, as shown in Figure 10-13, or by entering **sync center** in the Start Search box.

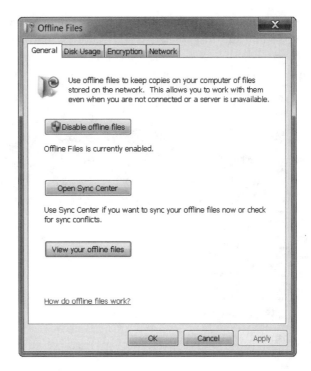

FIGURE 10-13

The Offline Files
dialog box

Text Editors

A type of application called a text editor allows you to create and edit text files using only the simplest of formatting codes (like carriage return, line feed, and end-of-document codes). A text editor uses only one set of characters, and does not use or understand codes for special character fonts or special paragraph formatting.

As a technician or support person, understanding text editors and knowing how to create and edit text files is helpful. The reason is that the operating system and certain applications use some text files. Although these files may not have the standard filename extension (TXT) used for text files, you can still use a text editor to view and modify them.

One such file is the BOOT.INI file in Windows XP. This important system file is actually a text file containing startup instructions for Windows versions beginning with Windows NT and continuing through Windows XP. It is not used beginning with Windows Vista.

Windows comes with two text editors. The first, Notepad, is a Windows application and is the preferred text editor when working in the Windows GUI. The second, Edit, is a DOS application. When you call up Edit in Windows, it is loaded in a text-mode window. Compare the two programs, shown here.

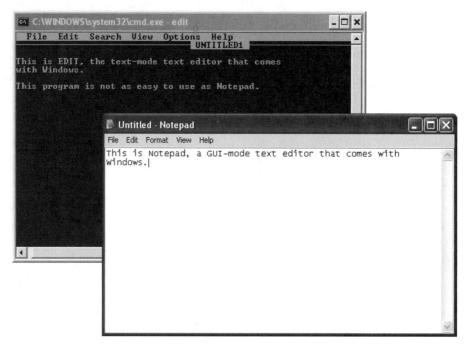

Notepad is a typical Windows GUI application that uses the standard Windows commands and mouse actions. Other applications (WordPad and Microsoft Word) can create and edit text files, but they are primarily word processors, which can create documents with fancy formatting instructions included. To create a text file with a word processor, you must choose to save the file as a text file. Notepad and Edit create only simple text files without the extra formatting.

Organizing Files Using Folders

All information on a computer is stored in files. Typically, you organize those files by separating them into folders containing related files. It's important to understand how to organize files and folders properly so you can easily access important files, and so you know which files you should not touch. And because even the best file organization won't guarantee that you'll always remember the name of that very important file, or even where you saved it, you should practice searching for files.

Any filing system needs a level of organization if it is to be useful. If you use a filing cabinet to hold a number of important documents, most likely you organize those documents into separate file folders and use some sort of alphabetical arrangement of the folders so you can locate the documents quickly when you need them. Imagine what a difficult time you would have finding your tax-related documents if all year you simply threw everything into a large box and then had to sort through each piece of paper to find the few important ones.

In Windows, you do not need to alphabetize your folders; Windows will sort them for you in the GUI. Simply give the folders names that make sense to you. You might simply name a top-level data folder "data." Subfolders below this level should have more meaningful names, perhaps a department name, such as "accounting," or a project or customer name.

As your data files grow in number, you will want to make more folders to organize them more logically. You will soon find that you have created an entire hierarchy of folders. Having them all under one or more top-level folders will make them easier to back up. You can select the top folder and have the backup program back up all subfolders and files.

As you work with Windows, you will develop your own filing system. The only caution is to never save data files in the *root folder* (root directory). Oh yes, the NTFS file system has the notion of the root directory, even though NTFS has a different file system structure on disk. From either the Command Prompt or the GUI, the folder and file organization looks the same across all the file systems. The root folder is at the top level of any drive, and you should never use it for saving data files. In My Computer/Computer, when you double-click one of the drive icons, it opens to the root folder, showing the top level.

Basic File Operations

Before we get into how to work with files in Windows, let's talk about the basic file operations: copy, move, and delete. When you *copy* a file, the original stays in the source location, and a duplicate is created in the target location. When you *move* a file, a copy is created in the target location, and then the original is deleted from the source location. When you *delete* a file on a hard drive or an SSD drive volume, the file is usually moved to the Recycle Bin, rather than actually being deleted. This file can be recovered if you open the Recycle Bin, right-click on the file and select Restore. You can permanently delete the contents of the Recycle Bin by selecting Empty the Recycle Bin. You can permanently delete selected files by pressing the SHIFT key and DELETE key at the same time. This permanent delete is so named because Windows will display a warning message saying that you are about to permanently delete the file and requiring that you click OK to proceed. It turns out that even this type of delete may not truly destroy files, so in Chapter 19 you will learn how to permanently delete files so that they are not recoverable.

GUI Techniques

If you are already familiar with Windows GUI techniques and tools for file management, you will be tempted to skip this section. But don't! Take the time to check out the drag-and-drop rules and to practice basic file management tasks.

EXERCISE 10-3

CertCam

Managing Files and Folders

In this exercise, you will practice some common file management tasks. First, you will create a folder, and then, you will copy, move, and delete files. Finally, you will open a file from its shortcut and edit it in Notepad.

1. Open the My Documents/Documents folder.

2. Position your cursor over an empty area of the Contents pane (right pane) of the window and then right-click. From the context menu, select New | Folder. Name the folder **data1**. Repeat this step to create a folder named **data2**.

3. Double-click the data1 folder to open it, and then right-click the Contents pane, and select New | Text Document. Name the document **report1.txt**.

4. Drag the file report1.txt from the Contents pane, and drop it on the data2 folder in the Folders pane. This moves the file so it no longer exists in the data1 folder.

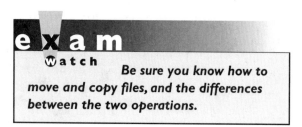

ⓦatch   *Be sure you know how to move and copy files, and the differences between the two operations.*

5. Open the data2 folder and confirm that report1 moved to this folder.

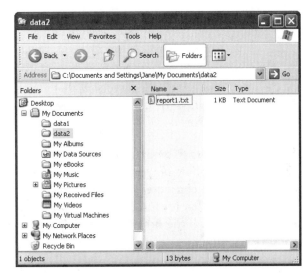

6. Press and hold the right mouse button while dragging the file back to the data1 folder. When you release the mouse button over the data1 folder, a context menu pops up that gives you the choice of copying, moving, or creating a shortcut to the file. Select the option to create a shortcut.

7. Expand the data1 folder and double-click Shortcut To report1.txt. This link is a shortcut to a text file, so double-clicking it causes Notepad to open, because that is the program associated with text files.

8. Now type a few sentences describing what happens when you drag a file from one folder to another folder on the same drive. Then save the file by selecting File | Save. Exit from Notepad.

9. Open the data2 folder and double-click the report1 file. The sentence you typed should be in the file. Exit from Notepad.

A drag-and-drop operation between folders on the same drive is a move operation, and a drag-and-drop operation between folders on different drives is a copy operation. In both cases, you are using the primary mouse button (usually the left button) for the drag operation. If you drag while holding down the secondary mouse button (usually the right button), a context menu will pop up with the options to move, copy, or create a shortcut.

File Management at the Command Prompt

The Command Prompt in Windows is a place in which you can enter commands in a simple command-line interface (CLI). If you run a GUI program from the Command Prompt, it will load into a separate Window, but if you run a character-mode program, it will run within the Command Prompt, displaying any associated output or messages. We strongly suggest that under normal circumstances you not do file management from the Command Prompt because you can only use text-mode commands that give you very little feedback, and a minor typo can result in disaster.

on the
Job

From a Command Prompt, you can launch any program that will run in Windows (depending on your permissions and User Account Control [UAC]). If the program is a character-mode program, it will run within the command-line interface. If written for text mode, the program will remain in the Command Prompt window. If the program is a GUI program, it will launch in a separate window.

However, as a support person, you might find yourself working at a special command-line interface—either the Recovery Console or Safe Mode with Command Prompt, designed as tools for recovering from serious damage to the OS. Therefore, prepare for the time when you may need to work with these command-line interfaces by practicing now with the Windows Command Prompt. In Chapter 13 you will learn about working with the Command Prompt in the Recovery Console and in Safe Mode with Command Prompt.

Opening the Command Prompt

You will find a shortcut to the Command Prompt in Windows XP at Start | All Programs | Accessories. Similarly, in Windows Vista and Windows 7, you will find it at Start | All Programs | Accessories.

When you work at the Command Prompt, you are still subject to Windows security, and if you attempt to run a command on a Windows Vista, Windows 7, or Windows 8 computer and receive the message, "The requested operation requires elevation," then close the Command Prompt and go back and run it using the Run As Administrator option. To do this, navigate to its shortcut. If you recently ran it, the shortcut will be on your Start menu (except in Windows 8, which does not have a Start menu). Otherwise, it lives in the Accessories folder in All Programs. Right-click the shortcut and select Run As Administrator. The title of the Command Prompt window will be "Administrator: Command Prompt," and anything you run in this window will run with elevated privileges.

In Windows 8, when you right-click the bottom left of the screen, a context menu appears as shown in Figure 10-14. From this menu, you can select either Command Prompt or Command Prompt (Admin). The second choice will run Command Prompt as an administrator.

Practicing at the Command Prompt

There are two commands for creating and deleting directories at the Command Prompt: MD (Make Directory) and RD (Remove Directory). Use the DIR (Directory) command to view listings of files and directories. Move around the directory hierarchy at the Command Prompt using the CD (Change Directory) command. Use two dots together (..) to indicate the directory immediately above the current directory. You can use these in many command-line commands. For instance, if you only want to move up one level, type **cd ..** and press ENTER.

You can use wildcards from the Command Prompt. The most useful one is the asterisk (*). Use the asterisk to represent one or more characters in a filename or extension. For instance, enter the command **dir *.exe** to see a listing of all files in the current directory ending with "exe." Using *.* will select all files and directories.

When you are working at the Command Prompt, the previous commands and messages remain on the screen until they scroll off. To clear this information from the screen, use the clear screen command (CLS).

FIGURE 10-14

The Windows 8 Start context menu shows two choices for running Command Prompt.

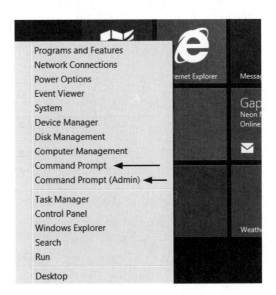

When you want to copy files, you have a choice of commands. The simplest is COPY, which is a very, very old command that does not understand directories. To use this command on files in different directories, you must enter the path to the directory or directories in the command. It helps to first make either the source directory or the target directory current before using this command. We rarely use COPY because of its limits. We prefer the XCOPY command, because it is a more advanced command that understands directories. In fact, you can tell XCOPY to copy the contents of a directory simply by giving the directory name. The simple syntax for both of these commands is *<command> <from_source> <to_destination>*. COPY and XCOPY will both accept either filenames or folder names in the source and destination arguments. For instance, the command xcopy monday tuesday can be entered to copy the contents of the folder Monday into the folder Tuesday.

A far more advanced command is *Robust File Copy*, which has the command name *ROBOCOPY*. It is a folder copier, meaning that you must enter folder names as the source and destination arguments. It will not accept filenames or wildcard characters in the source or destination arguments, although it copies all the files within the specified folder. In addition, ROBOCOPY has a list of advanced features, such as the ability to stop a copy operation that is interrupted by a disconnected network. It then resumes upon reconnection with the network. It also allows you to mirror two entire folder structures. This is a handy but tricky feature, because those files on the destination that are no longer present on the source will be deleted from the destination. There are many more ROBOCOPY features—all of which are accessed with the appropriate arguments. A simple example of a command that would mirror the DATA folder on two different drives is robocopy c:\data d:\data /mir.

Exercise 10-4 demonstrates the use of several file management commands as it walks you through creating and removing a directory. You will also move around the directory structure and copy and delete files. For the last, you will use the DEL command.

EXERCISE 10-4

Managing Directories and Files at the Command Prompt

Practice working with directories and files from the Command Prompt. This exercise requires the folders and files you created in Exercise 10-3.

1. Open the Command Prompt window, type **dir,** and press ENTER. A listing of files and directories within the directory will display. If they scrolled off the screen, type the command again with the pause switch: **dir /p**.

2. Type the clear screen command, **cls**, and press ENTER to clear the screen.

3. In Windows XP, change to the My Documents directory by typing **cd my documents** and pressing ENTER.

4. In Vista or Windows 7, to change to the directory containing the Documents directory, type **cd %homepath%** and press ENTER. To change to the Documents directory itself, type **cd documents** and press ENTER.

5. Create a new directory in the My Documents or Documents directory. At the Command Prompt, type **md testdata** and press ENTER.

6. Enter the command **dir /ad /p** to confirm that it created the new folder within the current folder. The switch /ad will only display directories; the /p switch will pause the screen.

7. To make the data2 directory current, type **cd data2** and press ENTER.

8. Copy the report1.txt file to the testdata directory. Type **copy report1.txt ..\ testdata**.

9. Use the more advanced XCOPY command to copy the contents of the data1 folder into testdata. Type **xcopy ..\data1 ..\testdata** and press ENTER. Figure 10-15 shows Steps 5 through 9.

10. Change the current directory to the My Documents directory, which is the parent directory of the data1, data2, and testdata directories. To do this, type **cd ..** and press ENTER.

11. Use the DIR command to view the contents of testdata. Type **dir testdata** and press ENTER.

12. To delete the testdata folder, first move into that folder, type **cd testdata**, and press ENTER.

13. Now delete all of the files within that folder. Type **del *.*** and press ENTER.

14. Now the testdata directory is empty, but it is the current directory, and you cannot delete the current directory so you must move out of the directory. Type **cd ..** and press ENTER.

15. Now remove the directory. Type **rd testdata** and press ENTER.

16. Confirm that it removed the testdata folder. Type **dir /ad** and press ENTER.

17. Close the Command Prompt window.

FIGURE 10-15

Creating a directory and copying files at the Command Prompt

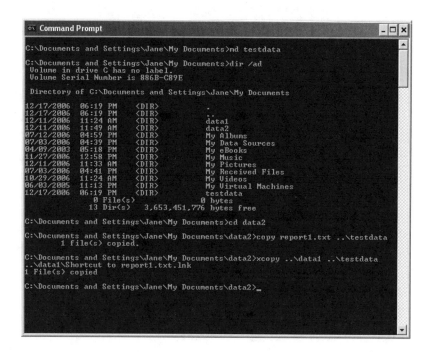

Windows Utilities

Windows comes with many utility programs, which are specialized programs that support people and that technicians use to configure, optimize, and troubleshoot Windows and networks. So far in the book, we have introduced you to some of these utilities, such as Device Manager, Disk Defragmenter, and Disk Management, and we even consider the Readiness Analyzer and Upgrade Advisor to be utilities.

In this section, we will look at some of the command-line and GUI utilities that come with Windows. As you continue through the book, you will encounter more of these, where appropriate. Here, you will learn certain command-line utilities used in troubleshooting problems in Windows, and in the chapters on networking (Chapters 14, 15, and 16), you will use utilities for testing network configuration and connectivity.

Command-Line Utilities

We believe it is important for an IT professional to understand a few other Command Prompt commands, including ATTRIB, DEFRAG, and DIR for file management; and the simple command-line editor, EDIT. Further, you should understand TELNET and the very useful NET commands if you are working with Windows on a network.

You have already learned to use the most common file management utilities at the Command Prompt, but a few more are used for disk management. Some of these commands have strong roots in MS-DOS but have been updated and modified to run from a Windows Command Prompt. Some may be traditional DOS commands, such as DIR, XCOPY, ATTRIB, DEFRAG, and FORMAT. There are also specialized command-line commands, such as the IPCONFIG and PING commands that you will use in Chapter 15 to view the network configuration and to test connectivity, respectively.

One of the handiest commands when you are working at the Command Prompt is the HELP command, which, when entered alone at the Command Prompt, gives a list and brief description of commands. A handy trick for a command that sends a great deal of information to the screen, like the HELP command, is to use the pipe (|) symbol and the MORE filter. Exercise 10-5 will demonstrate the use of the HELP command, the pipe, the MORE filter, and the /? switch that you can use to quickly see the syntax for any single command. You will also use the DEFRAG command.

EXERCISE 10-5

Using the DEFRAG command

In this exercise, you will run some simple file management and disk maintenance commands from the Command Prompt.

1. Open the Command Prompt window.

2. Type the HELP command with the MORE filter: **help | more**, and press ENTER to display a list of commands. As you finish reading each page, press SPACEBAR to display a new page. Continue until you are finished. If you wish to end without viewing all the pages, press the CTRL-C key combination.

3. Check out the syntax for the DEFRAG command by using the /? switch. Type **defrag /?** and press ENTER.

4. Now enter the command to run an analysis of drive (volume) C:. To do this, type **defrag c: -a** and press ENTER. This command returns the analysis results much faster than the GUI version of this program (see Figure 10-16).

5. Close the Command Prompt window.

Run the DEFRAG
command to
quickly analyze a
disk.

```
C:\Documents and Settings\Jane>defrag /?
Usage:
defrag <volume> [-a] [-f] [-v] [-?]
    volume   drive letter or mount point (d: or d:\vol\mountpoint)
    -a       Analyze only
    -f       Force defragmentation even if free space is low
    -v       Verbose output
    -?       Display this help text

C:\Documents and Settings\Jane>defrag c: -a
Windows Disk Defragmenter
Copyright (c) 2001 Microsoft Corp. and Executive Software International, Inc.

Analysis Report
    14.94 GB Total,  7.82 GB (52%) Free,  27% Fragmented (52% file fragmentation
)

You should defragment this volume.

C:\Documents and Settings\Jane>
```

As you can see, these programs quickly perform a task and then disappear from memory. Other commands, such as EDIT, may start programs called applications, which stay in memory, have a user interface, and allow you to do work such as creating and modifying text or word processing documents, or creating, modifying, and manipulating data with a database.

In addition to these methods of working at the Command Prompt, Windows has startup options that allow you to start at a Command Prompt. Accessing the Command Prompt in this way is valuable for troubleshooting startup problems. You will have a chance to look at the startup options in Chapter 13.

CHKDSK

The CHKDSK command (Check Disk) is the text-mode version of the GUI Error-Checking program you can access from the Tools page of the Properties dialog for a disk. It checks disks for physical and logical errors.

Running CHKDSK without the /f parameter is like running DEFRAG with the −a parameter—it only analyzes the disk. If errors are found, rerun the command with the /f parameter and it will fix disk errors. Use the /r parameter together with the /f parameter, and CHKDSK will both fix the disk errors and attempt to recover the data in the bad space by moving it. If the volume is in use (as is always the case with drive C:), you will see a message asking if you would like to schedule the volume to be checked during the next system restart. See Figure 10-17. Press y and ENTER to schedule this. Be aware that CHKDSK can take as much as an hour or more to check and repair a large hard drive.

FIGURE 10-17

If you see this message, press Y to let Windows schedule CHKDSK for the next time the system restarts.

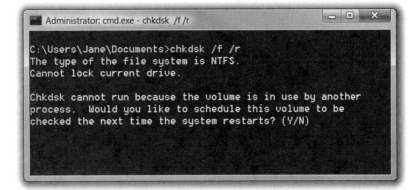

ATTRIB   The ATTRIB command lets you view and manipulate the file attributes read-only, archive, system, and hidden. As a technician, you may encounter a situation in which you need this command.

In one scenario, you may want to modify a file that has the read-only attribute turned on. If this attribute is on, you can open and read the file, and even modify it, but you will not be able to save it with the new changes. The solution is to turn off the attribute, which is something that you would normally do in the GUI by deselecting the read-only attribute in the Properties dialog box of the file. However, you may encounter situations in which you need to do this from a command line.

FORMAT   The FORMAT command will allow you to format a hard drive or other media, such as the rare floppy disk or the more common SSD from a Command Prompt. Once again, the preferred way is to format from the GUI, where you are less likely to make an error when doing this. The correct GUI tools are either the Disk Management console or Windows Explorer.

Figure 10-18 shows the command for formatting the D: drive. Notice that it does not proceed until you press Y. Press N to cancel. This command will wipe out the contents of the drive. Using the proper syntax, you can format a hard drive with any of the file systems supported by Windows for the target disk.

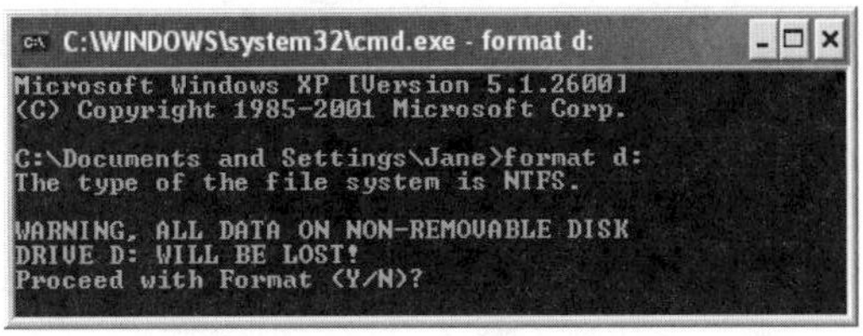

FIGURE 10-18

Press Y to continue with the formatting of drive D.

```
C:\WINDOWS\system32\cmd.exe - format d:
Microsoft Windows XP [Version 5.1.2600]
(C) Copyright 1985-2001 Microsoft Corp.

C:\Documents and Settings\Jane>format d:
The type of the file system is NTFS.

WARNING, ALL DATA ON NON-REMOVABLE DISK
DRIVE D: WILL BE LOST!
Proceed with Format (Y/N)?
```

SFC   System files have very privileged access to your computer. Therefore, malicious software targets system files so that malware can have the same access (more on malware when we describe security threats in Chapter 17). At one time, system files were fair game for such software, but recent versions of Windows come with protections, both at the file system level through assigned permission and through the use of a service that protects system files.

In Windows XP this service is called *Windows File Protection (WFP)*, and it maintains a cache of protected files. If a file is somehow damaged, WFP will replace the damaged file with the undamaged file from the cache. WFP will allow digitally signed files to replace existing system files safely as long as the replacement files are introduced into Windows using one of the following methods:

- Windows service packs
- Hotfix distributions
- Operating system upgrades
- Windows Update
- Windows Device Manager

Beginning in Windows Vista, WFP has been replaced by *Windows Resource Protection (WRP)*, which includes the features of WFP, plus it extends protection to registry keys. Learn more about the Windows registry in Chapter 13.

The *System File Checker (SFC)* is a handy utility that uses the WFP or WRP service to scan and verify the versions of all protected system files. You can choose to have it run after you restart your computer. The syntax for this program is as follows:

```
sfc [scannow] [scanonce] [scanboot] [revert] [purgecache]
[cachesize=x]
```

When you run SFC with the /scannow parameter, you will see a message box showing a progress bar while it checks that all protected Windows files are intact and in their original versions. If SFC finds any files that do not comply, it will replace them with the correct signed file from the cache.

SHUTDOWN   Strictly speaking, the SHUTDOWN command is not a disk or file management tool. It is also not limited to running within a Command Prompt. It will run from the Run Line (Run Box) or a Windows shortcut. It is a handy utility to use when you need to quickly shut down or restart a local or remote computer. We used it when we were testing the Developer Preview of Windows 8 until we became more comfortable with shutting down that OS from the GUI.

You can create one or more shortcuts for using the SHUTDOWN command with various options. Right-click an empty area of the desktop and select New, and then select Shortcut. In the Create a Shortcut wizard, enter the string for the SHUTDOWN command with the parameters you desire, then click Next and enter a name for the shortcut. You can research the SHUTDOWN command on your own or you can use one of the commands shown next. The first logs the user off and shuts down the computer in 20 seconds (the default). To have it shut down immediately, add –t 00. The second example logs off the user and restarts the computer immediately. We named the shortcut using the first command "Shutdown" and named the shortcut using the second command "Restart." We pinned both to the Windows 8 desktop taskbar. You may want to add these to any version of Windows.

- **shutdown.exe –s**
- **shutdown.exe –r –t 00**

The following command shuts down the remote computer named Server01 after a pause of 60 seconds, forces running apps to close, and reboots the computer.

- **shutdown -r -f -m \\Server01 -t 60**

Run Line Utilities

Certain Windows utilities are very important for a technician to know, but potentially dangerous in the hands of the ordinary user. Some of these programs are GUI programs that an experienced technician depends on for various administrative tasks. Some of these programs do not have shortcuts within the Windows GUI, whereas others do have shortcuts in the GUI from which you may run them. In either case, technicians find it handy to know the executable name and usually launch these programs from the Start menu's Run line (or Run box). The following are the Run-line utilities you must know for the A+ exams:

- CMD.EXE
- DXDIAG.EXE
- EXPLORER.EXE
- MMC.EXE
- MSCONFIG.EXE
- MSINFO32.EXE
- MSTSC.EXE

- NOTEPAD.EXE
- REGEDIT.EXE
- SERVICES.MSC

CMD.EXE is used to call up the Command Prompt from the Run line. Then, of course, you are in the Command Prompt. The Command Prompt is accessible as a shortcut on the Start menu, so this is just another way to call it up. The rest of the listed programs are described in Chapter 13.

e x a m

ⓦ a t c h
When extensions are hidden and you rename a file, you only rename the file, not the extension, preserving the extension so that the file is easily identified by Windows and applications. When you clear the Hide Extensions For Known File Types check box you defeat that protection.

CERTIFICATION SUMMARY

As a computer support professional, you need to arm yourself with knowledge of operating system disk and file management. Disk management in Windows begins with understanding both basic and dynamic storage types. Technicians working with Windows PCs should understand the differences between basic and dynamic storage types while focusing on creating primary partitions on basic disks.

Most file management tasks remain the same across all the file systems supported by Windows. NTFS is the preferred file system for Windows, providing more advanced file storage features and file and folder security. You should perform file management from the GUI tools, but a technician should be familiar with command-line file management methods for certain troubleshooting scenarios. You should understand file-naming conventions, file attributes, file types, and text file editors, and be able to organize files into folders. You should know the techniques and rules for moving and copying files in the GUI.

Windows comes with a number of utilities, specialized programs used to configure, optimize, and troubleshoot Windows and networks. A technician should be familiar with both GUI tools and command-line tools.

TWO-MINUTE DRILL

Here are some of the key points covered in Chapter 10.

Disk Management

❑ Disk management in Windows begins with the underlying storage types: basic or dynamic.

❑ Dynamic disks have features not available on basic disks; these features are mainly for use on network server computers, not desktop computers, which are the focus of this book and the A+ exams.

❑ Basic disks use the same partition table used by older versions of Windows.

❑ A basic disk can have up to four partitions. Either all four partitions can be primary, or the disk can have a combination of up to three primary and one extended partition. Primary partitions are preferred.

❑ A PC with one or more basic disks must have at least one primary partition in order to boot Windows.

❑ Windows Setup will create a basic disk with a primary, active (bootable) partition and format the partition with a file system.

❑ After installing Windows, use Disk Management to create or modify additional partitions and to format hard drive partitions.

❑ A spanned volume includes areas of unallocated space from multiple physical disks into one volume and can only exist on dynamic disks.

❑ A striped volume includes at least two physical disks, and the data is saved across the disks in a stripe, meaning that every time data is written to the volume, a portion is written on the first disk, then on the second disk, and so forth.

❑ A mirrored volume consists of identically sized volumes on two physical disks—both dynamic disks—that are created as identical twins, with all disk activity occurring on both disks as a mirrored set.

❑ While New RAID 5 Volume is an option in Disk Management, it is not available in the consumer versions of Windows.

❑ A quick format does not actually overwrite or test the entire volume, but simply puts the file system components on the disk, refreshing the directory and allocation information so that the disk appears empty, whether it is or not. A full format overwrites all the data space, as well as the directory information.

Understanding Windows Startup

❑ The Windows startup phases are power-on self-test, initial startup, boot loader, detect and configure hardware, kernel loading, and logon.

❑ The boot loader for Windows Vista, Windows 7, and Windows 8 is BOOTMGR, which loads the Boot Configuration Database (BCD), an extensible database that replaces the old BOOT.INI file. BCD then loads WINLOAD.EXE, the OS loader boot program. Together, BOOTMGR and WINLOAD.EXE replace the major functions of NTLDR and complete the startup phases for Windows Vista, Windows 7, and Windows 8.

❑ The Windows XP NTLDR, BOOT.INI, and NTDETECT.COM files are located in the root of drive C:. On a Windows Vista, Windows 7, or Windows 8 system, the BOOTMGR file is located in the root of drive C:. These files are hidden so that they are not visible by default when you try to view them in Windows Explorer.

❑ Windows places important boot settings in a location that is available before the OS is fully loaded. In Windows XP that location is the BOOT.INI file, and in Windows Vista and later, it is the BCD file.

❑ The Boot Configuration Database is actually a hidden part of the registry, stored in a registry file named BCD, located in C:\BOOT. If you have administrator-level privileges, you can view the contents using the BCDEdit program, a command-prompt utility.

File Management

❑ Most file management tasks remain the same across all the file systems available in Windows: FAT12, FAT16, FAT32, and NTFS.

❑ Of these file systems, NTFS is preferred because it works with larger hard drives, is more stable, and offers file and folder security and compression that is not available in the FAT file systems.

❑ Knowing the naming conventions, common file extensions, and file types is important to file management in Windows.

❑ Windows supports the standard file attributes of read-only, archive, system, and hidden. It also supports additional file attributes in NTFS, including index, compress, and encrypt.

❑ Never move program files from their folders in Windows. Most users should manage only data files.

❑ By default, Windows hides system files from view in My Computer/Computer or Windows Explorer. This does not depend on the hidden file attribute, and you can change it through the View page in the Folder Options dialog box.

❑ You can use text file editors to modify certain text files used by Windows and other programs.

❑ Use the Windows GUI to organize data files into folders containing related files.

❑ Offline files and folders are useful if your computer does not always have access to the network. You can configure Windows to save files to local storage so that when your computer is disconnected from the network, you can continue to work on the files.

❑ Do not perform normal file management from the Command Prompt, but instead, familiarize yourself with command-line file management commands for use in extreme troubleshooting scenarios.

❑ Windows includes a variety of command-line utilities, some for simple file management, but many others as well. Use the HELP command to display a list of command-line utilities.

❑ Command-line disk management utilities include DEFRAG and CHKDSK.

❑ Use the ATTRIB utility to view and modify file attributes.

❑ The FORMAT command will allow you to format a hard disk, floppy disk, or other media from the Command Prompt.

SELF TEST

The following questions will help you measure your understanding of the material presented in this chapter. Read all of the choices carefully, because there might be more than one correct answer. Choose all correct answers for each question.

Disk Management

1. Which disk storage type should you use on a typical Windows desktop PC?
   A. Dynamic
   B. Basic
   C. Primary
   D. Extended

2. Which of the following describes a partition from which Windows can boot?
   A. Primary extended
   B. Active extended
   C. Primary active
   D. Simple extended

3. Which GUI tool should you use to create a partition on a new drive after installing Windows?
   A. My Computer
   B. Device Manager
   C. Disk Defragmenter
   D. Disk Management

4. How many logical drives are on a typical primary partition?
   A. 1
   B. 2
   C. 3
   D. Up to 24

5. What is the maximum number of volumes allowed on a dynamic disk?
   A. One
   B. Two
   C. Three
   D. There is no limit.

6. Which of the following volume types combines areas of unallocated space from multiple physical disks?

A. striped

B. spanned

C. mirrored

D. RAID 5

Understanding Windows Startup

7. This startup phase, common to all PCs, tests system hardware, determines the amount of memory present, verifies that devices required for OS startup are working, and loads configuration settings from CMOS into memory.

A. Boot loader

B. POST

C. Detect and configure hardware

D. Kernel loading

8. In Windows XP, this file holds information used by NTLDR during the boot loader stage to locate the kernel and other operating system files.

A. BOOTMGR

B. BCD

C. NTOSKRNL.EXE

D. BOOT.INI

9. What is the name of the boot loader in Windows Vista and Windows 7?

A. BOOTMGR

B. BCD

C. NTOSKRNL.EXE

D. BOOT.INI

10. Beginning with Windows Vista, which file contains important boot settings available to Windows at startup before the OS is fully loaded?

A. BOOTMGR

B. BCD

C. NTOSKRNL.EXE

D. BOOT.INI

File Management

11. Which file system supports file and folder security?
- A. FAT12
- B. NTFS
- C. FAT16
- D. FAT32

12. Which of the following file attributes cannot be changed in a file's Properties dialog box?
- A. Read-only
- B. Archive
- C. System
- D. Hidden

13. Which file system supports file compression and encryption?
- A. FAT32
- B. FAT12
- C. FAT16
- D. NTFS

14. What feature of the NTFS file system stores a transaction–based database, with all file accesses treated as transactions?
- A. MFT
- B. FAT
- C. Boot sector
- D. Cluster

15. Which feature of NTFS makes file searches faster?
- A. .Compression
- B. Encryption
- C. Indexing
- D. MFT

16. Which of the following can you use for managing files and folders?
- A. Control Panel
- B. Notepad
- C. My Computer/Computer
- D. Disk Management

17. Which of the following best describes the type of files you should not move, delete, edit, or try to manage directly?

   A. Text

   B. Spreadsheet

   C. Program

   D. Data

18. What is the correct syntax (command plus switch combination) that will analyze drive C:, looking for file fragmentation, without changing anything on the drive?

   A. dir /ad

   B. help | more

   C. defrag c: –a

   D. defrag a:

19. If your data is saved onto a Microsoft domain server, but you do not always have access to the network, which option should you enable?

   A. Archive

   B. Copy

   C. Offline Files

   D. Mirrored volume

20. What disk error-checking program can you run from the Command Prompt to analyze the disk for physical and logical errors?

   A. CHKDSK

   B. DEFRAG

   C. FORMAT

   D. ATTRIB

SELF TEST ANSWERS

Disk Management

1. ☑ **B.** Basic is the disk storage type you should use on a typical Windows desktop PC.
   ☒ **A,** dynamic, is incorrect because this disk type is more suited for a network server. **C,** primary, is incorrect because this is a partition type, not a disk storage type. **D,** extended, is incorrect because this is a partition type, not a disk storage type.

2. ☑ **C.** Primary active describes a partition from which Windows can boot.
   ☒ **A,** primary extended, is incorrect because it describes two different partition types. **B,** active extended, is incorrect because you cannot mark an extended partition as active; only a primary partition can be marked as active. **D,** simple extended, is incorrect because Windows cannot boot from an extended partition (and "simple extended" is not a term that is normally used).

3. ☑ **D.** Disk Management is the GUI tool you should use for creating a partition on a new hard drive after installing Windows.
   ☒ **A,** My Computer, is incorrect because this is not a tool for creating a partition. **B,** Device Manager, is incorrect because this utility is for managing devices. **C,** Disk Defragmenter, is incorrect because this is a tool for defragmenting files on a drive.

4. ☑ **A.** One, because it is the only number of logical drives that you can create on a primary partition.
   ☒ **B, C,** and **D** are all incorrect because a primary partition can only contain one logical drive.

5. ☑ **D.** There is no limit (theoretically) to the number of volumes allowed on a dynamic disk.
   ☒ **A, B,** and **C** are all incorrect because they are placing a limit on the number of volumes allowed.

6. ☑ **B.** Spanned volume is the type that combines areas of unallocated space from multiple physical disks.
   ☒ **A, C,** and **D** are incorrect because, although they are all volume types, they are not the volume type described in the question.

Understanding Windows Startup

7. ☑ **B.** POST is the startup phase, common to all PCs, that tests system hardware, determines the amount of memory present, verifies that devices required for OS startup are working, and loads configuration settings from CMOS into memory.
   ☒ **A, C,** and **D** are incorrect because, although they are startup phases, they are not the startup phase described in the question. They all come after POST.

8. ☑ **D.** BOOT.INI is the file that holds information used by NTLDR during the boot loader phase to locate the kernel of the operating system in Windows XP.
☒ **A,** BOOTMGR, is incorrect because this file is the boot loader for Windows Vista and Windows 7. **B,** BCD, is incorrect because Windows Vista and Windows 7 use it, not earlier versions. **C,** NTOSKRNL.EXE, is incorrect because this is the kernel of the Windows operating system, which is loaded during the kernel-loading phase of Windows startup.

9. ☑ **A.** BOOTMGR is the name of the boot loader in Windows Vista and Windows 7.
☒ **B,** BCD, is incorrect because this is the Boot Configuration Database, which replaced the BOOT.INI file beginning in Windows Vista. **C,** NTOSKRNL.EXE, is incorrect because this is the kernel of the Windows operating system, which is loaded during the kernel-loading phase of Windows startup. **D,** BOOT.INI, is incorrect because this is a file used by the boot loader in earlier versions of Windows.

10. ☑ **B.** BCD, is correct because this is the Boot Configuration Database that contains important boot settings and that replaced the BOOT.INI file beginning in Windows Vista.
☒ **A.** BOOTMGR is the name of the boot loader in Windows Vista and Windows 7. **C,** NTOSKRNL.EXE, is incorrect because this is the kernel of the Windows operating system, which is loaded during the kernel-loading phase of Windows startup. **D,** BOOT.INI, is incorrect because this is a file used by the boot loader in earlier versions of Windows.

File Management

11. ☑ **B.** NTFS is the file system that supports file and folder security.
☒ **A, C,** and **D** are incorrect because none of these file systems support file and folder security.

12. ☑ **C.** System is the file attribute you cannot change in the file's Properties dialog box.
☒ **A, B,** and **D** are incorrect because they can all be changed in the file's Properties dialog box.

13. ☑ **D.** NTFS supports file compression and encryption.
☒ **A, B,** and **C** are all incorrect because none of these supports compression or encryption.

14. ☑ **A.** MFT, the Master File Table of NTFS, stores a transaction–based database with all file accesses treated as transactions.
☒ **B,** FAT, or file allocation table, is a feature of the FAT file system, not NTFS. **C,** Boot sector, is incorrect because it is the first sector on a disk, not strictly a part of a file system. **D,** cluster, is incorrect because this is an allocation unit used by a file system as the minimum disk space a file can use.

15. ☑ **C.** Indexing, an NTFS feature, makes file searches faster.
☒ **A,** Compression, is an NTFS feature, but does not make file searches faster. **B,** Encryption, is an NTFS feature. It does not make file searches faster. **D,** MFT, although a core components of NTFS, does not make file searches faster.

16. ☑ **C.** You can use My Computer/Computer for managing files and folders.

    ☒ **A,** Control Panel, is incorrect because this is a special folder containing applets for con-figuring many aspects of the Windows system. Although you can adjust hidden file and folder settings from the Folder Options applet, this is not the correct answer. **B,** Notepad, is incorrect because this is simply a text file editor. **D,** Disk Management, is incorrect because this tool is used for managing disk partitions.

17. ☑ **C.** You should not move, delete, edit, or manage program files.

    ☒ **A,** text, is incorrect because it is generally acceptable for a user to manage text files, except for those that are created and used by the operating system and stored with the boot files or sys-tem files. **B,** spreadsheet, is incorrect because this is a type of data file that the user can manage. **D,** data, is incorrect because the user can and should manage data files.

18. ☑ **C.** defrag c: -a is the command that will analyze drive C:, looking for file fragmentation, but without changing anything on the drive.

    ☒ **A,** dir /ad, is incorrect because this will only display a list of all the directories within the current directory. **B,** help | more, is incorrect because this will display a list of command-line commands with a brief description. **D,** defrag a:, is incorrect because the question asked the syntax for analyzing drive C:, and this command would defrag drive A:.

19. ☑ **C.** Offline Files is the feature you should enable if your data is saved onto a Microsoft domain server, but you do not always have access to the network, because it will save a copy to your local hard drive and synchronize when you have a network connection.

    ☒ **A,** archive, is incorrect because archive, as described in this chapter, is a file attribute used by backup programs. **B,** copy, is incorrect because it simply means to leave a file in place while creating a copy. This does not fully describe the Offline Files feature. **D,** mirrored volume, is incorrect because this is a disk technology that makes a simultaneous copy of one disk volume onto another. This would not help in the scenario described.

20. ☑ **A.** CHKDSK is the disk error-checking program that you can run from the Command Prompt to do an analysis of the disk for physical and logical errors.

    ☒ **B,** DEFRAG, is incorrect because this command analyzes the disk for fragmentation. With the correct switch, DEFRAG will defragment a disk. **C,** FORMAT, is incorrect because this will overwrite the contents of a drive with file-system components. **D,** ATTRIB, is incorrect because this command displays and manipulates file attributes.

11

Troubleshooting, Repair, and Maintenance of PCs

The most common procedures you will perform as a computer technician are trouble-shooting and resolving computer problems. The more familiar you are with a computer's components, the easier it will be for you to find the source of a problem and implement a solution. Build your comfort level by studying the previous chapters in this book and by gaining experience. In this chapter, you will first learn troubleshooting theory and then you will progress to basic diagnostic procedures and troubleshooting techniques, practice isolating PC component issues, discover the appropriate troubleshooting tools, and become proactive using common preventive maintenance techniques.

CERTIFICATION OBJECTIVES

- **802: 4.1** *Given a scenario, explain the troubleshooting theory*

- **802: 4.2** *Given a scenario, troubleshoot common problems related to motherboards, RAM, CPU, and power with appropriate tools*

> For 802 A+ Exam Objective 4.1, CompTIA requires that you understand the troubleshooting theory, procedures, and techniques that this section details. Also in this section is a list of the tools included in CompTIA Exam 802 Objective 4.2. That objective also lists common symptoms, which we will describe in the section that follows this.

Preparing for Troubleshooting

> *Troubleshooting* is the act of discovering the cause of a problem and correcting it. It sounds simple, and if you watch an experienced technician, it may appear to be. However, troubleshooting a PC requires patience, instinct, experience, and a methodical approach. In this section, we will explore a methodical approach to troubleshooting theory and techniques. You will need to acquire the experience on your own, and you will find that your experiences will hone your instincts.

Protecting Systems and Gathering Tools

When faced with a computer-related problem, resist the urge to jump right in and apply your favorite all-purpose solution. Rather, take time to do the following:

1. Before working on a problem computer, verify that you have a recent set of backups of the user's data. If you find there isn't one, perform backups of data (at minimum) and the entire system—providing the system is functional enough for these tasks. If backups are not available and there is no way to do a backup, inform the customer that they may lose all their data. Bad news is best served up immediately, but gently.

2. Always have a pad and pencil, tablet PC, smartphone, or other means to record your actions, findings, and outcomes. A digital camera or device with a camera built in is also handy for documenting the hardware before and after and at various stages of disassembly. These will be critical to the documentation you create at the end of the entire process.

3. Assemble troubleshooting tools—both hardware and software tools. Check out the hardware toolkit described in Chapter 3. Many software troubleshooting tools are built into Windows, and we will describe some in this chapter, and more in Chapter 13 where we list important software tools.

4. Apply the troubleshooting theory, described next.

Troubleshooting Theory

Experienced IT professionals find that six procedures, taken in order, are important for solving most problems and for documenting the problems and solutions in order to learn from each experience. CompTIA A+ 802 Exam Objective 4.1 lists the following procedures, and we describe each in more detail in the following paragraphs.

1. Identify the problem.
2. Establish a theory of probable cause (question the obvious).
3. Test the theory to determine the cause.
4. Establish a plan of action to resolve the problem, and then implement the solution.
5. Verify full system functionality and, if applicable, implement preventative measures.
6. Document findings, actions, and outcomes.

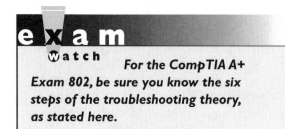

Protecting Systems and Gathering Tools

Clearly identify the problem. Always gather as much information as you can about the computer and its peripherals, applications, operating system, and history. Do this even when the solution seems obvious.

Examine the Environment   Ideally, you will be able to go onsite and see the computer "patient" in its working environment so you can gather information from your own observations. Once onsite, you may notice a situation that contributed to the problem or could cause other problems. If you cannot go onsite, you may be able to diagnose and correct software problems remotely, using Remote Assistance or Remote Desktop, methods you will explore in Chapter 13. Otherwise, you must depend solely on the user's observations. Whether onsite or remote, you are looking for the cause of the problem, which is often a result of some change, either in the environment or to the computer directly.

o n   t h e
j o b   *When troubleshooting a system that is not functioning properly, make it a practice to always perform a visual inspection of all cables and connectors, making sure all connections are proper before you invest any time in troubleshooting.*

Question the User: What Has Happened?

The best source for learning what happened leading up to a problem is the person who was using the computer when the problem occurred. Your first question to the user should be, "What happened?" This question will prompt the user to tell you about the problem—for example, "The printer will not work." Ask for a specific description of the events leading up to the failure and the symptoms the user experienced.

Do other devices work? This will help you isolate the problem. If one or more other devices also do not work, you know you are dealing with a more serious, device-independent problem.

Ask about a problem device's history. Did this device ever work? If the user tells you that it is a newly installed device, you have a very different task ahead of you than if you learn that it has worked fine until just now. The former indicates a flawed installation, whereas the latter points to a possible failure of the device itself.

If the user mentions an error message, ask for as much detail about the error message as possible. If the user cannot remember, try to re-create the problem.

Ask if this error message is new or old and if the computer's behavior changed after the error. For example, the computer might issue a warning that simply informs the user of some condition. If the error code points to a device, such as an optical drive, ask device-related questions.

The Event logs in Windows save many error messages, so if the user cannot remember the error messages, check the Event logs. Learn more about the Windows Event logs in Chapter 13.

on the **job** *Sometimes customers are reluctant to give you all the details of the problem because they fear being embarrassed or held responsible. Treat the customer in a respectful manner that encourages trust and openness about what may have occurred. In Chapter 1, you learned how important good communication skills are and how to apply them every day.*

Question the User: What Has Changed?   You should also find out about any recent changes to the computer or the surroundings. Ask if a new component or application was recently installed. If so, has the computer worked at all since then? The answer to this question could lead you to important information about application or device conflicts. For example, if the user tells you the audio has not worked since a particular game was loaded, you can surmise that the two events—the loading of the new game and the audio failure—are related. When troubleshooting, remove the software or any other upgrades installed shortly before the problem occurred.

Establish a Theory of Probable Cause

When you have determined the symptoms of a problem, try to replicate the problem and begin an analysis from which you will develop your theory of probable cause. Question the obvious. That is, if the user says the printer does not work, have him send another print job to the printer. Watch closely as he performs the task. Take note of any error messages or unusual computer activity that he may not have noticed. Observation will also give you a chance to see the process from beginning to end. Looking over the user's shoulder (so to speak) gives you a different perspective, and you may see a mistake, such as an incorrect printer selection or the absence of an entry in the Number Of Copies To Print field, that caused the problem.

e x a m

watch   *CompTIA A+ Exam 802 Objective 4.1 explicitly states "question the obvious." Be prepared for scenario-based questions in which the answer may not be exactly "question the obvious," but a choice that could be an example of doing that, as described here.*

Vendor Documentation   As you work to pinpoint the source of the problem, check out any vendor documentation for the software or hardware associated with the problem. This may be in the form of hard copy or information posted on the vendor's Website.

Hardware or Software   From your observations and the information you gather from the user, try to pinpoint the cause of the problem. It may be obvious that a device failed if the device itself will not power up. If the source of the problem is not yet apparent, however, you need to narrow down the search even further by determining whether the problem is hardware or software related. We consider a hardware problem to include the device as well as its device drivers and configuration. Software problems include applications, operating systems, and utilities.

One of the quickest ways to determine if hardware or software is at fault is to use Windows *Device Manager,* a Windows GUI utility for viewing the status of devices and installing, removing, and updating devices. The list available to Device Manager, called the *hardware profile*, is a list in the registry of all devices that have been installed on Windows and not uninstalled (drivers have not been removed), even if the physical devices are removed or disabled. This gives Device Manager access to the listed hardware and their status. Device Manager will indicate any conflicting or "unknown" devices. But even if Device Manager offers no information about the problem, it does not mean it is not hardware-related; it only means Windows has not recognized it. Exercise 11-1 shows you how to open Device Manager and look for problem devices, an important task when troubleshooting hardware.

EXERCISE 11-1

CertCam

Troubleshooting with Device Manager

1. Open the Run box (Windows key + R) and enter **devmgmt.msc**.

2. In Device Manager's window, you will see the devices on your computer organized under types of hardware, such as Computer, Disk Drives, Display Adapters, DVD/CD-ROM Drives, and Human Interface Devices, as Figure 11-1 shows.

3. If Windows detects a problem with a device, it expands the device type to show the devices. In the case of a device with a configuration problem, you will see an exclamation mark on both the device type icon and the device icon. When Windows recognizes a device but does not understand its type, it places the device under a type named Other Devices, and you will see a question mark.

Device Manager, showing the types of devices installed

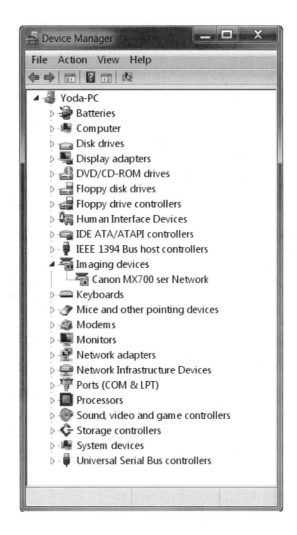

Probable Causes   From your observations and research, compile a list of probable causes, and if any of them has a simple solution, apply it first. If one of those does not solve the problem, then investigate the other items on your list.

Test the Theory to Determine Actual Cause

After establishing a theory of probable cause, test the theory. You may need to do this on a test system, isolated from the rest of the network, or, if that is not an option, simply test the theory on the problem system. Whatever you do, you need to find a way to test your theory in a manner that does not endanger the user's data and productivity. Does this solution extend beyond a single user's desktop or beyond your scope of responsibility? If so, you must escalate the problem to another department, such as network administration. Once you have tested the theory and found it to be successful, you can move to the next step.

Establish an Action Plan to Resolve the Problem and Implement the Solution

After successfully testing your theory of probable cause, you now move on to the planning stage. Now you need to think through both the actions you must take and the possible consequences of those actions, involving people from all areas affected by the problem and by the effects of the solution. Business areas can include accounting, billing, manufacturing, sales, and customer service. You also need to check with all IT support areas that must take part in the solution. The plan should then include the steps to take, the order in which to take them, and all testing and follow-up needed. This will include steps required to minimize any possible bad effects.

Verify Full System Functionality and Implement Preventative Measures

Whether the problem and solution involve a single computer or an entire enterprise, you must always verify full system functionality. If you are dealing with a single desktop system, once you have applied the solution, restart the system and the device (if appropriate), and test to be sure everything works. If your solution seems to have negatively affected anything, take additional steps to correct the problem—you may find yourself back in the troubleshooting loop.

Once you have successfully tested a solution, have the user verify and confirm that your solution solved the problem. This verification should begin just like the user's workday begins: with the user restarting the computer and/or logging on and opening each application used in a typical day and then using all peripherals such as printers. Have the user confirm that everything is working.

This is a very important step to take, regardless of the scope of the problem and solution. Our experience has been that once you touch a problem system, even though you might solve the problem, the person in charge or individual user will associate you with the next thing that goes wrong. Then you will receive a call stating that "such and such" has not worked since you were there, even though "such and such" does not relate to any changes you made.

Therefore, once everything is working normally and both you and the client have tested for full system functionality, have them sign off on it to document the satisfactory results. If this last is not an accepted procedure in your organization, you should suggest adopting it because it adds commitment to both sides of this transaction. You are committed to testing and confirming a successful solution, and the user is committed to acknowledging the solution worked.

Document Findings, Actions, and Outcomes

Document all findings, actions, and outcomes! Take notes as you work, and once you have resolved the problem, review the notes and add any omissions. Sit down with the client and review what you did. This is your statement to the client that you made certain changes. You should be clear that you made no other changes to the system.

These notes, whether informal or formal, such as comments entered into a help desk database, will be useful when you encounter identical or similar problems. It's a good idea to incorporate some of the lessons learned during troubleshooting into training for both end users and support personnel.

Training

Well-trained personnel are the best defense against problems. Therefore, an important troubleshooting technique is ongoing training for both end users and support personnel. The delivery methods and training materials should suit the environment, as many options are available for high-quality online training, starting with the help programs available in most operating systems and applications, user manuals, installation manuals, and Internet or intranet resources. All personnel involved should know how to access any training resources available. End users can often solve their own problems by checking out the help program or accessing an online training module, cutting down on the number of service calls and associated loss of productivity.

SCENARIO & SOLUTION

What should I do before making any changes to a computer?	Verify there is a recent set of backups; if a set does not exist, perform a backup of data and the operating system.
If I believe I know the solution, then why should I question the user before trying the solutions I know?	To learn what happened and what has changed and to gather all the information before jumping to any conclusions about the solution.
You have found a solution, applied it, and successfully tested it. What is the final step you need to take?	Document the troubleshooting activities and outcomes.

■ **802: 4.2**   *Given a scenario, troubleshoot common problems related to motherboards,* *RAM, CPU, and power with appropriate tools*

> The CompTIA A+ 802 Exam Objective 4.2 requires that you have important troubleshooting skills. It requires that you be able to explain and interpret common symptoms and, when faced with a scenario, know how to detect problems, troubleshoot, and repair or replace computer components.

Troubleshooting Motherboards, RAM, CPUs, and Power

> This section discusses procedures for troubleshooting common component problems, physical symptoms that can occur with various devices, power on self-test (POST) audio and text error codes, and, for certain components, specific symptoms and solutions. For each component problem, we describe scenarios, probable causes, and solutions.

Procedures

> When troubleshooting PC components, first do all that you can without opening the PC. If you do not find the source of the problem and a potential solution through nonintrusive methods, then you will have to open the PC. Follow these steps, which will take you from the least intrusive to the most intrusive:

1. Check for proper connections (external device).
2. Check for appropriate external components.
3. Check installation: drivers, driver settings, and physical settings.
4. Check proper seating of components (internal adapter card, memory, and so on).
5. Simplify the system by removing unneeded peripherals. If the problem goes away, then you must isolate the problem peripheral.

> While the traditional PC cases—towers and desktop system units—are convenient to open for adding or replacing components, the same is not true of the newer

all-in-ones. These systems resemble the Apple iMacs in that all the components normally found inside a computer case are inside the display case, and opening the case in most cases voids the warranty, and is very difficult to do without causing damage. This makes it even more imperative that you make every effort to troubleshoot using the least intrusive tactics.

Even the most knowledgeable technician cannot repair some problems with computers or components. That is why it is important to pay attention to warranties on equipment. In large organizations, warranties are managed through contracts with companies that provide the hardware and support it. In those cases, the contractor removes the failed equipment and replaces it. But if you, or your company or school, do not have such an arrangement, someone needs to be tracking the computer equipment as managed assets, and they must pay close attention to warranties—whether they are the basic warranty that comes with the item or a purchased extended warranty.

Manufacturers allow for returns of in-warranty equipment, but you need to contact the manufacturer and make arrangements, which will usually involve reporting the failure, and receiving what amounts to permission to return the equipment. This permission is a *returned materials authorization (RMA)*, which now often comes by email, and you must wait to receive this before packing up and returning the item. The RMA will usually have a number that must be displayed somewhere on the packaging.

General Symptoms

Inspect a computer and its peripherals for physical symptoms. Several symptoms can apply to any of several components, such as excessive heat, loud noise, odors, status light indicators, and visible damage to the device itself or cabling. When one of these symptoms occurs, take appropriate action based on the symptom and the device.

System Lockups, System Shutdowns, Unexpected Shutdowns, or BSOD

There are many possible causes of system instability problems with symptoms like system lockups, system shutdowns, unexpected shutdowns, and the dreaded Blue Screen of Death (BSOD). We tend to suspect software, especially device drivers, but these symptoms can and do occur after a failure of a motherboard component. We will discuss troubleshooting software-caused problems in Chapter 13. However, if you see any of these symptoms, first do basic troubleshooting of your hardware, especially the motherboard and associated components. Here are descriptions of these system instability symptoms so that you recognize them:

- **System lockups**   These appear as a screen that will not change or show any response to mouse movement. Often the mouse pointer will show an hourglass, or whatever symbol it normally shows when the system or an app is busy and cannot respond to input.

- **System shutdowns/unexpected shutdowns**   These are just what the terms imply: the system simply shuts down—usually without any warning. You may see an error message beforehand, but not necessarily.

- **Blue Screen of Death (BSOD)**   This blue error screen, more conventionally called the stop screen, appears when the Windows operating system detects a critical error and literally stops the system so that the error doesn't cause loss of data (or further loss of data). All operating systems have some form of the stop screen, and the Windows stop screen displays an error message indicating what software component failed. You can use this information to troubleshoot the cause of the problem. Learn more about working with the BSOD error information in Chapter 13.

Excess Heat/Overheating

If a device is giving off excessive heat, smoke, a burning smell, or other odors, or if wires or cables are hot, turn it off until you can replace it or otherwise solve the problem. Later in this chapter, we will discuss power supplies and cooling systems—components related to these symptoms. Unusual noises may occur if a device has moving parts, such as a fan or printer. In these cases, a new or different noise usually means a component, such as a fan bearing, is failing. This will reduce the fan's effectiveness and cause an unusual noise.

Indicator Lights

Many devices, such as printers and network adapters, have one or more *status light indicators*—usually a *light-emitting diode (LED)*, a semiconductor resembling a tiny light bulb. These usually indicate a problem with the device by changing the color of the light, by blinking or remaining steady, or by a combination of both. Look for labels on the device itself defining the function of each light. For example, a network interface card (NIC) may have a light with a label of "ACT" for "activity," indicating the card is indeed transmitting data. A multispeed NIC might have a different colored light for each of its speeds. These same indicators are often duplicated as icons in the status area (also called the notification area) of the taskbar on the Windows desktop. The applet associated with the icon will issue alerts when a device malfunctions.

Other physical symptoms include damage to a device, such as an area of melted plastic on a case or cable, a broken cable or connector pin, or a socket device not getting the appropriate signals (often due to a loose connection). Of course, when inspection of a device or cabling shows physical damage, such as a break or the appearance of melted plastic, you need to determine the extent of the damage and the right solution for the problem, such as replacing the device or cable.

Only the Fan Works

If you can hear the power supply fan and/or a case fan, but nothing else seems to work, including the display, then power the system off, open the case, and check out all power connectors between the power supply and the motherboard, reseating all of them. Also, look for some sort of debris that could be shorting out the motherboard and remove it. Something else that can cause the motherboard to short out is an incorrectly installed standoff—a washer-like part made of nonconducting material designed to keep the motherboard from coming in contact with the case. Yet another possible cause of this symptom is a failed CPU.

Intermittent Device Failure

If one device fails periodically, there are several causes to investigate. First, there could be an incorrect BIOS system setting or wrong device driver. Heat can cause such symptoms, in which case the device works fine until the system heats up. Because people use computers in all types of environments, we often forget that they work best in a low-to-moderate ambient temperature, around 75 degrees Fahrenheit. Of course, the internal temperature is higher than that, so the computer's own cooling system has to work harder as the environment gets hotter. If you witness intermittent device failure that coincides with a rise in ambient temperature, take steps to cool the environment and/or to augment the internal cooling system, or replace the entire system with a more rugged system designed to survive the higher temperatures.

Another possible cause of intermittent device failure could be the power supply unit providing too little or too much power or not maintaining a constant supply to the system. Test the power supply, as described later in this chapter.

Troubleshooting Motherboard Problems

A properly configured motherboard will typically perform flawlessly for several years. Things that can change that happy state include power problems, actual component failure, and incorrect changes to the system. A major motherboard failure will prevent the computer from booting properly. However, if the BIOS can run a POST, it might report a problem with the motherboard. In either case, consult the motherboard manual and the manufacturer's Website for solutions to the problem.

POST Audio and Visual Errors

A faulty motherboard can cause many different symptoms and can even make it appear that a different component is at fault. This is because a motherboard problem might manifest in one particular area, such as a single circuit or port, causing the failure of a single device only. For example, if the video card's expansion slot on the motherboard stops working, it will appear that the display system has a problem. In this case, you are likely to discover the motherboard as the point of failure only after checking all other components in the video system.

In Chapter 3 we briefly described the POST that occurs when a PC starts up. The POST checks for the presence and status of existing components. A visual (text) error message on the screen or POST code-beeps typically indicate errors found during the POST. A single beep or two quick beeps at the end of the POST normally mean that it detected no errors and the system should continue booting into the operating system. If you hear any other combination of beeps, or if the system does not continue the normal bootup, consult the motherboard manufacturer's documentation. If present, POST text error messages appear in the upper-left corner as white characters on a black screen, and should point you in the right direction for troubleshooting an error at bootup. For instance, if a BIOS manufacturer uses the traditional codes 1*xx*, 2*xx*, and 3*xx* (where *xx* = a range of numbers from 00 to 99), they can indicate system board, memory, or keyboard failures, respectively. Similarly, the 17*xx* error codes may indicate a hard disk controller or hard drive problem. These are the original POST error codes. If you see numeric digits during a failed startup, check out the Website of the BIOS manufacturer to find a list of codes so that you can interpret them.

If you believe a motherboard component is failing but no type of error code displays (perhaps because it is video or another vital component), a POST card (one of the tools listed in the hardware toolkit in Chapter 3) will give you more information. Consider buying one if you support many computers with the same or similar motherboard. Install a POST card into a motherboard expansion slot, then power up the computer. A small two-character LED display will show hexadecimal codes for errors detected on bootup, and the documentation that comes with the POST card will help you decipher the error codes. Then you will know what component is failing and you can make a decision about how to fix it. If it is an embedded component that is not easily replaced, such as a problem with the chipset, you may need to replace the motherboard. You can usually remedy a problem with an embedded video adapter or drive controller by installing a replacement into an expansion slot.

on the
! o b

Sometimes called PC analysis cards, POST cards come in a wide range of prices and with connectors for one or two types of expansion slots. Check out the specifications before purchasing, but an inexpensive card will usually suffice.

Physical Changes

Physical sources of motherboard problems can include jumper or switch settings, front panel connectors, back panel connectors, sockets, expansion slots, and memory slots. Because jumpers and switches are mechanical elements, they won't change unless someone has opened the system and fiddled with them. If you think someone has opened the system, double-check the jumper and switch settings and compare them with the manufacturer's documentation. If you are 100 percent sure that someone made a change that caused the present problems, determine the correct settings and then return the jumpers or switches to those settings. Note the BIOS may support jumper-free settings, meaning settings are BIOS defined rather than defined by jumpers or switches. In this case, you will need to run the BIOS Setup program to correct the situation.

Another possible physical motherboard problem source is loose or improperly made connections. These could include improper insertion of adapter cards into expansion slots, or of memory sticks into memory slots, or of the cables connecting onboard I/O ports to front or back panel connectors.

BIOS/CMOS Problems

Most motherboards come with a small coin-sized battery, such as a 3-volt lithium battery, to support the nonvolatile RAM, called CMOS RAM, where the BIOS settings are stored. We discussed this briefly in Chapter 3. Since this battery supports the date and time tracking, the classic symptoms of a failed complementary metal-oxide semiconductor (CMOS) battery is a system that does not keep the correct time after turning it off. If that occurs, open the case and remove the battery, much as you would remove a watch battery. Then find a replacement for it that matches the voltage and designation number of the old battery.

If the system repeatedly loses track of time when turned off, you probably need to replace the battery. This is usually a simple process, requiring opening the case and exchanging the old battery for a new one.

Problems associated with the CMOS chip include lost or incorrect BIOS system settings, and those that refer to BIOS time and settings resets. Lost settings can occur when the CMOS battery begins to lose power. You may discover this problem by a text error message at startup, or by a prompt to enter the correct time and date. A computer that does not maintain the date and time when powered off probably has a failing CMOS battery that is responsible for maintaining the system clock. Because these batteries only last between two and ten years, you probably have to replace a computer's battery before the computer becomes obsolete. To replace the battery properly, follow the steps in Exercise 11-2. Note you cannot follow this procedure in all computers, and you must consult the documentation before doing this.

EXERCISE 11-2

Replacing the CMOS Battery

1. Enter the computer's Setup program and make a backup copy of the current BIOS settings, using whatever method is available to you. You may want to take a digital picture with your camera, smartphone, or other device. Or simply write down the settings.

2. Turn off the computer and remove the cover, ensuring you carry out the proper electrostatic discharge (ESD) procedures.

3. Locate the CMOS battery on the motherboard.

4. Slide the battery out from under the retaining clip. The clip uses slight tension to hold the battery in place, so you do not need to remove the clip or bend it outward.

5. Note the battery's orientation when installed, and install the new battery the same way.

6. Restart the computer. Enter the system's Setup program again and restore the BIOS settings you recorded in Step 1.

If your system will not support a new device, you may need a BIOS firmware update. Before doing this, be sure to back up the BIOS settings or make note of them in some way—even with a digital camera. Then, using the manufacturer's utility, install the BIOS update, either from a local drive or from a source over the Internet. How is it possible to update something that is "read-only"? The answer is that you actually can change many modern ROMs, but only by special means. Today, that is normally a special program from the manufacturer that may also require changing a system setting or a dip switch just before performing the procedure so the BIOS accepts the changes. This is why reading the documentation before changing the BIOS is important. We often call upgrading BIOS *flashing the BIOS*. This applies to system-level BIOS, as well as to the BIOS on an individual adapter.

Become familiar with the system BIOS Setup menu screens and practice navigating through these menus, as described in Exercise 3-4 in Chapter 3. This means booting the system and selecting the keyboard option after the POST that lets you access BIOS system setup. The first thing you should then do is look for the help hints, usually at the bottom or in a sidebar on every screen. Then find out how you can exit from the BIOS without saving changes. Knowing this is important, because almost everyone who explores these menus gets confused about whether they have inadvertently made a change, and the best way to back out of that situation is to select Exit Without Saving, if it is available. If not, look for two exit methods. For instance, you might use the F10 function key for Save and Exit and the ESC key for Exit. Now you know how to exit without saving.

Although the exact BIOS menu organization varies by manufacturer, the main menu will have the most basic settings, such as system date and time, detected drives, and drive interfaces. An advanced menu will often have the settings for the CPU, the chipset, onboard devices, the expansion bus configuration, and overclocking, an option that boosts CPU performance. You do not need to use overclocking on computers designated for simple office tasks, but people often use it for computers requiring higher CPU performance, such as for gaming and other tasks requiring maximum performance. Other advanced BIOS settings may involve adjusting bus speeds, including the two main components of the system's chipset, the front-side bus and the Northbridge. Here, you may also find settings for the PCIe bus and configuration options for Universal Serial Bus (USB) and other interfaces.

Incorrect BIOS settings can have many permutations because there are BIOS settings for a great variety of system elements, including the hard drives, floppy drive, the boot sequence, keyboard status, and parallel port settings. An incorrect setting will manifest as an error relating to that particular device or function, so pinpointing the CMOS battery, for example, as the source of the problem can be difficult. However, when you need to change or update BIOS settings, enter the BIOS Setup menu at startup, make the appropriate change(s), save the new setting(s), and restart the computer.

Troubleshooting RAM Problems

As with CPUs, physical damage or failure of memory is fatal, meaning when such a problem occurs, the computer will not boot at all. However, you should be aware of some nonfatal error indicators.

If you turn on the computer and it does not even complete the POST, or it does nothing at all, and you have eliminated power problems, the main memory might have a problem. The solution to a memory problem is to remove the offending component and replace it with a new one. If the error persists, the memory might be in a damaged slot or socket on the motherboard. In this case, replace the motherboard, or the entire PC.

On a final note: The computer does not report some RAM errors at all. That is, if an entire memory module does not work, the computer might just ignore it and continue to function normally without it. At startup, watch the RAM count on the screen (if BIOS configuration allows this) to ensure the total amount available matches the capacity installed in the machine. If this amount comes up significantly short, you will probably have to replace a memory module.

Troubleshooting CPUs

In most cases, CPU problems are fatal, meaning the computer will not boot at all. These problems also closely relate to motherboard problems, such as CPU socket failure. However, you should be aware of some nonfatal error indications.

If you turn on the computer and it does not complete the POST, or it does nothing at all, and you have eliminated power problems, you might discover the processor has a problem. A persistent error indicates a possible problem with the slot or socket that the processor connects to the motherboard with. In this case, you need to replace the motherboard. Check the system warranty before taking any action, because the warranty could cover motherboard failure. If you determine the problem is isolated to the CPU, then you will have to replace it, in which case you must replace it with an exact match for the motherboard, including the socket type, speed, number of cores, internal cache, power consumption, and other features. This ensures it matches the front-side bus portion of the chipset that includes the Northbridge/memory controller chip (MCC). Use the motherboard documentation or information for the motherboard at the manufacturer's site to determine the exact requirements before purchasing a new CPU.

on the
Job

Considering today's low PC prices, if you encounter a CPU or motherboard problem on a computer not covered by a warranty, consider replacing the entire system. First, however, check to see if it is a leased computer and what the lease agreement says about component failures, service, and replacement.

A computer that has become slower can be a symptom of overheating. The CPU may have reduced its clock speed in response to overheating, a practice called *throttling*. A processor that has activated thermal throttling will run slower. Why is the computer overheating? Perhaps because of dust, blocked vents, or a failed cooling fan. Check out these possibilities and remedy any that you find.

Troubleshooting Power Supplies

Power supplies can experience either total or partial failures, resulting in inconsistent or displaced symptoms. However, to pinpoint the problem, you can check a few common symptoms of power supply failure; we discuss those symptoms here. When the power supply fails, replace it. Never try to open or repair a power supply because it can hold enough charge to injure you seriously, and the time spent on such a repair is more valuable than the replacement cost of a power supply.

When installing a new power supply in a PC, check the wattage and capacity, the availability and types of connectors, and the output voltage required by the computer components to ensure it will have sufficient power and the correct connections.

As suggested in Chapter 3, you can use either a multimeter or a power supply tester to make sure that a power supply is putting out the correct voltages. A multimeter requires more knowledge of electricity to use and is a more sophisticated instrument, measuring resistance, voltage, and/or current in computer components. To use a multimeter, you insert two probes (red and black) into sockets in the meter that correspond to what you want to measure, and set the control to the same measurement. For instance, set it to AC to measure wall line voltage, DC to measure the voltage coming from the power supply, or Ohms to measure resistance.

Once the multimeter is set to volts, you can measure voltage by touching the ends of the probes to power wires in the equipment you are testing. To measure resistance, you touch the probes to the circuit you want to measure. To measure current, you must break the circuit so the electricity goes through the meter. Most meters today are auto-ranging, meaning you don't have to choose a specific range; they change ranges on their own, but to test power connectors with more than one pin, you must know the purpose of each pin, requiring you to read labels or documentation.

A power supply tester tests voltage output from a power supply unit and is much easier and safer to use than a multimeter. Even an inexpensive power supply tester has several types of sockets to accommodate the variety of plugs available on power supplies. Simply connect the output connectors from a power supply to the matching socket, turn on the power supply, and LEDs or a liquid crystal display (LCD) display indicates whether the power supply is functioning correctly.

Symptoms Associated with Power Supply Problems

Failed or failing power supplies have many symptoms. A failed power supply is dormant, and so is the entire computer, so the cause is not hard to determine once you have eliminated the simpler causes, such as the power button being in the off position or an unplugged power cord. A failing power supply will cause symptoms in other components, leading you down the wrong troubleshooting path.

Nothing Happens When the Computer Is Turned On   A few things can cause a total lack of activity at system startup. These include a bad processor or memory, but the most likely suspect is the power supply.

First, check that the power supply connects properly to an electrical outlet. In addition, check the power selector (on the back of the computer near the power cord connection and the on/off switch) to ensure it has the right setting for your geographic region. Because you can switch many power supplies to use either 120 or 230 volts, verify that someone did not change the supply to the wrong voltage setting. North America is 110–120 VAC at 60 Hz and Europe is 220–240 VAC at 50 Hz.

When the power supply stops working, so does the computer's fan, which is typically the first thing you hear (along with the hard drive) when you turn on the computer. Therefore, if you do not hear the power supply fan at startup (or any fan or hard drive noise), you should suspect a power supply problem and turn off the computer immediately. Some power supplies will shut down if the fan is not working.

If only the power supply fan failed, then once the computer is off, try cleaning the fan from the outside of the case using an antistatic vacuum. Dust, lint, or hair can cause the fan to stop rotating. If cleaning does not resolve the problem, you must replace the entire power supply.

If the problem is not so easily isolated to the power supply fan because the system simply will not turn on, try removing all the power supply connections to internal components and turning the PC back on.

Also, check that the power cables attach properly to the motherboard and other necessary devices, including the computer's power button.

Memory Errors   Yes, a memory error can be an indication of a failing power supply because the error can be an indication of inadequate power to the RAM sticks. If on each reboot, the memory error identifies a different location in memory, then it is more likely to be a power problem than a memory error. A real memory error would identify the same memory location on each reboot.

The Computer Reboots Itself, or Some Components Sporadically Stop Working   A computer with a bad power supply may continuously reboot itself without warning. If the power supply provides power only to some devices, the computer will behave irregularly; some devices will seem to work, whereas others will work only part of the time or not at all. Check that all power plugs connect properly.

Cooling Systems

Excessive heat can be a symptom of cooling system failure. Inadequate cooling will cause components to overheat, in which case they might work sometimes but not at other times, and very commonly, an overheated computer will simply shut down or spontaneously reboot. Try cleaning the power supply fan without opening the power supply itself by vacuuming the fan vents. If this does not solve the problem, replace the power supply or consider adding another case fan, if one will fit in your computer. Many cases come with brackets to add one or more case fans.

Missing Slot Covers

Believe it or not, the removable slot covers at the back of the computer are not there solely to tidy up the appearance of the computer. They keep dust and other foreign objects out of the computer, and if you leave the slot covers off, you run the risk of allowing dust to settle on the PC's internal components, especially the empty expansion slots (which are notoriously difficult to clean). Missing slot covers can also cause the computer to overheat. The design of the computer places the devices that generate the most heat in the fan's cooling air flow. Missing slot covers mean the cooling air's path through the computer could be changed or impeded, resulting in improper cooling of the components inside.

Noisy Fan

There are more cooling fans inside a computer than the one on the power supply. Today's computers have one (slot) or two cooling fans on the CPU. There can also be one or more strategically placed cooling fans inside the case.

When a fan begins to wear out, it usually makes a whining or grinding noise. When this happens, replace the fan, unless it is inside the power supply. In that instance, replace the entire power supply.

CPU Cooling Issues

Considering the reliability of computer circuitry, you do not expect a CPU to fail, but modern CPUs generate a great deal of heat and they must be properly installed. Proper installation requires high standards for applying thermal compound and correctly inserting the CPU into the CPU socket on the motherboard and attaching a heat sink and/or a CPU fan. Systems assembled in tightly controlled facilities by experienced technicians who practice excellent quality control methods should not fail due to overheating during normal operation. Normal computer operation usually means the CPU and/or busses are not modified to operate beyond their default system settings, or in an environment with temperature and humidity beyond the manufacturer's specified operating range for the system.

---

e x a m

ⓦ a t c h   *Memory failures may not cause a system to appear to malfunction at all. Most modern systems will simply ignore a malfunctioning memory module and* *normal operations will continue. The user may note performance loss, however, which is a key symptom of a memory module failure.*

SCENARIO & SOLUTION

The computer does not maintain the date and time when powered on. What should I do?	Replace the CMOS battery.
What should I do with a computer that keeps rebooting itself?	Test the power supply. You may need to replace it.

CERTIFICATION OBJECTIVE

■ **802: 4.3** *Given a scenario, troubleshoot hard drives and RAID arrays with appropriate tools*

Troubleshooting Storage Devices

The steps you take when troubleshooting problems with storage devices vary based on the type of storage device. We will look at hard disk drives (HDD), floppy disk drives (FDD), optical drives, and solid-state drives (SSDs).

Hard Disk Drives

Many things can go wrong with a hard drive, each of which can result in a number of different symptoms, so it can be difficult to determine the cause of the problem. You should replace a hard drive that begins corrupting data before all the information stored on it is lost. In Chapter 13, you will learn about using specialized utilities to correct data problems on hard drives, including corrupted and fragmented files. We discuss the most common hard drive symptoms and problems in the sections that follow.

Computer Attempts to Boot to Incorrect Device

If a computer attempts to boot from the incorrect device and will not boot from the system drive (usually drive C:), the cause could be as simple as you inadvertently pressed a key as the system was starting up and it attempted to boot from the optical drive, or it could be a more serious cause. Therefore, once this occurs, restart the system, taking care not to touch the keyboard until the system has completed the startup. We have even found that a messy desk can be the root cause, because a book, papers, or other detritus on a desk touches the keyboard as the system boots up. If the system still fails to boot up from the correct drive, then go into the BIOS setup program and check out the boot order settings. Put the usual boot device first in the order and restart your computer. If this still does not work, you may have a failed disk controller or hard drive, or the operating system is corrupt. Troubleshoot for the hardware problems first, reseating any existing connections and try to boot once again. Chapter 13 describes how to recover from damage to the operating system. Try one of those methods before replacing the hard drive, which will require reinstalling or restoring the OS, your applications, and your data.

Failure to Boot

If your computer fails to boot due to a hard drive or controller failure, you might receive a POST error message with an error code in the 1700 to 1799 range if your BIOS POST uses the traditional error codes. You could also get a message stating that there is no hard drive present. Typically, these errors are not fatal, and you can still boot the computer using a special bootable floppy, USB drive, or optical disc.

This type of error means the computer does not recognize, or cannot communicate with, the hard drive. First, restart the computer and go into the CMOS settings. In the BIOS drive configuration, check that it lists the proper hard drive type. If not, enter the appropriate settings (usually only an option in older BIOSs), or use the system's hard drive detection option.

If the BIOS settings are correct and the drive still will not work, or if the BIOS cannot detect the hard drive, the system could have a cabling problem. To check on cabling and other physical configurations, perform the steps in Exercise 11-3.

EXERCISE 11-3

Troubleshooting a Drive Failure

1. Reboot the computer, start the BIOS system setup program, and check the settings for the drive and the interface (PATA, SATA, etc.), as appropriate. If you make any changes, restart and check to see if the problem is resolved. If it is not resolved, continue to the next step.

2. Turn off power to the computer and open the case.

3. If the drive connects to a Parallel Advanced Technology Enhancement (PATA) channel, ensure it has the proper master or slave setting. Read the

drive manual, or the labels on the drive, to determine whether you make the master or slave setting through jumpers or through the drive's position on the cable (cable select).

4. If the drive connects to a Serial Advanced Technology Enhancement (SATA) channel, ensure the connections are all secure, including an External SATA (eSATA) connection to the onboard SATA controller.

5. Check to see if the drive connects to a Small Computer System Interface (SCSI) controller, which may be the source of the problem. In this case, locate another computer with an identical working controller and swap the problem drive into the second computer.

6. Check that data and power cables are securely attached. If the drive has a PATA interface with the conventional ribbon cable, check the hard drive ribbon cable to ensure the red stripe aligns with pin 1 on both ends.

7. If possible, replace the ribbon cable with a known good one, even if it passed your physical inspection.

8. If the cables, jumpers, and BIOS settings all check out, the problem is with the hard drive itself and you must replace it.

Read/Write Failure

If you see a message containing the words "read/write failure," it means that the BIOS cannot find the information it needs in the first sector of the disk, where it expects to find information for either booting up from the disk or reading data from the disk. The possible causes can include a "head crash"—a collision that can occur in a classic hard drive system between the disk drive's read/write heads and the platters containing the data. This is often unrecoverable if it occurs in a critical portion of the disk, such as in the first few sectors, but recoverable if it occurs elsewhere, depending on how extensive the damage is. If the read/write error message appears as you boot up, the error is most likely in a critical area, but if it occurs after the operating system is running and does not cause any other problem with the OS, it is in a less critical area.

In this section we will talk about the hardware tactics you can use, and in Chapter 13, we will address the possible software solutions.

The first step you should take is to power the system off and check any connections to the disk in question; then replace any problem cables and reseat connectors. Then, repeat the actions that resulted in the message, such as restarting your computer or attempting to open a file. If the system returns to normal, then flip ahead to Chapter 13 and read up on how to run the CHKDSK command to identify and fix bad sectors on a disk.

If the problem will not allow the OS to start normally, then check out the information in Chapter 13 on various Windows OS recovery options, such as FIXBOOT and FIXMBR. Learn more about FORMAT and FDISK and learn about options for file recovery.

On the hardware side, check to see if the drive manufacturer has a diagnostic utility, which may be accessible from the drive's ROM via special instructions from the manufacturer or on their Website, to be run from a bootable disc.

Next, if the drive is on a PATA interface, check the configuration in BIOS. Is it cable select or master/slave? Did it work previously with this configuration? If it did, leave it alone. If you suspect it was changed, then switch it from one to the other. A master/slave arrangement will require that you configure the jumpers on the hard drive itself to be either master or slave. If you choose cable select, you will need to put the drive in the correct position on the PATA cable, which has two connectors. The connector on the end of the cable is the first (master) drive. The connector in the middle is for the second (slave) drive.

With a SATA drive, each drive is the only one on each SATA interface. If you have an extra SATA connector in the computer, move the drive to it.

Slow Performance

Slow performance can be a symptom that is difficult to quantify in a casual way, because what may seem like a slow hard drive may be a slow system caused by overheating or other problems. However, if you or a client perceive that the hard drive is slow and you have eliminated system performance as a symptom, then the problem is most likely with the file system, which we will address in Chapter 13.

Loud Clicking Noise

A loud clicking noise is a very ominous symptom for a hard drive. If you can isolate this noise to your drive and the drive is not functioning, it is probably physically damaged beyond repair. The smartest thing to do if you cannot access any data on the drive is to replace it and restore your data from the latest backup.

Drive Not Recognized

If you installed a drive and it is unrecognized, even in BIOS setup, recheck your installation. If it connects to a PATA controller, check that the PATA cable connects properly to the drive, as well as to the controller (some can be reversed). Is there another drive on the PATA controller? Recheck your installation and the BIOS for master/slave versus cable select settings. Some hard drives do not work well together on the same PATA controller. If you have room on another PATA controller, move the unrecognized drive to that controller. Finally, is the PATA power cable connected correctly? Reversing this can damage the drive.

If the unrecognized drive is using a SATA interface, check the connections to the interface, as well as the SATA power cable, to be sure they are firmly in place. Reversing the connector is not possible with SATA. It is possible that the drive is incompatible with the computer's BIOS, especially if you are adding a SATA drive to an older computer via a SATA bus card, although the bus card should add the needed BIOS support. Check the SATA card manufacturer's documentation for system BIOS requirements. If you find a BIOS incompatibility, determine if the computer manufacturer has a BIOS upgrade available.

OS Not Found

Once BIOS finishes the POST, it looks for the presence of an OS on the hard drive. If the BIOS does not find a special OS pointer in the drive's master boot record, it assumes that no OS exists and it will display a message that the OS was not found. If you have not yet installed an OS, you must do so at this point. Chapter 9 describes how to install Windows. If an OS exists but is not accessible, refer to Chapter 13 for steps to take to recover from this situation.

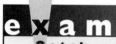

Knowing the features of the SATA and eSATA interfaces is important, especially such details as the L-type SATA connector versus the I-type eSATA connector.

When troubleshooting a disk-booting problem, unplugging all other devices not needed for the boot process and that are using the same interface (PATA or SATA) may be helpful. If the system boots with these devices disconnected, you may be able to isolate the problem. You can reconnect the devices one at a time until you find the problem device.

SATA and eSATA Interface

When planning to add a new SATA or eSATA drive to a system, first check that the operating system and motherboard will support it. Windows XP (if fully updated) and newer versions of Windows support SATA and eSATA, but older versions do not. At this writing, Mac OS X does not support some manufacturers' SATA interfaces. Check the device's documentation.

If you are connecting an external device, the eSATA cables must connect to an eSATA adapter card. You cannot use internal SATA cables to connect a removable eSATA device because the eSATA cables and their connectors are designed for thousands of connection and removal cycles, but the SATA cables and connectors are designed for only about 50 such cycles. Fortunately, the cables are keyed differently, with the I-type eSATA cable plug having a simple narrow oblong connector and the L-type SATA connector having a notch in the female connector and a corresponding key on the cable plug.

PATA Interface   Although round cables are available for PATA drives, you will normally see the standard wide-ribbon cables. These cables can block airflow, contributing to heat build-up within computers. They also can get in the way when a technician is working on other components, so any time you have a problem with a PATA-connected drive in a system that you know was opened recently, check that the cables were not accidently loosened or disconnected.

RAID Arrays and Controllers   If a single drive in a raid array fails, you will need to replace the drive with a comparable drive that will work in the array. After that, restart the computer and enter the RAID setup program, which may be part of the BIOS system setup program or, as in the case of a RAID bus adapter, may be a program in the adapter's BIOS that you can also enter during startup. Once in the RAID setup program, the steps you need to take depend on the level of RAID used.

If a drive in a RAID 0 array fails, you have lost the entire volume, because this type of RAID involves data written across the drives in the array, without any special algorithm for rebuilding the stripes in the array and recovering lost data should a drive fail. Therefore, once you replace a failed drive, run the RAID setup program, and re-create the array combining the drives into what appears to your operating system as a single logical drive. Then you must format the drive and restore your data from your latest backups. Chapter 10 discusses formatting disks and backup of data.

If a drive in a RAID 1 array fails, the system will continue working, writing to the surviving member of the array mirror, but it will no longer mirror the data. This may result in an error message at the time of the failure and at each startup, or you might find a record of a RAID error event in one of the computer's log files. Once you determine that one of the drives in the mirror failed, do a full backup, replace the failed hard drive, and re-create the mirror using the RAID setup program.

However, if you see a message such as "RAID not found" or the entire RAID array stops working without a clear message and you cannot access the drives at all, then you need to do some serious hardware troubleshooting, beginning with checking the connections. Then, if it is software-level Windows RAID, open Disk Manager and attempt to use it to determine if just one member of the array is failing, and if you can replace it and re-create the array.

If it is hardware-level RAID, check the manufacturer's documentation to see if there is a diagnostics procedure you can follow, along with diagnostic utilities—sometimes this is built into the controller. Or test the array in another computer, which can be problematic if the RAID is hardware-level RAID built into the first computer. Then you will need to find an identical system to test the drives in. If the hardware-level RAID is based on a separate RAID card, test the card and the drives in another computer.

w a t c h *When a RAID array fails with a RAID-specific error, troubleshoot the RAID controller or, if it is a Windows-based RAID, open Disk Management to see the status. Also remember to troubleshoot as you would any hard drive system.*

When a single drive in a RAID 5 array fails, an error message will appear, but the system will continue to write to the array in a stripe across the drives. The system will not be able to create a recovery block on one drive in each stripe, however, so you will have lost your fault tolerance, and reads will be slower, as it re-creates the lost data on each read. Do a backup before replacing the failed drive, and then restart the computer and run the RAID setup utility. The system will then rebuild the array without losing the data on the drive, re-creating the data on the replaced drive by using the data on the remaining drives and the algorithm block, when necessary.

Solid-state Storage Devices

When supporting SSDs, there are specific concerns for troubleshooting and caring for these devices. One is loss of data from incorrectly removing an external SSD from a computer. We describe this later in this chapter in "External Storage." Other issues are gradually degrading performance, exposure to dirt and grime, and recovering lost data from SSDs.

Performance Degradation   The issue of performance degradation in SSDs was reported in some of the first mass-marketed systems with internal SSDs in place of hard drives—mainly laptops. Although SSDs have much faster random access reads than traditional hard drives, the early drives had issues with random writes and overall performance. So far, the high-end SSDs manufactured for use in servers have not displayed this trend. It appears that internal SSDs in consumer-level computers, such as laptops, may be prone to degradation much sooner than their warranty period—a length of time that some manufacturers have kept in mind. If you support a system with an internal SSD and the user reports that the system seems slow, the internal SSD may be the source of the problem; contact the manufacturer to see if they have a fix. Our research shows that manufacturers have worked to correct this problem in systems developed in the last few years.

Dirt and Grime   Solid-state storage seems indestructible, or at least considerably more stable than conventional hard drives, which are sensitive to movement or being dropped while operating. But with external SSDs, the very portability of these devices makes them vulnerable to dirt, dust, and magnetic interference. People often carry thumb drives on lanyards around their necks, or on keychains, exposing them to a great deal of abuse—including food and beverage spills. Instruct your customers to always keep their solid-state storage devices protected. Thumb drives should always have a protected cap on when not connected to a computer. Each internal SSD has exposed connectors, and you should either install the SSD into a computer or portable device, or keep it in the plastic case it came in. Cleaning up one of these devices involves carefully removing dirt and debris from the contacts on the device's connectors.

Recovering Lost Data from SSDs   If you are helping someone who lost data on a solid-state storage device, either from deleting the data or from mishandling the device, all may not be lost. Programs are available for recovering files from solid-state devices, such as CompactFlash, SmartMedia, Memory stick, Secure Digital Card, Microdrive, and Multimedia Card. You must be able to access the device from your computer, and many of these utilities run in Windows.

Removable Storage

Removable media, as described in Chapter 4, includes all the storage types in which you can remove the media from the drive. These include optical discs, floppy disks, tape, and solid-state drives. We will discuss optical, floppy, and tape media here.

Optical Drives and Media

CD, DVD, and Blu-ray Disc drives and media are functionally similar, so you can use similar methods to troubleshoot them. A common problem with any of these devices is that the computer will report it cannot read the disc. First, check that you inserted the disc the correct way. If the drive is oriented horizontally, the label must be inserted face up so the drive can access the data on the underside of the disc. Next, visually inspect the disc. Scratches or smudges may prevent the computer from reading the disc. Learn how to clean optical discs later in this chapter when we explore maintenance issues in "Maintenance and Cleaning of Computer Components."

To rule out the media as the cause, try more than one disc in the optical drive. When you experience problems reading more than one disc in an optical drive, cleaning the lens may solve the problem. Sometimes a damaged optical disc will read in one drive but not in another, although the problem drive reads other discs just fine. If this is true, try making a copy of the disc, and then test the new disc in the original drive.

If the drive is the problem, check Device Manager to ensure the computer recognizes it. Reload the device's driver if necessary, and check its system resources. If the problem persists, check the cable connection and any jumper settings. Try the drive in another computer to confirm or rule it out as the cause of the problem.

Floppy Drives and Disks

The floppy disk, rather than the drive, is the cause of most floppy errors. The easiest way to check this is to eject the disk and insert another. If the problem goes away, the disk, not the drive, is the source of the problem. If you must have the information on a particular disk that is giving you trouble, try gently pulling the metal cover back and letting it snap back into place a few times, and then reinsert the disk in the drive and try to access the data again. Never touch the surface of a floppy disk (under the metal sliding cover), and do not attempt to clean the disk. Do try to use the disk in a different drive, however.

If you try to open the A: drive in Windows and receive this message: "Please insert a disk into drive A:" it means the drive cannot detect a floppy disk. The most common reason for this error is simply that there is no disk in the drive. Check to make sure a disk was inserted. If it was, remove the disk and reinsert it.

A floppy drive light that will not go off indicates an incorrectly attached data cable. Turn the computer off, remove the computer's cover, and reattach the cable the right way. Remember, you must align the red stripe on the cable with pin 1 on both the system board and on the drive.

Ensure the correct floppy drive configuration is present in the BIOS settings. If the computer still does not recognize the floppy drive, try replacing the cable. If that does not fix the problem, replace the drive with a working drive. A cheap and easy solution is to purchase an external floppy drive with a USB interface.

Tape Drives

If a newly installed drive does not work, review the installation procedure and make sure you did not skip a step. Make sure that the adapter card is properly seated and that any cable connectors are fully engaged. Check for damage to cables. If the drive is a SCSI tape drive, check to see that it has the correct SCSI configuration and that it is not in conflict with other devices on the chain. If no other devices on the chain work, check for proper termination per the manufacturer's instructions. If other devices work properly, the device itself may be the problem. Most manufacturers recommend cleaning the heads at regular intervals following instructions you will find in the documentation. Even a new tape drive may need to have the heads cleaned.

Check the tape media to be sure the drive manufacturer certified it. Any other tape could damage the tape drive heads. Only use tapes with the capacity recommended by the manufacturer. Test the drive with a new tape from a different box than the tape used when the problem occurred.

External Storage

External storage devices come in every storage type. A hard drive, floppy drive, or optical drive that has its own case and power supply and connects to a computer via an external cable is external storage. These devices can connect using USB, FireWire, eSATA, and even Ethernet (not discussed here) and still qualify as external storage. There are even external *media readers* (also called *card readers*) for reading a variety of solid-state cards. Of course, all forms of thumb drives are external storage.

Whatever the storage media, when experiencing problems with an external device first check the data cable and connectors between the device and computer as well as the power cable, unless the device is a very low-power USB device that is powered through the USB cable. Most drives, other than solid state, require more power than is available through USB, so check the power cable. If the cable and its connections are okay, restart the computer and see whether the situation changes. Connect the device to another computer—if it works, the problem is with the interface on the first computer.

Although newer external devices using USB or FireWire are plug and play, you should never disconnect an external storage device from a Windows computer while it is powered up unless you first close all applications that may be using the device. Then use the Safely Remove Hardware applet available as an icon in the notification area on the right of the taskbar (see Figure 11-2). A single click on this icon opens a list of removable devices. From this list, select the external drive you wish to remove,

FIGURE 11-2

The Safely Remove
Hardware icon in
the taskbar

wait for the Safe To Remove Hardware message to appear (see Figure 11-3), and then
disconnect the device.

SCSI Devices

The most common problems with SCSI devices involve incorrect installation or
configuration. This is more common than failure of the device itself. If the problem
occurs immediately after installation, begin by checking all connections. Then
check the two usual suspects: SCSI chain termination and SCSI device ID. Refer
back to Chapter 6 if you need help with these two issues.

Adapter Cards

If you must replace or upgrade an adapter card, follow the steps to remove the old
one in Exercise 6-8 in Chapter 6, followed by the instructions for installing a new
adapter card in Exercise 6-9 in Chapter 6. If the adapter card is a video card, ensure
the replacement card has the correct interface. Video cards currently come with
a choice of interfaces: Peripheral Component Interconnect (PCI), Accelerated
Graphics Port (AGP), and PCI Express (PCIe). If your computer supports both PCI
and AGP (a common configuration, until recently), purchase an AGP card, as it
performs better than a PCI card. In newer computers, both PCI and PCIe connectors
will be present. In this case, PCIe is the best choice.

FIGURE 11-3

The Safe
To Remove
Hardware
message

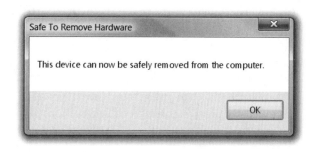

Thermally Sensitive Devices

Many components within a PC are thermally sensitive. These components should only operate within the recommended operating environment, as stated previously in this chapter. Transporting a PC or other thermally sensitive device requires being aware of the environment. For instance, if you live in a cold climate and bring a new PC home when it is 20 degrees Fahrenheit below zero, be sure to let it acclimate before plugging it in and turning it on. If the PC feels cold to the touch when you unpack it, this acclimation time should extended to several hours, because, as it warms up, some condensation will occur on internal components, and the PC needs time to dry out!

In addition, be sure to follow the procedures described later in "Maintenance and Cleaning of Computer Components" for cleaning dust and dirt from inside the PC to avoid heat build-up and to allow sufficient airflow around the PC and its peripherals.

Thermally sensitive devices include motherboards, CPUs, adapter cards, memory, and printers.

SCENARIO & SOLUTION

You have isolated a performance problem to your hard drive, but you would like to run more diagnostics tests to be sure. What programs should you look for?	Look for a hard drive diagnostics program from the drive's manufacturer, or obtain a third-party hard drive diagnostics program.
You are visiting a customer whose computer is running slowly. The computer is in a fabric store that generates a great deal of dust and fibers. In addition to your basic tools, what should you take along?	Be sure to take a vacuum—an antistatic vacuum, if possible. Overheating due to dust and fibers covering the internal components may cause the slow running.

CERTIFICATION OBJECTIVE

■ **802: 4.4** *Given a scenario, troubleshoot common video and display issues*

CompTIA Exam 802 Objective 4.4 lists several common symptoms of video and display problems, which we describe in this section, devoted to all types of I/O devices. Problems with video adapters and displays can be frustrating because many of the symptoms leave you with no visual means to troubleshoot in the operating system, so we provide common solutions for these problems that will help you on the job as well as in preparing for the exam.

Troubleshooting I/O Devices

Input/output (I/O) devices are our lifelines to our computers. The video system gives us our most important and immediate output, so we have devoted over half of the content of this section to video-related problems. Then, we detail troubleshooting symptoms and solutions for all other I/O devices.

Troubleshooting Video

A computer's video system includes, at minimum, the video adapter, one or more displays, and necessary cable and connectors. It may also include a video capture card or TV tuner, so diagnosing and resolving problems can be a bit tricky. Another difficulty in resolving video problems is that, without a working display, you cannot see the OS or BIOS settings in order to remedy the problem. Flat panel displays (FPDs) are now the norm for desktop PCs, and all laptops have this type of display. Regardless of the actual technology of an FPD, it is not user serviceable, because they are not repairable except by highly trained professionals at great cost. The same is true of cathode ray tubes (CRTs)—maybe even more so. There is a serious danger to doing such repairs yourself, regardless of the instructions and videos you may find on the Internet. They are so inexpensive today that just replacing them is the best course of action if you aren't trained in how to safely repair one of these devices. Of course, the display is only a part of a computer's video system, and therefore not the only source of problems. Therefore, we will talk about problems tied to all video components, including the device drivers, video adapters, displays, and cables and connectors. Following are some common video system symptoms and their most likely causes and solutions.

No Image on Screen

If, during the POST, the computer sounds the audio error code for a video problem and the display remains blank, the video adapter may not connect to a display or the adapter may be damaged. First, check the connection between the display and the video adapter. Next, check the video card function. If the video adapter is not a motherboard-integrated adapter, and if you have a spare computer, install the adapter in another computer to determine whether it is functioning. If it does not work in another computer, install a new adapter into the problem computer.

If the video adapter is integrated into the motherboard—a common configuration today—check the motherboard documentation for how to disable it. It may be a simple jumper that needs repositioning. Then, install a replacement video adapter card. If you cannot get the new adapter to work, you may need to replace the motherboard or the computer system itself, if it isn't cost effective to replace the motherboard.

The Computer Goes into Low-Resolution VGA Mode

If a display goes into a low-resolution Video Graphics Array (VGA) mode (640 × 480), first determine if it is in Safe Mode, which is pretty hard to miss, since the words "Safe Mode" are displayed right on the screen in the corners. If it is in Safe Mode, and if you did not purposely put it into Safe Mode, then flip forward to Chapter 13 to learn how to solve problems in Safe Mode.

If the display is in low resolution but not in Safe Mode, determine what has changed. Go back to questioning all that happened. Perhaps the user actually made changes that put the video into low resolution. If that is the case, use Control Panel to change the screen resolution. Perhaps Windows updated and is now not compatible with the video adapter. In Windows XP, right-click the desktop and select Properties to bring up the Display Properties dialog box, and then open the Settings tab where you can change the resolution. In Windows Vista or Windows 7, right-click the desktop and select Personalize to open the Personalization control panel. Then select Display from the left pane, and in the Display page, select Adjust Resolution at the top of the left pane. This opens the Screen Resolution control panel where you can make changes. We showed a Screen Resolution control panel in Chapter 5 in Figure 5-16.

Another cause for this symptom is a corrupted or incorrect video driver. If the driver was recently updated, there may be a problem with the update. First make sure you have tried to change the resolution to a higher resolution. If not, then troubleshoot for a bad driver update. Whenever Windows updates a device driver, it saves a copy of the previous version of the device driver. To check if this is a possible cause, open the properties dialog box of the display adapter, as shown in Figure 11-4. You can access this dialog box by opening Device Manager, expanding the Display Adapters node, and double-clicking the display adapter. In Figure 11-4, the Roll Back Driver button is grayed out, indicating that the driver has not been updated. If this button is active and you are troubleshooting a video problem, click it to remove the updated video driver, restart the computer, and see if the video returned to normal. You may need to go in and adjust the resolution settings.

If the Roll Back
Driver button is
active, the driver
was updated.

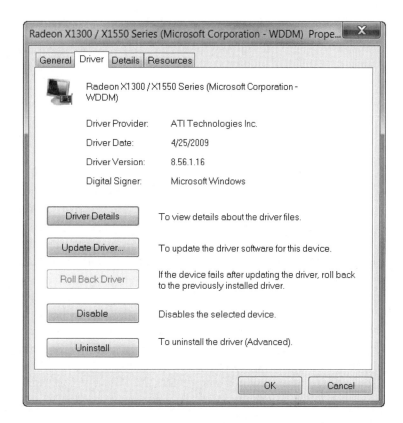

Blank Screen on Bootup

If the display shows no image at all and the computer does not issue a beep code,
check the video system components. Start with the display's connection to the
power supply and ensure the display is on. Check the data cable and verify that none
of the pins on the connector are bent; straighten them if necessary. Also, ensure the
brightness is set at an adequate level.

You can determine if the display itself is at fault by swapping it with a known
good one. If the new display works in the system, you can assume the original display
is the problem. Again, because display costs have decreased so much in the last few
years, it is less expensive to simply replace the display with a new one than to have
a technician professionally repair it. It seems counterintuitive, and you still have to
dispose of the old display appropriately, but that's today's reality. Chapter 1 describes
proper disposal of PCs and their components.

If a problem continues after you have eliminated the display as a cause, and if the video adapter is a bus card, check for proper seating of the video card in the expansion slot. Some video cards do not seat easily, so press the card firmly (but not too hard), and listen for an audible click to tell you the card seats properly.

Screen Suddenly Shuts Down

If the screen seems to be functioning normally and then suddenly shuts down, the first thing you should do is move the mouse or press a key on the keyboard. This will reactivate the system if the screen is blank because of a screen saver or a power mode setting that causes it to go blank after a specified period. For any other component, we would have you check the connections first, but it takes so little effort to move the mouse or press a key, that it is the best first step in this case.

If moving the mouse or pressing a key does not solve the problem, the screen may be overheated—perhaps due to a very hot environment. If that is the case, do whatever you can to lower the temperature in the room where the computer resides. If the ambient temperature is reasonable (around 75 degrees Fahrenheit), then troubleshoot for a problem with either the display or the video adapter. Switch out the display and see if the same problem occurs on a different display. If it does, then the video adapter is the source of the problem. If switching the display solves the problem, then the original display is damaged or defective and you should replace it, since displays are not user serviceable.

Screen Artifacts

Screen artifacts that randomly appear and disappear may look like pixel-sized spots. You know they are not physical, permanent spots because they come and go. Determine the software in use at the time, because the video adapter overheating can cause this symptom—in particular, the graphics processing unit (GPU) overheats when using software that is very video graphics intensive, such as photo-editing software. Test it by closing any photo-editing or other graphics-intensive software. If the artifacts disappear, then find a way to supplement the system's cooling system and/or replace the GPU or the entire video adapter with one designed for better cooling.

Flickering Image

A flickering image on a display has causes that depend on whether the display is a traditional CRT or an FPD.

Flickering on a CRT   A flickering CRT display may be a symptom of a faulty one. But before you jump to that conclusion, check to see if there is a motor or a fluorescent light very close to the display causing electromagnetic interference (EMI). Workers often have fluorescent lights in their office cubicles, and many add small fans to cool their workspace. Either of these can cause flickering, which goes away as soon as you remove or turn off the motor or fluorescent light. If possible, look on the other side of the wall partition, where you might find a source of EMI, such as an electrical panel. If you cannot remove the source from the display, move the display away from the source.

An inappropriate refresh rate setting, such as a rate too low for the video system you are using, can cause the display to flicker. On a Windows-based system, you can access the Control Panel's Display icon and choose a different refresh rate. Replace the display with another to see if the problem still exists.

on the **job**   *The standard refresh rate for CRT displays is 75 Hz. Older displays may not work at this rate, but may require a refresh rate of 60 Hz. An older display will usually blank out if run at faster speeds.*

Flickering on an FPD   A flickering FPD display is a sign of a failing component within the display—either the backlight or the inverter. Both are reasons to replace the display, but before you go to that expense, perform a small experiment. Test a known good display on the computer. If the test display has the same problem, the video adapter is the cause—if the test display works just fine, then replace the flickering display. Only open an FPD display if you were trained on how to do it, because there is a serious risk of electrical shock if you do. The inverter supplies alternating current (AC) power at a high voltage, and to make it worse, an inverter may still retain a charge after you remove power—whether unplugging the power cord or, in the case of a laptop, both unplugging the power cord and removing the battery.

Screen Image Is Dim

Something as simple as a maladjusted brightness control on the display itself can cause a dim screen image. Most displays have buttons on the case in addition to the power button. Pressing one of these opens a hardware-level menu for adjusting the display. One of the many options on the menu is brightness. Related to this are the special keys on a laptop that control brightness on the display. Therefore, if your FPD on your desktop or laptop seems too dim, check these controls. And while you are at it also use the display's controls to adjust contrast, which can also contribute to a perception that the display is dim.

A more serious case of a dim display is a bad inverter that simply isn't providing enough power to the display's light source. Once again, this may be justification for replacing the display. Recall the cautions in the previous section concerning attempting to open and repair an FPD.

Pixilation Problems on FPDs

Flat panel display LCD screens, described in Chapter 5, have special pixilation problems related to the LCD or related technology. These screens have three transistors per pixel, one transistor each for red, green, and blue, called subpixels. The transistors turn on and off to create a combination of colors. When a transistor turns off permanently (not by design, but through failure), it shows as a dark spot on the screen called a *dead pixel*. Another, nearly opposite problem is a *lit pixel* (also called a *stuck pixel*). This occurs when a transistor is permanently turned on, causing the pixel to constantly show as red, green, or blue. When pixels contiguous to each other are all in this lit-pixel state, they show as the color derived from their combination.

on the **Job** *Before you decide you have a defective FPD, be sure to wipe it clean with a soft, antistatic cloth, very slightly dampened with mild nonammonia glass cleaner. It wouldn't pay to try to troubleshoot a dirty screen!*

You may have bad or lit pixels on your FPD without noticing it because the dead pixels are not visible when displaying an image with dark colors in the defective area, and lit pixels may not show when displaying an image showing the colors that result from the dark pixels. A few defective pixels are normal; it is nearly impossible to find an FPD without some. It only becomes a problem if many bad pixels are located together and cause the image to be distorted or unreadable. To test for dead or lit pixels, you need to configure the desktop with a plain white background, close all windows, and configure the taskbar so it hides. This will give you a completely empty, white screen. Now examine the screen, looking for nonwhite areas. These may appear as the tiniest dot, about the size of a mark made by a fine-point pen on paper. Black dots indicate dead pixels, whereas any other color indicates a lit pixel. You will need to determine if the number you find is acceptable and what, if any, actions you will take.

Display Color Problems

If your display shows color problems, such as an incorrect color pattern, it may be a device driver problem, in which case you will want to update or replace the video adapter driver. But before going to that trouble, first see if adjustments in Windows Control Panel and using the Windows Display Color Calibration utility, along with the display's built-in settings menu, will solve the problem. *Calibration* is the adjustment of the color on a device, such as a video display, to ensure the accuracy of the colors.

on the

*j**o**b*

The calibration method described here depends on your own visual perception of colors. For best results, use a display calibration device with color measurement capabilities, as well as the specialized software that comes with it.

Before calibrating your display, ensure that your display is using the highest recommended resolution by opening the Screen Resolution page in Windows Control Panel, as described earlier in the discussion about low-resolution VGA mode. Then open the Advanced Settings dialog box, and select the Monitor tab, shown in Figure 11-5. Ensure that you are using the highest color mode supported by your display, which in our example is True Color (32-bit). Then click the Color Management tab and click the Color Management button. In the Color Management dialog box, shown in Figure 11-6, if you have multiple displays, you

FIGURE 11-5

The Monitor tab shows that this display is set to True Color.

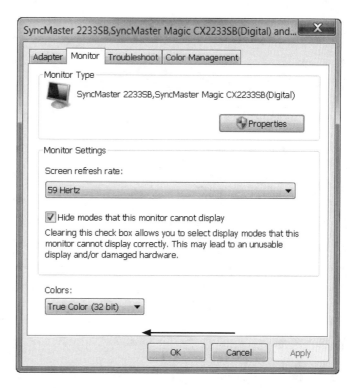

FIGURE 10-6 The Color Management dialog box

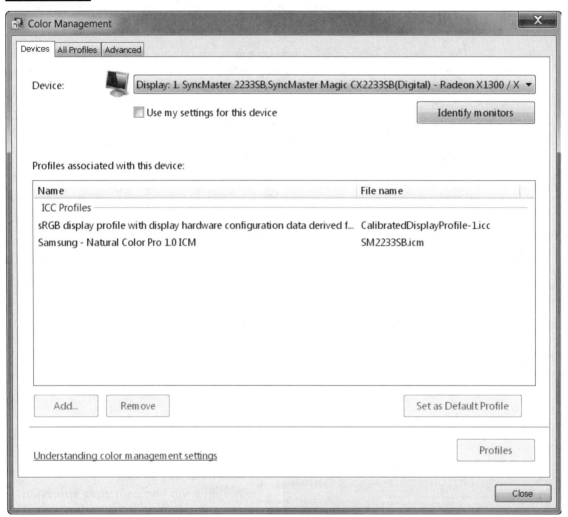

will need to select each display in turn and repeat the remaining steps. Select the Advanced tab and click the Calibrate display button, which opens the Display Color Calibration utility. Proceed with the calibration by clicking the Next button at the bottom of the window and following the instructions, which will require that you locate and use the physical buttons on your display for opening the display's menu and adjusting the colors as you proceed through the Display Color Calibration program.

Image Is Distorted   Improper display resolution or a driver issue can cause a distorted image. However, first check the display cable for damage or a bad connection. Check the manual settings on the display itself and reset it to the original settings (a common option). If this still doesn't resolve the problem, check the display resolution, and if it is at the correct resolution, then check the manufacturer's site for a driver update. If an update is available, install and test the display with the update.

Discoloration of CRT Screen

If a CRT display has discoloration problems, it may need to be degaussed. CRT displays have a metal plate—the *shadow mask*—at the front of the tube that focuses electron beams. A shadow mask is vulnerable to external electrical fields, causing color distortion. To counteract this effect, most CRTs have a copper degaussing coil used to create a rapidly oscillating magnetic field, reducing and randomizing the magnetic field on the shadow mask and correcting the color distortion. This process is called *degaussing*. Many CRT monitors and TVs will automatically perform a degauss when powered on or have a button you can press to initiate it. If a CRT monitor does not have an internal degaussing coil, you can use a handheld degaussing device.

Screen Elements Duplicated All Over the Screen

The problem of repeated screen elements is more common in older video systems. This problem is usually due to the use of an improper resolution setting for your video system. This setting results in multiple copies of the same image, including the mouse pointer, all over the screen. To solve this problem, go into the display settings and reduce the resolution setting. This task can be difficult because more than one mouse pointer appears on the screen, making it nearly impossible to work with the mouse. To navigate through the appropriate screens, we suggest using the keyboard.

Problems with TV Tuners and Video Capture Cards

Although a TV tuner card and a video capture card are two different devices, some manufacturers may combine them into one device, or they may be separate but work closely together. A TV tuner receives television signals for display on a PC's monitor, and a capture card can save video data to hard disk. When troubleshooting one of these devices, make sure you understand the features and capabilities of the device in question. How does it interface to the computer? The options vary, including all the usual buses and external I/O interfaces. Determine if the problem is with the interface. Check the connection where the TV tuner card receives the

TV signal. If all necessary connections are correct, then troubleshoot the drivers and software. A recent update to the operating system may have created a conflict with the drivers or software. Some TV tuners can receive only analog signals; some can receive only digital signals; and some can receive both. Another type of TV tuner card contains both an analog and a digital video tuner and can receive both types of signals simultaneously. In the latter scenario, you can watch one while recording the other. Considering all these variations, ensure the user is not expecting the device to do more than it is capable of doing. Then troubleshoot as you would any hardware device.

Troubleshooting Nonvideo I/O Devices

Now let's consider troubleshooting common I/O devices and cards, including serial, parallel, PS/2, sound, USB, IEEE 1394/FireWire ports, and specialized communications devices, such as NICs and modems. Today these devices, like all PC components, are plug and play so problems with them are rarely due to configuration. However, in the past, configuration errors involved a group of resources called system resources (I/O addresses, IRQs, and DMA channels). While we doubt you will encounter problems related to system resources in modern computing equipment, you may encounter a very old PC or very old component that serves a critical purpose in your work environment and needs to keep running, at almost all costs. For that you will need some knowledge of system resources, which we will describe first. Beyond that unlikely source of problems, we will look at other problems and solutions for I/O devices. We will begin that discussion with the oldest technologies (serial ports, parallel ports, and PS/2 ports). Then we will move on to audio devices (old and new), USB, IEEE 1394/FireWire, and NICs and analog modems.

System Resources

System resources are a finite set of resources controlled by the operating system and critical to the use of all computer components. These resources include memory addresses, I/O addresses, IRQs, and DMA channels. A *memory address* is a logical memory address defined in a processor's address bus that allows the system to access physical RAM or ROM memory locations. A memory address is required by a device that has its own RAM memory or ROM memory and that requires an address on the system bus (subtracting usable addresses from the system RAM) in order to use this memory and make it accessible to the processor. An *I/O address* is an assigned address or range of addresses on a system's address bus that allows the system's processor to recognize a device. An *interrupt request line (IRQ)* is an assigned channel over which a device can send a signal to the processor to get its attention (hence, the term "interrupt"). A direct memory access (DMA) channel, as described in Chapter 3, is a system resource that certain devices, such as sound cards and hard drives, can use to move data between the device and system RAM without involving the processor. A specialized chipset component, called the DMA controller, manages the use of the DMA channels. In Device Manager, if you open the View menu and select Resources By Type, you will see nodes for the four resource types. Figure 11-7 shows Device Manager with the Memory node expanded to show memory assignments to various computer components.

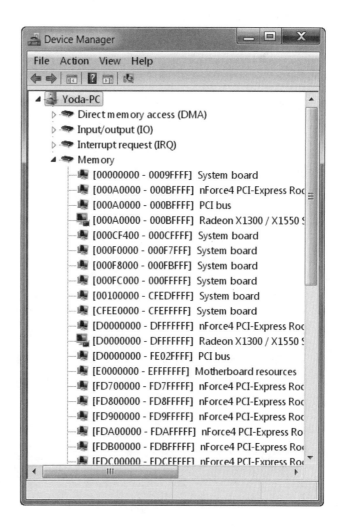

FIGURE 11-7

Device Manager showing system resources

All devices require the use of one or more types of system resources to interact with the processor. Although all devices require I/O ports, the use of other system resources varies from device to device. Configuring a device to use its own unique set of system resources was once part of installing a device and its device driver into a system. Today, this assignment is automatic, thanks to plug and play technologies. Only when things go terribly wrong will you need to make changes manually, and this is very rare.

Serial Ports

The USB interface has largely replaced the classic RS-232-C serial ports that were once the norm on PCs. Even the devices that once had serial ports built in, such as internally installed analog modems, have all but disappeared. Therefore, if you do encounter serial ports, they will be on older computers and/or analog modems or some other special-use device that uses an external or built-in-to-the-device serial port. That is why we include this topic in this book.

If a serial port is not functioning, first check the connections and cable. Serial connectors and the interface behind them can be defective. If visual inspection does not show problems, you can test a physical serial port using a loopback plug, as described in Chapter 3. Whether you have these tools or not, open Device Manager and confirm that the device is recognized and enabled. If it is not recognized, run the BIOS system setup program and try turning it on.

Another problem area with serial ports involves incorrect configuration. This problem is rare today, thanks to plug and play, but you may encounter it with an older computer or older serial device. To understand configuration issues, knowing the difference between a physical serial connector and a COM port in a PC is important. A physical serial connector (or "serial port") will not work unless it is assigned to a logical COM *port,* which is a logical device with an assigned I/O address range and an IRQ. COM ports have recognizable names, even at the BIOS level. These names are COM1, COM2, COM3, and COM4 (generically referred to as COM*x*). A serial device, such as an internal modem, requires a COM port before you can use it, as does any external serial connector. Table 11-1 shows the traditional COM port resource assignments with the beginning I/O address and the IRQ. Figure 11-8 shows Device Manager and the Resources tab in the Properties dialog box for COM1. Notice that COM1 has the standard assignments of I/O address range 03F8-03FF and IRQ 4. The COM1 address range includes eight bytes beginning at the I/O base address. This assignment of resources is entirely up to the plug and play process in your computer. You should only attempt to override these settings through this dialog box after researching the problem device and finding that the manufacturer or another reliable source recommends this step.

	Port	I/O Base Address	IRQ
TABLE 11-1	COM1	03F8	4
The Standard	COM2	02F8	3
COM Port	COM3	03E8	4
Assignments	COM4	02E8	3

Parallel Ports

Like RS-232-C serial ports, parallel ports have disappeared from the computing landscape, except when older equipment continues to be used and must be supported. As with other components, if a parallel port is not functioning, first check the connectors and cable, and then open Device Manager and ensure the

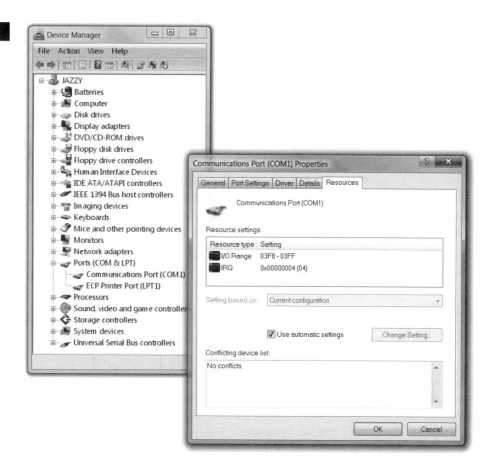

FIGURE 11-8

Device Manager showing a working COM1 port with its resource assignments device is recognized and enabled. When you look for it in Device Manager, you will notice that parallel ports also have names recognized by the system. *Line printer terminal (LPT)* describes any parallel port, while *LPT1* and *LPT2* describe the first and second parallel ports on the system. In Figure 11-8, the parallel port is labeled ECP Printer Port (LPT1). If your system has a parallel port but it is not visible in Device Manager, run the BIOS system setup program and try enabling the device. Like serial ports, to operate, parallel ports must have an I/O address and IRQ assignment, normally assigned automatically by the operating system. The standard assignments for LPT1 are I/O base address 0378 and IRQ 7; the assignments for LPT2 are traditionally I/O base address 0278 and IRQ5.

Resource assignments are rarely the issue with a parallel port problem. Rather, you should look at the parallel port mode, as described in Chapter 21. The BIOS Setup program assigns this, so you must check that it is using the correct mode for the device you are connecting to the parallel port. BIOS Setup usually describes these modes as standard parallel (the original, unidirectional mode), bidirectional parallel, *enhanced capability port (ECP) mode*, and *enhanced parallel port (EPP) mode*. Most parallel printers require ECP mode, which is usually the default mode. If your device requires a different mode, you will need to change the setting in BIOS Setup.

PS/2

The *Personal System/2 (PS/2) connector* is for input devices, including keyboards and mice. Many motherboards have two of these connectors—one dedicated to keyboard input and the other for a mouse. Problems with a keyboard or mouse are usually with the device itself, not with the interface, but a physical inspection is always in order. To do that, turn off the computer and unplug the keyboard or mouse. Inspect the cable plug for bent pins. If one is bent, try to straighten it, reconnect the device, restart the computer, and test it. If this does not solve the problem, substitute another keyboard or mouse to determine if the problem is with the device. If the problem is with a keyboard, check for loose or missing keys. Reseat any loose keys, and replace the keyboard if keys are missing.

e x a m
w a t c h

While you may never encounter the classical serial, parallel, or PS/2 interfaces (the last is more likely than the previous two), be sure you know the acronyms in the previous discussion *because they are included in the Acronyms list for both the CompTIA 801 and 802 exams. The acronyms include COMx, IRQ, Line Printer Terminal (LPT), ECP, EPP, and PS/2.*

Sound

Today's PCs, and not just those dedicated to home entertainment systems, have a huge variety of sound output available to them. The most common configuration is stereo speakers—either built in, as with laptops; integrated into the monitor; or separated as external stereo speakers, sometimes including a woofer. So, if a problem appears to be with the sound system, you first need to determine what type of sound output exists, whether it is using the correct cables, and if the speakers themselves are powered on—a common issue with external speakers. Then check to see if the problem is with a single program or with all programs, and make sure the program you are using is correctly configured for the sound system.

Today, computers come with multiple sound connectors, so be sure the speakers connect to the active sound output connector. For instance, video adapters often have sound output built in, as do many motherboards. Installing the drivers for a bus video adapter usually disables the onboard sound output of the motherboard, so when you plug the speakers into the onboard sound connectors, you won't hear anything! Further complicating this is the multiple output and input connectors that come on a single sound card. Make sure you are using the proper connector for the appropriate device. Here are the common sound card connectors:

- **Joystick**   This port is traditionally a DB15 connector and is disappearing from video adapters because the devices that use this, mainly joysticks and MIDI devices, have transitioned to USB.
- **Microphone**   This port connects to an external microphone.
- **Line out**   This port connects to an external device, such as a CD player, to send sound output to the device.
- **Line in**   This port is for connecting to an external device, such as a CD player, to send sound input to the computer (and, therefore, out the computer's speakers).
- **Analog/digital out**   This connector outputs analog sound signals to external center or subwoofer channels on an external speaker system. Alternatively, use it to output digital sound to external digital devices or digital speaker systems.
- **Rear out**   This connector outputs signals for the rear speakers in a surround-sound system.

Input Devices

A number of different symptoms are associated with input devices, especially the mouse, which provides a common source of computer problems. Fortunately, most procedures to resolve such problems are quite simple. Now look at two common mouse-related problems.

The Pointer Does Not Move Smoothly Across the Screen

A common mechanical mouse or trackball problem is irregular movement of the pointer across the screen. Some mice even appear to hit an "invisible wall" on the screen. These symptoms indicate dirty rollers, in the case of a traditional mouse, or dirt on the lens of an optical mouse or trackball. This problem is very common because as the mouse moves across a desk or table it picks up debris, which then gets on the internal rollers. You may still need to clean an optical or electronic motion-sensing trackball or mouse, but they are much more reliable than the older mechanical mouse. Learn how to clean a mouse later in this chapter when we explore preventive maintenance techniques in "Maintenance and Cleaning of Computer Components."

The Pointer Does Not Move on the Screen

The problem could be that the mouse driver is either corrupted or missing altogether. If you suspect a missing driver, you need to load the driver manually from the setup disc that came with the mouse.

If there is no driver disc, try simply restarting the computer. Most mice are plug and play, so the OS might automatically detect your mouse and load the appropriate driver for it at startup. If you suspect that a mouse driver does exist but is corrupted, use Device Manager or the Mouse icon in Control Panel to remove the existing driver and reload it. Learn about working with Device Manager in Chapter 13.

on the **job**

USB connectors are now the most common ones used for pointing devices.

Digitizer Problems

When using a digitizer, the user draws or writes on the tablet with the stylus and can even select "ink" of various colors and textures with which to draw. When the user is writing, a handwriting recognition program converts the writing into a text document, but it also saves the handwritten page as a graphic.

Problems with digitizers often involve the use and appearance of the ink while working in various applications. You can often resolve problems common to all applications by updating the digitizer driver. Many digitizers use the Wacom driver, as Wacom is the major manufacturer of digitizer tablets—both freestanding and those integrated into tablet PCs.

Digitizer problems associated with only one application, or two or more applications from the same manufacturer, need to be resolved through the application. Sometimes an application update will take care of the problem. A damaged or defective stylus may cause other digitizer problems. Whereas on a handheld computer you can use anything from a pen to your finger to work with a touch screen, on a digitizer you must use a stylus that sends a signal to the digitizer, giving it the position of the stylus on the tablet. The stylus, therefore, must receive power somehow, either by a battery or by an outside source like a USB port.

Further, the stylus used with a digitizer or tablet PC must be compatible with the digitizer. When replacing a stylus, the general rule is that a Wacom stylus will work with any digitizer or tablet PC using the Wacom tablet. Therefore, you will need to research the digitizer installed in the tablet PC you are troubleshooting.

Wireless digitizer tablets are subject to radio frequency interference, which can distort the created image. Some digitizers have additional insulation to block this interference. If you are having problems writing or drawing on a tablet, move it away from any possible sources of interference and try again.

USB

Most common peripherals are now available with a USB interface. We have found this plug and play interface to be the least troublesome of any we have worked with in the past. However, you may encounter problems even with these devices. One handy tool for diagnosing problem USB ports and devices is a USB loopback plug and the diagnostics software that comes with one. The sections that follow describe some common problems you may encounter with USB devices.

USB 2.0 and 3.0 Compatibility Problems   Have you noticed that the old connectors (parallel, serial, mini-DIN-6, and FireWire), as well as some not-so old connectors (eSATA), have virtually disappeared from new computers? USB has replaced them. New laptop and desktop computers seem to come with as many USB ports as will fit on the case. As of this writing, new computers come with both USB 2.0 and USB 3.0 ports, which brings up some compatibility issues.

If you add a USB device to a computer and it does not work, you should first look at the version of the standard used by both the USB device and the USB port on the computer. Your main concerns today will be between the Hi-Speed USB 2.0

standard and the SuperSpeed USB 3.0 standard. We described these standards in Chapter 4, and we will address how they work together using two scenarios:

■ Can I use a SuperSpeed USB 3.0 device connected via a USB 2.0 cable to a computer that only supports HighSpeed USB 2.0? Yes. Mostly. Many, but not all, USB 3.0 devices will work through a USB 2.0 port, but not at the higher speed of the 3.0 standard. The standard requires that all SuperSpeed USB 3.0 devices have connectors that are compatible with both the old (USB 2.0 with fewer pins) and the new (USB 3.0 with more pins). One known exception is that the male USB 3.0 B connector cannot physically connect to a female USB 2.0 port on a computer. It must connect to a USB 3.0 port. This is necessary because a USB 3.0 device requires more power than a USB 2.0 port can supply, and this guarantees that no one can accidentally connect a Powered USB 3.0 device to a USB 2.0 port.

■ Can I connect a Hi-Speed USB 2.0 device to a computer that supports Super-Speed USB 3.0? All USB 2.0 devices will work through a USB 3.0 port.

You can discern the differences by looking at the labeled computer ports. In addition, if you open Windows 7 (or newer) Device Manager on a recent computer and expand the Universal Serial Bus Controllers node, you should see the USB hubs and controllers with version labels, as shown in Figure 11-9.

USB Device Seems Not to Have Power   Low-power USB devices get their power from the USB system or, more specifically, from the root or external hubs. Other devices require external power and come with their own power supplies that switch on separately from the computer. If this is a new installation, check the documentation and packaging to be sure they did not overlook an external power cord. Check that a self-powered device has power and is on. Next, make sure the data cable is securely connected. You should also make sure the device plugs into the proper type of hub. You can plug "low-powered" USB devices into any type of USB hub, but "high-powered" devices (USB 2.1 or later), which use over 100 milliamps, must only plug into self-powered USB hubs.

USB Keyboard Not Functioning   The BIOS typically controls the keyboard's drivers and resources. When you install a USB keyboard, you must inform the BIOS so it will hand keyboard control over to the USB system. At startup, go into the CMOS settings program, ensure the USB keyboard option is turned on, and the BIOS will provide a generic driver for USB keyboards. On an older computer, this

Device Manager, showing both USB 2.0 and USB 3.0

option may not exist, in which case you might need to upgrade the BIOS in order to use a USB keyboard.

Some USB devices require installation of the driver before connecting the device to a USB port. This is especially true of USB printers. If you plug in the device before installing the driver, you may *not be able to use the device until you uninstall the driver, disconnect the device, reinstall the driver, and reconnect the device. Be sure to read the documentation before installing any device.*

"USB Device Is Unknown" Message, or the Device Is Not Functioning

A message stating that the USB device is unknown, or the device simply does not work, means the computer cannot communicate with the device. First, to make sure the device is properly attached and receiving power, try switching it to another port.

Also, check that the device's cable is less than five meters long. Although most USB devices are plug and play, the operating system may still not have the specific device driver, so make sure you load a driver for this device.

You should also check that the device is using the proper communications mode. On startup, the USB controller assigns an ID to all devices and asks them which type of data transfer (interrupt, bulk, or continuous) they will use. If a device is set to use the wrong type of transfer mode, it will not work. Finally, check the device by swapping it with a known good one.

None of the USB Devices Will Work   If none of the USB devices works, you could have a problem with the entire system or just with the USB controller. First, make sure your OS is USB-compliant, which is the case for all versions of Windows since Windows 98. Next, make sure the number of devices does not exceed 127 and that no single cable length exceeds five meters. The USB system is also limited to five tiers (or five hubs) in a single chain. Check the cable length and cable connections, especially from the root hub to the first external hub. A loose connection will prevent all devices attached to the external hub from functioning.

If the problem is not in the USB physical setup, turn your attention to the USB hub. In an older, pre-Windows XP OS, make sure the proper driver has been loaded and that the new device does not have a conflict with another device. You should also check the BIOS for USB support to determine if you can even use USB in this system. You may also want to uninstall the USB hub or controller driver. When you restart the system, the operating system will notify you to reinstall these drivers. This may fix the problem.

IEEE 1394/FireWire

Troubleshoot IEEE 1394/FireWire problems just as you would any interface problem. First, check the connections and cabling, and ensure the peripheral device has power. Also check any status indicator lights. Use Device Manager to make sure the IEEE 1394 bus host controller is listed and functioning. As with many of the other standard I/O interfaces, a device driver that comes with Windows fully supports IEEE 1394/FireWire. Devices such as hard drives will not need an additional driver, but for other types of devices, check the documentation. If a high-speed device seems to be running slowly, check to see if a slower device is on the same bus. For instance, as described in Chapter 4, one 1394a device in a chain will cause any 1394b device to operate at the lower speed of a 1394a.

NICs and Analog Modems

We will discuss installing and troubleshooting network interface cards (NICs) and analog modems in Chapters 15 and 16. You can begin troubleshooting one of these devices by treating it like any other device. First, check the connections, cables, and the status indicator lights, and then open Device Manager to see if the device is recognized.

CERTIFICATION OBJECTIVES

- **802: 1.7** *Perform preventive maintenance procedures using appropriate tools*

- **802: 4.1** *Given a scenario, explain the troubleshooting theory*

While preparing for the CompTIA A+ exams, be sure to study and practice preventive maintenance techniques. CompTIA understands that good preventive maintenance will cut down on the time spent solving problems. Preventive maintenance can involve both the physical aspects of computer equipment maintenance and the software tasks, such as backups. In this section we provide mostly the physical aspects of preventive maintenance, while in Chapter 13 we will discuss the software tasks, including scheduled disk maintenance, Windows updates, patch management, driver/firmware updates, and antivirus updates, which are listed in CompTIA Exam 802 Objective 1.7. CompTIA Exam 802 Objective 4.1 only includes a single mention of preventive maintenance: "Verify full system functionality and if applicable implement preventive measures." While this is a bit vague, we have compiled basic preventive maintenance information for the computer technician.

Preventive Maintenance Techniques

The old adage "an ounce of prevention is worth a pound of cure" applies to computers as much as it does to anything else. Begin by providing each computer and all peripherals with a well-ventilated location. Then take time to schedule and perform preventive maintenance on the PCs for which you are responsible. This includes regular visual and aural inspections, driver and firmware updates, and component cleaning.

Visual and Aural Inspection

Frequent visual inspections will alert you to problems with cables and connections. This is true of your own personal computer as well as other people's computers. Make yourself consciously look at a computer for connection problems and environmental problems. Things change. You may discover that you have inadvertently piled papers on top of a powered USB hub in a corner of your desk, and it is getting hot. You may find that a computer or peripheral moved, which stretched the data cable or power cables to the point of nearly coming out of the sockets.

An aural inspection involves listening for a noisy fan or hard drive. A squealing fan or hard drive may be a sign of a pending problem. Correct it before you lose the fan or hard drive. Clean and/or replace the fan. Immediately back up a hard drive that makes an unusual noise, and take steps to replace it.

Driver and Firmware Updates

Keep current on driver and firmware updates. When you move from an old computer to one with a newer operating system, or upgrade the operating system on an existing computer, obtain new device drivers from the manufacturers. Also, be sure to install all critical operating system and security updates (more on security in Chapters 17 and 18). Similarly, when you upgrade to a new operating system, you may need to update the firmware, which, as you learned earlier in "BIOS/CMOS Problems," means flashing the system BIOS and sometimes the device BIOSs.

Maintenance and Cleaning of Computer Components

Computer components will last longer and function better with some basic and regular maintenance and cleaning. For example, by regularly cleaning the fans in the power supply and case, you can ensure they properly cool the computer's internal components, preventing system slowdown and potential damage to components.

Cleaning Products

A variety of cleaning products are available for PCs. The following list includes some of the most common:

- Disposable moistened cleaning wipes
- Canned compressed air
- Antistatic vacuum cleaner
- Nonabrasive liquid cleaning compound, such as isopropyl alcohol

When using any cleaning products, first ensure that you are protected from any dangers involved in their use, as described in Chapter 1, and wear eye protection when doing any work that could stir up dust. Use compressed air to blow dust out of components, ensuring that you are not blowing it into other components.

Internal Components

One of the most common reasons to clean the insides of a computer is to remove dust build-up to protect the system from overheating. Recall that the power supply's fan draws air out of the computer. Outside air comes in through ports and is distributed over the internal components, bringing with it dust. Because dust can cause ESD and lead to overheated components, cleaning the inside of the computer regularly is important. Pay particular attention to the system board, the bottom of the computer chassis, and all fan inlets and outlets on both the power supply fan and case fans. Of course, make sure you turn off and unplug the computer before you start cleaning it.

One of the easiest ways to remove dust from the system is to use compressed air to blow the dust out. Compressed air comes in cans roughly the size of spray-paint cans. Typically, liquid Freon in the can compresses the air and forces it out when you depress the can's nozzle. Do not tilt the can because this can cause Freon to spill onto your skin or components. Liquid Freon can cause freeze burns on your skin and can damage the computer's components.

You can also use compressed air to blow dust out of the keyboard, expansion slots, and ports. Use only canned compressed air, not high-pressure air from a compressor. Whatever you use to blow out dust from a computer, be aware of where you are blowing the dust so that you are not blowing the dust off one component only to have it settle on or in another.

Another common method for removing dust from inside a computer is to use an antistatic vacuum cleaner—one that has a conductive path to ground to protect against causing electrostatic discharge damage to a computer during use. This has the advantage of removing dust without allowing the dust to settle elsewhere. It is best to use a handheld vacuum that allows you to get into smaller places and clean the computer without accidentally hitting and damaging other internal components. Take the nozzle out of the computer, and move the vacuum cleaner away before turning it off.

External Components

Finally, you can use a lint-free cloth to wipe off dusty surfaces, such as displays, keyboards, printers, and the outside of the PC case. Use a clean antistatic cloth to remove dust and dirt from display screens. Avoid using the newer dust cloths that work by "statically attracting" dust. Remember, static is harmful to the computer.

For dirt you cannot dust off, use disposable moistened cleaning wipes on optical discs and most plastic, metal, and glass exterior surfaces, such as display screens. A liquid cleaning compound, such as isopropyl alcohol, can come in handy for cleaning gummy residue from the surface of the PC case or a peripheral. Manufacturer's instructions may also suggest using this for cleaning components inside the PC or other device, but only do this per the manufacturer's instructions.

Storage Devices

Common storage devices also require regular maintenance for better performance. The following sections describe simple tasks for maintaining hard drives, optical drives, and floppy drives.

Hard Drives   Hard drive maintenance includes running a utility called a disk defragmenter (Defrag) or disk optimizer to reorganized fragmented files on disk, and Check Disk (CHKDSK) or Scandisk to discover problems with the disk. Run these utilities on a regular basis, perhaps once a week on a drive in which you save many new files and delete old files. Chapter 13 will explain the details of the problems both types of utilities resolve.

Optical Media and Drives   You can prevent damage to your optical drives by keeping the discs clean. Commercial optical disc cleaning and repair kits are readily available to restore optical discs. But you can simply wipe any type of optical disc (CD, DVD, or Blu-ray) clean with an antistatic cloth. For more stubborn dirt, use plain water or isopropyl alcohol on the cloth. Ensure the disc is completely dry before inserting it into a drive. The Blu-ray Discs (also called "BD") have a hard coating—beyond what you will find on older types of optical discs—that resists scratches.

If a disc is too badly scratched, you may need to replace it, or if it is irreplaceable or too expensive to replace and you have nothing to lose, consider polishing the disc.

Never clean an optical drive that is working properly, but if you find you must clean a drive, use compressed air to blow dirt out of the drive. If your optical drive has the lens in the disc tray, you will see it when the tray extends. You can carefully clean this type of drive with an antistatic cloth dampened with isopropyl alcohol. Be careful that you do not use too much alcohol and damage the drive. "Dampened" does not mean "dripping."

Be wary of kits for cleaning optical drives, because some of these use a small brush or felt pad to clean the lens of the drive, which can have unintended consequences, such as scratching the lens. If you decide to use one of these kits, make sure you follow the directions carefully, as improper use may cause more problems than it solves.

Cleaning Input Devices   For input devices, such as keyboards, mice, and trackball devices, schedule frequent cleaning. For the keyboard, this involves vacuuming the crevices between the keys. Simply turning a keyboard upside down over a wastebasket and shaking it will remove a surprising amount of dust and debris, depending on the environment and the habits of the user. You may need to protect a keyboard in a dirty environment, such as an auto repair shop, with a special membrane cover that allows use of the keyboard, but keeps dirt, grease, solvents, and other harmful debris out of it. You can find such covers on the Internet or in computer supply catalogs under the keyboard protector category. For devices that are rarely used, consider using dust covers that remain on the device until needed.

To clean an optical mouse, simply turn the mouse over, locate the tiny lens, and wipe it with a soft, static-free cloth. To clean a trackball, simply remove the ball, and wipe the socket with a soft, static-free cloth. To clean rollers on a traditional mouse, carefully dismantle it, remove the ball, and clean the inside, including the rollers.

CERTIFICATION SUMMARY

Understanding troubleshooting theory and taking a structured and disciplined approach will not only help you arrive at a solution, but also will help you quickly resolve similar problems in the future. If you determine that you have a software problem, check the application's configuration, or try uninstalling and then reinstalling the program. If the problem is hardware related, identify the components that make up the failing subsystem. Starting with the most accessible component, check for power and that the component properly attaches to the computer. Check the device's configuration and the presence of a device driver. Finally, swap suspected bad components with known good ones.

Assemble the right tools for troubleshooting and maintenance before you need them. Take time to perform regular maintenance tasks on computers and peripherals to prevent future problems.

As a computer technician, you will be required to locate and resolve the source of computer problems. If you have a good knowledge of the functions of the computer's components, you will be able to quickly troubleshoot problems that occur.

However, there are other telltale signs of failed components. For example, you can use POST error codes to determine a problem's cause. Although the troubleshooting procedures differ from component to component, and even for different problems within the same component, many of the procedures involve cleaning the component, ensuring it is properly attached to the computer, or finally, replacing the component.

TWO-MINUTE DRILL

Here are some of the key points covered in Chapter 11.

Preparing for Troubleshooting

❑ Arm yourself with appropriate troubleshooting tools, including software and hardware tools.

❑ The six steps of the troubleshooting theory include: Identify the problem; Establish a theory of probable cause (question the obvious); Test the theory to determine the cause; Establish a plan of action to resolve the problem and then implement the solution; Verify full system functionality and, if applicable, implement preventative measures; and finally, Document findings, actions, and outcomes.

❑ If you must service a large number of PCs, consider investing in a specialized diagnostic toolkit.

❑ Protect computers and data by performing backups of data and the operating system before making any changes to try to resolve problems.

❑ Ongoing user training can prevent many problems and ensure that users know how to respond to common problems.

Troubleshooting Motherboards, RAM, CPUs, and Power

❑ Procedures should move from least intrusive to most intrusive, checking proper connections, appropriate components, drivers, settings, and component seating for internal devices.

❑ General symptoms, such as excessive heat, noise, odors, and visible damage, can apply to any of several components.

❑ Various system instability problems are most likely to be software-related, but they also may have a hardware-based cause. These include system lockups, system shutdowns, unexpected shutdowns, and the BSOD.

❑ Never open a power supply because there is a danger of severe shock.

❑ POST error codes, such as 1xx, 2xx, and 3xx, can indicate system board, memory, or keyboard failures, respectively.

❏ Most CPU problems are fatal, which requires replacing the CPU or system. Check your warranty if you suspect a problem with the CPU because it may require replacing the motherboard.

❏ Incorrect CMOS settings can affect a variety of system components. Check and correct these problems by running the system setup and changing the settings.

❏ CMOS batteries last from two to ten years. A computer that does not maintain the date and time when powered off is a symptom of a failed CMOS battery.

❏ Most system board, processor, and memory errors are fatal, meaning the computer cannot properly boot up.

❏ Motherboard errors can be the most difficult to pinpoint and, due to the cost and effort involved in replacement, should be the last device you suspect when a subsystem or the entire computer fails.

Troubleshooting Storage Devices

❏ Replace a hard drive that begins to develop corrupted data before all the information stored on it is lost.

❏ USB device problems may involve power connections for external devices that require external power. Consider using a USB loopback plug to diagnose a stubborn USB problem.

❏ Problems with SCSI devices, beyond failure of the device itself, most often involve termination of the SCSI chain and SCSI device ID.

Troubleshoot I/O Devices

❏ When a system goes into low-resolution VGA Mode, first determine if it is in Safe Mode. If it is in Safe Mode, follow the instructions in Chapter 13. If the display is in low resolution VGA Mode but not in Safe Mode, determine what has changed, looking for a recently updated device driver or other newly installed software.

❏ If no image appears on the screen, first check all connections and then check the video card functionality.

❏ Some displays automatically shut down when overheated. Check ambient temperature and cool it down, if possible. Switch displays to see if the problem is in the display or video adapter.

❏ Dead pixels are pixels that are off, creating dark spots on the screen. This is only a problem if bad pixels cause the image to be distorted or unusable.

❑ An overheating video adapter can cause screen artifacts that randomly appear and disappear—in particular, the GPU overheats when using software that is very video graphics intensive, such as photo-editing software. Find a way to supplement the system's cooling system and/or replace the GPU or the entire video adapter with one designed for better cooling.

❑ To correct display color problems, use the Windows Display Calibration utility.

❑ Something as simple as a maladjusted brightness control on the display can cause a dim display image. Troubleshoot by adjusting the brightness control on a PC or laptop display. A more serious cause is a bad inverter, in which case, it may be wise to replace the display rather than try to repair it.

❑ A flickering image on a CRT may be due to EMI from a nearby motor. Remove the source. Or, it can be that the refresh rate setting for the CRT is incorrect.

❑ A flickering FPD display is a sign of a failing component within the display—either the backlight or the inverter. Replace the display.

❑ Improper display resolution or a driver issue can cause a distorted image. You should first check the display cable for damage or a bad connection.

❑ If a CRT shows discoloration, it needs degaussing, which may only require that you press a button, or may require that you use a handheld degaussing device.

❑ The most common mouse problem is irregular movement, which can be resolved by cleaning the internal rollers of a mechanical mouse or the bottom surface of an optical mouse.

Preventive Maintenance Techniques

❑ Schedule regular preventive computer maintenance, such as visual and aural inspections, driver and firmware updates, cleaning, and verifying a proper environment.

❑ Schedule regular preventive component maintenance for displays, power devices, and drives. Protect thermally sensitive devices by cleaning regularly and ensuring proper airflow.

❑ Acquire and learn how to use appropriate cleaning products, such as cleaning wipes, canned compressed air, an antistatic vacuum cleaner, and nonabrasive cleaning compounds, such as isopropyl alcohol.

SELF TEST

The following questions will help you measure your understanding of the material presented in this chapter. Read all of the choices carefully because there might be more than one correct answer. Choose all correct answers for each question.

Preparing for Troubleshooting

1. Which of the following is an advanced hardware diagnostics tool that you insert into an expansion slot?

    A. POST card

    B. Loopback plug

    C. Video adapter

    D. Nut driver

2. What should you do before making any changes to a computer?

    A. Turn off the computer.

    B. Use a grounding strap.

    C. Restore the most recent backup.

    D. If no recent backup of data and/or the operating system exists, perform a backup.

3. According to troubleshooting theory, what should you do after establishing a theory of probably cause?

    A. Identify the problem.

    B. Test the theory to determine the cause.

    C. Document findings, actions, and outcomes.

    D. Establish a plan of action to resolve the problem.

Troubleshooting Motherboards, RAM, CPUs, and Power

4. Reorder the following troubleshooting steps from the least intrusive to the most intrusive.

    A. Check proper seating of internal components.

    B. Check for proper connections to external devices.

    C. Check installation: drivers, driver settings, and physical settings.

    D. Check for appropriate external components.

5. You want to narrow down the source of a problem to one of what two broad categories?

    A. Power or data

    B. Operating system or application

    C. Motherboard or component

    D. Hardware or software

6. How do you narrow down the problem to one hardware component?
   A. Remove the data cables.
   B. Run specialized diagnostics.
   C. Swap each suspect component with a known good one.
   D. Restart the computer.

7. After you apply and test a solution, what should you have the user do as part of evaluating the solution? Select all that apply.
   A. First, restart the computer and device (if appropriate).
   B. First, disconnect the problem component.
   C. Test the solution and all commonly used applications.
   D. Print out the user manual.

8. What should you do if you are unsure if a problem is limited to the single application that was in use at the time the problem occurred?
   A. Remove and reinstall the application.
   B. Upgrade the application.
   C. Use more than one application to perform the actions that resulted in the problem.
   D. Upgrade the driver.

9. A customer reports that the computer spontaneously reboots and sometimes will not start at all. Furthermore, even when the computer does start, the fan does not make as much noise as before. What is the likely cause of these problems?
   A. The power supply
   B. The system board
   C. The processor
   D. The RAM

10. Which of the following is the safest and easiest device for measuring the voltage output from a power supply?
    A. Multimeter
    B. Power supply tester
    C. UPS
    D. Power Options

11. Your computer consistently loses its date and time settings. Which procedure will you use to solve the problem?

    A. Replace the battery.

    B. Flash the battery using a manufacturer-provided disk.

    C. Use the computer's AC adapter to recharge the battery.

    D. Access the CMOS setting programs at startup and select the low-power option.

12. Which component is typically associated with a 3*xx* BIOS error code?

    A. Motherboard

    B. Keyboard

    C. Processor

    D. RAM

Troubleshooting Storage Devices

13. Which of the following symptoms is not caused by a RAM error?

    A. The POST cannot be completed.

    B. When you turn on the computer, nothing happens.

    C. The system reports a read/write failure.

    D. The RAM count at bootup does not match the capacity of the installed RAM.

Troubleshooting I/O Devices

14. Your video display is blank. Which of the following should you do first?

    A. Swap the display with a known good one.

    B. Replace the video adapter with a known good one.

    C. Check the power and data cables.

    D. Check the seating of the video adapter.

15. A user reports that the mouse pointer does not move smoothly across the screen. Which of the following is most likely to remedy the problem?

    A. Reinstall the mouse driver.

    B. Ensure that the mouse cable connects securely to the computer.

    C. Replace the mouse with a trackball. Ensure there are no IRQ conflicts between the mouse and another device.

    D. Clean the mouse.

16. Which of the following is a possible cause of a display going into low-resolution VGA Mode?

    A. Incorrect brightness setting

    B. Lit pixel

    C. Corrupt video driver

    D. Disconnected cable

17. Which of the following is a possible cause of a display suddenly shutting down?

    A. Overheating

    B. Incorrect resolution

    C. EMI

    D. Incorrect brightness setting

18. Which of the following corrects display color problems?

    A. EMI

    B. Inverter

    C. Rollback Driver

    D. Calibration

19. Which of the following can cause flickering on a CRT display?

    A. EMI

    B. Inverter

    C. Rollback Driver

    D. Calibration

Preventive Maintenance Techniques

20. Which cleaning product blows dirt and dust out of PC components?

    A. Antistatic display cleaner

    B. Canned compressed air

    C. Liquid cleaning compound

    D. Antistatic vacuum cleaner

SELF TEST ANSWERS

Preparing for Troubleshooting

1. ☑ **A.** POST card is correct. You must install this into an expansion slot. Then, when the computer boots up, it performs advanced diagnostics and displays the results on a LED and through indicator lights.

   ☒ **B** and **D** are incorrect because, although these are examples of hardware tools, neither is insertable into an expansion slot. **C,** video adapter, is incorrect because this is not a hardware diagnostics tool, but a common PC component.

2. ☑ **D.** If no recent backup of data and/or the operating system exists, perform a backup. This is correct because you do not want to risk losing the user's data.

   ☒ **A,** turn off the computer, is incorrect because it is rather irrelevant, although after taking care of the backup, you may want to restart the computer. **B,** use a grounding strap, is incorrect because until you have narrowed down the cause, you do not know if this will be necessary. You must do a backup before you reach this point. **C,** restore the most recent backup, is incorrect because you have no idea if this is even necessary at this point.

3. ☑ **B.** Test the theory to determine the cause.

   ☒ **A,** identify the problem, is incorrect because you should do this before you establish a theory of probable cause. **C** is incorrect because documenting findings, actions, and outcomes is the very last procedure (sixth) of troubleshooting theory, while the procedure in question is the third procedure. **D,** establish a plan of action to resolve the problem, is incorrect because this comes after testing the theory to determine the cause.

Troubleshooting Motherboards, RAM, CPUs, and Power

4. ☑ **B.** Check for proper connections to external devices. **D,** Check for appropriate external component. **C,** Check installation: drivers, driver settings, and physical settings. **A.** Check proper seating of internal components.

   ☒ Any other order is incorrect.

5. ☑ **D.** Hardware and software are the two broad categories of problem sources.

   ☒ **A,** power or data, is incorrect because, although you may have problems in these areas, they are not the two broad categories of problem sources. **B,** operating system or application, is incorrect because these are both types of software, and software is just one of the two broad categories of problem sources. **C,** motherboard or component, is incorrect because these are both types of hardware, and hardware is just one of the two categories of problem sources.

6. ☑ **C.** Swapping each suspect component with a known good one is correct because this will narrow down a hardware problem to one component.

☒ **A,** remove the data cables, is incorrect because, although this may be part of removing a component, this alone will not help you narrow down the problem to one component. **B,** run specialized diagnostics, is incorrect because specialized diagnostics lead to general areas, not specific components. **D,** restart the computer, is incorrect because restarting will not indicate one component, although it might cause the problem to disappear.

7. ☑ **A,** first, restart the computer and device (if appropriate), and **C,** test the solution and all commonly used applications, are both correct. The user should perform these steps to confirm the fix works and to assure herself that the changes you made were not harmful.

☒ **B,** first, disconnect the problem component, is incorrect because without the problem component you cannot evaluate the solution. **D,** print out the user manual, is incorrect because that has little to do with evaluating the solution.

8. ☑ **C.** Use more than one application to perform the actions that resulted in the problem is correct. If the problem only occurs in the one application, then focus on that application.

☒ **A,** remove and reinstall the application, is incorrect because, although this may be a fix for the problem, you must first determine that the problem only occurs with that application before doing something so drastic. **B,** upgrade the application, is incorrect because, although this may be a fix for the problem, you must first narrow it down to the one application. **D,** upgrade the driver, is incorrect because, although this may be a solution, you must first narrow down the cause to specific hardware before upgrading the driver.

9. ☑ **A.** The power supply is the most likely cause of these symptoms. When a power supply begins to fail, it often manifests in a number of different, sporadic symptoms. If the power supply's fan stops working, the computer will overheat and spontaneously reboot itself. If the components are still excessively hot when the system restarts, the computer may not start at all.

☒ **B,** the system board, **C,** the processor, and **D,** the RAM, are all incorrect. Failure of these components does not cause the specific set of symptoms mentioned in the question. A RAM failure will not cause the computer to reboot (unless all RAM fails). Although an overheated processor could cause the system to reboot, it would not be associated with the lack of noise from the power supply fan.

10. ☑ **B.** A power supply tester is the safest and easiest device for measuring the voltage output from a power supply.

☒ **A,** multimeter, is incorrect because it requires much more knowledge of electricity to use and is a more complex device. **C,** UPS, is incorrect because a UPS is not a device for measuring voltage output from a power supply, but an uninterruptible power supply device. **D,** Power Options, is incorrect because Power Options is a Windows Control Panel applet for managing the power-saving features of your computer.

11. ☑ **A.** You should replace the battery. When the computer "forgets" the time and date, it is most likely because the CMOS battery, which normally maintains these settings, is getting low on power and you must replace it.

    ☒ **B** is incorrect because it suggests flashing the battery. This procedure (flashing) applies to the upgrade of a BIOS chip, not a CMOS battery. **C** is incorrect because it suggests recharging the battery with the computer's AC adapter. Although this procedure will work with a portable system battery, you cannot recharge CMOS batteries with an AC adapter. **D** is incorrect because it suggests selecting a "low-power" option in the CMOS settings program. Any low-power setting in the CMOS settings refers to the function of the computer itself, not to the CMOS battery. You cannot adjust the amount of power the CMOS chip draws from its battery.

12. ☑ **B.** The keyboard is typically associated with a 3xx BIOS error code. When the computer is started, the BIOS performs a POST test, which checks for the presence and function of certain components. If a keyboard error, such as a missing cable or stuck key, is detected, the BIOS typically reports a 3xx error code.

    ☒ **A,** motherboard, and **C,** processor, are incorrect because a 1xx error code typically indicates these errors, if detected by the BIOS. **D,** RAM, is incorrect because memory errors are typically associated with 2xx error codes.

Troubleshooting Storage Devices

13. ☑ **C.** The system reports a read/write failure. This message is not associated with a memory error, but with a disk error.

    ☒ **A, B,** and **D** are incorrect because these are all typical symptoms of bad memory. If the memory has totally failed, the BIOS cannot conduct or complete the POST—it is also possible that the BIOS might not even be able to initiate the processor. This problem might make it appear that the computer does absolutely nothing when turned on. A bad memory stick may not cause an error, but will not work, and if you watch the memory count during bootup, you may notice the count does not match the installed RAM.

Troubleshooting I/O Devices

14. ☑ **C.** Check the power and data cables is correct because it is the least intrusive action. If this does not resolve the problem, check the brightness setting, and then continue to **A, D,** and **B,** in that order.

    ☒ **A,** swap the display with a known good one, is incorrect because this is more trouble than simply checking the cables. **B,** replace the video adapter with a known good one, and **D,** check the seating of the video adapter, are incorrect because these very intrusive actions and should wait until you have performed less intrusive actions.

15. ☑ **D.** Cleaning the mouse is most likely to remedy the problem of a mouse pointer that does not move smoothly on the screen.
☒ **A,** reinstalling the mouse driver, is incorrect because if the mouse does not have a proper driver, it will not work at all. Driver problems for any device will cause that device to stop functioning altogether or to work sporadically. **B,** ensuring the mouse cable connects securely to the computer, is also incorrect. If the mouse does not connect to the computer, it will not respond at all. If the mouse connector is loose, the operation of the mouse could be sporadic, working at some times, and not working at all on other occasions. **C,** replacing the mouse with a trackball, is also incorrect. Although this solution may actually resolve the problem caused by a dirty mouse, it is more extreme than cleaning the mouse.

16. ☑ **C.** A corrupt video driver can cause a display to go into low-resolution VGA mode.
☒ **A,** incorrect brightness setting, is incorrect because this would only cause the display to be too bright or too dim. **B,** lit pixel, is incorrect because this would only cause a pixel to constantly display just one of its three colors; it would not result in VGA Mode. **D,** a disconnected cable, would simply result in a blank display.

17. ☑ **A.** Overheating can cause a display to suddenly shut down.
☒ **B,** incorrect resolution, is incorrect. This would not cause the display to shut down. **C,** EMI, is incorrect because this can cause flickering problems with a CRT; it does not cause a display to shut down. **D,** incorrect brightness setting, is incorrect because this would only cause the display to appear too dim or too bright.

18. ☑ **D.** Calibration is the adjustment of the color on a device, such as a video display, to ensure the accuracy of the colors.
☒ **A,** EMI, is incorrect because this is a cause of flickering problems, not a solution for color problems. **B,** inverter, is incorrect because this component of an FPD converts AC power to DC power. **C,** Rollback Driver, is incorrect because this just removes an updated driver.

19. ☑ **A.** EMI (electromagnetic interference) is a cause of flickering on a CRT display.
☒ **B,** inverter, is incorrect because this component of an FPD converts AC power to DC power. **C,** Rollback Driver, is incorrect because this just removes an updated driver. **D,** calibration, is the adjustment of the color on a device, such as a video display, to ensure the accuracy of the colors.

Preventive Maintenance Techniques

20. ☑ **B.** Canned compressed air is the cleaning product used to blow dirt and dust out of PC components. The drawback to this is that it can also blow dirt and dust into components, and if used improperly, the liquid Freon within the can could spill onto the skin or computer components, causing injury or damage.

☒ **A,** antistatic display cleaner, and **C,** liquid cleaning compound, are both incorrect because you use these wet cleaning products to wipe off the screen and other surfaces. **D,** antistatic vacuum cleaner, is incorrect because it draws the dust in, rather than blowing it out. This more expensive product is preferred for cleaning out a PC.

12

Troubleshooting and Preventive Maintenance for Laptops

A s with desktop computers, the most common procedures that computer technicians perform on laptops are troubleshooting and resolving problems. Understanding the technologies of PCs in general, as well as troubleshooting theory, diagnostic techniques, procedures, and use of tools, are all required to work with laptop computers. We presented these in earlier chapters, and Chapter 7 described the components installed in laptops and how to repair or replace many of them. Chapter 7 also detailed an important area for the CompTIA A+ Exam 802 Objective 4.8: the disassembly and reassembly of a laptop. In this chapter, you will explore the remaining topics in that exam objective, which include how to detect and troubleshoot common symptoms of problems related to laptops.

CERTIFICATION OBJECTIVE

■ **802: 4.8** *Given a scenario, troubleshoot and repair common laptop issues while adhering to the appropriate procedures*

In Chapter 7 we covered a portion of CompTIA Exam 802 Objective 4.8 when we described the disassembly and reassembly processes for laptops. Then, as we described installing and upgrading laptops and how to use Power Options, we could not seem to resist dropping little troubleshooting hints. For instance, when describing the use of FN keys, we just had to explain that if your display or wireless doesn't work, you should check the appropriate laptop function key before looking for other causes. Now we are left with tying the laptop troubleshooting objectives together, which we will do here. The troubleshooting topics left to cover are 12 common symptoms. This seems simple, except that some of these symptoms have more than one possible cause, so we decided to incorporate these symptoms under subtopics that make sense to us, and we hope it is helpful to you. We also added some troubleshooting symptoms and solutions that are beyond the exam topics. We hope these are helpful to you on the job.

Troubleshooting Laptops

Laptops are much more difficult and costly to repair than desktop PCs, and to make matters worse, they are also much more likely to need repairs because they

exam

ⓦatch

Be sure you understand laptop disassembly and reassembly processes, including documenting and labeling cable and screw locations, organizing parts, and using manufacturer documentation, as well as appropriate tools.

get in harm's way more often than the typical desktop computer. The busy traveler can easily drop one, bang it into things, and so on, all of which can cause damage. When it comes to troubleshooting laptops, you will use the same skills and procedures described in Chapter 11. So, you will want to refer back to that chapter from time to time while reading this chapter. In particular, read through the section titled "Preparing for Troubleshooting." Chapter 11 also includes many symptoms and probable solutions

involving components common to both PCs and laptops. They concern system lockups, shutdowns, overheating, and problems related to major components, so we'll examine the laptop-specific problems you may encounter when working with alternating current (AC) adapters and batteries, displays, input devices, and built-in wireless adapters.

Power Problems

Laptops are vulnerable to the same power problems that plague desktop PCs, but they are also susceptible to a group of problems unique to laptops involving rechargeable batteries and the external AC power adapters that help put the portability into laptops.

AC Adapter Power Problems

Symptoms listed in CompTIA Exam 802 Objective 4.8 that are possibly caused by AC adapters include no display (blank display), battery not charging, and no power. AC adapter problems fall into two areas: damage or failure of the original AC adapter, and damage to the computer due to use of the wrong AC adapter. To understand these problems, we will first consider the requirements for the correct AC adapter in terms of voltage, amperage, and polarity, and then look at power-related problem scenarios.

Never, under any circumstances, casually substitute another AC adapter for the one that came with your laptop unless you are sure it will not harm your computer. The most important features you are looking for are the laptop's direct current (DC) input voltage, amperage, and polarity requirements.

DC input requirements may be in the neighborhood of 19.5 volts and 2.15 amps. Labels on the laptop and the AC adapter show the positive or negative polarity of the laptop power connector, which must be compatible with the AC adapter's connector polarity. Figure 12-1 shows the engraved label by a laptop's AC connector indicating that it requires DC input of 19.5 volts and the outer portion of the plug must have negative polarity, while the inner plug must have positive polarity.

Now look for a label on the AC adapter, and ensure that the output from this device, and the polarity of its connector, match those of the laptop. Figure 12-2 shows the label on an AC adapter that is a match for the AC connector shown in Figure 12-1. Connecting an adapter that does not meet the laptop's requirements will damage the laptop. Depending on just which parameter is wrong, you may destroy the laptop's power components or the laptop motherboard and its components.

Some power adapters include an automatic circuit breaker that trips when it detects an input power overload. This breaker works like the circuit breaker in your home; you need to reset it before it will allow power through again. With some AC adapters, you do this simply by unplugging the adapter for a few minutes before reconnecting it. Some laptops have a reset button that you may use. If so, follow the instructions, which may include unplugging the power cord from the laptop and removing the laptop's battery before resetting.

FIGURE 12-1

The laptop power connector is labeled for polarity.

FIGURE 12-2

The label on
an AC power
adapter

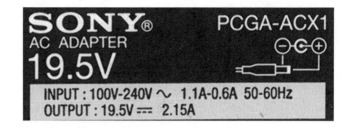

Recall that the AC adapter converts the AC input from the wall outlet to DC current, and the laptop's DC controller monitors and regulates the power usage, allocating the correct voltage (typically 5 volts, 12 volts, or 3.3 volts) to the various internal components. The laptop handles power to the liquid crystal display (LCD) display separately within the laptop, using an inverter to convert the DC input to the AC power required by the display backlight. Therefore, if you believe power has failed to the LCD display but you can hear the fan running in the main system, you will focus on how power gets to the display and troubleshoot the inverter and power connectors between the main system and the display.

Hardware Power Switch Issues

Do not assume that pressing the power button on a laptop (or desktop PC, for that matter) automatically turns it off. One of the many configuration options available through Windows' Power Options is a setting for what occurs when you press the power button. In Windows XP, the choices are Do Nothing, Ask Me What To Do, Standby, and Shut Down. If you have enabled Hibernate through Power Options, Hibernate replaces Standby. Beginning in Windows Vista, the choices are Do Nothing, Sleep, Hibernate, or Shut Down. Imagine how each of these settings might confuse an unwary laptop user. For instance, if the power button puts the laptop into a sleep mode other than Hibernate, the laptop is not truly powered down and still requires battery power. In some laptops, this situation comes to light when a user complains that the laptop is warm even when turned off, especially if it is in a carrying case. Ask this user if he is simply pressing the power off button and what he sees when he does press it. If he sees a message about preparing for Standby or Sleep, then his laptop is not configured to shut down when the power button is pressed.

Someone who is on the go all day, needing to access her laptop quickly between visits to clients, will prefer having the power button configured for a sleep mode. This user must learn that this state still requires power, however, and if she is running the laptop on battery power alone, she should watch the battery level and be sure to plug the laptop in to recharge the battery when it gets low. Learn about the battery alarms in the next section.

Battery Problems

Like the average car owner, the typical laptop owner doesn't worry much about the battery until it becomes a problem. On a daily basis, that means watching the battery indicator and recharging the battery when it gets low. To help you keep track of the battery level, turn on and configure the battery alarms. You can set an action for each of these alarms, such as sounding an alarm, displaying a message, putting the computer into a power-saving mode, shutting it down, or having it run a program before shutting down. You can use most of these options together, with the exception of the choice of a sleep mode or shut down.

Another way to track the battery level is by using the power meter normally appearing in the system tray on a laptop. You can turn this feature on or off in the Power Options applet. Power meter shows the power state. It will show a power plug when the computer is running on AC power and a battery-shaped meter when it is running on battery.

When you believe the laptop has a battery problem, first make sure the battery is installed properly and is charging. A rechargeable battery has a limited lifetime, beyond which its ability to hold a charge diminishes until it cannot hold a charge at all. In this case, the power meter may show a Not Present status, even when a battery is physically present. If a battery fails to fully charge and is about two years old or older, you may need to replace it.

If a newer battery fails, check your warranty or extended warranty, which will cover a laptop battery for a longer period than the standard warranty. You may be entitled to a replacement battery from the manufacturer. If the battery is one that has only two or three connections, you can test it with a multimeter set to read DC volts. A reading much less than the battery rating probably indicates a bad battery. Unfortunately, many laptop batteries have multiple power connectors and no guidance as to which connectors should provide what power, so testing them can be difficult. Sometimes the laptop's manual will indicate the voltages at the various terminals, but not always. If you determine that a battery has failed, replace it as described in Chapter 7.

Power-Related Scenarios

Understanding the basics of AC adapters and batteries will serve you well when faced with symptoms pointing to power problems. The most obvious is when the laptop will not power up. As you learned in Chapter 11, you should always approach troubleshooting systematically, and be sure you observe all the symptoms.

If a laptop will not power up at all when plugged into an AC power source, suspect the AC power adapter. But before you go down that road, first ask, "What has changed since it last successfully started up?" If the hardware has changed, then remove any new hardware devices installed since the laptop last started up normally. This is especially true of memory modules.

If the laptop starts up after removing any new hardware, then check with the manufacturer of the new hardware and/or with the manufacturer of the laptop. The hardware may be incompatible with the laptop.

If no new hardware was added since the last time the laptop started up normally, check out one of the usual suspects: an external display unit. Do you hear normal fan sounds from your laptop? If you are using an external display, keyboard, and mouse with the laptop screen toggled off, the computer may be powering up, but because no image appears on the external display, you may have jumped to the conclusion that the computer failed. Troubleshoot the display by asking these questions:

- Is it simply in a sleep mode?
- Is it turned off?
- Is the contrast or brightness control set too dark?
- Is it connected? Is it powered up?
- Is the display mode switch set to an external display?

If you are using the laptop's integrated display, use similar questions to eliminate it as the problem area.

If you have eliminated new hardware or display problems, continue through the following list of actions until you have either found the source of the problem or resolved it and the computer starts normally:

- Make sure the AC adapter is the one that came with your computer. Using the wrong AC adapter can damage your laptop or other device.
- An AC adapter may (but not always) have a light-emitting diode (LED) indicator light to show that it is receiving power. Check for this light on the adapter as a way to verify it is receiving AC power from the power source.
- Check that the adapter is securely plugged into the laptop, connected directly to a working power outlet (without an extension cord or other device while troubleshooting), and that the power switch is turned on. Check the power indicator light on the laptop to see that it is receiving power.

- If the laptop worked when connected directly to a power outlet but was previously plugged into a power strip or a power protection device, such as a surge protector or uninterruptible power supply (UPS), troubleshoot that device. Ensure it, too, is plugged in and the power to this device is turned on. If the circuit breaker in a power strip has tripped, you may need to reset it. After resolving a problem with the device, reconnect the laptop and test again.

- Make sure power cords show no sign of damage. If there are such signs, replace the cord or the entire device if the cable is not removable.

- Another way to verify that your AC adapter is or is not working is to swap it with another identical power supply. If the laptop works with the swapped AC adapter, then you have isolated the problem to the AC adapter.

- Use a multimeter and test the computer end of the AC adapter cable to check the output that the computer is receiving. It should be producing the DC voltage specified on the label or very close to it (see Exercise 12-1 and Figure 12-3).

FIGURE 12-3

A multimeter testing the power from the input line to the AC adapter

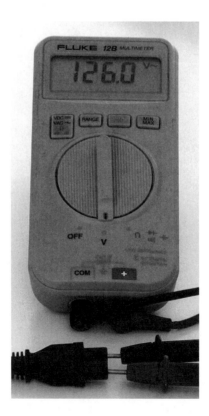

- In order to protect itself and the computer, an AC adapter may turn itself off after detecting a power overage. This depends on the AC adapter's design. Check your user manual for how to reset the AC adapter.

- If you suspect the power outlet is bad, test it simply by plugging in another device, such as a lamp. You may also check it with a multimeter by inserting the probes into the socket and checking the voltage. Typical voltage in the United States is 115–120 Volts/60 Hz cycle (see Figure 12-3).

on the
()o b

The typical voltage mentioned in the text is based on the present North American power standard—the old standard was 110 V. European and Asian countries have different power standards, but most have moved from 220 V to the present standard of 230–240 V/50 Hz.

- If you have not been able to isolate the problem after performing the preceding checks, disconnect the AC adapter and remove the battery. Wait an entire minute, reinstall the battery, reconnect the AC adapter, and then turn on the power and see if the laptop starts up.

- If it still fails to start up, disconnect the AC adapter and remove the battery. Leave the battery out but close the compartment door, if there is one, reconnect the AC adapter to both the laptop and the power outlet, and try to start the computer again.

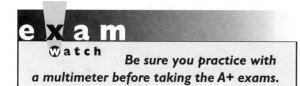

ⓦatch **Be sure you practice with a multimeter before taking the A+ exams.**

EXERCISE 12-1

Using a Multimeter to Test an AC Adapter

In this exercise, you will verify the DC power output of an AC adapter. For this exercise, you will need a multimeter and an AC adapter with a single plug on the computer end.

1. Unplug the AC adapter from the laptop, but leave it plugged into the wall outlet.

2. Examine the label on the AC adapter and write down the voltage output. Note the polarity and which is positive and negative: the tip of the plug versus the outside of the plug.

FIGURE 12-4

Using a
multimeter to
test the output of
an AC adapter

3. Set the multimeter to "Volts DC."

4. Place the positive probe on the positive portion of the plug and the negative probe on the negative portion of the probe (see Figure 12-4).

5. The voltage should be close to that shown in the AC adapter label or just one or two volts more.

Other Startup Problems

A laptop can fail at startup for reasons other than loss of power. Failure can be due to a variety of causes, both hardware- and software-related. In this section, we will look at hardware errors, limiting our examination of software errors to those related to BIOS setup. Learn about startup problems related to Windows operating systems in Chapter 13.

Laptop Fails at Startup

When a laptop fails at startup, take the following steps:

1. If you have added a new peripheral, remove the peripheral.
2. If you have eliminated power as a problem, remove all unneeded peripherals and add them back one at a time, attempting to restart after each addition.
3. If you cannot isolate the problem, the motherboard or one of its integrated components may be failing. Laptops are not user serviceable. Check your warranty to see if the suspected component is still under warranty. If you purchased an extended warranty that is still in effect, this is the time to use it.
4. If you do not have a warranty in effect but have a persistent problem that you cannot solve, check with the manufacturer. The easiest way to do this is to locate its Website and research problems associated with your laptop. You may discover your laptop is part of a recall involving the component that has failed.

on the job

Although we emphasize that you should have a laptop serviced by the manufacturer or authorized service center, it is not always practical to do so. If your laptop does not have a warranty and you feel it is worth the extra effort, check out local or Web-based repair services. Some businesses even specialize in replacement LCD panels for many laptop models. If you choose to go this route, know that there are no guarantees the repair will be worth the cost or that it will be successful, especially if you choose to do the repair yourself.

Laptop Fails During POST

If Windows fails to start and a text-mode screen displays, do not panic. The power-on self-test (POST) detected a problem. Simply read the information on the screen and follow any instructions. In the example shown in Figure 12-5, the BIOS hardware monitor found a problem, and the message on the error screen directs you to enter the power setup menu to see the details. Perhaps the hardware monitor detected a high temperature in the CPU or motherboard, which can indicate a failing cooling fan that is allowing the system to overheat.

on the job

This scenario can also occur on a desktop PC.

FIGURE 12-5

An error detected during the POST

```
BIOS v10.0
Copyright (c) 1984-2006

ACPI BIOS Revision 1205

Intel (R) Pentium 4 3000 MHz
Memory Test: 524288K OK

BIOS Extension V2.0A
Initialize Plug and Play Cards...
PNP Init Completed

Detecting Primary Master ...    MaxDrive 5D090H5
Detecting Primary Slave ...     None
Detecting Secondary Master ...  DVD-RW
Detecting Secondary Slave ...   CD-RW

Hardware Monitor found an error. Enter Power setup menu for details

Press F1 to continue, F2 to enter SETUP
```

Video Symptoms and Possible Causes and Solutions

Video issues with laptops are especially problematic because the user is often away from the office with little control over the environment and with many distractions—making it even more difficult to troubleshoot the problem. Therefore, become familiar with common symptoms and their causes.

External Display Is Blank

When an external display is blank, first move the mouse or press a key on the keyboard to ensure the computer is not simply in a power-saving state that has turned off the monitor. Then check that the display properly connects to the laptop, is plugged into power, and is powered on. If it is properly connected and powered on (look for a power indicator light on the display), then press the FN key while also pressing the function key that doubles as the DISPLAY MODE toggle key, as described in Chapter 7.

No Display

When a laptop LCD display fails, as with an external display, check that the display is not in sleep mode by moving the mouse or pressing a key, and check the DISPLAY MODE toggle key. Then assure yourself that it is not a power problem (see the preceding section). If the display is still not working, check for other sources, as described next.

Damaged Wiring   The wires for a laptop LCD panel must pass through the hinge of the lid and are subject to a great deal of flexing. Therefore, in some cases, the wiring comes loose at this point. Loose wires can cause a dim or blank display. Manufacturers of conventional laptops have generally solved the wire-through-the-hinge problem, but some older tablet PCs still have issues with this. They resembled very small laptops, and the hinge on these systems was more complex than on a standard laptop to allow the lid to both open and rotate into "tablet" position to cover the keyboard so the user can hold the PC like a physical clipboard. The manufacturer or a qualified repair center must correct these problems. Most newer tablets do not have a keyboard, and so do not have these problems.

Temperature Problems   Is the laptop operating in a very hot or very cold room? The liquid crystal material in an LCD panel is sensitive to extremes of hot and cold. If a display that is exposed to temperature extremes goes blank, move the laptop to a heated or air-conditioned room with a moderate temperature and wait an hour before trying it again. If the display appears to work correctly after adjusting the temperature, take steps to avoid the problem in the future.

   If you must transport a laptop in extremely cold or extremely hot conditions, do not power it up until you can place it in a room with a moderate temperature and allow it to warm up or cool down.

Backlight Problems   The backlight in a laptop LCD screen consists of several components. These include *cold cathode fluorescent lighting (CCFL)* tubes, positioned at the top, sides, and sometimes behind the screen, and a white diffusion panel behind the LCD that scatters the light evenly. The fluorescent tubes are thinner than a pencil and very fragile. For this reason, if you handle a laptop roughly or drop it, one or more of these tubes can break, causing the display to dim or go totally dark if all the tubes break. Replacing a fluorescent tube is a very difficult task; you also face the task of removing the broken tubes, which may contain mercury or other heavy metal that is equally dangerous to work with. For this reason, we do not recommend that anyone but a highly trained technician take on this task. Newer laptops are lit by LEDs that are much less susceptible to physical shock damage. LEDs have a very long service life and have become the screen illumination of choice.

Video Adapter Problems   The easiest way to test a laptop's integrated video adapter is to plug in an external display and see if it works. Plug it in, power it up, and wait a minute. If nothing appears on the screen, press the FN key and the DISPLAY MODE toggle key. If you have the same problems with the external display, then you have isolated the problem to the video adapter. Check your warranty to see if this problem is covered. If it is covered, then take the steps to have the laptop serviced by the manufacturer or an authorized repair site. If not covered by warranty, you must decide whether the laptop is worth taking it to a repair center at your or your company's expense or whether you want to attempt to replace it. See the discussion on replacing a video adapter in Chapter 7.

Problems with Display Quality

If you have display quality symptoms, such as screen artifacts, flickering image, or dim display, refer to the description in Chapter 11 of these symptoms and their possible causes and solutions.

Input Devices

If you have problems with an external mouse, refer back to Chapter 11, where we described some common problems and solutions. The specialized laptop input devices, such as touchpads and the integrated keyboard, can have certain problems described here.

Touchpad

Touchpad problems fall into two categories: problems with touchpad functionality and problems with accidental use of the touchpad.

Problems with Touchpad Functionality   Sometimes the touchpad will fail to work, or the touchpad control of the pointer will become erratic. In these cases, restart the computer and try again. Rebooting often takes care of the problem. If it occurs frequently, make note of the application software in use at the time. The software may be incompatible with the touchpad driver and the application. Check the laptop manufacturer's Website for any updates to the touchpad driver.

Problems with Accidental Use of the Touchpad   The touchpads on laptops cause problems for some users who cannot seem to avoid unintentionally resting their hands on the touchpad or brushing their hands or fingers over it when using the keyboard. This can cause a variety of problems, depending on what application is open and has the focus at the time. For instance, while the user is typing in a document, the pointer may suddenly jump to another part of the page, and you will insert the typed text where it does not belong. Or it may overwrite or delete text, or applications may even open or close without the user intending them to. The result

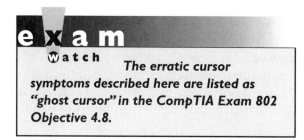

The erratic cursor symptoms described here are listed as "ghost cursor" in the CompTIA Exam 802 Objective 4.8.

is confusing to the user who is not aware of touching the touchpad.

Check the Mouse applet in Control Panel, which opens the Mouse Properties dialog box. On a laptop with a touchpad, this should include settings to control how the touchpad works. Check for a setting that controls the sensitivity of the touchpad, so it does not respond to a soft, accidental contact. You may find one such setting under a Tapping tab in a section labeled Typing. Selecting Tap Off When Typing will disable the touchpad when keys are pressed and provides for a configurable delay after the last key is pressed. Manufacturers use different terminology for this, so you will have to look for it and experiment. Figure 12-6 shows the Properties dialog box for the Synaptics touchpad, accessed via the Settings button on the Device Settings tab of Mouse Properties.

FIGURE 12-6 The Properties dialog box for the Synaptics touchpad

If nothing else works, disable the touchpad and attach a more conventional pointing device, such as a mouse or trackball. For the user who travels, this means one more piece of equipment to take along, but it may be well worth the trouble to avoid this annoyance. Check the laptop's documentation to find out how to disable the touchpad; some laptops actually have a switch next to the touchpad to disable it. If you cannot disable the touchpad, just tape a piece of card stock over it as a means of mechanically disabling it.

Keyboard Failure

If a laptop keyboard fails completely, or if some of the keys fail, you may need to replace it. However, some problems that appear to be keyboard related are actually not. For instance, when pressing a key has an unexpected result, such as displaying the wrong character or multiple characters, first check with the manufacturer to see if this is a problem related to your laptop, because in the past some models had such a problem, and the manufacturer offered a BIOS update. Alternatively, the problem may be that the computer is overheating. Check out the section later in this chapter titled "Cooling Issues."

Sticking Keys

If a key on your laptop physically stays depressed, it will cause a single character to repeat across the screen. If the key will not return to its normal raised position, it may simply be dirty, in which case, you should clean the keyboard carefully to release the key. First try turning the laptop upside down over a waste basket and very gently shaking it to remove the dirt. If that doesn't help, use canned air, taking the normal precautions to not tilt the can too far and spill the propellant, and being careful where you are blowing the dust. After which, you may want to try the waste basket procedure again to make sure that dislodged dirt doesn't stay on the keyboard. Alternatively use an antistatic vacuum—no need for a waste basket then, until the bag is full.

 on the **Job**

Don't remove the individual keys from a keyboard because they are very difficult to reinstall. Of course, if you have a laptop that is badly soiled and unusable, you may want to take the chance. First, look online for a technical manual for the laptop for instructions.

Keyboard Usage Issues

Laptop keyboards present special problems: first, because some keys have more functions than desktop keyboards, and second, because these functions are squeezed into a smaller space. Problems with laptop keyboards often result from users not remembering that they have turned a certain feature on or off (recall the DISPLAY MODE key problem discussed previously) or have accidentally pressed a combination of keys that enables or disables some function. If strange things are happening as you type, take a look at the keyboard, looking for indicator lights. If a Num Lock light is lit, you may have turned on the embedded keypad feature available on some laptops, as described in Chapter 7, and you find yourself entering numbers in place of some of the letters you thought you were entering.

When using a laptop for the first time, familiarize yourself with the special function keys by experimenting with them. Close all open applications before using any of these key combinations. At the very minimum, be sure to click an empty area of the desktop so your keystrokes do not affect an open application. We describe here a few common keys and their associated problems next. The names provided here are not standard, and keys with similar functions may have different names.

Display Mode Key   We described problems with the DISPLAY MODE key earlier in this chapter. Any time the display is blank but you can clearly hear the fan and see indicator lights, press the DISPLAY MODE key combination to switch modes and see if this is the cause of the problem. When you first attach an external display, it should be automatically detected and used, but if not, try toggling the DISPLAY MODE key.

Speaker On/Off Key   Another common special key is the speaker on/off key. Some laptop keyboards identify the speaker key by a speaker icon with an "X" over it. This may appear in blue on one of the function keys, such as the F3 key. When the FN key is combined with the speaker on/off key, it toggles the speaker on and off. This feature is handy on a trip when you want to quickly turn off the speaker so you do not bother your fellow travelers. The problem comes when you either forget that you toggled the speakers off or you accidentally toggled them off. Therefore, if you believe the inboard speakers are not working, first look for the speaker on/off key.

Speaker Volume Key   Similarly, some laptops include a speaker volume key. When the FN key is combined with the speaker volume key and either the up (↑) or right (→) arrow key, the volume will get louder. To lower the volume, press the FN key and the speaker volume key along with either the left (←) or down (↓) arrow key. This changes the speaker volume at the hardware level, bypassing Windows' volume control. Therefore, if you have no sound and using the Windows volume control has no effect, try turning the volume up using the speaker volume key.

Display Brightness Key The DISPLAY BRIGHTNESS key may appear as a sun icon on one of the function keys. Pressing the FN key and this key plus either the up (↑) or right (→) arrow key will brighten the display. Pressing the FN key and the DISPLAY BRIGHTNESS key plus either the left (←) or down (↓) arrow key will darken the display.

exam
watch

Pay special attention to the problems caused by the laptop's portability features, such as the special FN key combinations that change modes for *the display, speaker, and other components. If these modes have been changed, it may appear to be a more serious problem.*

Wireless Problems

Wireless cards in laptops can have many of the same problems as other types of cards. Unless the card is built in and not physically accessible, you should always check that it is connected properly. Beyond the physical connections and complete failure of a wireless adapter, wireless problems specific to laptop computers come in two main categories: antenna problems and interference problems.

Antenna Problems

Many laptops today come with built-in wireless Wi-Fi and Bluetooth network adapters, with a built-in antenna usually located in the lid. They will usually have a hardware switch at the side or front to turn on or turn off the internal Wi-Fi and Bluetooth adapter, or at least the antenna. Accidently turning this switch on or off is easy. Therefore, if a laptop user reports that he suddenly does not have a wireless signal, check the hardware switch. Its label may read "Wi-Fi" or it may have a radiating antenna symbol on the laptop case. Change the switch position, open the wireless configuration utility, and ensure that the configuration is correct. More on configuring and troubleshooting Wi-Fi in Chapters 15 and 16.

Bluetooth uses short-range signals for use with peripherals, such as keyboard and mice, and for synchronizing with various handheld devices. Therefore, if you are having a problem with one of these devices connecting, first ensure that the laptop's antenna is enabled, and then check the battery and on-off switch (if present) on the device.

As for Wi-Fi connection problems, a laptop's built-in antenna may be adequate in many instances, but it usually lacks the flexibility and power of some add-on external antennas. Therefore, if the problem with a laptop's wireless connection is a weak signal, the solution may be a more powerful antenna to increase the signal range. Attaching an external antenna to a built-in adapter is nearly impossible, so you may need to disable the built-in Wi-Fi adapter and replace it with an adapter that will solve that weak signal problem. The replacement should be a USB Wi-Fi card with an antenna at the end of the USB cable. Several manufacturers make such a USB Wi-Fi card and antenna. Learn more about troubleshooting wireless networks in Chapter 16.

Interference Problems

Interference problems are not limited to laptops, and we will look at interference problems common to all computers using wireless networks in Chapter 15. However, using a Bluetooth device with a laptop that also has a Wi-Fi adapter introduces a conflict, because both Bluetooth and some Wi-Fi implementations use the same 2.4 GHz radio band. You may have to choose which wireless devices you will use or when you will use them. Because Bluetooth is only for very short distances, it works for keyboards, pointing devices, printers, and headphones. Wi-Fi connects to a local area network and, in many cases, connects through that network to the Internet. You may need to choose between uninterrupted Wi-Fi access or wireless connections between your local devices and the laptop.

SCENARIO & SOLUTION

When I am typing on my laptop, the pointer seems to jump all over the document. How can I prevent this from happening?	This problem is common when a hand or finger contacts a touchpad while typing. If the laptop has a touchpad, try to turn it off, or tape a piece of cardboard over the touchpad and use an external pointing device.
I attached an external display to my laptop, but after I powered it up, no image appeared on the external display, only on the integrated display. What have I done wrong?	Try toggling the DISPLAY MODE key to set the laptop to use the external display.
I upgraded the memory in my laptop with a new SODIMM module. Now the laptop fails to power up at all. What should I do?	Remove the SODIMM module and power up again. If the laptop powers up without the new module, the module may be defective, incompatible, or perhaps not installed correctly. Try reinstalling it.

Preventive Maintenance for Laptops

In general, laptops and desktop PCs have much in common. Therefore, the preventive maintenance information in Chapter 11 applies to laptops and other portable devices. However, certain issues are either unique to portable computers or more common to them because they use certain technologies not used in most desktop PCs. The following sections cover these issues. Although we discuss laptops specifically, most of these issues also apply to other portable devices.

Transporting and Shipping a Laptop

Portability is the key feature of any laptop. However, moving sensitive equipment is fraught with opportunity for damage. Therefore, when transporting a laptop, always use a proper carrying case or bag to protect it from damage. Select a case that feels comfortable to carry, because a laptop is something that you should normally keep with you whenever you are traveling.

When purchasing a case, try it out in the store with the laptop in it. Look for a case with a wide, padded, adjustable shoulder strap. You will also want adequate compartments for any accessories, such as the AC adapter, an extra battery, a pointing device, and compartments to carry a few optical discs and a flash drive. Some traveling bags have a laptop compartment that will lie flat next to the bag while it is passing through the x-ray machine. This keeps you from having to take it out of the bag and hand-carry it through security checkpoints.

People tend to overstuff their laptop bags with books and other equipment. The danger in this practice is that it will put enough pressure on the back of the laptop display to crack the LCD panel. Therefore, refrain from packing bulky or nonessential items in the laptop case, even if you must use a second carrying case for books and other items.

Never check a laptop as baggage unless you pack it in a case especially designed to protect it while the airline is treating it like, well, baggage. This will not be your typical laptop carrying case, but a metal case with molded foam padding to protect it.

If you must ship a laptop via a package service or the U.S. Postal Service, do not pack it in its carrying case, because this will not be adequate. Nothing beats the original packing material and box. Always save these, because you never know when you may have to ship the laptop for service, in which case manufacturers recommend that you ship it in the original box.

Never leave a laptop in a vehicle for extended periods, especially when the laptop is powered on. Even in mild weather, on a sunny day, the interior temperature can climb into a range that could damage the laptop. The LCD display is especially sensitive to temperature extremes that can damage the laptop, either heat or cold.

Cooling Issues

There are several cooling issues specific to laptops. The fact that a laptop has a great deal of circuitry packed in a very small space makes it more likely to overheat and compounds the problem. All but the LCD display is in the bottom of the laptop case, and this small area contains all the heat-generating components. Therefore, you should pay attention to the work environment and consider supplemental cooling when possible.

The Work Environment

When operating a laptop, be sure ventilation around the laptop is adequate. Using your laptop while on the go means you must often improvise a workspace. In fact, you may see travelers who simply unzip the case and run the laptop while it is still nestled in the case. The problem with this practice is that it blocks the air vents and the fan, which can cause the laptop to overheat. Ideally, you should never place an operating laptop on soft, conforming surfaces like couches, beds, or even laps.

Another issue, especially for the mobile laptop user, may be air quality. A project manager on a construction site may necessarily expose her laptop to all the dirt and dust of a construction site, whether working out of a pickup truck or an onsite office. Because this cannot be avoided, this user should have the inside of the laptop cleaned frequently, and keep it powered off, closed, and in its case when not in use.

Supplemental Cooling

Supplemental cooling for a laptop can come in the form of a special laptop stand that holds the laptop off the surface of the desk to allow airflow underneath. This alone will help, but these stands also often contain one or more fans. Some of these can take power from the laptop's USB hub, whereas others require 110 VAC power and, therefore, have a power adapter. If you plan to use this device while traveling, look for the lightest one you can find, which means you want to avoid one with an AC adapter. If this device will remain on your office desktop, then weight is no problem, and you should buy the one that you judge will be most effective.

exam
ᗯatch　*Be sure you understand how to protect a laptop during storage, transportation, and shipping.*

Hardware and Video Cleaning Materials

When it comes to cleaning the laptop case and display, treat a laptop just like a desktop PC. Follow the suggestions and instructions in Chapter 11 for materials and techniques to use.

CERTIFICATION SUMMARY

Laptops and other portable computers have much in common with desktop PCs. However, the form factors and technologies that make these computers portable also make them vulnerable to certain problems. When troubleshooting problems with portable computers, a computer technician must apply the same procedures and techniques presented in Chapter 11. In addition, he or she must understand the special problems associated with laptops and other portables.

When it comes to preventive maintenance, a similar approach is required. Everything that applies to desktop PCs also applies to portable computers. Portable computers also have issues that are either unique or more common to them because they use technologies not used in most desktop PCs. Therefore, the technician must apply these special preventive maintenance and care procedures to portable computers.

TWO-MINUTE DRILL

Here are some of the key points covered in Chapter 12.

Troubleshooting Laptops

❑ Laptop-specific power problems involve rechargeable batteries and the external AC power adapters.

❑ AC adapter problems fall into two categories: damage or failure of the original AC adapter and damage to the computer due to using the wrong AC adapter.

❑ A battery not properly inserted or charged, an old battery that can no longer hold a charge, or a defective new battery can cause laptop power problems.

❑ Before troubleshooting an AC adapter problem, remove any hardware devices installed since the laptop last powered up normally.

❑ Eliminate the other usual suspects, such as an external display that is in a sleep mode or not powered up, or a blank integrated display that has been switched off accidently via the display toggle keys.

❑ Check with the manufacturer if you are unable to solve the problem. A warranty may cover the problem, or there may be a recall on the laptop that will resolve it.

❑ Like a desktop PC, if a laptop fails at POST, you may have to enter the BIOS Setup program to discover the cause and possibly apply a solution.

❑ A laptop display may appear to have failed because the DISPLAY MODE function key has switched it to external display only. Try pressing the DISPLAY MODE key combination to change the mode.

❑ The wires for a laptop LCD panel must pass through the lid's hinge and, therefore, the wiring can come loose at this point. Contact the manufacturer or authorized repair center for help with this problem.

❑ The LCD panel in a laptop and other portable devices is vulnerable to temperature extremes, in which case it may go blank. Remove the laptop from exposure to extreme temperatures.

❑ The CCFL tubes that backlight the LCD screen in a laptop are fragile and can break if the laptop is handled roughly. Rough handling will cause the display to dim or go totally dark.

Preventive Maintenance for Laptops and Portable Devices

❑ The portability of laptops makes them more vulnerable to damage than desktop computers.

❑ Use a proper carrying case for transporting a laptop.

❑ A laptop should not be shipped as baggage, but if it must be, pack it in an adequate case, preferably a metal case with molded foam padding to protect it.

❑ Save the original carton and packing material in case you need to ship the laptop for repair.

❑ Never leave a laptop in a vehicle for extended periods.

❑ The very compactness of laptops makes them vulnerable to overheating.

❑ Be sure to provide adequate ventilation. If this is not possible, consider buying supplemental cooling in the form of a laptop stand with one or more fans installed.

❑ If you must use the laptop in a dirty, dusty environment, power it off, close it, keep it in its carrying case when not in use, and have it cleaned frequently.

❑ Clean the laptop case and display surfaces as you would a computer case and display, which was described in Chapter 11.

SELF TEST

The following questions will help you measure your understanding of the material presented in this chapter. Read all of the choices carefully because there might be more than one correct answer. Choose all correct answers for each question.

Troubleshooting Laptops

1. What two components must you check when a laptop experiences power problems?
   A. LCD panel
   B. AC adapter
   C. Power-on self-test
   D. Battery

2. When replacing an AC adapter for a laptop, match these three characteristics.
   A. Voltage, amperage, and polarity
   B. Voltage, amperage, and current
   C. Inverter, converter, and generator
   D. AC, DC, and amps

3. What type of power does a laptop's display require?
   A. DC
   B. Battery
   C. Auto-switching
   D. AC

4. You watch the battery indicator in Windows to determine when this is needed.
   A. Replacement
   B. Recharging
   C. Rebooting
   D. Testing

5. A laptop plugged into an AC power source will not power up. What component should you suspect as the source of the problem, assuming the power source is working?
   A. Battery
   B. LCD panel
   C. AC adapter
   D. Keyboard

6. What is a simple way to test an AC power outlet?

    A. Use an inverter.

    B. Plug in a converter.

    C. Plug a generator into the outlet.

    D. Plug a lamp into the outlet.

7. What action will some AC adapters take when they detect a power overage?

    A. Turn on

    B. Automatically restart

    C. Shut down

    D. Beep

8. When testing the power output of an AC adapter, what should you set your multimeter to test?

    A. Volts DC

    B. Volts AC

    C. Amps

    D. MHz

9. What should you do if your laptop fails to start after you have installed a new memory module?

    A. Reboot.

    B. Power off, and then power on.

    C. Remove the memory module and restart.

    D. Update the device driver.

10. What should you do if a laptop fails during the POST?

    A. Restart.

    B. Return it to the manufacturer.

    C. Remove the battery.

    D. Read the information on the screen and follow any instructions.

11. A user reports that his laptop remains warm even after he turns it "off" with the power button. What option is configured for his power button in Windows?

    A. Shut Down

    B. Standby or Sleep

    C. Screen Off

    D. Hibernate

12. Why would the power meter in Windows show a Not Present status for a laptop's battery, even though the battery is present?

   A. The battery is only half charged.

   B. The battery has failed.

   C. The power meter is turned off.

   D. The computer is plugged into an AC outlet.

13. What is a very-easy-to-resolve cause for a blank display?

   A. Broken fluorescent lamp

   B. Power-saving mode

   C. Damaged wiring

   D. Temperature extremes

14. How do you bring a display screen out of power-saving mode?

   A. Move the mouse or press a key.

   B. Unplug the laptop.

   C. Reset the AC adapter.

   D. Restart the computer.

15. You left your laptop in your car for several hours while visiting Minnesota in the winter. What should you do?

   A. Power it up in the car and run it on battery.

   B. Allow it to warm up before turning it on.

   C. Replace the battery.

   D. Clean the display screen.

16. After you dropped your laptop, you powered it up and the display screen was blank, although you could hear the fan. What may be the problem?

   A. Pixilation problems

   B. Temperature extremes

   C. Failed touchpad

   D. Broken fluorescent tubes

17. What do the plus (+) and minus (−) symbols indicate on a label on an AC adapter or next to a laptop's AC connector?

   A. Volts

   B. Amps

   C. Polarity

   D. Direct current

18. You recently connected an external mouse to your laptop, and soon after, while typing a report you notice that you are suddenly entering text into a different area of the document. Which component is the most likely source of this problem?

A. Mouse

B. Keyboard

C. Touchpad

D. Video adapter

Preventive Maintenance for Laptops and Portable Devices

19. How should you prepare a laptop to ship via UPS?

A. Pack it in a laptop case.

B. Pack it in its original box and packing material.

C. Remove the LCD panel and pack it in a case.

D. Clean the LCD panel.

20. What should you do for a laptop that seems to run hot, in addition to having it cleaned and keeping it in a well-ventilated area?

A. Turn off the display and use an external display.

B. Purchase a laptop stand.

C. Close some applications.

D. Turn down the display's brightness.

SELF TEST ANSWERS

Troubleshooting Laptops

1. ☑ **B** and **D.** The AC adapter and the battery are the two components you must check when a laptop experiences power problems.

☒ **A,** LCD panel, is not correct because you would not check this when troubleshooting a power problem. **C,** power-on self-test, is not correct because if the power is off, the self-test will not occur.

2. ☑ **A,** voltage, amperage, and polarity, is correct. These values must match for the AC adapter and the laptop.

☒ **B,** voltage, amperage, and current, is not correct. Although voltage and amperage is correct, the third requirement, polarity, is missing. **C,** inverter, converter, and generator, is incorrect because an inverter is a device that converts DC current to AC current; a converter is a device that converts AC current to DC current; and a generator is a device that creates electrical current. **D,** AC, DC, and amps, is incorrect. Only one of these, amps, is one of the characteristics that should match in a laptop and an AC adapter.

3. ☑ **D.** A laptop display requires AC power.

☒ **A,** DC, is incorrect, although other laptop components do require DC power. **B,** battery, is incorrect because, although the battery may be the source of the laptop's power, it is not the type of power required by the display. **C,** auto-switching, is incorrect because it describes a type of power supply.

4. ☑ **B.** Recharging is correct because this is what you do when the battery indicator in Windows says the battery is low.

☒ **A,** replacement, is incorrect because the battery indicator does not explicitly tell you when to replace the battery. **C,** rebooting, is incorrect because the battery indicator does not tell you when to reboot the computer. **D,** testing, is incorrect because the battery indicator does not tell you when to test the battery.

5. ☑ **C.** The AC adapter is the component you should suspect as the source of a problem if a laptop plugged into an AC power source will not power up.

☒ **A,** battery, is incorrect because if the laptop is plugged into an AC power source, it does not need the battery to power up. **B,** LCD panel, is incorrect because, although a failed LCD panel will make the laptop appear to be off, the laptop should still power up if it can receive power. **D,** keyboard, is incorrect because this has nothing to do with the laptop's ability to power up.

6. ☑ **D,** plug a lamp into the outlet, is correct, as this is a simple way to test an AC power outlet.
   ☒ **A,** use an inverter, is incorrect because this device uses DC power as its input and, therefore, cannot be used to test an AC power outlet. **B,** plug in a converter, is incorrect because, although a converter uses AC power as its input, this is not a simple test, as a lamp is more common than a converter. **C,** plug a generator into an outlet, is incorrect because most common generators convert a fuel, such as diesel or gasoline, to AC power. You would not plug one into an AC outlet.

7. ☑ **C.** Shut down is the action some AC adapters take when they detect a power overage.
   ☒ **A,** turn on, is incorrect because this is not the action of an AC power adapter when a power overage is detected. **B,** automatically restart, is incorrect because this action would not protect the AC adapter or the computer from damage from a power overage. **D,** beep, is incorrect because this, in itself, would not protect the AC adapter or the laptop.

8. ☑ **A,** volts DC, is correct because the AC adapter converts volts AC to volts DC (output).
   ☒ **B,** volts AC, is incorrect because the AC adapter converts volts AC to volts DC (output). **C,** amps, is incorrect because although many multimeters can measure amps, in this case, you want to measure volts. **D,** MHz, is incorrect because this is not something most multimeters measure. MHz was mentioned in this book as a measurement of CPU speed.

9. ☑ **C,** remove the memory module and restart, is the correct answer because this component was changed since the computer last successfully powered up.
   ☒ **A,** reboot, is incorrect because rebooting will not change anything in this case. **B,** power off and then power on, is incorrect because this would also not change anything. **D,** update the device driver, is incorrect because memory does not require a device driver.

10. ☑ **D,** read the information on the screen and follow any instructions, is the correct answer because the POST may have detected a problem, in which case it will display an error message.
    ☒ **A,** restart, is incorrect, although you may be instructed to do this by the message on the screen. **B,** return it to the manufacturer, is incorrect because this is a drastic step to take when you have not tried to discover the problem first. **C,** remove the battery, is incorrect because you have no indication that the battery is the problem.

11. ☑ **B.** Standby or Sleep is correct. Standby in Windows XP or Sleep in Windows Vista or later would put the computer into a sleep mode that would still require a battery and would generate some heat.
    ☒ **A,** Shut Down, and **D,** Hibernate, are both incorrect because they would power the computer off. **C,** Screen Off, is not an option for configuring the power button in Windows.

12. ☑ **B.** A failed battery will show as Not Present in the power meter settings.
    ☒ **A,** the battery is only half charged, is incorrect because if it had any charge, the battery would show as present. **C,** the power meter is turned off, is incorrect, and **D,** the computer is plugged into an AC outlet, is incorrect.

13. ☑ **B.** Power-saving mode is a cause of a blank display that is very easy to resolve: simply move the mouse or press a key.
☒ **A,** broken fluorescent lamp, is incorrect because, although a broken lamp can cause a blank display, it is not an easy-to-resolve cause. **C,** damaged wiring, is incorrect for a similar reason. **D,** temperature extremes, is also a possible cause, but not a simple one.

14. ☑ **A,** move the mouse or press a key, is correct because this will bring a display screen out of power-saving mode.
☒ **B,** unplug the laptop, is incorrect because this will not bring the display out of power-saving mode. **C,** reset the AC adapter, is incorrect because this will not bring the display out of power-saving mode. **D,** restart the computer, is incorrect because, although once it restarts the display will be out of power-saving mode, this is simply not necessary and not recommended.

15. ☑ **B,** allow it to warm up before turning it on, is correct because running the laptop in extremely cold temperatures can damage it, especially the display.
☒ **A,** power it up in the car and run it on battery, is incorrect because running the laptop in the extreme cold can damage it. **C,** replace the battery, is incorrect because there is no indication that this is necessary. **D,** clean the display screen, is incorrect because this will not address the problem of temperature extremes.

16. ☑ **D,** broken fluorescent tubes, is correct because the backlight consists of fluorescent tubes.
☒ **A,** pixilation problems, is incorrect because pixilation would not make the screen go blank. **B,** temperature extremes, is incorrect because we did not mention temperature in the question. **C,** failed touchpad, is incorrect because this would not make the screen go blank.

17. ☑ **C.** Polarity of the plug and connector is indicated by the plus (+) and minus (−) symbols.
☒ **A, B,** and **D** are all incorrect, although volts, amps, and DC are also shown, as appropriate, on these labels.

18. ☑ **C.** The touchpad is the most likely component because the user is probably inadvertently touching it while typing.
☒ **A,** mouse, **B,** keyboard, and **D,** video adapter, are all incorrect because none of them is the most likely cause of the problem.

Preventive Maintenance for Laptops and Portable Devices

19. ☑ **B,** pack it in the original box and packing material, is correct.
☒ **A,** pack it in a laptop case, is incorrect because a laptop case will be inadequate. **C,** remove the LCD panel and pack it in a case, is incorrect because you should never remove the lid. **D,** clean the LCD panel, is incorrect because this in no way prepares the laptop for shipping.

20. ☑ **B,** purchase a laptop stand, is correct because a stand will allow air to circulate underneath the laptop and many stands have one or more fans.

☒ **A,** turn off the display and use an external display, is incorrect because the heat is usually generated in the bottom of the laptop case. **C,** close some applications, is incorrect because this has not proven to have any significant effect on heat generation. **D,** turn down the brightness of the display, is also incorrect because this has also not proven to have any significant effect on heat generation and does not affect the main case of the laptop, which generates the most heat.

13

Troubleshooting and Preventive Maintenance for Windows

Y ou are now familiar with the major functions of the Windows operating systems. You understand how to install Windows, and know how to manage files and disks. It is time to learn how to troubleshoot common problems. Your best troubleshooting tool is knowledge. The previous chapters have given you a strong foundation regarding PCs and Windows operating systems. In this chapter, you will learn a set of skills and tools for modifying startup failures, and how to diagnose and solve common operational problems, including instability, Stop errors, application failures, and other problems.

Finally, in order to minimize your risk of problems and increase your ability to quickly recover from failures, you will learn preventive maintenance for Windows operating systems.

CERTIFICATION OBJECTIVE

■ **802: 4.6** *Given a scenario, troubleshoot operating system problems with appropriate tools*

This brief section introduces the first things you should consider for solving a potential software problem—whether it is an OS problem or an app problem, and therefore covers the intent of CompTIA A+ Exam Objective 802: 4.6, if not its specific objectives. We use it as an introduction to troubleshooting Windows and include the first things you should consider before you do some serious digging into the cause.

Overview of Troubleshooting Software Problems

Software problems can involve application programs, operating system components, or a combination of both in cases where interaction between an application and the operating system is the cause. Here we look at the most basic procedures for identifying and solving software problems.

The Quick Fixes: Rebooting, Uninstalling, and Reinstalling

You can use several techniques to troubleshoot software problems. Begin with rebooting the computer, which you may have already done. In some cases restarting solves an occasional problem because it releases resources that a device or app needs but which another device or app is tying up. Restarting the computer also forces the operating system to reestablish the presence of existing devices and clear information out of its memory, which may include a transient problem with software interactions. If rebooting the computer does not solve the problem, you should then try to narrow the source to a single program and look at minimum requirements, updates, and compatibility. If all of these check out, try uninstalling and reinstalling a newly added app or device.

Pinpointing the Problem Application

Pinpoint a possible problem application by testing several apps under the same conditions. Many applications can use most hardware devices. Therefore, by using more than one application to access the suspect device, you can narrow the search when hardware appears to be the problem.

Suppose, for example, that a user was unable to scan an image using a particular scanning program. Try using a different application to access the scanner. If it works, you can conclude the scanner is physically sound and turn your attention to software as the problem.

If you have determined the problem is software related, and the problem still occurs after a reboot, focus on the application's configuration. Most applications or utilities include a Preferences, Tools, or Options feature, through which you can configure their operation and the devices they can access.

Minimum Requirements

Check to make sure the computer meets the application's minimum requirements. It is possible the computer simply will not support the application—in which case, you may need to upgrade the hardware or replace the computer in order to use the application.

CERTIFICATION OBJECTIVES

- **802: 1.3** *Given a scenario, use appropriate command-line tools*

- **802: 1.4** *Given a scenario, use appropriate operating system features and tools*

- **802: 1.5** *Given a scenario, use Control Panel utilities.*

- **802: 4.6** *Given a scenario, troubleshoot operating system problems with appropriate tools*

- **802: 4.7** *Given a scenario, troubleshoot common security issues with appropriate tools and best practices*

This section will familiarize you with many of the troubleshooting tools listed in CompTIA A+ Exam Objectives 802: 1.3, 1.4, and 4.6. While some of the command-line tools in Objective 1.3 were introduced in early chapters, as were some administrative tools listed in Objective 1.4, in this section we look at other tools in these categories you will need familiarity with for troubleshooting Windows. The majority of the CompTIA A+ Exam Objectives 802: 4.7 is detailed in Chapter 18. However, in this section, we describe the role that System Restore plays in malware removal.

Windows Troubleshooting Tools

In this section, learn about the many Windows tools for troubleshooting operating system problems. Begin with a discussion of the Windows registry—not exactly a tool in itself, but something at the core of the Windows OS that you may need to modify—and the tools you use to modify it. Then learn about the Microsoft Management Console (MMC), a user interface for many administrative tools. You have actually worked with some MMC-based tools, such as Device Manager and Disk Management, in earlier chapters. Now you'll tour a collection of tools, including those accessed within an MMC and those in other Windows environments, such as the Command Prompt, Safe Mode, Recovery Options, and the Recovery Console. Learn which tools are available in Windows XP, and which are available in Windows Vista, Windows 7, and Windows 8.

Troubleshooting Tools for Windows Vista and Newer Versions

Microsoft added some troubleshooting tools in Windows Vista and later that were not available in Windows XP. They actually save you time and effort in troubleshooting and resolving problems with Windows, so we will look at them first and then look at the many other troubleshooting tools.

The *Problem Reports and Solutions* Control Panel applet only exists in Windows Vista. It gives you feedback and possible solutions for security issues and problems your computer reports to Microsoft using the Windows Error Reporting service. Click a solution to have it applied to Windows. Then, manually remove the resolved items.

Windows 7 and Windows 8 have an improved reporting tool, called *Action Center*, a Windows 7 and Windows 8 Control Panel applet that reports security and maintenance status, and includes links to troubleshooting and recovery tools. Open Action Center when you want to take a quick look at the beginning of the troubleshooting process to see if it shows any problems in the Security or Maintenance areas (which pretty much cover everything). Once you identify a problem area, click a link to open a helpful tool, such as Performance and Information, Backup and Restore, Windows Update, System Restore, and the new (beginning in Windows 7) Troubleshooting tool.

Select the Troubleshooting link in Action Center and it opens a menu of categories with troubleshooters that walk you through a solution. For instance, the Programs category contains a link that opens the Program Compatibility Troubleshooter in which you identify the older program that will not run properly, and then the Troubleshooter walks you through a variety of settings for that application. You handled this task manually in Windows XP using the Compatibility tab on the Properties dialog box for a program.

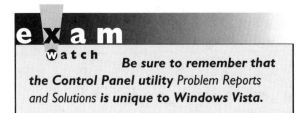

Be sure to remember that the Control Panel utility *Problem Reports and Solutions* **is unique to Windows Vista.**

In addition to the Programs category, Troubleshooting has Troubleshooters for Hardware and Sound, Network and Internet, System and Security, and Appearance and Personalization. The last category is not included in this tool in Windows 8 because the Appearance and Personalization troubleshooter in Windows 7 addresses problems with Windows Aero, which is not included in Windows 8.

System Information (MSINFO32.EXE)

You sit down at a Windows computer you have never touched before. You know little about it, but you need to gather information to troubleshoot a problem. Where do you start? One of the first things you should do is learn as much as you can as quickly as you can. What version, edition, and service pack of Windows are installed? How much memory is installed? What CPU? This information and more is displayed as a summary of the hardware, operating system, and other installed software in *System Information*, shown here. You can access it through the graphical user interface (GUI), but we prefer to simply start it from the Run line with its executable name, *MSINFO32.EXE.*

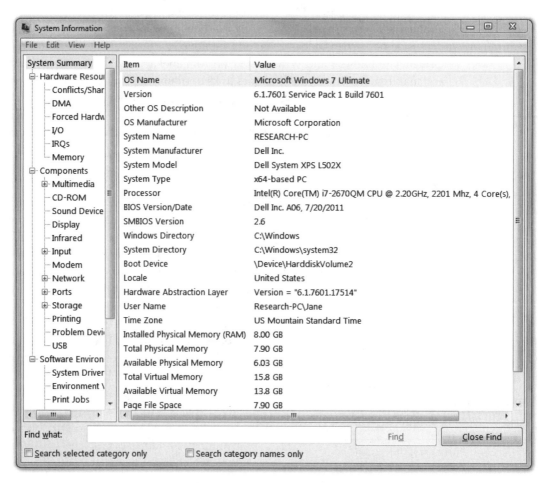

The Registry

A basic knowledge of the registry is required of anyone supporting Windows. As defined in Chapter 9, the Windows registry is a database of all Windows configuration settings for both hardware and software. As Windows starts up, it reads information in the registry that tells it what components to load into memory and how to configure them. After startup, the OS writes any changes into the registry and frequently reads additional settings as different programs load into memory.

Categories of Registry Settings

The registry includes settings for

- Device drivers
- Services
- Installed application programs
- Operating system components
- User preferences

Changing the Registry

The registry is created when Windows installs; however, configuring Windows and adding applications and devices continually modifies it. Here are the actions that cause registry changes:

- Windows starts up or shuts down
- Windows Setup runs
- Changes are made through a Control Panel applet
- Installing a new device
- Any changes made to the Windows configuration
- Any changes made to a user's desktop preferences
- Installing or modifying an app
- Any changes made to an app's user preferences

Using Registry Editor

The best way to change the registry is indirectly, using various tools in the GUI, such as the Control Panel applets and some MMC consoles. You should directly edit the registry only when you have no other choice and you have specific instructions from a very reliable source. Then the tool to use is Registry Editor, which you can start from the Run line by entering **regedit**.

In the Registry Editor, you can navigate the registry folders with your mouse in the same way you navigate disk folders. Each folder represents a *registry key*, an object that may contain one or more settings as well as other keys, each of which is a *subkey* of its parent key. The top five folders, as seen in Figure 13-1, are *root keys*, often called *subtrees* in Microsoft documentation. Each of these subtrees is the top of a hierarchical structure.

A setting within a key is a *value entry*. When you click the folder for a key, it becomes the active key in Registry Editor. Its folder icon opens, and the contents of the key appear in the right pane, as shown in Figure 13-1. Here is an overview of each subtree and its contents:

- **HKEY_LOCAL_MACHINE**   Information about detected hardware and software, security settings, and the local security accounts database.
- **HKEY_CLASSES_ROOT**   The relationships (associations) between applications and file types. Shown as a root key, it is actually all the information located in HKEY_LOCAL_MACHINE\Software\Classes.
- **HKEY_CURRENT_CONFIG**   Configuration information for the current hardware profile, which are settings defining the devices, the list of files associated with each device, and configuration settings for each. It also contains a set of changes to the standard configuration in the Software and Systems subkeys under HKEY_LOCAL_MACHINE.

FIGURE 13-1

Use the Registry Editor (REGEDIT) to view the registry components.

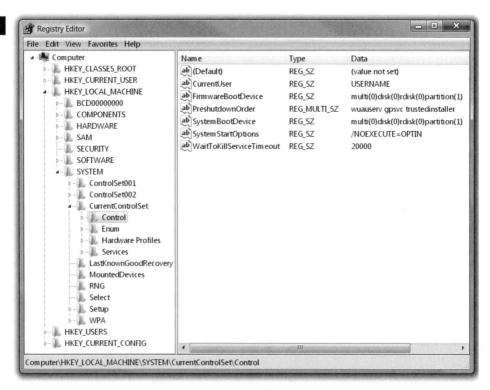

- **HKEY_CURRENT_USER** The user profile for the currently logged-on user, which consists of the NTUSER.DAT file for the user, along with any changes since logon.
- **HKEY_USERS** All user profiles that are loaded in memory, including the profile of the currently logged-on user, the default profile, and profiles for special user accounts for running various services.

Registry Files

Although considered a single entity, the registry is actually stored on disk in a number of binary files. A binary file contains program code, as opposed to a file containing data. Here is a list of the Windows registry files, along with a description of their contents:

- **SYSTEM** Information used at startup, including a list of device drivers to be loaded, as well as the order of their loading and configuration settings. It also contains various operating system settings, including those for the starting and configuring of services.
- **SOFTWARE** Configuration settings for software installed on the computer.
- **SECURITY** The computer's local security policy settings.
- **SAM** The local security accounts database containing local user and group accounts and their passwords.
- **DEFAULT** The user profile used when there is no logged-on user. On a Windows computer that requires an interactive logon, these settings affect the appearance before someone logs on.
- **NTUSER.DAT** The user profile for a single user. Each user who logs onto the computer has a separate NTUSER.DAT file, as well as one located in the DEFAULT USER folder. The NTUSER.DAT file is in the top-level personal folder for each user.

All changes to the registry saved from one session to the next are in these registry file extensions. With the exception of NTUSER.DAT, these registry files do not have file extensions and live in a disk folder named CONFIG. The default location of this folder is C:\WINDOWS\SYSTEM32. Figure 13-2 shows the CONFIG folder and its contents.

FIGURE 13-2

This view of the
CONFIG folder
shows registry
files.

The Microsoft Management Console (MMC)

The *Microsoft Management Console (MMC)* is a user interface for Windows
administration tools that is flexible and configurable. Most Control Panel applets
and administrative applets that run within the Windows GUI open in an MMC
window. The multipurpose tool set of MMCs is Computer Management, which you
can access by opening the Start menu and right-clicking Computer/My Computer
and selecting Manage (see Figure 13-3). Notice the grouping of tools on the left.
The tools (such as Task Scheduler, Event Viewer, Shared Folders, Local Users
and Groups, Performance, Device Manager, and Disk Management) are all *snap-
ins* to the Computer Management console, meaning they are MMC nodes that
can be added to an MMC console. An administrator can build his own custom
consoles, consisting of individual snap-ins. To do this, you enter the command
mmc.exe in the Run line, which opens a blank console window on the desktop.
Using the Add Or Remove Snap-ins option on the File menu, you can select one
or more administrative snap-ins to create your custom console. Consoles have
an .msc file extension, and you can call up your favorite tool directly from the
Run line by entering the correct filename and extension. For instance, to start

FIGURE 13-3

The Computer
Management
Console

Computer Management, shown here, from the Run line simply enter the command
compmgmt.msc. In Windows Vista and Windows 7, start it from the Start Search
line by entering **computer management**. Following are overviews of three MMC-
based tools that are useful in both troubleshooting and preventing problems. They
are Device Manager, Task Scheduler, and a performance-monitoring tool that has
undergone a name change, as well as feature upgrade from Windows XP to the
newer Windows versions.

Device Manager

Chapter 11 featured Device Manager as a troubleshooting tool for several types of
hardware problems, so we will only briefly revisit it here to emphasize that it is an MMC
snap-in. Device Manager allows an administrator to view and change device properties,
update device drivers (you normally will use the manufacturer's program to update a
driver), configure device settings, roll back an updated driver that is causing problems,
and uninstall devices. Recall that to access Device Manager in versions of Windows
from Windows XP through Windows 8, you open the Run line (Windows Key+R) and
enter **devmgmt.msc.** This will open it into a separate MMC console window.

Task Scheduler

The *Task Scheduler* is included in all versions of Windows covered in this book. This
console allows you to view and manage tasks that run automatically at preconfigured
times. Use Task Scheduler to automate daily backups and updates. In Windows XP, it

is not an MMC, but a Control Panel applet called *Scheduled Tasks*. In newer versions of Windows it is an MMC, so you can open Task Scheduler from the Run line by entering **taskschd.msc**; then expand the Task Scheduler Library to see folders for the many categories of tasks. You will be surprised at the number of scheduled tasks. Most, if not all of the tasks you will find there, were not created by you directly, but were added to Task Scheduler when you installed a new app and configured it to automatically check for updates.

<table>
<tr><td colspan="2">

e x a m

Ⓦatch

CompTIA A+ Exam Objective 802: 1.3 requires that you understand the KILL command. While current versions of Windows do not have a KILL command, they do have a TASKKILL command that will stop a running program.

This command-line command has many options that you can explore with the /? switch. Here is an example that will stop the Microsoft Paint program, assuming it will not stop normally: *taskkill /f /t /im mspaint.exe*.

</td></tr>
</table>

Monitoring Performance

Performance monitoring is something that has long been an important task for administrators of network servers to ensure maintenance of the quality of service and as an early warning of potential problems that show up first as performance problems. Desktop computers don't usually require the close monitoring of servers. The desktop versions of Windows come with several tools for monitoring performance and the overall health of your system, and for future troubleshooting. Familiarize yourself with a few of the monitoring tools in Windows for the exam.

We'll start with one of the simplest monitoring tools that leads to more advanced ones. Open Search in Windows 7 and Windows 8 (Settings Search) and search on **performance info**. From the results list select Performance Information And Tools. Figure 13-4 shows the *Performance Information And Tools* window in Windows 7. Every time you open this Control Panel applet it runs the Windows Experience Index assessment, which scores computer components on a scale of 1 to 7.9, with higher being better. The base score (right column) is that of the lowest subscore. Good thing we only use this old computer for email, word processing, and surfing the Web, because it would make a disappointing gaming computer. Run this on a new computer and record the information for later reference. Degradation in one of these figures means a change in the system that you may want to investigate. According

FIGURE 13-4 Windows 7 Performance Information And Tools

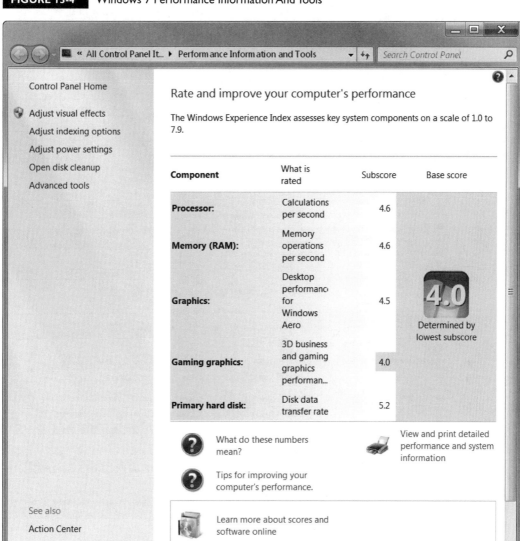

to Microsoft, you can use the base score to buy software that matches or is less than your computer's base score. A score of 2 is adequate for very basic word processing and Web browsing tasks, while graphics-intensive apps require a score of 4 or higher.

Select Advanced Tools in Performance Information And Tools to see a long list of links to performance tools, as Figure 13-5 shows. We discussed some of these

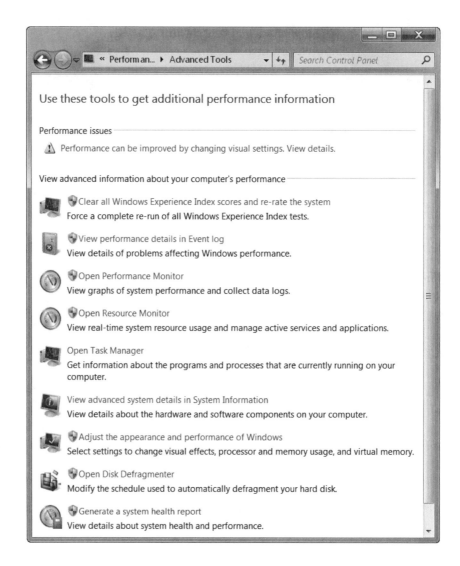

Use these tools to get additional performance information

Performance issues

⚠ Performance can be improved by changing visual settings. View details.

View advanced information about your computer's performance

🛡Clear all Windows Experience Index scores and re-rate the system
Force a complete re-run of all Windows Experience Index tests.

🛡View performance details in Event log
View details of problems affecting Windows performance.

🛡Open Performance Monitor
View graphs of system performance and collect data logs.

🛡Open Resource Monitor
View real-time system resource usage and manage active services and applications.

Open Task Manager
Get information about the programs and processes that are currently running on your computer.

View advanced system details in System Information
View details about the hardware and software components on your computer.

🛡Adjust the appearance and performance of Windows
Select settings to change visual effects, processor and memory usage, and virtual memory.

🛡Open Disk Defragmenter
Modify the schedule used to automatically defragment your hard disk.

🛡Generate a system health report
View details about system health and performance.

tools previously in this book, and we will cover some later. For now, let's look at Performance Monitor, as it is specifically named in the CompTIA A+ Exam 802 objectives.

The main Windows desktop performance-monitoring utility will track and gather performance data for memory, disks, processors, networks, and more so that you can see if one of these items is showing performance problems. This tool, *Performance Monitor*, has evolved and has had a variety of names. In fact, even today you will

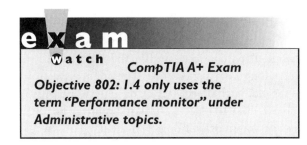

see more than one name for the same utility in different locations within the Windows GUI. In the Computer Management console in Windows Vista, the Performance Monitor snap-in is *Reliability and Performance Monitor*, but it was known as *System Monitor* in Windows XP, and in Windows 7 and Windows 8 we are back to Performance Monitor, the original name from the ancient days of Windows NT. From Windows XP through Windows 8, you can open Performance Monitor by entering its executable name, **perfmon.msc**, in the Run line.

Each item you can monitor, such as physical disks, memory, processor, and network interface, is an *object* and it has one or more characteristics, called *counters*, that you may select for monitoring. Performance Monitor displays the data in real time in a report, line graph, or histogram (bar chart) format. Figure 13-6 shows Performance Monitor displaying processor performance information.

FIGURE 13-6   Windows 7 Performance Monitor

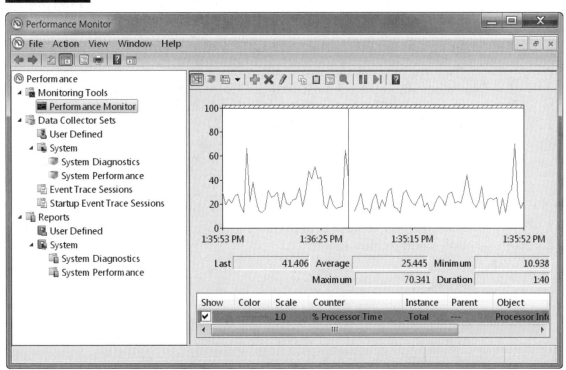

Resource Monitor, a tool listed in Advanced Tools shown in Figure 13-5, will help you find apps that are using up the most resources, as it measures each app's use of CPU, memory, disk, and network. The Image column lists the executable filename for each program monitored, along with a check box. The graph pane on the right shows the cumulative usage for each object (CPU, disk, network, or memory). Back in the pane for an object, click to place a check in an image box, and a colored line will appear in the line graph for that object in the pane on the right, showing you how much of that resource it is using.

Component Services

Windows has methods by which apps can work together. Applications called COM apps use *Component Object Model (COM)*. They use groups of COM components that work cooperatively. A COM app will have an executable program that opens the app for the user and various components in the form of pieces of code called *dynamic link libraries (DLLs)* that are brought into memory as needed for special functions. The next complexity level includes the *Component Object Model Plus* (COM+) apps, which come in two types: server and client. This changes the model from working cooperatively to one of a component (a server) providing a service to another component (a client). These server components provide the client components with services such as transactions, queuing, and role-based security through DLLs associated with the service.

When apps install, such as the various Microsoft Office apps, they normally automatically install and configure their COM and COM+ applications, and you are neither aware of nor concerned about these tasks. However, if you see an error message that includes the words "COM Server" or "missing dll," contact the source of the software involved or enter the error message (including the actual names of components or DLLs) into an Internet search engine. Using a reliable source, you will probably see instructions for correcting the problem using Component Services, a Microsoft Management console. But before you attempt this, back up your computer! Make sure you are logged on as an administrator, and then open Component Services by entering **compexp.msc** in the Run line and follow the instructions you found for resolving the problem.

Services

A *service* is a program that runs in background, has no GUI, and supports other programs. For instance, there are specialized services associated with various devices, such as smart cards, printers, displays, digital tablets, and audio devices. Many services support networking and security, and the list goes on. Open the Services console by entering **services.msc** in the Run line. The Services console, shown in Figure 13-7, lets you manage services. You normally should not need to make any changes to services, but if you must make changes, use this tool rather than others. In the Services console, you can start, stop, pause, resume, and disable services. You can also configure the recovery options for what should occur when an individual service fails. To access that feature, you need to right-click a service in the Services console and select Properties. In the Properties dialog box for the service, click the Recovery tab, as shown in Figure 13-8. The recovery options include Take No Action, Restart The Service, Run A Program, and Restart The Computer.

REGSVR32

As with Component Services, described earlier, you can use the *Register Server tool* to resolve problems with software components, but this is something you would only use with explicit instructions from a good source, such as the company that

FIGURE 13-7   The Windows 7 Services console

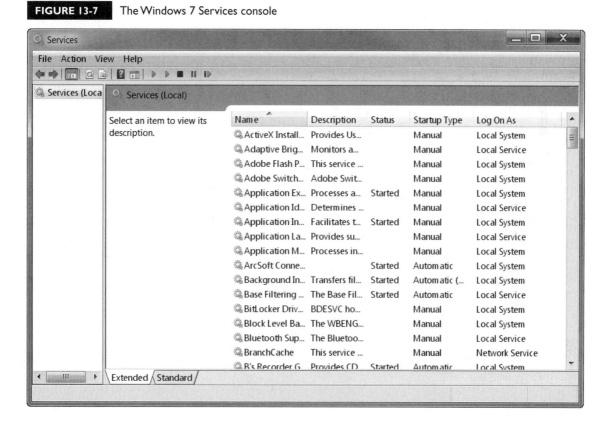

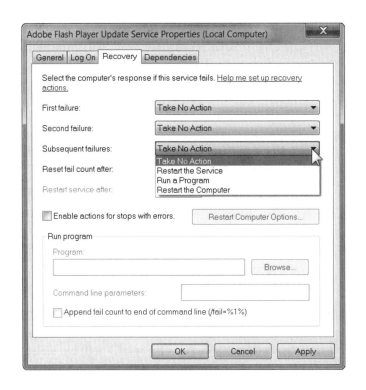

FIGURE 13-8

The Recovery
tab on a service's
Properties dialog
box

developed the software. Register Server is a command-line tool, and is mainly known by its executable name, *REGSVR32*, and it is used to register or unregister software components, such as DLLs and ActiveX Controls (OCX). If a software publisher recommends that you use this tool, you will need the exact command-line options and instructions from them. First do a complete backup of your system; then open the Command Prompt as administrator and carefully enter the command with options. Follow the software publisher's instructions for interpreting any resulting error messages and do testing to see if the problem is resolved.

exam

Watch

CompTIA A+ Exam Objective 802: 4.6 lists "REGSRV32" under the Tools topic. This is a typo, because the name of this tool is REGSVR32 (notice the "VR" in the correct spelling).

Data Sources

Yet another tool you would only use with explicit instructions is the *ODBC Data Source Administrator*. You can launch it from Administrative Tools in Control Panel or from the Run line by entering **odbcad32.exe**. This opens a tabbed dialog box where you can manage database drivers and data sources. To understand why you would use this tool, we need to define a few terms. *Open Database Connectivity (ODBC)* is program code for connecting to *database management systems (DBMS)*. A DBMS is a program that manages the creation, storage, retrieval, and modification of data on a computer. Theoretically, ODBC can be used with any operating system and any DBMS through the use of a special driver that, like a driver for a hardware component, acts as a translator. In the case of a hardware driver, it translates between the hardware component and the operating system, whereas an ODBC driver translates between the application and the DBMS.

As long as the correct ODBC driver is installed, a DBMS-compliant app can access any DBMS. Common data sources on Windows computers are Microsoft Excel spreadsheet files, Microsoft Access database files, and dBase files. When an ODBC-compliant program installs, it will normally install the correct ODBC driver. If you see an error message that an ODBC connection cannot be made, first back up data on that computer, and then reinstall the problem application. If that does not correct the problem, contact the software publisher and obtain a new ODBC driver or instructions for changes you can make in the ODBC Data Source Administrator.

Task Manager

Task Manager is a utility that each successive version of Windows has improved upon. The current Task Manager does not resemble the simple tool we used only to remove a program from memory that was not responding to mouse or keyboard actions before Windows XP, and it has improved with each version since then. Task Manager now opens as a tabbed window and is a very sophisticated program that allows you to end an unresponsive program and do other tasks involving applications, processes, services, and users. It also allows you to view system and networking performance.

Knowing how to start Task Manager and how to stop an unresponsive program are important tools. Our preferred method of opening this tool is with the keyboard shortcut, CTRL-SHIFT-ESC, which starts Task Manager directly. Task Manager in Windows 7, shown in Figure 13-9, has several tabbed pages that we'll explore next. Task Manager for Windows 8 is similar, but has a very simplified view (Figure 13-10) that only shows the current apps. Click More Details for a tabbed view similar to Windows 7.

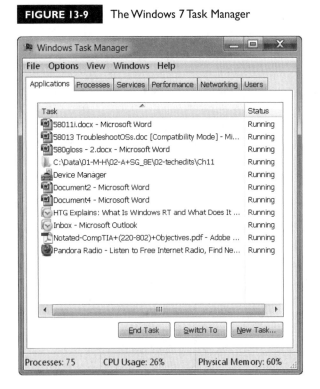

FIGURE 13-9 The Windows 7 Task Manager

FIGURE 13-10 The Windows 8 Task Manager in a simplified view

Applications Tab

The Applications tab is the one from which you view and manage GUI applications. If an application is not responding, and you cannot close the application any other way, open Task Manager, select the nonresponding application, and click End Task.

Processes Tab

Select the Task Manager Processes tab to see the Process list, showing each active process currently running in memory. A program runs in memory as one or more processes. A single *process* consists of memory space, program code, data, and the system resources required by the process. Each process has at least one thread, which is the program code executed by the process. An operating system has many active processes at any given time. Add to that the processes for such programs or applications as Windows Explorer and Microsoft Word, and you have dozens of active processes running in memory at one time performing various functions. A *background process* is one that runs "behind the scenes" and has a low priority, does not require input, and rarely creates output. Many of the processes in the Process list are background processes. In Task Manager, the image name (filename) and *Process ID (PID)* identifies a process, which is a number dynamically assigned by the operating system as it starts each process. The Processes tab also shows the amount of memory and the CPU usage of the process.

When a programmer creates a program, she gives it a *process priority level,* also called a *base priority level,* which determines the order in which the program code's process or processes execute in relation to other active processes. There are six levels, listed from the lowest to the highest: Low, Below Normal, Normal, Above Normal, High, and Real Time. A program that has a High priority level has the potential to tie up the processor, and one with a Real Time priority level can cause system crashes. The operating system can adjust these levels to some degree, and you can temporarily adjust the level of an active process by right-clicking a process and selecting Set Priority. We do not recommend that you do this.

To view all running process, select Show Processes From All Users at the bottom left of the window. To view the priority level of active processes, first select the Processes tab, and then open View | Select Columns. In the Select Process Page Columns dialog, click to place a check mark in the Base Priority box. This adds the Base Priority column. Most of the processes will have a Base Priority level of Normal, with a few High priorities and perhaps one or two Below Normal. The High Priority processes should be part of the operating system, such as csrss.exe, dwm.exe, or some (but not all) programs associated with a specialized device, such as a digital tablet.

So how do you use this knowledge of processes in troubleshooting? If a system is slow, noting which processes are running with a high priority at the times of slow performance may tell you which ones are taking processing time away from others. Perhaps the answer is to evaluate the need for that app. If it is critical that you continue to use it, and the software publisher does not have a solution, you may need to run it on a more powerful computer.

exam
Watch

CompTIA A+ Exam Objective 802: 1.3 requires that you understand the TLIST command-line command. In the versions of Windows included in the exam, TLIST has been replaced by TASKLIST.EXE. Run the TASKLIST command without parameters

to see a list of process IDs for all running tasks. Use the /? switch to learn more. If you encounter a question on the exam that you know is correctly answered by TASKLIST, but that answer is not provided as an option, then look for TLIST and select it.

Services Tab

Click the Services tab to see the list of services loaded into Windows. If you look at the status in Task Manager, you will see that not all of the listed processes are actually running. Many are stopped because they are only started when needed. Some processes and services are associated, and when you right-click a service that is running and select Go To Process, it will open the Processes tab and highlight the associated process. However, if you do that on a running service and no process is highlighted, the process may be hidden and you will need to select Show Processes From All Users, as described earlier. You can learn more about the current services by clicking the Services button on the bottom right of this page. This will open the Services MMC.

Performance Tab

The Performance tab is a "lite" version of Performance Monitor. Open this for a quick look at the current performance of CPU and memory. The most important object to check here is CPU, which you'll see in a real-time line graph. The graph measures the percentage of CPU usage in a separate window for each CPU or core. CPU usage usually bounces up and down as various processes execute. However, sustained usage above about 80 percent indicates that the CPU is inadequate for the task. This may indicate a problem with the CPU from overheating or another cause, or it may simply mean it is time to upgrade the CPU or entire computer.

Networking Tab

The Networking tab in Task Manager gives performance and state information about your network connections. If a network seems slow, open Task Manager, click Networking, and you will find a real-time line chart showing the bandwidth usage for each network connection. With this open, do whatever type of networking function seems to slow things down, such as a large download from a file-sharing site. Even that should not tax the network connection much. Network bottlenecks are usually beyond your local connection at an Internet router. Chapter 16 will show you how to find such a bottleneck.

Users Tab

The Users tab in Task Manager shows the currently logged-on users, including you, in a Session type of console, along with any users who are connected to a share on your computer over a network. When a network user is connected, their computer name will show up under the Client Name column. What will not show up are the various special user's accounts that run services on your computer. From this tab you can disconnect or log off a user. If it is a network user, you should click the Send

Message button to send them a warning so that they can close any files they have open on your computer.

CompTIA A+ Exam Objective 802: 1.4 specifically lists Task Manager and the tabs just mentioned.	**You should be familiar with the functions associated with each of these tabs for the exam.**

System Configuration Utility (MSCONFIG.EXE)

Beginning with Windows XP, and continuing through later versions of Windows, Microsoft includes the *System Configuration* utility, also known as *MSCONFIG*, that allows you to modify and test startup configuration settings without having to alter them directly. This allows you to first isolate the source of a problem. Once you determine what program or service is causing a problem, you can uninstall the program or permanently disable the service so it will not run when the computer boots. When you make such changes from within System Configuration and then restart the computer, it will start up and reflect the change you made. You can also use System Configuration to test a startup configuration change before making it permanent to make sure it won't negatively affect your computer. While you can call this program up from the GUI, the quick way to launch it from any version is by entering **msconfig.exe** in the Run line (WINDOWS KEY+R).

CompTIA A+ Exam Objective 802: 1.4 lists this utility twice: under the Administrative topic it is listed by its GUI name, System Configuration,	**and then the next topic is titled MSCONFIG. Be prepared to see either name in CompTIA's A+ Exam 802.**

General Tab

The General tab contains quick startup options to help you isolate a cause of a startup problem. Normal startup will simply start up Windows normally, and is what you should choose after you have used other options. Diagnostic startup will temporarily disable all but basic services and drivers before starting up. If the problem persists after using Diagnostic startup, then the source is within Windows base components, not in an installed driver or service. Selective startup lets you choose three categories of items to disable or enable at startup. Use this to isolate the problem to system services or other programs that normally start up with Windows.

on the *Take time to practice using the System Configuration utility before you need*
job *to use it for troubleshooting.*

Boot Tab

From the Boot tab, you can also use restart Windows In Safe Mode by selecting the Safe Boot option and clicking OK. Then a message box displays, giving you the opportunity to either restart or exit without restarting. If you restart, you will be in Safe Mode where you can continue your troubleshooting. When finished working in Safe Mode, open System Configuration again, clear the Safe Mode option from the Boot page, return to the General page, and select Normal Startup. You will see the same prompt, where you will need to click the Restart button, and Windows will restart normally. Figure 13-11 shows System Configuration open to the Boot tab page.

FIGURE 13-11

The System
Configuration
Boot tab

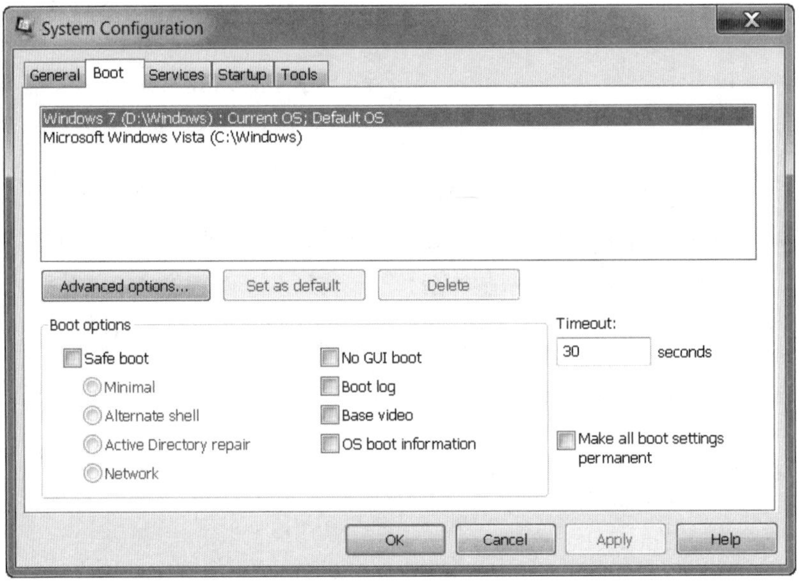

Services Tab

The System Configuration Services tab lets you select services to disable for a restart. This is one way to test if a certain service is causing a problem. Like the other tabs, when you click OK you will be prompted to restart or cancel. Do not consider this the place to manage services, because there is a full-featured Services MMC (services.msc).

Startup Tab

The Startup tab lists every program started when Windows starts up. System Configuration is great to use when you want to prevent a program from launching at startup to see if it is the cause of a problem. Using System Configuration saves you from needing to search all the possible startup locations. The value of System Configuration today is that it will let you test "what-if" scenarios for startup. For instance, you can temporarily disable the startup of one or more programs using MSCONFIG, restart and see if that eliminated the program; if it did, make the change permanent so that the problem will not reoccur.

Tools Tab

The Tools tab in System Configuration contains a long list of troubleshooting and administrative tools, giving you yet another way to launch them. This may be the only place in Windows that lists this group together. Select a tool in the list, and then click the Launch button.

Windows Memory Diagnostic

The *Windows Memory Diagnostic* tool (see Figure 13-12) is actually a memory diagnostics scheduler. You can open it by entering **mdsched.exe** in the Run line. Then, either choose to have the computer restart immediately to run the diagnostics or have it run them on the next restart. When the system shuts down and restarts the diagnostics, run in character mode on a blue background. It can take several minutes to run the tests, and then the computer will automatically restart. The next time you log on the results will display. By default, it runs a standard set of tests, but if you press F1 while the diagnostics are running, you can select to either run a basic set that won't take as long, or a more rigorous extended set that runs several more tests. While it is running, the screen will occasionally look as if it has stalled, but be patient, let it complete, and restart your computer.

FIGURE 13-12

Schedule a
memory scan
using Windows
Memory
Diagnostic.

Troubleshooting with Modified Startups

If a Windows computer fails to start up normally or behaves oddly after startup, you can modify the startup with certain components disabled. You saw how to do this earlier with the System Configuration utility; now learn how to use a special menu. We will refer to it as the Advanced Boot Options menu, as that is its name in Windows Vista, Windows 7 (see Figure 13-13), and Windows 8. In Windows XP, it was the Windows Advanced Options menu.

To access a list of startup options in all versions of Windows except Windows 8, restart the computer and press F8 before the graphical Windows start screen appears. In Windows 8, this menu is rather difficult to access, and we recommend you use the System Configuration tool to modify a Windows 8 restart for troubleshooting, as described earlier in this chapter.

Following is a brief description of the startup options available from the Advanced Boot Options menus.

Repair Your Computer (Windows 7 and Windows 8 Only)

Repair Your Computer is available on the Advanced Boot Options menu in both Windows 7 and Windows 8, but this description is specific to Windows 7, and varies a bit from Windows 8. When you select this option, Windows PE (the Windows Preinstallation Environment defined in Chapter 9) loads and first requires that

FIGURE 13-13 The Windows 7 Advanced Boot Options menu

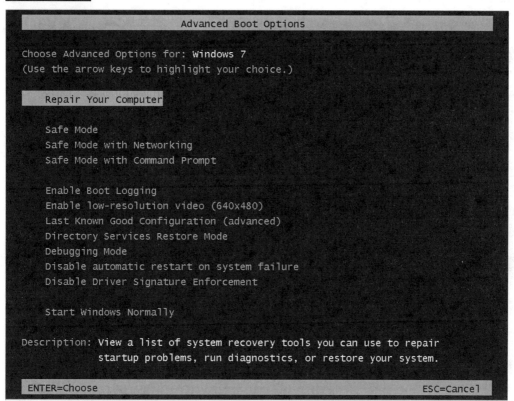

```
                            Advanced Boot Options

Choose Advanced Options for: Windows 7
(Use the arrow keys to highlight your choice.)

    Repair Your Computer

    Safe Mode
    Safe Mode with Networking
    Safe Mode with Command Prompt

    Enable Boot Logging
    Enable low-resolution video (640x480)
    Last Known Good Configuration (advanced)
    Directory Services Restore Mode
    Debugging Mode
    Disable automatic restart on system failure
    Disable Driver Signature Enforcement

    Start Windows Normally

Description: View a list of system recovery tools you can use to repair
            startup problems, run diagnostics, or restore your system.

ENTER=Choose                                              ESC=Cancel
```

you supply a keyboard input method, and then requires that you log on, and finally displays the System Recovery Options screen, described later in this chapter under "Recovery Options."

Safe Mode

Safe Mode is a startup mode for starting Windows with certain drivers and components disabled, but many troubleshooting and recovery tools do work in Safe Mode. Figure 13-14 shows Safe Mode in Windows 7. Notice that the background is all black and the words "Safe Mode" appear in the corners. If Windows will not start normally but starts just fine in Safe Mode, use Device Manager within Safe Mode to determine

FIGURE 13-14 The Windows 7 Safe Mode screen

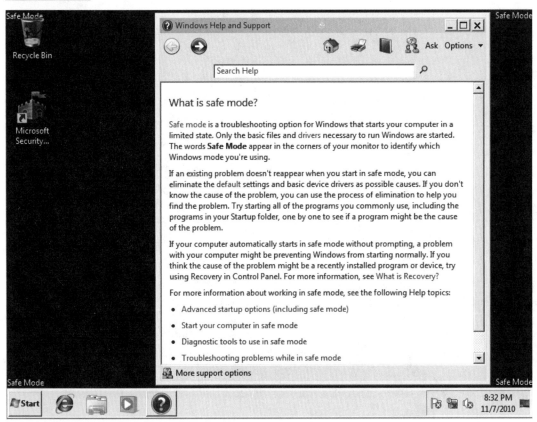

if the source of the problem is a faulty device. In Windows Vista, Windows 7, and Windows 8, you can run System Restore while in Safe Mode and roll back the entire system to before the problem occurred. Safe Mode does not disable Windows security. You are required to log on in all three variants of Safe Mode, and you can only access those resources to which you have permissions.

There are actually three Safe Mode variants available:

■ *Safe Mode* starts up without using several drivers and components that it would normally start, including the network components. It loads only very basic, nonvendor-specific drivers for mouse, video (loading Windows' very basic VGA.sys driver), keyboard, mass storage, and system services.

■ *Safe Mode with Networking* is identical to plain Safe Mode, except that it also starts the networking components. Use the following debug sequence with Safe Mode with Networking:

　■ If Windows will not start up normally but it starts fine in plain Safe Mode, restart and select Safe Mode With Networking.

　■ If it fails to start in Safe Mode with Networking, the problem area is network drivers or components. Use Device Manager to disable the network adapter driver (the likely culprit), and then boot up normally. If Windows now works, replace your network driver.

　■ If this problem appears immediately after upgrading a network driver, use Device Manager while in Safe Mode to roll back the updated driver. When an updated driver is available, install it.

■ *Safe Mode with Command Prompt* is Safe Mode with only a Command Prompt as a user interface. Windows would normally load your GUI desktop, but this depends on the program EXPLORER.EXE, the GUI shell to Windows. In place of this GUI shell, Safe Mode with Command Prompt loads a very limited GUI with a Command Prompt (CMD.EXE) window. This is a handy option to remember if the desktop does not display at all. Once you have eliminated video drivers as the cause, corruption of the EXPLORER.EXE program itself may be the problem. From within the Command Prompt, you can delete the corrupted version of EXPLORER.EXE and copy an undamaged version. This requires knowledge of the command-line commands for navigating the directory structure, as well as knowledge of the location of the file that you are replacing. You can launch programs, such as the Event Viewer (eventvwr.msc), the Computer Management console (compmgmt.msc), or Device Manager (devmgmt.msc), from the Command Prompt.

Enable Boot Logging

While boot logging occurs automatically with each of the three Safe Modes, selecting *Enable Boot Logging* turns on boot logging and starts Windows normally. Boot logging causes Windows to write a log of the activity (programs loaded into memory and programs started) during Windows startup in a file named NTBTLOG.TXT, and it saves it in the *systemroot* folder (usually C:\Windows). This log file contains an entry for each component in the order in which it loaded into memory. It also lists drivers that were not loaded, which alerts an administrator to a possible source of a problem.

Enable VGA Mode/Enable Low-resolution Video (640 × 480)

Titled "*Enable VGA Mode*" in Windows XP, but changed to *Enable Low-resolution Video* beginning in Windows Vista and continuing today, this option starts Windows normally, except that the video mode is changed to the lowest resolution (640 × 480), using the currently installed video driver. It does not switch to the basic Windows video driver. Select this option after making a video configuration change that the video adapter does not support and that prevents Windows from displaying properly.

Last Known Good Configuration (Not Available in Windows 8)

Last Known Good Configuration is a startup option that starts Windows normally and selects the configuration that existed at the last successful user logon (the "last known good configuration"), ignoring changes made after the last logon. This works if you made changes that caused obvious problems. On the very next restart selecting this option will discard the changes. The problem is that if you have logged on since the changes occurred, those changes will be part of the last known good configuration, so it won't work. This rather crude system-restore method only works if you did not restart and log on since making the change.

Directory Services Restore Mode (Not Available in Windows 8)

The *Directory Services Restore Mode* option only works on Windows Servers acting as domain controllers, and Microsoft finally removed it in Windows 8.

Debugging Mode

The *Debugging Mode* is a very advanced option in which Windows starts normally, and information about the activity (programs loaded and programs started) during Windows startup is sent over a serial cable to another computer that is running a special program called a debugger. We consider this option to be obsolete.

Disable Automatic Restart on System Failure

The default setting for Windows is for it to restart after a system crash. However, depending on the problem, restarting may simply lead to another restart—in fact, you could find yourself faced with a continuous loop of restarts. If so, access the Advanced Boot Options menu and select the *Disable Automatic Restart On System Failure* option. Then, Windows will attempt to start normally (just once for each time you select this option) and may stay open long enough for you to troubleshoot. Do not attempt to work with any data file after restarting with this option, because the system may be too unstable. If you are not able to solve the problem, then you will need to restart in Safe Mode to troubleshoot.

Disable Driver Signature Enforcement (Not Available in Windows XP)

If you are unable to install a driver because it has not been digitally signed and is being disabled by driver signing and you trust the manufacturer, select *Disable Driver Signature Enforcement,* which will start Windows normally, disabling driver signature enforcement just for one startup.

Disable Early Launch Anti-Malware Driver (Windows 8 Only)

While it is a good thing to have your anti-malware driver launch early so that it is ready to protect your computer, this very behavior may be tied to a startup problem. To eliminate this as the possible cause, select the *Disable Early Launch Anti-Malware Driver* option in Windows 8, which will only apply to one startup.

Start Windows Normally

Use the *Start Windows Normally* option to start Windows normally with no change in behavior. You would use this after accessing the Advanced Boot Options menu and deciding to continue with a normal startup. It does not restart the computer, but continues the startup.

Reboot (Windows XP Only)

This option restarts the computer, acting like a warm reboot (CTRL-ALT-DELETE) from MS-DOS or Restart Windows from the Windows Shut Down menu. You may then choose to allow Windows to start normally or to open the Advanced Options menu with the F8 key.

Return to OS Choices Menu (Multiboot Only)

Selecting the *Return to OS Choices Menu* option on a multiboot computer will return to the OS Choices Menu (OS Loader menu) where you can select the OS you want to load.

EXERCISE 13-1

Working in Safe Mode

In this step-by-step exercise, you will start Windows in Safe Mode. Although we will use Windows 7 in the steps, the steps are similar in Windows XP and Windows Vista. If you wish to use Windows 8 for this exercise, we recommend that you use the System Configuration utility and select Safe Boot from the Boot tab. The screens will not be identical, but you can experience Safe Mode in any of these OSs. Be prepared to provide credentials to access Safe Mode because security is still in place in Safe Mode. Once in Safe Mode, you can run most Windows troubleshooting tools just as you would after a normal start.

1. Restart the computer, pressing F8 as soon as the power-down completes and before the splash screen appears.

2. On the Advanced Boot Options menu, use the UP and DOWN ARROW keys to move the cursor around. Position the cursor on Safe Mode and press ENTER.

3. When prompted, provide credentials. Safe Mode loads with a black desktop background and the words "Safe Mode" in the corners of the screen. It also opens Windows Help and Support to the page on Safe Mode. Browse through the help information and click the link labeled Diagnostic Tools To Use In Safe Mode.

4. On the resulting page, locate links to start several very handy tools in Safe Mode. In the following steps, practice opening some of these utilities.

5. Click the link labeled Click To Open Recovery. On the Recovery page, notice the links to other tools. Click the button labeled Open System Restore. On the page labeled Restore Files And Settings, click Next to see a list of the restore points on your computer. Click Cancel to leave System Restore, and close the Recovery windows to return to Help and Support.

6. Next use the link that will open Control Panel. You can open most tools you would need from this page.

7. When you finish exploring Safe Mode, close all open windows, and either shut down or restart Windows, allowing it to start normally.

System Restore

If you have ever added the latest software or new device to your Windows computer, only to find that nothing seems to work right after this change, System Restore will come to your aid. In Windows XP you must be able to get into the Windows GUI (normal or Safe Mode) to use this great recovery tool, but later versions include this in both the GUI and outside of Windows via the System Recovery Options menu (described later in this chapter in "Recovery Options").

System Restore creates restore points, which are snapshots of Windows, its configuration, and all installed components. Windows creates restore points automatically when you add or remove software or install Windows updates and during the normal shutdown of your computer. You can also choose to force creation of a restore point before making changes. If your computer has nonfatal problems after you have made a change, or if you believe it has a malware infection, you can use System Restore to roll it back to a restore point.

During the restore process, only settings and programs are changed—no data is lost. Your computer will include all programs and settings as of the restore date and time. This feature is invaluable for overworked administrators and consultants. A simple restore will fix many user-generated problems.

To restore a Windows system to a previous time point, start the System Restore Wizard, which you can launch from Start Search in Windows Vista and Windows 7 and from Search Settings in Windows 8. In Windows XP choose Start | All Programs | Accessories | System Tools | System Restore, and then select the first radio button, Restore My Computer To An Earlier Time, and then click Next. In Windows Vista and later, choose either Recommend Restore or Choose A Different Restore Point, in which case you can select a restore point from a list similar to the one in Figure 13-15. In both cases, click Next and follow the instructions.

You don't have to just rely on the automatic creation of restore points. You can create a restore point at any time. In Windows 7 do this by clicking the Start button and entering **create** in the Search box. Then select Create A Restore Point from the results list. This will open System Properties. On the System Protection tab, click the Create button (at the bottom). Type a description for your restore point and then click Create. This is something to consider doing before making changes that might not trigger an automatic restore point, such as directly editing the registry.

System Restore is on by default and uses some of your disk space to save information on restore points. To turn System Restore off (disable) or change the disk space, open the System Properties applet and select the System Restore tab in Windows XP, or the System Protection tab in Windows Vista or later. Disabling System Restore is

FIGURE 13-15

Select a restore point.

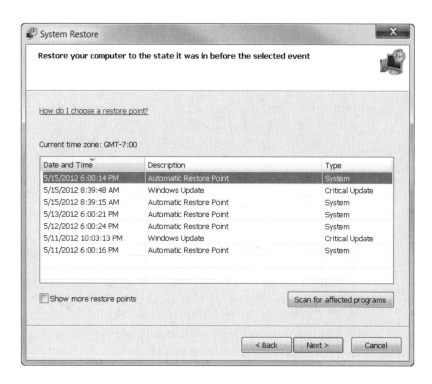

now a common part of cleaning off many malware infections to ensure that a virus isn't hiding in the restore files. But be aware that turning System Restore off, even for a moment, deletes all old restore points. After the malware removal process is complete, enable System Restore and immediately create a new restore point.

In Windows Vista you could delete an old restore point, but that feature is not available in Windows 7 or Windows 8, both of which automatically manage the old restore points, deleting them when space is needed. However, you can put limits on the maximum percentage of disk space used.

Shadow Copy

While System Restore tracks and maintains snapshots of the Windows files, it is not concerned with user data files, or it wasn't until Microsoft added Shadow Copy to System Restore in Windows Vista. Shadow Copy was briefly defined in Chapter 2. Previously only available on Microsoft Windows Server systems, Shadow Copy tracks and maintains backup copies of versions of data files. As long as System

Restore is on, Shadow Copy is also on for the volume containing the Windows OS, providing that it is a New Technology File System (NTFS) volume. While Microsoft calls this feature Shadow Copy, in the GUI the two features, System Restore and Shadow Copy, are called *System Protection*. In Windows Vista and Windows 7, Shadow Copy, like System Restore, is only turned on for the system drive—the drive containing the operating system files, and only if that drive is formatted with NTFS, which is the default.

Windows 8 includes the ability to add drives other than the system drive to Shadow Copy. To create or configure Shadow Copy in Windows 8, open the System Control Panel applet and select System Protection from the task list on the left. This will open the System Properties dialog box with the System Protection tab current. By default, System Protection (Shadow Copy) is only turned on for the system drive, but you may also turn it on for any other NTFS-formatted drive.

With Shadow Copy/System Protection turned on in any of these versions of Windows, you can right-click a file on the protected drive in Windows Explorer and select Restore From Previous Versions. This brings up a Properties dialog box for the file opened to the Previous Versions tab page. It may take several seconds for the list of previous versions to be populated. Once it is, select a version and restore it.

Recovery Options

Two sets of recovery tools exist for the Windows versions this book covers. First is the Recovery Console, available in Windows XP. In Windows Vista and Windows 7, the System Recovery Options menu replaces the Recovery Console. Windows 8 has a mix of the old and new recovery options, with the new options appearing in the Windows 8 GUI in the PC Settings page, and the old options appearing in a desktop Control Panel applet called Recovery.

Windows XP Recovery Console

The Recovery Console allows you to recover from an OS failure when all else has failed. It is a totally non-GUI command-line interface. If you have the Windows XP Professional installation disc, you can start the Recovery Console by booting from the disc, running Setup, selecting Repair, and then selecting Recovery Console.

However, if you like to be proactive, you can install the Recovery Console on your hard drive so it is one of your startup options and does not require the Windows disc to run. To do this, first log on as an administrator and insert the Windows XP Professional disc into the drive. If Autorun starts the Setup program, click No.

Then open a Windows Command Prompt by selecting Start | Run and typing **CMD** in the dialog box. At the Command Prompt, enter the following command:

```
d:\i386\winnt32 /cmdcons
```

where *d* is your optical media drive letter.

Just follow the instructions on the screen. If connected to the Internet, allow the Setup program to download updated files. After the Recovery Console installs, at each restart, the OS Selection menu will display two choices: Windows XP or the Microsoft Windows Recovery Console. It may also show other choices if your computer is dual-boot. When you select the Recovery Console, it will start and then you will see the Recovery Console Command Prompt.

The cursor is a small, white rectangle sitting to the right of the question mark on the last line. If only one installation of Windows is on your computer, type **1** at the prompt, and then press ENTER. If you press ENTER before typing a valid selection, the Recovery Console will cancel and the computer will reboot. Once you have made your selection, a new line appears on the screen prompting you for the administrator password.

Enter the administrator password for that computer and press ENTER. The screen still shows everything that has happened so far, unless something has caused an error message. The screen now looks like this.

```
Microsoft Windows XP(TM) Recovery Console.
The Recovery Console provides system repair and recovery functionality.
Type EXIT to quit the Recovery Console and restart the computer.

1: C:\WINDOWS

Which Windows installation would you like to log onto
(To cancel, press ENTER)? 1
Type the Administrator password: ********
C:\WINDOWS>_
```

Now what do you do? Use the Recovery Console commands, of course. Recovery Console uses Command Prompt utilities. To see a list of Recovery Console utilities, simply enter **help** at the prompt. To learn more about an individual command, enter the command name followed by /? Here is a brief description of a few handy commands:

- **DISKPART**   Performs disk partitioning
- **EXIT**   Exits the Recovery Console and restarts your computer
- **FIXBOOT**   Writes a new partition table from the backup master file table on disk

- **FIXMBR**   Repairs the master boot record (MBR)
- **HELP**   Displays a Help screen
- **LOGON**   Logs on to a selected Windows installation (if more than one is installed).
- **SYSTEMROOT**   Sets the current directory to the location of the Windows system files—usually C:\Windows

The files that make up the Recovery Console reside on drive C:, making the Recovery Console unavailable if this partition is badly damaged. The Recovery Console shines in allowing an administrator to restore registry files manually, stop problem services, rebuild partitions (other than the system partition), or use the EXPAND program to extract uncorrupted files from a disc to replace corrupted files.

You can reconfigure a service so it starts with different settings, formats drives on the hard disk, reads and writes on local FAT or NTFS volumes, and copies replacement files from a floppy or optical media. The Recovery Console allows you to access the file system, but it is still constrained by the file and folder security of NTFS. Recovery Console is a very advanced tool—definitely not for amateurs!

Windows XP Automated System Recovery

To recover from damage that prevents the operating system from starting up in any way, Windows XP has *Automated System Recovery (ASR)* available from the Backup Utility (NTBACKUP.EXE). ASR replaces the *Emergency Repair Disk (ERD)* process of even earlier versions of Windows, which required that you create an ERD while the system was healthy and then use it, along with the Windows Setup CD, to repair the OS. ASR, in contrast, uses a backup of the entire system partition (where the OS is installed) and, therefore, provides a more holistic repair, restoring the entire operating system to a certain point in time.

exam

watch   *CompTIA Exam 802 Objective 4.6 lists "repair disks." While Windows has not used that exact language since Windows NT, and Windows 2000 used the Emergency Repair Disk, the ASR option is effectively a repair disk. However, CompTIA is looking for "repair discs"*   *(as in optical discs), so the Windows 7 and Windows 8 option (described later under "Preventive Maintenance for Windows OSs") to create a system repair disc meets this criterion, and you need to understand these options.*

Using ASR requires some planning. You must use the Advanced Mode of the Windows XP Backup Utility (NTBACKUP.EXE) to create an ASR backup set, which includes an ASR disk to initiate a bootup into the ASR state, and a system partition backup to media such as tape, another local hard disk, or a network location accessed via a drive letter (a mapped drive).

The Welcome page of the Advanced Mode of the Backup Utility contains the option for running the Automated System Recovery Wizard to create an ASR set.

An ASR backup set does not include a backup of other partitions, nor does it allow you to select data folders. Therefore, your Windows XP Professional backup strategy should include occasional creation of an ASR set and frequent backups to save data and changes to the OS since the last ASR set.

Automated System Recovery and the Backup Utility are not included in Windows XP Home Edition. You can install the Backup Utility (NTBACKUP.EXE) from the Windows XP Home distribution CD, however. Some computer manufacturers include a custom system recovery tool for preinstalled original equipment manufacturer (OEM) Windows, but they may not include a backup utility.

Windows Vista and Beyond: Preinstallation Environments

In Chapter 9, you learned about the Windows Preinstallation Environment (Windows PE), a scaled-down Windows operating system with limited drivers for basic hardware and support for the NTFS file system, TCP/IP, certain chipsets, mass storage devices, and 32-bit and 64-bit programs. That description belies the power of this environment, because when needed, it supports a powerful group of diagnostics and repair tools called the *Windows Recovery Environment (Windows RE)*. Computer manufacturers have the option of adding their own repair tools to Windows RE.

Windows RE Startup at Failure   When a Windows Vista, Windows 7, or Windows 8 computer fails to start, if the damage is not too extensive, Windows Recovery Environment (RE) will start and load the Windows Error Recovery page with two options: Launch Startup and Repair (Windows RE's built-in diagnostics and recovery tool), and Start Windows Normally. It is always worth trying the second option to see if the cause of the problem was something transient. Then, if it still doesn't start up normally, select the Launch Startup Repair and follow the instructions on the screen.

Starting Windows RE from the Advanced Options Menu   You can also call up Windows RE from the Advanced Options menu. Earlier in this chapter, you learned about the Advanced Boot Options menu. Windows 7 and later include the

Repair Your Computer options, which loads the Windows RE System Recovery Options menu. This option requires a local administrator password.

Starting Windows RE from Windows Disc   Another option is to start Windows RE by inserting the Windows disc in the drive and restarting the computer. When prompted, press a key to start from disc. Select language, time and currency format, keyboard or input method, and click Next. On the following page, click Repair Your Computer (on the bottom left). This brings up the Windows RE System Recovery Options dialog box. Select the operating system you want to repair and click next, and the System Recovery Options menu appears.

If Windows came preinstalled on your computer, the manufacturer may have installed this menu as is or customized it, or they may have replaced it with their own recovery options. Like the Windows XP Recovery Console, these tools are useful to you when Windows Vista or Windows 7 will not start normally and you must attempt to recover from an environment outside of Windows. The individual tools on this menu are

- **Startup Repair**   This tool replaces missing or damaged system files, scanning for such problems and attempting to fix them.
- **System Restore**   This tool restores Windows using a restore point from when Windows was working normally.
- **System Image Recovery (Windows Vista)/Windows Complete PC Restore (Windows 7)**   If you previously created a complete PC image backup, this tool will let you restore it. This replaces the Automated System Recovery (ASR) that appeared in Windows XP.
- **Windows Memory Diagnostic Tool**   This tool, described earlier, tests the system's RAM (a possible cause for failure to start). If it detects a problem with the RAM, replace the RAM before trying to restart Windows.
- **Command Prompt**   This tool replaces the Recovery Console by providing an improved 32-bit or 64-bit (depending on the installation) character-mode interface where you can use Command Prompt tools to resolve a problem.

Windows RE Command Prompt   In the Windows RE Command Prompt, you can run some (but not all) commands you normally run within the Windows Command Prompt. The value of this Command Prompt is the ability to run such tools to repair the disk or BCD file when Windows will not start. Flip back to Chapter 10 and the discussion about two such repair tools: BCDEDIT and DISKPART. You can also run a tool, BOOTREC, which is not available to you from within a normal Windows Command Prompt. BOOTREC is a more capable disk repair tool than the Windows XP Recovery Console commands. Following are the BOOTREC commands you can run at the Windows RE Command Prompt for repairing a system partition:

- **bootrec /fixmbr**   Repairs the master boot record (MBR) without overwriting the partitionable portion of the disk.
- **bootrec /fixboot**   Overwrites the boot sector with one compatible with the Windows version installed.
- **bootrec /scanos**   Scans all disks looking for compatible Windows installations and then displays the results.
- **bootrec /rebuildbcd**   In addition to the scanning performed by /scanos, this option lets you select an installation to add to the BCD store. Do this if an installation on a multiboot system does not show as an option in the Boot Management menu.

The CompTIA 802 Exam expects you to be familiar with the tools included in the Windows XP Recovery	**Console and Windows Vista and Windows 7 System Recovery Options menu.**

DirectX Diagnostic Tool

The *DirectX Diagnostic Tool (DXDIAG)* is a Run line utility. Launch this program when experiencing video problems, such as the inability to take advantage of DirectX video, sound, and input support required by DirectX applications and evidenced by either poor performance in the inability to display video motion in two dimensions or three dimensions. Start up DXDIAG from the Run box. The utility was dumbed down a bit beginning in Windows Vista because it no longer allows you to run tests of the DirectX systems, just view status information. However, in Windows XP, you can run several tests of your multimedia system, including testing both the DirectDraw and Direct3D support for each video adapter and connected display, DirectSound support, Direct Music (synthesizer and any connected sound devices), input and output, and testing network performance for working with interactive DirectPlay applications.

CERTIFICATION OBJECTIVES

■ **802: 4.6** *Given a scenario, troubleshoot operating system problems with appropriate tools*

This section details the possible solutions for the symptoms listed in CompTIA A+ Exam Objective 4.6, along with appropriate tools for diagnosing and solving problems.

Symptoms and Solutions

Operating system failures occur for a variety of reasons, but just a few types—startup, device driver, and application failures—account for the majority. These often occur at startup. Operational problems are those that occur while Windows is running, as opposed to those that occur during startup. These may be instability problems, and they may involve OS components, including drivers, or application components. Regardless of the source of the problem, watching for error messages and familiarizing yourself with common error messages is important.

OS Instability Problems

What does OS instability look like? Instability includes a variety of symptoms, such as

- Slow system performance
- Inability to open programs
- Failure of running programs
- System lockup
- Missing graphical interface or graphical interface fails to load
- Complete failure of the OS, resulting in a Stop error on a bluescreen

Let's examine how you would approach an instability problem that results in a bluescreen error. When a system malfunctions due to a fatal error, it results in a text-mode screen with white letters on a blue background. This screen is officially a Stop screen, but unofficially people call it the Blue Screen of Death (BSoD). It displays a message and multiple numbers that are the contents of the registers and other key memory locations. This information is usually not overly useful to a computer technician, but it can provide a great deal of information to developers and technical support professionals as to the nature of the failure. It is a good idea to capture that information before you contact customer support.

A fatal error is one that could cause too much instability to guarantee the integrity of the system. Therefore, when the operating system detects a fatal error, it will stop and display the Stop screen.

Preparing for Stop Errors

To prepare for a Stop error, you should decide how you want your computer to behave after one occurs. You do this by modifying the System Failure settings on the Startup And Recovery page. You can find these settings by opening the System applet in Control Panel, selecting the Advanced System Settings tab, and clicking the Settings button under Startup And Recovery:

- ■ **Write An Event To The System Log** causes Windows to write an event to the System log, which is one of several log files you can view using Event Viewer (found under Administrative Tools). We highly recommend this setting, because it means that even if the computer reboots after a Stop screen, you can read the Stop error information that was on the screen in the System log.

- ■ **Send An Administrative Alert** is a setting that appears in Windows XP. It sends an alert message to the administrator that will appear on the administrator's screen the next time he or she logs on. This is a useful setting for alerting a domain administrator if your computer is part of a domain.

- ■ **Automatically Restart** is a setting we recommend, as long as you have also selected the first option, which preserves the Stop error information in the System log file.

- ■ **Write Debugging Information** contains a drop-down list, a text box, and a check box. The drop-down list allows you to control the existence and size of the file containing debugging information. This file, called a dump file, has settings that include None, Small Memory Dump (64 KB), Kernel Memory Dump, and Complete Memory Dump. A complete memory dump contains an image of the contents of memory at the time of the fatal error. You can send this file to Microsoft for evaluation of a problem, but this amount of effort and cost (Microsoft charges for these services) is normally only expended on a critical computer, such as a network server. For a desktop computer, a small memory dump should be adequate, unless a support person advises you otherwise. The text box allows you to specify the location of the dump file. The default is %SystemRoot%\ followed by the dump filename. The operating system uses the variable %SystemRoot% to point to the folder containing the Windows system files. The final setting is the check box labeled Overwrite Any Existing File. We recommend selecting this option so dump files do not accumulate on your computer's hard drive.

Troubleshooting a Stop Error

If you are present when a Stop error occurs, read the first few lines on the screen for a clue. If the system reboots before you can read this information, you can view it in the System log after the reboot. Open Event Viewer and look in the System log for a Stop error.

For example, say the error message looks something like this: "STOP [several sets of numbers in the form 0x00000000] UNMOUNTABLE_BOOT_VOLUME." If you search www.microsoft.com using just the last part of this message (UNMOUNTABLE_BOOT_VOLUME), you may find sufficient information to determine the cause and the action to take by examining the values that preceded it. One possible solution offered is to reboot using the Windows disc and start the Recovery Console (XP) or System Recovery Options menu (Vista/7) and to run a command from the Command Prompt. Now, you see the value of understanding how to work with the Recovery Console or System Recovery Options.

Spontaneous Shutdown or Restart

A spontaneous shutdown or restart can occur due to overheating problems and a failing power supply. If this happens, troubleshoot for heat problems in the system and also check out the power supply.

Improper Shutdown

While not a symptom, an improper shutdown can cause instability problems. All operating systems require a proper shutdown in order to close and save all open files. An improper shutdown can cause damage to open system and data files. Windows has controls built in that make this less likely to occur, such as the ability to configure the power button on your computer to not actually power down the computer but to send a shutdown command to the OS. Use the Power Options utility, described in Chapter 7, to configure your power button to shut down, hibernate, or put the computer to sleep.

Windows Boots to Safe Mode

If Windows spontaneously boots to Safe Mode, there is a failure with an operating system component and you can troubleshoot from Safe Mode. All of the recovery tools described earlier in this chapter that normally run in Windows also run within Safe Mode. First try using System Restore to restore the system to a previous point in time. If that doesn't help, then follow the instructions in the "Troubleshooting with Modified Startup" section earlier in this chapter.

RAID Not Detected During Installation

If you attempt to install Windows on a computer with a hardware-level RAID array in place, but Windows setup cannot see the resulting drive created by the array, you may have a firmware problem with the RAID controller. Recall what you learned about RAID in Chapters 4 and 6. Once configured, the physical hard drives in a hardware-level RAID are not seen separately by the Windows operating system. Windows only sees the resulting volume or volumes created by the array. This is also true of the Windows setup program. However, Windows does use a set of low-level drivers to communicate with drives and will install updated drivers during setup. Since drivers are an extension of the controller BIOS, the failure of Windows setup to see a RAID volume may be due to an incompatible BIOS. The solution is to contact the manufacturer of the controller (or motherboard, if the controller is embedded) and determine if you need a BIOS firmware upgrade for the Windows version you are attempting to install.

Troubleshooting Applications

Common problems with applications include the failure of an application to start and problems when running legacy applications in Windows.

Application Fails to Start

Imagine that you have spent days preparing a presentation for work. Your computer is running Windows, and you have several applications open. The presentation consists of a complex Excel spreadsheet, a Word report, and a PowerPoint slide presentation.

In researching a topic for this report, you locate source information in a file on the Internet. The file is in Portable Document Format (PDF) format. You double-click the file, expecting it to load into the Acrobat Reader program. The hourglass appears briefly, but Acrobat does not start up, and no error message appears. You open the Task Manager, which shows current tasks. You expect to see Acrobat listed with a status of Not Responding, but instead it is not listed. The possible problem is that there is not enough memory to run the additional program. The solution is to close one or more applications and then attempt to open Acrobat. The long-term solution to this problem is to add more RAM to your computer.

An Old Application Will Not Run

Let's say you start an old application in a new version of Windows and it does not run correctly. Maybe the screen doesn't look quite right, or perhaps the program frequently hangs up. To solve this problem, first check for program updates from the manufacturer and install those. If this does not help, try reinstalling the program. If that also does not work, then use the Program Compatibility Wizard for the version of Windows you are running. We described the Program Compatibility Wizard in Chapter 2. After running the Program Compatibility Wizard, test the program to see if there is an improvement. If Compatibility Mode does not solve the problem for a program that ran well under Windows XP, and if you are running Windows 7, you have another option, which is Windows XP Mode, described in Chapter 8. Use this option before doing something that would be less desirable, such as creating a dual-boot configuration. That would require booting the computer into Windows XP just to run the old app and back into Windows 7 for other tasks. If Windows XP Mode does not work, consider dual-booting or finding an alternate app that will run in Windows 7.

File Fails to Open

To troubleshoot why a file fails to open, first look at the method used for opening the file. There are two frequently used methods for opening files. One is to locate the file using Windows Explorer and double-click the file to launch it in the associated program. Another is to first open the app, such as Microsoft Word, and open a file from within the app. For instance, in Microsoft Word click the Office orb (or the File tab) in the upper-left corner of the window and either select the file from the Recent Documents list or select Open and browse to the file's location.

When a file fails to open when you use the first method, it is most likely that the file type is not associated with any installed program. This happens frequently on a brand-new computer when someone attempts to open a PDF file. The reason it cannot open is most likely because the computer does not have a PDF reader, such as Adobe Acrobat Reader. Locate a free PDF reader on the Web, download it, and install it. Caution: Only download from a site you trust, and be careful because a Web page containing free download will often have a bigger and more obvious button for downloading something you may not even want, and it is easy to click the wrong button.

If a file fails to open from a recent list—whether it is the Recent list within the application or the Recent Items list on the Start menu—suspect that the file got moved or renamed since the last time it was opened in an app. Open Windows Explorer and do a search for the filename you recall. If that fails to locate your file, do another search for a string of characters you know are contained in the document.

Common Error Messages

An IT professional must recognize and interpret common error messages and codes. These range from messages that appear during the early stages of a failed startup, through a variety of operational error messages. Once-fleeting messages that were not available after the fact are now logged in many cases, and a knowledgeable person learns where to find them, as you will see in the sections that follow.

Startup Error Messages

When an OS fails in the early stages of startup, the problem often stems from corruption or loss of essential OS files. If this is the case, you may need to reinstall the OS, but before you take such a drastic step, consider other actions, such as the recovery options detailed earlier in this chapter.

NTLDR or NTDETECT.COM Is Missing (Windows XP)   If Windows XP startup fails and you see a message that NTLDR or NTDETECT.COM is missing when you boot from your hard disk, simply boot with your Windows startup diskette (also called a bootable floppy), and copy the missing file from A:\ to C:\. If you support computers running Windows XP, and if they have floppy drives, we recommend that you create one of these disks for each OS. The Microsoft Support Website has several articles on doing this. Check out "How to create a bootable floppy disk for an NTFS or FAT partition in Windows XP" if you would like to learn more.

NTOSKRNL Is Invalid or Missing (Windows XP)   The error message "NTOSKRNL is invalid or missing" does not occur too often, but when it does, this message is usually incorrect and misleading because it is highly unlikely that this file is either invalid or missing. What is more likely is that NTOSKRNL is not where NTLDR expects it to be. NTLDR finds this location by reading the BOOT.INI file.

If a BOOT.INI file is not present, NTLDR attempts to locate this file in the default location for the version of Windows you are using.

In Windows XP the default location for NTOSKRNL is C:\WINDOWS\ SYSTEM32. If Windows was not installed in the default location, and if the BOOT .INI file is damaged or missing, Windows will fail to start and will display the "NTOSKRNL is invalid or missing" error.

Similarly, if the BOOT.INI file is present but contains incorrect information, NTLDR will look in the wrong location and once again display the error message. If the computer previously started without failure, and if you have a Windows startup diskette for the computer, use the disk to start Windows. If Windows starts when using the startup diskette, correct the problem by copying the BOOT.INI file from the startup diskette to the root of C:. If Windows does not start properly with the disk, then you have a more serious problem. It may still relate to the BOOT.INI file, but it may involve a change to the disk partitioning. In this case, research the Microsoft site for articles on the BOOT.INI file and how it describes the location of NTOSKRNL.EXE.

Invalid Boot or Invalid System Disk   An error message that reads "Invalid system disk" or "Invalid boot disk" can have several causes. This error message is more likely to occur on a very old version of Windows, such as Windows 98, than on any newer version of Windows. But if you see this message on a newer Windows system, here are a few possible causes and their solutions:

- A boot-sector virus may have infected your computer. Learn more about boot-sector viruses at support.microsoft.com.
- Third-party hard drive drivers did not copy to the hard disk during setup. You will need to obtain updated drivers and follow the manufacturer's instructions. This may require reinstalling Windows.
- Specialized security software is preventing access to drive C:. Check the documentation for the security software.

Inaccessible Boot Drive   This error may show as a bluescreen Stop error, in which case the exact wording is Inaccessible Boot Device. This fatal error has several possible causes and solutions. Here are just a few:

- A boot-sector virus has infected the computer. Learn more about boot-sector viruses at support.microsoft.com.
- A resource conflict exists between the two disk controllers. This conflict is most likely to occur after the installation of an additional controller. In that case,

remove the new controller and reboot. If Windows starts up normally, then troubleshoot the new controller for a configuration that conflicts with the boot controller.

■ The boot volume is corrupt. If you have eliminated other causes, then remove the boot hard drive system and install it in another computer that has a working installation of the same version of Windows. Configure it as an additional drive, boot into the existing operating system, and then run the CHKDSK (Check Disk) program on the hard drive to diagnose and fix errors.

Missing Operating System   "Missing operating system" or "Operating system not found" may appear on a black screen when you start Windows. Then, because you cannot start up from the hard drive at all, you can try to boot from the Windows Setup disc and start the Recovery Console (Windows XP) or Repair Your Computer (Windows Vista and Windows 7). At that point, if you see the message "Setup did not find any hard drives installed on your computer," the cause is most likely one of the following:

■ BIOS did not detect the hard drive.

■ The hard drive is damaged. See the last part of the previous paragraph.

■ The MBR (located in the first physical sector) is damaged.

■ An incompatible partition is marked as Active.

To troubleshoot for this, restart the computer and access the BIOS setup menu. Check to see that the BIOS recognizes the hard drive. If it is not recognized, check the computer or motherboard manufacturer's documentation to enable the BIOS to recognize the hard drive and learn how to run diagnostics once the drive is recognized.

If it still does not recognize the hard drive, power down, open the computer case, and check the data cable and power cable connections to the hard drive. If you found and corrected a problem with the connectors, close the system up, restart and run the BIOS setup again, and see if the drive is recognized. If it still fails, then the drive may be irreparable. But before you give up on the drive, restart again with the Windows Setup disc in the drive.

When using the Windows XP setup disc, follow the prompts and at the text-based screen that offers Repair or Recovery, press R and provide the Administrator password to access the Recovery Console where you can use command-line commands. For a full list of the commands, type **help**. We will describe the recommended commands for this problem after the instructions for accessing the Windows Vista and Windows 7 System Recovery Command Prompt.

In Windows Vista or Windows 7, boot from the setup disc and select Repair Your Computer; this loads the System Recovery Options dialog box. Select your operating system (unless your computer multiboots, there will only be one option). Then the System Recovery Options list will open. Select Command Prompt.

Regardless of the version of Windows you are attempting to repair, there are two utilities that are most useful for this problem. One is CHKDSK and the other is FIXMBR.

CHKDSK will check for damage to the file system within the logical drive. We recommend using this before trying FIXMBR. Run the CHKDSK command by entering **chkdsk c: /f /r**.

The CHKDSK command can take hours to run, but we have been able to recover hard drives that seemed hopeless. After the command completes, restart the computer. If it boots into the operating system, you are good to go, but if not, repeat the steps to get back to the Command Prompt through the Recovery Options menu and then run FIXMBR. To run FIXMBR, it is best to specify the exact hard drive with the problem unless there is only one. If there is only one, you simply enter **fixmbr** at the Command Prompt, and the program will locate the backup copy of the master boot record and overwrite the damaged one. Hard disks are numbered beginning with zero (0). So, if the disk is the second hard disk in the computer, run FIXMBR by entering **fixmbr \device\harddisk0**. If this fails to correct the problem, the disk may simply be too damaged to repair.

Device Has Failed to Start   If you see the message "Device has failed to start" or a similar message, open Device Manager and double-click the device name to open the device's Properties dialog box. On the General tab, look in the Device Status box for an error code. Troubleshoot in accordance with the error code. You may search the Microsoft Website for this error code and find a recommended solution.

If the driver is corrupted, you will need to uninstall the driver, click the Action menu in Device Manager, and select Scan For Hardware Changes to reinstall the driver. Another common solution is to select Update Driver in Device Manager. This will start the Hardware Update Wizard, which will walk you through the update process.

Sometimes, you do not see an associated error message when a device fails to start. This usually happens just as you attempt to use a device, such as a camera, scanner, or printer, and Windows does not recognize it and cannot install a driver (assuming this is the first time it was connected). First check that the device is properly connected and powered on, and then try again. Recall the quick fixes at the beginning of this chapter and power down the device and Windows. Turn power on to the device and power up the computer and try again. If the problem persists, contact the manufacturer and/or do a search on the problem.

Service Has Failed to Start   If you see the error message "Service has failed to start" or a similar message, open the Services console (enter **services.msc** in the Run line). In the contents pane, scroll down until you see the service that failed to start and right-click it. From the context menu, click Start. It may take several minutes for the service to start. If it starts normally, without any error messages, then do not take any further steps unless the problem recurs, in which case you will need to research the problem. Do this by searching the Microsoft site on the service name, adding the word "failed" to the search string.

Device Referenced in Registry Not Found   If you see an error message stating that a device referenced in the registry was not found, use the instructions given in the earlier section, "Device Has Failed to Start," to either update the driver or uninstall and reinstall the driver.

Program Referenced in Registry Not Found   If you see an error message stating that a program referenced in the registry was not found, uninstall and reinstall the program.

Missing DLL File   This error message may occur during startup or after you call up an application. Record the name of the DLL file, such as DIRECTX.DLL OR MS-VCR100D.DLL, and then use a search engine to research the error, or go to support .microsoft.com and enter a search string including "missing" and the filename. This error occurs when a program install or uninstall did not complete properly. You may need to reinstall a program or manually uninstall a program, based on instructions from either Microsoft or the publisher of the program, if it is a third-party program.

In a related but less common problem, the files in the DLL cache become corrupt, in spite of being in a protected location. The files in the DLL cache folder (%systemroot%\system32\dllcache) are used as a backup set in case the DLLs in the default location (%systemroot%\system32) become corrupt. In spite of many protections put in place to preserve both the installed DLL files and this cache of "spares," the cache location can be damaged. To repair it, use the System File Checker command-line command. There are three ways to use this command to repair the DLL cache. They are sfc /scannow, sfc /scanonce, or sfc /scanboot.

Viewing Error Messages in Event Viewer

You may think of error messages as something fleeting that you must write down so you can troubleshoot the problem to relay the information to a support person. However, Windows automatically saves most error messages in Event logs for later viewing in Event Viewer.

Become familiar with Event Viewer before a problem occurs, so you will be comfortable using it to research a problem. Use Event Viewer to view logs of system, security, and application events, paying attention to the warning and error logs for messages you can use to solve problems.

Event Viewer has three standard categories of events: system, application, and security. Other Event logs may exist, depending on the Windows configuration. For instance, Internet Explorer creates its own Event log. You can open Event Viewer from Administrative Tools or by using its filename, EVENTVWR.MSC, and starting it from the Run line.

Beginning in Windows Vista, the organization of the Event Viewer console changed quite a bit, displaying Administrative events, which is a selection of events from all the log files that show a status of Warning or Error. This saves scrolling through all the Information events to find an event indicating a problem. To see the individual logs, select the Windows Logs folder in the left pane and select each Event log in turn:

- The System log records events involving the Windows system components (drivers, services, and so on). The types of events range from normal events, such as startup and shutdown (called Information events), through warnings of situations that could lead to errors, to actual error events. Even the dreaded "Blue Screen of Death" error messages show up in the System log as Stop errors. The System log, shown in Figure 13-16, is the place to look for messages about components, such as a driver or service. In the newer versions of Windows, details for the selected event, including the actual message, display in the pane below the events list. In Windows XP double-click an event to see the details. The message itself may lead you to the solution. Each event also has an ID number. Search the Microsoft Website for a solution, using either a portion of the error message or the event ID.

- The Application log shows events involving applications. These applications may be your office suite of applications or Windows components that run in the GUI, such as Windows Explorer or Document Explorer. If you see an error on your screen that mentions an application, you will find the error listed in the Application log.

FIGURE 13-16 Windows 7 Event Viewer showing the System log

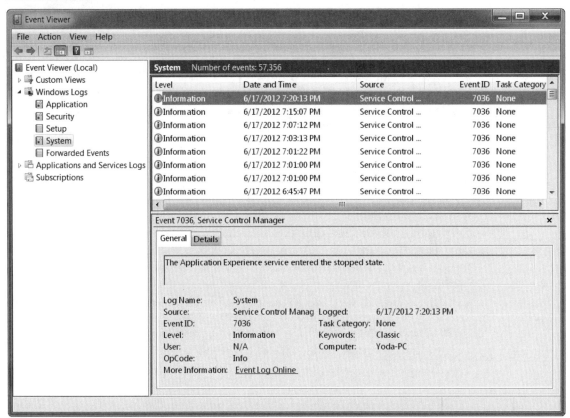

■ The Security log will log events such as a successful and/or failed logon attempt. It will also log events relating to access to resources, such as files and folders. Several types of security events are logged by default, and an administrator can enable and disable logging of security events on a computer with Windows 7 Ultimate or Windows 7 Enterprise using Local Security Policy, an MMC console you can open from a shortcut on the Administrative tools menu (if this menu is available) or by entering **secpol.msc** in the Run line. One small group of Local Security Policy settings that controls what is logged is in Security Settings | Local Policies | Audit Policy. These events will show in the Security log in Event Viewer as Success Audits or Failure Audits. Another much larger group of settings that affect what appears in the Security log are found in Security Settings | Local Policies | Security Options.

To learn more about Event Viewer, use the help program from within Event Viewer.

CERTIFICATION OBJECTIVES

■ **802 1.7** *Perform preventive maintenance procedures using appropriate tools.*

CompTIA Exam Objective 802: 1.7 describes a list of best practices for preventive maintenance of Windows computers. You should know how to schedule important maintenance tasks, such as backups, check disks, defragmentation, updates, patch management, driver or firmware updates, and antivirus updates. Also listed are the tools you should use for many of these tasks, including backup, system restore, check disk, recovery image, and defrag. The following section will describe how you use these tools to perform important maintenance tasks.

Preventive Maintenance for Windows OSs

Preventive maintenance for Windows operating systems includes tasks that either prevent certain problems from occurring or guarantee that you can quickly recover from a problem or disaster with a minimum loss of time or data.

Preventive maintenance best practices include the following:

■ Scheduled backups
■ Scheduled check disks
■ Scheduled defragmentation
■ Windows updates
■ Patch management
■ Driver/firmware updates
■ Antivirus updates

Scheduled Backups

The data created and stored on computers is far more valuable for individuals and organizations than is the computer hardware and software used to create and store the data. So your backup strategies, the hardware and software used for backup, and the actual habit of backing up are critical to maintaining both data and computers.

In case of the accidental destruction of data, and/or the disks containing the data, having a recent backup on removable media can be the difference between personal or professional disaster and the relatively minor inconvenience of taking the time to restore the data. Therefore, most versions of Windows include backup programs.

Backup in Windows XP

The executable name of the backup program that comes with Windows XP Professional is NTBACKUP.EXE. The GUI calls this the Backup Utility and Windows Backup. Running NTBACKUP opens the Backup Or Restore Wizard. You can access it through a shortcut in the System Tools folder, or from Start | Run or Windows Key+R using the executable name NTBACKUP. It will back up to a tape drive, to a local hard disk, or to a network location available as a drive letter (a "mapped" drive).

NTBACKUP is not included in Windows XP Home. If you find yourself working with Windows XP Home Edition, you may still install Windows Backup if you have the distribution CD. NTBACKUP and its installation program are located under VALUEADD\MSFT\NTBACKUP. Simply launch the installation program located in this directory (it has an MSI extension), and NTBACKUP will install. If your computer came preinstalled with XP Home and you do not have the distribution CD, search for this folder on your hard drive, because it may be there along with the other distribution files.

Backup in Windows 7 and Windows 8

Backup And Restore in Windows 7 includes the use of network locations, as well as internal and external drives. Open it by entering **backup** in the Start Search box and selecting Backup And Restore from the results. Figure 13-17 shows Backup And Restore with settings for the location and information about the next scheduled backup, the last scheduled backup, the contents of the backups, and the schedule. All of this information is missing when you first open Backup And Restore. In its place is a simple statement, "Windows Backup has not been set up," and a shortcut labeled Set Up Backup. Click this to select what you want to back up and to choose a location for the backups. You can have Backup And Restore back up files in certain folders (and you choose the types of files you want backed up from those folders), and you can have it create a system image. We do both (files and system), and

FIGURE 13-17 Click Change Settings to make changes to the backup settings.

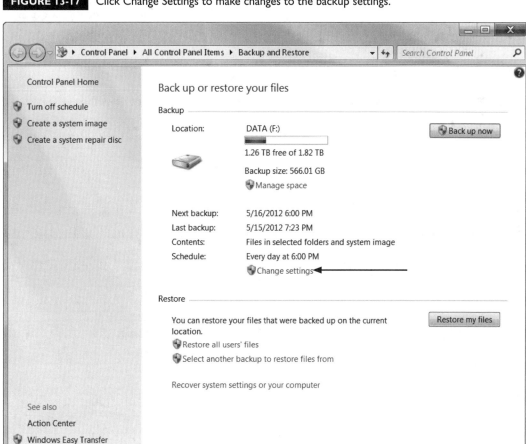

we recommend that you do this also. The computer in the example backs up to an external hard drive, and has been backing up to the drive for the last several months. We allow Windows Backup And Restore to manage the space, automatically deleting old backups as necessary to preserve space, and we still have 1.26 TB of space free on the backup disk. We also configured backup to run every evening at 6 P.M.

If you have Windows 7 Professional or Ultimate, you have the options of telling Backup And Restore to save to a network location by clicking Change Settings and then in the Set Up Backup dialog box, click the Save On A Network button. In the resulting dialog box, shown in Figure 13-18, either enter a network location or browse to it and then enter the user name and password you would normally use to access this location.

FIGURE 13-18   Enter a network location and a user name and password for accessing that location.

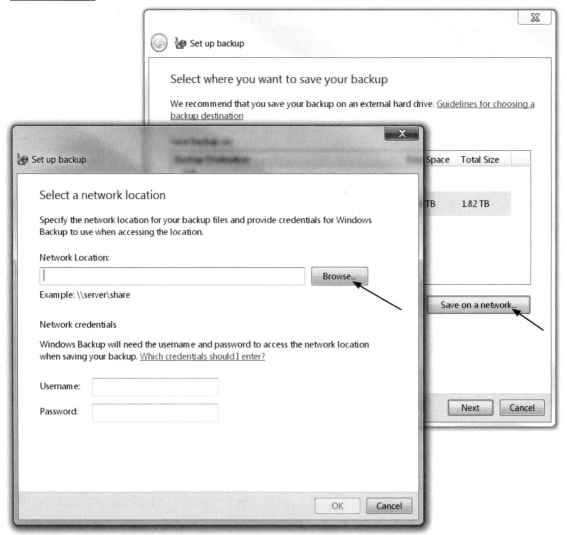

Testing Restore

If possible, occasionally test your backups by restoring them. Now, you need to be careful when doing this, because if the backup is even minutes old and you have made changes to files since the backup, you will end up restoring on top of the changed files and lose your new work. Therefore, if possible, test your backups by restoring to another identically configured computer—perhaps one you use for testing or training purposes.

Create a System Image

A *system image* is a complete backup of the hard drive containing an operating system. There are third-party tools that you can use to create a system image for previous versions of Windows without this option, but Windows 7 Backup And Restore includes the option Create A System Image. You can create an image backup on a hard disk, one or more DVDs, or a network location. Start the Create A System Image wizard from the task list in the left pane of the Backup And Restore utility (see Figure 13-17). In the wizard, select the location, and follow the instructions. If you choose to use DVDs, you may need a stack of them to complete the image backup.

Create a System Repair Disc

Windows 7 and Windows 8 have a utility that will create a *system repair disc*, an optical disk that you can use to boot your computer when Windows will not boot normally, and it contains system recovery tools that you can use to restore a system image (providing you created a system image beforehand) or do other repairs to Windows without restoring the image. Create a system repair disc ahead of time and keep it on hand for an emergency. To do this, type **system** in the Start search box and select Create A System Repair Disc from the results list. This opens the Create A System Repair Disc dialog box where you can choose an optical drive to use to create a repair disc.

Scheduled Check Disks

The Windows GUI tool that is the equivalent of the CHKDSK command-line tool is Check Disk. Find this tool by right-clicking a drive icon in Windows Explorer, selecting Properties, and then opening the Tools tab where you will see Error-checking. Click the Check Now button, and the Check Disk dialog box will open (Figure 13-19) with two choices: They are Automatically Fix File System Errors and Scan For And Attempt Recovery Of Bad Sectors. You may choose one or both options. The first will mark damaged space as unusable so that it will not be used

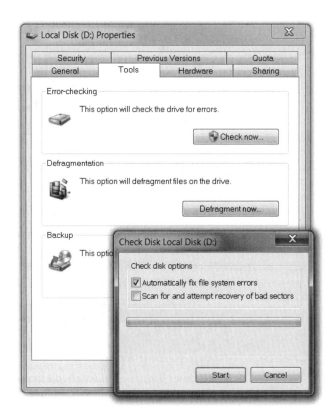

FIGURE 13-19

Tools tab in the Properties dialog box for a drive in Windows 7

again, whether parts of files are sitting on that space or not, so you will lose any data in that space if you choose only this option. The second will attempt to move data from bad sectors to good sectors. Even this does not always have good results, and depends on the file type. A data file can lose data that was in bad sectors, but apps can still open the file so that you can work with the remaining data. However, some file types, especially those that contain program code, will not be usable with some of the contents gone. Once you have selected options, click Start. You will see the message shown in Figure 13-20, and you can click Schedule Disk Check. The next time the computer restarts, a Check Disk will run.

Scheduled Disk Defragmentation

A common, and easily corrected, cause of system slowness is fragmented files. Windows writes files in available space beginning near the outside of the disk platters. Over time, as you delete files, this leaves open space into which new files can be written, but large files may require more space than is available in the first

FIGURE 13-20

Click to schedule
a disk check.

available contiguous open space. The OS then places in this space what will fit and
seeks the next available space.

This practice causes files—especially large ones—to be fragmented, meaning that
the various pieces of one file are in several locations on the disk. Reading or writing
a fragmented file takes much longer than it does for the same file written into one
contiguous space. Therefore, over time, a system will slow down simply because of the
large number of fragmented files on a volume.

A simple preventive task is defragmenting the hard drive. You can run Disk
Defragmenter as described in Chapter 9. You can also run it from the command-line
program, DEFRAG.EXE, as described in Exercise 10-5 in Chapter 10, or use a third-
party defragmenter. Whichever program you use, defrag your hard drive volumes
on a regular basis—once a week or once a month.

There are certain tasks you should perform before defragmenting a drive. Because
Disk Defragmenter cannot work on the Recycle Bin, consider emptying it before
running the program. This will open up more space. It also cannot defrag any open
files, so close all other applications before starting Disk Defragmenter. This program
also requires 15 percent free space on the drive in which to work as it moves files
around. If you start defragmenting when there is insufficient space, it will stop and
display an error message. Therefore, before beginning, check on the available disk
space on the volume you wish to defrag. You can do this from within the GUI Disk
Defragmenter program. Look at the value at the right of the drive to confirm it has
more than 15 percent free space before selecting it.

If you find that you do not have enough free space, delete files. Use the Disk
Cleanup program to free up adequate space. We described this program in Chapter 9.

Patch Management

Patch management is the management of all the important updates that are
necessary to keep operating systems and applications secure and functional.
These include updates to firmware, drivers, the operating system, applications,

and antivirus and other security software. Large organizations have procedures for how they test updates before deploying them; then they use server-based patch management systems that automatically distribute updates to all the computers on the network. However, everyone needs to manage these updates in some fashion— even for your home computer. Individuals should, at minimum, enable automatic updates for Windows and all applications that allow it, including antivirus and other security programs. As for driver and firmware updates, it simply isn't practical for an individual or personnel in a small office to keep tabs on driver and firmware updates. So, at least be aware that problems with computers and devices, especially when they occur when you add a new device or program to an older computer, may require a firmware or driver update.

CERTIFICATION SUMMARY

An IT professional must have a foundation of knowledge about Windows in order to troubleshoot common problems, beginning with a few quick fixes to try before going any further in researching symptoms. Then, attempt to pinpoint the problem's source to a single application or to the operating system in general. Ensure that a computer meets the minimum requirements for the installed OS and apps.

Familiarize yourself with the utilities and tools for troubleshooting. Begin with documentation resources available to you for troubleshooting and training yourself in using and supporting Windows and applications. Practice using Registry Editor, Device Manager, Task Manager, Task Scheduler, Performance Monitor, System Configuration Utility (MSCONFIG), and Windows Memory Diagnostics. Also practice modified startups using the various Safe Mode options. Ensure that you know the recovery options for Windows XP, Windows Vista, and Windows 7.

You should recognize common symptoms and understand the possible causes and solutions to these problems. Recognize common error messages and codes, and understand how to work with Event Viewer.

Practice preventive maintenance on Windows computers, including defragmenting hard drive volumes, turning on automatic updates for both Windows and applications, scheduling backups, testing restores, and configuring System Restore.

TWO-MINUTE DRILL

Here are some of the key points covered in Chapter 13.

Overview of Troubleshooting Software Problems

❑ Try quick fixes, such as rebooting, uninstalling, and reinstalling software that you suspect is causing a problem.

❑ Pinpoint a problem application by testing several apps under the same conditions.

❑ Verify that a computer meets the minimum requirements for the installed OS and apps.

Windows Troubleshooting Tools

❑ Use the System Information Utility (MSINFO32.EXE) to quickly learn about a system you must troubleshoot or support.

❑ The registry is a database of all Windows configuration settings that is best modified indirectly through many configuration tools, although administrators can use Registry Editor (REGEDIT) to view and directly edit it.

❑ The GUI for many Windows utilities is an MMC window. Some tools available in MMCs are Device Manager, Task Scheduler, Performance Monitor, Component Services, and Services.

❑ REGSVR32 is a command-line tool for resolving problems with software components.

❑ Use Task Manager to stop a program that has stopped responding and that cannot be stopped any other way.

❑ Use the System Configuration Utility (MSCONFIG.EXE) to modify startup configuration settings without having to alter the settings directly. You can test startup settings without making them permanent until you are satisfied with the results.

❑ Windows Memory Diagnostic is a tool that will schedule a group of diagnostic tests of your memory after a reboot.

❏ You can access the Windows Advanced Boot Options menu (Advanced Options in Windows XP) by pressing F8 as the computer is restarting. It contains many alternative ways to start Windows when you are troubleshooting startup problems.

❏ Select from three Safe Mode options to troubleshoot and solve Windows problems. They are Safe Mode, Safe Mode with Networking, and Safe Mode with Command Prompt.

❏ System Restore creates restore points, or snapshots that Windows created automatically, including its configuration and all installed programs. If your computer has nonfatal problems after you make a change, you can use System Restore to roll it back to a restore point.

❏ Windows Shadow Copy is turned on when System Restore is, adding the ability to track and maintain backup copies of data file versions for files on an NTFS volume. Windows Vista and Windows 7 can only use Shadow Copy on the system volume, while Windows 8 allows you to add other NTFS volumes.

❏ Start the Recovery Console, a command-line interface, from the Windows XP CD by running Setup, selecting Repair, and then selecting Recovery Console.

❏ Beginning in Windows Vista, the System Recovery Options menu gives you very powerful recovery tools that you can use to recover or restore Windows after a failure.

❏ In Windows XP, ASR allows you to create a backup of the system partition, which will include a bootable disk and backup media. Use this to recover from a complete failure when all other options have failed.

❏ If your computer cannot take advantage of DirectX video, sound, and input required by some applications, use the DirectX Diagnostic Tools (DXDIAG) from the Run line to diagnose the problem.

Symptoms and Solutions

❏ OS instability problems include extreme slowness, inability to open programs, failure of running programs, system lockup, and complete failure of the OS, resulting in a Stop error.

❏ When an application fails to start but there are no other obvious symptoms, suspect that insufficient memory is the problem.

❑ If an old application will not run and that application was for an earlier version of Windows, use the Program Compatibility Wizard to modify the environment in which the program runs in Compatibility Mode. If you are running Windows 7, you have another option, which is Windows XP Mode.

❑ Be familiar with command error messages and their possible solutions. Use Event Viewer to see error messages you missed.

Preventive Maintenance for Windows OS

❑ Schedule regular backups of both the OS and data files using either the Backup utility in Windows or a third-party backup program. Test a restore of your data to ensure that it will work when you really need it.

❑ Schedule Check Disks to automatically fix file system errors and scan for and attempt recovery of bad sectors.

❑ Defragment files on your hard drives on a regular basis to prevent the slowdowns that can result from file fragmentation.

❑ Test your backups with an occasional restore.

❑ Create a system image and a system repair disc.

❑ Do patch management, including automatic updates for both Windows and your applications, driver and firmware updates, and antivirus updates.

SELF TEST

The following questions will help you measure your understanding of the material presented in this chapter. Read all of the choices carefully because there might be more than one correct answer. Choose all correct answers for each question.

Overview of Troubleshooting Software Problems

1. All but one of the following is a quick fix that you should at least consider before further investigation of a problem. Select the quick fix.
   A. Reboot the computer
   B. Restore a system image
   C. Uninstall a recently installed app
   D. Uninstall a recently installed device

Windows Troubleshooting Tools

2. Where can you access Safe Mode?
   A. Start menu
   B. Advanced Boot Options menu
   C. Control Panel
   D. System Properties

3. In what startup mode should you attempt to start Windows after making a change to the video settings that result in the Windows GUI not displaying properly, making it impossible to work in the GUI?
   A. Software Compatibility Mode
   B. System Restore
   C. Boot logging
   D. Enable VGA Mode/Enable Low-resolution Video

4. Last Known Good (LKG) only works within a narrow window of opportunity that ends when the following occurs.
   A. A user logs on.
   B. The computer reboots.
   C. The disk is defragmented.
   D. A restore point is created.

5. This Windows XP recovery tool creates a backup of the entire system partition, as well as a boot disk to start the recovery process.
   A. System Restore
   B. Automated System Recovery
   C. Last Known Good
   D. Safe Mode

6. Beginning with Windows Vista, you can access this entire menu of software tools that you can use outside of Windows if it fails to start up.
   A. System Recovery Options
   B. Windows Memory Diagnostic Tool
   C. Startup Repair
   D. Windows Complete PC Restore

7. What Run box command opens up a GUI utility with a lot of information about the computer and its Windows installation, including memory, processor, Windows version, and more?
   A. MSINFO32
   B. MSCONFIG
   C. SYSINFO
   D. REGEDIT

8. Which of the following is a Run line tool that should only be used when you cannot make a change to system settings by any other means?
   A. MSINFO32
   B. MSCONFIG
   C. REGSVR32
   D. REGEDIT

9. If a Windows XP application will not run in Compatibility Mode in Windows 7, what can you try next?
   A. Compatibility Mode Plus
   B. Dual-boot
   C. Windows XP Mode
   D. A Windows 7–compliant application

10. What can cause an application to fail to start without issuing an error message?
    A. A Stop error
    B. Hibernation turned off
    C. Sleep Mode
    D. Insufficient memory

11. What mode can you try to allow a legacy application to run well in Windows Vista?
   A. GUI Mode
   B. Legacy Mode
   C. Compatibility Mode
   D. Virtual Mode

12. What GUI tool will you use to stop an application that is not responding to mouse and keyboard commands?
   A. Startup disk
   B. Task Manager
   C. System Configuration Utility
   D. Device Manager

13. What GUI tool will allow you to modify and test Windows startup configuration settings without having to alter them directly? Once you are satisfied, you can use this tool to make the settings permanent.
   A. Device Manager
   B. Safe Mode
   C. Notepad
   D. MSCONFIG

14. If you upgrade a device driver only to find it causes problems, use this feature in Device Manager to return to the old device driver.
   A. Roll Back Driver
   B. Update Driver
   C. Uninstall
   D. Driver Details

15. Where does System Restore store its restore points?
   A. In RAM
   B. On the local hard disk
   C. On a network share
   D. On removable drives

Symptoms and Solutions

16. How can you control Windows' automatic behavior after a Stop error?

- **A.** Power off and power up.
- **B.** Modify System Failure settings.
- **C.** Open Event Viewer.
- **D.** Use System Restore.

17. After receiving an error message in Windows, you searched for the error message using the Help program and the Microsoft Knowledge Base. It failed to find a solution. What should you do now?

- **A.** Locate the paper documentation for Windows.
- **B.** Call Microsoft's free 24-hour support line.
- **C.** Search the Internet using the error message.
- **D.** Locate the Windows Read Me file.

18. What command-line tool can you use to repair the DLL cache?

- **A.** Taskkill
- **B.** REGSVR32
- **C.** SFC
- **D.** TASKLIST

Preventive Maintenance for Windows OS

19. What utility should I run to free up more disk space before using Disk Defragmenter on a drive?

- **A.** Format
- **B.** Task Manager
- **C.** Disk Cleanup
- **D.** System File Checker

20. Taken together, when you are tasked with centrally handling updates to OSs and apps, as well as to firmware and device drivers, for computers in an organization of any size, what is the name for this overall responsibility?

- **A.** Automatic update
- **B.** Patch management
- **C.** System restore
- **D.** System image

SELF TEST ANSWERS

Overview of Troubleshooting Software Problems

1. ☑ **B.** Restore a system image is not a quick fix, when compared to the other three options, which are quick fixes that would not have further impact. You would need much more investigation before you would restore a system image.

   ☒ **A,** reboot the computer, **C,** uninstall a recently installed app, and **D,** uninstall a recently installed device, are all incorrect answers because they are quick fixes, as opposed to restoring a system image.

Windows Troubleshooting Tools

2. ☑ **B.** The Advanced Boot Options menu is the place where you can access Safe Mode. Get to this menu by pressing the F8 key immediately after restarting your computer.

   ☒ **A,** Start menu, **C,** Control Panel, and **D,** System Properties, are all incorrect because these are all part of the Windows GUI, and the Advanced Options menu is something you use before you start Windows.

3. ☑ **D.** Enable VGA Mode/Enable Low-resolution Video is the startup mode you should attempt after making a change to the video settings that result in Windows not displaying properly.

   ☒ **A,** Software Compatibility Mode, is incorrect because this is not a startup mode, but a mode for running a legacy application. **B,** System Restore, is incorrect because this is not a startup mode, but a tool for restoring the operating system to a previous point in time. **C,** Boot Logging, is incorrect because this startup option will cause the system to create a log of all components as they are loaded and started.

4. ☑ **A.** A user logon is the event that terminates the window of opportunity for using Last Known Good.

   ☒ **B,** the computer reboots, is incorrect because you must restart the computer and press F8 to access the Advanced Options menu from which to select Last Known Good Configuration. **C,** the disk is defragmented, is incorrect. This has no bearing on the use of Last Known Good. **D,** a restore point is created, is incorrect because this has no effect on using Last Known Good.

5. ☑ **B.** Automated System Recovery is the Windows XP recovery tool that creates a backup of the entire system partition, as well as a boot disk to start the recovery process.

   ☒ **A,** System Restore, is incorrect because this does not create a backup of the entire system partition, nor does it create a boot disk. **C,** Last Known Good, is incorrect because Last Known Good only uses a set of registry keys; it does not back up the entire system partition. **D,** Safe Mode, is incorrect because this is simply a special startup mode, not a backup of the system partition.

6. ☑ **A.** System Recovery Options is the menu of recovery options in Windows Vista and later versions that includes an entire set of software recovery tools you can run outside of Windows.
   ☒ **B,** Windows Memory Diagnostic Tool, **C,** Startup Repair, and **D,** Windows Complete PC Restore, are all incorrect because these are all individual tools available through the System Recovery Options menu.

7. ☑ **A.** MSINFO32 is the Run box command that opens up the System Information page with information about the computer and its Windows installation.
   ☒ **B,** MSCONFIG, and **D,** REGEDIT, although both Run box utilities, do not provide the information that MSINFO32 does. **C,** SYSINFO, is not a Run box utility.

8. ☑ **D.** REGEDIT is a registry-editing tool that you should only use to make a change to system settings when you cannot do it by any other means.
   ☒ **A,** MSINFO32, is incorrect because this is a tool for viewing information about the hardware and software on a computer. **B,** MSCONFIG, is incorrect because this is a utility for testing alternate startup settings. **C,** REGSVR32, is incorrect because it is a command-line tool for resolving a certain type of software problem.

9. ☑ **C.** Windows XP Mode is correct.
   ☒ **A,** Compatibility Mode Plus, is incorrect because there is no such mode. **B,** dual-boot, is incorrect because although you could configure the system to dual-boot into Windows XP and Windows 7, this would be rather clumsy and you would try Windows XP Mode first. **D,** a Windows 7–compliant application, is incorrect because although this is ideal, we often do not have a choice and must find a way to use old applications.

10. ☑ **D.** Insufficient memory can cause an application to fail to start without issuing an error message.
    ☒ **A,** a Stop error, is incorrect because although this will only display the Stop error message, it is not necessarily the cause of the problem described. **B,** hibernation turned off, is incorrect because this is not related to the problem described. **C,** Sleep Mode, is incorrect because this will not cause the problem described.

11. ☑ **C.** Compatibility Mode may allow a legacy application to run well in Windows Vista.
    ☒ **A,** GUI Mode, is incorrect because this is not used to allow a legacy application to run well in Windows 8. **B,** Legacy Mode, is incorrect because this is not the mode described. **D,** Virtual Mode, is incorrect because this is not the mode described.

12. ☑ **B.** Task Manager is the GUI tool used to stop an application that is not responding to mouse and keyboard commands.
    ☒ **A,** Startup disk, is incorrect because this is neither a GUI tool nor the tool to use to stop a nonresponsive application. **C,** System Configuration Utility, and **D,** Device Manager, are incorrect because neither is the correct GUI tool to use to stop a nonresponsive application.

13. ☑ **D.** MSCONFIG is the tool that will allow you to modify and test startup configuration settings without having to alter them directly.
☒ **A,** Device Manager, is incorrect because this GUI tool works solely with device drivers, not with the Windows startup settings. **B,** Safe Mode, is incorrect because this is simply a startup mode that allows you to troubleshoot and make changes using a variety of tools. **C,** Notepad, is incorrect because this is simply a Windows text editor.

14. ☑ **A.** Roll Back Driver is the feature in Device Manager that will allow you to return to an old device driver after upgrading.
☒ **B,** Update Driver, is incorrect because this feature installs an updated driver; it does not remove an updated driver and return to the old driver. **C,** Uninstall, is incorrect because this will completely uninstall the driver for the device. **D,** Driver Details, is incorrect because this will only display information about the driver files.

15. ☑ **B.** System Restore stores its restore points on the local hard disk.
☒ **A,** in RAM, is incorrect because you would not want restore points to be stored in volatile RAM. **C,** on a network share, and **D,** on removable drives, is incorrect because a network share and removable drives may not always be available.

Symptoms and Solutions

16. ☑ **B.** Modify System Failure settings is correct.
☒ **A,** power off and power up, is incorrect because this will not change the System Failure settings. **C,** open Event Viewer, is incorrect because this does not control Windows' automatic behavior after a Stop error. **D,** use System Restore, is incorrect because this will not alter Windows' automatic behavior after a Stop error.

17. ☑ **C.** Search the Internet using the error message is correct.
☒ **A,** locate the paper documentation for Windows, is incorrect because this is not as searchable as the Microsoft site or the Internet. **B,** call Microsoft's free 24-hour support line, is incorrect because the Microsoft phone support is a service for which it charges. If it is available to the user, that user will either pay per incident or be part of a paid subscription plan. **D,** locate the Windows Read Me file, is incorrect because it holds very limited information.

18. ☑ **C.** SFC (System File Checker) is a command-line tool that you can use to repair the DLL cache.
☒ **A,** TASKKILL, is incorrect because this is a command-line tool for stopping a running program. **B,** REGSVR32, is incorrect because it is a command-line tool that is used to register or unregister software components, such as DLLs, and ActiveX Controls. **D,** TASKLIST, is a command-line tool for viewing running tasks.

Preventive Maintenance for Windows OS

19. ☑ **C.** Disk Cleanup will free up more disk space to be defragmented.

☒ **A,** Format, is incorrect because this will remove all files from the drive. **B,** Task Manager, is incorrect because this utility will not free up more disk space. **D,** System File Checker, is incorrect because this command-line utility (described in Chapter 10) is used to scan and verify the versions of all protected system files.

20. ☑ **B.** Patch management is the name for this overall responsibility.

☒ **A,** automatic update, is incorrect because this is a very small part of patch management. **B,** system restore, is incorrect because this is a feature on an individual computer, and has nothing to do with updates. **D,** system image, is incorrect because this is also a feature on a single computer.

14

Network Basics

Computer networks provide users with the ability to share files, printers, resources, and email globally. Networks have become so important that they provide the basis for nearly all business transactions.

Obviously, a discussion of the full spectrum of network details and specifications is too broad in scope to be contained in this book. However, as a computer technician, you should be aware of basic networking concepts so you can troubleshoot minor problems on established networks. This chapter focuses on basic concepts of physical networks; Chapter 15 guides you through simple small office/home office (SOHO) network installation, and Chapter 16 provides the basis for troubleshooting common network problems.

CERTIFICATION OBJECTIVES

■ **801: 2.5** *Compare and contrast wireless networking standards and encryption types*

■ **801: 2.7** *Compare and contrast Internet connection types and features*

■ **801: 2.8** *Identify various types of networks*

This section begins by describing the types of networks based on how they are connected (topology) and based on the area they service (LAN, WAN, PAN, and MAN) as required by CompTIA 801 Exam Objective 2.8. The coverage in this section on wide area network (WAN) technologies details Internet connection types and features to prepare you for the CompTIA 801 Exam Objective 2.7. The discussion of the wireless networking standards contains the information as required by CompTIA 801 Exam Objective 2.5, but a portion of that objective, Encryption Types, is not in this chapter, but in Chapter 15.

Network Topologies, Classifications, and Performance

For a computer professional working with PCs, the networked computer is the norm, not the exception. A computer not connected to a network is a *standalone computer,* and this has become a nearly extinct species, as more and more PCs network together—even within homes.

To understand networks, you must first be familiar with common physical network topologies and basic network performance and classifications, which describe networks by speed, geography, and scale, beginning with the smallest networks up to globe-spanning ones.

Network Topologies

You can connect network devices together in a number of ways, and each of these methods is called a *topology*. All but one topology—the hybrid topology—are named for the geometric pattern the connected components create. The geometric topologies are bus, ring, star, and mesh.

Bus

The *bus topology* gets its name from the fact that all computers in this topology connect to a central transmission line (simply called the *bus* or *backbone*) with the appropriate type of connector. The computers are strung out along a single cable (see Figure 14-1) with a *terminator* at each end. A terminator is a device that absorbs the signals so that they don't bounce or reflect, causing traffic problems. The bus topology has drawbacks because a problem with the central transmission line will take down the entire network. Another drawback is that signals from different devices can collide and create problems.

The most common wired local area network (LAN) implementation, Ethernet, is built on the bus topology, and small Ethernet networks in the 1980s used a physical bus. Today Ethernet is more of a hybrid topology, which we will describe later.

FIGURE 14-1

Bus topology

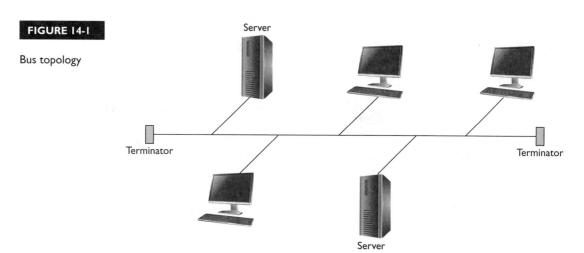

Star

By far the most common physical topology used in today's networks, the *star topology* (see Figure 14-2) resembles a star since each network device connects directly to a central device called a hub or switch (more on hubs and switches later in the section titled "Devices for Connecting to LANs and the Internet"). Thus, a cable problem with one device affects only that device. However, if the hub or switch fails, all of the devices are affected.

Ring

In a *ring topology*, each computer connects to the next device in the ring and the last device connects to the first, as shown in Figure 14-3. Each device regenerates and retransmits signals it receives to the next device in the ring in one direction, thus avoiding the collision issues of a bus or star topology. However, a break anywhere in the ring could bring down the entire network.

Mesh

A *mesh topology* provides redundant paths to each device on the network because each connects directly with every other device. This topology gives each device on the network access to every other device, as shown in Figure 14-4, and the redundancy eliminates downtime if one device fails. Mesh topologies are expensive and lack scalability, so they are rare.

FIGURE 14-2

Star topology

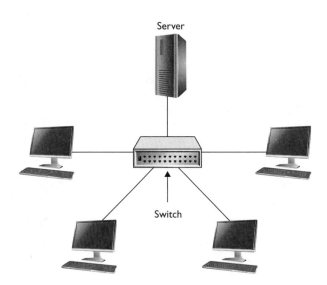

FIGURE 14-3

Ring topology

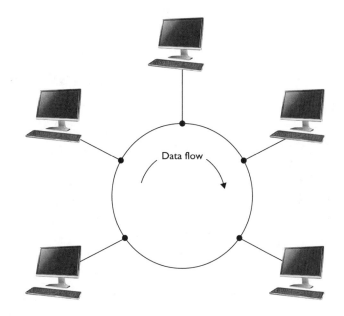

FIGURE 14-4

Mesh topology

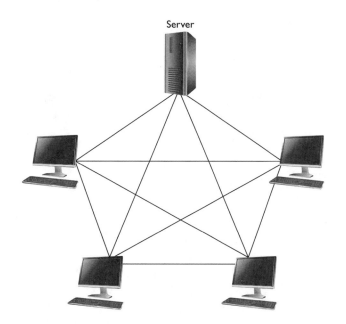

Hybrid

A *hybrid topology* is one that uses a combination of the topologies described earlier. It may include bus or star topologies, with connecting devices between the topologically different networks. Or, one network may combine topologies. For example, an Ethernet network is basically a bus inside the box (hub or switch), but outside the box, what you see is a central connecting point that looks like a star. So it is a physical star (what you see from outside the box) with a logical bus. The physical topology follows the media, while the logical topology follows the data. Ethernet hubs and switches (more on these later) are at central points for connection of wires, resembling the star topology, but the data actually travels on a bus within the hub or switch.

e x a m

ⓦ a t c h *Be sure you can differentiate the bus, star, ring, mesh, and hybrid network topologies for the CompTIA A+ 220-801 Exam.*

Geographic Network Classifications and Technologies

We classify networks by geographic area types, and there are specific technologies designed for each of them. Network builders select these technologies for the capabilities that match the distance needs of the network.

Personal Area Network

You may have your own *personal area network (PAN)*, if you have devices such as smartphones, tablets, or printers that communicate with each other and/or your desktop computer. A PAN may use a wired connection, such as Universal Serial Bus (USB) or FireWire, or it may communicate wirelessly using one of the standards developed for short-range communications, such as Infrared Data Association (IrDA) or Bluetooth. Both were defined in Chapter 7.

Recall that any two IrDA-enabled devices can communicate with each other over a very short distance (one meter), and because IrDA uses an infrared light, the communicating devices must maintain line-of-sight between the IrDA ports on the two devices.

Bluetooth uses radio waves, which do not require line-of-sight, but the signal can be disrupted by physical barriers as well as

e x a m

ⓦ a t c h *The term PAN is included in the objectives for the CompTIA A+ 220-801 Exam; the wireless technologies used in a PAN are also included, so be familiar with them and their distance limit, which is 1 meter for IrDA and 10 meters for Bluetooth (see Chapter 7).*

interference from other signals. The Bluetooth standard describes three classes, with power requirements and distance limits. The Bluetooth standard commonly used with computer peripherals and mobile devices is Class 3, limited to a distance of 1 meter, or Class 2, limited to about 10 meters.

Local Area Network

A *local area network (LAN)* is a network that covers a much larger area than a PAN, such as a building, home, office, or campus. Typically, distances measure in hundreds of meters. A LAN may share resources such as printers, files, or other items. LANs operate very rapidly, with speeds measured in megabits or gigabits per second, and have become extremely cost effective. While there are many LAN technologies, the two most widely used in SOHO network installations are Ethernet and several Wi-Fi standards.

Ethernet   Most wired LANs use hardware based on standards developed by the 802.3 subcommittee of the Institute of Electrical and Electronics Engineers (IEEE). *Ethernet* is the word created to describe the earliest of these networks, and we continue to use this term, although there really are many Ethernet standards—all under the 802.3 umbrella. These standards define, among other things, how computer data is broken down into small chunks, prepared, and packaged before the Ethernet network interface card (NIC) places it on the Ethernet network as a chunk of data called an Ethernet frame. Ethernet standards also define the hardware and medium that control and carry the data signals.

Early implementations of Ethernet were half-duplex, meaning that while data could travel in either direction, it could only travel in one direction at a time. Later implementations are capable of full-duplex communication, in which the signals travel in both directions simultaneously, but they usually auto-negotiate and automatically use either half- or full-duplex, depending on what is in use on the network. Networks today are usually full-duplex, unless a network has very old hardware.

Depending on the exact implementation, Ethernet supports a variety of transmission speeds, media, and distances. All Ethernet standards using copper cabling, either unshielded twisted pair or shielded twisted pair, support a maximum cable length of 100 meters between a NIC and a hub or switch. Learn more about hubs and switches later in this chapter in the section titled "Devices for Connecting to LANs and the Internet." The maximum distances for fiber installations vary, depending on the exact fiber-optic cabling in use. Here is a summary of several Ethernet levels and their speeds:

- **10BaseT/Ethernet** For many years the most widely used implementation, 10BaseT transfers data at 10 Mbps over unshielded twisted-pair (UTP) copper cabling in half-duplex mode with a maximum cable length of 100 meters.

- **100BaseT/Fast Ethernet** Using the same cabling as 10BaseT, 100Base-T or *Fast Ethernet* operates at 100 Mbps and uses different network interface cards, many of which are also capable of the lower Ethernet speeds, auto-detecting the speed of the network and working at whichever speed is in use. Early 100BaseT NICs were half-duplex, but later ones support full-duplex.

- **1000BaseT/Gigabit Ethernet** Supporting data transfer rates of 1 Gbps over UTP, there are several *Gigabit Ethernet* standards, but the most common one is 1000BaseT. It is capable of full-duplex operation using four-pair UTP cable with standard RJ-45 connectors (see the description of cable later in "Transmission Medium").

- **10 GbE/10-Gigabit Ethernet** WANS and very high-end LANs use one of the many standards of *10-Gigabit Ethernet,* which operates at speeds of up to 10 Gbps in full-duplex mode over either copper (10GBaseT) or fiber. There are many 10-Gigabit Ethernet fiber standards for both WANs and LANS, and we will only briefly mention two of them here. The *10GBaseSR* standard is one of the standards used for fiber-optic LANs, whereas *10GBaseSW* is one of the standards used for fiber-optic WANs.

Wireless LAN (WLAN) *Wireless LAN (WLAN)* communication (local area networking using radio waves) is very popular. The most common wireless LAN implementations are based on the IEEE 802.11 group of standards, also called *Wireless Fidelity (Wi-Fi)*. There are several 802.11 standards, and more were proposed. These wireless standards use either 2.4 GHz or 5 GHz frequencies to communicate between systems. The range on these systems is relatively short, but they offer the advantage of not requiring cable for network connections.

In many homes and businesses, Wi-Fi networks give users access to the Internet. In these instances, the wireless communications network uses a wireless router connected to a broadband connection, such as a cable modem or digital subscriber line (DSL) modem.

Wi-Fi, long a standard feature on laptops, is now also available on most smartphones and tablets. In large corporations, users with wireless-enabled laptops and other devices can move around the campus and continue to connect to the corporate network through a Wi-Fi network that connects to the corporate wired network. And many public places, such as libraries, restaurants, and other business, offer free or pay access to Wi-Fi networks that connect to broadband Internet services. Such a point of connection to the Internet through a Wi-Fi network is called a *hotspot*. On an interesting twist on this concept, cellular providers and manufacturers of cellular-enabled mobile devices have cooperated to provide a newer type of service called a *mobile hotspot*. When you purchase a device that supports this, an optional fee-based feature of your cellular service lets you enable the *mobile hotspot* capability that turns your device into a wireless Internet router for other Wi-Fi–enabled devices within range of the device hosting the mobile hotspot.

Here is a brief description of several 802.11 standards and their features:

- **802.11a** The *802.11a* standard was developed by the IEEE at the same time as the slower 802.11b standard, but the "a" standard was more expensive to implement. Manufacturers, therefore, tended to make 802.11b devices. 802.11a uses the 5 GHz band, which makes 802.11a devices incompatible with 802.11b and the subsequent 802.11g devices. Because 802.11a devices do not provide downward compatibility with existing equipment using the 802.11b or newer 802.11g standards, they are seldom used. An 802.11a network has speeds up to 54 Mbps with a range of up to 150 feet.

- **802.11b** The *802.11b* standard was the first widely popular version of Wi-Fi, with a speed of 10 Mbps and a range of up to 300 feet. Operating in the 2.4 GHz band that is also used by other noncomputer devices such as cordless phones and household appliances, these devices are vulnerable to interference if positioned near another device using the same portion of the radio spectrum.

- **802.11g** *802.11g* replaced 802.11b. With a speed of up to 54 Mbps and a range of up to 300 feet, it also uses the 2.4 GHz radio band. 802.11g devices are normally downward compatible with 802.11b devices, although the reverse is not true.

- **802.11n** The *802.11n* standard has speeds of up to 100+ Mbps and a maximum range of up to 600 feet. The standard defines speeds of up to 600 Mbps, which actual implementations do not achieve. *MIMO (multiple input/multiple output)* makes 802.11n speeds possible using multiple antennas to send and receive digital data in simultaneous radio streams that increase performance. Some manufacturers of wireless NICs, signal boosters, and access points manufactured before the release of the full specification used terms such as 802.11pre-n to describe their equipment.

When considering a wireless network, determining its speed and range can be nebulous at best. In spite of the maximums defined by the standards, many factors affect both speed and range. First, there is the limit of the standard, and then there is the distance between the wireless-enabled computer and the *wireless access point (WAP)*, a network connection device at the core of a wireless network. Finally, there is the issue of interference, which can result from other wireless device signals operating in the same band or from physical barriers to the signals. In Chapter 15, you will learn about installing a WLAN to avoid interference and devices that will extend the range of the signals. You will also learn about the configuration options for wireless networks, including the use of identifiers for the wireless devices, secure encryption settings, and settings for keeping intruders out.

e x a m

ⓦ a t c h   Be sure you understand that Wi-Fi alone does not give you a connection to the Internet, because it is a LAN technology. The reason people are able to connect to the Internet through a

Wi-Fi connection is that the Wi-Fi network connects to a broadband connection through a device called a *wireless router,* a combination WAP and router.

Metropolitan Area Network

A *metropolitan area network (MAN)* is a network that covers a metropolitan area, connecting various networks together using a shared community network, and often providing WAN connections to the Internet. A MAN usually runs over high-speed fiber-optic cable operating in the gigabits-per-second range. *Synchronous Optical Networking (SONET)* is one long-established fiber-optic WAN technology. Although people tend to be less aware of MANs, they nonetheless exist. In fact, a MAN may well be somewhere between you and the Internet.

e x a m

ⓦ a t c h   For the CompTIA A+ 220-801 Exam, be sure that you understand the distinctions between the various network types, including PAN, LAN, MAN, and WAN.

Wide Area Network

A *wide area network (WAN)* can cover the largest geographic area. A *WAN connection* is the connection between two networks over a long distance (miles). The term WAN is used to describe a wired WAN connection versus a wireless wide area network (WWAN): a wireless connection between two networks over a long distance. The generic term for these connected networks is an *internetwork,* if it is a public network. The most famous, and largest, internetwork is the *Internet* itself. An *intranet* is a private internetwork, generally owned by a single organization. Your Internet connection from home is a WAN connection, even when the network at home consists of but a single computer. WANs, which traditionally used phone lines or satellite communications, now also use cellular telecommunications and cable networks.

WAN speeds range from thousands of bits per second up into the billions of bits per second. At the low end today are 56 Kbps analog modems (56,000 bits per second). At the high end of WAN speeds are parts of the Internet backbone, the connecting infrastructure of the Internet, running at many Gigabits per second.

on the **job** ***The speed of your communications on any network is a function of the speed of the slowest part of the pathway between you and the servers you are accessing. The weakest link affects your speed.***

Dial-Up WAN Connections   A *dial-up* network connection uses an analog modem (described in Chapter 2) rather than a network card, and uses regular phone cables instead of network cables. In a dial-up connection, you configure the client computer to dial the remote host computer and configure the host computer to permit dial-up access. Once a dial-up connection is established, the client communicates with the host computer as though it were on the same LAN as that computer. If the host computer is already part of a LAN, and if the host configuration allows it, the client computer can access the network to which the host is connected. Some home PCs still use a modem connection for dial-up Internet access. In this case, the host computer is just a gateway to the Internet. This is the slowest, but cheapest, form of Internet access, and in some areas, it may be all that is available.

Broadband WAN   WAN connections that exceed the speed of a typical dial-up connection come under the heading of *broadband WAN*. Broadband speeds are available over cellular, Integrated Services Digital Network (ISDN), DSL, cable, and satellite technologies. WAN connections can connect private networks to the

Internet and to each other. Often, these connections are "always on," meaning that you do not have to initiate the connection every time you wish to access resources on the connected network, as you do with dial-up. If you wish to browse the Web, you simply open your Web browser. Unless you are using dial-up, your connection to the Internet is a broadband WAN connection, and we will explore your Internet connection options here:

■ **Line-of-sight wireless** As implied by the name, *line-of-sight wireless* technology cannot tolerate obstructions such as forests, mountains, or buildings between the service provider tower and the Internet-connecting site. On-site equipment includes a dish to receive and transmit microwave signals to and from the tower, as well as a modem device connected to a computer. One technology that uses both line-of-sight and non-line-of-site is *Worldwide Interoperability for Microwave Access (WiMAX)*. Line-of-sight is much faster than non-line-of-site, and both types of WiMAX are used in cellular networks (see next) as well as by various Internet service providers (ISPs) and carriers as a wireless "last mile" connection option for homes and businesses, in which case, it is line-of-sight wireless service.

■ **Cellular** Long used for mainly voice, the cell networks provide cellular WAN Internet data connections, also referred to as wireless WAN (WWAN). These data services vary in speed from less than dial-up speeds (28.8 Kbps) to a range of broadband speeds, depending on the cellular provider and the level of service you have purchased. Because the trend in cellular is to provide broadband speeds, we include it under broadband WAN. In the United States, the move away from the original analog cellular networks (the first and second generations) to all-digital cellular networks supports this trend to higher speeds. The first two common digital cellular networks in the United States were based on two standards: *Code Division Multiple Access (CDMA)*, used by Verizon and Sprint-Nextel, and *Global System for Mobile Communications (GSM)*, used by T-Mobile and AT&T. Cell providers add other technologies that speed things up. For instance, both Verizon and Sprint-Nextel have used *Evolution Data Optimized (EVDO)* on their networks in the past. Both CDMA and GMS are *Third Generation (3G)* digital mobile broadband technologies. A later and faster 3G technology is High Speed Packet Access (HSPA), with various implementations. The earlier 3G ran at a minimum of 144 Kbps, but eventually 3G service ranged from 400 Kbps to over 4 Mbps. The next big technology leap was *Fourth*

Generation (4G), which is less of a standard and more of a marketing term associated with several different standards with a range of speeds. The expectation is that a 4G network provides many megabits per second, but the actual speeds vary by cellular provider (carrier). At this writing, a number of large cities in the United States enjoy 4G access offered by several cell providers. The 4G technologies include HSPA+, WiMAX, and LTE. T-Mobile and AT&T both use HSPA+ 21/42. The 21 and 42 indicate maximum speeds of 21 Mbps and 42 Mbps, but actual tests are usually much lower—around 10 Mbps. Sprint's 4G service for mobile devices is called Worldwide Interoperability for Microwave Access (WiMAX), with speeds around 10 Mbps over a maximum distance of 30 miles. Metro PCS and Verizon use *Long Term Evolution (LTE)*; both call their offering *4G LTE*. More carriers are moving to LTE.

■ **ISDN**   *Integrated Service Digital Network (ISDN)* was an early international standard for sending voice and data simultaneously over digital telephone wires. These days, newer technologies such as DSL and cable have largely replaced it. ISDN uses existing telephone circuits or higher-speed conditioned lines to get speeds of 64 Kbps or 128 Kbps. In fact, the most common ISDN service, Basic Rate Interface (BRI), includes three channels: two 64 Kbps channels, called B-channels, that carry the voice or data communications, and one 16 Kbps D-channel that carries control and signaling information. ISDN connections use an ISDN modem on both ends of the circuit. Figure 14-5 shows an ISDN connection between two computers. This connection uses a conditioned phone line provided by the phone company.

■ **DSL**   *Digital subscriber line (DSL)* uses existing copper telephone wire for the communications circuit. A DSL modem splits the existing phone line into two bands to accomplish this; voice transmission uses the frequency below 4000 Hz, and data transmission uses everything else. Figure 14-6 shows the simplest configuration with a single computer connected directly to the

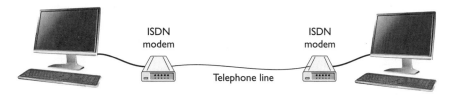

FIGURE 14-5

An ISDN network connection between two computer systems

FIGURE 14-6

A DSL connection

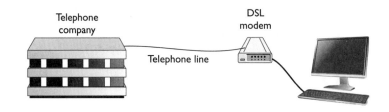

DSL modem. If you have multiple computers, you would connect a router between the computer and the modem and either plug wired computers into it, and/or if the router is a Wi-Fi router, you would connect computers and devices via Wi-Fi, and if there are available Ethernet ports on the router, you can also connect computers via Ethernet. Not shown in the figure is that you can also connect your phones, adding a special filter to each phone jack in your house or office and connecting the phones via phone cable and RJ-11 connectors. DSL separates the total bandwidth into two channels: one for voice, the other for data. Voice communications operate normally, and the data connection is always on and available. DSL service is available through phone companies, which offer a large variety of DSL services, usually identified by a letter preceding DSL, as in ADSL, CDSL, SDSL, VDSL, and many more. Therefore, when talking about DSL in general, the term *xDSL* is often used. Some services, such as *asymmetrical digital subscriber line (ADSL)*, offer asymmetric service in that the download speed is higher than the upload speed. The top speeds, including the newer variations of ADSL (ADSL2 and ADSL2+), can range from 1.5 Mbps to 25 Mbps for download and between 0.5 Mbps and 3.3 Mbps for upload. An inexpensive version of DLS, Consumer DSL (CDSL) service, targets the casual home user with lower speeds than this range. CDSL service is limited to download speeds of up to 1 Mbps and upload speeds of up to 160 Kbps. It is now rare to see a provider offer a service labeled "CDSL." Other, more expensive services aimed at business offer much higher rates. Symmetric DSL offers matching upload and download speeds. Table 14-1 shows some DSL services and their maximum data transfer speeds. Most of these services are available as second-generation services with higher speeds, indicated with a "2" at the end of the name, as in ADSL2, ADSL2+, VDSL2, and HDSL2.

| TABLE 14-1 | DSL Services with Maximum Download and Upload Speeds |

Service	Maximum Speed Download	Maximum Speed Upload	Comments
ADSL	1.5–12 Mbps	0.5–1.8 Mbps	Speeds vary among versions approved between 1998 and 2007
ADSL2	1.5–12.0 Mbps	0.5–3.5 Mbps	Speeds vary among versions approved between 2002 and 2007
ADSL2+	24 Mbps	1.3–3.3 Mbps	Speeds vary among versions approved between 2003 and 2008
Consumer DSL (CDSL)	1 Mbps	16–160 Kbps	Different upload and download speeds. Also called DSL-Lite (G.Lite)
High-data-rate DSL (HDSL)	1.544 Mbps in North America; 2.048 Mbps elsewhere	1.544 Mbps in North America; 2.048 Mbps elsewhere	Same upload and download speeds
Symmetric DSL (SDSL)	1.544 Mbps in North America; 2.048 Mbps elsewhere	1.544 Mbps in North America; 2.048 Mbps elsewhere	Same upload and download speeds
Very high data-rate DSL (VDSL)	13–52 Mbps	1.5–6.0 Mbps	Different upload and download speeds

■ **Cable**   Cable television service has been around for several decades offering *subscription channel (SC)* television service. Most cable providers have added Internet connection services with promised higher speeds of up to 30 Mbps, which is three times the practical maximum for the typical DSL service. Whereas DSL service is point-to-point from the client to the ISP, a cable client shares the network with their neighboring cable clients. It is like sharing a LAN that, in turn, has an Internet connection, so speed degrades as more people share the local cable network. You still get impressive speeds with cable, depending on the level of service you buy. Cable networks use coaxial cable to connect a special cable modem to the network. The PC's Ethernet NIC connects to an integrated switch in the cable modem with twisted-pair cable.

- **T-carrier**   Developed by Bell Labs in the 1960s, the T-carrier system multiplexes voice and data signals onto digital transmission lines. Where previously one cable pair carried each telephone conversation, the *multiplexing* of the *T-carrier system* allows a single pair to carry multiple conversations. Over the years, the T-carrier system has evolved, and telephone companies have offered various levels of service over the T-carrier system. For instance, a *T1* circuit provides full-duplex transmissions at 1.544 Mbps, carrying digital voice, data, or video signals. A complete T1 circuit provides point-to-point connections, with a *channel service unit (CSU)* at both ends. On the customer side, a T1 multiplexer or a special LAN bridge, referred to as the *customer premises equipment (CPE)*, connects to the CSU. The CSU receives data from the CPE and encodes it for transmission on the T1 circuit. T1 is just one of several levels of T-carrier services offered by telephone companies over the telephone network.

- **Satellite**   *Satellite communications* systems have come a long way over the last several years. Satellite communications systems initially allowed extensive communications with remote locations, often for military purposes. These systems usually use microwave radio frequencies and require a dish antenna, a receiver, and a transmitter. Early satellite communications systems were very expensive to maintain and operate. Today, a number of companies offer relatively high bandwidth at affordable prices for Internet connections and other applications. Satellite connections are available for both fixed and mobile applications, and these systems offer download speeds of up to 2 Mbps (upload speeds typically range from 40 to 90 Kbps). Satellite providers offer different levels of service. The highest speeds require a larger dish antenna. The authors formerly used a 0.74-meter dish (larger than modern TV dish antennas) with a special digital receiver/transmitter referred to as a modem. This dish-and-modem combination gives a certain range of speeds, and larger and more expensive dishes provide greater speeds. As with TV satellite service, you must have a place to mount the dish antenna with a clear view of the southern sky. One plan designed for homes and small business has a download speed of 700 Kbps and an upload speed of 128 Kbps. The next higher level of service offers speeds of 1000 Kbps for downloads and 200 Kbps for uploads.

- **Fiber**   In order to compete with cable companies, AT&T, Verizon, and a few other telecommunications companies offer fiber-optic cabling to the home in most areas. Where available, subscribers can have the combined services of phone, Internet, and television. The Internet access speeds vary by provider and service level, but look for speeds greater than 100 Mbps.

- **Permanent virtual circuit (PVC)**   A *virtual circuit (VC)* is a communication service provided over a telecommunications network or computer network. A VC logically resembles a circuit passing over a complex routed or switched network, such as the phone company's *frame relay* or *asynchronous transfer mode (ATM)* network. A *permanent virtual circuit (PVC)* is a virtual circuit, created and remaining available, between two endpoints that are normally some form of data terminal equipment (DTE). Telecommunications companies provide PVC service to companies requiring a dedicated circuit between two sites that require always-on communications.

- **Virtual private network (VPN)**   A *virtual private network (VPN)* is not in itself a WAN connection option, but rather a way to create a simulated WAN-type point-to-point connection across a complex unsecured network. For instance, at one time, if you wanted to connect the computers in a small district office to your employer's private internetwork, you either used a very slow dial-up connection or a fast but expensive physical point-to-point connection. Today, you would connect a single computer or network to the private internetwork over the Internet in a way that keeps your data secure and appears to be a point-to-point connection. You would still need a physical connection to the Internet, preferably a WAN connection, and on top of that you run special software on both ends of the connection that create a VPN. This is one of several *tunneling* techniques used to secure network traffic by encapsulating the original packets within other packets. A VPN uses special tunneling protocols for this purpose, and each endpoint of the tunnel must be assigned an IP address.

EXERCISE 14-1

Testing Broadband Speeds

Regardless of the broadband service you use, they all vary in the actual speeds they provide from moment to moment. Connect to one of the many broadband speed-testing sites on the Internet and test yours now.

1. Open your favorite search engine and enter a search string. We used **network speed test**.

2. From the results listed in the search engine, select a site (we chose www .internetfrog.com). Often sites suggest downloading and running other software to test your computer, so be careful to only select the speed test and not to download or run programs you do not want.

3. Follow the instructions for testing your connection. Some sites test as soon as you connect, and some test sites ask you to select a city near you. The test may take several minutes.

4. View the results (see Figure 14-7). Are the results congruent with the service you expect from your broadband connection?

5. Time permitting, try this at another time, or even on another day.

FIGURE 14-7 The speed of a broadband Internet connection can vary.

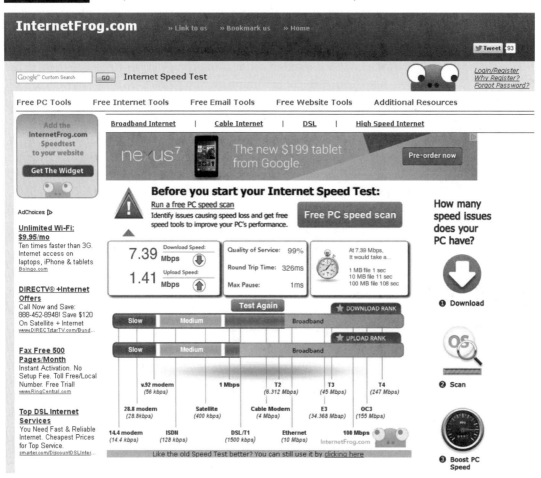

Bandwidth and Latency

While the range of a network, the distance over which signals are viable, is one important defining characteristic of a network, bandwidth is another. *Bandwidth* is the amount of data that can travel over a network within a given time. It may be expressed in kilobits per second (Kbps), kilobytes per second (KBps), megabits per second (Mbps), and even gigabits per second (Gbps); that is, thousands of bits per second, thousands of bytes per second, millions of bits per second, and billions of bits per second, respectively.

Another network characteristic related to bandwidth is latency. *Latency* is the amount of time it takes a packet to travel from one point to another. In some cases, latency is determined by measuring the time it takes for a packet to make a round trip between two points. This can be a more important measurement, as it is does not measure the speed at which the packets travel, but the length of time it takes a packet to get from point A to point B. It is like measuring the actual time it takes you to travel by car from Los Angeles to San Francisco. The actual time of travel varies by the amount of traffic you encounter and the interchanges you pass through. The same is true for a packet on a network.

CERTIFICATION OBJECTIVES

■ **801: 2.3** *Explain properties and characteristics of TCP/IP*

■ **801: 2.4** *Explain TCP and UDP ports, protocols, and their purpose*

This section details the topics required for CompTIA 801 Exam Objective 2.3, including IP address class, a comparison of IPv4 and IPv6, the types of IP addresses based on usage (public, private, and APIPA), the two methods for assigning IP addresses (static and dynamic), and such important TCP/IP terms as client-side DNS, DHCP, subnet mask, and gateway. Coverage of CompTIA 801 Exam Objective 2.4 is also included in this section because it is part of the TCP/IP story. It includes an explanation of both TCP and UDP protocols, as well as other TCP and UDP protocols and related services, and the ports used by TCP and UDP.

Network Software

The software on a network is what gives us the network that we know and use. This is the logical network that rides on top of the physical network. In this section, we'll explore several aspects of networking that are controlled by software, including the network roles, protocol suites, and network addressing of the logical network.

Network Roles

You can describe a network by the types of roles played by the computers on it. The two general computer roles in a network are clients, the computers that request services, and servers, the computers that provide services.

Peer-to-Peer Networks

In a *peer-to-peer network*, each computer system in the network may play both roles: client and server. They have equal capabilities and responsibilities; each computer user is responsible for controlling access, sharing resources, and storing data on their computer. In Figure 14-8, each of the computers can share its files, and the computer connected to the printer can share the printer. A typical peer-to-peer network is very small, with users working at each computer. Peer-to-peer networks work best in a very small LAN environment, such as a small business office, with fewer than a dozen computers and users. Microsoft calls a peer-to-peer network a *workgroup*, and each workgroup must have a unique name, as must each computer.

Client/Server-Based Networks

A *client/server-based network* uses dedicated computers called *servers* to store data and provide print services or other capabilities. Servers are generally more powerful computer systems with more capacity than a typical workstation. Client/server-based models also allow for centralized administration and security. These types of

FIGURE 14-8

A peer-to-peer network

Laser printer

FIGURE 14-9 A client/server environment where dedicated or special-purpose servers perform assigned functions

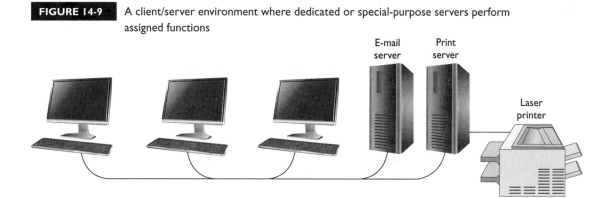

networks are scalable in that they can grow very large without adding administrative complexity to the network. A large private internetwork for a globe-spanning corporation is an example of a client/server-based network. When configuring the network, the network administrator can establish a single model for security, access, and file sharing. Although this configuration may remain unchanged as the network grows, the administrator can make changes, if needed, from a central point. Microsoft calls a client/server network with Microsoft servers, a *domain*. The domain must have a unique name, and each client or server computer must have a unique name.

Organizations use client/server environments extensively in situations that need a centralized administration system. Servers can be multipurpose, performing a number of functions, or dedicated, as in the case of a Web or mail server. Figure 14-9 shows a network with servers used for email and printing. Notice in this example that each of the servers is dedicated to the task assigned to it.

Network Operating System

A *network operating system (NOS)* is an operating system that runs on a network server and provides file sharing and access to other resources, account management, authentication, and authorization services. Microsoft Windows Server operating systems, Novell Server operating systems, and Linux are examples of network operating systems. The distinction is clouded somewhat by the ability of desktop operating systems, such as Windows XP, Vista, Windows 7, and Windows 8, to allow file sharing, but these operating systems do not provide the robust services that, coupled with high-performance servers and fast network connections, add up to reliable server operating systems.

Network Client

A *network client* is software that runs on the computers in a network and that receives services from servers. Windows, Mac OS, and Linux, when installed on desktop computers that have a network connection, automatically install a basic network client that can connect to servers and request file and print services. In each case, the automatically installed clients can only connect to a certain type of server. In the case of Windows, it is a Windows server. Novell has client software that comes in versions the Linux and Windows operating systems can use for accessing Novell servers.

Beyond a basic file and print client, Windows and other OSs usually come with an email client, a browser (Web server client), and other clients, depending on the options you select during installation. You can add other clients. For instance, if you install an office suite such as Microsoft Office 2010, you will have a more advanced email client than the one that comes with the OS. Outlook is the Microsoft email client for business use.

TCP/IP

Every computer network consists of physical and logical components controlled by software. Standards, also often called *protocols,* describe the rules for how hardware and software work and interact together. Ethernet, detailed earlier in this chapter, is a standard for the physical components, such as cabling and network adapters, as well as for the software that controls the hardware, such as the ROM BIOS in the network adapters and device drivers that allow the network adapters to be controlled from the operating system.

However, in most discussions about networks and related documentation, the term "protocol" describes certain software components that work on top of such underlying protocols as Ethernet. These protocols control communication at a higher level, including the addressing and naming of computers on the network, among other tasks. They combine into suites that include a group of protocols built around the same set of rules, with each protocol describing a small portion of the tasks required to prepare, send, and receive network data.

The CompTIA exams require that A+ candidates understand the basics of the *TCP/IP* protocol suite because it is the most common protocol suite used on LANs and WANs, as well as on the Internet. It actually involves several protocols and other software components, and together, we call these a "protocol stack."

In recent years, TCP/IP has largely replaced two other protocol suites for use on most computer networks, namely Microsoft's NetBEUI and Novell's IPX/SPX.

You may encounter these in some organizations or hear about them from long-time network techs.

Transmission Control Protocol/Internet Protocol (TCP/IP) is by far the most common protocol suite on both internal LANs and public networks. It is the Internet's protocol suite. TCP/IP requires some configuration, but it is robust, usable on very large networks, and routable (a term that refers to the ability to send data to other networks). At each junction of two networks is a router that uses special router protocols to send each packet on its way toward its destination.

Although the TCP/IP suite has several protocols, the two main ones are the Transmission Control Protocol (TCP) and the Internet Protocol (IP). There are many subprotocols, such as UDP, ARP, ICMP, and more. We'll describe UDP later in the discussion about common ports; *Address Resolution Protocol (ARP)* is used to resolve an IP address to a MAC address; and Internet Control Message Protocol (ICMP) is described in Chapter 16.

on the
job

Although TCP/IP is actually a protocol suite, techs commonly refer to this suite as "the TCP/IP protocol." On the job, take your cue from the experienced techs, and use the terms they use for easy communication. Hey, that sounds like a protocol!

exam
watch   *The A+ Exams only expect you to understand the basics of TCP/IP, how to configure IP, and the purpose of the various protocols and their associated ports.*

TCP/IP allows for cross-platform communication, meaning that computers using different OSs (such as Windows and Linux) can send data back and forth, as long as they are both using TCP/IP. We now briefly describe the two cornerstone protocols of the TCP/IP suite as well as NetBIOS, a leftover from the NetBEUI suite.

Internet Protocol

Messages sent over a network are broken up into smaller chunks of data, and each chunk is placed into a logical container called a *packet*. Each packet has information attached to the beginning of the packet, called a *header*. This packet header contains the IP address of the sending computer and that of the destination computer. The *Internet Protocol (IP)* manages this logical addressing of the packet so that routing protocols can route it over the network to its destination. We will describe addressing later in "Network Addressing."

Transmission Control Protocol

When preparing to send data over a network, the *Transmission Control Protocol* (*TCP*) breaks the data into chunks, called datagrams. Each *datagram* contains information to use on the receiving end to reassemble the chunks of data into the original message. TCP places this information, both a byte-count value and a datagram sequence, into the datagram header before giving it to the IP protocol, which encapsulates the datagrams into packets with addressing information.

When receiving data from a network, Transmission Control Protocol (TCP) uses the information in this header to reassemble the data. If TCP is able to reassemble the message, it sends an *acknowledgment* (*ACK*) message to the sending address. The sender can then discard datagrams that it saved while waiting for an acknowledgment. If pieces are missing, TCP sends a *non-acknowledgment* (*NAK*) message back to the sending address, whereupon TCP resends the missing pieces.

An excellent 13-minute movie describing how TCP/IP works in an amusing and interesting fashion is available for viewing at www.warriorsofthe.net and is well worth watching.

NetBIOS versus NetBEUI

Networked Basic Input/Output System (*NetBIOS*) and *Networked Basic Input/Output System Extended User Interface* (*NetBEUI*) are very old technologies that you may never encounter. However, the CompTIA A+ 801 and 802 Exam objectives include both of these in their Acronyms list, so here is the short lecture. People often confuse NetBEUI with NetBIOS, perhaps because NetBEUI was the original protocol suite within which NetBIOS was a single protocol. NetBEUI was the default protocol suite on Microsoft networks in the 1980s and 1990s. It was only appropriate for small networks because it was limited to a single network segment and could not route network traffic beyond that segment. TCP/IP has replaced NetBEUI as well as other outdated network protocol suites.

NetBIOS is a single protocol for managing names on a network. In a Windows network, you can use NetBIOS names and the NetBIOS protocol with the TCP/IP suite. NetBIOS only requires a computer name and a workgroup name for each computer on the network. NetBIOS naming has limited value in modern networks, and the Internet-style names of the DNS protocol (which requires TCP/IP) have replaced it. Learn more about DNS later in the topic "DNS Server."

NetBT

NetBIOS over TCP/IP (*NetBT*) is a software component that supports the NetBIOS naming system and name resolution on a TCP/IP network. While even Microsoft has pretty much abandoned the use of the NetBIOS naming system, some organizations are still using old apps that depend on finding network resources based on the old NetBIOS system. Since virtually all networks today use the TCP/IP protocol suite, these systems must have NetBT enabled, as do the servers or networked printers that are being accessed by the old software. Then NetBT on the client computer uses several methods to resolve a NetBIOS name to an IP address. First, it looks in the local computer's local NetBIOS cache of recently resolved NetBIOS names. If it does not find the name in the cache, it then sends a query to the WINS server. If the WINS server does not have the name in its list of NetBIOS names and IP addresses, the client sends out a NetBIOS broadcast on the local network querying for the name. If the server/computer in question has NetBT enabled and it is functioning, it will respond and the client is done searching. That may be more than you will ever need to know about NetBT, but in Chapter 16 we revisit this topic and how to troubleshoot for NetBT problems

Network Addressing

Identifying each computer or device directly connected to a network is important. We do this at two levels: the hardware level, in which the network adapter in each computer or network device has an address, and the logical level, in which a logical address is assigned to each network adapter.

Hardware Addressing

Every NIC, and every device connected to a network, has a unique address, placed in ROM by the manufacturer. This address, usually permanent, is called by many names, including *Media Access Control (MAC) address*, physical address, Ethernet address (on Ethernet devices), and NIC address. For the sake of simplicity, we will use the term "physical address" in this book.

A MAC address is 48 bits long and usually expressed in hexadecimal. You can view the physical address of a NIC several ways. It is usually, but not always, written on a label attached to the NIC. Figure 14-10 shows the label on a wireless USB NIC. The words "MAC Address" appear above the physical address. The actual address on this NIC is six two-digit hexadecimal numbers, but on this label, the numbers are not separated. It is easier to read these numbers if separated by a dash, period, or space, like this: 00-11-50-A4-C7-20.

Locating this address is not always so easy. You can also discover the address of a NIC through Windows. Use the *IPCONFIG* command-line utility that is installed on a Windows computer with the TCP/IP protocol suite. This command lets you view the IP configuration of a network connection and perform certain

The physical
address of a NIC,
labeled "MAC,"
and shown on
the NIC

administrative functions. To see the physical address as well as the rest of the IP
configuration for a connection, simply open a Command Prompt and type the
ipconfig /all command. The physical address is in the middle of the listing. Notice
that it shows six two-digit hexadecimal numbers, each separated by a dash.

This physical address identifies a computer located in a segment of a network.
However, you use logical addresses to locate a computer that is beyond the local
network segment.

Logical Addressing/IP Addressing

In addition to the hardware address, a computer in a TCP/IP network must have a
logical address that identifies both the computer and the network. This address comes
under the purview of the IP protocol. The Internet Protocol version 4 (IPv4) and its
addressing scheme have been in use for over the past three decades. It offers almost
4.3 billion possible IP addresses, but the way they were allocated throughout the world
reduces that number. The Internet is currently transitioning to Internet Protocol
version 6 (IPv6) with a new addressing scheme that provides many more addresses.

An IP address identifies both a computer, a *host* in Internet terms, and the logical
network on which the computer resides. This address allows messages to move from
one network to another on the Internet. At the connecting point between networks, a
special network device called a router uses its routing protocols to determine the route
to the destination address before sending each packet along to the next router closer to
the destination network. Each computer and network device that directly attaches
to the Internet must have a globally unique IP address. Both versions of IP have this
much and more in common. Following are explanations of these addressing schemes
to help you distinguish between them.

IPv4 Addresses An IPv4 address is 32 bits long, usually shown as four decimal numbers, 0–255, each separated by a period, for example: 192.168.1.41. Called *dotted-decimal notation*, this format is what you see in the user interface. However, the IPv4 protocol works with addresses in binary form, in which the preceding address looks like: 11000000.10101000.00000001.00101001.

IPv4 addresses are routable because an IP address contains within it both the address of the host, called the *host ID*, and the address of the network on which that host resides, called the *network ID (netid)*. A mask of 1s and 0s separates the two parts. When you put the mask over an address, the 1s cover up the first part, or network ID, and the 0s cover up the remaining part, or host ID. The address portion that falls under the 1s is the network address, and the address portion that falls under the 0s is the host address. In the preceding example, with a mask of 11111111.111 11111.11111111.00000000, or 255.255.255.0, the network ID is 11000000.101010 00.00000001.00000000, and the host ID is 00101001 (see Figure 14-11). In dotted decimal form, the network ID is 192.168.1.0, and the host ID is 41. Often called a subnet mask, this mask is an important component in a proper IP configuration. After all, the IP address of a host does not make any sense until masked into its two IDs. When you enter the subnet mask into the Windows user interface in the Properties dialog box of the NIC, you will enter it in dotted decimal notation, but we commonly use a shorthand notation when talking about the subnet mask, and you will see this notation in some user interfaces. For instance, a subnet mask of 255.255.255.0 is easily represented as /24. Therefore, using our example address from earlier, rather than saying the IP address is 192.168.1.41, with a subnet mask of 255.255.255.0, you can put it together as 192.168.1.41 /24.

The *Internet Assigned Numbers Authority (IANA)* oversees the allocation of IP addresses for use on the Internet. They did this directly in the early years, and now do it through a group of *Regional Internet Registries (RIRs)* that allocate IP addresses to the largest Internet service providers. In the early years of IPv4, they divided the IP address pool up into groupings of addresses, called *Class IDs*, with five classes, each defined by the value of the first octet of the IP address, as Table 14-2 shows.

FIGURE 14-11	
The subnet mask defines the network ID and host ID portions of an IP address.	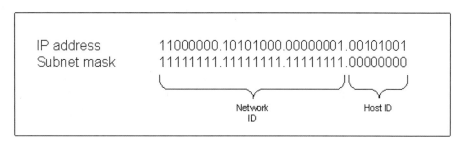

TABLE 14-2

IPv4 Class IDs

Class	First Octet (Network ID)	Address Range	Hosts per Network
A	1–126	1.0.0.0–126.255.255.255	16,277,214
B	128–191	128.0.0.0–191.255.255.255	65,534
C	192–223	192.0.0.0–223.255.255.255	254
D	224–239	224.0.0.0–239.255.255.255	N/A because this is a multicast class
E	240–255	240.0.0.0–255.255.255.255	Reserved

e x a m

ⓦ a t c h   *For the A+ exams, be sure you can recognize the class of an IPv4 address by examining the first octet and understand the number of hosts available for the Class A, B, and C networks.*

So, the organization that received a Class A network ID of 12 actually has more than 16,277,214 host IDs. Obviously, this scheme is a very inefficient way to allocate IP addresses. In fact, they can subnet this Class A network into smaller networks, wasting individual host IDs in the process. Today some organizations have returned all or part of their original allotment, and the large ISPs give out portions of these classful networks using subnetting rules called Classless Inter-Domain Routing (CIDR).

IPv6 Addresses   In preparation for the day when ISPs and the Internet routers are fully IPv6 ready, Windows Vista, Windows 7, and Windows 8 support both IPv6 and IPv4, as do most new network devices. In fact, some high-speed internetworks already use IPv6. IPv6 has 128-bit addressing, which theoretically supports a huge number of unique addresses—340,282,366,920,938,463,463,374,607,431,768,211,456 to be exact. We show an IPv6 address in eight groups of hexadecimal numbers separated by colons, such as this: 2002:470:B8F9:1:20C:29FF:FE53:45CA. Sometimes the address will contain a double colon (::), for example, 2002:470:B8F9::29FF:FE53:45CA. This means there are consecutive groups of all 0s, so :: might be shorthand for :0000:0000:0000. *Global unicast*, the public IPv6 addresses, have a prefix of 001.

IPv6 addresses use a network mask the same way IPv4 addresses do—to distinguish which portion of the address identifies the network. As is often done with IPv4, the mask is expressed with a front slash (/) and the number of bits in the mask; for example, 2002:470:B8F9:1:20C:29FF:FE53:45CA / 64 implies a 64-bit network mask.

June 6, 2012, was international World IPv6 Launch Day. Major Websites such as Google, Facebook, Yahoo!, and others enabled IPv6 on their Websites to assess real-world connectivity for a 24-hour period, but until ISPs around the globe enable IPv6 routing, true end-to-end IPv6 connectivity on the Internet will not be realized.

When you use the IPCONFIG command in Windows Vista, Windows 7, or Windows 8, you will see the configuration for both protocols, but you can also see these details in the graphical user interface (GUI). In Windows Vista or Windows 7, access this by opening Start Search and entering **network connections**. From the results list, select View Network Connections. Then in the Network Connections control panel, double-click the connection you wish to view. This opens the status box for the connection. In the Connection Status box, click the button titled Details to display the Network Connection Details dialog box. Figure 14-12 shows the details for a single network connection as seen in the Windows 7 Network Connection Details dialog. Notice that this connection has both IPv4 (dotted decimal) and IPv6 (hexadecimal) addresses. Only the IPv4 protocol has addresses for the default gateway, DHCP server, and DNS server, indicating that this computer is configured for a IPv4 network.

FIGURE 14-12

The Network
Connection
Details dialog box
in Windows 7

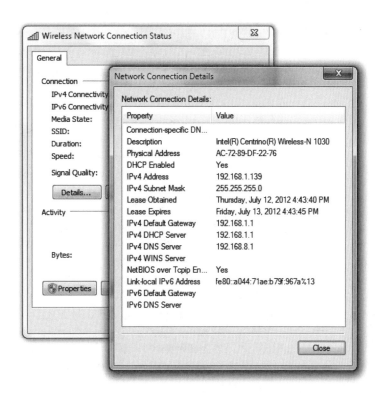

Addresses for IP Configuration

When you view the IP configuration for the NIC on your PC, you may be surprised to see other IP addresses besides that of the NIC. These include addresses labeled Default Gateway, DHCP Server, DNS Servers, and (sometimes) Primary WINS Server.

Default Gateway   When your IP protocol has a packet ready to send, it examines the destination IP address and determines if it is on the same IP network (in the earlier example, this is 192.168.1.0) as your computer. If it is, then it can send the packet directly to that computer (host ID 41 in the example). If the destination IP address is on another IP network, then your computer sends it to the IP address identified as the *default gateway*. This address is on your network (same IP network ID), and it belongs to a router that will send the packet on to the next router in its journey to its destination. Without a default gateway, your computer does not know what to do with packets that have a destination address beyond your IP network. IPv6 also requires a default gateway setting to route packets to remote networks. This can be configured manually or delivered via a Dynamic Host Configuration Protocol (DHCP) device that supports IPv6.

DNS Server   A *DNS client* uses the DNS server IP address for name resolution. The *Domain Name Service (DNS)* manages access to Internet domain names, like mcgraw-hill.com. The server-side service maintains a database of domain names and responds to queries from DNS clients (called resolvers) that request resolution of Internet names to IP addresses. A client will do this before sending data over the Internet, when all it knows is the domain name. For instance, if you wish to connect to a McGraw-Hill Web server, you might enter **www.mcgraw-hill.com** in the address bar of your browser. Then, your computer's DNS client (the *resolver*) sends a request to a DNS server, asking it to resolve the name to an IP address. Once the DNS server has the answer (which it most likely had to request from another DNS server), it sends a response to your computer. The IP protocol on your computer now attaches the address to the packets your computer sends requesting a Web page. IPv4 clients query a DNS server for "A" records, which map, for example, www.mcgraw-hill.com, to an IPv4 address. IPv6 clients query an IPv6 DNS server for "AAAA" (quad A) records to resolve names to IP addresses. Note that an IPv6 address (128 bits) is four times longer than an IPv4 address (32 bits)!

Primary WINS Server   *Windows Internet Name Service (WINS)* has a function similar to that of DNS, but it resolves NetBIOS names rather than DNS host names. WINS works in Microsoft networks, but the need for it has diminished over the years.

Newer versions of Windows and its client/server environment, Active Directory, can locate computers strictly by DNS name. Sometimes the WINS service is required on a network because of old operating systems or applications that only know how to work with NetBIOS names and depend on querying the WINS service. In that case, the address of the WINS server must be included in the IP configuration.

Assigning IP Addresses to NICs   There are two ways to assign an IP address to a network host: manually (or statically) and automatically (or dynamically). We will discuss assigning an address manually here and automatically in the next section when we discuss DHCP. When you assign an address manually in Windows, you must open the Properties dialog box for the NIC and enter the exact IP address (obtained from your network administrator), subnet mask, and other configuration information, which includes the addresses for the default gateway, DNS server, and (if necessary) WINS server. An IP address configured in this manner is a static address. This address is not permanent, because an administrator can easily change it, but some documentation uses the term permanent rather than static.

e x a m

ⓦ a t c h   *Be sure you understand how the subnet mask divides the host ID and network ID of an IP address and that you understand the purpose of the following addresses as used in an IP configuration: default gateway, DNS server, WINS server, and DHCP server.*

DHCP Server   When you install any nonserver version of Windows, the Setup program installs the TCP/IP protocol suite and configures the computer (or its network card to be more specific) as a *DHCP client,* meaning it configures it to obtain an IP address automatically from a DHCP server. A NIC configured as a DHCP client will send a special request out on the network when Windows starts.

Now, you would think that a client computer without an IP address would not be able to communicate on the network, but it can in a very limited way. Using a special protocol called *BOOTP,* the computer sends a very small message that a *Dynamic Host Configuration Protocol (DHCP)* server can read. It cannot communicate with other types of servers until it has an IP address. A properly configured *DHCP server* will respond by sending the DHCP client an IP address and subnet mask (also using BOOTP). This configuration is the minimum it will assign to the client computer. In most cases, the server will provide the other IP configuration addresses, including default gateway, DNS server, and primary WINS server. Only Windows networks that require this last address get that one.

A DHCP server does not permanently assign an IP address to a client. It leases it. *Lease* is the term used, even though no money changes hands in this transaction between a DHCP client and a DHCP server. When one-half of the leased time for an IP address (and its associated configuration) has expired, the client tries to contact the DHCP server in order to renew the lease. As long as the DHCP server has an adequate number of unassigned IP addresses, it will continue to reassign the same address to the same client each session. In fact, this happens every day for a computer that is turned off at the end of the workday, at which point the DHCP client will release the IP address, giving up the lease.

Exercise 14-2 will walk you through using a command that will display the physical address, as well as the IP address for your network card. This command is very handy to use because, although you can see the manually configured IP addresses in the properties of a dialog box, you cannot see the automatically configured IP information in this box for a DHCP client running Windows prior to Windows Vista.

EXERCISE 14-2

CertCam

Viewing the Physical and IP Addresses of a NIC

To view the physical and IP addresses of a NIC, follow these steps:

1. Open a Command Prompt.
2. In the Command Prompt window, enter the command **ipconfig /all** and press ENTER.
3. The result should look something like Figure 14-13 (Windows 7), only with different addresses.
4. The address of the NIC is in the middle, labeled Physical Address. Notice that the physical address is six pairs of hexadecimal numbers separated by hyphens.
5. Three lines below that is the NIC's IPv6 address, and one line below that is the IPv4 address.
6. Locate the other addresses discussed in the preceding text, including default gateway, DNS server, DHCP server (if present), and WINS server (if present).
7. When you run this command on a Windows Vista, Windows 7, or Windows 8 computer, you will also see IPv6 information.

FIGURE 14-13

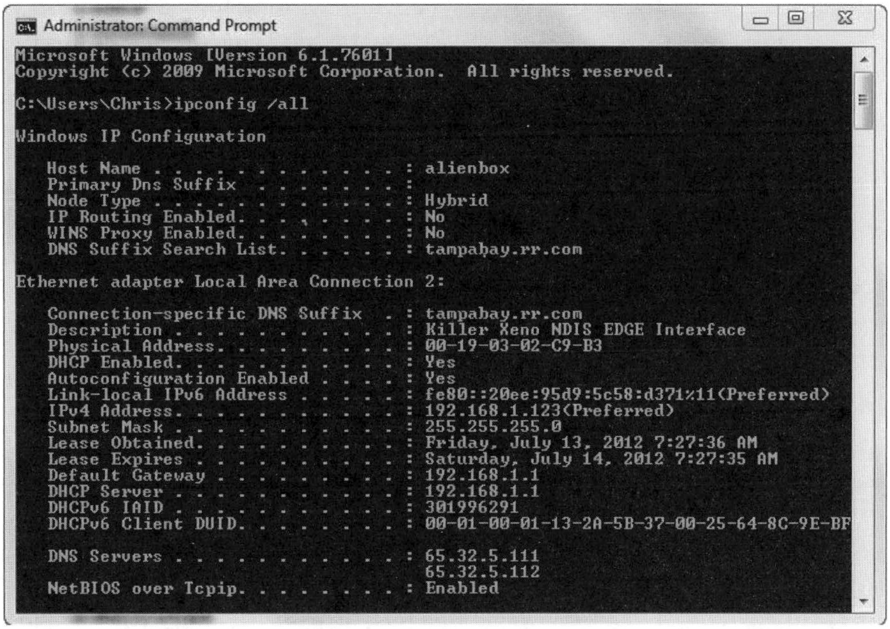

Use the
IPCONFIG /
ALL command
to view the
physical address
and the IP
address of a NIC
and the other
addresses that
are part of the
IP configuration.

```
Administrator: Command Prompt

Microsoft Windows [Version 6.1.7601]
Copyright (c) 2009 Microsoft Corporation.  All rights reserved.

C:\Users\Chris>ipconfig /all

Windows IP Configuration

    Host Name . . . . . . . . . . . . : alienbox
    Primary Dns Suffix  . . . . . . . :
    Node Type . . . . . . . . . . . . : Hybrid
    IP Routing Enabled. . . . . . . . : No
    WINS Proxy Enabled. . . . . . . . : No
    DNS Suffix Search List. . . . . . : tampabay.rr.com

Ethernet adapter Local Area Connection 2:

    Connection-specific DNS Suffix  . : tampabay.rr.com
    Description . . . . . . . . . . . : Killer Xeno NDIS EDGE Interface
    Physical Address. . . . . . . . . : 00-19-03-02-C9-B3
    DHCP Enabled. . . . . . . . . . . : Yes
    Autoconfiguration Enabled . . . . : Yes
    Link-local IPv6 Address . . . . . : fe80::20ee:95d9:5c58:d371%11(Preferred)
    IPv4 Address. . . . . . . . . . . : 192.168.1.123(Preferred)
    Subnet Mask . . . . . . . . . . . : 255.255.255.0
    Lease Obtained. . . . . . . . . . : Friday, July 13, 2012 7:27:36 AM
    Lease Expires . . . . . . . . . . : Saturday, July 14, 2012 7:27:35 AM
    Default Gateway . . . . . . . . . : 192.168.1.1
    DHCP Server . . . . . . . . . . . : 192.168.1.1
    DHCPv6 IAID . . . . . . . . . . . : 301996291
    DHCPv6 Client DUID. . . . . . . . : 00-01-00-01-13-2A-5B-37-00-25-64-8C-9E-BF

    DNS Servers . . . . . . . . . . . : 65.32.5.111
                                        65.32.5.112
    NetBIOS over Tcpip. . . . . . . . : Enabled
```

Special IP Addresses   You use public IP addresses on the Internet, and each address is globally unique. But there are some special IP addresses that are never allowed for computers and devices connected directly to the Internet. They are as follows:

■ **Loopback addresses**   Although it is generally believed that the address 127.0.0.1 is the IPv4 loopback address, any Class A address with a network ID of 127 is a loopback address, used to test network configurations. If you send a packet to a loopback address, it will not leave your NIC. Sounds like a useless address, but you will use it for testing and troubleshooting in Chapters 15 and 16. Also, note that the IPv6 loopback address is ::1 (0:0:0:0:0:0:0:1).

■ **Private IPv4 addresses**   If a network is not directly connected to the Internet, or if you wish to conceal the computers on a private network from the Internet, you use private IP addresses. Millions of locations all over the world use these addresses and they are, therefore, not globally unique because they are never used on the Internet. In Chapter 15, we will describe how you can use these addresses on your private network, yet still access resources on the Internet, thanks to methods that hide your address when you are on the Internet. The private address ranges include the following:

- 10.0.0.0 through 10.255.255.255 (1 Class A network)
- 172.16.0.0 through 172.31.255.255 (16 Class B networks)
- 192.168.0.0 through 192.168.255.255 (256 Class C networks)

- **Private IPv6 addresses**   The FC00::/7 range has been set aside for private IPv6 network addressing. These addresses will not be routable by IPv6 Internet routers, but internal routers within an organization can route them much like they do IPv4 private addresses. The proper term for this type of address is a Unique Local Address (ULA).

- **Automatic private IP address (APIPA)**   If a DHCP client computer fails to receive an address from a DHCP server, the client will give itself an address with the 169.254 /16 network ID. If a computer uses this range of addresses, it will not be able to communicate with other devices on the network unless they also have addresses using the same network ID, which means the other computers must also be using an APIPA address. These clients will not have a default gateway address and, therefore, will not be able to communicate beyond the local network. IPv6 behaves similarly, except that the self-assigned IPv6 address will have a prefix of FE80 and is always present, even if a routable IPv6 address was configured either statically or via DHCP. This is referred to as a "link local address."

Common Ports

It isn't enough for a packet to simply reach the correct IP address; each packet has additional destination information, called a port, which identifies the exact service it is targeting. For instance, when you want to open a Web page in your browser, the packet requesting access to the Web page includes both the IP address (resolved through DNS) and the port number of the service. In this case, it would be HTTP for many Web pages and HTTPS for a secure Web page where you must enter confidential information. All the services you access on the Internet have port numbers. These include the two services just mentioned, plus FTP, POP3, SMTP, TELNET, SSH, and many more. Each port is also associated with a protocol. The most common protocols for communicating with Internet applications are TCP and UDP. TCP is used for communications that are connection-oriented, which is true of most services you are aware of using, whereas *Universal Datagram Protocol (UDP)* is used for connectionless communications, in which each packet is sent without establishing a connection. Therefore, in Table 14-3, we identify the protocol along with the port number for common TCP/IP services.

exam

ⓦ**atch**   *For the CompTIA 801 Exam, be sure you understand the common TCP and UDP ports and protocols mentioned in this section.*

TABLE 14-3	Service	Port	Descriptions
Protocol and Port Numbers for Common Internet Services	Domain Name System (DNS)	UDP 53	Used by DNS clients to perform DNS queries against DNS servers
	File Transfer Protocol (FTP)	TCP 20/21	Transfers files between an FTP client and FTP server
	Hypertext Transfer Protocol (HTTP)	TCP 80	Web page transmission to Web browser
	Hypertext Transfer Protocol over Secure Sockets Layer	TCP 443	Secure transmission of Web pages
	Internet Message Access Protocol Version 4 (IMAP4)	TCP 143	Retrieves email; advanced features beyond POP3, such as folder synchronization
	Lightweight Directory Access Protocol (LDAP)	TCP 389	A standard method of accessing a network database; often used for authenticating user accounts during user logon
	Post Office Protocol Version 3 (POP3)	TCP 110	Retrieves email from a POP3 mail server
	Remote Desktop Protocol (RDP)	TCP 3389	Used to remotely access a Windows desktop
	Secure File Transfer Protocol (SFTP)	TCP 22	Uses an SSH-encrypted connection to transfer files
	Secure Shell (SSH)	TCP 22	Secure (encrypted) terminal emulation that replaces Telnet
	Server Message Block (SMB)	TCP 445	Windows file and print sharing service
	Simple Mail Transfer Protocol (SMTP)	TCP 25	Sending email
	Simple Network Management Protocol (SNMP)	UDP 161	Queries network devices for status and statistics
	Telnet	TCP 23	Terminal emulation; all data sent in clear text
	Trivial File Transfer Protocol (TFTP)	UDP 69	Differs from FTP in that there is no option for authentication

CERTIFICATION OBJECTIVES

■ **801: 2.1** *Identify types of network cables and connectors*

■ **801: 2.2** *Categorize characteristics of connectors and cabling*

■ **801: 2.9** *Compare and contrast network devices, their functions, and features*

In this section we will detail the features and characteristics of network cabling, including fiber optic, twisted pair, and coaxial cabling, as well as their connectors, as required by CompTIA 801 Exam Objectives 2.1 and 2.2. We will also survey the various hardware devices used on networks—some of them for connecting networks to each other, and some for allowing client computers and devices to access networks. These are required for the CompTIA 801 Exam Objective 2.9.

Network Hardware

Network hardware includes many network connection devices that are part of the infrastructure of small networks, as well as large internetworks, and of the largest internetwork, the Internet itself. We limit the hardware we describe in this section to the network adapters used in PCs, the medium that connects these adapters to the network, the devices that connect networks to one another, and a few miscellaneous devices included in the CompTIA 801 Exam Objectives.

Network Adapters

While we previously mentioned network interface cards in this chapter, we now focus on this particular type of network hardware device. Each computer on a network must have a connection to the network provided by a NIC, also called a network adapter, and some form of network medium that makes the connection between the NIC and the network. NICs are identified by the network technology used (Ethernet or Wi-Fi) and the type of interface used between the card and the PC, such as the PCI and PCIe interfaces, or the USB or FireWire interfaces defined in Chapter 4, or for a laptop, the PC Card or ExpressCard interfaces explored in Chapter 7.

Most NICs come with status indicators, as lights on the card itself, and/or software that displays the status on the notification area of the taskbar. You can use these when troubleshooting, as described in Chapter 16.

Transmission Medium

The transmission medium for a network carries the signals. These signals may be electrical signals carried over copper-wire cabling, light pulses carried over fiber-optic cabling, or infrared or radio waves transmitted through the atmosphere. In these examples, the copper wire, fiber-optic cable, and atmosphere are the media. When it comes to wired media, one important issue is plenum versus PVC, which we will explore next, and then we'll look at the basics of twisted-pair, coaxial, and fiber-optic cabling.

Plenum vs. PVC

Many commonly used network cables use a *polyvinyl chloride (PVC)* outer sheath to protect the cable. PVC is not fire resistant, and, by code, you cannot use it in overhead or *plenum* areas in offices, those spaces in a building through which air conditioning and heating ducts run. *Plenum cable* uses a special fire-resistant outer sheath that will not burn as quickly as PVC. Plenum cable frequently costs more, but most areas require it. Most of the standard cables discussed in this chapter are available in plenum-grade ratings.

Twisted Pair

Twisted-pair cable is the most popular cable type for internal networks. The term "twisted pair" indicates that it contains pairs of wires twisted around each other. These twists help "boost" each wire's signals and make them less susceptible to *electromagnetic interference (EMI)*. The most common type of twisted-pair wiring is *unshielded twisted-pair (UTP)*, which, although it has a plastic sheathing, does not have actual metal shielding.

There are several standards for twisted-pair cables, each with a different number of wires, certified speed, and implementation. We often refer to these standards as CAT (short for "category") followed by a number, for example, CAT3 or CAT4. Currently, CAT5, CAT5e, and CAT6 are the most common twisted-pair cable types. Table 14-4 summarizes twisted-pair cable standards. CAT 5e is an enhanced and more stringently tested version of CAT5 that offers better transmission characteristics than CAT5. CAT6 cable offers even higher bandwidth and improved signal-handling characteristics.

The telecommunications standards organization, *Telecommunication Industry Association/Electronics Industry Alliance (TIA/EIA)*, developed the *TIA/EIA 568* standards for telecommunications cabling. TIA/EIA standards are now labeled per the standards group, the American National Standards Institute (ANSI), with an ANSI prefix. A portion of these standards, now called *ANSI/TIA/EIA-568-B* standard, includes pin assignments for connecting eight-wire cabling to Ethernet connectors. One pin assignment is called *T568A*, and the other is *T568B*. Technically, as long as you standardize on one pin assignment, either is fine. However, T568B is recommended, and the use of T568A is only recommended if you want to create a cross-over cable, which you can accomplish by using the T568A standard on one end and the T568B standard on the other, as the main difference is in the assignment of the two wires that these two standards reverse.

According to the ANSI/TIA/EIA standard for category 5e copper cable (TIA/EIA 568-5-A), the maximum length for a structured wiring cable segment, is 100 meters (328 feet) without need for a switch or a hub (repeater). With a repeater, you can run up to five segments for 10Base-T. For 100Base-T, you can use two hubs for a cable run of up to 200 meters (656 feet). Using modern switches with 100M and Gigabit LANs raises these limits. Consult the switch vendor's specifications for details.

Twisted-pair cable is also available as *shielded twisted-pair (STP)*, with an extra insulating layer that helps prevent data loss and blocks EMI. However, due to the expense of STP, UTP is more commonly used.

You can identify a twisted-pair cable by its use of RJ-45 connectors, which look like regular RJ-11 phone connectors but are slightly larger, as they contain eight wires, whereas RJ-11 connectors contain four wires.

on the
ⓞb
The oldest cabling you should normally encounter in a business is CAT5, although it is certainly possible to find very old installations of CAT3 cabling, which is not adequate for modern networks running 100 Mbps or faster.

TABLE 14-4	Type	Speed	Common Use
Cable Categories	CAT1	1 Mbps	Phone lines
	CAT2	4 Mbps	Token Ring networks
	CAT3	16 Mbps	Ethernet networks
	CAT4	20 Mbps	Token Ring networks
	CAT5	100 Mbps	Ethernet networks
	CAT5e	1 Gbps	Ethernet networks
	CAT6	10 Gbps	Ethernet networks

Coaxial Cable

The type of cabling used to connect a cable modem to a cable network is coaxial cable, which consists of a central copper wire surrounded by an insulating layer, which is itself surrounded by a braided metal shield that protects the signals traveling on the central wire from outside interference. We also described coaxial cabling in Chapter 5, with a drawing of a cable and its components shown in Figure 5-14. A plastic jacket encases all of this. Coaxial cable used for standard cable television and high-definition TV (HDTV), as well as cable-modem Internet access, is usually RG-6 cable with a 75 Ohm rating. Theoretically, signals can travel up to 300 meters at 500 Mbps over RG-6 coax cables, but the practical limit is 50 Mbps, which still makes this medium very popular for broadband Internet connections. The specific distance and speed vary, depending on the type of signal and the devices generating the signal. Sometimes people use RG-59 cable to carry closed-circuit TV (CCTV) signals, although modern CCTV implementations use standard network cabling such as CAT5e UTP. Compared to RG-59, RG-6 cabling has a thicker conductive core and as a result can transmit data over longer distances. Expect an RG-6 cable to connect to the cable wall jack and cable modem with either F-connectors that you must securely screw on or BNC connectors that lock with a simple quarter-turn twist.

Fiber-Optic Cable and Connectors

Until recently, LANs seldom used fiber-optic cable (fiber for short), but fiber is often used to join separate networks over long distances. Increasingly, however, many new homes, apartments, and businesses have both fiber and copper wiring installed when being built. Also, some phone companies are using fiber to connect to homes and businesses.

Fiber transmits light rather than electrical signals, so it is not susceptible to EMI. It is capable of faster transmission than other types of cable, but it is also the most expensive cable.

A single light wave passing down fiber cabling is a *mode*. Two variants of fiber used in fiber-optic cables are *single-mode fiber* (SMF) and *multimode fiber* (MMF). Single-mode fiber allows only a single light wave to pass down the cable, but supports faster transmission rates over longer distances. Multimode fiber allows multiple light waves to pass simultaneously and is usually larger in diameter than single-mode fiber; each wave uses a certain portion of the fiber cable for transmission. There are many Ethernet standards for fiber-optic cabling, with a wide range of maximum speeds and distances. Multimode fiber is used most often in LANs with speeds up to 1 Gbps and a maximum range of 1000 meters, whereas single-mode fiber has a range of dozens of miles with speeds in the terabits per second.

Fiber-optic data transmission requires two cables: one to send and another to receive. Connectors enable fiber-optic cable to connect to transmitters, receivers, or other devices. Over the years, the various standards for connectors have continued to evolve, moving toward smaller connectors. Here are brief descriptions of four types of connectors used with fiber-optic cable:

- **Straight-tip (ST)**   The *straight-tip (ST) connector* is a straight, round connector used to connect fiber to a network device. It has a twist-type coupling.

- **Subscriber connector (SC)**   The *subscriber connector (SC)* is a square snap coupling, about 2.5 mm wide, used for cable-to-cable connections or to connect cables to network devices. It latches with a push-pull action similar to audio and video jacks.

- **Lucent connector (LC)**   The *Lucent connector (LC)*, also called local connector, has a snap coupling and, at 1.25 mm, is half the size of the SC connector.

- **Mechanical Transfer Registered Jack (MT-RJ)**   The *Mechanical Transfer Registered Jack (MT-RJ) connector* resembles an RJ-45 network connector and is less expensive and easier to work with than ST or SC.

Figure 14-14 shows ST and SC connectors.

Devices for Connecting to LANs and the Internet

Most LANs now connect to other LANs or through WAN connections to internetworks, such as the Internet. A variety of network connection devices connects networks. Each serves a special purpose, and a single device may contain two or more of these functions.

FIGURE 14-14	
The ST and SC connectors used with fiber-optic cable	

Repeater

A *repeater* is a device used to extend the range of a network by taking the signals it receives from one port and regenerating (repeating) those signals to another port. Repeaters are available for various networks. For instance, on an Ethernet network, you would use an Ethernet repeater, and on a Wi-Fi network, you would use a wireless repeater (often called a signal booster) to boost the signal between wireless networks. In both cases, the repeater must be at the appropriate level and speed for the network (Ethernet, Fast Ethernet, Gigabit Ethernet, 802.11b, 802.11g, 802.11n, etc.).

Bridge

A *bridge* is a device used to connect two networks, and it passes traffic between them using the physical address of the destination device. Bridges segment large networks into smaller networks and only forward network traffic to the segment where the recipient station resides. A bridge is specific to the hardware technology in use. For instance, an Ethernet bridge looks at physical Ethernet addresses (MAC addresses) and forwards Ethernet frames with destination addresses that are not on the local network. Bridges are now seldom used since a switch functions as both a bridge and a hub.

Hub

A *hub* is a device that is the central connecting point of a classic 10BaseT Ethernet LAN. It is little more than a multiport repeater, because it takes a signal received on one port and repeats it on all other ports. An *active hub* will regenerate the signal and send it on to all devices connected to the network. A *passive hub* is simply a wiring panel or punch-down block for connecting or disconnecting devices.

Router

Connections between networks usually require some form of routing capability. In the case of a connection to the Internet, each computer or device connected to the network requires a TCP/IP address. In order to reach a computer on another network, the originating computer must have a means of sending information to the other computer. To accomplish this, routes are established, and a *router*, a device that sits at the connection between networks, stores information about destinations.

A router is specific to one protocol suite. The type of router used to connect TCP/IP networks is an *IP router*, using routing protocols that work with the IP protocol. Routers use several specialized router protocols to update their list of routes dynamically, such as *routing information protocol (RIP)*, a protocol that dates to the 1980s and is now essentially obsolete even though it has been updated a few times

A router con-
necting a LAN to
a T1 network

and most routers still support it. An IP router knows the IP addresses of the networks
to which it connects and the addresses of other routers on those networks. At the
least, a router knows the next destination to which it can transfer information.

Many routers include bridging circuitry, a hub, and the necessary hardware to
connect multiple network technologies together, such as a LAN and a T1 network,
or a LAN to any of the other broadband networks. The Internet has thousands of
routers managing the connections between the millions of computers and networks
connected to it. Figure 14-15 shows a router between a LAN and a WAN.

Switch

After the introduction of 100BaseT, the *switch* replaced the classic hub. This is
a more intelligent device that takes an incoming signal and sends it only to the
destination port. This type of switch is both a bridge and a hub. At one time
switches were very expensive, but now small eight-port switches are inexpensive
and commonly used, even in very small LANs. As always, each computer or other
device in a network attaches to a switch of the type appropriate for the type of LAN.
For example, computers using Ethernet cards must connect to an Ethernet switch;
wireless devices attach wirelessly to a wireless hub, more often called a *wireless access
point* (WAP) or wireless router. Devices may combine these functions, as in the case
of a WAP or wireless router that includes an Ethernet switch (look for one or more
RJ-45 connectors). This last is very common.

Wireless Access Point

A wireless access point allows wireless clients to connect to a wired network. Most
access points also have built-in routing capability and as such are called wireless
routers. Modern access points are configurable in "isolation mode," which isolates
wireless clients from one another, usually for security or privacy purposes.

Modem

Note that this discussion does not apply to DSL or cable modems. Computers are
digital devices. Most local telephone lines are still analog. A modem allows computer-
to-computer communication over analog telephone lines. Modems can be external

devices that connect to a piece of computing equipment via a serial cable, or they could be internal expansion cards. Either way, they have at least one RJ-11 telephone jack so that they can plug into an analog phone line. Many network administrators still use modems today to remotely connect to network equipment (such as a router) in case the Internet connection fails or the router is misconfigured!

Firewall

A *firewall* restricts or allows the flow of network traffic based on a set of rules. A firewall can be a hardware device or it can be software. Hardware firewalls run on network devices such as dedicated firewall appliances or routers or on a dedicated computer. Software firewalls run within an operating system and apply *IP packet filtering*, a service that inspects (or filters) each packet that enters or leaves the network; apply a set of security rules defined by a network administrator; and do not allow packets that fail inspection to pass between networks. When you change the rules to allow a certain type of traffic through a firewall, you are making an *exception*. To allow or deny traffic, you can base a firewall rule on many attributes, including:

■ **Type of packet**   Defined by port, TCP 80 (HTTP Website) traffic might be allowed where TCP 25 (SMTP outbound email) traffic might be denied.

■ **Source/destination**   SMTP traffic to a specific host might be allowed, but all other destination SMTP hosts could be denied.

EXERCISE 14-3

Identifying Network Hardware

See what network hardware you can identify in your home, office, or school.

1. If you have a PC in your home and it has a connection to the Internet, locate and identify the network components.

2. If you use a dial-up connection, look for the modem, the telephone cable between the modem and the phone jack on the wall, and the RJ-11 connectors at either end of the telephone cable.

3. If you have a DSL connection, look for the Ethernet cable that runs between your computer and the hub/switch or modem. Examine the RJ-45 connectors on either end of the cable. The cable may connect to a single box that performs all of these functions.

4. If you have cable Internet service, look for an Ethernet cable between your computer and the cable modem, and then look for a coaxial cable between the modem and the wall connector.

5. At school or work, all you may find is an Ethernet cable connecting your computer to a wall jack that connects to the cable in the walls that connects to the network. Ask the network administrator to describe how you connect to the Internet through the network.

Other Network Devices

Beyond the typical desktop, laptop, server, and even mobile computing devices, there are devices that do not fit easily into the categories we have covered so far. Three of these listed in CompTIA A+ Exam 801 objectives are Internet appliance, network attached storage, and VoIP phones.

Internet Appliance

An *Internet appliance* is a device designed to allow a nontechnical person to easily access Internet resources. Today these take the form of smartphones, tablets, and gaming and entertainment consoles such as the Wii or Xbox.

Network Attached Storage

Instead of storing data on disks in a desktop or server computer, a *network attached storage (NAS)* device consists of an enclosure that contains hard disks, plugs directly into a network, and has its own IP address. It has an embedded firmware operating system designed only to service file requests. Unlike a traditional file server, it does not have a keyboard or monitor, nor does it allow configuration of services that are not file related.

VoIP Phones

Voice over IP (VoIP) is a set of technologies that allows voice transmission over an IP network specifically used for placing phone calls over the Internet, rather than using the *public-switched telephone network (PSTN)* or *plain-old telephone service (POTS)*. Both terms describe the worldwide network that carries traditional voice traffic. You can make phone calls over the Internet with little or no cost, as compared to regular long-distance phone service. Skype is a very popular VoIP application that uses the peer-to-peer technology used in the Kazaa file-sharing system.

VoIP phones come in more than one form. One example is a physical phone with a network connector (usually RJ-45) instead of an analog phone connector (RJ-11). They can also come in the form of a "softphone," which is nothing more than a software application that mimics a phone interface—a *softphone* requires a headset (microphone and headphones) to use. Both transmit voice data inside of TCP/IP packets over a TCP/IP network instead of over a traditional telephone network. Instead of a phone number, each VoIP phone has an IP address. When using a VoIP phone to call an analog telephone, a translation device is required. This is offered as a for-pay service by most phone companies.

SCENARIO & SOLUTION

My computer is part of a large corporate network. What role is my desktop computer most likely playing in this network?	A large corporate network is a client/server network. A desktop PC in this network has the role of a client.
What is the protocol suite of the Internet?	The protocol suite of the Internet is TCP/IP.
I understand that NetBEUI is very easy to install and use. Why does our corporate internetwork not use it?	A corporate internetwork consists, by definition, of interconnected networks requiring a protocol suite routable between networks. NetBEUI, as a nonroutable protocol, is therefore not used.

CERTIFICATION SUMMARY

IT professionals preparing for the CompTIA A+ exams must understand the basic concepts of computer networks. More in-depth knowledge is required for other exams, such as the CompTIA Network+, Security+, and Server+ exams. Basic concepts include network topologies—the geographic classifications of networks into LANs, MANs, and WANs. You must understand LAN technologies, such as Ethernet and Wi-Fi, and the various WAN connection methods, including dial-up and broadband WAN connections like ISDN, cable, DSL, satellite, and cellular. Be able to identify the most common cabling types, connectors, and common network adapters used in PCs.

Understand that TCP/IP is a protocol suite designed for the Internet and now used on most LANs and interconnected networks. Understand network-addressing concepts, including physical addresses assigned to network adapters and logical addresses assigned and used through the network protocols.

Understand the various addresses that are part of an IP configuration and their roles. These include the IP address and subnet mask of the network adapter, default gateway, DNS server, DHCP server, and WINS server addresses.

Be prepared to distinguish between various network hardware, including adapters, the transmission medium, network-to-network connection devices (repeater, bridge, and router), and devices for connecting computers to a network (hub and switch). Also, ensure that you can describe the purpose of an Internet appliance, NAS, and VoIP phone.

TWO-MINUTE DRILL

Here are some of the key points covered in Chapter 14.

Network Topologies, Classifications, and Performance

- ❏ The common network topologies are bus, star, ring, mesh, and hybrid.
- ❏ Networks fall into several network classifications, including PAN, LAN, MAN, and WAN.
- ❏ PAN technologies include the use of standards for wireless transmissions over very short distances. These include infrared (IrDA), limited to about 1 meter, and Bluetooth, which has a range of up to 10 meters.
- ❏ Common LAN technologies include Ethernet in wired LANs and Wi-Fi in wireless LANs.
- ❏ Ethernet has several implementations, each with increasing speeds, including 10Base-T at 10 Mbps, 100Base-T at 100 Mbps, 1000Base-T at 1 Gbps over UTP, and 10-GBaseT with speeds up to 10 Gbps. In addition, fiber-optic cable supports very high speeds.
- ❏ The Wi-Fi standard 802.11a supports speeds up to 54 Mbps using the 5 GHz frequency. Other Wi-Fi standards are more popular. These include 802.11g, which also supports speeds of up to 54 Mbps but uses the same frequency (2.4 GHz) as its predecessor, 802.11b. 802.11g equipment is usually downward compatible with the slower and older 802.11b equipment.
- ❏ The 802.11n Wi-Fi standard provides speeds of up to 100 Mbps and beyond. The standard actually defines speeds of up to 600 Mbps.
- ❏ Dial-up WAN connections are the slowest and require initiation of the connection every time a user wishes to connect to a remote resource.
- ❏ Broadband WAN connections, all offering speeds faster than dial-up, include cellular, ISDN, DSL, cable, T-carrier, satellite, and fiber.

Network Software

- ❏ The roles played by the computer on the network describe the network. The two most general roles are those of clients and servers.
- ❏ A network in which any computer can be both a client and a server is a peer-to-peer network.

❑ A client/server network is one in which most desktop computers are clients and dedicated computers act as servers.

❑ An NOS is an operating system that runs on a network server and provides file sharing and access to other resources, account management, authentication, and authorization services. Examples of NOSs are Microsoft Windows Server operating systems, Novell Server operating systems, and Linux.

❑ A network client is software that requests services from compatible servers. Windows, Mac OS X, and Linux, when installed on desktop computers that have a network connection, automatically install a basic network client.

❑ A protocol suite is a group of related protocols that work together to support the functioning of a network. TCP/IP is the dominant protocol suite as well as the protocol suite of the Internet.

❑ TCP/IP supports small-to-large networks and interconnected networks called internetworks. The Internet is the largest internetwork.

❑ Network addressing occurs at both the physical level and the logical level. Every Ethernet network adapter from every Ethernet NIC manufacturer in the world has a unique physical address, also called a MAC address, which is 48 bits long and is usually shown in hexadecimal notation.

❑ Internet Protocol is concerned with logical addresses. An IPv4 address is 32 bits long and is usually shown in dotted decimal notation, as in 192.168.1.41. IPv6 has 128-bit addressing, which theoretically supports a huge number of unique addresses.

❑ An IPv4 and IPv6 address configuration includes a subnet mask, which determines the host ID and network ID portions of the address. In addition, the IP configuration may include addresses for a default gateway, DNS server, primary WINS server, and DHCP server.

❑ In addition to an IP address, a packet will contain a port number identifying the service on the target computer that should receive the packet's contents.

Network Hardware

❑ A network adapter provides the connection to the network medium. Network adapters are available for the various networking technologies, such as Ethernet and Wi-Fi.

❑ Physical transmission media include twisted-pair, fiber-optic, and coaxial cable.

❑ Networking requires various network connection devices. A repeater is a device used to extend the range of a network by taking the signals it receives from one port and regenerating (repeating) those signals to another port.

❑ A bridge is a device used to connect two networks and pass traffic between them based on the physical address of the destination device.

❑ A hub is a device that is the central connecting point of a 10BaseT Ethernet LAN, with all network devices on a LAN connecting to one or more hubs.

❑ More intelligent devices called switches or switching hubs now replace hubs on Ethernet networks. These take an incoming signal and send it only to the destination port.

❑ An IP router sits between networks and routes packets according to their IP addresses.

❑ Many routers combine routing and bridging, and connect multiple network technologies, such as a LAN and a T1 network.

❑ An Internet appliance is a device designed to allow a nontechnical person to easily access Internet resources. Examples are smartphones, tablets, and gaming and entertainment consoles such as the Wii or Xbox.

❑ An NAS device consists of an enclosure that contains hard disks, plugs directly into a network, and has its own IP address. It has an embedded firmware operating system designed only to service file requests.

❑ VoIP phones allow you to make voice calls over an IP network (the Internet). They come in two types: a physical VoIP phone with a network connector (usually RJ-45) instead of an analog phone connector (RJ-11), and a softphone which is a software application that mimics a phone interface and requires a headset with a microphone and headphones.

SELF TEST

The following questions will help you measure your understanding of the material presented in this chapter. Read all of the choices carefully because there might be more than one correct answer. Choose all correct answers for each question.

Network Topologies, Classifications, and Performance

1. Which network topology directly connects each device on a network to every other device?
   A. Bus
   B. Star
   C. Ring
   D. Mesh

2. Which of the following statements is true about a LAN versus a WAN?
   A. A LAN spans a greater distance than a WAN.
   B. A WAN spans a greater distance than a LAN.
   C. A LAN is generally slower than a WAN.
   D. A WAN is used within a home or within a small business.

3. Which of the following is a PAN technology?
   A. Ethernet
   B. Satellite
   C. Bluetooth
   D. 802.11a

4. What is the type of network that connects many private networks in one metropolitan community?
   A. PAN
   B. MAN
   C. WAN
   D. LAN

5. Of the following technologies, which is downward compatible with 802.11b?
   A. 802.11a
   B. 802.11g
   C. Bluetooth
   D. IrDA

6. Which of the following is usually the slowest WAN connection?

A. Dial-up

B. DSL

C. Cable

D. Satellite

7. Which of the following WAN technologies uses a network originally created for television transmissions?

A. DSL

B. Cellular

C. Cable

D. Dial-up

8. Which of the following is a term that describes the amount of time it takes a packet to travel from one point to another?

A. Bandwidth

B. KBps

C. Latency

D. MBps

Network Software

9. Which statement describing IPv4 vs. IPv6 differences is correct?

A. IPv6 uses a subnet mask, while IPv4 uses 128-bit addressing.

B. IPv4 uses 128-bit addressing, while IPv6 uses 32-bit addressing.

C. IPv4 uses 32-bit addressing, while IPv6 uses 128-bit addressing.

D. IPv4 uses double colons to indicate consecutive groups of 0s.

10. Which port is the correct one for Hypertext Transfer Protocol (HTTP) and Web page transmission to a browser?

A. TCP 80

B. UDP 53

C. TCP 443

D. TCP 110

11. What protocol used on the Internet is concerned with the logical addressing of hosts?

    A. TCP

    B. IP

    C. UDP

    D. ARP

12. What protocol adds the old Microsoft naming system to TCP/IP?

    A. NetBEUI

    B. NetBIOS

    C. DHCP

    D. DNS

13. What divides an IP address into its host ID and network ID components?

    A. Default gateway

    B. DNS server

    C. DHCP server

    D. Subnet mask

14. A NIC has this type of a permanent address assigned to it by the manufacturer.

    A. IP address

    B. Physical address

    C. Host ID

    D. Automatic address

15. A packet with a destination address not on the local network will be sent to the address identified by which label in the IP configuration?

    A. Default gateway

    B. DNS server

    C. DHCP server

    D. Subnet mask

Network Hardware

16. Which of the following questions about CAT5 vs. CAT5e vs. CAT6 cable speed and length is correct?

    A. CAT5 cable can transmit 1 Gbps.

    B. CAT6 cable can transmit 10 Gbps.

    C. All three categories of cable can be 200 meters long.

    D. CAT5e cable can transmit 10 Gbps.

17. Which of the following is not a network medium?

    A. Plenum

    B. Twisted-pair cable

    C. Fiber-optic cable

    D. Atmosphere

18. Which type of cable uses ST, SC, LC, or MT-RJ connectors?

    A. STP

    B. UTP

    C. Fiber-optic

    D. Coaxial

19. Thousands of this type of device exist on the Internet between networks, direct the traffic of the Internet using the destination IP address of each packet, and pass the packets to their destinations along the interconnected networks of the Internet.

    A. Router

    B. Modem

    C. NIC

    D. Hub

20. A Wii game console is an example of this type of network hardware.

    A. Internet appliance

    B. NAS

    C. VoIP phone

    D. Modem

SELF TEST ANSWERS

Network Topologies, Classifications, and Performance

1. ☑ **D.** The mesh topology directly connects each device on a network to every other device.
   ☒ **A,** bus, **B,** star, and **C,** ring, are all incorrect because none of these topologies directly connects all devices.

2. ☑ **B.** A WAN spans a greater distance than a LAN.
   ☒ **A,** that a LAN spans a greater distance than a WAN, is not true. **C,** that a LAN is generally slower than a WAN, is not true. **D,** that a WAN is used within a home or a small business, is not true.

3. ☑ **C.** Bluetooth is a personal area network (PAN) technology used to connect devices and computers over very short distances.
   ☒ **A,** Ethernet, **B,** satellite, and **D,** 802.11a, are all incorrect because none of these is a PAN technology. Ethernet is a wired LAN technology; satellite is a WAN technology; and 802.11a is a set of WLAN standards.

4. ☑ **B.** MAN, a metropolitan area network, is the type of network that connects many private networks in one community.
   ☒ **A,** PAN, is incorrect because this is a very small personal area network that only connects devices in a very small (usually a few meters) area. **C,** WAN, is incorrect because this type of wide area network connects over long distances. **D,** LAN, is incorrect because this local area network type is limited to a distance of hundreds of meters that would not span an entire metropolitan community.

5. ☑ **B.** 802.11g is downward compatible with the slower 802.11b standard because they both use the 2.4 GHz bandwidth.
   ☒ **A,** 802.11a, is incorrect because this Wi-Fi standard operates in the 5 MHz band, which makes it totally incompatible with 802.11b. **C,** Bluetooth, is incorrect because it is a standard for very short distances and is not downward-compatible with 802.11b. **D,** IrDA, is incorrect because this is a standard for very short-range infrared communications, which is totally incompatible with 802.11b.

6. ☑ **A.** Dial-up is usually the slowest WAN connection at an advertised rate of 56 Kbps, but with a top actual rate of about 48 Kbps.
   ☒ **B,** DSL, **C,** cable, and **D,** satellite, are all incorrect because each of these is a broadband service with maximum speeds that go up to many times that of dial-up.

7.   ☑   **C.** Cable is the WAN technology that uses a network originally created for television transmissions.
☒   **A,** DSL, is incorrect because it uses the telephone network, not a network created for television transmissions. **B,** cellular, is incorrect because it uses the cellular network, originally created for voice transmissions but which was upgraded to digital and can be used for broadband data transmissions. **D,** dial-up, is incorrect because it uses the telephone network, not a network created for television transmissions.

8.   ☑   **C.** Latency is the term for the time it takes a packet to travel from one point to another.
☒   **A,** bandwidth, is incorrect because this is the amount of data that can travel over a network within a given time. **B,** KBps, and **D,** MBps, are incorrect because these terms mean kilobytes per second and megabytes per second, respectively, which describe the amount of data that can travel over a network.

Network Software

9.   ☑   **C.** IPv4 uses 32-bit addressing, while IPv6 uses 128-bit addressing.
☒   **A,** IPv6 uses a subnet mask, while IPv4 uses 128-bit addressing, is incorrect because IPv4 uses 32-bit addressing. IPv6 can use a subnet mask also. **B,** IPv4 uses 128-bit addressing, while IPv6 uses 32-bit addressing, is incorrect because it is just the opposite. **D,** IPv4 uses double colons to indicate consecutive groups of 0s, is incorrect because it is IPv6 that uses the double colons to indicate consecutive groups of zeroes.

10.   ☑   **A.** TCP 80 is the correct port number for HTTP and Web page transmission to a Web browser.
☒   **B,** UDP 53, is incorrect because it is the port for Domain Name Service used by clients to perform DNS queries against DNS servers. **C,** TCP 443, is incorrect because it is the port for secure Web page transmission. **D,** TCP 110, is incorrect because it is the port for Post Office Protocol that retrieves email from a POP3 mail server.

11.   ☑   **B.** IP is the protocol used on the Internet that is concerned with the logical addressing of hosts.
☒   **A,** TCP, is incorrect because this protocol is not concerned with the logical addressing of hosts. **C,** UDP, is incorrect because this protocol, which we only mentioned and did not describe, is not concerned with the logical addressing of hosts. **D,** ARP, is incorrect because this protocol is not concerned with the logical addressing of hosts.

12.   ☑   **B.** NetBIOS is the protocol that adds the old Microsoft naming system to TCP/IP.
☒   **A,** NetBEUI, is incorrect because this old Microsoft network protocol suite had NetBIOS as just a part. **C,** DHCP, is incorrect because this is the protocol used for automatically allocating IP addresses. **D,** DNS, is incorrect because this protocol supports Internet-style names.

13. ☑ **D.** A subnet mask divides an IP address into its host ID and network ID components.
     ☒ **A,** default gateway, is incorrect because this is the name of the router address to which a computer directs packets with destinations beyond the local network. **B,** DNS server, is incorrect because this is where a network client sends queries to resolve DNS names into IP addresses. **C,** DHCP server, is incorrect because this is what automatically assigns IP addresses to DHCP client computers.

14. ☑ **B.** The physical address is the type of permanent address assigned to a NIC by the manufacturer.
     ☒ **A,** IP address, is incorrect because this is not a permanent address but a logical address not permanently assigned to a NIC. **C,** host ID, is incorrect because this portion of an IP address identifies the host. **D,** automatic address, is incorrect because this usually refers to an IP address assigned to a PC by a DHCP server.

15. ☑ **A.** The default gateway is the address to which the router sends packets that have addresses not on the local network.
     ☒ **B,** DNS server, is incorrect because this server resolves DNS names. **C,** DHCP server, is incorrect because this server assigns IP addresses automatically. **D,** subnet mask, is incorrect because this is not an address but a mask used to divide an IP address into its host ID and network ID components.

Network Hardware

16. ☑ **B.** CAT6 can indeed transmit 10 Gbps.
     ☒ **A,** CAT5 cable can transmit 1 Gbps, is incorrect because it can only transmit 100 Mbps. **C,** all three categories of cable can be 200 meters long, is incorrect because each of these cable categories requires a repeater or a switch at 100 meters. Even with a switch, CAT6 cable can only be 200 meters in length, while the others can be up to 600 meters with repeaters or switches. **D,** CAT5e cable can transmit 10 Gbps, is incorrect because it can only transmit 1 Gbps.

17. ☑ **A.** Plenum is not a network medium, but rather a characteristic of certain network media (cables), indicating the cable sheath is fire resistant and appropriate to run in plenum space.
     ☒ **B,** twisted-pair cable, **C,** fiber-optic cable, and **D,** atmosphere, are all networking media.

18. ☑ **C.** Fiber-optic cable uses ST, SC, LC, or MT-RJ connectors.
     ☒ **A,** STP, **B,** UTP, and **D,** coaxial cabling, do not use ST, SC, LC, or MT-RJ connectors.

19.   ☑   **A.** A router is the device that exists on the Internet and passes IP packets from many sources to destinations along the Internet.
☒   **B,** modem, is incorrect because it does not pass packets along the Internet, although it is a beginning point for a single computer to send packets. **C,** NIC, is incorrect because this is simply a device for connecting a single computer to a network. **D,** hub, is incorrect because this is an older device used at the heart of a LAN but not an Internet device.

20.   ☑   **A.** A Wii console is an example of an Internet appliance.
☒   **B,** NAS, is incorrect because network attached storage consists of an enclosure that contains hard disks, plugs directly into a network, and has its own IP address. **C,** VoIP phone, is incorrect because it does not describe a Wii console. **D,** modem, is incorrect because it does not describe a Wii.

15

Installing a Small Office/ Home Office (SOHO) Network

I n this chapter, you will learn the tasks required to install and configure client computer access to a local area network (LAN) or wireless local area network (WLAN), focusing on a small network, such as you would find in a small office or home office (SOHO).

CERTIFICATION OBJECTIVES

- **801: 2.5** *Compare and contrast wireless networking standards and encryption types*

- **801: 2.6** *Install, configure, and deploy a SOHO wireless/wired router using appropriate settings*

- **802: 1.5** *Given a scenario, use Control Panel utilities*

- **802: 1.6** *Set up and configure Windows networking on a client/desktop*

- **802: 2.5** *Given a scenario, secure a SOHO wireless network*

- **802: 2.6** *Give a scenario, secure a SOHO wired network*

- **802: 4.5** *Given a scenario, troubleshoot wired and wireless networks with appropriate tools*

An A+ certification candidate must know how to connect desktop and laptop computers to a LAN, wide area network (WAN), or WLAN. This requires understanding how to install and configure common network hardware, and how to configure the OS to recognize and work with the hardware. The coverage of tools for installing wired and wireless networks described in this section includes the hardware tools listed in Objective 802: 4.5. Certain Windows Control Panel utilities listed in CompTIA Objective 802: 1.5 are useful when installing and configuring a network, and we describe them in this section. Also included is a very small subset of CompTIA Objective 802: 1.6 concerning working with wired and wireless network cards, while Objective 801: 2.6 covers a long list of knowledge and skills required to install and configure a small office/home office network, all of which are included in this chapter. We also cover the five topics in Objective 801: 2.6 on securing a wired SOHO network, although some of it is provided under the wireless topic, because many of the necessary security technologies and tasks for both wired and wireless networks are the same.

Installing and Configuring Networks

A *small office/home office (SOHO)* is an office consisting of a single computer or just a few computers. The location may be in a home or in a commercial office. Computers in a SOHO environment need to connect to the Internet, requiring the same steps you would take in a larger environment. A connection to a LAN requires a network interface card (NIC) for each computer—whether it is a wired NIC (Ethernet), a Wi-Fi NIC, or an analog modem for making a dial-up connection. Therefore, the first step in connecting a computer to a network is to install a NIC appropriate for the type of network—wired or wireless. Once you've installed the NIC and driver, you need to configure the NIC with an appropriate IP configuration, along with any other settings appropriate to the type of network. In this section, we describe the tools required for installing and configuring a network and then describe the steps for configuring a typical SOHO network.

Using Networking Tools

Networking tools—at least the hardware ones—are mainly required to make wired connections and test those connections. We described those tools in Chapter 3, and we explain their role in installing networks here. As you read through the descriptions for using these tools, and the discussion in the next section on connecting a wired NIC to a network, recall the information in Chapter 5 in the section titled "Cable Basics: What's Inside a Cable?"

Crimper

To create your own UTP network cables, you will need bulk unshielded twisted-pair (UTP) cabling, RJ-45 connectors, and a crimper. Use a wire stripper (often built into the crimper) on each end of the cable to expose the four wire pairs. Ensure the wires are in the correct order and place them into an RJ-45 connector. Insert the RJ-45 connector into the crimper and squeeze the crimper handles. The RJ-45 connector has eight small metal probes or needles, each of which will pierce one of the eight wires. Figure 15-1 shows a crimper with a crimped network cable.

Using a wire-crimping tool to attach an RJ-45 connector to a UTP cable

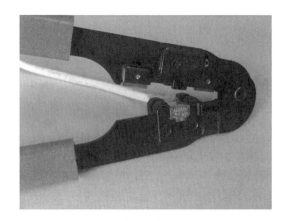

Punchdown Tool

Wall jacks for shielded twisted-pair (STP) or UTP network cables have an RJ-45 port. First run the cabling through the walls and ceilings between the wall jack and the wiring room. Then use a punchdown tool to connect the eight wires in an STP or UTP cable to the inside of an RJ-45 wall jack port. The other end of the same cable goes through walls, ceilings, and perhaps floors, back to a wiring room where you again use the punchdown tool to connect the eight wires to a *punchdown block* (a wiring panel), which also has RJ-45 ports. Shorter cables then connect from the punchdown block to network switches.

Multimeter

You can test the electrical properties of a cable or circuit with a multimeter. You could test, for example, the continuity of a power cable, or you could test that a power supply Serial Advanced Technology Attachment (SATA) hard disk connector is supplying the proper voltage.

Toner Probe

Wiring rooms can sometimes look like a packrat's nest—complete and utter chaos. To determine exactly which cable in the wiring room maps to a network jack in another room, use a toner probe (defined in Chapter 3). A toner is an audible tone generator that connects to a cable or network jack. In the wiring room, for example, we use the probe to amplify the tone emitted by the toner. As you pass the probe near the cable carrying the tone, the probe gets louder. This helps you isolate a specific cable in a cable bunch.

Cable Tester

Sometimes network cables look fine, but some wires inside may be bent and broken. Testing STP and UTP network cable continuity is easy with a cable tester; it has two RJ-45 ports where you plug in each end of the cable. Indicator lights tell you whether wires inside the cable are broken or not.

Loopback Plug

A loopback plug connects to a port, such as a serial or RJ-45 port. Inside the device, it reverses the receive and transmit wires so you can determine whether a port is functional.

Installing a NIC

When installing any NIC into a PC or laptop, there are two connections to consider—the connection to the computer and the connection to the network. You must first decide how the NIC will interface with the computer based on the choices available in the computer. NICs are available for all of the expansion bus types for desktop PCs described in Chapter 3. If you need a NIC for a laptop, you will also find NICs for the various laptop expansion slots described in Chapter 7. Similarly, if you need an external NIC, a large selection of Universal Serial Bus (USB) NICs is available.

Installing an Analog Modem

If you are connecting via dial-up, the modem is, in effect, your NIC. Analog modems are disappearing from laptops as standard equipment, and are even rarer in desktop computers. If you need to install a modem in a computer, first decide if you want a bus modem or an external modem. At one time an external modem had to use a serial interface, but today they use the USB interface. Installing a bus modem is no different from installing any other bus adapter card. Once you have physically installed either type, start Windows and provide the driver disc if prompted. After that, you will connect the modem to a telephone wall jack, using a phone cable with RJ-11 connectors, which is similar to connecting an Ethernet cable to a NIC, as described in Exercise 15-1. Once you connect it, you are ready to configure the modem, as described later in this chapter in "Configuring Dial-up and Cellular Connections."

Installing a Bus NIC

Because of the array of expansion slots in PCs and laptops, before choosing a NIC to install, you must first determine what expansion bus type or types are available in the computer. Once you have selected and purchased the appropriate NIC for the computer, follow the manufacturer's instructions for installing it. Then, in the case of an Ethernet NIC, connect the network cable (described in Exercise 15-1: "Connecting an Ethernet Cable") and boot the computer.

Installing a USB, FireWire, PC Card, or ExpressCard NIC

Before installing a USB, FireWire, PC Card, or ExpressCard NIC, check the manufacturer's instructions. In most cases, you will connect the NIC to the USB or FireWire port or PC Card or ExpressCard slot and connect the NIC to the network, and then let Windows recognize it. When prompted, provide the disc or location of driver files.

on the job

ExpressCard has replaced the outdated PC Card.

Enabling Wake on LAN

Imagine that your computer at your desk at work was powered off and you are about to give a presentation far from your office when you realize you forgot a file that you need. A feature in many modern network adapters might save you from going back to your desk. Called Wake On LAN, it allows a powered-off computer to be powered on when someone connects to it over the network. To enable or disable Wake On LAN, open Device Manager and double-click your network adapter to open its Properties dialog. Click the Advanced tab, and scroll down in the list until you see Wake On LAN (or a similar description), as shown in Figure 15-2. If it isn't listed, your network adapter does not support it. If it is there, select it, and enable or disable it using the Value drop-down box.

PoE

A few recently manufactured NICs support a feature called Power over Ethernet (PoE) that supports both Ethernet signals and power signals over the same Ethernet cable. You may see this type of NIC in specialized equipment, such as surveillance cameras, in locations where power is not available but where you can run Ethernet cabling. The original PoE standard, IEEE 802.3af-2003, only supported up to 15.4 Watts of direct current (DC) power, but the latest standard, IEEE 802.3at-2009, is called *Power over Ethernet Plus (PoE+)*, and it provides up to 25.5 watts of power. We will describe a use of PoE in the section titled "Creating a Wi-Fi Network."

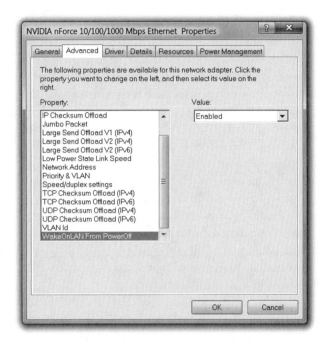

FIGURE 15-2

Look for Wake on LAN settings in the Properties dialog for your network adapter.

QoS

When you receive an email, the message is fully assembled before you open it, so your experience is okay as long as the message is complete, which means it can arrive out of order, but gets reassembled before you see it. Using a service like Skype to talk to your Aunt Sally, you need a very stable and reliable signal that delivers time-sensitive traffic like video and sound intact, with packets in order, and in real time. Similarly, when watching streaming video or listening to streaming music, you need everything delivered in the correct order and with the least delay. Of course, a certain amount of buffering occurs with streaming traffic, so you may not notice a problem, but more help is needed all along the path the signals travel. *Quality of Service (QoS)* includes many techniques and technologies that attempt to solve the problem of delivering content that cannot suffer delays and lost packets over not just a network, but an internetwork. A variety of QoS features are found in NICs and other network equipment, including features that prioritize types of traffic, giving higher priority to traffic like your Skype call. If you open the Local Area Connection Properties dialog box for your NIC, you will see a feature called QoS Packet Scheduler, which should be turned on by default.

Connecting to a Wired Network

Connecting a wired Ethernet NIC to a network is a task you will perform many times—whether you are connecting to a simple LAN or to a broadband router. In both cases, you will connect the cable from the PC to a switch, either a simple Ethernet switch or a switch integrated with a broadband router. An Ethernet NIC will need to connect to the LAN using UTP CAT5/5e/6 cabling that has RJ-45 connectors and does not exceed the 100-meter distance limit between the computer and the switch for UTP or STP cable. Before connecting the cable, turn off power to the PC and the switch, if applicable. This step may seem a bit extreme, and is generally not required, but we have found that some SOHO Ethernet switches include this instruction, which ensures that the switch will properly detect the new connection upon repowering. Connect one end to the NIC and the other to a wall jack, or directly to a hub (rarely) or switch. In a large organization, a network administrator or technician will tell you where to connect to the LAN, which will probably be to a wall jack with an RJ-45 connector. At home or in a small office, you will normally connect directly to a small switch or to a broadband router with an integrated switch.

Figure 15-3 shows a device that acts as an Ethernet switch, as well as a router to a cable or Digital Subscriber Line (DSL) WAN connection. The cable on the left connects to a cable modem, whereas the center cable connects to the PC. The cord on the right provides power to the device. The manufacturer calls this device a router, although it is a multifunction device, as described in Chapter 14.

FIGURE 15-3

A device that performs the functions of an Ethernet switch and an IP router between WAN and LAN networks

EXERCISE 15-1

Connecting an Ethernet Cable

You can easily connect an Ethernet cable to an RJ-45 outlet on a PC, switch, or hub.

1. Align the RJ-45 cable connector with the RJ-45 outlet on the computer so the clip on the cable connector lines up with the notch in the center of one side of the outlet.

2. Push the connector into the outlet until you hear the clip click into place. Doing this secures the cable so it makes a good connection and cannot accidentally fall out of the outlet.

3. Use the same technique to connect the cable to an outlet on an Ethernet switch or wall-mounted plate. (See Figure 15-4, in which the cable connector is in front of the outlet on the router.)

4. If this is the first time you have connected an Ethernet cable, practice unplugging it by grasping the connector, pressing on the clip, and gently pulling the connector out. Never force it, or you will break off the clip and then your cable will be not be securely connected. Now plug it back in.

FIGURE 15-4

The clip on the RJ-45 connector must align properly with the RJ-45 outlet.

The next step is to configure the TCP/IP properties of the connection in Windows. Since this configuration is common to both wired Ethernet connections and Wi-Fi connections, we will explore the IP configuration after we examine how to create a Wi-Fi network.

Creating a Wi-Fi Network

Before you install a wireless network, you must consider some special issues for selecting and positioning wireless hardware. These issues include obstacles between the computers and the WLAN, the distances involved, any possible interference, the standards supported by the devices on the Wi-Fi network, and the wireless mode for your WLAN. Then you should take steps to update the firmware on the wireless access point (WAP), if necessary.

Obstacles and Interference

Certain devices emit radio signals that can interfere with Wi-Fi networks. These devices include microwave ovens and cordless telephones that use the 2.4 GHz radio band, as well as other nearby WAPs. WAPs normally support channel selection. Therefore, if you have a 2.4 GHz cordless phone that supports channel selection, configure the phone to use one channel (channel 1, for instance), and the WAP and each wireless NIC to use another channel, like channel 11. In addition, metal furniture and appliances, metal-based ultraviolet (UV) tint on windows, and metal construction materials within walls can all block or reduce Wi-Fi signals.

on the
j o b

When a computer or other physical device connects to a network, it is called a node.

Certain businesses and organizations require a professional site survey, a set of procedures to determine the location of obstacles and interference that would disrupt wireless signals. WAP placement is then determined from this site survey. Although a professional site survey is too costly for a small business or home owner, you can use the site survey feature of your wireless NIC to discover which channel nearby wireless networks are using. The name of the site survey feature may simply be Available Network, which shows a list of wireless networks. Clicking a network in the list reveals the channel in use and other important information. Alternatively, use a wireless locator.

Wireless networks can be detected using a *wireless locator*. The tool displays discovered WLANs and their characteristics, such as the SSID, channel, signal strength, encryption type, geographical coordinates (working in conjunction with GPS), and many other details. Used often during wireless site surveys to detect nearby WLANs and their channels, the tool can also be used during a security audit to test WLAN visibility, distance, and security. A wireless locator can be a specialized handheld device or software installed on a smartphone, tablet, laptop, or PC.

Distances and Speeds

A huge issue with wireless networks is the signal range of the communicating devices. All of the Wi-Fi standards used give maximum outdoor signal ranges of 75 to 125 meters, but that is for a signal uninterrupted by barriers, such as walls that may contain signal-stopping materials like metal lath. Position a WAP in a central location within easy range of all devices, NICs, and access points.

The farther a wireless NIC is from a WAP, the more the signal degrades and the greater the chance of slowing down the connection speed. Actual ranges for these devices once in place vary greatly. For instance, the documentation for our 802.11g WAP shows that the outdoor range of this device is 40 meters at 54 Mbps and 300 meters at 6 Mbps or less. Indoor range is 15 meters at 54 Mbps and 120 meters at 6 Mbps. Compare that with the ranges for the standards shown in Table 15-1.

In the past, we preferred to use USB NICs attached to a USB cable (Figure 15-5) rather than bus or PC Card NICs that were internal to the computer. The cable gives you more flexibility in positioning the wireless antenna for best signal reception. However, unless you can find a Wi-Fi NIC with a USB 3.0 interface, the 480 Mbps speed of USB 2.0 is slower than the maximum data rate for 802.11n. Alternatively, you can find bus Wi-Fi NICs with antennas attached via a cable to the NIC, allowing you some flexibility for positioning the antenna.

When a wireless network spans buildings, you encounter special problems. For instance, the material in the building's walls may interfere with the signal. Now you need to get creative. For instance, consider a wireless NIC with a directional dish antenna (see Figure 15-6) that you can position in a window and point directly

TABLE 15-1 Summary of Common Wi-Fi Standards	IEEE Standard	Operating Frequency	Typical Data Rate	Maximum Data Rate	Indoor Range	Outdoor Range
	802.11b	2.4 GHz	6.5 Mbps	11 Mbps	~35 meters	~100 meters
	802.11g	2.4 GHz	25 Mbps	54 Mbps	~25 meters	~75 meters
	802.11n	2.4 GHz or 5 GHz	200 Mbps	540 Mbps	~50 meters	~125 meters

You can position a USB wireless NIC like this for better signal strength.

toward the WAP. Another option is a wireless range extender—a device that resembles a WAP but is designed to boost the signals from a WAP and extend its coverage distance.

Once you find the ideal location for each WAP, you may discover that you do not have a power connection available to each one, but you do have a nearby run of Ethernet cabling to tap into so that the WAP/router can connect to an Ethernet

A USB wireless NIC with a directional dish antenna

network. It requires the correct Ethernet cable and *PoE splitter*. The Ethernet cable from the network plugs into the splitter, which splits the signal and sends it to two connectors: an Ethernet jack and a power connector. You then connect the WAP by Ethernet cable to the jack, and by power cable to the power connector.

In addition to WAPs and wireless routers, all types of networked devices, such as security cameras, IP phones, and Ethernet switches, use PoE.

Compatibility

Another issue is the standard supported by each device. If possible, for each wireless network installation, select NICs and WAPs that comply with the exact same Wi-Fi standard. Even though 802.11g, which is faster than 802.11b, is downward compatible with the slower standard, even a single 802.11b device on the wireless network will slow down the entire WLAN. Similarly, an 802.11n device is downward compatible with 802.11a, 802.11b, and 802.11g devices. However, a single, slower, non-802.11n device may slow down the entire WLAN.

In addition, use devices from the same manufacturer, when possible, because some manufacturers build in special proprietary features—support for higher speeds or greater range—that are only available in their device. However, this rule is difficult to enforce in practice, especially when you add a laptop with a built-in wireless NIC to your network.

Wireless Modes

Once you have physically installed a wireless NIC or NIC, the steps required to set up a wireless network depend on the wireless mode you select—ad hoc mode or infrastructure mode. Before we discuss the differences between these two modes, it is important to note that when a WAP or wireless router is present, a modern network card will auto-configure for infrastructure mode, so there is less need to distinguish between these two modes.

Ad Hoc Mode   If you do not have a WAP or wireless router available, and your goal is to have just two or three PCs communicate with each other wirelessly, and they do not need connections to other LANs or the Internet, you can consider having these computers communicate directly—without the use of a WAP—in *ad hoc mode*. In this case, each computer will require a wireless NIC, which you must position within range of the others. The first time you start Windows after the NIC is connected, the Found New Hardware Wizard will run and install the software for your NIC. If prompted for configuration information, select Ad Hoc Mode.

The NIC will now communicate peer-to-peer with other ad hoc wireless NICs within range. Configure ad hoc mode on the other computers to also work in ad hoc mode. The wireless nodes communicating together in this mode make up an *Independent Basic Service Set (IBSS)*. This small group of computers is similar to the peer-to-peer model of Microsoft workgroup administrative models.

on the
j o b
The use of ad hoc mode has just about disappeared because WAPs and wireless routers are very common, and the same two or three computers would then communicate through those devices using infrastructure mode (explained next).

Infrastructure Mode

Ad hoc is a minimal configuration. Even in a small home network, when you wish to use a Wi-Fi connection to gain access to an Internet connection, you will not use this mode. In most cases, the reason for a wireless network is to have access to a wired network or to connect to a broadband connection to the Internet. For this, you will use *infrastructure mode*, which requires a WAP that acts as a hub for a wireless network.

Many wireless nodes can connect to a single WAP. In fact, the WAP itself may be a multifunction device, acting as a WAP, an Ethernet switch, and an IP router. It, in turn, can connect to a wired Ethernet network, a cable, or a DSL modem. Figure 15-7

FIGURE 15-7

A wireless access point

shows a WAP. Many manufacturers refer to these as wireless routers. The one pictured is a WAP that you can use to share a broadband connection; it includes a dedicated Ethernet port for connecting to a broadband modem, plus a four-port Ethernet switch. The wireless nodes (including the WAP) communicating together in infrastructure mode make up a *Basic Service Set (BSS)*.

Infrastructure Setup: WAP

Position a WAP in the center of all the computers that will participate in the wireless network. If there are barriers to the wireless signals, you will need to determine if you can overcome them with the use of an enhanced antenna on the WAP, as shown in Figure 15-8, or a wireless signal booster to reach computers that are beyond the WAP's range. A wireless signal booster physically resembles a WAP.

FIGURE 15-8

A wireless access point with an enhanced antenna attached

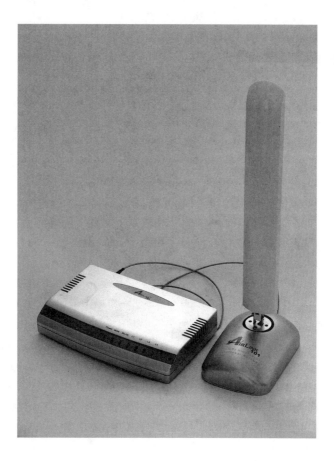

In order to configure a new WAP, you normally connect to it using an Ethernet cable between a computer with an Ethernet NIC and the WAP. Check the documentation that comes with the WAP in case you need to use a special cable. Direct connection via the Ethernet port is only required for initial setup of the WAP. Once it is up and running, you can connect from any computer on the network and modify the configuration.

It only takes a few minutes to set up a WAP physically and then to configure it to create your wireless LAN. You will need a WAP and its user manual, a computer with an Ethernet NIC, two Ethernet cables (one may have come with the WAP), and the WAP's IP address, obtained from the user manual. If you are setting this up as a broadband router, you will need the DSL or cable modem. With all the materials assembled, follow these general instructions for connecting and configuring a WAP that is a DSL/cable router, commonly called a wireless router. The actual steps required to configure a WAP may vary from these steps. These general instructions work for most WAPs we have used:

- Before connecting the WAP, turn off the computer and the DSL or cable modem.
- Connect one end of an Ethernet cable to the WAN port of the WAP, and connect the other end of the cable to the DSL or cable modem.
- Take another network cable and connect one end of the cable to your computer's Ethernet NIC and the other end to one of the Ethernet ports on the WAP.
- Turn power to the modem on, and wait for the lights on the modem to settle down.
- Turn the WAP's power on by connecting the power cable that came with the WAP, first to the WAP and then to an electrical outlet. If the WAP has a power switch, turn it on now.
- Turn the computer's power on.
- Now look at the WAP and verify that the indicator lights for the WAN and WLAN ports light up. Ensure that the indicator light for the LAN port to which the computer connects is lit as well.

Once you have completed these steps, you can test the connection to the WAP, and if all works well, you can configure the WAP settings. Exercise 15-2 will walk you through testing the WAP connection and then using your Web browser to connect and configure the WAP settings.

exam
watch

For CompTIA Exams 801 and 802 be aware that most of the topics discussed here under "Securing a Wireless Network" apply to both wired and wireless networks. Those that only apply to a wireless network include Wi-Fi Protected Setup (WPS), changing the Service Set Identifier (SSID), disabling SSID broadcasts, and the wireless standards discussed under the topic "Wireless Encryption." You can apply much of what you learn here to configure a router/firewall on a wired network, although the examples given here and in Exercise 15-2 are of a wireless network.

Securing a Wireless Network

There are several techniques for protecting a wireless network—both through maintaining physical security and through the configuration utility for a WAP or wireless router. Even devices designed for the consumer market have sophisticated security technologies, and any technology or feature that applies rules to control access between networks is a firewall technology. On top of that, many of them automatically and securely configure themselves while walking you through the process.

We will review important tasks for securing a wireless network next, and in Exercise 15-2, you will see the steps required to configure settings for most of these.

Physical Security   Ensure that you physically protect the heart of the wireless network, the WAP or wireless router, both from theft and from harmful conditions. Then consider the physical security of the computers and devices that connect to the network; because many of them are small mobile devices, those two characteristics make them vulnerable to theft. Therefore, consider taking steps to protect those devices and the data on them. For instance, using Apple's iCloud service, you can configure an iPad so that if it is lost or stolen, you can see its location via the Internet and the use of the network of terrestrial navigation satellites called the *Global Positioning System (GPS)*. You can remotely lock it or erase it. Learn more about mobile devices in Chapter 20.

Wi-Fi Protected Setup (WPS)   Newer wireless routers support an automatic configuration method called *Wi-Fi Protected Setup (WPS)*. WPS makes connecting wireless clients to a wireless network easy, because you can simply press a button on the wireless router and on any compatible wireless NIC to allow access. This automated configuration is very secure. However, if a wireless device is not WPS enabled, you will need to manually configure it with the settings, including the password to access the wireless network.

Changing SSID and Disabling SSID Broadcast   A *Service Set ID (SSID)* is a network name used to identify a wireless network. Consisting of up to 32 characters, the SSID travels with the messages on the wireless network, and all of the wireless devices on a WLAN must use the same SSID in order to communicate. Therefore, assigning a SSID is part of setting up a wireless network. A WAP or wireless router comes from the manufacturer with a preconfigured SSID name. You must change this name in the WAP; in fact, some configuration programs assign a random new name for you every time you run the configuration utility, but allow you the option to provide a different name if you wish. You can also disable SSID broadcast through the configuration menus on a WAP or wireless router. This means that before any clients can connect, someone must manually enter the WLAN name into the configuration for that client's NIC.

Changing Default Administrator User Name and Password   WAPs and wireless routers come with a default administrator user name and password, which you must change immediately so that no one can easily log on to the WAP and change its configuration. Here again, the configuration program in many wireless routers will prompt you to do this.

Enabling MAC Filtering   Another way to limit access is by enabling and configuring *MAC filtering* on the WAP or wireless router. As you learned in Chapter 14, a Media Access Control (MAC) address is a unique hardware address assigned to every NIC, including Wi-Fi and Bluetooth NICs. The MAC address of the sending NIC is contained within each packet that travels the network. You can enable MAC filtering to allow or deny specific MAC addresses from connecting to your wireless network. One way to see the MAC address for a NIC is to open a Command Prompt and enter **ipconfig /all**.

Disabling Ports   Recall the section in Chapter 14 titled "Common Ports" and the description of the services that use each port. A wireless broadband router limits incoming traffic from the Internet that was not initiated from inside the wireless network. It does this by disabling incoming ports in the router's settings. By default, most wireless broadband routers have all incoming ports disabled, requiring a request from the local wireless network to open a port. For instance, when you browse to Web pages on the Internet, the router recognizes that the Website is responding to your requests.

Port Forwarding   If you have a server on your private network that you would like to receive traffic from the Internet, then you will need to enable *port forwarding*, which you do through the router's settings, mapping the port to the IP address of the server (a static IP address). Then outsiders can access that server. A situation in which you may need to enable port forwarding that does not involve what you normally think of as a server is when you want to allow Remote Desktop (RDP) access from a computer beyond the router to an internal host. Exercise 15-2 includes instructions for configuring this on the router.

Port Triggering   While port forwarding requires that the host within the private network have a static address, you can use *port triggering* to allow incoming traffic to reach a host that receives its address via Dynamic Host Configuration Protocol (DHCP) and is behind a network address translation (NAT) router (true of wireless broadband routers). See the later section in this chapter titled "NAT Routing." To enable port triggering, you specify a range of outgoing ports, and when an interior host makes an outgoing connection through a port in that range, a specified incoming port will open for a brief period of time. Exercise 15-2 shows an example of port triggering to enable Internet Relay Chat (IRC).

Wireless Encryption   Wireless transmissions are vulnerable because they travel over radio waves, which are easy for anyone with the right equipment to pick up and read the data. Therefore, you should take steps to encrypt any data sent over a wireless network. There are three sets of standards for this: WEP, WPA, and WPA2. One concept to understand is that wireless encryption (as well as other encryption methods) depend on the use of a code called an *encryption key* (also simply called a *key*) that is issued automatically by the encryption software. The key is used by other devices or users for decrypting the encrypted data. The types of keys and how they are used is one of the features that distinguishes the standards.

Wired Equivalent Privacy (WEP) is the oldest of the Wi-Fi encryption standards. It uses 64- or 128-bit encryption that is easily broken. It does not encrypt the actual data in a packet, just the portion that contains the source and destination information. Another security issue with WEP is that it issues a single static key that is not changed from session to session and that all network clients share. Further, WEP has no way to perform user authentication on the packet, something added to later standards. Consider WEP obsolete and do not use it unless it is the only wireless encryption standard supported by your hardware, which would make your hardware very old.

Wi-Fi Protected Access (WPA) is a data encryption standard based on the IEEE 802.11i security standard for wireless networks. It corrects many of the problems with WEP. It issues keys per-user and per-session and includes encryption key integrity checking. On top of the WPA data encryption, it uses a *Temporal Key Integrity Protocol (TKIP)* with a 128-bit encryption key for authentication. WPA was considered transitional because it supported most older NICs, and, once hackers broke the TKIP encryption key, it, too, became obsolete.

At this time, the latest wireless encryption standard is *Wi-Fi Protected Access 2 (WPA2)*, which complies with the 802.11i security standard in that it does not support older network cards and offers both secure authentication and encryption, thus providing true end-to-end data encryption with authentication. It uses *Extensible Authentication Protocol (EAP)*, which defines a type of wrapper for a variety of authentication methods. A *wrapper* is program code that acts as a logical container for other code or data. Wireless devices generally use *EAP with Personal Shared Key (EAP-PSK)*, which involves using a string of characters (a shared key) that both communicating devices know. WPA2 uses an encryption standard approved by the U.S. government—*Advanced Encryption Standard (AES)*.

Each computer that connects must have a wireless NIC that is compatible with the version of wireless encryption in use on the WAP/router, and will be required to enter a password.

Normally, you can configure your wireless NIC to remember the password and use it every time it connects to that Wi-Fi network. Learn how to do this in Exercise 15-2: "Configuring a WAP or Wireless Router."

NAT Routing   In a home or small business, a broadband router (wired or wireless) is the connection point between the wired or wireless LAN. This router will contain a DHCP server that automatically assigns a private IP address on the LAN, and the device will also act as *a NAT router*, although you can turn this on or off without affecting the DHCP settings. The default is to turn on *NAT routing*, a firewall technology that uses the *network address translation (NAT)*, a TCP/IP protocol that hides IP addresses on a private network from hosts beyond the router—usually on the Internet. When you access the Internet through a router using NAT routing (almost everyone does), it "remembers" your internal address, but changes the source address in each IP packet from your computer to the router's external address. When packets come back from the Internet in response to your computer's requests, the NAT router recalls that your computer made that request and sends the return packet to your computer. Therefore, malicious code outside your network does not know your internal address and cannot target you directly using your IP address.

Assigning Static IP Addresses   Any NIC accessing a Wi-Fi network must be assigned an IP address with the same network ID as the Wi-Fi network. The DHCP server on most WAPs and wireless routers will do this by default. However, you can configure static addresses—either through the WAP or router's DHCP settings or in the settings for the NIC on each computer. If you assign a static address through the DHCP settings on a WAP or router, you will need the MAC address for each NIC you wish to allow to connect to the network. Sometimes the WAP or router helps in this regard, displaying the MACs of detected NICs, and you can then associate a static IP address to the NIC. Technically, this isn't a static address, since it is assigned through DHCP, but it has the same result in that the same address is always given to the same MAC address (which DHCP tries to do anyway), but it also keeps a NIC with a different MAC address from connecting.

DMZ   A standard firewall feature is support for something called a *demilitarized zone (DMZ)*, a network between firewalls. The way it works is one firewall is at the gateway between an internal network and the Internet, and another firewall is at the connecting point between the first internal network and another internal network. You place servers you want accessible from the Internet on the first network, the DMZ, and you open ports on the external firewall for the services on these servers.

Then, on the internal firewall, you close those ports. An inexpensive broadband router (wireless or wired) will have a DMZ feature that opens ports just for certain MAC addresses on the internal network.

Updating the Firmware

Occasionally, manufacturers release firmware updates for their equipment, and WAPs and NICs are not immune to this. These updates can be crucial to the successful operation of your WLAN. Therefore, even if you purchased your wireless equipment yesterday, it is worth taking the time to check out the manufacturer's Website, using the model number and serial number for your devices. Then follow the instructions for updating the firmware on each device. You can update a WAP through its Ethernet port before creating the WLAN, and update wireless NICs through their PC interface, providing the connected PC has access to the Internet through another network. Otherwise, you may have to update the wireless NICs after installing the WLAN.

EXERCISE 15-2

Configuring a WAP or Wireless Router

You will need to obtain the IP address for the WAP and then use the PING command to test the connection between the computer and the WAP. Once you determine that the connection works, you can connect and configure the WAP.

1. Open a Command Prompt window in Windows.
2. Test the connection using the PING command. Type **ping *ip_address_of_WAP***. A successful test will show results similar to those shown in Figure 15-9.

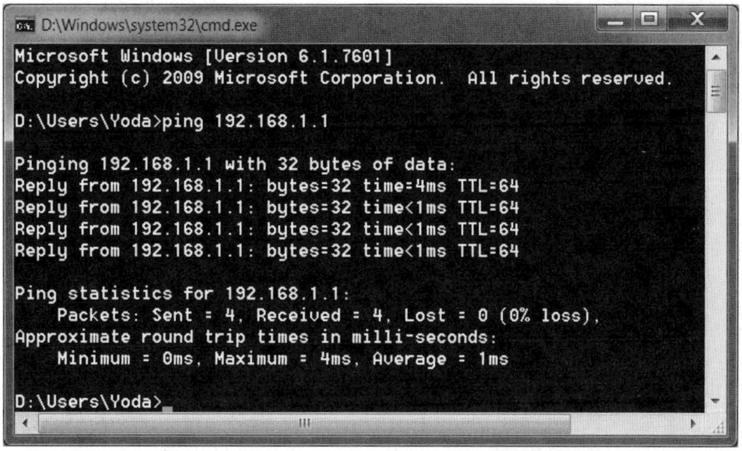

FIGURE 15-9

A successful test of the Ethernet connection to the WAP.

```
D:\Windows\system32\cmd.exe

Microsoft Windows [Version 6.1.7601]
Copyright (c) 2009 Microsoft Corporation.  All rights reserved.

D:\Users\Yoda>ping 192.168.1.1

Pinging 192.168.1.1 with 32 bytes of data:
Reply from 192.168.1.1: bytes=32 time=4ms TTL=64
Reply from 192.168.1.1: bytes=32 time<1ms TTL=64
Reply from 192.168.1.1: bytes=32 time<1ms TTL=64
Reply from 192.168.1.1: bytes=32 time<1ms TTL=64

Ping statistics for 192.168.1.1:
    Packets: Sent = 4, Received = 4, Lost = 0 (0% loss),
Approximate round trip times in milli-seconds:
    Minimum = 0ms, Maximum = 4ms, Average = 1ms

D:\Users\Yoda>
```

3. Then open the browser, and in the address box, enter the address you successfully tested in Step 2.

4. If prompted for a user name and password, use the one provided in the WAP's user manual. At your first opportunity, change this user name, as well as the password, so no one else familiar with the default settings can connect and change the settings.

5. The next screen should be a setup utility for the WAP. Follow the instructions and provide the type of Internet access, using information from your Internet service provider (ISP). Perform other steps appropriate to your type of Internet access, and provide the user name and password required for Internet access so the router can connect to the Internet.

6. Most WAPs, by default, act as DHCP servers, running the DHCP service and giving out private IP addresses to computers on the internal WLAN and LAN (if appropriate). If there is no other DHCP server on your network, leave this as the default. If there is a DHCP server for your LAN, disable DHCP for the LAN (all Ethernet connections), but leave it enabled for the WLAN (all wireless connections).

7. A screen will appear, such as in Figure 15-10, in which you can configure other settings for the wireless router. The Network Mode setting determines if older Wi-Fi clients can connect. A setting of "Mixed" means the wireless router will allow connections from 802.11b, 802.11g, and 802.11n clients. Look for the SSID setting, and change it from the default name to a unique name; for additional security, consider disabling SSID broadcast. You can also change the standard channel if there is interference from other devices.

FIGURE 15-10

WPS, network
mode, channel,
and SSID wireless
configuration
settings

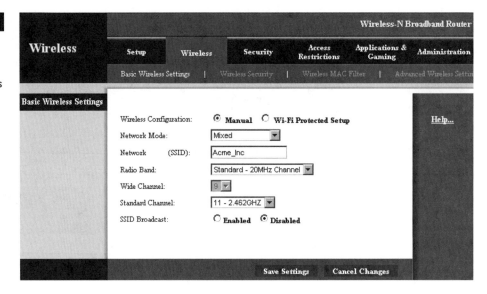

8. Figure 15-11 shows how you can permit specific device access using MAC address filtering.

9. Figure 15-12 shows a port-forward configuration allowing RDP access to an internal host (192.168.1.166) on port 3389. By default, the wireless router does not allow inbound traffic to internal hosts.

FIGURE 15-11

Wireless access
point MAC
address filtering

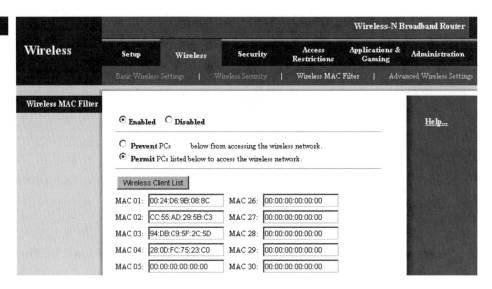

Wireless access
point port
forwarding
configuration

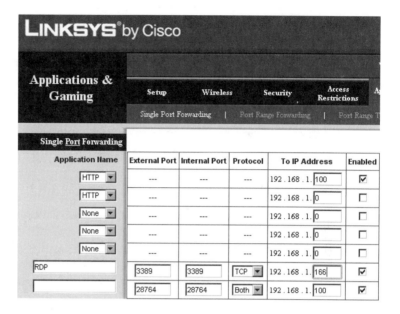

10. In Figure 15-13, we see a port-triggering configuration for IRC. In this example, the wireless router will monitor internal clients that connect to IRC servers between ports 6660–7000 and open an inbound port (113) since IRC servers authenticate users by connecting back to them on port 113, which, by default, will not work through most firewalls.

Wireless
access point
port triggering
configuration

11. Next we can configure wireless encryption. In Figure 15-14, we enabled WPA2 encryption with the passphrase of P@$$w0rd. Connecting stations (see Figure 15-15) must use this same passphrase to connect to the wireless network. If your connecting devices support it, choose Advanced Encryption Standard (AES); it is considered more secure than Temporal Key Integrity Protocol (TKIP).

12. If you want to prioritize certain types of Internet traffic, use your wireless router QoS settings. Figure 15-16 shows that Jane's Voice over IP (VoIP) phone has priority over playing the game Counter Strike on the Internet since VoIP network traffic is time-sensitive; Counter Strike network traffic will have to wait if Jane is using her VoIP phone at the same time.

13. After completing the configuration, save your settings and back up the configuration to a file on your computer (an option in many WAPs or broadband routers), and then log out of the setup program.

FIGURE 15-14

Configuring WPA2 wireless encryption

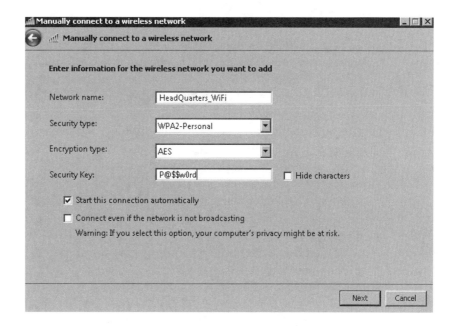

FIGURE 15-15

Connecting to a WPA2-encrypted wireless network from Windows 7

FIGURE 15-16

QoS configuration on a wireless access point

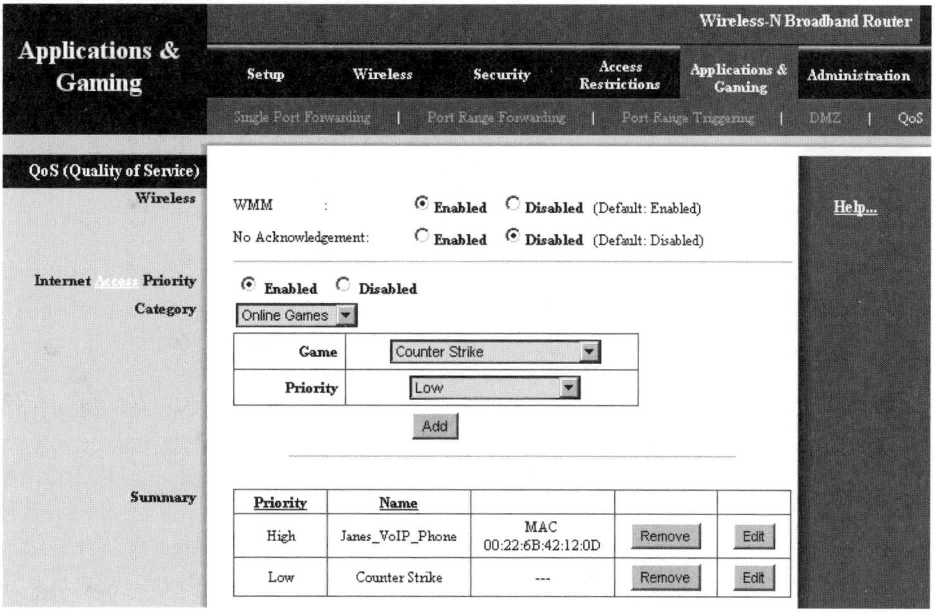

Infrastructure Setup: Wireless NIC

Follow the manufacturer's instructions for installing, connecting, and configuring your wireless NIC. After the NIC is connected, Windows will detect the new hardware, and the Windows Found New Hardware Installation Wizard will display. Select the option Install The Software Automatically and click Next. Follow the instructions to install the NIC, including providing the SSID of your wireless network. Once the installation is complete, an icon for the wireless NIC will appear on the notification area of the taskbar.

Once you have installed the software, you can change the configuration by double-clicking the notification area icon for your wireless NIC. This program will let you search for available wireless networks, change the mode in which your wireless NIC is operating, set security settings for encryption of the data transmitted, change channels, and much more.

As shown here, status messages will appear over your notification area when a wireless connection is first established and when a wireless connection fails. These messages only display briefly, so most NICs also change the appearance of the icon, showing perhaps a blue or green icon when the NIC is connected and a red icon, or an icon with an x over it, when the NIC is disconnected. A laptop with an integrated wireless adapter will usually have a hardware switch to enable or disable the wireless connection. Be sure you have this turned on.

IP Configuration

By default, Windows assumes that each network connection will receive an IP address automatically via a DHCP server on your network. This is true of connections made via an Ethernet NIC as well as through a wireless NIC.

You may need to set up a computer on a LAN in which all the computers are assigned static IP addresses. In that case, you will obtain the configuration information from a LAN administrator and then manually enter an IP configuration into Windows. This information should include the IP configuration addresses described in Chapter 14. The list will resemble Table 15-2, although the actual addresses will be unique to your network. Notice that these are private IP addresses. Add the address for a WINS server only if the computer is part of a routed network that requires Windows Internet Naming Service (WINS).

	IP Configuration Setting	Setting Value
TABLE 15-2	IP address	192.168.227.138
	Subnet mask	255.255.255.0
Sample IP	Default gateway	192.168.227.2
Configuration	DNS server	192.168.227.3
Settings	WINS server (rarely used)	192.168.227.4

If you need to manually configure IP settings, make a list similar to that in Table 15-2, showing the required settings that you received from your network administrator. Then open the IP configuration dialog for your network adapter. Exercise 15-3 describes how to do this in Windows XP, and Exercise 15-4 describes the steps used in Windows Vista and Windows 7.

EXERCISE 15-3

Manually Configuring IP Settings in Windows XP

The following steps will guide you through entering IP configuration settings into Windows XP.

1. Open the Network Connections applet in Control Panel, and then select and right-click the icon for the network connection you wish to configure. Select Properties from the context menu.

2. The resulting dialog box will vary based on the type of connection. The General tab of an Ethernet or wireless connection will have a Connect Using field showing the NIC and the list of protocols and services used by that NIC (called Items), whereas a dial-up or cellular connection will have the list of protocols and services on the Networking tab.

3. Locate the list of items used by the connection and double-click Internet Protocol (TCP/IP) to open the Properties dialog box. Click the radio button labeled Use The Following IP Address.

4. Enter the IP address, subnet mask, and default gateway settings.

5. If you have a DNS server address, click the radio button labeled Use The Following DNS Server Addresses and enter the Preferred DNS Server. If you have an address for the Alternate Server, enter that address, too.

FIGURE 15-17

Test the configuration by pinging the gateway.

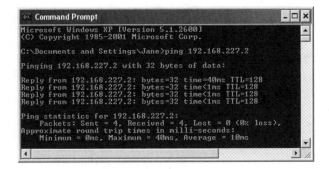

```
C:\ Command Prompt                                         _ □ ×
Microsoft Windows XP [Version 5.1.2600]
(C) Copyright 1985-2001 Microsoft Corp.

C:\Documents and Settings\Jane>ping 192.168.227.2

Pinging 192.168.227.2 with 32 bytes of data:

Reply from 192.168.227.2: bytes=32 time=40ms TTL=128
Reply from 192.168.227.2: bytes=32 time<1ms TTL=128
Reply from 192.168.227.2: bytes=32 time<1ms TTL=128
Reply from 192.168.227.2: bytes=32 time<1ms TTL=128

Ping statistics for 192.168.227.2:
    Packets: Sent = 4, Received = 4, Lost = 0 (0% loss),
Approximate round trip times in milli-seconds:
    Minimum = 0ms, Maximum = 40ms, Average = 10ms
```

6. Check the numbers you entered, click OK to accept these settings, and then click the Close button in the Properties dialog box.

7. To test your settings, open a Command Prompt window and ping the gateway address to ensure that your computer can communicate on the LAN. If your configuration is correct, and if the gateway router is functioning, you should see four replies. Figure 15-17 shows the results of pinging a gateway address of 192.168.227.2.

EXERCISE 15-4

CertCam

Manually Configuring IP Settings in Windows Vista and Windows 7

The following steps will guide you through entering IP configuration settings into Windows Vista. The steps are very similar in Windows 7.

1. Open the Network And Sharing Center in Control Panel, and in Vista, select Manage Network Connections from the list of tasks in the left pane to open the Network Connections window. In Windows 7, select Change Adapter Settings.

2. Select and right-click the icon for the network connection you wish to configure. Select Properties from the context menu.

3. Locate the list of items used by the connection and double-click Internet Protocol Version 4 (TCP/IPv4) to open the Properties dialog box. Click the radio button labeled Use The Following IP Address.

4. Enter the IP address, subnet mask, and default gateway settings.

5. If you have a DNS server address to use, click the radio button labeled Use The Following DNS Server Addresses and enter the Preferred DNS Server. If you have an address for the Alternate Server, enter that address, too.

6. If you have a WINS server address, click the Advanced button, select the WINS tab, click the Add button, and enter the address. Click Add and click OK to close the Advanced TCP/IP Settings dialog box.

7. The Internet Protocol Version 4 (TCP/IPv4) Properties dialog box should resemble Figure 15-18. Check the numbers you entered, click OK to accept these settings, and then click the Close button in the Properties dialog box for the connection.

8. To test your settings, open a Command Prompt window and ping the gateway address to ensure your computer can communicate on the LAN. If your configuration is correct, and if the gateway router is functioning, you should see four replies.

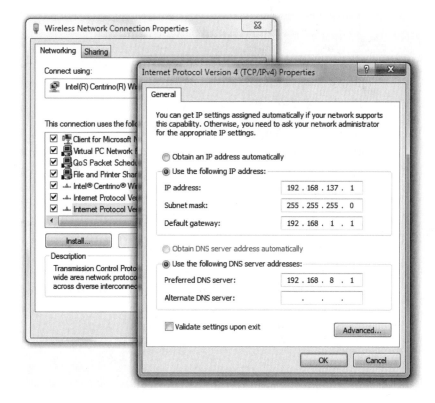

FIGURE 15-18

Static IP information in the Windows 7 Internet Protocol Version 4 (TCP/IPv4) Properties dialog

Configuring a WAN Connection

Of the various WAN connections, dial-up and cellular connections have similar configuration steps, and DSL, cable, and satellite WAN configurations have common steps. A virtual private network (VPN) is not, strictly speaking, a WAN connection, as it depends on an existing network connection, but because VPNs are used to make WAN connections more secure and are part of the connection configuration for many users, we include VPN configuration here.

Configuring Dial-up and Cellular Connections

The steps to configure dial-up and cellular connections are very similar because, in both cases, the WAN connection device connects directly to the computer, and it provides a point-to-point connection, requiring a phone number or similar address to connect. First, you install the analog or cellular modem, which creates a connection object in the Windows Network Connections dialog box.

For a dial-up connection, you either manually enter the connection information using the appropriate Control Panel applet for your version of Windows, or you use a configuration utility received from the ISP. In either case, enter the phone number, logon name, and other configuration information. In Windows XP, open the Network and Internet Connections app in Control Panel, and then from the Pick A Task menu, select Set Up Or Change Your Internet Connection. This opens the Internet Properties dialog box to the Connections tab. Click the Setup button, and enter the information provided by your ISP. You can view the status of a modem (disabled, enabled, etc.) by double-clicking the connection object in the Network Connections window.

The server that accepts the incoming connections from dial-up clients is a server running some form of *remote access service (RAS)*. This server authenticates the users before allowing access to the private network.

A cellular modem will come directly from your cellular service provider, and you will install and configure it in one operation. When you run the installation disc to install the device driver and other software for the cellular connection, it will prompt you to enter the connection information you received for your connection from the ISP. When you wish to view the configuration of a cellular connection, you will use the cell provider's software, but you will also normally be able to view it through the connection's Properties dialog box from the Network Connections window. In fact, attempting to do this through the Network Connections window may result in an error message similar to this one that came up when we double-clicked the Verizon modem.

Clicking the Advanced button opens the Properties dialog, where we can view and change the settings.

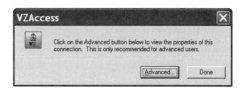

Configuring DSL, Cable, and Satellite Connections

The configuration of a client computer for DSL, cable, and satellite connections is very similar. Connect a cable between the client's Ethernet NIC and a switch that connects to the broadband router. In many cases, the broadband router will have an integrated switch. Then the broadband router will have a DHCP server enabled, and it will give the client computer an appropriate IP configuration. If DHCP is disabled on the router, then you will need to know the address of the LAN interface of the router versus the WAN interface. Once you know this, you can configure the client's NIC with an IP address with the same NetID, and provide it with the LAN address of the router as the client's default gateway. The final piece of IP configuration is the address of a DNS server. Your ISP will give you this.

Configuring a VPN Connection

Regardless of how you connect to the Internet, if you connect over the Internet to your work network, you are at risk because your messages are traveling over an unsecured network. Therefore, you and your employer will want to protect that connection with a virtual private network (VPN), which is defined in Chapter 14. A VPN creates a virtual tunnel that encapsulates your traffic using special protocols.

e x a m
w a t c h

Many protocols support VPNs, but there are three you should know for the A+ exams. The first is Point-to-Point Protocol (PPP), *which allows two devices to connect, authenticate, and negotiate what protocols they will use (almost always TCP/IP). The second is* Point-to-Point Tunneling Protocol (PPTP), *an enhanced version of PPP, which adds the ability to secure the point-to-point connection with encryption. The third is* IP Security (IPSec), *which is actually a point-to-point encryption method used for some VPNs and in Microsoft networks between client and server computers.*

FIGURE 15-19

The Windows XP
New Connection
Wizard

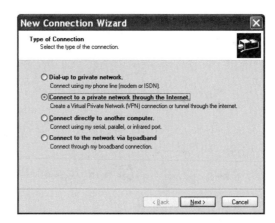

Before you can configure a VPN, you must have the specific configuration information, which you will obtain from whoever is providing the VPN connection. You will need the host name or IP address of the VPN. Then, to configure the VPN connection in Windows XP, open the Internet Options applet from Control Panel, and select the Connections page. Then click the Add button to open the New Connection Wizard (see Figure 15-19), in which you will select the radio button labeled Connect To A Private Network Through The Internet. Continue through the wizard, entering the required information.

In Windows Vista and Windows 7, you can access the Create A VPN Connection Wizard through the Connection page in Internet Options, or open it more quickly from Start Search by entering **VPN** and selecting the option Set Up A Virtual Private Network (VPN) Connection. In the Create A VPN Connection Wizard, shown in Figure 15-20, follow the instructions and continue through the wizard using the information you have for the VPN connection.

Configuring Bluetooth

If your computer does not have Bluetooth, you can purchase and install a Bluetooth transceiver, exactly as you would install any device in your PC, depending on the PC's interface. The one corollary to this is that the Bluetooth driver packaged with the device may be better than the one installed with Windows, especially with Windows XP, in which case, you may be wise to install the driver before installing the Bluetooth transceiver into the computer. Look for the Bluetooth Devices applet in Control Panel, as seen here.

FIGURE 15-20

The Windows
Vista and
Windows 7 VPN
Connection
Wizards are
identical.

When installing and configuring a Bluetooth device, you should not have version problems, even though there have been four major Bluetooth standards, 1.0, 2.0, 3.0 + HS, and 4.0, as well as 1.0B, 1.1, 1.2, and 2.1. Each new version has improved discovery and connection, as well as speed, with the latest versions increasing the speed and/or reducing the power consumption of the devices. New devices should be at version 3.0, and each version beginning with 1.2 is backward compatible. The Bluetooth 4.0 standard was adopted and is awaiting products; at this writing it is on the edge of mass adoption, with some smartphones already including it. If you are connecting two devices that comply with different versions of the standard, the connection will only support the speed and features of the older version.

The most common Bluetooth device you may need to connect to a PC is a cell phone or smartphone; in which case, you will need to first access the phone's Bluetooth configuration menu and make sure it has a name and is discoverable. If your computer has Bluetooth installed, and it is enabled, then simply turn on the Bluetooth device within range of the PC's Bluetooth transceiver, and then open the Bluetooth Devices applet and click Add (Windows XP) or Add Wireless Device (Windows Vista and Windows 7). Then follow the steps in the wizard, including entering a password and enabling encryption. Bluetooth security is not very strong; therefore, if you keep sensitive information on your phone, never use Bluetooth communications if it is possible for someone who might be able to crack the passkey and encryption to pick up your signals. The very short range of Bluetooth devices is probably the best security they offer.

Installing Basic VoIP

Once a rogue technology used by people trying to avoid telephone company long-distance call charges, Voice over IP (VoIP) has now been embraced by those same telephone companies. If you live in an area where one of these companies offers the service, you can purchase it from them. Look for it under the title of "broadband phone service." Qwest, for instance, offers it in some areas where they can provide connections of at least 1.5 Mbps. We recommend a higher speed.

If you have connected your computer to a broadband router, or connected a modem to a phone line, you have the skills necessary for installing VoIP in your home or small office. If you sign up for this service, the company provides a broadband modem and a broadband phone adapter. You must have the company's broadband Internet service to subscribe to its broadband phone service. The modem, a conventional DSL modem, connects to the wall jack with phone wire and an RJ-11 connector, and you connect the broadband phone adapter via Ethernet cable to an Ethernet port on the broadband modem. You then connect an analog phone to the RJ-11 connector on the broadband phone adapter, which acts as an *Integrated Access Device (IAD)*, a device that converts digital signals from the broadband connection to voice for the analog phone, and the analog voice signals to digital signals for the digital network. A computer is not necessary for this service. The basic broadband phone service costs about $20 a month in some cities.

Similarly, cable providers offer this service in some areas, and it is as easy to install it as it is to install a cable Internet connection because, of course, that is required for the service. On a cable network, the generic name for the device used at the customer site for the analog/digital conversion is *Multimedia Terminal Adapter (MTA)*, and it sits between an analog phone and the cable modem. An MTA is unnecessary if you connect a digital IP telephone set directly to the cable modem. Cisco, among others, manufacturers these phones.

There are many VoIP services, including the very popular Skype, which offers free service between Skype users, but charges for calling outside their network. You will need speakers and a microphone (headset preferred) and a broadband connection. A Webcam is optional. Simply point your browser to www.skype.com and download the program. The installation takes several minutes, and after the setup screen closes, the Skype Create Account window opens. Here, you must provide your name, a Skype name, and a password. Once you complete this information, you log on and the Welcome screen displays over the Skype console window. From the Welcome screen, you can browse the services offered by Skype; check your microphone, headset, and Webcam; find friends; and import contacts. If all checks out, then close this window and make your first call from the Skype window. The Echo/Sound Test Service is automatically included in your contacts list, so this is a good first call. You hear a recorded voice and then you respond. Skype records your voice and then plays it back to you. You are now ready to use Skype.

These VoIP services are the most basic and generally for only one or two phones. If you need to provide this service for many phones at a single site, you may need to purchase a piece of equipment called a, SMB IP PBX, designed for small to medium businesses. A *Private Branch Exchange (PBX)* is a device with functions that provide services similar to the equipment in the phone company's central office. An *SMB IP PBX* connects to either one or more standard phone lines, or to a T-1 line or better. Then, you connect an Ethernet cable to this device and to your LAN switch. Finally, you connect special IP phones with Ethernet connections to the network. Further configuration is required for this type of setup—some of it by the phone company and some of it by you following the company's instructions for configuring the PBX. After you have configured VoIP, the only charges are for the connections.

Configuring Remote Desktop

Since Windows XP, Microsoft has included *Remote Desktop* as a feature that depends on the *Remote Desktop Protocol (RDP)*. Remote Desktop allows you to connect remotely to a computer running Windows XP or higher and log on to the desktop, just as if you were physically sitting at that computer. It does not require an "invitation," but it does require that you configure the computer to which you will connect with Remote Desktop beforehand. While connected, the local computer screen is logged out; only the Remote Desktop user sees the Windows desktop. Not every edition of Windows supports connection via Remote Desktop—Windows 7 Home Premium edition does not, whereas Windows 7 Professional does. To be clear, Windows 7 Home Premium can connect to other Remote Desktop hosts, but you cannot use Remote Desktop to connect to it.

Remote Desktop is disabled by default in Windows Vista, Windows 7, and Windows 8. Figure 15-21 shows the Remote tab of the System Properties dialog box in Windows 7 (it is nearly identical to dialog box in Windows XP and Windows

Vista), where you can configure Remote Desktop settings. The setting Allow Connections from Computers Running Any Version Of Remote Desktop (Less Secure) means computers running older versions of the Remote Desktop client software (for example, from a Linux computer) will still be able to connect.

In Windows 8, the Remote tab of the System dialog box is modified so that the second radio button reads simply Allow Remote Connections To This Computer, with the more secure former third radio button demoted to a check box under this setting.

Members of the local Administrators group can always connect via Remote Desktop, but you can click the Select Users button to add any user account. Enabling Remote Desktop will allow inbound port 3389 traffic in the Windows Firewall on that computer, and if the incoming Remote Desktop connection is coming from within your LAN, you will not need to do anything else. If it is coming over the Internet, or any other location on the other side of a router, you will need to configure the router, as described back in Exercise 15-2.

Figure 15-22 shows the Remote Desktop client connection software. You can connect to either the friendly host name (Toronto_Server1) or the IP address.

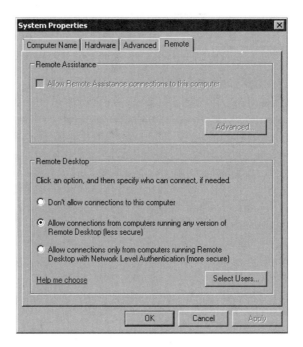

FIGURE 15-21

Enabling Remote Desktop in Windows 7

FIGURE 15-22

The Remote
Desktop
connection client

Configuring Remote Assistance

Remote Assistance is another service that is available for connecting to computers
running Windows XP or later. Like Remote Desktop, it relies on the RDP protocol,
and the major difference between Remote Assistance and Remote Desktop is that
Remote Assistance requires that the user needing assistance send an invitation.
A remote assistant cannot connect without this invitation.

There are three requirements for using Remote Assistance:

- Both computers must be running Windows XP or a newer version of Windows.
- Both computers must be connected via a network.
- Windows Messenger must be running for Remote Assistance in Windows XP
  (but not for later versions).

Preparing for Remote Assistance

The computer seeking assistance must have Remote Assistance turned on. Do
this on the requesting computer by opening the System applet in Control Panel,
selecting the Remote tab, and placing a check in the box labeled Allow Remote

Assistance Invitations To Be Sent From This Computer (Windows XP) or Allow Remote Assistance Connections To This Computer (Windows Vista, Windows 7, and Windows 8). Click OK to close the dialog box.

Before requesting remote assistance, check your firewall settings—both your computer's software firewall and any firewall between the two computers, such as a wireless broadband router—and configure it to allow this traffic through as an exception.

Requesting Remote Assistance

You request remote assistance by sending an invitation. In Windows XP, you do this by first opening Windows Help And Support, available from the Start menu. Under Ask For Assistance, click Invite A Friend To Connect To Your Computer With Remote Assistance; on the next page, select Invite Someone To Help You. This will open the Remote Assistance page with three choices for contacting your assistant: Windows Messenger, email, or a file. Select one of the first two, and the wizard will guide you through the process of creating and sending the invitation. If you must send an invitation through Web mail, choose to create a file. The wizard will create the file, and then you must attach it to an email message and send it.

To make a request for assistance, you need to open the Windows Remote Assistance Wizard. To do this in Windows Vista or Windows 7, simply enter **remote assistance** in the Start Search box. In Windows 8, open the Control Panel and enter **remote** in the Search box, and then from the results select Invite Someone To Connect To Your PC And Help You, Or Offer To Help Someone Else. One big change from Windows XP to all the newer versions is that, in addition to requesting assistance, you can offer remote assistance help to someone from this wizard. To request assistance, click the option labeled Invite Someone You Trust To Help You (in all versions). Then continue through the wizard, choosing to send an email invitation or to create a file that you will manually send to the assistant.

CERTIFICATION OBJECTIVES

- **801: 2.4** *Explain common TCP and UDP ports, protocols, and their purpose*

- **802: 1.5** *Given a scenario, use Control Panel Utilities*

- **802: 1.6** *Setup and configure Windows networking on a client/desktop*

While Chapter 14 included an explanation of Transmission Control Protocol (TCP) and User Datagram Protocol (UDP) ports and protocols, as required in CompTIA Exam 801 Objective 2.4, this section adds more to that explanation. This section also returns to Objective 802: 1.5 in its explanation of the use of Internet Options to configure many settings that affect Web browsers. The discussion on proxy servers satisfies one topic within Objective 802: 1.6 by defining the function of a proxy server and describing how to configure one.

Internet Concepts

We have established that the vast majority of computers connect to some type of network. We can go a step further and say that most computers connect to the Internet, and most of us spend a good part of our lives on the Internet with our computers or other devices. Therefore, it is important to understand Internet concepts and technologies. Some of these have been mentioned earlier but not explained, and others not included here, such as the TCP/IP protocol stack, have been fully covered in previous chapters. In this section, we will explore some of the services and protocols that run on the Internet and any TCP/IP network.

Internet Service Providers

An *Internet service provider (ISP)* is a company in the business of providing Internet access to users. When you connect to the Internet from your home or office, you connect through your ISP. While you are on the Internet, your ISP relays all data transfers to and from locations on the Internet. Traditionally, ISPs were phone companies, but now ISPs include cable companies and organizations that lease phone or cable network usage.

The ISP you select will depend on the type of connection available to you. For instance, a cellular provider will be your ISP if you chose to connect to the Internet via the cellular network, and a cable company will be your ISP if you connect over the cable network. As for DSL, at first local phone companies mainly offered this service, but many other companies now offer DSL using the telephone network, and some telephone companies are now offering Internet access via their fiber-optic networks. Meanwhile, some ISPs specialize in satellite Internet access.

There are also levels of ISPs, with the highest-level ISPs only serving very large corporations and providing Internet access to the ISPs at the next lower level. The ISP you use from home or a small business may be at the bottom of several layers of ISPs.

In addition to Internet connection services, ISPs now provide a huge number of other services. Some of these services, such as email, are free, and they base the cost of others, such as hosting Web servers, on the complexity of the Web services provided. For example, an e-commerce site in which you sell products and maintain customer lists is a service that would come at additional cost. You also are not limited to purchasing Internet services from your ISP. You now have a huge variety of sources for all of these services.

Internet Services and Protocols

There are a large number of Internet services. You may use many every day if you frequent the Internet. In this section, we will describe a few of these services.

Simple Mail Transfer Protocol (SMTP)

Simple Mail Transfer Protocol (SMTP) transfers email messages between mail servers. Clients also use this protocol to send email to mail servers. When configuring a computer to access Internet email, you will need the address or name of an SMTP server to which your mail client software will send mail.

Post Office Protocol (POP)

Post Office Protocol (POP) is the protocol used to allow client computers to pick up (receive) email from mail servers. The current version is POP3.

Internet Message Access Protocol (IMAP)

Internet Message Access Protocol (IMAP) is a protocol used by email clients for communicating with email servers. IMAP allows users to connect to email servers and not only retrieve email, which removes the messages from the server as they do with the POP protocol, but also manage their stored messages without removing them from the server. The current version is *IMAP4*.

Hypertext Markup Language (HTML)

Hypertext Markup Language (HTML) is the language of Web pages. Web designers use the HTML language to create Web page code, which your Web browser converts into the pages you view on your screen.

Hypertext Transfer Protocol (HTTP)

The *World Wide Web (WWW)* is the graphical Internet consisting of a vast array of documents located on millions of specialized servers worldwide. The *Hypertext Transfer Protocol (HTTP)* is the information transfer protocol of the Web. Included in HTTP are the commands Web browsers use to request Web pages from Web servers and then display them on the screen of the local computer.

Secure Sockets Layer (SSL)

The *Secure Sockets Layer (SSL)* is a protocol for securing data for transmission by encrypting it. Encryption is the transformation of data into a code that no one can read unless they have a software key or password to convert it back to its usable form (decrypt it). When you buy merchandise online, you go to a special page where you enter your personal and credit card information. These Web merchants almost universally use some form of SSL encryption to protect the sensitive data you enter on this page. When you send your personal information over the Internet, it is encrypted and only the merchant site has the key to decrypt it. As with most computing technologies, there are improvements to SSL, and a newer encryption technology, *Transport Layer Security (TLS)*, for secure transmission over the Internet.

Hypertext Transfer Protocol Secure (HTTPS)

Hypertext Transfer Protocol over Secure Sockets Layer (HTTPS) is a protocol that encrypts and decrypts each user page request, as well as the pages downloaded to the user's computer. The next time you are shopping on a Website, notice the address box in your browser. You will see the Uniform Resource Locator (URL) preceded by "HTTP" until you go to pay for your purchases. Then the prefix changes to "HTTPS," because the HTTPS protocol is in use on the page where you will enter your personal information and credit card number.

Telnet

At one time, all access to mainframes or minicomputers was through specialized network equipment called *terminals*. At first, a terminal was not much more than a display, a keyboard, and the minimal circuitry for connecting to the mainframe. People called it a "dumb terminal." With the growing popularity of PCs in the 1980s, it wasn't unusual to see both a terminal and a PC on a user's desktop, taking up a great deal of space. Eventually, by adding both software and hardware to a PC, the PC could emulate a terminal and the user would switch it between terminal mode and PC mode.

The *Telnet* utility provides remote terminal emulation for connecting to computers and network devices running responsive server software, and it works without concern for the actual operating system running on either system. The original Telnet client was character based, and it was a popular tool for network administrators who needed to access and manage certain network equipment, such as the routers used to connect networks.

Secure Shell (SSH)

Although Telnet supports the use of credentials for a terminal emulation session, it sends those credentials in clear text that many methods can pick up, such as a device that connects to the network and collects the traffic. To overcome that limit, the *Secure Shell (SSH)* service has replaced Telnet because it secures all traffic using a tunneling technique similar to a VPN (described earlier). It is used to connect to terminal servers that require sophisticated security protocols.

File Transfer Protocol (FTP)

File Transfer Protocol (FTP) is a protocol for computer-to-computer (called host-to-host) file transfer over a TCP/IP network. The two computers do not need to run the same operating system; they only need to run the FTP service on the server computer and the FTP client utility on the client computer. FTP supports the use of user names and passwords for access by the FTP client to the server. FTP is widely used on the Internet for making files available for download to clients.

Secure Copy and SFTP

Another file transfer method is *secure copy (SCP)*, which uses Secure Shell (SSH) for encrypting data. SCP lacks the file management capabilities of other methods, such as SFTP. Therefore, SFTP, which also uses SSH, is often preferred.

exam
ᴡatch

The Acronym list for the for the CompTIA 801 and 802 Exams, lists "secure copy protection (SCP)", but this acronym is more commonly known as "secure copy (SCP)," as described in this section.

Proxy Servers

In many instances, an Internet connection includes a *proxy server*, a network service that handles the requests for Internet services, such as Web pages, files on an FTP server, or mail for a proxy client, without exposing that client's IP address to the Internet. There is specific proxy server and client software for each type of service. Most proxy servers combine these services and accept requests for HTTP, FTP, POP3, SMTP, and other types of services. The proxy server will often cache a copy of the requested resource in memory, making it available for subsequent requests from clients without having to go back to the Internet.

If your network has a proxy server, you can configure your browser to send requests to the proxy server, which will forward and handle all requests. You can do this within Chrome or Firefox, or let Windows manage your proxy settings, which is a good idea if you have multiple browsers. To configure Windows to use a proxy server, open Control Panel's Internet Options applet and click the Connections tab. This tab has two places for configuring a proxy server, depending on how you connect to the Internet.

If you have a configured dial-up connection, click the Settings button under Dial-Up, and then select Virtual Private Network Settings. Follow the instructions for configuring the proxy server, which will include entering the server's IP address.

If your computer connects to the Internet through a LAN, go to the bottom of the Connection page, and click the LAN Settings button to open the Local Area Network (LAN) Settings dialog. Under Proxy Server, click to place a check in the box labeled Use A Proxy Server For Your LAN. (These settings will not apply to dial-up or VPN connections.) Then enter the IP address in the Address box and the port number (obtained from your network administrator or from the documentation for the proxy server) in the Port box. Click Advanced if you need to add more addresses and ports for other services. Figure 15-23 shows this dialog box in Windows 7, which is similar to that in Windows XP and Windows 8.

However, Windows only provides options for four types of proxy servers: HTTP, Secure (HTTPS), FTP, and Socks. You should be familiar with all but the last of these terms. Socks is a proxy server protocol. If you have a proxy server for other services not supported by Windows, you will need to install a proxy client provided by the vendor of the server software.

Internet Relay Chat

The *Internet Relay Chat (IRC)* protocol supports text messaging over a TCP/IP internetwork in real time, something commonly called *chat*. The latest version is

FIGURE 15-23

Proxy settings for
Windows

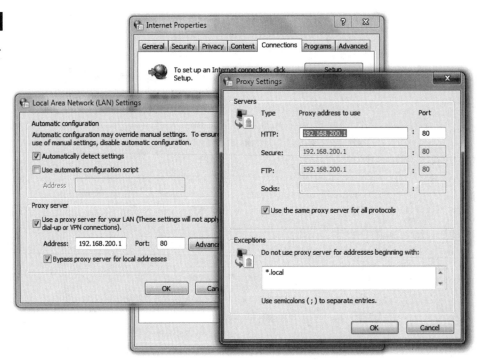

Internet Relay Chat web extension (IRCwx), but it is still widely referred to as IRC. Groups of people can chat simultaneously using IRC, or it can be used between just two people.

News Service

The *Network News Transfer Protocol (NNTP)* is used by *news servers* that support newsgroups, to which users can subscribe. Using *news reader* software, the client to the news server, a subscriber connects and selects articles to read.

Keeping Time

Windows computers (and many others worldwide) keep their date and time settings up-to-date thanks to a time service. *Network Time Protocol (NTP)* is an Internet protocol that has been improved upon over its thirty-year life span as a service that synchronizes a computer's real-time clock (described in Chapter 3) with a network time server. Windows is configured to synchronize with an Internet-based time server.

To view the time server settings on your computer, open the Control Panel Data and Time applet and click the Internet Time tab. The time server for the Windows computers in our office is time-a.nist.gov. You can select another time server by clicking the Change Settings button on the Internet Time tab.

CAPTCHA

Often, when you create a new account of almost any type on the Internet, after you have created your user name (often an email address) and password, you encounter a *Completely Automated Public Turing test to tell Computers and Humans Apart (CAPTCHA)*, a test that only a human can pass. A CAPTCHA usually consists of an image of one or two hard-to-read words, or at least a string of characters. To pass the test and proceed with creating your new account, you must enter the characters you see into a box. This ensures that a computer program is not attempting to automatically create accounts for nefarious reasons, such as for creating an account for sending SPAM. To learn more about CAPTCHA, point your browser to www.captcha.net.

Web Servers

While the World Wide Web (the Web) is just one on the many services that exist on the Internet, it alone is responsible for most of the huge growth in Internet use that began after the Web's introduction in the 1990s. Web technologies changed the look of Internet content from all text to rich and colorful graphics. A *Web server* provides the graphical content we call Web pages, that is accessed by client software, called a *Web browser*. There are many choices of Web server software, but the most popular may be *Apache HTTP Server*, open source software that runs on a wide range of operating systems including Windows and several versions each of Linux and UNIX.

Microsoft's Web server software, *Internet Information Services (IIS)*, only runs on Windows and supports the traditional HTML content as well as the transfer services Hypertext Transfer Protocol (HTTP) and Hypertext Transfer Protocol over Secure Sockets Layer Web services. It also supports other services, such as File Transfer Protocol (FTP), Simple Mail Transfer Protocol (SMTP), and Network News Transfer Protocol (NNTP).

Web Browsers

The two top Web browsers as of June 2012 are Google Chrome at 27.06 percent market share and Microsoft Internet Explorer (IE) at 24.42 percent. Mozilla's Firefox is not far behind at 19.69 percent. Other browsers, such as Apple Safari, Opera, and others, have smaller market shares. In this section, learn how to configure and install Internet Explorer, Chrome, and Firefox; how to install and manage browser add-ons; and how to configure proxy settings. All three top browsers have security features built in, are very configurable, and the three publishers work to add new attractive features in each edition of their products.

The Web browser's ease of use hides the Internet's complexity because it uses protocols to transfer the contents from a Web page to the user's computer, where the Web browser translates the plaintext language into a rich, colorful document that may contain links to other pages—often at disparate locations on the Internet. We'll describe Internet Explorer and Mozilla Firefox in the next sections, and we will describe security settings for these two Web browsers in Chapter 18.

Internet Explorer

In August 1995, Microsoft introduced the *Internet Explorer (IE)* Web browser when they launched the Windows 95 operating system. IE was included (or bundled) free with the operating system, and it has been included in each subsequent Windows version. Free updates to newer versions of IE for Windows and Mac OSs are available at the Microsoft Website.

Upgrading Internet Explorer   IE comes installed into Windows, so you do not need to install it, but expect to upgrade IE as Microsoft releases a new version every few years. If you have Automatic Updates turned on, it will download and install security updates to IE automatically, but you will need to agree to upgrading to an entirely new version. You can also use Windows Update from the Start menu (or the Search charm in Windows 8), or go directly to the Microsoft download site at www.microsoft.com/downloads.

The latest version of Microsoft's browser is *Internet Explorer 10 (IE 10)*, which comes with Windows 8 in two graphical user interfaces (GUIs): a full-screen Windows 8 version and a windowed desktop version. We (the authors) distinguish between these two Windows 8 GUI versions as Windows 8 IE 10 and Desktop IE 10, due to a lack of official names for them currently.

In spite of the release of this new version, expect to see the three previous versions, *Internet Explorer 7 (IE 7)*, *Internet Explorer 8 (IE 8)*, and *Internet Explorer 9 (IE 9)*, on Windows desktops that have not upgraded to a newer browser.

If you install a third-party Web browser into Windows, we recommend that you not uninstall IE because it is so integrated into Windows. Not only is it not advisable to uninstall IE, but some Web pages do not display correctly in other browsers and only look fine in IE. This functionality has to do with Web page content that is running small programs in ActiveX, which run best in IE. ActiveX is a technology developed by Microsoft for making Web pages more interactive by downloading small programs from Websites and running them in an ActiveX-enabled browser—mainly Internet Explorer. These programs include sound files, Java applets, and animation.

Conversely, some Web pages may not display properly in IE but will work fine in other Web browsers. In this scenario, the problem may be one or more Java scripts that are not compatible with IE.

Configuring Internet Explorer   There are two places to configure Internet Explorer: through the Tools menu in all desktop versions, shown in Figure 15-24 (press ALT-X or click the gear icon on the top right), and in the Internet Options Control Panel applet. In the Windows 8 version of IE 10, you access all IE configuration options through the Settings charm. Figure 15-24 shows the IE 9 Tools menu. In the Tools menu in IE 8 or 9, you can turn on and configure the Pop-up Blocker, turn on and configure the SmartScreen Filter antiphishing tool (called Phishing Filter in IE 7),

FIGURE 15-24

The Internet
Explorer 9
Tools menu

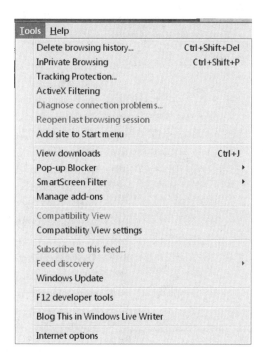

run Windows Update, diagnose connection problems, and open the Internet Options dialog box, which has pages of settings to further control IE's behavior. You can also manage add-ons such as Adobe PDF Reader, Link Helper, Diagnose Connection Problems, Sun Java Console, and Windows Messenger. Learn about the security features in IE and other browsers, including phishing filters, pop-up blockers, deleting browsing history, InPrivate Browser, Tracking Protection, and more, in Chapter 18.

Chrome

Chrome, by Google, is now the number one Internet browser. It is considered a safer Web browser than Internet Explorer because malicious attacks do not target it as much as they do the Microsoft browser.

Installing and Upgrading Chrome   To download and install Chrome, point your browser to www.google.com and look for the Install Google Chrome button. Click this and then click the Download Chrome button. On the next page read

the terms of service and decide if you want Chrome as your default browser. This means that when you click a link in a document or email message it will open in Chrome. If this is okay, keep the check in that box. If not, click to remove that check. When ready, accept the terms of service by clicking the Accept And Install button. A Security Warning box will display, and the installation will not continue until you click the Run button. Click it and then you will see the Welcome To Chrome page where you must either sign in with a Google Gmail account or create one and sign in. Once you do, Chrome will synchronize bookmarks, history, and other settings with the Chrome browser on any other computer you have logged onto with the same account.

Configuring Chrome   To configure Chrome, click the wrench button on the far-right side of the navigation bar (the bar that includes the address box), and the menu shown here will display. Click Settings (near the bottom of the menu), and a new browser tab will open with Chrome Settings, shown in Figure 15-25. This is a limited list. To see more settings, scroll to the bottom of the page and click Show Advanced Settings. This is where you will find most settings, including those for security and privacy.

Firefox

Firefox, by Mozilla, second in popularity only to Microsoft's IE until the rapid emergence of Google's Chrome, is still a popular free Web browser. Some consider it a safer Web browser than Internet Explorer because malicious attacks do not target

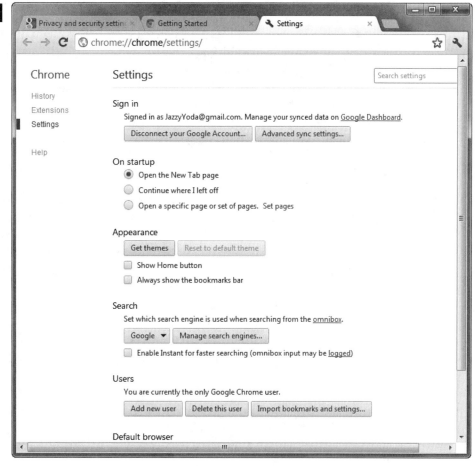

FIGURE 15-25

The Chrome browser Settings page

it as much as they do the Microsoft browser. You still need to have security in place when you use Firefox.

Installing and Upgrading Firefox   To download Firefox, point your browser to www.mozilla.com and follow the instructions for downloading and installing Firefox. The installation process will copy your Favorites from Internet Explorer. You will have an opportunity to select Firefox as your default browser during installation. The default browser is the browser Windows opens when the user clicks a URL.

Configuring Firefox   There are many options for configuring Firefox. You should do the first configuration task as soon as Firefox installs, and that is to open the Options dialog box from the Tools menu, select Advanced, and then select the Update tab. Make sure Firefox is set to check for Firefox updates automatically. Choose between having Firefox ask what you want to do when it discovers an update or having Firefox automatically download and install the update.

The General tab includes settings for accessibility, browsing, and system defaults. The Startup settings allow you to configure the home page—the page that appears when you first open the browser. The Downloads settings let you choose what happens when you are downloading files, including the display of the Downloads window and where to save the files.

Browser Add-ons

You can add functionality to a browser by installing an *add-on*, a small program inserted into an app (such as a browser), but not fully controlled by the app. Also called a plug-in or *browser helper object (BHO)*, an add-on is usually free and available as a download. For instance, most of us depend on being able to open Adobe PDF files within our browsers. Doing this is possible only if you have installed the Adobe Acrobat add-on. Videos and animation on a Website may require Adobe Flash Player or JavaScript. Some add-ons change the browser interface by adding toolbars, such as those from Yahoo! and Google. There are add-ons for quickly accessing one or more social networking sites, helping you track the bidding on eBay, keeping up to date on the latest news, and much more. Some programs that you install for other purposes, such as security suites, also include browser add-ons. Therefore, when you install programs, watch for options to install a browser toolbar and decide if you really need another add-on to your browser.

Because the "host" program—usually a browser—does not fully control an add-on, they are malware targets. As a result, the trend is moving away from using add-ons and using HTML5 instead to create rich, interactive Web page content that does not require an add-on. Internet Explorer 10 (IE 10) does not allow add-ons, but because many Websites depend on Adobe Flash for their content, Adobe and Microsoft worked together to integrate Adobe Flash Player into IE 10—not as an add-on. Similarly, Adobe and Google programmers collaborated to incorporate Adobe Flash Player into the Google Chrome browser. In each case, the integrated Adobe Flash Player also automatically receives security fixes and patches.

While IE 10 does not allow add-ons, other browsers do. View and manage the installed add-ons in Internet Explorer 8 or 9 by opening the Tools menu and selecting Manage Add-ons; in Firefox, open the Tools menu and select Add-ons. You can disable or enable add-ons in this dialog. Our favorite add-on is the FireFTP add-on to Firefox, which we use for FTP file transfers with various FTP servers.

SCENARIO & SOLUTION

I plan to use Google Chrome as my Web browser. Should I uninstall Internet Explorer?	No. Do not uninstall Internet Explorer. You can still make Chrome your default browser.
I connect to the Internet via the company LAN, and my LAN administrator has emailed me proxy server addresses. Where do I enter these in Windows?	Open Control Panel | Internet Options. On the Connections page, click the LAN Settings button at the bottom. In the Local Area Network Settings dialog, place a check in the box under Proxy Server and enter the settings provided by your administrator.
At home, we have two computers and a broadband Internet connection. We have decided that we want our two computers to connect to the WAN connection via WLAN. Can we use ad hoc mode and save the cost of a wireless router?	No, an ad hoc WLAN cannot connect to another network. Use a wireless router and infrastructure mode to connect these computers to the Internet.

CERTIFICATION SUMMARY

An A+ certification candidate must be able to identify and describe basic Internet concepts, including the role of ISPs and the basic functions of Internet services and protocols, such as SMTP, POP3, IMAP, HTML, HTTP, HTTPS, SSL, FTP, and VoIP.

Understand the tasks required to install, configure, and upgrade networks for client computers on a small office/home office network. Installation and upgrade tasks include physically installing all types of NICs, setting up a wired or wireless LAN, configuring IP settings, and configuring both dial-up and broadband WAN connections.

The three most popular Web browsers are Chrome, Microsoft Internet Explorer, and Mozilla Firefox. A PC technician should be familiar with each and know how to install, configure, and update them. Finally, a technician must know how to configure settings for a proxy server for HTTP, FTP, POP3, SMTP, and other types of services using the Connection tab of the Internet Options applet.

TWO-MINUTE DRILL

Here are some of the key points covered in Chapter 15.

Installing and Configuring Networks

❑ Crimpers are used to create network cables. Use a punchdown tool to connect network cabling to the inside of an RJ-45 wall jack and to a punchdown block.

❑ A multimeter tests the electrical properties of a cable or circuit. Cable testers test for broken wires inside network cables. Toner probe sets identify cable ends by sending a signal through the cable that the toner probe receiver can pick up.

❑ A loopback plug reverses the receive and transmit wires on a port so you can test if the port is functional.

❑ Each computer on a network requires a NIC (wired or wireless) in order to connect. NICs may be Ethernet NICs, Wi-Fi NICs, or the NIC is an analog modem when using a dial-up connection.

❑ Decide how a NIC should interface with your computer (bus, USB, or other interface), and select a NIC for the type of network you require—LAN or WLAN.

❑ For a bus NIC installation, first install the NIC; then, if it is an Ethernet NIC, connect the cable, and finally, start the computer and install the drivers.

❑ When installing a NIC, you will connect the NIC to the port or slot, connect the NIC to the network, and then start the computer and let Windows recognize the NIC. When prompted, provide a disc or the location of driver files.

❑ Some NICs support PoE for some special equipment, such as surveillance cameras, that are located far from power outlets but in reach of Ethernet cabling.

❑ If required, enable a NIC's Wake on LAN feature.

❑ QoS is a feature that supports stable and reliable transmission of time-sensitive content, such as streaming music or video.

❑ When connecting to a wired Ethernet network, use CAT5/5e/6 UTP cabling with an RJ-45 connector. Connect one end to the NIC and the other to the wall jack, or directly to a hub or switch.

❏ When creating a Wi-Fi network, check for possible obstacles and interference sources that can block the signal. Signals degrade over distance, causing slower data speeds, so verify that the distances between the wireless devices are well within the published signal range for the devices.

❏ A Service Set ID (SSID) is a network name used to identify a wireless network. All of the wireless devices on a WLAN must use the same one.

❏ Ad hoc wireless mode is useful for only a very few computers and cannot connect directly to another network.

❏ To connect a wireless network directly to another network, you need to use a wireless access point (WAP) and infrastructure mode for all nodes on the network.

❏ You normally do the initial setup of a WAP with a directly wired Ethernet connection between a PC and the WAP. You can make subsequent changes over the wireless network.

❏ With a single press of a button, Wi-Fi Protected Setup (WPS) automatically sets up a secure wireless network.

❏ Most WAPs run the DHCP service to give out IP addresses on the WLAN. Most can also do the same over their Ethernet port or ports.

❏ Change the default SSID of a WAP to a unique name, change the default user name and password to ones that will not be easily guessed, enable MAC address filtering and wireless encryption, and set other security options, as appropriate for your WLAN.

❏ Once a NIC connects to the network and the drivers are installed, configure the TCP/IP properties. If your network has a DHCP server, you can leave these settings at their default, and your computer will acquire an IP address automatically from the DHCP server.

❏ If you do not use a DHCP server and wish to communicate beyond a single network, you must configure IP settings manually (static IP), including IP address, subnet mask, default gateway, DNS server, and (rarely) WINS server.

❏ Although there are many types of WAN connections, some of them have common configuration steps. Configuring a dial-up connection is very similar to configuring a cellular WAN connection, whereas the steps for configuring several broadband services are almost identical. They include DSL, cable, and satellite.

❏ Configure a VPN for a secure connection over the Internet to a private network. It requires a VPN server on the private network, but Windows has a wizard that will walk you through the configuration for a VPN.

❏ Although many laptops have Bluetooth capabilities, desktop PCs usually do not. If you need to connect a PC to a Bluetooth device, such as a cell phone or smartphone, you may need to install a Bluetooth transceiver into the PC. Once a PC or laptop has Bluetooth turned on, use the Bluetooth Devices applet in Windows Control Panel to configure the connection.

❏ There are many VoIP service providers, including telephone companies, cable companies, and even Internet-based services, such as Skype. The configuration and costs will vary based on the type of service.

❏ Port forwarding allows external stations to connect through a wireless router to internal network services such as Remote Desktop.

❏ Port triggering dynamically opens inbound ports when certain outbound port traffic is detected.

❏ Remote Desktop is disabled by default in Windows Vista, Windows 7, and Windows 8. Members of the local Administrators group always have Remote Desktop access.

Internet Concepts

❏ An ISP is a company in the business of providing access to the Internet.

❏ There are a large number of Internet protocols and services.

❏ SMTP transfers email messages between mail servers. Clients also use this protocol to send their mail to mail servers.

❏ POP is the protocol used to allow client computers to pick up email from mail servers. The current version is POP3.

❏ IMAP is a protocol used by email clients for communicating with email servers. The current version is IMAP4.

❏ HTML is the language of Web pages that your browser converts into the pages you view on your screen.

❏ HTTP is the transfer protocol used to transmit browser-requested Web pages over the Internet to your computer.

❏ SSL is a protocol for securing data for transmission by encrypting it. When you pay for merchandise over the Internet, you connect to a page that uses SSL to encrypt your personal and financial data before sending it to the Website where it is decrypted.

❏ HTTPS is a protocol that uses SSL to encrypt data and then transports it to the Website for decryption.

❏ Telnet is a utility that provides remote terminal emulation for connecting to computers and network devices that are running the Telnet server software.

❏ FTP is a file transfer protocol for computer-to-computer transfer of files over a TCP/IP network.

❏ VoIP is a set of technologies that allows voice transmission over an IP network. You use it to place phone calls over the Internet rather than using the public-switched telephone network.

❏ A proxy server is a network service that handles the requests for Internet services, such as Web pages, for a proxy client without exposing the client's IP address to the Internet. You can configure a proxy server in the Windows Internet Options Control Panel applet.

❏ A Web browser is software that transfers the contents of a Web page to a computer and translates the plain-text language into a rich, colorful document. Google Chrome, Microsoft Internet Explorer (IE), and Mozilla Firefox are three common Web browsers for Windows.

❏ IE is installed in Windows by default, and, although you can and should upgrade it as updates and new versions are available, do not try to uninstall it from Windows—even if you install a second browser.

❏ Configure IE through its Tools menu where you can turn on and configure the Pop-up Blocker, turn on and configure a Phishing Filter or SmartScreen Filter, manage add-ons, run Windows Update, diagnose connection problems, and open the Internet Options dialog box, which has pages of additional settings.

❏ Download Chrome from www.google.com. Click the wrench button on the far side of the navigation bar to open a menu of Chrome's settings inside the browser window. Scroll to the bottom of the page and select Advanced Settings to see the complete list of settings.

❏ Download Firefox from www.mozilla.com. Configure Firefox from Tools | Options. Be sure to configure it to update automatically.

SELF TEST

The following questions will help you measure your understanding of the material presented in this chapter. Read all of the choices carefully because there might be more than one correct answer. Choose all correct answers for each question.

Installing and Configuring Networks

1. What is the first step in connecting a client computer to a LAN?
   A. Finding an ISP
   B. Installing a proxy server
   C. Configuring TCP/IP
   D. Installing a NIC

2. What are the two connections required for every PC NIC?
   A. Computer and network
   B. USB and FireWire
   C. Bus and PC Card
   D. Wi-Fi and Ethernet

3. What type of connector is used on both ends of the cable connecting an analog modem to the wall jack?
   A. RJ-45
   B. USB
   C. RJ-11
   D. FireWire

4. Which Wi-Fi radio band is most likely to experience interference from microwave ovens and cordless telephones?
   A. 5.0 GHz
   B. 5.4 GHz
   C. 2.4 GHz
   D. 2.0 GHz

5. What is the maximum UTP/STP cable distance between an Ethernet NIC and a switch?
   A. 300 meters
   B. 100 meters
   C. 300 feet
   D. 100 feet

6. What secures an RJ-45 connector to an outlet on a PC or switch?
   A. A torx screw
   B. A clip on the connector
   C. A latch on the outlet
   D. A slot cover

7. Which of the following is the acronym for the name that identifies a wireless network?
   A. BSS
   B. IBSS
   C. SSID
   D. WAP

8. What radio band do three Wi-Fi standards use?
   A. 2.4 GHz
   B. 4.2 GHz
   C. 5 GHz
   D. 7 GHz

9. What happens as you move a wireless NIC and host computer farther away from a WAP?
   A. Signal increases
   B. Connection speed increases
   C. No change
   D. Connection speed decreases

10. Use this wireless mode if you wish to connect a Wi-Fi network to a wired network.
    A. Infrastructure
    B. Ad hoc
    C. IBSS
    D. SSID

11. Even a new NIC or wireless access point may need this updated if the manufacturer makes certain changes after the device has been released for sale, and you can usually download it from the manufacturer's Website.
    A. Cabling
    B. Password
    C. Firmware
    D. Admin user name

12. Not a WAN connection in itself, you use this to make a connection over the Internet to a private network more secure, and it is part of the connection configuration for many users.
    A. Bluetooth
    B. DSL
    C. Cable
    D. VPN

13. If this one address is missing from your IP configuration, you will be able to communicate on your LAN but will not have access to the Internet.
    A. DHCP
    B. Default gateway
    C. WINS
    D. Subnet mask

14. Which of the following pairs of WAN connections are similar because the WAN connection device is installed in the computer, and it provides a point-to-point connection between the computer and the other end of the WAN connection?
    A. Cellular and cable
    B. Dial-up and DSL
    C. Dial-up and cellular
    D. Wi-Fi and satellite

15. If you subscribe to your phone company's VoIP service over DSL, what device is used to make the analog/digital signal conversion between your analog phone and the DSL network?
    A. Multimedia Terminal Adapter (MTA)
    B. Modem
    C. Smartphone
    D. Integrated Access Device (IAD)

16. Which wireless mode is appropriate for two computers that only need to communicate with each other peer-to-peer and do not need to connect to the Internet through a Wi-Fi connection?
    A. Ad hoc
    B. Infrastructure
    C. 802.11g
    D. 802.11n

17. Which of the following wireless standards operates at 2.4 GHz or 5 GHz and has a typical data rate of 200 Mbps?
    A. 802.11a
    B. 802.11b
    C. 802.11n
    D. 802.11g

Internet Concepts

18. What Internet service allows users to connect to a mail server and manage their messages, giving them the option to leave the messages they have read on the server?
    A. SMTP
    B. IRC
    C. FTP
    D. IMAP

19. Which of the following acronyms represents an alternative term to describe an add-on to an app, such as a Web browser?
    A. BHO
    B. ARP
    C. IMAP
    D. ISDN

20. Which of the following is an acronym for a protocol that supports text messaging over a TCP/IP internetwork in real time?
    A. SMTP
    B. IRC
    C. FTP
    D. IMAP

SELF TEST ANSWERS

Installing and Configuring Networks

1. ☑ **D.** Installing a NIC is the first step to connecting a client computer to a LAN.
   ☒ **A,** finding an ISP, is incorrect because it is not necessary to have an ISP in order to connect to a LAN. **B,** installing a proxy server, is incorrect because you would not normally install a proxy server on a client computer, and it is definitely not the first step in connecting a computer to a LAN. **C,** configuring TCP/IP, although an important step, is not the first step in connecting a computer to a LAN.

2. ☑ **A.** A computer connection and a network connection are the two required for every PC NIC.
   ☒ **B,** USB and FireWire, is incorrect because both of these are computer connections, and with each, a connection to a network (wired or wireless) is required. **C,** bus and PC Card, is incorrect because both of these are computer connections, and with each, a connection to a network (wired or wireless) is also required. **D,** Wi-Fi and Ethernet, is incorrect because both of these are network connections, and with each, a connection to a computer is also required.

3. ☑ **C.** RJ-11 is the type of connector used to connect an analog modem to a telephone wall jack.
   ☒ **A,** RJ-45, is incorrect because this connector is used on Ethernet cable. **B,** USB, and **D,** FireWire, are both incorrect because these are not used to connect an analog modem to a telephone wall jack.

4. ☑ **C.** The 2.4 GHz radio band is most likely to experience interference from microwave ovens and cordless telephones.
   ☒ **A,** 5.0 GHz, is incorrect, although it is a Wi-Fi radio band. **B,** 5.4 GHz, and **D,** 2.0 GHz, are both incorrect because neither of these are Wi-Fi radio bands.

5. ☑ **B.** 100 meters is the maximum distance for an Ethernet UTP/STP cable running between a NIC and switch.
   ☒ **A,** 300 meters, **C,** 300 feet, and **D,** 100 feet, are all incorrect distances.

6. ☑ **B.** A clip on the connector secures an RJ-45 connector to an outlet on a PC or switch.
   ☒ **A,** a torx screw, is incorrect because this is not used to secure an RJ-45 connector to an outlet on a PC or switch. **C,** a latch on the outlet, is incorrect because although the outlet has a notch into which the connector clip fits, this is not a latch. **D,** a slot cover, is incorrect because this covers an empty slot in the back of a PC and does not secure an RJ-45 connector to an outlet on a PC or switch.

7. ☑ **C.** SSID, or Service Set ID, is the term that describes a name that identifies a wireless network.
   ☒ **A,** BSS, or Basic Service Set, is incorrect because this term describes the wireless nodes (including the WAP) communicating together in infrastructure mode. **B,** IBSS, or Independent

Basic Service Set, is incorrect because this term describes the wireless nodes communicating together in ad hoc mode. **D,** WAP, or wireless access point, is incorrect because this is a hub for a wireless network.

8. ☑ **A.** 2.4 GHz is the band used by three Wi-Fi wireless standards: 802.11b, 802.11g, and 802.lln (just one of two bands used by this last standard).
    ☒ **B,** 4.2 GHz, and **D,** 7 GHz, are both incorrect because none of the Wi-Fi wireless standards use these radio bands. **C,** 5 GHz, is incorrect because only two of the Wi-Fi wireless standards use it: 802.11a and 802.11n (just one of two bands used by 802.11n).

9. ☑ **D.** Connection speed decreases as you move a wireless NIC and host computer farther away from a WAP.
    ☒ **A,** signal increases, is incorrect because the opposite happens as you move a wireless NIC and host computer farther away from a WAP. **B,** connection speed increases, is incorrect because the opposite happens as you move a wireless NIC and host computer farther away from a WAP. **C,** no change, is incorrect because connection speed definitely decreases because the signal degrades as distance increases.

10. ☑ **A.** Infrastructure mode is the wireless mode to use if you wish to connect a Wi-Fi network to a wired network.
    ☒ **B,** ad hoc mode, is incorrect because it will not allow you to connect a Wi-Fi network to a wired network. **C,** IBSS, and **D,** SSID, are both incorrect because neither of these are wireless modes.

11. ☑ **C.** Firmware may need to be updated on a NIC or wireless access point.
    ☒ **A,** cabling, **B,** password, and **D,** admin user name, are all incorrect because these are not things that the manufacturer would update.

12. ☑ **D.** VPN is correct.
    ☒ **A,** Bluetooth, is incorrect because this is a PAN network technology, not something used to make a connection over the Internet to a private network more secure. **B,** DSL, and **C,** cable, are both incorrect because these are WAN connection technologies, not something that would make a connection more secure.

13. ☑ **B.** Default gateway is the address used to send messages beyond your LAN.
    ☒ **A,** DHCP, is incorrect because it is not really a single address in the IP configuration. **C,** WINS, is incorrect because it is an address in the IP configuration, used by WINS clients for resolving NetBIOS names. **D,** subnet mask, is incorrect because this is actually part of the IP address, and if it is missing, you will not be able to communicate at all.

14. ☑ **C.** Dial-up and cellular WAN connections are similar configurations because in both cases, the WAN connection device is installed in the computer and it provides a point-to-point connection, requiring a phone number or similar address to connect.

☒ **A,** cellular and cable, and **B,** dial-up and DSL, are incorrect because only one of each of these pairs of WAN connections matches the description. **D,** Wi-Fi and satellite, is incorrect because Wi-Fi is not a WAN connection.

15. ☑ **D.** Integrated Access Device (IAD) is the device used to make the analog/digital signal conversions.

☒ **A,** Multimedia Terminal Adapter (MTA), is incorrect because this device performs the signal conversion between an analog phone and a cable VoIP service. **B,** modem, and **C,** smartphone, are both incorrect because these are not the correct devices.

16. ☑ **A.** Ad hoc is the wireless mode used for peer-to-peer wireless networking.

☒ **B,** infrastructure, is incorrect because this mode goes beyond peer-to-peer, allowing many computers to communicate and to also access a network through a connection to the wireless WAP. **C,** 802.11g, and **D,** 802.11n, are both incorrect because these are Wi-Fi standards, not modes, although the modes are part of the standards.

17. ☑ **C.** 802.11n is the wireless standard that operates at 2.4 GHz and 5 GHz and has a typical data rate of 200 Mbps.

☒ **A,** 802.11a, **B,** 802.11b, and **D,** 802.11g, are all incorrect because each of them only supports a single frequency and none of them comes close to the 200 Mbps typical data rate, even at their theoretical maximum.

Internet Concepts

18. ☑ **D.** IMAP is an Internet service that allows users to connect to a mail server and manage their messages, giving them the option to leave messages they have read on the server.

☒ **A,** SMTP, is incorrect because this is a service used to send email, not to pick it up or manage it. **B,** IRC, is incorrect because it is the Internet Relay Chat protocol. **C,** FTP, is incorrect because this service has nothing to do with email but is for transferring files over the Internet.

19. ☑ **A.** BHO, short for browser helper object, is an alternative term to describe an add-on to a Web browser.

☒ **B,** ARP, is incorrect because it is short for Address Resolution Protocol. **C,** IMAP, is short for Internet Message Access Protocol, used for email service. **D,** ISDN (Integrated Service Digital Network), is a type of broadband service.

20. ☑ **B.** IRC (Internet Relay Chat), is an acronym for a protocol that supports text messaging over a TCP/IP internetwork in real-time.

☒ **A,** SMTP, is a service for sending email, which is not done in real time. **C,** FTP, is a service for transferring files, which is not real-time messaging, and **D,** IMAP, is another type of email service, which is not real-time messaging.

16
Troubleshooting Networks

A lthough there are many network problems only a trained network specialist can resolve, there are also many common and simple network problems that you will be able to resolve without extensive training and experience. You can also run certain tests that will give you important information to pass on to more highly trained network specialists, such as those in a large corporation or at your local Internet service provider (ISP).

In this chapter, you will explore the tools and techniques for troubleshooting common network problems. You will also learn about preventive maintenance tasks for networks.

CERTIFICATION OBJECTIVES

- **802: 1.3** *Given a scenario, use appropriate command-line tools*

- **802: 4.5** *Given a scenario, troubleshoot wired and wireless networks with appropriate tools*

For CompTIA Exam Objectives 802: 1.3 and 802: 4.5, be prepared to identify hardware and software tools for basic network troubleshooting and demonstrate that you understand how they are used. You should practice and review troubleshooting techniques for networks.

Troubleshooting Common Network Problems

To troubleshoot networks, a PC professional must call on all the skills required for hardware and software support, applying a structured approach to determining the problem, applying solutions, and testing. However, keep in mind that if you make all the connections properly, and all the hardware is working properly, the most common problems will involve the TCP/IP configuration of network interface cards (NICs).

Tools for Network Troubleshooting

The tools you will use for network troubleshooting include hardware tools and software tools The hardware tools and some software tools were described in Chapter 15 as tools needed to create a network, but you also need them to troubleshoot network problems.

exam

Be sure you know how each of the following hardware tools is used for troubleshooting networks: cable tester, toner probe, loopback plug, punchdown tool, and crimper.

In this chapter, as we visit troubleshooting problems, we will describe which of those tools to use and how to use them. But first, we would like to briefly talk about a group of software tools—Windows command-line utilities—that play a big role in troubleshooting.

When the TCP/IP protocol suite installs into Windows, it also installs a variety of command-line tools, such as IPCONFIG, PING, TRACERT, NETSTAT, NBTSTAT, and NSLOOKUP. These are the handiest and least expensive tools you can use for network troubleshooting or a variety of problems—those both local to and far removed from the computer, such as Domain Name Service (DNS) and Dynamic Host Configuration Protocol (DHCP) problems.

Each utility provides different information and is most valuable when used appropriately. For instance, you should first view the IP configuration using the *IPCONFIG* utility and verify that the configuration is correct for the network to which you are connected. If you discover any obvious problems when you view the IP configuration, correct them before proceeding. Then, select the tool that will help you diagnose and—in some instances—resolve the problem.

Most of these utilities have many optional parameters you can enter at the command line to change the command's behavior. In this book, we provide the simplest and/or most often used syntax. If you would like to learn more about each command, in Windows, simply open a Command Prompt window and enter the command name followed by a space, a slash, and a question mark, and then press ENTER. For the IPCONFIG command, enter the following: **ipconfig /?**.

A *parameter* is a string of characters entered at the command line along with the command. Some parameters are data, such as the IP address you enter with the PING command, and other parameters are switches, which alter the behavior of the command, such as the "/?" switch that requests help information about a command. Most command-prompt commands will accept either a hyphen (–) or a slash (/) character as part of a switch. When entering commands at the command line, separate the command name, such as "ipconfig," from any parameters with a space. In the case of **ipconfig /?**, the slash and question mark together comprise a parameter and are separated from the command name with a space. Do not insert a space between the slash or hyphen and what follows, such as "?" or "all." If additional parameters must be used, separate each parameter with a space.

Now that you understand some of the basics of command-line tools, we will look at some common network problems. Some require hardware tools, but most require that you use command-line tools—both to test for a problem and to resolve a problem.

Connectivity Problems

Connectivity problems are more obvious because the user simply fails to connect to a computer and usually receives an error message. For the PC technician troubleshooting connectivity problems involving the Internet, there are literally worlds of possible locations for the problems. When you suspect that a computer does not have network connectivity, check the network hardware, and use a variety of utilities to determine the cause, as described in the following sections. Learn how to pinpoint the location of a connection problem, from the local computer to Internet routers.

Checking Network Hardware

When there is a connectivity problem, first check the hardware. Check the NIC, cables (for a wired network), hub, switch, wireless access point (WAP), and router. Check the NIC by examining the status indicator lights on it, if available. On a bus NIC, the lights are on the card's bracket adjacent to the RJ-45 connector. Status indicator lights typically indicate link (a connection to a network), activity, and speed. Since most NICs (bus or USB) receive power from the PC, any light is a good indication that the NIC's connection to the PC is working (or at least the power lines are). Look closer to check the connection. The Link light (usually green), when steady, indicates the connection to the network is live, and it will usually blink when sending or receiving. Multispeed NICs may have a separate Link light for each speed the NIC supports, and the lights may be labeled 100M for 100 Mbps and 1000M for 1000 Mbps (1Gbps). If a Link light is off, there is either no power to the NIC or the connection is broken, which may be caused by a broken connector or cable.

Indicator Lights on NICs and Switches
Status indicators for network hardware include light-emitting diode (LED) lights on the physical device itself and/or software installed along with the device driver. With a quick glance at the lights on a device, or at the icons and messages on your computer screen, you will know that the device is powered up, that it is receiving and transmitting data, and (in the case of wireless devices) the strength of the signal. Many NICs have at least an *activity (ACT)* light that blinks to indicate network activity. These lights also indicate problems when they flash or change color. Read the device's documentation so you understand what these lights mean when troubleshooting.

Most NICs—both Ethernet and Wi-Fi—install with a configuration utility that can be opened from an icon in the taskbar's system tray. A balloon message may appear over the notification area when the status of one of these devices changes.

The icon may also change to indicate the device's current status, and you can pause your mouse over one of these icons to display the status of the devices. The status message shown here appeared when we passed a mouse over the status icon for the Local Area Connection. The icon for this connection also had a red "X" over it, so we knew there was a problem.

> Local Area Connection
> A network cable is unplugged.

If you see an amber light, especially on an older NIC, this may be a collision light, flashing as collisions are detected on the network. It will usually be on an older NIC because modern Ethernet switches make the need for this light obsolete, since a switch is designed to minimize collisions. If you do see a collision light on an old NIC on an old Ethernet network, then pay attention to it, because if it is blinking so excessively that it almost appears steady, this means there are excessive collisions on the network, and it could indicate that there is more traffic than the network can handle. The solution is to swap out the hub (which allows collisions) for a switch.

In addition, some wireless NICs have five LEDs that indicate signal strength, much like the bars on a cell phone. One lit light indicates a poor connection, and five lit lights indicate an excellent connection.

With many Ethernet and wireless NICs now built into computers, you often do not have physical status lights but must rely on status information provided in Windows. Check the notification area on the taskbar for an icon for the NIC.

If you have determined that a NIC has power, but there is no evidence of a connection (Link lights or status icon), take steps to correct this. In the case of a wired Ethernet NIC, check for a loose or damaged cable and examine the RJ-45 connectors for damage. Follow the cable to the hub or switch. We recommend the use of a cable tester since broken wires inside the cable are not revealed by visual inspection.

If the cable tests okay, check that the hub, switch, WAP, and router are functioning. Check for power to each device. These devices also have status lights similar to those of NICs. If all the lights are off, check the power supply. In the case of an Ethernet hub or switch, if it has power, look at the status light for each Ethernet connection on the device. If the light is out for the port to which the computer connects, swap the cable with a known good cable, and recheck the status. Also check the cable standard that is in use. You may still find very old CAT3 cabling in use on a Fast Ethernet network. Upgrade the cabling to, at minimum, CAT5e. Remember that network devices such as switches and WAPs are computers. So, for example, if all users connected to the same WAP have the same network problem, consider restarting the WAP.

Check for any source of electrical interference affecting the cabling. Unshielded twisted-pair (UTP) cabling does not have shielding from interference, relying instead on the twists in the cable pairs to resist electromagnetic interference (EMI). Many things can cause EMI. Heavy power cables running parallel to network cabling emit signals that can cause interference, especially if there are intermittent loads on the power cable, such as when a large electric motor starts and stops. *Radio frequency interference (RFI)* can also affect networks if a source of RFI, such as a poorly shielded electronic device, is located near network cabling. If you find such a situation, take steps to move the cabling or the source of the interference.

If you cannot find any physical problems with the NIC, cabling, hub, switch, or WAP, and cannot find a source of interference, check the status of the NIC in Network Connections.

Figure 16-1 shows the Status dialog from a Windows 7 computer with a connection problem (left) and a Windows Vista computer with no problem indicated. This does not necessarily mean there is absolutely no problem with the NIC on the Vista computer, but when you are first troubleshooting a network problem, accept this opinion at least temporarily, and perform other tests before doing anything drastic, like replacing

FIGURE 16-1   Check the status of the NIC.

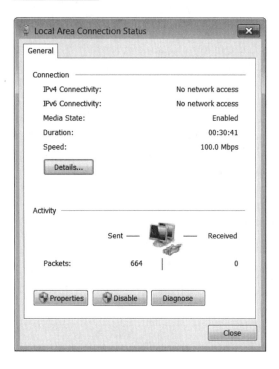

the NIC. In the case of the Windows 7 computer, we eventually found that we had a problem with the device driver. Installing the correct driver solved the problem.

Testing a Cable   To test for a broken cable, use a cable tester, such as the one shown in Figure 16-2. Notice that there are two separate components: a master unit and a smaller remote terminator. This makes it possible to connect to each end of a cable when those ends are in separate rooms or even on separate floors, in which case, you will need a troubleshooting partner on the other end. Of course, before you can test for a broken cable, you must locate both ends of the same cable. If the far end is connected to a punchdown block, you will need to connect a tester to the correct RJ-45 socket, which can be a challenge if the punchdown block in the wiring closet is not properly labeled. That is where a toner probe comes in handy. Chapter 15 described how to use a toner probe. Of course, this assumes you can access the cable bunch near the punchdown block.

Once you find both ends of a cable, plug one end into the master unit and the other end into the remote unit. Turn on the master unit and watch the lights on the remote unit (it helps to have a helper on one end). The LEDs on the remote terminator will light up in turn as the master unit sends signals down each pair of wires. If the cable wiring is intact, the LEDs corresponding to each pair will be

FIGURE 16-2

A cable-testing tool

green. If there is damage to the cable wiring, the LEDs will not light up at all, or may first be green and then turn red. This is true for each pair of wires tested.

Some cable testers will test more than one type of cabling, but in most LANs, being able to test Ethernet cable is very useful and may be all you need.

on the
Job

If you use your favorite search engine to query cable tester, *you will find a large selection of cable testers. You are sure to find one that fits your budget and needs. Some vendors, such as LANshack (www.lanshack.com), publish free tutorials on working with various types of cables.*

If you find problems with a cable, you may need to run a new cable, which also means getting out the punchdown tool for attaching cable to a punchdown block and digging into your supply of spare RJ-45 connectors and crimping new ones onto the ends of cables before connecting to the ends to the hubs/switches and NICs.

Testing Network Ports   Loopback plugs test whether or not a physical port, such as an RJ-45 port on a switch, or the RJ-45 port in a wall jack, are working. Some variations of this device are essentially a single plastic RJ-45 connector with two very short internal looped wires—one connecting pin one to pin three, and the second wire connecting pin two to pin six, all within the same RJ-45 connector. Indicator lights may be present to let you know if the connection is good or not.

Troubleshooting Wireless Connectivity

When you encounter connectivity problems on an existing wireless network that involve more than one computer, try the easier fix: restart the WAP/broadband router. In our home office, this is an almost guaranteed solution. If this is a new wireless network, wireless connectivity problems may be the result of too great a distance between the wireless NICs and a WAP or it could be interference problems. The farther a Wi-Fi NIC is from a WAP, the lower the radio frequency (RF) signals. This translates to slower network speeds. But what if you are within a reasonable distance that had a much better signal before? The three most likely suspects are changes to the environment, new signal-impeding obstructions, or interference. Snow storms in the winter and thick foliage in the summer can affect your signal. Higher-gain antennae on the WAP and the Wi-Fi clients (if feasible) can help.

Using an *RF spectrum analyzer,* a generally expensive hardware device, you can do an RF spectrum analysis to discover interference from other nearby devices using the same frequency range, be they wireless local area networks (WLANs), cordless phones, microwave ovens, and so on. Assuming you don't have the budget for an RF spectrum analyzer, there are many inexpensive or free wireless locators (defined in Chapter 15) that only detect Wi-Fi networks. Figure 16-3 shows the result of using a free software wireless locator called inSSIDer (http://www.metageek.net/products/inssider). It discovered six wireless networks and displays information it detected by analyzing the signals from each network. Because a software wireless locator like inSSIDer depends on your Wi-Fi adapter to detect signals, it will not detect the broad range an RF spectrum analyzer can, but it will detect nearby Wi-Fi networks.

Once you run one of these tools, the solution here is to configure the WAP to use a channel as far away from the interfering frequencies as possible. Each channel actually uses a different frequency, although adjacent channels—for example, channels 2 and 3—are so close together that changing from channel 2 to 3 will not make a difference.

Limited Connectivity

Limited connectivity should mean that you only have a local LAN or WLAN connection, but a router of some sort is present and you cannot communicate beyond the LAN. However, network connection status messages vary depending on the version of the installed operating system. For Windows Vista, limited "local

FIGURE 16-3

Scanning for wireless networks using inSSIDer

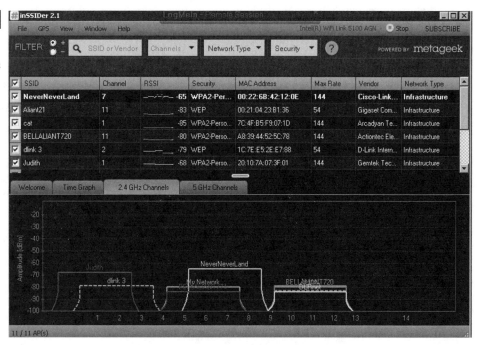

connectivity" sometimes means an IPv4 address could not be acquired via DHCP but there is a local IPv6 address (prefix of FE80). In this case, open the Properties dialog box for the NIC involved and deselect Internet Protocol Version 6 (TCP/IPv6). Click OK to accept that change and then open a Command Prompt window. Then, in the Command Prompt window, type **ipconfig /release** followed by **ipconfig /renew**. This command forces the DHCP client to release any IP address it may have and request a new IP address. It may take several seconds before you see a response, but it should receive a new address if it is able to reach the DHCP server. The output from the command will make it clear whether the computer receives an address. Remember this command because it is very useful, and we will recommend this command as a solution at least two more times in this chapter.

If your computer is a member of a HomeGroup, you will want to enable IPv6 after solving the limited connectivity problem because IPv6 is required for a HomeGroup. Learn more about HomeGroups in Chapter 19.

There are other possible causes for "limited or no connectivity" messages, and we will review some scenarios and possible solutions:

■ For encrypted wireless networks, ensure your wireless NIC supports the encryption method. For example, your card only supports Wired Equivalent Privacy (WEP) but the wireless network is using Wireless Protected Access (WPA). Check the configuration on both ends of the wireless connection. You may need to upgrade your NIC. If they both are using the same encryption method, ensure you have correctly entered the wireless encryption passphrase.

■ From the Command Prompt, type **ipconfig**. If the NIC's IP address begins with 169.254, this means it issued itself an Automatic Private Internet Protocol Addressing (APIPA) address because it did not reach a DHCP server to receive a valid IP configuration. If other stations are experiencing the same issue, consider restarting the DHCP server—bear in mind, however, the DHCP server might be your wireless router. If only this station is having problems, type **ipconfig /release** and then type **ipconfig /renew**.

■ Ensure you have the latest stable driver for your wireless NIC and that Device Manager is not reporting a problem. Consider uninstalling and reinstalling the driver.

■ Use **ipconfig /all** to ensure you have a valid default gateway and DNS server configured.

■ If your computer has more than one NIC (for example, a wired NIC and a wireless NIC), consider enabling one at a time and testing network connectivity individually.

- In Windows XP, navigate to the Windows Control Panel network adapters and right-click your NIC to disable it; then right-click it once again to enable it.

- In Windows Vista, Windows 7, and Windows 8, open Network Connections in Control Panel. Then to reset the NIC, right-click it, select Disable, and when that completes, right-click again and select Enable. Wait a few minutes before testing connectivity.

- If disabling and enabling the network adapter does not resolve the problem, then run diagnostics. In Windows XP, right-click the NIC and select Repair. In Windows Vista, Windows 7, or Windows 8, right-click the NIC and select Diagnose. In both cases, Windows will attempt to detect and repair the problem.

- On a wireless network, interference usually causes intermittent connectivity problems. Try configuring the wireless router to use a different channel.

- Check that the configuration of installed anti-malware or firewall programs is not interfering with network operations.

- Check the router to see if Media Access Control (MAC) address filtering is preventing WLAN connections.

on the
job

As the Internet and the world in general move to IPv6, you will want to learn more about working with it. Some of the traditional command-line commands work with IPv6—some requiring special parameters. For instance, to release and renew an IPv6 DHCP address, the commands to enter are ipconfig /release6 and ipconfig /renew6. Use the /? switch with IPCONFIG and look for more IPv6 options.

Testing IP Configuration and Connectivity

If you have eliminated obvious and easy-to-check connectivity issues, then use IPCONFIG to first check that the IP configuration is correct and then use PING to test connectivity. To test for slow communications over a routed network, use the TRACERT command, and use the NETSTAT command to troubleshoot some connection errors.

Verifying IP Configuration with IPCONFIG   When you are troubleshooting network connectivity problems on an IP network, after eliminating an obviously disconnected or failed NIC, use the IPCONFIG command to verify the IP configuration. Ensure that the IP address is within the correct range and has the appropriate subnet mask and DNS settings. If you completed Exercise 14-2 in Chapter 14, you already saw what this command can do, but you will now learn how to use the information.

Remember that IP addresses must be unique on a subnet. DHCP servers are smart enough to only assign unused IP addresses to clients, but it is possible for somebody to manually configure an IP address already in use on the network—Windows is not shy about telling you there is an IP address conflict. When you see this message, first check the IP configuration on the computer reporting that problem. If it has a static address and there is no good reason for that, change it to automatic (DHCP) and use the command **ipconfig /release** followed by **ipconfig /renew**. If that does not solve the problem, check the IP addresses in use on the DHCP server (or in your WAP or router). If you have more than a handful of computers on the network, this can be a tedious task.

When you open a Command Prompt and enter **ipconfig /all**, it will display the IP configuration of all network interfaces on the local computer, even those that receive their addresses and configuration through DHCP. In fact, if your NIC is a DHCP client, this is the best way to see the resulting IP configuration quickly in all versions of Windows. Previously, there were no good graphical user interface (GUI) options for displaying this information in Windows, since the TCP/IP Properties dialog for a DHCP client connection will only show that it is configured to receive an IP address automatically, and it will not show its IP configuration. Windows Vista, Windows 7, and Windows 8 display the IP configuration information, regardless of how the NIC received it, in the Network Connection Details box, as shown in Figure 14-12 in Chapter 14. You can only view this information for one connection at a time, so techs still like to use **ipconfig /all** to see information about all connections at once. Figure 16-4 shows an example of running the **ipconfig /all** command on a Windows 7 computer with multiple network adapters.

When the output from the IPCONFIG command shows an IP address other than 0.0.0.0, you know that the IP settings have been successfully bound to your network adapter. "Bound" means that there is a linking relationship, called a "binding," between the network protocol and the adapter. A binding establishes the order in which each network component handles network communications.

In addition, when viewing the IP configuration information, verify that each item is correct for the IP network segment on which the NIC is connected. There are three rules to keep in mind when evaluating an IP configuration:

- The network ID and the subnet mask of each host on an IP segment must match.
- The default gateway address must be the IP address of a router on the same subnet.
- Each host on an IP segment must have a unique host ID.

```
D:\Windows\system32\cmd.exe                                                    ─ □  ✕

Microsoft Windows [Version 6.1.7601]
Copyright (c) 2009 Microsoft Corporation.   All rights reserved.

D:\Users\Yoda>ipconfig /all

Windows IP Configuration

    Host Name . . . . . . . . . . . . : Yoda-PC
    Primary Dns Suffix  . . . . . . . :
    Node Type . . . . . . . . . . . . : Hybrid
    IP Routing Enabled. . . . . . . . : No
    WINS Proxy Enabled. . . . . . . . : No

Ethernet adapter Local Area Connection 3:

    Connection-specific DNS Suffix  . :
    Description . . . . . . . . . . . : Realtek PCI GBE Family Controller
    Physical Address. . . . . . . . . : 00-27-19-CD-2F-C2
    DHCP Enabled. . . . . . . . . . . : Yes
    Autoconfiguration Enabled . . . . : Yes
    Link-local IPv6 Address . . . . . : fe80::40dc:bc77:14ee:9cf3%18(Preferred)
    IPv4 Address. . . . . . . . . . . : 192.168.1.134(Preferred)
    Subnet Mask . . . . . . . . . . . : 255.255.255.0
    Lease Obtained. . . . . . . . . . : Friday, July 13, 2012 7:26:28 AM
    Lease Expires . . . . . . . . . . : Saturday, July 14, 2012 7:26:33 AM
    Default Gateway . . . . . . . . . : 192.168.1.1
    DHCP Server . . . . . . . . . . . : 192.168.1.1
    DHCPv6 IAID . . . . . . . . . . . : 452994841
    DHCPv6 Client DUID. . . . . . . . : 00-01-00-01-14-2D-C9-A0-00-27-19-CD-2F-C2

    DNS Servers . . . . . . . . . . . : 192.168.8.1
    NetBIOS over Tcpip. . . . . . . . : Enabled

Ethernet adapter VirtualBox Host-Only Network:

    Connection-specific DNS Suffix  . :
    Description . . . . . . . . . . . : VirtualBox Host-Only Ethernet Adapter
    Physical Address. . . . . . . . . : 08-00-27-00-98-C5
    DHCP Enabled. . . . . . . . . . . : No
    Autoconfiguration Enabled . . . . : Yes
    Link-local IPv6 Address . . . . . : fe80::bc35:1a2:a311:2433%14(Preferred)
    IPv4 Address. . . . . . . . . . . : 192.168.56.1(Preferred)
    Subnet Mask . . . . . . . . . . . : 255.255.255.0
    Default Gateway . . . . . . . . . :
    DHCPv6 IAID . . . . . . . . . . . : 336068647
    DHCPv6 Client DUID. . . . . . . . : 00-01-00-01-14-2D-C9-A0-00-27-19-CD-2F-C2

    DNS Servers . . . . . . . . . . . : fec0:0:0:ffff::1%1
                                        fec0:0:0:ffff::2%1
                                        fec0:0:0:ffff::3%1
```

Therefore, if there are other hosts on the same subnet, run IPCONFIG on each
of them to determine if all the hosts comply with these rules. If not, correct
the problem.

Finally, if the computer in question has an IP address that begins with 169.254,
this is an Automatic Private IP Address (APIPA)—an address that a DHCP client
can assign to itself when it cannot reach a DHCP server. If this is a very small network

of just a few computers in which all of the computers use APIPA, this may be okay, but in most cases, consider this address a sign of a failure. If possible, check to see if the DHCP server is available. For a large network, you will need to contact a network administrator.

In a small office or home network, the DHCP server may be part of a broadband router. In that case, reset the router. If you wait long enough, the DHCP server should assign an address to the DHCP client computer, and if you wish to take control of the process, use the command **ipconfig /release** followed by **ipconfig /renew**.

Troubleshooting Connection Errors with the PING Command The *PING* command is useful for testing communications between two hosts. The name of this command is an acronym for Packet Internet Groper. We prefer to think (as many do) that it was named after the action of underwater sonar. Instead of bouncing sound waves off surfaces, the PING command uses data packets, sending them to specific IP addresses and requesting a response (hence, the idea of pinging). Then, PING listens for a reply.

If you completed Exercise 15-2 or 15-3 in Chapter 15, you know the simplest syntax of the PING command, which is **ping *target-IP-address***. However, you do not always need to know a target's IP address. You can also ping a domain name, such as mcgraw-hill.com, and on a network running Windows computers, you can ping the computer name. Use the PING command to test a new network connection and, for troubleshooting, a connection failure. The following is a suggested order for doing this.

1. Ping the local NIC using the command: **ping localhost**. The standard host name *localhost* is assigned by the IP protocol to the loopback network interface and no packets will leave the NIC, and if it is functioning, it will send the normal response back. Recall the discussion of loopback in Chapter 15. If the ping results in four responses, move on to the next step. If this fails, troubleshoot the NIC as you would any hardware component. If you have another identical NIC known to work, swap it with the current NIC. If the replacement NIC works, replace the original NIC.

2. Ping the IP address of the default gateway. If this does not work, verify that the gateway address is correct. If there are other computers on the network, compare the IP configuration settings. If the address for the default gateway matches those of other hosts on the network, ping the default gateway address from another computer.

3. Ping the IP address or DNS name of a computer beyond the default gateway.

This order tests, first, if the NIC is working. It also tests that the address works within your LAN, because the default gateway address is on the LAN and has the same network ID as the local NIC. Finally, successfully pinging an address beyond the gateway confirms at least two things: the router works, and the NIC of the target host is functioning and can respond to ping requests. If you cannot ping any computer beyond the router, the problem may be in the router itself.

PING has several switches. Use the –t command when you want to ping an address repeatedly. The default is to ping an address four times. It will continue until you stop it. Pressing the CTRL-BREAK key combination will cause it to display statistics and then continue. To stop this command, press the CTRL-C key combination. Figure 16-5 shows the output from this command.

Another default of the PING command is the size (or length) of the data it uses. The default size is 32 bytes, which is not a very heavy load for any connection. Therefore, administrators sometimes test a connection by sending more data. Do this with the –l switch followed by a space and the size, such as 1024. For instance, type

FIGURE 16-5

Using the PING command with the –t parameter

```
Command Prompt

C:\Users\Jane>ping 192.168.1.1 -t

Pinging 192.168.1.1 with 32 bytes of data:
Reply from 192.168.1.1: bytes=32 time<1ms TTL=64
Reply from 192.168.1.1: bytes=32 time<1ms TTL=64
Reply from 192.168.1.1: bytes=32 time<1ms TTL=64
Reply from 192.168.1.1: bytes=32 time<1ms TTL=64
Reply from 192.168.1.1: bytes=32 time<1ms TTL=64
Reply from 192.168.1.1: bytes=32 time<1ms TTL=64

Ping statistics for 192.168.1.1:
    Packets: Sent = 6, Received = 6, Lost = 0 (0% loss),
Approximate round trip times in milli-seconds:
    Minimum = 0ms, Maximum = 0ms, Average = 0ms
Control-Break
Reply from 192.168.1.1: bytes=32 time<1ms TTL=64
Reply from 192.168.1.1: bytes=32 time<1ms TTL=64
Reply from 192.168.1.1: bytes=32 time<1ms TTL=64

Ping statistics for 192.168.1.1:
    Packets: Sent = 9, Received = 9, Lost = 0 (0% loss),
Approximate round trip times in milli-seconds:
    Minimum = 0ms, Maximum = 0ms, Average = 0ms
Control-C
^C
C:\Users\Jane>_
```

the command **ping 192.168.1.1 -l 1024.** A connection that can easily handle the 32-byte size with zero percent loss of data may show some data loss with the 1024-byte size.

Now for some technical information about PING and related commands. The PING command uses a subprotocol of IP called the *Internet Control Message Protocol (ICMP)*. This little protocol has a big job in a TCP/IP internetwork. It detects problems that can cause errors. Such problems include congestion and downed routers. When ICMP detects these problems, it notifies other protocols and services in the TCP/IP suite, resulting in routing of packets around the problem area.

When you use PING, it sends *ICMP echo packets* to the target node. An echo packet contains a request to respond. Once the target node receives the packets, it sends out one response packet for each echo packet it receives. You see information about the received packets in the lines that begin with "Reply from." Pay attention to the time information on this line. It should be below 200 ms; if the time is greater than 500 ms, there is a connectivity issue between the two hosts. Of course, a little common sense may tell you that it will take a longer time to receive a response from the other side of the world.

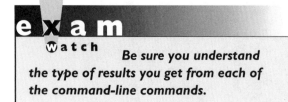

on the job

Practice working with these command-line tools before your network has a problem. Then you will be more comfortable with the tools and their screen output.

Using TRACERT to Troubleshoot Slow Communications

You may have situations in which you can connect to a Website or other remote resource, but the connection is very slow. If this connection is critical to business, you will want to gather information so a network administrator or ISP can troubleshoot the source of the bottleneck. You can use the TRACERT command to gather this information. *TRACERT* is a command-line utility that traces the route taken by packets to a destination.

exam

Watch *Be sure you understand the type of results you get from each of the command-line commands.*

When you use TRACERT with the name or IP address of the target host, it will ping each of the intervening routers, from the nearest to the farthest. You will see the delay at each router, and you will be able to determine the location of the bottleneck. You can then provide this information to the people who will troubleshoot it for you.

Understanding *time to live (TTL)* is also important. Each IP packet header has a TTL field that shows how many routers the packet can cross before being discarded. Like PING, TRACERT creates ICMP echo packets. The packet sent to the first host or router has a TTL of one. The TTL of each subsequent packet is increased by one. Each router, in turn, decreases the TTL value by one. The computer that sends the TRACERT waits a predetermined amount of time before it increments the TTL value by one for each additional packet. This repeats until the destination is reached. This process has the effect of pinging each router along the way, without needing to know each router's actual IP address.

Consider a scenario in which your connection to the Google Website (www.google.com) is extremely slow. You are working from a small office that has a cable modem connection to the Internet, and you are accustomed to very fast responses when you browse the Web. You have connected in the last few minutes to other Websites without significant delay, so you believe there is a bottleneck between you and Google.

Use TRACERT as described in Exercise 16-1 and report the results to your ISP. TRACERT will reveal the address of the router that is the bottleneck between you and a target host. Normally, the first and last numbered lines in the output represent the source IP address and the target IP address. Every line in between is a router located between your computer and the target. You can verify that the last line is the target by matching the IP address to the one you entered at the command line. If you entered a DNS name at the command line, the IP address will display below the command line.

EXERCISE 16-1

CertCam

Using TRACERT

In this exercise, we use Google as the target, but you can substitute another domain name or IP address.

1. Open a Command Prompt.
2. Type **tracert www.google.com.**
3. In Figure 16-6, one of the routers shows a value that is much greater than the others, but it is not greater than 500 ms, so there is a bottleneck relative to the others, but it is not a serious one. If your test shows a router with a much greater value, report this to your ISP or to a network professional in your company, if appropriate.

Using TRACERT to trace the route to www.google.com

```
Command Prompt                                          [ _ ][ □ ][ ✕ ]
Microsoft Windows [Version 6.0.6002]
Copyright (c) 2006 Microsoft Corporation.  All rights reserved.

C:\Users\Jane>tracert www.google.com

Tracing route to www.l.google.com [209.85.225.106]
over a maximum of 30 hops:

  1      3 ms      2 ms      3 ms  192.168.8.1
  2     16 ms     17 ms     15 ms  12.52.41.97
  3     25 ms     27 ms     28 ms  12.88.37.77
  4     85 ms     81 ms     72 ms  cr1.phmaz.ip.att.net [12.123.206.142]

  5     68 ms    142 ms    113 ms  cr1.dlstx.ip.att.net [12.122.28.181]
  6     74 ms     77 ms     66 ms  cr2.kc9mo.ip.att.net [12.122.28.86]
  7     71 ms     97 ms     81 ms  cr2.sl9mo.ip.att.net [12.122.28.90]
  8     70 ms    139 ms     96 ms  cr2.cgcil.ip.att.net [12.122.2.21]
  9     74 ms     73 ms     85 ms  cr84.cgcil.ip.att.net [12.123.7.249]
 10     69 ms     70 ms     89 ms  gar27.cgcil.ip.att.net [12.122.132.1]

 11     90 ms    157 ms    139 ms  12.88.249.234
 12    134 ms     87 ms     84 ms  209.85.254.128
 13     77 ms     84 ms     85 ms  209.85.240.224
 14     75 ms     90 ms     77 ms  72.14.232.141
 15     86 ms     83 ms     96 ms  209.85.241.29
 16    287 ms    359 ms    362 ms  72.14.239.18
 17    121 ms    134 ms    114 ms  iy-in-f106.1e100.net [209.85.225.106]

Trace complete.

C:\Users\Jane>
```

Using NETSTAT to Troubleshoot Connection Errors   The *NETSTAT* command will give you statistical information about the TCP/IP protocols and network connections involving your computer, depending on the parameters you use when you enter the command. Although NETSTAT has many options, there are a few you should remember. For instance, running netstat without any parameters, as shown in Figure 16-7, will show the current connections by protocol and port number. NETSTAT by itself can show you a connection that is not working— perhaps because an application has failed. Running netstat -s displays statistics on outgoing and incoming traffic on your computer. If this test shows there is no traffic in one direction, you may have a bad cable.

Troubleshooting with the NET Command

The Windows *NET* command is a command-prompt utility that can be used to perform a variety of administrative and troubleshooting tasks. We have even used

FIGURE 16-7

The NETSTAT command shows current connections.

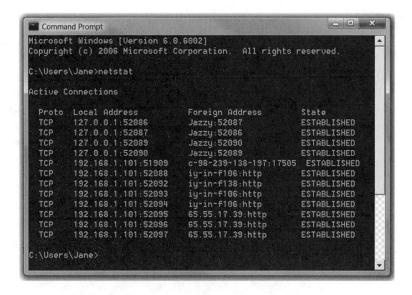

this command to create scripts for automating the creation of user accounts in a Windows domain—an advanced task. You can use the NET command to start and stop network services. To learn more about the NET command, enter **net help** to display a list of subcommands, such as those shown in Figure 16-8. You can then learn more about a single subcommand. For instance, the command for starting network services is **net start** *service*, where *service* is the name of the network service you wish to start. Enter **net stop** *service* to stop a service. To see a list of the services you can start, enter this command: **net help start**. To see a list of the services you can stop, enter this command: **net help stop**. You will see fewer services listed for the STOP command because some services cannot be stopped.

Use the NET command with the **use** subcommand to connect to a network *share*. A network share is a resource, such as a file folder or printer, that is available to you over the network. For instance, to connect to a shared folder named DATA on the computer named Wickenburg, enter **net use \\Wickenburg\data.** Use this command if you have determined that you can ping another computer but are not able to access a shared folder on that computer.

on the **job**

At the command line, you can enter net /? *to view information about the NET command. However, this version is really a condensed version of* net help *and gives you less information. So, remember* net /? *for the exam, but use* net help *on the job.*

Viewing the
subcommands
for the NET
command

```
Command Prompt                                                   _ □ x

C:\Users\Jane>net help
The syntax of this command is:

NET HELP
command
        -or-
NET command /HELP

    Commands available are:

NET ACCOUNTS            NET HELPMSG            NET STATISTICS
NET COMPUTER            NET LOCALGROUP        NET STOP
NET CONFIG             NET PAUSE             NET TIME
NET CONTINUE           NET PRINT             NET USE
NET FILE               NET SESSION           NET USER
NET GROUP              NET SHARE             NET VIEW
NET HELP               NET START

NET HELP NAMES explains different types of names in NET HELP syntax lines.
NET HELP SERVICES lists some of the services you can start.
NET HELP SYNTAX explains how to read NET HELP syntax lines.
NET HELP command | MORE displays Help one screen at a time.

C:\Users\Jane>
```

Resolving Insufficient Bandwidth

Chapter 14 described bandwidth as the amount of data that can travel over a network at a given time. That is deceptively simple when what is important is the user's perception of network slowness. Therefore, when a user perceives a network to be slow, increasing the bandwidth will improve its speed. The more data you can send at once, the faster data will move from beginning to end, and the faster the network will run overall. There are two ways to increase bandwidth. One is the low-cost method of reducing the broadcast sources, and the second, more costly, method is a hardware upgrade. Remember that wireless networks are shared bandwidth; 150 Mbps for an 802.lln wireless network feels fast for a single user but feels slower for 100 simultaneous network users.

Reducing Sources of Network Broadcasts

Most protocol suites have at least a few subprotocols that rely on network broadcasts. A broadcast is a transmission of packets addressed to all nodes on a network.

Broadcast traffic is, to some extent, unavoidable within a network segment, but too much of it takes up bandwidth needed for other traffic. Although broadcasts do not cross routers, they still persist within the network segments between routers, thus taking up valuable bandwidth. Reduce these sources by searching for the unnecessary protocol suites, and then look within the suites that are necessary and reduce the amount of broadcasting within them.

Why do unnecessary protocols exist on a network? First, more than one protocol suite can be active on a Windows computer, but that is rarely necessary anymore. If you have a TCP/IP network, and you find another protocol suite on a computer and there is no good reason to have it, remove it. Likely unnecessary (and outdated) protocol suites are Microsoft's NetBEUI, Novell's IPX/SPX, or Microsoft's NWLink (a version of IPX/SPX).

Of course, as you learned in Chapter 15, you can turn off the Service Set Identifier (SSID) broadcast from a WAP. This is not only more secure, but it reduces broadcasts. However, when it comes to the use of excess protocol suites, the most common offenders are not usually computers, but old print servers, which may have come with several protocol suites enabled. Whether a print server is a separate box or integrated into a network printer, find out how to access the print server configuration. In the case of a separate print server box, you will normally enter the print server's IP address into a Web browser's address box and access it remotely. You will need the administrative user name and password to access it. For a print server integrated into a printer, it all depends on its design. The documentation for the printer will give instructions on how to access its configuration—usually through a Web browser or through a control panel on the printer. In both instances, look for protocols and remove protocol suites that are not required on your network.

Today's Internet users enjoy streaming audio and video, which means that users listening to Internet radio or Internet TV can have a negative impact on network throughput for others. This is a serious problem in a working environment because aside from the ethical problem of spending work time for personal activities, using shared network bandwidth for downloading and uploading questionable content such as movies and music using a Bit Torrent client can also seriously degrade network performance.

Upgrading Network Hardware

Once you have eliminated unnecessary protocol suites and unnecessary broadcasting, if there is still a bandwidth problem, increase the bandwidth by upgrading the network's components. If the network has any Ethernet hubs, replace them with switches. Recall that a hub takes a signal received on one port and repeats it on all other ports. This consumes bandwidth. A switch, on the other hand, is a more intelligent device, which takes an incoming signal and only sends it to the destination port. This saves bandwidth.

If the network already has switches, then consider upgrading to faster equipment. For example, a LAN with Ethernet (10 Mbps) or Fast Ethernet (100 Mbps) equipment can be upgraded to Gigabit Ethernet (1 to 10 Gbps).

Be sure that when you upgrade to increase bandwidth, the upgrade is thorough. That is, all the NICs, switches, and routers must support the new, higher speed. Although the faster equipment is downward compatible with the slower equipment, the network will only be as fast as its slowest hardware component. Also, on an Ethernet network, do not forget to upgrade the cabling to the grade required for the network speed you want to achieve. So, if you want to achieve Gigabit Ethernet speeds, you need a Gigabit Ethernet NIC, cable, and switch.

Similarly, to upgrade a wireless network, replace slower equipment with newer, faster equipment. Increase signal strength with proper placement of the wireless antenna, and install signal boosters, if necessary. Newer wireless equipment will also have better security.

Troubleshooting DNS Problems

DNS problems show themselves as messages such as "Server not found." These messages can appear in your Web browser, your email client, or any software that attempts to connect to a server. How do you know it is a DNS problem? You do not know this until you eliminate other problems, such as a failed NIC, a broken connection, a typo, or an incorrect IP configuration. But once you have eliminated these problems, use the following tests to troubleshoot DNS problems.

Using PING to Troubleshoot DNS Problems

Notice that in the steps provided for using both the PING and TRACERT commands in the previous sections, you can use either the IP address or the DNS name. When you use the DNS name with either of these commands, you are also testing DNS. For instance, if you open a Command Prompt window and enter the following command: ping www.mcgraw-hill.com, before the PING command can send packets to the target, www.mcgraw-hill.com, the DNS client must resolve the DNS name to an IP address. This is exactly what happens when you enter a Uniform Resource Locator (URL) in the address box of a Web browser. The DNS client resolves the name to an IP address before the browser can send a request to view the page.

When pinging a DNS name is successful, you know several things: your DNS client is working, your DNS server is responding and working, and the target DNS

name has been found on the Internet. Now, notice that the name we used (www
.mcgraw-hill.com) has three parts to it. Reading from right to left, "com" is the *top-
level domain (TLD)* name, and mcgraw-hill is the *second-level domain (SLD)* name
within the com TLD. Both of these together are usually referred to as a domain
name. So what is "www"? The owner of the second-level domain name defines
everything else you see in the URL.

For instance, www.mcgraw-hill.com is listed in DNS servers that are probably
under the control of McGraw-Hill or its ISP. The entry points to a server, named
"www," are where Web pages can be found. So, to the left of the second-level
domain name are the names of servers or child domains of McGraw-Hill.com. This
allows McGraw-Hill to organize their portion of the DNS name space and help
client computers locate resources on these servers. Another example is support
.microsoft.com that points to the Microsoft Support Website.

And what about all those letters, numbers, slashes, and other characters to the
right of the TLD? They point to specific documents on the servers. Simple? To the
casual observer, yes, because DNS hides the complexity of the organization and
the locations of servers and documents. Understanding this much will help you to
work with DNS and perform basic troubleshooting.

So, the next time you cannot connect to a Website from your browser, first double-
check your spelling. If you entered the URL correctly, then open up a Command
Prompt and ping the portion of the URL that contains the TLD and SLD. In our first
example, you would open a Command Prompt and type **ping mcgraw-hill.com**. If
the PING is not successful, you should immediately ping another domain name and/
or try connecting to another URL through your browser. If you are successful pinging
another location, then the problem may be with a router in the path to the first
location. Use TRACERT, described earlier, to pinpoint the problem router.

Using IPCONFIG to Flush the DNS Cache

Before a DNS client queries a DNS server for a specific name, it checks a little chunk
of memory, the *DNS cache*, where it retains a list of previously resolved DNS names
and IP addresses. If the DNS client finds the name in the cache, it does not query
the DNS server. However, if the server address has changed since it was recorded
in the DNS cache, the DNS client will return an error and you will not be able to
connect to the server. So, if you recently were able to connect to a server through
your browser, but have a "server not found" error, an easy solution to try is to flush the
DNS cache so that the client will query the DNS server rather than use the address in
the cache. To do this, open a Command Prompt and enter this command: **ipconfig /
flushdns**. Then open your browser and attempt to connect to the server again.

Using **NSLOOKUP** to Troubleshoot DNS Problems

To further troubleshoot DNS problems, use the *NSLOOKUP* command, which lets you troubleshoot DNS problems by allowing you to query DNS name servers and see the result of the queries. In using NSLOOKUP, you are looking for problems such as a DNS server not responding to clients, DNS servers not resolving names correctly, or other general name resolution problems. NSLOOKUP bypasses the client DNS cache and talks directly to the DNS server and is thus more reliable than PING for DNS troubleshooting. NSLOOKUP has two modes: *interactive* and *noninteractive*:

■ **Interactive mode** In interactive mode, NSLOOKUP has its own command prompt, a greater than sign (>) within the system Command Prompt. You enter this mode by typing **nslookup** without any parameters, or **nslookup** followed by a space, a hyphen, and the name of a name server. In the first instance, it will use your default name server, as shown here, and in the second instance, it will use the name server you specify. While in interactive mode, enter commands at the NSLOOKUP prompt, and type **exit** to end interactive mode and return to the system Command Prompt, as shown here.

■ **Noninteractive mode** In noninteractive mode, you enter the NSLOOKUP command plus a command parameter for using one or more NSLOOKUP subcommands. The response is sent to the screen, and you are returned to the Command Prompt. Exercise 16-2 uses noninteractive mode.

EXERCISE 16-2

Using **NSLOOKUP** to Troubleshoot DNS

Use NSLOOKUP to resolve any Internet domain name to an IP address.

1. Open a Command Prompt window, and enter the following command: **nslookup mcgraw-hill.com**. If the name server is working, the result will resemble Figure 16-9.

FIGURE 16-9

The NSLOOKUP
command queries
the default name
server.

■ The server and address in the first and second lines of the output are the
name and IP address of the DNS server that responded to your request.
This will be the name server used by your ISP or your company.

■ The second group of lines shows the result of the query. It is called a non-
authoritative answer because the name server queried had to query other
name servers to find the name.

2. The results in Figure 16-9 show that DNS name resolution is working. Therefore,
if you are unable to connect to a server in this domain, the server may be
offline, or a critical link or router between it and the Internet has failed. If
you were troubleshooting a connection problem to this domain, you would
pass this information on to a network administrator or ISP.

Troubleshooting WINS Problems

The Windows Internet Name Service (WINS) is nearly extinct because it was a
Microsoft NetBIOS naming system used on pre-Windows 2000 clients and servers,
and Microsoft networks now use DNS. However, if your TCP/IP network has older
versions of Windows, you may still need WINS, and error messages on these older
Windows clients will refer to WINS and/or NetBIOS.

In such a scenario, if you have eliminated TCP/IP configuration problems and
hardware problems, then suspect a WINS problem. WINS problems involve NetBIOS
names within Microsoft networks, so first check the client computer's NetBIOS name.
It may be a duplicate of another on the network, which happens when someone tries
to enter the name manually. If that is not the cause, then verify that the problem is not
due to two computers having the same NetBIOS name. Once you have eliminated that
as the problem, make sure that the WINS server is online.

If the WINS server is online, then another possible cause is that NetBIOS over TCP/IP (NetBT) has not been enabled on the WINS server. This service supports the NetBIOS name system on a TCP/IP network. At the server, open a Command Prompt and enter the command **ipconfig /all**. If the server has more than one network adapter, be sure to check the information listed under the one connected to the network the server has in common with the client. The line you are looking for is "NetBIOS over Tcpip" and its status should be "enabled." If not, you will need to enable NetBIOS on that server in the Advanced TCP/IP Settings dialog box.

If the server is located on the same IP network, then the Windows clients will use NetBIOS broadcasts to contact the server. If it is on another IP network, the intervening routers will block broadcasts, and the client will need to contact a WINS server to resolve the name. In that case, check that the IP network has a WINS server enabled and that the client's TCP/IP configuration includes the address of a WINS server. If the client is receiving its IP address through a DHCP server, that same server may not be configured to give that client the WINS server address. Also, the DHCP server is very likely also functioning as the WINS server, especially if it is a Microsoft Windows server.

Back in the day when most of our Windows network clients and their installed software required NetBIOS, we found that simply restarting the computers (client for sure, server only in a pinch) in question would resolve this problem. This was an okay fix when you could not actually visit the computer and had to give a user the quickest fix. However, what restarting Windows did was to flush the NetBIOS cache (and everything else in memory). If we were able to sit at the computer, we used the *NBTSTAT* command-line utility, entering the following at the Command Prompt: **nbtstat R** (the "R" is uppercase). This command purged and refreshed the local NetBIOS cache. The NBTSTAT command lets you see a variety of statistics for the NetBIOS protocol, including BIOS name tables and caches—both local and remote. To see more NBTSTAT options, run the command by itself.

exam
watch
Practice using network troubleshooting commands so that you understand what parameters to use with each and what each does. The commands listed in CompTIA Exam Objective 4.5 are PING, IPCONFIG, TRACERT, NETSTAT, NBTSTAT, and NET.

Troubleshooting with Terminal Software

Telnet is character-based terminal software that has a server component that allows a Telnet client to connect. The connected client works in a character-mode environment and can enter commands. Windows XP and earlier versions have a Telnet client installed. Historically, network devices like routers contained a Telnet server service to which router administrators connected and used cryptic commands to configure the router. In today's small office/home office (SOHO) network equipment, the Telnet server has been replaced by a Web server, and a technician connects to the device by entering the IP address of the device in a browser.

However, Telnet still has its uses as an advanced troubleshooting tool. Recall in Chapter 14 that you learned about ports and how a port identifies the exact service targeted at a certain IP address. When you use Telnet, it uses TCP port 23, but you can direct it to use a different port number—say, TCP port 25—which is normally used by Simple Mail Transport Protocol (SMTP). Here is the scenario: Your email client is unable to send messages. You have used the ping command to ping the mail server successfully. Therefore, it is possible that the physical server is up and running on the network but the SMTP service is not working. If you direct Telnet to connect to the IP address/port for the SMTP server and are unable to connect, then notify the mail server administrator because this can indicate the SMTP service is down.

Rather than use the cryptic character-based Telnet client, which has the added disadvantage of not being secure, consider downloading a GUI-based terminal client with security features. Secure Shell (SSH), described in Chapter 15, has replaced Telnet as a terminal client. It can be used to connect to terminal servers that require sophisticated security protocols. Many free terminal clients are available—many with "Telnet" in their name—but most of them are some form of SSH. One free terminal client is PuTTY, which is described on the Website (http://www.chiark.greenend.org .uk/~sgtatham/putty/) as "a free Telnet/SSH client."

Troubleshooting Modem Problems

When an analog modem fails, without even attempting to make a connection, first check all the connections, as you would for any network device, and then check the modem configuration. If it is a bus or Universal Serial Bus (USB) modem, plug and play allocates resources, and there should not be any resource conflicts, meaning the OS avoids such conflicts among devices by managing their allocation and use. The old conflicts were with the COM port, IRQ settings, or I/O addresses. Find out if the person who installed the modem manually configured the modem or any other device and undo these changes, allowing Windows to allocate them without interference.

If a modem actually dials up but fails to connect, make sure the sound is turned on, and test it again, if necessary. If you hear the dial tone, dialing, and some beeps in response, followed by a dropped connection, suspect that the modem you are using is not compatible with the modem on the other end of the connection. There are actually still some very old 33.6 Kbps modems out there that are no longer supported by ISPs, or old 56 Kbps modems that were manufactured before standards for this speed were established. ISPs that still support dial-up support 56 Kbps modems using the latest set of standards, so if the modem is the right speed, check with the ISP for any special configuration information you may have overlooked.

Open the Control Panel's Phone And Modem Options applet. Here is where you can resolve configuration issues, especially by checking out the Dialing Rules tab. A common configuration issue is getting a modem to dial out through a private branch exchange (PBX), which will not give you a dial tone for an outside line until you "request" it, usually by dialing a 9 and waiting for the dial tone. The dialing program you use, whether it is a special utility from an ISP or the Phone And Modem Options applet in Windows, will allow you to program this, along with a short pause, so the modem requests a line before attempting to dial. The Dialing Rules tab is where you enter the phone number and other dialing settings. If you are dialing through a PBX and you neglect to provide the number that gives you an outside line, then, when the modem attempts to dial, it will return a "no dial tone detected" message. The Vista Phone And Modem Options applet is shown in Figure 16-10, and it is very similar across all the versions of Windows listed in the objective for the CompTIA A+ Exams.

SCENARIO & SOLUTION

My network has a DHCP server. I need to see if the NIC received an IP address, but when I look at the properties of the Local Area Connection, the IP address is empty. What can I do?	Open a Command Prompt and enter the following command: **ipconfig /all**. This will display the IP configuration.
I have connected to a certain Website many times, but today the connection to this one Website is very slow. I would like to talk to my ISP about this, but I need more information. How can I tell where the problem is?	Because other Websites do not seem as slow, use the TRACERT command to trace the route to the Website and determine where the bottleneck may be.

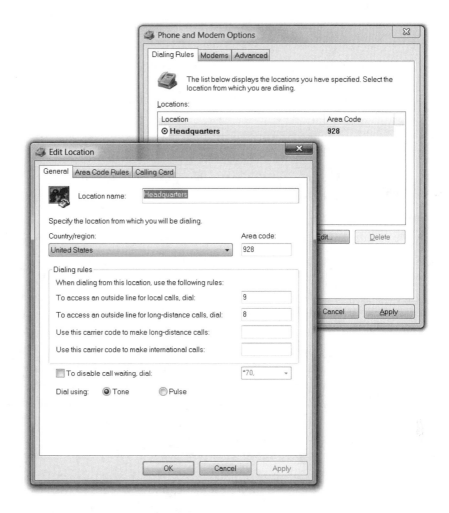

FIGURE 16-10

The Windows Vista Phone And Modem Options applet looks much like the one in Windows 7 and in earlier versions of Windows.

Preventive Maintenance for Networks

It is always better to prevent problems than to spend your time solving them. In this section, you will learn the basic maintenance tasks specific to networks, which include maintaining all the equipment directly attached to the network and the media over which the signals travel. However, the value and usability of a network also depend on proper functioning of the attached computers (clients and servers), as well as other shared devices, such as printers. In Chapter 11, you learned preventive maintenance for computers. Preventive maintenance for network devices, such as NICs, hubs, switches, WAPs, and routers, is identical to that for computers.

A network also depends on the maintenance of an appropriate and secure environment for both the equipment and data. Chapters 17 and 18 explore security issues for computers and networks, and Chapter 1 presented safety and environmental issues.

Therefore, although this chapter presents some network-specific maintenance tasks, keep in mind that a computer professional must look beyond the components and software that are specific to a network and approach network maintenance holistically.

Maintaining Equipment

Network equipment, from the NICs in the computers to the bridging and routing devices that connect networks together, all have similar requirements. For instance, they all require sufficient ventilation and cooling systems to maintain the appropriate operating environment.

Reliable Power

All computer and network components must have electrical power. Providing reliable power begins with the power company supplying the power, but your responsibility begins at the meter. Do not assume that the power will always be reliable. Most of us have experienced power outages and can understand how disrupting they are. However, bad power, in the form of surges, spikes, and voltage sags, can do a great deal of damage. Prevent damage and disruption from these events by using uninterruptible power supply (UPS) devices or other protective devices discussed in Chapter 1. Versions of these power protection devices come in a form factor for mounting in equipment racks. Equipment racks are discussed in the following section.

Be aware of the number and location of circuits in the building, and the total power requirements of the equipment you have on each circuit. If you have network equipment unprotected by a UPS, be sure this equipment is not sharing a circuit with a device that has high demands, such as a laser printer or photocopier.

Consider using a dedicated circuit for the most critical equipment. A dedicated circuit has only one, or very few, outlets.

Housing Servers and Network Devices

Servers and network devices such as switches and routers should be in a physically secure room or closet with proper climate controls. The humidity should be at or near 40 percent, and the temperature should be no higher than 70 degrees. Provide adequate spacing around the equipment for proper ventilation. When dealing with more than a few servers plus network equipment, use rack-mounted servers that fit into the specially designed equipment racks for holding servers and other devices, such as UPSs, routers, and switches. These take up less space and, unlike tables and desks, allow more air to flow around the equipment.

Dedicate the room or closet to the equipment. Do not make this a multipurpose room for storage or office space because that is inviting disaster, especially if the space is readily accessible by people who have no professional reason to be in contact with the servers or network equipment. The unintended consequences of such an arrangement can damage the equipment.

on the **()ob** | *As a new technician, you may find yourself in a new and growing company. Take a professional approach to organizing and protecting the networking equipment from the beginning. This will make the changes required to accommodate a larger network easier.*

Securing and Protecting Network Cabling

Regardless of the size of the network, keep network cabling neat and labeled. In the equipment room or closet, use patch panels. A patch panel is a rack-mounted panel containing multiple network ports. Cables running from various locations in the building connect to ports on the back of the patch panel. Then shorter cables, called patch cables, connect each port to switches and routers in the closet or equipment room. This keeps cables organized and even allows for labeling the ports. This will help prevent damaged cables and confusion when troubleshooting a cable run.

on the **()ob** | *Secure and protect network cabling to avoid damage from mishandling or mischief and ensure that it is well labeled so that it is easier to add new equipment and to troubleshoot.*

Horizontal runs of cabling often must run through suspended ceilings. Resist the urge to simply lay the cabling on the top of the ceiling tiles. This arrangement may be okay for a very small number of cables, but it only takes a few cables to make a tangle. Further, running additional cables into this space can be very difficult. Therefore, bundle cables together and run them through channels where possible. If the budget allows, specialized cable management systems are worth the investment. Use cable trays for running cables in the ceiling. A cable tray is a lightweight, bridge-like structure for containing the cables in a building.

watch
An IP address conflict (called an "IP conflict" in the list of topics under CompTIA Exam 802: Objective 4.5) will keep a computer from communicating on a network and will result in an IP address conflict error message.

CERTIFICATION SUMMARY

This chapter explored the tools and techniques for troubleshooting networks and preventive maintenance for networks. The tools discussed included physical and software status indicators, command-line utilities, toner probe, loopback plugs, punchdown tools, crimpers, and cable testers. In this chapter, you learned strategies for using commands to analyze network problems.

A problem that may appear to be caused by insufficient bandwidth may actually be caused by inefficient use of bandwidth, and you solve this by removing unnecessary protocol suites from computers and network devices, such as print servers.

Analyze network connectivity problems based on error messages or other symptoms. If you see no obvious source for the problem, check the hardware, beginning with the NIC, cables, hubs, switches, WAPs, and routers. Check for any source of EMI. If you detect no physical source of a problem, check the IP configuration of the NIC and correct any errors you find.

Use command-prompt utilities to reveal the IP configuration, test connectivity, locate a bottleneck on the Internet, reveal statistics about the TCP/IP protocols and network connections involving the local computer, and detect DNS and WINS problems.

Most preventive maintenance for network devices is identical to that for computers. There are some special considerations for the servers, network devices, and the cabling, for which preventive maintenance begins with providing a proper and secure environment and carefully organizing the cabling and the cable runs through ceilings and walls. Restrict access to network-specific devices to protect them from people with no professional reason to be in contact with the servers or network equipment.

TWO-MINUTE DRILL

Here are some of the key points covered in Chapter 16.

Troubleshooting Common Network Problems

❑ Status indicators for network hardware include LED lights on physical devices and/or status information from software installed along with the driver.

❑ A quick glance at indicator lights on a device or icons and messages on the computer screen reveals valuable information.

❑ The typical NIC installs with a configuration utility that you can open from an icon in the notification area of the taskbar. A change in status or hovering your mouse over this icon will cause a message to appear over the notification area.

❑ A group of command-prompt utilities installs with the TCP/IP protocol suite. Among them are IPCONFIG, PING, TRACERT, NETSTAT, NBTSTAT, and NSLOOKUP.

❑ Use the /? switch with any command-prompt utility to learn about the variety of subcommands and parameters that alter the behavior of the utility.

❑ A cable tester connects to the ends of a cable and sends a signal down the cable in order to detect breaks in it.

❑ You can use a wireless locator to identify the source of wireless interference and to optimize WAP configuration.

❑ One way to increase network bandwidth is to remove unnecessary protocol suites from the network. Check computers for unneeded protocol suites and other network devices, such as print servers, which may come with several protocols enabled.

❑ A more costly method of increasing network bandwidth is to upgrade hardware. Consider changing all the network hardware (NICs, switches, cabling, etc.) to hardware capable of higher speeds than the existing equipment.

❑ If you eliminate physical connection as the source of a modem problem, check out the configuration and dialing properties.

❑ When troubleshooting network connectivity problems, physically check the local network hardware. Next, check the status of the NIC driver in the Properties dialog for the NIC.

❑ Use the IPCONFIG command to check the IP configuration.

❑ Use the PING command to test for connectivity to another host.

❑ Find a network bottleneck on a routed network (like the Internet) using the TRACERT command.

❑ Use the NETSTAT command to view statistics about connections to the local computer.

❑ Troubleshoot DNS problems with PING and NSLOOKUP.

❑ WINS problems involve NetBIOS names within Microsoft networks. Check for duplication of NetBIOS names or problems with the WINS server, and use NBTSTAT to flush the NetBIOS cache and do other tasks.

❑ Sometimes simply restarting the WAP/broadband router solves connectivity issues.

❑ Media Access Control (MAC) address filtering might be preventing WLAN connections.

❑ Wireless encryption settings and passphrases must match on both the WAP and the wireless client.

❑ Make sure you are using the correct updated wireless NIC driver.

❑ A degraded wireless signal could be due to interference in the same frequency range, atmospheric conditions, or physical obstructions.

❑ Some anti-malware and firewall programs can cause problems with wireless connections—check their configuration.

Preventive Maintenance for Networks

❑ Preventive maintenance for network devices, such as NICs, hubs, switches, WAPs, and routers, is identical to what we described in Chapter 11 for computers.

❑ Do not overload circuits, and provide reliable power using power protection devices, as described in Chapter 1. Consider using a dedicated circuit for the most critical equipment.

❑ Locate servers and network devices in a dedicated space, such as a room or closet. Make sure the environment in this space is appropriate, and restrict access to the equipment.

❑ Secure, protect, and organize network cabling by using patch panels in the closet or room housing the network devices and by using cable management systems, such as cable trays for horizontal runs through ceilings.

SELF TEST

The following questions will help you measure your understanding of the material presented in this chapter. Read all of the choices carefully because there might be more than one correct answer. Choose all correct answers for each question.

Troubleshooting Common Network Problems

1. You suspect a network port on a switch is not functioning correctly. The indicator lights for the switch port look correct. How can you determine whether or not the switch port is working?
   A. Test with a loopback plug
   B. Use a toner probe
   C. Reboot the switch
   D. Use a wireless locator

2. What category of tool is the handiest and least expensive for troubleshooting problems with a variety of causes from those local to the computer to sources on the Internet?
   A. Status indicators
   B. Command-line utilities
   C. Ethernet NICs
   D. Cable testers

3. Which of the following is a command-line utility you would use to release a DHCP-allocated IP address from a local NIC?
   A. NBTSTAT
   B. PING
   C. IPCONFIG
   D. NSLOOKUP

4. What tool would you use if you suspected that a cable contained broken wires?
   A. Cable ping
   B. Cable tester
   C. Status indicator
   D. LED

5. When you see a blinking green LED (labeled "Link"), what does it usually mean?
   A. 1000 Mbps connection
   B. 100 Mbps connection
   C. Network activity
   D. Broken cable

6. What should you look for first on a network that seems to have a bandwidth problem?

   A. Unnecessary protocol suites

   B. Unnecessary servers

   C. Unnecessary network printers

   D. Unnecessary print servers

7. How can you quickly view the IP configuration information for all the network adapters in your computer?

   A. Open Network Connections Detail

   B. Run **netstat**

   C. Run **ipconfig /renew**

   D. **Run ipconfig /all**

8. Which of the following devices reduces network traffic within an Ethernet LAN?

   A. Hub

   B. Switch

   C. Router

   D. NIC

9. How would you check the signal strength received by a wireless NIC? Select all that apply.

   A. Check indicator lights on the wireless NIC.

   B. Check indicator lights on the WAP.

   C. Open the NIC's program from the notification area.

   D. Run IPCONFIG.

10. Which tool will show you the status of nearby Wi-Fi networks?

   A. Punchdown tool

   B. NETSTAT

   C. Toner probe

   D. Wireless locator

11. What is the result of mixing Ethernet and Fast Ethernet hardware?

   A. Transmissions at 100 Mbps

   B. Transmissions at 10 Mbps

   C. Transmissions at 1 Gbps

   D. Transmissions at 10 Gbps

12. The distance between a WAP and one group of wireless hosts causes the signal to degrade so badly that the transmissions are too slow and users are complaining. What can you do?

    A. Install a signal booster.

    B. Upgrade all the wireless devices to a faster speed.

    C. Install an Ethernet network.

    D. Install a router.

13. Which type of server automatically assigns IP addresses to hosts?

    A. DHCP

    B. WINS

    C. DNS

    D. APIPA

14. What command can you use to force a DHCP client to request an IP address assignment?

    A. **ping localhost**

    B. **ipconfig /renew**

    C. **ipconfig /all**

    D. **tracert**

15. A user complains that an Internet connection to a Website she needs to access for her work is extremely slow. Which of the following commands will you use first to analyze the problem?

    A. NETSTAT

    B. IPCONFIG

    C. TRACERT

    D. NSLOOKUP

16. Which of the following command-line utilities would *not* help when troubleshooting a possible DNS problem?

    A. NBTSTAT

    B. PING

    C. IPCONFIG

    D. NSLOOKUP

17. How do you stop the output from a PING command in which you used the –t switch?

    A. Type **exit**.

    B. Press the CTRL-C key combination.

    C. Type **pause**.

    D. Press the CTRL-BREAK key combination.

18. When you PING this name, you are pinging the loopback network interface as a test of the local NIC to see if it is functioning.

   A. server

   B. echo

   C. localhost

   D. gateway

Preventive Maintenance for Networks

19. Which of the following is the preferred environment for network equipment and servers in a law office?

   A. A broom closet

   B. A reception desk

   C. A dedicated, climate-controlled room

   D. A conference room

20. You need to run a group of wires through a suspended ceiling. What should you use to keep the wires organized within the ceiling area?

   A. An equipment rack

   B. A UPS

   C. Cable wraps

   D. Cable trays

SELF TEST ANSWERS

Troubleshooting Common Network Problems

1. ☑ **A.** You should use a loopback plug to test a questionable switch port. It will need an RJ-45 connector.

   ☒ **B,** use a toner probe, is incorrect because it is used to identify unlabeled cables. **C,** rebooting the switch, is incorrect. This will not identify a faulty switch port. **D,** use a wireless locator, is incorrect because this can only identify wireless networks.

2. ☑ **B.** Command-line utilities are the handiest and least expensive network troubleshooting tools for a wide range of problems.

   ☒ **A,** status indicators, is incorrect because although these are handy for detecting problems local to the computer (NIC) or its local connection, they are not useful for problems far removed from the computer. **C,** Ethernet NICs, is incorrect because these are network devices, not troubleshooting tools. **D,** cable testers, is incorrect because although these are good troubleshooting tools for local problems, they are not the handiest or least expensive compared to the command-line utilities.

3. ☑ **C.** Use IPCONFIG to release a DHCP-allocated IP address from a NIC (**ipconfig /release**, which you would normally follow with **ipconfig /renew** to renew the address).

   ☒ **A,** NBTSTAT, is incorrect because this command lets you work with the NetBIOS name lists and caches, but does not release an IP address. **B,** PING, is incorrect because this tests a connection between two hosts. **D,** NSLOOKUP, is incorrect because this tests for DNS problems.

4. ☑ **B.** You would use a cable tester if you suspected that a cable had broken wires.

   ☒ **A,** cable ping, is incorrect because such a tool was not even mentioned and may not exist. **C,** status indicator, and **D,** LED, are incorrect because neither is a tool you would use if you suspected that a cable was bad, although they would supply the clue that such a problem exists.

5. ☑ **C.** Network activity is usually indicated by a blinking green LED.

   ☒ **A,** 1000 Mbps connection, and **B,** 100 Mbps connection, are incorrect, although a multispeed NIC may have a separate Link light for each speed. **D,** broken cable, is incorrect and would probably result in the Link light being off.

6. ☑ **A.** Unnecessary protocol suites are what you should look for first in a network that seems to have a bandwidth problem.

   ☒ **B,** unnecessary servers, **C,** unnecessary network printers, and **D,** unnecessary print servers, are all incorrect because none of these contribute to bandwidth as much as unnecessary protocol suites.

7. ☑ **D.** Run **ipconfig /all** to quickly see the IP configuration information for all the network adapters in a computer.
   ☒ **A,** open Network Connections Detail, is incorrect because this Windows Vista and 7 GUI only shows a single network connection at a time. **B,** run **netstat,** is incorrect because this command displays information on the open connections by protocol and port number. **C, ipconfig /renew,** is incorrect because this command forces a DHCP client to send an IP address renewal request to a DHCP server.

8. ☑ **B.** A switch is the device that reduces network broadcasts in an Ethernet network.
   ☒ **A,** hub, is incorrect because a hub sends a packet to every port, which increases traffic, whereas a switch only sends packets to the destination port. **C,** router, is incorrect because a router connects LANs, whereas a switch is within a LAN. It is true that a router will keep broadcast traffic from traveling between LANs. **D,** NIC, is incorrect because this is a network adapter, which is not a device that reduces network traffic.

9. ☑ **A and C.** The indicator lights on the wireless NIC and the NIC's program, available from the notification area, are both correct as places where you look for the signal strength received by a wireless NIC.
   ☒ **B,** check indicator lights on the WAP, is incorrect because since the WAP is the source of the signals, these do not indicate the strength of the signal received by a wireless NIC. **D,** run IPCONFIG, is incorrect because it is not how you check the signal strength received by a wireless NIC.

10. ☑ **D.** A wireless locator will show you the status of nearby Wi-Fi networks.
    ☒ **A,** punchdown tool, is incorrect because this is used to connect cabling to a punchdown block. **B,** NETSTAT, is incorrect because this is a command-line utility that provides statistical information about the TCP/IP protocols and network connections. **C,** toner probe, is incorrect because this is a hardware tool for locating both ends of a cable.

11. ☑ **B.** The result of mixing Ethernet (10 Mbps) and Fast Ethernet (100 Mbps) is transmissions at 10 Mbps.
    ☒ **A,** transmissions at 100 Mbps, is incorrect because the presence of the slower Ethernet devices will cause communications between the slower and faster devices to run at the slower rate. **C,** transmissions at 1 Gbps, and **D,** transmissions at 10 Gbps, are both incorrect because neither Ethernet nor Fast Ethernet runs at these speeds.

12. ☑ **A.** The solution to the degraded signal due to distance is to install a signal booster.
    ☒ **B,** upgrade all the wireless devices to a faster speed, is incorrect because the question does not mention the standard of the device in use, and it may be at the highest level available. **C,** install an Ethernet network, is incorrect because a wireless network is often installed where it is not possible or practical to install a wired network. **D,** install a router, is incorrect because this would not solve the problem of the weak signal within the wireless LAN.

13. ☑ **A.** DHCP is the type of server that automatically assigns IP addresses to hosts.
    ☒ **B,** WINS, is incorrect because a WINS server resolves NetBIOS names to IP addresses.
    C, DNS, is incorrect because the DNS server resolves Internet domain names to IP addresses.
    D, APIPA, is incorrect because this does not describe a server, but an IP address (beginning with 169.254) that a DHCP client can assign to itself if it does not get a response from a DHCP server.

14. ☑ **B.** You use the **ipconfig /renew** command to force a DHCP client to request an IP address assignment.
    ☒ **A, ping localhost,** is incorrect because this command is used to ping the local NIC.
    C, ipconfig /all, is incorrect because this command is used to look at the TCP/IP configuration.
    D, tracert, is incorrect because this command displays a trace of the route taken by packets to the destination.

15. ☑ **C.** TRACERT is the command to use to analyze the problem of a slow connection to a Website.
    ☒ **A,** NETSTAT, **B,** IPCONFIG, and **D,** NSLOOKUP, are all incorrect because none of these is the correct command to analyze the problem described.

16. ☑ **A.** NBTSTAT would not help when troubleshooting a possible DNS problem because NBTSTAT is for working with the NetBIOS naming system.
    ☒ **B,** PING, **C,** IPCONFIG, and **D,** NSLOOKUP, are all useful when troubleshooting a possible DNS problem.

17. ☑ **B,** press the CTRL-C key combination, is correct, as this will stop the command and return you to the prompt.
    ☒ **A,** type **exit, C,** type **pause,** and **D,** press the CTRL-BREAK key combination, are all incorrect because none of these will not stop the command output.

18. ☑ **C.** localhost is the name of the loopback network interface, and pinging it tests the NIC.
    ☒ **A,** server, **B,** echo, and **D,** gateway, are all incorrect because none of them is the name of the loopback network interface.

Preventive Maintenance for Networks

19. ☑ **C.** A dedicated, climate-controlled room is the preferred environment for network equipment and servers in any organization.
    ☒ **A,** a broom closet, **B,** a reception desk, and **D,** a conference room, are all unsuitable locations because they do not restrict access to the equipment and do not provide the correct climate-controlled environment.

20. ☑ **D.** You should use cable trays to keep the wires organized within the ceiling area.
    ☒ **A,** an equipment rack, is incorrect because an equipment rack is not used within ceiling areas. **B,** a UPS, is incorrect because this is a power protection device, not something for organizing cables. **C,** cable wraps, is incorrect because although you could use these to organize cables, they are not mentioned in the chapter and are not the best solution for organizing cables within the ceiling.

17

Computer Security Fundamentals

W indows and other modern operating systems have a long list of security features, as well as other features we add to our operating systems. Chapter 15 described many security features and steps required to secure both a wireless and wired small office/home office (SOHO) network, covering all the topics in CompTIA Exam 802 Objectives 2.5 and 2.6. In addition, vendors update their software (OS, apps, and drivers) as they discover new vulnerabilities, and an entire multibillion-dollar industry has grown up to provide security products for home and business computers worldwide. It is a dangerous world out there, and today "out there" is everywhere.

No form of computing is safe from threats as long as a computer connects to any network; malicious code on flash drives—and even optical disks—can still infect those few that do not connect to networks. In this chapter, learn what the threats to your identity, to your data, and even to your hardware are. Prevention of threats to physical security will be covered in the second section in this chapter, while prevention of threats to data security will be included in Chapter 18.

CERTIFICATION OBJECTIVES

■ **802: 2.2** *Compare and contrast common security threats*

CompTIA Exam 802 Objective 2.2 requires that you compare and contrast common security threats, including social engineering, malware, rootkits, phishing, shoulder surfing, spyware, and viruses. Learn about these threats in this section.

Security Threats

We need to understand security threats in order to put security concepts, technologies, and features into context and then to implement strategies for protecting against those threats. What are the threats? In this section, we list and describe some that affect individuals and entire organizations, beginning with hardware theft and disaster threats. Then we look at threats to individuals in the form of inappropriate content and invasion of privacy that can also include identity theft. You'll learn about malicious software attacks and the long list of vectors (methods) they use to infect our computers, and then consider a list of threats that may or may not do damage that are called grayware. Finally, you'll consider the various methods used to gain access or gather information.

Computer Hardware Theft

People steal an astounding number of computers, especially laptops, tablets, and other mobile devices, each year from businesses, homes, and automobiles. The result is loss of important tools and valuable data files—and perhaps even a loss of identity, not to mention the downtime until equipment is replaced and programs and data are restored. At one time, most computer equipment thieves simply wanted to sell the hardware quickly for cash—at a fraction of the value of your computer and data to you or your business. Today, thieves realize the value of the data itself, so the data may be their main objective in stealing hardware; they will go through your hard drive looking for bank account, credit card, and other financial data so they can steal your identity.

Disasters, Big and Small

Accidents and mistakes happen. It seems as if everyone has at one time or another accidentally erased an important file, pressed the wrong button at the wrong instant, or created a file and thereafter forgotten its name and location. To the person who made the error, this is a disaster.

Disasters happen in many forms. Just to name a few, there are fires, earthquakes, and weather-induced disasters resulting from tornados, lightning strikes, and floods. There is, of course, the possibility of a disaster of an even greater magnitude, such as a nuclear explosion, with the obvious consequences of a bomb, but also with the resulting electromagnetic pulse (EMP). This huge burst of electromagnetic energy has the potential to damage communications and power lines over a large geographic area, depending on the size of the pulse and the proximity to electrical lines and equipment. Predicting such events is imperfect at best. The principal protection against accidents, mistakes, and disasters is to make frequent, comprehensive backups.

Threats to Individuals

All the threats described in this chapter affect individuals, but certain threats specifically target them. These threats include exposure to inappropriate content and invasion of privacy, which includes the worst threat: identity theft.

Exposure to Inappropriate Content

The Internet, and especially the World Wide Web, is a treasure trove of information. It is hard to imagine a subject that cannot be found somewhere on the Internet. However, some of this content is inappropriate or distasteful. What is inappropriate or distasteful content? To some extent, only an individual can judge, but there are many circumstances in which an individual or groups should be shielded from certain content.

Invasion of Privacy and Identity Theft

Many of the threats are also clearly invasions of privacy. Protecting against privacy invasion includes protecting your personal information at your bank, credit union, retail stores, and Websites, health clinics, and any organization where you are a customer, member, patient, or employee. Every step you take to make your computer more secure contributes to the protection of your privacy.

Perhaps the worst form of invasion of privacy is *identity theft,* which occurs when someone collects personal information belonging to another person and uses that information to fraudulently make purchases, open new credit accounts, and even obtain new driver's licenses and other forms of identification in the victim's name. All the thieves need is your Social Security number and other key personal information to steal your identity. They can do this by physically accessing your computer, by accessing it via the Internet, or by many other low-tech means. Several Websites maintained by the U.S. government offer valuable information for consumers who wish to protect themselves from identify theft.

Malicious Software Attacks

Malicious software, or *malware,* attacks are, sadly, now common on both private and public networks. Someone who initiates these malicious attacks is commonly called a *hacker* or *cracker.* They make an avocation or vocation out of creating ways to invade computers and networks. At one time, this term "hacker" described a clever programmer, or anyone who enjoyed exploring the software innards of computers.

You probably have heard of many types of software threats against computers, such as viruses, worms, Trojan horses, or spam. But have you ever heard of pop-up downloads, drive-by downloads, war driving, Bluesnarfing, adware, spyware, rootkits, backdoors, spim, phishing, or hoaxes? Do you know the difference between a vector and malware? Read on to learn about the many vectors and the various forms of deliberate attacks.

Viruses

A *virus* is a program installed and activated on a computer without the knowledge or permission of the user. At the least, the intent is mischief, but most often, the intent is malicious. Like a living virus that infects humans, a computer virus can result in a wide range of symptoms and outcomes. Loss of data, damage to or complete failure of an operating system, and theft of personal and financial information are just a few of the results of viruses infecting an individual computer. If you extend the range of a virus to a corporate or government network or portions of the Internet, the results can be devastating and costly in lost productivity, lost data, lost revenues, and more.

Denial-of-Service Attacks

Hackers and others with malicious intent have many methods for attacking network servers, and most of these techniques are beyond the scope of the CompTIA A+ Exams. However, two types of threats to servers are in the CompTIA A+ Acronyms list at the end of both the CompTIA A+ 220-801 and 220-802 Objectives. They are DoS and DDoS. A *denial-of-service (DoS) attack* occurs when someone sends a large number of requests to a server, overwhelming it so it stops functioning on the network, and therefore, denying service to all other traffic. A *distributed denial-of-service (DDoS) attack* occurs when a massive number (as many as hundreds of thousands) of computers send DoS attacks to a server, making it unavailable to legitimate users.

Rootkits

A *rootkit* is malware that hides itself from detection by anti-malware programs by concealing itself within the operating system (OS) code or any other program running

on the computer. Someone with administrator (root) access to the computer first installs a rootkit; then the rootkit is used as a vector to install any type of malware to quietly carry out its mission. "Rootkit" also refers to the software components of a rootkit.

W a t c h *For CompTIA Exam 802 Objective 2.2, be sure you know that a rootkit hides within the OS code.*

Malware Vectors

A *vector* is any method by which malware gains access to a computer or network. While some malware may use just a single vector, multivector malware uses an array of methods to infect computers and networks. Sometimes it is difficult to separate the vector from the malware, but we'll try. Let's look at a few well-known vectors. The first two, Trojan horses and worms, are each both a vector and virus.

on the
j o b *"Vector" is not a term you will see in the objectives for the CompTIA 801 and 802 Exams, but it is part of what you need to understand about how computers become infected so that you can work to educate yourself and others.*

Trojan Horse   A *Trojan horse*, often simply called a Trojan, is both a type of malware and a vector. The modern-day Trojan horse program gains access to computers much like the ancient Greek warriors who, in Homer's famous tale, *The Iliad*, gained access to the city of Troy by hiding in a large wooden horse, presented as a gift to the city (a Trojan horse). A Trojan horse program installs and activates on a computer by appearing to be a harmless program that the user innocently installs. It may appear as just a useful free program that a user downloads and installs, but it is a common way for malware to infect your system. One common example is a pop-up window that looks very official, like it is part of your OS, especially since it is titled Windows Advanced Security Center. This is an example of a *rogue antivirus*. It pretends to be an antivirus, but is actually a Trojan horse hiding malware. It states that it is scanning your computer and has already found threats. Then you may see a message box with a button labeled "Prevent Attack" or a message that you are using a trial version and must purchase the full version to ensure protection. Click Activate Ultimate Protection, and you'll go to a Website where you actually pay to install a Trojan on your computer. Some sources say this Trojan will steal your personal financial information. It also may install a proxy server to prevent access to the Internet.

Worm   A *worm* is a self-replicating virus. Worms travel between machines in many different ways. In recent years, several worms have moved from one computer to another as compressed (zipped) attachments to email, but they can also be executable files. The file might have an innocent-sounding or enticing name to tempt the user to open and execute the program. Some of these worms, upon execution, scan the local address book and replicate themselves to the addresses. Variants of such worms as Netsky and MyDoom slowed down entire networks just through the amount of network traffic they generated.

exam
Watch   *CompTIA Exam 802 Objective 2.2 lists just two types of viruses: worms and Trojans. Be sure you can distinguish between how each infects, even if the exam does not use the term "vector."*

Sneakernet   As old as PCs, if not older, *sneakernet* does not rely on networks but on removable storage inserted into a computer by someone simply walking up to it (in sneakers or other footwear). Sneakernet still exists today, but the storage device of choice is the flash drive, and the computers are usually also on a real network, which extends the risk when malware infects a single computer via a flash drive. In

August 2010 the U.S. Deputy Defense Secretary revealed that a flash drive, inserted into a U.S. military laptop in 2008 on a military post in the Middle East, was the vector for malicious code that caused a significant breach of military computers. News outlets reported the breach and cited anonymous Defense Department officials as stating that this attack originated from outside the United States.

Email   Some malware infects computers via email—mainly when the recipient opens an attachment or clicks a link. You may have believed it was always safe to open email as long as you didn't open attachments, but the simple act of opening an email containing the Nimda virus can infect a computer, depending on the software you are using to read the message. While most recent email programs have protections against that particular virus and other known viruses, email is still a potential vector, as long as people open attachments and click links.

The email vector often depends on convincing you that it is in your interest to click a link, perhaps by stating that Microsoft or another software publisher is sending you an update. Don't fall for this; Microsoft never sends out updates through email!

on the **()** o b

Remember that Microsoft never sends out updates through email!

Malware Installation Code on Websites   Some malware infects computers by lurking in hidden code on Websites. When an unsuspecting user browses to that site and clicks a link, it launches and installs malware on her computer without her knowledge. Clicking the link gives the program permission to run.

Searching for Unprotected Computers   An unprotected computer becomes a vector when discovered by malware that searches for computers with security flaws, takes advantage of the flaws to install itself on the computer, and then uses that computer to gain access throughout a private network.

Backdoor   In computing, a *backdoor* bypasses authentication security so someone can gain access to a computer. Sometimes a program's author installs a backdoor into a single program so she can easily access it later for administering and/or troubleshooting the program code. Or an attacker may create a backdoor by taking advantage of a discovered weakness in a program. Then any program using the backdoor can run in the security context of the invaded program and infect a computer with malware. In one well-known situation, the Code Red worm took advantage of a specific vulnerability in Microsoft's Internet Information Server (IIS) to install a backdoor. The result was that the worm displayed a message on every Web page on the IIS server. The message included the phrase, "Hacked by Chinese." Then, the Nimda worm took advantage of the backdoor left by the Code Red worm to infect computers.

Pop-up Download   A *pop-up* is a separate window that displays (pops up) uninvited from a Web page. The purpose of a pop-up may be as simple as an advertisement, but some pop-ups can be vectors for malware. A *pop-up download* is a program downloaded to a user's computer through a pop-up page. It requires an action on the part of a user, such as clicking a button that implies acceptance of something such as free information, although what that something may actually be is not usually clear. The program that downloads may be a virus or a worm.

Drive-by Download   A *drive-by download* is a program downloaded to a computer without consent. Often the simple act of browsing to a Website, or opening a Hypertext Markup Language (HTML) email message, may result in such a surreptitious download. A drive-by download may also occur when installing another application. This is particularly true of certain file-sharing programs that users install to share music, data, or photo files over the Internet. Some drive-by downloads may alter your Web browser home page and/or redirect all your browser searches to one site. A drive-by download may also install a virus, a worm, or even more likely, adware or spyware (described later in this chapter).

Spam and Spim   *Spam* is unsolicited email. This includes email from a legitimate source selling a real service or product, but if you did not give the source permission to send such information to you, it is spam. Too often spam involves some form of scam—a bogus offer to sell a service or product that does not exist or that tries to include you in a complicated moneymaking deal. If it sounds too good to be true, it is! We call spam perpetrators spammers, and spam is illegal. Some corporate network administrators report that as much as 60 percent of the incoming email traffic is spam. Most often, spam is a vector for social engineering, but it can also be used to deliver malware to your computer. Spam accounts for a huge amount of traffic on the Internet and private networks, and a great loss in productivity as administrators work to protect their users from spam and individuals sort through and eliminate spam. Use the steps in Exercise 17-1 to research spam statistics.

EXERCISE 17-1

Research Spam Statistics

Find out the latest bad news on the amount of Internet email identified as spam. Try this:

1. Open your browser and connect to your favorite search engine, such as Google, Bing, or Chrome.

2. Search on the words "spam statistics." For a more targeted search, include the current year in your search string.

3. In the results list, many of the links will be for antispam programs that provide individual statistics. Review the results and select a link that appears to give actual statistics on spam occurrences for Internet email users. Discuss the results with your classmates.

Spim is an acronym for *spam over instant messaging*, and the perpetrators are spimmers. Small programs, called bots (short for robot, a program that runs automatically) and sent out over the Internet to collect information, often collect instant messaging screen names. The spimbot then sends unsolicited instant messages to the screen names. A typical spim message may contain a link to a Website, where, like spam, the recipient will find products or services for sale, legitimate or otherwise.

Browser Hijacking   We received a call the other day from Dave, a finance officer at a large farm-implement company. Every time he opened Internet Explorer, the home page pointed to a site advertising adware removal software. This is an example of *browser hijacking* (also called *browser redirection*), a practice that has been growing. *Browser hijacker* malware infected his Internet browser, changing or redirecting the home page. It is not all about selling you adware removal software; there can be many reasons for browser hijacking. Sometimes they do it so that a Website will register more visitors and the owners of the site can raise their rates to advertisers.

Dave was able to reverse this by changing the default page in Internet Options, but it was very annoying. He was lucky; sometimes hijackers make it very difficult to defeat the hijack by modifying the registry so that every time you restart Windows or Internet Explorer the hijack reinstates. Or you may even find that a registry change makes Internet Options unavailable.

Email Hijacking Every week it seems like another friend or two has their email account hijacked, and these accounts are most often with one of the main Internet-based email providers, such as Yahoo! or Gmail. Email hijacking occurs when someone gains access to your email account by using some method to obtain the password, and then uses the account to send messages out to your entire contact list. This may be a one-time occurrence, or it may happen over and over again.

What are the symptoms? To the recipients of the email, the symptoms are most often a message with no subject line and the only content is a link. This is the most primitive use, but it can be effective, since if the hijacker does this on hundreds or thousands of accounts (they seem to have automated systems), sending messages out to all the contacts, the odds are many will click the link. This could result in installing malware, or it may simply be that the hijacker is being paid for the number of clicks on a page.

Other email hijackers are more sophisticated and send out messages with compelling subject lines, posing as your friends and claiming that they are stranded in a foreign country and need money wired to them immediately.

Grayware

The term *grayware* describes threats that are not truly malicious code, but which have indirect negative effects, such as decreasing performance or using up bandwidth. They are still undesirable, and computers should have protection against grayware, which includes spyware, adware, spam, and spim.

Spyware

Spyware is a category of software that runs surreptitiously on a user's computer in order to gather information without his or her permission and then sends that information to the people who requested it. Internet-based spyware, sometimes called "tracking software" or "spybots," may be installed on a computer by one of many means of secretly installing software. A company may use spyware to trace users' surfing patterns in order to improve its marketing efforts. Some individuals use it for industrial espionage. With appropriate legal permissions, law enforcement officers use it to find sexual predators and other criminals. Governments use forms of spyware to investigate terrorism.

Adware

Adware, which also installs on a computer without permission, collects information about a user in order to display targeted advertisements, either in the form of inline banners or pop-ups. Inline banners are advertisements that run within the context of the current page, just taking up screen real estate. Pop-ups are a greater annoyance, because each ad runs in a separate browser window that you must close before you can continue with your task. Clicking an offer presented on an inline banner or pop-up may trigger a pop-up download that can install a virus or worm.

Dialers

A *dialer* is a program that surreptitiously causes a modem to dial phone numbers. These are often pay-per-call or international numbers charged to the user's phone bill and benefitting the entity originating the dialer program.

Prank Programs

A *prank program*, also called a joke program, produces strange behavior, such as screen distortions, erratic cursor behavior, or strange icons on the screen. Even though normally these programs do not directly harm data, they are costly in lost productivity and time to rid the computer of the problem.

Methods for Gaining Access and Obtaining Information

People can gain access to computers and networks through a variety of techniques that include both physical access and malicious software and grayware. Here are just a few methods.

Piggybacking and Tailgating

Physical security can include restricting access to any area by having doors guarded, requiring security badges, and using a passkey of some sort to access the area. *Piggybacking* is when someone follows an authorized person into a secure area with their consent. When someone does the same thing without the authorized person's consent, perhaps slipping into a door behind the authorized person, it is *tailgating*.

Shoulder Surfing

One method people use to gain access to your bank account, computer and corporate network, and secure physical areas is by *shoulder surfing* to steal your security code, passcode, or other security credentials as you enter them, or even as you write them on a form. The most primitive example is someone peering over your shoulder to see the keystrokes you enter at the checkout counter, ATM cash machine, or the entrance to a secure building. The thief may literally be standing at your shoulder, or may be at a distance using binoculars. More sophisticated implementations

watch   *CompTIA Exam 802 Objective 2.2 specifically lists the term "shoulder surfing." Be sure you understand how thieves use this to steal security credentials.*

include using cameras or devices attached to the security keypad itself to log the keystrokes and either save the information for later retrieval, or transmit it wirelessly to the thief.

When sitting at your desk, your computer screen may also be a target of shoulder surfing, and the methods are the same as those used on ATM terminals.

Cookies—the Good and the Bad

Cookies are good—mostly. Under some circumstances people can use them for the wrong purposes, but for the most part, their benefits far outweigh the negatives. There is a great deal of misinformation about cookies, the small files a Web browser saves on the local hard drive at the request of a Website. The next time you connect to that same site, it will request the cookie saved on a previous visit. Cookies are text files, so they cannot contain viruses, which are executable code, but they may contain the following information:

- User preferences when visiting a specific site
- Information a user entered into a form at the Website, including personal information
- Browsing activity
- Shopping selections on a Website

The use of cookies is a convenience to users. Thanks to cookies, you do not have to reenter preferences and pertinent information on every visit to a favorite Website. The cookies act as electronic notes about your preferences and activities within a Website, remembering selections you have made on each page so when you return to the page you do not have to reselect them. Just one example of this is when you are at a retail site and make selections that you add to your "shopping cart." In all likelihood, cookies save these selections, and when you decide to check out, the checkout page reads the cookie files to calculate your order.

Although users are not overtly aware when the Website saves or retrieves cookies on the local hard disk, most good Websites clearly detail whether they use cookies and what they use them for. Look for this information in the site's privacy policy statement.

Normally, only the Website that created the cookies can access them; these are called first-party cookies. However, some advertisers on Websites have the browser create cookies, and then other sites that include this advertiser can use them. These are third-party cookies.

If you dig around in your browser's settings, you will find not only the settings for controlling cookies, but a list of the cookies themselves. In Chapter 18 you will learn how to configure cookie settings in your browser. Figure 17-1 shows a list of Websites with cookies saved by the Chrome browser. We expanded one to show more information. To find this list in Chrome, do the following:

1. Click the wrench icon on the right of the navigation bar to open a menu.
2. Select Settings, which opens a Settings page within the browser window.
3. Scroll to the bottom and select Show Advanced Settings.
4. Scroll down to Privacy and click the Content Settings button.
5. On the Content Setting page, click All Cookies And Site Data.

FIGURE 17-1

A list of saved cookies by site, with one site expanded

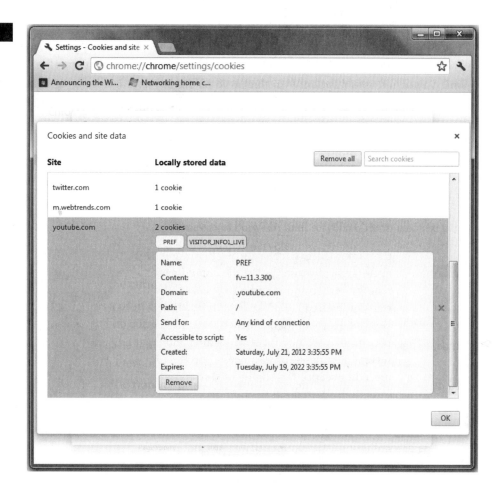

Password Theft

People use a huge number of programs and techniques to steal passwords, and once they have one password, they have access to at least one source of information or money, and maybe more. We will explain a few of those techniques.

Unsecured Websites   One commonly used technique is to invade an unsecured Website to access information unwitting users provide to the site, such as user names and passwords, and such personal information as account numbers, Social Security number, birthdate and place, and much more.

Password Crackers   A huge number of programs and techniques are available to people who want to discover passwords. In addition to invading an unsecured Website, another technique is to use a *password cracker*, a program used to discover a password. Some password crackers fall into the *brute-force* category, which simply means the program tries a huge number of permutations of possible passwords. Because most people tend to use simple passwords such as their initials, birthdates, addresses, pets' names, and so on, the brute-force method often works. Other password crackers use more sophisticated statistical or mathematical methods to discover passwords.

on the
① o b

If you enter the words "password cracker" into your favorite search engine, you will discover that there are password crackers for every operating system, every type of computing device, and all the social networking services in use today.

Keystroke Loggers   A *keystroke logger* (also called a *keylogger*) is either a hardware device or a program that monitors and records a user's every keystroke, usually without their knowledge. In the case of a hardware logger, the person desiring the keystroke log must physically install it on the computer before recording keystrokes, and must then remove it afterward in order to collect the stored log of keystrokes. Some keyloggers transmit pressed keystroke data in real time wirelessly to a receiver unit. A software keystroke logger program may not require physical access to the target computer, but simply a method for downloading and installing it on the computer. Any one of several methods—for instance, a pop-up downloader or drive-by downloader (see the preceding sections)—can be used to install a keystroke logger. A keystroke logger can send the collected information over a network to the person desiring the log.

Some parents install keystroke loggers to monitor children's Internet activity, but such programs have the potential for abuse by people with less benign motives, including stalking, identity theft, and more.

Social Engineering

Social engineering encompasses a variety of persuasion techniques used for many purposes—both good and bad. People with malicious intent use social engineering to persuade someone to reveal confidential information or give something else of value to the perpetrator. The information sought may be confidential corporate data, personal identifying or financial information, user names and passwords, or anything you can imagine that could be of value to another person.

Social engineering is as old as *Homo sapiens*, and there are countless techniques employed; everyone should learn to recognize these techniques, all of which depend on the natural trusting behavior of the targeted people. Once you understand the forms of social engineering threats, you are less likely to become a victim. We will now explore social engineering threats and appropriate responses. On the Internet, the most common vehicle for social engineering communications is email.

The best response to any form of social engineering is to not respond and/or not reveal any information. And you should never send money in response to a communication from a stranger, no matter how enticing the offer may be.

Fraud   *Fraud* is the use of deceit and trickery to persuade someone to hand over money or valuables. Fraud is often associated with identity theft, because the perpetrator will falsely pose as the owner of the victim's credit cards and other personal and financial information.

Phishing   *Phishing* is a fraudulent method of obtaining personal and financial information through pop-ups, email, and even letters mailed via the Postal Service, that purport to be from a legitimate organization, such as a bank, credit card company, retailer, and so on. They often (falsely) appear to be from well-known organizations and Websites, such as various banks, eBay, PayPal, MSN, Yahoo!, Best Buy, or America Online. As such, the typical phishing attack relies on a *hoax*, meaning that it uses deception and lies to gain your confidence.

In a typical phishing scenario, the message will contain authentic-looking logos, and an email may even link to the actual site, but the link specified for supplying personal financial information will take recipients to a "spoofed" Web page that asks them to enter their personal data. The Web page may look exactly like the company's real Web page, but it's not the legitimate site. A common practice is for a phisher to use the credit card information to make purchases over the Internet, choosing items that are easy to resell, and having them delivered to an address unconnected to the phisher, such as a vacant house to which he has access.

Be very suspicious of emails requesting personal financial information, such as access codes, Social Security numbers, or passwords. Legitimate businesses will never ask you for personal financial information in an email.

To learn more about phishing, and to see the latest examples, point your Web browser to www.antiphishing.org, the Website of the Anti-Phishing Working Group (APWG), which reports that every possible measurement of phishing activity shows huge increases. For instance, the number of unique phishing Websites detected in February 2012 was 56,859. You can report phishing attacks at this site.

Would you recognize a phishing email? There are Websites that work to educate people to recognize a phishing scam when they receive it in email or other communications. Exercise 17-2 describes how to use just one of these sites.

EXERCISE 17-2

What Is Your Phishing IQ?

You can test your Phishing IQ and learn to identify phishing scams.

1. Use your Web browser to connect to the Phishing IQ test at www.sonicwall.com/phishing.

2. You will see ten emails, one at a time. You must decide whether each is legitimate or phish.

3. When you finish, you can review the correct answers, along with a detailed explanation as to why each is either legitimate or phish.

If you completed Exercise 17-2, you will have noticed that phishing emails look very official, but in some cases, careful scrutiny reveals problems. Although the signs identified in these messages are not the full extent of the problems you can find in a phishing email, this type of test helps to educate people so they do not become victims of phishing.

Although not all phishing emails have the same characteristics, the following lists just a few problems detected in phishing emails:

- The "To:" field is not your address, even though it appeared in your inbox.
- There is no greeting, or the greeting omits your name.
- The message text shows bad grammar or punctuation.
- When you click a link, the Uniform Resource Locator (URL) you are directed to does not match what appears in the email.

■ A link does not use Hypertext Transfer Protocol Secure (HTTPS).

■ The title bar reveals that a foreign character set (e.g., Cyrillic) is used.

■ What appears to be a protected account number (revealing only the last four digits) is not your number at all.

■ What appears to be an account expiration date is not the correct expiration date for your account.

■ A URL has a slightly misspelled domain name that resembles the legitimate domain name.

■ There is no additional contact information, such as a toll-free phone number and a name and title of a contact person.

Now, to make things more confusing, some legitimate emails may show some of these problems or practices, and not all phishing emails have all of these negative characteristics.

A safer way to include a URL in a legitimate email is not to make it a link, but to include it in the email as unformatted text, with instructions to cut and paste it into a Web browser. This way, malware cannot redirect you to a bogus Website, but you must still be diligent and examine the URL before using it.

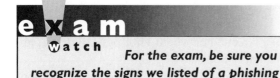

For the exam, be sure you recognize the signs we listed of a phishing email.

Phone Phishing   Phone phishing is another form of phishing. In order to gain the intended victim's confidence, a phishing email will urge the reader to call a phone number to verify information, at which point the person on the phone will ask the victim to reveal the valuable information.

What makes this so compelling to the user is that phone phishing often involves a very authentic-sounding professional Interactive Voice Response (IVR) menu system, just like a legitimate financial institute would have. It may ask the user to enter his password or personal identifying number (PIN). To ensure that the system captures the correct password or PIN, the system may even ask the victim to repeat it. Some systems then have the victim talk to a "representative" who gathers more information.

on the
job

Keep yourself up to date on the latest threats. Microsoft, Symantec, Trend Micro, and other software vendors, particularly those who specialize in security products, offer a wealth of information on their Websites. You can also subscribe to newsletters from these same organizations.

Enticements to Open Attachments   Social engineering is also involved in the enticements—called "gimmes" in emails, either in the subject line or the body of the email—to open the attachments. Opening the attachment then executes and infects the local computer with some form of malware. There are a huge number of methods used. Sadly, enticements often appeal to basic characteristics in people, such as greed (an offer too good to be true), vanity (physical enhancements), or simple curiosity. Some bogus enticements appeal to people's sympathy and compassion by way of a nonexistent charity. Or the author of the email will pose as a legitimate charity—anything to get you to open the attachment.

War Driving

War driving is the name given to the act of driving or walking through a neighborhood in a vehicle or on foot, using either a laptop equipped with Wi-Fi wireless network capability or a simple Wi-Fi sensor available for a few dollars from many sources. War drivers are searching for open hotspots, areas where a Wi-Fi network connects to the Internet without using security to keep out intruders. Using a practice called *war chalking,* a war driver may make a mark on a building where a hotspot exists. People "in the know" look for these marks to identify hotspots for their use.

People who use these hotspots without permission are trespassing, and, in addition to gaining Internet access, they can prey on unprotected computers on the wireless network. With this access to the network, the intruder can capture keystrokes, passwords, and user names. Further, if the wireless network connects to an organization's internal wired network, the intruder may gain access to the resources on that network.

Intentionally created hotspots are increasing in number as more and more are made available for free or for a small charge by various businesses, such as coffee shops, bookstores, restaurants, hotels, and even campgrounds and truck stops. In fact, city-sized areas are now hotspots made with overlapping Wi-Fi signals.

Bluesnarfing

Similar to war driving, *Bluesnarfing* is the act of covertly obtaining information broadcast from wireless devices using the Bluetooth standard. Using a cell phone with Bluetooth enabled, a Bluesnarfer can eavesdrop to acquire information, or even use the synchronizing feature of the device to pick up the user's information without being detected by the victim.

SCENARIO & SOLUTION

What type of threat uses deceit and trickery to gain money or valuables?	Fraud is the use of deceit and trickery to persuade a person to give up money or valuables. Fraud is a crime.
What is the term used to describe a software attack that captures keystrokes, usually without the user's knowledge?	Keystroke logger
Phishing, phone phishing, hoaxes, and enticement to open attachments are all examples of techniques used to persuade someone to reveal confidential information or give something else of value to the perpetrator. What is the term used for this?	Social engineering

CERTIFICATION OBJECTIVES

- **802: 2.1**   *Apply and use common prevention methods*

- **802: 2.4**   *Given a scenario, use the appropriate data destruction/disposal method*

CompTIA Exam 802 Objective 2.1 has four topic areas. We will detail physical security in this section and describe user education, digital security, and the principle of least privilege, the other three topics in that objective, in Chapter 18.

CompTIA Exam 802 Objective 2.4 includes tasks required to destroy the old data on a computer when you no longer need that computer. Whether you are giving it away to be used again, moving it to another user's desk in your organization, or disposing of the equipment, you need to ensure that you are not giving away personal or organizational data. A portion of this objective is the physical destruction of the storage device, and we describe those tasks in this section. This objective also includes the use of software in the form of formatting, overwriting, and drive wipe, which we will cover in Chapter 18.

Defense Against Threats: Physical Security

Physical security begins when an individual approaches the entrance to a building or campus. The level of security and the lengths to which an organization will go to secure an area depend on what they are protecting. Many organizations do not require any type of authentication until an employee is logging onto their computer—which is digital security. Others secure only small areas of their buildings, while some require authentication before you can access a campus or larger geographic area. Think of a government installation, manufacturing facility, or research institute. In this section we will look at some methods used to prevent unauthorized physical access to areas ranging in size from a computer closet to an army base.

If an unauthorized person manages to gain access to one of these areas—how do they secure the documents? We will discuss the methods for securing digitally stored documents in Chapter 18, but what about the data visible on screens and on paper documents? That is another facet of physical security, and we will address that in this section as we examine methods to secure access to paper documents and on-screen data.

Lock Doors and Enforce Policies

Locked doors and physically secured computers are the best protection from computer hardware theft. You can achieve locked doors against unauthorized access with low-tech methods ranging from limiting distribution of keys to the physical locks to other methods as low tech as human guards at entrances examining conventional badges as people enter and leave, to high-tech solutions for authentication at entrances using smart cards, radio frequency identification (RFID) badges, key fobs, Rivest, Shamir, Adleman (RSA) tokens, or biometric authentication.

You can secure special equipment such as switches, routers, and servers inside locked areas, but the typical desktop computer or laptop cannot always be physically secured. There are devices for physically securing computers, such as kiosk enclosures, but you rarely see them in use except in high-risk environments, such as schools and public buildings.

Preventing Piggybacking and Tailgating

Campuses and buildings with restricted areas need to guard against piggybacking and tailgating practices, mentioned earlier in the description of threats. If using guards, an organization must train them to not allow this. Authorized employees must agree not to participate in piggybacking (bringing in unauthorized people) and to watch out for people following them closely in the hopes of tailgating. Using surveillance video may be necessary, along with having personnel monitor the video and taking action, watching both who comes in and who leaves.

Badges

A simple paper or plastic ID badge, with photo, is a traditional method for gaining access to areas with security guards at entrances. But unless the badge also contains one of the other technologies discussed here, such as a smart card, or RFID, it is not very good security, especially in a large facility where the guards may not recognize individuals well enough to challenge badge holders.

Smart Card Authentication

A *smart card* is a plastic card, often the size of a credit card, that contains a microchip. The microchip can store information and perform functions, depending on the type of smart card. Some smart cards only store data, whereas others may have a variety of functions, including security cards for gaining physical access to facilities or logging on to computers and networks. If configuration of the Windows domain and local Windows computers allows acceptance of smart card logons, users may use this method of presenting credentials and logging on. The domain controllers require certain software security components, and the local computer must have a special piece of hardware called a *smart card reader* or card terminal. When the user inserts the card into the reader, the reader sends commands to the card in order to complete the authentication process. As is true of a bank cash card, the user may also need to enter a PIN into the keyboard in conjunction with the smart card. The two together comprise two-factor authentication.

on the **job**

A user cannot use a smart card when required to join his or her Windows XP computer to a domain, but smart cards are supported in Windows Vista and Windows 7.

Setup will require the device itself and the drivers and other software for the device. Further, you must install a special service called *Certificate Services* on the domain controllers for the Windows domain. Once you have installed the reader and configured the domain controllers to support Certificate Services, users can log on to the computer. Inserting the card into the reader has the same effect as pressing the CTRL-ALT-DELETE key combination, which is normally required on a Windows computer logging onto a domain. Either action constitutes a *secure attention sequence* (*SAS*) that clears memory of certain types of viruses that may be lurking and waiting to capture a user name and password. Smart cards are a very secure and tamper-resistant method of authentication.

Modern debit and credit chip cards are smart cards. While American banks have been slow to move away from the old magnetic-strip technology for credit and debit cards, Europe moved to smart cards for debit and credit several years ago. These are considered safer than the magnetic-strip cards, which only require a signature.

RFID Badges

Another variation of smart card authentication includes *radio frequency identification (RFID) badges*. These cards contain an RFID chip (also called an RFID tag) with a radio antenna that can be carried by employees to allow access to secured facilities or computer systems, and which can also be used to track user activity and location. These badges work wirelessly within a few meters and do not depend on line-of-sight communication—this tends to be more convenient than swipe cards. More important, no physical contact with the authenticating device is required, as long as the RFID badge is within range of the device. You can also tie RFID badge authentication to the user network account to simplify administration.

Key Fobs

Much like a smart card, a *key fob* is a small device containing a microchip, and you can use it for gaining access to a secure facility or for logging on to a computer or a network. Also called a security token, it has a form factor that suggests something you might attach to a key chain, as its name implies. A common procedure for using a key fob is to enter the PIN, which identifies the user as the owner of the key fob. Then, the key fob displays a string of characters, and the user enters the string into a keypad terminal or computer to gain access. This string is a *one-time password (OTP)*. The key fob generates a different password at a prespecified interval, and this guarantees that the user has a unique, strong password protected from the vulnerabilities of ordinary user-generated passwords, which may be too easy to guess, or which the user may write down somewhere to avoid having to memorize.

Examples of key fobs are the RSA SecurID hardware security tokens from RSA Security, referred to in CompTIA Exam 802 Objective 2.1 as *RSA tokens*. These are very popular for authenticating to virtual private networks (VPNs), although you can also use them to authenticate to email, your Windows desktop, and so on. To authenticate to a server, the user enters their PIN, and the device generates a numeric value every 60 seconds that corresponds to a server-side numeric value. RSA Security owns the *Rivest Shamir Adleman (RSA)* encryption and authentication system, named for the creators Ron Rivest, Adi Shamir, and Leonard Adleman.

It is used in the company's key fobs and in many apps, such as Web browsers and accounting systems.

Installing support for a key fob involves installing an agent that runs on the local computer and a service on the Active Directory domain controllers. The agent acts as a front end to the authentication process, passing encrypted authentication information to the domain controller that responded to the authentication request. On the domain controller, the service decrypts the password and provides the password and the user name to the Active Directory security components for authentication. If the password and user name match a domain user account, the user is allowed access to the resources that she has been granted permissions and rights to.

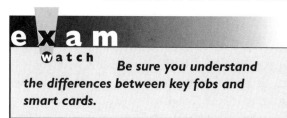

Be sure you understand the differences between key fobs and smart cards.

Biometric Authentication

Users can easily forget passwords or PINs and lose smart cards. But each person can be uniquely identified by measurements of body parts—a biometric. These are used both for physical access to buildings or areas and for logging into computer networks. A logon based on one of these measurements is a biometric logon. Commonly used biometrics include fingerprints, handprints, and *retinal scans* (a scan of the retina in a person's eye). A hardware device, such as a *retina scanner* or *fingerprint scanner* (also called a *fingertip scanner*), performs that scan. A fingerprint scanner is the least expensive of the biometric devices. The built-in fingerprint scanners are the size of a Universal Serial Bus (USB) port, with a slender scanning slot. External USB fingerprint scanners are available from several vendors.

Biometric scanners require both drivers and software to integrate with the computer's or network's security system to send the scanned information to the security components for processing. If the computer is a member of a domain, you must install special software on the domain controller servers. The software will update the domain accounts database with the biometric information for each user account for which this type of logon is enabled. Anyone traveling with a laptop with sensitive data should look into purchasing a laptop with a built-in fingerprint scanner.

Follow the manufacturer's instructions for installing the software and hardware. After installing the software, configure it to recognize your fingerprint and associate it with your user account. To do this, you will need to provide a user name and password. If your computer is a member of a workgroup, you will need to provide either the computer name or the workgroup name. If your computer is a member of a domain, you must provide the domain name and your user name and password in the domain. When the configuration utility is ready to scan your fingertip and associate it with your user account, it will prompt you. To do this, swipe your finger across the scanner's sensor. You can scan one or more fingers and use any one of them for login. In most cases, the scanner's associated software will also save passwords for applications and Websites and associate them with your profile.

Securing Physical Access to Documents

Securing physical access to documents can begin with the access to a building or area, described earlier, requiring some form of authentication with a password or one of the authentication devices. In addition, there are methods for guarding against shoulder surfing, securing documents in locked storage, shredding documents, and disposing of used equipment after removing all data and then following environmentally safe disposal methods.

Guarding Against Shoulder Surfing

The low-tech way to guard against shoulder surfing is to attach a privacy filter to any screen that may be targeted, including ATMs, desktop PCs, and laptops. Privacy filters narrow the screen's viewing angle, which ensures that only the person sitting directly in front of the system can view the screen contents.

Locked Storage for Documents

Confidential documents should be in a secure area or in locked containers. You should also control access to these areas with the methods discussed earlier.

Shredding Paper Documents

Private individuals and organizations combined generate many tons of waste paper each year. Much of that is in the form of documents holding confidential information of some sort, from credit card information on receipts to individual health status information to corporate secrets. The answer is to be diligent about shredding these paper documents and properly disposing of them. Individuals and small companies can purchase inexpensive cross-shredding devices that render the documents nearly impossible to reassemble and can feel safe disposing of this with the rest of their trash, as long as they comply with any recycling ordinances or regulations. It is, after all, a great deal of paper waste. Government agencies must use more sophisticated shredding devices and then usually dispose of the shredded documents by having them burned.

Equipment Disposal and Removal of Data

How does your organization dispose of old computer equipment? This is a topic described in Chapter 1 in regard to keeping discarded computer equipment out of the waste stream, recycling components, and disposing of hazardous waste contained in computers and related equipment. Whatever the policy on equipment disposal, it should include thorough removal of all data from hard drives and destruction of optical media containing data. The best practice is to destroy all the data on the hard drives before sending them to a recycler. Ordinary deletion of the files in Windows will not permanently delete these files, even if you reformat the hard drives. Therefore, use a program that will truly erase all the data from the hard drives so it is not recoverable, even with very sophisticated tools. We call this process drive sanitation, and we will describe tools you can use for this in Chapter 18 as part of digital security.

If you do not have the option of using a software tool to destroy data on old equipment, then you have other options for physically destroying the data, depending on your budget. A hand power drill is something everyone can buy from a hardware store, and unless your drives contain government secrets or data that is worth millions (or at least hundreds of thousands) of dollars, aggressively attacking a hard drive (or SSD storage) will render the data irretrievable. Of course, the power drill method will cause metal bits and pieces to fly out of the target, so it does pose some risks to the individual doing it. Wear safety glasses, gloves, and protective clothing.

Yet another tactic is to use an electromagnetic device such as a degaussing tool to remove storage from hard drive platters. These devices are costly, running from several hundred for a simple handheld wand to several thousand dollars for a powerful device into which you insert a hard drive or tape drive; it first erases the data through degaussing and then physically crushes the storage device.

exam
watch
CompTIA Exam 802 Objective 2.4 lists both electromagnetic and degaussing tools as if they are two separate methods for physically destroying *data. Be prepared for questions that discuss electromagnetic data destruction as well as degaussing tools.*

CERTIFICATION SUMMARY

A computer professional must understand the threats to people, computers, and networks. These include malicious software, social engineering tactics, and many others. To that end, this chapter began with an overview of the various threats.

Also, old hardware should be disposed of in a way that is environmentally sound (described in Chapter 1), but before disposing of old hardware, remove sensitive data previously stored on hard drives and other storage devices.

TWO-MINUTE DRILL

Here are some of the key points covered in Chapter 17.

Security Threats

❑ Hardware theft results in the loss of important tools and valuable data files—and perhaps even a loss of identity, not to mention the downtime until equipment is replaced and programs and data are restored.

❑ Disasters that affect computers, networks, and data come in many forms, including accidents, mistakes, and natural and unnatural disasters.

❑ Identity theft occurs when someone collects personal information belonging to another person and uses that information to fraudulently make purchases, open new credit accounts, and even obtain new driver's licenses and other forms of identification in the victim's name.

❑ The wealth of information on the Internet also includes information that is generally distasteful or inappropriate for some individuals, such as children.

❑ Malicious software attacks are common on both private and public networks. Some forms include viruses, password crackers, worms, Trojan horses, keystroke loggers, pop-up downloads, and drive-by downloads.

❑ Grayware is a term for threats that are not true malicious code but which can have indirect negative effects, such as decreasing performance or using up bandwidth. Grayware includes spyware, adware, spam, spim, dialers, and prank programs.

❑ Perpetrators use a variety of methods for gaining access and obtaining information. Some common methods include backdoors, war driving, and Bluesnarfing.

❑ Cookies are small files a Web browser saves on the local hard drive at the request of a Website. Most cookies are harmless first-party cookies that are not program code but small text files, and they can normally only be read by the Website that created them.

❑ Some advertisers on Websites create cookies that the program code from the same advertiser can read from other Websites. These are third-party cookies, and you can configure a Web browser to disable third-party cookie reading.

❑ Social engineering involves a variety of techniques used to persuade someone to reveal confidential information or give something else of value to the perpetrator. Phishing, phone phishing, hoaxes, and enticements to open attachments all employ persuasive social engineering tactics.

❑ Fraud is the use of deceit and trickery to persuade someone to hand over money or valuables.

Defense Against Threats: Physical Security

❑ Campuses and buildings with restricted areas need to guard against piggybacking and tailgating practices.

❑ A smart card is a plastic card, often the size of a credit card, that contains a microchip. The microchip can store information and perform functions, depending on the type of smart card.

❑ Another variation of smart card authentication includes radio frequency identification (RFID) badges. These cards contain an RFID chip (also called an RFID tag) with a radio antenna that can be carried by employees to allow access to secured facilities or computer systems, and which can also be used to track user activity and location.

❑ Commonly used biometrics include fingerprints, handprints, and retinal scans.

❑ A key fob is a small device containing a microchip that you can use for gaining access to a secure facility or for logging on to a computer or a network. Examples of key fobs are the RSA SecurID hardware security tokens from RSA Security that are very popular for authenticating to VPNs.

❑ Government agencies must use more sophisticated shredding devices and then usually dispose of the shredded documents by having them burned.

❑ A smart card reader requires software and drivers on the local computer and Certificate Services installed on the domain controllers for the Windows domain.

❑ A user cannot use a smart card when required to join his or her Windows XP computer to a domain; Windows Vista and Windows 7 supports smart cards.

❑ Both the built-in and external biometric devices require drivers and software to integrate with the computer's security system.

❑ Control access to restricted spaces, equipment, files, folders, and other resources of the organization.

❑ Privacy filters narrow the screen-viewing angle, which ensures that only the computer user can view the screen contents.

❑ A variety of authentication technologies is available. Just a few include ordinary logons using the standard keyboard, smart-card logons, key-fob logons, and biometric logons. RFID badges wirelessly authenticate the carrying user to secured resources such as floors within a building or locked doors.

❑ When disposing of old computer equipment, be sure to remove all data from hard drives using an acceptable disk-wiping program and destroy optical media containing confidential data. Recovery from an attack depends on how well you prepared by making good backups and protecting against the threats outlined in this chapter.

SELF TEST

The following questions will help you measure your understanding of the material presented in this chapter. Read all of the choices carefully, because there might be more than one correct answer. Choose all correct answers for each question.

Security Threats

1. What is the term for the activity that results in someone using your personal information to obtain new credit or credentials?
    A. Virus
    B. Identity theft
    C. Trojan horse
    D. Social engineering

2. Netsky and MyDoom were this type of virus, which replicates itself, moving from computer to computer.
    A. Trojan horse
    B. Password cracker
    C. Worm
    D. Keystroke logger

3. What is the term used to describe the delivery of malicious code to a user's computer through a pop-up window in a Web browser?
    A. Worm
    B. Grayware
    C. Trojan horse
    D. Pop-up download

4. Which of the following is a category of software that runs surreptitiously on a user's computer to gather personal and financial information without the user's permission, and then sends that information to the people who requested it?
    A. Spam
    B. Spyware
    C. Adware
    D. Spim

5. Which of the following is a term for unsolicited email?
    A. Spyware
    B. Spam
    C. Backdoor
    D. Worm

6. What type of program attempts to guess passwords on a computer?
    A. Keystroke logger
    B. Password cracker
    C. Virus
    D. Fraud

7. What type of malware is installed by an administrator and hides from detection by anti-malware programs by concealing itself within the OS code or other program code?
    A. Rootkit
    B. Bluesnarfing
    C. Cookies
    D. Phishing

8. Web browsers save these small text files on the local computer at the direction of programs on a Website.
    A. Backdoor
    B. Spam
    C. Cookies
    D. Prank programs

9. Someone using this method may steal your password or key code as you enter it at the ATM, grocery store checkout, or security door.
    A. Trojan Horse
    B. Bluesnarfing
    C. Tailgating
    D. Shoulder surfing

10. This threat installs on a computer without permission and collects information about a user in order to display targeted advertisements.
    A. Spam
    B. Spyware
    C. Adware
    D. Spim

11. The symptom of this threat is that your Web browser home page changed from the one you selected, pointing to a site advertising some product.
    A. Rootkit
    B. Sneakernet
    C. Spam
    D. Browser hijack

12. This term describes the practice of closely following someone into a restricted area without the authorized person's permission.
    A. Piggybacking
    B. Sneakernet
    C. Tailgating
    D. Trojan horse

13. This is the general term for any method malware uses to gain access to a computer or network.
    A. Vector
    B. Trojan horse
    C. Worm
    D. Sneakernet

14. You may install this type of malware because it appears to be a harmless program.
    A. Spam
    B. Worm
    C. Trojan horse
    D. Rootkit

15. This type of attack overwhelms a server with so much traffic that it stops functioning.
    A. DoS
    B. Worm
    C. Backdoor
    D. Pop-up download

16. This term describes the questionable practice of an authorized person bringing an unauthorized person into a restricted area.
    A. Piggybacking
    B. Sneakernet
    C. Tailgating
    D. Trojan horse

Defense Against Threats: Physical Security

17. In its most common use, this device uses a PIN and generates a new password every time a PIN is entered.

   A. Smart card

   B. Key fob

   C. Biometric logon

   D. Keyboard

18. What type of device will allow people access to secured facilities or computer systems as long as the device is within several feet of the authenticating device?

   A. Key fob

   B. RFID badge

   C. Badge

   D. Fingerprint scanner

19. Which of the following is a simple physical-security device for protecting on-screen data from prying eyes?

   A. Privacy filters

   B. Shredding

   C. Key fob

   D. Degaussing

20. Which of the following is a popular encryption and authentication system used in key fobs as well as many apps, such as Web browsers and accounting systems?

   A. RSA

   B. SPIM

   C. DoS

   D. Degaussing

SELF TEST ANSWERS

Security Threats

1. ☑ **B.** Identity theft is the term for activity that results in someone using your personal information to obtain new credit or credentials.

   ☒ **A** and **C** are incorrect because they are both malicious code, not an activity. **D,** social engineering, is incorrect because it is the use of persuasion techniques for many purposes. Social engineering may be involved with identity theft, but the two terms do not identify the exact same behavior.

2. ☑ **C.** A worm (Netsky and MyDoom were worms) is a type of virus that replicates itself, moving from computer to computer.

   ☒ **A,** Trojan horse, is incorrect because this is a type of virus that hides within an apparently harmless program. A worm, like any other virus, can transfer to a computer as a Trojan horse. **B,** password cracker, is incorrect because this program attempts to discover passwords. **D,** keystroke logger, is incorrect because this program logs the user's keystrokes.

3. ☑ **D.** Pop-up download describes the delivery of malicious code to a user's computer through a pop-up window in a Web browser.

   ☒ **A** and **C** are both incorrect because they are types of viruses, not the method for delivering a virus. **B,** grayware, is incorrect because this describes threats that are not truly malicious code but that still have indirect negative effects.

4. ☑ **B.** Spyware is a category of software that runs surreptitiously on a user's computer to gather personal and financial information without the user's permission.

   ☒ **A** and **D** are both incorrect because they represent unwanted messages—spam being unwanted email and spim being unwanted instant messaging messages. **C,** adware, is incorrect because, although it also installs on a computer without permission and collects information, it collects information in order to display targeted advertisements.

5. ☑ **B.** Spam is a term for unsolicited email.

   ☒ **A, C,** and **D** are all incorrect because they are examples of malicious program code and grayware, not email. The email could contain malicious code, but that is not part of the definition.

6. ☑ **B.** Password crackers attempt to guess passwords on a computer.

   ☒ **A** is incorrect because a keystroke logger does not try to "guess" passwords—it tries to *steal* passwords by capturing keystrokes. **C,** virus, is incorrect because a virus is a very general term for malicious code. **D,** fraud, is incorrect because this is the use of deceit and trickery to persuade someone to hand over money or valuables. It does not match the narrow definition of guessing passwords.

7. ☑   **A.** Rootkit is malware installed by an administrator that hides from detection by anti-malware programs by concealing itself within the OS code or other program code.

☒   **B,** Bluesnarfing, is incorrect because this is the act of covertly obtaining information broadcast from wireless devices using the Bluetooth standard. **C,** cookies, is incorrect because cookies are not program code, and they do not allow access to an operating system. **D,** phishing, is incorrect because phishing is a fraudulent method of obtaining personal and financial information through pop-ups or email messages that purport to be from a legitimate organization.

8. ☑   **C.** Cookies are small text files saved by a Web browser on the local computer at the direction of programs on a Website.

☒   **A,** backdoor, is incorrect because this program code is used for an entirely different purpose. **B,** spam, is incorrect because spam is unsolicited email. **D,** prank programs, is incorrect because these are programs, and they do not serve the same purpose as cookies.

9. ☑   **D.** Shoulder surfing is the method of watching over your shoulder (from nearby or long range with binoculars) while you enter a password or key code.

☒   **A,** Trojan horse, is incorrect because this program appears to be a harmless and desirable program that you install, but malware is installed with it. **B,** Bluesnarfing, is incorrect because this is the act of covertly obtaining information broadcast from wireless devices using the Bluetooth standard. **C,** tailgating, is incorrect because this is the practice of following an authorized person into a secure area without permission.

10. ☑   **C.** Adware is a threat that installs on a computer without permission and collects information about a user in order to display targeted advertisements.

☒   **A** and **D** are both incorrect because they represent unwanted messages—spam being unwanted email and spim being unwanted instant messaging messages. **B,** spyware, is incorrect; spyware is software that runs surreptitiously on a user's computer and gathers personal and financial information without permission.

11. ☑   **D.** Browser hijack is a change in your Web browser home page.

☒   **A,** rootkit, is incorrect because an administrator installs rootkit malware. **B,** sneakernet, is a term for infecting computers by walking up to them and using infected removable drives, and **C,** spam, is unwanted email.

12. ☑   **C.** Tailgating is the practice of closely following someone into a restricted area without the authorized person's permission.

☒   **A,** piggybacking, is incorrect because it describes the practice of an authorized person bringing an unauthorized person into a restricted area. **B** and **D** are incorrect because both describe malware vectors.

13. ☑ **A.** Vector is the general term for how malware gains access to a computer or network.
    ☒ **B, C,** and **D** are all incorrect because Trojan horse, worm, and sneakernet are individual examples of vectors.

14. ☑ **C.** Trojan horse is correct because it appears to be a harmless program.
    ☒ **A,** spam, is incorrect because this is unwanted email. **B,** worm, is incorrect because a worm is malware that self-replicates over a network. **D,** rootkit, is incorrect because an administrator installs a rootkit, which often resides in the OS code, giving access to malware.

15. ☑ **A.** A denial-of-service (DoS) attack sends so much traffic to a server that it stops functioning.
    ☒ **B, C,** and **D,** are all incorrect because worm, backdoor, and pop-up download are examples of vectors.

16. ☑ **A.** Piggybacking is the practice of an authorized person bringing an unauthorized person into a restricted area.
    ☒ **B,** sneakernet, is incorrect because it is a term for infecting computers by walking up to them and using infected removable drives. **C,** tailgating, is incorrect because it is the practice of closely following someone into a restricted area without the authorized person's permission. **D,** Trojan horse, is incorrect because it is a vector for infecting computers.

Defense Against Threats: Physical Security

17. ☑ **B.** A key fob is a device that uses a PIN and generates a new password every time a PIN is entered.
    ☒ **A,** smart card, is incorrect because, although it may be similar to a key fob, people don't generally use it in the manner described in the question. **C,** biometric logon, is incorrect because it uses a body measurement for authentication. **D,** keyboard, is incorrect because you cannot use a keyboard in the manner described in the question.

18. ☑ **B.** RFID badges authenticate users to secured resources wirelessly as long as the RFID badge is within range of the authentication device.
    ☒ **A,** key fob, is incorrect because it commonly requires that the person carrying it enter a PIN, and then it displays a one-time password (OTP) to enter for access. **C,** badge, is incorrect because a traditional badge would require that a guard inspect it before allowing someone access. **D,** fingerprint scanner, is incorrect because it is a hardware device, interfaced with a computer, which scans a fingerprint and transmits the scan for authentication.

19. ☑ **A.** A privacy filter is a simple device that fits over a screen and prevents unauthorized screen viewing.

☒ **B,** shredding, is the destruction of paper documents. **C,** key fob, is a device for gaining physical access to a building or logging onto a computer. **D,** degaussing, is the electromagnetic erasure of magnetically stored data.

20. ☑ **A.** Key fobs and many apps use the RSA (Rivest Shamir Adleman) encryption and authentication system.

☒ **B,** spim, is unwanted email over instant messaging. **C,** DoS (denial of service), is an attack that sends so much traffic to a server that it stops functioning. **D,** degaussing, is the electromagnetic erasure of magnetically stored data.

18

Implementing Digital Security

T he security story is complex, which is why we spread it out over several chapters. We mentioned security topics, at least briefly, in every chapter, with more detail in some, such as Chapter 15, which detailed how to install a small office/home office network. An important part of installing a network includes immediately securing it. Therefore, we detailed all the topics of CompTIA A+ Exam 802 Objectives 2.5 and 2.6 in Chapter 15. Then, Chapter 17 described all the security threats listed in CompTIA A+ Exam 802 Objectives 2.2, plus a portion of other security objectives. We continue the security story in this chapter, in Chapter 19, and in Chapter 20, with a small coverage of security for printers in Chapter 21.

CERTIFICATION OBJECTIVES

- **802: 1.4** *Given a scenario, use appropriate operating system features and tools*

- **802: 1.5** *Given a scenario, use Control Panel utilities*

- **802: 1.8** *Explain the differences among basic OS security settings*

- **802: 2.1** *Apply and use common prevention methods*

- **802: 2.3** *Implement security best practices to secure a workstation*

    Chapter 17 described a long list of security threats. Then it detailed options for physical security and how to implement them, a topic of the CompTIA Exam 802: 2.1 Objective. In this section, we will look at more (but not all) of the remaining topics in that objective, including user education, user authentication, strong passwords, and the principle of least privilege. CompTIA Exam 802: 2.3 lists seven best practices to secure a workstation, and we describe them in this section. In this section, we will also address one topic in CompTIA A+ Exam 802 Objective 1.5 when we describe the User Accounts Control Panel applet, common to all versions of Windows that are included in the CompTIA A+ 801 and 802 Exams. Then, we will detail several topics from the CompTIA 802: Objective 1.8. They include users and groups and user authentication.

Implementing Authentication for Digital Security

In Chapter 17, you learned the options for implementing physical security. In this section, learn how to implement the various methods of digital security, authentication, and data security.

Security Policies and Education

In Chapter 1, you learned about acceptable-use policy, also called a *security policy*, which defines what is acceptable use of all resources of the organization, of which computer equipment and data are important parts. It includes both physical and digital security, whether employees are on the organization's property or not. Therefore, a small part of this policy will be a remote access policy for how you access the network when out of the office. If you have not been informed about an acceptable-use or security policy, inquire about it because all organizations should have this spelled out and should educate all employees on the exact policies. In the United States, the *Health Insurance Portability and Accountability Act (HIPAA)* and other government regulations have made security policies mandatory for many organizations in the healthcare or finance industries. For instance, HIPAA includes a Privacy Rule that defines what medical information is protected and how and when it can be used and disclosed. There are significant civil and criminal consequences to organizations and individuals who fail to comply.

There is a category of information, called *personally identifiable information (PII)*, that can be used to uniquely identify an individual. PII includes many pieces of information ranging from the obvious, such as name, birthdate, and Social Security Number, to a person's email address, home address, telephone number, schools attended, family pets, and much more. This information is scattered all over the Internet on social networking sites, as well as in what should be private databases, such as those maintained by healthcare providers, schools, and businesses. People use various means to gather this information and then use it for their own gain. This is yet another reason for a security policy that protects this information—whether it is your own information or that of clients, customers, and patients.

A security policy is not effective if no one is informed about the policy and the consequences of not complying. Flip back to Chapter 1 and review this information. As an IT professional, whenever you interact with client users you have an opportunity to educate them about threats, symptoms, protections, and recovery. In Chapter 17, we placed a few reminders within the text and one On-the-Job note reminding you to do just that. This is a bigger reminder that an educated user actively participates in the security policy and is aware of how to behave to avoid certain threats and how to notice symptoms and take action to recover on their own. This means better security and privacy for the client and fewer calls for help.

Implementing Authentication Security

Windows requires authentication for access to a PC, and that is usually accomplished by authenticating using a local account or a domain account. A *local account* is a security account in the local accounts database, while a *domain account* resides in a database on a Windows domain controller server. However, you can also set a password that must be entered before a PC launches an operating system—a basic input/output system (BIOS) password. In this section, you will look at how these are set. We also describe how to use the Lock Computer option in Windows to protect your computer.

Authentication and Authorization

Access control to resources on a local computer or over a network involves *authentication* (verifying a user's identity) and *authorization* (determining the level of access an authenticated user has to a resource). One of the first defenses against security threats is authentication and authorization by security systems built into the operating systems on your local computer and network servers. Windows desktop operating systems (OSs) support authenticating with a local account on a Windows computer that is a member of a workgroup. Recall from Chapter 14 that a workgroup is a term used by Microsoft for a peer-to-peer network in which each computer can be either a file-and-printer sharing client or server or both. There is no central authentication with a workgroup. To have central authentication, a Windows computer, must be a member of a Microsoft domain, which we will describe in Chapter 19.

Passwords   We have used the term password many times in the previous chapters of this book, but until now, we have not stopped to define it. A *password* is a string of characters that a user enters, along with an identifier, such as a user name, in order for authentication to take place. This security tool is an important one for anyone who uses a computer, especially one connected to any network, including the Internet. Do not take your passwords for granted! You may have habits or practices that make you vulnerable to identity theft and other threats. Consider the following questions:

- Do you have too many passwords to remember?
- When you have an opportunity to create a new password, do you use your favorite password?

- Do you have your password written on sticky notes or your desk calendar at school or work?
- Have you used the same password for more than a few months?

If you answered "yes" to any of these questions, you are at risk, and you need to change your behavior.

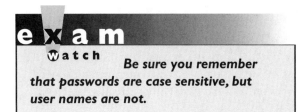

w a t c h *Be sure you remember that passwords are case sensitive, but user names are not.*

The Windows authentication system does not require case sensitivity for user names, but it does for passwords. So, as long as you enter the correct characters for your user name, case does not matter. Case is very important for passwords, which is why Windows login will warn you when the CAPS LOCK key is turned on.

Authentication Technologies   In the vast majority of cases, especially in a small office/home office environment, people are authenticated to computers and networks with a user name and password. This is a standard interactive logon and does not require any special hardware, as the user name and password can be entered using the keyboard or, in the case of someone with special needs, an adaptive input device.

Organizations requiring more stringent authentication practices for protecting digital access will use specialized technologies, such as smart cards, radio frequency identification (RFID) badges, key fobs, and biometric scanners. All of these technologies, discussed in Chapter 17 as methods to use for physical security, also apply to digital security and provide more secure authentication at an additional cost, but the costs are decreasing, and the technologies are becoming more widespread. Chapter 17 described how to install each type.

Authentication Factors   The actual information or device used for authentication verification is an *authentication factor*. There are three categories of authentication factors: something you know, something you have, and something you are. An example of something you *know* is a user name and password or a personal identification number (PIN). Something you *have* may be a smart card, and something you *are* may be a measurement of a body part (a biometric), such as a fingerprint or retina scan. Authentication involves one or more of these factors, so you can have one-factor, two-factor, or three-factor authentication.

Local User and Group Accounts

Windows requires authentication and authorization and, therefore, requires that each user have an account. In a Windows network, the account can be a local account or a centralized domain account. Of course, whenever possible, use centralized accounts so each user only needs to log on to the centralized database for authentication, and, as he or she attempts to access resources on other computers in the domain, the system performs authorization to verify the user's level of access to the resource.

Each installation of Windows for desktop PCs, laptops, and tablets maintains a local accounts database containing *local user accounts* and *local group accounts*. A user account represents a single person, whereas a local group account can contain multiple users and other groups. When the computer is a member of a Windows domain, a local group may contain domain users or domain group accounts to give domain users and groups access to resources on the local computer. Logging on with a local account only gives you access to the resources on that computer, although you may have access to other resources on your network through relationships we will describe in Chapter 19.

Windows 8 allows you to sign in with a *Microsoft Account,* which is an email and password that are your credentials to an account with one of Microsoft's online services, such as Xbox LIVE or SkyDrive. You are still signing on with a local account because the Microsoft Account is associated with the local account. The benefit is that you have access to local resources as well as all online resources granted to the Microsoft Account.

When any user logs on to a Windows computer for the first time, a local user profile is created for that user as well as a set of personal folders for that user's data. A *user profile* includes registry settings for all personal settings for that user.

Each version of Windows surveyed in this book, from Windows XP through Windows 8, has two graphical user interface (GUI) tools for administering local accounts—one that is very simplified and hides many accounts and the complexity from you, and another that lets you see all local user and group accounts. As you read this section, you may want to open one or both of these tools. In Windows XP, Windows Vista, and Window 7, the simple tool is User Accounts. User Accounts is similar, but not identical across these versions. They have added many more features in the Windows 7 version, shown in Figure 18-1. The contents pane on the right contains links to allow you to make changes to your account. Because the logged-on user is an administrator, the contents pane also includes two links that only an administrator can use: Manage Another Account and Change User Account Control Settings (learn about User Account Control Settings later in this chapter). The task pane on the left contains links to more tasks.

The simpler tool in Windows 8 is the Users page of the PC Settings tool in the new Windows 8 user interface. In all versions, the more complex tool has remained much the same, and it is the Local Users and Groups node of the Computer Management console, shown in Figure 18-2. To open this in Windows XP, Windows Vista, or Windows 7, click Start, right-click My Computer/Computer, and select Manage.

Windows 7 User
Accounts

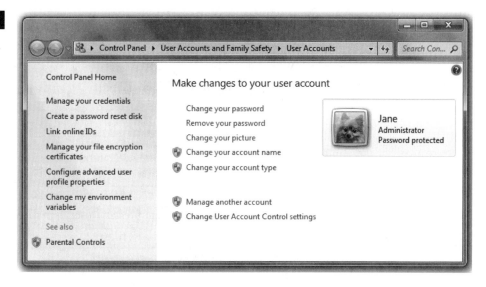

Built-in Accounts Windows also has several built-in user and group accounts, plus the installation of certain services and applications automatically creates some users and groups needed for the service or program, but not necessarily directly used by a human user. While there are several built-in groups, the important group accounts to understand are Administrators, Users, Guests, and Power Users.

The *Administrators* group has full control over the entire system and can perform all tasks on a computer, from installing a device driver to creating other security accounts. Any account added to this group gains those permissions. *Administrator*

The Windows 7
Computer
Management
console showing
the Local User
and Groups node

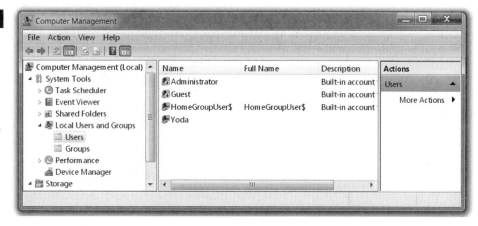

is a built-in account that is a member of the Administrators group. It cannot be renamed, disabled, or deleted. Administrators can

- Create any type of local user account
- Change permissions for any local user account
- Modify any local user account
- Install new hardware and software
- Run any program
- Modify all system settings
- Upgrade and repair Windows
- Back up and restore Windows system files and user data files
- Take ownership of any other local user's files
- Manage security and auditing logs

When you allow multiple users to perform administrative functions on a computer (or network), rather than use the built-in Administrator account, make their individual account a member of the Administrators group. Then, if you ever need to find out who performed a certain administrative action (most are automatically logged), they will be identified in the logs by their unique user name.

The built-in *Users* group has limited permissions, preventing members of this group from making system-wide changes, although they can run most applications that do not try to change system settings.

The *Guests* group has the same limited permissions of the Users group, but the default member of this group, the built-in *Guest* account, is further restricted to have fewer privileges than granted by the Guests group and it is disabled by default. You cannot delete this account, but you can rename and disable it. Another name for this type of account is *anonymous,* as used with older File Transfer Protocol (FTP) sites that did not require a user logon to upload and download files. When a member of the Guests group logs on, a user profile and personal folders are created for that user, but are immediately deleted when the user logs off.

on the **job**

Do you wonder why there is a Guest account? The notion of a Guest account began many years ago as a way to give individuals access without having them enter a user name or password and with very limited privileges. Use of the Guest account is discouraged, since, for audit logging purposes, it is difficult to determine who performed which action.

Next learn about account types and your personal Windows user account.

The *Power Users* group was created before Windows had the protection of User Account Control, and it therefore was useful in Windows 2000, Windows XP, and Windows Server 2003. Since Windows Vista and the introduction of User Account Control, this group is only included for backward compatibility. The Power Users group has more permissions than the Users group, much less than the Administrators group, and has no default members. A member of Power Users can

- Create local users and groups
- Modify local user and group accounts created by that power user
- Remove users from the Power Users, Users, and Guests groups
- Install most applications
- Create, manage, and delete local printers
- Create and delete file shares

Account Types   Windows has the notion of types of user accounts that it uses to simplify account creation when you use the User Accounts utility on Windows XP, Windows Vista, and Windows 7. A *standard user account* (called a *limited account* in Windows XP) is appropriate for an "ordinary" user without administrator status. This account is a member of the local Users group. A user logged on with a standard account can change her password and other personal settings, but cannot change computer settings, install or remove software and hardware, or perform other system-wide tasks. In contrast, a user logged on with an account that is an *administrator account* type, called a computer administrator in Windows Vista and Windows 7, can perform system-wide tasks. Windows 8 does not mention standard user account, but when you log on as a member of the Administrators group and use the Users page of PC Settings, the only type of new account you can create is a member of the local Users group, even if you choose to create a new Microsoft Account. Of course, if you logged on as an administrator in Windows and convert your local account to a Microsoft Account, that account will be associated with your existing account, which is a member of the local Administrators group.

Your User Account   The rule has been that a user should not use the Administrator account as a day-to-day account. This is because prior to Windows Vista, if you logged on with an account belonging to the Administrators group (the Administrator account or other account), a program could install without your knowledge and run with full administrative rights to your computer. That is how a lot of malware infected Windows. Beginning in Windows Vista, Microsoft added User Account Control (UAC), a feature that alerts the user—even an administrator—when a program attempts to install or make other unauthorized changes to Windows. Later in this chapter, you will learn more about UAC, including how it works and how to configure it. Because UAC guards against the old threat, Windows Vista, Windows 7, and Windows 8 now keep the Administrator account hidden in User Accounts, but create another account during installation that is a member of the Administrators group and seen in User Accounts. This is the account for which you provide a user name and password as you install Windows. In Windows XP, you are asked to provide a password for the Administrator during Windows installation, and this is the account you first log on with, but you should create a separate user account for yourself, make it a limited user, and use it for day-to-day work, logging off and logging on as an administrator when you need to do advanced tasks.

exam
⓪atch *Local accounts always exist on Windows computers, whether the computer is a member of a workgroup or in a domain.*

Windows Vista, Windows 7, and Windows 8 automate the process of creating the third account at the end of setup, or in the case of preinstalled Windows, you will be prompted to provide a user name and password the first time you start up your new computer. This account is a member of the Administrators group.

Special Groups   *Special groups* are groups created by the Windows' security system, and no user can create or modify these accounts. The membership of a special group is predefined, and the group is available to you only when you assign permissions or rights. A few important special groups are *Creator Owner* (membership consists of the user who created a file or folder), *System* (the operating system), and the *Everyone* group, which includes all users on a network, even those who have not been authenticated.

Windows Logon

The versions of Windows included on the A+ exams always require a logon, meaning you must provide a user name and password that are verified against a security database, either local or on a server on the network. Even your home computer that perhaps boots up right to the Windows desktop without asking for a user name or password is actually performing a logon. If your computer is not a member of a Windows domain, but rather a member of a workgroup (a Windows computer must be a member of one or the other), and you are only logging on to the local computer, then it is possible to configure it to start up right to the desktop. This scenario occurs when there is only one user account on a computer and it does not have a password assigned to it—a very unsecure situation, but typical for a home computer. The system simply supplies the user name and blank password to the Windows security system during logon.

The next step up, security-wise, is the Welcome screen, introduced with Windows XP and continuing in Windows Vista and Windows 7, which says "Welcome." This screen is only available if the computer is not a member of a Windows domain. The Welcome screen shows the names of all the local user accounts (except Administrator and Guest) and only requires that you select the user name and enter the password. Windows 8 has a sign-in screen similar to the Welcome screen, where you enter your user name and password.

The last logon method is the Security dialog box. If a computer is a member of a domain, it uses the Security dialog box by default, and another level of security requires the user to press the CTRL-ALT-DELETE key combination before this dialog box will appear. To log on, you enter your user name, password, and (when appropriate) domain name into this box. Figure 18-3 shows the Windows XP Log On To Windows dialog including the Log On To box, in which you can select to log on locally to the computer or use the down arrow to select a domain to log onto.

Figure 18-4 shows the log-on screen for Windows 7 in which the user, Administrator, is logging on to the domain Lachance.local. Do not be confused by the use of

FIGURE 18-3

This Windows XP dialog box allows the user to log on to the local computer or to a domain.

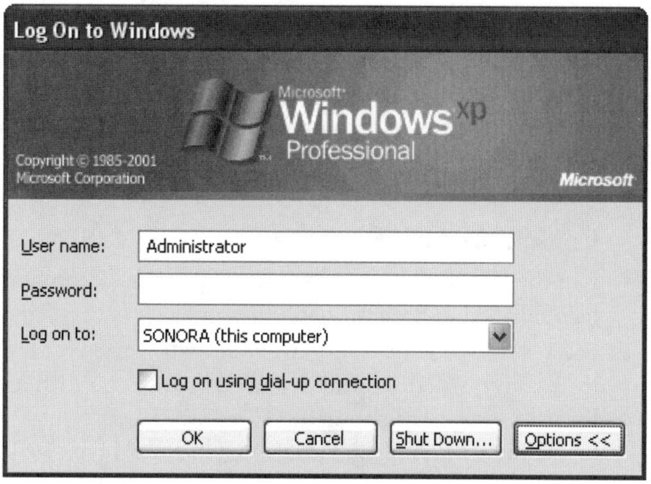

FIGURE 18-4

The Windows 7 log-on screen showing the user Administrator logging on to the domain Lachance.local

"local" in the domain name. For a domain that is restricted to a private network, an organization may use an invalid top-level domain name (TLD) that Internet DNS servers will not allow, such as "local," in place of a valid TLD (such as .com, .biz, and so on) to distinguish and separate the private network from the publicly accessible network. The public network can use a domain name that is identical to the internal domain, with the exception of the TLD name, which must be a valid top-level domain name.

Lock Computer

Use the Windows Lock Computer option to secure your desktop quickly, while leaving all your programs and files open. It is very simple to do. Before leaving your computer unattended, simply press WINDOWS KEY-L. This will lock the computer; the desktop will disappear, replaced by a screen with a message that the computer is locked. Figure 18-5 shows the Windows 7 lock screen. The word "Locked" appears below the user name and above the password box. When you return to your desk,

This Windows 7 computer is locked until someone enters the correct password.

simply enter your password and your desktop appears. Use this when you must leave your desk for a little while, like when you go to lunch. Do not use this when you leave for the day, unless that is required by your employer's security policy.

on the *job*

Remember that Lock Computer is a better practice than enabling the password for the screen saver, even though a screen saver–required password is listed as a best practice in the CompTIA 802 Exam Objective 2.3.

BIOS Passwords/DriveLock/TPM

As described in Chapter 3, you can set one or more passwords in system BIOS. For example, BIOS may have three types of passwords: one type restricts access to the computer itself; another type restricts access to the BIOS Setup; and a third, less common type, restricts access to hard drives, a feature called "DriveLock" on HP computers. We will use this term to apply to all such implementations. As a further enhancement, an embedded Trusted Platform Module (TPM) chip restricts access to hard drives, providing more advanced security.

BIOS Passwords for Setup and Startup   Recall from Chapter 3 that many BIOSs allow you to set a password that must be given before anyone can change

BIOS settings, and many allow you to set a separate password required to start up the computer. The first is reasonable if a computer is in an environment where people may tend to tamper with the BIOS settings. An example would be in a student lab. The second is a bit extreme unless security requirements dictate this.

To set a BIOS password for setup or startup, check the manual for the motherboard, and then go into the BIOS Setup program and navigate to the correct setting; it may simply be called "Set Password." Selecting this option will open a password dialog, in which you enter the new password. On another screen, you configure the password requirement for setup and/or startup.

DriveLock   Some manufacturers provide a BIOS DriveLock feature that allows you to set a password that you must provide at startup. This password is stored on the hard drive, which means that even if you move the drive to another computer, it will be inaccessible. With some implementations, if you use the same password for BIOS startup and DriveLock, you will only need to enter the password once to complete the startup; otherwise, you will need to enter two passwords.

TPM   A more sophisticated method is to store the cryptographic keys for encrypting and decrypting disk volumes in an embedded Trusted Platform Module (TPM) chip as described in Chapter 3. With TPM enabled, the user might optionally have to enter a PIN at bootup. If the PIN is correct, TPM decrypts the disk volume and allows the bootup to continue. If the drive is removed from the computer and installed into another computer, it will not be accessible unless the encryption data was transferred from the original TPM chip to the new TPM-enabled computer. TPM can also verify that the hardware boot sequence has not been tampered with.

The Windows BitLocker Drive Encryption feature (available in Windows Vista and Windows 7 Enterprise and Ultimate editions) works with TPM to secure drive contents, although this is just an option, and you can choose to use a password or smart card for unlocking the drive. The Windows BitLocker To Go feature that encrypts flash drives does not use TPM, but lets you configure it to use either a password or smart card to store the password.

When you install the Ultimate or Enterprise versions of Windows Vista or Windows 7 or Windows 8 Pro on a computer with a TPM 1.2 chip on the motherboard, Windows Setup will automatically enable

---

e x a m

ⓦ a t c h   *Make sure you don't confuse BitLocker with Microsoft's Encrypting File System (EFS); EFS encrypts specified files and folders on NTFS disk partitions, whereas BitLocker encrypts entire disk drives. For the utmost data storage security, consider using both.*

BitLocker and install the BitLocker applet in Control Panel; otherwise, you will need to enable it yourself.

Windows Credential Manager

Windows Vista, Windows 7, and Windows 8 allow storage of credentials to automatically log on to servers, Websites, and certain applications. These are stored in local folders, called *vaults*. The user of these locally stored credentials provides a *single sign-on (SSO)*, meaning that a user only need provide credentials (usually user name and password) once and have access to multiple resources. They added the *Credential Manager* Control Panel applet in Windows 7 to allow you to directly manage your credentials. Figure 18-6 shows the Windows 7 Credential Manager. We expanded one of the credentials—for connecting to a computer named W8-64-LAPTOP in a HomeGroup—so that you can see the links to edit or remove these credentials. The

FIGURE 18-6

Credential
Manager in
Windows 7

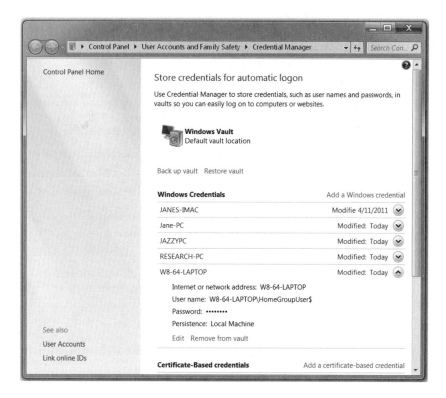

Edit option allows you to change the user name and password. In Chapter 19, you will learn how to create and connect to a HomeGroup.

Best Practices to Secure a Workstation

Here are some best practices for securing a Windows workstation. They are listed in CompTIA A+ Exam 802 Objective 2.3.

Require and Set Strong Passwords   Require and use passwords wherever possible, and there is no reason to use passwords if you are not going to use strong passwords. A *strong password* is one that meets certain criteria in order to be difficult to crack. The criteria change over time as people with malicious intent (hackers) create more and more techniques and tools for discovering passwords. One definition of a strong password is one that contains at least eight characters; includes a combination of letters, numbers, and other symbols (_, -, $, and so on); and is easy for you to remember but difficult for others to guess.

For instance, some people take a song title or part of the lyrics from a favorite song, remove the spaces, and substitute numbers for some of the letters. For instance, the lyrics "Dance while the music goes on" (from the ABBA song "Dance") would turn into the password "dan2ewh1lethemu3i2g0es0n." The longer the better, and if nonalphanumeric characters are permitted, throw in a few of them, too, to make it even stronger.

Use strong passwords for the following account types:

- Banks, investments, credit cards, and online payment providers
- Email
- Work-related
- Online auction sites and retailers
- Sites where you have to provide personal information

Every account should have a unique user name (if possible) and a unique password (always). Many Websites require your email address as the user name, so these will not be unique.

Enable Screen Saver Password   If you have sensitive data on your computer, or available to your user account over a network, and if you use a screen saver, be sure to require that you must log on again to resume. You should also shorten the wait period if you are using your screen saver rather than locking your computer (in our view, Lock Computer is a better practice). Then if you walk away from your computer and the screen saver turns on, it will require a password to return to the desktop. Otherwise, anyone passing by your desk can simply touch the mouse and keyboard, and then access everything on your local computer and network that you can access.

To enable this in Windows Vista and Windows 7, open Control Panel and type **screen saver** in the Search box. In the results list, select Change Screen Saver. This will open the Screen Saver Settings dialog shown in Figure 18-7. Click to place a check in the check box in the middle of the dialog box labeled On Resume, Display Logon Screen.

To enable the screen saver password in Windows XP, right-click an empty area of the desktop, and select Properties. In the Display Properties dialog box, click the Screen

Enable On
Resume, Display
Logon Screen.

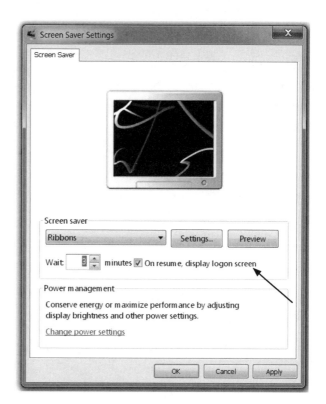

Saver tab. On the Screen Saver page, select a screen saver and click to place a check in the check box in the middle of the dialog box labeled On Resume, Password Protect.

Restrict User Permissions   Use of the HomeGroups method in Windows 7 or Windows 8 for sharing files in a small office/home office (SOHO) network gives those who have access to your computer complete control over the folders or printers to which they are granted access. However, there are other methods you will learn about in which you may apply permissions in such a way that someone has less than full control to a file, folder, or printer, giving each person or group just the level of permission they need to accomplish their work without giving them too much. This is the *principle of least privilege*. Learn more about the different methods for sharing resources over a network and about applying levels of permissions in Chapter 19.

Change Default User Names   You learned in Chapter 15 that when configuring a wireless access point (WAP) or broadband router, you should change the default administrator user name and password. These devices usually come with an administrator user name of Admin, and changing it and the password makes access to that device more secure because someone would need to guess the user name as well as the password. Unfortunately, you cannot do this on the many Websites that require that you use your email address as a user name, but you do have this option on devices, such as those mentioned, and you should always change such default user names.

Disable Guest Account   By default, Windows disables the local Guest account. However, it doesn't hurt to know how to disable it in case you discover it enabled on a computer. In Windows XP, Windows Vista, and Windows 7, open the User Accounts Control Panel applet and select Manage Another Account. The Manage Accounts page will normally only display two accounts: the account created when installing Windows, and the Guest account, as shown in Figure 18-8, in which the status of the Guest account is off. If the account is on (enabled), there will be no mention of that status in this dialog box. Notice that the other user account does not indicate that it is on, but it is. If you discover that the Guest account is turned on, double-click it and select Turn Off in the Turn Off Guest Account dialog box.

Disable Autorun/AutoPlay   The feature called *Autorun* in earlier versions of Windows, but now called *AutoPlay*, enables Windows to automatically find and run the content on removable media when it connects to a computer. Over the years, this feature was expanded so that if you open the AutoPlay applet in Control Panel, you will find a long list of media and content types, and you can choose exactly how each is treated when it is placed in your computers. However, this can make you

FIGURE 18-8

This Guest
account is
disabled.

vulnerable to malware infections, because removable media is a vector for malware. The safest thing to do is to disable AutoPlay, and simply choose the action you want each time you place removable media in your computer. Figure 18-9 shows the Windows 7 AutoPlay Control Panel applet with an arrow pointing to the check box you should clear to disable this feature.

FIGURE 18-9

To turn off
AutoPlay in
Windows 7,
clear the check
box labeled Use
AutoPlay For
All Media And
Devices.

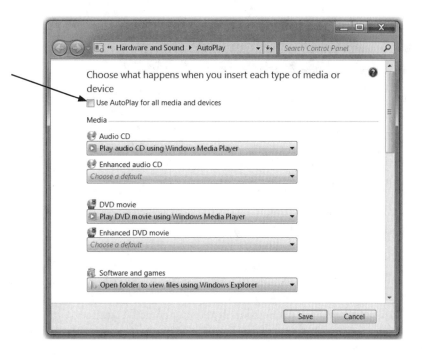

SCENARIO & SOLUTION

I am preparing a new computer for a computer lab. How can I configure the computer so students will not be able to access the system setup and change the BIOS settings, making the computer unusable?	Check out the manufacturer's documentation on the computer's system settings and look for the password settings. Set the password to the BIOS Settings menu only. Do not set the password on system startup unless the security policy for the computer lab requires this.
We are getting ready to order ten laptops for traveling auditors who will have sensitive data on the hard drives. We are looking for a secure authentication method beyond a simple user name and password for basic interactive logon to a Windows domain. What do you recommend?	Since you are in the process of purchasing the laptops, check out biometric devices, such as fingerprint scanners. These are more secure than the basic interactive logon and work with a Windows domain.
Our employees' computers are in a public area where customers and others can easily wander in and out. Employees must frequently leave their computers unattended during the workday for brief periods. How can they keep their desktops secure without shutting down their applications and Windows?	We suggest you show the employees how to use Windows' Lock Computer option.

CERTIFICATION OBJECTIVES

- **802: 1.5** *Given a scenario, use Control Panel utilities*

- **802: 2.1** *Apply and use common prevention methods*

- **802: 4.7** *Given a scenario, troubleshoot common security issues with appropriate tools and best practices*

In this section we will continue the coverage of topics from CompTIA Exam 802: Objective 2.1, including antivirus, firewalls, and antispyware. The last topic from this objective, directory permissions, is included in Chapter 19. In this section, we will also address one topic in CompTIA A+ Exam 802 Objective 1.5 when we describe the security functions in the Internet Options Control Panel applet, a utility common to all versions of Windows that are included in the CompTIA A+ 801 and 802 Exams. Finally, learn about the common symptoms listed in CompTIA Exam 801 Objective 4.7 as well as the best practices for malware removal, also listed in that objective.

Implementing a Defense Against Malware

There are many small building blocks to an effective defense against malicious software. It begins with educating yourself about threats and defenses and setting up a foundation of secure authentication and data protection techniques, and continues with placing a firewall and related technologies at the junction between a private network and the Internet. Then, each computer in the private network must use a group of technologies, such as software firewalls and programs that detect and remove all types of malware, to protect it from attacks.

Self-education

Research malware types, symptoms, and solutions to keep yourself informed. Check out the many *virus encyclopedias* on the Internet sponsored by many different organizations, including security software manufacturers such as Trend Micro, Kaspersky, and Symantec. Despite the use of the word "virus," these lists contain all types of known threats and are always up to date. Threat Encyclopedia is the title of the list maintained by Trend Micro, a security software manufacturer. Also look for antivirus support forums, which include information about threats other than viruses.

Such resources categorize the malware by type and describe symptoms and solutions. The Website www.av-comparatives.org contains lists of antivirus support forums and virus encyclopedias. The U.S. government maintains excellent general information on all types of threats to computers at the United States Computer Emergency Readiness Team (US-CERT) Website at www.us-cert.gov/cas/tips/.

Network Access Control

A significant percentage of workers access their employer's network from outside—often over the Internet. Similarly, many organizations have temporary contractors working for them. Allowing access from outside the private network can open an organization to all types of threats, and an organization with very high security needs may implement some form of *network access control* (NAC). A NAC is a group of practices for securing a private network from outside access by restricting the resources available, beginning with a specialized server called a *network access server (NAS)*. Connection to a NAS is often via a secure virtual private network (VPN), and the NAS performs authentication and authorization services. Several vendors offer NAC solutions, including both hardware and software, which include several security functions. At minimum, a NAC solution includes firewall, antivirus, antispyware, authentication, and authorization functions.

Protecting Windows Files and Programs

Windows has many built-in protections as described in Chapter 10. Windows XP protects essential system files and programs using the Windows File Protection (WFP) service. Windows Vista/7 use the Windows Resource Protection (WRP) service, which also protects critical registry keys. Then again, Windows itself also has features that can be pathways for malware infections. The Autorun/AutoPlay feature described earlier in this chapter is one of them, and disabling it is a recommended best practice.

User Account Control

Malware often runs in the background without user consent, making system changes and installing itself. To prevent this, Microsoft added User Account Control (UAC) in Windows Vista, and improved it in Windows 7 and Windows 8. UAC can prompt the user when this happens to prevent malicious code from running unknown in the background. With UAC enabled, you can expect two scenarios. In the first, a user logged on with a name and password that is a member of the Administrators group only has the privileges of a standard account (member of the Users group), until the user (or a malicious program) attempts to do something that requires higher privileges. At that point, UAC makes itself known, graying out (dimming) the desktop, and displaying the *Consent Prompt* (see Figure 18-10), with a message concerning the action. Click Continue or Yes (depending on the message) to allow the action. You can choose to cancel the action by clicking No. If you click Yes, the task runs with your administrative privileges, and you return to working with standard privileges in other programs.

on the **job**

UAC does not remove the need for antivirus and antispyware tools.

In the second scenario, a user logs on with the privileges of a standard user and attempts to do something that requires administrative privileges. In this case, UAC displays the *Credentials Prompt* (Figure 18-11) requiring the user name and password of an account with administrative privileges. If you provide these, the program or task will run with these elevated privileges, but you will return to the standard user privileges for all other activities. In either case, if you do not respond in a short period of time, UAC will time out, cancel the operation, and return control of the desktop to you. By default, UAC is turned on in Windows Vista and Windows 7, although Microsoft made changes to Windows 7 that reduce the number of prompts you will see because they changed the number of Windows programs that require approval to run.

FIGURE 18-10

The Windows 7
UAC Consent
Prompt

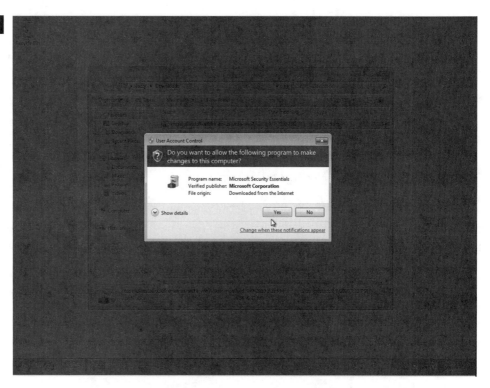

FIGURE 18-11

The Windows 7
Credentials
Prompt

Even with UAC turned off, you will not be allowed to perform all tasks and will see a message such as "The requested operation requires elevation" when you attempt to perform certain functions. Windows Vista only allows you to turn UAC on or off through the User Accounts Control Panel applet. Windows 7 lets you modify User Account Control settings in the Action Center in the Control Panel. The Windows 7 Action Center includes security, troubleshooting, and recovery options, as shown in Figure 18-12. To modify the UAC settings, click the link labeled Change User Account Control Settings, which will open a dialog box with a slider control that lets you select a range of four settings, from Never Notify (effectively turns off UAC) to Always Notify. The settings are

- **Always Notify**   Notify when programs try to install software or make changes to the computer, or when the administrator user attempts to make changes to Windows settings. The desktop will dim when the prompt appears.
- **Notify Me Only When Programs Try To Make Changes To My Computer**   The desktop will dim. This is the default setting.
- **Notify Me Only When Programs Try To Make Changes To My Computer (Do Not Dim My Desktop)**   Only choose this option if it takes a long time to dim the desktop.
- **Never Notify**   Not recommended.

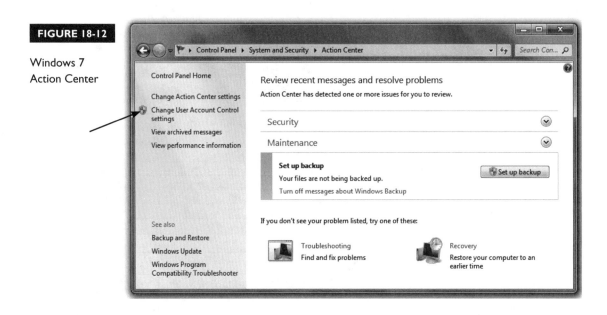

FIGURE 18-12

Windows 7 Action Center

System Protection

As you learned in Chapter 13, System Protection is the feature we most often call System Restore, although it also includes Shadow Copy in Windows Vista, Windows 7, and Windows 8. From the System Control Panel page, select System Protection from the task list, which opens the System Properties page to the System Protection tab. From this page, you can start System Restore and undo recent system changes and you can configure system restore settings. You can also create a new restore point.

Software Firewalls

In Chapter 15, you learned that a firewall is a hardware device or software that uses several technologies to prevent unwanted traffic from entering a network. If your computer is behind a well-configured hardware firewall, it will be protected against attacks coming from outside the private network. However, many attacks come from within a private network. Therefore, whether your computer is behind an expensive well-managed hardware firewall or an inexpensive SOHO broadband router, you still need to install and configure a software firewall on every Windows computer. The best strategy is to start with the most restrictive settings and then make exceptions to allow the required traffic to pass through the firewall. Since one of the main jobs of a firewall is to maintain port security, exceptions are in the form of port numbers and can even include specific IP addresses or domain names associated with port numbers.

Windows Firewall

Windows Firewall is included in Windows XP Service Pack 2 or greater, Windows Vista, Windows 7, and Windows 8. Windows Firewall is on by default, and you can open the Windows Firewall dialog box through its Control Panel applet. This was a simple multi-tabbed dialog box in Windows XP (shown here). The General page (not shown) has the status information, and the Exceptions page lets you open ports on the firewall without needing to know the protocol and port number; Windows knows the port numbers of the listed programs.

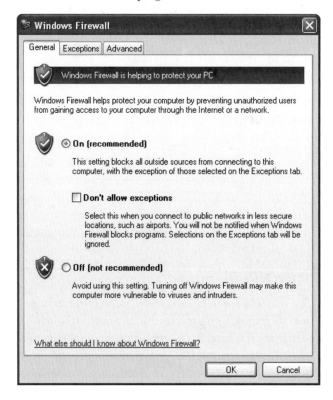

Beginning in Windows Vista, the Firewall applet is a newer-style Control Panel applet, although when you need to select exceptions in Windows Vista, clicking the link Allow A Program Through Windows Firewall will open the Windows XP–style dialog box to the Exceptions page. Figure 18-13 shows the Windows Firewall page in Windows 7 that contains simple status information and has links if you need to make any changes to the Firewall. In Windows 7, clicking the link labeled Allow Program Or Feature Through Windows Firewall will open a new page, shown in Figure 18-14. You will need to do this to allow traffic for certain apps or services

FIGURE 18-13

Windows Firewall
in Windows

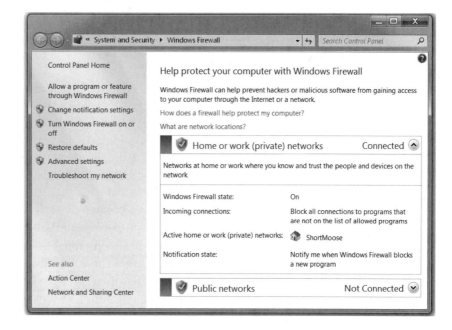

in. For instance, File And Printer Sharing must be allowed in if you need to share folders or printers from your computer. Similarly, allow Remote Assistance when you want to request remote assistance, and turn on Remote Desktop if you plan to connect to your computer over the Internet when you are away from the office. Of course, these three examples are turned on automatically when you enable these services, but it doesn't hurt to check when you have problems with sharing, Remote Assistance, or Remote Desktop.

Exercise 18-1 will help you learn more about the Windows Firewall. You must log on as a member of the local Administrators group to work with the Windows Firewall (and to complete this exercise). If you installed a third-party firewall, you should turn off Windows Firewall, because multiple firewalls on the same computer do not cooperate. Therefore, when you do Exercise 18-1, if you find that Windows Firewall is turned off, do not turn it on unless you are sure that no other firewall is installed. The exercise is for Windows 7, but the steps are very similar in Windows Vista and Windows 8.

EXERCISE 18-1

Configuring the Windows Firewall in Windows 7

In this exercise, you may encounter UAC prompts. If you are logged on with an administrator account, simply choose to continue. If you are logged on with a standard account, you will need to enter credentials to continue, in which case, you should obtain these credentials before you begin.

1. Open Control Panel and type **fire** in the Control Panel Search box. Select Windows Firewall from the results.

2. If the Windows Firewall is on, proceed to step three. If it is not on, find out why. If you have another firewall, you can look at the settings for that firewall. If Windows Firewall is turned off but no other firewall is enabled, then locate the link Turn Windows Firewall On Or Off in the Task pane and turn it on. There may be more than one location showing, so be sure you have it turned on for all locations. Then click the OK button to accept the change and return to the main Windows Firewall page.

3. On the main Windows Firewall page, select Allow A Program Or Feature Through Windows Firewall (a task item on the left). In Windows 7 this will open the Allowed Programs page, shown in Figure 18-14.

4. You can select or deselect programs to allow through the firewall, and you can look at details that describe the program and the protocols it uses. Only place a check in boxes next to services you need to use.

5. To make any other changes, you may need to first click the Change Settings button near the top of the page. This makes two more buttons active: Remove and Allow Another Program. We do not recommend adding a program unless you are confident that this exception is required and will not cause harm. The Remove button lets you remove an item from the list.

6. When you have finished with the Allowed Programs page, if you have made changes, click the OK button. If you have not made any changes, or wish to discard your changes, use the Cancel button. This will bring you back to the main Windows Firewall page; close this page.

FIGURE 18-14

The Windows
Firewall Allowed
Programs Page in
Windows 7

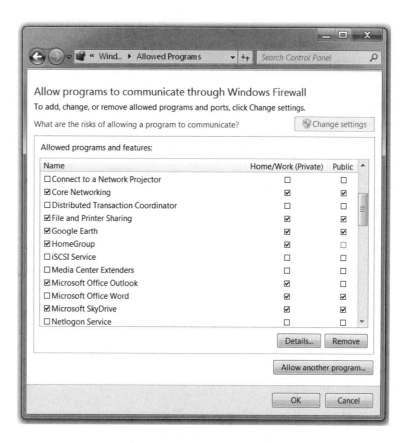

<table>
<tr><td colspan="3">Allowed programs and features:</td></tr>
</table>

Name	Home/Work (Private)	Public
☐ Connect to a Network Projector	☐	☐
☑ Core Networking	☑	☑
☐ Distributed Transaction Coordinator	☐	☐
☑ File and Printer Sharing	☑	☑
☑ Google Earth	☑	☑
☑ HomeGroup	☑	☐
☐ iSCSI Service	☐	☐
☐ Media Center Extenders	☐	☐
☑ Microsoft Office Outlook	☑	☐
☐ Microsoft Office Word	☑	☑
☑ Microsoft SkyDrive	☑	☑
☐ Netlogon Service	☐	☐

e x a m

ⓦatch   *So far, you have been using simple tools for working with Windows Firewall, and these will work for you most of the time. For a look at a more advanced* *tool, click Advanced Settings. This will open a Microsoft Management Console titled Windows Firewall With Advanced Security.*

Third-party Software Firewalls

There are many inexpensive third-party software firewalls—some commercial and some free. Examples of personal firewalls are ZoneAlarm and ZoneAlarm Pro by CheckPoint, Norton Personal Firewall by Symantec, and Sunbelt Personal Firewall from Sunbelt (previously named Kerio Personal Firewall). Each of these is available as a separate product or as part of a security software bundle. ZoneAlarm is a free program with fewer features than ZoneAlarm Pro.

Antivirus

An antivirus program can examine the contents of a disk and random access memory (RAM), looking for hidden viruses and files that may act as hosts for virus code. Effective antivirus products not only detect viruses in incoming files before they can infect your system, but also remove existing viruses and help you recover data that has been lost because of a virus.

To keep an antivirus program up to date, always enable the update option you will find in all popular antivirus programs. Configure it to connect automatically to the manufacturer's Website, check for updates, and install them. An antivirus program will update at least two components: the antivirus engine (the main program) and a set of patterns of recognized viruses, usually contained in files called definition files. Manufacturers of antivirus software commonly charge an annual fee for updates to the antivirus engine and to the definitions. Common commercial antivirus manufacturers with both home and business solutions include Symantec, TrendMicro, CA, McAfee, Kaspersky, and Grisoft. There are excellent free services for home users. One example is AVG Anti-Virus from Grisoft. Even the commercial vendors who do not offer a completely free product often allow you to try their product for a period, usually 30 days.

Antispyware/Anti-adware

As you learned in Chapter 17, spyware and adware are types of programs that install on your computer and perform functions on behalf of others. The intent of spyware can be very malicious, including identity theft, whereas the intent of adware is generally less malicious, even if the people responsible for the adware hope to profit by advertising their products.

How spyware and adware get installed on your computer is yet another issue. Users have a hard time believing that their actions invite in malicious programs, but that is how it happens. Perhaps you installed a wonderful free program. You may be very happy with the program itself, but you may have also installed spyware, adware, or worse along with the program.

The most insidious method used to install spyware and adware on your computer comes in the form of a pop-up window resembling a Windows alert. These bogus messages may warn you that spyware was installed on your computer and you must take some action, such as clicking OK in the pop-up window. By clicking OK, you supposedly start downloading software from Microsoft or another credible source to install on your computer to rid you of the threat. In reality, it is only a disguised method for installing spyware or adware.

Do not fall for these tricks. Fighting these threats begins with being very careful about how you respond to messages in pop-up windows and what you install on your computer while browsing the Web. If you are unsure of a message, do not click any buttons or links within the window, but close it using the Close button at the upper-right. Be aware that you can infect your computer by simply viewing a Website, without clicking anything.

Many free and commercial programs are available that effectively block various forms of spyware and adware, especially pop-ups. These are the easiest to block, and the most annoying because a pop-up advertisement appears in its own window and must be closed or moved before you can see the content you were seeking. Such a blocking program is a *pop-up blocker*. Configure a pop-up blocker so it will block pop-ups quietly. You can also opt to configure it to make a sound and/or display a message, allowing you to decide whether to block each pop-up.

Several years ago Microsoft offered *Windows Defender* antispyware as a free download, and they later came out with *Microsoft Security Essentials (MSE)* (antivirus and more), also offered free. Then they combined the features of both into Microsoft Security Essentials, and it is available to Windows XP, Windows Vista, and Windows 7 at www.microsoft.com/security_essentials/.

In Windows 8, Microsoft renamed Microsoft Security Essentials back to Windows Defender and bundled it with the OS.

on the
ǒ o b   *We have installed the free Microsoft security utilities many times, and we prefer them over others because they work for us and you are not required to give any information before you download. Others require at least an email address, and you usually must click through a minefield of links to things you do not want to download.*

Configuring Browser Security

There are many security settings and features in the current browsers. While you can configure some security settings directly in your browser, the *Internet Options* Control Panel applet is a central place to configure Internet Explorer security settings, as well as general browser settings, such as the home page and appearance. We'll use

Internet Explorer as the example browser, but the settings we suggest are available in other browsers such as Chrome and Firefox.

Cookies and Other Temporary Files

On the General page of Internet Options, the Browsing History section lets you manage cookies and other temporary files saved by your browser. The Settings button controls when Internet Explorer (IE) checks for newer versions of stored pages and the maximum disk space to use for these files. This is also where you can change the location of temporary Internet files and control how many days IE will save the list of visited Websites.

We described cookies in Chapter 17, including the differences between first-party cookies and third-party cookies. In general, third-party cookies are more of a threat than first-party cookies. An important settings page for controlling first-party and third-party cookies is almost hidden. To find it, click the Privacy tab in Internet Options, and then click the Advanced button. In the Advanced Privacy Settings dialog box, you can configure the handling of first-party cookies to accept, block, or prompt (this third is very annoying). You have the same choices for third-party cookies. The default is to accept first-party cookies and to block third-party cookies.

Security Zones

Many Websites are notorious for attempting to install all types of malware when users browse to them. Therefore, Internet Explorer (and other Web browsers) can detect and block this type of behavior as well as block sites known for attacking browsers. In IE, the Security page contains settings for blocking sites, letting you configure zones for various levels of security. A *zone* may be any area such as the Internet or local intranet or a list of sites grouped together, as in trusted sites and restricted sites. You can configure a different security level for each zone.

Private Browsing

During a normal browser session, your browser tracks information and saves it when you close the session (by closing the window or tab). This information includes browsing history, cookies, passwords, form data, addresses entered into the address box, and temporary Internet files. Normally, Websites can use this locally stored data for good or evil, retrieving it via your browser. All popular Internet browsers include a private browsing feature that changes this behavior. In Microsoft Internet Explorer, it is InPrivate Browsing. Other browsers call it Private Browsing or Incognito Mode.

An *InPrivate Browsing* session in Windows IE works like a normal browsing session, except when you close the tab you were using for InPrivate browsing, it saves none of the gathered information, and so your browsing behavior cannot be tracked. However, at some sites, it is a convenience to you to allow this. For instance, have you ever visited a shopping site like Amazon, not logged in with an account, and selected items for your shopping cart, then, without completing the transaction, you left the site? Did you notice that the next time you returned to that site from the same computer that things you looked at show up and your shopping list is still there? If you considered that a convenience, then you would not want to do InPrivate browsing to that site. But you may want it turned on for other sites or when using someone else's computer. That is when you select InPrivate browsing.

When you start an InPrivate session, you are protected until you leave the tab page that was opened for InPrivate. Turn on an InPrivate Browsing session from the Tools menu or, if the Command toolbar is visible, click the Safety button and select InPrivate Browsing. Figure 18-15 shows the Internet Explorer InPrivate Browsing home page. From here, enter a Uniform Resource Locator (URL), and it will not

FIGURE 18-15

The InPrivate Browsing home page in Internet Explorer

save your browsing information when you close the tab or window. By default, InPrivate browsing also disables toolbars and extensions during a private browsing session. This makes it more secure, but if you find you need to disable this, open the Internet Options Control Panel applet, select the Privacy page, and ensure that the bottom check box is deselected: Disable Toolbars And Extensions When InPrivate Browsing Starts.

Tracking Protection

Many Websites contain content provided by another Website, a third-party Website, that may track your browsing across multiple sites. *Tracking Protection* blocks third-party sites from tracking you by blocking requests for your tracking data from any site on a list of suspect sites. To turn on Tracking Protection for Internet Explorer, open Internet Options and select the Programs tab. Then click the Manage Add-Ons button. This opens the Manage-Add-Ons dialog box. In the Add-on Types area on the left, select Tracking Protection; then in the right pane, if a list is not enabled, select a list and click the Enable button at the bottom. Figure 18-16 shows this dialog box with Tracking Protection turned on.

FIGURE 18-16

Turn on Tracking Protection in Manage Add-Ons.

Managing Add-ons

In the last two decades Web content has become ever more complex and the original programming language for Web pages, Hypertext Markup Language (HTML), did not keep up with the features people wanted in Web content. Today Web servers often include other types of program code to create active content. So, browsers don't just interpret HTML code, but must be ready to interpret other types of code on Web pages so that you can view animation and videos and interact with programs on the Website. You are able to view and interact with such content on Web servers thanks to add-ons. An add-on (also called an *add-in*, *plug-in*, or *extension*) is a small program that you add to your Web browser to bring the enhanced content, such as animation, to you. These add-ons include JavaScript, CSS3, QuickTime, Adobe Flash Player, and others. One problem with how add-ons traditionally work within browsers is that once you've activated an add-on to play Web page content it operates independently outside the control of the browser. This has made add-ons a security hole, and the trend is to change that model of add-on independence. Today the latest version of HTML, HTML5, supports animation and interactive content, and many believe it is more secure to use HTML5 than add-ons. You install add-ons by downloading them from Websites. In fact, when you attempt to run content that requires an add-on, it will usually prompt you to download the required add-on. To disable an add-on in Windows Explorer, open the Manage Add-Ons dialog box, as described in the previous section, and select the type of add-on, locate the add-on you wish to remove, and click the Disable button. To remove an add-on, open the Add Or Remove Programs Control Panel applet, locate the add-on in the list, and double-click it. Then click the Uninstall button.

Pop-up Blockers

We have found a few Websites where blocking all pop-ups has blocked much of the content we were seeking. If you find that to be the case, configure the pop-up blocker to allow pop-ups for that session or configure it to display a message. You can also configure it to always allow pop-ups from specified sites.

Pop-up blockers are now the norm in Web browsers, and third-party pop-up blockers are available. If your Web browser does not have a pop-up blocker option, you may simply need to update the browser to a newer version.

To configure the pop-up blocker for Internet Explorer, open the Internet Options Control Panel applet, select the Privacy page, and first ensure that Turn On Pop-Up Blocker is turned on. Then click the Settings button to open the Pop-Up Blocker Settings dialog box. In this box you can add or remove Websites you trust to allow pop-ups, configure it to show a notification bar when a pop-up is blocked, and select a blocking level.

Phishing Filter

In Chapter 17, you learned about the dangers of phishing, a practice in which authentic-looking communications attempt to fool you into providing personal financial information. Phishing is often very difficult to detect for what it truly is. Along with educating yourself on what to look for, be sure to install or enable a phishing filter for your Web browser. You may already have a disenabled one. Keep in mind that even with a phishing filter, you must still be alert to possible phishing attacks. A phishing filter will check for suspicious behavior on the Websites you visit. It will also usually maintain a list of reported phishing sites. Here is how a phishing filter works:

- The filter manufacturer, such as Microsoft for Windows Internet Explorer 7 and 8, maintains a list of legitimate Websites, which it downloads to your computer on a regular basis. As you browse the Web, the phishing filter compares each site you visit with the list.

- A phishing filter looks at the information posted on Websites and compares it to traits typical of phishing Websites on each site you visit. If it detects these traits, it will warn you and flag the Website as suspicious. If you receive a message that a site is suspicious, do not submit any personal information.

- Depending on how you configure a phishing filter, it may automatically send addresses of Websites you visit to the manufacturer, which compares them to a list of reported phishing Websites. The information sent includes your IP address (encrypted using SSL) and only the domain and path of the Website. It sends no other information identifying your activities at the Website.

To configure Phishing Filter in Internet Explorer 7, open Internet Options. Internet Options is a Control Panel applet. You can open Internet Options from Control Panel or from within IE by selecting Tools | Phishing Filter | Phishing Filter Settings. In Internet Options, select the Advanced tab, and scroll down to Phishing Filter in the Settings list.

While browsing the Web, selecting the Tools | Phishing Filter option on the Tools menu in IE will allow you to check the current Website, turn off (or on) automatic Website checking, report a site, or open the Internet Options menu to change Phishing Filter settings.

In Internet Explorer 8, 9, and 10, the SmartScreen Filter replaces Phishing Filter, but it does more. SmartScreen prevents you from opening links and Website content based on the reputation of the source, as reported by the online Microsoft SmartScreen service, comparing sites you visit with known phishing and malware sites. In Internet Explorer 10 they added reputation protection for apps, so when you attempt to open an app, SmartScreen will check something it calls Application Reputation. Enable or disable SmartScreen for IE through the Safety menu on the IE Command bar.

Keep one thing in mind: a phishing filter or similar tool is only an aid. You must educate yourself, and the people whose computers you support, about the tactics phishers employ. Never provide your Social Security number or other financial information in response to an unsolicited message—no matter how official the message or the method of transmitting it appears to be. Phishing attacks can come to you via any means—through the mail (postal service) or via email.

Implementing Security Suites

Today's security software is very different from a decade ago because today's threats are more diverse than a decade ago. Therefore, you are not as likely to install a simple antivirus program, but rather an entire security suite, so we'll talk in terms of a multifunction security suite. Symantec, Trend Micro, and many other software manufacturers offer such suites, which normally offer a full range of security products, including antivirus, antispyware, phishing filters, and even firewalls. As with these third-party security suites, Microsoft Security Essentials protects against all known malicious software.

Installing a security suite that includes a firewall will normally disable the Windows Firewall. Installing this into Windows Vista or Windows 7 automatically disables Windows Defender. Before installing a security suite in Windows XP, you must uninstall Windows Defender.

Part of the installation of a security suite is a thorough scan of your computer, including memory contents and all portions of all storage devices, examining all types of files, and the parts of the disk where viruses can hide, such as the boot sector or boot block. Also, as part of the installation, you can choose to turn on automatic scans (the normal default) and the frequency of those scans. Even when you configure automatic scans, you can choose to initiate a scan when you detect possible malware symptoms. In this case, boot the computer to Safe Mode, as described in Chapter 13, and run a complete antivirus scan, then follow the instructions under the section titled "Removing Malware."

Microsoft Baseline Security Analyzer (MBSA) is a free Windows security auditing tool. You can analyze a single computer, computers in Active Directory, or you can specify an IP address range to scan, and you can configure credentials to use for the scanning of remote computers. MBSA checks for security updates and the lack of valid security configurations.

You do not always have obvious symptoms of malware infections because some malware is not detectable under normal computer operation. These infections are often, but not always, ones that occurred before a system is adequately protected. They can also occur if you have not kept up to date with updates—both to the operating system and to the security programs. If you suspect that a computer is infected, but a normal scan from within Windows does not detect malware, then you should try a special technique for detecting and removing malware. For such a scenario, the top security programs have a special Safe Mode Scan that runs in Windows Safe Mode. To do this, restart Windows in Safe Mode, and then locate the security program and have it run a full scan. If it detects malware, have it quarantine or remove it, and then restart the computer and see if the symptoms have gone away.

Although the top security programs claim to protect against all types of malware, including boot sector viruses, these are rather difficult viruses to detect and remove once they have infected a computer. Therefore, security software will, by default, scan all removable media upon insertion, not allowing access to it or programs to run from it until the scan is complete. Never disable this option.

If you suspect a boot sector virus in Windows XP, repair the boot block with the Recovery Console. In Windows Vista or Windows 7, use the System Recovery Options menu described in Chapter 13.

Removing Malware

When malware is detected, you must remediate the infected systems, removing the malware and repairing any damage it may have done. Following are the best practices for malware removal, as listed in CompTIA A+ Exam 802 Objective 4.7.

Identifying Malware Symptoms

Malware symptoms range from no symptoms to overt, but not too obvious, symptoms, such as sudden slowness, unusual cursor movements, and unusual network activity (indicated by status lights or messages) when you are not actively accessing the network. Following is a list of other symptoms that can be associated with a malware infection or other threat. In some cases, it is a true symptom of a security problem or actual malware infection. Other symptoms can have other causes that you will need to eliminate before taking direct action against malware.

Security Alerts   Windows Security Alerts (Windows XP) or Windows Action Center will display warning messages when Windows detects a security problem. Some common problems these tools detect include no antivirus or spyware protection detected or a disabled Windows Firewall. Respond to the message, for instance, by installing antivirus and antispyware software. In the case of a no-firewall message, open Windows Security Center (Windows XP) or Windows Action Center (Windows Vista and newer) and enable Windows Firewall, or, if you have another firewall installed, select the option that informs Windows of this.

Slow Performance   Slow performance can have several causes, depending on what there is about the computer that is actually slow. Chapter 11 described this symptom and solutions related to hard drives; Chapter 13 described slow system performance and some solutions. Chapter 16 described slow network transfer speeds and some solutions. After eliminating other causes for slow performance, follow the instructions under the topics "Quarantine Infected System," "Disable System Restore and Create a Restore Point," and "Remediate Infected Systems."

Internet Connectivity Issues   Internet connectivity issues are more likely to be from the causes described in Chapter 15 than from a malware infection. Troubleshoot using the methods described in that chapter, and if you cannot find the cause and solution, boot the computer to Safe Mode, described in Chapter 13, and run a complete antivirus scan.

PC Locks Up   This term can cover several symptoms, but is usually associated with a screen that looks normal, but the system does not respond to any input from keyboard or mouse. First, restart the computer using the power button, and then see if it will start normally. If Windows does not start normally, then follow the instructions in Chapter 13. If Windows starts up normally, immediately run a complete scan with your security software. If it detects no malware, then try to duplicate the problem and see which software or device may have been associated with the lock-up. Once you isolate it to a single program or device, remove the program or device and device driver, restart your computer, and see if the system remains stable. You may need to contact the software publisher or hardware manufacturer for a solution.

Windows Update Fails   Update failures can be a sign of a malware infection because they often disable Windows Updates so that your computer will not become more secure through security updates. When an update failure occurs, read the message, and research the cause. It may have been a network connection problem, or an incompatibility issue. If it is not clearly a network connection problem, use the error message to do an Internet search for a solution. Look at solutions from both the Microsoft site and other technical sites that you trust.

Rogue Antivirus   In Chapter 17, we described one example of a rogue antivirus when we discussed Trojan horses. A rogue antivirus is a Trojan horse masquerading as an antivirus program. Education and prevention are the best defenses, because rogue antiviruses look like the real thing, and we know several people who installed the malware. Again, the best solution is to boot the computer to Safe Mode, described in Chapter 13, and run a complete antivirus scan.

Renamed System Files   Renamed system files are less of a threat, because malware can simply infect the system files themselves. Both renaming the system files and directly infecting system files are less likely with many of the protections built into Windows. You can solve this by booting the computer to Safe Mode, described in Chapter 13, and running a complete antivirus scan. If removal of the virus leaves your system unbootable, then run the recovery options from a Windows installation disc.

Files Disappearing   Disappearing files is a malware symptom, but before you assume malware has caused it, look at how it was discovered and what you or the client was doing at the time the files disappeared. Sometimes, we just forget where we stored files. However, it never hurts to run a security scan, even from Safe Mode. If you discover malware, remove it and restore your files from the latest backup.

File Permission Changes   File permission changes are also not as likely to happen in the newer versions of Windows as in Windows XP because of User Account Control. If you notice that permissions have changed, change them back (if your permissions allow), then boot the computer to Safe Mode, described in Chapter 13, and run a complete antivirus scan.

Access Denied   If access is denied to a resource a user previously was able to access, troubleshoot it as a file permission change, described earlier.

Hijacked Email   In the event of a hijacked email, described in Chapter 17, you should do three things: immediately change your password, change your security question and answer, and verify that you are the owner of your alternate email address (most email accounts ask you to provide an alternate email address). Hopefully the people you email know that you're not stranded in Ireland and need money to get home, or whatever message the hijacker sent out from your account. You should probably send everyone an email telling them what happened, reminding them not to click anything and to delete anything strange coming from your address.

Sometimes the hijacker changes your password and locks you out. In that case, contact the email provider for help in resolving the problem.

Quarantine Infected System

When you suspect a computer of infection with malware, remove it from the network in order to quarantine it and keep other computers from being infected. In addition, your security program may quarantine the malware file or it may remove it entirely. It all depends on the security software configuration. A quarantined file is disabled, but not removed from the computer. Some security software talks about the malware being in a "vault," which is the same as quarantining. Since security software can make mistakes and identify critical and uninfected files as malware, consider configuring your security program to quarantine detected malware so that you have the opportunity to review the file and decide what action to take.

Disable System Restore and Create a Restore Point

Because System Restore keeps snapshots of your computer configuration and system files, the malware can be included in those files, and your computer would be reinfected when you restored from a restore point. Therefore, after you have removed malware, disable System Restore and create a new restore point.

Remediate Infected Systems

Part of the removal process should include remediating the infected system by updating the antivirus and other security programs. As we have said several times in this book, it is best to turn on automatic updates for any program that supports it. This is the best way to ensure that your system gets security updates in a timely fashion.

SCENARIO & SOLUTION

I support computers in a large organization that uses Cisco routers and firewalls at all connections to the Internet. Why should we use personal firewalls on all our Windows computers?	A properly configured hardware firewall will protect against invasions to the network, but it will not protect each computer from invasion from within the private network.
Now that I have a phishing filter enabled in Windows, do I need to be on the watch for phishing?	Yes, you still must watch for phishing attempts. Educate yourself on the techniques phishers use to obtain your personal financial information.

Preventive Maintenance for Security

As all steps you take to implement security are preventive steps, we do not need to add a long description of preventive security maintenance. There are, however, certain tasks that we should add to those described so far in this chapter that fall under preventive maintenance, beginning with backing up data, keeping up to date on service packs and patches, training users, and recognizing social engineering.

Implementing Data Backup Procedures

An important part of data security is a backup policy that includes frequent backups of data to removable media. Storage of the media should also be part of the policy. Although backup media should be handy for quick restores, a full backup set should also be stored offsite in case something occurs to the building in which the computer is housed, as well as to the computer. For offsite storage, consider encrypting the backup media. The frequency of the backups, and of the full backup that is stored offsite, depends on the needs of the organization. It is not possible to overemphasize how important it is to back up data. We discussed backup in Chapter 10. We will talk about who has the permission to back up here.

Users can back up files they created on their local NTFS volume, including the My Documents or Documents folder, in their own profile and its contents. Users can restore files and folders to which they have the Write permission on an NTFS volume. Members of the local Administrators and Backup Operators groups have the right to back up and restore all files. Individual users in these groups can back up and restore files that they do not normally have permissions to access. This ability does not give them any other access to these files and folders. If someone is only doing the backup function for a computer that contains other users' data, and that person does not need to do other administrative tasks, make them a member of the Backup Operators group rather than the Administrators group. This is an example of applying the principle of least privilege.

Installing Service Packs and Patches

Although this point was made previously in this book, it is important to the security of your computer and your confidential data that you keep your computer updated with the latest service packs and patches. If you have Internet access, turn on Automatic Updates in Windows. In addition, any security software you install will normally have an automatic update feature. Be sure to turn this on.

Training Users

Knowledge of the danger of threats and ways to prevent malicious software from invading computers is important to both the computer professional and to each PC user. Do your part to keep yourself current on security technologies. Depending on your role in an organization, take all opportunities to educate users. Make them aware of the company's security policy and the role they need to play in preventing attacks.

Recognizing Social Engineering

In Chapter 17, you learned about social engineering and ways to recognize social engineering when you encounter it in emails and other messages. Do your part to inform other users about social engineering by sharing what you have learned and by directing them to look at a site that educates people about these threats. We gave an example in Exercise 17-2.

CERTIFICATION SUMMARY

There are no easy answers or quick fixes when it comes to computer security. Security threats go beyond simple computer invasions to inflict damage to threats against your very identity. Therefore, computer security must be multifaceted to protect computers, data, and users.

On a Windows computer, this multifaceted approach begins with implementing authentication and creating accounts using your understanding of local users and groups and how group membership gives a user his or her level of access. In Chapter 19, we will look at how you modify this level of access to files, folders, and printers. Also implement best practices to secure a workstation.

Be aware of the built-in security features in Windows and how to configure them, including but not limited to User Account Control, antivirus software, phishing filters, antispyware, anti-adware, and pop-blockers. Configure firewalls on your network as well as on individual computers using Windows Firewall or another personal firewall.

✓ TWO-MINUTE DRILL

Here are some of the key points covered in Chapter 18.

Implementing Authentication for Digital Security

❑ Each organization must have a security policy, sometimes dictated by government regulations, to protect equipment, people, and data. Among the many types of data that must be protected is personally identifiable information (PII) that uniquely identifies an individual.

❑ Access control to resources on a computer or network begins with authentication (verifying a user's identity) and authorization (determining the level of access an authenticated user has to a resource).

❑ Two types of BIOS passwords can be set—one that must be entered at startup before an operating system is loaded, and another that is required for access to the BIOS system settings (also known as CMOS settings).

❑ Windows Credential Manager can store user names, passwords, and certificates in the Windows Vault to automate logging on to various network services.

❑ When a user needs to walk away from a PC for short periods, the Lock Computer option will hide the desktop until the user returns and enters his or her account password.

Implementing a Defense Against Malicious Software

❑ User Account Control prevents malware from modifying your computer by prompting for your consent; this behavior can be configured in Windows 7 and Windows 8. With Windows Vista, UAC is either on or off.

❑ A properly configured hardware firewall will protect a network from certain types of invasions from the Internet or other untrusted networks, but personal firewalls on each computer will protect from attacks that originate on the private network.

❑ The Windows Firewall that comes with Windows XP Service Pack 2, Windows Vista, Windows 7, and Windows 8 is enabled by default, but if you install a third-party firewall, Windows Firewall will be turned off.

❑ Antivirus programs examine the contents of a disk and RAM, looking for hidden viruses and files that may act as hosts for virus code.

❑ Always enable the update option in an antivirus program and configure it to automatically connect to the manufacturer's Website, check for updates, and install them. These updates will include changes to both the antivirus engine and definition files.

❑ Private browsing in Internet Explorer is InPrivate Browsing, and when you are in an InPrivate Browsing session, it does not save your browsing information.

❑ Tracking Protection blocks third-party sites from tracking you by blocking requests for your tracking data from any site on a list of suspect sites. Turn it on using the Manage Add-Ons dialog box that you can open from the Programs tab in Internet Options.

❑ Disable an add-on in Windows Explorer in the Manage Add-Ons dialog box. Remove an add-on from the Add or Remove Programs applet in Control Panel.

❑ A pop-up blocker can prevent unwanted windows from opening in your browser. Configure the pop-up blocker for Internet Explorer through the Privacy page in Internet Options.

❑ Install or enable a phishing filter for your Web browser. This filter will check for suspicious behavior on the Websites you visit. You will still need to watch out for possible phishing attacks. In IE 7, it is Phishing Filter. In IE 8, 9, and 10, it is SmartScreen. Enable or disable SmartScreen through the Safety menu on the Command bar.

❑ Microsoft Baseline Security Analyzer (MBSA) is a free tool that checks for weak security configurations.

SELF TEST

The following questions will help you measure your understanding of the material presented in this chapter. Read all of the choices carefully because there might be more than one correct answer. Choose all correct answers for each question.

Implementing Authentication for Digital Security

1. On a computer that has DriveLock or a similar feature, the password to access the hard drive at startup can either be stored on the hard drive itself or in this special type of chip, if present.
   - A. Key fob
   - B. TPM
   - C. CMOS
   - D. Biometric

2. When you use a smart card with a PIN, this is an example of which of the following?
   - A. RFID
   - B. One-factor authentication
   - C. TPM
   - D. Two-factor authentication

3. Which of the following is a best practice to apply to passwords?
   - A. Short passwords
   - B. Memorable passwords
   - C. Strong passwords
   - D. Blank passwords

4. This feature is quite handy, but you should disable it because it potentially could allow malware on removable media to infect your computer.
   - A. Creator Owner
   - B. DriveLock
   - C. Screen Saver
   - D. AutoPlay

5. Set this on a school lab computer to protect from tampering with hardware settings, but still allow students normal access with just their student ID password.
   - A. Lock Computer
   - B. Screen Saver password
   - C. BIOS startup password
   - D. BIOS settings password

6. This local built-in Windows account, disabled by default, is restricted in what it can do if enabled.
- **A.** Administrator
- **B.** Guest
- **C.** Anonymous
- **D.** Power User

7. This feature, introduced in Windows Vista, protects against programs running in the background, changing settings, and installing malware when a logged-on user is a member of the Administrators group.
- **A.** DriveLock
- **B.** TPM
- **C.** UAC
- **D.** Autorun

8. If you use a screen saver, you should really take this action for added security.
- **A.** Use personal photos
- **B.** Enable screen saver password
- **C.** Disable Lock Computer
- **D.** Lengthen the wait period

9. Before walking away from your computer, press WINDOWS KEY-L to enable this security feature.
- **A.** DriveLock
- **B.** Lock Computer
- **C.** Screen Saver
- **D.** TPM

10. Your company, Acme, has several Web servers that you use on daily basis. You would like authentication to these servers to be transparent after logging on to Windows. What should you configure?
- **A.** BitLocker To Go
- **B.** Credential Manager
- **C.** UAC
- **D.** EFS

11. Which of the following authentication methods is considered the most secure?
- **A.** Smart card
- **B.** User name and password
- **C.** Fingerprint scanner
- **D.** Credential Manager

Implementing a Defense Against Malicious Software

12. What hardware device or software program uses several technologies to prevent unwanted traffic from entering a network?

A. Proxy server

B. Firewall

C. Router

D. Switch

13. What two antivirus components are frequently updated?

A. Antispyware

B. Engine and definitions

C. Engine and spam filter

D. Definition files and phishing filter

14. What type of security software examines Website content for certain social engineering traits and warns you if it detects one of these traits while you are browsing?

A. Antispyware

B. Spam filter

C. Phishing filter

D. Antivirus

15. What service do popular Web browsers, such as IE, Firefox, and Chrome, offer to prevent unwelcome browser windows from opening on your desktop?

A. Phishing filter

B. Spam filter

C. Pop-up blocker

D. Personal firewall

16. What security software examines the contents of a disk and RAM, looking for hidden viruses and files that may act as hosts for virus code?

A. Phishing filter

B. Antivirus

C. Personal firewall

D. Pop-up blocker

17. What Control Panel applet allows you to manage temporary Internet files?

    A. Internet Options

    B. Computer Management

    C. Event Viewer

    D. Administrative Tools

18. Your IT security office is concerned that network computers do not have the latest security updates installed. Which tool can determine this?

    A. Security center

    B. Local security policy

    C. UAC

    D. MBSA

19. If files are saved on an NTFS volume, members of this group can only back up files they created, including the contents of the My Documents or Documents folder in their own profile.

    A. Administrators

    B. Backup Operators

    C. Guests

    D. Users

20. Jason needs correct permission to back up and restore a computer containing confidential data saved by other users into their own Documents folders on an NTFS volume from other users. Assuming he does not need to perform other administrative tasks, select the group you would put him into so that he can do these tasks. Apply the principle of least privilege.

    A. Administrators

    B. Backup Operators

    C. Guests

    D. Users

SELF TEST ANSWERS

Implementing Authentication for Digital Security

1. ☑ **B.** TPM, or Trusted Platform Module, is a chip that DriveLock can use to store passwords or keys for accessing a computer's hard drive.
☒ **A,** key fob, is incorrect; although a key fob contains a microchip, DriveLock-type systems do not use one. **C,** CMOS, is incorrect; although this is a type of chip, DriveLock does not use it to store passwords. **D,** biometric, is incorrect because this term describes a type of device that uses a scan of (usually) a fingerprint for authentication.

2. ☑ **D.** Two-factor authentication. In this case, you are using something you have (the smart card) and something you know (the PIN).
☒ **A,** RFID, is radio frequency ID, and does not require entering a PIN, or even touching a computer or keypad. **B,** one-factor authentication, is incorrect because it depends on only one factor, which could be a password. **C,** TPM (Trusted Platform Module), is incorrect because it is a chip that can be used to store passwords or keys.

3. ☑ **C.** Strong passwords are a best practice for passwords. This means a password should be both long and complex, with numbers, letters, and symbols.
☒ **A, B,** and **D** are all incorrect because none of them is a best practice, and you could call blank passwords a worst practice.

4. ☑ **D.** AutoPlay (or Autorun in older versions) enables Windows to automatically find and run the content on removable media when it is connects to a computer. Removable media is a potential vector for malware.
☒ **A,** Creator Owner, is incorrect because this is a special Windows group. **B,** DriveLock, is incorrect because it is a drive protection feature on some computers. **C,** Screen Saver, is incorrect because this is simply a picture or animation that displays on your screen after a period of inactivity.

5. ☑ **D.** BIOS settings password will prevent people from changing the BIOS settings for hardware.
☒ **A,** Lock Computer, is incorrect because it does not prevent access to BIOS settings. **B,** Screen Saver password, is incorrect because it does not prevent access to BIOS settings. **C,** BIOS startup password, is incorrect because it would not allow normal access unless every student knew the BIOS startup password.

6. ☑ **B.** Guest is built in, disabled by default, and restricted in what it can do.
☒ **A,** Administrator, is incorrect because it is not disabled and is not restricted. **C,** Anonymous, while similar, is not a Windows account. **D,** Power User, is incorrect because there is no built-in Power User account, although there is a built-in Power Users group.

7. ☑ **C.** UAC (User Account Control) prevents programs from running in the background, changing settings, and installing malware when a logged-on user is a member of the Administrators group.

☒ **A,** DriveLock, is incorrect because it just allows you to set a password that you must provide at startup. **B,** TPM, is incorrect because it is a chip that can store passwords or keys. **D,** Autorun, is incorrect because this feature enables Windows to automatically find and run the content on removable media when it connects to a computer.

8. ☑ **B.** Enable screen saver password requires entry of a password when a screen saver is activated.

☒ **A,** use personal photo, would not provide added security. **C,** disable Lock Computer, is incorrect. **D,** lengthen the wait period, is incorrect because this would decrease security because the screen contents would be visible for longer.

9. ☑ **B.** Lock Computer is enabled when you press WINDOWS KEY-L, requiring authentication before anyone can access your computer.

☒ **A,** DriveLock, is a feature on some computers that locks access to hard drives. **C,** Screen Saver, is incorrect because WINDOWS key-L does not enable it. **D,** TPM, is incorrect because it is a chip that can store passwords or keys for accessing a computer's hard drive.

10. ☑ **B.** Credential Manager allows you to enter user names and passwords for Windows servers and Websites, and it lets you specify use of PKI certificates for automatic authentication.

☒ **A,** BitLocker To Go, is used to encrypt the contents of USB flash drives. **C,** UAC, can prevent malicious code from modifying your computer without your consent. **D,** EFS, encrypts individual files and folders.

11. ☑ **A.** Smart cards represent multifactor authentication: something you have and something you know.

☒ **B** and **C** represent only single-factor authentication. **D,** Credential Manager, is used to automate logon to specified network hosts.

Implementing a Defense Against Malicious Software

12. ☑ **B.** A firewall is the hardware device or software program that uses several technologies to prevent unwanted traffic from entering a network.

☒ **A,** proxy server, is incorrect because although this is one of the technologies used by a firewall, it does not fully describe a firewall. **C,** router, is incorrect because this is a separate device (or software), although it may use one or more of the technologies associated with a firewall. **D,** switch, is incorrect because this device or software does not prevent unwanted traffic from entering a network. A switch is a cable-connecting device used within a network.

13. ☑ **B.** The engine and definitions are the two frequently updated antivirus components.

    ☒ **A,** antispyware, is incorrect because this is not a component of antivirus, although antispyware and antivirus software may both be part of a security bundle. **C,** engine and spam filter, is incorrect because although the antivirus engine is one of the updated components, the spam filter is not part of antivirus software, even though it may be bundled with antivirus software in a security package. **D,** definition files and phishing filter, is incorrect because although definition file is part of the correct answer, phishing filter is not part of an antivirus program, but a Web browser add-on or feature.

14. ☑ **C.** A phishing filter is the type of security software that looks at Website contents for certain traits and warns you if it detects one of these traits while you are browsing.

    ☒ **A,** antispyware, is incorrect because antispyware looks for spyware on your computer, not social engineering traits. **B,** spam filter, is incorrect because this does not look for social engineering traits but for spam in your email. **D,** antivirus, is incorrect because this does not look for social engineering traits, but for viruses.

15. ☑ **C.** A pop-up blocker is the service offered by Web browsers to prevent unwanted windows from opening on the desktop.

    ☒ **A,** phishing filter, is incorrect because although this filter works within a browser, it scans Websites for certain social engineering traits. **B,** spam filter, is incorrect because this scans incoming emails for suspected spam messages. **D,** personal firewall, is incorrect because it does not work within a Web browser, but blocks certain types of incoming messages based on information in the packet header.

16. ☑ **B.** Antivirus is security software that examines the contents of a disk and RAM, looking for hidden viruses and files that may act as hosts for virus code.

    ☒ **A,** phishing filter, is incorrect because this filter works within a browser and scans Websites for certain social engineering traits. **C,** personal firewall, is incorrect because this firewall blocks certain types of incoming messages based on information in the packet header, but does not look at the contents to determine if it is virus code. **D,** pop-up blocker, is incorrect because it only works within a browser to prevent unwanted browser windows from opening.

17. ☑ **A.** Internet Options is where you can manage temporary Internet files.

    ☒ **B,** Computer Management, **C,** Event Viewer, and **D,** Administrative Tools, are all incorrect because none of these administrative tools allows you to manage temporary Internet files.

18. ☑ **D.** The Microsoft Baseline Security Analyzer (MBSA) can scan one or more computers for update compliance.

    ☒ **A, B,** and **C** are incorrect. The Security Center in Windows Vista (Action Center in Windows 7) allows configuration of components such as the Windows Firewall and automatic updates. Local security policy is used to configure security settings on a single computer. UAC prevents programs from running without your consent.

19. ☑ **D.** Users group members can only back up files they created, including the contents of the My Documents or Documents folder, in their own profile.

☒ **A** and **B** are incorrect. Members of the Administrators group as well as members of Backup Operators can back up anything on an NTFS volume. **C**, Guests, is incorrect because this group has very limited capabilities.

20. ☑ **B.** Backup Operators group gives the person the right to back up and restore files to which he would not normally have access, but does not give him permissions to access and open these files.

☒ **A** is incorrect. A member of the Administrators group could do the tasks, but the question assumes that the person does not need to do administrative tasks. **C**, Guests, is incorrect because these users cannot perform these tasks. **D** is incorrect because a member of the Users group can only back up their own files.

19

Configuring and Troubleshooting Windows Clients

At work, at school, and at home, computer users depend on client software components to accomplish work—whether they are doing research over the Internet, playing an Internet game, using email, or transferring files from a server to the desktop computer. Making files and devices available to network users has led to the need for securing those resources, possibly the most important set of tasks on a network. Implementing security in this environment involves many different tasks, such as implementing authentication and data security, taking all necessary steps to prevent the invasion of malicious software, and discovering if malicious software is already on a system. This chapter continues the discussion of authentication begun in Chapter 17 where we described methods for authenticating access to buildings and campuses. Here we look at authentication of digital access to computers and networks. We begin with configuring Windows clients for file and printer sharing; then we look at how to apply permissions on NTFS volume for both local and network users, and how to apply share permissions, which combine with NTFS permissions for network users. Learn about file and folder encryption on NTFS volumes versus BitLocker drive encryption and how to thoroughly remove data from drives. We end the chapter with a section on troubleshooting security problems.

CERTIFICATION OBJECTIVE

■ *802: 1.6 Set up and configure Windows networking on a client/desktop*

In this section learn how to configure Windows clients for file and printer sharing, using the three methods listed in CompTIA Exam 802 Objective 1.6: HomeGroup, workgroup, and domain (Microsoft Active Directory domain). Learn how to configure a client for each type and how the methods differ.

Configuring Windows Clients for File and Printer Sharing

In this section we will examine three methods for sharing files and printers from a Windows client computer. Two methods are ideal for a home or small office network that does not require a great deal of security. They are HomeGroups and workgroups. The third method is for the Windows client to join a Windows domain, which is a common method used in medium to large-size organizations and small organizations with a greater need for security and a need for better services in-house, such as using Microsoft's email server, Exchange Server, for employees' email accounts.

HomeGroups

The *HomeGroup* feature, new in Windows 7 and also supported in Windows 8, is an easy-to-configure form of Microsoft's peer-to-peer file and print sharing, with only a single password protecting the HomeGroup shares on all Windows computers that join a HomeGroup. With HomeGroup enabled, you can choose to share local printers and selected Windows library folders (Documents, Music, Pictures, and/or Videos.) You can configure a Windows 8, Windows 8 Pro, or Windows 7 computer running any edition of this operating system (OS) as clients to join a HomeGroup, but only certain Windows 7 editions can create and host a HomeGroup. Those versions are Windows 7 Home Premium, Professional, Ultimate, and Enterprise editions. After you create a HomeGroup on one computer, you only have to enter the password once on each client computer in the HomeGroup when the client joins the HomeGroup.

Microsoft created HomeGroup to make it simple for people on a very small network to share their data with one another. It is ideal for a family or small business. In this section, we will first describe Windows Network locations, something that is important to understand in order to participate in a peer-to-peer network in Windows 7 and Windows 8. Then we will summarize the rules for HomeGroups and detail how to create, configure, leave, or join a HomeGroup. Finally, we will look at the notion of Libraries, and Public Libraries, in particular, because these are the folders through which you share files and folders in a HomeGroup.

Microsoft documentation, and even the graphical user interface (GUI) tools, capitalize the term HomeGroup inconsistently. We have decided to go with HomeGroup, and have tried to be consistent in its use.

Windows Network Locations

It is important to understand Microsoft's notion of a network location, which you need to select when you first connect to a network in Windows Vista and newer editions, because Windows will configure appropriate firewall and security settings based on the network location. This setting has an impact on your ability to use the file and printer sharing methods we discuss in this chapter. To view this setting, open Network And Sharing Center, shown in Figure 19-1. Your choices in Windows 7 are Home Network, Work Network, Public Network, or Domain. In Windows 8 the word "private" is used in place of the home location used in Windows Vista and Windows 7.

FIGURE 19-1

ShortMoose is a
Home network.

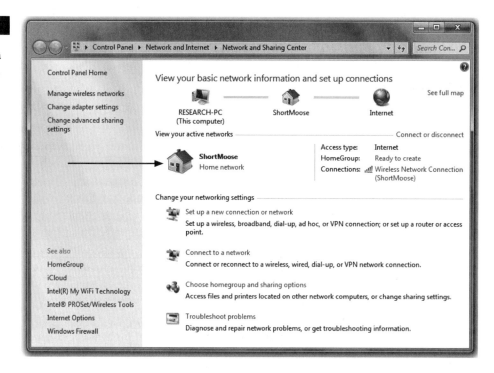

Home Network Choose Home Network as your location when you trust all the computers on your network, as you would at home. When you choose this, the *Network Discovery* feature is turned on, your computer will be visible to other users on the network, and you will see other computers on the network.

To manually turn Network Discovery on or off in Windows 7, open Network And Sharing Center and in the task list on the left, select Change Advanced Sharing Settings and expand the current network profile. Then simply click the appropriate radio button.

Work Network The Work Network location is your choice if you are connecting to a small network at work. Network Discovery is turned on for this setting also. While you cannot create or join a HomeGroup when in a Work network, you can participate in a workgroup, Microsoft's older form of peer-to-peer networking.

Public Network The Public Network location is your choice for untrusted locations, such as public waiting rooms and coffee shops. It is also your preferred choice if you are using a mobile broadband connection or if your computer connects directly to the Internet without going through a router. You will not be visible to other computers on the network because Network Discovery is automatically turned off for this location and the HomeGroup feature is disabled while on a public network. This is also your safest choice if you do not want to share your local files or printers with others on your network.

e x a m

ⓦatch   *Be sure you understand   setting is the safest. Network Discovery is*
that Windows will configure Windows   turned on for Home and Work networks,
Firewall settings based on the network   and turned off for Public networks.
location and that the Public Network

Domain   Domain is not a network location you can select, but it is automatically configured when your computer is joined to a Windows domain at your workplace or school. You cannot change this network location as long as your computer is part of the domain.

Creating and Configuring a HomeGroup

As discussed earlier, a HomeGroup requires the Home network location. It also requires that IPv6 be enabled, even on a network that also supports IPv4. That is just part of the picture. Here are rules and guidelines for HomeGroups in Windows 7 and Windows 8:

- HomeGroups are only supported in Windows 7 and Windows 8.
- A computer can belong to only one HomeGroup at a time, and there can only be one HomeGroup on a local area network (LAN) or wireless local area network (WLAN).
- Computers that are part of a Windows Active Directory domain cannot create a HomeGroup but can join one.
- Your computer's network location, selected in Network And Sharing Center, must be Home Network.
- HomeGroup requires that IPv6 be enabled on the local computer. This is turned on by default in Windows 7 and Windows 8, but if it is disabled, HomeGroup will not work.

- All firewalls between HomeGroup computers must support IPv6 and allow file and printer sharing. Windows Firewall supports both.

- Routers that forward IPv6 and multicast traffic allow HomeGroups to exist beyond a LAN.

- A HomeGroup lets you share local printers and Public folders within your Windows 7 or Windows 8 Libraries.

Before creating a HomeGroup, check that IPv6 is enabled and that your computer is on a Home network type. To check that IPv6 is enabled, open Network And Sharing Center, and in the task list on the left, select Change Adapter Settings. This opens the Network Connections page. In many cases, there will be just one, but you may have two or more. For instance, a laptop with both an Ethernet network interface card (NIC) and a Wi-Fi NIC will show both connections. The choice is simple if, for instance, the Ethernet NIC network connection is unplugged and you are connected to a Wi-Fi network. Double-click the network connection you will use for the HomeGroup, and this will open the Status box for that connection. Click the Properties button, and on the Networking page of the Properties dialog box, ensure that a check is in the box for Internet Protocol Version 6 (TCP/IPv6).

Now you are ready to create and configure a HomeGroup. Exercise 19-1 will walk you through the steps using Windows 7.

EXERCISE 19-1

Creating a HomeGroup

Practice creating and configuring a HomeGroup. The steps were written for Windows 7 Home Premium/Professional/Ultimate/Enterprise editions. If you are using Windows 8, the steps are different because you begin in the PC Settings page opened from the Settings Charm | Change PC Settings menu.

1. From the Start menu type **home** in the Search box and select HomeGroup from the results list.

2. If your computer is not on a Home network, you will see the message shown in Figure 19-2. In that case, open Network And Sharing Center, select your network, and change it to Home Network.

3. On the HomeGroup page click Create A HomeGroup.

4. The first page of the Create A Homegroup Wizard (Figure 19-3) lists printers and the names of the libraries on your computer that you can select to share. Click to place a check by the items you wish to share, and click Next.

5. Windows will generate a password for your HomeGroup, shown in Figure 19-4. Write it down or use the link to print the password and instructions. You will need to enter the password on the other computers on your network as you join them to the HomeGroup. After writing down or printing out the password, click the Finish button. Note that if you lose the password, you can open HomeGroup and view it again.

Joining or Leaving a HomeGroup

Go to another Windows 7 or Windows 8 computer on your network, and open HomeGroup. To do this on a Windows 7 computer from the Start menu, enter **HomeGroup** in the Search box. On a Windows 8 computer, open the Charms menu (swipe to bottom right and up to the Settings Charm), and then select Change PC Settings to open the PC Settings page. From there, select HomeGroup.

FIGURE 19-2

This error message appears when you open the HomeGroup applet when your computer is using a network location other than Home.

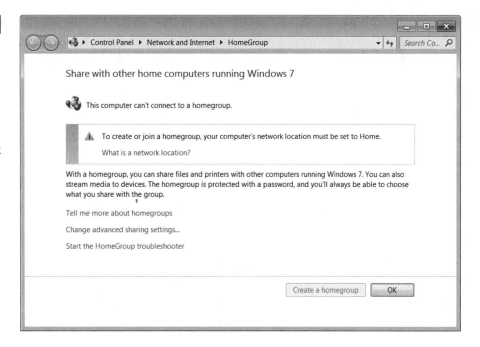

Select the Public libraries and printers you want to share with others on your HomeGroup.

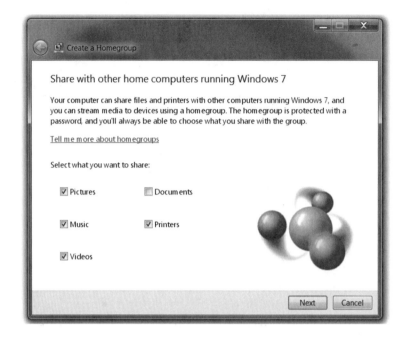

This password must be entered in the Home-Group applet on Windows 7 or Windows 8 computers as they join the HomeGroup.

If the computer is already a member of a different HomeGroup, then select the Leave The HomeGroup option in Windows 7 or click the Leave button in Windows 8.

To join a HomeGroup, click Join Now (Windows 7) or Join (Windows 8) and follow the instructions to enter the HomeGroup password. This will include selecting which library folders to share and choosing to share your local printers with the HomeGroup.

Populating Your Public Libraries

Now that you've joined a HomeGroup, anytime you wish to share files and folders simply place them in the Public libraries. Libraries are very special folders in Windows 7 and Windows 8. A *library* looks like a folder that contains other folders and files, but it is not a conventional storage folder, because it only contains pointers to the actual locations of each folder or file. A single library can point to various locations on local storage or network storage. Libraries make it easier for you to organize related information or types of files. Libraries also make it easier to back up related files because you can simply point to one library and back up files from all locations. Figure 19-5 shows the Libraries folder with four libraries: Documents, Music, Pictures,

FIGURE 19-5

Each library contains a private folder and a Public folder and any others added by the user.

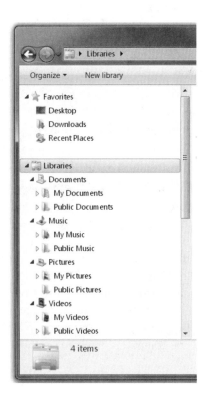

and Videos. Each library has a Public folder in addition to the base folder for that library. Each of these points to a different location. Users can add more locations to the libraries, and they will appear as folders under the library folders.

Anyone using a computer in the HomeGroup has full control in the Public library folders that you shared. As such, they can copy, edit, delete, and move within those folders. Put anything you wish to share under those conditions into the Public folders.

To add folders or files to a library, copy or move them directly into one of the library folders, or add a folder to a library as a location—then you do not need to move or copy the files and folders. Consider the Documents library. By default, it includes two locations, My Documents (C:\Users\<user_name>\Documents) and Public Documents (C:\Users\Public\Documents). The first location is not shared through HomeGroups, but the second location is as long as you enabled HomeGroup sharing for Documents in the HomeGroup applet. In this case, simply copy or move folders and files into the second location to make them available to the HomeGroup. Figure 19-6 shows the Documents Library Locations dialog, which we opened by clicking the locations link, seen just above it in the Documents library contents pane.

Connecting to a HomeGroup Computer

Once you are a member of a HomeGroup, you can use Windows Explorer to browse to other computers in the HomeGroup and connect to the Public folders that were selected to share. The computer you are using will not show in the HomeGroup, just the other members. Figure 19-7, created at the computer RESEARCH-PC, does not show that computer listed under HomeGroup, but does show YODA-PC. The opposite is true when we do this from YODA-PC. Notice that YODA-PC is identified by both the user name, Yoda, and the computer name in the HomeGroup listing. Also, notice the Network group at the bottom of the folders pane where it lists all the computers detected on the network. There are three computers,

FIGURE 19-6

Click the locations link to see the actual locations of the libraries.

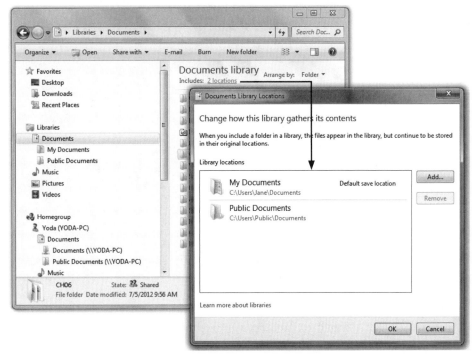

JAZZYPC, RESEARCH-PC, and YODA-PC. We know that RESEARCH-PC and YODA-PC are in the HomeGroup, so JAZZYPC is not a member. This could be because it is not running a Windows version that supports HomeGroups or that it has not joined the HomeGroup.

After browsing to YODA-PC, we opened the Public Pictures folder, which has been populated with many subfolders. HomeGroup members have full control over the files and folders shared through Public folders. Therefore, you can browse among them and perform all the file operations you would on your own computer.

Workgroups

Windows Vista and Windows XP computers cannot participate in a HomeGroup. A workgroup is the solution when you want to share files with these older versions of Windows, because it is supported by all versions of Windows included in the CompTIA A+ exams. In fact, Microsoft Windows workgroup support has been around for over 20 years since Windows 3.11: Windows for Workgroups. HomeGroups are

FIGURE 19-7

Browse to a
Public folder on
a HomeGroup
computer.

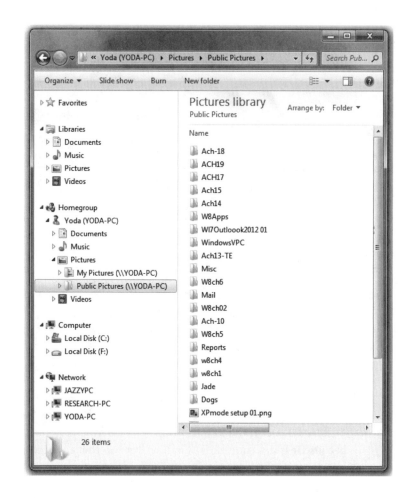

essentially wizard-driven simplified workgroups,
but they only work for Windows 7 and Windows 8
computers. A workgroup is a uniquely named
collection of networked computers participating
in file and print sharing, but with no central
administration. From a Windows XP computer,
this named collection makes browsing the
network for shared resources easier, especially
if there are multiple workgroups. For example,
a group of accounting computers might be in

exam

watch   *Windows Vista and Windows XP computers cannot participate
in a HomeGroup. A workgroup is the
solution when you want to share files
with these older versions of Windows.*

the "Acct" workgroup, while a group of marketing computers might be in the "Mktg" workgroup.

The actual workgroup name is less important in Windows 7 and Windows 8, as Microsoft has actually put the workgroup feature in the background, encouraging use of HomeGroups. Although you can still change the workgroup name, when you view workgroup computers in Windows Explorer (File Explorer in Windows 8) there is no mention of workgroups or their names. In Windows Vista, there is a Workgroup tab in Windows Explorer, but the workgroup name does not display when you are browsing. In Windows XP, you see computers organized under workgroup names.

Creating and Joining a Workgroup

It is very simple to join a workgroup; in fact, if your computer is not a member of a domain, it is automatically a member of a workgroup, and the default workgroup name is "Workgroup." Joining a workgroup is as simple as changing your workgroup name using a maximum of 15 characters:

■ To change a workgroup name in Windows XP, you simply enter a new workgroup name in the Computer Name Changes dialog box. Open this box from the Windows XP System Properties dialog box Computer Name tab by clicking the Change button.

■ To change a workgroup name in Windows Vista, Windows 7, and Windows 8, open Control Panel. In the Search box type **computer name**. In the results list select Rename This Computer. If a User Account Control message pops up (by default, it will in Windows Vista; it won't in Windows 7), click Continue or enter an administrator's password. On the Computer Name page click the Change button. In the Computer Name/Domain Changes dialog click in the Workgroup box and enter a workgroup name. When you click OK, a dialog box will pop up, as shown in Figure 19-8. Click OK and you will be prompted to restart your computer. Click OK, and then click Close in System Properties. Close all open files and programs and restart your computer.

As a member of a workgroup, you log on to the local computer with a local user name and password, not to the workgroup. Figure 19-9 shows the Windows 7 logon screen for a workgroup computer; the workgroup name is never specified during logon.

Workgroups simply organize the way we browse for network resources. Unlike HomeGroups, you do not have to set the network location to Home, IPv6 is not required, and there can be more than one workgroup on the LAN.

FIGURE 19-8

Joining a
computer to
the ACCT
workgroup

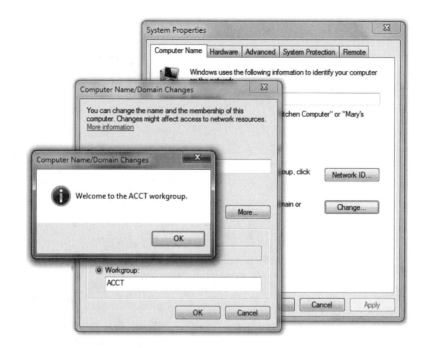

FIGURE 19-9

Logging into
a workgroup
computer

e x a m

ⓦ a t c h   *In Windows XP the first time you connect to a network, run the Network Setup Wizard. Open this wizard from Start | Control Panel | Network* ... *and Internet Connections | Network Connections | Network Setup Wizard (under Common Tasks).*

Workgroup Administration

Functionally, computers in different workgroups behave as if they were in the same workgroup; they can access shared folders and printers in precisely the same way. And that way depends on each computer in a workgroup that is sharing its files and/or printers having a local user account for each person in the workgroup to whom they want to give access. This is decentralized administration, because if ten computers in a workgroup wish to share resources from their computer with other users, a local account must be created for each user on each computer.

The trick here is to decide if you want each user to manually provide credentials every time they connect or if you want them to connect without having to enter credentials. If the answer is that you want them to enter credentials, then create an account that does not match the account they use to log in on their own computer. Then, a user browsing to the other workgroup computer is greeted with a log-in dialog box requiring credentials.

If the answer is that you want it to happen seamlessly, then on each workgroup computer that will share its resources, for each person create an account with a user name and password identical to the one on their individual computers. As they browse to the workgroup computer, the credentials will automatically be sent to the computer for authentication. Then, the user will have access to shared folders to which they have been manually given permissions. In the section on data security, we will explore how to create shares, how to apply permissions to those shares, and how to apply permission to the underlying files and folders. Since those tasks are nearly identical for sharing files and printers in a workgroup and in a domain, we will delay the details until after we talk about joining a Microsoft Active Directory domain.

Active Directory Domains

A Microsoft *Active Directory (AD) domain* is a collection of workstations and servers under single administrative control. The security accounts database is much more sophisticated than that on local Windows computers and resides on at least one special Windows Server computer called a domain controller. The securities database, or directory, is replicated across all domain controllers in the domain, allowing for more efficient access to the domain controllers from many locations. A medium-sized organization might consist of a single AD domain, where a large multinational firm might consist of many AD domains. When a computer joins a domain, a computer account is created for that computer and the computer itself logs on to the domain when it starts up. This is separate from a user logon. Joining a computer to a domain (Figure 19-10) requires local administrative rights, and when prompted for AD domain credentials, any valid AD user account may be specified; every AD user can join up to ten computers to the domain by default. Windows XP Professional and Windows Vista Business, Ultimate, and Enterprise editions can join a domain as can Windows 7 Professional, Enterprise, and Ultimate editions. Windows 8 Pro and Enterprise editions can join a domain.

Joining a computer to a domain provides the following benefits:

- You can log on to the computer using any valid user account that exists in Active Directory or any local account.

- You will not be asked to authenticate again to resources to which you have permissions in the domain.

FIGURE 19-10

Joining a computer to an Active Directory domain

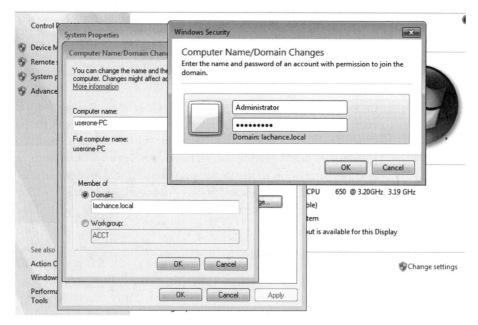

- The domain administrator can create centralized *Group Policy settings* for both your domain user account and your local computer that apply every time you log on (in the case of user settings) and every time the computer logs on (in the case of computer settings).

- The AD "Domain Admins" group is automatically added to the local computer "Administrators" group. This means members of "Domain Admins" have full control over every computer joined to the domain.

Users of nondomain-joined computers can still access network resources in an AD environment as long as they have valid AD credentials. The AD credentials of mobile laptop users will be cached locally (no expiration) so that these users can use the same credentials to authenticate to the laptop whether they are connected to the network or not. When logging on to a domain-joined computer, you can specify either a local user name and password or an AD user name and password. Remember that only passwords are case sensitive.

Domain-joined computers have the ability to share folders and printers in the same way that workgroup computers do. The only difference shows up when selecting the users and groups to which you are granting share permissions; you can select local users and groups, or you can select users and groups that exist in the AD domain.

CERTIFICATION OBJECTIVES

- **802: 1.5**   *Given a scenario, use Control Panel utilities*

- **802: 1.8**   *Explain the differences among basic OS security settings*

- **802: 2.1**   *Apply and use common prevention methods*

- **802: 2.4**   *Given a scenario, use the appropriate data destruction/disposal method*

This section includes coverage of pieces and parts of the four CompTIA Exam 802 objectives listed here. Objective 1.5 mentions the Control Panel Folder Options applet, which we described in Chapter 10, but there is a Sharing option in Folder Options that turns on a Sharing Wizard, not previously described. In addition, we describe how to create network shares and how to map drives. In a closely related topic, part of Objective 1.8 concerns NTFS and share permissions, which we describe and contrast and explain how they interact, as well as how moving and copying affects permissions. Learn about administrative shares and permission propagation and inheritance. The piece of Objective 2.1 covered in this section concerns directory (folder) permissions and how they affect the contents of directories (folders). For Objective 2.4, learn about low-level format, standard format, and hard drive sanitation methods.

Implementing Data Security

Now that you have learned about the ways you can configure your Windows computer for file and printer sharing, we will move on to ways we then protect data—shared or otherwise. In this section we will look at the file and folder-level permissions you can set on an NTFS volume and how they apply to both local users and users connecting over a network. We will detail how to share and map resources, and then how to apply NTFS file and folder encryption as compared to BitLocker drive encryption. Finally, when taking a storage device out of service, learn how to remove all data before reusing or recycling it. Learn about all these data protection functions in the following sections.

NTFS Permissions

NTFS permissions apply to both the local user sitting at the computer, as well as to someone accessing a file or folder over a network. It is not necessary to understand permissions if you are only sharing files through a HomeGroup, but if you use a workgroup or AD domain, you need to understand permissions and how to apply them. Set NTFS permissions at the most restrictive level that will allow users to accomplish their work. This is an application of the principle of least privilege described in Chapter 18.

The NTFS file system in Windows supports file and folder permissions through *discretionary access control (DAC)*, in which the creator of each file or folder is the owner and can control access. Additionally, NTFS permissions are also controlled by any account that is a member of the Administrators group. NTFS permissions should be assigned based on the principle of least privilege, using an *access control list (ACL)* on each file and folder. This list is a table containing at least one *access control entry (ACE)*, which in turn is a record containing just one user or group account name and the permissions assigned to that account. Administrators, the owner, or anyone with permission to create ACEs for the file or folder, can create ACEs. You manage permissions using the Security page in the Properties dialog box of a file or folder. The permissions to a file are slightly different from those applied to a folder. The standard folder permissions are

- Full Control
- Modify
- Read and Execute
- List Folder Contents
- Read
- Write

The standard file permissions are

- Full Control
- Modify
- Read and Execute
- Read
- Write

Allow and Deny

Each NTFS permission can be allowed or denied. Permissions explicitly denied always override allowed permissions. For example, if the Sales group is given the List Folder Contents NTFS permission to D:\Reports, and Bob is a member of Sales, Bob can list the contents of D:\Reports. If we deny Bob (or any group of which he is a member) the List Folder Contents permission for D:\Reports, Bob cannot list the contents of D:\Reports even though he is a member of a group that can.

Permission Propagation and Inheritance

When folder permissions and the permissions on the files within the folder are combined, the least restrictive permissions apply. But we also need to address the issue of the permission propagation throughout the folder hierarchy, also called *inheritance*. When you create a new folder or file, it inherits the permissions of the parent folder, unless you choose to block propagation of permissions to child objects.

When you view permissions on a file or folder, the permissions inherited from the parent will be grayed out, and you will not be able to modify those permissions at the child (inherited) level. You can assign new permissions, but you cannot alter inherited permissions unless you modify them in the folder in which they originated. You can block inheritance on a folder or file to which you wish to assign different (usually more restrictive) permissions.

Further, you can bypass inheritance with the Allow and Deny permissions for a file or folder. For instance, if you explicitly allow one of the standard permissions, such as Full Control, the user will have full control to the file or folder, even if inheritance would have given the user a lesser permission. If you explicitly deny a permission, the user will be denied a permission, even if it was granted to the user at a higher level in the folder hierarchy or through membership in a group. When a conflict occurs, Deny overrides Allow, and Deny creates the one exception to the rule that when NTFS folder and file permissions, including all inherited permissions, are combined, the least restrictive permission applies.

Permissions and Moving and Copying

When a file or folder is created on an NTFS volume, it inherits permissions from its parent folder; this is also true when a file or folder is copied or moved to a folder on an NTFS volume. There is one important exception to this rule that occurs when you move a file or folder to a different folder on the same NTFS volume: in this case, the file or folder takes its permissions with it.

Permissions on System Files and Personal Folders

Windows assigns permissions automatically to certain files and folders. They include system files and each user's personal folders.

System Files and Folders   Windows assigns restrictive permission on the folders in which the system files and other critical files are stored. In addition, the default setting in Windows Explorer (File Explorer in Windows 8) is to hide these files and folders. To view hidden files and folders you need to open the Tools menu, select Folder Options (a Control Panel applet), then select the View tab, and then expand the Hidden Files And Folders node and click the radio button next to Show Hidden Files, Folders, And Drives. In addition, to view system files, go down just a few items in that same list and click to clear the check box by Hide Protected Operating System Files. This is fine for learning about the hidden and system files, but for normal everyday use, we strongly recommend that you set these to the default to hide hidden files and folders and hide protected operating system files.

Personal Folders When a user logs on to a computer for the first time, Windows creates personal folders on the local hard drive for that user. If that local drive is an NTFS partition (the default file system), Windows will assign a default set of permissions to those folders designed to keep other users out. The user has full control over his personal folders, as does the Administrators group and the SYSTEM (operating system). No other user has permissions to these folders, nor can they view their contents.

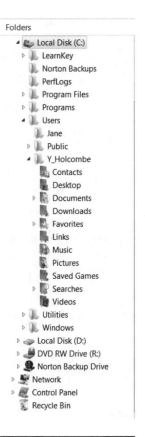

The default location for personal folders in Windows XP is in a folder that Windows assigns to the user's logon name and places in C:\Documents and Settings.

The default location for personal folders in Windows Vista, Windows 7, and Windows 8 is in a folder that Windows creates, names with the user's logon name, and places in C:\Users. As shown, the Users folder in Windows can contain personal folders for several users.

If you have a computer running Windows and with an NTFS drive C:, use the steps in Exercise 19-2 to view permissions on your personal folders.

EXERCISE 19-2

Viewing Folder Permissions in Windows

View the permissions on your personal folders. In order to complete this exercise, you need to use the Security tab on the Properties dialog of a folder on an NTFS volume. If this tab is not available on an NTFS volume in Windows XP, turn off Simple File Sharing. If you do not know how to do this, search for it in Windows Help.

1. Open Windows Explorer (File Explorer in Windows 8) and browse to C:\ Documents and Settings in Windows XP or C:\Users in all the newer versions. Notice the folders. There should be one for each user who has logged on, plus one titled "All Users" in Windows XP or "Public" in the newer versions.

2. Open the folder with the user name that you used when you logged on. View the contents of this folder. These folders make up the user profile for your user account on this computer. Close the folder.

3. Right-click the folder with the user name that you used to log on. Select Properties, and then select the Security tab. Examine the list of users and groups that have permissions to the folder.

4. Figure 19-11 shows this dialog box with the user Y-Holcombe highlighted in the list of user names and the permissions for that user listed below. These permissions amount to full control, which is also true for the Administrators group and SYSTEM (the Windows operating system). No other user or group has full control permissions to access these folders. Close the window when you are finished.

Applying Share Permissions

While we use the term "file sharing," sharing is actually done at the folder level. A share is a folder or printer that is available to network users. *Share permissions* are permissions set on a share, and they only apply to network users. If a shared folder is on an NTFS volume, a network user is affected by both share and NTFS permissions,

The default permissions on personal folders

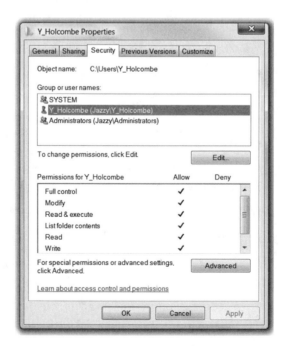

but local users are only affected by NTFS permissions. When preparing to share a folder with network users, the recommended order is

1. Create the folder.
2. Set the appropriate NTFS permissions on the folder and individual files (if needed).
3. Create the share.
4. Set the share permissions.

To create a file share on your PC, browse to a folder you wish to share, right-click that folder, and select Properties. Click the Sharing tab in the folder's Properties dialog. In Windows XP, select Share This Folder and complete the rest of the settings. In Windows Vista/7, from the Sharing tab, click the Advanced Sharing button, and then select Share This folder, as shown in Figure 19-12 in which we share the SalesReports folder. A share has three permissions—Full Control, Change, and Read—and each permission has an explicit Allow or Deny permission level. The default permissions on

FIGURE 19-12

In the Advanced Sharing dialog, click to place a check by Share This Folder.

a share give the Read permissions to the Everyone group. If you wish to change the default permission, click the Permissions button to access the Permissions dialog for the share, as shown in Figure 19-13.

Advanced sharing is simply a term for managing shares the old-fashioned way—one share at a time—turning on sharing for a folder or printer and giving users access to that share.

on the
j o b

Windows 7 Home Premium, with simpler dialog boxes that protect you from some of the complexity you will see with Windows 7 Ultimate, is the version we use for our examples.

Now, consider what happens when a user connects to files through a share. First, the NTFS file and folder permissions (inherited and otherwise) are combined with the resulting least-restrictive permission applying at the NTFS level, and then the resulting effective NTFS permission is combined with the share-level permission, and the most restrictive permission is applied.

Because you are depending on the NTFS permissions to provide file security to a shared folder, and you know that when NTFS and share permissions are combined,

FIGURE 19-13

The default
permission
on a shared
folder gives the
Everyone group
only the Read
permission.

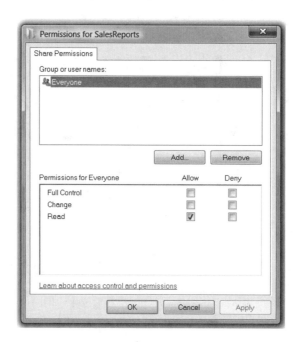

the most restrictive permission applies, it follows that the default Everyone Read Only permissions on a share will be both too permissive ("everyone" can read the contents) and yet too restrictive if you wish to allow network users to modify files in the shared folder. Exercise 19-3 walks through the steps to modify the share permissions in Windows 7 so only the users or groups you wish to give access to have the Full Control permission, and the Everyone group is completely removed from the share. Modifying the permission actually simplifies your administrative tasks by allowing you to assign the specific permission at the NTFS level.

EXERCISE 19-3

CertCam

Creating a Share and Modifying Share Permissions in Windows Vista/7

These instructions are specific for Windows Vista/7, but they are very similar to those in Windows XP. If your Windows 7 computer is a member of a HomeGroup, you will need to leave the HomeGroup in order to do this exercise.

1. From Windows Explorer, right-click a folder you wish to share and select Properties.

2. Select the Sharing tab, and then click the Advanced Sharing button. This step is important because you wish to modify the permissions on the share you will create.

3. In the Advanced Sharing dialog, most of the options will be dimmed until you click to place a check in the check box labeled Share This Folder.

4. Click the Permissions button. Notice that the Everyone group has Read permissions. We want to assign permissions to specific users or groups rather than to the Everyone group.

5. Click the Add button. Then click the Advanced button.

6. In the Select Users or Group box, click Find Now and the local accounts will appear in the Search results box at the bottom.

7. Select the user or group you wish to give permissions to the share. Click OK twice to return to Close the Select Users Or Groups box and return to the Permissions dialog for the selected folder. The name or group should now be included.

8. In the Group Or User Names box at the top of the Permissions dialog, select each added user or group in turn, and then click the Full Control box in the Permissions list.

9. Once you have assigned the desired permission, select the Everyone group and click the Remove button.

Administrative Shares

Windows has special hidden administrative shares that it creates automatically and uses when administrators, programs, and services connect to a computer over a network to perform special tasks that are mainly for use in a Microsoft domain network. Before Windows Vista, you could connect to an administrative share using a valid local account, but that feature is disabled beginning in Windows Vista, only allowing access to users with domain accounts. You cannot modify the permissions on an administrative share.

An administrative share has a special name that ends in the $ character, which marks the share as being hidden as well as being administrative. You can create a hidden share by appending the dollar sign to its name, but only the operating system can create administrative shares. These are the administrative shares:

- **Root partitions or volumes** Only internal storage is shared, no removable drives (optical, USB flash drives, etc.). The administrative share for drive C: is C$. The complete network path to this share is \\*computername*\C$, which is a Universal Naming Convention (UNC) path, described later in the section titled "Connecting with a UNC Path."

- **System root folder** This share points to the folder in which Windows was installed, which usually is C:\Windows. The UNC path to this share is \\computername\admin$.

- **FAX$ share**   This share points to a shared fax server.
- **IPC$ share**   This share is used for temporary connections for remotely administering a computer.
- **PRINT$ share**   This share is used for remote administration of shared printers.

---

e x a m

w a t c h

CompTIA A+ Exam 802 Objective 1.8 lists "administrative shares vs. local shares." This is not an equal comparison, since administrative shares

on your local Windows computer are local shares, as are nonadministrative shares that you create for sharing files and printers with network users.

Connecting to a Shared Folder

There are three ways to connect to a shared folder: browse to it for one-time use, map a drive letter to it, or connect using the UNC path.

Browsing for One-Time Use

Browsing to a share is simple—you open Windows Explorer (File Explorer in Windows 8) and first navigate to the computer and then to the share, open it, and access files.

Mapping a Drive Letter

Mapping a drive letter requires that you associate a local, unused drive letter with the share on another computer. This can be automated in a logon script or through settings in Group Policy, or it can be done manually. In the latter case, you can do it in the GUI or from the command line. Figure 19-14 shows the result of browsing the network for a shared folder called Shared_Files on a computer named LAPTOP in the GUI and then right-clicking that folder and choosing Map Network Drive.

Mapping a drive from the command line is done using NET USE—for example, **net use s: \\192.168.1.222\shared_files /persistent:yes** (see Figure 19-15). The Internet Protocol (IP) address or the host name can be used. The **/persistent:yes** parameter ensures that drive S: is mapped each time the user logs on. Take note that **net use * \\192.168.1.222\Shared_Files** would consume the next available drive letter.

FIGURE 19-14

Mapping a drive letter to a shared folder in the GUI

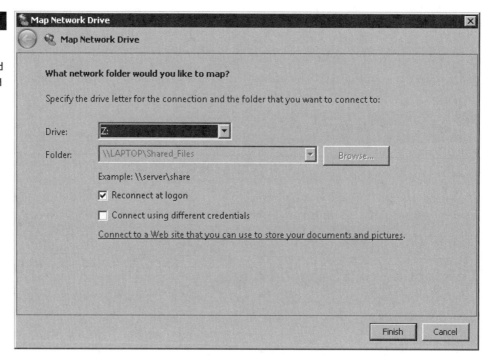

FIGURE 19-15

Mapping a drive letter to a shared folder from the command line

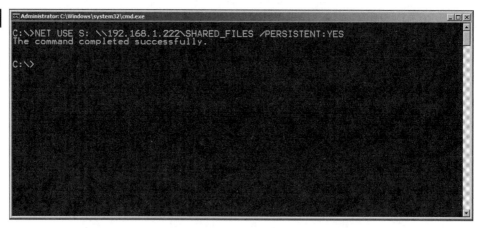

Connecting with a UNC Path

You can also map to a network share using a UNC path. *Universal Naming Convention (UNC)* is a method for pointing to shares on a network that begins with two backslashes (\\) followed by the name or IP address of the server, followed by a single backslash and the name of the share on the server. Do this in the Windows GUI by opening Windows Explorer, clicking in the address/navigation bar, and entering the UNC path. For instance, you would enter **\\yoda-pc\research** to create a mapping to the RESEARCH folder on the computer named YODA-PC. Figure 19-16 shows an example in which the IP address of the server is used in place of the name and the share name is SHARED_FILES. This method does not consume a local drive letter. In a workgroup, you will be prompted for credentials unless the target computer has the same user name and password you are currently using.

Applying NTFS File and Folder Encryption

Encrypting a folder using the Encrypting File System (EFS) on a Windows NTFS volume does not actually encrypt the folder itself, but all files in the folder are encrypted, and any new files saved in the folder are automatically encrypted. NTFS encryption only applies to files when they are saved in the encrypted folder and when they are moved or copied into unencrypted folders on NTFS volumes that support encryption. This is true, even if the folder to which the files are moved does not have encryption turned on. The files are not encrypted if they are copied to non-NTFS volumes or if they are emailed to someone.

FIGURE 19-16

Connecting to a shared folder using the UNC path

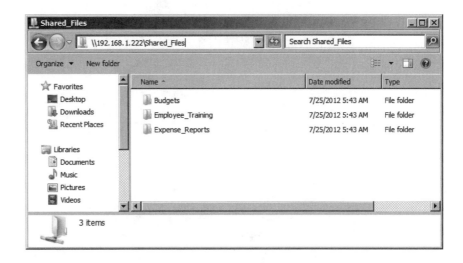

It is simple to encrypt a folder. Simply open the Properties dialog box of the folder and click Advanced. In the Advanced Attributes dialog box, click Encrypt Contents To Secure Data (see Figure 19-17), and then click OK.

You can only decrypt a file when logged on with the account used to encrypt it. Knowing this is important. Then decryption is transparent; simply open the file using the usual application for that file type. Both normal permissions and a special authorization to decrypt are applied. Even when logged on with another account with Full Control permissions to the file, you will not be able to decrypt the file, and, therefore, you will not be able to use it in any way.

EFS in Windows has the following features:

- A user can share encrypted files with other users.
- A user may encrypt offline files, which are files that are stored on a network server but cached in local memory when the local computer is disconnected from the server.

FIGURE 19-17

To encrypt files within a folder, turn on the Encrypt attribute.

The only person who can decrypt a file or folder is the person who encrypted it, or an EFS Recovery Agent. By default, only the local or Active Directory Administrator account is an EFS Recovery Agent.

on the job

While the CompTIA A+ Exam objectives require that you understand NTFS encryption, this encryption has shortcomings that you will learn about later in this chapter in the section "Troubleshooting Security."

BitLocker

BitLocker, briefly described in Chapter 2, will encrypt your entire boot volume. It requires that the boot volume be separate from the system volume, and when you install Windows Vista or Windows 7 on a blank hard disk, Windows Setup will create two volumes in case you later decide to enable BitLocker. BitLocker is supported in the Ultimate and Enterprise editions of Windows Vista and Windows 7, and in Windows 8 Pro. The system volume is the active primary partition containing the boot loader accessed by the basic input/output system (BIOS) during startup. Traditionally, the system and boot volumes are one and the same, but they must be separate because BitLocker cannot encrypt the system volume since it must be accessible by the BIOS startup, which cannot access an encrypted drive. On Windows Vista computers previous to Service Pack 1 this was a problem, because when Windows Vista installed, the system and boot volumes were together. Figure 19-18 shows Disk Management on a Vista computer on which the system and boot volumes (seen on Disk 0) are one and the same: Volume C:. Realizing that two volumes on the same physical disk are required, not two physical disks, is important. Further, beginning with Windows Vista Service Pack 1, and, of course, in Windows 7 and Windows 8, drives other than the boot volume can be encrypted with BitLocker.

Beginning in Windows 7 Microsoft changed how Windows partitions a drive during installation. If you install Windows 7 on an unpartitioned hard drive, it will create a small (approximately 100 MB) system partition and a second partition containing the balance of the drive space as the boot partition, as shown in Figure 19-19, in which Disk 0 contains a 100 MB NTFS volume identified as System, Active, and Primary. The boot volume is drive C:. This configuration will allow BitLocker to store the encryption key on the hard drive.

You can configure BitLocker to install the encryption key in one of several locations, including a Universal Serial Bus (USB) drive, a Trusted Platform Module (TPM) chip, or on the system volume (Windows 7 and Windows 8). If storing encryption keys on a USB drive, this USB drive must be plugged in during computer

FIGURE 19-18

The system and boot partitions are combined on Drive 0.

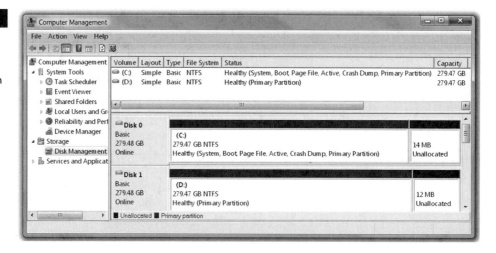

startup for decryption to succeed. To turn on BitLocker, open Windows Explorer or File Explorer and right-click the drive. Then select BitLocker, which opens the BitLocker Drive Encryption Wizard. Select how you want to unlock the drive, and then click Next and follow the instructions.

Windows 7 and Windows 8 also have a new feature called BitLocker to Go, which encrypts external hard drives and flash drives. While older versions of Windows cannot create a BitLocker to Go volume, Windows XP and Windows Vista computers can read BitLocker to Go–encrypted removable drives using the

FIGURE 19-19

The system volume and boot volume are separate on Disk 0.

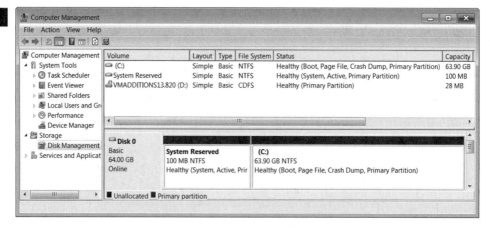

BitLocker to Go Reader, a program named BITLOCKERTOGO.EXE that is added to a drive that is encrypted with BitLocker to Go. To encrypt a removable drive, locate it in Windows Explorer or File Explorer and right-click the drive. Then select Turn On BitLocker, and after it encrypts the drive, choose how you want to unlock the drive. This page is different from that shown in Figure 19-20 in that it does not have the third choice, Automatically Unlock This Drive On This Computer.

Digital Data Wiping

In many organizations, the permanent removal of data is an important security function, but in too many organizations removing data from storage devices is overlooked. Further, the ordinary user deletes data every day that is not really deleted but saved in the Recycle Bin. Suppose you delete confidential files and then walk away from your computer without logging off. Someone with malicious intent could sit at your computer in your absence, open the Recycle Bin, restore the deleted files, and copy them to a flash drive.

FIGURE 19-20

BitLocker to Go
Drive Encryption
settings page

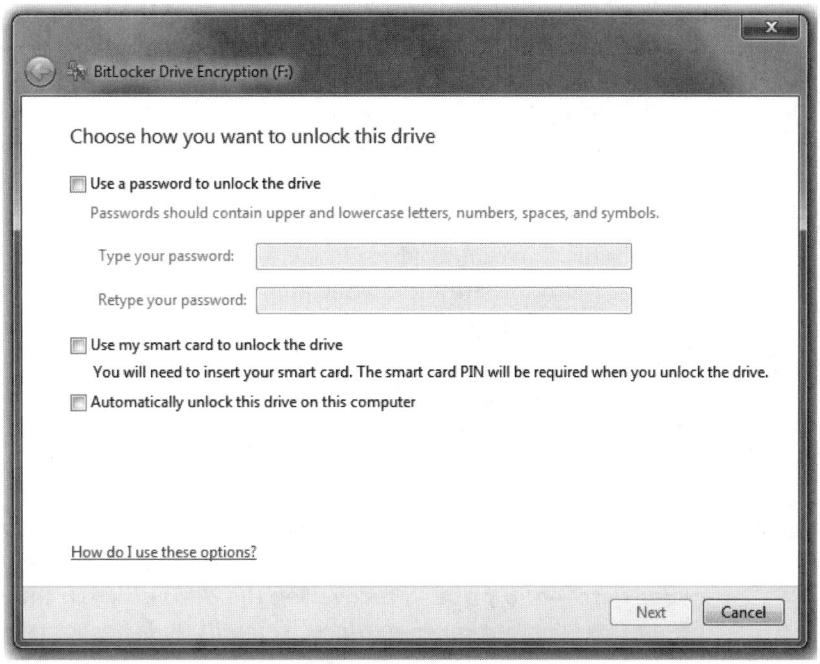

What Does Not Work

In a scenario in which you remove computers from service, thoroughly removing the data from the hard drives is important because not only is delete not a permanent delete but a format, and even partition programs do not truly destroy the data saved on hard drives. Therefore, a determined person can recover the data or even remnants of data files. So whether it is your personal financial data or your employer's super-secret research and development information, start being smarter about removing data from hard drives before it falls into the wrong hands. In Chapter 18 we described how to physically destroy drives. Most of us do not need this extreme measure, but can use one of the many inexpensive software tools for permanently removing data from hard drives.

What Does Work

To begin with, be smarter about deleting files from your hard drive in Windows. A simple delete from any menu in Windows will only move the file from its present folder into the Recycle Bin folder. There are conditions under which normally deleted files do not go to the Recycle Bin. These include files stored on removable media, files stored on network drives, and files deleted from compressed folders. These files are said to be "permanently" deleted, but even they can be recovered, although not quite as easily as from the Recycle Bin. Emptying the Recycle Bin prevents casual Windows users from undeleting data, but freely available tools can easily make this data recoverable.

Recovering a file from the Recycle Bin is easy. This is great for those times when you change your mind after deleting a file—or accidentally delete the wrong file. It is also a security hole. So, when you are absolutely sure that you want to permanently delete a file, you can avoid sending it to the Recycle Bin by selecting the file and holding down the SHIFT key while pressing the DELETE key.

This only protects you from the user who gains access to your computer and uses the Recycle Bin to recover deleted files. It does not protect you from someone who gains access to your computer or hard drive and uses specialized software (and hardware) to recover deleted files or files from a reformatted or repartitioned partition.

on the job

Use the staying power of data on a hard drive to your advantage. If a hard drive with valuable data fails or somehow is damaged so you cannot access the data on the drive, you can send the drive to a company that will recover your data—at a price. If recovering the data is worth thousands of dollars, then this is an option to explore. You will find these services by searching on "hard drive data recovery" in a search engine. Remember the bad guys can do this, too.

Shredding and Wiping

To protect your data from malicious attempts to recover it, use a data-wiping program that removes the data from the hard drives and other writable storage devices. The most recent name for this class of program is "shredder." A *shredder* overwrites deleted files using random data, and it can overwrite the same space multiple times, although this is not technically necessary. You can choose to shred an entire disk or just any one or more documents. Most of these programs will protect your data from all but the most aggressive attempts to recover data using very high-end software and equipment. Several free shredders such as Darik's Boot and Nuke as well as several commercial products are available.

Use a shredder program to wipe out a hard drive before moving a computer to another user, donating it, or sending it to a recycler.

Consider using a shredder program on a regular basis to ensure that deleted files are truly deleted. Beginning with XP, Microsoft Windows comes with CIPHER, a Command Prompt utility for encrypting files and folders. However, one option of this command, the /w (wipe) switch, makes it work like a shredder, permanently removing all deleted files from a folder or an entire volume. When you enter the command **cipher /w<drive>:\<folder_name>**, all the empty space (which includes deleted files) in the folder specified will be overwritten. If you enter the command with this syntax and only specify a drive, it will overwrite all the "empty" space on the drive. Figure 19-21 shows the CIPHER command with the correct syntax to overwrite the deleted files in D:\SalaryReview. The line of dots acts as a progress bar, with more dots showing as the program works until it is finished. CIPHER makes three passes: In the first pass, it writes all zeros onto the empty space; on the second pass, it writes the hexadecimal value FF over the same space; and on the final pass, it writes random numbers. This technique is the same one used by shredder programs.

Neither the CIPHER command nor third-party shredder programs should be used without taking the precaution of first backing up any data on the same drive, because the way these programs manipulate data on the drives has the potential of damaging good files if anything goes wrong during the shredding process.

Low-Level Format

The normal Windows FORMAT command—whether selected as an option within the GUI or run from the Command Prompt—does not directly overwrite data, and files can be recovered from a formatted drive if someone is willing to devote time, effort, and even money to do it. A better alternative is a physical format program, which is available sometimes in a hard drive's BIOS and/or the disc that comes with a hard drive system. You can also find some online for free from Hewlett Packard and other sources.

```
D:\>cipher /w:d:\salaryreview
To remove as much data as possible, please close all other applications while
running CIPHER /W.
Writing 0x00
.............................................................................
.....................
Writing 0xFF
.............................................................................
.....................
Writing Random Numbers
.............................................................................
.....................

D:\>
```

File Attributes

While not strictly part of security, file attributes, as you learned in Chapter 10, can affect your access to files on both File Allocation Table (FAT) and NTFS volumes. The use of hidden and system attributes is the closest thing you have to file security on a FAT volume. Attributes can be viewed, and in some cases set, by right-clicking a file or folder and choosing Properties (for advanced attributes, click the Advanced button). The ATTRIB.EXE command is the command-line equivalent. Figure 19-22 depicts applying the hidden and read-only attributes to a file from the command line using the ATTRIB command.

```
Administrator: C:\Windows\system32\cmd.exe

C:\>ATTRIB +H +R D:\BUDGETS\BUDGET-2013.XLS
```

CERTIFICATION OBJECTIVE

■ **802: 4.7** *Given a scenario, troubleshoot common security issues with appropriate tools and best practices*

Technically, all the listed topics for CompTIA Exam 802 Objective 4.7 were covered in Chapters 17 and 18. However, we decided to include some security troubleshooting issues not listed in the topics, but definitely knowledge an A+ technician should have.

Troubleshooting Security

Troubleshooting security follows the same path as all computer troubleshooting. Gather information, perform an analysis, arrive at possible solutions, and apply the solution and test it. Once you are successful, document the process so you or your coworkers will not have to "solve" the same problem twice. There are certain problems that are specific to PC security, and you will explore some of these in the following sections.

BIOS Password Problems

Earlier in this chapter, we explored the issue of setting passwords in BIOS. As with all passwords, forgetting a BIOS password is easy. How this will affect the user depends on the type of BIOS password that was set.

If a BIOS password is set on the system at startup, no one will be able to get beyond the BIOS password prompt and boot up the computer until the password is provided. Forget the password, and you are locked out of using the computer.

If a BIOS password is set on the System Setup menu, and only on this menu, the computer will boot up normally without requiring a BIOS system startup password. Forget the password, and you can start up the computer just fine, but you will not be able to access the System Setup menu and make changes. As we mentioned earlier, this password is necessary in situations in which people have physical access to computers, as in a computer lab.

In both cases, documenting the password or passwords is very important, and you should maintain and keep them in a safe place available to all authorized personnel. The password should not be something only the head techie knows but does not share with anyone else. There are better ways to gain job security.

If you set a password and later forget it, you will have to find out how to reset the BIOS in order to access BIOS Setup. Finding this in the motherboard manual can be difficult, as we have never seen one with an index. Fortunately, motherboard manuals are usually short, and the instructions for resetting or clearing the BIOS settings are usually near the back in a troubleshooting section. Alternatively, search the motherboard manufacturer's Website. What you must do after that depends on the system and can range from temporarily removing the battery that supports CMOS to changing a jumper setting and restarting the computer. Then, you can enter Setup without providing a password. Your work is not yet done, however, because you will have lost all custom settings and will need to reconfigure the BIOS settings. Recall Exercise 3-4 in Chapter 3, in which you learned how access the BIOS settings. This was followed by a paragraph titled "Backing Up BIOS Settings" containing suggestions for how to do this. If you have access to a copy of the BIOS settings for the computer, the configuration process will be far easier than trying to guess what the settings were. If you do not know the previous BIOS settings, accept the default settings, but you may face more than one choice here, such as Fail-Safe Defaults and Optimized Defaults. If you have such a choice, select Optimized Defaults first and see if everything functions. If not, you will have to change to the Fail-Safe Defaults. The moral to this story is either don't set a BIOS password or, if you do, don't lose the password.

Anyone who knows how can remove a BIOS password from a physically unlocked computer case. This demonstrates the futility of setting BIOS passwords on physically unsecured computers.

Biometric Authentication Problems

Sometimes users cannot log on to a Windows XP computer using biometrics when the computer resumes from Standby or Hibernate. Microsoft solved this problem in a hotfix. A hotfix is program code that fixes a specific problem. A hotfix is normally only available from Microsoft Product Support Services to persons who identify the problem. In these cases, Microsoft usually waives the normal charges for Microsoft Product Support Services. When we last checked, contacting Support Services was the only manner in which this fix was available. However, it is worth running Windows Update to see if this hotfix was added to the updates that are available free through this service. If you support one or more Windows computers that are using biometric authentication, check to see if they were updated, and update them before this becomes a problem.

When this problem occurs, the computer will still accept a basic interactive logon from the keyboard. Therefore, enter a user name and password from the keyboard. Then take steps to update the computer.

Forgotten Windows Password

If you have forgotten your password, there is help. For one thing, if you are part of a Windows domain, tell the domain administrator about your problem. Lost passwords are at the top of the list of things administrators must fix, especially in an environment where people log on with a standard interactive logon—entering user names and passwords at their keyboard. The administrator can log on with the Domain Administrator account (or any account with appropriate rights), access the Domain User account, and reset the password. The administrator can assign a password and configure your account so you will sign on with the assigned password but then must change it during that logon.

Now, if you are not part of a Windows domain, there is still some hope if you can log on with the Administrator account. If you know the local Administrator password, or an account that is a member of the local Administrators group, simply log on with this user name and password and modify the password setting for the user.

If you do not know the Administrator password and you are working with Windows XP, your installation of Windows may possibly have a hidden Administrator account without a password, and unless someone assigned a password to the account, you should be able to access it—in Safe Mode. To do that, restart your computer in Safe Mode. If you need help with Safe Mode, flip back to Chapter 13 and read about Safe Mode. Log on with the Administrator account. Unless the password was changed, you can leave the password blank when you log on. After logging on as the administrator, run the User Accounts applet, and then reset the password on the user account.

No Permissions on FAT32

You would like to set permissions on a folder that you plan to share. You first notice that there is no Security tab in the Properties dialog box for the folder. Perhaps you don't have Simple File Sharing turned on. Then you notice that the volume is not NTFS but FAT32. FAT32 does not support file- and folder-level permissions. The only permissions in this case will be at the share level, and you want to set NTFS permissions so you can assign permissions to each subfolder under the shared folder. What can you do?

If there is no compelling reason for using FAT32 on the volume, convert it to NTFS. Before doing this, back up the entire drive that you plan to convert, just in case something goes wrong during the process. Once the backup is completed, convert the volume using the Disk Management node of the Computer Management console, or by opening a Command Prompt window and running the CONVERT program. The syntax for running the CONVERT program is **convert *d*: /fs:ntfs**

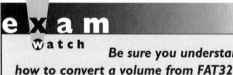

Be sure you understand how to convert a volume from FAT32 to NTFS. Remember, you cannot reverse this without losing the data on the drive.

where *d*: is the drive you wish to convert. Whether you use Disk Management or the CONVERT program, if the drive you are converting is not being used by the OS or any other program, the conversion will occur immediately. If the drive is in use, as is always the case with the system drive (normally drive C:), you will see a message that the conversion will occur the next time Windows is restarted.

This conversion is one-way. You cannot convert back from NTFS to FAT32 unless you reformat the drive, and then you lose all the data on the hard drive.

Once you have converted the file system from FAT32 to NTFS, you can assign permissions to files and folders and use other NTFS features not available in FAT32.

Encryption Issues

If you, or the users you support, encrypt files using EFS encryption, you risk having the encryption defeated or being locked out of your own encrypted files. Sometimes we leave the worst news for last.

EFS Encryption Can Be Broken

One way in which someone can break EFS encryption is by guessing your password. Once someone does that, that person can log on with your user name, which is often displayed in the logon dialog box as the last logged-on user. Once logged on, the invader has access to everything on your computer, including your encrypted files. Imagine what can happen if an attacker discovers the password for an EFS Recovery Agent account!

The key is to not allow any unauthorized person physical access to your computer. With physical access, someone can use a variety of tools to access your encrypted files. There are free software tools, classified as password recovery software, that can crack passwords on Windows accounts—both local and domain. If you need such a tool, use an Internet search engine to search on this category of software.

Encrypted Files Can Become Inaccessible

You have been careful to encrypt sensitive data files and to back up your computer. Then, one day your computer crashes. After trying many recovery options, you reformat the hard drive, reinstall Windows, and restore your data from the most recent backup set. Your new installation of Windows has an account with the same user name as your old one. You believe you did everything you were supposed to do, but you cannot access the encrypted files you restored to your computer. What can you do?

Starting with Windows Vista, EFS uses Public Key Infrastructure (PKI) certificates. You can back up (export) your PKI certificate using the graphical Certificate Manager tool, or you can use the CIPHER.EXE command-line tool with the /X option. You can then import this certificate if your computer is reinstalled. In an enterprise, certificates can be stored with your user account in Active Directory. If your computer is joined to a domain, yet another option is to have an EFS Recovery Agent decrypt your files for you.

Software Firewall Issues

A firewall may prompt a pop-up message that a program running on your computer is trying to access the Internet; the firewall then requires that you make a decision to allow this action or not. When this happens, use a search engine to discover if the program is harmful. A wealth of information is on the Web about problem programs. If your firewall has blocked a program, you can be sure that others' firewalls have also. Your search will normally result in many hits, and some of the Websites it discovers may not be well monitored, or the advice may not be from experienced and qualified people. Do not make a decision based on just one Website. Check out several. If you know and trust the company posting the information, such as one of the top security software companies, you may accept their answer as authoritative.

Some personal firewalls provide additional information on blocked files with a recommended action you may choose to take. Still, you often have to make a decision without being absolutely sure of the safety of the program, even when it appears to be one you are familiar with. Windows does protect certain operating system files with safeguards in the form of digital signatures. If Windows indicates that a program is digitally signed, you can usually trust the program.

Wireless Access Point Compromised

You are the administrator of a wireless LAN and find that although you could once access the wireless access point's Web page, you no longer can do this from any computer on the WLAN. You also fear that someone has gotten into the wireless access point (WAP)/broadband router and made changes in the security settings, compromising the WAP and the private network. What can you do? You will need to reset the WAP using the manufacturer's instructions. Then, because resetting the WAP erases all your settings, you will need to reconfigure it. Be sure to set a complex password on the Administrator account to keep intruders out, and set all the security settings on the WLAN.

CERTIFICATION SUMMARY

An IT tech must know the differences between HomeGroups, workgroups, and Microsoft AD domains and how to configure Windows clients in each of these resource-sharing models. A closely related topic is the differences and features of NTFS permissions, including how NTFS permissions apply to resources for the local user as well as network users. Another important topic is NTFS permission propagation and inheritance. Compare NTFS versus share permissions, and be sure you understand how both share permissions and NTFS permissions are combined to apply to network users.

An A+ candidate should also practice and understand methods for creating shares on the server side and for mapping shares from the client side. Windows creates special hidden shares, called administrative shares, mainly for use in an AD domain.

Understand the differences between NTFS Encrypted File System (EFS) as a file encryption tool and BitLocker and BitLocker to Go as disk encryption tools. Be sure you can explain the various methods for destroying data before donating, selling, or disposing of old computers.

Approach security troubleshooting as you would any PC troubleshooting. Some special security issues are BIOS passwords, biometric devices, forgotten Windows passwords, lack of permissions on FAT32 volumes, problems with NTFS encryption, software firewall messages, and preventive maintenance for security.

TWO-MINUTE DRILL

Here are some of the key points covered in Chapter 19.

Configuring Windows Clients for File and Printer Sharing

❏ HomeGroups are new in Windows 7 and facilitate sharing documents and printers on a small network.

❏ There can be only a single HomeGroup per LAN, the network location must be set to Home, and IPv6 is required.

❏ Libraries are central to how HomeGroups work, as they organize folders from different locations under a single entity and HomeGroup users can connect to Public libraries on HomeGroup computers where users have allowed this sharing.

❏ Workgroups are a peer-to-peer file and print sharing option, with decentralized administration, requiring creating both shares and user accounts on each computer in the workgroup that will share resources.

❏ A Microsoft Active Directory (AD) domain is a collection of workstations and servers under single administrative control, meaning that access to all computers and other resources in the domain is centrally managed.

❏ Windows XP Professional and Windows Vista Business, Ultimate, and Enterprise editions can join a domain as can Windows 7 Professional, Enterprise, and Ultimate editions. Windows 8 Pro and Enterprise editions can join a domain.

Implementing Data Security

❏ NTFS permissions that are explicitly denied always take precedence over any allowed permissions.

❏ UNC paths and drive letter mappings can be used to access shared folders.

❏ File and folder attributes are flags used by software to treat those files and folders in a specific manner.

❏ Use EFS encryption on the most sensitive data files. BitLocker encrypts entire volumes and is supported in the Ultimate and Enterprise editions of Windows Vista and Windows 7, and in Windows 8 Pro. In addition, BitLocker in Windows 7 and Windows 8 includes BitLocker to Go for encrypting removable hard disks or flash drives.

❑ Permanent data removal is an important security task, required when moving a computer from one user to another in an organization or when removing the computer from service within the organization.

❑ Data deleted by users is not truly deleted but saved in the Recycle Bin and easily recovered. Even after you remove data from the Recycle Bin and "permanently" delete it, it can be recovered unless the disk has been wiped with a disk-wiping program. Do not confuse the Microsoft disk-formatting utility with disk wiping; data can be recovered from a disk after formatting, but not after disk wiping. A special low-level format, available from disk manufacturers and other sources, will also destroy existing data on a disk.

❑ File attributes, described in Chapter 10, are not strictly part of security, but the use of hidden and system attributes is the closest thing you have to file security on a FAT volume.

Troubleshooting Security

❑ A BIOS password, depending on its function, will keep users from starting up the OS, or just keep everyone out of the System Settings menu.

❑ To remove a BIOS password, follow the manufacturer's instructions, which may require opening the computer and setting jumpers to erase the contents of CMOS where the BIOS password is saved.

❑ If you remove the BIOS password by erasing the contents of CMOS, you will need to run the system Setup program and enter the correct settings for the system.

❑ If users cannot log on to a Windows computer using biometrics as the computer resumes from Standby or Hibernate, check to see if the computer has the latest updates, because this problem was resolved in an update. Until you solve the problem, the short-term fix is to log on with a basic interactive logon from the keyboard.

❑ You have several options if you forget your password, depending on the situation. If your logon account is in a Windows domain, ask the domain administrator to reset the password.

❑ If the forgotten password is for a local user account, you also have several options. Log on as the local administrator if you know that password. Then reset the password for the user account. Or perhaps your installation of Windows XP has a hidden Administrator account. Access this account by restarting in Safe Mode and logging on with the Administrator account. Unless the password was changed, you can leave the field blank. Then reset the password for the user account.

❑ If the Security tab is missing from the Properties dialog of a file or folder on an NTFS volume, Simple File Sharing is probably on. Turn this off, and the Security tab will appear.

❑ FAT32 does not support file and folder permissions. Therefore, unless there is a special reason for having a FAT32 volume, convert FAT32 volumes to NTFS using the CONVERT command at the Command Prompt.

❑ Two major problems with EFS file encryption are that it can be broken and that encrypted files can become inaccessible. Third-party programs may be able to recover the encrypted files.

❑ A message from the firewall may pop up that a program running on your computer is trying to access the Internet. The firewall then requires that you decide to allow this action or not. You should research the filename displayed in the message to determine the action you should take. Use a search engine and/or information available from the firewall.

❑ If you cannot access a WAP Web page and you previously could, reset the WAP using the manufacturer's instructions. This will erase the WAP's settings, so you will need to reconfigure it. Be sure to set a complex password on the administrative account to keep intruders out, and set all the security settings on the WLAN.

SELF TEST

The following questions will help you measure your understanding of the material presented in this chapter. Read all of the choices carefully because there might be more than one correct answer. Choose all correct answers for each question.

Configuring Windows Clients for File and Printer Sharing

1. You are the Windows technician for a large organization. An employee, Francesca, brings her personal laptop with Windows 7 Starter edition to work but cannot create a HomeGroup. Which of the following is the cause?
   A. Multicast forwarding must be enabled on the router.
   B. IPv6 must be disabled.
   C. IPv4 must be disabled.
   D. Wrong Windows 7 edition.

2. Which network location, when selected in Windows 7, will cause Windows to disable both Network Discovery and HomeGroup?
   A. Home
   B. Work
   C. Public
   D. Workgroup

3. Which editions of Windows 7 can join a HomeGroup? (Choose all that apply.)
   A. Ultimate
   B. Home Premium
   C. Professional
   D. Enterprise

4. When someone enables sharing of documents in a HomeGroup, what is actually shared from that person's computer?
   A. Public Documents
   B. C:\Users\Public
   C. \\computername\C$
   D. Personal folders

5. Your home network consists of a Windows XP Professional computer and two Windows 7 Home Premium computers. You would like to share music and video files among all computers. What should you configure?

   A. HomeGroup

   B. Active Directory domain

   C. Streaming server

   D. Workgroup

6. A tax auditor is at your office for the next three days. She requires access to resources stored on servers in your AD domain. What should you do to grant her access to those resources she needs?

   A. Join her computer to the domain.

   B. Provide domain administrative credentials to her.

   C. Enable the AD guest account.

   D. Create an AD account for her, grant permissions, and set the account expiration date to four days in the future.

Implementing Data Security

7. What strategy should you use when setting NTFS permissions? Hint: This is an application of the principle of least privilege.

   A. Set the least restrictive level for all users.

   B. Set the most restrictive level that still allows users to accomplish their work.

   C. Give the Everyone group Read permissions.

   D. Use Allow or Deny on every permission.

8. What permission, applied directly to a file, defeats inheritance?

   A. Deny

   B. Allow

   C. Full Control

   D. Modify

9. What simple rule does Windows apply to inherited NTFS permissions to determine effective permissions?

   A. Most restrictive applies.

   B. Least restrictive applies.

   C. Full Control is calculated first.

   D. Read is calculated first.

10. What is the recommended order of tasks for creating shares and applying permissions?
   A. Create the share, apply NTFS permissions, and apply share-level permissions.
   B. Give Everyone Read access, apply NTFS permissions, apply share-level permissions, and create the share.
   C. Apply NTFS permissions, create the share, and apply share-level permissions.
   D. Apply NTFS permissions, apply share-level permissions, and create the share.

11. When a user connects over a network to a file share, how are the effective NTFS permissions and the share permissions combined for that user?
   A. Most restrictive.
   B. Least restrictive applies.
   C. Full Control is calculated first.
   D. Read is calculated first.

12. If an encrypted file is moved or copied into an unencrypted folder on an NTFS volume, which of the following will occur?
   A. It will be decrypted.
   B. It will remain encrypted.
   C. It will be read-only.
   D. Encrypted files cannot be moved or copied.

13. Which encryption feature comes with the Ultimate and Enterprise editions of Windows Vista and Windows 7, as well as Windows 8 Pro, and encrypts an entire volume?
   A. NTFS encryption
   B. WPA2
   C. DriveLock
   D. BitLocker

14. Which of the following identifies the administrative share that points to the system root folder?
   A. C$
   B. IPC$
   C. \\computername\admin$
   D. PRINT$

15. Jerome is the IT director for Acme. He must dispose of used hard drives and is concerned about sensitive data that may have been stored on them in the past. What should Jerome do to ensure the data is not recoverable?
   A. Empty the Recycle Bin.
   B. Wipe the hard disks.
   C. Format the hard disks.
   D. Encrypt the hard disks.

16. Which of the following commands will map G: to the root of drive C: on a laptop called PC424?
   A. NET USE C: \\G:\PC424
   B. NET USE G: \\PC424\C$
   C. NET USE G: \\PC424\C:
   D. NET USE G: \\PC424\C:$

Troubleshooting Security

17. What are the direct consequences of forgetting the password on the System Settings menu?
   A. Inability to launch Windows.
   B. All system settings will be reset.
   C. The Windows password will be reset.
   D. Inability to access the System Settings menu.

18. Because users frequently forget their passwords, administrators have the right to take this action.
   A. Reset the account.
   B. Restrict the account.
   C. Reset the password.
   D. Remove the password from the account.

19. You discover that a Windows XP computer on your network is sharing files with others, but only has FAT32 on the sole disk volume, C:. You want to assign a variety of permissions to the five people accessing this computer for which you need NTFS. What is the quickest solution that will not destroy data?
   A. Reinstall Windows XP and select NTFS.
   B. Open a Command Prompt and enter **format c: /fs:ntfs**.
   C. Open a Command Prompt and enter **convert c: /fs:ntfs**.
   D. Open a Command Prompt and enter **cipher c: /fs:ntfs**.

20. If you find yourself locked out of the administrative screens on your WAP/broadband router because someone has changed the administrator password, what should you do? All of the following are correct; you must put them in the correct order.
   A. Assign a strong password.
   B. Change the administrator user name.
   C. Reset the WAP.
   D. Configure appropriate security settings.

SELF TEST ANSWERS

Configuring Windows Clients for File and Printer Sharing

1. ☑ **D.** Only Windows 7 Home Premium edition and later can create a HomeGroup.
   ☒ **A** is incorrect. Multicast forwarding can allow a HomeGroup to exist on different sides of a router, but it is clear that Francesca has the wrong Windows 7 edition. **B** and **C** are both incorrect. HomeGroups require IPv6 even if your network also uses IPv4.

2. ☑ **C.** Public, when selected as a network location in Windows 7, causes Windows to disable both Network Discovery and HomeGroup support.
   ☒ **A** and **B** are both incorrect because choosing Home or Work will turn on Network Discovery and allow you to enable HomeGroup (as long as other requirements are met). **D** is incorrect because workgroup is not a network location.

3. ☑ **A, B, C, and D.** All Windows 7 editions can join a HomeGroup.

4. ☑ **A.** Public Documents, a folder in the Documents library, is shared.
   ☒ **B,** C:\Users\Public, is incorrect. **C,** \\<*computername*>\C$, is incorrect. **D,** personal folders, is incorrect.

5. ☑ **D.** Workgroups allow you to share folders and printers to computers running any version of Windows.
   ☒ **A** is incorrect. HomeGroups only apply to Windows 7. **B** is incorrect; Active Directory is not required on this small home network. **C** is a generic answer, and the question does not ask about streaming; it asks about sharing files.

6. ☑ **D.** When accessing domain resources, she will be prompted for domain credentials, which she will supply to get access to network resources.
   ☒ **A** is incorrect; her computer does not have to be in the domain. **B** is incorrect because you should never give somebody much more access than they require to perform a task. **C** is not recommended since audit tracking becomes difficult.

Implementing Data Security

7. ☑ **B.** Set the most restrictive level that still allows users to accomplish their work.
   ☒ **A,** set the least restrictive level for all users, is incorrect because this would expose data to unauthorized users. **C,** give the Everyone group Read permission, is incorrect because this would often be too permissive. **D,** use Allow or Deny on every permission, is incorrect because this was not stated as a good strategy and it defeats inheritance, which is not always a good thing.

8. ☑ **A.** Deny explicitly defeats an inherited permission.
☒ **B,** Allow, is incorrect because this defeats all inherited permissions except Deny. **C,** Full Control, and **D,** Modify, are both defeated if they are explicitly set to Deny.

9. ☑ **B.** Least restrictive applies is the rule Windows uses for determining effective permissions on a file or folder on NTFS.
☒ **A,** most restrictive applies, is incorrect, as this is not the rule used. **C,** Full Control is calculated first, and **D,** Read is calculated first, are both incorrect.

10. ☑ **C.** Apply NTFS permissions, create the share, and apply share-level permissions is correct.
☒ **A,** create the share, apply NTFS permissions, and apply share-level permissions, is incorrect because if you create the share before applying NTFS permissions, the share-level default permissions will leave the shared files and folders too vulnerable. **B,** give Everyone Read access, apply NTFS permissions, apply share-level permissions, and create the share, is incorrect for two reasons: Everyone Read is too open for most situations, and you cannot apply share-level permissions before you create a share. **D,** apply NTFS permissions, apply share-level permissions, and create the share, is also incorrect because you cannot apply share-level permissions before you create the share.

11. ☑ **A.** Most restrictive is how effective NTFS permissions and share permissions combine for a user.
☒ **B,** least restrictive, is incorrect, although this is how the effective NTFS permissions are applied. **C,** Full Control, is calculated first, and **D,** Read is calculated first, are both incorrect.

12. ☑ **B.** The file will remain encrypted if moved or copied into an unencrypted folder on an NTFS volume.
☒ **A,** it will be decrypted, is incorrect because as long as the move or copy is not performed as a drag-and-drop operation, an encrypted file will remain encrypted. **C,** it will be Read-Only, is incorrect because this is not the result of moving or copying an encrypted file into an unencrypted folder on an NTFS volume. **D,** encrypted files cannot be moved or copied, is incorrect because encrypted files can be moved or copied.

13. ☑ **D.** BitLocker is the encryption that comes with the OS and protects an entire volume on a computer running the Ultimate and Enterprise versions of Windows Vista and Windows 7, or Windows 8 Pro.
☒ **A,** NTFS encryption, is incorrect because it only encrypts at the folder level on an NTFS volume. **B,** WPA2, is incorrect because this is a Wi-Fi encryption standard. **C,** DriveLock, is incorrect because it is not an encryption technology, but a system for controlling access to an entire hard drive without data encryption.

14. ☑ **C.** *computername**admin$* identifies the system root folder administrative share.
     ☒ **A,** C$, **B,** IPC$, and **D,** PRINT$, although all administrative shares, do not point to the system root folder.

15. ☑ **B.** Disk wiping means overwriting the entire hard disk with either zeroes or random values.
     ☒ **A, C,** and **D** are incorrect. Files are easily restored from the Recycle Bin. Formatting a hard disk does not actually destroy the data stored on the disk; it simply prepares it with a new file system; the data is recoverable. Encrypting the hard disk is less secure because if you have the decryption keys, you can get to the data. This is not true if you've wiped the disk.

16. ☑ **B.** Drive C: is a hidden share (suffixed with a $).
     ☒ **A, C,** and **D** are incorrect variations of drive letters, computer names, and share names.

Troubleshooting Security

17. ☑ **D.** Inability to access the System Settings menu is the direct consequence of forgetting the password on the System Settings menu.
     ☒ **A,** inability to start up Windows, is incorrect because forgetting the password on the System Settings menu will have no effect on starting Windows. **B,** all system settings will be reset, is incorrect because this will not happen just because you forget the System Settings menu password. **C,** the Windows password will be reset, is incorrect because the password on the System Settings menu will not affect the Windows password for any user account.

18. ☑ **C.** Resetting the password is something an administrator can do to help a user who forgot his password.
     ☒ **A,** reset the account, **B,** restrict the account, and **D,** remove the password from the account, are all incorrect actions when a user forgets her password.

19. ☑ **C.** Open a Command Prompt and enter **convert c: /fs:ntfs**. This will convert drive C: to NTFS without overwriting data.
     ☒ **A,** reinstall Windows XP and select NTFS, is incorrect because it would not be a quick solution and would depend on migrating the data to the new installation. **B,** open a Command Prompt and enter **format c: /fs:ntfs**, is incorrect because this would effectively wipe out everything on the hard drive, requiring reinstalling Windows and restoring the data. **D,** open a Command Prompt and enter **cipher c: /fs:ntfs**, is incorrect because CIPHER will not place NTFS on the volume.

20. ☑ **C, B, A,** and **D.** Reset the WAP to return it to factory settings, change the administrator user name from the default, assign a strong password, and configure appropriate security settings.

20

Supporting Mobile Devices

Mobile computing was once solely the territory of the business traveler with laptop in tow, resting what was sometimes a hefty computer on knees in waiting rooms and on trays on airliners. Today that model of mobile computing seems rather quaint as more and more ordinary people are doing mobile computing with smaller, faster devices in more places—many of them not far from home. We confess, we even do mobile computing at home, texting from our smartphones, to keep up with family, friends, business associates, and each other. Tablets are issued to schoolchildren of all ages for delivering courseware content. And let's not even begin to talk about the use of smartphones among even the youngest of children. In this chapter we will explore mobile devices from the A+ technician's perspective, focusing on the smartphones and tablets, and making comparisons between these devices and laptops, which were previously covered in Chapters 7 and 12.

CERTIFICATION OBJECTIVES

- **802: 1.5**   *Given a scenario, use Control Panel utilities*

- **802: 3.1**   *Explain the basic features of mobile operating systems*

- **802: 3.4**   *Compare and contrast hardware differences in regard to tablets and laptops*

As described in Chapter 7, a typical laptop is a portable computer that has an all-in-one component layout and includes a keyboard as part of its physical construction as well as a touchpad. Laptops are essentially portable versions of traditional desktop computers. Recent variations on the laptop theme are physically scaled-down devices such as netbooks and Ultrabooks. A netbook is a smaller laptop with less capability, primarily used for accessing the Web and using email. The newest laptop variant, Ultrabooks, are powerful, full-featured laptops using all solid-state components but focusing on slimness, light weight, and high power (with associated high cost). Most laptops still use hard disk drives for storage and most still include built-in disc drives. Ultrabooks feature solid-state storage. Although they are truly portable computers, they are not nearly as portable as tablets and smartphones, and therefore are not considered mobile devices in the same sense. Keep these features of laptops in mind as we explore the world of smartphones and tablets.

Overview of Mobile Devices

The most popular mobile devices today are smartphones and tablets—both of which can perform a huge number of computer functions, depending on the apps you install. A *smartphone* fits in the palm of your hand and functions as a cell phone handset, as well as your personal Jack-of-all gadgets. When you select a smartphone, you are also selecting a certain operating system (OS), as well as committing to a contract to use that smartphone on a certain cellular network for a specific length of time. There are numerous smartphone manufacturers, but only a handful own a significant share of those sales, with Apple showing the most growth and overtaking all the others. They are, to date (each listed with a recent model line), Apple (iPhone), Samsung (Galaxy), HTC (One X), and Motorola (Droid RAZR).

A *tablet* (less often called a *tablet* PC), is a portable computer without an integrated keyboard. A tablet is smaller than most laptops, larger than a cell phone, and has a touch screen display. One thing a tablet is not is a cell phone, because it is simply too big and heavy to use as a handset, although it may have an optional connection (with service fee) to a cellular data network for Internet connectivity. So, it is mainly size and the fact that a smartphone is first a cell phone that separates these two types of mobile devices. There are numerous tablet manufacturers, but the top tablet manufacturers and their most popular models are Apple (iPad), Amazon (Kindle, Kindle Fire, and Kindle Fire HD), Google (Nexus 7), and Samsung (Galaxy Tab 10.1). In this section we will give a user's perspective on smartphones and tablets, and then look at the hardware and software features that set each type of mobile device apart from the others.

Smartphones and Tablets in Everyday Life

We own and use many computing devices. We have two PCs we use daily (plus one "spare"), a very powerful laptop, an Apple iMac, a new iPad (commonly called the iPad3) with a wireless keyboard, two powerful smartphones, and two Kindles. We've discovered real differences in what they're good for and how to use them.

We do a lot of research online, and find that smartphones and tablets don't have nearly the search capabilities of the desktops or the laptop simply because of the small screen size and the lack of a physical keyboard. When you're searching for information, you tend to move rapidly from site to site, and typing on the tablet or smartphone screen is more difficult.

When you're trying to read a screen on a smartphone, you must move your focus around the document in order to read it all, as opposed to having a large portion of the Website showing on a monitor. With software designed for mobile use, the tablet and smartphones become much more usable. The ability to access literally thousands of apps that can convert a smartphone or tablet into almost any kind of tool you can think of is unprecedented. We love our apps!

We do a lot of reading, and since we got the Kindles, we are hooked on reading books via Kindle, but not always from the original devices. The Kindles are wonderful to use, but they require that you be in a lighted area. We installed the Kindle app on our desktop machines, on our smartphones, and on the iPad. Surprisingly, we discovered that we prefer reading books on our smartphones in certain situations. They are very small, pocketable, and have backlit screens that let us use them in low light. The iPad is relatively heavy; reading a book on a big bright screen is tiring; and if you like to read at bedtime, you only need to drop the tablet on your face once to switch to the smartphone. For researching texts, we like using the Kindle app on a desktop because of the powerful search capabilities.

A great deal of attention is being paid to the use of smartphones and tablets as tools for training and for performance support on the job. There is no doubt that these kinds of uses are growing in many industries for on-the-job or just-in-time training.

All that being said, however, huge numbers of people use smartphones and tablets for music, videos, texting, and staying in touch with each other. Although you can do these things on desktop and laptop computers, the "take with you anywhere" capability of these mobile devices is wonderful.

Hardware Features

While there are exceptions, the user should not open up smartphones and tablets, and they rarely allow for hardware upgrades, especially as far as memory and networking connections. Laptops remain more expandable than smartphones and tablets. Among the few peripherals available for mobile devices, the most common may be a headset for listening to music. Depending on how you use your device, you may also want an external keyboard, attached to a Universal Serial Bus (USB) or proprietary USB connection or wirelessly via Bluetooth. Whatever you wish to add, first determine what ports are available on the mobile device. That requires learning more about the hardware features.

on the
job

Nothing is impossible, and if you search YouTube, you will find videos of people dismantling a variety of tablets, including Apple's latest iPad (on the first day it was available). Although possible, there is risk in dismantling a $600 tablet. You can easily render it useless, and even opening one up voids the warranty!

Screens

All popular smartphones and tablets now have touch interfaces in the form of touch screens that accept and interpret multiple touch gestures at a time—something called *multi-touch*. The touch screen is the main input device on a smartphone or tablet, while currently touch screens are on few laptop models. This may change as manufacturers bring out a range of laptops and tablets running Microsoft's Windows 8, which contains remarkable support for touch screens.

Of course, the screen is also the main output device on smartphones and tablets. Most smartphones and tablets use some form of liquid crystal display (LCD) screens that are further modified to be touch sensitive, although some smartphones use some form of organic light-emitting diode (OLED) technology described in Chapter 5. The benefit of OLED over LCD technology is that OLED is lighter and uses less power because it does not use backlighting. The present technology for OLED is too expensive to produce screens larger than the size of a smartphone.

e x a m

ⓦatch

CompTIA Exam 802 Objective 3.4 lists touch flow along with multi-touch. However, the closest reference you will find to this is Touch-FLO, a touch screen user interface (UI) manufacturer

HTC used several years ago in their Pocket PCs and subsequently phased out. It was tied to a gesture in which you dragged your finger up and then moved it left and right.

The touch screens in current smartphones and tablets are *capacitive screens* that sense capacitance (the electrical charge) from your body when you touch the screen.

Capacitive touch screens really work best when you use your finger. However, several manufacturers make a pen-shaped device called a *stylus* just for these screens. This stylus is very different from the stylus you may use with an input device like a Wacom tablet, because they work passively, using a special material, such as rubber that mimics a finger. We have tried them with our smartphones and tablet, and find they work okay on a tablet, and are a bit more helpful on the smaller screen of a smartphone. A stylus keeps the screen cleaner, but it is one more thing to keep track of and easy to misplace!

on the
ⓙob *Older smartphone touch screens used a different noncapacitive technology that responded better to a stylus than to a finger.*

Older screen technology required screen calibration to align touch actions, and you may encounter some smartphones that still require this. When you need to do that you start the calibration program and then touch a symbol that appears sequentially in each corner of the screen and then one in the screen's center. The software then adjusts the touch calibration to match.

All modern mobile devices support *screen rotation,* a feature also called *screen orientation,* that keeps the image on the screen upright no matter how the device rotation changes. This is based on the angle at which you hold the device, and it is made possible by an *accelerometer,* a built-in component that measures tilt and acceleration of the smartphone or tablet. Figure 20-1 shows the screen of an iPad when held in "landscape" orientation, and Figure 20-2 shows the same screen in "portrait" orientation.

If you perceive that a smartphone or tablet is not responding correctly to change in orientation, consult the manufacturer because the phone may be defective or may need to be calibrated to respond to rotation. Some Android devices have a program

FIGURE 20-1

The iPad home page in "landscape" orientation

The iPad home page in "portrait" orientation

to calibrate for screen orientation. For instance, on a Galaxy Tab, you place it on a level surface with the screen up and start the screen orientation calibration program from Settings. Then you tap Calibrate and an image of a ball moves to the center of the screen. Supposedly that solves the problem.

Presently a few smartphones have a *gyroscope*; these gyroscopes are not of the mechanical variety we studied in middle school science class or had as toys, but are digital devices. The advantage of a gyroscope over an accelerometer is that a gyroscope detects an additional type of motion, and therefore can detect if a device made a full 360-degree turn. This is not important when you only care about the orientation of the screen display for reading, but it is a desired trait if you want your smartphone to act like a game controller for a flight game. You will see and hear more about these devices, if you haven't already.

There are a variety of touch gestures, and we will look at the most common. A *tap* gesture is a firm, but brief, touch to the screen. This will open the tapped app or other object. When you want to move the contents of the screen to see what is outside the viewing area, touch the screen and flick your finger right, left, up, or down. This gesture is called a *swipe* or a *flick*. There are several multi-touch gestures that use two or more fingers. If you place two fingers on the screen at a small distance from each other and draw them together, this is a *pinch*. Reverse that gesture, and it is still called a pinch. *Press and hold* is a touch without releasing. On some mobile devices, this will open a context menu; on others it allows you to move the icon you pressed—or some other action. Where you touch the screen is also significant.

Our last word on screens is about keyboards. The operating system on a smartphone or tablet provides you with a *virtual keyboard*, an on-screen keyboard that appears when you tap inside a box requiring text or number entry, as shown in Figure 20-3.

Storage

Recent smartphones and tablets exclusively use solid-state drives (SSDs) for installed programs and for storing your data. They do not use hard drives due to the bulk, weight, slower speed, and vulnerability to head crashes that can occur when the hard drive read/write heads come in contact with the disk platters due to the motion of the device. Ultrabooks use SSDs in order to attain their very thin profiles, and an SSD is an option in some more conventional laptop models. The cost of SSDs is dropping even as their capacity increases, and it probably won't be too long before most new laptops will use them instead of or in addition to hard drives, eliminating yet another difference between laptops and tablets. Optical drives are disappearing from the smaller laptops, but are still standard on most other laptop models.

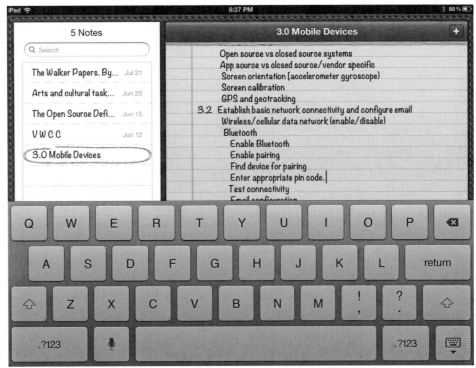

FIGURE 20-3

A virtual keyboard opens on the screen when you need it.

Multimedia Support

While individual device models vary, multimedia support in smartphones and tablets includes built-in speakers and connectors for headsets, microphones, and speakers, and these are also included on laptops, but the speakers on a laptop may be a higher quality because the larger size can accommodate them. Smartphones and tablets also have feature-rich digital cameras for photos and videos, including optical zoom and flash. In fact, many have two cameras: one on the back of the device to be aimed away from the user, and one aimed at the user, handy for taking self-portraits and for participating in video conferencing. This is where laptops, in comparison to smartphones and tablets, have less because they normally have a single camera mounted in the lid above the screen and aimed at the user. This is not a great loss, as it would be very awkward to aim a camera mounted on the back of a laptop screen. Finally, while virtually all laptops have a connector for an external display, not all smartphones or tablets have this feature.

Network Options

Smartphones and tablets today offer several network connection options. To begin with, a smartphone, by definition, connects to a cellular network as a phone, but also, as an option, will connect to the cellular data network. This depends mainly on what level of service you subscribe to from a cellular provider.

A tablet would make a rather awkward cell phone, but a tablet may come with a cellular modem installed so that it can connect to a cellular data network. You pay extra for this option—both for a cellular modem and for the cellular data service.

Today both types of devices normally come with two other wireless network options: Bluetooth and Wi-Fi. New laptops compare to tablets in regard to wireless networking, where a cellular data modem is optional, but Bluetooth and Wi-Fi are pretty standard. However, a laptop usually also has an Ethernet interface with an RJ-45 connector.

watch   *Smartphones and tablets have no field-serviceable parts and are typically not upgradeable, while you can replace or upgrade the memory and drives in most laptops.*

Mobile Operating Systems

While there are several mobile operating systems, we will concentrate on the most important ones. Smartphone operating systems include Apple iOS, Google Android, and Microsoft Windows Phone. On tablets, it is almost the same lineup, except for Windows Phone. Microsoft Windows is on some tablets, and Microsoft has built Windows 8 with a new touch-enabled UI for both conventional PCs and laptops, as well as for tablets. Each of these operating systems has an easy-to-use graphical user interface (GUI) optimized for touch screens, and each has a home page (expandable to multiple pages) where icons for settings, utilities, and apps reside. We will talk about some differences among these OSs.

watch   *Be sure you understand that versions of Windows previous to Windows 8 run on some tablets. CompTIA Exam 802 Objective 1.5 lists two Control Panel applets that were introduced in Windows Vista. They are Tablet PC Settings and Pen and Input Devices. The first allows you to configure tablet buttons, if supported by the tablet, and the second has many options for both pen and touch, including allowing you to configure settings for tablets and other input devices.*

The operating system on Apple's iPhone and iPad is *iOS*, Apple's operating system for Apple mobile devices. You will only find iOS on devices manufactured by Apple, making it a vendor-specific, *closed-source* operating system. It is vendor specific because it is only offered on Apple hardware. It is closed source because Apple does not publish iOS source code and does not allow others to modify it in any way. There are closed-source applications as well as operating systems.

The *Android* mobile OS runs on devices from many manufacturers worldwide. This is *open source* software, meaning that the source code is available to anyone to use or modify, and the software is not controlled by a single entity. Android is a very popular OS for non-Apple mobile devices. Manufacturers do make some vendor-specific changes to the OS, some even change the GUI.

e x a m

ⓦatch *As with the hardware, the Android operating system is generally not upgradable. You are expected to buy a new device. This may change, at least on tablets, as consumers demand the ability to upgrade mobile operating systems.*

While standard Microsoft Windows runs on some tablets, Microsoft has a long history of mobile versions, going back to the 1990s. More recently, they have Windows 8 that runs on everything from PCs to tablets, and Windows Phone for smartphones. The most recent versions of Windows Phone are Windows Phone 7.5 and Windows Phone 8. These are closed-source, because only Microsoft can modify the OS, although they allow computer manufacturers to add software into the OS using sanctioned methods, but not to modify the source code. The Windows operating systems for mobile devices are not single-vendor, as Microsoft sells the appropriate versions to manufacturers of tablets and phones.

Mobile Apps

All mobile devices come with some built-in apps, and you can customize your device by choosing from the huge number of available apps—some free and many for sale. There are literally hundreds of thousands of mobile apps. Apps are OS specific, so you must find apps that work with your OS and device. Among the mobile devices, the biggest difference is in how the apps are available and what apps are available. The home screens on these mobile devices will normally have an icon for connecting to an online retail site for buying apps. The differences in your choices for sources depend on the operating system. As you browse through apps for any mobile device, you will find that many of them have requirements to install—mainly that certain services are turned on—so read through the description of each app and pay attention to the requirements. You may need to give the app full control of your device or turn on the locator service and/or global positioning system (GPS) service.

Apps for Apple iOS

For Apple iPhones and iPads, the only source of apps is Apple via the online App Store or the brick-and-mortar Apple Stores, selling only Apple-sanctioned software from many publishers. Apps written for iOS run on both types of Apple devices, but apps display best on the device for which they were written because of the screen size differences. There is no other Apple-sanctioned source of apps for iOS systems. Tap the App Store on the home page of an iPhone or iPad to connect to the App Store; the first time you connect you will need to provide your Apple ID and password. Figure 20-4 shows the App Store. Your apps are updated through the App Store, and when one or more updates are ready, the number of updates will appear on the App Store icon. When you open the App Store, the updates will display, and if you decide to update, you will need to enter your Apple ID and password before it will download and update.

FIGURE 20-4   The Apple online App Store

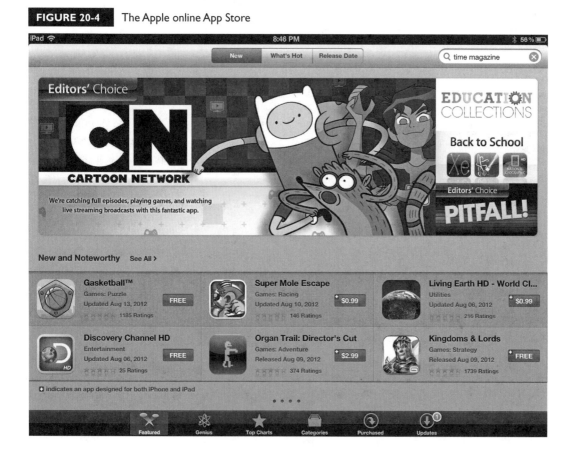

Apps for Android

Play is an Android app that connects you to the Google Play online app store. Google Play is Google's official source for Android apps, but since this is an open OS, there are other sources in the open-source market, such as the Android Market at www.androidpit.com. Pay very close attention to the specs for an app, as there are many versions of Android, with features that are only supported on some devices. Figure 20-5 shows a small sampling of the Android apps at the Play Store.

Apps for Microsoft Windows

The Microsoft Store has apps from many publishers for all their Windows OSs on all devices, including those for devices running Windows 8 and smartphones running Windows Phone. Some are free, but there is a charge for most of them. The Microsoft model is, in part, like the Apple model. Apps written for the new Windows 8 GUI (regardless of the device it is intended for) must be purchased exclusively through the Microsoft Store; apps written for traditional Windows or the Windows 8 Desktop GUI are available at the Microsoft Store and through other sources that sell software.

FIGURE 20-5

A small sampling of apps at the Google Play online app store

Path
PATH, INC.
★ ★ ★ ★ ★ (33,663)
INSTALL

Ocean Tower
FLAREGAMES
★ ★ ★ ★ ★ (5,327)
INSTALL

The Art of Rap
PURESOLO LTD
★ ★ ★ ★ ★ (1,064)
INSTALL

Fantasy Kingdom De...
TEQUILA MOBILE
★ ★ ★ ★ ★ (6,201)
INSTALL

Justin Bieber BELIEV...
CELLFISH STUDIOS
★ ★ ★ ★ ★ (194)
INSTALL

Monster Park
KIWI, INC.
★ ★ ★ ★ ★ (50,884)
INSTALL

Monster Park
KIWI, INC.
★ ★ ★ ★ ★ (50,884)
INSTALL

9 Innings: 2013 Pro B...
COM2US ✦
★ ★ ★ ★ ★ (42,616)
INSTALL

AutoRap
SMULE
★ ★ ★ ★ ★ (14,591)
INSTALL

TuneIn Radio
TUNEIN INC ✦
★ ★ ★ ★ ★ (202,057)
INSTALL

Shake Spears!
ALAWAR ENTERTAINME...
★ ★ ★ ★ ★ (22,899)
INSTALL

Endomondo Sports T...
ENDOMONDO ✦
▪ EDITORS' CHOICE
$4.99 BUY

All Talk FREE
POCKET GEMS
★ ★ ★ ★ ★ (1,725)
INSTALL

Apps that Track Your Location

Some apps and utilities for mobile devices track your location with the help of the Internet, and you can turn this feature on or off. Go into Settings on any mobile device and look for any setting that includes the word "location." For instance, Location Services on the Apple iPad will determine the iPad's physical location by using Wi-Fi hotspot locations. This is enabled in the Settings app on the Locations Services page, shown in Figure 20-6.

The Locations and Security settings in Android devices include several location-specific settings, including Google Location Services, which uses a location service supplied by Google over the Internet. It also includes standalone GPS services based

FIGURE 20-6   Turning on Location Services on an iPad

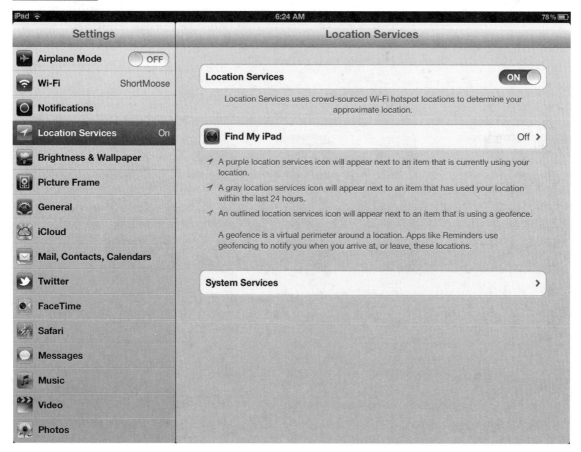

on third-party software and/or a peripheral device. You would need to enable this if you wanted to use a mapping app, most of which tie into the GPS through the Internet. In addition, in all devices that connect to a cellular network for voice or data, look for a setting to enable or disable location services over that network.

on the Job *Enabling Location Services in iOS and Google Location Service or GPS Services also means that technically you can be tracked through your device, a practice called geotracking. **To do it legally would require government action, and in some cases, the cooperation of the phone company.***

CERTIFICATION OBJECTIVES

■ **802: 3.2** *Establish basic network connectivity and configure e-mail*

■ **802: 3.5** *Execute and configure mobile device synchronization*

To prepare for CompTIA 802 Exam Objective 3.2, this section details how to enable or disable Wi-Fi or cellular connections and how to configure them. It also describes how to enable Bluetooth for pairing with another device or computer, including the use of a PIN code for some devices and how to test the connectivity. For the CompTIA 802 Exam Objective 3.5, you need to know the options for mobile device synchronization, including the software requirements to install synchronization apps on a PC, the connection types for synchronization, and the types of data to synchronize.

Configuring Mobile Devices

In this section we will describe how to connect your mobile device to three types of wireless networks: cellular, Wi-Fi, and Bluetooth. Once your device is connected, there are two important tasks: configuring email and data synchronization, and we will detail your options and how to do these tasks.

Connecting to Wireless Networks

As described earlier, smartphones and tablets come with network adapters for cellular data networks, Wi-Fi networks, or both. They also have Bluetooth connections for connecting to nearby devices. Now learn how to connect to these wireless networks.

Connecting to Cellular Networks

When you buy a smartphone or a tablet with cellular data capability, you make the choice at the point of sale concerning the cellular network to which you will subscribe, and you normally sign a contract for a certain level of service before you gain possession of the device (whether in person or over the Internet). Therefore, the actual configuration is done in the store; or in the case of a purchase over the Internet, all you need to do is enter credentials received from the cellular provider on the first use.

However, there is an important feature in devices with both cellular and Wi-Fi connections. By default, when you attempt to connect to the Internet, the device will first connect to an available Wi-Fi network. If a Wi-Fi network is not available, or if one is available that you cannot connect to or choose not to connect to, the device will connect using an available cellular data network.

Connecting to Wi-Fi Networks

To connect to a Wi-Fi network for the first time, open the Settings app on your device. Then select the option for Wireless (or Wi-Fi) and turn on Wi-Fi, if necessary. In the list of available cellular networks, displayed by SSID, select one and enter the required password. It will remember this network, maintaining a list of Wi-Fi networks it has successfully connected to, as shown in Figure 20-7, and providing the password whenever it detects a network. If you travel, you will need to do this for each new Wi-Fi network you connect to.

e x a m
ⓦatch

All radio frequency (RF) signals coming from mobile devices must be turned off when you fly on a commercial airliner. Therefore, smartphones and tablets have a mode called *airplane mode* **that does** just that, allowing you to continue using your device for access to locally stored data, while complying with the regulations. Look for it in the Settings app.

Connecting to Bluetooth Devices

Bluetooth, as described in Chapter 7, is a wireless standard used for communicating over very short distances. You might want to use Bluetooth to connect a Bluetooth keyboard to your mobile device, or to connect a mobile device to a PC or Mac to

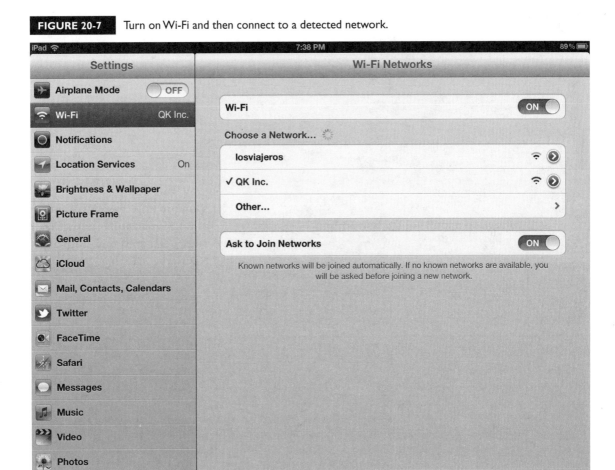

FIGURE 20-7   Turn on Wi-Fi and then connect to a detected network.

synchronize data. Bluetooth consumes battery power, so it is disabled by default. When you want to use Bluetooth, you first need to go into the Settings app on your mobile device and enable Bluetooth. Then enable it on your computer or Bluetooth device with which you wish to connect to so that they can discover (find) each other, which they will attempt to do as soon as Bluetooth is enabled. A connection between two Bluetooth devices is called a *pairing*. When both devices have discovered each other, go to the Settings screen on each one and select the other device for pairing. After a short pause, a message will display with a pairing code (also called a PIN code), as shown in Figure 20-8.

FIGURE 20-8 Pairing a Bluetooth keyboard with an iPad

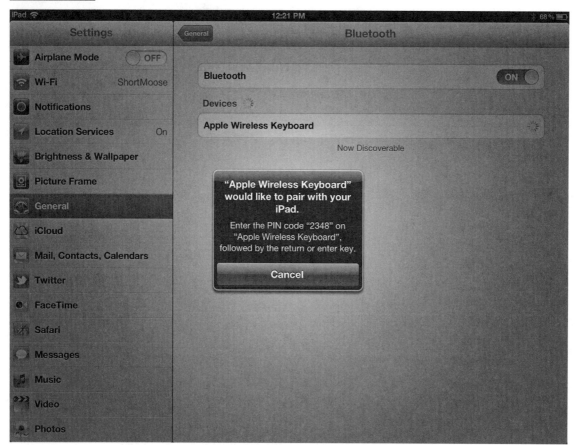

When connecting a keyboard, you will need to enter the code using the keyboard. When pairing a computer with a mobile device, you may simply need to confirm that the same pairing code shows on the screen for both devices. Finally, test connectivity between the devices. We have found that just entering the pairing code on a keyboard is not enough confirmation that the connection is working. You wouldn't want to set up a Bluetooth connection for a client and then find out after you leave that it didn't work for them. So in the case of a keyboard, open an app, such as an Internet browser, click in a box requiring text (such as an address box), and then start typing on the keyboard. If it does not work, you may not have confirmed the pairing on both sides (not always necessary). Although we have found that a failure to connect is often a case of impatience, if you have a problem with the pairing, disable Bluetooth on both devices and start over again.

Email Configuration

If you would like to use your mobile device to access your email, you begin by adding the account, which requires first that you select the type of account. Mobile devices support several types of accounts for email, social networking, data backup, and more—for which they know the basic connection information. Therefore, for these accounts, you only need to provide your personal login, which is usually an email address and password to the account. Figure 20-9 shows a list of account types supported on an iPad. For all account types, you need your email address and a password for your account that allows your device to send and receive email using that account.

Online Email Accounts

For online email accounts, such as Hotmail or Gmail, you do not have to specify a sending and receiving server. All you need to enter is your user name and password.

Other Internet Domain Accounts

If you want to use an account type other than an online email service, you will need server addresses obtained from your email server administrator. To receive mail you will need either an address for a Post Office Protocol 3 (POP3) or Internet Message Access Protocol 4 (IMAP4) server that receives your incoming mail and forwards it to you. An email client uses one or the other of these. To send mail you usually need the address of your Simple Mail Transfer Protocol (SMTP) server that accepts your outgoing mail and forwards it to an email server.

FIGURE 20-9   A list of supported account types

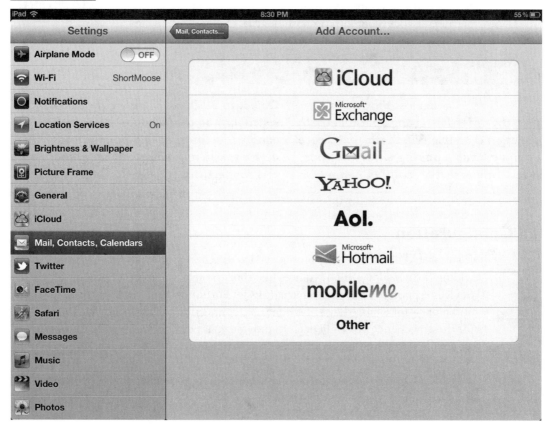

on the
job

To complicate matters, the name of the server is irrelevant, as long as it points to the email server.

The addresses for these servers are not numerical. A POP3 address will simply be the name of a mail server in an Internet domain, and may resemble this: pop. domainname.com. While the address for an IMAP4 server might look something like this: imap.domainname.com. Then, we probably don't need to say this, but the SMTP address might look like this: smtp.domainname.com. These are just examples, so you need to get the actual addresses for these servers from your email administrator.

Armed with the needed information, locate the email settings on your mobile device and carefully enter the information. On an iPad open the Settings app and

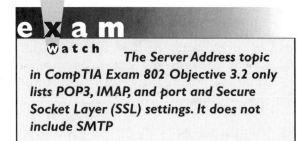

The Server Address topic in CompTIA Exam 802 Objective 3.2 only lists POP3, IMAP, and port and Secure Socket Layer (SSL) settings. It does not include SMTP

tap Mail, Contacts, Calendars. Then, in the right pane, tap Add Account. Is the type of email account you need to use listed? If it is, tap it and continue. If not, tap Other at the bottom of the list and then tap Add Mail Account. The New Account dialog box will display, along with the virtual keyboard (unless you have an external keyboard connected). Enter your name (not a user account name), email address, password for that email account, and a description for the email account that will identify it for you in the list of accounts. Tap Next and follow the instructions, using the addresses you obtained from your email server administrator. Figure 20-10 shows the configuration for a POP account being verified for the first time (notice the word "Verifying" at the top of the box).

FIGURE 20-10   Configuring a POP email account

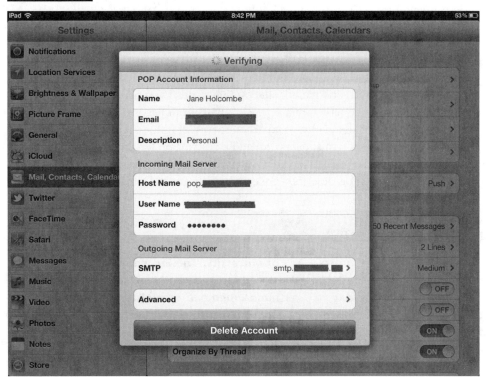

On an Android device, you will have a Google account for accessing Google services, as well as a required Gmail account. In fact, the Email icon on the desktop opens to Gmail. To configure another type of account in Android, open Settings, select Accounts, and then select Add Account. This opens the Setup Accounts screen that lists a variety of account types, not just email accounts but social networking sites, photo sharing sites, data backup sites, and other accounts added as you install certain apps.

Tap Email and enter the account information described earlier. If your administrator indicates that your account requires a different port setting or needs a special SSL setting, tap Advanced Settings at the bottom of the Outgoing Server page. This will bring up a page for the port settings, as well as the security settings. The default port is 25 for outgoing email. This page shows settings for Transport Layer Security (TLS), which is a protocol based on SSL. Do not change these settings, unless your administrator requires it.

Configuring an Exchange Client

Many organizations use internally maintained Microsoft Exchange email servers for employee email accounts and for sending email within the organization as well as over the Internet. Also, many hosting services for Internet domain names offer Exchange email services to their clients. Exchange gives the organization full administrative control, while providing users with a central location for their email history, contacts, tasks, and many collaborative tools. If you need to connect your device to an Exchange server, first open Accounts from Settings and see if your device lists Microsoft Exchange as an account type. If it does, select it and enter the email address, user name, password, and a description for the list of accounts. If Microsoft Exchange is not listed as a supported account type, you will need to manually configure it, as described under "Other Internet Domain Accounts."

exam

ⓦatch   *All Exchange accounts stored in one Exchange accounts database are centrally managed by and belong to the organization owning the Exchange server and domain, such as a manufacturer*   *or university. The individual accounts stored in Gmail and Hotmail are centrally maintained and administered by Google and Microsoft, respectively.*

Synchronization

It has become common for people to have multiple computing devices. At the "Holcombe World Headquarters," we each have a desktop computer, a laptop, and a smartphone. In addition, we have an iMac and iPad that we grudgingly share between us. With so many devices (and we know lots of people with more), it is a challenge to keep track of our data. What we do is *synchronize*, or *sync*, certain data. When data is synchronized between two locations, the files are examined and newer files replace the older files—sometimes, but not always, in both directions. When you sync mobile devices, it may simply be a backup to ensure against data loss if the device is lost or stolen.

We don't do this between the two users, but each of us syncs our own data between mobile devices and PCs and between mobile devices and a cloud service. Some devices can sync through Wi-Fi connections or with a direct connection via the USB cable that came with the device. Syncing to a cloud-based service occurs through an Internet connection—whether it is via a Wi-Fi connection or through a cellular connection.

When you make a USB cable connection between your device and a PC, it is called *tethering,* and sometimes there is software that you install on the PC side, which will have a requirement for the operating system and version. There are many options to choose from, and you should select one or two and use them regularly. If you keep your devices synced, then when you buy a new device, you can sync it and download all your data to the new device.

Connecting Mobile Devices for Syncing

You can sync your smartphone or tablet with your computer, either locally with a USB cable or over the Internet using a cloud-based service. For the local option, use the USB cable that came with the smartphone, usually attached to an alternating current (AC) adapter for charging. Disconnect it from the AC adapter. Connect the end previously connected to the power supply (usually a standard USB connector) to the computer and connect the other end to the device. On smartphones, this will usually be a micro USB connector; on an iPad and some other tablets it is a proprietary 30-pin connector. On some devices, this connection will usually cause two programs to run on the PC—one from your cell provider (if the device has cellular service) for configuring your online account (if you already have one, you simply log in). The second program will be device-specific to aid in transferring files.

Syncing iPhones and iPads

Use Apple iTunes for syncing an iPhone and iPad with a Mac or PC. It comes with all Apple computers, and is a free download for Windows PCs. The current requirements are a PC with 1 GHz Intel or AMD processor and 512 MB of RAM, Windows XP Service Pack 2 or later, or 32-bit editions of Windows Vista or Windows 7. The 64-bit editions require the 64-bit iTunes installer. It also requires 200 MB of free disk space. There are other requirements for playing music and video through iTunes on a PC, but these are requirements to synchronize your contacts, email, pictures, music, and videos from the device to the Mac or PC. You cannot copy files from the Mac or PC to the mobile device. You can also back up (not sync) your apps using iTunes.

Another option that is more of a backup than a syncing option is iCloud, an Apple Internet-based service for backing up your data from any Apple device to the iCloud service. This data is available to all devices from any location with Internet access.

Syncing Android Devices

When you connect an Android device to your computer, it is treated like an external drive, and you can copy files back and forth. Strictly speaking, this isn't syncing. There are individual solutions for various types of data. For instance, when you create a contact in Android, it asks you to pick an account to store (or backup) the contact information. The choices are Google or one provided by your cellular carrier. Select Google and they will be automatically backed up and synced to Google over the Internet, either through a cell connection or via Wi-Fi. After all, who do you expect to have the longest relationship with, Google or your cell provider? We use Google to back up our contacts because it will be available to use if we cancel the contract with the cell provider.

Securing Mobile Devices

Mobile devices have become a security issue in many organizations for the very reason mobile devices are part of the CompTIA A+ exams: they have become ubiquitous and have come into the workplace, both by invitation when required for work and as party crashers when users bring their favorite mobile devices to work, even connecting them to the corporate intranet against policy.

Under those circumstances, how do you protect a mobile device from malware? How do you keep the wrong people from logging on to a device they stole or found? How do you keep mobile operating systems up to date? How can you find lost devices? We will answer those questions and more after we look at why mobile devices keep security officers awake at night—and not because they're playing computer games.

Today's IT Challenge: BYOD

Bring Your Own Device (BYOD) is the practice (condoned or otherwise) of employees connecting to employers' networks with personal mobile devices. Here is an overview of this practice and how IT may support it.

The Advantages of BYOD

Do you have a personal smartphone or tablet? How many of your friends, coworkers, or fellow students have such mobile devices? If you purchase a tablet or smartphone and invest time learning to use all its features, the next logical step is to want to use it for all your personal and work email and data access when away from work. Some experts say that there are great advantages to allowing people to access work email and data using their personal devices. Here are a few that may or may not be reason enough to condone BYOD:

- The user is comfortable using the device and does not require training in its use, so there are fewer help desk calls.
- The employer doesn't need to buy the device. Some jobs either require or are greatly aided by the use of personal mobile devices, and so if the employee is willing to use their own, it is a savings to the employer.
- Allowing the use of the latest mobile device (regardless of who owns it) attracts more tech-savvy young people.
- Employers may hope that employees will be inclined to work outside of normal hours.

There are many sorts of hybrids of the BYOD phenomenon. For instance, you might use your own device, but be reimbursed for cell charges. Or, your employer may give you a certain amount of money to buy a mobile device, leaving it up to you to purchase either within that budget or to upgrade. This is sometimes called shared ownership, and this sharing allows you to use the device for both work and play.

BYOD Risks

Do you or any of your friends connect to a school or work network via a mobile device? At school this may not be an issue, but at work using a mobile device for both work and personal email, as well as using it to connect to corporate data, may be in conflict with corporate policy. Of those you know who do that, how many are using those devices outside the security policy of their employer?

Data of all types is at risk from many types of threats. Employers have a legal obligation to protect various types of data, including their employees' personal data, customers' personal and financial data, and, in the case of the healthcare industry, confidential medical data. On the other side of that equation, employees have a legal obligation to protect the organization's data. What happens when a BYOD device containing sensitive files is lost or stolen? What about devices in the possession of terminated employees? Some of these questions are only answered by security policies and enforcement of those policies, while other issues are addressed by enabling and configuring security features available for mobile devices. We will explore them next.

Meeting the Challenge

To meet the challenges of supporting mobile devices in the workplace, you need to know what security software is available for those devices, if the mobile OS can be patched or updated, how to enable passcode locks and restrictions for failed login attempts, how to configure and use remote backups, and how to use locator applications to find a lost or stolen device.

Security Software

Many security programs are available for Android systems with such features as antivirus, antispam, browsing protection, and privacy features that will alert you if an app attempts to access your private information (e.g., location, contacts, and messages). These inexpensive security suites also include backup and missing device features. If a device is missing, you can use this software to locate it (if location services is enabled), initiate a loud alarm on the device, and/or do a *remote wipe* (deleting all contents) of your device, making it effectively unusable by anyone who steals or finds it.

Apple iOS devices do not come with antivirus software, and the Apple Store at this time does not have antivirus software. While we question the lack of antivirus software, iOS devices are not totally lacking in security, as described next.

Patching and OS Updates

As with any computer, you need to keep your device updated with operating system patches and security updates, when available through the manufacturer of the device. Enable automatic updates. For instance, they are automatic on an Apple iOS device, but to check on them, open Settings, then tap General, and on that page, locate and tap Software Update to see the current state. Figure 20-11 shows the General page

The General page of the iPad's Settings app has several security settings.

from the iPad's Settings app. There are several security settings on this page that we will discuss next.

Passcode Locks

Mobile devices usually have a setting for a passcode lock. A *passcode lock* restricts access to a device by requiring a login to the device using a pattern (screen gestures you choose), a PIN, or password. On Android devices look for Set Up Screen Lock Settings under Location and Security Settings.

The iPad has Passcode Lock as an option on the General page of the Settings app. You should require a login for access to your mobile device. Then make it more secure. On an iOS device turn on Passcode Lock from the General page of Settings, and create a complex password, turning off Simple Passcode. Note the Auto-Lock option only sets the amount of time of inactivity before a device locks, but this does not, on its own, require a passcode. If you don't require a passcode, you simply use a swipe to close the lock screen and access the device.

Restrictions for Failed Login Attempts and Remote Wipes

Some devices put restrictions (or consequences) on multiple consecutive failed password attempts. For instance, on an iOS device if you have enabled Passcode Lock, and if you can guarantee that you will never forget your passcode and you want to protect your data from someone successfully guessing your passcode, turn on Erase Data. This will erase all data on the device (wiping out the data) after ten failed passcode attempts. You can also do a remote wipe through iCloud if your device is lost or stolen. On an Android device, install a security suite like Lookout that includes a remote-wipe capability.

Remote Backup Applications

On an Android device, you can have several sources for backing up. First, a device with a cellular connection will usually have a backup option through the cellular provider. Next, you have backup through Google, and finally you may have a backup through an app.

You can back up your data from all your iOS devices to the iCloud service, which also provides you with both remote lock and remote wipe options.

Locator Applications

Locator applications allow you to find your lost or stolen mobile device using a map on another device or computer. On an iPad, if you turn on the locator services, you can use the built-in locator app, Find My iPad, to locate your device on a map from another computer if it is lost or stolen.

On an Android device, there are several location services—one from Google, one based on a standalone GPS (usually an app), and another from your cell provider. If you turn on the locator service and then use an app, such as the security app Lookout, it will locate your lost or stolen device. In the case of Lookout, you would log on to www.mylookout.com and locate the device on a map.

CERTIFICATION SUMMARY

Because mobile devices have come into all areas of our daily life and are used more and more at work (officially and unofficially), an A+ Certification candidate needs to be prepared to support users of these small but useful devices. Understand their hardware features and the sources of apps for the most popular devices, which run the Apple iOS or Android OS. Mobile devices have locator and GPS services that you can enable for pinpointing the location of the device. This is handy for using mapping programs, but is also useful for finding your device, should it be lost or stolen. It also means that you could be tracked through your device, if necessary.

A smartphone, because it is first of all a cell phone, comes configured with a connection to a cellular network, including both voice and data services. Tablets do not function as phones, so a connection to a cellular network for data access is optional. Beyond that, both smartphones and tablets come with Wi-Fi and Bluetooth options. Know how to configure a device to receive and send email through email accounts, and synchronize devices with computers or cloud-based services.

There are many options for securing mobile devices, from security apps for Android devices to a variety of security settings on both Android and iOS devices.

TWO-MINUTE DRILL

Here are some of the key points covered in Chapter 20.

Overview of Mobile Devices

❑ Current mobile devices have a touch screen that accepts and interprets multiple simultaneous touch gestures, a feature called multi-touch. Manufacturer HTC had a touch screen Pocket PC with a Touch-FLO UI that was tied to specific gestures and does not apply to today's devices, but the CompTIA 802 Exam Objective 3.4 lists touch flow as a topic.

❑ Screen rotation (also called screen orientation) is a feature that changes the screen orientation based on the angle at which you hold the device. This is accomplished with an on-board accelerometer in most devices, but some devices aimed at gamers use a gyroscope.

❑ Modern touch screens are capacitive screens and do not need calibration, although that was required in many older devices.

❑ Mobile devices have no field-serviceable parts and are usually not upgradeable.

❑ Mobile devices use SSDs for storage.

❑ Android is an open-source operating system for mobile devices, while Apple iOS is closed source and vendor specific.

❑ Mobile devices have location services that use Internet-based tracking services and/or GPS, allowing for use of mapping programs and also allowing geotracking of the device.

❑ Apps for Apple iOS are only available from the Apple Store. The Google Play online app store is Google's official source for Android apps, but since this is an open OS, there are other sources in the open-source market, such as the Android Market at www.androidpit.com.

Configuring Mobile Devices

❑ When you purchase a smartphone, it has a configured cell connection, but you need to configure Wi-Fi and Bluetooth separately.

❑ When traveling by commercial airliner, use airplane mode to turn off all RF broadcasts.

❑ Tablets may optionally have a cellular connection only for data, and you separately enable and configure Wi-Fi and Bluetooth.

❑ The steps for configuring a Bluetooth connection must be done on both devices that will communicate as a pairing. First you enable Bluetooth, have the devices discover each other, then enable pairing, then either enter a PIN code on one side or confirm that the same code displays on both devices, and finally test connectivity.

❑ To configure email on a mobile device, you need certain information that you may need to obtain from an email administrator if you do no already have it. For connection to Gmail or Hotmail or similar service, you only need the email address and password. For other email connections, you may need a user name (definitely for Exchange), but you always need an email address and password. In addition, you may need server addresses for POP3 or IMAP4 and SMTP, and port and SSL settings.

❑ You can synchronize devices by tethering the device to a computer or over an Internet connection to a cloud-based service. Data you should sync includes contacts, programs, email, pictures, music, and videos.

Securing Mobile Devices

❑ Securing mobile devices is a challenging, but necessary, task for a support person, especially since so many people use their personal mobile devices at work, a practice (sanctioned or not) called bring your own device (BYOD).

❑ Antivirus software is available for Android devices; in fact, security suites are available with a long list of features. Antivirus software is not currently available for iOS devices, but iOS includes a long list of other security features.

❑ Apple iOS allows you to update the OS, but this is not a feature in current versions of Android.

❑ As with any computer, you need to keep your device updated with operating system patches and security updates.

❑ Most mobile devices have passcode locks, a feature that restricts access to a device by requiring that someone use a pattern (screen gestures you choose), PIN, or password to log in to the device.

❑ Before a device is lost or stolen, enable remote backups and be prepared to do a remote wipe. For iOS devices, keep data synced to iCloud, and use its remote-wipe feature on the lost or stolen device. On an Android device, install a security suite that includes remote wipe.

❑ If you enable locator features, you can use a locator app to find your lost or stolen mobile device using a map on another device or computer.

❑ Enable a passcode lock for your device, and also enable a setting that will either lock up your system or remotely wipe the data after a predefined number of failed login attempts.

SELF TEST

The following questions will help you measure your understanding of the material presented in this chapter. Read all of the choices carefully because there might be more than one correct answer. Choose all correct answers for each question.

Overview of Mobile Devices

1. Current mobile devices use this type of touch screen that detects the human touch.
   A. Calibration
   B. Accelerometer
   C. Capacitive
   D. Virtual

2. What component in most mobile devices is responsible for the screen orientation feature that keeps the image upright no matter how the device is rotated?
   A. Calibration
   B. Accelerometer
   C. Stylus
   D. Virtual keyboard

3. A typical mobile device uses this component for local storage.
   A. Virtual disk
   B. Tethering
   C. Hard drive
   D. SSD

4. What three words best describe a major difference between the two most popular mobile operating systems, Google Android and Apple iOS?
   A. Easy-to-use versus difficult-to-use
   B. Robot versus fruit
   C. Open versus closed
   D. CLI versus GUI

5. If you want to use an app that employs geotracking of your mobile device, you must enable this type of service on the device.
   A. Locator
   B. Mapping
   C. Gyroscope
   D. Accelerometer

6. Where can you find apps for an iOS device?
- **A.** Amazon
- **B.** Play Store
- **C.** Software retailer
- **D.** Apple Store

Configuring Mobile Devices

7. When you purchase a smartphone, it has this type of connection configured for you.
- **A.** Wi-Fi
- **B.** Cell
- **C.** Bluetooth
- **D.** Tethered

8. What type of service is not available on a typical tablet?
- **A.** Cellular voice
- **B.** Cellular data
- **C.** Wi-Fi
- **D.** Bluetooth

9. What is the correct order for pairing Bluetooth devices?
- **A.** Enter a PIN or confirm a code.
- **B.** Enable pairing.
- **C.** Let the devices discover each other.
- **D.** Enable Bluetooth.

10. What mode on mobile devices turns off all RF broadcasts?
- **A.** Pairing
- **B.** Airplane
- **C.** Tethering
- **D.** Wi-Fi

11. What information do you need to configure your mobile device to connect to a Gmail account?
- **A.** Server addresses for IMAP4 and POP3
- **B.** User name and password
- **C.** Email address and password
- **D.** SSL settings

12. What additional settings for security protocols may be needed to configure some email accounts?
    A. IMAP4 server address and POP3 server address
    B. User name and password
    C. Email address and password
    D. Port and SSL settings

13. What type of email service is internally maintained for an organization's employees and all accounts are centrally administered by the organization's email administrator?
    A. Gmail
    B. Hotmail
    C. Microsoft Exchange
    D. Work

14. Which of the following is not a connection type for syncing a mobile device?
    A. USB cable
    B. Ethernet
    C. Wi-Fi
    D. Cellular data network

Securing Mobile Devices

15. Which of the following statements is false?
    A. Antivirus software is available for Android.
    B. Antivirus software is available for iOS.
    C. Android has security settings.
    D. There are security settings in iOS.

16. Which of the following statements is true?
    A. Apple iOS automatically updates.
    B. Android automatically updates.
    C. There are no security settings in iOS.
    D. There are no security settings in Android.

17. What should you enable and configure to restrict access to a device by requiring a login using a pattern (screen gestures you choose), a PIN, or password?
    A. Remote wipe
    B. Failed login attempts restrictions
    C. Multi-touch
    D. Passcode lock

18. If you enable this on an iOS device, a drastic measure will be taken after ten failed passcode attempts.
    A. Passcode Lock
    B. Auto-Lock
    C. Erase Data
    D. Remote wipe

19. What Apple service will allow you to both back up your mobile device data and perform a remote wipe?
    A. iCloud
    B. iTunes
    C. iChat
    D. iOS

20. Enable this service on your device, and you can find it after it has been lost or stolen using a locator app to tell you where it is.
    A. Remote wipe
    B. Bluetooth
    C. Location
    D. GPS

SELF TEST ANSWERS

Overview of Mobile Devices

1. ☑ **C.** Capacitive touch screens detect the human touch by detecting an electrical charge from the finger.
    ☒ **A,** calibration, is not correct. This is a process that had to be applied to very old touch screens. **B,** accelerometer, is incorrect because an accelerometer affects the orientation of the image on a screen. **D,** virtual, is incorrect because this implies a virtual, or pretend, screen, and that does not describe a touch screen.

2. ☑ **B.** Accelerometer is correct, as this is the component in most mobile devices that is responsible for the screen orientation feature.
    ☒ **A,** calibration, is incorrect because this is not a component in a mobile device. **C,** stylus, is incorrect because a stylus is simply a device you can use in place of a finger on a touch screen. **D,** virtual keyboard, is incorrect because this is an on-screen keyboard that appears on a mobile device when an app requires text input.

3. ☑ **D.** SSD (solid-state drive) is used in a mobile device for local storage.
    ☒ **A,** virtual disk, is incorrect because it is not a component of mobile devices. **B,** tethering, is incorrect because that describes a cable connection between a mobile device and a PC. **C,** hard drive, is incorrect because they are too bulky, heavy, slow, and vulnerable to head crashes.

4. ☑ **C.** Open versus closed best describes a difference between Google Android and Apple iOS.
    ☒ **A,** easy-to-use versus difficult-to-use, is incorrect because they are both easy to use. **B,** robot versus fruit, is incorrect, although, if you are observant, you know that a robot is the symbol for Android, while an apple is the symbol for everything Apple. Yet, this does not describe a major difference between the two. **D,** CLI (command-line interface) versus GUI (graphical user interface), is incorrect because both of these are GUIs.

5. ☑ **A.** Locator service must be enabled in order to use an app that uses geotracking.
    ☒ **B,** mapping, is not correct, although mapping apps also take advantage of locator services. **C,** gyroscope, and **D,** accelerometer, are both incorrect because these are components for detecting the orientation of a device.

6. ☑ **D.** Apple Store is the only source for apps for iOS.
    ☒ **A,** Amazon, **B,** Play Store, and **C,** software retailer, are all incorrect because the Apple Store is the only source for iOS apps.

Configuring Mobile Devices

7. ☑ **B.** When you purchase a smartphone, it has a configured cell connection.
    ☒ **A, C,** and **D** are all incorrect because you need to configure Wi-Fi, Bluetooth, and a tethered connection separately.

8. ☑ **A.** Cellular voice service is not available on a typical tablet.
    ☒ **B,** cellular data, **C,** Wi-Fi, and **D,** Bluetooth, are all available on a typical tablet.

9. ☑ **D, C, B, A.** Enable Bluetooth, let the devices discover each other, enable pairing, and enter a PIN or confirm a code.

10. ☑ **B.** Airplane mode turns off all RF broadcasts.
    ☒ **A,** pairing, is incorrect because this is done between two Bluetooth devices. **C,** tethering, is incorrect because this term describes a cable connection between a mobile device and a computer. **D,** Wi-Fi, is incorrect because this describes a wireless network using one of the 802.11 standards.

11. ☑ **C.** Email address and password are all you need to configure your mobile device to connect to a Gmail account.
    ☒ **A,** server addresses for IMAP4 and POP3, **B,** user name and password, and **D,** port and SSL settings, are all incorrect because a mobile device only needs an email address and password to connect to a Gmail account.

12. ☑ **D.** Port and SSL settings involving security protocols such as TLS may be required for some email accounts.
    ☒ **A,** IMAP4 server address and POP3 server address, is incorrect because, while this information is needed for some email accounts, they are not security protocols. **B,** user name and password, are also not additional security settings. **C,** email address and password, while required for all email accounts, are not security settings.

13. ☑ **C.** Microsoft Exchange is a type of email service that is internally maintained for an organization's employees, and all accounts are centrally administered by the organization's email administrator.
    ☒ **A,** Gmail, is incorrect because this is not maintained internally, nor is it centrally administered by anyone other than Google. **B,** Hotmail, like Gmail, is not internally maintained within an organization for their employees; it is administered by Microsoft. **D,** work, is incorrect, because this is not a type of email service.

14. ☑ **B.** Ethernet is not a connection type for syncing mobile devices.
    ☒ **A,** USB cable, **C,** Wi-Fi, and **D,** cellular data network, are all incorrect, as they are connection types for syncing mobile devices.

Securing Mobile Devices

15. ☑ **B.** Antivirus software is available for iOS is false, and therefore the correct answer.
☒ **A,** antivirus software is available for Android, **C,** Android has security settings, and
D, there are security settings in iOS, are all true, and therefore incorrect answers.

16. ☑ **A.** Apple iOS automatically updates is correct.
☒ **B,** Android automatically updates, is incorrect because Android does not update. **C,** there
are no security settings in iOS, and **D,** there are no security settings in Android, are incorrect
because both mobile OSs have security settings.

17. ☑ **D.** Passcode Lock is a setting that restricts access to a device by requiring login using a
pattern (screen gestures you choose), a PIN, or a password.
☒ **A,** remote wipe, is incorrect because this does not restrict access by requiring a login.
B, failed login attempts restrictions, is incorrect because this is simply a setting for consequences
of entering the wrong password too many times. **C,** multi-touch, is incorrect because this just
describes a feature of a touch screen.

18. ☑ **C.** Erase Data is the setting to enable on an iOS device (found under Passcode in the
General page of settings) that will result in a drastic measure after ten failed passcode attempts.
☒ **A,** Passcode Lock, is incorrect because you can enable Passcode Lock without enabling
Erase Data. **B,** Auto-Lock, is incorrect because this only sets the amount of time of inactivity
before a device locks. **D,** Remote wipe, is incorrect because this is not a setting in iOS.

19. ☑ **A.** The Apple iCloud service will allow you to back up your mobile device data and
perform a remote wipe.
☒ **B,** iTunes, is incorrect because, while it lets you sync your data to a Mac or PC, it does
not have a remote wipe feature. **C,** iChat, is incorrect. This service was not mentioned in the
chapter and will not do a remote wipe. **D,** iOS, is incorrect because this is the name of Apple's
mobile OS, not a service that will do a remote wipe.

20. ☑ **C.** Location is the service to turn on before you can use a locator app to find it.
☒ **A,** Remote wipe, is incorrect; this is simply a feature that wipes out the data remotely, but
does not tell you where the device is. **B,** Bluetooth, is not the service that must be enabled for a
locator app. **D,** GPS, while a type of locator service, is not the answer because a locator app can
work using methods other than GPS.

21

Using and Supporting Printers

I n this chapter, you will examine printers to understand the types in use and the technologies, components, and consumables involved. You will learn about the typical issues involved with installing and configuring printers, the typical upgrading and optimizing options, and preventive maintenance and troubleshooting.

CERTIFICATION OBJECTIVE

■ *801: 4.1* *Explain the differences between the various printer types and summarize the associated imaging processes*

CompTIA requires that A+ certification candidates recognize the various types of printers available for use with PCs, and understand the differences among these device types so you can make purchasing decisions and determine the consumables required for each.

Printer Basics

Printers are the most common peripherals used with PCs. Understanding such printer basics as printer types and their related technologies, paper-feeding technologies, printer components, and printer interfaces is important to your success on the exams and on the job.

Windows Print Processing

You've just created a report in Word and click Print. Normally you see your printer spring to life and you hear the hum of a busy printer. Then, you reach over and snatch the paper as it leaves the printer. However, there's more to the print story than a mouse click and an instant printout. Windows plays a big part in this frequent and ordinary transaction, doing some processing to prepare the job for the printer via the printer driver that controls how the document is prepared for the capabilities of the printer. Once Windows has the print job ready to send, it doesn't leave the computer right away, but is sent to the *print spooler,* a Windows component that uses memory or disk to store print jobs in a queue, sending each one to the printer as it is ready to print. This feature is on by default, and is especially important when sending several jobs to a printer at once, whether to a local printer or to a network printer. Once a job is sent to the printer, additional processing is done by the printer before the document is printed. The extent of that processing depends on the printer, so we will look at printer types and technologies next.

Printer Types and Technologies

There are several types of printers in use, including impact, laser, inkjet, and thermal printers. Laser and inkjet printers may be the most commonly used by the average home or business user, but the other types have their place in the world, and we will describe the characteristics of all types. Each has its own set of steps for taking output from your computer (or a scanned image) and printing it for you, called an *imaging process*.

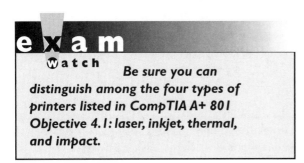

e x a m

ⓦ **a t c h** *Be sure you can distinguish among the four types of printers listed in CompTIA A+ 801 Objective 4.1: laser, inkjet, thermal, and impact.*

Impact

An *impact printer* has a roller or platen the paper presses against and a *print head* that strikes an inked ribbon in front of the paper, thus transferring ink to the paper. This impact of the print head is often very loud, and the wear and tear of the repeated hammering makes these printers prone to mechanical failures. Today, an impact printer is a dot matrix printer, but originally impact printers also included daisy wheel printers, line printers, and others. The average office or home user does not use an impact printer, but will almost certainly have an inkjet or laser printer.

A *dot matrix printer* uses a matrix of pins to create dots on the paper, thus forming alphanumeric characters and graphic images. Each pin is attached to an actuator, which, when activated, rapidly pushes the pin toward the paper. As the print head (containing the pins) moves across the page, different pins move forward to strike a printer ribbon against the paper, causing ink on the ribbon to adhere to the paper. Because they create printouts one character at a time, we call dot matrix printers character printers.

The dot matrix impact printer is the original basic printer used with PCs. The most common use for dot matrix impact printers today is for printing multiple-page receipts or forms that require an impact to make an impression on the second and third sheet of the form. We often refer to them as "receipt printers," and we see

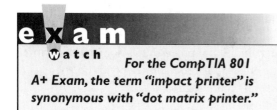

them in use in retail stores and service centers connected to point-of-sale systems (cash registers).

Impact printers do not provide very good resolution. Text and images appear grainy, and you can usually see each individual printed dot. Furthermore, impact printers are limited in their ability to use color, and they usually can only use one printer ribbon color (typically black, although you can substitute another color available for that printer, if available). Even if you manage to find am impact printer that can use ribbons with up to four colors and/or up to four printer ribbons, it will not have as many color combinations as other printer types.

Laser

Most *laser printers* use a coherent, concentrated light beam (called a *laser beam* because a laser generates it) in the imaging process. Some less expensive ones use light-emitting diodes (LEDs) for this purpose. They are generally faster than other types of printers, provide the best quality, and have the most complex structure and process. Laser printers use very small dots of toner, so they are able to provide excellent resolution, and because of this and their speed, these are perhaps the most commonly used printers in business environments, especially for shared network printers. Figure 21-1 shows a typical laser printer for a home or small office. Laser printers are also the most expensive to operate.

FIGURE 21-1

A desktop laser printer with the manual tray open. The toner cartridge is hidden behind the panel above the paper feeder.

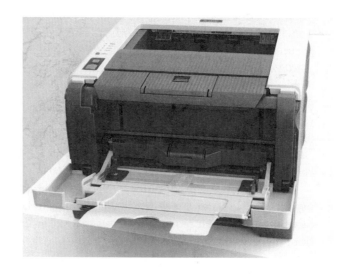

A laser printer is a nonimpact printer, because it does not require any form of physical impact to transfer an image to a printout. Because it creates printouts one page at a time (rather than one character or line at a time), a laser printer is called a "page printer."

Laser Printer Imaging Process   Although some laser printers use a slightly different imaging process, we'll describe a typical order of events that occurs in the laser imaging process. Note that these events occur in repeating cycles, so it is not as important to know which step is first or last, as it is the sequence of events. For example, some sources list charging as the first step, whereas others list cleaning as the first step.

In a laser printer, the *imaging drum* (the technical term is *electro-photosensitive drum*) is made of metal with an electro-photosensitive coating. The drum is actually more like a slender tube, with a typical circumference of less than an inch, so the imaging process must repeat several times per printout page. Both the drum and the primary corona wire are often contained within the toner cartridge. When printing a page, the feed mechanism moves the paper into the printer and the drum rotates. The steps that follow occur repeatedly while the paper is moving and the drum is turning, although even the processing step will need to repeat for large, multipage documents.

1. **Processing**   During the *processing* stage, the printer takes the file sent from a computer (or a scanned image) and creates a bit-mapped image (consisting of dots), called a *raster image*. Then it breaks this image up into its individual horizontal lines of dots, called *raster lines*, and the imaging process prints each raster line in turn until completing the page, processing each page in the document in turn.

2. **Charging**   In the *charging* step, the printer's high-voltage power supply (HVPS) conducts electricity to a *primary corona wire* that stretches across the printer's photosensitive drum, not touching it, but very close to the drum's surface. The charge exists on the wire and in a corona (electrical field) around the length of the wire. The high voltage passes a strong negative charge to the drum. In more recent printers, a primary charge roller is used for this purpose.

3. **Exposing**   The surface of the electro-photosensitive drum now has a very high negative charge. In the *exposing* (also called *writing*) stage, the printer's laser beam moves along the drum, creating a negative of the image that will eventually appear on the printout. Because the drum is photosensitive, each place that the laser beam touches loses most of its charge. By the end of the writing step, the image exists at a low voltage while the rest of the drum remains highly charged. The laser that generates this laser beam is normally located within the printer body itself, rather than in the toner cartridge.

4. **Developing**   In the *developing* stage, the "discharged" areas on the drum attract microscopic toner particles through the open cover on the printer's toner cartridge. By the end of this stage, the drum contains a toner-covered image in the shape of the final printout.

5. **Transferring**   During the *transferring* step, *pickup rollers* extract a single page of paper, and the paper moves through the printer close to the drum. The *transfer corona wire*, located within the body of the printer and very close to the paper, applies a small positive charge to the paper as it passes through on the *transfer roller*. This positive charge "pulls" the negatively charged toner from the drum onto the paper. At this point the only thing holding the toner to the paper is an electrical charge and gravity.

6. **Fusing**   As the paper leaves the printer it enters the *fusing* stage, passing through a set of *fusing rollers* that presses the toner onto the paper. These rollers are heated by a *fusing lamp*. The hot rollers cause the resin in the toner to melt, or fuse, to the paper, creating a permanent nonsmearing image. These components, collectively called the *fuser assembly*, are normally located within the body of the printer rather than in the toner cartridge.

7. **Cleaning**   There are two parts to the *cleaning* stage. First, when the image on the drum transfers to the paper, a *cleaning blade* (normally located within the toner cartridge) removes residual toner, which drops into a small reservoir or returns to the toner cartridge. Next, one or more high-intensity *erasure lamps* (located within the body of the printer) shine on the photosensitive drum, removing any remaining charge on that portion of the drum. The drum continues to rotate, and the process continues.

Imaging Process Variations in Color Laser Printers   Color laser printers are able to blend colors into practically any shade, typically using four toner cartridges. Therefore, the writing and developing stages take place four times (once for each color: black, cyan, magenta, and yellow) before the image transfers to the paper. Some color laser printers use a *transfer belt* to transfer colors from each cartridge to the final printed page.

Ozone and Laser Printers   The side effect of a laser printer's use of coronas in the imaging process is the creation of ozone (O_3), which can harm other printer parts, and if at sufficient levels in a closed area has the potential to be harmful to humans. Therefore, laser printers that produce ozone above certain levels have an *ozone filter* to remediate this, but others do not. If a printer has an ozone filter, your printer documentation will identify it. Ozone is only created when a printer is printing, and only some laser printers produce an amount of ozone requiring an ozone filter.

Inkjet

The printers categorized as *inkjet* printers use several technologies to apply wet ink to paper to create text or graphic printouts. Inkjets use replaceable *ink cartridges*—one for each color. Some combine multiple ink reservoirs into a single cartridge, and other inkjet printers have a separate cartridge for each ink reservoir. An inkjet cartridge will only fit certain printer models. These printers provide much better resolution than impact printers, and many of them create wonderful color output because, unlike impact printers, inkjets can combine basic colors to produce a wide range of colors. Inkjet printers are very quiet, compared to impact printers and even laser printers.

The *print head* in an inkjet ink cartridge is an assembly of components, including a tiny pump that forces ink out of the reservoir, through nozzles, and onto the page. There are many kinds of nozzles that make microscopic droplets measured in picoliters (one-millionth of a millionth of a liter); a typical droplet measures 1.5 picoliters. Ink cartridges move back and forth across the page. They sit in a cartridge *carriage* mechanism driven by a *carriage belt* that allows the print heads to move over the paper.

When printing text inkjet printers print a character at a time, so they are character printers, and their print mechanisms do not contact the page, making them nonimpact printers as well. They are usually inexpensive, but the significant operating costs of these printers are the ink cartridges, which can cost between 10 and 25 cents per printed color page. Black and white pages are less expensive. So, although these printers are inexpensive to buy, the cost of the consumables (ink) can be high.

Thermal

A *thermal printer* uses heat in the image transfer process. Thermal printers for PCs fall into two categories: direct thermal printers and thermal wax transfer printers.

In a *direct thermal printer,* a *heating element* heats a print head that burns dots into the surface of *thermochromic paper,* commonly called *thermal paper.* Early fax machines used this technology for printing, and direct thermal printers are commonly used as receipt printers in retail businesses. Thermal paper has a coating consisting of a dye and an acid in a suitable stable matrix. When the matrix heats above its melting point, the dye reacts with the acid and shifts to its colored form in the areas where it is heated, producing an image. Thermal printers are actually dot-matrix printers, although no one calls them that. Thermal printers are roll fed with a *feed assembly* that moves the paper appropriately past the print head.

In thermal wax transfer, printers use a film coated with colored wax that melts onto paper. These printers are similar to dye-sublimation printers but differ in two major ways: the film contains wax rather than dye, and these printers do not require special paper. Thermal wax transfer printers are, therefore, less expensive than most dye-sublimation printers, but the dye-sublimation printers create higher-quality output.

All-in-One Printers

Not many years ago, a printer and a scanner were two separate devices. Today combination devices abound. These types of devices, often categorized as a *multi-function device (MFD)* or an *all-in-one printer,* combine the scanner, printer, and copier in one box, often with a built-in fax as well. Although an MFD can function like a copier or a fax machine (when you place an image to copy on the platen and the copied image comes out or a fax is sent over a phone line), there are significant differences between the old and the new. An MFD shines as a PC-connected device that provides all the functionality of a printer as well as a copier and scanner while using up the desk space of just one of these devices. The printing component of an all-in-one printer is usually either a laser or inkjet printer. Figure 21-2 shows an MFD combining an inkjet printer, scanner, copier, and fax in one machine.

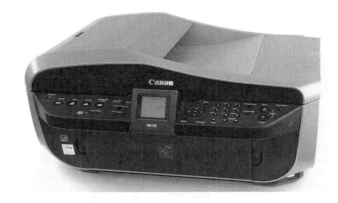

FIGURE 21-2

An all-in-one inkjet printer that combines scanner, printer, fax, and copier in one machine

e x a m
watch

The printer types included in the CompTIA 801 A+ Exam are laser, inkjet, thermal, and impact. We include the MFDs simply because you will encounter *them frequently in homes and offices. Also, MFD is included in the CompTIA 801 and 802 Exam Objectives Acronyms list.*

Paper-Feeding Technologies

While each type of printer has unique qualities, each one has a set of components called the feed assembly that moves paper through the printer so that the image can be placed on it.

The two most common paper-feeding technologies are friction feed and tractor feed. A printer using *friction feed* prints on individual pieces of paper, moving the paper by grasping each piece of paper with rollers. *Tractor feed* requires *continuous form paper,* sheets of paper attached to each other at perforated joints, with perforations on the sides that fit over sprockets that turn, pulling the paper through the printer. Further, continuous-form paper has about a half-inch-wide border at each side that contains holes that accommodate the sprockets on the tractor feed mechanism, thus pulling the paper through the printer. These borders are removable. When using continuous form feed, you must disable the friction feed. Checks, receipts, and other forms, including multiple-part forms, use continuous form feed paper. Because these forms often have specific areas in which the information must print, a necessary step when inserting this paper into the printer is to register or align the perforation accurately between each form with a guide on the printer.

All the printer types discussed here can and usually do use friction feed to move paper through the printer. Some, especially laser printers, use more than one set of rollers to keep the page moving smoothly until ejecting it. Many laser printers use a *separation pad* to get proper feeding of a single sheet of paper. The pickup rollers press down on the paper to move it through the printer, while the separation pad keeps the next sheet from advancing. The separation pad is a replaceable item when paper stops feeding properly. Friction-fed printers usually have more than one paper source available: one tray that can hold a lot of paper, and another that holds a smaller amount of paper. These trays can hold from a few pages up to several reams in the large paper feeders of high-end network printers.

Once in the printer, the path the paper takes during friction feed varies from printer model to printer model. Normally, *rollers* pick paper from the feed stack one sheet at a time and move it to the *feeder* mechanism that controls movement of the paper through the printer. The feeder moves the paper one line at a time either past a fixed point for printing, or in some printers, past a print head that moves back and forth printing each line.

Some friction feed assemblies are designed to allow selection of single-sided or double-sided printing. Some printers contain a *duplexing assembly* to print on both sides of the page, but many will require you to feed pages already printed back into the printer again to print on the other side of the page.

All printers eventually deposit the printed page in a tray where the user can retrieve it, and some support the *collating* of documents, placing them in page order—sometimes even for multiple copies.

on the Job *Prevent paper jams and component wear and tear by using the proper paper for your printer. Read the documentation for the printer to determine the best paper for the results you desire.*

Printer Components

The actual printer components vary, depending on the printing and paper-feed technology of the printer. However, regardless of the printing technology used, all printers have a certain set of components in common, which include the system board, memory, driver and related software, firmware, and consumables.

System Board

Each printer contains a system board that serves the same purpose as a PC's motherboard. Often referred to simply as a printer board, this circuit board contains a processor, read-only memory (ROM), and random access memory (RAM).

The processor runs the code contained in the ROM, using the RAM memory as workspace for composing the incoming print jobs (in most printers) and storing them while waiting to print them.

Firmware

A printer, like a computer and most devices, has its own firmware code, including basic input/output system (BIOS) code that contains the low-level instructions for controlling it. Printer BIOS code is accessed by the driver, which is installed into the operating system. Another type of firmware code in printers is an interpreter for at least one printer language.

Driver

A new printer comes packaged with a disc containing drivers, usually for several operating systems. Like drivers for other devices, a print driver allows you to control a printer through the operating system.

Printer Language

Beyond a driver that physically controls the action of a printer, the computer must also have special software printer language that translates the characters and graphics of your computer-generated document into a form that the printer can compose and print out. Common printer languages include PostScript, Hewlett-Packard Printer Control Language (PCL), Windows GDI, and other vendor-specific printer languages.

CERTIFICATION OBJECTIVES

- **802: 1.4** *Given a scenario, use appropriate operating system features and tools*

- **802: 1.5** *Given a scenario, use Control Panel utilities*

- **801: 4.2** *Given a scenario, install and configure printers*

    In this section we tie up more loose ends by including one item in CompTIA Exam 802 Objective 1.4, Print Management. We also describe the use of two Control Panel applets listed in CompTIA Exam 802 Objective 1.5: Printers and Faxes in Windows XP and Printers in Vista. We thoroughly cover CompTIA Exam 801

Objective 4.2, which requires that you understand printer drivers, print interfaces, and printer device sharing options, and how to install a local printer versus a network printer.

Installing and Configuring Printers

The plug and play nature of Windows, as well as of printers and scanners, makes installing and configuring these devices quite easy, even for the ordinary PC user. Before you install a printer, make sure that you have a print driver for that printer that will run in the version of Windows running on the computer. Not only must the version level be correct (Windows XP, Windows Vista, Windows 7, Windows 8), but you must also match 32-bit Windows with 32-bit drivers and 64-bit Windows with 64-bit drivers. In this section, we will begin with an overview of printer interfaces, and then explore the issues related to installing and configuring printers.

Printer Interfaces

There are a number of interfaces for connecting a printer to a computer. For example, you can configure a printer so it attaches directly to a computer or indirectly through a network. You can also configure a printer so it is accessible to only one person or to an entire network of people. Printers use the common interfaces described in Chapter 4, and the following text describes usage of each of these interfaces with printers and scanners.

Parallel

For many years after the introduction of the IBM PC in 1981, the most common way to attach a printer to a computer was through the computer's parallel port. The parallel interface requires a significant amount of space on the PC case for its 25-pin connector, needs an even larger 36-pin Centronics connector on the printer or other device, and a heavy cable with appropriate connectors on each end. A Centronics connector on a printer has 36 pins and is about 2" long, as shown here above the much smaller Universal Serial Bus (USB) connector.

The parallel interface dominated for a long time and was the hands-down favorite over another common, but slower, interface, serial, that shared its long history. While the parallel interface transfers eight bits at a time (in parallel), it originally only supported one-way communication. For this reason, it was best suited for early printers, sending print data to the printer, but not capable of receiving status data from the printer. The speed of the standard one-way parallel port is 150 Kbps. Today's printers send status data back to the PC, alerting you when you are out of paper or low on ink or toner. This requires two-way communications.

When you buy a new parallel cable, its label will show it as compliant with the IEEE 1284 standard introduced in the 1990s. This standard defines a parallel interface backward compatible with the original parallel port in the early IBM PCs:

- **Compatibility mode**   Data only travels in one direction, from the PC to the device, in compatibility mode (also called "Centronics mode"). This mode ties up the PC's central processing unit (CPU). Its speed is 150 Kbps.

- **Nibble mode**   Used together with compatibility mode, nibble mode offers limited bidirectional communications. Because this mode depends on software to send each eight-bit byte in two chunks of four bits (a "nibble"), nibble mode uses more CPU cycles than compatibility mode. Its top speed is 50 Kbps.

- **Byte mode**   Also called "Enhanced Bidirectional Port mode," byte mode, used together with compatibility mode, supports two-way, eight-bit data communications with a device. This configuration can communicate at speeds close to 150 Kbps.

- **Enhanced Parallel Port (EPP) mode**   Enhanced Parallel Port (EPP) mode offers high-speed, bidirectional speeds of between 500 Kbps and 2 Mbps. This speed is possible because the IEEE 1284 parallel interface hardware does most of the work of data transfer, requiring less CPU involvement. This mode is not for printers but for network adapters, portable hard drives, and other devices that require high transfer speeds, such as data acquisition hardware used to collect data automatically from special sensors and readers used in factories, test laboratories, scientific research, and medical equipment.

- **Extended Capability Port (ECP) mode**   The fastest parallel port mode for use with printers and scanners is Extended Capability Port (ECP) mode. Like EPP, ECP requires hardware that supports its features, and like EPP, ECP supports speeds of 500 Kbps to 2 Mbps and bidirectional communications. This is the mode you should use for a parallel printer whenever it is supported by the printer and if you have an IEEE 1284 cable.

On some computers and peripherals, you may encounter parallel port modes that are not part of the IEEE 1284 standard. These come with names such as "Fast Centronics Mode" or "Parallel Port FIFO Mode." They are proprietary and not supported on all parallel devices or computers.

In the past several years, other, faster interfaces have become far more popular than the parallel interface. Where it was once considered a given that a parallel port was standard on a new PC, many new computers today, especially laptops, do not come with a parallel port. This omission goes unnoticed by most people because most new printers and scanners do not come with a parallel interface.

Serial

The serial interface, as described in Chapter 4, was once a common printer interface. But even the original parallel interface was, and is, faster than the traditional RS-232 serial ports. Therefore, even back in the day, parallel was more popular than serial. Serial interface does not natively support plug and play, and printers rarely use a serial interface; in fact, the serial port is disappearing from standard PC configurations.

USB

The Universal Serial Bus (USB) is the current dominant printer interface. As its name implies, data travels one bit at a time over the USB interface. However, as described in Chapter 4, USB is fast and requires only a very small connector on each end. The PC end uses a USB type A connector, and the device end of the cable may be either a type A or type B connector, depending on what the device requires. Printers do not always come with a USB cable, and you may need to supply your own.

A USB interface can only provide a small amount of electrical power from the PC, but printers normally require more power than that and, therefore, use an external power supply. To attach a USB device, simply plug it into a USB external socket or root hub. There is no need to even turn off the computer for this plug and play interface, but be sure to read the instructions first, because for some USB printers, you must install the device driver before plugging in the device.

IEEE 1394/FireWire

The IEEE 1394 interface, also known as FireWire, was popular for a while, but few manufacturers include it on new printers, and even Apple, who originated this standard, no longer includes FireWire on their devices. Virtually all new printers come with USB, and the CompTIA A+ 801 Printers domain does not list this interface.

Network Printer vs. Local Printer

A printer connected to your PC for your own use is a local printer. A printer connected directly to the network is a *network printer*. However, this line blurs because it has long been common to share locally connected printers over a network or to connect one or more printers to a network-connected hardware print server. We will examine these three ways to connect a printer to a network.

- Use a *hardware print server*, a device connected to a network that controls the printing jobs to one or more printers, which are usually connected directly to the print server. Using the manufacturer's instructions, you configure this type of print server much as you do a wireless access point (WAP), by connecting your computer and the print servers with an Ethernet cable and entering its Internet Protocol (IP) address into a browser and configuring the device. As with a WAP or router, be sure to change the password.

- Use a true network printer that contains a network interface card (NIC) and that you configure in the same manner as any computer on the network. The printer acts as a print server, accepting print jobs over the network. If the printer is powered on and online, it is available to network users. The NIC may be an Ethernet NIC or a wireless NIC, or the printer may contain both types. Although this is not a hard-and-fast rule, high-end network printers most often have Ethernet NICs for use in businesses and large installations.

  The most common wireless printers use one of the 802.11x standards for Wi-Fi technology, although some may use infrared (IR) or Bluetooth. We described infrared and Bluetooth in Chapter 7, and Wi-Fi in Chapter 14.

- A computer with a network connection can share a local printer attached to that computer's local interface (parallel, USB, or other). This computer becomes the print server. In this case, you can only access the printer from the network if the computer attached to it is on and has network access.

exam
watch

In each method of sharing printers over a network, there is a print server. However, the CompTIA Exam 801 *Objective 4.2 only lists a hardware print server.*

Installing a Printer

Before installing any printer, you need to unpack it (if new) and test it. The actual steps you take to install it will depend on the individual printer and whether it is plug and play or non–plug and play. Any new printer today is plug and play, but on the job, you may run into some old printers that are not plug and play and be asked to install them on new computers.

Some Windows terminology is helpful at this point. To Windows, a *printer* is the software installed in Windows that controls a physical printer (or more, if other similar printers are available). To Windows, a physical printer is a *print device*. So, when you install a printer into Windows, you are installing a software printer as well as the print driver. The printer uses the driver and spooler to process and send your print jobs to the print device.

Unpacking and Testing a Printer

Follow the manufacturer's instructions to unpack a new printer, removing all the shipping material. Normally a disc is packed with the printer containing the printer driver (usually several for different operating systems) and additional software for working with the printer's features. Immediately check that you have a correct print driver for the operating system on the computer it will be connected to, or computers if it will be shared.

Next, plug in the power cable, but do not connect the printer to the computer, and follow the instructions to install toner or ink cartridges and to load paper. You must power up some printers before you can install the cartridges. Follow the manufacturer's instructions for printing a test page directly from the printer. Then move on to installing the printer, as per the next two sections on plug and play printers and non–plug and play printers.

Installing a Plug and Play Printer

Windows includes extensive plug and play support for printers. As with other plug and play devices, if a printer connects to a plug and play interface on the PC (USB or IEEE 1394), Windows automatically detects the printer, installs the printer driver, and configures it. If the printer uses an infrared interface, this will require turning the printer on and pointing its infrared port at your computer's infrared port. When Windows detects a printer, it briefly displays a Found New Hardware message from the notification area of the taskbar, as shown here. Then it installs the driver and configures the printer, displaying another message after completing these tasks.

Installing a Non–Plug and Play Printer

In the event that you attach a non–plug and play printer, you will have to install it manually. A non–plug and play printer is most likely an old printer with a parallel or serial interface. After connecting the printer to a power source and testing it, connect it to the PC, power it up, and install the print driver and associated software. Each of the Windows versions discussed here has a slightly different path to opening the folder for working with printers. They are as follows:

- In Windows XP, select Start | Printers And Faxes.
- In Windows Vista, select Start | Printers.
- In Windows 7, select Start | Devices And Printers.
- In Windows 8, open Control Panel and under Hardware And Sound select View Devices And Printers.

For the sake of simplicity, we will refer to the window that opens as the "Printers folder" across all these versions of Windows, and we will discuss the small differences within the Printers folder, which in all cases contains links to printers connected to your computer.

Once in the Printers folder in Windows XP, you will select Add Printer, and in Windows Vista, Windows 7, and Windows 8, select Add A Printer, which opens the Add Printer Wizard, shown in Figure 21-3.

Be prepared to make selections on each page of the wizard. You will need to know the following:

- Is it a local printer or a network printer?
- For a local printer, you will need to know the port it uses.
- For a network printer, you will need to know its location on the network.
- For a local printer and some network printers, to install the printer driver and other software, either select the printer manufacturer and model number from a list provided by the wizard, or provide a disc or a location for the driver files.

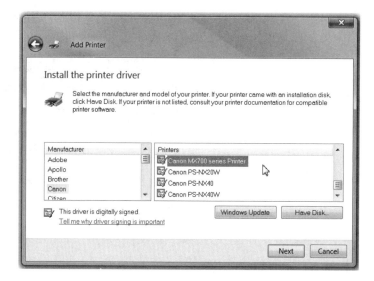

FIGURE 21-3

Use the Add
Printer Wizard to
install a non–plug
and play printer.

■ For a network printer, the printer software may automatically install over the network from the print server.

■ Give the printer a user-friendly name to better identify it if you want to.

■ For both local and network printer installation, you will be asked if you want to set the printer as the default printer.

■ You will be asked if you wish to share the local printer over the network.

■ You will be asked if you wish to print a test page to confirm proper printer installation and functions. We recommend you always do this to ensure that you can print from Windows.

If you are prepared with the answers to the questions it asks, the Windows Add Printer Wizard makes installing a non–plug and play printer easy, as demonstrated in Exercise 21-1.

EXERCISE 21-1

Installing a Non–Plug and Play Printer

1. In the Printers folder, select Add A Printer from the Printer Tasks list or bar.

2. In the Add Printer Wizard, Local or Network Printer page, select Local Printer Attached To This Computer and also select Automatically Detect And Install My Plug And Play Printer. Windows XP will detect a parallel

plug and play printer, and you won't have to configure the port. For newer versions of Windows you will need to configure the parallel port.

3. Complete each page, using the responses you prepared from the list that precedes this exercise. When prompted, choose to print a test page to confirm that the printer installation is working correctly.

4. Click Finish to close the Add Printer Wizard, and it will copy the files, the installation will finish, and the test page will print out.

5. After successfully installing a printer, the Printers folder will display. Look for the icon for the new printer.

Installing a Network Printer

When preparing to connect a printer directly to a network via the printer's built-in NIC, first unpack the printer, install ink or toner cartridges, load the paper, connect to a power source, and then connect the appropriate cable to a switch. If the printer has a Wi-Fi NIC, ensure that an appropriate wireless router is configured and within signal range of the printer. Then power up the printer and follow these general steps.

1. **Configure the IP address for the printer's network adapter**. Networks come with network protocols, including Transmission Control Protocol/ Internet Protocol (TCP/IP) built in, and on most networks, you will need to configure an IP address for the printer's NIC. You usually do this through a menu on the printer's control panel, or via special software on a PC directly connected to one of the printer's ports, such as a USB port. The manufacturer's instructions will give you the details on the method, but you may want to talk to a network administrator to discover the correct IP address to assign to the printer's network adapter.

2. **Test the IP address**. Once you have assigned the IP address, test that you can reach the printer over the network. Testing will require going to a computer proven to be connected to the network and running the following command from a command line: **ping <*ip_address*>**, where <*ip_address*> is the IP address assigned to the printer. IP addresses were described in Chapter 14.

3. **Prepare each network computer**. Install the printer driver and other utilities on each computer that will print to the printer. After installing the printer, open the Properties page for the printer in Windows and select the Ports tab. Scroll down and check that the port for the network printer

is installed. You will need to check the manufacturer's documentation. For instance, the port for the Canon MX700 does not install automatically; you need to add it, and you need to assign the IP address of the printer to the port on each computer. To add a port, click the Add Port button and scroll down through the Printer Ports list until you see the port for your printer. For instance, the Canon port, shown here, is listed as "Canon BJNP Port." Select the port, and click the New Port button. In the Add Port dialog box, either select IP Address and manually enter the address of the printer, or select Auto Detection, in which case you will need to wait until the printer is detected and the correct IP address appears in the box. Once the IP address is either entered or detected, click the Next button. If you manually entered the address, the wizard will not proceed until it detects the printer on the network. Then follow the instructions to complete the wizard.

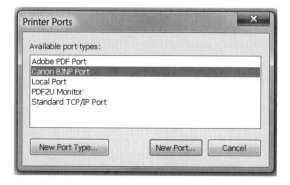

If you have a printer connected directly to your computer, whether the network is an Ethernet wired network or Wi-Fi, you can print to a printer only known to you by its IP address if you have the correct software installed in Windows to support this. Prior to Windows Vista, the client software that allowed a computer to print to an "IP printer" was the Line Printer Remote (LPR) client software, also called the LPR Port Monitor. It prints to a server with the Line Printer Daemon (LPD) service installed. Both the LPR and LPD software can be installed on any of the Windows versions studied here. In versions prior to Vista, LPD is known as Print Services for Unix. In Windows XP, you add and enable LPD or LPR through the Add/Remove Programs applet in Control Panel.

Beginning in Windows Vista, Microsoft added an improved and preferred alternative to LPR: the Internet Printing Client. This client is installed and enabled by default along with TCP/IP protocols and services. In Windows Vista, Windows 7, and Windows 8, you install and enable the Internet Printing Client in the Windows

Features dialog box, accessed by first opening the Programs applet in Control Panel, then locating Programs And Features, and selecting the task labeled Turn Windows Features On Or Off. Then open the Print Services node (Print and Document Services in Windows 8), and select the check box for Internet Printing Client. The LPD Print Service and LPR Port Monitor (the new names for the old services) are also available there, but you will normally use the new client service.

Testing a Printer for Compatibility

The printer test you perform at the end of printer installation in Windows will print a test page and verify the compatibility of your printer and its software with Windows. The Windows printing system eliminates most problems with incompatibility between individual applications and a printer. However, there are the rare instances in which output from an application does not produce the expected results. Therefore, to further test the compatibility of your applications with the new printer, open each application and print a document to the printer.

Installing an All-in-One Printer

When installing an all-in-one printer containing a scanner, copier, and fax, you will have a few additional tasks. When unpacking a new device, pay extra attention to the setup instructions because the scanner in the all-in-one may have a lock to secure the fragile internal components from damage during shipping. Release this lock once you have the device positioned properly on a clean surface. The installation program on the disc that comes with the device will have all the software for the three types of devices.

If the all-in-one includes a fax, and if you plan to use that feature, then you will need to connect a phone cable to the device's RJ-11 connector and connect this to a phone wall jack. Then follow the manufacturer's instructions for configuring the fax to send and receive fax messages.

Configuring a Printer

Windows has two sets of printer settings: Printer Properties and Printing Preferences.

Printer Properties

Open a printer's Properties dialog box to configure settings for the printer itself, such as single-sided versus double-sided printing, sharing the printer on a Microsoft network, which computer or network port the printer uses, color management, security, and maintenance tasks. Right-click the appropriate printer's icon and select Properties (in Windows 7, select Printer Properties). This will open a window similar to Figure 21-4. The tabs may vary, depending on the printer's capabilities and Windows' configuration.

on the job

The actual tabs on the Printer Properties dialog box vary by printer. Tabs, such as Accessories, Device Settings, and Maintenance, will display only if the printer's device driver supports them. Also, the Sharing tab disappears when your computer joins a HomeGroup.

You will be able to control a variety of settings, such as resolution, paper type, color use, and print density. You can also print a test page from this dialog box and, in some printers, use one or more cleaning and diagnostic modes for the printer.

Printing Preferences

Another group of options, Printing Preferences, controls how documents are printed, and these settings vary from printer to printer. This dialog is where you

---

FIGURE 21-4

Configure a printer using the printer's Properties dialog box.

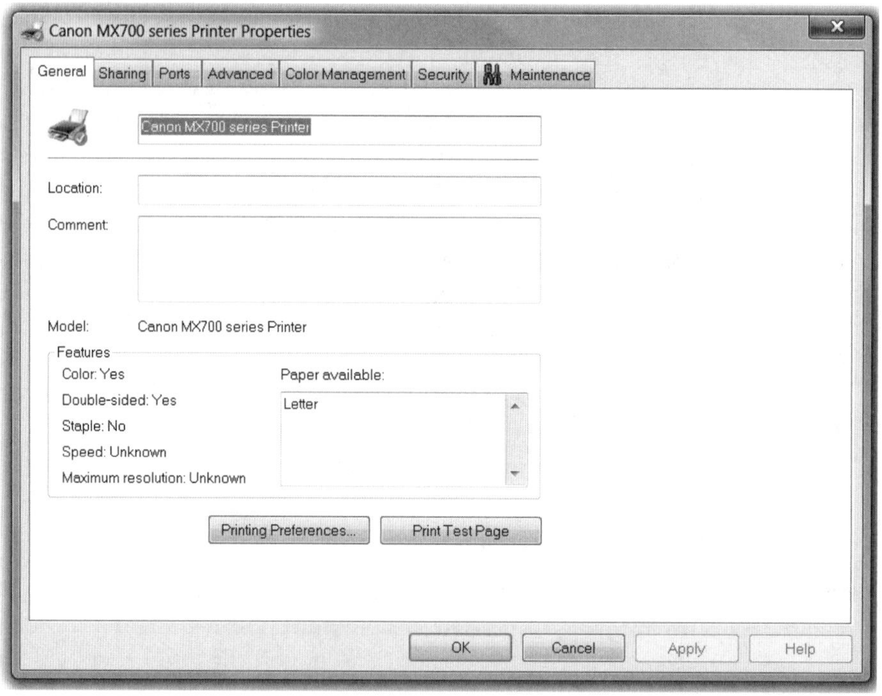

Canon MX700 series Printer Properties

General | Sharing | Ports | Advanced | Color Management | Security | Maintenance

Canon MX700 series Printer

Location:

Comment:

Model: Canon MX700 series Printer

Features
Color: Yes
Double-sided: Yes
Staple: No
Speed: Unknown
Maximum resolution: Unknown

Paper available:
Letter

Printing Preferences...   Print Test Page

OK   Cancel   Apply   Help

select the number of copies, paper orientation, paper source, paper size, paper type, graphic options, output mode (number of pages per side, duplex printing, etc.), print order (front to back, back to front, etc.), printed overlays, and watermarks. To access printing preferences, right-click a printer in the Printers folder, and select Printing Preferences, or access it from the Printing Preferences button in the Properties dialog.

Print Management

Microsoft introduced a new Microsoft Management Console (MMC), Print Management, in Windows 7 (not included in Windows 7 Home Premium). Print Management gives you a central location for administering all printers—both local and network. It is listed in Administrative Tools in both Windows 7 and Windows 8, but you can easily open it in Windows 7 by entering **print management** in Start Search. Figure 21-5 shows the Print Management console showing one of the filtered views, All Printers. You can also view all print drivers, printers that are not ready, and printers with jobs. Notice that the local computer, because it is sharing printers, is listed as a print server.

If your Windows 7 or Windows 8 computer is joined to a HomeGroup and you open the Properties dialog box from Devices and Printers, you may be surprised to see that there are only a few tabs—usually General and Hardware. All the other tabs are removed when you join a HomeGroup because it hides administrative tasks in order to simplify file and printer sharing.

FIGURE 21-5

The Print Management Console in Windows 7

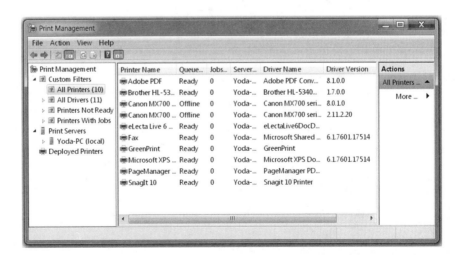

If your computer is a member of a workgroup or domain, you will see many tabs in a printer's Properties dialog box. However, even when your computer is in a HomeGroup, you can access all of a printer's properties tabs by opening the Print Management console, locating the printer in All Printers, and double-clicking the printer. This opens the Properties dialog box with all tabs displayed. What you can do here depends on your permissions for each printer.

Sharing a Printer

If you are sharing a local printer, how you enable printer sharing depends on how you configured your client for file and printer sharing in a HomeGroup, workgroup, or in a Microsoft Active Directory domain. These methods were described in Chapter 19.

Sharing a Printer in a HomeGroup

If your computer is part of a HomeGroup and you wish to share a local printer, open the HomeGroup app in Control Panel and click to place a check mark in the box labeled Printers (as shown in Chapter 19 in Figure 19-3). If you are using Windows 8, use the HomeGroup page in PC Settings and make sure the setting labeled Printers And Devices is turned on.

Sharing a Printer in a Workgroup or a Microsoft Active Directory Domain

If your computer is part of a workgroup or Microsoft Active Directory domain, you can share printers through the Sharing tab on the printer's Properties dialog box, shown in Figure 21-6. Click to place a check mark in the box labeled Share This Printer. If you have administrative rights and your computer is a member of a domain, there will be another check box labeled List In The Directory. Checking this will publish the printer in Active Directory, making it available to others in the domain to search Active Directory for your shared printer.

Render Print Jobs On Client Computers should be selected by default. If not, ensure that it is, because it moves the task of preparing a document for the printer to the client computer, saving your computer's processing power. Also, click Additional Drivers if computers that will be connecting to access the printer are running versions of Windows other than the one on this computer. Then select drivers for those printers, and when they connect, the correct driver will automatically be sent to their computer and installed.

FIGURE 21-6

The Sharing tab
in a Printer's
Properties
dialog box

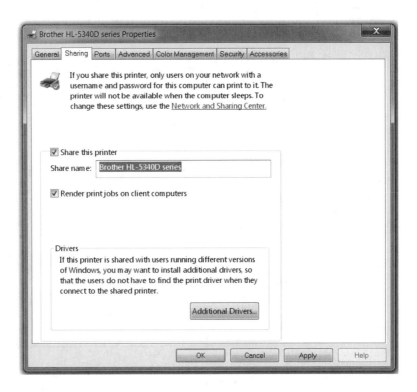

As with file sharing, when you share a printer in a workgroup or domain, you must assign permissions manually to the users connecting over the network, unless you leave the default permissions. In the case of a printer, the default permission gives the Everyone group Print permission, as shown on the Security tab in Figure 21-7. Creator Owner has Manage document permission, the user Yoda is a member of the Administrators group, and therefore has Print, Manage this printer, and Manage Documents permissions.

exam
ⓦatch *The Sharing tab will not be visible if your computer is a member of a HomeGroup. You must leave a HomeGroup to use this method of sharing.*

The four printer permissions are as follows:

■ **Print**   Allows a user to print, cancel, pause, and restart only the documents that they send to the printer.

■ **Manage This Printer**   Allows a user to rename, delete, share, and choose printer preferences. Also permits a user to assign printer permissions to other users and manage all print jobs on that printer.

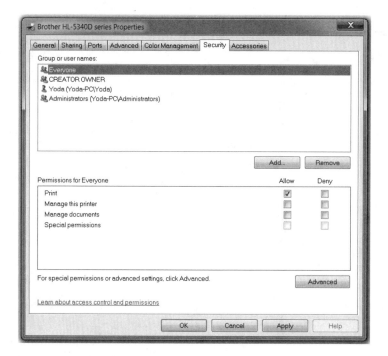

- **Manage Documents**   Permission to manage all jobs (for all users) in the printer's print queue.
- **Special Permissions**   Primary use of specials printers is by an administrator in order to change the printer owner. The person who installs a printer is the Creator Owner, who is automatically assigned the Manage documents permission.

Upgrades

Printers are somewhat limited in how you can upgrade them, unlike computers, which you can upgrade in many ways, such as by adding memory, installing a large selection of new peripherals, upgrading the ROM BIOS, and upgrading the software. We will describe some possible software and hardware upgrades for printers.

Device Driver and Software Upgrades

Like other software, software associated with printers and scanners calls for occasional upgrades, with drivers being the most frequently upgraded. When an updated driver is available for your printer, follow the manufacturer's instructions to install it. If it comes with its own installation program, run it. Alternatively, the instructions may tell you to use the Update Drivers option. To update a printer driver in this fashion, open the printer's Properties, select the Advanced tab, click New Driver, and follow the instructions in the Add Printer Driver Wizard.

Hardware Upgrades

Popular hardware upgrades for printers and scanners are automated document feeders for scanners and larger-capacity paper trays for laser printers. Higher-end devices in both categories are most likely to have upgrade options, usually offered by the manufacturer.

Another popular hardware upgrade is memory, particularly for laser printers. Adding memory can increase the speed when printing complex documents or graphics. A search of the Internet will turn up many manufacturers of memory upgrades for laser printers.

Firmware Upgrades

Some printers—in particular, laser printers—support firmware upgrades. This, of course, depends on the manufacturer releasing firmware upgrades. First, determine the firmware version currently in your printer, and then check on the manufacturer's Website for notices of upgrades. Instructions from the manufacturer will guide you through upgrading the firmware, which you do from your computer.

Optimizing Printer Performance

The average user is happy if a printer is reliable and creates reasonable printouts, but a growing number of users have more discerning tastes and more exacting needs. For them, printers offer a variety of optimizing choices.

Tray Selection

If a printer has multiple trays, there are ways to optimize their use. One is to load plain paper in one tray and special stationery in another. Then instruct users on which tray to select for the types of jobs they send to the printer.

Tray Switching

You should use a different strategy when users send a large volume of printing to a multiple-tray printer using just one kind of paper. With this, you set the printer's

SCENARIO & SOLUTION

We need a printer that will print an image to multipart forms for retail receipts. What should we buy?	Buy an impact printer, which will be able to print to carbon-copy forms.
In a laser printer, how does the image get from the drum to the paper?	The transfer corona wire applies a positive charge to the paper. As the paper passes the drum, the negatively charged toner is attracted to the page.
What cleans the photosensitive drum in a laser printer?	A cleaning blade removes residual toner from the drum, and an erasure lamp removes any remaining charge from the drum.
I am trying to install a printer on a parallel port, but when I plug it in, it is not recognized. What can I do?	Use the Add Printer Wizard in Windows to install the printer and configure the port.

preferences for tray switching so it will use the first tray until it is empty and then automatically switch to the second tray.

Deleting a Printer

When you no longer use a printer, delete it from Windows by opening the Printers folder, right-clicking the printer, and selecting Delete Or Remove Device. Respond to the confirmation dialog box ("Are you sure...?"), and the printer will be deleted.

CERTIFICATION OBJECTIVE

■ **801: 4.3** *Given a scenario, perform printer maintenance*

Printer Maintenance

Because of the frequency with which printers are used, they require almost constant maintenance. Fortunately, the maintenance procedures are usually easy—the most frequent tasks involve consumables. Consider scheduling regular maintenance, such as cleaning, based on the amount of usage for each printer and scanner. Manufacturers may provide a list of other maintenance tasks, such as vacuuming or replacing the ozone filter in laser printers, which should occur along with a regular cleaning, but not at the same frequency.

Check with the manufacturer for recommendations for how to maintain the ozone filter. Some can be vacuumed, while others must be replaced at a specified interval.

Maintenance Tools

The basic tool set that you use for maintaining a computer is appropriate for printers too. It includes using compressed air from pressurized cans for blowing out the paper dust and debris inside a printer and a small vacuum cleaner. Because the particles of toner in a laser printer are so microscopic, it isn't a good idea to use a conventional vacuum because the toner can clog it up. Manufacturers do make special vacuums for laser printers, but they tend to be expensive. Laser printer manufacturers do make maintenance kits for replacing aging parts at predetermined intervals.

Replacing Consumables

The most common maintenance tasks involve replacing consumables. Printer consumables include the printer medium, some components, and paper. The printer medium is a consumable that contains the pigment for the image that a printer creates. The medium comes in a special form for the technology and is specific to the model of printer. The most common forms are ink ribbons, ink cartridges, and laser printer toner cartridges. A printer cannot work without consumables, such as paper and ink or toner cartridges. If you are the one responsible for purchasing and storing these products, letting these supplies run out is bad for your career!

For the best results, use the manufacturer's recommended consumables. This includes ink and toner cartridges as well as paper for printers. In the case of the major printer manufacturers, their branded ink and toner products may only be available at premium prices. To save money, consider third-party sources, but be prepared to buy and test one set of cartridges before ordering quantities.

Shelf Life The shelf life of both laser printer toner cartridges and inkjet cartridges is similar, and is usually two years from production date or six months from when you first open the package or first put it into use. Even printer paper has a shelf life because paper for friction-feed printers must contain a certain range of moisture content in order to feed properly without causing jams. Old paper also may discolor unless it is of very high quality. Used printer consumables can negatively affect the environment and should be disposed of in a manner that is both legal and respectful of the environment, as described in Chapter 1.

Paper   All printers have the dreaded "paper out" light and Windows desktop error message (if connected to a computer). A printer in a cash register, a point-of-sale (PoS) printer, typically has an alarm. Replacing paper is the most frequent maintenance task. So, be prepared for this, and aid any user who does not know how to do this, because support techs simply can't be available at every printer.

With the exception of thermal printers and some impact printers that require tractor-feed paper, most printers, including laser and inkjet, can use standard-sized sheets of ordinary copier paper for drafts and everyday casual printing. For the best results, however, consult the printer documentation for the type and quality of paper to use. Paper should be stored in its packaging and in a cool, dry place. For instance, copier paper often comes in paper-wrapped one-ream (500-page) packages, but is also available in bulk boxes, in which the paper is not wrapped. Do not unwrap or remove paper from its container until ready to install in a printer. If you are using a tray to feed a friction-feed printer, simply pull out the appropriate paper tray. Gently ripple a stack of fresh paper and then insert it into the tray. If there is a lid for the tray, replace that before inserting the tray into the printer.

Tractor-feed impact printers printing multiple copies use either carbon paper or *impact paper* that contains encapsulated ink or dye on the back of each sheet except the last one so that the impact of the print head on the first sheet breaks the encapsulation on all sheets and causes a character image to appear on the subsequent sheets.

To replace paper in a tractor-feed printer, you will need to lift the printer lid, feed the first sheet of the new stack through the paper path, and line up the holes with the sprockets on the feed wheels. As this procedure varies from model to model, consult the manufacturer's documentation. Finally, stack the continuous form paper in a bin or next to the printer neatly so that it can easily feed into the printer.

on the Job   *When feeding card stock or sheets of labels through a printer, be sure to use the straightest paper path to avoid jams. And never feed a sheet of labels through a laser printer if one or more labels have been removed, because the "Teflon-like" material on the paper carrier will melt on the fusing roller and ruin it. A fusing roller is an expensive component to replace because you normally must replace the entire fusing assembly.*

Adding paper to any printer should only take a few seconds because it does not involve turning off the printer's power. The error message should go away on its own. If you do not close or insert the tray properly, a Tray Open or Close Tray message may appear. If the printer uses an upright friction feed, follow the steps in Exercise 21-2 to add more paper.

EXERCISE 21-2

Adding Paper to an Upright Friction-Feed Tray

If you have access to a printer with an upright friction-feed tray, you can follow these instructions.

1. Release the tray lever at the back of the printer (if so equipped). This will cause the paper tray to drop away slightly from the friction rollers.
2. Place a small stack of paper in the tray, using the paper guides.
3. Engage the tray lever to bring the paper closer to the feed rollers.
4. The printer might automatically detect the paper and continue the print job. If not, look for and press the Paper Advance button on the printer. This instructs the printer to detect and try to feed the paper.

Multipart forms are not always available as continuous-feed paper, in which case, you need an impact printer capable of friction feed. Usually, this only requires removing the tractor feed assembly and making sure that the friction-feed mechanism is engaged (it is disengaged while tractor feed is in use).

Paper for a thermal printer comes in rolls. Perhaps the most common thermal printers are in cash registers; you have probably witnessed a cashier changing thermal paper while you waited in line with a shopping basket full of frozen food. To change the thermal paper roll, you first open the feed assembly compartment and remove the plastic or cardboard roll from the spent roll and remove any torn paper or debris in the compartment. Then place the new roll on the spindle, taking care to have the paper feed in the correct direction from the roll, and thread it through the assembly (look for directions mounted in the compartment or arrows on the components), making sure to thread the end of the roll outside. Close the door, give a gentle tug to the paper, and tear off the leading edge. Most thermal printers have a paper cutter where the paper exits.

Ink   The most common forms of ink for printers are ink ribbons for impact printers and ink cartridges for inkjet printers.

An impact printer uses a fabric ribbon embedded with ink. The ribbon is usually a closed loop on two spools (for unused and used ribbon) enclosed within a cartridge. This cartridge is either a movable cartridge mounted on the print head assembly, or a stationary cartridge that stretches the ribbon the width of the paper, allowing the moving print head assembly to move back and forth. The used portion of the ribbon simply spools back into the ribbon cartridge. To install, follow the manufacturer's instructions, which will include carefully bringing the ribbon over the print head.

The medium for inkjet printers is ink contained in reservoirs. In the case of inkjet printers, this reservoir is part of a small cartridge that also may contain the print head that sprays the ink on the paper. Figure 21-8 shows an open inkjet printer with the cartridges exposed. You must turn this model on when you change the cartridges because when it is turned off, the cartridges are "parked" out of sight. Lights on each cartridge give the status of the cartridge: steady when there is adequate ink, blinking when ink is low.

If you search the documentation or the manufacturer's Website, you can discover the expected yield of a cartridge. The yield of a typical inkjet cartridge is in the hundreds of pages. One printer shows a black ink cartridge yield of 630 pages of text and 450 pages for graphic printouts that have 5 percent coverage. The same printer shows a color ink yield of 430 pages with 5 percent coverage per color. If your printouts use more ink per page, then the yield will be smaller.

Toner Toner cartridges for a typical noncolor desktop laser printer run around $50 and up, but they last for several thousand pages, making these printers relatively inexpensive per page to use. Color laser cartridges are several hundred dollars a set, but they offer very high quality, and they, too, print thousands of pages before you need to replace the cartridges.

FIGURE 21-8

An open inkjet printer with the ink cartridges exposed

Many companies take used printer cartridges, recondition the drum and other components, refill the toner reservoir with fresh toner, and offer them at significantly lower cost than the manufacturer's fresh cartridges. We have had mixed experiences with these "refilled" cartridges. Some refilled/reconditioned cartridges have performed as well as the best brand-name new toner cartridges, whereas others have been very poor. Caveat emptor!

The brand-name cartridges from your printer's manufacturer will normally produce the highest quality and demand the highest price. We often buy new cartridges from a company that sells both new and reconditioned cartridges. No matter what vendor we use for our toner cartridges, we always buy from one that takes our old toner cartridges for recycling at no cost to us.

The yield of a laser cartridge for a typical desktop monochrome black laser printer is several thousand pages. Numbers such as 3,000 to 8,000 pages are common. The yield for a color laser printer generally runs over 1,000 pages per cartridge. For instance, the documentation for one printer estimates the yield for a standard-capacity black toner cartridge at 4,000 pages, whereas the estimate for each of the standard cyan, magenta, yellow, and black (CMYK) cartridges is 1,500 pages. The high-capacity color toner cartridges show an expected yield of 4,000 pages.

To replace a toner cartridge, first turn off the printer, unplug it, and gently remove the old cartridge. This last is not required for replacing the cartridge, but we recommend doing it because this is a good time to give the printer a quick cleaning, removing paper and toner debris, as described later in this chapter. After cleaning the printer, remove the new cartridge from its packaging and set it aside while you insert the old cartridge into the packaging for disposal. Then remove any tape or plastic components labeled to be removed before installing. Gently rock the cartridge from side to side, and then insert into the printer, per the manufacturer's instructions.

Cleaning a Printer

The best thing you can do to prolong the life of a printer and prevent problems from occurring is to clean it regularly. In all printers, whether laser, thermal, or impact, small particles of paper and other debris can be left behind and cause a potentially harmful build-up. As mentioned earlier, this build-up can hold a static charge, which can, in turn, damage components through electrostatic discharge (ESD) or cause pages to stick together.

We do not recommend using any solvents to clean a printer, and never spray a liquid on or into a printer for any reason. Use a very dilute mixture of water and white vinegar to dampen a cloth, and thoroughly wring it out before wiping off the exterior. Do not use liquids inside the printer unless following the advice of the manufacturer.

Before opening up a printer for cleaning, power it down and unplug it. Do not touch the printer's power supply, and allow the fusing roller in a laser printer to cool down before you clean inside.

Removing the build-up will also keep the paper path clear, thus reducing paper jams and ensuring there is no inhibition of moving parts. You can remove dust and particle build-up using compressed air or a vacuum. As you clean the printer, be on the lookout for small paper corners left behind during the print process or after you cleared a paper jam.

In an inkjet printer, you should look for and remove ink from the inside of the printer. Ink can leak and cause smudges on the paper. As the ink dries, it can cause moving components or paper to stick.

Laser printers can accumulate toner. Remove excess toner using a paper towel or cotton swab, but beyond that, only clean laser printer internal components using the manufacturer's instructions, which may include using a *toner vacuum*, a vacuum with filters to protect you from inhaling the super-fine toner particles. This is essential if you support many laser printers.

You may have to replace the ribbon and the print head in an impact printer, and in a thermal printer you should clean the heating element. Figure 21-9 shows the interior of a laser printer.

A desktop laser printer opened and ready for cleaning

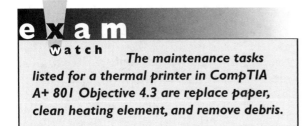

Some manufacturers add a Maintenance tab to the Printer Properties dialog box for tasks such as those shown in Figure 21-10 for an inkjet printer. Notice the four buttons for cleaning various components, plus the buttons for Print Head Alignment and Nozzle Check.

Replacing Print Heads

The print head is the hardest working component in an impact printer, so be prepared to replace one if necessary. We will describe symptoms of problems with print heads later in "Troubleshooting Printers." If the solutions provided there do not eliminate the symptoms, then replace the print head. Contact the manufacturer for a replacement, and follow the instructions for removing the old print head and installing the new one.

FIGURE 21-10

A Printer Properties dialog box showing maintenance options

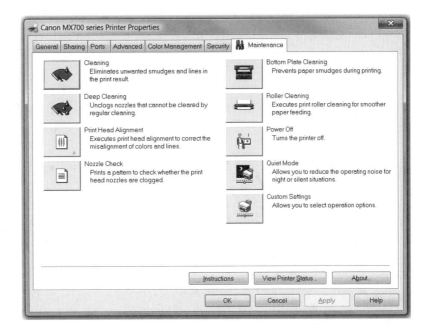

Maintenance Kits and Page Counts

Some printers, mainly professional-quality and high-production laser printers, have "maintenance counts." The printer counts the number of pages printed over the lifetime of the printer, and when this page count reaches a certain number, called the maintenance count (in the hundreds of thousands), a service message will appear on the printer's display. This message indicates that the printer has reached the end of the expected service life for some of its internal components, such as the various types of rollers, pads, and entire assemblies. When this occurs, you must install the manufacturer's maintenance kit of replacement parts, after which you must reset the page count so it can track the expected life of the parts in the new maintenance kit.

If you do not reset the page count, the printer will continue to issue the maintenance warning. Use the manufacturer's instructions for resetting the page count. In the rare instance when you must install a new maintenance kit before the page count reaches the maintenance count, on some models you must reset the maintenance count to match the page count. Then, when the next page is printed, you will receive the maintenance message and can proceed with the maintenance and reset the page count.

Calibration

Calibration is a process that matches colors seen on the screen to colors printed on paper. To get the best quality out of a color printer, look for a calibration tool in the Color Management tab of the printer's Properties dialog box. We opened

FIGURE 21-11

The Color
Management
dialog box

the Color Management dialog box shown in Figure 21-11 by selecting the Color Management tab, and then clicking the Color Management button. Notice the list (two items) in the box under ICC Profiles. These are sets of specifications used by your printer to print color, per *International Color Consortium (ICC)* standards. ICC is a standards organization for color management systems. Find additional profiles on the All Profiles tab, which in this case contains *Windows Color System (WCS)* profiles. WCS is a color management system that Microsoft is promoting as a standard. You can select profiles from this list and add them to the printers list on the Devices page. Then print out samples and compare the screen image of each sample with the printed image. Using a utility like this, you are depending on your eyes to judge the correct settings. Of course, none of these profiles will work if your display's color is not right. So, click the Advanced tab and click Calibrate Display. Follow the instructions for calibrating the display.

e x a m

w a t c h
    The maintenance tasks for a laser jet printer listed in CompTIA A+ 801 Objective 4.3 are replacing toner (cartridge), applying maintenance kit, calibration, and cleaning. Note that for laser printers calibration only applies to color laser printers.

Ensuring a Suitable Environment

Prevent a myriad of problems with your printer by providing a suitable environment. Be sure the printer is on a level surface, close to the computer to which it is connected, and convenient for the user. Temperature extremes, dirt, and dust will negatively affect either type of device. Dirt and dust will affect the quality of scanned documents, and, if they infiltrate the case, can cause heat build-up in any device.

CERTIFICATION OBJECTIVE

■ **802: 4.9**   *Given a scenario, troubleshoot printers with appropriate tools*

Troubleshooting Printers

When troubleshooting printers, apply the same troubleshooting theory and procedures used with other computer components and use the same toolkit, as described in Chapter 3. When a printer needs a major repair, first evaluate the cost benefit of the repair by finding out how much it would cost to replace the printer versus the cost of the repair. In this section, learn about common printer problems and their solutions.

on the
job
    Printers are one of the most commonly accessed network resources and are the cause of a majority of network-related trouble calls.

Printer Troubleshooting Tools

Troubleshooting tools for printers include a subset of the tools described in Chapter 3 for installing, maintaining, and troubleshooting computers. A subset of those tools will be your most useful tools, including an assortment of screwdrivers, a selection of printer-specific field replaceable units (FRUs), multimeter (for testing wall outlets), and printer-specific tools, such as those listed in CompTIA A+ Exam Objective 802: 4.9, which include a maintenance kit, toner vacuum, compressed air, and printer spooler. We'll discuss each of these last four in context with specific printer problems.

Understanding Print Spooling for Troubleshooting

Since the print spooler is included in the list of tools for troubleshooting printers, we will explain why that is. The correct print spooler settings for a printer will avoid potential problems. These settings are found on the Advanced tab in all versions of Windows included in the CompTIA A+ Exams.

Enable spooling by selecting Spool Print Jobs So Program Finishes Printing Faster. The alternative to spooling is to select the Print Directly To The Printer option. If you have enabled spooling, you will be able to decide whether the printer begins printing after the first page is spooled or after the last page is spooled.

You can also select the spool data format. In Windows XP and later, this setting is contained in a dialog box that opens from the Print Processor button on the Advanced page of the printer's Properties dialog box, as shown in Figure 21-12.

The three print processors in Figure 21-12 are shown in the Print Processor box. Each print processor has a selection of data types. There are several versions of *Enhanced Metafile Format (EMF)*, a Windows graphic-rendering language. When you use an EMF data type, the printing application builds an EMF file representing the print job, and Windows sends this file to the spooler. When the RAW data type is used, Windows translates each print job into printer-specific code. It actually takes Windows longer to do this than to create an EMF file. Windows then sends the resulting RAW file to the spooler. RAW is not an acronym, although Microsoft shows it in all caps. The output will look the same with either file format, but not all printers can print EMF print jobs. The printer's installation program will normally select its own software print processor and the RAW spool data format, and you should not select a different format unless you experience problems, such as the computer slowing down when you print a file. Then experiment with keeping the printer's print processor and using an EMF format before trying the Windows print processor, and use whichever solves the problem.

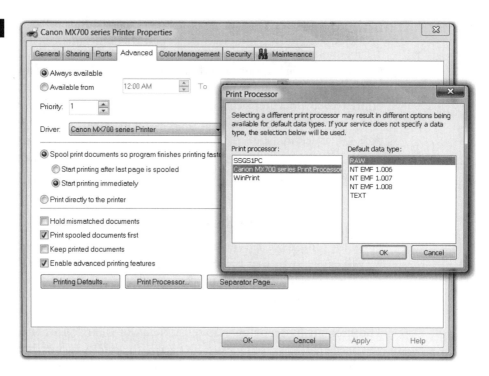

FIGURE 21-12

Select the data
type from the
Print Processor
dialog box.

Unable to Install a Printer

With plug and play and Windows' ability to discover network printers, you will
have fewer instances in which a printer will not install. In all cases of printer
installation problems, check that you are using the correct driver version for your
version of Windows, including 32 bit versus 64 bit. Then concentrate on the type
of connection. If you are unable to install a local printer with a USB connection, be
sure that the print device is not connected to the computer until after you install the
printer driver. Then connect the printer and turn it on.

If the problem is with a print device connected via parallel printer, ensure that
the port is configured correctly in Windows and BIOS settings.

For a network printer, go to the print device itself and make sure it is turned on
and connected. Check connections to it from other computers. If you receive an
access denied message when trying to install a printer, you will need to have the
administrator of the printer share give you administrative access to the printer. After
doing this, repeat the steps for installing the printer.

Access Denied to an Installed Printer

If a user attempts to print to a local or network printer and sees an access denied message, the printer administrator will need to change the permissions on the printer or printer share for your account or group so that the user can print. Recall that to print requires the Print permission. A user who has the responsibility of managing all jobs on a printer needs Manage Document permission, and someone who does all printer management tasks must have the Manage This Printer permission.

Non-Windows Clients Cannot Connect to a Shared Printer

If you need to share a printer connected to a Windows computer with computers on your network running other operating systems, such as Mac OS X, you may need to enable the line printer daemon (LPD) service on the Windows computer. On a Windows 7 computer, open Control Panel, select Programs And Features, and then select Turn Windows Features On Or Off. In the Turn Windows Features On Or Off dialog box, browse to the Print And Document Service node and expand it. Then enable the LPD Print Service.

On an Apple computer running Mac OS X, open an app that you would normally print from and then open the Print menu (File | Print in Microsoft Word for Mac). From the Print dialog box, open the Printer pop-up menu and select Add Printer. In the Add Printer dialog box, click the IP button. In the Protocol box, select Line Printer Daemon. In the Address box, enter the IP address of the Windows computer to which the printer is connected. It will then attempt to detect the printer and the Print Using box will suggest a printer (a driver). For our laser printer, it will select a Generic PostScript Printer. Click Add. On the Installable Options page, select the options you wish to use, such as duplex printing, and click Continue. Then send a print job to the printer as a test.

e x a m
ⓦ a t c h   *The Acronyms List includes*
line printer daemon/line printer remote (LPD/
LPR) and Internet Printing Protocol (IPP). **Both**
are protocols for printing to a networked
printer over TCP/IP networks, using the

IP address of the printer. LPD/LPR itself
is also sometimes broken down into the
two named protocols. IPP is a newer,
more secure protocol that supports
authentication and encryption.

Paper Feed Problems

Common to all printers, paper feed problems have a variety of causes, and the symptoms are not just paper jamming and stopping the printing. Paper feed problems result in creased paper and paper simply not feeding at all because it never leaves the paper tray. Here are just a few possible causes and solutions:

- **Too much paper in a paper tray**   Too much paper can cause more than one page to feed through the printer at a time. The extra page can cause problems with the print process itself and jam within the printer. To avoid this, reduce the amount of paper you place in the tray.

- **Static electricity**   If static builds up within the pages, it can cause the pages to stick together. Use your thumb to "riffle," or quickly separate, the pages before you load them into the paper tray. Riffling allows air between the pages and can reduce "static cling." Remove dust from the printer, as this can also cause static build-up.

- **Moisture in the paper**   Moisture can cause pages to stick together or not feed properly. To protect paper from moisture changes, keep it in its packaging until needed. Store paper in a cool, dry place.

- **Worn out friction-feed parts**   Worn parts will fail to move the paper smoothly. Check feed rollers for wear. Feed rollers are often rubber or plastic, and you should replace them (depending on the cost of replacing parts versus replacing the printer). You may also need to replace the separation pad.

- **The wrong paper**   Use paper that is not too thin, not too thick, and that has a certain range of moisture content to avoid static build-up. Try using a different weight paper. Try feeding from an alternative (straight-through) paper path. Most printers have the option of a more direct paper path that can handle heavier-weight paper than the standard path.

- **Too few sheets in an upright paper tray**   If the stack of paper in an upright paper tray is too small, the friction rollers might not be able to make good contact with the top page. Try putting a larger stack of paper in (without making it too large).

- **Broken parts in the paper path**   Inspect for any broken parts in the paper path. If you find any, you will have to investigate repairing or replacing the printer. If necessary, clean the printer, and once you have finished clearing the jam, either resume the print job or send another print job. Most printers will not resume operation until you have completely cleared the jam. Many printers also require you to press the reset or clear button to restart the printer.

■ **Misalignment of paper in tractor feed**   Tractor feed has its own problems. These feed mechanisms are notorious for feeding paper incorrectly through the printer. Misalignment of the paper in the printer usually causes the problem. Tractor feeds require special continuous-form paper, in which each page of paper attaches to the one before it, much like a roll of paper towels. If the perforations between pages do not line up properly, the text for one page will print across two pages. When this happens, look for a Paper Advance button on the printer that will incrementally advance the paper until it is properly aligned. If you do not have the documentation for the printer, this task may take trial and error.

■ **Friction feed not disabled for tractor feed**   Another problem with tractor feeds occurs when the friction-feed mechanism is not disabled. The most obvious symptom of this problem will be torn paper if the tractor pulls faster than the friction feed moves, or bunched paper if the opposite condition exists.

Clearing a Paper Jam

Most paper jams will stop the current print job. If you suspect a paper jam, consult your printer documentation. In general, turn off and open the printer, and carefully remove any paper jammed in the paper path, following the manufacturer's instructions. Some printers include levers that you can release to more easily remove jammed paper. Normally, you will need to gently pull the paper in the direction the paper normally moves through the printer. Pulling in the opposite direction could damage internal components, such as rollers. This is especially true of the fusion roller in a laser printer. Avoid tearing the paper. If it tears, be sure you locate and remove all pieces from the printer.

ⓦatch   *Paper-feed problem symptoms listed in CompTIA A+ Exam 802 Objective 4.9 include creased paper, paper not feeding, and paper jam.*

No Connectivity to Printer

A problem with printer connectivity begs the question, "Was it ever connected?" If this is the first time you are attempting to connect the printer, then troubleshoot based on the connection method you are attempting. This is rarely a problem with USB, unless the connector is not properly connected. USB is the least troublesome of your connection options. If this is a parallel printer connection (we'll try not to ask "Why parallel?), check the cable connection, and verify that the cable is an IEEE 1284-compliant cable. Then check the computer's parallel port settings in BIOS settings to ensure that the port is enabled, and that it is using the correct mode, which is ECP mode if you have an IEEE 1284–compliant cable and printer. See Chapter 4 to review how to enter BIOS Settings. If connecting via Ethernet, Wi-Fi, or Bluetooth, troubleshoot the network connection.

Unable to Install Printer

If you attempt to install a printer and are unable to do so, there are several possible causes and solutions, depending on the printer model and the version of Windows. Note any error messages and if you cannot interpret them or do not understand what action you should take, contact the manufacturer, or check out the support page on their Website for a solution. If you are using the driver disc that came with the printer, the problem may be with the installation program itself rather than the printer driver, and the manufacturer's support personnel may give you instructions on how to install the driver manually, bypassing the installation program. Another possible cause is that the printer did not come with a driver for the version of Windows you are using, and you will need to request an appropriate driver from the manufacturer. If they do not have an exact match, they may be able to recommend a similar driver from one of their models that will allow you to use most of the printer's capabilities.

Printer Will Not Print

If you send a print job to a printer and nothing happens, check the connection first (local connection or network connection), and check to see that the printer is powered on. Check the printer status lights or display, if it has one, to see if there are any printer errors and is perhaps out of paper, ink, or toner. If you see errors, troubleshoot the errors.

If everything about the printer seems normal except for it failing to print (or stopping in the midst of a print job), then treat it like a print spooler problem. Print spooler problems can cause a print job to not arrive at a printer or a job in progress to inexplicably stop. The print queue may be backed up because it is overwhelmed, or the print spooler service may have stopped. When this service stops, nothing prints until it is restarted. This is referred to as a "stalled print spooler."

You need to determine if the spooler is stalled. For this, you must have the Manage Documents permission to the printer. Assuming you logged on as a member of the

Administrators group, which is automatically assigned this permission, open the Printers folder and double-click the printer. Doing this opens the user interface for the print queue from which you can manage the print jobs the print spooler is holding. Check the status of the print job. If the print job status is Paused, right-click it and select Restart. If this fails, attempt to cancel the print job. Sometimes canceling the first job in the queue will allow the other jobs to print.

If this does not help, then cancel each job in the queue. If you are not able to restart or cancel jobs in the queue, you will need to restart the Print Spooler service. Follow the steps in Exercise 21-3 to restart this service.

EXERCISE 21-3

CertCam

Restarting the Print Spooler Service

Use the Services node in Computer Management to restart a stalled print spooler.

1. Right-click My Computer or Computer, and select Manage from the context menu.
2. In the Computer Management Console, select Services And Applications, and then double-click Services.
3. In the contents pane, scroll down to Print Spooler.
4. Right-click Print Spooler and select Restart (see Figure 21-13).
5. If restarting the service fails, then close all open windows and restart the computer. When Windows restarts, the Print Spooler service will restart.
6. Restart the printer.
7. Resend the print jobs to the printer.

Blank Pages

If a printer produces blank pages, troubleshoot the possible cause based on the type of printer.

Blank Pages from an Impact Printer   If an impact printer produces blank pages, pay attention to the sound coming from the printer. If the pins are striking the page but not printing, you have a ribbon problem. Make sure the ribbon lines up

FIGURE 21-13

Right-click the
Print Spooler
service and select
Restart.

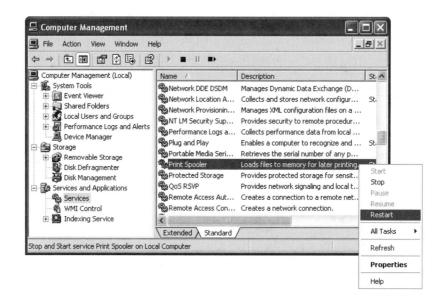

with the print head; if it does not, move it into position. You may have to find a way
to remove slack from the ribbon, which you can do by removing the ribbon cartridge
and manually rewinding the ribbon before reinserting it into the printer. If the
ribbon does line up properly but there is no print or just very faint print, the ribbon
has probably worn out, and replacing the ribbon will resolve the problem.

If carbon copies printed on an impact printer are blank or dim, consult the
documentation to adjust the distance between the print head and the paper. If you
cannot hear the pins striking the page, try replacing the print head.

Blank Pages from an Inkjet   If an inkjet printer produces blank pages, the likely
cause is an ink cartridge. Use the printer software to determine the amount of ink left
in an ink cartridge. The printer software may be a separate program that you will
start from an icon in the Windows GUI, or it may be integrated into the Windows
Printer Properties dialog box. If the printer software is integrated into the Printer
Properties dialog box, it may be in the form of a custom tab or a special button.

A warning that the printer is running low on ink, as shown on the next page, does
not necessarily mean that you should immediately replace the cartridge. We go for
weeks with this status showing and warnings popping up when we print. We simply
tell it to continue. We normally only replace a cartridge if the quality of the printout is
not adequate for our purposes, or if the print job will not continue without changing it.

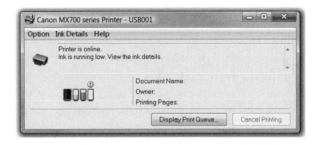

If there is ink, the problem could be clogged nozzles. Follow the printer manufacturer's instructions for cleaning the nozzles in the print head. Software installed with the printer driver usually does this and should be available on the Maintenance tab of the printer's Properties dialog. If it isn't, check the documentation for a way to initiate this from the printer's controls. In the extreme, follow the manufacturer's instructions for manually cleaning the print head, perhaps with a lint-free cloth slightly dampened with distilled water.

Blank Pages from a Laser Printer   If a laser printer is producing blank pages, suspect some component of the printing process. For instance, a blank page can result if the image fails to transfer to the paper, which could be a problem with the transfer corona wire. Shut down the printer, disconnect the power cable, open the printer, and inspect the corona wire (consult your manual for its location). You may find dirt or debris (like a staple) shorting out the wire. You may discover that the wire itself is broken, although it would take rough treatment indeed to do this. If the wire is intact but has debris on it, it could be shorting out. Clean the printer, and then try to print again.

It is rare for a laser cartridge to be the cause of a completely blank page, unless it contains a drum and the drum has failed. If it has, you must replace it. If the drum is part of the cartridge, replace the cartridge. You are more likely to see some of the other problems described next when the cartridge has a problem.

Print Quality

Print quality problems are very common with all types of printers. In laser printers, print quality problems are most often (but not always) associated with a component in the toner cartridge. When troubleshooting a print quality problem on a laser printer, swapping the toner cartridge often solves many of the problems listed here. Following are several common print quality problems and their suggested solutions.

Faded Prints

Several things can cause faded prints from a laser printer. The toner in the cartridge could be low, the corona wire could be dirty and not passing the correct charge to the paper, or the drum could be dirty or defective. If the drum is part of the toner cartridge, replacing the cartridge could solve the problem. If the drum is separate from the toner cartridge, try replacing it. Most laser printers include a way to clean the corona wires. You must first power off the printer and disconnect the power cable. Then, using either a special felt-lined tool or a built-in slider, gently move the tool along the wire.

Faded prints on an impact printer are almost always due to ribbon problems. Replace the ribbon cartridge.

Printouts from thermal printers have a unique problem, especially since thermal printers are frequently used to print receipts. The paper darkens over time, and the image fades and becomes unreadable. There are several solutions to this, but thermal paper quality varies, so you may completely lose the image when you try some of these techniques. The best action to take is to immediately scan or copy all receipts before they fade. Then you either have a paper copy or an image of the receipt stored in your computer. Even this proactive technique has its risks, since the light from the copier can darken the thermal printout.

Another technique used after an image has faded is to copy or scan it after adjusting the contrast settings to try and recover the image. And yet another technique uses a laminating machine with the hope that the heat from the laminator will restore the image. None of these techniques is guaranteed to work.

Ghost Image from the Previous Page

A ghost image occurs when a usually very faint image from a previous page appears on subsequent pages. This problem occurs only in laser printers and indicates a cleaning stage failure. The drum might have lost the ability to drop its charge in the presence of light. Replace the drum to resolve the problem. If the drum is not the cause, it could be either the cleaning blade or the erasure lamps. Because both the cleaning blade and drum are inside the toner cartridge in many laser printers, you can resolve this problem by replacing the toner cartridge. The erasure lamps are always (to our knowledge) in the printer itself, and they are not easy to replace. You will probably have to send the printer back to the manufacturer or to a specialized printer repair shop.

Toner Not Fused to the Paper

If the toner is not sticking to the paper, the fusing roller is defective or the fusing lamp (inside the roller) is burned out and not heating the roller enough to melt the toner to the paper. Similarly, a scratched nonstick coating on the fusing roller, or baked-on debris on it, can cause smeared toner on the printout. Either way, replace the fusing lamp and/or the fusing roller to fix the problem.

Random Speckles, Smudging, Smearing, and Streaking

Ribbon ink, cartridge ink, and toner residue can be within the printer itself and transfer onto the paper. If any type of printer produces a page with speckles, smudging, smearing, or streaking of the ink or toner, try cleaning the printer. This includes manually cleaning it and/or using the printer software to instruct the printer to perform cleaning and other maintenance tasks. We described printer cleaning in this chapter in "Printer Maintenance."

If an impact printer produces a smudged, smeared, or streaked printout, check the pins on the print head. Stuck pins can cause printouts to have a smudged appearance as they continue to transfer ink to the page, even when they do not create a character or image. If this is the case, notify the manufacturer, and replace the print head or the entire printer.

If the output from an inkjet printer appears smudged or smeared, the most likely cause is someone touching the printed page before the ink dries. The ink used in an inkjet printer must totally dry before it is touched, or it will smear. Most inkjet printers do not use permanent ink, and even after it has dried, these inks may smear if they become wet.

The heat and pressure of the fusion stage in a laser printer creates a smudge-proof permanent printout. Smudged or streaked laser printouts could be caused by a dirty corona wire, but are usually the result of a failed fusing stage. Depending on the exact source of the problem, you may need to replace the fusing rollers, the halogen lamp, or the entire fuser assembly.

Repeated Pattern of Speckles or Blotches

A repeated but unintended pattern on a printout is another indication of ink or toner residue in the printer. Clean the printer, paying attention to the feed rollers in an inkjet and the transfer corona wire in a laser printer. If a repeated pattern is on the printout of a laser printer, suspect the drum. A small nick or flaw in the drum will cause toner to collect there, and it will transfer onto each page in a repetitive pattern. In addition, some drums lose their ability to drop their charge during the cleaning step. The drum has a very small diameter, so this same pattern will repeat several times down the length of the page. In either case, replacing the drum should solve the problem.

Wrong Colors

Wrong colors may be a problem with the ink or toner cartridges, or it may be a software problem of some sort. Modern color printers don't allow you to print if a cartridge is out of ink or toner, so we can usually rule out an empty color cartridge. However, open up the printer and take a look at the cartridges. Things have improved in this area, but if a color cartridge is low, some printers cannot produce the correct shades. To get the desired results in a printout, you may simply need to replace the cartridges.

Also, if the nozzles on an inkjet clog, the colors may come out "dirty" or might not appear at all. Follow the manufacturer's instructions for cleaning the nozzles.

Wrong colors can be an application-related issue, and you should test a document using similar colors from another application. If the colors print out correctly from another app, there may be a problem with a setting in the first app.

Lines

If lines appear in a printout from an impact printer, the print head may have a malfunctioning pin, in which case, replace the print head. In any printer, parallel lines of print can indicate an incompatible driver, a problem you may solve by updating or replacing the driver. This symptom can also be a sign of a malfunction in the printer's electronics, so you need to repair or replace the printer, depending on its value and the cost of repair.

In a laser printer, a leaking toner cartridge or a dirty printer that has toner where the paper can pick it up as it passes through can cause vertical lines. Remove the toner cartridge, set it on a paper towel to see if it's leaking, clean it with a small vacuum cleaner, and then clean the interior of the printer until all the toner and paper dust are removed.

Garbled Output

Garbled output—often called "garbage"—usually indicates a communications problem between the computer and printer. The most common cause of this is an incorrect or corrupted print driver, but first check that the data cable is firmly and properly attached, and then try doing a power cycle (turning the printer off and then back on) because it may have simply experienced a temporary problem. Restarting the computer may also solve the problem.

If there are no connection problems and a power cycle of the printer and computer does not improve the printing, then check that the computer is using the correct printer driver. Look at the printer settings by opening the Printers folder. Ensure that the physical printer matches the printer shown in this dialog box. If the driver is not correct, uninstall it and reinstall the correct driver. If the driver appears to be correct, look at the manufacturer's site for an update and install the update. If the version of the driver is the most current, try reinstalling the driver.

Finally, this problem could be the result of insufficient printer memory. You can test this by trying to print a very small document. If it works, there is a chance that the original document was too large for the printer's memory. You can add more RAM. Check the documentation to find out how to check on the amount of memory, what type of memory to install, and how to install the memory.

Printer Error Messages

Printers generate a variety of error messages. They often come with their own configuration and monitoring utility installed on your computer when you install the printer driver. We'll describe some of the more common error messages that could appear on the computer screen or the printer's console, or both. The OS generates some of these messages. Any time you get a printer error message that you do not understand, check the message or error code number in the manufacturer's documentation. You may need to do a search on the manufacturer's Website, where a more complete list is often available.

Paper Out

A paper out message normally indicates that there is no paper in the printer, and the solution is simple: add paper. However, it can also appear on an older printer when there is paper in the tray. Over time, the surface of the rollers used to feed the paper may lose their ability to grip and move the paper. This issue occurs especially as the paper becomes low in the tray and the rollers cannot benefit from the pressure of a full stack of paper to grip and feed the paper. Locate the rollers and clean them, first wipe the dust and grime off, and then use isopropyl alcohol to clean any residue that may make the rollers slippery.

Out of Memory/Lost Memory Errors

A laser printer composes each page of a print job, using its own memory as it creates the raster image. This can require a great deal of memory, depending on the complexity and resolution of the page. Therefore, if an out of memory, lost memory, or memory overflow error appears on a printer's display, the printer does not have enough memory for the print job. For the short term, reduce the resolution of the image or reduce the dimensions of graphics on a page and try again. In most cases, the more permanent solution is to add more RAM to the printer, as described previously when we discussed the symptom of garbage or "garbled" printing.

Processing Error

If a printer has a processing error, such as the error 21 displayed on an HP laser printer, the cause is a document that is too complex for the printer's print processor. Adding memory will not help this problem. If the printer cannot print it as is, simplify the document by minimizing the number of fonts, reducing the resolution, and making graphics images smaller. Since you still want the best quality document possible, experiment by making one change that affects your document the least and testing to see if it will print out. Go with the fewest changes that result in a successful printout.

I/O Error or Connectivity Problem

An I/O error message can take many forms, including "Cannot communicate with printer" or "There was an error writing to LPT# or USB#." Windows typically reports this message, and it indicates that the computer cannot properly communicate with the printer, clearly identifying it as a connectivity problem. Or is it? Start by ensuring that the printer is on. If it is not, turn it on, and then try to print. Next, make sure the printer data cable firmly and properly attaches to both the printer and the computer and that a proper driver is loaded. If you suspect the driver is corrupt, remove it, and then reload it. Ensure that the driver uses the correct port by checking the Ports tab in the Properties dialog for the printer.

Incorrect Port Mode

An incorrect port mode error applies to parallel ports. Wording of this message may vary, but it indicates that the parallel port the printer attaches to is using the wrong mode. This message usually appears on the computer screen rather than on the printer's display. Enter the computer's BIOS system setup program, and change the parallel port to the proper mode (unidirectional, bidirectional, or ECP). If the error message does not indicate the correct mode, consult the printer manufacturer's documentation.

No Default Printer Selected

The first printer installed in Windows gets the default printer designation. A default printer is the printer that automatically receives a print job when you select the Print command from within a program but do not specify which printer you want to use. If you install one or more printers after that, the first one will remain the default printer until you change its status. A small solid-color circle containing a white check mark indicates the default printer in the Printers folder, as shown here on the Canon MX700 series printer. Make the printer you use most often the default printer by right-clicking the desired printer. From the context menu, select Set As Default Printer.

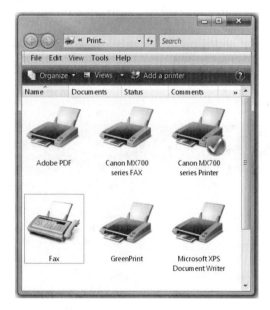

If there is no installed printer and you attempt to print, Windows will issue the error message "No default printer selected." Once you install at least one printer, this error message is rare, but it is not totally extinct. Corrupted printer drivers and utility files can disable the printer and cause this message to appear, but it will probably appear before or after another message that begins "Rundll has caused an error in..." This message will include a filename and will end with "Rundll will now close." If this occurs, attempt to uninstall the printer software, and then reinstall it. If this occurs immediately after installing a new printer, contact the manufacturer for another copy of the printer software, as the one that came with the printer may be corrupted.

Low Toner or Ink

The low toner (or similar) message applies to laser printers, and it appears well before the toner is completely gone as an early warning. The printer should continue to print normally. You can often make the error message go away by removing the toner cartridge and gently rocking the cartridge back and forth. This will resettle and redistribute the toner within the cartridge. Note, however, that this is not a solution to the problem. The reason for the error is to warn you to replace the toner cartridge soon. Most laser printers will not work at all if the toner cartridge is empty.

When you are using an inkjet, the ink low (or similar) message will appear on your computer screen or an ink level bar will be displayed. Replace the cartridge.

on the *When an ink cartridge gets low, you should replace rather than refill it. By*
job *refilling an old cartridge, you are reusing old, possibly worn-out components.*

SCENARIO & SOLUTION

The output from my laser printer is smeared. What should I do?	Clean the printer, especially the fusion roller. If this doesn't work, replace the drum. If the drum is in the toner cartridge, replace the toner cartridge. If none of this works, the problem may be with the fuser assembly, which will need replacing.
I am careful not to handle the printouts from my inkjet printer, but they are coming out with smudges. What can I do?	Check the paper path. Something may be contacting the page before the ink has had a chance to dry, or people may be handling the printout before it is dry.
Why do printouts from my color inkjet printer have the wrong colors?	The printer is probably low in one or more colors or has a clogged nozzle.

CERTIFICATION SUMMARY

This chapter explored printer issues for IT professionals. The focus of this chapter was the components, procedures, troubleshooting, and maintenance procedures for common printer types. Impact printers provide the lowest quality, and today they mainly print multiple-part forms. Laser printers, the most expensive, can provide excellent printouts and are the most common type used in offices. For this reason, you are likely to deal with laser printers in businesses more frequently than with other printer types. Inkjet printers are extremely popular as inexpensive desktop color printers.

Before installing a printer, carefully read the manufacturer's instructions. When working with printer problems, apply the troubleshooting procedures learned in Chapter 11, and become familiar with the symptoms and problems common to the printer or scanner. Printers require maintenance to replenish paper and, less frequently, ink or toner. Clean printers regularly to ensure high-quality results, and to avoid many problems that dirt, dust, and grime can create.

TWO-MINUTE DRILL

Here are some of the key points covered in Chapter 21.

Printer Basics

❑ Printers are the most common peripheral used with PCs.

❑ Impact printers are usually of low quality, use a ribbon, move paper with friction feed or tractor feed, and their most common use is for printing multiple-part forms, such as retail receipts.

❑ Laser printers use laser light technology in the printing process. The stages of the laser printing imaging process are charging, exposing, developing, transferring, fusing, and cleaning.

❑ The term "inkjet" refers to printers that use one of several technologies to apply wet ink to paper to create text or graphic printouts.

❑ Thermal printers use heat in the image transfer process.

❑ The two most common paper-feed technologies are friction feed and continuous form feed.

❑ The typical printer has a system board, ROM (containing firmware), and RAM memory, as well as various components related to the specific printing technology and paper-feed mechanism. Additional components include the device driver and related software, and consumables in the form of paper, ink ribbons, ink cartridges, or toner cartridges.

❑ Manufacturers offer all-in-one printers, multifunction products that include a scanner, printer, copier, and fax integrated within the same case.

❑ Printer interfaces include parallel, serial, USB, IEEE 1394/FireWire, Ethernet, and wireless.

Installing and Configuring Printers

❑ Before installing a printer, be sure to read the manufacturer's instructions.

❑ Installing a printer in Windows is a simple job, especially for plug and play printers. Even non–plug and play printers are easy to install using the Add Printer Wizard.

❑ After installing a printer, perform a test print, and then print from each installed application to ensure compatibility.

❑ Configure a printer through the printer's Properties dialog box and through the Printing Preferences dialog box.

❑ There are a few common upgrades to printers, including device drivers and other software, document feeders, memory, and firmware.

❑ Ways to optimize a printer's performance include tray selection for different stationery and enabling tray switching.

Printer Maintenance

❑ Some laser printers track the number of pages printed in a page count and require that critical components be replaced using a maintenance kit. After installing the maintenance kit, you must reset the page count.

❑ Clean each printer according to the manufacturer's recommendations to avoid poor output and other problems.

❑ Provide a suitable environment for each printer to avoid problems that dirt and temperature extremes can cause in these devices.

❑ For the best results, use the recommended consumables in printers. This may require using the media and paper provided by the manufacturer or less expensive substitutes of equal quality from other sources.

Troubleshooting Printers

❑ The troubleshooting process for printers is identical to that used for computers.

❑ Common printer problems include those involving paper feed and print quality. Printer error messages on your computer screen or the printer display panel will alert you to common problems, such as paper out, I/O errors, and print spooler problems.

SELF TEST

The following questions will help you measure your understanding of the material presented in this chapter. Read all of the choices carefully, because there might be more than one correct answer. Choose all correct answers for each question.

Printer Basics

1. What is a common use for impact printers?
    A. High-quality color images
    B. High-speed network printers
    C. Multipart forms
    D. UPC code scanning

2. What type of printer is the most often-used shared network printer in businesses?
    A. Laser
    B. Impact
    C. Thermal
    D. Inkjet

3. In what stage of the laser printing process does a laser beam place an image on the photosensitive drum?
    A. Cleaning
    B. Developing
    C. Charging
    D. Exposing

4. Which stage in the laser printing process is responsible for creating a permanent nonsmearing image?
    A. Cleaning
    B. Fusing
    C. Transferring
    D. Exposing

5. What type of printer applies wet ink to paper?
    A. Laser
    B. Impact
    C. Thermal
    D. Inkjet

6. What is the unit of measure used to describe the size of droplets created by the nozzles in an inkjet printer?

    A. Millimeter

    B. Meter

    C. Picoliter

    D. Liter

Installing and Configuring Printers

7. What Windows GUI tool can you use to install a non–plug and play printer?

    A. Add Printer Wizard

    B. Device Manager

    C. My Computer/Computer

    D. Add or Remove Programs

8. What important configuration task must you perform on a network printer before it will be recognized on the network?

    A. Install TCP/IP.

    B. Assign an IP address.

    C. Give it the address of each client.

    D. It must be detected by the clients.

9. Which of the following would you use to turn on sharing local printers in a HomeGroup?

    A. Devices and Printers

    B. Printer Properties

    C. Printing Preferences

    D. HomeGroup applet

10. Which of the following is a Windows 7 and Windows 8 tool for viewing and centrally administering all local and network printers?

    A. Devices and Printers

    B. HomeGroup applet

    C. Printer Properties

    D. Print Management

Printer Maintenance

11. What should you do after installing a maintenance kit in a laser printer?

A. Reset the maintenance count.

B. Reset the page count.

C. Reset the printer.

D. Call the manufacturer.

12. What simple maintenance task for printers helps maintain high-quality results?

A. Performing a memory upgrade

B. Installing a maintenance kit

C. Replacing the fuser

D. Cleaning

Troubleshooting Printers

13. When a print job will not print, check to see if this Windows service is still holding it in its queue.

A. Printer

B. Spooler

C. Print driver

D. Print device

14. What can contribute to static build-up in a printer?

A. Dust

B. Ink

C. Overloaded paper tray

D. Paper jams

15. You have shared a printer on your Windows 7 computer, and the Windows clients on your network can connect and print, but your Apple computer running Mac OS X cannot. What service should you enable on your Windows 7 computer?

A. IPP

B. Network Discovery

C. LPD

D. Printer

16. What component on an inkjet printer may clog with ink?
    A. Nozzles
    B. Hammers
    C. Friction-feed rollers
    D. Tractor feeder

17. What is a possible source of a problem causing blank pages to print out on a laser printer?
    A. Paper path
    B. Transfer corona wire
    C. Power supply
    D. Paper tray

18. What component in a laser printer could be the source of a repeated pattern of speckles?
    A. Fusion roller
    B. Drum
    C. Toner
    D. Primary corona wire

19. When a ghost image from a previous page occurs on subsequent pages printed on a laser printer, what component is a probable source of the problem?
    A. Fusion roller
    B. Drum
    C. Toner
    D. Primary corona wire

20. Of all the possible solutions for "garbage" printing, these two are the first ones you should try. Select the two correct answers.
    A. Check for loose data cable.
    B. Upgrade driver.
    C. Power-cycle the printer and computer.
    D. Uninstall and reinstall driver.

SELF TEST ANSWERS

Printer Basics

1. ☑ **C.** Multipart form printing is a common use for impact printers.
☒ **A,** high-quality color images, is incorrect because impact printers do not create high-quality color images. **B,** high-speed network printers, is incorrect because impact printers are not high-speed printers. **D,** UPC code scanning, is incorrect because no standalone printer can scan.

2. ☑ **A.** The laser printer is the most often-used shared network printer in businesses.
☒ **B,** impact, **C,** thermal, and **D,** inkjet, are all incorrect because these types of printers seldom are shared network printers in businesses.

3. ☑ **D.** Exposing is the laser printing stage in which the laser beam places an image on the photosensitive drum.
☒ **A,** cleaning, is incorrect because it is the stage in which the drum is cleaned. **B,** developing, is incorrect because it is the stage in which toner is attracted to the image on the drum. **C,** charging, is incorrect because it is the stage in which a charge is applied to the drum.

4. ☑ **B.** Fusing is the stage in the laser printing process in which the image permanently fuses to the paper.
☒ **A,** cleaning, **C,** transferring, and **D,** exposing, are incorrect because none of these is the stage that creates a permanent nonsmearing image.

5. ☑ **D.** Inkjet is the type of printer that applies wet ink to paper.
☒ **A,** laser, is incorrect because in this type of printer dry toner is fused to the paper. **B,** impact, is incorrect because this type of printer uses an ink ribbon. **C,** thermal, is incorrect because this type of printer uses heat to print an image.

6. ☑ **C.** Picoliter is the unit of measure used to describe the size of droplets created by the nozzles in an inkjet printer.
☒ **A,** millimeter, and **B,** meter, are both incorrect because neither one is the unit of measure used for the size of droplets from the nozzles in an inkjet printer, which is a measurement of liquid volume. Both millimeter and meter are units of distance measure. **D,** liter, although a measure of liquid volume, is far too large a volume for such small drops.

Installing and Configuring Printers

7. ☑ **A.** The Add Printer Wizard is the Windows GUI tool for installing a non–plug and play printer.
☒ **B,** Device Manager, **C,** My Computer/Computer, and **D,** Add or Remove Programs, are incorrect because none of these is the GUI tool for installing a non–plug and play printer.

8. ☑ **B.** Assign an IP address is the important configuration task you must do on a network printer before it will be recognized on the network.

   ☒ **A,** install TCP/IP, is incorrect because a network printer comes with TCP/IP installed. **C,** give it the address of each client, is incorrect because the network printer does not need the address of each client; each client needs the address of the network printer. **D,** it must be detected by the clients, is incorrect because the network printer must have an IP address before it can be recognized on the network.

9. ☑ **D.** HomeGroup applet is where you turn on sharing of local printers.

   ☒ **A,** Devices and Printers, and **B,** Printer Properties, are incorrect because once your computer is joined to a workgroup, you cannot turn on sharing by going into Devices and Printers, selecting your printer, and opening the Printer Properties, as you would if the printer belonged to a workgroup or domain. **C,** Printing Preferences, is incorrect because this dialog box only controls how documents are printed and has nothing to do with sharing.

10. ☑ **D.** Print Management is a Windows 7 and Windows 8 tool for viewing and centrally administering all local and network printers.

    ☒ **A,** Devices and Printers, is incorrect because it does not give you access to centrally administer all local and network printers. **B,** HomeGroup applet, is incorrect because it hides file and print sharing administrative tasks. **C,** Printer Properties, is incorrect because this only gives access to the properties on a single printer.

Printer Maintenance

11. ☑ **B.** Reset the page count of a laser printer after installing a maintenance kit.

    ☒ **A,** reset the maintenance count, is incorrect because resetting this count will set the number at which the printer should receive maintenance to zero pages. **C,** reset the printer, is incorrect because this will not turn the page count to zero, and the printer will display a maintenance warning. **D,** call the manufacturer, is incorrect because this step is unnecessary when all you need to do is reset the page count.

12. ☑ **D.** Cleaning is the simple maintenance task for printers that helps maintain high-quality results.

    ☒ **A,** performing a memory upgrade, is incorrect because this is not a simple maintenance task, and it will not help maintain high-quality results. **B,** installing a maintenance kit, is incorrect because this is not a simple maintenance task. **C,** replacing the fuser, is incorrect because it is not a simple maintenance task but a complex repair task.

Troubleshooting Printers

13. ☑ **B.** Spooler is the Windows component that holds print jobs in its queue before sending them to the printer. The spooler can be stalled, preventing a job from printing.
    ☒ **A,** printer, is incorrect, although this is the software in Windows that manages print jobs and sends them to print devices via the spooler. **C,** print driver, is incorrect, as this is a device driver for the printer. **D,** print device, is incorrect, as this is the physical printer.

14. ☑ **A.** Dust can contribute to static build-up in a printer.
    ☒ **B,** ink, is incorrect because, although ink residue may build up in a printer, it does not appreciably contribute to static buildup. **C,** overloaded paper tray, is incorrect because this is not a cause of static build-up in a printer. **D,** paper jams, is incorrect because, although static build-up in a printer may occasionally cause a paper jam, it is not a primary cause.

15. ☑ **C.** LPD is correct. You must enable the line printer daemon (LPD) service on the Windows computer for the Apple computer running Mac OS X.
    ☒ **A,** IPP, is incorrect. Although Internet printing protocol (IPP) is also a service for printing over a TCP/IP network, it is not the one that will correct the problem described. **B,** Network Discovery, is incorrect because it is also not the service that will correct the problem described. **D,** printer, is incorrect because this is not a service.

16. ☑ **A.** Nozzles in an inkjet printer can become clogged with ink.
    ☒ **B,** hammers, **C,** friction-feed rollers, and **D,** tractor feeder, are incorrect because these components do not become clogged with ink.

17. ☑ **B.** The transfer corona wire is a possible source of a problem causing blank pages to print on a laser printer.
    ☒ **A,** paper path, **C,** power supply, and **D,** paper tray, are incorrect because they are not considered possible sources for blank pages printing out on a laser printer.

18. ☑ **B.** The drum could be the source of a repeated pattern of speckles on printouts from a laser printer.
    ☒ **A,** fusion roller, **C,** toner, and **D,** primary corona wire, are incorrect because none of these is a probable source of repeated pattern of speckles on printouts from a laser printer.

19. ☑ **B.** The drum is the probable source of a ghost image printing on subsequent pages from a laser printer.
    ☒ **A,** fusion roller, **C,** toner, and **D,** primary corona wire, are incorrect because none of these is a probable source of a ghost image.

20. ☑ **A,** check for loose data cable, and **C,** power cycle the printer and computer, are the first two solutions you should try for "garbage" printing because they are simple and easy to try.
    ☒ **B,** upgrade the driver, and **D,** uninstall and reinstall the driver, are incorrect because they are not as simple and fast to try as the first two.

Appendix

About the CD-ROM

The CD-ROM included with this book comes complete with two MasterExam practice exams, MasterSim interactive labs, CertCam video clips, the Glossary, Session #1 of LearnKey's Online Training, and a link to download the Adobe Digital Editions eBook version of the book. The MasterExam and MasterSim software is easy to install on any Windows 2000/XP/Vista/7 computer and must be installed to access the MasterExam and MasterSim features. You may, however, browse the CertCams and Glossary directly from the CD-ROM without installation. To register for LearnKey's Online Training and the two bonus MasterExam practice exams, simply click the Bonus MasterExam link or the LearnKey Online Training link on the CD-ROM's main launch page and follow the directions for the free online registration.

System Requirements

The MasterExam and MasterSim software requires Windows 2000 or higher and Internet Explorer 6.0 or later and 20 MB of hard disk space for full installation. The Glossary requires Adobe Reader. To access the Online Training from LearnKey, you must have Windows Media Player 9 or later and Adobe Flash Player 9 or later. The Adobe Digital Editions eBook requires the Adobe Digital Editions software.

LearnKey Online Training

The LearnKey Online Training link will allow you to access online training from Osborne.OnlineExpert.com. The first session of this course is provided at no charge. An additional session of this course and other courses may be purchased directly from www.LearnKey.com or by calling 1-800-865-0165.

The first time you click the LearnKey Online Training link, you will be required to complete a free online registration. Follow the instructions for a first-time user. Please make sure to use a valid email address.

Installing and Running MasterExam and MasterSim

If your computer's CD-ROM drive is configured to autorun, the CD-ROM will automatically start up upon inserting the disk. From the CD-ROM's main launch page, you may install MasterExam or MasterSim by clicking the MasterExam or MasterSim links. This will begin the installation process and create a program group named LearnKey. To run MasterExam or MasterSim use Start | All Programs | LearnKey. If the autorun feature did not launch your CD-ROM, browse to the CD-ROM and click the LaunchTraining.exe icon.

MasterExam

MasterExam provides you with a simulation of the multiple-choice portion of the actual exams. You have the option to take open-book exams, including hints, references, and answers; closed book exams; or timed MasterExam simulations.

When you launch MasterExam, a digital clock display will appear in the bottom-right corner of your screen. The clock will continue to count down to zero unless you choose to end the exam before the time expires.

w a t c h　　　*MasterExam does not provide simulations of the exams' performance-based question type. For*　　　*further discussion on this question type, please see the book's Introduction.*

MasterSim

MasterSim offers a set of interactive labs that will provide you with a wide variety of tasks to allow you to experience the software environment even if the software is not installed. Once you have installed MasterSim, you may access it quickly through the CD-ROM main launch page, or you may also access it through Start | All Programs | LearnKey | MasterSim.

w a t c h　　　*The MasterSim interactive labs are not intended to be simulations of the exams' performance-based question*　　　*type. These labs are provided to allow you to practice what you've learned in a hands-on environment.*

CertCam Video Clips

The CertCam video clips walk you through a selection of the exercises included in the book. These videos show what occurs on the screen in Windows step by step, while a voice-over provides helpful commentary. You can access the clips directly from the CertCam table of contents by clicking the CertCam link on the CD-ROM's main launch page.

Glossary

The Glossary is provided in Adobe PDF. From the CD-ROM's main launch page, you may view the Glossary by clicking the Glossary link. The Glossary is also included in the Adobe Digital Editions eBook.

Adobe Digital Editions eBook

The contents of this book are available as a free downloadable eBook in the form of a secured Adobe Digital Editions file.

The CD-ROM contains links to both the Adobe Digital Editions software and the eBook download Web page.

1. First, download and install Adobe Digital Editions on your computer.
2. Next, follow the link listed below to the eBook download Web page. You are required to provide your name, a valid email address, and your unique access code in order to download the eBook.
3. Your unique access code can be found on the label that is adhered to the inside flap of the CD-ROM envelope. The CD-ROM envelope is inside the paper sleeve bound into the back of this book.
4. Upon submitting this information on the eBook download Web page, an email message will be sent to the email address you provided. Follow the instructions included in the email message to download your eBook.

To download your Adobe Digital Editions eBook, please visit:

http://books.mcgraw-hill.com/ebookdownloads/9780071795784

NOTE Your unique access code entitles you to download one copy of the eBook to one personal computer. The unique access code can only be used once. Unless you set up additional computers in Adobe Digital Editions prior to downloading the eBook, the eBook will only be viewable on the computer to which it was downloaded.

You must have the Adobe Digital Editions software installed to open, view, and navigate the eBook. You can download the latest version of Adobe Digital Editions for free from the Adobe Website, www.adobe.com, or use the version included on the CD-ROM.

Remember, you must download and install the Adobe Digital Editions software before attempting to download the eBook. Please review the Adobe Digital Editions FAQ on the Adobe Website before installing the software to check computer and device compatibility, and system requirements (minimum system requirements are listed next). Adobe Digital Editions does not support Apple's iPad at the time of publication, but workarounds are available that may allow you to view the eBook on an Apple device (the Bluefire application, for example). Customer support for Adobe Digital Editions should be directed to Adobe. McGraw-Hill does not warrant that use of any workaround solution will work, and McGraw-Hill does not provide technical support for any workaround solution using nonsupported devices with Adobe Digital Editions.

Minimum System Requirements for Adobe Digital Editions

Windows: Microsoft Windows XP with Service Pack 2 (Service Pack 3 recommended), Windows Vista (32-bit or 64-bit), Windows 7 (32-bit or 64-bit); Intel Pentium 500 MHz processor; 128 MB of RAM; 800×600 monitor resolution.

Mac: PowerPC: Mac OS X v10.4.10 or v10.5; PowerPC G4 or G5 500 MHz processor; 128 MB of RAM. Intel: Mac OS X v10.4.10, v10.5 or v10.6; 500 MHz processor; 128 MB of RAM.

Supported browsers and Adobe Flash versions for Windows: Microsoft Internet Explorer 8, Mozilla Firefox 3, Google Chrome for Windows; Adobe Flash Player 9 or 10. For Mac: Apple Safari 4, Mozilla Firefox 3; Adobe Flash Player 9 or 10.

Help

A help file is provided through the Help button on the CD-ROM's main launch page in the lower-left corner. Individual help features are also available through MasterExam, MasterSim, and LearnKey's Online Training.

Removing Installations

MasterExam and MasterSim are installed to your hard drive. For best results removing LearnKey programs, use the Start | All Programs | LearnKey | Uninstall option to remove MasterExam or MasterSim.

Technical Support

For questions regarding the operation of the Adobe Digital Editions eBook download, email techsolutions@mhedu.com or visit http://mhp.softwareassist.com.

For questions regarding the book content, email customer.service@mcgraw-hill.com. For customers outside the United States, email international_cs@mcgraw-hill.com.

LearnKey Technical Support

For technical problems with the software (installation, operation, removing installations) and for questions regarding LearnKey Online Training and MasterSim content, visit www.learnkey.com, email techsupport@learnkey.com, or call toll-free at 1-800-482-8244.

INDEX

D

N

O